HUTCHINSON
GALLUP

# INFO 92

HUTCHINSON
GALLUP
# INFO 92

**Hutchinson**

London · Melbourne · Sydney · Auckland · Johannesburg

© Random Century Group 1991

Maps copyright © Random Century Group 1990

*All rights reserved*

Random Century Ltd
20 Vauxhall Bridge Road
London SW1V 2SA

Random Century Australia (Pty) Ltd
20 Alfred Street
Milsons Point
Sydney
NSW 2061, Australia

Random Century Group New Zealand Ltd
P O Box 40–086 Glenfield
Auckland 10, New Zealand

Random Century Group South Africa (Pty) Ltd
P O Box 337, Bergvlei 2012, South Africa

*Set in* Century Old Style and Trade Gothic

*Data prepared on* Telos

*Printed and bound in England*

ISBN 0 09 174999 9

*Editorial Director* Michael Upshall

*Project Editor* Anne-Lucie Norton

*Coordinating Editor* Denise Dresner

*Editors* Penny Hext, Sara Jenkins-Jones

*Researcher* Anna Farkas

*Design* Terry Caven, Edna A Moore, Tek Art Ltd

*Design Consultant* Malcolm Smythe

*Database Software* BRS Software Products Ltd

*Page Make-up* Helen Bird, Rosalia Pardina

*Picture Research* Jane Lewis

*Index* Fiona Barr

*Jacket Design* Jude Fletcher

*Illustration and artwork* Anneset and Ian Foulis
Associates

*We would like to thank the following for their help:*
Bryan Alvey, Jane Anson, John Coles, Peter D James,
Jonathan Wainwright

*Contributors* Paul Bahn, Tia Cockrell, Mike Corbishley,
Susan Cusworth, Caroline Dakers, Ian Derbyshire,
Dr J D Derbyshire, Col Michael Dewar, Dougal Dixon,
Denise Dresner, Nigel Dudley, Robert Dyer, Graham Edge,
Caroline Evans, Anna Farkas, Barry Fox, Wendy Grossman,
Michael Hitchcock, Stuart Holroyd, Stephen Kite,
Peter Lafferty, Mike Lewis, Graham Littler, Morven
MacKillop, Robin Maconie, Tom McArthur, Joanna
O'Brien, Maureen O'Connor, Robert Paisley, Martin
Palmer, Carol Place, Tim Pulleine, John Pym, Chris Rhys,
Ian Ridpath, John Rowlinson, Kate Salway, Jack
Schofield, Mark Slade, Steve Smyth, Joe Staines,
Prof Ian Stewart, Ingrid von Essen, Prof Trevor Watkins,
Imogen Stooke-Wheeler, Charles Wintour

# CONTENTS

# PREFACE

INFO 92 is an entirely new annual compilation from Hutchinson. It aims to give concise but informed coverage of the essential topics and issues of today as they affect us: from the unification of Germany to the continuing dissolution of the USSR, from global warming to the preservation of wilderness areas.

It has been compiled with the help of more than forty subject specialists, and written to inform and explain without pedantry or obscure technical jargon.

INFO 92 is designed for use by everyone: home, office, school and college, and library. We have made every effort to include the most up-to-date, best-informed expert opinion, together with the salient fact. It is equally for the student, the curious, and the quiz game buff.

**How it is different**
Of course INFO 92 includes the major events of the year — who died (pp 29–51), what happened when (pp 11–20), even who said what (pp 3–10) — but it is more than just a yearbook. It provides a concise overview of more than forty subjects, including dates (when was platinum first isolated? p 364), facts (the latest Wimbledon champions, p 566), figures (the size of the UK national debt, p 234), and background information.

And INFO 92 goes beyond this to provide analysis and insight — what led to the abortive Soviet coup? p 157; how did the Gulf War begin? p 641; who are the Estonians? p 131; are crop circles a trick played on an unsuspecting public? p 405. INFO 92 also sets out to guide and explain — where do you put the apostrophe? p 142; should we be worried about food additives? (p 448); how can we contribute to a cleaner environment? (p 435). We have tried in every section not simply to include an undigested mass of figures, but to present information in a clear, easily understandable way.

In addition to this, with the aid of the extensive resources of Gallup Opinion Poll material, INFO 92 provides statistical information on hundreds of topics ranging from the top-selling LPs of all time (p 312) to views on computer hacking (p 395).

It covers events in a European and world context, ranging from endangered species (Africa's mountain gorilla, p 499) to endemic species (Australia's cane toad, p 470), from baseball (p 548) to sumo wrestling (p 550); from the European Community (p 99) to the Andean Pact (p 96).

**How to use INFO 92**
INFO 92 can be used in two ways. Look in the contents for the five major sections — Society, Economics and Business, The Arts, Science and Technology, and Sport and Leisure — which are in turn divided into forty-one topics, each one forming a compact, logically arranged outline of a single subject from astronomy to warfare, and including key terms, dates, and people. Use the index, which includes over 12,500 items, for a detailed guide to individual entries. The index contains many additional references to topics in the book, enabling you to find, for instance, information on CFCs in both the Chemistry and Environment sections.

**How you can help**
Writing and compiling INFO 92 showed us convincingly that an encyclopedic yearbook can be fun; it can inform while being entertaining, and need not be a dull compilation of official titles and statistics. But with your help it can become much better. Please write to us and let us know what you liked, what you didn't use, and what you think should be included next time. Your letters will enable us to produce a bigger, better second edition which corresponds more closely with what you, the reader, want to know.

# ACKNOWLEDGEMENTS

We would like to thank the following for photographs supplied: Rex Features; Popperfoto; Philips Medical Systems, The Bristol Cancer Help Centre; Olympia & York Ltd; Jane Lewis; NCEER/SUNY, Buffalo, N Y, USA; Reuters; The Game Conservancy, Fordingbridge, Hampshire; The Press Complaints Commission; Panasonic UK; W Industries; University of Wales College, Cardiff; Mitsubishi UK; S M Alexander (Plastics) Ltd; Renewable Energy Promotion Department; Phil Starling: The National Gallery; Natural History Museum, London; Marysia Woroniecka; COI, London; The Trustees of the British Museum; Vatican Museum; BOF/OGA.

**Gallup**
Gallup, Social Surveys (Gallup Polls) Limited, have provided all the polls and surveys which appear in the book, generally at the end of each subject section. All Gallup material is based on a sample of approximately 1000 adults in the UK and all figures are percentages of people sampled unless stated otherwise.

**Statistics**
It should be borne in mind that official statistics take a full year or more to compile. We have provided the latest figures available at the time of going to press.

# THE YEAR

# QUOTES OF THE YEAR

Space is out of this world.
**Helen Sharman** *first Briton in space.*
May 1991.

It's kind of a coincidence that this guy's getting ready to testify and he turns up as a cadaver.
*Lawyer for Ramon Navarro, who died in a car crash, who was chief witness against Manuel Noriega.*
March 1991.

It's very difficult to interview witnesses after all these years, particularly when some of them are dead.
**Ronald Hadfield** *West Midlands Chief Constable on the new Birmingham bomb inquiry.*
March 1991.

The English are all right. They're quiet, they're slow, they count things carefully, they hesitate. I'm switching to their track.
**Lech Walesa** *president of Poland.*

Once, to avoid hitting a kitten with my car, I braked sharply. I was shaking all over. And I'm supposed to have cut someone I was fond of into tiny pieces.
**Simone Weber** *defendant in France's murder trial of the decade.*

It is because people sometimes make the wrong choice, fall for temptation—often in a way that is not thought through but on the spur of the moment—that we have a criminal justice system at all, costing the taxpayer in England and Wales more than £7 billion a year; protecting the good, helping victims, punishing and hopefully rehabilitating the bad.
**John Patten** *UK Home Secretary writing on the Criminal Justice Bill.*

Judges should be independent of loud-mouthed politicians.
**Lord Hailsham** *former UK Lord Chancellor on the petition of 102 MPs calling for Lord Lane's resignation.*

Blaming the judges for the system is like blaming the sticking plaster for the wound.
**Steve Haywood** *producer of the BBC TV programme Rough Justice in a letter to* The Times.
An ancient dinosaur living in the wrong age.
**Judge Pickles** *describing Lord Lane, Lord Chief Justice. He was publicly rebuked for the remark by Lord Mackay, Lord Chancellor.*

The police told us from the start that they knew we hadn't done it.
**Patrick Hill** *a member of the 'Birmingham Six' on his release.*
March 1991.

It is easy to judge matters in retrospect.
**Lord Lane** *Lord Chief Justice in the Court of Appeal.*
March 1991.

Since China has a population of 1.1 billion, it won't feel lonely even if it becomes the only socialist country.
**Li Peng** *Chinese Prime Minister on the world's dwindling number of socialist governments.*

There are no jobs, no money, no apartment, no car and no good women.
**Pavel Novgorotsky** *Soviet émigré, on his prospects in Israel.*

Perhaps I failed as a father.
**Marlon Brando** *at the trial of his son Christian.*

They accuse us of working for foreign powers. Democracy is indeed foreign to them.
**Zoran Djindjic,** *leader of the opposition Democratic Party at an anti-government demonstration in Belgrade.*
March 1991.

Well hello. It's very nice to be here after five years ... I want to go home, to be with my family, to try to make up the time I have lost.
**John McCarthy** *released after five years as a hostage in Lebanon.*
August 1991.

The idea of peaceful development in Europe does not include NATO troops up to the borders of the USSR.
**Pravda** *about post-Communist Eastern Europe joining NATO.*
March 1991.

Organizers of strikes are breaking the law. Strikes interfere with Poland.
**Lech Walesa**
June 1991.

One is short of all-male preserves in present-day England.
**Roger Hearn** *member of MCC*
May 1991.

We have to have something better than parliament. All they ever do in parliament is attack the Ministers.
**Sheik Saad al-Sabah** *Crown Prince of Kuwait, speaking to Kuwaitis.*
March 1991.

Gentlemen in this country do get drunk, but they don't get disorderly with it.
**Geoffrey Noel** *London magistrate, addressing two German brothers arrested for rowdiness.*
March 1991.

Germany is our fatherland, the united Europe our future.
**Helmut Kohl** *Chancellor of West Germany, on the unification of the two Germanies.*
October 1990.

It is very different, I discover, being Prime Minister, from having any other position.
**John Major** *British prime minister from Nov 1990*

We have to take a certain amount of care about what we say to each other.
**Douglas Hogg** *Foreign Office minister whose wife, Sarah, is head of the Prime Minister's policy unit.*
March 1991.

It is said that when a fish deteriorates, the rot sets in at the head. It is the same with government departments.
**Frank Dobson** *Shadow energy secretary*
March 1991.

I've never been over impressed with academic qualifications ... I know an awful lot of people who have an armful of academic qualifications ... they are wholly useless, most of them. They have no common sense at all.
**John Major**

If you fix the exchange rate, then interest rates and domestic monetary conditions go where they will. And finance ministers are left like innocent bystanders at the scene of an accident.
**Margaret Thatcher** *on the ERM*
*June 1991.*

Any reference to class distinctions is a Marxist concept.
**Margaret Thatcher** *British Prime Minister from 1979–1990*

The destruction of life is not a social democratic policy.
**Oskar Lafontaine** *leader of Germany's Social Democratic Party, on the Gulf war.*
1991.

Historians will one day look back and think it a curious folly that just as the Soviet Union was forced to recognize reality by dispersing power to its separate states and by limiting the powers of its central government, some people in Europe were trying to create a new artificial state by taking powers away from national states and concentrating them at the centre.
**Margaret Thatcher**
June 1991.

I'm going to try as hard as I can. But I'm very young, and if it goes wrong, I can always do something else.
**John Major** *reported by Jilly Cooper,* Hello!

He stands for nothing; he is nothing. He is grey. He has no ideas. I have been totally deceived.
**Margaret Thatcher** *on her successor, John Major 1991.*

What intrigued me was the distortion of reality that was necessitated by Margaret Thatcher's elegant argument. The United States was founded on two ideas—not one. Like her great friend President Reagan, Margaret Thatcher conveniently forgets that the Declaration of Independence began with affirmations of both equality and liberty, and that the tension between them has shaped American history.
**David Broder** *Washington Post*

It's like asking someone: 'Would you like to have dinner and jump out of a third floor window?' The only way you can answer safely is 'No'.
**Leonid Batkin** *a leader of the radical Democratic Russia movement, on the referendum about the future of the Soviet Union.*
March 1991.

Everybody has a vote. That's a big problem as far as I'm concerned.
**Fianna Fáil** *party activist*

Stalin was right when he said that regardless of who votes and how they vote, the only thing that matters is who counts the vote.
**Anatoly Alexeyev** *head of the predominantly Russian Interfront movement, in response to the 77% vote in Latvia for independence.*
1991.

I want us to be where we belong: at the very heart of Europe.
**John Major**
March 1991.

You can acquire all you want and still feel empty. It took a deadly illness to bring me eye to eye with that truth, but it is a truth that the country, caught up in its ruthless ambitions and moral decay, can learn on my dime.
**Lee Atwater** *President Bush's campaign manager.*

If you're a genuine artist you have a very powerful vision of most situations, whether or not they're painful, as in my case they most often are.
**Morrissey**
November 1990.

Parliament must not be told a direct untruth, but it's quite possible to allow them to mislead themselves.
**Norman Tebbit**
March 1991.

We don't want to dominate anyone, really we don't.
**Helmut Kohl** *responding to Margaret Thatcher's renewed warnings about monetary union with the Bundesbank.*
March 1991.

I nearly went elsewhere, but if I was there, I wouldn't be here. I might say it's far nicer to be here.
**Brian Lenihan,** *explaining his presence at the Fianna Fáil Ard Fheis.*
March 1991.

The public have not been persuaded that the community charge is fair.
**Michael Heseltine**
March 1991.

I think we had better start again somewhere else.
**John Major** *during the war cabinet meeting which was interrupted by an IRA mortar bomb attack.*
February 1991.

Making capitalism out of socialism is like making eggs out of an omelette.
**Vadim Bakatin** *first candidate in Russian presidential election.*
May 1991.

Comrade democrats, you have scattered. The reformers have gone to ground. Dictatorship is coming. I state it with complete responsibility. No one knows what kind of dictatorship this will be.
**Eduard Shevardnadze** *in his dramatic resignation speech delivered to the USSR Congress of People's Deputies.*
December 1990.

The war in the Gulf is not a Christian war, a Jewish war, a Muslim war, it is a just war.
**George Bush**
February 1991.

I fight, I fight.
**Margaret Thatcher** *in an interview with the* Sunday Times *after failing to achieve an outright victory in the first ballot of the Conservative Party's leadership contest.*
November 1990.

I do believe that once it is fully understood ... then it will be seen to be a very much fairer system and more acceptable system than was the old rating system.
**John Major** *on the community charge/poll tax, in a letter to a constituent.*
April 1990.

The time has come for others to consider their own response to the tragic conflict of loyalties with which I have myself wrestled for perhaps too long.
**Geoffrey Howe** *after his resignation from Margaret Thatcher's cabinet.*
November 1990.

Thatcherism is not for a decade. It is for centuries!
**Margaret Thatcher** *in an interview with* Newsweek *a month before her resignation.*
October 1990.

It's a funny old world that I have won a majority of the party, and yet I feel I have to go.
**Margaret Thatcher** *to cabinet colleagues after announcing that she would not contest the second ballot for the Conservative Party's leadership and would resign as Britain's prime minister.*
November 1990.

To govern is to choose ... to appear to be unable to choose is to appear to be unable to govern.
**Nigel Lawson** *in a House of Commons speech concerning the government's uncertain plans for replacing the Poll Tax.*
March 1991.

You bring in your wake destruction, ruin, famine, cold, blood and tears ... Amid the applause of the West, Mikhail Sergeievich has forgotten whose President he is.
**Sazhi Umalatova** *a Soviet parliament deputy from the North Caucasus, who proposed a motion of no confidence in President Gorbachev.*
December 1990.

I separate myself from the position and policies of Gorbachev, and I call for his immediate resignation. He has brought the country to dictatorship in the name of presidential rule.
**Boris Yeltsin** *president of the Russian republic in a television interview.*
February 1991.

To be perfectly honest, the last thing we expected was a poll tax bill.
**Darren Barker** *Gulf military policeman*
February 1991.

It might seem a paradox but I regard fascism as a less dangerous ideology than communism.
**Yelena Bonner** *widow of Soviet dissident scientist Andrei Sakharov.*
April 1991.

Those who are able most effectively to undermine national security are those who least appear to constitute any risk to it.
**Lord Donaldson** *Master of the Rolls*

By God, we kicked the Vietnam syndrome once and for all.
**George Bush**
March 1991.

I gave warning that it is part of Gorbachev's character to search for absolute personal power. Everything he has done has been aimed at bringing the country to dictatorship, to presidential rule as they call it. I distance myself from the position and policies of the president. I call for his immediate resignation and the transfer of power to a collective body, the Council of the Federation.
**Boris Yeltsin** *speaking on Soviet television.*
February 1991.

Gorbachev is a president without a people—just an army, a party and a KGB.
**Vitaly Korotich** *editor of the radical magazine* Ogonyok
March 1991.

We must remember, this certainly was not the prize for economics.
**Gennady Gerasimov** *Soviet foreign ministry spokesman commenting on the lukewarm reception of Soviet parliamentarians to the announcement that President Gorbachev had been awarded the 1990 Nobel Peace Prize.*
October 1990.

Physicists are useless, they just like to play with their toys and when they grow tired with them they want more money for new ones.
**David Phillips** *Chairman of the Advisory Board of Research Councils.*
April 1991.

I always wondered about that taping equipment. But I'm damn glad we have it.
**Richard Nixon** *speaking on newly released Watergate tapes.*
June 1991.

No credible trade union believes in strike action.
**Doug McAvoy** *general secretary of British National Union of Teachers*

The daggers were not only struck from the front, which one expects, but also from the side, as well as from the back. But sometimes it is better to die like that than to take poison.
**V P Singh** *on the collapse of his government at the hands of rival members of his own Janata Dal party.*
November 1990.

If I had to do it over again, I would not even be a Communist, and if Lenin were alive today, he would say the same thing.
**Todor Zhivkov** *Bulgaria's former Communist Party leader.*
December 1990.

Anyone who has been educated in an English public school and survived in the ranks of the British army feels at home in a third-world prison.
**Roger Cooper** *British businessman, released after being held in Iran since 1985 on charges of espionage.*
April 1991.

It's like a business. We are cutting back because our market has shrunk.
*Belgian NATO official commenting on 500 job cuts at Supreme Headquarters Allied Powers Europe.*
April 1991.

It is easier to obstruct peace than to promote it.
**James Baker** *US Secretary of State*
*April 1991.*

For many centuries sovereignty was used to wage war in Europe. That era is over. Thank God it is.
**Edward Heath** *former UK prime minister*
June 1991.

The army sees no reason to say sorry for having taken part in this patriotic task.
**General Pinochet** *in response to a government-sponsored report on human rights abuses under his regime.*
March 1991.

The paradox in South Africa is that after all these years of white racism, oppression and injustice there is hardly any anti-white feeling.
**Archbishop Desmond Tutu** *in his foreword to Black Sash: The Beginning Of A Bridge in South Africa.*

Are our trials contested to find a loser and a winner, rather than a search for the truth.?
**Lord Scarman** *English judge*
*March 1991.*

In our country, I know that there are fears of another Vietnam. Let me assure you, should military action be required, this will not be another Vietnam. This will not be a protracted, drawn-out war.
**George Bush** *in his address to the nation*
December 1990.

America does not seek conflict .. The mission of our troops is wholly defensive ... They will not initiate hostilities, but they will defend themselves, the Kingdom of Saudi Arabia and other friends in the Gulf.
**George Bush** *in a televised address to the nation, explaining the decision to send ground forces to the Gulf region.*
August 1990.

This is not, as Saddam Hussein would have it, the United States against Iraq, it is Iraq against the world.
**George Bush** *in his address to a joint session of Congress.*
September 1990.

Iraq will not be permitted to annex Kuwait. That's not a threat, not a boast. That's just the way it's going to be.
**George Bush** *in his address to a joint session of Congress.*
September 1990.

Out of these troubled times ... a new world order can emerge: a new era, free from the threat of terror, stronger in the pursuit of justice, and more secure in the quest for peace. An era in which the nations of the world, East and West, North and South, can prosper and live in harmony.
**George Bush** *in his address to a joint session of Congress.*
September 1990.

I'm not brave enough to be a woman.
**Sting** *pop singer*
April 1991.

I bet the Queen doesn't remember all the people she meets either.
**Betty Boo** *pop singer*
March 1991.

We now have the chance to build the world envisioned by the founders of the UN. We have the chance to make the council and this United Nations true instruments for peace and justice across the globe.
**James Baker** *in a UN Security Council debate over Resolution 678, authorizing member governments to use 'all necessary means' to secure Iraq's complete withdrawal from Kuwait after a 15 January deadline.*
November 1990.

Hindsight is not an attractive thing.
**John Major**
March 1991.

The Americans will come here to perform acrobatics like [in] Rambo movies. But they will find here real people to fight them. We are a people who have eight years of experience in war and combat.
**Saddam Hussein**
January 1991.

There are times in life when we confront values worth fighting for. This is one such time.
**George Bush**
January 1991.

Should the Americans become embroiled, we will make them swim in their own blood, God willing.
**Saddam Hussein**
January 1991.

I felt we were making rock music with some art in it.
**Johnny Marr** *remembering the Smiths.*
April 1991.

They could excommunicate half the world.
**Matilde Fernández** *Spanish Social Affairs Minister on the possibility of the Spanish Church excommunicating women who consider abortion.*
April 1991.

People have described me as a 'management bishop' but I say to my critics, 'Jesus was a management expert too.'
**Dr George Carey**
March 1991.

We're the sort of group that had our own T-shirts way before we had our own records.
**Tim Burgess** *The Charlatans*
April 1991.

The market came with the dawn of civilization and is not the invention of capitalism. If the market leads to the improvement of people's daily lives, then there is no contradiction with socialism.
**Mikhail Gorbachev** *rebutting the complaints of his conservative rivals that he was attempting to restore capitalism in the Soviet Union.*
June 1990.

I'm 24, hoping to be 25.
**Corporal Dave Hoernle** *of 14th Military Police Brigade in Saudi Arabia after being asked his age by a reporter.*
February 1991.

It was three and a half hours of boredom and 10 minutes of stark terror.
**Lt Tyler Kearly** *a naval pilot describing his first combat mission.*
February 1991.

There is no other course than the one we have taken, except the course of humiliation and darkness.
**Saddam Hussein**
March 1991.

He is neither a strategist, nor is he schooled in the operational art, nor is he a tactician, nor is he a general, nor is he a soldier. Other than that, he is a great military man.
**General H Norman Schwarzkopf** *on his adversary, Iraq's Saddam Hussein.*
March 1991.

Who could not be moved by the sight of that poor, demoralized rabble, outwitted, outflanked, outmaneuvered by the US military? Yet, given time, I think the press will bounce back.
**James Baker**
March 1991.

It's a lot more humiliating to sing a bad line than it is to play one on a guitar.
**Michael Stipe** *member of rock group REM*
April 1991.

Mitterrand has 100 lovers. One has AIDS, but he doesn't know which one. Bush has 100 bodyguards. One is a terrorist, but he doesn't know which one. Gorbachev has 100 economic advisers. One is smart, but he doesn't know which one.
**President Mikhail Gorbachev** *sharing a joke with reporters after an all-day session of parliament.*
December 1990.

We must fight against animal overpopulation. I call on all cat and dog owners to have their pets sterilized.
**Brigitte Bardot** France-Soir
June 1991.

If you can get it out of sight and down the sewer, people think you don't have to do anything about it. As for incineration, that's just landfill in the sky. It's just pollution as usual. The real solution is to go back into the [chemical] plants and ask why they're producing the things in the first place.
**Tim Birch** *Greenpeace*
May 1991.

Removing cashew nuts from the mixed nuts will save about £40,000 a year.
*British Airways spokesman on catering arrangements for first-class passengers.*
1991.

We live in an age where the artist is forgotten. He is a researcher. I see myself that way.
**David Hockney**
June 1991.

Naturally, I had other men in mind.
**Fay Wray** *actress of King Kong fame, on how her co-star was first described to her as 'the tallest, darkest leading man in Hollywood'.*

I have this in common with Mickey Mouse—big ears and a long tail.
**Serge Gainsbourg** *French popular songwriter, actor and film-maker.*
March 1991.

The independent film maker is independent of one thing, which is money.
**Alexander Mackendrick** *director*
March 1991.

My whole career is based on systematic destruction. You destroy what you did before and you're free to carry on.
**Neil Young** *rock musician*
May 1991.

A classless society? England will always be a class-ridden society, there is no social mobility, there really isn't.
**Sting**
April 1991.

We have avoided a catastrophe. What we have is just a grave accident.
**Girogia Ruffolo** *Italian Environment Minister, on the Haven oil-tanker sinking.*
April 1991.

I've thought to myself—how long can I keep on doing this? Somebody has got to find out how far you can take this thing, so it might just as well be me.
**Keith Richards** *The Rolling Stones*
June 1991.

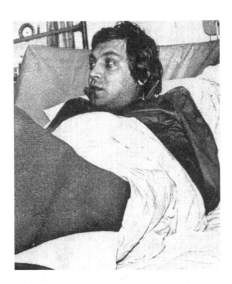

The KGB is a great group of guys.
**Alexander Nevzorov** *Leningrad television presenter recovering in hospital in April 1991 after being lured to a nightclub and attacked.*
April 1991.

I think it's helpful to address the audience. You have to consider them allies or else I don't know who the hell they are.
**Jerry Garcia** *leader of rock group The Grateful Dead*
March 1991.

Part of music's primary function has always been to get people to celebrate or to produce changes of consciousness.
**Jerry Garcia**
March 1991.

I've always known that Catholicism is a completely sexist, repressed, sin-and-punishment-based religion.
**Madonna**
June 1991

I'm sick to death of explaining our game. There's a lot more to us than kick and hump.
**Jack Charlton** *Republic of Ireland football team manager.*
March 1991.

I don't feel guilty as long as the Queen and Prince Charles are swimming about. I've just got more money than I need. I give it away, it's as simple as that.
**Robert Smith** *The Cure*
April 1991.

I don't think she is a natural peer. She is a natural commoner. She would find the Lords too relaxed.
**Lord Hailsham** *on reports that Margaret Thatcher may be destined for the Upper House.*
March 1991.

When I pass a belt I cannot resist hitting below it.
**Robert Maxwell** New York Times
March 1991.

You are an amiable figure but you've a tendency to demagoguery and you are sometimes irresponsible.
**Jean-Pierre Cot** *chairman of the European Parliament's socialist group, on the Russian President, Boris Yeltsin.*
April 1991.

The sort of people you step on when you come out of the opera.
**Sir George Young** *on London beggars.*
June 1991.

Shrugging the (telephone) receiver between cheek and shoulder places an enormous strain on the sternocleidomastoid muscles, the prominent bulges on each side of your neck, and on the splenius capitis, the muscle that runs up to the base of your skull.
**Esquire Magazine** *on a new condition known as 'phone neck'.*
March 1991.

Irish people must learn to be intellectuals outside the confines of a public house.
**Emmanuel Sweeney** *leader of the new Irish Christian Democrats who are demanding an inquiry into why the Republic has 11,000 pubs.*
April 1991.

I'm the most irritating person you could hope to hear of. I know this because people write and tell me.
**Morrissey**
November 1990.

In life generally you can get hurt. Life is dangerous ... look at sex today. Sex is getting more danger warnings than boxing at the moment.
**Frank Bruno** *British boxer*
March 1991.

It is not helpful to help a friend by putting coins in his pockets when he has got holes in his pockets.
**Douglas Hurd** *on aid to Russia.*
June 1991.

Rising unemployment is the price we have to pay to get inflation down, and it is a price well worth paying.
**Norman Lamont**
May 1991.

The merchant bankers sowed the seeds of this recession when they said anybody who was not highly leveraged was a fool.
**Richard Duggan** *Trade Indemnity plc*
March 1991.

# CHRONOLOGY

**JUNE 1990**
**INTERNATIONAL**

1 Presidents Bush and Gorbachev signed more than a dozen bilateral agreements, protocols and understandings in Washington DC. Included among these was an agreement to reduce their arsenals of chemical weapons.

7 Soviet troops were rushed to the republic of Kirghizia and sealed the border with Uzbekistan, where the ethnic violence had been centred. The official toll was 148 dead and 885 injured.

7 South African President F W de Klerk announced that he was lifting the four-year-old nationwide state of emergency in three of the country's four provinces.

8 Israeli Prime Minister Yitzhak Shamir formed a right-wing coalition government, ending six years of 'national unity' coalitions.

11 Alberto Fujimori, a political outsider, easily won Peru's presidency over Mario Vargas Llosa and instituted a market-oriented anti-inflation programme.

21 A major earthquake, measuring 7.3 on the Richter scale, struck northern Iran, devastating scores of towns and villages. The Iranian government placed the death toll at more than 35,000, with more than 100,000 people injured and 400,000 left homeless.

**NATIONAL**

3 The executive committee of the Social Democratic Party, led by David Owen, voted to effectively disband the struggling party.

5 The House of Lords rejected a bill passed in the Commons allowing trials of suspected World War II criminals living in Britain.

18 Defence Minister Tom King announced that the government would cut defence expenditure by £600 million, beginning with the cancellation of orders for 33 Tornado strike and fighter aircraft.

25 Eight people were injured when a bomb exploded at a central London social club frequented by high-ranking members of the Conservative party. The Provisional Irish Republican Army claimed responsibility for the blast.

**GENERAL**

8 The 14th World Cup football championship opened in Milan, Italy.

25 The USA Supreme Court ruled that a person had the right to refuse life-sustaining medical treatment.

27 NASA reported a major flaw in the Hubble Telescope's main light-gathering mirrors which would curtail the space project's ability to probe the universe for several years.

29 Representatives of 93 nations agreed in London to banish, by the end of the 20th century, production of chemicals that destroy the atmosphere's protective ozone layer.

**JULY 1990**
**INTERNATIONAL**

1 A state treaty establishing a unified economy and monetary system for East and West Germany went into effect.

2 The Soviet Union announced a complete lifting of its economic embargo on the rebellious Lithuanian republic, which had begun in April.

2 An estimated 1,426 Muslim pilgrims were killed when a stampede occurred in a pedestrian tunnel leading to the holy city of Mecca.

3 The foreign ministers of Iran and Iraq in Geneva held their first direct talks since a UN cease-fire ended the Persian Gulf War in August 1988.

6 At a NATO summit held in London leaders backed major strategy changes, reflecting the changing face of Europe and the close of the Cold War.

16 The Soviet Union agreed to conditions that would allow a reunified Germany to become a member of NATO.

16 An earthquake struck the main Philippines island of Luzon; at least 1,621 people died.

17 Iraqi president Saddam Hussein threatened to use force against Kuwait and the United Arab Emirates, to stop them from driving oil prices down by overproduction. Baghdad's wartime ally Kuwait was accused of having stolen $2.4 billion worth of petroleum over the past decade from Iraq's southern Rumaila border.

**NATIONAL**

4 Prime Minister Margaret Thatcher met Nelson Mandela at Downing Street for the first time in the highest level contact yet between the ANC and the British government.

12 Secretary of State for Trade and Industry Nicholas Ridley retracted damning statements he had made against the European Community and West Germany, but the opposition Labour Party nonetheless demanded his resignation.

24 A Catholic nun and three policemen were killed by an IRA landmine hidden at the side of a road in County Armagh.

30 Ian Gow, Conservative MP for Eastbourne, a close personal friend and advisor to Prime Minister Thatcher, was killed by a car bomb at his home in East Sussex.

GENERAL

2      Imelda Marcos, the former first lady of the Philippines, was acquitted in federal court in New York City of fraud and other charges,

7      Martina Navratilova won a record ninth Wimbledon singles title.

8      West Germany won the World Cup football championship in Italy with a 1–0 victory over Argentina in the finals.

21     Rock performers staged a large-scale concert in East Berlin to celebrate the dismantling of the Berlin Wall. More than 150,000 people attended the concert, which included performances by Pink Floyd member Roger Waters, Sinead O'Connor, and Phil Collins.

## AUGUST 1990
INTERNATIONAL

2      Iraqi troops and tanks stormed across the border into Kuwait and quickly seized effective control of the oil-rich nation.

6      The UN voted to impose a sweeping trade and financial embargo of Iraq and Kuwait.

6      Pakistani Prime Minister Benazir Bhutto was removed from office amid charges of corruption and nepotism.

6–7    ANC leaders and the South African government held talks for the first time. The ANC announced that it was suspending its 30-year armed struggle against the white minority regime.

7      Washington ordered troops, planes, and armour to Saudi Arabia and deployed thousands of troops.

10     The Arab League voted to send troops to defend the Saudis.

12–23  Factional civil fighting between Zulus and Xhosas in South Africa spread to black townships in Transvaal province. More than 500 blacks were killed in the violence.

20     Iraqis began moving westerners and other non-Iraqis to strategic sites as human shields.

21     The Western European Union agreed to increase its naval operations in the Persian Gulf region and coordinate its efforts with the USA.

24     Irish hostage Brian Keenan, who had been held a prisoner for over four years, was released in Beirut by his pro-Iranian captors.

28     Iraq's president Saddam Hussein ordered the release of all foreign women and children as a 'humanitarian gesture'.

31     Rebels in Liberia killed 200 civilians of nations whose governments contributed to the five-nation force that had been sent to end the civil war. An estimated 5,000 people, mostly civilians, were killed in the eightmonth conflict.

31     Representatives of East and West Germany signed a treaty establishing the political and social terms for the reunification of Germany, with Berlin as the new capital.

NATIONAL

2      More than 4,000 contract workers took part in a 24-hour wildcat strike on North Sea oil platforms. Work stoppages and sit-ins continued until 9 August.

23     The British government announced that it would proceed with plans to sell off the state-owned electricity generator PowerGen, through a public flotation of stock.

25     Bishop George Carey was nominated as the next Archbishop of Canterbury.

27     Four prominent British executives were convicted of conspiracy, theft and fraud in connection with Guinness PLC's 1986 takeover bid for Distillers Co PLC.

GENERAL

3      Britain recorded the highest temperature ever measured there, 37°C/99°F.

10     A jury in Washington DC failed to reach a verdict on 10 of the 12 drug and perjury charges against DC mayor Marion S Barry. Barry was convicted on one drug possession charge and sentenced to six months in jail.

26     Jose-Maria Olazabal of Spain won the World Series of Golf in Akron, Ohio.

## SEPTEMBER 1990
INTERNATIONAL

1      UN Secretary General Pérez de Cuéllar met with Iraqi Foreign Minister Aziz for two days of inconclusive talks in Jordan.

4      New Zealand Prime Minister Geoffrey Palmer resigned, as his Labour Party prepared for federal elections scheduled in Oct.

7–22   A series of 'freedom flights' carried Western women, children, and a handful of men out of Kuwait and Iraq.

9      Presidents Bush and Gorbachev held a summit in Helsinki. The two leaders displayed unity on the Persian Gulf crisis.

10     The four warring Cambodian factions ended two days of talks in Jakarta, agreeing to accept a UN plan to end the civil war.

10     Former Prime Minister Benazir Bhutto was formally charged by a special Pakistani court with abuse of power.

10     President Samuel Doe of Liberia was killed by rebels fighting to overthrow him in a civil war marked by atrocities on both sides.

12     Representatives of the World War II Allied powers, East Germany, and West Germany signed a treaty in Moscow granting full sovereignty to a unified Germany and setting Soviet troop withdrawals from East Germany.

14     Iraqi troops raided several Western dip-

lomatic missions in Kuwait City.

14 British Defence Secretary, Tom King, announced the sending of the 'Desert Rats'—the 7th Armoured Brigade—to the Gulf.

15 The French began sending troops, aircraft, and tanks to Saudi Arabia to protest about Iraqi moves against diplomats.

15 Iraq opened the southern border between Kuwait and Saudi Arabia, allowing thousands of Kuwaitis to flee into exile.

24 South African President de Klerk met with President Bush at the White House, in the first official visit to the USA by a South African head of state in 45 years.

24 The Soviet parliament voted to give President Gorbachev new powers to rule by decree.

25 The UN Security Council voted to extend its land and sea blockade of Iraq to include an embargo on air traffic.

27 Britain and Iran announced that they would restore diplomatic relations.

30 The Soviet Union established full diplomatic relations with South Korea and also significantly upgraded its ties with Israel.

## NATIONAL

3 The Trades Union Congress voted in Blackpool to back the Labour Party's new policies on employment and unions.

6 The House of Commons met after being recalled for an emergency debate on the Persian Gulf crisis. The last time that Parliament had been recalled from a recess was in 1982, over the Falkland Islands.

12 The government launched £18 million campaign to sell off the twelve regional electricity boards of England and Wales.

19 The IRA claimed responsibilty for an attack on Peter Terry, the former governor of Gibraltar. Terry had been shot nine times in his home near Derby the previous night.

## GENERAL

8–9 19-year-old Pete Sampras and Gabriela Sabatini of Argentina won the men's and women's titles respectively at the USA Open tournament in Flushing, New York.

14 A four-year-old Cleveland girl suffering from a rare immune deficiency became the first person to undergo experimental treatment using a genetically engineered human gene.

18 The city of Atlanta, Georgia was chosen as the site for the 1996 Summer Olympic Games.

30 71 world leaders attended the first World Summit for Children at the UN General Assembly in New York City.

## OCTOBER 1990

### INTERNATIONAL

3 Germany became a united nation.

3 USA Secretary of State Baker and Soviet Foreign Minister Shevardnadze announced that they had reached agreement on the main points of a Conventional Forces in Europe Treaty, following negotiations held at the Soviet mission to the UN in New York.

3 Soviet President Gorbachev dispatched one of his advisers, Primakov, to the Gulf region, where he met Iraq's Foreign Minister, Aziz, and Jordan's King Hussein.

5 Britain announced that it would join the exchange rate mechanism of the European Monetary System, linking the pound to other European currencies.

8 Israeli police opened fire on stonethrowing Palestinian protesters at Jerusalem's Temple Mount, killing 21 and wounding more than 100.

9 Saddam Hussein, responding to the killings in Jerusalem, repeated his threats to attack Israel to defend Iraq and the Palestinian cause.

10 About 360 people, most of them Americans of Arab descent, were allowed by Iraqi officials to leave Kuwait.

12 The UN Security Council adopted a USA backed resolution criticizing Israel for the Temple Mount killings of 8 Oct.

13 General Aoun, the renegade Christian army commander who had defied the Syrian-backed Lebanese army for more than two years, surrendered power.

16 The Supreme Soviet adopted Gorbachev's long-awaited economic reform programme.

21 In the worst of a series of attacks by Arabs apparently seeking revenge for the Temple Mount killings, a Palestinian labourer stabbed three Israelis to death in West Jerusalem.

24 The Islamic Democratic Alliance defeated Bhutto's Pakistan People's Party at national elections, and Nawaz Sharif became prime minister.

27 The opposition National Party won New Zealand's general election. Party leader Jim Bolger became prime minister.

28 Leaders of the European Community gave their support to the creation of a central bank for the community in 1994. Only prime minister Margaret Thatcher opposed the plan.

29 The UN Security Council passed a resolution making Iraq liable for damages, injuries and financial losses resulting from its invasion and occupation of Kuwait.

### NATIONAL

10 Two leading members of the IRA were shot dead near the town of Loughall,

in County Armagh by an army under-cover team.

11    Patrick Nicolls, UK government minister who had been behind an official campaign against drinking at work, resigned after being arrested for drunken driving.

19    The Liberal Democrats won the byelections at Eastbourne, previously considered one of the safest Tory seats in the country, with a majority of 4,550.

20    Demonstrators clashed with police outside Brixton prison in south London, following an anti-poll-tax meeting.

23    Edward Heath, UK former prime minister, took off from Baghdad with 33 Britons whose release he had won from Saddam Hussein in 48 hours of negotiations.

24    Using a new tactic, the IRA forced three men to drive car bombs to British security targets in Northern Ireland. One of the men driving the cars and six British soldiers were killed.

GENERAL
1     The Supreme Soviet voted, 341–2, to pass a landmark law guaranteeing religious freedom to all citizens.

2     At least 132 people were killed and 50 others injured, when a hijacked Chinese passenger jet crashed into two other planes while attempting to land at Baiyum Airport in Canton province.

6–10  The US Space Shuttle *Discovery* successfully ran a four day mission to deploy the *Ulysses* spacecraft on a surveying project to the Sun's polar regions.

25    (James) Buster Douglas, in his first defence of his title as world heavyweight boxing champion, was knocked out by Evander Holyfield.

**NOVEMBER 1990**
INTERNATIONAL
7     The government of Prime Minister Vishwanath Singh of India was ousted. A breakaway faction of Singh's party took a shaky hold under Prime Minister Chandra Shekhar.

8     The USA announced plans to increase the number of its armed forces in the Gulf region to more than 400,000 by early 1991.

9     Mary Robinson became the first woman elected to the Irish presidency.

14    Representatives of Germany and Poland signed a treaty guaranteeing the current border between the two nations.

18–19 Iraq offered to release all of its remaining foreign hostages over a three-month period beginning at the end of the year provided there was no outbreak of war with the US-led military forces in the Gulf region. The next day, Iraq said it would add 250,000 troops to bolster the 430,000-strong army it had already

deployed in occupied Kuwait and southern Iraq.

21    Leaders of 34 European and North American nations signed the Charter of Paris, bringing a formal end to the Cold War. At the same summit member states of NATO and the Warsaw Pact signed a treaty on Conventional Forces in Europe, which would limit the non-nuclear armaments of the two military alliances.

22    Britain announced that it would send 15,000 more troops to the Gulf.

26    Poland's first non-Communist premier since the 1940s, Tadeusz Mazowiecki, resigned.

26    Lee Kuan Yew, Singapore's prime minister for 31 years, announced that he was stepping down. He was replaced by his deputy prime minister, Goh Chok Tong.

29    The UN Security Council, at the urging of the USA, authorized the use of force against Iraq if it did not withdraw totally from Kuwait by 15 Jan, 1991.

29    Andrei Lukanov, Bulgaria's acting premier, resigned along with his entire cabinet amid an opposition-led general strike.

NATIONAL
2     In an attempt to end a costly struggle for market share, Britain's two satellite television systems, Sky Television and British Satellite Broadcasting, agreed to merge.

11    Police seized an IRA arms cache in London and arrested two men.

22    Prime minister Margaret Thatcher, who had led Britain since 1979, announced her resignation after failing to defeat decisively a challenge for the Conservative Party leadership from ex-minister Michael Heseltine.

28    John Major became the new prime minister of Great Britain by winning a three-way contest for the Conservative Party leadership against foreign secretary Douglas Hurd and former cabinet minister Michael Heseltine.

30    British Aerospace announced the loss of 5,000 jobs in the military aircraft division, and Rover announced the closure of two assembly lines in Cowley.

GENERAL
5     Rabbi Meir Kahane, founder of the militant Jewish Defense League and Israel's extremist anti-Arab Kach party, was assassinated after giving a talk in a New York City hotel. He was shot by an Egyptian who claimed to be acting on his own.

12    Emperor Akihito was formally enthroned as the 125th monarch of Japan.

26    Matsushita Electric Industrial Co. of Japan agreed to acquire MCA Inc. for $6.59 billion in the largest acquisition ever of a

USA company by a Japanese one.

## DECEMBER 1990
INTERNATIONAL
1    Iraq accepted President Bush's offer to hold talks between USA Secretary of State Baker and Iraq's Foreign Minister Aziz.
1    Chadian President Habre fled to Cameroon, after his army was defeated in a fierce three-week rebel offensive.
2    West German Chancellor Helmut Kohl was elected chancellor of a united Germany.
4    President Ershad of Bangladesh resigned after eight weeks of antigovernment protests.
6    President Saddam Hussein said he would free all of the foreign hostages being held in Iraq and occupied Kuwait.
7    Bulgaria's Grand National Assembly elected Dimitar Popov, a political independent, to the post of premier.
7    The General Agreement on Trade and Tariffs (GATT) Uruguay Round of multilateral talks was suspended after negotiators failed to agree on a plan to reduce farm subsidies.
7–15  Violent clashes between Hindus and Muslims in several Indian cities left about 300 people dead, and 3,000 under arrest.
8–13  Most of the 2,000 Western hostages who had been held in Iraq and Kuwait for over four months, were flown to freedom.
8–18  The planned talks between the USA and Iraq over the Persian Gulf crisis foundered, as both sides argued over scheduling.
9    Lech Walesa, chairman of the onceoutlawed Solidarity labour movement, was elected president of Poland.
16   Jean-Bertrand Aristide, a leftist priest, was elected president in Haiti's first democratic elections.
17   Former East German Premier Lothar De Maziere resigned as vice chairman of Germany's Christian Democratic Union following renewed charges that he had cooperated with the former East German Communist security agency known as Stasi.
20   Soviet Foreign Minister Shevardnadze announced his resignation, complaining of conservative attacks on his policies. He issued warnings about a wave of conservatism and the approach of a dictatorship that threatened the government.
21   Saddam Hussein, in a German television interview, declared that he would not withdraw from Kuwait by the UN deadline.
23   Elections in Yugoslavia ended, leaving four of its six republics with nonCommunist governments.
27   Gennadi Yanayev was elected Soviet vice president by the Congress of People's

Deputies.

NATIONAL
2–4   The Conservative Party's selection of black barrister, John Taylor, as its candidate for a predominantly white district aroused some outspoken local opposition.
5    Environment Secretary Heseltine proposed a wide-ranging review of the community charge, or poll tax.
11   Trading of newly issued shares in 12 regional distributors of electricity in England and Wales began. The government sold the company shares in a privatization worth £5.18 billion.
15   Police arrested Asil Nadir, chairman of struggling Polly Peck PLC. He was charged with 18 counts of theft and false accounting in connection with the company's affairs.

GENERAL
2–10  The US Space Shuttle *Columbia* completed an astronomy mission bedevilled with plumbing problems, computer burnout and a bulky $60 million pointing device for its telescopes.
6    A 39-nation conference on the environmental protection of Antarctica ended without agreement.
31   Titleholder Gary Kasparov of the USSR won the world championship chess match against his countryman Anatoly Karpov.

## JANUARY 1991
INTERNATIONAL
1–2   Rebels of the Revolutionary Armed Forces of Colombia (FARC) killed at least 17 security agents in a two-day offensive.
4    The UN Security Council voted unanimously to condemn Israel's treatment of the Palestinians in the occupied territories.
6    Jorge Serrano Elias, an engineer and educator, was elected president of Guatemala in a runoff vote.
9    USA Secretary of State Baker and Iraqi Foreign Minister Aziz met for 6½ hours in Geneva, but failed to reach any agreement that would forestall war in the Persian Gulf.
12   US Congress passed a resolution authorizing President Bush to use military power to force Iraq out of Kuwait.
13   UN Secretary General Pérez de Cúellar left Baghdad after making no progress toward peace in talks there.
13   Soviet troops killed 15 protesters in Vilnius, capital of Lithuania, in a crackdown on pro-independence forces.
14   Two high-ranking PLO leaders were shot dead in Tunis. The PLO said that a bodyguard once linked to the Abu Nidal terrorist organization was the assassin.

| | |
|---|---|
| 15 | The Supreme Soviet confirmed Aleksandr A Bessmertnykh as the new foreign minister, succeeding Shevardnadze. |
| 15 | President Bush signed a National Security Directive committing the USA military to war with Iraq—to be revoked only in the event that Iraq began withdrawing from Kuwait. |
| 16 | A US-led international force launched air and missile attacks (in operation 'Desert Storm') on Iraq and Iraqi occupied Kuwait less than 17 hours after the expiration of the UN deadline for Iraqi withdrawal. |
| 17 | Iraq responded to attack by firing one Scud missile at Saudi Arabia and eight Scuds into Israel. More than 1,000 Allied air sorties took place in the first 14 hours of battle. |
| 17 | More than 100,000 antiwar protesters marched through Germany in the sixth straight day of protests there. |
| 20 | At least four Latvians were killed when elite Soviet 'black beret' interior ministry troops stormed the headquarters of the Latvian interior ministry in Riga. |
| 21 | Economic ministers of the Group of Seven (G-7) nations said that they would cooperate to keep the world markets stable for the duration of the Persian Gulf war. |
| 24 | More than 15,000 Allied air sorties flown in the Gulf War, with 23 aircraft lost. |
| 29 | Iraq began its first major ground offensive into Saudi Arabia. |

NATIONAL

| | |
|---|---|
| 3 | The government announced that seven Iraqi diplomats, another embassy staff member and 67 other Iraqis were being expelled from Britain. |
| 6 | Prime Minister John Major left for a tour of the Middle East to visit troops in the Gulf region as the UN deadline for Iraqi withdrawal from Kuwait approached. |
| 8 | One person was killed and 248 people injured when a commuter train from Kent crashed into the buffers of London's Cannon Street station. |
| 30 | The Confederation of British Industry (CBI) predicted a loss of 89,000 jobs in the first quarter of 1991. The CBI said no recovery was in sight for the current year. |

GENERAL

| | |
|---|---|
| 9 | A UN agency reported that drug abuse in many areas of the world appeared to be on the rise. |
| 10–11 | An auction of silver and paintings that had been acquired by the late Ferdinand Marcos and his widow, Imelda, brought in a total of $20.29 million at Christie's in New York City. |
| 13 | At least 40 South Africans were killed and 50 injured when fighting erupted during a football match at Orkney between two popular black teams from Soweto. |
| 24 | The USA federal Centers for Disease Control said that of the 161,073 persons in the USA reported to have developed AIDS since June 1981, a total of 100,777 had died by the end of Dec 1990. |

## FEBRUARY 1991
INTERNATIONAL

| | |
|---|---|
| 1 | The Israeli government of Prime Minister Shamir signed an agreement with the extremist Moledet (Homeland) Party to allow it into the ruling coalition. |
| 1 | President de Klerk announced plans to abolish the remaining laws on which South Africa's apartheid system was based. |
| 2 | The ANC welcomed de Klerk's proposals, but urged the international community to maintain sanctions against South Africa until fundamental changes take place. |
| 8 | Colombian officials reported that at least 63 people had died in rebel attacks around the country 5–7 Feb. |
| 9 | The republic of Lithuania, still reeling from the Kremlin crackdown on the Baltic region, held a nonbinding plebiscite on independence which showed overwhelming support for secession. |
| 12 | China handed out its harshest punishments yet for activities associated with the prodemocracy demonstrations of 1989. The two defendants were each given sentences of 13 years. |
| 19 | The president of the Russian Federation, Boris Yeltsin, in his strongest criticism of Gorbachev to date, demanded the Soviet president's resignation. |
| 22 | Albanian President Ramiz Alia announced an assertion of emergency presidential rule and appointed a new government to end a wave of prodemocracy protests that had shaken his regime. |
| 23 | The rebel Ethiopian People's Revolutionary Democratic Forces launched an offensive against government troops in an effort to overrun the northwestern Gondar and Gojam provinces. |
| 25 | Ministers of the six Warsaw Pact nations signed an agreement to disband the alliance's military structure by 31 March. |
| 26 | Khaleda Zia, widow of the general who had ruled Bangladesh from 1976 to 1981, was elected prime minister. |

NATIONAL

| | |
|---|---|
| 2 | An antiwar protest was held in London's Hyde Park, attended by more than 40,000 people. |
| 7 | Prime Minister Major and his senior cabinet ministers escaped an apparent assassination attempt when three mortar shells were fired at 10 Downing Street from a parked van. The IRA later claimed responsibility for the attack. |

13 The Bank of England engineered a decrease in commmercial banks' base lending rates, to stimulate the weak economy.

14 The government reported that the number of unemployed Britons rose by almost 110,000 in Jan (the largest monthly gain in five years) bringing the total number to 1.9 million.

18 A bomb exploded at the Victoria Station railway terminal in London, killing one man and injuring 40 other people. The IRA later claimed responsibility for the attack. Following the attack all mainline railway stations in London were temporarily closed, affecting an estimated 500,000 commuters.

19 An Iranian newspaper reported Iraqi war casualties at more than 20,000 dead, and 60,000 wounded.

21 The USSR announced that Iraq agreed to a proposal for withdrawal from Kuwait.

22 In the wake of the Soviet-Iraqi peace initiative, President Bush set a noon Feb 23 deadline for Iraq to commence a large-scale withdrawal from Kuwait, or face a ground assault from the Allied forces.

23 The deadline was not met, and the Allied ground offensive on Iraq began.

24 Large numbers of Iraqi soldiers surrendered.

25 Baghdad announced orders for Iraqi soldiers to withdraw from Kuwait.

26 Kuwait resistance leaders claimed control over Kuwait City. Approximately 600 Kuwaiti oil wells were reported ablaze.

27 US Army VII Corps engaged the Iraqi Republican Guard in a major tank battle. President Bush announced at 9.00 pm that Kuwait was liberated, and that the Allies would cease fire.

28 Iraq announced a cease-fire. Total allied combat fatalities were 141. Estimates of Iraqi troops and civilians killed and wounded ranged up to 100,000.

GENERAL

4 Richard W Miller, a former FBI agent, was sentenced in Los Angeles to 20 years in prison for espionage. He had been arrested after it was discovered that he had been having an affair with a Soviet agent, Svetlana Ogorodnikova.

6 Debris from Salyut 7, a Soviet space station abandoned in 1986, reentered the Earth's atmosphere. Much of the craft was believed to have landed in the Atlantic Ocean, but some pieces were reportedly found in Argentina.

9 World Boxing Council Superwelterweight Champion Terry Norris won a unanimous 12-round decision over Sugar Ray Leonard in New York City.

**MARCH 1991**
INTERNATIONAL

1 The first reports of a revolt led by Shi'ite

Muslims and other opponents of the regime in Basra, Iraq began to emerge.

3 Iraqi military commanders accepted the cease-fire terms imposed by the multinational coalition forces.

3 The peoples of the republics of Estonia and Latvia voted for independence from the Soviet Union in non-binding plebiscites.

4 Kuwait's crown prince and premier Sheik Saad Al-Abdallah Al-Sabah returned to Kuwait.

4–7 About 20,000 Albanians sought political asylum in Italy. Most of the Albanians arrived by boat, in what was the third major exodus from Albania in eight months.

5 Iraq freed the last 45 Allied prisoners of war.

6 Indian Prime Minister Chandra Shekhar resigned following the withdrawal of support for his government by the Congress Party.

7 Anti-government unrest or hostilities were reported in more than 15 different Iraqi cities. In northern Iraq, minority Kurdish rebels claimed control over several areas.

7–8 Iraq freed about 1,200 Kuwaiti prisoners of war, the first of some 2,000 detainees the Red Cross said Iraq would release.

7–14 US Secretary of State Baker toured the Middle East seeking to promote a new dialogue between Arabs and Israelis.

9 The final draft of Gorbachev's proposed union treaty was made public. The revised document called for a transformation of the nation into a 'federative democratic state.'

12 South African President de Klerk introduced a legislative package that would scrap all racial discrimination in land ownership and allow South Africans to live where they chose.

13 As unrest continued in at least two dozen Iraqi cities, it was reported that unrest had begun in Baghdad.

14 Ethiopian rebel armies made key advances in several regions against government troops.

15–19 Yugoslavia was plunged into political chaos, as the federal collective presidency was crippled by resignations, the republic of Serbia renounced obedience to the national government and the threat of a military takeover increased.

22 An American F-15C fighter jet downed an Iraqi SU-22 warplane in northern Iraq, in the second such attack in three days. The two incidents of air combat came amid continuing widespread antigovernment unrest in Iraq and following USA warnings that the use of military aircraft by Iraq would be a violation of the preliminary cease-fire terms.

26 The Bush administration formally indicated that the USA would not aid rebels

seeking to overthrow the Iraqi government.

26 Kurdish rebels fighting against loyalist troops in northern Iraq seized a military base and airfield near Kirkuk.

NATIONAL

7 The Conservative Party was dealt a surprising defeat in a by-election for the parliamentary seat in Ribble Valley, Lancashire. The Liberal Democratic candidate Michael Carr bested Conservative Nigel Evans by 4,601 votes.

8 The bodies of 17 British troops killed in the Gulf war were flown home to a sombre ceremony at Brize Norton Air Base.

14 Six men born in Northern Ireland were freed from prison after serving 16 years of a life sentence for the 1974 bombing of two pubs in Birmingham. The appeal that won their freedom had been their third.

21 The government announced that it would scrap the unpopular year-old poll tax system. Environment Secretary Heseltine said that a successor to the poll tax would be based on both property values and the size of households.

GENERAL

11 A British family planning agency created a stir when it confirmed that it had been providing artificial insemination treatment to an unidentified woman who was a virgin and who said she had no intention of ever having sex.

20 British publisher Robert Maxwell took ownership of the New York *Daily News*.

25 *Dances with Wolves*, a film which Kevin Costner directed and starred in, won seven Academy Awards including that for best film.

27 The Commission on Apartheid and Olympism announced that South Africa would be readmitted to the Olympic Games if it met five key conditions, which included the abolition of apartheid laws, within the next six months.

**APRIL 1991**
INTERNATIONAL

1 The Iraqi Kurdistan Front issued a statement urging the USA, the UK, and France to take action on behalf of the insurgents in Iraq.

3 The UN Security Council approved a resolution to establish a permanent cease-fire in the Gulf war and bring about a gradual halt to international sanctions against Iraq. Resolution 687 set forth stern financial and military conditions intended to limit Iraq's ability to make war on its neighbours.

3–10 At least one million Iraqi civilians, most of them Kurds, fled to Turkey and Iran to escape the Iraqi army.

4 President Bush conferred with Japanese Premier Kaifu in an effort to smooth frictions over world trade and the Gulf war.

5 President Bush said he planned to authorize the release of $10 million from refugee relief funds to benefit the Kurds.

5 The ANC issued an ultimatum to South African President de Klerk warning that it would pull out of negotiations on a new constitution unless the government met seven demands aimed at stopping the factional violence in black townships by 9 May.

6 The Iraqi government accepted the cease-fire terms of UN Resolution 687, bringing a formal end to the Gulf war.

8 The European Community pledged 150 million Ecu (about $187 million) in aid to the Kurds.

9 The parliament of the southern republic of Georgia unanimously voted to declare independence from the Soviet Union.

9 Iraq announced that it would reject any attempt to establish special protective zones for Kurdish refugees in northern Iraq.

9 The Soviet Union began withdrawing its military forces from Poland.

10 Israeli Housing Minister Sharon announced that he would continue to foster Jewish settlement in occupied territories.

15 The main opposition group in Albania, the Democratic Party, boycotted the opening of the newly elected People's Assembly.

17 Christian Democrat Giulio Andreotti presented his new coalition government, the 50th for Italy since 1945.

17–19 Soviet President Gorbachev and Japanese Premier Kaifu met in Tokyo during the first ever visit by a Soviet president to Japan. In three days of talks the two leaders failed to resolve the key territorial dispute (the Kurile Islands) dividing their nations.

17–23 US, French, and British soldiers crossed from Turkey into northern Iraq to secure a 'safe zone' and build camps for some of the 850,000 Iraqi refugees who were stranded along the Iraq-Turkey border.

30 Taiwanese President Lee Teng-hui formally declared an end to the 43-year period of emergency rule that had perpetuated a state of war with mainland China.

30 Thousands of people were drowned and millions left homeless when a cyclone struck coastal areas and offshore islands in the Ganges Delta of Bangladesh. The official death toll was 125,730.

NATIONAL

1 Iranian authorities released British businessman Roger Cooper from prison in Tehran. Cooper had been held in Iran since Dec 1985 on charges of espionage.

12 The UK government and the Bank of England engineered a 0.5% cut in commercial banks' base lending rates. The government also announced a sharp decline in the country's annual inflation rate.

23 The government outlined its plan for a system to replace the poll tax. The new 'council tax' would be based on property values, rather than on the per capita principle of the poll tax.

30 Secretary of State for Northern Ireland Peter Brooke held the first round of talks in Belfast on the question of the future governance of Northern Ireland.

GENERAL

6 Diego Maradona, considered one of the world's top football players, was suspended from international football for 15 months. The Argentine star had tested positive for cocaine and had recently been questioned in Naples in connection with a prostitution and drug-smuggling operation.

11 The supertanker *Haven*, carrying one million barrels of heavy crude oil exploded in the Mediterranean Sea, three miles off the coast of Genoa, Italy. Three members of the Greek ship's crew were killed and an oilslick 10–24 km/6–15 mi long resulting from the explosion threatened pollution of the nearby French and Italian rivieras.

11 The USA Space Shuttle *Atlantis* completed a six-day mission in which astronauts launched into orbit an astronomy satellite, practised techniques for assembling a space station and logged a total of 22 hours of spacewalking.

**MAY 1991**
INTERNATIONAL

1 The Angolan government and the rebel National Union for Total Independence of Angola (UNITA) initialled an agreement to end their civil war of 16 years and to hold the nation's first elections.

6–7 A 1,440 member UN peacekeeping force took control of a demilitarized zone along the Iraq-Kuwait border in compliance with UN Resolution 687, ending US occupation of southern Iraq.

7 Bangladeshi officials said the country would need a total of $1.41 billion for relief and reconstruction, of which $670 million was needed for immediate relief.

8 At least 47 people were killed in clashes between Indian army troops and proindependence demonstrators in Jammu and Kashmir.

9 Yugoslavia's collective presidency voted to give the military sweeping powers to end the ethnic fighting in Croatia.

9 Albanian Premier Fatos Nano unveiled a 25-member cabinet made up entirely of members of the ruling Albanian Workers' Party.

10–16 USA Secretary of State Baker returned to the Middle East for the fourth time in 10 weeks, in an attempt to reach an Arab-Israeli agreement on the terms of a US and Soviet sponsored peace conference. Both Israel and Syria rejected compromises regarding the UN's role in such a conference and other issues.

13 Officials from the UN Office of the High Commissioner for Refugees took over from USA military personnel the administration of an encampment of Kurdish refugees in the allied 'safe zone' near Zakho, Iraq.

15 French Premier Michel Rocard resigned, and President Mitterrand named Socialist Edith Cresson to replace him, thus becoming France's first female premier.

18 The ANC broke off power-sharing talks with the government until more progress was made on meeting ANC demands to do with curbing violence in black townships.

21 Indian Congress (I) Party leader and former Prime Minister Rajiv Gandhi was killed by a bomb blast on an election campaign stop in Sriperumbudur, 40 km/25 mi southwest of Madras.

21 Ethiopia's president, Lt Col Mengistu Haile Mariam, resigned and fled the country as government forces failed to check an advance by rebel forces on Addis Ababa, the capital.

27–30 The Ethiopian government surrendered to the rebel forces. Despite a ban on public demonstrations imposed by the new interim government, disturbances and violence in Addis Ababa continued.

29 India's Congress (I) Party named the veteran loyalist P V Narasimha Rao as leader and successor to Rajiv Gandhi to see the party through a crucial second round of elections.

NATIONAL

2 Local elections in England and Wales produced surprisingly strong support for the Liberal Democrats. According to a BBC analysis of the voting, Labour won 37% of the votes cast to 36% for the Conservatives and 21% for the Liberal Democrats.

9 The former publicity director of Sinn Fein, Danny Morrison, was convicted in Belfast on a charge of false imprisonment and was sentenced to eight years in jail. He had been charged with complicity in the false imprisonment of an IRA informer, Alexander Lynch.

16 The Coservative Party lost a by-election in Monmouth. Labour candidate Huw Edwards defeated Tory Roger Evans by 2,406 votes.

28 Transport Secretary Malcolm Rifkind announced that private firms would be able to compete with British Rail to provide

passenger and freight service.

GENERAL

2      Pope John Paul II, in a papal encyclical, expressed support for the economic concept of capitalism.

3      The Swiss Federal Banking Commission announced regulations that would phase out most of the nation's famed secret bank accounts by Sept 1992.

5–6    Riots erupted in the largely Hispanic neighbourhood of Mount Pleasant in Washington DC, after the shooting of a Hispanic man by a police officer.

14     Winnie Mandela, the controversial wife of ANC leader Nelson Mandela, was convicted of charges arising from the abduction and beating of four black youths at her Soweto home in 1988. She was sentenced to six years in prison.

26     A Lauda Air Boeing 767, on flight from Bangkok to Vienna, exploded in a fireball and crashed in jungle in Thailand. The 223 people on board were killed.

# ON THIS DAY

## JANUARY

1   Queen Victoria was proclaimed Empress of India in Delhi. *1887*
2   Cardinal Richelieu established the Académie Française. *1635*
3   English explorer Howard Carter discovered the sarcophagus of Tutankhamun in the Valley of the Kings, near Luxor, Egypt. *1924*
4   The attack on Monte Cassino was launched by the British Fifth Army in Italy. *1944*
5   Charles the Bold was killed by the Swiss at the battle of Nancy. *1477*
6   The Committee of Inquiry on the South Sea Bubble published its findings. *1720*
7   Calais, the last English possession on mainland France, was recaptured by the French. *1558*
8   The final withdrawal of Allied troops from Gallipoli took place. *1916*
9   New York State introduced a bill to outlaw flirting in public. *1902*
10  The first meeting of the United Nations General Assembly took place in London. *1946*
11  Leonard Thompson became the first person to be successfully treated with insulin. *1922*
12  Kwang-su was made emperor of China. *1875*
13  The Independent British Labour Party was formed by Keir Hardie. *1893*
14  The king of Denmark ceded Norway to the king of Sweden. *1814*
15  President Nixon called a halt to the USA's Vietnam offensive. *1973*
16  Ivan the Terrible was crowned first Tsar of Russia. *1547*
17  Captain Cook's *Resolution* became the first ship to cross the Antarctic Circle. *1773*
18  The Versailles Peace Conference opened. *1919*
19  John Wilkes was expelled from the House of Commons for seditious libel. *1764*
20  Hong Kong was ceded by China and occupied by the British. *1841*
21  Louis XVI, King of France, was found guilty of treason and guillotined. *1793*
22  Insurgent workers were fired upon in St Petersburg, resulting in 'Bloody Sunday'. *1905*
23  The first British Labour government was formed, under Ramsey McDonald. *1924*
24  Beer in cans was first sold, in Virginia, by the Kreuger Brewing Company. *1935*
25  King Henry VIII and Ann Boleyn were secretly married. *1533*
26  Vincente Yanez Pinzon discovered Brazil and claimed it for Portugal. *1500*
27  The US Air Force carried out its first bombing raid on Germany. *1943*
28  The US Space Shuttle *Challenger* exploded shortly after liftoff from Cape Canaveral, killing five men and two women on board. *1986*
29  The first successful petrol-driven motor car, built by Karl Benz, was patented. *1886*
30  The Commonwealth of England was established upon the execution of Charles I. *1649*
31  The Soviet government expelled Leon Trotsky and he went into exile. *1929*

## FEBRUARY

1   Ayatollah Khomeini returned to Iran after 14 years of exile in France. *1979*
2   Greece declared war on Turkey. *1878*
3   The first rocket-asssisted controlled landing on the moon was made by the Soviet space vehicle Luna IX. *1966*
4   Roosevelt, Churchill, and Stalin met at Yalta. *1945*
5   Glenn Miller recorded 'Tuxedo Junction' with his orchestra. *1940*
6   Britain declared war on France. *1778*
7   Edward Caernarvon (later King Edward II) became the first Prince of Wales. *1301*
8   Odessa was taken by Bolshevik forces. *1920*
9   Lieutenant Dawson's expedition in search of Dr Livingstone began. *1872*
10  Canada was ceded to Britain by the Peace of Paris. *1763*
11  The Virgin Mary is said to have appeared to three young girls in Lourdes. *1858*
12  Independence was proclaimed by Chile. *1818*
13  Britain, Prussia, Austria, Holland, Spain and Sardinia formed an alliance against France. *1793*
14  Captain Cook was stabbed to death by natives in the Sandwich Islands (now Hawaii). *1779*
15  The first shipment of frozen meat left New Zealand for England. *1882*
16  Fidel Castro became Cuban premier. *1959*
17  The British parliament voted to join the European Common Market. *1972*
18  The planet Pluto was discovered by Clyde Tombaugh at Lowell Observatory in the USA. *1930*
19  Napoleon Bonaparte established himself in the Tuileries as First Consul. *1800*
20  Austria announced that it was bankrupt. *1811*
21  The Germans launched an all-out attack on the French fortress of Verdun. *1916*
22  Florida was purchased by the United States from Spain. *1819*
23  Captains Speke and Grant announced the discovery of the source of the Nile. *1863*
24  Louis-Philippe of France abdicated. *1848*
25  Cassius Clay (later Muhammad Ali) won the world heavyweight boxing title for the first time in Miami. *1964*
26  A severe earthquake in Lisbon resulted in the loss of an estimated 20,000 lives. *1531*
27  The British were defeated by the Boers at the battle of Majuba, South Africa. *1881*
28  Albert Berry made the first parachute jump

from a plane over Missouri. *1912*

29   Hugh Heffner opened the first Playboy Club in Chicago. *1960*

## MARCH

1   Mozambique, on the southeastern coast of Africa, was discovered by Vasco de Gama. *1498*

2   Nicholas II, the last Russian tsar, was forced to abdicate. *1917*

3   Beethoven's Moonlight Sonata was published. *1802*

4   The *Nautilus*, USA atomic submarine, passed under the North Pole ice cap. *1958*

5   The Nazis won almost half the seats in the German elections. *1933*

6   The Alamo fell to Mexican forces commanded by Santa Anna. *1836*

7   Alexander Graham Bell patented the first telephone capable of relaying sustained articulate speech. *1876*

8   Queen Anne acceded to the British throne. *1702*

9   The first battle of iron-clad ships took place during the American Civil War. *1862*

10   A Japanese soldier was discovered on Lubang Island in the Philippines who believed that World War II was still continuing. *1974*

11   A Maori uprising against the British in New Zealand began. *1845*

12   Mahatma Gandhi began a campaign of civil disobedience in India. *1930*

13   The planet Uranus was discovered by the German-born English astronomer William Herschel. *1781*

14   The first telephone cable was laid across the British Channel. *1891*

15   Julius Caesar was assassinated by Brutus and others in Rome. *44 BC*

16   The first liquid-fuelled rocket was launched, by Dr Robert Goddard in the USA. *1926*

17   The British were forced to evacuate Boston by George Washington. *1776*

18   Napoleon Bonaparte was proclaimed Emperor of France. *1804*

19   The USA Senate rejected the Versailles Treaty. *1920*

20   The Dutch East India Company was founded by the Netherlands government to trade with the East Indies. *1602*

21   The 'Sharpeville Massacre' took place when South African police opened fire on demonstrators, killing 56 and injuring 162. *1960*

22   The English were defeated by the Scots at Anjou. *1421*

23   The Fascist Party was founded by Benito Mussolini. *1919*

24   Greece was formally declared a republic. *1924*

25   Tuscany was occupied by French Troops. *1799*

26   The seven men accused of the £2.5 million 'Great Train Robbery' (8 Aug 1963) were found guilty in London. *1964*

27   The world's worst aviation disaster took place, when two jumbo jets collided on the ground at Tenerife airport killing 574 people. *1977*

28   The Irish parliament passed the Act of Union with England. *1800*

29   The Battle of Towton took place in north Yorkshire in a snowstorm during the War of the Roses—the bloodiest battle ever fought on British soil, in which it was said that over 28,000 died. *1461*

30   Alaska was sold by Russia to the USA for $7.2 million (approximately two cents an acre). *1867*

31   The 300 m/884 ft Eiffel Tower was completed in readiness for the Universal Exhibition in Paris. *1889*

## APRIL

1   The invasion of Okinawa by USA forces began. *1945*

2   The British annexed the Punjab. *1849*

3   Stalin was appointed as General Secretary of the Communist Party. *1922*

4   Eleven countries signed the North Atlantic Treaty in Washington DC. *1949*

5   Kissing was banned on the French railways because it would cause delays. *1910*

6   Robert Peary became the first man to reach the North Pole, at his sixth attempt in 15 years. *1909*

7   The notorious highwayman Richard Turpin was hanged in York. *1739*

8   The first Home Rule for Ireland bill was introduced by WE Gladstone. *1886*

9   Confederate General Robert E Lee surrendered to General Grant at Appomattox Court House in Virginia, bringing the American Civil War to an end. *1865*

10   The Prussians defeated the Austrians at Molwitz, *1741*

11   Napoleon abdicated as Emperor, and was exiled to the island of Elba. *1814*

12   The Fourth Crusade was diverted by the Venetians to the riches of Constantinople. *1204*

13   The Anti-Semitic League was founded and a petition presented to Bismarck demanding restrictions on the liberty of Prussian Jews. *1882*

14   USA President Abraham Lincoln was assassinated in Ford's Theatre in Washington by John Wilkes Booth. *1865*

15   The SS *Titanic* sank on its maiden voyage and over 1,500 people were drowned. *1912*

16   The Senate in Rome appointed two emperors, D Caelinus Balbinus to run civil affairs, and M Clodius Pupierus Maximus to commmand the legions. *238*

17   The sea broke through the dykes at Dort in Holland and an estimated 100,000 people were drowned. *1421*

18   The first launderette was opened in Fort Worth, Texas by JF Cantrell, and called a 'Washeteria'. *1934*

19   Halley's Comet reappeared. *1910*

20   The Spanish fleet was destroyed in the harbour of Santa Cruz by the English under

Admiral Blake. *1657*

21 Over 100,000 Chinese students poured into Tiananmen Square, ignoring government warnings of severe punishment. *1989*

22 Pedro Alvarez Cabral discovered Brazil and claimed it on behalf of the King of Portugal. *1500*

23 The USA announced the discovery of the AIDS virus. *1984*

24 Captain Joshua Slocum set sail, in his sloop *Spray*, on his single-handed voyage around the world (completed 27 June 1898). *1895*

25 Work began on the construction of the 161 km/100 mi Suez Canal, under the direction of Ferdinand de Lesseps. *1859*

26 The largest underground nuclear device ever to be tested in the USA exploded in Nevada. *1968*

27 Guernica in northern Spain was destroyed in a blitz by German planes. *1937*

28 Captain Cook, Sir Joseph Banks and others landed in Australia, in what is now known as Botany Bay, and named the country New South Wales. *1770*

29 Women were first admitted to Oxford University examinations. *1885*

30 Galerius Valerius Maximianus issued an edict at Nicomedia which gave legal recognition to Christians by the Roman Empire. *311*

**MAY**

1 The German Army in Italy surrendered to the Allies. *1945*

2 The Emperor Haile Selassie and his family fled from the Abyssinian capital, Addis Ababa, three days before it fell to Italian forces. *1936*

3 The first duel fought from two hot air balloons took place above Paris. *1808*

4 The Geneva Conference on arms, poison gas, and related matters began. *1925*

5 The next conjunction of the Sun, Moon, Mercury, Venus, Mars, Jupiter, and Saturn will take place. *2000*

6 Manhattan Island, now a borough of New York City, was bought from the native indians by Peter Minuit for trinkets worth no more than $25. *1626*

7 A German submarine torpedoed and sank the *Lusitania* off the coast of Ireland; around 1,400 people were drowned. *1915*

8 Dr Pemberton first produced the world's top-selling soft drink, Coca-Cola, in Atlanta, Georgia. *1886*

9 Disguised as a clergyman, Colonel Thomas Blood attempted to steal the Crown Jewels from the Tower of London. *1671*

10 The Sepoy Revolt broke out in Meerat, triggering the Indian mutiny against British rule. *1857*

11 The first printed book, known as the *Diamond Sutra*, was published in China. *868*

12 The Russian blockade of Berlin, which had lasted 11 months, was lifted. *1949*

13 A state of emergency was declared in Kuala Lumpur, Malaysia, after continued fighting between Malays and Chinese. *1969*

14 Louis XIV ascended the throne of France, aged 4 years, and reigned for over 72 years. *1643*

15 Soviet troops began their evacuation from Afganistan after more than eight years of occupation. *1988*

16 The first meeting of Dr Johnson and James Boswell took place at Tom Davie's bookshop in Russell Street, London. *1763*

17 The first 'package holiday', arranged by Thomas Cook, set out from London Bridge on a six-day trip to Paris. *1861*

18 Ville Marie (Montreal) was formally founded. *1642*

19 Ann Boleyn, Henry VIII's second wife and mother of Queen Elizabeth I, was beheaded. *1536*

20 The Spanish Armada, under the command of the Duke of Medina, set sail from Lisbon in an attempt to invade England. *1588*

21 Charles Lindbergh became the first to fly the Atlantic solo, from New York to Paris in 33.5 hours. *1927*

22 Ceylon was declared a republic and changed its name to Sri Lanka. *1972*

23 Marlborough defeated the French at the battle of Ramilles in Belgium. *1706*

24 The first morse message over a telegraph line was transmitted from Washington to Baltimore by Samuel Morse, its inventor. *1844*

25 The Philadelphia Convention met under George Washington to draw up the USA constitution. *1787*

26 The last public execution in England took place, outside Newgate Prison in London. *1868*

27 Tsar Peter the Great proclaimed St Petersburg the new capital of Russia. *1703*

28 Belgian King Leopold III surrendered to Germany. *1940*

29 Constantinople fell to the Turkish army after a year's seige. *1453*

30 Joan of Arc was burned at the stake in Rouen. *1431*

31 The colonies of the Cape of Good Hope, Natal, Transvaal and the Orange River Colony became united to form the Union of South Africa. *1910*

**JUNE**

1 The first attack on London by Zeppelins took place. *1915*

2 The coronation of Queen Elizabeth II, the first to be televised, took place. *1953*

3 The first 'bikini' bathing suit was unveiled in Paris. *1946*

4 The evacuation of allied forces from Dunkirk, which had begun 27 May, was completed. *1940*

5 The 'Six Day War' between Israel and Egypt, Jordan, Syria, and Iraq began. *1967*

6 'Operation Overlord', the allied landings on the coast of Normandy, took place. *1944*

7 The Addled Parliament was dissolved without having passed a Bill since it first sat on

5 April—hence its name. *1614*

8 George Mallory, on his third attempt to climb Mount Everest, was last seen at a point some 244 m/800 ft below the summit. *1924*

9 Hong Kong was leased by Britain from the Chinese for 99 years. *1898*

10 The first of 19 people were hanged at Salem at the end of the hysterical witch hunt trials conducted by Judge Corwin. *1692*

11 Henry VIII married Spanish Princess Catherine of Aragon, the first of his six wives. *1509*

12 Abner Doubleday invented baseball in Cooperstown, New York. *1839*

13 The Boxer Rebellion, led by a secret society originally formed to promote boxing, began in China to end foreign domination. *1900*

14 Argentinian forces formally surrendered to the British task force in the Falkland Islands. *1982*

15 The Magna Carta was stamped with the Royal seal by King John at Runnnymede, near Windsor. *1215*

16 A Cathay Pacific's Catalina flying boat on a scheduled flight to Hong Kong was the first plane to be hijacked, by a gang of Chinese bandits. *1948*

17 Sir Francis Drake anchored the *Golden Hind* just north of what would later be named San Francisco Bay. *1579*

18 The combined forces led by the Duke of Wellington and von Blucher defeated Napoleon at the Battle of Waterloo. *1815*

19 Ethel and Julius Rosenberg were executed in New York, the first US civilians to go to the electric chair for espionage. *1953*

20 146 British subjects were imprisoned by the Nawab of Bengal in a dungeon known as the 'Black Hole of Calcutta'; only 23 survived overnight. *1756*

21 Tobruk fell to Rommel with the capture of 25,000 Allied troops. *1943*

22 The first cricket match was played at the present Lord's ground in London. *1814*

23 General Nasser became Egypt's first president, after an election in which voting was compulsory, and he was the only candidate. *1956*

24 The first Freemason Lodge was inaugurated in London. *1717*

25 General Custer led US troops against the Sioux Indians at the Little Bighorn in Montana, and he and his 264 soldiers of the 7th Cavalry were massacred. *1876*

26 The first Grand Prix took place at Le Mans, and was won by the Hungarian Ferenc Szisz, driving a Renault at an average speed of 63 mph. *1906*

27 The *Ladies' Mercury*, the first magazine for women, was published. *1693*

28 The Archduke Ferdinand of Austria and his wife were assassinated in Sarajevo, by terrorist Gavrillo Princip. *1914*

29 Tahiti was annexed by France. *1880*

30 Montezuma, the last Aztec ruler, was killed by his own subjects in Mexico City during the Spanish Conquest of Mexico under Cortes. *1520*

**JULY**

1 Charles Darwin, together with Alfred Russell Wallace, presented a paper to the Linnean Society in London, on his theory of the evolution of the species. *1838*

2 President Johnson signed the USA Civil Rights Bill prohibiting racial discrimination. *1964*

3 French explorer, Samuel Champlain, founded Quebec. *1608*

4 The Philippine Islands were given independence by the USA. *1946*

5 Israel annexed Gaza. *1967*

6 Sir Thomas More was beheaded in London. *1535*

7 The unseeded 17-year-old Boris Becker became the youngest ever men's singles champion at Wimbledon. *1985*

8 Vasco de Gama left Lisbon for a voyage on which he discovered the Cape route to India. *1497*

9 Argentina declared independence from Spain. *1816*

10 The Yorkists defeated the Lancastrians and captured Henry VI at the battle of Northampton. *1460*

11 America's *Skylab I* returned to earth after 34,981 orbits and six years in space. *1979*

12 President Wilson opened the Panama Canal. *1920*

13 Queen Victoria became the first sovereign to move into Buckingham Palace. *1837*

14 The Bastille was stormed by the citizens of Paris and razed to the ground as the French Revolution began. *1789*

15 Jerusalem was captured by the Crusaders with troops led by Godfrey and Robert of Flanders and Tancred of Normandy. *1099*

16 The first atomic bomb developed by Robert Oppenheimer and his team at Los Alamos was exploded in New Mexico. *1945*

17 The British royal family changed their name from 'House of Saxe-Coburg-Gotha' to 'House of Windsor'. *1917*

18 The Spanish Civil War began with an army revolt led by Francisco Franco against the Republican government. *1936*

19 At a convention in Seneca Falls, New York, female rights campaigner Amelia Bloomer introduced 'bloomers' to the world. *1848*

20 Charles Sturt became the first white man to enter Simpson's Desert in Central Australia. *1845*

21 The lunar module from *Apollo 11* landed on the Moon, and US astronauts Armstrong and Aldrin took their first exploratory walk. *1969*

22 American bank robber and 'public enemy no. 1', John Dillinger, was gunned down by an FBI squad in Chicago. *1934*

23 Dr Livingstone returned to England. *1864*

24 Admiral Sir George Rooke captured Gibraltar from the Spaniards. *1704*

25 Magarethe Geertruida Zelle, the Dutch spy known as 'Mata Hari', was sentenced to death. *1917*

26 Liberia became the first African colony to secure independence. *1847*

27 The Korean armistice was signed at Panmunjom, ending three years of war. *1953*

28 The first potato arrived in Britain, brought from Colombia by Thomas Harriot. *1786*

29 The Spanish Armada was defeated by the English fleet under Howard and Drake, off Plymouth. *1588*

30 The world's first radar station was opened, to assist shipping at the port of Liverpool. *1948*

31 The Weimar Republic was established in post-war Germany. *1919*

---

**AUGUST**

1 The first savings bank was opened, in Hamburg. *1778*

2 Iraq invaded Kuwait causing an international crisis. *1990*

3 La Scala Opera House opened in Milan. *1778*

4 Britain declared war on Germany after the Germans had violated the Treaty of London, and the First World War began. *1914*

5 The first transatlantic cable was opened when Queen Victoria exchanged greetings with US President Buchanan. *1858*

6 An atomic bomb was dropped on the Japanese city of Hiroshima from a US Boeing B29 bomber. *1945*

7 Queen Victoria chose Ottawa as the capital of the Dominion of Canada. *1858*

8 Richard Nixon became the first US president to resign from office in face of threats to impeach him for his implication in the Watergate scandal. *1974*

9 The frontier between Canada and the USA was defined by the Webster-Ashburton treaty, signed by the USA and Britain. *1842*

10 Mozart completed his popular 'Eine kleine Nachtmusik'. *1787*

11 Canton was entered by Chiang Kai-shek and his supporters. *1963*

12 The first communications satellite was launched—America's *Echo I*. *1969*

13 The Battle of Blenheim took place in southern Germany, in which the Anglo-Austrian army inflicted a decisive defeat on the French and Bavarian armies. *1704*

14 The first British troops were deployed in Northern Ireland to restore order. *1969*

15 The Tivoli Pleasure Gardens were opened in Copenhagen. *1843*

16 The Peterloo Massacre took place in Manchester when militia opened fire on a crowd gathered to hear discussion of reform, killing eleven people. *1819*

17 Gold was discovered at Bonanza Creek in Canada's Yukon Territory, leading to the great gold rush of 1898. *1896*

18 The first oral contraceptive was marketed by the Searle Drug Company in the USA. *1960*

19 France and Spain formed an alliance against Britain. *1796*

20 Russian and troops of other communist countries invaded Czechoslovakia. *1968*

21 Leonardo da Vinci's painting the *Mona Lisa* was stolen from the Louvre in Paris—it was recovered two years later. *1911*

22 The Civil War in England began, between the supporters of Charles I (Royalists or Cavaliers) and of Parliament (Roundheads), when the king raised his standard at Nottingham. *1642*

23 The Blitz began as German bombers launched an all-night raid on London. *1940*

24 The Visigoths, led by Alaric, sacked Rome. *410*

25 Daily flights between Paris and London began, starting the first scheduled international air service. *1919*

26 The French Assembly adopted the Declaration of the Rights of Man. *1789*

27 Krakatoa, a volcanic island in the Sunda Strait between Sumatra and Java, erupted with thousands killed by the resulting tidal waves. *1883*

28 Venice was taken by the Austrians after a seige. *1849*

29 The 100-ton battleship HMS *Royal George* sank off Spithead while at anchor, with the loss of 900 lives. *1782*

30 The seige of Leningrad by German forces began (ended in Jan 1943) *1941*

31 Mary Ann 'Polly' Nichols, the first victim of Jack the Ripper, was found mutilated in Buck's Row. *1888*

---

**SEPTEMBER**

1 Germany invaded Poland, starting World War II. *1939*

2 The Great Fire of London started; it destroyed 13,000 buildings in four days. *1666*

3 Britain recognized US independence with the signing of a treaty in Paris. *1783*

4 Emperor Napoleon III, Bonaparte's nephew, was deposed and the Third Republic was proclaimed. *1870*

5 The world's longest road tunnel, the St Gotthard, was opened; it ran ten miles from Goschenen to Airolo, Switzerland. *1980*

6 After three years voyaging the *Vittoria*, which had set out under the command of Ferdinand Magellan, sailed into San Lucar harbour in Spain with 17 surviving crew members having completed the first circumnavigation of the world. *1522*

7 Bishop Desmond Tutu was appointed Archbishop of Capetown, the first black head of South African Anglicans. *1986*

8 The Dutch colony of New Amsterdam was surrendered to the British who renamed it New York in 1669. *1664*

9 North Korea declared its independence. *1948*

10 Hungary opened its border to the West allowing thousands of East German refu-

gees to leave, much to the anger of the East German government. *1989*

11 A military junta, with USA support, overthrew the elected government of Chile. *1973*

12 Cleopatra's Needle, the obelisk of Thothmes II, was erected on London's Embankment. *1878*

13 *The Mousetrap* became Britain's longest-running play, reaching its 1,998th performance. *1957*

14 Miguel Primo de Riviera became dictator of Spain. *1923*

15 The civil war in Beirut began between Christians and Muslims. *1975*

16 The USA Buick and Oldsmobile car manufacturers merged to become General Motors. *1908*

17 The British airborne invasion of Arnhem, Holland began as part of 'Operation Market Garden'. *1944*

18 France abolished the use of the guillotine. *1981*

19 Led by Edward, the Black Prince, the English defeated the French at the Battle of Poitiers in the Hundred Years' War. *1356*

20 The US embassy in Beirut was attacked by a suicide bomber who drove into the compound with a lorry full of explosives and set them off killing 40 people. *1984*

21 Bonnie Prince Charles and his Jacobite army defeated the English at the Battle of Prestonpans in Scotland. *1745*

22 Idi Amin gave the 8,000 Asians in Uganda 48 hours to leave the country. *1972*

23 German astronomer Johann Galle discovered the planet Neptune. *1846*

24 The Iraqis blew up the Abadan oil refinery, turning the Iran-Iraq conflict into a full-scale war. *1980*

25 The first blood transfusion using human blood, as opposed to earlier attempts with animal blood, took place at Guy's Hospital in London. *1818*

26 The Parthenon was severely damaged by mortar bombs fired by the Venetian army which was beseiging the Turkish-held Acropolis. *1687*

27 Constantine I, King of Greece, abdicated following the Greek defeat in Turkey. *1922*

28 Pope John Paul I, pope for only 33 days, was found dead. *1978*

29 The first British monarch to abdicate, Richard II, was replaced by Bolingbroke who ascended the throne as Henry IV. *1399*

30 The first performance of Mozart's *The Magic Flute* took place in Vienna. *1791*

## OCTOBER

1 The Arab forces of Emir Faisal, with British officer T E Lawrence, captured Damascus from the Turks. *1918*

2 Saladin, the Muslim sultan, captured Jerusalem after an 88-year occupation by the Franks. *1187*

3 The Kingdom of Serbs, Croats, and Slovenes was renamed Yugoslavia. *1929*

4 Orville Wright became the first to fly an aircraft for over 33 minutes. *1905*

5 Bulgaria declared its independence from Turkey. *1908*

6 One day after the 11th anniversary of his election to office, Egyptian President Anwar Sadat was assassinated by Muslim extremists. *1981*

7 The Battle of Lepanto between Christian allied naval forces and the Ottoman Turks attempting to capture Cyprus from the Venetians, took place. *1571*

8 St Mark's Cathedral in Venice was consecrated. *1085*

9 Henry VI was restored to the English throne after being deposed in 1461. *1470*

10 Mrs Emmeline Pankhurst formed the Women's Social and Political Union to fight for women's emancipation in Britain. *1903*

11 The Anglo-Boer War began. *1899*

12 President Theodore Roosevelt renamed the Executive Mansion 'The White House'. *1901*

13 Sigmund Freud's *The Interpretation of Dreams* was published. *1904*

14 The Battle of Hastings was fought on Senlac Hill, where King Harold was slain as William the Conqueror's troops routed the English army. *1066*

15 The first major ballet was staged at the request of Catherine de' Medici at the palace in Paris. *1581*

16 Nazi war criminals, including von Ribbentrop, Rosenberg and Streicher, were hanged at Nuremberg. *1946*

17 British commander General Burgoyne surrendered to General Horatio Gates at Saratoga, a victory for the American colonists. *1777*

18 Germany's anti-terrorist squad stormed a hijacked Lufthansa aircraft at Mogadishu Airport, Somalia, killing three of the four Palestinian highjackers and freeing all of the hostages. *1977*

19 The first company to manufacture internal combustion engines was formed in Florence. *1860*

20 Mao Zedong's Long March ended in Yenan, north China. *1935*

21 Mao Zedong's Long March with his 100,000 strong Communist army began, after they had fought their way out of the seige mounted by Chiang Kai-shek's Nationalist armies in Funkien. *1934*

22 The first parachute jump was made by Andre-Jacques Garnerin from a balloon 6,000 feet above the Parc Monceau, Paris. *1797*

23 The Hungarian revolt against Soviet leadership began, in which thousands of demonstrators called for the withdrawal of Soviet forces. *1956*

24 The first football club was formed by a group of Cambridge University Old Boys meeting in Sheffield. *1857*

25 Lord Cardigan led the Charge of the Light Brigade during the Battle of Balaclava in the Crimean War. *1854*

26 Sweden and Norway ended their union and Oscar II, the Norwegian king, abdicated. *1905*

27 Charles II sold Dunkirk to Louis XIV for 2,500,000 livres. *1662*

28 The Statue of Liberty, designed by Auguste Bartholdi, was presented by France to the USA to mark the hundredth anniversary of the Declaration of Independence. *1886*

29 The Wall street crash known as 'Black Tuesday' took place, leading to the Great Depression. *1929*

30 P'u-i, the boy emperor of China aged five, granted a new constitution on the advice of the regent Prince Chun, officially ending three centuries of Manchu domination over China. *1911*

31 The Battle of Britain ended. *1940*

**NOVEMBER**

1 An earthquake reduced two-thirds of Lisbon to rubble and resulted, according to contemporary accounts, in the death of 60,000 people. *1755*

2 The Balfour Declaration, stating British sympathies for Jewish Zionist aspirations for a homeland in Palestine and promising aid to support efforts to achieve this goal, was sent to Lord Rothschild. *1917*

3 The Russian dog, Laika, became the first in space aboard Sputnik II. *1957*

4 Iranian students stormed the US Embassy in Tehran and held over 60 staff and US marines hostage. *1979*

5 The combined British and French armies defeated the Russians at the Battle of Inkerman during the Crimean War. *1854*

6 The construction of the Kariba High Dam began on the Zambezi River between Zambia and Zimbabwe. *1956*

7 The *Marie Celeste*, the ill-fated brigantine, sailed from New York to be found mysteriously abandoned near the Azores. *1872*

8 The Louvre was opened to the public by the revolutionary government, although only part of the collection could be viewed. *1793*

9 The SS (Schutzstaffel or 'Protection Squad') was formed in Germany. *1922*

10 Bulldozers began demolishing the 28-year-old Berlin Wall, the day after the East German government had announced that it would lift the 'iron curtain' and allow free travel between East and West Germany. *1989*

11 The armistice was signed between the Allies and Germany in Compeigne. *1918*

12 Leotard, the daring young man on the flying trapeze, made his debut in Paris. *1859*

13 The first helicopter rose 2 m/6.5 ft above ground in Normandy, powered by two motor-driven propellers above the pilot. *1907*

14 Scottish explorer James Bruce discovered the source of the Blue Nile in northeastern Ethiopia, then considered the main stream of the Nile. *1770*

15 Winston Churchill was captured by the Boers while covering the war as a reporter for the *Morning Post*. *1899*

16 The USSR launched *Venus III*, an unmanned spacecraft that successfully landed on Venus. *1965*

17 The last sultan of Turkey was deposed by Kemal Ataturk. *1922*

18 St Peter's in Rome was consecrated. *1626*

19 President Lincoln delivered his famous Gettysburg address, during the American Civil War. *1863*

20 The lights of Piccadilly Circus and the Strand were switched back on after five years of blackout. *1944*

21 The discovery of the 'Piltdown Man' skull by Charles Dawson in Sussex in 1912 was finally revealed as a hoax. *1953*

22 Portuguese navigator Vasco de Gama rounded the Cape of Good Hope in his search for a route to India. *1497*

23 The first jukebox was installed in Palais Royal Saloon in San Francisco. *1889*

24 Dutch navigator Abel Tasman discovered Van Diemen's Land which he named after his captain, but it was later renamed Tasmania. *1642*

25 Evaporated milk was patented by John Mayenberg of St Louis, Missouri. *1884*

26 The Soviet forces counterattacked at Stalingrad, ending the seige and forcing General von Paulus's Sixth Army to retreat. *1942*

27 President de Gaulle rejected British entry into the Common Market. *1967*

28 The Irish political party Sinn Fein was founded by Arthur Griffith in Dublin. *1905*

29 USA admiral Richard Byrd became the first man to fly over the South Pole, with his pilot Bernt Balchen. *1929*

30 Napoleon I's remains were returned from St Helena to Paris. *1840*

**DECEMBER**

1 The Spanish were driven out of Portugal and the country regained its independence. *1640*

2 The rebuilt St Paul's Cathedral, work of Sir Christopher Wren, was opened. *1697*

3 At Groote Schurr Hospital, Cape Town, Dr Christaan Barnard carried out the world's first heart transplant. *1967*

4 The only Englishman to become a pope, Nicholas Breakspear, became Adrian IV. *1154*

5 The Russian fleet was almost totally destroyed by the Japanese at Port Arthur. *1904*

6 Austria became the first nation to introduce a state education system. *1774*

7 The Japanese attacked the US fleet in Pearl Harbor. *1941*

8 Pope Pius IX declared the dogma of the Im-

maculate Conception of the Blessed Virgin Mary to be an article of faith. *1854*

9 The first martyrs of the 'intifada' in the Gaza Strip were created when an Israeli patrol attacked in the Jabaliya refugee camp. *1987*

10 Cuba became independent of Spain following the Spanish-American War. *1898*

11 The first wildlife preservation society was formed in Britain, called the Society for the Preservation of Wild Fauna of the Empire. *1903*

12 Bill Haley and the Comets recorded 'See You Later Alligator' at Decca Recording Studios, New York. *1955*

13 The Metropolitan Underground railway in London went electric. *1904*

14 US *Mariner II* sent the first close-up pictures of the planet Venus back to Earth. *1962*

15 A meteorological office established in Tuscany began recording daily temperature readings. *1654*

16 The first immigrant ship, the *Charlotte Jane*, arrived at Lyttleton, New Zealand. *1850*

17 *A Christmas Carol* by Charles Dickens was published. *1843*

18 The USA officially abolished slavery with the ratification of the 13th Amendment. *1865*

19 Henry II became King of England. *1154*

20 General Noriega, Panama's former military leader, dictator and alleged drug baron, was overthrown by a US invasion force invited by the new civilian government, headed by Guillermo Endara. *1989*

21 Charles de Gualle became President of France. *1958*

22 Alfred Dreyfus, the French officer who was falsely convicted for selling military secrets, was sent to Devil's Island. *1894*

23 English architect Joseph Hansom patented his 'safety cab', better known as the Hansom cab. *1834*

24 The War of 1812 between the USA and Britain was brought to an end with the signing of the Treaty of Ghent. *1814*

25 The Nicaraguan capital Managua was devastated by an earthquake which killed over 10,000 people. *1972*

26 Marie and Pierre Curie discovered radium while experimenting with pitchblende. *1898*

27 Charles Darwin set sail in the *Beagle* on his voyage of scientific discovery. *1831*

28 An earthquake killed over 75,000 at Messina in Sicily. *1908*

29 Sun Yat Sen became the first president of a republican China following the Revolution. *1911*

30 A petition to Queen Victoria with over one million names of women appealing for public houses to be closed on Sundays was handed to the Home Secretary. *1887*

31 The first Huguenots set sail from France for the Cape of Good Hope, where they would escape religious persecution and create the South African wine industry with the vines they took with them on the voyage. *1687*

# OBITUARIES

**Anderson** Carl David 1905–1991. US physicist, who discovered the positive electron (positron) in 1932; he shared the Nobel Prize for Physics in 1936.

Carl Anderson was one of the pioneers in cosmic ray physics. He made two of the first discoveries in the field and launched what is now known as 'elementary particle physics'. The first discovery in 1932 was the positive electron or positron, a particle whose existence had been predicted by English theorist Paul Dirac. Anderson found that positrons were present in cosmic rays, energetic particles reaching Earth from outer space. For this discovery, Anderson shared the 1936 Nobel Prize for Physics with Victor Hess, the discoverer of cosmic rays. In 1937, Anderson discovered a new particle in cosmic rays, one with a mass between that of an electron and a proton. The new particle was first called a mesotron and then a meson muon. The discovery of the muon was a great step forward in physics; the muon was the first elementary particle to be discovered beyond the constituents of ordinary matter (proton, neutron, and electron). This could be said to be the birth of elementary particle physics.

**Ashcroft** Peggy 1907–1991. English actress. Her many leading roles included Desdemona in *Othello* (with Paul Robeson), Juliet in *Romeo and Juliet* 1935 (with Laurence Olivier and John Gielgud), and appearances in the TV play *Caught on a Train* 1980, the series *The Jewel in the Crown* 1984 (BAFTA Award) and the film *A Passage to India* 1985.

Ashcroft made her professional stage debut playing opposite Ralph Richardson in a Birmingham Repertory revival of *Dear Brutus*

*Peggy Ashcroft*

1926. During her 60-year-career on stage and later in television and film, she played a wide variety of roles. She worked with the English Stage Company, the Royal Shakespeare Company, and the National Theatre, and was always at the forefront of developments on the English stage through her work with (among others) John Gielgud, Theodore Komisarjevsky, George Devine, and Trevor Nunn. Her later television work (for example, playing Queen Mary in *Edward and Mrs Simpson* 1978) and film work won her several awards, including an Oscar for best supporting actress for her performance in *A Passage to India*. Two months prior to her death she appeared at the Olivier Awards, London, and was given a special award to mark her life's service to the theatre.

**Balfour** Eve 1898–1990. English agriculturalist and pioneer of modern organic agriculture. Balfour established the Haughley Experiment, a whole farm research project at New Bells Farm near Haughley, Suffolk, to demonstrate that a more sustainable agricultural alternative existed. The experiment ran for almost 30 years, comparing organic and chemical farming systems. The wide-ranging support it attracted led to the formation of the Soil Association 1946; one of the first environmental organizations, it was established to show that 'health, whether of soil, plant, animal or man, is one and indivisible'.

Lady Eve lived to see her ideas progress from being regarded as fringe crankiness to becoming a respected agricultural policy option. She was also a qualified pilot, experienced yachtswoman, wrote mystery novels and played saxophone in a jazz band.

**Bardeen** John 1908–1991. US physicist who won a Nobel Prize for Physics in 1956, with Walter Brattain and William Shockley, for the development of the transistor in 1948.

In 1972 he became the first double winner of a Nobel Prize in the same subject (with Leon Cooper and John Schrieffer) for his work on superconductivity.

John Bardeen is one of only two people who have received two Nobel Prizes in the same subject (the other is English biochemist Frederick Sanger). Bardeen's two Nobel Prizes for quite different achievements in theoretical physics mark him out as one of the greatest physicists of the twentieth century.

The first Nobel Prize was awarded for work done at the Bell Telephone laboratory in New Jersey in the years following the Second World War. A team led by Bardeen, William Shockley and Walter Brattain undertook an intensive study of semiconductors, especially germanium, which were used in radar receivers in the same way that 'crystals' had been used in the earliest radio sets. The work led to the development in 1956 of the transistor, which was equivalent to the 'cat's whisker' of early radios.

The second Nobel Prize was won for explaining superconductivity, the total loss of electrical resistance by some metals when cooled within a few degrees of absolute zero. The theory developed in 1957 by Bardeen, his student Robert Schrieffer and Leon Cooper, his research associate, is a triumph for its imaginative insight. Superconductivity arises, according to the Bardeen-Cooper-Schrieffer theory, because of the way in which electrons travelling through a metal interact with the vibrating atoms of the metal.

Bardeen's influence on the world of science was immense. After leaving the Bell Laboratory in 1951, he formed a major research group in the physics and applications of semiconductors at the University of Illinois. Under his leadership, the University became a world centre for research into quantum liquids.

**Bell** John 1928–1990. Irish physicist who in 1964 devised a test to decide an important philosophical point concerning quantum theory: whether two particles that were once connected are always afterwards interconnected even if they become widely-separated. As well as investigating fundamental problems in theoretical physics, Bell contributed to the design of particle accelerators.

John Bell was one of the most profound thinkers in physics, widely regarded as one of the few physicists of modern times to equal the pioneers of quantum theory, such as Max Born, Werner Heisenberg and Niels Bohr.

Bell worked as a laboratory assistant at Queen's University in Belfast before taking his first degree. He then moved to CERN, the European laboratory for particle physics near Geneva, where he worked for 30 years. He demonstrated how to measure the continued interconnection of particles which had once been closely connected. Bell put forward mathematical criteria which had to be obeyed if such a connection existed, as required by quantum theory. Hence, his work amounted to a test of quantum ideas. In the early 1980s, a series of experiments by a French team led by Alain Aspect tested Bell's criteria, and a connection between widely-separated particles was detected.

**Benavides** Felipe 1917–1991. Peruvian conservationist, director of the zoo at Lima, Peru, which he designed as an ecological park. Born into an aristocratic family, Benavides followed a diplomatic career in Europe and the USA before becoming a full-time conservationist. He helped create several national parks, but concentrated his efforts to protect the vicuna, a small camel found in the Andes Mountains.

The vicuna faced extinction through constant poaching for its exceptionally fine and valuable wool. Benavides established a number of vicuna reserves in the southern Andes, and attempted to establish domestic stock for shearing, thus probably saving the vicuna from extinction. Numbers have recovered well and there are now estimated to be more than 80,000 vicunas in the wild.

As a result of his work, Benavides became Latin American representative on the Convention on International Trade in Endangered

*Leonard Bernstein*

Species (CITES); an international convention regulating the wildlife trade. He was an ardent Anglophile, and was awarded a Member of the Order of the British Empire (MBE) for his services to Anglo-Peruvian relations.

**Bernstein** Leonard 1918–1990. US composer, conductor, and pianist. Bernstein was one of the most energetic and versatile of US musicians in the 20th century. His works, which established a vogue for realistic, contemporary themes, include symphonies such as *The Age of Anxiety* 1949; ballets such as *Fancy Free* 1944; scores for musicals including *Wonderful Town* 1953 and *West Side Story* 1957; and *Mass* 1971 in memory of President J F Kennedy.

Born in Lawrence, Massachussetts, he was educated at Harvard University and the Curtis Institute of Music. From 1958 to 1970 he was musical director of the New York Philharmonic. Among his other works are the symphony *Jeremiah* 1944, the ballet *Facsimile* 1946, the musical *Candide* 1956, and the *Chichester Psalms* 1965.

He was eager to share his appreciation of music, writing several books, including *The Joy of Music* 1959, and becoming something of a missionary in this respect through his series of television lectures that reached about 11 million listeners. Throughout his career Bernstein was a supporter of liberal causes and was active in the civil rights movements, sympathies which gained him a degree of notoriety during the 1960s.

**Bettelheim** Bruno 1904–1990. Austrian pioneering psychoanalyst whose work in childhood development and disorder made him highly regarded in the field of child psychology. His work as director of the Sonia Shankman Orthogenic School at the University of Chicago laid the basis for current approaches to the treatment of emotionally disturbed children, by emphasising the need to provide children with a warm, respectful and supportive environment. His books included *Love Is Not*

*Enough* 1950, *The Uses of Enchantment: The Meaning and Importance of Fairy Tales* 1976 and *A Good Enough Parent: A Book on Child-Rearing* 1987.

Bettelheim's experiences as an inmate of the concentration camps of Dachau and Buchenwald during the years before the war were crucial to his development of a view of the human personality which later came through in his work. In 1939 his release was petitioned for by Eleanor Roosevelt and Governor Lehman of New York and he emigrated to the US. He became the director of the Sonia Shankman Orthogenic School, a residential and treatment centre for disturbed children, in 1944. Bettelheim strongly believed in the innate goodness of children, and was able to treat children so severely disturbed that they were considered beyond any person's or institution's reach. He recognised in the mental agonies of disturbed children similarities with the nature of the agonies of the camps and became convinced that the construction of a warm and positive environment—the antithesis of the degrading regime of the camps—would have the power to repair shattered psyches. His institution claimed the remarkable results of an 85% return to normal life.

**Bevan** Brian 1924–1991. Australian-born rugby league player. Bevan's total of 796 tries for Warrington, Blackpool Borough and representative sides is an unequalled record. Lean and almost scrawny in appearance, his remarkable sportsmanship lay in his speed, swerve and characteristic sidestep which enabled him to score many of his tries untouched.

Born into a family that was deeply committed to rugby in Sidney, Bevan had played a handful of games with his father's team, Eastern Suburbs, when World War II began. He joined the Australian Navy and arrived in Britain in 1945. However he never played for his native country and almost all his rugby was played in his adopted country. It is said that Bevan perfected his baffling sidestep by weaving around telegraph poles on his way home from the playing ground in Sidney. He confirmed that this story was true, but added that he would also make use of passers-by for this purpose. He played his last game for Warrington in 1962, but was persuaded to come out of retirement for two seasons with Blackpool Borough.

**Blacking** John 1928–1990. English anthropologist and ethnomusicologist. He is acclaimed for research on the relationship between music and body movement, and the patterns of social and musical organisation. Blacking was appointed to the Chair of Social Anthropology Queen's University, Belfast, in 1970, where he established the influential centre for ethnomusicology. His most widely-read book is *How Musical is Man?* (1973).

Following a degree in anthropology at Cambridge, Blacking—who was also a pianist and choirmaster—joined the staff of the International Library of African Music in South Africa in 1954. Two years later he commenced fieldwork among the Venda of Transvaal, leading to the publication of *Venda Children's Songs* (1967). Blacking, a strong opponent of apartheid, came into conflict with the South African authorities, and eventually left the country. Between 1981 and 1983 Blacking was the chairman of the Society for Ethnomusicology, the only non-North American resident to have been elected to the post. He also founded the European Seminar on Musicology.

**Blakey** Art. Muslim name Abdullah Ibn Buhaina 1919–1990. US jazz drummer and bandleader whose dynamic, innovative style made him one of the jazz greats. He contributed to the development of bebop in the 1940s and subsequently to hard bop, and formed The Jazz Messengers in the mid-1950s, continuing to lead the band for most of his life and discovering many talented musicians.

Blakey was born in Pittsburgh, Pennsylvania, and worked in New York from 1942. During the formative years of bebop, 1944–47, he was a member of a band that at various times included Charlie Parker, Dizzy Gillespie, and Miles Davis, and recorded with the pianist Thelonius Monk. Blakey visited Africa in 1947, but later denied any musical influence. Together with the pianist Horace Silver (1928– ) in the early 1950s, Blakey developed hard bop, a sparse, blues-based jazz style. Among those whose talents the Jazz Messengers subsequently nurtured were the saxophonist Wayne Shorter (1933– ), the pianist Keith Jarrett (1945– ), and on trumpet 1980–82 Wynton Marsalis (1961– ). Blakey also recorded with other bandleaders during his career, and for two years, 1970–71, was part of the Giants of Jazz, a supergroup that included Gillespie and Monk. 'Music washes away the dust of humdrum existence' Blakey once said.

*Art Blakey*

*Aaron Copland*

**Breker** Arno 1900–1991. German classical sculptor. He assisted his father, also a sculptor, before enrolling at the art academy in Düsseldorf. He was based in Paris from 1924, where his friends included French poet and playwright Jean Cocteau and French painter Maurice de Vlaminck. French sculptor Aristide Maillol, whose pupil he became, helped to develop his style, a muscular neo-classicism.

Returning to Germany, Hitler saw and admired Breker's statue of Dionysus, a 3.65 m/ 12 ft figure created for the Berlin Olympics Committee in 1935. While working on the German Pavilion at the 1938 Paris Exhibition, he met Nazi architect Albert Speer, who commissioned two statues for the entrance to the new Berlin chancellery. After World War II, with much of his work destroyed, Breker was forbidden to sculpt for the next five years. After this, despite frequent invitations from Stalin and Franco, commissions were infrequent. The artistic isolation embittered him but, unlike Speer, he never expressed any regret for his contribution to the Nazi cause.

**Clark** (Harold) Gene 1941–1991. US rock and folk singer, songwriter, and guitarist, a founder member 1964–66 of the influential rock group the Byrds; he was a member of the New Christy Minstrels (a folk group) 1963–64, and later of Dillard & Clark, a bluegrass duo; he also recorded solo.

Clark, born in Missouri, played in various college bands before joining the New Christy Minstrels, who at the time had some chart success ('Green Green' 1963). After 18 months he left for Los Angeles, where he met and formed the Jet Set with Jim McGuinn and David Crosby; with the addition of Chris Hillman and Michael Clarke they became the now legendary Byrds. Heavily influenced by the Beatles, Clark was initially the main songwriter and strongly

contributed to the group's vocal sound. He left at the height of the Byrds' fame, in April 1966, citing fear of flying (though he wrote the lyrics to 'Eight Miles High': 'and when you touch down you'll find that it's stranger than known'). His solo albums include *No Other* 1974, and he made two albums with the banjo player Doug Dillard. Clark participated in various Byrds reunion projects and for a time in the late 1970s teamed up with two former Byrds in McGuinn, Clark & Hillman. His last album was *So Rebellious a Lover* 1987 with Carla Olson.

**Copland** Aaron 1900–1990. US composer whose work popularized and fostered the phenomenal growth of music appreciation in the US after 1940. Copland's early works, such as the piano concerto of 1926, were in the jazz idiom but he gradually developed a gentler style with a regional flavour drawn from American folk music.

Born in New York, he studied in France with Nadia Boulanger, and in 1940 became instructor in composition at the Berkshire Music Center. After 1945 he was the assistant director. He took avant-garde European styles and gave them a distinctive American accent. By making use of folk music and old American hymns as the basis for many of his works in the 1930s and 1940s he created the symphonic style now recognised as 'American'. His eight film scores set new standards for music's dramatic effectiveness for Hollywood, and became much imitated classics of film-score composition. Copland's film scores included those for *Our Town* 1940, *Of Mice and Men* 1939, and *The Heiress* 1949, which won him an Oscar. Besides numerous articles and lectures, Copland wrote three books: *Our New Music* 1941, *Music And Imagination* 1952, and *Copland On Music* 1960. Among his later works are the ballets *Billy the Kid* 1939; *Rodeo* 1942; and *Appalachian Spring* 1944, based on a poem by Hart Crane; and *Inscape for Orchestra* 1967. He won the Pulitzer Prize 1945 and the Presidential Medal of Freedom in 1964.

**Coveri** Enrico 1952–1990. Italian fashion designer who set up his own business 1979. A bold designer of young, fun-loving clothes, he was best known for knitted tops and trousers in strong colours, and for incorporating comic characters and Pop art in his designs.

Coveri was born in Florence and studied at its Accademia delle Belle Arti. He started working freelance for several companies, creating knitwear and sportswear under the Touche label, in 1973, and five years later moved to Paris to work at the Espace Cardin. By the time of his death, his own business had achieved a turnover of £100 million ($165 million).

**Doc Pomus** (Jerome Solon Felder) 1925–1991. US pop-music songwriter who worked primarily in partnership with Mort Shuman (1936–  ). The team had its greatest successes in the early 1960s with hits for the Drifters ('Save the Last Dance for Me' 1960) and Elvis Presley ('Little Sister' and 'His Latest Flame' 1961). Fluent in a number of styles, they were innovators in none.

Pomus, born in New York, began as a blues singer in the style of Big Joe Turner, and made some recordings for Chess and other labels in the early 1950s. Through Turner, Pomus came in contact with Atlantic Records, who gave his composition 'Lonely Avenue' to Ray Charles in 1956. Soon afterwards he teamed up with Shuman. Their songs usually had a bluesy feel but the lyrics were conventional and sentimental, and much of their material was written for prefabricated pop stars like Fabian ('I'm a Man' 1959). 'Teenager in Love' for Dion and the Belmonts 1959 capitalized successfully on the formula of Frankie Lymon's 1956 hit 'Why Do Fools Fall in Love'. Between 1960 and 1963 Pomus and Shuman were on contract to Atlantic's publishing arm.

This was the age of the Brill Building, the New York Tin Pan Alley hit factory, where songwriters were employed by music-publishing firms to turn out songs custom-tailored to particular acts. (Another such team, Leiber and Stoller, wrote for some of the same artists, including the Drifters, and they cowrote 'She's Not You' 1962 for Presley with Pomus.) After an accident 1965, the team split up.

**Dunne** Irene 1904–1990. US actress. From 1930 until 1952 she appeared in a wide variety of movies, including musicals and comedies, but was perhaps most closely associated with the genre of romantic melodrama. After Dunne retired from acting, she was for many years active in support of the Republican Party and also on behalf of charitable causes.

Starring in the road-show production of *Show Boat*, Dunne was signed to a film contract on the strength of it. She made her name in musical comedy in the 1920s, but the 1930s was the decade of her greatest success, when she brought a poised vitality and an instinctive sense of timing to 'screwball' comedies like *The Awful Truth* 1937 and to such musicals as *Roberta* 1935. Complementing these qualities was a sense of gravity, which came to the fore when she played the self-sacrificing heroines of films such as *Back Street* 1932 and *Magnificent Obsession* 1935.

**Elton** Charles 1900–1991. English ecologist and zoologist who pioneered the science of animal ecology in Britain. Amongst many other innovations, he defined the concept of 'food chains' (the patterns of 'who eats whom' that aid understanding on how natural systems operate. Elton was also an early conservationist, instrumental in establishing the Nature Conservancy Council, and was much concerned with the impact of introduced species on natural systems.

Elton's theories on ecology were shaped during expeditions looking at the relatively simple animal communities within the Arctic Circle. The resulting book *Animal Ecology*, published 1927, is still in use. Later, he studied a highly complex animal community on a large estate near Oxford, and his 20-year research project

of interrelationships of animals in meadows, woods, and water is arguably the most comprehensive ever attempted. Even in retirement he continued to break new ground, studying animal communities in tropical forests. He was a Senior Research Fellow at Corpus Christi College, Oxford, and a member of the Royal Society.

**Erim** Kenan Tevfig 1929–1990. Turkish-born US historian and archaeologist. Erim taught classics at New York University from the late 1950s until his death. He was both a classicist and historian specializing in art history, and a field archaeologist. From 1961 he chose to excavate the city of Aphrodisias in Turkey while teaching at New York University. In his efforts to conserve and protect the site, the excavation took 30 years to complete. Erim took over work previously begun by Turkish archaeologist Ahmet Donmez, and excavated the Temple of Aphrodite which he showed had been converted into a Byzantine basilican church. He also uncovered some sculptures, including a statue of Aphrodite.

**Erté** adopted name of Romain de Tirtoff 1893–1990. Russian born Art Deco designer and illustrator of fashion magazine covers and theatrical costumes. He was highly successful in many branches of design, including graphics, bronze scupture, clothes and theatre, and created designs whose turnover now reach close to $100 million (£62.5 million) a year. Erté (the name was derived from the French pronunciation of his initials) designed hundreds of covers for *Harper's Bazaar* magazine between 1915 and 1937 and created costumes for musicals, films, operas and ballets, as well as for the Folies-Bergères and the Ziegfeld Follies. His lithographs, which mostly featured elegant women, became very popular in the 1970s and 1980s.

*Erté*

After studying portraiture with Russian painter Ilya Repin in St Petersburg, Russia Erté continued his studies in Paris, where he arrived in 1912. In 1913 he was hired by French fashion designer Paul Poiret, as a studio assistant. When Poiret closed his business at the outbreak of World War I, Erté began selling his designs directly to US fashion houses and gained his contract with *Harper's Bazaar* for monthly covers. His theatrical career commenced in 1915 and led eventually to his association with the Folies-Bergères and Broadway's Ziegfield Follies. His first work for cinema was commissioned in 1920 by US newspaper publisher William Randolph Hearst. Erté designed individual costumes for a number of stars, including Norma Shearer, Eileen Pringle, and Lillian Gish. After World War II he designed many popular theatre productions throughout the world. Erté continued to design, both for fashion and the theatre, into advanced age, and enjoyed a second period of fame in the last decade when exhibitions and reproductions of his works gave him almost superstar status.

**Fender** (Clarence) Leo 1909–1991. US inventor of the solid-body electric guitar 1948 and the electric bass guitar 1951. Although not a musician, he had a greater influence than all but a handful of performers. His instruments have been played by countless rock guitarists and bassists and their designs have been adapted by other manufacturers.

Fender began making amplifiers and Hawaiian-style guitars in 1945, and built solid-body guitars for several country musicians. The guitarist and producer Les Paul was working independently on a solid-body electric guitar around this time, but Fender was the first to get his model on the market. Initially called the Broadcaster, it underwent a name change in 1950 to Telecaster. The design was totally new, with a one-piece neck bolted on to a wooden body, and could easily be mass-produced. Its clear trebly sound was particularly suited to country music; rock guitarists have generally preferred its successor, the futuristically streamlined Stratocaster introduced 1954, whose three pickups made possible various electronic modifications of tone and volume. Even more of an innovation, the Fender Precision bass guitar was not only louder and more portable than a standup acoustic but also cheaper, and could be played by any guitarist. The basic rock-band line-up then remained unchallenged from 1951 until the introduction of synthesizers. In 1965 he sold the Fender name to CBS, which continues to manufacture the instruments.

**Flett** John 1963–1991. English fashion designer who achieved international recognition while still training at St Martin's School of Art, London. In the late 1980s his collections were bought by top fashion houses, but an attempt to set up his own business ran into financial difficulties. In 1989 he moved to Paris to join Claude Montana, and from there went to the Italian house Enrico Coveri. He was

*Margot Fonteyn*

in Florence to sign a rainwear and knitwear contract with manufacturer Zuccoli when he died suddenly of a heart attack.

**Fonteyn** Margot. Stage name of Margaret Hookham 1919–1991. English ballet dancer. She made her debut with the Vic-Wells Ballet in *Nutcracker* 1934 and first appeared as Giselle 1937, eventually becoming prima ballerina of the Royal Ballet, London. Renowned for her perfect physique, musicality, and interpretive powers, she created many roles in Frederick Ashton's ballets and formed a legendary partnership with Rudolf Nureyev.

During the course of her extraordinarily long career Fonteyn reached ever wider audiences, awakening a love of dance in spectators who saw her stage performances in many parts of the world, and in the millions who watched her on television and films. She created many leading roles with choreographers Ninette de Valois, and Frederick Ashton, among them *The Haunted Ballroom* 1939, *Symphonic Variations* 1946, and *The Fairy Queen* 1946. Although she was surpassed by many dancers in virtuosity she never lacked the technique or balanced interpretation required of her roles. She continued dancing until after her sixtieth birthday, giving her final performances during Nureyev's 1979 summer season.

**Freeman** (Lawrence) Bud 1906–1991. US jazz saxophonist who took part in developing the Chicago style in the 1920s. His playing was soft and elegant, and he worked and recorded with a number of bands, as well as cofounding the World's Greatest Jazz Band in the 1970s.

Freeman was a member of the Austin High School Gang with Jimmy McPartland. The saxophone at that time was not regarded as a solo instrument, but the pioneering work of Coleman Hawkins inspired Freeman to use the tenor sax as a soloist, and his playing in turn was an influence on Lester Young. 'The Eel' 1933 was a hit record that featured Freeman. As a member of Benny Goodman's orchestra 1936–39 he was given insufficient freedom to improvise; he left to form his own Summa cum Laude 1939–40, and then to work with a variety of line-ups. In the 1960s he recorded again with McPartland. A dandy who affected an English accent, he was based in London 1974–84.

**Fröhlich** Herbert 1905–1991. German-born English theoretical physicist who helped lay the foundations for modern theoretical physics in the UK. He was Professor of theoretical physics at Liverpool University from 1948 to 1973. He made important advances in the understanding of low-temperature superconductivity and biological systems.

Fröhlich studied in Munich under Arnold Sommerfeld, one of Germany's foremost theoretical physicists. The start of his academic career was spoiled by the Nazis, who engineered his dismissal from his teaching post in 1933. Frohlich was one, many German scientists who left Germany at the time of World War II. He went to Bristol where he became a lecturer in theoretical physics. His main research interest was in solid state physics, but he also became familiar with quantum field theory—the application of quantum theory to particle interactions.

In 1948 Fröhlich accepted a newly created chair of Theoretical Physics at Liverpool University. He revolutionized solid state theory by importing into it the methods of quantum field theory. In particular, he proposed a theory to explain superconductivity using the methods of field theory. His theory was later developed by John Bardeen, Leon Cooper and John Schrieffer, an effort for which they received the Nobel prize for Physics in 1972. His work also led him to the idea that quantum methods might elucidate some aspects of biological systems, and he ranged over such subjects as the electrical properties of cell membranes.

**Fuller** Peter 1947–1990. English art critic who, from the mid-1970s relentlessly attacked the complacency of the art establishment. He began at the left-wing magazine *New Society*, where he was deeply influenced by its regular critic, the Marxist John Berger. But gradually Fuller came to reject doctrinaire arguments. His friendship with abstract painter Robert Natkin, and his reading of art critic John Ruskin strenthened his belief that art was a craft rooted in, and developing through tradition: ideas which put him at variance with the artists and movements of the 1960s. He repeatedly attacked, amongst other issues, the reputation and influence of US pop artist Andy Warhol; the selection policy of the Tate Gallery; and the laissez-faire approach of modern art education—attitudes which he felt were fashionable, rather than true to art. From 1988 these views, and an increased interest in the

spiritual power of art, were voiced in his own magazine *Modern Painters*.

**Gaillard** Slim (Bulee) 1916–1991. US jazz singer, songwriter, actor, and musician. A light humourous performer, he claimed to have invented his own language,: Vout, (nonsense syllables as in scat singing). His first hit was 'Flat Foot Floogie' 1938.

Gaillard was a hipster for the fun of it. His career began in partnership with the bass player Slam (Leroy) Stewart (1914–1987) as Slim and Slam 1937–43, and their 'Flat Foot Floogie' was covered by well-known acts from the Mills Brothers to Benny Goodman. On the West Coast in the mid-1940s the Slim Gaillard Quartette, which included the jazz drummer Zutty Singleton, recorded novelty numbers like 'Atomic Cocktail' 1945, 'Penicillin Boogie', and the hit 'Cement Mixer' 1946. 'Down by the Station' 1949, a song for children, is said to have inspired the books about Thomas the Tank Engine. In New York from 1947, Gaillard witnessed at close hand the early days of bop and recorded with Charlie Parker and Dizzy Gillespie. He also influenced the beat-generation writers and features in Jack Kerouac's 1957 novel *On the Road*. From the 1960s Gaillard appeared in films and TV series. Vout his brand of jive talk, consisted largely of adding 'vouty' and 'oroony' to words; it could last be heard 1990 in his guest spot on the Canadian rap group Dream Warriors' number 'Easy to Assemble but Hard to Take Apart'.

**Gandhi** Rajiv 1944–1991. Indian politician, prime minister from 1984, following his mother Indira Gandhi's assassination, to Nov 1989. As prime minister, he faced growing discontent with his party's elitism and lack of concern for social issues. He was assassinated by a bomb at an election rally.

Elder son of Indira Gandhi and grandson of Nehru, Rajiv Gandhi was born into the Kashmiri-Brahmin family which had governed

*Rajiv Gandhi*

India for all but four years since 1947. He initially displayed little interest in politics and became an airline pilot with Indian Airlines. But after the death in a plane crash of his brother *Sanjay* (1946–80), he was elected to his brother's Amethi parliamentary seat 1981. In the Dec 1984 parliamentary elections he won a record majority. In 1985 he reached a temporary settlement with the moderate Sikhs which failed, however, to hold. His reputation was tarnished by a scandal concerning alleged kickbacks to senior officials from an arms deal with the Swedish munitions firm Bofors and, following his party's defeat in the general election of Nov 1989, Gandhi was forced to resign as premier. He returned to fight a vigorous campaign in the 1991 elections, responding to earlier criticisms of aloofness and mixing closely with the electorate. The discarding of tight security resulted in his own assassination, at a rally near Madras, in the middle of the campaign.

**Garbo** Greta. Stage name of Greta Lovisa Gustafsson 1905–1990. Swedish-born US film actress. She went to the USA in 1925, and her captivating beauty and leading role in *The Torrent* 1926 made her one of Hollywood's first stars in silent films. Her later films include *Mata Hari* 1931, *Grand Hotel* 1932, *Queen Christina* 1933, *Anna Karenina* 1935, *Camille* 1936, and *Ninotchka* 1939. Her qualities of ethereality and romantic mystery on the screen intermingled with her much proclaimed desire for seclusion in private life. She was noted for her reclusiveness after her retirement from films.

**Gardner** Ava 1922–1990. US film actress, a sensuous star of such films as *The Killers* 1946 and *Pandora and the Flying Dutchman* 1951. Her greatest success was *The Barefoot Contessa* 1954. Perhaps the best of her later appearances

*Greta Garbo*

was as Lily Langtry in *The Life and Times of Judge Roy Bean* 1972. She remained active in films until the 1980s, when she retired to London.

A brief early marriage 1942–43 to Mickey Rooney had much publicity value, and as the femme fatale of *The Killers* 1946, she ascended to leading roles. she remained a leading star for the next decade, with added publicity accruing to her attachment to the international jet set and her marriages to bandleader Artie Shaw 1945–47, and to Frank Sinatra 1951–57. The film for which she is best remembered *The Barefoot Contessa* 1954 tells a tragically slanted Cinderella story about a gypsy girl who becomes an international celebrity, which plays to ironic but also resonant effect upon Gardner's own public and professional identity. The film also presaged Gardner's gravitation toward a European base, but many of her subsequent roles were in unrewarding spectaculars.

**Gauquelin** Michel 1928–1991. French astrologist. Gauquelin trained as a psychologist and statistician, but became widely known for neoastrology or the scientific measurement of the correlations between the exact position of certain planets at birth and individual fame. His work attracted strong criticism as well as much interest. His book *Neo-Astrology: a Copernican Revolution* was published posthumously 1991.

Gauquelin studied the relationship between planet and personality, proposing the 'Mars effect' that sports personalities were more likely to be born with Mars in the crucial positions, actors with Jupiter, and scientists and doctors with Saturn. Gauquelin studied thousands of eminent people to obtain his data, likewise using thousands of non-eminent people as a control group.

**Getz** Stan 1927–1991. US jazz tenor saxophonist. Often regarded as a precursor of 'cool' jazz, his lyrical style won a wide following and went beyond the confines of jazz itself. He was not an innovator, but was known for his highly distinctive 'sound' and wide range of expression. In the 1960s he latched onto the 'bossa nova' craze, giving jazz a new popularity and assuring himself of the kind of financial security that jazz musicians rarely find. He continued to play 'straight jazz' until the late 1980s.

He made his recording debut at 16 with the band of Jack Teagarden. In 1947, Getz joined the reeds section of Woody Herman's band, the 'Second Herd', playing in the celebrated 'Four Brothers' saxophone team. By 1949 he was able to form the first of his quartets of tenor, piano, bass and drums, the format he was to depend on for the rest of his life. Because of the instant commercial success of jazz samba in the 1960s, Getz could afford to limit his touring and go back to a traditional line up, performing and recording with musicians such as Chick Corea and Albert Dailey. Getz fell out with many people during his career

*Martha Graham*

and had the reputation of being a difficult, temperamental man.

**Goddard** Paulette. Stage name of Marion Levy 1911–1990. US actress. She starred as leading lady in *Modern Times* 1936 and *The Great Dictator* 1940, where her gamine quality, together with a mixture or practicality and pathos, showed through. Both films were directed by Charlie Chaplin, to whom she was married from 1936 until 1942. During the 1940s she continued to make a strong impression in both comedies and costume melodramas, making a notable appearance as Mrs Cheveley in the British-made version of Oscar Wilde's play *An Ideal Husband* 1948. She made only a few minor films in the 1950s, and, after her fourth marriage to German novelist Erich Maria Remarque 1958, she retired from acting.

**Gow** Ian 1937–1990. English Conservative politician. After qualifying as a solicitor, he became member of Parliament for Eastbourne 1974. He became parliamentary private secretary to the prime minister, Margaret Thatcher 1979, and her close ally. He secured steady promotion but resigned his post as minister of state 1985 in protest at the signing of the Anglo-Irish Agreement. A strong critic of terrorists, he was killed by an IRA car bomb.

**Graham** Martha 1894–1991. US dancer and choreographer. She helped to establish modern dance as an art form and created a distinctive technique that represented the first substantive alternative to classical ballet. Her purpose was to express inner emotion and intention through dance forms. Graham's achievements as an innovator remain unsurpassed.

The first concert of her own works was given in New York in 1926. During the following few years she evolved a starkly expressive style, which audiences found increasingly puzzling. Her prestige gradually built up during the 1930s and her success was consolidated with *American Document* 1938. Her 180 works included several on American themes, notably *Letter to the World* 1940 and *Appalachian Spring* 1944, for which US composer Aaron Copland wrote the music. She also created a series of dances inspired by Greek tragic heroines and Judaic myths which inevitably expressed the woman's point of view.

Her innovations also influenced other aspects of dance production by, for example, selecting sculptor Isamu Noguchi as designer in the 1930s, and by making use of adventurous costuming which presented the body as moving sculpture. She continued dancing until 1970 and directed her company until her death; her last creation, 'Maple Leaf Rag', premiered October 1990 was critically acclaimed. She won numerous awards for her work, including the first Medal of Freedom, the US's highest civilian honour, in 1976.

**Graziano** Rocky (Thomas Rocco Barbella) 1922–1990. US middleweight boxing champion who fought in the 1940s and 1950s. Although he was not noted for his boxing skills or finesse—he was a fighter of the kill-or-be-killed school with little use for the defensive arts—his colourful, brawling style made him a popular favourite. He compiled a record of 67 wins, 10 losses and 6 draws between 1942 and 1952. Three of his bouts, with Tony Zane in 1946,1947, and 1948, were considered classics.

Born in New York's Lower East Side, Graziano began stealing as a child. A hardened criminal by 19, he went from jail straight to the US Army in 1941. He soon deserted, was caught, dishonourably discharged from the army and given a prison sentence. It was while he was in hiding following his desertion that he began boxing. After his release from prison he pursued his boxing career, becoming a world title contender by 1946. Graziano won the middleweight title from Zane in 1947, but lost it to him the following year. His criminal record and background of hard living led to rumours that he was involved in fixed fights and bribery, and in 1948 the New York State Athletic Commission took his licence away for failing to report the offer of a bribe to lose against Rueben Shank. Graziano retired in 1953 and made a lucrative living as an entertainer and actor. In 1956 his autobiography, *Somebody Up There Likes Me*, was made into a film starring US actor Paul Newman. He was almost certainly the model for Sylvester Stallone's *Rocky* films of the 1970s and 1980s.

**Greene** (Henry) Graham 1904–1991. English writer. An astounding storyteller, Greene was exceptionally versatile; he wrote plays, film scripts and was also a film critic and contributed to children's literature. His novels of guilt,

Graham Greene

despair, and penitence include *The Man Within* 1929, *Brighton Rock* 1938, *The Power and the Glory* 1940, *The Heart of the Matter* 1948, *The Third Man* 1950, *The Honorary Consul* 1973, *Monsignor Quixote* 1982, and *The Captain and the Enemy* 1988.'

It was with *Stamboul Train* 1932 that Greene was first recognised as a writer of originality and power with a special sensitivity to the world of urban seediness. This interpretive setting became known as 'Greeneland,' an imaginary country which extended its boundaries to mid-century Africa, Latin America, the Far East, the Caribbean, Vienna and Brighton Pier. His conversion to Catholicism when a young man supplied the intellectual and moral intensity which, alongside his concern with politics and corruption, gave his work its individual character. *The Power and the Glory*, which won the Hawthornden Prize for 1940, established Greene as a writer of international importance. Greene continued to write and publish works of varying success until the last decade (his final novel, *The Captain and the Enemy*, was published in 1988), but his high literary reputation rested on his serious religious novels, of which *The Power and the Glory* is considered his masterpiece.

**Halston** Roy Halston Frowick 1932–1990. American fashion designer. Born in Evansville, Indiana, Halston trained in millinery and joined Bergdorf Goodman in 1958, where he produced highly successful and innovative hat designs. His cachet grew in the 1960s and Bergdorf offered him the chance to design clothes.

Halston opened his own company in New York in 1968 making made-to-measure clothes; his first collection was shown in 1969. In the 1960s he was known for his knitwear designs—long cashmere dresses and sweaters tied over the shoulder—and in the early 1970s he shot to fame with his response to the American fitness cult. He created a vogue for easy-to-wear clothes that emphasized the body but left it free to move. In 1973 Norton Simon paid $12 million for the Halston label, and Halston diversified into loungewear, luggage, and cosmetics.

**Hammer** Armand 1898–1990. US entrepreneur. Hammer visited the USSR 1921 and acquired the first private concession awarded by the Soviet government: an asbestos mine. He built up fortunes in several business areas, including the import-export business, and was chair of the US oil company Occidental Petroleum until his death. He was renowned for his dynamism, his championing of East–West relations, and his many philanthropic and cultural activities.

Having graduated in medicine from Columbia University, Hammer wanted to use his skills to aid victims of starvation and typhus in the Ural Mountains. While in the USSR, he developed the idea of importing food from the US grain surplus in exchange for luxury goods. Lenin approved, and Hammer established a large import-export business. During the next quarter of a century, he made a fortune in, among other things, livestock feed and cattle.

In 1956, he and his wife each put $50,000 (£30,000) into a struggling oil company, Occidental Petroleum, which became one of America's largest. He ruled it with what has been described as 'a whim of iron'—the annual meeting was held on his birthday.

**Harrison** Rex (Reginald) Carey Harrison 1908–1990. English film and theatre actor. He appeared in over 40 films and numerous plays, often portraying sophisticated and somewhat eccentric characters. He won a Tony Award and an Academy Award for his performance in *My Fair Lady* 1964 and was nominated for an Oscar for his role as Julius Caesar in *Cleopatra* 1963. His other films included *Blithe Spirit* 1945, *The Ghost and Mrs Muir* 1947 and *Dr Doolittle* 1967. He was renowned for his theatre and film portrayals of the waspish Professor Higgins in *My Fair Lady*, the musical version of Irish dramatist George Bernard Shaw's play *Pygmalion*.

Harrison made his first stage appearance in London in 1927 and New York in 1939. His films in the 1930s and 1940s showed his ability to give his characters personality and the speed, ease and elegance of his acting were equally impressive. After the end of the war, he became the quintessential English gentleman of Hollywood films, with a gift for understatement and precise timing. At the same time, he was given important and challenging roles on the New York stage, such as that of Sir Henry Harcourt-Reilly in T S Eliot's *The Cocktail Party*. He had been appearing in a Broadway production of *The Circle* until a month before his death. Professor Higgins in *My Fair Lady*, however, marked the apex of Harrison's career. He apparently took on some of the professor's personality in private life, and tended to use the alias of Higgins when booking seats at the theatre or making a restaurant reservation.

**Heffer** Eric 1922–1991. English Labour politician. In 1960 Heffer was elected to Liverpool city council, and became a member of Parliament for the Walton division of Liverpool, retaining his seat there from 1964–91. A brutally honest churchman, his refusal to compromise his principles won him many admirers but blighted his ministerial career. In 1974 Harold Wilson appointed him minister of state, in the Department of Industry, but he resigned 1975 over a disagreement with the government's European policies. He joined Michael Foot's shadow cabinet 1981, and was regularly elected to Labour's National Executive Committee, but found it difficult to follow the majority view.

Born in Liverpool, Heffer left school at 15 and entered an apprenticeship as a carpenter and joiner, becoming a member of the Amalgamated Society of Woodworkers. He soon joined the Labour Party, beginning a life-long association with socialism. After war service with the Royal Air Force, Heffer returned to his trade, but became steadily more involved in party politics. Although lacking a strong formal education, Heffer was a voracious reader and, as he advanced his self-education, a successful journalist and author. He was a hard-working parliamentarian and constituency representative and regularly attended the House of commons until the severity of his illness, some few months before his death, prevented it.

**Henson** Jim (James) Maury 1936–1990. US puppeteer who created the popular television Muppet characters, including Kermit the Frog, Miss Piggy and Fozzie Bear. The Muppets became popular through the children's television series 'Sesame Street' which first appeared in 1969. The educational series soon became compulsive viewing in over 80 countries. In 1976 Henson created 'The Muppet Show', which ran for five years and became one of the world's most widely seen television programmes, reaching 235 million viewers in 100 countries.

Henson claimed that he became a puppeteer by accident when he needed a job between high school and college. His Muppet figures (he said the name was a cross between 'marionette' and 'puppet') first appeared in 1954 in a five-minute, late-night television show called 'Sam and His Friends'. The Muppets later appeared in television advertisements and variety shows, but did not become universally known until they became the mainstays of 'Sesame Street' and 'The Muppet Show'. Henson's feature films included three Muppet movies, *The Dark Crystal* (1982), *Labyrinth* (1986) and the blockbuster *Teenage Mutant Ninja Turtles* (1990). In 1989, Henson sold the production company, Henson Associates Inc., to Walt Disney Co. for about $100 million.

*Jim Henson*

**Hill** Austin Bradford 1897–1991. English epidemiologist and statistician. He pioneered the need for a rigorous statistical approach to study patterns of disease, and together with Richard Doll was the first to demonstrate the important connection between cigarette smoking and lung cancer.

Hill took a degree in economics, and in 1923 began working for the Medical Research Council as a statistician. In 1933 he moved to the London School of Hygiene and Tropical Medicine, where he later became professor of medical statistics. His work on smoking and lung cancer, which involved collecting data on the smoking habits and health of over 30,000 British doctors for several years, in the pre-computer age, is considered to be among the great medical achievements of the century.

**Hofstadter** Robert 1915–1990. US nuclear physicist who made pioneering studies of nuclear structure and the elementary nuclear constituents, the proton and the neutron. He established that the proton and neutron were not point-like, but had a definite volume and shape. He shared the 1961 Nobel Prize for Physics.

Born in Manhattan, Hofstadter held positions at the National Bureau of Standards, Washington DC, and Princeton University, New Jersey, before moving in 1950 to Stanford University, California, to start the work which was to earn him a Nobel Prize. His early work at Stanford involved bouncing, or scattering, electrons from complex nuclei, such as gold. This work produced accurate pictures of the charge distribution within nuclei. Gradually, smaller nuclei were studied by Hofstadter and his team, using electrons of increasing energy. By 1960, accurate data had been obtained for the proton and neutron, revealing the spatial distribution within nuclei. Gradually, smaller nuclei were studied by Hofstadter and his team, using electrons of increasing energy. By 1960, accurate data had been obtained for the proton and neutron, revealing the spatial distribution of charge and magnetization within these particles. Hofstadter was awarded the 1961 Nobel Prize for Physics, which he shared with Rudolf Mössbauer, for his work on nuclear structure. His work was carried on, and extended by others, revealing that point-like objects—quarks—are the constituents of protons and neutrons. Physicists Jerome Friedman, Henry Kendall, and Richard Taylor, who made this discovery at Stanford about 20 years ago, were awarded the 1990 Nobel Prize for Physics.

**Holmes à Court** Robert 1937–1990. Australian entrepreneur. At the peak of his financial strength, before the stock-market crash 1987, he owned 30% of Broken Hill Proprietary, Australia's biggest company; 10% of Texaco; and also had substantial media, transport, and property interests. His personal fortune was about A\$1.3 billion/(£555) million, making him the richest individual in Australia. His fortune halved in a matter of weeks after the stock-market crash. Having sold his master company, the Bell Group 1988, to Alan Bond, he retired becoming a private investor.

When Holmes à Court began to rebuild his fortune after the sale of the Bell Group, instead of using high-profile public companies, he chose to invest in companies that appealed to his personal interests—the theatre and the arts, including Andrew Lloyd Webber's Really Useful Company.

**Jiang Qing** formerly *Chiang Ching* 1914–1991. Chinese communist politician, wife of the party leader Mao Zedong. In 1960 she became minister for culture, and played a key role in the 1966–69 Cultural Revolution as the leading member of the Shanghai-based Gang of Four, who attempted to seize power 1976. Jiang was imprisoned.

Jiang was a Shanghai actress when in 1937 she met Mao Zedong at the communist headquarters in Yan'an; she became his third wife 1939. She emerged as a radical, egalitarian Maoist. Her influence waned during the early 1970s and her relationship with Mao became embittered. On Mao's death Sept 1976, the Gang of Four with Jiang as a leading figure, sought to seize power by organizing military coups in Shanghai and Beijing. They were arrested for treason by Mao's successor Hua Guofeng and tried 1980–81. The Gang were blamed for the excesses of the Cultural Revolution, but Jiang asserted during her trial that she had only followed Mao's orders as an obedient wife. This was rejected, and Jiang received a death sentence Jan 1981, which was subsequently commuted to life imprisonment Mar 1983 in Qincheng Prison. She eventually died in her home, allegedly committing suicide after suffering from lung cancer.

**Joyce** Eileen 1912–1991. Australian concert pianist. Internationally recognised as a charismatic artist, her playing combined subtlety with temperamental fire and a rare ardour. She made a London debut in 1930. Her immense repertoire included over 70 works for piano and orchestra. After 25 years of relentless work and travel, Joyce decided to end her career, for she had found that 'having lived totally for music, there was nothing else in my life.'

The daughter of an itinerant labourer in Western Australia, she studied in Leipzig, East Germany for three years before moving to London, where her brilliant talent soon won acclaim. Joyce became a household name during the 1930s and 1940s, reaching a much broader section of the public than generally listened to classical music at that time. It was during this period that she made her stylish recordings for Parlophone. However, the pace of work became overtaxing, and Joyce withdrew in the early 1960s to escape the tension she had lived with incessantly for 25 years.

**Kerr** John Robert 1914–1990. Australian lawyer. After graduating at the University of Sydney, he embarked on a legal career on the New South Wales circuit, becoming a judge of the Australian Supreme Court 1966–72, and chief justice of the Supreme Court of New South Wales 1972–74. He was appointed governor-general of Australia 1974. He achieved notoriety when he controversially dismissed the prime minister, Gough Whitlam, and his government 1975. The government had suffered a defeat in the Senate, but retained a majority in the House of Representatives. Kerr called upon the leader of the opposition, Malcolm Fraser, to form an administration. Kerr subsequently resigned as governor-general 1977.

**Kosinski** Jerzy 1933–1991. Polish-born US author. His childhood experiences as a Jew in Poland during World War II are recounted in *The Painted Bird* 1965, a popular success. Later novels include *Being There* 1971, filmed 1979 with Peter Sellers, and *Pinball* 1982.

After many unsuccessful attempts to leave Poland, Kosinski finally reached the USA in 1957 and was offered a place at Columbia University in New York. His first novel *The Painted Bird* 1965, was a novel of raw experience: told through the eyes of a small boy, it drew much of its popularity from its ability to shock American readers who were unaccustomed to such cold accounts of wartime atrocities. The book's success was followed by that of *Steps* 1968, which won the National Book Award, and of *Being There* 1971, which mocked the rampant media fascination of Americans. The success of his early novels made him a celebrity; he came to enjoy New York high society and to display a growing and unattractive interest in the very rich, appearing on the cover of the *New York Times Sunday Magazine* in polo gear. His later novels were largely unsuccessful and his fame as a novelist gradually eroded.

**Land** Edwin 1909–1991. US inventor of the Polaroid camera 1947, which developed the film in one minute inside the camera and produced an 'instant' photograph. Land established the Polaroid Corporation 1937–80. His research also led to a process for 3-D pictures, 'instant' colour film, 'instant' motion pictures, and a

*Archbishop Marcel Lefebvre*

new theory of colour perception, the 'retinex' theory 1977.

Polaroid sunglasses and 60-second photography were only two of the better known inventions through which Land revolutionized the field of optics in a career during which he amassed over 500 patents. He made his first discovery, the polarizing filter, at the age of 20, while a student at Harvard. It eventually became the mainstay of the Polaroid Corporation which he set up in 1937 to market his inventions. Many discoveries in the optical field followed, embracing work for gun sights and aerial surveillance during World War II and afterwards. Land's patents were used to build the camera in the U2 spy plane. The instant X-ray photograph was another of his achievements. His investigations into instant photography had been inspired by his 5 year old daughter who, in 1941, had asked why she could not see the photograph immediately after it was taken. The Polaroid system of instant photography was put on sale in 1948, but it was bulky and the process messy. Land spent the next 30 years developing and refining the system until, in 1972, the SX-70 system provided the first pocket sized instant camera able to deliver dry colour photographs.

**Lean** David 1908–1991. English film director. His films, noted for their atmospheric quality, include early work codirected with Noël Coward. On his own Lean directed *Blithe Spirit* 1945, *Brief Encounter* 1946, (which established him as a leading talent), *Great Expectations* 1946, and *Oliver Twist* 1948. His later films included such accomplished epics as *The Bridge on the River Kwai* 1957 (Academy Award), *Lawrence*

*of Arabia* 1962 (Academy Award), *Dr Zhivago* 1965, and *A Passage to India* 1984.

Lean's films are distinguished more by a flair for visual storytelling than by a consistent personal vision. Certain themes recur in his work, particularly that of a protagonist who is in some way out of step with his or her surroundings. But the most striking aspect of his work is its progressive widening of scale, from the suburbia (redolent of Lean's own background, from which the cinema afforded an escape) of *Brief Encounter*, via the crowded historical canvasses of the Dickens' films *Great Expectations* 1946 and *Oliver Twist* 1948, to the daunting scale of *Bridge on the River Kwai* 1957, *Lawrence of Arabia* 1962, and *Dr Zhivago* 1965. The critics' antipathy to *Ryan's Daughter* 1970, in which he failed to reconcile physical sweep with intimacy, caused him to withdraw from filmmaking for over a decade, but a *Passage to India* represented return to form. At the time of his death he was beginning a film based on Joseph Conrad's novel *Nostromo*.

**Lefebvre** Marcel 1905–1991. French Catholic priest in open conflict with the Roman Catholic Church. In 1976, he was suspended by Pope Paul VI for the unauthorized ordination of priests at his Swiss headquarters. He continued and in June 1988 he was excommunicated by Pope John Paul II, in the first formal schism within the church since 1870.

Ordained in 1929, Lefebvre was a missionary and an archbishop in West Africa until 1962. He opposed the liberalizing reforms of the Second Vatican Council 1962–65 and formed the 'Priestly Cofraternity of Pius X'.

**Lockwood** Margaret. Stage name of Margaret Mary Lockwood 1919–1990. English actress. She achieved stardom notably as the determined heroine of Alfred Hitchcock's *The Lady Vanishes* 1938. Between 1937 and 1949 she acted exclusively in the cinema, achieving success in *The Wicked Lady* 1945. After 1955 she made only one, much later film *The Slipper and the Rose* 1976, though she periodically appeared on the stage and on television until her retirement in 1980.

Lockwood attended the Royal Academy of Dramatic Art (RADA), and made her stage and film debut 1934. She had some modest early successes, playing a variety of minor roles in films during the latter 1930s, and achieving stardom, notably as the determined heroine of Alfred Hitchcock's *The Lady Vanishes* 1938. Her lustrous good looks were accompanied by flexible performing skills within a somewhat narrow range. During the war years she starred in several of the melodramas made by the Gainsborough studio (an English film company of the 1930s), making headlines with her plunging necklines as the female highwayman of *The Wicked Lady*. Her film career subsequently faltered, but she achieved renewed success on television, particularly as a barrister in the courtroom series *Justice* 1972–73. The last years of her life, however, were spent as a virtual recluse. Her daughter is the actress

Julia Lockwood (1941– ). She published an autobiography *Lucky Star* 1955.

**Lubetkin** Bertholdt 1901–1990. Russian-born architect whose effect upon avant garde English architecture was far reaching. He moved to England in 1930 and formed, with six young architects, a group called Tecton. During the 1930s Tecton was responsible for many of the public buildings erected in England in the new style of architecture then flourishing on the Continent, including the Gorilla House, 1937 at the London Zoo and a health centre for the London borough of Finsbury, 1938. The group was also a training ground for the forward looking architects of the next generation, such as Denys Lasdun.

Lubetkin studied architecture in Moscow and Paris. His work in England with the Tecton group was met with a very favourable response from the public because it showed that modern functional design could incorporate gaiety. During World War II the group dispersed and Lubetkin became a farmer in Gloucestershire. During the early part of the war Lubetkin, at the request of the London Zoo, provided a temporary home to a number of rare birds and animals, adding exotic animals to the common ducks and poultry that inhabited his farm yard. Lubetkin resumed his practice in London after the war and continued to show a strong sense of social as well as architectural responsibilty in his designs. In 1948 he was appointed architect-planner of Peterlee, a new post war town. But his plan was ahead of the times and, after much dispute, was rejected; his resignation followed soon after. Lubetkin retired at the age of 52 and thereafter led a secluded life.

**Luria** Salvador Edward 1912–1991. Italian-born US physician who was a pioneer in molecular biology, internationally known for his research in the field of virology and genetics. With fellow biologists Max Delbrueck and Alfred Hershey, the three were cited for their 'discoveries concerning the replication mechanism and the genetic structure of viruses,' which 'set the solid foundation on which modern molecular biology rests.' In the same year, Luria and Delbruek also received the Louisa Gross Horwitz Prize for their work on genetics of bacteria and bacteriophage. Nobel Prize in Medicine 1969.

Luria was born in Turin, Italy, into a distinguished Northern Italian Jewish family. He went to Paris in 1938, where he became a research fellow at the Institut du Radium. In 1940 Luria emigrated to the US. From 1943 he taught at a number of universities and in 1959 became a professor at the Massachusetts Institute of Technology (MIT), where he taught until his death. After joining MIT he organised a new teaching and research programme in the field of microbiology and later founded the MIT Center for Cancer Research which he directed from 1972 to 1985. He urged his students to form a strong world view and for some time taught a course in world literature to graduate students at MIT and at Harvard Medical School to ensure their involvement in the arts. Luria was an ardent pacifist and was identified with efforts to keep science humanistic.

**McCone** John Alex 1902–1991. US industrialist and civil servant. Early successes in the steel and construction industries made him a multimillionaire on the strength of winning several government contracts. He became chairman of the US Atomic Energy Commission 1958, and was chosen by President Kennedy to succeed Allen Dulles as director of the Central Intelligence Agency (CIA) 1961. A devout Catholic and a fervent opponent of communism, he declined to use extreme measures to secure some of the political ends his political masters sought. He was eventually removed from his post by President Johnson. He returned to his successful, lucrative business career as a director of the International Telephone and Telegraph Corporation (ITT).

**McCrea** Joel 1905–1991. US film actor. Beginning as an extra, McCrea rapidly graduated to romantic leads in the 1930s, and played in several major productions of the 1940s, such as *Sullivan's Travels* 1941. In the postwar years he was associated almost exclusively with the western genre, notably *Ride the High Country* 1962, now recognized as a classic western film. He retired to become a rancher.

McCrea's career stretched from 1928 to 1976. By the time of *Dead End* 1937 and *Union Pacific* 1939, he was starring in major films. Alfred Hitchcock who cast him in *Foreign Correspondent* 1940 described him as too 'easygoing', yet this aspect of his playing was both deceptive and the key to his skill, and contributed significantly to his success in the comedies of Preston Sturges, such as *The Palm Beach Story* 1944, which were the high point of his career.

**McPartland** Jimmy (James Duigald) 1907–1991. US cornet player, one of the founders of the Chicago school of jazz in the 1920s. He was influenced by Louis Armstrong and Bix Beiderbecke, whom he replaced in a group called the Wolverines in 1924. He also recorded with the guitarist Eddie Condon, and from the late 1940s often worked with his wife, the British pianist Marian McPartland (1920– ).

Originally McPartland, Bud Freeman, Frank Teschemacher (1906–1932), and others were known as the Austin High School Gang, after the school in Chicago they all attended (McPartland played an anniversary concert for the school in 1965). Chicago's riverboat link to New Orleans made the city a focus of early jazz developments from the Dixieland style, and in the northern city the music became harder and faster. In the mid-1930s McPartland was in a band with his brother, a guitarist; later he toured widely with bands of his own.

**Manzù** Giacomo 1908–1991. Italian sculptor who, from the 1930s, worked mostly in bronze. Though a left-wing agnostic, he received many religious commissions. His figures reveal a belief in the innate dignity of the human form.

*Steve Marriott*

Born in Bergamo, he trained as a carpenter and gilder but was largely self-taught as a sculptor. In Milan in the 1930s he was associated with progressive, anti-fascist intellectuals, but he was never a Modernist. French sculptors Auguste Rodin, Edgar Degas, and Aristide Maillol were among those whom he most admired. 1938 saw the first of a recurring series of Cardinals whose form became increasingly simplified. His work for the Vatican included portraits of Pope John XXIII, and the renowned Door of Death, completed in 1964 for St Peter's cathedral, Rome. His later years produced painting and occasional theatre designs, notably for Stravinsky's *Oedipus Rex*. His former studio, at Ardea, near Rome, is now a museum of his work.

**Marriott** Steve 1947–1991. UK pop singer and guitarist, successful in the mid-1960s as lead singer with the Small Faces, a mod group; less successful with Humble Pie 1969–1975; and subsequently reduced to playing the pub circuit. The Small Faces had a number-one hit in 1966 with 'All or Nothing'.

Marriott's show-business career began with the part of the Artful Dodger in the musical *Oliver!*. His first recordings imitated Buddy Holly, and he was briefly in a band called the Moments before forming the Small Faces in 1965 with Ronnie Lane, Ian McLagen, and Kenny Jones. They were popular on the London mod scene and soon had a hit with 'Watcha Gonna Do About It?' 1965, followed by TV appearances on *Ready Steady Go!*, 'Sha La La La Lee', and 'My Mind's Eye'. The band came third in a 1966 popularity poll after the Beatles and the Rolling Stones.

**Mortensen** Stanley 1921–1991. English football player. He joined the Blackpool Football Club shortly before World War II. As Blackpool's dashing centre forward 1946–55, Mortensen either led the attack or supported the leader, scoring 197 goals in 317 appearances. In the 1953 FA Cup Final when Blackpool defeated Bolton 4–3, Mortensen scored three goals—a feat never accomplished before or since in a FA Cup Final. He won 25 international caps while playing for the England team and scored 14 goals, four of which were scored on his debut, against Portugal, in 1947.

**Michelucci** Giovanni 1891–1990. Italian architect. He produced numerous urban projects which combined a restrained modernism with sensitive contextualism, for example, the Santa Maria Novella Station in Florence 1934–37. He departed from his rationalist principles in the design of the church of San Giovanni (1961) by the Autostrada del Sole near Florence.

Michelucci was born in Pistoia and graduated in Florence in 1914. He built his first work, a chapel at Caporetto, 1916. Michelucci's rationalism is apparent in his Bank and Commodities Exchange at Pistoia 1950–52 which, however, was also seen as an idealization of the local vernacular. The church of San Giovanni was a fluid, sculptural composition in poured concrete, dedicated to the men who died in the construction of the motorway. The move towards a more organic and expressionist building was in line with Michelucci's ideas about architecture, its relation to craft and society, and the lessons of nature. As well as continuing to build, Michelucci spent a large part of his remaining years working on imaginary projects, largely inspired by natural forms.

**Muggeridge** Malcolm 1903–1990. English journalist and author. He worked for *The Guardian*, *The Calcutta Statesman*, and the *Evening Standard*. In World War II he distinguished himself in the Intelligence Corps and returned to journalism on *The Daily Telegraph* before becoming editor of *Punch* 1953–57.

His many books reflected the complex soul-searching which dominated so much of his life, two examples were *The Earnest Atheist* 1936, and his autobiography *Chronicles of Wasted Time* 1982. He converted to Roman Catholicism in 1982.

**Namuth** Hans 1915–1990. German-born US photographer who specialized in portraits and documentary work. He began as a photojournalist in Europe in the 1930s and opened a portrait studio in New York in 1950. His work includes documentation of the Guatemalan Mam Indians (published as *Los Todos Santeros* 1989) and of US artists from the 1950s (published as *Artists 1950–1981*). He also carried out assignments for magazines.

**Noyce** Robert Norton 1927–1990. US scientist and inventor, together with Jack Kilby, of the silicon microchip that revolutionized the computer and electronics industries in the 1970s and 1980s. The device, also known as the integrated circuit (IC), quickly became the basis for such products as the personal computer, the pocket calculator, and the programmable microwave oven.

Noyce was an entrepreneur as well as a scientist and was equally at ease in the research laboratory as he was in the office of the venture capitalist. Noyce was awarded a patent for the integrated circuit in 1959. The device was capable of handling far more information than individual transistors and proved a vital catalyst in technological change and industrial development. In 1961 Noyce founded his first company, Fairchild Camera and Instruments Corporation, from which emerged the seedlings of Silicon Valley. The company was the first in the world to understand and exploit the commercial potential of the integrated circuit. In 1968 he and six colleagues founded Intel Corporation, which became one of the USA's leading semiconductor manufacturers. At the time of his death, he was president of Sematech Incorporated, a government-industry research consortium created to help US firms regain a lead in semiconductor technology that they had lost to Japanese manufacturers.

**Oakeshott** Michael 1901–1990. English political philosopher, author of *On Civilization* 1969. A conservative, he was praised by the right for emphasizing experience over ideals, summed up as 'Tory anarchism'. He was professor of politics at the London School of Economics 1951–69.

Oakeshott was a fellow of Gonville and Caius College, Cambridge for 65 years. He was editor of the *Cambridge Journal*, in which he developed, in the 1940s, his polemic against the ethos of collectivism and ideological politics which he regarded as rationalist politics bearing no relation to the practice of politics. However, he made his main public impact as Professor of Political Science at LSE. The LSE had traditionally been associated with left-wing causes, and his arrival was a major innovation in the school. His weekly lectures were highly popular, and his arrival at the lectern was usually met with applause. In the 1960s he established a one-year masters degree devoted to historiography which attracted students from all parts of the world and which he continued to run after his retirement. Included among his major works are *Experience and its Modes* 1933, *Rationalism in Politics* 1962 and *On Human Conduct* 1975.

**O'Faolain** Sean (John Whelan) 1900–1991. Irish novelist and biographer. His first novel *A Nest of Simple Folk* 1933, was followed by an edition of translated Gaelic *The Silver Branch* 1938. He also wrote many biographies including *Daniel O'Connell* 1938, and *De Valera* 1939, with whom he fought during the Irish civil war.

The son of a police constable in the Royal Irish Constabulary, O'Faolain was brought up in a home sympathetic to the established order. He was converted to Irish republicanism when he was 17 and was active in the Irish Republican Army during the war of independence. He opposed the Anglo-Irish Treaty of 1921 and acted as an intelligence officer and later as director of publicity for the republicans who took up arms against the new government of the Irish Free State. He was disillusioned and embittered by the republican defeat and remained active in the movement for a totally independent Ireland.

O'Faolain was educated at the National University of Ireland and Harvard University, USA. Following a period of self-imposed exile in the US and a short stay in England, he returned to Ireland in 1933, full of hope. His first book of short stories was published 1933. O'Faolain's novels and Irish historical biographies were written during a period in which he was intensely involved in social issues, reflecting the hopes of the revolution and the subsequent disillusionment with society which emerged. When his six year editorship of the magazine he had founded, *The Bell*, ended in 1946 O'Faolain became more detached from Irish social and national issues. He continued to live in Ireland, writing short stories, travel books and an autobiography.

**Olav V** Prince Edward Christian Frederick 1903–1991. King of Norway, after his father, Haakon VII, who reigned from 1905 (when Norway's union with Sweden was dissolved), until 1957. After the German invasion of Norway in 1940 Olav, as crown prince, became a rallying point for his countrymen by holding out against German air raids for two months and later, in exile in England, by playing an important part in liaison with resistance movements in Norway and in building up the Free Norwegian forces in Britain. Olav became king following his father's death in 1957 and won wide respect and affection among his people.

Olav V was born in London, the son of Prince Carl, a member of the Danish royal family, and of Princess Maud, a daughter of King Edward VII. From 1924 to 1926 he studied political economy and international law at Balliol; the Oxford college made him an honorary fellow in 1937. He always retained strong personal ties with England. He was an avid sportsman and won an Olympic gold medal in 1928 for yachting. The image he conveyed throughout his reign was that of a public-spirited, democratic monarch, who was not reluctant to mingle with ordinary people.

**O'Neill** Terence, Baron O'Neill of the Maine 1914–1990. Northern Irish Unionist politician. In the Ulster government he was minister of finance 1956–63, then prime minister 1963–69. He resigned when opposed by his party on measures to extend rights to Roman Catholics, including a universal franchise.

Born in London into an Irish family, O'Neill's early life took him from Eton into the Irish Guards and war service. He entered the House of Commons 1946. He was made a life peer 1970.

**Pandit** Vijaya Lakshmi 1900–1990. Indian politician. A former Indian ambassador to the USSR 1947–49 and the USA 1949–52, she was the first woman to serve as president of the United Nations General Assembly 1953–54. Pandit was involved, with her brother Jawaharlal Nehru, in the struggle for India's independence and was imprisoned three times by the British.After her brother became the first prime minister of India in 1947, she filled a series of political and diplomatic posts, including that of high commissioner to Britain 1954–61, with great distinction. She retired from public life in 1968.

In 1962 she became governor of the state of Maharashta and, after her brother's death in 1964 she took over his constituency, with a large majority. She resigned in 1968, saying that she felt 'out of tune' with the new parliament. During the 1970s she became alarmed by the increasingly authoritarian regime of her niece Indira Gandhi, and became a staunch critic of Gandhi's government. Pandit's last years were clouded by continuing disagreements with Mrs Gandhi.

**Parkinson** Norman 1913–1990. (adopted name of Ronald William Parkinson Smith) English fashion and portrait photographer who caught the essential glamour of each decade from the 1930s to the 1980s. Chiefly associated with the magazines *Vogue* and *Queen*, he was best known for his colour work, and from the late 1960s took many official portraits of the royal family.

**Penney** William 1909–1991. English scientist. A mathematician by training, Penney became an explosives expert. He worked at Los Alamos, New Mexico 1944–45, designed Britain's first atomic bomb, and directed the initial tests at the Monte Bello Islands off Western Australia 1952. He developed the advanced gas-cooled nuclear reactor used in some UK power stations.

The turning point of Penney's career came in 1944, when his investigations regarding blast waves sent him to Los Alamos to join

*William Penney*

the British team working on the atomic bomb. Penney soon established a high reputation there; he made blast measurements at the first nuclear explosion in the USA and was one of two British observers to accompany the flight when the second atom bomb was dropped on Nagasaki. Penney was also one of the British party at the Bikini tests in 1946, where his determination of the blast power, at a time when the USA's more sophisticated gauges failed to operate, earned him the US Medal of Freedom.

Upon his return to England in 1946 Penney was appointed chief superintendent of armament research in the Ministry of Supply. He became responsible for the design and development of Britain's nuclear weapons without the benefit of US cooperation since the US Atomic Energy Act of 1946 prohibited the release of any information. The successful testing of Britain's first atomic bomb in 1952 and of its first hydrogen bomb in 1957 were largely made possible by Penney's outstanding abilities and leadership. This achievement had far reaching consequences in that it paved the way for the bilateral treaty, signed in 1958 between the US and the UK for mutual assistance in nuclear defence.

**Penston** Michael 1943–1990. English astronomer at the Royal Greenwich Observatory since 1965; he became known as the man who weighed the black hole. From observations made with the Ultraviolet Explorer Satellite of hot gas circulating around the core of the galaxy NGC 4151, Penston and his colleagues concluded that a black hole of immense mass lay at the galaxy's centre. Penston calculated the mass of this black hole as about 100 million Suns. However, in an amusing postscript, a number of amateur astronomers spotted a simple mathematical error in the published paper which meant that Penston had to revise the estimated mass of the black hole upwards to 1 billion Suns.

NGC 4151 is the brightest of a class of objects known as Seyfert galaxies, which are like scaled-down versions of quasars. Supermassive black holes had long been suspected to lie at the centres of such objects to explain their strange behaviour, but Penstons result was the first direct observational evidence in favour of this theory. Penston was leading an international team engaged in observations of the nuclei of other galaxies at the time of his death from intestinal cancer in December 1990.

**Perls** Laura (born Lore Posner) 1906–1990. German born psychotherapist who, together with her husband, Fritz, helped develop the Gestalt method of psychotherapy. The Gestalt treatment relied on a wide range of techniques to treat emotional illness, including some derived from theatre and dance movement. Perls and her husband emigrated to the US in 1948 and founded the New York Institute for Gestalt Therapy 1952.

Gestalt therapy is a non-interpretive psychotherapy which emphasises awareness and personal responsibility and adopts a holistic approach, giving equal emphasis to mind and body. It began to achieve prominence towards the end of the 1960s, after it had acquired a radical tinge because it was considered to embody aspects of the free 'hippy' spirit. It has become one of the leading therapies in the USA and has been developing strongly in the UK.

**Pierce** Webb 1926–1991. US country singer and songwriter who developed the honky-tonk style and enjoyed two decades of hit records in the US country-music charts. He was one of the first artists to have a pedal-steel guitar on his own recordings (inconspicuous on his debut 'Wondering' 1952, strongly featured on 'Slowly' 1954), an instrument that later became almost ubiquitous in country music.

Born in Louisiana, Pierce became known in 1950 through a live radio show called the *Louisiana Hayride* (an early showcase, four years later, for Elvis Presley). Pierce was a regular on the programme until 1954, when he moved to the more prestigious and more conservative *Grand Ole Opry* in Nashville, Tennessee. The honky-tonk music that he and his band, the Wandering Boys, made their own, used electric guitars, pedal steel, and fiddle, and dealt as often as not with bars and broken hearts, usually in uptempo numbers. Hits like 'Back Street Affair' 1952, 'There Stands the Glass' 1953 (both written by Pierce), and 'In the Jailhouse Now' 1955 bought Pierce a guitar-shaped swimming pool that became a Nashville tourist attraction. By the 1970s his sound had dated and he was largely neglected until a duet album with Willie Nelson 1982 revived his fortunes.

**Powell** Michael 1905–1990. English film director and producer. Some of his most memorable films were made in collaboration with screenwriter Emeric Pressburger (1902–1988). Their richly imaginative films include *A Matter of Life and Death* 1946, *Black Narcissus* 1947, and *The Red Shoes* 1948. He was the author of several books, including his autobiography *A Life in Movies* 1986.

After a public school education, Powell worked in France as assistant to director Rex Ingram. Returning to Britain he graduated from assistant to director, learning his craft on sundry low-budget 'quickies'. His meeting with Pressburger, who scripted *The Spy in Black* 1939 coincided with Powell's elevation to more prestigious films. The two men formed a company, The Archers 1942, which produced a succession of ambitious films which engaged provocatively with cultural and ethical values. The films ranged from *The Life and Death of Colonel Blimp* 1943 to the opera movie *The Tales of Hoffman* 1951, but after the partnership was amicably dissolved Powell went on to make generally less rewarding films. The most distinctive was the horror tale *Peeping Tom* 1960, which was so vituperously received as to blight his subsequent options.

*Lee Remick*

**Remick** Lee 1935–1991. US film and television actress. Although often typecast as a teasing but obliging flirt, she delivered intelligent and affecting portrayals of an extensive range of characters in her career. Among her best known films were *Anatomy of a Murder* 1959, *The Long Hot Summer* 1958 and *Sanctuary* 1961. Her best performances were perhaps in two 1962 films by Blake Edwards, *Experiment in Terror* and *Days of Wine and Roses*; she earned an Oscar nomination for her role in the latter.

She began her career in musical comedy and then in television. Remick made her screen debut in *A Face in the Crowd* 1957, in which she was cast as a nubile drum majorette. Although she later portrayed a number of diverse characters it proved difficult for her to shake off the image determined by this first casting. During the late 1960s and early 1970s she appeared in a series of films, including *The Hallelujah Trail* 1965 and *The Omen* 1976, which did little to bolster her already faltering reputation. Her last film role was in *The Europeans* 1979, in which she gave a warm and amusing performance.

**Rohwedder** Detler 1932–1991. German Social Democrat politician and businessman. In Aug 1990 he became chief executive of Treuhand, the body that owned some 8,000 East German businesses and that is now concerned with their privatization or liquidation. He was one of the few top German managers thought to have the ability to force market-oriented solutions on Treuhand. This approach was controversial, many preferring a more interventionist stance. He was assassinated the following April.

A former state secretary in the West German economics ministry, Rohwedder was on loan to Treuhand from the Hoesch steel company, which he had turned round and headed for 11 years. Despite the obvious dangers from the Red Army Faction or former members of the Stasi (East German secret police), he refused full-time personal protection. He was shot dead at his home in Düsseldorf.

**Rothschild** Nathaniel Mayer Victor, 3rd Baron 1910–1990. English scientist and public servant. After working in military intelligence during World War II he joined the zoology department at Cambridge University 1950–70, at the same time serving as chairman of the Agricultural Research Council 1948- -58 and Shell Research 1963–70. In 1971 he was asked by prime minister Edward Heath to head his new 'think tank', the Central Policy Review Staff (CPRS), a post which he held until 1974.

The choice of Rothschild to run the 'think tank' proved to be inspired as he quickly began applying the technocratic, efficient methods to social problems he had admired at Shell. However, his unconventionality also brought him trouble. In 1973, he made a public speech warning that 'unless we give up the idea that we are one of the wealthiest, most influential and important nations in the world...we are likely to find ourselves in increasingly serious trouble.' This unfortunately coincided with ministerial speeches declaring that Britain was such a country. He resigned soon after Harold Wilson became prime minister. Rothschild's last major public service was his chairmanship of a Royal Commission on Gambling.

**Ruffin** David 1941–1991. US pop singer, member of the vocal group the Temptations 1962–68 and lead baritone on many of their hits, including 'My Girl' 1965. The Temptations were Motown Records' most popular male group.

Born in Mississippi, Ruffin 'heard gospel before I could think'; in Detroit he recorded on local labels before joining the Temptations. Their first hit 'The Way You Do the Things You Do', 1964, was written by Smokey Robinson, with Eddie Kendricks on lead vocal. Ruffin became lead singer starting with 'My Girl' 1965, which sold a million copies, followed by 'Since I Lost My Baby' and 'It's Growing' the same year, and many others. 'I Wish It Would Rain' 1968 also has Ruffin on lead, but he left after 'Cloud Nine' that year.

He had a few solo hits, notably 'My Whole World Ended' 1969 and 'Walk Away From Love' 1975. When the Temptations reformed for varius projects, including the LP *Reunion* 1982, Ruffin took part. But his voice was damaged by cocaine use and he spent some time in prison for possession and tax evasion. He died of a drug overdose.

**Scott** Douglas 1913–1990. English industrial designer. Scott produced a remarkable variety of classic designs, including the London Transport Routemaster bus, the red double-decker which has been in service since 1968; the 'Roma' wash basin, designed 30 years ago, and still being installed in houses and hotels around the world; and the Raeburn cooker. He set up Britain's first professional product design course, and Mexico's first design school.

He was awarded an RDI (Royal Designer in Industry) in 1970.

Scott was born in Lambeth, London, in 1913 and trained from the age of 13 to be a silversmith. His first work was with a succession of lightning manufacturers, producing Art Deco and Neo-Greek light fittings for town halls and cinemas. His streetlamp designs are still in use in Australia and Cyprus. He then moved to the office of Raymond Loewy, a French war hero and illustrator who almost singlehandedly created the profession of product designer. After World War I, Scott set up his own practice, designing a succession of rugged yet streamlined household, including hand whisks, television cameras, buses, power boats, and wash basins.

**Seebohm** Frederick, Baron Seebohm of Hertford 1909–1990. English banker and philanthropist. Seebohm joined Barclays Bank at 20, progressing to become deputy chairman of Barclays Bank, and chairman of Barclays Bank International 1965–72. He was highly influential in the banking world, and chaired numerous governmental and quasi-governmental committees. A notable philanthropist, he was made a life peer 1972.

Seebohm's Quaker origins led him to take a lifelong interest in improving society as a whole. He was chairman of the Joseph Rowntree Memorial Trust for 15 years, and chaired a government-commissioned inquiry into social work, the Committee on Local Authority and Allied Personal Social Services. The committee's report, published in 1968, was the foundation of the present Department of Social Services. Seebohm was knighted in 1970 for his contribution to banking, and later contributed to House of Lords debates on social services. Following his retirement in 1972 he was president of Age Concern, The National Institute for Social Work, The Royal African Society and Project Fullemploy.

**Serkin** Rudolf 1903–1991. Austrian pianist and teacher, renowned for the quality and sonority of his energetic interpretations of works by J S Bach and other Viennese classics. He first appeared at the age of 12 with the Vienna Symphony. Serkin made his major American debut with the New York Philharmonic orchestra in Switzerland 1936. He emigrated to the USA 1939 and joined the piano faculty of the Curtis Institute in Philadelphia, where he taught until 1975, serving as director from 1968 to 1975. He founded, with German violinist Adolf Busch, the Marlboro Festival for chamber music in Vermont; he served as its director from 1952 until his death.

Serkin's talent was apparent at a very early age and, on the advice of the Emperor Franz Josef's court pianist, his whole family moved to Vienna. During this period he studied composition with German composer Arnold Schoenberg, whom he regarded as one of the three main influences in his life; the other two were Italian conductor Arturo Toscanini and Busch. Busch and Serkin formed a successful duo in the 1920s and also worked together in the Busch's Berlin based chamber orchestra. Following Serkin's US debut, Toscanini helped further his solo career. Serkin led an active concert career while teaching in Philadelphia and understood the significance of the influx of musical talent to the US in altering that country's perception of music's contribution to cultural life. He did much to further this development by serving on the National Council of the Arts and establishing the Marlboro Music School and Festival.

**Siegel** Don(ald) 1912–1991. US film director of thrillers, Westerns, and police dramas. Siegel began as head of the montage unit at the Warner Studio, with *Casablanca* 1942 representing the most celebrated example. He went on to make low-budget features, two of which, the prison film *Riot in Cell Block 11* 1954 and the science-fiction story *Invasion of the Body Snatchers* 1956 were widely recognized for transcending their lack of resources. Siegel moved on to bigger budgets, but retained his taut, acerbic view of life in such films as the Clint Eastwood vehicles *Coogan's Bluff* 1969 and *Dirty Harry* 1971.

**Singer** Isaac Bashevis 1904–1991 Polish novelist and short story writer. Singer's works, written in an often magical storytelling style, reached a wider readership than those of any other Yiddish writer. His novels were set in the Jewish enclaves in which he grew up and combined a deep psychological insight with dramatic and visual impact, they included *The Family Moskat* 1950, *The Slave* 1960, and *Shosha* 1978. Among his short stories are *Gimpel the Fool and Other Stories* 1957, and *The Spinoza of Market Street* 1961. He was awarded the Nobel Prize for Literature 1978.

The son of a penniless rabbi, he followed the path of his brother, Israel Joshua, an aspiring novelist who rejected his father's form of unquestioning faith and emigrated to the USA. It was not until after his brother's death in 1944 that Singer felt free to begin his creative life. He emigrated to the US from Warsaw in 1935, and initially had his work published only in New York Yiddish journals. His short stories and books were later published in translations which he painstakingly supervized. Many of his novels were written for newspaper serialization, and he often held a huge audience spellbound as he read episodes aloud. He continued to write until shortly before his death, adhering to a regular, exacting schedule.

**Siskind** Aaron 1903–1991. US art photographer who began as a documentary photographer and in 1940 made a radical change towards a poetic exploration of forms and planes, inspired by the Abstract Expressionist painters.

Siskind was given a camera as a wedding present in 1929 and took his first pictures while on his honeymoon. He was soon obsessed by photography's creative potential and joined the left wing Film and Photo League. During the Depression years of the 1930s he shot documentary essays, notably his *Harlem Document*, later published as a book. However, his distinctive expressionist style did not emerge until 1943 when he began photographing still lifes of ropes and beach detritus while in a Massachusetts fishing village. Through his use of close ups he discovered a visual ambivalence, expressing a recognisable subject within a formal content of shape and texture which accurately evoked his innermost feelings. He became committed to locating evidence of abstract form in everyday places. Siskind was accepted by avant-garde painters as an equal and participated in heated theoretical discussions held with other members of the abstract expressionist group, such as Adolph Gottlieb, Mark Rothko, and Franz Kline.

**Skinner** B(urrhus) F(rederic) 1904–1990. US psychologist who was a pioneer in the field of behaviorism. Skinner's achievement, by means of his radical approach, was to create a science of behaviour in its own right. His influential work in the theoretical validation of behavioural conditioning attempted to explain even complex human behaviour as a series of conditioned responses to outside stimuli. He created the 'Skinner Box', an enclosed experimental environment for laboratory animals, which was widely adopted by scientists for the assessment of the effects of drugs as well as for more theoretical analyses of behavioural processes.

Skinner opposed the use of punishment, arguing that it did not effectively control behaviour and had unfavourable side effects. However, his vision of a well ordered, free society, functioning in the absence of punishment was one which failed to have much appeal. His research and writings had great influence, attracting both converts and critics. Skinner was the author of several books, including a novel, *Walden Two* 1948, and *Beyond Freedom and Dignity* 1971. He taught at Harvard University from 1947 to 1974, and was active in research until his death.

**Stanwyck** Barbara. Stage name of Ruby Stevens 1907–1990. US film actress. Stanwyck made her first film appearance 1927 after early experience in vaudeville and on Broadway, rapidly assumed star status and continued to be active in the cinema until 1965. She was equally at home in comedy or melodrama and was well suited to the roles of dependently minded women, however perverse. She excelled as the confidence trickster of *The Lady Eve* 1941, and as the temptress of *Double Indemnity* 1944. In later years she appeared frequently on television, notably as the matriarchal star of *The Big Valley*. She never achieved the top rung of stardom, but in 1944 was said to be the highest-paid woman in the US.

**Stewart** Michael, Baron Stewart of Fulham 1906–1990. English Labour politician. Stewart became member of Parliament for Fulham 1945. He soon entered Clement Attlee's government, rising from a junior whip in 1945 to secretary of state for war in 1951. His quietly-spoken, schoolmasterish image disguised a strong political determination, a quality recognized by Harold Wilson who made him education secretary 1966–67, and then foreign secretary 1968. He remained in the House of Commons until 1979, when he accepted a life peerage.

**Stirling** (Archibald) David 1915–1990. English army colonel and creator of the Special Air Service which became the elite regiment of the British Army from 1942. Stirling lived in Rhodesia and Kenya from 1945, but returned to England 1959, where he started Television International Enterprises. However, he was soon drawn into advising units countering terrorism and subversion in countries where Britain had interests. In 1967 he and his friends created the Watchguard organization which, based in Guernsey, employed ex-SAS soldiers to provide bodyguards for Middle East rulers and others. He resigned from this organization in 1972.

Educated at Trinity College, Cambridge, Stirling served, on the outbreak of World War II, with the Scots Guards before transferring to the Commandos. He then created his own special force, after gaining the approval of General Auchinleck, commander in chief in the Middle East. After some abortive initial efforts, he developed the Long Range Desert Group which used jeeps to strike deep behind enemy lines in the North African desert. Stirling was captured in Northern Tunisia 1942, and eventually, after four escape attempts, interned at Colditz. The SAS was given the status of a full regiment 1942 (Stirling himself designed the regiment's cap badge bearing the motto 'Who Dares Wins'), and played a leading part in disrupting German communications in France.

**Taylor** A(lan) J(ohn) P(ercivale) 1906–1990. English historian and television lecturer. International history lecturer at Oxford University 1953–63, he was author of *The Struggle for Mastery in Europe 1848–1918* 1954, *The Origins of World War II* 1961, and *English History 1914–1945* 1965.

Born in Southport and educated in York and at Oriel College, Oxford, A J P Taylor lectured at Manchester University 1930–38 and then returned to Oxford, as a fellow of Magdalene College 1938–76. He established himself as an authority on modern British and European history. He did much to popularize the subject, giving the first televised history lectures, usually standing in front of the cameras, without the use of props or notes.

**Thunders** Johnny. Stage name of John Anthony Genzale 1952–1991. US rock guitarist and singer. Lead guitarist with the trash-glam cult band the New York Dolls 1971–75, he fronted his own group, the Heartbreakers, 1975–77. Moving to London in 1976, they became part of the burgeoning punk scene. Thunders's subsequent solo work includes the album *So Alone* 1978.

*Paul Tortlelier*

The tattered lurex outfits, teased hair, and make-up flaunted by the New York Dolls were influenced by the drag queens at Andy Warhol's Factory, and Thunders remained a flamboyant figure all his life. ('I'll retire if I lose my hair or grow it on my chest,' he vowed.) Songs like 'Pills' and 'Trash' convey their ethos, but the albums *New York Dolls* 1973 and *Too Much Too Soon* 1974 disappointed fans of their live show, and the brief management of Malcolm McLaren in 1974 failed to prevent the breakup of the band. Thunders's newly formed Heartbreakers combined full-tilt hedonism with a sense of irony, as evidenced by the poster slogan 'Check them out while they're still alive'.

After changes in line-up, the band moved to London, where their song 'Chinese Rocks' became a punk favourite. The album *LAMF* 1977 reflects this period; *Too Much Junkie Business* 1983 followed a five-year silence.

**Tortelier** Paul 1924–1990. French cellist, who came to prominence in 1947 as soloist in Richard Strauss's *Don Quixote* in London under British conductor Thomas Beecham. A powerfully intuitive style brought him widespread fame as a soloist and, from 1956, influence as a teacher at the Paris Conservatoire, where his pupils included English cellist Jacqueline du Pré. An unredeemed Romantic in temperament, his fame rested on a wide range including the standard 19th century repertoire, Bach's solo suites, as well as Edward Elgar, William Walton, Zoltán Kodály.

Tortelier played cello for silent film shows and in restaurants while still in his teens. After studies at the Conservatoire he freelanced until appointed principal cellist with the Monte Carlo Orchestra in 1935. Contracts in Boston and Paris followed, and he was becoming established as a soloist after World War II when an encounter with Beecham brought the London engagement and fame. Like Catalan cellist Pablo Casals, in many respects his role model, Tortelier composed occasional pieces against the trend of modern music, which he also viewed as symptomatic of a wider social pathology. His son Yan Pascal Tortelier is conductor-designate of the BBC Philharmonic Orchestra. He left a large legacy of recordings, including a number of his own compositions.

**Tower** John 1925–1991. US Republican politician, a senator from Texas 1961–83. Despite having been a paid arms-industry consultant, he was selected in 1989 by President Bush to serve as defence secretary, but the Senate refused to approve the appointment because of Tower's previous heavy drinking.

Tower, in 1961 the first Republican to be elected senator for Texas, emerged as a military expert in the Senate, becoming chair of the Armed Services Committee in 1981. After his retirement from the Senate in 1983, he acted as a consultant to arms manufacturers and chaired the 1986–87 *Tower Commission*, which investigated aspects of the Irangate arms-for-hostages scandal.

**Valentino** Mario 1927–1991. Italian shoe designer who built an international empire of boutiques and shops, leather-goods, cosmetics, and ready-to-wear ranges. He was instrumental in furthering the careers of the designers Giorgio Armani and Gianni Versace, employing both of them on his leather ranges, and Karl Lagerfeld still designs Valentino shoes.

Valentino was born in Naples and began his career designing specialist shoes, a sector in which he reached fame in the 1950s. His commercial flair steered him towrds many areas. By 1956 he had a shoe-manufacturing company in Naples and a number of shops around the world. He attracted custom from international socialites such as Sophia Loren, Ava Gardner, and Jacqueline Onassis.

**Vaughan** Sarah Lois 1924–1990. US jazz vocalist noted for the remarkable range of her voice (nearly three octaves) and her mastery of such vocal techniques as vibrato, vocal leaps, 'skat' singing and improvization. Her career began in the 1940s; amongst her numerous popular recordings were 'Make Yourself Comfortable' 1954, 'Mr Wonderful' 1956 and 'Broken-Hearted Melody' 1959. She began by singing be-bop with such musicians as Dizzie Gillepsie and Charlie Parker, and later moved effortlessly between jazz and popular music, interpreting pop songs such as 'Misty' and 'Send in the Clowns'.

At the age of 18 she entered a talent contest at the Apollo Theatre in Harlem and impressed Billy Eckstine, whose newly formed band she joined in 1944. From her first recording sessions with Eckstine emerged 'It's Magic,' a smash hit in 1947, which sold over two million copies. In 1955 she left Eckstine's band and made a career for herself as a solo singer. Charlie Parker and Dizzie Gillepsie, who had become great enthusiasts for her voice, helped

further her career, as did a recording contract with Musicraft. She toured indefatigably during the 1960s and 1970s, appearing in 60 countries. In 1982 she won a Grammy Award for the best female jazz vocal performance for the album *Gershwin Live!*. Her vocal control and the beauty of her tone were the hallmarks of her singing in any musical genre, and her vocal contribution to the development of be-bop was certainly of the first importance. She remained a popular performer in nightclubs, at jazz festivals and with symphony orchestras around the world until shortly before her death.

**Walker** Sebastian 1942–1991. English publisher. Formerly a salesman, Walker worked his way up to director of Chatto and Windus Publishing house 1977–79, and founded Walker Books Ltd 1978. Walker Books produce some 300 children's books a year, with an emphasis on high-quality, following a broadly anti-sexist and anti-racist line. In 1989, Walker Books won four of the five major children's books awards.

**Wang An** 1920–1990. Chinese-born engineer, who emigrated to the USA in 1945 and founded Wang Laboratories 1951; it subsequently became one of the world's largest suppliers of word-processing equipment. In 1948 he invented core memory, the world's most common computer memory in the 1950s.

Wang developed Wang Laboratories, with the funds he received from the sale of his patent on core memory. His invention, which was the most common device used for storing computing data before the invention of the microchip, gained him $500,000 from computing company IBM. The company's success began with Wang's custom-made electronic components. An example of one of his early contracts was the first electronic scoreboard, installed at New York's Shea Stadium. However, his company really began to

*An Wang*

take off in 1964 with the introduction of a desktop calculator. With the advent of cheap computer chips Wang switched with great success to the newly emerging market for word processing systems, turning Wang Laboratories into a multi-billion dollar company. When it came to the advent of the personal computer the company was slow in picking up on the trend, a misjudgment which led to financial trouble. The company experienced a slump in the 1980s and posted a loss of more than $400/(£246 million) million in 1989. In response, Wang sold off some of the company's assets and eased out his son, who had become president of the firm in 1986, in favour of an outsider.

**White** Carrie 1874–1990. US centenarian. Born in Gadsden, Florida, as Carrie Joyner, she lived to become, in her 116th year, the oldest authenticated person in the world. Although that was her only claim to fame, she enjoyed a happy family life and died peacefully in a nursing home.

**White** Patrick Victor Martindale 1912–1990. Australian novelist. His internationally acclaimed novels and short stories explored the lives of early settlers in Australia and often masterfully evoked the mental processes of inarticulate and 'abnormal' people. White did more than any other writer to put Australian literature on the international map. His novels include *The Tree of Man* 1955, *Voss* 1957 and *The Solid Mandala* 1966. Nobel Prize for Literature 1973.

White was born in London, but spent his childhood in the Australian countryside. 'Whatever has come since,' he said of this period, 'I feel that the influences of this strange, dead landscape of Australia predominate.' He studied and worked in Australia and England, alternating his residency between the two countries, travelling extensively in Europe when based in England. His first novel *Happy Valley* 1939, won the Australian Literature Society's gold medal. His early novels were compared to James Joyce by critics who, though sometimes finding him difficult to read, recognised his visionary power and willingness to deviate or take risks. In 1940 he joined the Royal Air Force and served as an intelligence agent in Sudan and Egypt. He returned to Australia in 1945, where he resumed his writing and continued to live until his death.

*Patrick White*

**Woolcott** Marion Post 1910–1990. US documentary photographer best known for her work for the Farm Security Administration (with Walker Evans and Dorothea Lange), showing the conditions of poor farmers in the late 1930s in Kentucky and the deep South.

Woolcott had become active in radical politics by the early 1930s. She joined the League Against War and Fascism, photographed at the Group Theatre and attended meetings of the Photo League. In 1937, disappointed by her small earnings from freelancing, she took a job as staff photographer at the *Philadelphia Evening Bulletin*. However, she soon grew impatient with constant assignments from the Ladies' Page and went to Washington where she successfully applied for a post with the Farm Security Agency (FSA). Through her FSA assignments she became a vital, energizing and influential iconographer of America in the 1930s. Her photographs appeared simple, yet were full of political subtleties and stylistic sophistication.

# SOCIETY

# DESIGNERS OF TODAY

**Anthony** John 1938– . US fashion designer with his own business from 1971, noted for cardigans, trousers, and evening dresses in satin and sheer wool. He designs couture collections rather than ready-to-wear ranges, and uses only natural fabrics.

**Armani** Giorgio 1935– . Italian fashion designer. He launched his first menswear collection 1974 and the following year started designing women's clothing. His work is known for fine tailoring and good fabrics. He designs for young men and women under the Emporio label.

**Banks** Jeff 1943– . English textile, fashion, and interior designer. He helped establish the Warehouse Utility chain in 1974 and combines imaginative designs with inexpensive materials to provide stylish but affordable garments for the younger market.

**Bohan** Mark 1926– . French fashion designer who joined the Dior firm 1958, replacing Yves St Laurent, to design couture and ready-to-wear ranges. In 1990 he moved to the English couture house Hartnell. He is noted for refined, romantic clothes, soft prints, and flattering colours.

**Conran** Jasper 1959– . English fashion designer known for using quality fabrics to create comfortable garments. He launched his first collection 1978 and has rarely altered the simple, successful style he then adopted.

**Courrèges** André 1923– . French couturier. Originally with Balenciaga, he founded his own firm 1961 and is credited with inventing the miniskirt in 1964.

**Emanuel** David 1953– and Elizabeth 1953– . English fashion designers who opened their own salon 1977. They specialize in off-the-shoulder, feminine, bouffant-style (puffed out) evening wear. In 1981 Diana, Princess of Wales, commissioned the Emanuels to design her wedding dress.

**Gaultier** Jean-Paul 1952– . French fashion designer who, after working for Pierre Cardin, started his own company 1977, designing collections that went against the fashion trends, inspired by London's street style. Humorous and showy, his clothes are among the most influential in the French ready-to-wear market.

## MONEY WOMEN SPEND ON CLOTHING IN THE UK (1989)

|  | Number (m) | Value in £m |
|---|---|---|
| costumes and suits | 11.5 | 117 |
| skirts | 42.2 | 337 |
| dresses | 37.1 | 354 |
| blouses | 67.3 | 348 |
| corsets and bras | 68.6 | 178 |
| tights | 601.9 | 235 |
| Source: Bulletin of Textile and Clothing Statistics | | |

## MONEY MEN SPEND ON CLOTHING IN THE UK (1989)

|  | Number (m) | Value in £m |
|---|---|---|
| suits | 5.8 | 219 |
| woven trousers | 45.9 | 339 |
| jackets | 7.5 | 178 |
| t-shirts, sweatshirts | 93.7 | 380 |
| Source: Bulletin of Textile and Clothing Statistics | | |

**Hamnett** Katharine 1948– . English fashion designer with her own business from 1979. She became known as an innovative designer, particularly popular in the UK and Italy. She specializes in producing oversized T-shirts promoting peace and environmental campaigns with slogans such as 'Save the World, 'Ban Pollution', and 'Stop Acid Rain'.

**Jackson** Betty 1940– . English fashion designer who produced her first collection 1981 and achieved an international reputation as a designer of young, up-to-the-minute clothes. She rescales separates into larger proportions and makes them in boldly coloured fabrics. In 1991 she launched her own accessories range.

**Karan** Donna 1948– . US fashion designer with her own label; for many years she worked for the Anne Klein company, producing Anne Klein sportswear from 1983. Karan produces trendy, wearable sportswear in bright colours, and also designs tight, clingy clothes, such as the bodysuit.

**Kenzo** trade name of Kenzo Takada 1940– . Japanese fashion designer, active in France from 1964. He opened his shop Jungle JAP 1970, and by 1972 he was well established, known initially for outrageous designs based on traditional Japanese clothing.

**Klein** Calvin (Richard) 1942– . US fashion designer whose collections are characterized by the understated, sophisticated look produced in natural fabrics. He set up his own business 1968 specializing in designing coats and suits, and expanded into sportswear in the mid-1970s.

**Klein** Roland 1938– . French fashion designer, active in the UK from 1968. He opened his own-label shop 1979 and from 1991 designed menswear for the Japanese market.

**La Croix** Christian 1951– . French fashion designer who opened his couture and ready-to-wear business 1986. He worked with Jean Patou 1981–87. He made headlines with his fantasy creations including the short puffball skirt, rose prints, and low décolleté necklines.

**Lagerfeld** Karl (Otto) 1939– . German-born fashion designer, active in France from 1953 and in the USA from 1985. He launched his first own-label collection 1984 while working for Chanel, designed sportswear from 1985, and still works for other fashion houses, designing sportswear for Fendi, shoes for Mario Valentino, and sweaters for Ballantyne.

**Lauren** Ralph 1939– . US fashion designer, producing menswear under the Polo label from 1968, women's wear from 1971, children's wear, and home furnishings from 1983. He

## SPORTSWEAR: HIGH FASHION FOR EVERYONE?

The fashion business is looking healthy. Models walk down the catwalk in Lycra skinsuits and launch their own glittering swimwear companies. But are the fashion and sports worlds getting their wires crossed?

For the last 20 years fitness and health have been 'in', but suddenly the synthetic materials and technologies of the sports world have crossed over into the fashion world, and sports shoe manufacturers are spending as much money decorating trainers with flourescent tongues, stripes and splashes as on serious developments for the serious athlete. Inspired by the developments in clothing for cyclists, skiers and gymnasts, couture fashion designers are working with new materials to create clothes which offer complete freedom of movement, comfort and a close fit. Inspired by the explosive interest in aerobics in the 1980s, manufacturers developed fashion leggings and skinsuits in bold colours. As it's still fashionable to be thin, the figure-hugging materials like nylon/Lycra mixes have proved as popular and attractive off the sports field as on it. And it's a healthy business—model Jerry Hall launched her own shop to fill a gap in the market, producing designer swimwear.

Most high street fashion stores sell wide ranges of Lycra clothing, while chains such as Olympus and Dash offer branded clothing which blurs the difference between fashion and leisurewear. So while you might not be able to survive 40 minutes in the gym or a 17 km/10 mi cycle, you can easily persuade yourself and your friends that because you look fit, you are fit.

Even genuine outdoor and mountainwear ranges, such as those sold by Rohan, have become popular. Polyester 'fleece' pullovers in vibrant sports colours are all the rage, as are Gore-Tex Berghaus jackets. Gore-Tex is one of a new generation of synthetic fabrics designed to improve performance in active outdoor pursuits. It has become as popular in fashion circles as on the mountains. The material is one of a number of 'breathable' fabrics, built up of thousands of tiny pores per square inch which create spaces small enough to stop water penetrating but large enough to allow vapour (or perspiration) to evaporate. Originally aiming at the serious mountaineer and hiker, Gore-Tex 'inventor' W L Gore has changed direction and is using the fabric to make jackets for Mulberry and a line of raincoats for women.

Of course, the trend goes from top to bottom. The sport shoe has been a fashion item since the mid-80s. But the training shoe's image as a high fashion item, which has its roots in the youth culture of the US, really took off in 1988 when it was 'imported' to Britain simultaneously by the street-wise and by couture designer Jean Paul Gaultier, who featured trainers in his 1988 catwalk show.

Now, sports shoes are big business. Designs originally intended to improve the performance and speed of athletes have gained a highly marketable 'street cred'. They have become part of the rapidly growing trend for casual and sports clothing. International sports-shoe manufacturers still design and produce advanced shoes for serious athletes, but around 80% of all sales are to fashion-conscious consumers.

The basic upper design of the shoes has changed little in the last 50 years, although major technical advances have dramatically improved the quality of running soles. The ever-increasing range of new materials (sorbathane, polyurethanes, and EVA as well as numerous foams and nylons) has given shoe designers much more scope to create comfortable and interesting trainers. Trainers and teenagers are a profitable combination. Last year, in North America alone, Nike sold over $1.7 billion worth of shoes and clothing. Some $56 million of the total was spent by 11 to 24-year-old consumers.

For many young New Yorkers, choice of footwear has become a matter of life and death. Everybody wants to walk on 'Air' in basketball boots or trainers, and plenty of style-conscious individuals are prepared to scrimp, save or steal $150 or more, to be able to buy the popular brands. Just a few are prepared to kill to get the required look, and a number of violent attacks related to sought-after training shoes prompted a New York City preacher to call for a boycott of all Nike shoes.

Yet, much of what you pay for has no function whatsoever. Top manufacturers like Adidas, Nike, Reebok and Puma employ some 80 people—rubber technologists, traditional shoe designers, bio-mechanics and fashion designers—working for about two and half years in the development of each new shoe. Most of the 30 or so pieces which make up a pair of trainers have no use other than creating the 'right look'.

*A model sports a black lycra dress with a real fur trim.*

## WHERE PEOPLE BUY THEIR CLOTHES (UK)

| | |
|---|---|
| Marks and Spencer | 16% |
| Multiples | 27% |
| Department stores | 7% |
| Other stores | 4% |
| Mail order | 10% |
| Independents | 18% |
| Others (including supermarkets) | 17% |

Source: BCG Research

## MONEY SPENT ON UNISEX CLOTHING IN THE UK (1989)

| | Number (m) | Value in £m |
|---|---|---|
| jeans | 42.5 | 274 |
| overalls | 22.9 | 145 |
| jumpers, pullovers | 153 | 815 |
| t-shirts, sweatshirts | 147.1 | 261 |

Source: Bulletin of Textile and Clothing Statistics

also designed costumes for the films *The Great Gatsby* 1973 and *Annie Hall* 1977.

**Missoni** knitwear fashion label established in the UK 1953 by Italian designers Rosita and Ottavio Missoni. It became an international business producing classic knitwear.

**Miyake** Issey 1938– . Japanese fashion designer, in France from 1965 and then in the USA. He established his own company in Japan 1970, first showed a collection in Paris 1973, and set up European and US companies from 1979. His designs combine Eastern and Western influences with exotic fabrics.

**Montana** Claude 1949– . French fashion designer who promoted the broad-shouldered look. He established his own business and launched his first collection 1977.

**Mugler** Thierry 1946– . French fashion designer who launched his first collection 1971 under the label Café de Paris. By 1973 he was designing under his own label. His work is strongly influenced by 1940s and 1950s fashion, and known for broad shoulders and well-defined waists.

**Muir** Jean 1933– . English fashion designer who produced her own label for Jaeger from 1962 and set up her own fashion house 1966. In 1991 she launched a knitwear collection. Her clothes are characterized by soft, classic, tailored shapes in leathers and soft fabrics.

**Oldfield** Bruce 1950– . English fashion designer, who set up his own business 1975. His evening wear has been worn by the British royal family, film stars, and socialites.

**Quant** Mary 1934– . English fashion designer. Her Chelsea boutique, Bazaar, revolutionized women's clothing and make-up in the 'swinging London' of the 1960s.

**Red or Dead** UK fashion design label established 1982 by Wayne Hemingway. Initially he sold clothing designed by his wife Geraldine, and customized heavy industrial footwear to make an anti-fashion statement, which was

## HOW MUCH PEOPLE SPEND ON CLOTHING AND SHOES (1987)

| | Spend per head ($) |
|---|---|
| US | 792 |
| Italy | 744 |
| West Germany | 634 |
| UK | 551 |
| France | 546 |
| Japan | 464 |

Source: OECD and NECD

partly responsible for the trend for Doc Martens workwear boots. In 1987 he designed his own-label footwear range, and in 1988 launched clothing collections for men and women, which became popular in London's clubland.

**Renta** Oscar de la 1932– . US fashion designer with his own luxury ready-to-wear label from 1965, later diversifying into perfumes, swimwear, and jewellery. He is noted for the use of opulent fabrics in evening clothes.

**Saint-Laurent** Yves (Henri Donat Mathieu) 1936– . French couturier, producing high quality, individually tailored garments. He was partner to Dior from 1954 and his successor 1957. He opened his own fashion house 1962. He pioneered the ready-to-wear market, creating the first 'power dressing' looks for men and women: classical, stylish city clothes.

**Storey** Helen 1959– . English fashion designer who launched her own label Amalgamated Talent to promote the work of young designers. She opened a shop in Soho, London, 1987 and in 1989 designed a range of shoes for Doctor Marten UK and her own jewellery collection. Her first fashion show was held 1990 and her first menswear collection launched 1991.

**Valentino** trade name of Valentino Garavani 1932– . Italian fashion designer who opened his own house in Rome 1959. Ten years later he had boutiques around the world. In 1975 he launched a ready-to-wear collection. His designs are characterized by simplicity—elegantly tailored suits and coats, usually marked with a V in the seams.

**Versace** Gianni 1946– . Fashion designer who opened his own business and presented a menswear collection 1979. He has diversified into women's wear, accessories, perfumes, furs, and costumes for opera, theatre, and ballet. He began as a buyer for his mother's couture business.

**Westwood** Vivienne 1941– . English fashion designer who first attracted attention in the mid-1970s as co-owner of a shop with Malcolm McLaren (1946– ), which became a focus for the punk movement in London. Early in the 1980s she launched her Pirate and New Romantics looks, which gave her international recognition. Westwood's dramatic clothes have had a wide influence on the public and other designers.

**Yamamoto** Kansai 1944– . Japanese fashion designer who opened his own house 1971. The presentation of his catwalk shows made him famous, with dramatic clothes in an exciting atmosphere. He blends the powerful and exotic designs of traditional Japanese dress with Western sportswear to create a unique, abstract style.

## What people think are 'in'

*(percentage of people asked)*

| | |
|---|---|
| Blue jeans | 85 |
| Bermuda shorts | 82 |
| Pierced ears for women | 77 |
| White weddings | 77 |
| Mini skirts | 71 |
| Wearing boxer shorts | 71 |
| Leather jackets | 69 |
| Women wearing stockings | 63 |
| One-piece swimsuits | 59 |
| Wearing slippers | 57 |
| Short hair for women | 56 |
| French knickers | 54 |
| Long hair for women | 53 |
| Tailor-made suits | 48 |
| Matching colour watches | 47 |
| Turn-ups on men's trousers | 47 |
| Bikinis | 47 |
| The Princess Diana look | 44 |
| Men wearing braces | 42 |
| Double-breasted jackets | 41 |
| Suede shoes | 41 |
| Pyjamas | 34 |
| Fluorescent colours | 34 |
| Hats for men | 34 |
| Lace tights | 33 |
| Pearls | 32 |
| Hats for women | 31 |
| Leg warmers | 31 |
| Bow ties | 31 |
| Flared trousers | 27 |
| Wearing aprons | 25 |
| Y-fronts for men | 21 |
| Fun-fur coats | 19 |
| Furry dice, etc in cars | 16 |
| Shirt cuff-links | 16 |
| Pocket watches | 12 |
| Real fur coats | 9 |
| Flying ducks on wall | 8 |

# RECENT CHANGES AND AREAS OF DEBATE

**city technology college** in the UK, a planned network of some 20 schools, financed jointly by government and industry, designed to teach technological subjects in inner-city areas to students aged 11–18. By 1991 only seven schools had opened, industry having proved reluctant to fund the scheme.

CTCs have caused controversy, (a) because of government plans to operate the schools independently of local education authorities; (b) because of selection procedures; and (c) because of their emphasis on vocational training at a time when there is also a drive towards a broader curriculum. The first college opened in Sept 1987 at Solihull, West Midlands. In 1990 the Treasury announced that the scheme would not be funded beyond the originally planned 20 schools.

**further education college** college in the UK for students over school-leaving age that provides courses of skills towards an occupation or trade, and general education at a level below that of a degree course.

**GCSE** (*General Certificate of Secondary Education*) in the UK, from 1988, examination for 16-year old pupils, superseding both GCE O level and CSE, and offering qualifications for up to 60% of school leavers in any particular

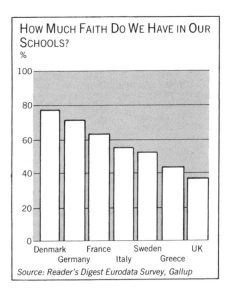

How Much Faith Do We Have in Our Schools?

Source: Reader's Digest Eurodata Survey, Gallup

subject.

The GCSE includes more practical and coursework than O level. GCSE subjects are organized as part of the national curriculum.

**grant-maintained school** in the UK, a state school that has voluntarily withdrawn itself from local authority support (an action called *opting out*), and instead is maintained directly by central government. The first was Skegness Grammar School in 1989. In this way, schools have more

Teacher Vacancies* in Secondary Schools† in England and Wales (1981 and 1990)

| Main teaching subject†† | 1981 | | 1990 | |
|---|---|---|---|---|
| | Numbers | % of filled teaching posts | Numbers | % of filled teaching posts |
| Science | 396 | 1.1 | 417 | 1.5 |
| Mathematics | 383 | 1.3 | 279 | 1.2 |
| English | 195 | 0.6 | 317 | 1.4 |
| Languages | 215 | 1.1 | 366 | 2.4 |
| Craft, design, & technology | 177 | 1.2 | 137 | 1.1 |
| Physical education | 110 | 0.6 | 223 | 1.6 |
| Home economics or needlework | 94 | 0.8 | 80 | 0.8 |
| Music | 91 | 1.3 | 131 | 2.7 |
| Geography | 57 | 0.4 | 90 | 1.0 |
| Commercial and business studies | 45 | 1.1 | 72 | 1.8 |
| Religious education | 58 | 0.8 | 102 | 2.2 |
| Art or light craft | 55 | 0.5 | 77 | 0.9 |
| History | 53 | 0.4 | 89 | 1.0 |
| Other | 258 | 1.2 | 376 | 1.9 |
| **Total vacancies** | 2,187 | 0.9 | 2,756 | 1.5 |

\* Vacancies for full-time teachers as at Jan in maintained schools.
† Includes middle deemed secondary schools.
†† The breakdowns of teachers in post by main teaching subjects have been estimated from the 1984 and 1988 English secondary school staffing surveys.
Source: Dept of Education and Science in Social Trends 21, 1991

## EDUCATION FOR WORK: A SYSTEM IN CHAOS

Vocational education has always been the weakest aspect of British education, particularly in comparison to the UK's European partners.

The structural base of vocational education in the UK is confused. Most non-degree level vocational education is provided in colleges of further education (FE). These cater for young people over the age of 16 who have decided to leave school, full or part-time, and for adults. They offer a wide range of vocational courses and also some academic GCSE and A level courses.

The majority of A level courses, and the new AS levels, worth half an A level, for 16 to 18 year olds are offered in school sixth forms. However two 'hybrid' types of college have been launched in some local authority areas: sixth form colleges, replacing school sixth forms and specializing mainly in academic courses, and tertiary colleges, which combine the functions of sixth form colleges and further education colleges, offering academic and vocational courses for all the over 16s in their area. Private schools have retained their sixth forms and do not normally offer any vocational education.

In 1991 the Conservative Government announced that it would take over the funding and control of all local authority colleges for the over 16s, but not of school sixth forms. The new sector, paid for directly by central government, will therefore include both vocational FE colleges, academic sixth form colleges and the 'mixed' tertiary colleges.

In 1987 the Government launched a programme to set up City Technology Colleges (CTCs), which were to be funded largely by industry and provide a more vocational education from the age of 11 in inner city areas. So far only seven CTSs have opened. The Treasury has announced that the programme will not be extended beyond the initial 20 colleges.

The structure of higher education (post 18) is equally confusing, with more than 40 universities offering mainly traditional academic but some vocational (medicine, engineering) courses, 32 polytechnics offering mainly vocational but some academic courses, and many colleges of higher education offering their own mixture of the two. Two separate funding councils deal with the university sector on the one hand and the polytechnic and college sector, in which the majority of undergraduates are now taught, on the other. The government announced in 1991 that the two funding councils will be merged in the near future, and that the polytechnics could in future opt for the title 'university'.

The separate academic and vocational sectors of education provide separate academic and vocational qualifications up to the age of 18 and beyond, with the BTEC (British Technical and Education Council) system of vocational diplomas running mainly in the FE colleges and A and AS levels mainly in the schools. For the 16- to 18-year olds, the Technical and Vocational Initiative was launched by the Department of Employment in the early 1980s to encourage pre-vocational education in schools. It had its funding sharply cut in 1991. However the Government is considering how it might offer a new system of vocational qualifications at 16 to run parallel with the GCSE as an optional element in the National Curriculum.

Work is going on to standardize vocational qualifications through the National Council for Vocational Qualifications. Critics argue that NCVQs are too heavily influenced by the current needs of employers and not sufficiently geared to the broader educational needs of a flexible workforce in the future.

There remains a distinct gap in status between vocational and academic education in the UK. The polytechnics have found it hard to convince employers that their degrees are of equal value to those offered by the universities, even though they are often more closely geared to employers needs. At 18, although a BTEC national diploma is in theory the equivalent of A Levels as an entry qualification for degree-level study, it is not widely regarded as such by parents or by some university admissions tutors. In the schools, although TVEI (Technical and Vocational Education Initiative) courses were intended to benefit pupils of all abilities, they have tended to be regarded as more suitable for less able young people.

All this is in contrast to the experience of some of the UK's European partners. Germany and the Netherlands run high-status systems of vocational education for 14- to 18-year olds. In France vocational options have been incorporated into the Baccalaureate examinations for 18-year olds while the most prestigious insitutions of higher education remain the vocational *écoles superieures* for administrators, engineers, and others.

Depending on political developments in the UK, the vocational-academic divide could be narrowed over the next few years in several ways. Many options are already under consideration by one or other of the political parties. Among these options are bringing A Level and BTEC qualifications closer together, possibly by means of a British Baccalaureate for 18 year olds; consolidating post-16 education in a college sector, which might supersede school sixth forms either compulsorily or by means of market forces; and providing a single certificate for 18-year olds in academic and vocational subjects.

opportunity to manage their own budgets.

**national curriculum** in the UK, scheme set up through the Education Reform Act 1988 to establish a single course of study in ten subjects common to all primary and secondary state schools. The national curriculum is divided into three core subjects—English, maths, and science—and seven foundation subjects: geography, history, technology, a foreign language (for secondary school pupils), art, music, and physical education. There are four key stages, on completion of which the pupil's work is

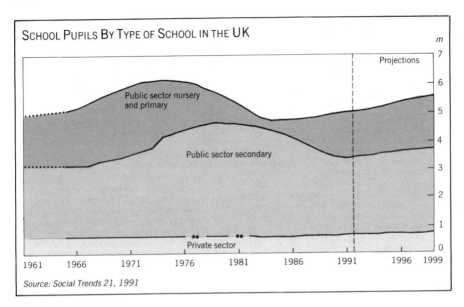

SCHOOL PUPILS BY TYPE OF SCHOOL IN THE UK

Public sector nursery and primary

Public sector secondary

Private sector

Projections

1961 1966 1971 1976 1981 1986 1991 1996 1999

Source: Social Trends 21, 1991

assessed. The stages are for ages 5–7, 7–11, 11–14, and 14-16.

The syllabus for each subject is proposed by a working party, which after consultation with the National Curriculum Council, consisting of 14 advisers from education, industry, and commerce, proposes a final report to the secretary of state for education, who publishes regulations setting out what is to be taught. The first final report was produced June 1988.

**opting out** in UK education, schools that choose to be funded directly from the Department of Education and Science are said to be opting out of local-authority control. The Education Act 1988 gave this option to all secondary schools and the larger primary schools, and in 1990 it was extended to all primary schools. By 1991 only 71 out of 17,000 schools had opted out.

**student finance** payment for higher education, whether by grants, loans, parents, or the student working part time. In the UK, students in higher education have their fees paid by their local education authority and are eligible for a maintenance grant, means-tested on their parents' income. In 1990 the government introduced a system of top-up loans intended gradually to replace 50% of the grant entitlement. At the same time students were debarred from previously available welfare benefits, and the National Union of Students argued that this left many worse off.

In the USA, private organizations called loan guarantors act as intermediaries between the federal government and banks providing the money. The guarantor repays the money if the student defaults, and the government then reimburses most or all the money to the guarantor.

**teacher training** in the UK, teachers are trained either by means of the four-year Bachelor of Education degree, which integrates professional training and the study of academic subjects, or by means of the postgraduate Certificate of Education, which offers one year of professional training to follow a degree course in a specialist subject. The majority of BEd students train to teach in primary schools; the majority of PGCE students to teach specialist subjects in secondary schools.

**vocational education** education relevant to a specific job or career.

The term refers to medical and legal education in the universities as well as higher and further education courses in professional and craft skills. In the UK, the TVEI (Technical and Vocational Education Initiative) was intended to expand pre-vocational education in schools but was in the early 1990s being run down.

# AN ABC OF TERMS

**adult education** in the UK, voluntary classes and courses for adults provided mainly in further-

TOTAL NET EDUCATION AND RELATED EXPENDITURE IN THE UK

| Financial year | Net expenditure | |
|---|---|---|
| | Cash (£m) | As a % of GDP |
| 1965–66 | 1,644 | 4.5 |
| 1970–71 | 2,740 | 5.2 |
| 1975–76 | 7,023 | 6.3 |
| 1980–81 | 13,051 | 5.5 |
| 1985–86 | 17,288 | 4.8 |
| 1987–88 | 20,401 | 4.7 |
| 1988–89* | 22,317 | 4.6 |

\* Provisional
Source: Dept. of Education & Science

# SHOULD YOU THANK THE TEACHER IF YOUR CHILD CAN READ?

Panics about the teaching of reading are a regular feature of educational life. In the early 1990s, experts in both France and the UK reported apparent falls in reading standards—in the UK amongst seven year olds and in France on transfer from primary to secondary school.

In the UK the debate has split into two strands—whether the results of reading tests genuinely do show a fall in standards since the 1980s and secondly over the cause of such a fall, if it exists. A great deal of heat has been generated, but little light.

The UK has no definitive record of reading standards over time. But recent research does indicate some decline since about 1985—although some academics argue the results cannot be regarded as unequivocal because both reading tests and child populations change over time.

What the tests cannot say is how declining standards may relate to teaching methods. The debate is part of the much wider one about 'traditional' and 'progressive' methods of primary school teaching.

Primary schools in the UK use three methods to teach reading, and research shows that the vast majority of schools use a combination of all three. These are:

## Phonics
This links letters, and combinations of letters, to sounds and is crucial to decoding unfamiliar words. The disadvantage of phonics is that it does not provide a complete key to English spelling which is notoriously irregular.

## Psycholinguistics

*Primary school children at a state school.*

This is the theory behind approaches known variously as 'real books' and the 'apprenticeship approach'. These are based on the theory that children learn to read the same way as they learn to speak through their increasing knowledge of the language. Reading partnership schemes involving parents have proved very effective in raising standards. The disadvantage of this approach is that it can be unstructured and provide no fall-back position when a child approaches a new word.

## Look and Say
This is based on the theory that children learn by acquiring a knowledge of the shape and 'look' of words, building up a 'sight vocabulary' over time. It is based on the knowledge that fluent adult readers do have a wide sight vocabulary of thousands of words which they recognize automatically, but used on its own, it does not provide a ready strategy for tackling unfamiliar words.

The increasing use of the 'real books' method of teaching reading was unequivocally blamed for the fall in standards by the educational psychologist who leaked the local authority test results which sparked concern in 1990. Other experts argue that as the apparent decline started in the mid-1980s this is a red herring as very few schools had even heard of 'real books' at that time.

In fact, surveys indicate that more than 90% of British primary schools use a combination of the three approaches to teaching. This is what is recommended to schools in the guidelines on the teaching of reading for the new National Curriculum.

It is the approach supported by the president of the UK Reading Association, Colin Harrison, who applauds the 'real books' advocates.

But Mr Harrison also believes that in order to become fluent children must understand the relationship between letters and sounds in order to decode new words (phonics) and will reach full fluency when they have built up an adult sight vocabulary (Look and Say). In other words the methods are complementary not antagonistic.

This leaves wide open the question of why standards of reading amongst seven-year-olds appear to have fallen in England and Wales (though not in Scotland) over the latter half of the 1980s while standards amongst 11-year olds have apparently not. Potential reasons could include cuts in educational spending (this particularly affects the amount of ancillary and remedial help available to infants' classes') increased child poverty, increasing numbers of children in school with special educational needs and with English as a second language, low teacher morale following industrial action in schools in the mid-1980s, and over-work amongst teachers because of the introduction of the National Curriculum.

One thing parents and all parties agree upon is that we should continue to develop a broader curriculum.

education colleges, adult-education institutes, and school premises. Adult education covers a range of subjects from flower arranging to electronics and can lead to examinations and qualifications. Small fees are usually charged. The Open College, Open University, and Workers' Educational Association are adult-education bodies.

**comprehensive school** in the UK, a secondary school which admits pupils of all abilities, and therefore without any academic selection procedure.

Most secondary education in the USA and the USSR has always been comprehensive, but most W European countries, including France and the UK, have switched from a selective to a comprehensive system within the last 20 years. In England, the 1960s and 1970s saw a slow but major reform of secondary education, in which most state-funded local authorities replaced selective grammar schools (taking only the most academic 20% of children) and secondary modern schools (for the remainder), with comprehensive schools capable of providing suitable courses for children of all abilities. By 1987, only 3% of secondary pupils were still in grammar schools. Scotland and Wales have switched completely to comprehensive education, while Northern Ireland retains a largely selective system.

**conductive education** specialized method of training physically disabled children suffering from conditions such as cerebral palsy. The method was pioneered at the Peto Institute in Budapest, Hungary, and has been taken up elsewhere.

**curriculum** in education, the range of subjects offered within an institution or course.

Until 1988, the only part of the school curriculum prescribed by law in the UK was religious education. Growing concern about the low proportion of 14- and 16-year-olds opting to study maths, science, and technology, with a markedly low take-up rate among girls, led to the government in the Education Reform Act 1988 introducing a compulsory national

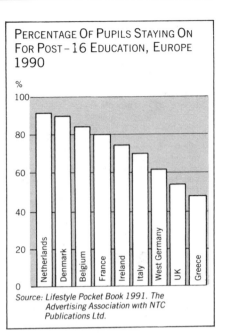

PERCENTAGE OF PUPILS STAYING ON FOR POST-16 EDUCATION, EUROPE 1990

Source: Lifestyle Pocket Book 1991. The Advertising Association with NTC Publications Ltd.

curriculum, which applied to all children of school age (5–16) in state schools. There are three core subjects in the curriculum: English, maths, and science, and seven foundation subjects: technology, history, geography, music, art, physical education, and a foreign language.

**health education** teaching and advice on healthy living, including hygiene, nutrition, sex education, and advice on alcohol and drug abuse, smoking, and other threats to health. Health education in most secondary schools is also included within a course of personal and social education, or integrated into subjects such as biology, home economics, or physical education.

**higher education** in most countries, education beyond the age of 18 leading to a university or college degree or similar qualification.

NUMBER OF STUDENTS* IN HIGHER EDUCATION IN THE UK

|  | '000s | | | 1988–89 | | | % change 1980–81 to 1988–89 | | |
|---|---|---|---|---|---|---|---|---|---|
|  | 1965–66 | 1975–76 | 1985–86 | Total | Men | Women | Total | Men | Women |
| Universities |  |  |  |  |  |  |  |  |  |
| Full-time | 173 | 269 | 310 | 334 | 193 | 141 | + 8 | + 1 | + 21 |
| Part-time† | 13 | 82 | 120 | 135 | 74 | 61 | +33 | +23 | + 48 |
| Total | 186 | 351 | 430 | 469 | 267 | 202 | +14 | + 6 | + 29 |
| Polytechnics and Colleges |  |  |  |  |  |  |  |  |  |
| Full-time | 133 | 247 | 290 | 311 | 159 | 152 | +36 | +25 | + 50 |
| Part-time | 110 | 137 | 217 | 251 | 157 | 93 | +30 | + 7 | +102 |
| Total | 243 | 383 | 507 | 562 | 316 | 245 | +33 | +15 | + 66 |
| Total | 429 | 734 | 937 | 1031 | 583 | 447 | +24 | +11 | + 47 |

*Includes students from abroad. Excludes students enrolled on nursing and paramedical courses at DHSS establishments, 83,600 (prov.) in 1988–89. Excludes students attending private sector colleges.
† Includes Open University.
Source: Dept. of Education and Science

# WHY AREN'T THERE ENOUGH TEACHERS?

The survey conducted by the UK teacher unions in the autumn of 1990 revealed an acute shortage of modern language teachers, in addition to longstanding problems over maths, science, technology and business studies teachers. The survey also revealed a growing shortage of primary teachers, and that special schools for disabled and 'difficult' children were badly hit by teacher shortages. When undergraduates were interviewed by the *New Statesman* about why they would not consider teaching as a career, poor pay and prospects were the major disincentives they mentioned. In the 15-year period to 1991 teachers' pay fell from 37% above the national average to a mere 5% above.

After the series of pay disputes in the mid-1980s which led to industrial action by some teachers, the government unilaterally removed teachers' negotiating rights and determined the profession's pay by means of an appointed advisory committee.

In 1991 the Government abandoned a Parliamentary Bill to restore negotiating rights and offered the profession instead a 'review body', on the lines of those operating for nurses, doctors, dentists, senior civil servants and judges, in return for pledges not to strike over pay. The survey by the six unions into teacher shortages indicates that it is not only pay which is depressing morale in the profession and acting as a disincentive to recruitment. In their comments to the unions, head teachers emphasize the high level of stress the profession was working under as the changes of the Education Reform Act were implemented. These involved substantial curriculum change, imposed from the centre, a new range of assessment procedures for children which proved extremely time-consuming to implement, and much greater financial autonomy for schools. By the autumn of 1990 it looked as though the lowest ebb of recruitment to teacher training courses had been reached and a slight upturn was recorded. Primary courses were over-recruited for the year. But although applications for secondary school training were also up, this disguised continuing shortages of recruits in specific subject areas.

Government measures to improve recruitment seemed to be having some effect. The addition of modern languages to the list of secondary subjects eligible for an extra student bursery boosted recruitment in 1990. However, when this happened with regard to maths, science, and craft, design, and technology (CDT) recruits in 1987, the increase in recruitment was short-lived.

In 1989 the Government introduced two new schemes to help attract recruits to the schools. The Articled Teacher Scheme allowed graduates to train 'on the job' for two years to gain a post-graduate certificate. 500 places were offered in 1990 and 400 licensed teachers recruited.

The Licensed Teacher Scheme allowed up to 500 mature entrants, not necessarily graduates, to move directly into schools as teachers. This scheme is generally opposed by the teacher unions as a dilution of the teaching profession and has so far attracted only a small number of entrants.

The government continued a £2.2 million national advertising campaign in 1991 and reported at the beginning of the year that applications for teacher training places were up by 7%. It also increased its grant to assist local education authorities to tempt former teachers back into the profession from 2 million to 10 million.

Whether and how the teacher shortage will be resolved in the medium term is not yet clear. So far the indicators are mixed. In the longer term, the school population is set to rise after its sharp 1980s dip, so demand for teachers, particularly in primary schools, will also rise. There is no sign yet that teaching will return to its former popularity as a career for young graduates.

## TEACHER SHORTAGES (1990)

| | No. of schools | No. of schools with vacant posts | % of schools with vacant posts | No. of FTE* posts vacant | % of FTE posts vacant in estab | No. of other FTE posts requiring cover | No. of posts either vacant or requiring cover | % of FTE posts either vacant or requiring cover |
|---|---|---|---|---|---|---|---|---|
| **General type of school** | | | | | | | | |
| Nursery and Primary | 11372 | 2583 | 22.7% | 3043 | 3.0% | 1760 | 4803 | 4.7% |
| Secondary | 2741 | 1316 | 48.0% | 2307 | 1.8% | 1111 | 3417 | 2.7% |
| Special | 714 | 278 | 38.9% | 383 | 4.7% | 182 | 565 | 6.9% |
| Other | 343 | 114 | 33.2% | 222 | 3.3% | 100 | 322 | 4.7% |
| *Total/Average %* | 15170 | 4291 | 28.3% | 5955 | 2.4% | 3152 | 9107 | 3.7% |

\* Full time equivalent

## CRISIS IN HIGHER EDUCATION?

The 1990s will inevitably be a period of great change for higher and further education in the UK. All the major political parties are committed to increasing participation in higher education—low by comparison with other industrialized countries—and to breaking down the present division into an elite university sector and a lower status polytechnic and college sector also teaching to degree level.

At present the UK system of higher education is a binary one. On one side of the divide 45 universities, ranging from the ancient (Oxbridge), through the 'redbrick' civic (Birmingham and Manchester), the technological (Loughborough and Surrey) and the modern 'plateglass' (Sussex and Lancaster), all of which provide degree courses which emphasize the theoretical and traditionally academic disciplines. On the other side of the divide are 32 polytechnics (shortly to be 34), and the colleges of higher education, which provide a bewildering range of vocational courses, including most teacher training and art and design courses, plus some more traditional offerings. The majority of British undergraduates are now taught in the public sector of polytechnics and colleges, although it is still true to say that the universities retain an elite status which few polytechnics can match in the eyes of the public or employers. University student numbers fell back in the early 1980s following spending cuts, and although they began to rise again in 1985, they were outstripped by the public sector in 1989, which pushed up its numbers by almost 50% between 1979 and 1989, leaving each sector with more than 300,000 degree level students.

However Government intentions are to double the proportion of students in higher education in the early part of the next century, an ambition shared by the other major political parties.

The question comes of how to attain this objective. A first step will be the amalgamation of the two separate funding organisations which currently serve the two sectors. But this will be only a formality. The more difficult task will be to find an equitable way of financing two sectors which have historically different unit costs. This can only be done by separating out the research funding of universities, which is currently allocated in part with their teaching budgets, and by finding a more equitable method of funding research in all institutions of higher education. A government White paper 1991 proposed both these reforms.

Major decisions will then have to be taken on the issue which concerns the research community: should all institutions of higher education in a new unified system have an equal right to bid for research funds, or should some attempt be made to concentrate research in a few elite institutions, as some scientists want. A second major question to be resolved concerns academic standards. In the public sector these have been overseen by the Council for National Academic Awards, until polytechnics were regarded as sufficiently experienced to oversee their own, and by Her Majesty's Inspectorate. The universities have guarded their academic independence jealously. In a unified system some unified system of quality control would be needed. This would be particularly true if the rapid expansion of higher education envisaged by the politicians does in fact happen over the next decade or more. Some universities and polytechnics are already 'franchising' courses to further education colleges to help students work their way through the vocational route to a degree. If this became common practice some sort of monitoring would be required to maintain standards.

The present binary system now boasts more than 150 institutions. The late 1980s saw a spate of amalgamations in the public sector as, freed from local authority control, very many smaller colleges secured their future by amalgamating with larger neighbours. By the end of the 1990s the first merger between a polytechnic and a university in mainland Britain, between the City University and the City of London Polytechnic, looked as though it was on the cards, and an amalgamation of Leicester and Loughborough Universities has been mooted. Amalgamation has occurred in Northern Ireland between the Polytechnic of Ulster and the University of Colraine.

At the same time the majority of polytechnic directors have welcomed the decision to allow them to call their institutions universities, on the grounds that they perform the same function as their older brethren, and that the polytechnic title confuses overseas recruits, who form an important part of the UK's higher education intake.

If the political will actually follows the political rhetoric it looks as though the UK will have a larger and very different community of universities by the end of the next decade, something much more on the lines of the American model.

**independent school** school run privately without direct assistance from the state. In the UK, just over 7% of children (1991) attend private fee-paying schools; the proportion has risen since the 1980s. The sector includes most boarding education in the UK. Although a majority of independent secondary schools operate a highly selective admissions policy for entrants at the age of 11 or 13, some specialize in the teaching of slow learners or difficult children and a few follow particular philosophies of progressive education. A group of old-established and prestigious independent schools are known as public schools.

The Labour Party is committed to the withdrawal of tax privileges for private education and the phasing-out of assisted places; the Conservatives have encouraged state funding of selected students within certain independent schools under the Assisted Places Scheme.

**literacy** the ability to read and write. The level at which functional literacy is set rises as society becomes more complex, and it becomes increasingly difficult for an illiterate person to find work and cope with the other demands of everyday life.

Nearly 1,000 million adults in the world, most of them women, are unable to read or write. Africa has the world's highest illiteracy rate: 54% of the adult population. Asia has 666 million illiterates, 75% of the world total. Surveys in the USA, the UK, and France in the 1980s found far greater levels of functional illiteracy than official figures suggest, as well as revealing a lack of basic general knowledge, but no standard of measurement has been agreed.

**magnet school** school that specializes in a particular area of the curriculum; for example, science, sport, or the arts. Magnet schools were established in the USA from 1954 in some inner cities, with the aim of becoming centres of excellence in their special field.

Critics say that magnet schools attract talented pupils and staff away from equally deserving schools in the surrounding neighbourhood. In the UK, the idea has been discussed since 1987 but no magnet schools have been established.

**nursery school** or **kindergarten** semi-educational establishment for children aged three to five. The first was established in Germany 1836 by Friedrich Froebel.

**Open University** an institution established in the UK 1969 to enable mature students without qualifications to study to degree level without regular attendance. Open University teaching is based on a mixture of correspondence courses, TV and radio lectures and demonstrations, personal tuition organized on a regional basis, and summer schools.

Announced by Harold Wilson 1963 as a 'university of the air', it was largely created by Jennie Lee, minister for the arts, from 1965. There are now over 30 similar institutions in other countries, including Thailand and South Korea.

**remedial education** special classes, or teaching strategies, that aim to help children with learning difficulties to catch up with children within the normal range of achievement.

**statement** in UK education, the results of an assessment of the special educational needs of a child with physical or mental disabilities. Under the Education Act 1981, less able children are entitled to such an assessment by various professionals, to establish what their needs are and how they might be met. Approximately 2.4% children were in receipt of statements in 1990.

---

## Science at school

*Which, if any, of these best describes your experience of science lessons in school*

| | |
|---|---|
| Boring | 20 |
| Hard | 9 |
| Badly taught | 17 |
| Irrelevant to everyday life | 14 |
| Interesting | 33 |
| Easy | 5 |
| Well taught | 15 |
| Improved understanding of the outside world | 9 |
| None of these | 3 |
| No experience | 11 |

*Do you think the Government should legislate to ensure that all children are taught some science and technology at school?*

| | |
|---|---|
| Yes | 86 |
| No | 10 |
| Don't know | 4 |

# MEDICAL TERMS

**abortion** the ending of a pregnancy before the fetus is developed sufficiently to survive outside the womb. Loss of a fetus at a later gestational age is termed premature stillbirth. Abortion may be accidental (miscarriage) or deliberate (termination of pregnancy).

Methods of deliberate abortion vary according to the gestational age of the fetus. Up to 12 weeks, the cervix is dilated and a suction curette passed into the uterus to remove its contents (*D and C*). Over 12 weeks, a prostaglandin pessary is introduced into the vagina, which induces labour, producing a miscarriage.

In 1989, there were 183,974 abortions performed in England and Wales (includes residents and non-residents). In April 1990 Parliament approved a measure to lower the time limit on abortions to 24 weeks from 28.

In 1991 the anti-progesterone abortion pill, mefipristone, was licensed in the UK. (See *Types of Drugs* in this section for more.)

**allergy** special sensitivity of the body that makes it react, with an exaggerated response of the natural immune defence mechanism, especially with histamines, to the introduction of an otherwise harmless foreign substance termed an *allergen*.

**amniocentesis** sampling the amniotic fluid surrounding a fetus in the womb for diagnostic purposes. It is used to detect Down's syndrome and other abnormalities.

**blood pressure** the pressure, or tension, of the blood against the inner walls of blood vessels, especially the arteries, due to the muscular pumping activity of the heart. Abnormally high blood pressure (see hypertension) may be associated with various conditions or arise with no obvious cause; abnormally low blood pressure occurs in shock.

**Caesarean section** surgical operation to deliver a baby by cutting through the mother's abdominal and intrauterine walls. It may be recommended for almost any obstetric complication implying a threat to mother or baby. In the USA in 1987, 24% of all births were by Caesarean section.

**cervical smear** removal of a small sample of tissue from the cervix (neck of the womb) to screen for changes implying a likelihood of cancer. The procedure is also known as the *Pap test* after its originator, George Papanicolau.

**chemotherapy** any medical treatment with chemicals. It usually refers to treatment of cancer with cytotoxic and other drugs. The term was coined by the German bacteriologist Paul Ehrlich for the use of synthetic chemicals against infectious diseases.

**contraceptive** any drug, device, or technique that prevents pregnancy. The contraceptive pill (the Pill) contains female hormones that interfere with egg production or the first stage of pregnancy. The 'morning-after' pill can be taken up to 72 hours after unprotected intercourse. Barrier contraceptives include condoms (sheaths) and caps (also called Dutch caps or diaphragms); they prevent the sperm entering the cervix. Intrauterine devices, also known as IUDs or coils, cause a slight inflammation of the lining of the womb; this prevents the fertilized egg from becoming implanted.

**convulsion** series of violent contractions of the muscles over which the patient has no control. It may be associated with loss of consciousness.

**dermatology** science of the skin, its nature and diseases. It is a rapidly expanding field owing to the proliferation of industrial chemicals affecting workers, and the universal use of household cleaners, cosmetics, and sun screens.

**dialysis** the process used to mimic the effects of the kidneys. It may be life-saving in some types of poisoning. Dialysis is usually performed to compensate for failing kidneys; there are two main methods, haemodialysis and peritoneal dialysis.

**endoscopy** examination of internal organs or tissues by an instrument allowing direct vision. An endoscope is equipped with an eyepiece, lenses, and its own light source to illuminate the field of vision. The endoscope that examines the alimentary canal is a flexible fibreoptic instrument swallowed by the patient.

**gallstone** pebblelike, insoluble accretion formed in the human gall bladder or bile ducts from cholesterol or calcium salts present in bile. Gallstones may be symptomless or they may cause pain, indigestion, or jaundice. They can be dissolved with medication or removed, along with the gall bladder, in an operation known as cholecystectomy.

**geriatrics** branch of medicine concerned with diseases and problems of the elderly.

**gynaecology** branch of medicine concerned with disorders of the female reproductive system.

**haematology** branch of medicine concerned with disorders of the blood.

**hormone-replacement therapy** (HRT) the use of oral oestrogen and progestogen to help lessen the side-effects of the menopause in women. The treatment was first used in the 1970s. (See feature in this section.)

**hospice** residential facility specializing in palliative care for terminally ill patients and their

UK INFANT MORTALITY RATES BY BIRTHWEIGHT
*(Deaths of infants under 1 year of age)*

| | (Infant mortality rates per thousand live births) | | |
|---|---|---|---|
| Birthweight (grams) | 1981 | 1986 | 1988 |
| Under 1,500 | 345.7 | 302.4 | 302.1 |
| 1,500–1,999 | 72.5 | 61.1 | 53.2 |
| 2,000–2,499 | 24.7 | 19.7 | 19.9 |
| Under 2,500 | 72.1 | 65.3 | 66.7 |
| 2,500–2,999 | 9.5 | 8.0 | 8.0 |
| 3,000–3,499 | 5.2 | 4.8 | 4.6 |
| 3,500–3,999 | 4.7 | 3.9 | 3.4 |
| 4,000 and over | 4.5 | 3.7 | 3.1 |

## NEW TECHNOLOGIES IN MEDICINE

Advances in computer technology mean that one field of medicine is likely to develop dramatically in the 1990s—diagnostic imaging. Twenty years ago doctors had to rely on bedside skills and simple X-rays to try to diagnose internal disorders, but now they have a battery of imaging tests at their disposal, using X-rays, ultrasound, magnetic resonance, and radio-isotopes to study not only structure but also function in all parts of the body. The images from different systems can be digitized and combined, and in the future the surgeon will be able to dissect a 3-D image of the body on the computer screen when planning a complicated operation.

One of the most exciting imaging developments of recent years has been MRI (magnetic resonance imaging) scanning, which produces beautifully detailed pictures of the body's soft tissues—brain, spinal cord, muscles, ligaments and so on, without exposing the patient to any harmful radiation. How does MRI work? The nuclei of atoms in the body are like tiny magnets, each of which is spinning like a top. These magnets can all be made to align using a strong magnetic field. When a pulse of radio waves is then sent through the patient, the magnets (nuclei) all change direction slightly. Once the pulse has passed, they return to their original orientation, emitting a different electromagnetic signal as they do so. These signals are then detected and analyzed by the imaging system, which can display the differences between different tissues. The emitted signal from an atom depends upon its local environment, and the total signal from a tissue is also dependent upon the concentration of the relevant atoms within it. For example, MRI scanning is able to demonstrate very clearly the difference between the white matter and the grey matter in the brain.

The great usefulness of MRI scanning lies in its ability to image clearly areas that are poorly visualized with CAT (computerized axial tomography) scanning, such as the cerebellum. In general, MRI produces good images of soft tissue, but cannot visualize bone, whereas CAT has the opposite strengths. This has led researchers to try to combine images from the two systems. They are first digitized into two data sets, and then a series of important anatomical landmarks is identified in each set (for example, the cochleas on each side). By matching the coordinates of the landmarks in each data set, the computer is able to calculate how much to shrink, expand, or rotate one image in order to superimpose it upon the other. Another algorithm then keeps the clearest parts from each image in order to produce a composite, which is known as a 'synergistic image'. Such images will be of great use, for example to neuro-surgeons and ear surgeons, enabling them to see with great clarity not only the bones of the skull but also the adjacent brain and nerves.

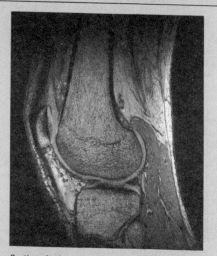

*Section of a knee as scanned by magnetic resonance gyroview—showing anatomical structures.*

### Surgery on the screen?

As the computer analysis of images from MRI and CAT becomes more sophisticated, it will be possible to display 3-D images of, say, the head on a video-display unit, and to orientate them as required. Researchers are currently developing computer programs to allow individual layers of tissue to be 'peeled' off the image. This will enable the surgeon to rehearse a difficult operation by seeing what the tissues will look like at each stage. Novice surgeons will be able to use the method in their training.

### PET—a new window on the brain.

CAT and MRI scanning may offer beautiful pictures of the structure of the body, but they can tell us little about its functioning—for this purpose radioisotope studies (collectively known as 'nuclear medicine') are much better. Nuclear medicine is not a new field, but in one area it has shown exciting developments. PET (positron emission tomography) is a technique in which a substance normally present in the body—for example, glucose—is labelled with a radioisotope that emits positrons (positive electrons), and injected into the patient's blood. As each positron is emitted within the body it collides with an electron and is annihilated, creating two gamma rays that leave the point of collision in opposite directions. A circular array of gamma-ray detectors surrounds the patient, and is used to build up an image of the distribution of the labelled substance, which corresponds to regions of active metabolism.

PET has been used extensively to study the brain, showing, for example, how opening the eyes increases the blood flow to the occipital cortex, the area responsible for visual processing. Studies of this kind are currently of great interest in psychiatry, where they may show how brain function is altered in mental illness.

relatives.

**hysterectomy** surgical removal of all or part of the uterus (womb). Instead of a full hysterectomy it is sometimes possible to remove the lining of the womb, the endometrium, using either diathermy or a laser.

**immunization** conferring immunity to infectious disease by artificial methods. The most widely used technique is vaccination.

**inflammation** defensive reaction of the body tissues to disease or damage, including redness, swelling, and heat. Denoted by the suffix *-itis* (as in appendicitis), it may be acute or chronic, and may be accompanied by the formation of pus. This is an essential part of the healing process.

**intrauterine device** IUD or coil, a contraceptive device that is inserted into the womb (uterus). It is a tiny plastic object, sometimes containing copper. By causing a mild inflammation of the lining of the uterus it prevents fertilized eggs from becoming implanted. It has a success rate of about 98%; there is a very small risk of a pelvic infection leading to infertility.

**in vitro fertilization** (IVF) literally, 'fertilization in glass', that is, allowing eggs and sperm to unite in a laboratory to form embryos. The embryos produced may then either be implanted into the womb of the otherwise infertile mother (an extension of artificial insemination), or used for research. In cases where the fallopian tubes are blocked, fertilization may be carried out by *intra-vaginal culture*, in which egg and sperm are incubated (in a plastic tube) in the mother's vagina, then transferred surgically into the uterus. The first baby to be born by IVF was Louise Brown in 1978 in the UK.

**mammography** X-ray procedure used to detect breast cancer at an early stage, before the tumours can be seen or felt. It is recommended that women have annual mammographies after the age of 35.

**nursing** care of the sick, the very young, the very old and the disabled. Nurses give day-to-day care and carry out routine medical and surgical procedures under the supervision of a physician. Organized training originated 1836 in Germany, and was developed in Britain by the work of Florence Nightingale (1820–1910), who, during the Crimean War, established standards of scientific, humanitarian care in military hospitals.

In the UK there are four National Boards (England, Scotland, Wales, and Northern Ireland) for Nursing, Midwifery and Health Visiting, and the Royal College of Nursing (1916) is the professional body.

**nutrition** the science of food, and its effect on human and animal life, health, and disease. Nutrition is the study of the basic nutrients required to sustain life, their bioavailability in foods and overall diet, and the effects upon them of cooking and storage. *Malnutrition* can be caused by underfeeding, an imbalanced diet, and over-feeding.

**obstetrics** branch of medicine concerned with the management of pregnancy, childbirth, and the immediate postnatal period.

**oncology** branch of medicine concerned with the diagnosis and treatment of neoplasms, especially cancer.

**ophthalmology** branch of medicine concerned with diseases of the eye and its surrounding tissues.

**orthopaedics** branch of medicine concerned with the surgery of bones and joints.

**pacemaker** medical device implanted in a patient whose heart beats irregularly. It delivers minute electric shocks to stimulate the heart muscles and restores normal heartbeat. The latest ones are powered by radioactive isotopes for long life and weigh no more than 15 grams/0.5 oz. They are implanted under the skin.

**paediatrics** or *pediatrics* branch of medicine concerned with the care of children.

**pain** the sense that gives an awareness of harmful effects on or in the body. It may be triggered by stimuli such as trauma, inflammation, and heat. Pain is transmitted by specialized nerves and also has psychological components controlled by higher centres in the brain. Painkillers are also known as analgesics.

**paraplegia** paralysis of the lower limbs, involving loss of both movement and sensation, usually due to spinal injury.

**physiotherapy** treatment of injury and disease by physical means such as exercise, heat, manipulation, massage, and electrical stimulation.

**poison** or *toxin* any chemical substance that, when introduced into or applied to the body, is capable of injuring health or destroying life. The liver is the organ that removes some poisons from the blood.

**prematurity** the condition of an infant born before term. In obstetrics, an infant born after less than 37 weeks' gestation is described as premature. In hospitals with advanced technology, special-care baby units (SCBUs) can save babies born as early as 24 weeks.

**prophylaxis** any measure taken to prevent disease, including exercise and vaccination. Prophylactic (preventive) medicine is an aspect of public-health provision that is receiving increasing attention.

**psychosomatic** descriptive term for any physical symptom or disease thought to arise from emotional or mental factors. The term 'psychosomatic' has been applied to many conditions, including asthma, migraine, hypertension, and peptic ulcers. Whereas it is unlikely that these and other conditions are wholly due to psychological factors, emotional states such as anxiety or depression do have a distinct influence on the frequency and severity of illness.

**radiotherapy** treatment of disease by radiation from X-ray machines or radioactive sources. Radiation, which reduces the activity of dividing cells, is of special value for its effect on malignant tissues, certain nonmalignant tumours, and some diseases of the skin.

**remission** temporary disappearance of symptoms during the course of a disease.

**resuscitation** steps taken to revive anyone on

the brink of death. The most successful technique for life-threatening emergencies, such as electrocution, near-drowning, or heart attack, is mouth-to-mouth resuscitation. Medical and paramedical staff are trained in cardiopulmonary resuscitation: the use of specialized equipment and techniques to attempt to restart the breathing and/or heartbeat and stabilize the patient long enough for more definitive treatment.

**retrovirus** any of a family (*Retroviridae*) of viruses containing the genetic material RNA rather than the more usual DNA. For the virus to express itself and multiply within an infected cell, its RNA must be converted to DNA; it does this by using a built-in enzyme known as reverse transcriptase. Retroviruses include those causing AIDS and some forms of leukemia.

**screening** or *health screening* the systematic search for evidence of a disease, or of conditions that may precede it, in people who are not suffering from any symptoms. The aim of screening is to try to limit ill health from diseases that are difficult to prevent and might otherwise go undetected. Examples are hypothyroidism and phenylketonuria, for which all newborn babies in Western countries are screened; breast cancer and cervical cancer; and stroke, for which high blood pressure is a known risk factor.

**spastic** person with cerebral palsy. The term is also applied generally to limbs with impaired movement, stiffness, and resistance to passive movement, and to any body part (such as the colon) affected with spasm.

**spermicide** any cream, jelly, pessary, or other preparation that kills the sperm cells in semen. Spermicides are used for contraceptive purposes, usually in combination with a condom or diaphragm. Sponges impregnated with spermicide have been developed but are not yet in widespread use. Spermicide used alone is only 75% effective in preventing pregnancy.

**sterilization** any surgical operation to terminate the possibility of reproduction. In women, this is normally achieved by sealing or tying off the Fallopian tubes (tubal ligation) so that fertilization can no longer take place. In men, the transmission of sperm is blocked by vasectomy.

**tomography** the obtaining of plane-section X-ray photographs, which show a 'slice' through any object. Crystal detectors and amplifiers can be used that have a sensitivity 100 times greater than X-ray film, and, in conjunction with a computer system, can detect, for example, the difference between a brain tumour and healthy brain tissue. In modern medical imaging there are several types, such as the CAT scan (computerized axial tomography).(See feature in this section.)

**transfusion** intravenous transfer of blood or blood products (plasma, red cells) into a patient's circulation to make up for deficiencies due to disease, injury, or surgical intervention.

**transplant** the transfer of a tissue or organ from one human being to another or from one part of the body to another (skin grafting). In most organ transplants, the operation is for life-saving purposes, though the immune system tends to reject foreign tissue. Careful matching and immunosuppressive drugs must be used, but these are not always sucessfull.

The 1990 Nobel Prize for Medicine and Physiology was awarded to two US surgeons, Donnall Thomas and Joseph Murray, for their pioneering work on organ transplants.

**trauma** a painful emotional experience or shock with lasting psychic consequences; any physical damage or injury.

**tumour** overproduction of cells in a specific area of the body, often leading to a swelling or lump. Tumours are classified as *benign* or *malignant*. Benign tumours are essentially harmless and can be cured by removal; a malignant tumour is cancerous.

**ultrasound** vibrations similar to sound waves but too rapid to be heard; it has limited use in diagnosis, and can be used in the treatment of disease. An ultrasonic beam can be aimed at a certain depth below the skin surface and the energy of the vibrations dissipated as heat (this is used to alleviate pain in joints and muscles).

**vaccine** any preparation of modified viruses or bacteria that is introduced into the body, usually either orally or by a hypodermic syringe, to induce the specific antibody reaction that produces immunity against a particular disease. In the UK, children are routinely vaccinated against diphtheria, tetanus, whooping cough, polio, measles, mumps, German measles, and tuberculosis (BCG).

**X-rays** rays with a short wavelength that pass through most body tissues. Dense tissues such as bone prevent their passage and show up as white areas on X-ray photographs. X-rays with very short wavelengths penetrate the tissues deeply and destroy them: these are used in radiotherapy.

# THE HUMAN BODY

**Achilles tendon** the tendon pinning the calf muscle to the heel bone. It is one of the largest in the human body.

**adenoids** masses of lymphoid tissue, similar to tonsils, located in the upper part of the throat, behind the nose. They are part of a child's natural defences against the entry of germs but usually shrink and disappear by the age of ten.

**adrenal gland** or *suprarenal gland* a gland situated on top of the kidney. The adrenals are soft and yellow, and consist of two parts: the cortex and medulla. The *cortex* (outer part) secretes various steroid hormones, controls salt and water metabolism, and regulates the use of carbohydrates, proteins, and fats. The *medulla* (inner part) secretes the hormones adrenaline

## HORMONE REPLACEMENT THERAPY (HRT): WOMAN'S SAVIOUR?

Hormone replacement therapy is prescribed for women to treat the symptoms and complications of the menopause. A change of use to natural rather than synthetic oestrogens in HRT has allayed worries about the putative association between HRT and cancer of the ovaries or uterus. There is now unequivocal evidence that HRT can reduce the incidence of hip fractures amongst postmenopausal women by up to 50%.

At the menopause, a woman's ovaries cease to produce the hormones oestrogen and progesterone. This causes a number of symptoms, including hot flushes, sweating, and drying and soreness of the vagina. In the absence of these hormones, the breasts and the lining of the womb, or endometrium, may shrink. These symptoms often lead to a loss of self-esteem in menopausal women, and consequent anxiety and depression, but they are usually self-limiting, ceasing after a few years.

Of greater concern medically are the effects of the menopause on a woman's bones and arteries. Oestrogen helps to keep the bones dense and strong, and the osteoporosis, which follows the menopause, can lead to a greatly increased risk of fractures, especially of the hip. In addition, it is oestrogen which, by increasing the levels of high-density lipoprotein, helps to protect women from the effects of atherosclerosis, so that after the menopause the risk of heart disease and stroke among women climbs rapidly to equal that among men.

HRT, by replacing the natural oestrogen and progesterone, can not only effectively treat the symptoms of the menopause, but also delay the long-term risks of fractures and heart disease. It may be given orally, in a calendar pack like the one used for the contraceptive pill, or several months' supply can be given by implanting a small, slow-release pellet under the skin. A third method is to wear a sticky plaster impregnated with the hormones, which then are absorbed through the skin. Vaginal dryness and soreness can be treated by oestrogen creams applied locally.

may actually protect women from cancer of the uterus. There may be a slightly increased risk of breast cancer, although no one has yet been able to prove this one way or another. The potential risk should be considered minimal. The dangers of hip fracture and heart disease among untreated women are certainly far higher. One side effect of HRT is the continuation of menstrual bleeding each month.

### How long should HRT be taken?
This is a controversial question. Until recently it was thought that, to protect bone density, HRT had to be continued for at least ten years, long after the unpleasant symptoms of the menopause had ceased. Few women were prepared to continue treatment for this length of time. Now, however, it has been shown that treatment for five years can offer significant protection from osteoporosis, so that most doctors would now recommend continuing for at least as long as this.

### Who is suitable for HRT?
Any woman suffering from the symptoms of the menopause can be offered HRT, except those who have had previous cancer of the breast or endometrium. It is also offered to women who have an early menopause (either because their ovaries have ceased to function or because they have been removed surgically) because they spend a greater proportion of their lives with lower hormone levels, and are therefore more likely to develop osteoporosis.

### Are there any disadvantages to HRT?
HRT was first given using synthetic oestrogens of the type used in the contraceptive pill. These are more powerful than natural hormones, and are associated with an increased risk of thrombosis and endometrial cancer. Modern preparations, however, use natural oestrogens, and carry no increased risk of thrombosis; they

and noradrenaline which constrict the blood vessels of the belly and skin so that more blood is available for the heart, lungs, and voluntary muscles, an emergency preparation for the stress reaction 'fight or flight'.

**alimentary canal** the tube through which food passes; it extends from the mouth to the anus. It is a complex organ, adapted for digestion. In human adults, it is about 9 m/30 ft long, consisting of the mouth cavity, pharynx, oesophagus, stomach, and the small and large intestines.

**antibody** protein molecule produced in the blood by lymphocytes in response to the presence of invading substances, or antigens, including the proteins carried on the surface of microorganisms. Antibody production is only one aspect of immunity in vertebrates. Many diseases can only be contracted once because antibodies remain in the blood after the infection

has passed, preventing any further invasion. Vaccination boosts a person's resistance by causing the production of antibodies specific to particular infections.

**aorta** the chief artery, the dorsal blood vessel carrying oxygenated blood from the left ventricle of the heart. It branches to form smaller arteries, which in turn supply all body organs except the lungs. Loss of elasticity in the aorta provides evidence of atherosclerosis, which may lead to heart disease.

**artery** vessel that conveys blood from the heart of a vertebrate to the body tissues. The largest of the arteries is the aorta, which leads from the left ventricle of the heart, up over the heart, and down through the diaphragm into the belly. Arteries are flexible, elastic tubes, consisting of three layers, the middle of which is muscular; its rhythmic contraction aids the pumping of blood around the body.

**blood** liquid circulating in the arteries, veins, and capillaries. Blood carries nutrients and oxygen to individual cells and removes waste products, such as carbon dioxide. It is also important in the immune response and, in many animals, in the distribution of heat throughout the body.

Blood consists of a colourless, transparent liquid called **plasma**, containing microscopic cells of three main varieties. **Red cells** (erythrocytes) form nearly half the volume of the blood, with 5 billion cells per litre. **White cells** (leucocytes) include phagocytes which ingest invading bacteria and so protect the body from disease; these also help to repair injured tissues. Others (lymphocytes) produce antibodies, which help provide immunity. Blood **platelets** (thrombocytes) assist in the clotting of blood.

**bone marrow** substance found inside the cavity of bones. In early life it produces red blood cells but later on lipids (fat) accumulate and its colour changes from red to yellow. Bone marrow may be transplanted using immunosuppressive drugs in the recipient to prevent rejection.

**brain** a mass of interconnected nerve cells, contained by the skull, forming the anterior part of the central nervous system, whose activities it coordinates and controls. (See **Life Sciences** for more.)

**bronchus** one of a pair of large tubes (bronchii) splitting off from the windpipe and passing into the lung. Apart from their size, bronchii differ from the bronchioles in possessing cartilaginous rings, which give rigidity and prevent collapse during breathing movements. The bronchus is adversely effected by several respiratory diseases and by smoking, which damages the cilia and therefore the lung cleaning mechanism.

**cranium** the dome-shaped area of the skull, consisting of several fused plates, that protects the brain. Fossil remains of the human cranium have aided the development of theories concerning human evolution.

**ear** the organ of hearing consisting of three parts: outer ear, middle ear, and inner ear. It responds to the vibrations that constitute sound, and these are translated into nerve signals and passed to the brain.

**eye** the organ of vision, a roughly spherical structure contained in a bony socket. Light enters it through the **cornea**, and passes through the circular opening (**pupil**) in the **iris** (the coloured part of the eye). The light is focused by the combined action of the curved cornea, the internal fluids, and the **lens** (the rounded transparent structure behind the iris). The ciliary muscles act on the lens to change its shape, so that images of objects at different distances can be focused on the **retina**. This is at the back of the eye, and is packed with light-sensitive cells (rods and cones), connected to the brain by the optic nerve.

**Fallopian tube** or **oviduct** one of two tubes that carry eggs from the ovary to the uterus. An egg is fertilized by sperm in the Fallopian tubes,

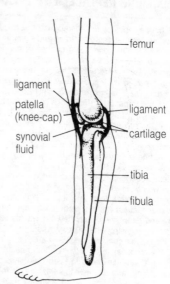

**Joint**   *hinge joint (knee)*

femur
ligament
patella (knee-cap)
synovial fluid
ligament
cartilage
tibia
fibula

which are lined with cells whose cilia move the egg towards the uterus.

**gall bladder** small muscular sac attached to the underside of the liver and connected to the small intestine by the bile duct. It stores bile from the liver.

**hair** threadlike structure growing from the skin. Each hair grows from a pit-shaped follicle embedded in the second layer of the skin, the dermis. The hair consists of dead cells impregnated with the protein keratin. There are about a million hairs on the average person's head. Each grows at the rate of 5–10 mm per month, lengthening for about three years before being replaced by a new one.

**heart** a muscular organ that rhythmically contracts to force blood around the body. The beating of the heart is controlled by the autonomic nervous system and an internal control centre or pacemaker, the sinoatrial node.

**joint** a point of movement or articulation in the skeleton. Joints between bones are fixed (**fibrous**, for example the bones of the skull) or mobile (**synovial**). Of the latter, some allow a gliding motion (one vertebra of the spine on another), some have a hinge action (elbow and knee), and others allow motion in all directions (hip and shoulder joints), by means of a ball-and-socket arrangement. In synovial joints, the ends of the bones are covered with cartilage for greater elasticity and smoothness, and enclosed in an envelope (capsule) of tough white fibrous tissue lined with a membrane which secretes a lubricating and cushioning synovial fluid. The joint is further strengthened by ligaments, however the stability of most joints depends more on muscles than on ligaments.

**kidney** one of a pair of organs responsible for water regulation, excretion of waste products,

**the human body**

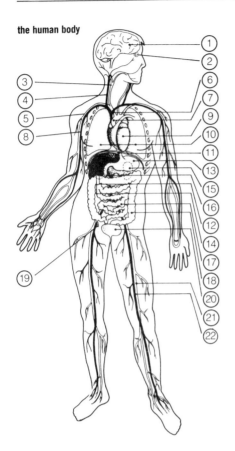

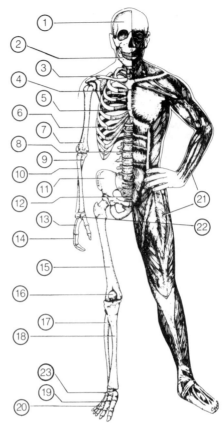

*Key*

| | |
|---|---|
| 1. brain | 12. liver |
| 2. eye | 13. stomach |
| 3. carotid artery | 14. gall bladder |
| 4. jugular vein | 15. kidney |
| 5. subclavian artery | 16. pancreas |
| 6. superior vena cava | 17. small intestine |
| 7. aorta | 18. large intestine |
| 8. subclavian vein | 19. appendix |
| 9. heart | 20. bladder |
| 10. lungs | 21. femoral artery |
| 11. diaphragm | 22. femoral vein |

*Key*

| | |
|---|---|
| 1. cranium (skull) | 13. metacarpals |
| 2. mandible | 14. phalanges |
| 3. clavicle | 15. femur |
| 4. scapula | 16. patella |
| 5. sternum | 17. fibula |
| 6. rib cage | 18. tibia |
| 7. humerus | 19. metatarsals |
| 8. vertebra | 20. phalanges |
| 9. ulna | 21. superficial (upper) |
| 10. radius | layer of muscles |
| 11. pelvis | 22. carpals |
| 12. coccyx | 23. tarsals |

and maintaining the ionic composition of the blood. It consists of a number of long tubules; the outer parts filter the aqueous components of blood, and the inner parts selectively reabsorb vital salts, leaving waste products in the remaining fluid (urine), which is passed through the ureter to the bladder.

The action of the kidneys is vital, although if one is removed, the other enlarges to take over its function. A patient with two defective kidneys may continue near-normal life with the aid of a kidney machine or continuous ambulatory peritoneal dialysis (CAPD).

**liver** a large organ which has many regulatory and storage functions, situated in the upper abdomen, and weighs about 2 kg/4.5 lbs. It receives the products of digestion, converts glucose to glycogen (a long-chain carbohydrate used for storage), and breaks down fats. It removes excess amino acids from the blood, converting them to urea, which is excreted by the kidneys. The liver also synthesizes vitamins, produces bile and blood-clotting factors, and removes damaged red cells and toxins such as alcohol from the blood.

**lung** organ of respiration, used for gas exchange.

The paired lungs are essentially sheets of thin, moist membrane that are folded so as to occupy less space, situated in the pleural cavities of the thorax (the upper part of the trunk). Lungs function by bringing inhaled air into close contact with the blood, so that oxygen can pass into the organism and waste carbon dioxide can be passed out; the oxygen is carried by haemoglobin in red blood cells. The principal diseases of the lungs are tuberculosis, pneumonia, bronchitis, emphysema, and cancer.

**lymph nodes** small masses of lymphatic tissue in the body that occur at various points along the major lymphatic vessels. Tonsils and adenoids are large lymph nodes. As the lymph passes through them it is filtered, and bacteria and other microorganisms are engulfed by cells known as macrophages.

**muscle** contractile tissue that produces locomotion and maintains the movement of body substances. Muscle is made of long cells that can contract to between one-half and one-third of their relaxed length. Muscle is the body's most abundant tissue, accounting for some two-fifths of the body weight.

An artificial muscle fibre was developed in the USA 1990. Besides replacing muscle fibre, it can be used for substitute ligaments and blood vessels and to prevent tissues sticking together after surgery. (See **Life Sciences** for more.)

**nerve** strand of nerve cells enclosed in a sheath of connective tissue joining the central and the autonomic nervous systems with receptor and effector organs. A single nerve may contain both motor and sensory nerve cells, but they act independently.

**oesophagus** the passage about 23 cm/9 in long by which food travels from mouth to stomach. Its upper end is at the bottom of the pharynx, immediately behind the windpipe.

**ovary** the organ that generates the ovum. The two ovaries are whitish rounded bodies about 25 mm/1 in by 35 mm/1.5 in, located in the abdomen near the ends of the Fallopian tubes. Every month, from puberty to the onset of the menopause, an ovum is released from the ovary. This is called ovulation, and forms part of the menstrual cycle.

**pancreas** an accessory gland of the digestive system located close to the duodenum. When stimulated by secretin, it secretes enzymes into the duodenum that digeest starches, proteins, and fats. In humans, it is about 18 cm/7 in long, and lies behind and below the stomach. It contains groups of cells called the *islets of Langerhans*, which secrete the hormones insulin and glucagon that regulate the blood sugar level.

**parathyroid** one of a pair of small endocrine glands located behind the thyroid gland. They secrete parathyroid hormone, which regulates the amount of calcium in the blood.

**pelvis** the lower area of the abdomen featuring the bones and muscles used to move the legs or hindlimbs. The *pelvic girdle* is a set of bones that allows movement of the legs in relation to the rest of the body and provides sites for the attachment of relevant muscles.

**penis** male reproductive organ, used for internal fertilization; it transfers sperm to the female reproductive tract. In mammals, the penis is made erect by vessels that fill with blood, and in most mammals (but not humans) is stiffened by a bone. It also contains the urethra, through which urine is passed.

**pharynx** the interior of the throat, the cavity at the back of the mouth. Its walls are made of muscle strengthened with a fibrous layer and lined with mucous membrane. The internal nostrils lead backwards into the pharynx, which continues downwards into the oesophagus and (through the epiglottis) into the windpipe. On each side, a Eustachian tube enters the pharynx from the middle ear cavity. The upper part (nasopharynx) is an airway, but the remainder is a passage for food. Inflammation of the pharynx is called pharyngitis.

**prostate gland** gland surrounding, and opening into, the urethra at the base of the bladder in male mammals. The prostate gland produces an alkaline fluid that is released during ejaculation; this fluid activates sperm, and prevents their clumping together. In humans, the prostate often enlarges and obstructs the urethra; this is treated by prostatectomy.

**red blood cell** or *erythrocyte* the most common type of blood cell, responsible for transporting oxygen around the body. It contains haemoglobin, which combines with oxygen from the lungs to form oxyhaemoglobin. When transported to the tissues, these cells are able to release the oxygen because the oxyhaemoglobin splits into its original constituents. Mammalian erythrocytes are disc-like with a depression in the centre and no nucleus; they are manufactured in the bone marrow and, in humans, last for only four months before being destroyed in the liver and spleen.

**rib** long, usually curved bone that extends laterally from the spine. Humans have 12 pairs of ribs; they protect the lungs and heart, and allow the chest to expand and contract easily. At the rear, each pair is joined to one of the vertebrae of the spine. The upper seven are joined by cartilage directly to the breast bone (sternum). The next three are joined by cartilage to the end of the rib above. The last two ('floating ribs') are not attached at the front.

**skull** the collection of flat and irregularly shaped bones (or cartilage) that enclose the brain and the organs of sight, hearing, and smell, and provide support for the jaws. The skull consists of 22 bones joined by sutures. The floor of the skull is pierced by a large hole for the spinal cord and a number of smaller apertures through which other nerves and blood vessels pass.

**spinal cord** major component of the central nervous system. It is enclosed by the bones of the spine, and links the peripheral nervous system to the brain, of which it is a continuation.

**stomach** the first cavity in the digestive system, between the lower end of the oesophagus and the beginning of the intestine. Food enters it from the oesophagus, is digested by the acid and enzymes secreted by the stomach lining, and then passes into the duodenum.

**testis** (plural **testes**) the organ that produces sperm in male (and hermaphrodite) animals. The paired testes (or testicles) descend from the body cavity during development, to hang outside the abdomen in a scrotal sac.

**throat** the passage that leads from the back of the nose and mouth to the trachea and oesophagus. It includes the pharynx and the larynx, the latter being at the top of the trachea; it is also used to mean the front part of the neck, both in humans and other vertebrates.

**thyroid** endocrine gland situated in the neck in front of the trachea. It secretes several hormones, among them thyroxin, a hormone containing iodine. This stimulates growth, metabolism, and other functions of the body. Excessive action produces Graves's disease, characterized by bulging eyeballs and an elevated metabolism, while deficient action produces myxoedema in adults and dwarfism in juveniles. *Goitre* is an enlargement of the thyroid gland, caused (in simple goitres) by lack of iodine in the diet.

**tongue** a muscular organ usually attached to the floor of the mouth, crucial for speech. It has a thick root attached to a U-shaped bone (hyoid), and is covered with a mucous membrane containing nerves and 'taste buds'. It directs food to the teeth and into the throat for chewing and swallowing.

**trachea** tube that forms an airway, also known as the **windpipe**. It runs from the larynx to the upper part of the chest; its diameter is about 1.5 cm/0.6 in and its length 10 cm/4 in. It is strong and flexible, and reinforced by rings of cartilage. In the upper chest, the trachea branches into two tubes: the left and right bronchi, which enter the lungs.

**uterus** (womb) hollow muscular organ in females, located between the bladder and rectum, and connected to the Fallopian tubes above and the vagina below. The embryo develops within the uterus, and is attached to it after implantation via the placenta and umbilical cord. The lining of the uterus (endometrium) is shed every month (menstruation) and replaced by a new one. During pregnancy menstruation does not occur and the endometrium remains intact. The outer wall of the uterus is composed of smooth muscle, capable of powerful contractions (induced by hormones) during childbirth.

**vagina** the front passage in females, linking the uterus to the exterior. It admits the penis during sexual intercourse, and is the birth canal down which the fetus passes during delivery.

# PSYCHOLOGICAL DISORDERS

**agoraphobia** a phobia involving fear of open spaces and crowded places. The anxiety produced can be so severe that some sufferers are confined to their homes for many years.

**anorexia** lack of desire to eat, especially the pathological condition of **anorexia nervosa**, usually found in adolescent girls and young women, who may be obsessed with the desire to lose weight. Compulsive eating, or bulimia, often accompanies anorexia. In anorexia nervosa, the patient refuses to eat and finally becomes unable to do so. The result is severe emaciation and, in rare cases, death.

**anxiety** emotional state of fear or apprehension. Anxiety is a normal response to potentially dangerous situations. Abnormal anxiety can either be free-floating, experienced in a wide range of situations, or it may be phobic, when the sufferer is excessively afraid of an object or situation.

**behaviour therapy** the application of behavioural principles, derived from learning theories, to the treatment of clinical conditions such as phobias, obsessions, sexual and interpersonal problems. For example, in treating a phobia the person is taken into the feared situation in gradual steps. Over time, the fear typically reduces, and the problem becomes less acute.

**claustrophobia** a phobia involving fear of enclosed spaces.

**clinical psychology** discipline dealing with the understanding and treatment of health problems, particularly mental disorders. The main problems dealt with include anxiety, phobias, depression, obsessions, sexual and marital problems, drug and alcohol dependence, childhood behavioural problems, psychoses (such as schizophrenia), mental handicap, and brain damage (such as dementia).

**cognitive therapy** a treatment for emotional disorders such as depression and anxiety, developed by Professor Aaron T Beck in the USA. This approach encourages the client to challenge the distorted and unhelpful thinking that is characteristic of these problems. The treatment includes behaviour therapy and has been most helpful for people suffering from depression.

**delusion** a false belief that is unshakeably held. Delusions are a prominent feature of schizophrenia and paranoia, but may also occur in severe depression and manic depression.

**depression** emotional state characterized by sadness, unhappy thoughts, apathy, and dejection. Sadness is a normal response to major losses such as bereavement or unemployment.

After childbirth, postnatal depression is common. However, clinical depression, which is prolonged or unduly severe, often requires treatment, such as antidepressant medica-

## LIFESTYLE, DISEASE AND THE MIND-BODY QUESTION

When Dean Ornish of the San Francisco Medical School sought funding from major foundations and government agencies for his Lifestyle Heart Trial, he was told the project would be a waste of money because it was impossible to reverse heart disease and impossible to motivate people to change their lifestyle.

He and his team of researchers conducted the Trial anyway, and their results, published in 1990, confounded rigid adherents of interventionist (drugs and surgery dependent) medical methodology, and delighted the alternative and natural medicine camp. Compared with a control group of 19 coronary patients who received conventional care, and just 8 of whom showed improvement over a year, in the experimental group, who made and sustained lifestyle changes involving diet, exercise and the practice of stress-management techniques, 18 out of the 22 patients showed improvement.

That there is a link between lifestyle and disease causation is no startling news. But that lifestyle change alone, unassisted by drugs can actually reverse a degenerative disease like coronary atherosclerosis certainly is. It shows that the body has great self-healing resources, that there are alternatives to the interventionist approach to disease, that patients can take responsibility for their own health, and that even when their condition is grave they need not become quiescent conformists with specialists' medical prescriptions and strategies. Which are things the alternative medicine people have been saying for years.

Dr Ornish isn't an alternative therapist, he's a professor of medicine, but he is something of an outsider within the orthodox medico-scientific community. As he points out, there are some 25 studies in progress worldwide to see whether coronary atherosclerosis can be reversed, and his is the only one that focuses on lifestyle changes rather than some kind of intervention. One could say that it is the only one that adopts a holistic approach. Dr Ornish himself doesn't use the term, perhaps out of deference to the biases of the funding bodies. At least his results have now secured him funding for a further three-year research programme.

People capable of sustaining lifestyle changes must exercise will and discipline to do so, and these are mind-directed efforts, so do we now have proof that there exists a positive mind-body link?

Any doctor will concede that there is a negative link, that body states affect mental states, that for instance people who are physically ill are prone to mental lethargy and depression. But to maintain that the influence can go the other way, that the mind can positively affect pathological body states, is something else, and too mystical and 'alternative' a view to get most doctors' assent.

Although Dr Ornish's results are encouraging for the advocates of alternative medicine, they don't go so far as to demonstrate a mind-over-matter effect, for it was clearly physical changes in body functions attributable to diet, exercise and stress- reduction that affected his patients' regression rates. There is no evidence that there was any mental contribution to the healing other than the maintenance of the will and discipline to stay with the programme.

But what is known as PNI research has made some recent progress that is more suggestive of a positive mind-body link. 'Psychoneuroimmunology' is a formidable word for an exciting new research area in medical science which studies the relations and interactions between the mind, the nervous system and the immune system.

In the October 1990 issue of the *Journal of Alternative and Complementary Medicine*, Oxford University physiologist Dr Clive Wood explained how the recent discovery of 'lymphocyte receptors' shows that there is interaction and information transmission between the nervous and immune systems, which were formerly thought to work completely independently. Lymphocytes are the active cells of the immune system, and the 'receptors' that have been discovered on their surface are designed to lock on to the 'messenger molecules' produced by the glands and the brain, respectively known as hormones and neuropeptides. Furthermore, the latest research indicates that lymphocyte cells themselves produce neuropeptides. That is to say, they have their own 'messengers', so they can not only receive information from the brain and the nervous system but also convey responses back.

These are early days for PNI research, but the clear indications are that mind and body have an efficient two-way information exchange system more complex and active than orthodox medical theory and practice have hitherto recognised. It seems that human-cell biochemistry may respond positively not only to physical lifestyle changes such as those effected by Dr Ornish's experimental group, but also to instructions direct from the brain. The rigid Cartesian mind-body demarcation, upon which orthodox medicine is based and that unorthodox medicine has always deplored, is now under scientific scrutiny, and may soon have to relinquish its predominance and credibility to a more 'holistic' theory.

tion, cognitive therapy, or, in very rare cases, electroconvulsive therapy (ECT), in which an electrical current is passed through the brain. **drug and alcohol dependence** physical or psychological craving for addictive drugs such as alcohol, nicotine (in cigarettes), tranquillizers, heroin, or stimulants (for example, amphetamines). Such substances can alter mood or behaviour. When dependence is established, sudden withdrawal from the drug can cause unpleasant physical and/or psychological reactions, which may be dangerous.

**dyslexia** malfunction in the brain's synthesis and interpretation of sensory information, popularly 'word blindness'. It results in poor ability to read and write, though the person may otherwise excel, for example, in mathematics. A similar disability with figures is called dyscalculus.

**electroconvulsive therapy** (ECT) or *electroshock therapy* a treatment for schizophrenia and depression, given under anaesthesia and with a muscle relaxant. An electric current is passed through the brain to induce alterations in the brain's electrical activity. The treatment can cause distress and loss of concentration and memory, and so there is much controversy about its use and effectiveness.

**hyperactivity** condition of excessive activity in young children, combined with inability to concentrate and difficulty in learning. The cause is not known, although some food additives have come under suspicion. Modification of the diet may help, and in the majority of cases there is improvement at puberty.

**hypnosis** an artificially induced state of relaxation in which suggestibility is heightened. The subject may carry out orders after being awakened, and may be made insensitive to pain. Hypnosis is sometimes used to treat addictions to tobacco or overeating, or to assist amnesia victims.

**hysteria** according to the work of Freud, the conversion of a psychological conflict or anxiety feeling into a physical symptom, such as paralysis, blindness, recurrent cough, vomiting, and general malaise. The term is little used today in diagnosis. schizophrenia.

**manic depression** mental disorder characterized by recurring periods of depression which may or may not alternate with periods of inappropriate elation (mania) or overactivity. Sufferers may be genetically predisposed to the condition.

**mental handicap** impairment of intelligence. It can be very mild, but in more severe cases, it is associated with social problems and difficulties in living independently. A person may be born with a mental handicap (for example, Down's syndrome) or may acquire it through brain damage. There are between 90 and 130 million people in the world suffering such disabilities.

**nervous breakdown** popular term for a reaction to overwhelming psychological stress. It has no equivalent in medicine: patients said to be suffering from a nervous breakdown may in fact be going through an episode of depression, manic depression, anxiety, or even schizophrenia.

**neurosis** in psychology, a general term referring to emotional disorders, such as anxiety, depression, and obsessions. The main disturbance tends to be one of mood; contact with reality is relatively unaffected, in contrast to the effects of psychosis.

**obsession** repetitive unwanted thought or compulsive action that is often recognized by the sufferer as being irrational, but which nevertheless causes distress. It can be associated with the irresistible urge of an individual to carry out a repetitive series of actions. For example, a person excessively troubled by fears of contamination by dirt or disease may engage in continuous handwashing.

**paranoia** mental disorder marked by delusions of grandeur or persecution.

**phobia** an excessive irrational fear of an object or situation, for example, agoraphobia (fear of open spaces and crowded places), acrophobia (fear of heights), claustrophobia (fear of enclosed places). Behaviour therapy is one form of treatment.

**postnatal depression** short-lived mood change occurring in many mothers four to five days after delivery, also known as 'baby blues'. Sometimes this is prolonged and the most severe form of depressive illness, puerperal psychosis, requires hospital treatment. In mild cases, antidepressant drugs and hormone treatment may help.

**psychiatry** the branch of medicine dealing with the diagnosis and treatment of mental disorder.

In practice there is considerable overlap between psychiatry and clinical psychology, the fundamental difference being that psychiatrists are trained medical doctors (holding an MD degree) and may therefore prescribe drugs, whereas psychologists may hold a PhD but do not need a medical qualification to practise.

**psychoanalysis** a theory and treatment method for neuroses, developed by Freud. The main treatment method involves the free association of ideas, and their interpretation by patient and analyst. It is typically prolonged and expensive and its effectiveness has been disputed.

**psychology** the systematic study of human and animal behaviour. The first psychology laboratory was founded 1879 by Wilhelm Wundt at Leipzig, Germany. The subject includes diverse areas of study and application, among them the roles of instinct, heredity, environment, and culture; the processes of sensation, perception, learning and memory; the bases of motivation and emotion; and the functioning of thought, intelligence, and language.

*Experimental psychology* emphasizes the application of rigorous and objective scientific methods to the study of a wide range of mental processes and behaviour, whereas *social psychology* concerns the study of individuals within their social environment; *clinical psychology* concerns the understanding and treatment of mental-health disorders, such as anxiety, phobias, or depression; treatment may include behaviour therapy, cognitive therapy, counselling, psychoanalysis, or some combination of these.

**psychosis** or *psychotic disorder* general term for a serious mental disorder where the individual commonly loses contact with reality and may experience hallucinations (seeing or hearing things that do not exist) or delusions (fixed false beliefs). For example, in a paranoid psychosis, an individual may believe that others are plotting against him or her. A major type of psychosis is schizophrenia (which may be biochemically induced).

**psychotherapy** treatment approaches for psychological problems involving talking rather than surgery or drugs. Examples include cognitive therapy and psychoanalysis.

**schizophrenia** mental disorder, a psychosis of unknown origin, which can lead to profound changes in personality and behaviour including paranoia and hallucinations. Modern treatment approaches include drugs, family therapy, stress reduction, and rehabilitation.

**senile dementia** a general term associated with old age. (See *dementia* and *Alzheimer's disease* in *Diseases*.)

**stress** any event or situation that makes demands on a person's mental or emotional resources. Stress can be caused by overwork, anxiety about exams, money, or job security, unemployment, bereavement, poor relationships, marriage breakdown, sexual difficulties, poor living or working conditions, and constant exposure to loud noise.

Many changes that are apparently 'for the better', such as being promoted at work, going to a new school, moving house, and getting married, are also a source of stress. Stress can cause, or aggravate, physical illnesses, among them psoriasis, eczema, asthma, stomach and mouth ulcers. Apart from removing the source of stress, acquiring some control over it and learning to relax when possible are the best treatments.

# DISEASES AND DISORDERS

**acne** skin eruption, mainly occurring among adolescents and young adults, caused by inflammation of the sebaceous glands which secrete an oily substance (sebum), the natural lubricant of the skin. Sometimes their openings become stopped and they swell; the contents decompose and pimples form on the face, back, and chest.

**alcoholism** dependence on alcoholic liquor. It is characterized as an illness when consumption of alcohol interferes with normal physical or emotional health. Excessive alcohol consumption may produce physical and psychological addiction and lead to nutritional and emotional disorders. The direct effect is cirrhosis of the liver, nerve damage, and heart disease, and the condition is now showing genetic predisposition.

**Alzheimer's disease** common cause of dementia, thought to afflict one in 20 people over 65. Attacking the brain's 'grey matter', it is a disease of mental processes rather than physical function, characterized by memory loss and progressive intellectual impairment.

The cause is unknown, although a link with high levels of aluminium in drinking water was discovered 1989. It has also been suggested that the disease may result from a defective protein circulating in the blood. There is no treatment, but recent insights into the molecular basis of the disease may aid the search for a drug to counter its effects. For example, one type of early-onset Alzheimer's disease has been shown to be related to a defective gene on chromosome 21.

**anaemia** condition caused by a shortage of haemoglobin, the oxygen-carrying component of red blood cells. The main symptoms are fatigue, pallor, breathlessness, palpitations, and poor resistance to infection. Treatment depends on the cause; untreated anaemia taxes the heart and may prove fatal.

**angina** or *angina pectoris* severe pain in the chest due to impaired blood supply to the heart muscle because a coronary artery is narrowed.

**appendicitis** inflammation of the appendix, a small, blind extension of the bowel in the lower right abdomen. In an acute attack, the pus-filled appendix may burst, causing a potentially lethal spread of infection. Treatment is by removal (appendectomy).

**arthritis** inflammation of the joints, with pain, swelling, and restricted motion. Many conditions may cause arthritis, including gout and trauma to the joint. More common in women, *rheumatoid arthritis* usually begins in middle age in the small joints of the hands and feet, causing a greater or lesser degree of deformity and painfully restricted movement. It is alleviated by drugs, and surgery may be performed to correct deformity. *Osteoarthritis*, a degenerative condition, tends to affect larger, load-bearing joints, such as the knee and hip. It appears in later life, especially in those whose joints may have been subject to earlier stress or damage; one or more joints stiffen and may give considerable pain. Joint replacement surgery is nearly always successful.

**asthma** difficulty in breathing due to spasm of the bronchi (air passages) in the lungs. Attacks may be provoked by allergy, infection, stress, or emotional upset. It may also be increasing as a result of air pollution and occupational hazards. Treatment is with bronchodilators to relax the bronchial muscles and thereby ease the breathing, and with inhaled steroids that reduce inflammation of the bronchi. Asthma sufferers may monitor their own status by use of a peak-flow meter, a device that measures how rapidly air is breathed out. Peak-flow meters are available on prescription in the UK.

Although the symptoms are similar to those of bronchial asthma, *cardiac asthma* is an unrelated condition and is a symptom of heart deterioration.

**atherosclerosis** thickening and hardening of the walls of the arteries, associated with atheroma.

**autoimmunity** condition where the body's immune responses are mobilized not against 'foreign' matter, such as invading germs, but

# GENE REPLACEMENT THERAPY: REPAIRING NATURE'S MISTAKES?

Gene replacement therapy (GRT) is a treatment for genetic diseases, in which affected cells from a sufferer would be removed from the body, the DNA repaired in the laboratory, and the functioning cells reintroduced. At present it is still only a theoretical treatment for humans, although one experimental attempt at treatment of a child suffering from severe combined immune deficiency (SCID) has been attempted, and several successful animal experiments have been performed.

Although it is now possible to detect some genetic diseases using prenatal screening, there are a number of reasons why this has not eradicated the problem: (1) only a small proportion of all known diseases is detectable; (2) it is not practical to screen all pregnancies for all diseases; and (3) many parents have ethical objections to abortion should a disease be detected. Developments in genetic engineering have made GRT a theoretical possibility, by enabling the genes responsible for certain diseases (for example cystic fibrosis) to be identified, sequenced and cloned. This in turn means that deletions or mutations can be detected. A copy of the working gene can then be spliced into a retrovirus, which can be used to infect deficient cells. The retrovirus will incorporate its own gene sequences, including that of the replacement gene, into the host cell's DNA using its reverse transcriptase enzyme, leaving the host cell 'repaired' by addition of the working gene.

There are several features that would make a genetic disease a suitable candidate for GRT: (1) it must be serious, having no effective existing treatment; (2) the gene responsible for the disease must have been identified; and (3) it must be possible to introduce working copies of the normal gene into affected cells. Ideally, affected cells should be easy to remove and replace, and, once repaired, must be capable of dividing and growing to restore normal functioning. It must be possible to grow the cells in tissue culture, in order to have enough to reintroduce successfully. Finally, diseases which are common obviously command a higher priority than those which are rare.

Using these criteria, genetic blood disorders like thalassaemia and sickle cell anaemia emerge as excellent candidates for GRT. Blood cells and their precursors are easy to remove, grow well in tissue culture, and will repopulate the bone marrow successfully following injection. These techniques form the basis of bone marrow transplantation, which is already well-established as a successful therapy. For these reasons it is possible to envisage the successful treatment of thalassaemia and sickle cell anaemia by GRT within the next decade.

By contrast, genetic diseases of the nervous system, like Huntingdon's chorea, are unlikely to become treatable by GRT. Brain cells are difficult to remove, to grow in culture and to reintroduce into the correct location.

The commonest genetic disease in western populations is cystic fibrosis (CF), a recessive disorder affecting about one in 2,000 people. The CF gene was identified in 1990, but because of the number of different gene mutations responsible for the disease, only about 70% of cases can be identified by genetic screening. CF produces a thickening of the secretions from all the exocrine glands, including sweat, mucus and pancreatic juice. The defect produces its most serious effects in the lungs, where difficulty in coughing up the thickened secretions leads to infection in the retained mucus. Eventually the lungs are destroyed by chronic infection, leaving lung transplantation as the only effective treatment. GRT in cystic fibrosis would have to involve changing the cells lining the airways, and it is at present difficult to envisage how this might be done.

In 1990 researchers in the USA attempted to treat a child suffering from SCID by GRT. In SCID the lymphocytes lack an essential enzyme, adenosine deaminase, leaving them powerless to fight infection, and the disease is invariably fatal. In the treated child, genetically repaired lymphocytes were reintroduced in an attempt to rebuild the damaged immune system. The outcome has not been reported.

A number of ethical problems may arise in relation to GRT. Attempts to interfere with DNA contained in the germ cells are forbidden under current regulations. Therefore, although individuals can be cured of a disease by GRT, they might still pass on that disease to their children. GRT is likely to be an extremely expensive therapy, which will strain the resources available for health care, and may widen the health divide between rich and poor nations.

Finally, certain genetic diseases offer a survival advantage to their sufferers. Sickle cell anaemia, for example, protects individuals in endemic areas from malaria, so that treatment may actually harm them.

against the body itself. Diseases considered to be of autoimmune origin include myasthenia gravis, pernicious anaemia, rheumatoid arthritis, and lupus erythematosus.

In autoimmune diseases T-lymphocytes reproduce to excess to home in on a target (properly a foreign disease-causing molecule); however, molecules of the body's own tissue that resemble the target may also be attacked (for example insulin-producing cells, resulting in insulin-dependent diabetes). In 1990 in Israel a T-cell vaccine was produced that arrests the excessive reproduction of T-lymphocytes attacking healthy target tissues.

**back pain** aches in the region of the spine. Low back pain can be caused by a very wide range of medical conditions. About half of all episodes of back pain will resolve within a week, but severe back pain can be chronic and disabling. The causes include damage to muscles, a prolapsed intervertebral disc, and vertebral collapse due to osteoporosis or cancer. Treatment methods include rest, analgesics, physiotherapy, and exercises.

## UK Aids Cases And Known Deaths By Exposure Category

| | AIDS cases | | Known AIDS deaths | |
|---|---|---|---|---|
| Exposure Category | Males | Females | Males | Females |
| Homosexual/bisexual male | 2,734 | | 1,481 | |
| Injecting drug user (IDU) | 90 | 27 | 37 | 14 |
| Homosexual/bisexual male and IDU | 50 | | 24 | |
| Haemophiliac | 204 | 3 | 135 | 2 |
| Blood or components recipient | 27 | 25 | 20 | 19 |
| Heterosexual contact | | | | |
|   Partners in above risk categories | 9 | 20 | 5 | 10 |
|   Known exposure abroad | 104 | 47 | 51 | 19 |
|   No evidence of exposure abroad | 11 | 10 | 5 | 3 |
|   Undetermined | 0 | 0 | 0 | 0 |
| Child of infected parent at risk | 10 | 15 | 5 | 10 |
| Multiple exposure | 2 | 1 | 1 | 1 |
| Other/undetermined | 39 | 5 | 25 | 2 |
| TOTAL | 3,280 | 153 | 1,789 | 80 |

Source: Public Health Laboratory Service, Communicable Disease Surveillance Centre; Communicable Diseases
(Scotland) Unit

**blindness** complete absence or impairment of sight. It may be caused by heredity, accident, disease, or deterioration with age. Aids to the blind include the use of the Braille and Moon alphabets in reading and writing, and of electronic devices now under development that convert print to recognizable mechanical speech; guide dogs; and sonic torches.

**blood poisoning** condition in which poisons are spread throughout the body by the bloodstream, such as those produced by pathogens.

**bronchitis** inflammation of the bronchi (air passages) of the lungs, usually caused initially by a viral infection, such as a cold or flu.

It is aggravated by environmental pollutants, especially smoking, and results in a persistent cough, irritated mucus-secreting glands, and large amounts of sputum.

**cataract** eye disease in which the crystalline lens or its capsule becomes opaque, causing blindness. Fluid accumulates between the fibres of the lens and gives place to deposits of albumin. These coalesce into rounded bodies, the lens fibres break down, and areas of the lens or the lens capsule become filled with opaque products of degeneration. The condition nearly always affects both eyes, usually one more than the other. In most cases, the treatment is replacement of the lens with an

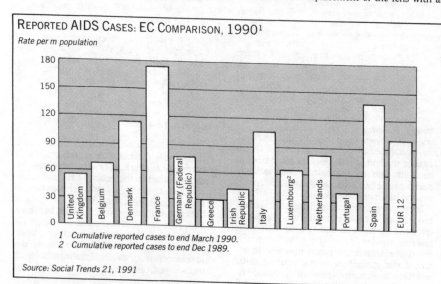

## Reported AIDS Cases: EC Comparison, 1990[1]

Rate per m population

1  Cumulative reported cases to end March 1990.
2  Cumulative reported cases to end Dec 1989.

Source: Social Trends 21, 1991

## AIDS

**AIDS** (acquired immune deficiency syndrome) is the newest and gravest of sexually transmitted diseases or STDs. It is caused by the human immunodeficiency virus (HIV), now known to be a retrovirus, an organism first identified 1981. HIV is transmitted in body fluids, mainly blood and sexual secretions.

Sexual transmission of the AIDS virus endangers heterosexual men and women as well as high-risk groups, such as homosexual and bisexual men, prostitutes; intravenous drug-users sharing needles, and haemophiliacs and surgical patients treated with contaminated blood products. The virus itself is not selective, and infection is spreading to the population at large. The virus has a short life outside the body, which makes transmission of the infection by methods other than sexual contact, blood transfusion, and shared syringes extremely unlikely.

Infection with HIV is not synonymous with having AIDS; many people who have the virus in their blood are not ill, and only about half of those infected will develop AIDS within ten years. Some suffer AIDS-related illnesses but not the full-blown disease. However, there is no firm evidence to suggest that the proportion of those developing AIDS from being HIV-positive is less than 100%.

The effect of the virus on those who become ill is the devastation of the immune system, leaving the victim susceptible to diseases that would not otherwise develop. In fact, diagnosis of AIDS is based on the appearance of rare tumours or opportunistic infections in unexpected candidates. Pneumocystic pneumonia, for instance, normally seen only in the malnourished or those whose immune systems have been deliberately suppressed, is common among AIDS victims and, for them, a leading cause of death.

The estimated incubation period is 9.8 years. Some AIDS victims die within a few months of the outbreak of symptoms, some survive for several years; roughly 50% die within three years. There is no cure for the disease, although the new drug zidovudine is claimed to delay the onset of AIDS and diminish its effects. The search continues for an effective vaccine.

In Britain, 2,256 people had died of AIDS by Dec 1990, and between 30,000 and 50,000 people were thought to be carriers of the disease. Altogether 1,276 new cases of AIDS were reported in the UK in 1990, a 51% increase over the 1988 figure. The rise was 44% among homosexual men, 78% among heterosexuals, and 102% among those who inject drugs. In the USA, 90,990 cases were reported up to Apr 1989, with 52,435 deaths; 58% of all cases. One million Americans are thought to be infected with the virus.

The HIV virus originated in Africa, where the total number of cases up to Oct 1988 was 19,141. In Africa, the prevalence of AIDS among high-risk groups such as prostitutes may approach 30%. Previous reports of up to 80% of certain populations being affected are thought to have been grossly exaggerated by inaccurate testing methods. By Feb 1991, 323,378 AIDS cases in 159 countries had been reported to the World Health Organization (WHO), which estimated that over 1.3 million cases might have occurred worldwide, of which about 400,000 as a result of transmission before, during, or shortly after birth. WHO also estimated that at least 8–10 million individuals had been infected with HIV, and about half of these would develop AIDS within ten years of infection. By the year 2000 WHO expects that 15–20 million adults and 10 million children will have been infected with HIV.

artificial implant.

**chickenpox** or **varicella** common acute disease, caused by a virus of the herpes group and transmitted by airborne droplets. Chickenpox chiefly attacks children under ten. The incubation period is two to three weeks. One attack normally gives immunity for life.

**cirrhosis** any degenerative disease in an organ of the body, especially the liver, characterized by excessive development of connective tissue, causing scarring and painful swelling. Cirrhosis of the liver may be caused by an infection such as viral hepatitis, by chronic alcoholism or drug use, blood disorder, or malnutrition. If cirrhosis is diagnosed early, it can be arrested by treating the cause; otherwise it will progress to jaundice, oedema, vomiting blood, coma, and death.

**coma** a state of deep unconsciousness from which the subject cannot be roused and in which the subject does not respond to pain. Possible causes include head injury, liver failure, cerebral haemorrhage, and drug overdose.

**cot death** death of an apparently healthy baby during sleep, also known as **sudden infant death syndrome** (SIDS). It is most common in the winter months, and strikes boys more than girls. The cause is not known.

**cystitis** inflammation of the bladder, usually caused by bacterial infection, and resulting in frequent and painful urination. Treatment is by antibiotics and copious fluids with vitamin C.

Cystitis is more common after sexual intercourse, and it is thought that intercourse encourages bacteria, especially *Escherichia coli*, which are normally present on the skin around the anus and vagina, to enter the urethra and ascend to the bladder. By drinking water before intercourse, and passing urine afterwards, the incidence of cystitis can be reduced, because the bacteria are driven back down the urethra.

**deafness** lack or deficiency in the sense of hearing, either inborn or caused by injury or disease of the middle or inner ear. Of assistance are hearing aids, lip-reading, a cochlear implant in the ear in combination with a special electronic processor, sign language (signs for concepts), and 'cued speech' (manual clarification of ambiguous lip movement during speech).

**dementia** a progressive loss of mental abilities such as memory and orientation as a result of physical changes in the brain. It may be due

to degenerative change, circulatory disease, infection, injury, or chronic poisoning. Typically a problem of old age, it can be accompanied by depression.

**dermatitis** inflammation of the skin, usually related to allergy. *Dermatosis* refers to any skin disorder and may be caused by contact or systemic problems.

**diabetes** the disease *diabetes mellitus* in which

## WATER IN BRITAIN—IS IT SAFE?

A clean, safe supply of drinking water, and hygienic sanitation, are fundamental to public health. In less developed countries over 8 million children die each year from diarrhoeal disease, principally cholera, as a consequence of inadequate sanitation. In recent years concern has been expressed in the UK about the quality of our drinking water. In an incident in 1988 the water supply in Camelford, Cornwall became contaminated with aluminium chloride, exposing local people to a theoretical long-term risk of developing Alzheimer's disease. In 1989 Britain was faced with the threat of legal action from the EC over a failure to meet a 1985 Community directive on water quality, and an outbreak of contaminated drinking water by *Cryptosporidium*, a food-poisoning bacterium, occurred in the area between Swindon and Oxford.

The dispute with the EC arose when the British government decided that the directive's requirements would be met provided the average quality of all its samples complied. In 1989 the failure rate was only two per thousand. Community officials, however, felt that *every* sample should comply, a demand that will cost the water industry about £3.8 billion by the year 2000.

### Who monitors water safety?

Until recently, there were no regulations governing the quality of drinking water in the UK, except that it should be wholesome, a property decided by the Secretary of State for Environment. In 1989 the Water Supply (Water Quality) Regulations were introduced under the Water Act. An independent drinking water inspectorate was established, and, under the rules of the privatization of the water industry, individual companies were obliged to make available to the public the results of their own tests on water quality. The complexity of the regulations, however, means that few consumers will be able to interpret the results.

Local authorities also have a responsibility to check water quality, through their environmental health officers. Currently, however, a further 400 officers are required in the UK. The National Rivers Authority is responsible for monitoring discharges of pollutants and sewage into rivers, the major source of British drinking water.

### Where does our water come from?

In the UK 99% of people receive drinking water from public supplies, of which 70%

comes from rivers and the remainder from underground sources. River water is stored in reservoirs before processing, which involves filtration to remove particulate debris, and disinfection with chlorine at a concentration of at least 0.5 parts per million. Before distribution most of the chlorine is then removed by treatment with sulphur dioxide, leaving a small residual concentration of chlorine to maintain the water free of bacteria.

### Is our sanitation adequate?

Although government figures suggest that over 99% of the population have access to a hygienic means of sewage disposal, a survey in 1986 found that nearly half a million houses lacked either a kitchen sink, a wash hand basin, shower/bath, or indoor toilet. (The rat population in surface sites in London increased by 30% in one recent year, a rise which has been blamed on a deterioration in the sewer network.)

### What are the main health hazards in water?

The incidence of waterborne infection in Britain is very low—the 1989 outbreak of *Cryptosporidium* being the only important recent example. Of more concern are the levels of certain metals in water—particularly lead, copper, zinc, and aluminium. Lead is present in obsolete pipework, and while more modern pipes use plastic or copper instead, lead is still present in solder. The new water companies are required to monitor the levels of lead, copper and zinc in the distribution system.

### Coastal bathing in Britain

There have been several recent press reports about the poor quality of sanitation around British beaches. Provisional results from a 1990 survey of bathing waters show that of 446 sites only 77% meet EC criteria for the levels of bacterial contamination.

Since the bacteria find their way into the sea via sewage outlets, this in turn suggests that an unacceptably high level of sewage is present around our beaches.

Water quality in the UK remains high, in spite of the apparent threat to uniformity of standard, posed by the privatization of the industry and the variety of monitoring agencies, at least one of which is seriously understaffed. Further action is needed, however, in order to improve the quality of British beaches.

## CANCER

**Cancer** is a group of diseases characterized by abnormal proliferation of cells. Cancer (malignant) cells are usually degenerate, capable only of reproducing themselves (tumour formation). Malignant cells tend to spread from their site of origin by travelling through the bloodstream or lymphatic system.

There are more than 100 types of cancer. Some, like lung or bowel cancer, are common; others are rare. The likely cause remains unexplained. Triggering agents (carcinogens) include chemicals such as those found in cigarette smoke, other forms of smoke, asbestos dust, exhaust fumes, and many industrial chemicals. Some viruses can also trigger the cancerous growth of cells, as can X-rays and radioactivity. Dietary factors are important in some cancers; for example, lack of fibre in the diet may predispose people to bowel cancer and a diet high in animal fats and low in fresh vegetables and fruit increases the risk of breast cancer. Psychological stress may increase the risk of cancer, more so if the person concerned is not able to control the source of the stress. In some families there is a genetic tendency towards a particular type of cancer.

Cancer is one of the leading causes of death in the industrialized world, yet it is by no means incurable, especially in the case of certain tumours, including Hodgkin's disease, acute leukaemia, and testicular cancer. Cures are sometimes achieved with specialized treatments, such as surgery, chemotherapy with cytotoxic drugs, and irradiation, or a combination of all three. Monoclonal antibodies have been used therapeutically against some cancers, with limited success. There is also hope of combining a monoclonal antibody with a drug that will kill the cancer cell to produce a highly specific magic bullet drug. In 1990 it was discovered that the presence in some patients of a particular protein, p-glycoprotein, actively protects the cancer cells from drugs intended to destroy them. If this action can be blocked, the cancer should become far easier to treat. However, at present public health programmes are more concerned with prevention and early detection.

a disorder of the islets of Langerhans in the pancreas prevents the body producing the hormone insulin, so that sugars cannot be used properly. Treatment is by strict dietary control and oral or injected insulin.

Sugar accumulates first in the blood, then in the urine; the patient experiences thirst, weight loss, and copious voiding, along with degenerative changes in the capillary system. Without treatment, the patient may go blind, ulcerate, lapse into diabetic coma, and die. Early-onset diabetes tends to be more severe than that developing in later years. Before the discovery of insulin, severe diabetics did not survive. It is still the most common cause of end-stage renal failure and there were 383 deaths per million population from *diabetes mellitus* in England and Wales in 1989. A continuous infusion of insulin can be provided via a catheter implanted under the skin, which is linked to an electric pump. This more accurately mimics the body's natural secretion of insulin than injections or oral doses, and can provide better control of diabetes. It is, however, very dangerous if the pump should malfunction.

In 1989, it was estimated that 4% of the world's population had diabetes, and that there were 12 million sufferers in Canada and the USA.

**diarrhoea** excessive action of the bowels so that the faeces are fluid or semifluid. It is caused by intestinal irritants (including some drugs and poisons), infection with harmful organisms (as in dysentery, salmonella, or cholera), or allergies.

Diarrhoea is the biggest killer of children in the world. The World Health Organization estimates that 4.5 million children die each year from dehydration as a result of diarrhoeal disease in Third World countries. It can be treated by giving an accurately measured solution of salt and glucose by mouth in large quantities. Since most diarrhoea is viral in origin, antibiotics are ineffective.

**Down's syndrome** condition caused by a chromosomal abnormality (the presence of an extra copy of chromosome 21) which in humans produces mental retardation; a flattened face; coarse, straight hair; and a fold of skin at the inner edge of the eye (hence the former name 'mongolism'). Those afflicted are usually born to mothers over 40 (one in 100); they are good-natured and teachable with special education. The syndrome is named after J L H Down (1828–1896), an English physician who studied it.

All people with Down's syndrome who live long enough eventually develop early-onset Alzheimer's disease, which led to the discovery in 1991 that some forms of early-onset Alzheimer's disease are caused by a gene defect on chromosome 21.

**drug misuse** the illegal use of drugs for nonmedicinal purposes.

Under the UK Misuse of Drugs Acts they comprise: (1) *most harmful* heroin, morphine, opium, and other narcotics; hallucinogens, such as mescalin and LSD, and injectable amphetamines, such as methedrine; (2) *less harmful* narcotics such as codeine and cannabis; stimulants of the amphetamine type, such as Benzedrine and barbiturates; (3) *least harmful* milder drugs of the amphetamine type. *Designer drugs*, for example ecstasy, are usually modifications of the amphetamine molecule, altered in order to evade the law as well as for different effects, and may be many

## DEATHS FROM MAJOR DISEASES (1989)

| Causes of death | All ages (Per m population) England and Wales | | Worldwide | |
|---|---|---|---|---|
| | Males | Females | Males | Females |
| All causes | 10,352 | 10,293 | 6,758 | 4,280 |
| Infectious and parasitic diseases | 47 | 47 | 39 | 28 |
| Benign and malignant tumours | 2,867 | 2,604 | 1,822 | 1,301 |
| Endocrine, nutritional and metabolic disorders, immunity disorders | 162 | 204 | 109 | 85 |
| Diseases of the nervous system, sense organs | 199 | 212 | 139 | 101 |
| Circulatory disease | 4,717 | 4,723 | 2,966 | 1,710 |
| Respiratory system (eg. asthma, bronchitis, pneumonia) | 1,176 | 1,114 | 747 | 413 |
| Complications of pregnancy, childbirth and puerperium | | 2 | | 2 |
| External causes of injury (eg. road traffic accidents) and poisoning | 434 | 233 | 385 | 153 |

times more powerful and dangerous. Crack, a smokable form of cocaine, became available to drug users in the 1980s. Sources of traditional drugs include the 'Golden Triangle' (where Myanmar, Laos, and Thailand meet), Mexico, Colombia, China, and the Middle East.

**eczema** inflammatory skin condition, a form of dermatitis, marked by dryness, rashes, itching, the formation of blisters, and the exudation of fluid. It may be allergic in origin and is sometimes complicated by infection.

**endometriosis** common gynaecological complaint in which patches of endometrium (the lining of the womb) are found outside the uterus. This ectopic (abnormally positioned) tissue is present most often in the ovaries, although it may invade any pelvic or abdominal site, as well as the vagina and rectum. Endometriosis may be treated with analgesics, hormone preparations, or surgery.

**epilepsy** medical disorder characterized by a tendency to develop fits, which are convulsions or abnormal feelings caused by abnormal electrical discharges in the cerebral hemispheres of the brain. Epilepsy can be controlled with a number of anticonvulsant drugs. Most epileptics have infrequent fits that have little impact on their daily lives. Epilepsy does not imply that the sufferer has any impairment of intellect, behaviour, or personality. Epilepsy is more common in the Third World, with up to 30 sufferers per 1,000 people in some areas; in industrialized countries the figure is 3–5 per 1,000.

**food poisoning** any acute illness characterized by vomiting and diarrhoea and caused by eating food contaminated with harmful bacteria (for example, listeriosis), poisonous food (for example, certain mushrooms, puffer fish), or poisoned food (for example, lead or arsenic introduced accidentally during processing). A frequent cause of food poisoning is salmonella bacteria. These come in many forms, and various strains are found in some cattle, pigs, poultry, and eggs. The most dangerous food poison is the bacillus that causes botulism. This is rare but leads to muscle paralysis and, often, death. Food irradiation is intended to prevent food poisoning.

Food poisoning has increased in the UK. In northern England there were 4,000 reported cases in 1990, up from 600 cases in 1982; East

Anglia and the Mersey area reported rises of 50% of the northern region.

**gastroenteritis** inflammation of the stomach and intestines, giving rise to abdominal pain, vomiting, and diarrhoea. It may be caused by food or other poisoning, allergy, or infection, and is dangerous in babies.

**German measles** (or **rubella**) mild, communicable virus disease, usually caught by children. It is marked by a sore throat, pinkish rash, and slight fever, and has an incubation period of two to three weeks. If a woman contracts it in the first three months of pregnancy, it may cause serious damage to the unborn child.

**glandular fever** or **infectious mononucleosis** viral disease characterized at onset by fever and painfully swollen lymph nodes (in the neck); there may also be digestive upset, sore throat, and skin rashes. Lassitude persists for months and even years, and recovery is often very slow. It is caused by the Epstein-Barr virus.

**glaucoma** condition in which pressure inside the eye (intraocular pressure) is raised abnormally as excess fluid accumulates. It occurs when the normal flow of intraocular fluid out of the eye is interrupted. As pressure rises, the optic nerve suffers irreversible damage, leading to a reduction in the field of vision and, ultimately, loss of eyesight.

**gout** a hereditary form of arthritis, marked by an excess of uric acid crystals in the tissues, causing pain and inflammation in one or more joints (usually of the feet or hands). Acute attacks are treated with anti-inflammatories. The disease, ten times more common in men, poses a long-term threat to the blood vessels and the kidneys, so ongoing treatment may be needed to minimize the levels of uric acid in the body fluids. It is worsened by drinking alcohol.

**haemophilia** any of several inherited diseases in which normal blood clotting is impaired. The sufferer experiences prolonged bleeding from the slightest wound, as well as painful internal bleeding without apparent cause.

Haemophilias are nearly always sex-linked, transmitted through the female line only to male infants; it has afflicted a number of European royal households. Males affected by the most common form are unable to synthesize Factor VIII, a protein involved in the clotting of blood. Treatment is primarily with Factor VIII (now mass-produced by recombinant techniques), but the haemophiliac remains at risk from the slightest incident of bleeding. The disease is a painful one that causes deformities of joints.

**haemorrhoids** distended blood vessels (varicose veins) in the area of the anus, popularly called piles.

**hay fever** allergic reaction to pollen, causing sneezing, inflammation of the eyes, and asthmatic symptoms. Sufferers experience irritation caused by powerful body chemicals related to histamine produced at the site of entry. Treatment is by antihistamine drugs.

**heart attack** sudden onset of gripping central chest pain, often accompanied by sweating and vomiting, caused by death of a portion of the heart muscle following occlusion of a coronary artery by thrombosis. Half of all heart attacks result in death within the first two hours, but in the remainder survival has improved following the widespread use of streptokinase and aspirin to treat heart-attack victims.

**heartburn** burning sensation below the breastbone (sternum). It results from irritation of the lower oesophagus (gullet) by excessively acid stomach contents, as sometimes happens during pregnancy and in cases of duodenal ulcer or obesity. It is often due to a weak valve at the entrance to the stomach that allows its contents to well up into the oesophagus.

**heart disease** disorder affecting the heart; for example, ischaemic heart disease, in which the blood supply through the coronary artieries is reduced by atherosclerosis; valvular heart disease, in which a heart valve is damaged; and cardiomyopathy, where the heart muscle itself is diseased.

**hepatitis** any inflammatory disease of the liver, usually caused by a virus. Other causes include alcohol, drugs, gallstones, lupus erythematosus and amoebic dysentery. Symptoms include weakness, nausea, and jaundice.
The viral disease **hepatitis A** (infectious or viral hepatitis) is spread by contaminated food, often seafood, and via the oro-faecal route. Incubation is about four weeks. Temporary immunity is conferred by injections of normal immunoglobulin (gamma globulin). The virus causing **hepatitis B** (serum hepatitis) was isolated in the 1960s. Contained in all body fluids, it is very easily transmitted. Some people become carriers. Those with the disease may be sick for weeks or months. The illness may be mild, or it may result in death from liver failure. Liver cancer is now recognized as a long-term complication of the disease. A successful vaccine was developed in the late 1970s.

**hernia** or **rupture** protrusion of part of an internal organ through a weakness in the surrounding muscular wall, usually in the groin or navel. The appearance is that of a rounded soft lump or swelling.

**herpes** any of several infectious diseases caused by viruses of the herpes group. **Herpes simplex I** is the causative agent of a common inflammation, the cold sore. **Herpes simplex II** is respon-

sible for genital herpes, a highly contagious, sexually transmitted disease characterized by painful blisters in the genital area. It can be transmitted in the birth canal from mother to newborn. **Herpes zoster** causes shingles; another herpes virus causes chickenpox. A number of antivirals treat these infections, which are particularly troublesome in patients whose immune system has been suppressed medically, for example, after a transplant operation.
The Epstein-Barr virus of glandular fever also belongs to this group.

**hypertension** abnormally high blood pressure due to a variety of causes, leading to excessive contraction of the smooth muscle cells of the walls of the arteries. It increases the risk of kidney disease, stroke, and heart attack.

**hypothermia** condition in which the deep (core) temperature of the body spontaneously drops. If it is not discovered, coma and death ensue. Most at risk are the aged and babies (particularly if premature).

**impotence** in men, failure to achieve an erection; this may be due to illness, the effects of certain drugs, or psychological factors.

**incontinence** failure or inability to control evacuation of the bladder or bowel (or both in the case of double incontinence). It may arise as a result of injury, childbirth, disease, or senility.

**infection** invasion of the body by disease-causing organisms (pathogens, or germs) that become established, multiply, and produce symptoms.
Most pathogens enter and leave the body through the digestive or respiratory tracts. Polio, dysentery, and typhoid are examples of diseases contracted by ingestion of contaminated foods or fluids. Organisms present in the saliva or nasal mucus are spread by airborne or droplet infection; fine droplets or dried particles are inhaled by others when the affected individual talks, coughs, or sneezes. Diseases such as measles, mumps, and tuberculosis are passed on in this way. The common cold is passed from hand to hand, which then touches the eye or nose.

**influenza** any of various virus infections primarily affecting the air passages, accompanied by systemic effects such as fever, chills, headache, joint and muscle pains, and lassitude. Depending on the virus strain, influenza varies in virulence and duration, and there is always the risk of secondary (bacterial) infection of the lungs (pneumonia). Treatment is with bed rest and analgesic drugs such as aspirin and paracetamol. Vaccines are effective against known strains but will not give protection against newly evolving viruses.

**jaundice** yellow discoloration of the skin and whites of the eyes caused by an excess of bile pigment in the bloodstream. Bile pigment is normally produced by the liver from the breakdown of red blood cells, then excreted into the intestines. A build-up in the blood is due to abnormal destruction of red cells (as in some cases of anaemia), impaired liver function (as in hepatitis), or blockage in the excretory channels (as in gallstones or cirrhosis). The jaundice gradually recedes following treatment of the underlying cause.

**laryngitis** inflammation of the larynx, causing soreness of the throat, dry cough, and hoarseness. The acute form is due to a virus or other infection, excessive use of the voice, or inhalation of irritating smoke, and may cause the voice to be completely lost. With rest, the inflammation usually subsides in a few days.

**leukaemia** any one of a group of cancers of the blood cells, with widespread involvement of the bone marrow and other blood-forming tissue. The central feature is runaway production of white blood cells that are immature or in some way abnormal. These rogue cells, which lack the defensive capacity of healthy white cells, overwhelm the normal ones, leaving the victim vulnerable to infection. Abnormal functioning of the bone marrow also suppresses production of red blood cells and blood platelets, resulting in anaemia and a failure of the blood to clot.

Leukaemias are classified into acute or chronic, depending on their known rates of progression. They are also grouped according to the type of white cell involved. Treatment is with radiotherapy and cytotoxic drugs to suppress replication of abnormal cells, or by bone-marrow transplantation.

**measles** acute virus disease (rubeola), spread by airborne infection. Symptoms are fever, severe catarrh, small spots inside the mouth, and a raised, blotchy red rash appearing for about a week after two weeks' incubation. Prevention is by vaccination. In industrialized countries it is not usually a serious disease, though serious complications may develop. Third World children particularly suffer a high mortality.

In the UK a vaccination programme is under way, combining measles, mumps, and rubella (German measles) vaccine; this is given to children at age 15 months. A total of 86,001 cases of measles were recorded in England and Wales in 1988.

**melanoma** mole or growth containing the dark pigment melanin. Malignant melanoma is a type of skin cancer developing in association with a pre-existing mole. Unlike other skin cancers, it is associated with brief but excessive exposure to sunlight. Once rare, this disease is now frequent, owing to the increasing popularity of holidays in the sun. Most at risk are those with fair hair and light skin, and those who have had a severe sunburn in childhood.

**meningitis** inflammation of the meninges (membranes) surrounding the brain, caused by bacterial or viral infection. The severity of the disease varies from mild to rapidly lethal, and symptoms include fever, headache, nausea, neck stiffness, delirium, and (rarely) convulsions. Many common viruses can cause the occasional case of meningitis, although not usually in its more severe form. The treatment for viral meningitis is rest. Bacterial meningitis, though treatable by antibiotics, is a much more serious threat. Diagnosis is by lumbar puncture.

**migraine** acute, sometimes incapacitating headache (generally only on one side), accompanied by nausea, that recurs, often with advance symptoms such as flashing lights. No cure has been discovered, but ergotamine normally relieves the symptoms. Some sufferers learn to avoid certain foods, such as chocolate, which suggests an allergic factor.

In 1990, Hammersmith Hospital in London, England, reported successful treatment with goggles that turn down beta waves in the brain (associated with stress) and stimulate alpha waves (whose effect is calming).

**multiple sclerosis** (MS) incurable chronic disease of the central nervous system, occurring in young or middle adulthood. It is characterized by degeneration of the myelin sheath that surrounds nerves in the brain and spinal cord. It is also known as disseminated sclerosis. Its cause is unknown.

Depending on where the demyelination occurs—which nerves are affected—the symptoms of MS can mimic almost any neurological disorder. Typically seen are unsteadiness, ataxia (loss of muscular coordination), weakness, speech difficulties, and rapid involuntary movements of the eyes. The course of the disease is episodic, with frequent intervals of remission.

**mumps** virus infection marked by fever and swelling of the parotid salivary glands (such as those under the ears). It is usually minor in children, although meningitis is a possible complication. In adults the symptoms are severe and it may cause sterility in adult men. An effective vaccine against mumps, measles, and rubella (MMR vaccine) is now offered to children aged 18 months.

**muscular dystrophy** any of a group of inherited chronic muscle disorders marked by weakening and wasting of muscle. Muscle fibres degenerate, to be replaced by fatty tissue, although the nerve supply remains unimpaired. Death occurs in early adult life.

The commonest form, Duchenne muscular dystrophy, strikes boys, usually before the age of four. The child develops a waddling gait and an inward curvature (lordosis) of the lumbar spine. The muscles affected by dystrophy and the rate of progress vary. There is no cure, but physical treatments can minimize disability.

**myalgic encephalitis** (ME) a debilitating condition still not universally accepted as a genuine disease. The condition occurs after a flulike attack and has a diffuse range of symptoms. These strike and recur for years and include extreme fatigue, muscular pain, weakness, and depression.

ME, sometimes known as *postviral fatigue syndrome* or *chronic fatigue syndrome* or *yuppie flu*, is not a new phenomenon. Outbreaks have been documented worldwide for more than 50 years. Recent research suggests that ME may be the result of chronic viral infection, leaving the sufferer exhausted, debilitated, and with generally lowered resistance. There is no definitive treatment for ME, but with time the symptoms become less severe.

**osteoarthritis** degenerative disease of the joints in later life, sometimes resulting in disabling stiffness and wasting of muscles. Formerly thought to be due to wear and tear, it has been shown to be less common in the physically active. It appears to be linked with crystal deposits (in the form of calcium phosphate) in cartilage, a discovery that suggests hope of eventual prevention.

**osteoporosis** disease in which the bone substance becomes porous and brittle. It is common in older people, affecting more women than men. It may occur in women whose ovaries have been removed, unless hormone-replacement therapy (HRT) is instituted. It may also be treated with calcium supplements and etidionate. Osteoporosis may occur as a side effect of long-term treatment with corticosteroids. Early menopause in women, childlessness, small body build, lack of exercise, heavy drinking, smoking, and hereditary factors may also be contributory factors.

**otitis** inflammation of the ear. *Otitis externa*, occurring in the outer ear canal, is easily treated with antibiotics. Inflamed conditions of the middle ear (*otitis media*) or inner ear (*otitis interna*) are more serious, carrying the risk of deafness and infection of the brain.

**Parkinson's disease** or *parkinsonism* or *paralysis agitans* degenerative disease of the brain characterized by a progressive loss of mobility, muscular rigidity, tremor, and speech difficulties. The condition is mainly seen in people over the age of 50.

Parkinson's disease destroys a group of cells called the *substantia nigra* ('black substance') in the upper part of the brainstem. These cells are concerned with the production of a neurotransmitter known as dopamine, which is essential to the control of voluntary movement. The almost total loss of these cells, and of their chemical product, produces the disabling effects. The introduction of L-dopa in the 1960s seemed at first the answer to Parkinson's disease. However, it became evident that long-term use of the drug brings considerable problems. At best, it postpones the terminal phase of the disease. Brain grafts with dopamine-producing cells were pioneered in the early 1980s, and attempts to graft Parkinson's patients with fetal brain tissue have been made. In 1989 a large US study showed that the drug deprenyl may slow the rate at which disability progresses in patients with early Parkinson's disease.

**pneumonia** inflammation of the lungs, generally due to bacterial or viral infection but also to particulate matter or gases. It is characterized by a build-up of fluid in the alveoli, the clustered air sacs (at the end of the air passages) where oxygen exchange takes place. Symptoms include fever and pain in the chest. With widespread availability of antibiotics, infectious pneumonia is much less common than it was. However, it remains a dire threat to patients whose immune systems are suppressed (including transplant recipients and AIDS and cancer victims) and to those who are critically ill or injured.

**polio** (*poliomyelitis*) viral infection of the central nervous system affecting nerves that activate muscles. The disease used to be known as infantile paralysis. The World Health Organization expects that polio will be eradicated by 2000.

**premenstrual tension** (PMT) popular name for *premenstrual syndrome*, a medical condition caused by hormone changes and comprising a number of physical and emotional features that occur cyclically before menstruation and disappear with its onset. Symptoms include mood changes, breast tenderness, a feeling of bloatedness, and headache.

**psoriasis** chronic, recurring skin disease characterized by raised, red, scaly patches, usually on the scalp, back, arms, and/or legs. It is a common disease, affecting 2% of the UK population. Tar preparations, steroid creams, and ultraviolet light are used to treat it, and sometimes it disappears spontaneously. Psoriasis may be accompanied by a form of arthritis.

**puerperal fever** infection of the genital tract of the mother after childbirth, due to lack of aseptic conditions. Formerly often fatal, it is now rare and treated with antibiotics.

**rabies** or *hydrophobia* disease of the central nervous system that can afflict all warm-blooded creatures. It is almost invariably fatal once symptoms have developed (fever, muscle spasm, delirium). Its transmission to humans is generally by a bite from a rabid dog. Injections of rabies vaccine and antiserum may save those bitten by a rabid animal from developing the disease.

**rheumatic fever** or *acute rheumatism* acute or chronic illness characterized by fever and painful swelling of joints. Some victims also experience involuntary movements of the limbs and head, a form of chorea. Rheumatic fever, which strikes mainly children and young adults, is always preceded by a streptococcal infection such as scarlet fever or a severe sore throat, usually occurring a couple of weeks beforehand. It is treated with bed rest, antibiotics, and painkillers. The most important complication of rheumatic fever is damage to the heart valve, producing rheumatic heart disease, which may lead to disability and death.

**rubella** technical term for German measles.

**scabies** contagious infection of the skin caused by the parasitic itch mite *Sarcoptes scaboi*, which burrows under the skin to deposit eggs. Treatment is by antiparasitic creams and lotions.

**sciatica** persistent pain in the leg, along the sciatic nerve and its branches. Causes of sciatica include inflammation of the nerve or pressure on, or inflammation of, a nerve root leading out of the lower spine.

**septicaemia** technical term for blood poisoning.

**shingles** common name for herpes zoster, a disease characterized by infection of sensory nerves, with pain and eruption of blisters along the course of the affected nerves.

## TROPICAL DISEASES: REPORTED CASES (1989)

| | Africa | Asia/Oceania | USA | Europe (not imported) |
|---|---|---|---|---|
| Malaria | 250,000 | 13,500 | 3,500 | — |
| Schistosomiasis | 160,000 | 25,000 | 8,000 | — |
| Leishmaniasis | 1,000 | 6,000 | 5,000 | 10 |
| River blindness | 17,000 | — | 100 | — |
| Leprosy | 2–3,000 | 7–8,000 | 500–1,000 | <50 |
| African sleeping sickness | 25 | — | — | — |
| TOTAL | 460,000 | 110,000 | 35,000 | <60 |

< = fewer than

**shock** in medicine, circulatory failure marked by a sudden fall of blood pressure and resulting in pallor, sweating, fast (but weak) pulse, and sometimes complete collapse. Causes include disease, injury, and psychological trauma. In shock, the blood pressure falls below that necessary to supply the tissues of the body, especially the brain. Treatment depends on the cause. Rest is needed, and, in the case of severe blood loss, restoration of the normal circulating volume.

**sickle-cell disease** hereditary chronic blood disorder common among people of black African descent; also found in the E Mediterranean, parts of the Gulf, and in NE India. It is characterized by distortion and fragility of the red blood cells, which are lost too rapidly from the circulation. This often results in anaemia.

**sinusitis** painful inflammation of one of the sinuses, or air spaces, that surround the nasal passages. Most cases clear with antibiotics and nasal decongestants, but some require surgical drainage.

**spina bifida** congenital defect in which part of the spinal cord and its membranes are exposed, due to incomplete development of the spine (vertebral column).

Spina bifida, usually present in the lower back, varies in severity. The most seriously affected babies may be paralysed below the waist. There is also a risk of mental retardation and death from hydrocephalus, which is often associated. Surgery is performed to close the spinal lesion shortly after birth, but this does not usually cure the disabilities caused by the condition.

**stroke** a sudden interruption of the blood supply to the brain. It is also termed a cerebrovascular accident or apoplexy. Strokes are caused by a sudden bleed in the brain (cerebral haemhorrhage) or interruption of the blood supply to part of the brain due to embolism or thrombosis. They vary in severity from producing almost no symptoms to proving rapidly fatal. In between are those (often recurring) that leave a wide range of impaired function, depending on the size and location of the event.

The disease of the arteries that predisposes to stroke is atherosclerosis. High blood pressure (hypertension) is also a precipitating factor. Strokes can sometimes be prevented by surgery (as in the case of some aneurysms), or by use of anticoagulant drugs or daily aspirin to minimize the risk of stroke due to blood clots.

**syphilis** venereal disease caused by the spiral-shaped bacterium (spirochete) *Treponema pallidum*. Untreated, it runs its course in three stages over many years, often starting with a painless hard sore, or chancre, developing within a month on the area of infection (usually the genitals). The second stage, months later, is a rash with arthritis, hepatitis, and/or meningitis. The third stage, years later, leads eventually to paralysis, blindness, insanity, and death.

With widespread availability of antibiotics, syphilis is now increasingly cured in the industrialized world, at least to the extent that the final stage of the disease is rare. The risk remains that the disease may go undiagnosed or that it may be transmitted by a pregnant woman to her fetus.

**tetanus** or *lockjaw* acute disease caused by the toxin of the bacillus *Clostridium tetani*, which usually enters the body through a wound. The bacterium is chiefly found in richly manured soil. Untreated, in seven to ten days tetanus produces muscular spasm and rigidity of the jaw spreading to the other muscles, convulsions, and death. There is a vaccine, and the disease may be treatable with tetanus antitoxin and antibiotics.

**thrombosis** condition in which a blood clot forms in a vein or artery, causing loss of circulation to the area served by the vessel. If it breaks away, it often travels to the lungs, causing pulmonary embolism. Thrombosis in veins of the legs is often seen in association with phlebitis, and in arteries with atheroma. Thrombosis increases the risk of heart attack (myocardial infarct) and stroke. It is treated by surgery and/or anticoagulant drugs.

**thrush** infection usually of the mouth (particularly in infants), but also sometimes of the vagina, caused by a yeastlike fungus (genus *Candida*). It is seen as white patches on the mucous membranes.

Thrush, also known as **candidiasis**, may be caused by antibiotics removing natural antifungal agents from the body. It is treated with a further antibiotic.

**tonsillitis** inflammation of the tonsils.

**toxic shock syndrome** condition marked by rapid

onset of fever, vomiting, and low blood pressure. It is caused by a toxin of the bacterium *Staphylococcus aureus* which may accumulate, for example, if a tampon used by a woman during a period remains unchanged beyond four to six hours.

**travel sickness** nausea and vomiting caused by the motion of cars, boats, or other forms of transport. Constant vibration and movement may stimulate changes in the fluids of the semicircular canals (responsible for balance) of the inner ear, to which the individual fails to adapt, and to which are added visual and psychological factors. Some proprietary cures contain antihistamine drugs.

**tropical disease** the most important tropical diseases worldwide are malaria, schistosomiasis, leprosy, and river blindness. Malaria kills about 1.5 million people each year, and produces chronic anaemia and tiredness in one hundred times as many, while schistosomiasis is responsible for one million deaths annually.

All the main tropical diseases are potentially curable, but the facilities for diagnosis and treatment are rarely adequate in the countries where they occur. There is evidence that malaria, which was eliminated from Norfolk, England only last century, will spread into more temperate regions as global warming develops.

**tuberculosis** (TB) formerly known as *consumption* or *phthisis* infectious disease caused by the bacillus *Mycobacterium tuberculosis*. It takes several forms, of which pulmonary tuberculosis is by far the most common.

In pulmonary TB, a patch of inflammation develops in the lung, with formation of an abscess. Often, this heals spontaneously, leaving only scar tissue. The dangers are of rapid spread through both lungs (what used to be called 'galloping consumption') or the development of miliary tuberculosis (spreading in the bloodstream to other sites) or tuberculous meningitis. The first antituberculosis drug, streptomycin, was developed in 1944. In England and Wales 478 people died of TB in 1988 out of 5,164 recorded cases.

**varicose veins** or *varicosis* condition where the veins become swollen and twisted. The veins of the legs are most often affected, although other vulnerable sites include the rectum (haemorrhoids) and testes.

**vomiting** the expulsion of the contents of the stomach through the mouth. It may have numerous causes, including direct irritation of the stomach, severe pain, dizziness, and emotion. Sustained or repeated vomiting is always a serious symptom, because it may indicate serious disease, and because dangerous loss of water, salt, and acid may result (as in bulimia).

**whooping cough** or *pertussis* acute infectious disease, seen mainly in children, caused by colonization of the air passages by the bacterium *Bordetella pertussis*. There may be catarrh, mild fever, and loss of appetite, but the main symptom is violent coughing, associated with the sharp intake of breath that is the characteristic 'whoop', and often followed by vomiting and severe nose bleeds. The cough may persist for weeks.

# TYPES OF DRUGS

**anaesthetic** drug that produces loss of sensation or consciousness; the resulting state is *anaesthesia*, in which the patient is insensitive to stimuli. Anaesthesia may also happen as a result of nerve disorder.

**analgesic** agent for relieving pain. Opiates alter the perception or appreciation of pain and are effective in controlling 'deep' visceral (internal) pain. Non-opiates, such as aspirin, paracetamol, and NSAIDs, relieve musculoskeletal pain and reduce inflammation in soft tissues.

Temporary or permanent analgesia may be achieved by injection of an anaesthetic agent into, or the severing of, a nerve. Implanted devices enable patients to deliver controlled electrical stimulation to block pain impulses. Production of the body's natural opiates, endorphins, can be manipulated by techniques such as relaxation and biofeedback. For the severe pain of, for example, terminal cancer, however, opiate analgesics are required.

**antibiotic** drug that kills or inhibits the growth of bacteria and fungi. It is derived from living organisms such as fungi or other bacteria, which distinguishes it from synthetic antimicrobials.

The earliest antibiotics, the penicillins, came into use from 1941 and were quickly joined by chloramphenicol, the cephalosporins, erythromycins, tetracyclines, and aminoglycosides. A range of broad-spectrum antibiotics, the 4-quinolones, was developed 1989, of which ciprofloxacin was the first. Each class and individual antibiotic acts in a different way and may be effective against either a broad spectrum or a specific type of disease-causing agent. Use of antibiotics has become more selective as side effects, such as toxicity, allergy, and resistance, have become better understood. Bacteria have the ability to develop immunity following repeated or subclinical (insufficient) doses, so more advanced and synthetic antimicrobials are continually required to overcome them.

**antidepressant** any drug used to relieve symptoms in depressive illness. The two main groups are the tricyclic antidepressants (TCADs) and the monoamine oxidase inhibitors (MAOIs), which act by altering chemicals available to the central nervous system. Both may produce serious side effects and are restricted.

**anti-inflammatory** a substance that reduces swelling in soft tissues. Antihistamines relieve allergic reactions; aspirin and NSAIDs are effective in joint and musculoskeletal conditions; rubefacients (counterirritant liniments) ease painful joints, tendons, and muscles; steroids, because of the severe side effects, are only prescribed if other therapy is ineffective, or if a condition is

## Is Aspirin Good For Your Heart?

There is evidence that low-dose aspirin—one tablet every other day—can help protect people from heart attacks. In a large trial in the USA, 22,000 men received either aspirin or a placebo tablet. Among the 11,000 who received aspirin there were 104 heart attacks (five fatal), but 189 (18 fatal) in the placebo group. This suggests that taking one aspirin every other day can cut your risk of a heart attack by approxi mately half. On the other hand, deaths from stroke were more common in the aspirin group in the trial, with the result that aspirin made no difference to the overall mortality. It is therefore not clear that aspirin

should be recommended to everyone.

For people who have already suffered a heart attack, the situation is much clearer. A large international trial involving 17,000 heart attack victims demonstrated clearly that aspirin given as soon as possible after the attack reduced the mortality at five weeks by about 25%, and when streptokinase was given as well, the reduction was by 40%. Following this trial streptokinase and aspirin are now routinely used in all heart attack patients, except those who are at risk from bleeding (for example, patients who have had a recent operation).

---

life-threatening. A corticosteroid injection into the affected joint usually gives long-term relief from inflammation.

**antiseptic** any substance that kills or inhibits the growth of microorganisms. The use of antiseptics was pioneered by Joseph Lister. He used carbolic acid (phenol), which is a weak antiseptic; substances such as TCP are derived from this.

**antiviral** any drug that acts against viruses, usually preventing them from multiplying. Most viral infections are not susceptible to antibiotics. Antivirals have been difficult drugs to develop, and do not necessarily cure viral diseases.

**aspirin** acetylsalicylic acid, a popular analgesic developed in the early 20th century for headaches and arthritis. It inhibits prostaglandins, and is derived from the white willow tree *Salix alba*.

**beta-blocker** any of a class of drugs that block impulses that stimulate certain nerve endings (beta receptors) serving the heart muscles. This reduces the heart rate and the force of contraction, which in turn reduces the amount of oxygen (and therefore the blood supply) required by the heart. Beta-blockers are banned from use in competitive sports. They may be useful in the treatment of angina, arrhythmia, and raised blood pressure, and following myocardial infarctions. They must be withdrawn from use gradually.

**codeine** opium derivative that provides analgesia in mild to moderate pain. It also suppresses the cough centre of the brain. It is an alkaloid $C_{18}H_{21}NO_3$, derived from morphine but less toxic and addictive.

**corticosteroid** any of several steroid hormones secreted by the cortex of the adrenal glands; also synthetic forms with similar properties. Corticosteroids have anti-inflammatory and immunosuppressive effects and may be used to. treat a number of conditions including rheumatoid arthritis, severe allergies, asthma, some skin diseases, and some cancers. Side effects can be serious, and therapy must be withdrawn very gradually.

**insulin** protein hormone, produced by specialized cells in the islets of Langerhans in the pancreas, that regulates the metabolism (rate

of activity) of glucose, fats, and proteins. Insulin was discovered by Canadian physician Frederick Banting, who pioneered its use in treating diabetes.

**L-dopa** chemical, normally produced by the body, which is converted by an enzyme to dopamine in the brain. It is essential for integrated movement of individual muscle groups.

L-dopa is a left-handed isomer of an amino acid $C_9H_{11}NO_2$. As a treatment, it relieves the rigidity of Parkinson's disease but may have significant side effects, such as extreme mood changes, hallucinations, and uncontrolled writhing movements. It is often given in combination with other drugs to improve its effectiveness at lower doses.

**mefipristone** abortion pill (previously known as RU 486), licensed in the UK in 1991. It is administered in conjunction with a prostaglandin to induce termination of pregnancy, which occurs within 24 hours. The procedure can be done at home.

The pill was introduced in France in 1989, and trials there showed that it was effective in 94% of patients up to 10 weeks pregnant. Up to March 1991, 60,000 abortions were carried out in France by this method.

**oxytocin** hormone that stimulates the uterus in late pregnancy to initiate and sustain labour. After birth, it stimulates the uterine muscles to contract, reducing bleeding at the site where the placenta was attached.

**paracetamol** analgesic, particularly effective for musculoskeletal pain. It is as effective as aspirin in reducing fever, and less irritating to the stomach, but has little anti-inflammatory action (as for joint pain). An overdose can cause severe, often irreversible, liver and kidney damage.

**penicillin** any of a group of antibiotic compounds obtained from filtrates of moulds of the genus *Penicillium* (especially *P. notatum*) or produced synthetically. Penicillin was the first antibiotic to be discovered (by Alexander Fleming), and it kills a broad spectrum of bacteria, many of which cause disease in humans.

The use of the original type of penicillin is limited by the increasing resistance of pathogens and by allergic reactions in patients. Since 1941, numerous other antibiotics of the penicillin family have been discovered, which are more selective against, or resistant to, specific microorganisms.

**placebo** any harmless substance, often called a 'sugar pill', that has no chemotherapeutic value and yet produces physiological changes.

Its use in medicine is limited to drug trials, where it is given alongside the substance being tested, to compare effects. The 'placebo effect', first named in 1945, demonstrates the control 'mind' exerts over 'matter', including causing changes in blood pressure, perceived pain, and rates of healing. Recent research finds the release of certain neurotransmitting substances in the production of the placebo effect.

**premedication** combination of drugs given before surgery to prepare a patient for general anaesthesia.

**steroid** any of a group of cyclic, unsaturated alcohols (lipids without fatty acid components), which, like sterols, have a complex molecular structure consisting of four carbon rings. Steroids include the sex hormones, such as testosterone, the corticosteroid hormones produced by the adrenal gland, bile acids, and cholesterol.

An **anabolic steroid** is any hormone of the steroid group of organic compounds that stimulates tissue growth. Its use in medicine is limited to the treatment of some anaemias and breast cancers; it may help to break up blood clots. Side effects include aggressive behaviour, masculinization. In 1988 the Canadian sprinter Ben Johnson was stripped of an Olympic gold medal for taking anabolic steroids.

**warfarin** poison that induces fatal internal bleeding in rats; neutralized with sodium hydroxide, it is used in medicine as an anticoagulant: it prevents blood clotting by inhibiting the action of vitamin K. It can be taken orally and begins to act several days after the initial dose.

Warfarin is a crystalline powder, $C_{19}H_{16}O_4$. Heparin may be given in treatment at the same time and discontinued when warfarin takes effect. It is often given as a preventive measure, to reduce the risk of thrombosis or embolism after major surgery.

**zidovudine** formerly **AZT** antiviral drug used in the treatment of AIDS. Developed in the mid-1980s and approved for use by 1987, it is not a cure for AIDS but is effective in suppressing the causative virus (HIV) for as long as it is being administered. Taken every four hours, night and day, it reduces the risk of opportunistic infection and relieves many neurological complications. However, frequent blood monitoring is required to control anaemia, a potentially life-threatening side effect of zidovudine. Blood transfusions are often necessary, and the drug must be withdrawn if bone-marrow function is severely affected.

# ALTERNATIVE MEDICINE

**acupuncture** ancient Chinese medical art based on a theory of physiology that posits a network of life-energy pathways or 'meridians' in the human body and some 800 'acupuncture points' where metal needles may be inserted to affect the energy flow for purposes of preventive or remedial therapy or to produce a local anaesthetic effect. Numerous studies and surveys have attested the efficacy of the method, which is widely conceded by orthodox practitioners despite the lack of an acceptable scientific explanation.

**Alexander technique** a method of correcting established bad habits of posture, breathing, and muscular tension which Australian therapist F M Alexander (1869–1955) maintained cause many ailments. Back troubles, migraine, asthma, hypertension, and some gastric and gynaecological disorders are among the conditions said to be alleviated by the technique, which is also effective in preventing disorders, particularly those of later life, and conferring a general health benefit, promoting relaxation and enhancing vitality.

**applied kinesiology** an extension of chiropractic developed in the USA in the 1960s and '70s, principally by US practitioner Dr George Goodheart. Relating to the science of kinesiology, or muscle testing, the Chinese principle that there exist energy pathways in the body and that disease results from local energy blockages or imbalances, Goodheart developed both diagnostic and therapeutic techniques, working on the body's musculature, which have proved particularly effective with stress-related ailments.

**aromatherapy** the medicinal use of oils and essences derived from plants, flowers, and wood resins. Bactericidal properties and beneficial effects upon physiological functions are attributed to the oils, which are sometimes ingested but generally massaged into the skin. Aromatherapy was practised in the ancient world and revived in the 1960s in France, where today it is an optional component of some courses available to postgraduate medical students.

**astrological diagnosis** the casting of a horoscope to ascertain a person's susceptibility to specific kinds of disease. From statistical evidence that offspring tend to have the same planetary positions in their charts as a parent, astrologers infer that there is a significant correlation between genetic and planetary influences, and that medical horoscopes, by pinpointing pathological tendencies, can be a useful tool of preventative medicine.

**aura diagnosis** ascertaining a person's state of health from the colour and luminosity of the aura, the 'energy envelope' of the physical body commonly claimed to be seen by psychics. A recent Charing Cross Hospital Medical School

## ALTERNATIVE MEDICINE AT THE CROSSROADS

The ideological war between practitioners of orthodox and alternative medicine came to a head and to public notice in the autumn of 1990. A research report published in *The Lancet* appeared to demonstrate that cancer patients receiving alternative therapy were twice as likely to die and three times as likely to suffer recurrence as those receiving conventional treatment. The report threatened the very existence of the Bristol Cancer Help Centre, one of Britain's best known alternative therapy institutions. A three-month waiting list evaporated virtually overnight. Whereas the medical establishment had previously tended to regard complementary therapies as merely ineffective, this report carried the implication that they were positively dangerous.

Advocates of alternative medicine launched a counterattack, pointing out flaws in the research protocols which totally invalidated the report's conclusions. In Nov the authors retracted, conceding that the patients who went to the Bristol Centre were originally more seriously ill than those in the control group.

But this was no storm in a teacup. It highlighted an antagonism that is at base ideological, some would say even religious in nature. Behind the extremist accusations on the one hand that alternative medicine is retrogressive and exploitative quackery, and on the other that orthodox medicine has become so narrowly specialized and technological that it is now counterproductive, contributing to a dependence on drugs and surgery that violates the fundamental principle of healing, there lies the age-old antagonism between magic and science, mysticism and rationalism, philosophies that emphasize the primacy of the spiritual or of the material in their views of man and the world.

Perhaps there can never be any rapprochement between these views on the philosophical-religious level. Perhaps they correspond with biases inherent in human psychology. But when they are applied in the field of medicine, ethical issues arise and take precedence. The patient values life and health above ideology,

*Dr Anne Pye counsels patient at the Bristol Cancer Help Centre, London.*

and wants the treatment that will best guarantee them.

Over recent years the medical orthodoxy has had to concede that some things work that have no rationale, at least none that it can acknowledge as such. Acupuncture and homoeopathy have been grudgingly admitted to be apparently effective. As increasing numbers of people voted with their feet and their fees for alternative therapies, some concessions had to be made. The wide adoption of the term 'complementary' to replace 'alternative' signalled an acceptance by both sides that they could work together.

Cooperation and complementarity were the touchstones of the Bristol Cancer Help Centre's philosophy. Its prospectus states: 'It does not profess to offer a cure...[or] an alternative programme to conventional cancer treatment ... the emphasis is on improving quality of life.' In fact, most of its patients were referred by orthodox medical practitioners. No wonder the hostile report and the media attention it attracted seemed like a backlash.

Now another and more swingeing backlash is feared. The principle of free consumer choice, and the plurality of available remedies and therapies, which have enabled alternative medicine to flourish in Britain in recent years despite establishment opposition, will be under threat in the 'harmonized' Europe of 1992. Natural remedies will have to comply with regulations governing standards, testing, labelling, licensing and marketing which were designed for pharmaceutical products, and for practical and economic reasons many will not be able to do so. Practitioners will probably have to belong to recognized professional organizations that endorse their qualifications and guarantee their competence.

The prognosis is not entirely gloomy, for in some European countries alternative medicine is already more integrated with the national health systems than it is in Britain. Homoeopaths, osteopaths, acupuncturists, and chiropractors have acknowledged status and self-regulating professional structures. But remedies and therapies further out on the fringe of alternative medicine have neither the quantifiably demonstrable efficacy nor the political lobbying power of these 'core' therapies. And there are more fundamental causes of concern: the principles of harmonization and pluralism are basically incompatible, and the bureaucratic mind has the same rational biases as the orthodox scientific mind.

An EC Commissioner recently stated: 'The growing interest of the general public in alternative medicine is not shared in competent scientific circles ... There is nothing in the medical literature to indicate that alternative remedies are any more effective than placebos.' Back-street herbalists and bootleggers of comfrey tea may be improbable figures, but such statements, and the backlash that surfaced in the Bristol Help Centre affair, do not bode too well for alternative medicine post-1992.

study confirmed that the aura can be viewed by high frequency electrophotography techniques and is broadly indicative of states of health, but concluded that aura diagnosis cannot identify specific abnormalities.

**autogenics** a system developed in the 1900s by German physician Johannes Schultz, designed to facilitate mental control of biological and physiological functions generally considered to be involuntary. Effective in inducing relaxation, assisting healing processes and relieving psychosomatic disorders, autogenics is regarded as a precursor of biofeedback.

**Ayuraveda** a basically naturopathic system of medicine widely practised in India and based on principles derived from the ancient Hindu scriptures, the Vedas. Hospital treatments and remedial prescriptions tend to be non-specific and to co-ordinate holistic therapies for body, mind, and spirit.

**Bach flower healing** an essentially homoeopathic system of therapy developed in the 1920s by English physician Edward Bach. Based on the healing properties of wild flowers, it seeks to alleviate mental and emotional causes of disease rather than their physical symptoms.

**Bates eyesight training** a method developed by US ophthalmologist William Bates (1860–1931) to enable people to correct problems of vision without wearing glasses. The method is of proven effectiveness in relieving all refractive conditions, correcting squints, lazy eyes, and similar problems, but does not claim to treat eye disease.

**biochemic tissue salts therapy** the correction of imbalances or deficiencies in the body's resources of essential mineral salts. There are 12 tissue salts in the body and the healthy functioning of cells depends on their correct balance, but there is scant evidence that disease is due to their imbalance and can be cured by supplements, as claimed by German physician W H Schuessler in the 1870s, though many people profess to benefit from the 'Schuessler remedies'.

**bioenergetics** an extension of Reichian therapy principles developed in the 1960s by US physician Alexander Lowen, and designed to promote, by breathing, physical exercise, and the elimination of muscular blockages, the free flow of energy in the body and thus restore optimum health and vitality.

**biofeedback** the use of electrophysiological monitoring devices to 'feed back' information about internal processes and thus facilitate conscious control. Developed in the USA in the 1960s, independently by neurophysiologist Barbara Brown and neuropsychiatrist Joseph Kamiya, the technique is particularly effective in alleviating hypertension and preventing associated organic and physiological dysfunctions.

**chiropractic** a technique of manipulation of the joints of the body, particularly the spine, based on the principle that pathology originates in disordered physiology attributable to aberrations in the functioning of the nervous system, which manipulation can correct.

**clinical ecology** a recent development in medical science which specializes in ascertaining environmental factors involved in illnesses, particularly those manifesting non-specific symptoms such as fatigue, depression, allergic reactions and immune system malfunctions, and in prescribing means of avoiding or minimizing these effects.

**colour therapy** the application of light of appropriate wavelength to alleviate ailments or facilitate healing.

**crystal therapy** the application of crystals to diseased or disordered physical structures or processes to effect healing or stabilizing.

**cupping** an ancient 'folk medicine' method of drawing blood to the surface of the body by applying cups or glasses in which a vacuum has been created, found to be effective in alleviating (though not curing) rheumatism, lumbago, arthritis, asthma, and bronchitis.

**dietetics** the prescription of dietary regimens to promote health or healing. Although no one quarrels with the general principle that diet affects health, the preventative or curative effects of specific diets, such as the 'grape cure' or raw vegetable diets sometimes prescribed for cancer patients, are disputed by orthodox medicine.

**electrocrystal diagnosis** a technique recently developed by British biologist Harry Oldfield, based on the finding that stimulated electromagnetic fields of the human body resonate at a particular frequency which varies with individuals, and that actual or incipient disease can be pinpointed by a scanning device responsive to local deviations from the person's norm.

**endogenous endocrinotherapy** the fostering of hormonal balance in the body by regulating the activities of the endocrine glands without recourse to introduced stimulants, suppressants or supplements.

**fasting** total abstinence from food for a limited period is prescribed by some naturopaths to eliminate body toxins or make available for recuperative purposes the energy normally used by the digestive system.

**Gerson therapy** a radical nutritional therapy for degenerative diseases, particularly cancer, developed by German-born US physician Max Gerson (1881–1959).

**hair analysis** a diagnostic technique for ascertaining deficiencies or excesses of mineral resources in the body, using a sophisticated analytic procedure called atomic-emission spectroscopy.

**hand healing** a form of *spiritual healing* in which apparently energy emanating from the healer's hands cures or alleviates a condition suffered by the healee.

**herbalism** the prescription and use of plants and their derivatives for medication.

**holistic medicine** umbrella term for an approach that virtually all alternative therapies profess, which considers the overall health and lifestyle profile of a patient, and treats specific ailments not primarily as conditions to be alleviated but rather as symptoms of more fundamental dis-ease.

**homoeopathy** system of medicine based on the principle that symptoms of disease are part of the body's self-healing processes, and on the practice of administering extremely diluted doses of natural substances found to produce in a healthy person the symptoms manifest in the illness being treated. Developed by German physician Samuel Hahnemann (1755–1843), the system is widely practised today as an alternative to allopathic medicine, and many controlled tests and achieved cures testify to its efficacy.

**hydrotherapy** the use of water, externally or internally, for health or healing.

**hypnotherapy** the use of hypnotic trance and post-hypnotic suggestions to relieve stress-related conditions such as insomnia and hypertension, or to break health-inimical habits or addictions.

**ionization therapy** enhancement of the atmosphere of an environment by instrumentally boosting the negative ion content of the air.

**iridology** a diagnostic technique based on correspondences between specific areas of the iris and bodily functions and organs, discovered over a century ago independently by a Hungarian and a Swedish physician, and later refined and developed in the USA by Dr Bernard Jensen.

**magnet therapy** the use of applied magnetic fields to regulate potentially pathogenic disorders in the electrical charges of body cells and structures.

**megavitamin therapy** the administration of large doses of vitamins to combat conditions considered wholly or in part due to their deficiency.

**music therapy** the use of music as an adjunct to relaxation healing, or in psychotherapy to elicit expressions of suppressed emotions by prompting patients to dance, shout, laugh, cry or whatever, in response.

**naturopathy** the facilitating of the natural self-healing processes of the body. Naturopaths are the GPs of alternative medicine and often refer clients to other specialists, particularly in manipulative therapies, to complement their own work of seeking, through diet, the prescription of natural medicines and supplements, and lifestyle counselling, to restore or augment the vitality of the body and thereby its optimum health.

**osteopathy** a therapy developed over a century ago by US physician Andrew Taylor Still, who maintained that most ailments can be prevented or cured by techniques of spinal manipulation. Osteopaths are generally consulted to treat problems of the musculo-skeletal structure such as back pain, and many doctors refer patients to them for such treatments, but the wider applicability of their skills is not generally recognized.

**psionic medicine** a system of medical diagnosis and therapy developed by British physician George Lawrence in the 1930s and subsequently. Diagnosis is effected by dowsing a small blood sample with the aid of a pendulum to ascertain deficiencies or imbalances affecting the body's vitality, and treatment by the administration of homoeopathic remedies to combat illness and restore the vital balance.

**pulsed high frequency (PHF)** the instrumental application of high frequency radio waves in short bursts to damaged tissue to relieve pain, reduce bruising and swelling, and speed healing.

**radionics** occult healing method said to work on the 'subtle energy' level of the organism, and the alternative therapy that the orthodox love to deride as of exemplary crankiness. Critics regard the radionic 'black box'—invented early in the century by US physician Albert Adams and later modified by his follower Ruth Drown—as a fraudulent quasi-scientific instrument, though practitioners maintain that it is an enabling device to effect psychic healing at a distance and can adduce numerous successes, both diagnostic and curative.

**reflexology** manipulation and massage of the feet to ascertain and treat disease or dysfunction elsewhere in the body.

**Reichian therapy** a general term for a group of body-therapies based on the theory propounded in the 1930s by Austrian/US psychiatrist Wilhelm Reich, that many functional and organic illnesses are attributable to constriction of the flow of vital energies in the body by tensions that become locked into the musculature. Bioenergetics and Rolfing are related approaches.

**relaxation therapy** entrainment in regular and conscious control of physiological processes and their related emotional and mental states, and of muscular tensions in the body, to avert or alleviate ailments attributable to such stresses. Meditation, hypnotherapy, autogenics, and biofeedback are techniques commonly employed.

**Rolfing** a technique of deep muscular manipulation developed in the 1960s and '70s by US physiologist Ira Rolf. Also known as 'structural integration', the technique is designed to correct gravitational imbalance in body postures and movements, and to relieve muscular rigidities and inflexibilities, thus enhancing general health and vitality.

**shiatsu** a Japanese method of massage derived from acupuncture and sometimes referred to as 'acupressure', which treats organic or physiological dysfunctions by applying finger or palm-of-the-hand pressure to parts of the body remote from the affected part.

**sound therapy** a therapy based on the finding that human blood cells respond to sound frequencies by changing colour and shape, and the hypothesis that therefore sick or rogue cells can be healed or harmonized by sound. Currently being developed and researched by French musician and acupuncturist Fabien Maman and US physicist Joel Sternheimer. It is claimed that sound frequencies applied to acupuncture points are as effective as needles.

**spiritual healing** (or *psychic healing*) the transmission of energy from or through a healer, who may practise hand healing or absent healing through prayer or meditation.

**thanatology** the study of the psychological aspects of the experiences of death and dying and its application in counselling and assisting the terminally ill. Pioneered by US psychiatrist Elizabeth Kübler-Ross in the 1970s.

**visualization** the use of guided mental imagery to activate and focus the body's natural self-healing processes. A component of integrated multi-method complementary techniques for the treatment of cancer patients to which some remarkable remissions have been attributed.

**vitalistic medicine** a generic term for a range of therapies that base their practice on the theory that disease is engendered by energy deficiency in the organism as a whole or dynamic dysfunction in the affected part. Such deficiencies or dysfunctions are regarded as antecedent to the biochemical effects in which disease becomes manifest and upon which orthodox medicine focuses. Acupuncture, crystal therapy, homoeopathy, magnet therapy, naturopathy, radionics, and Reichian therapy are all basically vitalistic.

**zone therapy** an alternative name for reflexology.

## National Health Service

*From what you have heard, do you broadly approve or broadly disapprove of the changes that are currently taking place in the way the National Health Service is run?*

| | |
|---|---|
| Approve | 16 |
| Disapprove | 75 |
| Don't know | 9 |

*Do you think they will lead to a better Health Service, or a worse one, or will they make no difference?*

| | |
|---|---|
| Better | 15 |
| Worse | 65 |
| No difference | 11 |
| Don't know | 8 |

*Do you agree or disagree with the statement: 'The National Health Service is safe in the hands of the Conservatives'?*

| | |
|---|---|
| Agree | 19 |
| Disagree | 73 |
| Don't know | 8 |

## Doctors and the NHS

*How many times, if at all, have you seen your GP (local doctor) in the last 12 months?*

| | |
|---|---|
| Not at all | 23 |
| Once | 18 |
| Twice | 16 |
| Three times or more | 42 |
| Don't know/can't remember | 1 |

*When it comes to factors such as getting a drug you want prescribed, obtaining a second opinion, or having an operation in your preferred hospital, how much influence do you think you have?*

| | |
|---|---|
| Quite a lot | 28 |
| Little | 23 |
| Very little | 18 |
| None at all | 14 |
| Don't know | 17 |

*Which of the following approaches comes closest to your doctor?*

| | |
|---|---|
| Prescribes drugs when what you want is someone to listen to and give advice | 17 |
| Offers advice when you would rather have a prescription | 12 |
| Offers the treatment you feel you need | 61 |
| Don't know | 10 |

*How would you describe the service you feel you get from your GP? Is it...*

| | |
|---|---|
| Good | 58 |
| Fairly good | 22 |
| Adequate | 12 |
| Fairly poor | 2 |
| Poor | 1 |
| Don't know | 4 |

*If you needed an operation and waiting lists had become too long, how would you respond?*

| | |
|---|---|
| I am covered by health insurance and would seek private treatment | 15 |
| I am not covered by health insurance and would consider paying for treatment | 13 |
| I am not covered by health insurance and would be willing to travel to a distant NHS hospital for treatment | 24 |
| I would wait my turn | 42 |
| Don't know | 6 |

*Have you been put on a waiting list for an operation in the past 5 years?*

*If yes: How long have you waited?*

| | |
|---|---|
| 3 months or less | 9 |
| 4–6 months | 3 |
| 7–12 months | 2 |
| More than a year | 4 |
| Not been on waiting list | 81 |
| Don't know | 1 |

# INTERNATIONAL ORGANIZATIONS

*(excluding United Nations and Economic Community)*

**Amazon Pact** treaty signed in 1978 by Bolivia, Brazil, Colombia, Ecuador, Guyana, Peru, Suriname, and Venezuela to protect and control the industrial and commercial development of the Amazon River.

**Andean Group** (Spanish *Grupo Andino*) South American organization aimed at economic and social cooperation between member states. It was established under the Treaty of Cartagena 1969, by Bolivia, Chile, Colombia, Ecuador, and Peru; Venezuela joined 1973, but Chile withdrew 1976. The organization is based in Lima, Peru.

**Antarctic Treaty** agreement signed 1959 between 12 nations with an interest in Antarctica (including Britain); 35 countries were party to it by 1990. It came into force in 1961 for a 30-year period. Its provisions (covering the area south of latitude 60°S) neither accepted nor rejected any nation's territorial claims, but barred any new ones; imposed a ban on military operations and large-scale mineral extraction; and allowed for free exchange of scientific data from bases. Since 1980 the treaty has been extended to conserve marine resources within the larger area bordered by the Antarctic Convergence.

**Arab League** organization of Arab states established in Cairo 1945 to promote Arab unity, especially in opposition to Israel. The original members were Egypt, Syria, Iraq, Lebanon, Transjordan (Jordan 1949), Saudi Arabia, and Yemen. In 1979 Egypt was suspended and the league's headquarters transferred to Tunis in protest against the Egypt-Israeli peace accord, but Egypt was readmitted as a full member May 1989, and in March 1990 its headquarters returned to Cairo.

**Asian and Pacific Council** (ASPAC) organization established 1966 to encourage cultural and economic cooperation in Oceania and Asia. Its members include Australia, Japan, South Korea, Malaysia, New Zealand, the Philippines, Taiwan, and Thailand.

**Asia-Pacific Economic Cooperation Conference** (APEC) trade group comprising 12 Pacific Asian countries, formed Nov 1989 to promote multilateral trade and economic cooperation between member states. Its members are the USA, Canada, Japan, Australia, New Zealand, South Korea, Brunei, Indonesia, Malaysia, the Phillipines, Singapore, and Thailand.

**Association of South East Asian Nations** (ASEAN) regional alliance formed in Bangkok 1967; it took over the nonmilitary role of the Southeast Asia Treaty Organization 1975. Its members are Indonesia, Malaysia, the Philippines, Singapore, Thailand, and (from 1984) Brunei; its headquarters are in Jakarta, Indonesia.

**Benelux** customs union of *Be*lgium, the *Ne*therlands, and *Lux*embourg (agreed 1944, fully effective 1960); precursor of the European Community.

**Caribbean Community and Common Market** (CARICOM) organization for economic and foreign policy coordination in the Caribbean region, established by the Treaty of Chaguaramas 1973 to replace the former Caribbean Free Trade Association. Its headquarters are in Georgetown, Guyana. The leading member is Trinidad and Tobago; other members are Antigua, Barbados, Belize, Dominica, Grenada, Guyana, Jamaica, Montserrat, St Christopher–Nevis, Anguilla, St Lucia, and St Vincent. From 1979, a left-wing Grenadan coup led to a progressive regional subgroup including St Lucia and Dominica.

**CERN** nuclear research organization founded 1954 as a cooperative enterprise among European governments. It has laboratories at Meyrin, near Geneva, Switzerland. It was originally known as the *Conseil Européen pour la Recherche Nucléaire* but subsequently renamed *Organisation Européene pour la Recherche Nucléaire*, although still familiarly known as CERN. It houses the world's largest particle accelerator (completed 1989), the Large Electron–Positron Collider (LEP) with which notable advances have been made in particle physics. In 1965 the original laboratory was doubled in size by extension across the border from Switzerland into France.

**Cooperative Council for the Arab States of the Gulf** (CCASG) Arab organization for promoting peace in the Persian Gulf area, established 1981. Its declared purpose is 'to bring about integration, coordination, and cooperation in economic, social, defence, and political affairs among Arab Gulf states. Its members include Bahrain, Kuwait, Oman, Qatar, Saudi Arabia and the United Arab Emirates; its headquarters are in Riyadh, Saudi Arabia.

**Council of Europe** body constituted 1949 at Strasbourg, France (still its headquarters) to secure 'a greater measure of unity between the European countries'. The widest association of European states, it has a *Committee* of foreign ministers, a *Parliamentary Assembly* (with members from national parliaments), and a *European Commission* investigating violations of human rights.

The first session of the *Consultative Assembly* opened Aug 1949, the members then being the UK, France, Italy, Belgium, the Netherlands, Sweden, Denmark, Norway, the Republic of Ireland, Luxembourg, Greece, and Turkey; Iceland, West Germany, Austria,

Cyprus, Switzerland, Malta, Portugal, Spain, and Liechtenstein joined subsequently.

**Council of the Entente** (CE, *Conseil de l'Entente*) organization of West African states for strengthening economic links and promoting industrial development. It was set up in 1959 by Benin, Burkina Faso, Ivory Coast, and Niger; Togo joined 1966 when a Mutual Aid and Loan Guarantee Fund was established. The headquarters of the CE are in Abidja'n, Ivory Coast.

**CSCE or *Helsinki Conference*** international conference 1975 at which 35 countries, including the USSR and the USA, attempted to reach agreement on cooperation in security, economics, science, technology, and human rights.

Some regarded the conference as marking the end of the Cold War; others felt it legitimized the division of Europe that had been a fact since the end of World War II. Human-rights groups contend that there have been many violations of the provisions of the accords. Its full title is the Helsinki Conference on Security and Cooperation in Europe (CSCE).

A second CSCE conference in Paris Nov 1990 was hailed as marking the formal end of the Cold War.

**Danube Commission** organization that ensures the freedom of navigation on the river Danube, from Ulm in Germany to the Black Sea, to people, shipping, and merchandise of all states, in conformity with the Danube Convention 1948. The commission comprises representatives of all the states through which the Danube flows: Germany, Austria, Czechoslovakia, Hungary, Bulgaria, and Romania. Its headquarters are in Budapest, Hungary.

**Economic Community of West African States** (ECOWAS, *Communauté Économique des États de l'Afrique de l'Ouest*) organization for the promotion of economic cooperation and development, established in 1975 by the Treaty of Lagos. Its members include Benin, Burkina Faso, Cape Verde, Gambia, Ghana, Guinea, Guinea-Bissau, Ivory Coast, Liberia, Mali, Mauritania, Niger, Nigeria, Senegal, Sierra Leone, and Togo. Its headquarters are in Lagos, Nigeria.

**European Free Trade Association** (EFTA) organization established 1960 and as of 1988 consisting of Austria, Finland, Iceland, Norway, Sweden, and Switzerland. There are no import duties between members. Of the original members, Britain and Denmark left (1972) to join the European Community, as subsequently did Portugal (1985). Its headquarters are in Geneva, Switzerland.

**European Space Agency** (ESA) an organization of European countries (Austria, Belgium, Denmark, France, Germany, Ireland, Italy, the Netherlands, Norway, Spain, Sweden, Switzerland, and the UK) that engages in space research and technology. It was founded 1975, with headquarters in Paris.

**Inter-American Development Bank** (IADB) bank founded in 1959, at the instigation of the Organization of American States, to finance economic and social development, particularly in the less wealthy regions of the Americas. Its membership includes Austria, Belgium, Canada, Denmark, Finland, France, Germany, Israel, Italy, Japan, the Netherlands, Spain, Sweden, Switzerland, and the UK, as well as the states of Central and Southern America, the Caribbean and the USA. Its headquarters are in Washington, DC.

**Latin American Economic System** (LAES) (*Sistema Economico Latino-Americana* SELA) organization founded by treaty 1975 as the successor to the Latin American Economic Co-ordination Commission, to create and promote multinational enterprises in the region, to provide markets, and to stimulate technological and scientific co-operation. It has 26 members, covering Central and South America and parts of the Caribbean. Its headquarters are in Caracas, Venezuela.

**Latin American Integration Association** (*Asociacion Latino-Americana de Integration* ALADI) organization aiming to create a common market in Latin America; to promote trade it applies tariff reductions preferentially on the basis of the different stages of economic development that individual member countries have reached. Formed 1980 to replace the Latin American Free Trade Association, it has 11 member countries, all in South America except for Mexico, with headquarters in Montevideo, Uruguay.

**Lomé Convention** convention 1975 that established economic cooperation between the European Community and African, Caribbean, and Pacific countries. It was renewed 1979 and 1985.

**North Atlantic Treaty Organization** (NATO) association set up 1949 to provide for the collective defence of the major W European and North American states against the perceived threat from the USSR. Its chief body is the Council of Foreign Ministers (who have representatives in permanent session), and there is an international secretariat in Brussels, Belgium, and also the Military Committee consisting of the Chiefs of Staff. The military headquarters SHAPE (Supreme Headquarters Allied Powers, Europe) is in Chièvres, near Mons, Belgium.

In 1990, after a meeting in London, NATO declared that nuclear weapons were 'weapons of last resort' rather than 'flexible response', and offered to withdraw all nuclear artillery shells from Europe if the USSR did the same. With the ending of the Cold War, the roles and military resourcing of NATO and its East European counterpart the Warsaw Pact are undergoing major revision.

**Organisation Commune Africaine et Mauricienne** (OCAM) organization founded 1965 to strengthen the solidarity and close ties between member states, raise living standards, and coordinate economic policies. The membership includes Benin, Burkina Faso, Central African Republic, Ivory Coast, Niger, Rwanda, Senegal, and Togo. Through the organization, members share an airline, a merchant fleet, and a common postal and communications system. The headquarters of OCAM are in Bangui in the Central African Republic.

**Organization for Economic Cooperation and Development** (OECD) Paris-based international organization of 24 industrialized countries, which coordinates member states' economic policy strategies. The OECD's subsidiary bodies include the International Energy Agency 1974, set up in the face of a world oil crisis.

**Organization of African Unity** (OAU) association established 1963 to eradicate colonialism and improve economic, cultural, and political cooperation in Africa; its headquarters are in Addis Ababa, Ethiopia. The secretary-general is Salim Ahmed Salim (deputy prime minister of Tanzania). The French-speaking *Joint African and Mauritian Organization/Organisation Commune Africaine et Mauritienne* (OCAM) works within the framework of the OAU for African solidarity.

**Organization of American States** (OAS) association founded 1948 by a charter signed by representatives of 30 North, Central, and South American states. Canada held observer status from 1972 and became a full member 1990. It aims to maintain peace and solidarity within the hemisphere, and is also concerned with the social and economic development of Latin America.

It is based on the International Union of American Republics 1890–1910 and Pan-American Union 1910–48, set up to encourage friendly relations between countries of North and South America. Its headquarters are in Washington DC.

**Organization of Arab Petroleum Exporting Countries** (OAPEC) body established 1968 to safeguard the interests of its members and encourage cooperation in economic activity within the petroleum industry. Its members are Algeria, Bahrain, Egypt, Iraq, Kuwait, Libya, Qatar, Saudi Arabia, Syria, and the United Arab Emirates; headquarters in Kuwait.

**Organization of Central American States** (OCAS) (*Organización de Estados Centro Americanos: ODECA*) international association promoting common economic, political, educational, and military aims in Central America. The first organization, established 1951, was superseded in 1962. Its members are Costa Rica, El Salvador, Guatemala, Honduras, and Nicaragua, provision being made for Panama to join at a later date. The permanent headquarters are in Guatemala City.

**Organization of the Islamic Conference** (OIC) association for the promotion of solidarity between Muslim countries, established 1971, with 45 member states in the Middle East, Africa, and Asia, plus the Palestine Liberation Organization. The OIC has its headquarters in Jeddah, Saudi Arabia.

**Organization of the Petroleum Exporting Countries** (OPEC) body established 1960 to coordinate price and supply policies of oil-producing states, and also to improve the position of Third World states by forcing Western states to open their markets to the resultant products. Its concerted action in raising prices in the 1970s triggered worldwide recession but also lessened demand so that its influence was reduced by the mid-1980s. OPEC members are: Algeria, Ecuador, Gabon, Indonesia, Iran, Iraq, Kuwait, Libya, Nigeria, Qatar, Saudi Arabia, United Arab Emirates, and Venezuela. Its headquarters are in Vienna, Austria.

**Preferential Trade Area for East and Southern Africa** (PTA) organization established 1981 with the object of increasing economic and commercial cooperation between member states, harmonizing tariffs, and reducing trade barriers, with the eventual aim of creating a common market. The current members include Burundi, Comoros, Djibouti, Ethiopia, Kenya, Lesotho, Malawi, Mauritius, Rwanda, Somalia, Swaziland, Tanzania, Uganda, Zambia, and Zimbabwe. The headquarters of the PTA are in Lusaka, Zambia.

**Rarotonga Treaty** agreement that formally declares the South Pacific a nuclear-free zone. The treaty was signed 1987 by Australia, Fiji, Indonesia, New Zealand, and the USSR.

**Southeast Asia Treaty Organization** (SEATO) former collective defence system (analogous to NATO in Europe) established 1954 by Australia, France, New Zealand, Pakistan, the Philippines, Thailand, the UK, and the USA, with Vietnam, Cambodia, and Laos as protocol states. After the Vietnam War, SEATO was phased out by 1977.

**Southern African Development Coordination Conference** (SADCC) organization of countries in the region working together to reduce their economic dependence on South Africa. It was established 1979 and focuses on transport and communications, energy, mining, and industrial production. The member states are Angola, Botswana, Lesotho, Malawi, Mozambique, Swaziland, Tanzania, Zambia, and Zimbabwe; headquarters in Gaborone, Botswana.

**South Pacific Bureau for Economic Cooperation** (SPEC) organization founded 1973 for the purpose of stimulating economic cooperation and the development of trade in the region. The headquarters of SPEC are in Suva, Fiji.

**South Pacific Commission** (SPC) organization founded 1947 to promote economic and social cooperation in the region. Its members include most of the sovereign and dependent states in the South Pacific, plus France, the UK, and the USA; headquarters in Nouméa, New Caledonia.

**South Pacific Forum** (SPF) association of states in the region to discuss common interests and develop common policies, created 1971 as an offshoot of the South Pacific Commission. Member countries include Australia, Cook Islands, Fiji, Kiribati, Nauru, New Zealand, Niue, Papua New Guinea, Solomon Islands, Tonga, Tuvalu, Vanuatu, and Western Samoa. In 1985 the forum adopted a treaty for creating a nuclear-free zone in the Pacific.

**Warsaw Pact** or ***Eastern European Mutual Assistance Pact*** military alliance 1955–91 between the USSR and East European communist states, originally established as a response to the admission of West Germany into NATO. Its military structure was dismantled in 1991 but a political structure remained, with member states divided over what to do with it.

Czechoslovakia, Hungary, and Poland announced in Jan 1991, and Bulgaria in Feb, that they would withdraw all cooperation from the Warsaw Treaty Organization from 1 July 1991. In response, the USSR announced that the military structure of the pact would be wound up by 31 March 1991, and a meeting of member countries convened for this purpose in Feb.

**Western European Union** (WEU) organization established 1955 as a consultative forum for military issues among the W European governments: Belgium, France, Holland, Italy, Luxembourg, the UK, West Germany, and (from 1988) Spain and Portugal. Its secretariat is in London; the assembly normally meets in the Hague, and sometimes in Paris.

Policy is agreed during meetings of the foreign ministers of the member nations, with administrative work carried out by a permanent secretariat and specialist committees. The WEU is charged under its charter with ensuring close cooperation with NATO. During its early years the WEU supervised the gradual rearmament of West Germany and the transfer of the Saarland back to West German rule 1957. In the early 1990s attempts were made to transform the WEU into a body to coordinate W European security policy either within NATO or within the European Community if the latter were to adopt a common security policy.

**World Council of Churches** (WCC) international organization aiming to bring together diverse movements within the Christian church. Established 1945, it had by 1988 a membership of more than 100 countries and more than 300 churches. The supreme governing body, the assembly, meets every seven or eight years to frame policy. A 150-member central committee meets once a year and a 22-member executive committee

twice a year. Its headquarters are in Geneva, Switzerland.

# THE EUROPEAN COMMUNITY (EC)

## Member states

Founder members, 1957: Belgium, France, West Germany, Italy, Luxembourg, Netherlands. 1971: Denmark, Ireland, United Kingdom. 1981: Greece. 1985: Portugal and Spain

## Background

Following World War II, those countries that had experienced the war first hand—France, Belgium, Luxembourg, Netherlands, West Germany, and Italy—took steps to set up institutions which would make another war in Europe virtually impossible. The first such institution to be established was the European Steel and Coal Community (ESC) in 1952, based on the premise that if the leading European nations shared coal and steel-making facilities (seen as the basic raw materials of war) future conflicts would be avoided. 1957 saw the momentous signing in Rome of the treaties which established the European Economic Community (EEC) and the European Atomic Energy Community (Euratom).

Other Western European countries remained aloof, resisting the prospect of eventual political integration, and, led by the UK, formed a purely economic association, the European Free Trade Association (EFTA). The EEC grew in strength and influence, while EFTA declined, leading the UK eventually to apply for membership. After two attempts at entry in 1963 and 1967, blocked largely by France, the UK became a full member in 1972, along with Denmark, Ireland, and Norway. Norway withdrew soon afterwards, but membership of the Community grew to 12, with other nations—including Austria, Cyprus, Sweden, and Turkey—applying to join. In 1990 the former East Germany was admitted as part of the unified Germany.

## Aims

The establishment of a closer union among European peoples; the improvement of their working and living conditions; the progressive abolition of trading restrictions between them; and the encouragement of free movement of capital and labour within the community.

EC institutions and policies collectively constitute an economic, social, and potentially political system which is still developing and which could become, if all member states eventually agree, a single European state. Steps towards monetary union have already been taken in the form of the EMS and the European currency unit (ECU), but the community remains divided over the question of political unity, the UK in particular resisting any move which may weaken national sovereignty and decision-making powers.

In 1990 there were 320 million people in the EC countries. Almost 60% of the EC's budget is spent on supporting farmers (about 4 million people); of this, £4 billion a year goes to dairy farmers, because the dairy quotas, which were introduced 1984, are 14% greater than EC consumption. The EC sheep policy cost over £1.7 billion in 1990, and 30 million tonnes of excess grain is exported every year at a subsidized price. Altogether it cost member countries' taxpayers almost £9 billion in 1989–90 to maintain the international competitiveness of the EC's overpriced produce under the Common Agricultural Policy.

In 1992 members will become one market with the free movement of goods and capital.

## Constituent institutions and policies

**Common Agricultural Policy** (CAP)
*established* 1962
*purpose* to ensure reasonable standards of living for farmers in member states by controlling outputs, giving financial grants, and supporting prices to even out fluctuations.
*base* Brussels

**European Atomic Energy Commission** (EURATOM)
*established* 1957
*purpose* the cooperation of member states in nuclear research and the development of large-scale nonmilitary nuclear energy.
*base* Brussels

**European Coal and Steel Community** (ECS)
*established* 1952
*purpose* the creation of a single European market for coal, iron ore, and steel by the abolition of customs duties and quantitative restrictions.
*base* Brussels

**European Court of Justice established** 1957
*purpose* to ensure the treaties that established the Community are observed and to adjudicate on disputes between members on the interpretation and application of the laws of the Community
*base* Luxembourg.

**European Economic Community** (EEC), popularly called the Common Market
*established* 1957
*purpose* the creation of a single European market for the products of member states by the abolition of tariffs and other restrictions on trade.
*base* Brussels

**European Investment Bank** (EIB)
*established* 1958
*purpose* to finance capital investment that will assist the steady development of the Community.
*base*: Brussels

**European Monetary System** (EMS)

*established* 1979
*purpose* to bring financial cooperation and monetary stability to the Community. Central to the EMS is the Exchange Rate Mechanism (ERM), which is a voluntary arrangement whereby members agree to their currencies being fixed within certain limits. The value of each currency is related to the European Currency Unit (ECU), which, it is anticipated, will eventually become the single currency for all member states. If the currency of any one member state moves outside the agreed limits, its government must buy or sell to avert the trend.

## Central organs and methods of working of the Community

**European Commission**
*membership* 16: two each from France, Germany, Italy and the UK, and one each from Belgium, Denmark, Greece, Ireland, Luxembourg, the Netherlands, Portugal, and Spain. The members are nominated by each state for a four-year, renewable term of office. One member is chosen as president for a two-year, renewable term. The post of president is a mixture of head of government and head of the European civil service
*operational methods* the commissioners are drawn proportionately from member states, and each takes an oath on appointment not to promote national interests. They head a comparatively large bureaucracy, with 20 directorates-general, each responsible for a particular department
*base* Brussels

**Council of Ministers**
*membership* one minister from each of the 12 member countries
*operational methods* it is the supreme decision-taking body of the Community. The representatives vary according to the subject matter under discussion. If it is economic policy it will be the finance ministers, if it is agricultural policy, the agriculture ministers. It is the foreign ministers, however, who tend to be the most active. The presidency of the Council changes hands at six-monthly intervals, each member state taking its turn
*base* Brussels

**Committee of Permanent Representatives** (COREPER)
*membership* a subsidiary body of officials, often called 'ambassadors', who act on behalf of the Council. The members of COREPER are senior civil servants who have been temporarily released by member states to work for the Community
*operational methods* COREPER receives proposals from the Council of Ministers for consideration in detail before the Council decides on action
*base* Brussels

**Economic and Social Committee**
*membership* representatives from member countries covering a wide range of inter-

## JACQUES DELORS AND THE NEW EUROPE: AN IDEA WHOSE TIME HAS COME?

Six years after the end of World War II the leaders of France, Germany, Italy, Belgium, Holland and Luxembourg met in Paris to sign a treaty to establish the European Coal and Steel Community (ECSC). This was to be the first step in creating a union of nations so mutually interdependent that the possibility of their embarking on another disastrous European war would be impossible. In the following year, 1957, the same countries signed the Treaty of Rome, establishing the European Economic Community (EEC). The signatories of the 1957 treaty in Rome had a vision of a truly united Europe, in which frontiers would be abolished, a common currency established, common political and judicial institutions founded, and common economic, social, defence, and foreign policies adopted.

Although much of that is still a vision, rather than a reality, many steps have already been taken down the road towards it. The original six members of the Community are now 12 and several more countries, including Sweden, Austria and Turkey, as well as smaller nations, are in the ante-room, waiting to join. The European Monetary System (EMS) came into force in 1979 and its full implementation, including

*Jacques Delors, president of the European Commission*

that of the Exchange Rate Mechanism (ERM), whereby member countries accept the discipline of holding the value of their national currencies within agreed, controlled bands, will soon take place, the UK committing itself to it in 1990. The Single European Act was signed in 1986 and in 1992 all barriers will be down and Europe will truly become a single market. But, as the president of the Commission, Jacques Delors, has remarked 'You cannot fall in love with a single market.' Delors, the 66-year-old son of a Paris banker, has a much wider and stronger vision of what Europe could become. Speaking to the European Parliament in Jan 1989, he said 'History is knocking at the door. Are we going to pretend that we cannot hear ? It will not be enough to create a large, frontier-free market, nor ... a vast economic and social area. It is for us, in advance of 1993, to put some flesh on the Community's bones and give it more soul.'

Although sometimes branded by his critics as a socialist, he is by no means an extremist or a believer in outright left-wing policies. After advising the French prime minister on social affairs, he joined the Socialist Party in 1973, at the relatively mature age of 48. He served as finance minister under President Mitterrand 1981–84, overseeing an austerity programme which produced a strong recovery in the French economy, and has shown himself by no means averse to marrying socialist policies with market forces. After failing to win the premiership in Mitterrand's government, he entered the field of international politics by becoming Commission president in 1984.

In this role he has led his team of ministers with great vigour, sometimes resulting in disagreements with national leaders, such as Margaret Thatcher, who preferred a slower pace of 'Europeanization'. Delors has, above everything, brought to the forefront this vision of Europe, recreating some of the enthusiasm and idealism of the Community's founding fathers.

His ultimate vision is, arguably, of a United States of Europe, and he is in good company, with former statesmen, such as Winston Churchill, also taking this view. But Jaques Delors is also a realist and knows that such a union will not come in his lifetime, or possibly those of his immediate successors. The failure of the Community members to agree on a common policy when faced with the Gulf Crisis in 1990 reminded everyone of the long road yet to be travelled before genuine unity is achieved.

It is certain that, inexorably, over the coming years national sovereignties of all EC members will be eroded. The way ahead towards the Delors vision is to avoid lost sovereignty passing to the largely unaccountable bureaucracy in Brussels, and to strengthen democratic institutions, such as the European Parliament, to ensure better accountability. A truly united Europe would be a dominant yet stabilizing force in a still uncertain world.

## UN MEMBERSHIP

| country | year of admission | contribution to UN budget (%) | country | year of admission | contribution to UN budget (%) |
|---|---|---|---|---|---|
| Afghanistan | 1946 | 0.01 | Haiti + | 1945 | 0.01 |
| Albania | 1955 | 0.01 | Honduras + | 1945 | 0.01 |
| Algeria | 1962 | 0.15 | Hungary | 1955 | 0.21 |
| Angola | 1976 | 0.01 | Iceland | 1946 | 0.03 |
| Antigua & Barbuda | 1981 | 0.01 | India + | 1945 | 0.37 |
| Argentina + | 1945 | 0.66 | Indonesia | 1950 | 0.15 |
| Australia + | 1945 | 1.57 | Iran + | 1945 | 0.67 |
| Austria | 1955 | 0.74 | Iraq + | 1945 | 0.12 |
| Bahamas | 1973 | 0.02 | Ireland | 1955 | 0.18 |
| Bahrain | 1971 | 0.02 | Israel | 1949 | 0.21 |
| Bangladesh | 1974 | 0.01 | Italy | 1955 | 3.99 |
| Barbados | 1966 | 0.01 | Jamaica | 1962 | 0.01 |
| Belgium + | 1945 | 1.17 | Japan | 1956 | 11.38 |
| Belize | 1981 | 0.01 | Jordan | 1955 | 0.01 |
| Benin | 1960 | 0.01 | Kenya | 1963 | 0.01 |
| Bhutan | 1971 | 0.01 | Kuwait | 1963 | 0.29 |
| Bolivia + | 1945 | 0.01 | Laos | 1955 | 0.01 |
| Botswana | 1966 | 0.01 | Lebanon + | 1945 | 0.01 |
| Brazil + | 1945 | 1.45 | Lesotho | 1966 | 0.01 |
| Brunei | 1984 | 0.04 | Liberia + | 1945 | 0.01 |
| Bulgaria | 1955 | 0.15 | Libya | 1955 | 0.28 |
| Burkina Faso | 1960 | 0.01 | Luxembourg + | 1945 | 0.06 |
| Burundi | 1962 | 0.01 | Madagascar | 1960 | 0.01 |
| Byelorussia + * | 1945 | 0.33 | Malawi | 1964 | 0.01 |
| Cambodia | 1955 | 0.01 | Malaysia | 1957 | 0.11 |
| Cameroon | 1960 | 0.01 | Maldives | 1965 | 0.01 |
| Canada+ | 1945 | 3.09 | Mali | 1960 | 0.01 |
| Cape Verde | 1975 | 0.01 | Malta | 1964 | 0.01 |
| Central African Republic | 1960 | 0.01 | Mauritania | 1961 | 0.01 |
| Chad | 1960 | 0.01 | Mauritius | 1968 | 0.01 |
| Chile + | 1945 | 0.08 | Mexico + | 1945 | 0.94 |
| China + | 1945 | 0.79 | Mongolia | 1961 | 0.01 |
| Colombia + | 1945 | 0.14 | Morocco | 1956 | 0.04 |
| Comoros | 1975 | 0.01 | Mozambique | 1975 | 0.01 |
| Congo | 1960 | 0.01 | Myanmar (Burma) | 1948 | 0.01 |
| Costa Rica + | 1945 | 0.02 | Namibia | 1990 | 0.01 |
| Cote d'Ivoire | 1960 | 0.02 | Nepal | 1955 | 0.01 |
| Cuba + | 1945 | 0.09 | Netherlands + | 1945 | 1.65 |
| Cyprus | 1960 | 0.02 | New Zealand + | 1945 | 0.24 |
| Czechoslovakia + | 1945 | 0.66 | Nicaragua + | 1945 | 0.01 |
| Denmark + | 1945 | 0.69 | Niger | 1960 | 0.01 |
| Djibouti | 1977 | 0.01 | Nigeria | 1960 | 0.20 |
| Dominica | 1978 | 0.01 | Norway + | 1945 | 0.55 |
| Dominican Republic + | 1945 | 0.03 | Oman | 1971 | 0.02 |
| Ecuador + | 1945 | 0.03 | Pakistan | 1947 | 0.06 |
| Egypt + | 1945 | 0.07 | Panama + | 1945 | 0.02 |
| El Salvador + | 1945 | 0.01 | Papua New Guinea | 1975 | 0.01 |
| Equatorial Guinea | 1968 | 0.01 | Paraguay + | 1945 | 0.03 |
| Ethiopia + | 1945 | 0.01 | Peru + | 1945 | 0.06 |
| Fiji | 1970 | 0.01 | Philippines + | 1945 | 0.09 |
| Finland | 1955 | 0.51 | Poland + | 1945 | 0.56 |
| France + | 1945 | 6.25 | Portugal | 1955 | 0.18 |
| Gabon | 1960 | 0.03 | Qatar | 1971 | 0.05 |
| Gambia | 1965 | 0.01 | Romania | 1955 | 0.19 |
| Germany ** | 1973/1990 | 9.30 | Rwanda | 1962 | 0.01 |
| Ghana | 1957 | 0.01 | St Christopher & Nevis | 1983 | 0.01 |
| Greece + | 1945 | 0.40 | St Lucia | 1979 | 0.01 |
| Grenada | 1974 | 0.01 | St Vincent & Grenadines | 1980 | 0.01 |
| Guatemala + | 1945 | 0.02 | São Tomé & Príncipe | 1975 | 0.01 |
| Guinea | 1958 | 0.01 | Saudi Arabia + | 1945 | 1.02 |
| Guinea-Bissau | 1974 | 0.01 | Senegal | 1960 | 0.01 |
| Guyana | 1966 | 0.01 | Seychelles | 1976 | 0.01 |

## UN MEMBERSHIP (cont.)

| country | year of admission | contribution to UN budget% | country | year of admission | contribution to UN budget% |
|---|---|---|---|---|---|
| Sierra Leone | 1961 | 0.01 | Turkey + | 1945 | 0.32 |
| Singapore | 1965 | 0.11 | Uganda | 1962 | 0.01 |
| Solomon Isles | 1978 | 0.01 | Ukraine + * | 1945 | 1.25 |
| Somalia | 1960 | 0.01 | USSR + | 1945 | 9.99 |
| South Africa + | 1945 | 0.45 | United Arab Emirates | 1971 | 0.19 |
| Spain | 1955 | 1.95 | United Kingdom + | 1945 | 4.86 |
| Sri Lanka | 1955 | 0.01 | United States of America + | 1945 | 25.00 |
| Sudan | 1956 | 0.01 | Uruguay + | 1945 | 0.04 |
| Suriname | 1975 | 0.01 | Vanuatu | 1981 | 0.01 |
| Swaziland | 1968 | 0.01 | Venezuela + | 1945 | 0.57 |
| Sweden | 1946 | 1.21 | Vietnam | 1977 | 0.01 |
| Syria + | 1945 | 0.04 | Western Samoa | 1976 | 0.01 |
| Tanzania | 1961 | 0.01 | Yemen | 1947 | 0.02 |
| Thailand | 1946 | 0.10 | Yugoslavia + | 1945 | 0.46 |
| Togo | 1960 | 0.01 | Zaire | 1960 | 0.01 |
| Trinidad & Tobago | 1962 | 0.05 | Zambia | 1964 | 0.01 |
| Tunisia | 1956 | 0.03 | Zimbabwe | 1980 | 0.02 |

+Founder members.
*Byelorussia and the Ukraine are integral parts of the USSR and not independent countries, but they have separate UN membership.
**Represented by two countries until unification in 1990.
   The sovereign countries that are not UN members are Andorra, Kiribati, North Korea, South Korea, Liechtenstein, Monaco, Nauru, San Marino, Switzerland, Taiwan, Tonga, Tuvalu, and Vatican City.

ests, including employers, trade unionists, professional people, and farmers
**operational methods** a consultative body advising the Council of Ministers and the Commission
**base** Brussels
**European Parliament**
**membership** determined by the populations of member states. The total number of seats is 518, of which France, Germany, Italy, and the UK have 81 each, Spain has 60, the Netherlands 25, Belgium, Greece, and Portugal 24 each, Denmark 16, Ireland 15, and Luxembourg 6. Members are elected for five-year terms in large Euro-constituencies. Voting is by a system of proportional representation in all countries except the UK.
**role and powers** mainly consultative, but it does have power to reject the Community budget and to dismiss the Commission if it has good grounds for doing so. It debates Community present and future policies and its powers will undoubtedly grow as the political nature of the Community becomes clearer
**base** Luxembourg and Strasbourg.

# UNITED NATIONS (UN)

The UN is an association of states for international peace, security, and cooperation, with its headquarters in New York. The UN was established 1945 as a successor to the League of Nations, and has played a role in many areas, such as refugee aid and resettlement, development assistance, disaster relief,

and cultural cooperation.
   Its total budget for 1991/92 was $2.5 billion. Javier Pérez de Cuéllar became secretary-general 1981.
   Members contribute financially according to their resources, an apportionment being made by the General Assembly, with the addition of voluntary contributions from some governments to the funds of the UN. These finance the programme of assistance carried out by the UN intergovernmental agencies, the **United Nations Children's Fund** (UNICEF), the UN refugee organizations, and the **United Nations Special Fund** for developing countries. There are six official working languages: English, French, Russian, Spanish, Chinese, and Arabic.

## Background

The UN charter was drawn up at the San Francisco Conference 1945, based on proposals drafted at the Dumbarton Oaks conference held in Washington DC in 1944 between the World War II allies—the USSR, the UK, and the USA. The original intention was that the UN's Security Council would preserve this alliance (with France and China also permanent members) in order to maintain the peace. This never happened because of the outbreak of the Cold War.
   The influence in the UN, originally with the Allied states of World War II, is now more widely spread. Although part of the value of the UN lies in the recognition of member states as sovereign and equal, the rapid increase in membership of minor—in some cases minute—states was causing concern by 1980 (154 members) as lessening the weight of voting decisions. Taiwan, formerly

a permanent member of the Security Council, was expelled 1971 on the admission of China. The USA regularly (often alone or nearly so) votes against General Assembly resolutions on aggression, international law, human-rights abuses, and disarmament, and has exercised its veto on the Security Council more times than any other member (the UK is second, France a distant third).

The UN suffers from a lack of adequate and independent funds and forces (the latter having been employed with varying success, for example in Korea, Cyprus, and Sinai), and, until recently, from the political polarization resulting from the Cold War, which divided members into adherents of the East or West and the uncommitted. However, since becoming UN secretary-general in 1982, Javier Pérez de Cuellar has been responsible for several successful peace initiatives, including the ending of the Iran–Iraq war and the withdrawal of South African and Cuban troops from Angola, paving the way for the independence of Namibia. He has also initiated talks between Greek and Turkish leaders in Cyprus.

The principal UN institutions (all based in New York except the International Court of Justice in The Hague) are:

**General Assembly** the UN parliament, of which all nations are members, each having one vote. Representatives from each of 159 member states meet annually for a session generally lasting from late Sept to the end of the year; it can be summoned at any time for an emergency session. Decisions are made by simple majority voting, but on certain important issues, such as the condemnation of an act by one of its members, a two-thirds majority is needed;

**Security Council** five permanent members (China, France, UK, USA, USSR, with the power of veto, so their support is requisite for all decisions), plus ten others, elected for two-year terms by a two-thirds vote of the General Assembly; retiring members are not eligible for re-election. Any UN member may be invited to participate in the Security Council's discussions (though not to vote) if they bear on its interests. The council may undertake investigations into disputes and make recommendations to the parties concerned and may call on all members to take economic or military measures to enforce its decisions; it has at its disposal a Military Staff Committee, composed of the chiefs of staff of the permanent member countries. The presidency of the Security Council is held for a month at a time by a representative of a member state, in English-language alphabetical order;

**Economic and Social Council** 54 members elected for three years, one-third retiring in rotation; presidency rotating on same system as Security Council. It initiates studies of international economic, social, cultural, educational, health, and related matters, and may make recommendations to the General Assembly. It operates largely through specialized commissions of international experts on economics, transport and communications, human rights, status of women, and so on, as well as regional commissions and hundreds of nongovernmental agencies that have been granted consultative status. It coordinates the activities of the *Food and Agriculture Organization* (FAO) (see below);

**Trusteeship Council** responsible for overseeing the administration of the UN trust territories. Its members are China, France, the USSR, the UK, and the USA. It holds one regular session a year and can meet in special sessions if required;

**International Court of Justice** 15 independent judges, elected by the Security Council and the General Assembly on the basis of their competence in international law and irrespective of their nationalities, except that no two judges can be nationals of the same state. They serve for nine years and may be immediately re-elected. The president and vice president are elected by the court for three-year terms. Decisions are by majority vote of the judges present, and the president has a casting vote. Only states, not individuals, can be parties to cases before the court. There is no appeal;

**Secretariat** the chief administrator of the UN is the secretary-general, who has under- and assistant secretaries-general and a large international staff. The secretary-general is appointed by the General Assembly for a renewable five-year term.

## UN SPECIALIZED AGENCIES

*(More information on financial agencies below can be found in the International Economics section.)*

**Food and Agriculture Organization** (FAO)
*established* 1945
*responsibilities* to raise levels of nutrition and standards of living, to improve the production and distribution of food and agricultural products particularly for the less developed parts of the world, and to sponsor relief in emergency situations
*headquarters* Rome

**General Agreement on Tariffs and Trade** (GATT) *established* 1948
*responsibilities* a multilateral treaty which lays down a common code of conduct in international trade, providing a forum for discussion of trade problems, with the object of reducing trade barriers
*headquarters* Geneva

**International Atomic Energy Agency** (IAEA) *established* 1957
*responsibilities* to accelerate and enlarge the contribution of atomic energy to peace, health and prosperity throughout the world and to prevent its diversion from peaceful purposes to military ends
*headquarters* Vienna

**International Bank for Reconstruction and Development (IRBD)—(World Bank)**
*established* 1945
*responsibilities* to provide funds and technical assistance to help the economies of the poorer nations of the world
*headquarters* Washington DC

**International Civil Aviation Organization (ICAO)**
*established* 1947
*responsibilities* to establish technical standards for safety and efficiency in air navigation, to develop regioinal plans for ground facilities and services for civil aviation, and generally provide advice to airline operators
*headquarters* Montréal

**International Development Association (IDA)**
*established* 1960
*responsibilities* as an agency of the World Bank, to provide financial and technical help to the poorest nations
*headquarters* Washington DC

**International Finance Corporation (IFC)**
*established* 1956
*responsibilities* as an affiliate of the World Bank, to make investments in companies, to assist their development, or provides loans
*headquarters* Washington DC

**International Fund for Agricultural Development (IFAD)**
*established* 1977
*responsibilities* to mobilize funds for agricultural and rural development
*headquarters* Rome

**International Labour Organization (ILO)**
*established* 1919, becoming part of the UN in 1946
*responsibilities* to improve labour conditions, raise living standards and promote productive employment through international cooperation
*headquarters* International Labour Conference, ILO's supreme deliberative body, meets annually in Geneva; International Labour Office and International Institute for Labour Studies, both based permanently in Geneva; a training institution, particularly concerned with the needs of developing countries, based in Turin

**International Maritime Organization (IMO)**
*established* 1948
*responsibilities* to promote cooperation between governments on technical matters affecting merchant shipping, with the object of improving safety at sea
*headquarters* London

**International Monetary Fund (IMF)**
*established* 1945
*responsibilities* to promote international monetary cooperation and to help remedy any serious disequilibrium in a country's balance of payments by allowing it to draw on the resources of the Fund while it takes measures to correct the imbalance
*headquarters* Washington DC

**International Telecommunication Union (ITU)**
*established* 1932
*responsibilities* to maintain and extend international cooperation in improving telecommunications of all kinds by promoting the developoment of technical skills and services and harmonizing national activities
*headquarters* Geneva

**United Nations Centre for Human Settlements (UNCHS; Habitat)**
*established* 1978
*responsibilities* to service the intergovernmental Commission on Human Settlements by providing planning, construction, land development, and finance
*headquarters* Nairobi

**United Nations Children's Emergency Fund (UNICEF)**
*established* 1953
*responsibilities* to meet the emergency needs of children in developing countries
*headquarters* New York

**United Nations Conference on Trade and Development (UNCTAD)**
*established* 1964
*responsibilities* to promote international trade, particularly in developing countries
*headquarters* Geneva

**United Nations Disaster Relief Coordinator (UNDRO)**
*established* 1972
*responsibilities* to provide a 24-hour service for monitoring natural disasters and emergencies; to promote disaster prevention; and to coordinate preparedness and relief
*headquarters* Geneva

**United Nations Educational, Scientific and Cultural Organization (UNESCO)**
*established* 1946
*responsibilities* to promote peace by encouraging international collaboration in education, science, and culture; the USA, contributor of 25% of its budget, withdrew 1984 on grounds of its repoliticization and mismanagement; Britain followed 1985.
*headquarters* Paris

**United Nations Environment Programme (UNEP)**
*established* 1972
*responsibilities* to monitor the state of the environment and to promote environmentally sound developments throughout the world
*headquarters* Nairobi

**United Nations Fund for Population Activities (UNFPA)**
*established* 1972
*responsibilities* to provide finance for projects in the areas of family planning, education, and research into population trends and the needs of particular age groups
*headquarters* New York

**United Nations High Commission for Refugees (UNHCR)**
*established* 1951
*responsibilities* to provide international protection for refugees and to find solutions to their problems
*headquarters* Geneva

**United Nations Institute for Training and Research (UNITAR)**
*established* 1965
*responsibilities* to improve the effectiveness of the UN through training and research
*headquarters* New York

# THE BRITISH COMMONWEALTH

The British Commonwealth is a voluntary association of 48 states that have been, or still are, ruled by Britain. Independent states are full 'members of the Commonwealth', while dependent territories, such as colonies and protectorates, rank as 'Commonwealth countries'. Small self-governing countries, such as Nauru, may have special status. The Commonwealth has no charter, treaty, or constitution, and is founded more on tradition and sentiment than political or economic factors.

As the successor to the British Empire, the Commonwealth was initially based on allegiance to a common Crown. However in 1949 India chose to become a republic and from that date the modern Commonwealth was born, based now on the concept of the British monarch being a symbol, rather than a legal entity; Queen Elizabeth II is thus the formal head but not the ruler of member states. Presently, 18 of the 48 members accept the Queen as their head of state, 26 are republics, and five have their own local monarchs. Heads of government of Commonwealth countries meet every two years to discuss international affairs and areas of cooperation. Finance ministers meet annually, and other ministers meet as and when the need arises. The Commonwealth is not a mutual defence organization and most member countries are committed to regional treaties.

The Commonwealth secretariat, headed from Oct 1989 by Secretary-General Chief Emeka Anyaoko of Nigeria, is based in London. The secretariat's staff come from a number of member countries which also pay its operating costs.

# ENVIRONMENTAL AND HUMAN RIGHTS GROUPS

**ActionAid**
*established* 1972
*objectives* to help children, families, and communities in the world's poorest countries to overcome poverty, and to secure lasting improvements in the quality of their lives
*areas of operation* 18 countries in Africa, Asia, and Latin America

*membership* over 110,000 sponsors and supporters
*annual budget* (1990) £20,216,000
*current projects* long-term integrated rural development in the areas of water, health, agriculture, education, and income generation
*headquarters* London

**Amnesty International**
*established* 1961
*objectives* to campaign for human rights, work for the release of political prisoners, the abolition of torture and the death penalty, and the observance of the Universal Declaration of Human Rights. Politically unaligned
*areas of operation* worldwide, with nationally organized headquarters in 46 countries (25 in Latin America, Asia, Africa, Middle East)
*membership* over 1,100,000 members; section offices in over 70 countries; more than 6,000 volunteer groups active in over 70 countries
*annual budget* (1990) £11m
*current projects* human rights in Mexico, Morocco, the UK; situation of juveniles in the USA
*headquarters* international secretariat, London

**Campaign for Nuclear Disarmament (CND)**
*established* 1958
*objectives* to campaign for the unilateral dismantling of nuclear weapons, bases, and alliances; also campaigns against nuclear power. Politically unaligned
*areas of operation* mainly the UK
*membership* 70,000
*annual budget* (1990) £842,000 and £477,000 (publications wing)
*current projects* campaigning against international arms trade and nuclear proliferation
*headquarters* London

**Friends of the Earth (FoE)**
*established* 1971
*objectives* to conserve the planet's resources and reduce pollution; campaigns, among other things, for recycling and renewable energy, and against the destruction of wildlife and habitat
*areas of operation* 44 countries worldwide
*membership* 38 groups internationally; 250 local groups in the UK
*annual budget* (1990) £6m
*current projects* participation in forthcoming international conference in Rio de Janeiro, Brazil
*headquarters* Amsterdam

**Greenpeace**
*established* 1971
*objectives* to persuade governments to protect and improve the environment; campaigns against pollution, whaling, nuclear power, and on many other issues, with a policy of nonviolent direct action backed by scientific research
*areas of operation* 25 countries worldwide

## The British Commonwealth

| country | capital | date joined | area sq km |
|---|---|---|---|
| **IN AFRICA** | | | |
| Botswana | Gaborone | 1966 | 582,000 |
| British Indian Ocean Terr. | Victoria | + | 60 |
| Gambia | Banjul | 1965 | 10,700 |
| Ghana | Accra | 1957 | 238,300 |
| Kenya | Nairobi | 1963 | 582,600 |
| Lesotho | Maseru | 1966 | 30,400 |
| Malawi | Zomba | 1964 | 118,000 |
| Mauritius | Port Louis | 1968 | 2,000 |
| Namibia | Windhoek | 1990 | 824,200 |
| Nigeria | Lagos | 1960 | 924,000 |
| St Helena | Jamestown | + | 100 |
| Seychelles | Victoria | 1976 | 450 |
| Sierra Leone | Freetown | 1961 | 73,000 |
| Swaziland | Mbabane | 1968 | 17,400 |
| Tanzania | Dodoma | 1961 | 945,000 |
| Uganda | Kampala | 1962 | 236,900 |
| Zambia | Lusaka | 1964 | 600 |
| Zimbabwe | Harare | 1980 | 390,300 |
| **IN THE AMERICAS** | | | |
| Anguilla | The Valley | + | 155 |
| Antigua | St John's | 1981 | 400 |
| Bahamas | Nassau | 1973 | 13,900 |
| Barbados | Bridgetown | 1966 | 400 |
| Belize | Belmopan | 1982 | 23,000 |
| Bermuda | Hamilton | + | 54 |
| Brit. Virgin Is. | Road Town | + | 153 |
| Canada | Ottawa | 1931 | 9,958,400 |
| Cayman Islands | Georgetown | + | 300 |
| Dominica | Roseau | 1978 | 700 |
| Falkland Is. | Stanley | + | 12,100 |
| Grenada | St George's | 1974 | 300 |
| Guyana | Georgetown | 1966 | 215,000 |
| Jamaica | Kingston | 1962 | 11,400 |
| Montserrat | Plymouth | + | 100 |
| St Christopher–Nevis | Basseterre Charlestown | 1983 | 300 |
| St Lucia | Castries | 1979 | 600 |
| St Vincent and the Grenadines | Kingstown | 1979 | 400 |
| Trinidad and Tobago | Port of Spain | 1962 | 5,100 |
| Turks and Caicos Is. | Grand Turk | + | 400 |
| **IN THE ANTARCTIC** | | | |
| Australian Antarctic Terr. | | + | 5,403,000 |
| Brit. Antartic Terr. | | + | 390,000 |
| Falklands Is. Dependencies | | | 1,600 |
| (NZ) Ross Dependency | | | 453,000 |
| **IN ASIA** | | | |
| Bangladesh | Dhaka | 1972 | 144,000 |
| Brunei | Bandar Seri Begawan | 1984 | 5,800 |
| Hong Kong | Victoria | + | 1,100 |
| India | Delhi | 1947 | 3,166,800 |
| Malaysia | Kuala Lumpur | 1957 | 329,800 |
| Maldives | Malé | 1982 | 300 |
| Pakistan * | Islamabad | 1947 | 803,900 |
| Singapore | Singapore | 1965 | 600 |
| Sri Lanka | Colombo | 1948 | 66,000 |

* left 1972 and rejoined 1989

THE BRITISH COMMONWEALTH (cont.)

| country | capital | date joined | area sq km |
|---------|---------|-------------|-----------|
| IN AUSTRALASIA AND THE PACIFIC | | | |
| Australia | Canberra | 1931 | 7,682,300 |
| Norfolk Island | | + | 34 |
| Kiribati | Tawawa | 1979 | 700 |
| Nauru * | Yaren | 1968 | 21 |
| New Zealand | Wellington | 1931 | 268,000 |
| Cook Islands | | + | 300 |
| Niue Islands | | + | 300 |
| Tokelau Islands | | + | 10 |
| Papua New Guinea | Port Moresby | 1975 | 462,800 |
| Pitcairn | | | 5 |
| Solomon Islands | Honiara | 1978 | 27,600 |
| Tonga | Nuku'alofa | 1970 | 700 |
| Tuvalu * | Funafuti | 1978 | 24 |
| Vanuatu | Villa | 1980 | 15,000 |
| Western Samoa | Apia | 1970 | 2,800 |

(Fiji was a Commonwealth member until 1987, when a military coup overthrew the elected government and declared the country a republic. Its future within the Commonwealth has yet to be

| country | capital | date joined | area sq km |
|---------|---------|-------------|-----------|
| IN EUROPE | | | |
| United Kingdom * | | 1931 | |
| England | London | | 130,400 |
| Wales | Cardiff | | 21,000 |
| Scotland | Edinburgh | | 79,000 |
| N. Ireland | Belfast | | 13,500 |
| Isle of Man | Douglas | | 600 |
| Channel Islands | | | 200 |
| Cyprus | Nicosia | 1961 | 9,000 |
| Gibraltar | Gibraltar | | 6 |
| Malta | Valletta | 1964 | 300 |
| total | | | 33,089,900 |

* special members
+ all dependent territories within the Commonwealth.

---

**membership** 5m
**current projects** protection of wildlife; disposal of toxics; civil nuclear energy; atmosphere and energy
**headquarters** Amsterdam
**Human Rights Watch**
**established** 1978
**objectives** to monitor and publicize human-rights abuses by governments, especially attacks on those who defend human rights in their own countries
**areas of operation** separate committees focus on one area each: *Africa Watch*, *Americas Watch*, *Asia Watch*, *Middle East Watch*; *Helsinki Watch* monitors compliance with the 1975 Helsinki accords by the 35 signatory countries
**annual budget** does not accept financial support from governments or government-funded agencies
**current projects** more than 100 investigative missions every year to some 60 countries around the world
**headquarters** New York
**Minority Rights Group**
**established** 1965
**objectives** to promote human rights and increase awareness of minority issues

**areas of operation** Europe, Australia, North America, India, USSR
**membership** non-membership organization
**current projects** publishing reports on minority groups worldwide; producing educational material for schools; making representations at the United Nations
**annual budget** (1990) £390,600
**headquarters** London
**Oxfam (Oxford Committee for Famine Relief)**
**established** 1942
**objectives** to relieve poverty, distress, and suffering in any part of the world
**areas of operation** worldwide, particularly in developing countries
**membership** non-membership organization
**annual budget** (1990) £62m
**current projects** 50th anniversary year, 'working for a fairer world'
**headquarters** Oxford
**The Red Cross**
**established** 1864 by the Geneva Convention; the Muslim equivalent is the Red Crescent
**objectives** to assist the wounded and prisoners in war, and war-related victims such as refugees and the disabled; to aid victims of natural disasters—floods,

earthquakes, epidemics, famine, and accidents—and to organize emergency relief operations worldwide
*membership* non-membership organization
*annual budget* £4.92m
*areas of operation* worldwide
*headquarters* Geneva, Switzerland

**Save the Children Fund**
*established* 1919
*objectives* to promote the rights of children to care, good health, material welfare, and moral, spiritual, and educational development, throughout the world
*areas of operation* more than 50 Third World countries and the UK
*membership* over 850 branches in the UK
*annual budget* (1990) £52m
*current projects* assistance in famine-affected areas; provision of health care, education, community development, and emergency relief
*headquarters* London

**Survival International**
*established* 1969
*objectives* to ensure the rights of threatened tribal peoples to survival, self-determination, ownership and use of land, and proper representation in all decisions affecting their future
*areas of operation* more than 60 countries worldwide
*membership* 12,000
*annual budget* (1990) £530,000
*current projects* lobbying against rainforest logging, huge dams, and industrial activity that displaces tribal people, and for the return of confiscated lands; emergency medical aid; protests against killing and intimidation of tribal people
*headquarters* London

**Voluntary Service Overseas** (VSO)
*established* 1958
*objectives* to help Third World development by providing opportunities for people with skills to make a practical contribution as volunteers
*areas of operation* 40 developing countries worldwide
*membership* 45 local groups
*annual budget* (1990) £15.7m
*headquarters* London

**War on Want**
*established* 1952
*objectives* to fight poverty throughout the world
*areas of operation* 40 developing countries worldwide
*membership* local groups throughout the UK; financial support from individuals, trade unions, and other organizations
*annual budget* (1990) £8.7m
*current projects* education and training projects in Bangladesh, Brazil, India, Jamaica, and Zimbabwe; agricultural and social development programmes in Bangladesh, Brazil, Cape Verde, Chile, Cuba, India,

Mozambique, Philippines, and Sri Lanka; projects in Angola for orphaned children, and cholera prevention
*headquarters* London

**World Conservation Monitoring Centre**
*established* 1983
*objectives* to support international programmes for conservation and sustainable development through the provision of information on the world's biological diversity
*areas of operation* provides information to the World Wide Fund for Nature, the World Conservation Union (IUCN), and the United Nations Environment Programme (UNEP) (*not* direct to the general public)
*membership* non-membership organization
*annual income* (1989–90) £1,307,180
*current projects* managing information holdings on threatened species, important habitats, national parks, wildlife trade, and conservation bibliography
*headquarters* Cambridge, England

**World Wide Fund for Nature** (WWF)
*established* 1961
*objectives* to protect endangered species and to tackle all environmental problems that threaten any form of life
*areas of operation* worldwide
*membership* 28 offices in 23 countries
*annual budget* (1990) £22m
*current projects* tropical rainforests; marine conservation; wetlands; pollution within EC member countries
*headquarters* Gland, Switzerland; UK hq, Godalming, Surrey

---

**Faith in organizations**

*Generally speaking, do you think that British membership of the European Community is a good thing, a bad thing, or neither good nor bad?*

| | |
|---|---|
| Good | 51 |
| Bad | 19 |
| Neither | 23 |
| Don't know | 8 |

*How important do you think it is that we try to make the United Nations a success—very important, fairly important or not so important?*

| | |
|---|---|
| Very important | 70 |
| Fairly important | 17 |
| Not so important | 5 |
| Don't know | 8 |

*In general, do you think the United Nations is doing a good job or a poor job in trying to solve the problems it has to face?*

| | |
|---|---|
| Good job | 39 |
| Fair job | 29 |
| Poor job | 19 |
| Don't know | 13 |

# LEGAL TERMS

**accessory** a party to a crime that is actually committed by someone else.

**accomplice** a person who acts with another in the commission or attempted commission of a crime, either as a principal or as an accessory.

**acquittal** the setting free of someone charged with a crime after a trial.

**action** any proceeding in a civil court of law, including an ecclesiastical court. Actions in the High Court are commenced by the plaintiff issuing a writ, which will usually include a concise statement about the nature of the claim and the damages which are being sought from the defendant.

**adjournment** the postponement of the hearing of a case for later consideration. If a hearing is adjourned *sine die* (without day) it is postponed for an indefinite period. If a party requests an adjournment the court may find the costs of the adjournment have been unnecessarily incurred and make an order for costs against that party.

**Act of Parliament** in Britain, a change in the law originating in Parliament and called a statute. Before an act receives the royal assent and becomes law it is a *bill*. The US equivalent is an act of Congress.

An Act of Parliament may be either public (of general effect), local, or private. The body of English statute law comprises all the acts passed by Parliament: the existing list opens with the Statute of Merton, passed in 1235. An Act (unless it is stated to be for a definite period and then to come to an end) remains on the statute book until it is repealed.

How an act of Parliament becomes law:

**1 first reading of the bill** The title is read out in the House of Commons (H of C) and a minister names a day for the second reading.

**2** The bill is officially printed.

**3 second reading** A debate on the whole bill in the H of C followed by a vote on whether or not the bill should go on to the next stage.

**4 committee stage** A committee of MPs considers the bill in detail and makes amendments.

**5 report stage** The bill is referred back to the H of C which may make further amendments.

**6 third reading** The H of C votes whether the bill should be sent on to the House of Lords.

**7 House of Lords** The bill passes through much the same stages in the Lords as in the H of C. (Bills may be introduced in the Lords, in which case the H of C considers them at this stage.)

**8 last amendments** The H of C considers any Lords' amendments, and may make further amendments which must usually be agreed by the Lords.

**9 royal assent** The Queen gives her formal assent.

**10** The bill becomes an act of Parliament at royal assent, although it may not come into force until a day appointed in the act.

**adoption** the permanent legal transfer of parental rights and duties in respect of a child from one person to another.

**adultery** voluntary sexual intercourse between a married person and someone other than his or her legal partner. It is one factor that may prove 'irretrievable breakdown' of marriage in actions for judicial separation or divorce in Britain.

**advocate** (Latin *advocatus*, one summoned to one's aid, especially in a lawcourt) pleader in a court of justice. A more common term for a professional advocate is barrister or counsel. In many tribunals lay persons may appear as advocates.

**affidavit** legal document, used in court applications and proceedings, in which a person swears that certain facts are true.

**alibi** a provable assertion that the accused was at some other place when a crime was committed.

**amnesty** the release of political prisoners under a general pardon, or a person or group of people from criminal liability for a particular action; for example, the occasional amnesties in Britain for those who surrender firearms that they hold illegally.

**appeal** an application for the judicial examination of the decision of a lower court by a higher court. In the UK, summary trials (involving minor offences) are heard in the magistrate's court and appeals against conviction and/or sentence are heard in the Crown Court. The appeal in the Crown Court takes the form of a full retrial but no jury is present. Appeals against conviction and/or sentence in the Crown Court are heard by the Criminal Division of the Court of Appeal.

In 1989 31% of the appeals before the Criminal Division of the Court of Appeal were successful.

**arrest** the apprehension and detention of a person suspected of a crime classified as sufficiently serious (an 'arrestable' offence).

**arson** the malicious and wilful setting fire to property. A capital offence in the UK until 1971, it still carries a maximum sentence of life imprisonment.

**assault** intentional act or threat of physical violence against a person. In English law it is both a crime and a tort (a civil wrong). The kinds of criminal assault are common (ordinary); aggravated (more serious, such as causing actual bodily harm); or indecent (of a sexual nature).

**Attorney General** in England, principal law officer of the Crown and head of the English Bar. The consent of the Attorney General is required for bringing certain criminal proceedings where offences against the state of public order are at issue, for example incitement to racial hatred. Under the Criminal Justice Act 1988, cases can be referred to the Court of Appeal by the Attorney General if it appears to him that the sentencing of a person convicted of a serious offence (e.g. murder, rape, robbery) has been unduly lenient.

## NOTIFIABLE OFFENCES RECORDED BY THE POLICE, ENGLAND AND WALES

| | Violence against the person | Sexual offences | Robbery and Burglary | Theft and handling stolen goods | Fraud and forgery | Criminal damage | Other | Thousands Total |
|---|---|---|---|---|---|---|---|---|
| 1985 | 121.7 | 21.5 | 894.2 | 1,884.1 | 134.8 | 539.0 | 16.7 | 3,611.9 |
| 1986 | 125.5 | 22.7 | 961.6 | 2,003.9 | 133.4 | 583.6 | 16.7 | 3,847.4 |
| 1987 | 141.0 | 25.2 | 932.7 | 2,052.0 | 133.0 | 589.0 | 19.3 | 3,892.2 |
| 1988 | 158.2 | 26.5 | 849.2 | 1,931.3 | 133.9 | 593.9 | 22.7 | 3,715.8 |
| 1989 | 177.0 | 29.7 | 859.1 | 2,012.8 | 134.5 | 630.1 | 27.6 | 3,870.7 |
| 1990 | 184.7 | 29.0 | 1042.7 | 2,374.0 | 147.9 | 733.3 | 31.1 | 4,542.8 |

Source: Home Office, in Monthly Digest of Statistics no. 543, March 1991

**bail** the setting at liberty of a person in legal custody on an undertaking, (usually backed by some security, given either by that person or by someone else), to attend a legal proceeding at a stated time and place. If the person does not attend, the bail may be forfeited.

**barrister** in the UK, a lawyer qualified by study at the Inns of Court to plead for a client in court. In Scotland they are called advocates. Barristers also undertake the writing of opinions on the prospects of a case before trial. They act for clients through the intermediary of solicitors. In the highest courts, only barristers can represent litigants but this distinction between barristers and solicitors seems likely to change in the 1990s. In the USA an attorney (lawyer) may serve both functions. When pupil barristers complete their training they are 'called to the bar': this is the name of the ceremony in which they are admitted as members of the profession. A Queen's Counsel (silk) is a senior barrister appointed on the recommendation of the Lord Chancellor.

**bigamy** the offence of marrying a person while already lawfully married to another. In some countries marriage to more than one wife or husband is lawful.

**blackmail** criminal offence of extorting money with menaces or threats of detrimental action, such as exposure of some misconduct on the part of the victim.

**blasphemy** written or spoken insult directed against religious belief or sacred things with deliberate intent to outrage believers.

**breathalyzer** an instrument for on-the-spot checking by police of the amount of alcohol consumed by a suspect driver. The driver breathes into a plastic bag connected to a tube containing a chemical that changes colour. Another method is to use a gas chromatograph, again from a breath sample.

Approximately 500,000 breath tests are carried out each year. Alcohol-related road traffic accidents result in 22,000 casualties each year; 50% of those injured are victims of drunk drivers.

**brief** the written instructions sent by a solicitor to a barrister before a hearing.

**burden of proof** in court proceedings, the duty of a party to produce sufficient evidence to prove that his or her case is true. In English and American law a higher standard of proof is required in criminal cases (beyond all reasonable doubt), than in civil cases (on the balance of probabilities).

**capital punishment** punishment by death; methods of execution include electrocution, lethal gas, hanging, shooting, lethal injection, garrotting, and decapitation. 44 countries have abolished the death penalty for all offences, and 17 (including the UK) have done so for all but exceptional crimes such as wartime crimes. 25 countries can be considered abolitionist *de facto*, that is they retain the death penalty in law but have not carried out any executions for the past ten years or more. Capital punishment is retained and used in 92 countries, including the USA (37 states), China, and the USSR.

In 1990, a record-breaking number of countries abolished the death penalty—Namibia, the Czech and Slovak Federative Republic, Ireland, Andorra, São Tomé and Príncipe, Mozambique, and Hungary abolished the death penalty for all offences; Nepal abolished the death penalty for ordinary offences.

The International Covenant on Civil and Political Rights 1977 ruled out imposition of the death penalty on those under the age of 18. The covenant was signed by President Carter on behalf of the USA, but in 1989 the US Supreme Court decided that it could be imposed from the age of 16 for murder, and that the mentally retarded could also face the death penalty. In 1990 there were over 2,000 prisoners on death row (awaiting execution) in the USA.

**care order** in Britain, a court order that places a child in the care of a local authority; this may be with foster parents or in a community home.

**child abuse** the molesting of children by parents and other adults. It can give rise to various criminal charges and has become a growing concern since the early 1980s. A local authority can take abused children away from their parents by obtaining a care order from a juvenile court under the Children's and Young Persons Act 1969 (replaced by the Children's Act 1989). Controversial methods of diagnosing sexual abuse led to a public inquiry in Cleveland, England 1988, which severely criticized the handling of such cases. The standard of proof required for criminal proceedings is greater than that required for a local authority to take children into care. This has led to highly publicized cases where children have been taken into care but prosecutions have eventually not

---

## COUNTRIES WHICH HAVE ABOLISHED THE DEATH PENALTY SINCE 1976

| | |
|---|---|
| 1976 | Portugal*; Canada ** |
| 1978 | Denmark*; Spain ** |
| 1979 | Luxembourg, Nicaragua, Norway*; Brazil (1), Fiji, Peru** |
| 1981 | France* |
| 1982 | The Netherlands* |
| 1983 | Cyprus, El Salvador** |
| 1984 | Argentina (2), Australia** |
| 1985 | Australia* |
| 1987 | The Philippines, Haiti, Liechtenstein, German Democratic Republic* |
| 1989 | Cambodia, New Zealand, Romania* |
| 1990 | Andorra, Czech and Slovak Federative Republic, Hungary, Ireland, Mozambique, Namibia, São Tomé and Príncipe*; Nepal** (3) |

\* for all offences ** for ordinary offences

1. Brazil had abolished the death penalty in 1882 but reintroduced it in 1969 while under military rule. 2. Argentina had abolished the death penalty for all offences in 1921 and again in 1972 but reintroduced it 1976 following a military coup. 3. Nepal had abolished the death penalty for murder in 1946 but reintroduced it in 1985 after bomb explosions killed several people.

---

been brought, as in Rochdale, Lancashire, and the Orkneys, Scotland in 1990.

**civil disobedience** the deliberate breaking of laws considered unjust, a form of nonviolent direct action; the term was coined by the US writer Thoreau in an essay of that name 1849. It was advocated by Mahatma Gandhi to prompt peaceful withdrawal of British power from India. Civil disobedience has since been employed by, for instance, the US civil-rights movement in the 1960s and the peace movement in the 1980s.

**civil law** the legal system based on Roman law. It is one of the two main European legal systems, English (common) law being the other. Civil law may also mean the law relating to matters other than criminal law, such as contract and tort. Inside the Commonwealth, Roman law forms the basis of the legal systems of Scotland and Québec and is also the basis of that of South Africa.

**commissioner for oaths** in English law, a person appointed by the Lord Chancellor with power to administer oaths or take affidavits. All practising solicitors have these powers but must not use them in proceedings in which they are acting for any of the parties or in which they have an interest.

**common law** that part of the English law not embodied in legislation. It consists of rules of law based on common custom and usage and on judicial decisions. English common law became the basis of law in the USA and many other English-speaking countries.

**compulsory purchase** in the UK the right of the state and authorized bodies to buy land required for public purposes even against the wishes of the owner. Under the Land Compensation Act 1973, fair recompense is payable.

**consumer protection** laws and measures designed to ensure fair trading for buyers. Responsibility for checking goods and services for quality, safety, and suitability has in the past few years moved increasingly away from the consumer to the producer.

**contempt of court** behaviour that shows contempt for the authority of a court, such as disobeying a court order, breach of an injunction, or improper use of legal documents. Behaviour that disrupts, prejudices, or interferes with court proceedings either inside or outside the courtroom may also be contempt. The court may punish contempt with a fine or imprisonment.

**contract of employment** the legal basis of an agreement between an employer and an employee.

**copyright** law applying to literary, musical, and artistic works (including plays, recordings, films, photographs, radio and television broadcasts, and, in the USA and Britain, computer programs), which prevents the reproduction of the work, in whole or in part, without the author's consent.

**coroner** official who investigates the deaths of persons who have died suddenly by acts of violence, or under suspicious circumstances, by holding an inquest or ordering a postmortem examination.

The coroner's court aims not to establish liability but to find out how, where, and why the death occurred. A coroner must be a barrister, solicitor, or medical practitioner with at least five years' professional service. In Scotland similar duties are performed by the procurator-fiscal. The coroner alone decides which witnesses should be called, and legal aid is not available for representation in a coroner's court. Nor may any of the parties make a closing speech to the jury.

**corporal punishment** physical punishment of wrongdoers, for example, by whipping. It is still used as a punishment for criminals in many countries, especially under Islamic law. It was abolished as a punishment for criminals in Britain 1967 but only became illegal for punishing schoolchildren in state schools 1986. Corporal punishment of children by parents is illegal in some countries, including Sweden, Finland, Denmark, and Norway.

## Highest Sentences 1990

| judicial area | murder | rape | severe assault | tax fraud | armed robbery | drunken driving | soft drugs |
|---|---|---|---|---|---|---|---|
| Canada | life | life | 4 years | 18 months | 5 years | n/a | n/a |
| Denmark | life | 3 years | 1 year | 10 months | 6 years | 20 days | fine |
| England and Wales | life | 15 years | 5 years | 3 years | 14 years | disqualification | 1 year |
| Greece | life | 20 years | 5 years | 5 years | 20 years | 1 year | 1 year |
| Hong Kong | death | life | 3 years | 3 years | life | 3 years | life |
| India | death | 10 years | 1 year | n/a | 7 years | n/a | n/a |
| Republic of Ireland | life | 18 months | suspended sentence | repayment | 5 years | n/a | n/a |
| Kenya | death | life | life | 3 years | death | n/a | n/a |
| Netherlands | life | 5 years | 2 years | 1 year | 6 years | n/a | n/a |
| New Zealand | life | 6 years | 4 years | large fine | 9 years | n/a | n/a |
| Nigeria | death | life | 7 years | 7 years | death | 6 months | 21 years |
| Norway | 21 years | 5 years | 18 months | 6 months | 2 years | n/a | n/a |
| Scotland | life | 10 years | 5 years | 3 years | 10 years | disqualification | 18 months |
| Spain | 30 years | 20 years | 6 years | 6 years | 6 years | 6 months | 4 years |
| United Arab Emirates | death | life | 5 years | n/a | life | 1 year | 10 years |
| Texas | death | 50 years | 10 years | 99 years | 99 years | 2 years | 1 year |

**court martial** court convened for the trial of persons subject to military discipline who are accused of violations of military laws.

**criminal law** the body of law that defines the public wrongs (crimes) that are punishable by the state and establishes methods of prosecution and punishment. It is distinct from civil law, which deals with legal relationships between individuals (including organizations), such as contract law.

In England and Wales crimes are either: *indictable offences* (serious offences triable by judge and jury in the crown court); *summary offences* dealt with in magistrates' courts; or *hybrid offences* tried in either kind of court according to the seriousness of the case and the wishes of the defendant. The crown court has power to punish those found guilty more severely than a magistrates' court. Punishments include imprisonment, fines, suspended terms of imprisonment (which only come into operation if the offender is guilty of further offences during a specified period), probation, and community service. Overcrowding in prisons and the cost of imprisonment have led to recent experiments with noncustodial sentences such as electronic tags fixed to the body to reinforce curfew orders on convicted criminals in the community.

The total cost of criminal justice services for England and Wales was £7 billion in 1990, an increase of 77% in real terms from 1980.

**custody** the state of being held by the police or prison authorities in confinement. Following an arrest, a person may either be kept in custody or released on bail. Custody is also the legal guardianship of a child; a parent, guardian, or authority who has custody of a child usually exercises all parental rights.

**damages** compensation for a tort (such as personal injuries caused by negligence) or breach of contract. Damages for personal injuries include compensation for loss of earnings, as well as for the injury itself. The court might reduce the damages if the claimant was partly

to blame. In the majority of cases, the parties involved reach an out-of-court settlement (a compromise without going to court).

**decree nisi** conditional order of divorce. A *decree absolute* is normally granted six weeks after the decree nisi, and from the date of the decree absolute the parties cease to be husband and wife.

**deed** legal document that passes an interest in property or binds a person to perform or abstain from some action. Deeds are of two kinds: indenture and deed poll. *Indentures* bind two or more parties in mutual obligations.

A *deed poll* is made by one party only, such as when a person changes his or her name.

**defamation** an attack on a person's reputation by libel or slander.

**defendant** a person against whom court proceedings are brought.

**defence** the defendant and his or her legal advisors and representatives are collectively known as the defence. The defence is also the case made in answer to the action or claim being made against the defendant.

**Director of Public Prosecutions** (DPP) in the UK, the head of the Crown Prosecution Service (established 1985), responsible for the conduct of all criminal prosecutions in England and Wales. The DPP was formerly responsible only for the prosecution of certain serious crimes, such as murder.

**divorce** the legal dissolution of a lawful marriage. It is distinct from an annulment, which is a legal declaration that the marriage was invalid. The ease with which a divorce can be obtained in different countries varies considerably and is also affected by different religious practices.

**easement** rights that a person may have over the land of another. A common example is a right of way; others are the right to bring water over another's land and the right to a sufficient quantity of light.

**ecclesiastical law** church law. In England, the Church of England has special ecclesiastical courts to administer church law. Each diocese has a consistory court with a right of appeal to the Court of Arches (in the archbishop of Canterbury's jurisdiction) or the Chancery Court of York (in the archbishop of York's jurisdiction). They deal with the constitution of the Church of England, church property, the clergy, services, doctrine, and practice. These courts have no influence on churches of other denominations, which are governed by the usual laws of contract and trust.

**employment law** law covering the rights and duties of employers and employees. During the 20th century, statute law has increasingly been used to give new rights to employees. Industrial tribunals are statutory bodies that adjudicate in disputes between employers and employees or trade unions and include complaints concerning unfair dismissal, sex or race discrimination, and equal pay.

Discrimination against employees on the ground of their sex or race are illegal under the Sex Discrimination Act 1975 and the Race Relations Act 1976.

**English law** one of the major European legal systems, Roman law being the other. English law has spread to many other countries, including former English colonies such as the USA, Canada, Australia, and New Zealand.

**equal opportunities** the right to be employed or considered for employment without discrimination on the grounds of race, gender, physical or mental handicap.

**equity** system of law supplementing the ordinary rules of law where the application of these would operate harshly in a particular case; sometimes it is regarded as an attempt to achieve 'natural justice'. So understood, equity appears as an element in most legal systems, and in a number of legal codes judges are instructed to apply both the rules of strict law and the principles of equity in reaching their decisions.

**escrow** a document sealed and delivered to a third party and not released or coming into effect until some condition has been fulfilled or performed, whereupon the document takes full effect.

**executor** a person appointed in a will to carry out the instructions of the deceased. A person so named has the right to refuse to act. The executor also has a duty to bury the deceased, prove the will, and obtain a grant of probate (that is, establish that the will is genuine and obtain official approval of his or her actions).

**extradition** the surrender, by one state or country to another, of a person accused of a criminal offence in the state or country to which that person is extradited.

**foreclosure** the transfer of title of a mortgaged property from the mortgagor (borrower, usually a home owner) to the mortgagee (loaner, for example a bank) if the mortgagor is in breach of the mortgage agreement, usually by failing to make a number of payments on the mortgage (loan).

**forgery** the making of a fake document, painting, or object with deliberate intention to deceive or

| PUBLIC EXPENDITURE ON LAW AND ORDER IN THE UK (£m) | | | | |
|---|---|---|---|---|
| | 1986 | 1987 | 1988 | 1989 |
| Police | 3,679 | 3,787 | 4,184 | 4,597 |
| Prisons | 1,071 | 1,240 | 1,176 | 1,430 |
| Legal Aid | 345 | 402 | 441 | 524 |
| Probation | 148 | 169 | 182 | 201 |
| Parliament | 530 | 487 | 638 | 709 |
| Law Courts | 1,241 | 1,570 | 2,044 | 2,367 |
| TOTAL | 7,014 | 7,655 | 8,665 | 9,828 |

Source: Central Statistical Office, in Monthly Digest of Statistics no. 543 March 1991

defraud. The most common forgeries involve financial instruments such as cheques or credit-card transactions or money (counterfeiting). There are also literary forgeries, forged coins, and forged antiques.

**fraud** an act of deception resulting in injury to another. To establish fraud it has to be demonstrated that (1) a false representation (for example, a factually untrue statement) has been made, with the intention that it should be acted upon; (2) the person making the representation knows it is false or does not attempt to find out whether it is true or not; and (3) the person to whom the representation is made acts upon it to his or her detriment.

A contract based on fraud can be declared void, and the injured party can sue for damages.

**freehold** in England and Wales, ownership of land which is for an indefinite period. It is contrasted with a leasehold, which is always for a fixed period. In practical effect, a freehold is absolute ownership.

**grievous bodily harm** (GBH) in English law, very serious physical harm suffered by the victim of a crime. The courts have said that judges should not try to define grievous bodily harm but leave it to the jury to decide.

**hearsay evidence** evidence given by a witness based on information passed to that person by others rather than evidence experienced at first-hand by the witness. It is usually not admissable as evidence in criminal proceedings.

**homicide** the killing of a human being. This may be unlawful, lawful, or excusable, depending on the circumstances. Unlawful homicides include murder, manslaughter, infanticide, and causing death by dangerous driving. Lawful homicide occurs where, for example, a police officer is justified in killing a criminal in the course of apprehension or when a person is killed in self-defence or defence of others.

**illegitimacy** the status of a child born to a mother who is not legally married; a child may be legitimized by subsequent marriage of the parents. The nationality of the child is usually that of the mother.

**indemnity** an undertaking to compensate another for damage, loss, trouble, or expenses, or the money paid by way of such compensation—for example, under fire insurance agreements.

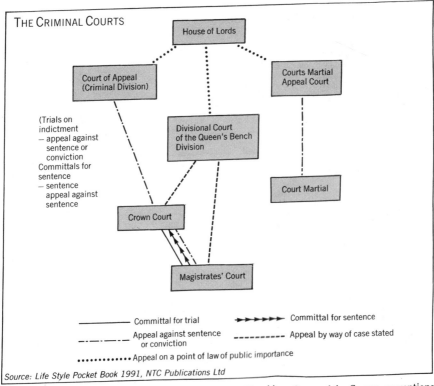

THE CRIMINAL COURTS

House of Lords

Court of Appeal
(Criminal Division)

Courts Martial
Appeal Court

(Trials on
indictment
— appeal against
sentence or
conviction
Committals for
sentence
— sentence
appeal against
sentence

Divisional Court
of the Queen's Bench
Division

Court Martial

Crown Court

Magistrates' Court

——————— Committal for trial          ►►►►►► Committal for sentence

—··—··— Appeal against sentence      – – – – – – Appeal by way of case stated
          or conviction

·············· Appeal on a point of law of public importance

Source: Life Style Pocket Book 1991, NTC Publications Ltd

**injunction** court order that forbids a person from doing something, or orders him or her to take certain action. Breach of an injunction is contempt of court.

**inquest** inquiry held by a coroner into an unexplained death. At an inquest, a coroner is assisted by a jury of between 7 and 11 people. Evidence is on oath, and medical and other witnesses may be summoned.

**international law** body of rules generally accepted as governing the relations between countries, pioneered by Hugo Grotius, especially in matters of human rights, territory, and war. The scope of the law is now extended to space – for example, the 1967 treaty that (among other things) banned nuclear weapons from space. *The Genocide Convention* 1948 declares that acts of killing, causing serious bodily harm, prevention of births, forcible transfer of children, the deliberate infliction of conditions of life calculated to bring about the physical destruction of a group, if those acts are 'committed with intent to destroy, in whole or in part, a national, ethnical, racial or religious group', are international crimes. *The Geneva Convention* is a series of international conventions on the laws of war. The Geneva Protocol of 1925 prohibits the use of gas and bacteriological warfare. The 1949 conventions include provision for the protection of sick and wounded soldiers, prisoners of war and certain groups of civilians; a protocol of 1977 extends such protection and further regulates the law

of bombing. Some of the Geneva conventions have been extended to cover civil wars and wars of national liberation.

**judge** a person invested with power to hear and determine legal disputes.

**judicial review** in English law, action in the High Court to review the decisions of lower courts, tribunals, and administrative bodies. Various court orders can be made: **certiorari** (which quashes the decision); **mandamus** (which commands a duty to be performed); **prohibition** (which commands that an action should not be performed because it is unauthorized); a **declaration** (which sets out the legal rights or obligations); or an **injunction**.

**jurisprudence** the science of law in the abstract – that is, not the study of any particular laws or legal system, but of the principles upon which legal systems are founded.

**jury** body of lay people (usually 12) sworn to decide the facts of a case and reach a verdict in a court of law. Juries, used mainly in English-speaking countries, are implemented primarily in criminal cases, but also sometimes in civil cases; for example, inquests and libel trials.

In July 1991 a jury at the Old Bailey acquitted Michael Randle and Pat Pottle of helping the Soviet agent George Blake escape from prison in 1966. The two defendants were prosecuted 25 years after the escape following publication of a book in which they admitted to their part in the escape. The judge told the

# INTERNATIONAL LAW AND THE GULF

When Iraqi forces invaded neighbouring Kuwait on 2 Aug 1990 their action was a violation of international law. On 8 Aug 1990, Iraq annexed Kuwait in breach of the right of self-determination, and in breach of the principle of the inadmissibility of the acquisition of territory by force.

The invasion caused widespread condemnation of Iraq. The United Nations issued a number of binding Security Council resolutions calling for immediate and unconditional withdrawal. The authority of the Security Council to restore international peace and security comes from the UN Charter which is founded on a determination to avoid the horrors of war. The Council, comprising five permanent members—the USA, Soviet Union, France, Britain and China—and ten members who are elected for periods of two years, can call for a variety of measures to restore peace and security. These include diplomatic, economic and other sanctions and, where necessary, the use of force.

While waiting to see if sanctions imposed against Iraq by the Security Council would work, the USA and her allies continued to send armed forces into the region. The majority of these were from America and by 7 November 1990 there were 230,000 American troops in Saudi Arabia. The last resolution of the Security Council before the outbreak of war, Resolution 678,authorized member states cooperating with the government of Kuwait to use all necessary means to uphold and implement all relevant

*Retreating Iraqi troops set fire to Kuwait's oil wells—international law could only condemn such crimes, not bring the perpetrators to justice.*

resolutions and restore international peace and security in the area if Iraq did not comply by 15 Jan 1991. But following the military offensive that began on Jan 16, principles of international law continued to be disregarded, with human rights abuses and crimes against humanity remaining unchecked.

The crisis in the Gulf re-emphasized both the importance and the complexity of the role of international law in providing regulatory principles within the international community. These principles embrace not only the conduct of hostilities but also include such issues as the prevention of genocide, respect for neutral rights and protected persons, reprisals, the interpretation and withdrawal from treaties, and the punishment of those guilty of war crimes.

It is claimed that the following breaches of international law have occurred over the past year in the Gulf:

—treatment of foreign civilians in Iraq in breach of the Geneva 'Red Cross' Convention which forbids the taking of hostages and the use of civilians to protect places against military attack;

—violation of Article 23 of the Geneva Convention which states that prisoners of war must be protected from attacks, violence and intimidation, and against insults and public curiosity by the parading of allied captives on Iraqi television;

—unlawful environmental damage inflicted on the region by the sabotage and destruction of Kuwaiti oil wells by Iraqi forces;

—violation of a number of international law principles forbidding abuse of fundamental human rights including the torture of Kuwaiti citizens and the use of chemical weapons against the Kurdish population of northern Iraq.

Following such blatant breaches of international law there have been calls for subjecting those responsible to war crimes trials. By international law individuals may be criminally responsible for violations committed by them, even if committed under order. Responsibility can also extend to those who gave the orders, be they military commanders, government officials or heads of state (as in the prosecution of those responsible for war crimes at the Nuremberg trials in occupied Germany in 1946). In the aftermath of the Gulf war such prosecutions seem remote. Despite the machinery which exists, such prosecution will be frustrated if the offenders have not been captured and remain in unoccupied territory. Obviously, Iraqis accused of war crimes will not give themselves up to any state intent on prosecuting them, or travel to countries where extradition is a possibility.

The 1991 Gulf war was not a unique instance of one country attempting to absorb another through the use of military force but it was the first major international crisis since the thawing of East-West relations. The crisis highlighted both the uses and defects of international law in setting out the rights and duties of States towards each other.

## MISCARRIAGES OF JUSTICE

**Birmingham Six**: Richard McIlkenny, Hugh Callaghan, John Walker, Patrick Hill, Billy Power, and Gerald Hunter were each sentenced to 21 life sentences following the bombing of the Mulberry Bush pub, Birmingham in Nov 1974. The Court of Appeal quashed the sentences in March 1991 after the men had spent nearly 17 years in prison.

**Guildford Four**: Carole Richardson, Patrick Armstrong, Gerald Conlon, and Paul Hill were convicted following two bomb explosions in separate pubs in Guildford which killed five people in Oct 1974. Their convictions were quashed by the Court of Appeal in Oct 1989 after they had spent 14 years in prison.

**Maguire Seven**: Anne Maguire, Patrick Maguire, Patrick Maguire (son), Vincent Maguire, Sean Smyth, Patrick O'Neill and Giuseppe Conlon went on trial in 1976 for providing bombs to the IRA. They were sentenced to between 7 and 14 years. Giuseppe Conlon died in prison. At their hearing before the Court of Appeal in May 1991, they were acquitted.

**Possible miscarriages...**

**Tottenham Three**: Winston Silcott, Mark Braithwaite, and Engin Raghip were convicted of murdering PC Blakelock on the Broadwater Farm Estate in 1985. The Court of Appeal is to review Raghip's case. The statements made by all three to the police have been disputed.

**Bridgewater Four**: Jimmy Robinson, Vincent Hickey, Michael Hickey (aged 16 at time of killing), and Pat Molloy (who died in prison) were imprisoned following the murder of Carl Bridgewater, a 13-year-old newsboy who was shot near Wordsley in Staffordshire in Sept 1978. The defendants' appeal in Jan 1989 failed.

**Judith Ward**: was jailed for life in 1974 after a bomb on a soldier's coach on the M62 near Bradford killed 12 people. Her involvement was denied by the IRA. The case continues to be questioned.

jury that the two men had no defence in law. However, in an instance of reaching a 'perverse judgment', the jury adopted a common-sense rather than strict letter-of-the-law approach and disobeyed the judge, acquitting both defendants. The case strengthened support for maintaining the jury system, in the face of abolitionist arguments.

**juvenile offender** term for young persons who commit offences. Young people under age 17 are commonly referred to by the law as juveniles, although for some purposes a distinction is made between children (aged under 14) and 'young persons' (14–16). Most legal proceedings in respect of juveniles are brought in specially constituted magistrates' courts known as juvenile courts, where the procedure is simpler and less formal than in an adult magistrates' court. Members of the public are not admitted to juvenile courts and the name of the juvenile may not be disclosed in any report of the proceedings. A juvenile under the age of ten may not be found guilty of an offence.

**King's Counsel** in England, a barrister of senior rank; the term is used when a king is on the throne and Queen's Counsel when the monarch is a queen.

**law lords** in England, the ten Lords of Appeal in Ordinary who, together with the Lord Chancellor and other peers, make up the House of Lords in its judicial capacity. The House of Lords is the final court of appeal in both criminal and civil cases. Law lords rank as life peers.

**leasehold** land or property held by a tenant (lessee) for a specified period, (unlike freehold, outright ownership) usually at a rent from the landlord (lessor).

**legacy** a gift of personal property made by a testator in a will and transferred on the testator's

death to the legatee. **Specific legacies** are definite named objects; a **general legacy** is a sum of money or item not specially identified; a **residuary legacy** is all the remainder of the deceased's personal estate after debts have been paid and the other legacies have been distributed.

**legal aid** public assistance with legal costs. In Britain it is given only to those below certain thresholds of income and unable to meet the costs. There are separate provisions for civil and criminal cases. Since 1989 legal aid is administered by the Legal Aid Board.

**libel** defamation published in a permanent form, such as in a newspaper, book, or broadcast.

**licensing laws** laws governing the sale of alcoholic drinks. Most countries have some restrictions on the sale of alcoholic drinks, if not an outright ban, as in the case of Islamic countries.

**lien** the right to retain goods owned by another until the owner has satisfied a claim against him by the person in possession of the goods. For example, the goods may have been provided as security for a debt.

**Lord Advocate** chief law officer of the Crown in Scotland who has ultimate responsibility for criminal prosecutions in Scotland. The Lord Advocate does not usually act in inferior courts where prosecution is carried out by proscurators-fiscal acting under the Lord Advocate's instructions.

**Lord Chancellor** UK state official, originally the royal secretary, today a member of the cabinet, whose office ends with a change of government. The Lord Chancellor acts as speaker of the House of Lords, may preside over the court of appeal, and is head of the judiciary.

**magistrate** in English law, a person who presides in a magistrates' court: either a justice of the

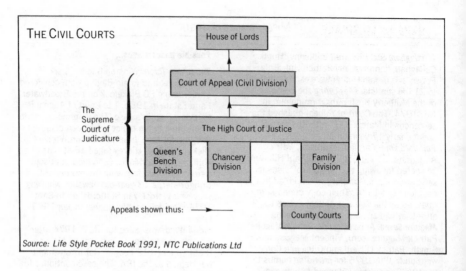

THE CIVIL COURTS

House of Lords

Court of Appeal (Civil Division)

The Supreme Court of Judicature

The High Court of Justice

Queen's Bench Division | Chancery Division | Family Division

Appeals shown thus: ⟶

County Courts

Source: *Life Style Pocket Book 1991, NTC Publications Ltd*

peace (with no legal qualifications, and unpaid) or a stipendiary magistrate. Stipendiary magistrates are paid, qualified lawyers largely used in London and major cities.

**maintenance** payments to support children or a spouse, under the terms of an agreement, or by a court order. In Britain, financial provision orders are made on divorce, but a court action can also be brought for maintenance without divorce proceedings. Applications for maintenance of illegitimate children are now treated in the same way as for legitimate children.

**malpractice** in US law, negligence by a professional person, usually a doctor, that may lead to an action for damages by the client. Such legal actions result in doctors having high insurance costs that are reflected in higher fees charged to their patients.

**manslaughter** the unlawful killing of a human being in circumstances less culpable than murder—for example, when the killer suffers extreme provocation, is in some way mentally ill (diminished responsibility), did not intend to kill but did so accidentally in the course of another crime or by behaving with criminal recklessness, or is the survivor of a genuine suicide pact that involved killing the other person.

**maritime law** that part of the law dealing with the sea: in particular, fishing areas, ships, and navigation. Seas are divided into *internal waters* governed by a state's internal laws (such as harbours, inlets); *territorial waters* (the area of sea adjoining the coast over which a state claims rights); the *continental shelf* (the seabed and subsoil that the coastal state is entitled to exploit beyond the territorial waters); and the *high seas*, where international law applies.

**martial law** the replacement of civilian by military authorities in the maintenance of order.

**minor** the legal term for those under the age of majority, which varies from country to country but is usually between 18 and 21. In the USA

(from 1971 for voting, and in some states for nearly all other purposes) and certain European countries (in Britain since 1970) the age of majority is 18. Most civic and legal rights and duties only accrue at the age of majority; for example, the rights to vote, to make a will, and (usually) to make a fully binding contract, and the duty to act as a juror.

**motoring law** the law affecting the use of vehicles on public roads. It covers the licensing of vehicles and drivers, and the criminal offences that can be committed by the owners and drivers of vehicles.

**murder** unlawful killing of one person by another. In the USA, first-degree murder requires proof of premeditation; second-degree murder falls between first-degree murder and manslaughter.

**negligence** negligence consists in doing some act that a 'prudent and reasonable' person would not do, or omitting to do some act that such a person would do. Negligence may arise in respect of a person's duty towards an individual or towards other people in general. Breach of the duty of care that results in reasonably foreseeable damage is a tort. *Contributory negligence* is a defence sometimes raised where the defendant to an action for negligence claims that the plaintiff by his or her own negligence contributed to the cause of the action.

**neighbourhood watch** local crime-prevention schemes. Under the supervision of police, groups of residents agree to increase watchfulness in order to prevent crimes such as burglary and vandalism in their area.

**oath** a solemn promise to tell the truth or perform some duty, combined with an appeal to a deity or something held sacred.

**obscenity law** law prohibiting the publishing of any material that tends to deprave or corrupt.

**parole** the conditional release of a prisoner from jail. The prisoner remains on licence until the date release would have been granted,

## RAPE IN MARRIAGE

The case of R v R , decided by a five member Court of Appeal in March 1990, ended 250 years of a husband's exemption from prosecution for the rape of his wife.

The authority for saying that husbands cannot rape their wives goes back to the seventeenth century and a statement made by the famous witch-hunting judge, Matthew Hale. In a commentary on the criminal law which has been followed ever since, the Chief Justice said a husband could not be guilty of raping his wife because by virtue of marriage 'the wife hath given up herself in this kind unto her husband which she cannot retract'. However, the Court of Appeal decided that this was not a ruling by which they were bound but merely a legal fiction—a poor basis for the criminal law.

The case concerned a husband and wife who separated in 1989 because the wife complained, among other things, that she was being forced to have sexual intercourse. The wife left the matrimonial home with the couple's young child and went to her parent's home. The husband told his wife that he was going to get a divorce. A month later he broke into the parent's house and coerced her into sex against her will and without her consent—the legal definition of rape.

Unlike previous test cases on the point there was no non-molestation order in force against the husband nor were the couple legally separated. According to Lord Lane, 'a rapist remains a rapist... irrespective of his relationship with his victim'. The court found that the rule that a husband cannot be guilty of raping his wife if he forces her to have sexual intercourse against her will is an anachronistic and offensive common law fiction which does not represent the position of a wife in present-day society.

This conclusion had already been reached by the Scottish Justiciary Appeal Court in 1989. Also the Law Commission in England and Wales provisionally recommended abolition of the rule in a working paper published a few months before the Court of Appeal ruling. Despite this backing not all commentators are happy with the decision.

Before the court's ruling the Criminal Law Revision Committee had advised against making all marital rape a crime as it would 'undermine the institution of marriage'. Other critics object that abolition of the exemption means that the privacy of marriage has been invaded and reconciliation of partners going through marital breakdown will be hindered, especially by a wife having to give evidence against her husband. This is because under a rule of evidence introduced in 1984, a wife is a compellable witness on any charge against her husband involving assault, injury or threat of injury. Although the rule prevents the wife frustrating the prosecution by refusing to give evidence and allegedly helps prevent intimidation, the rule has been criticised by women's groups who object that it takes all control of the case away from the victim and principal witness and hands it over to the prosecution, who are not always sympathetic to the victim's position. At present if a wife refuses to testify she may be found guilty of contempt of court and fined or sent to prison.

According to a nationwide survey published in 1990 of a representative sample of 1,007 married and divorced women in 11 cities in England and Wales and Scotland, one in seven said they had been coerced by their husbands into sex against their will and without their consent. In nearly half the cases the husbands had used or threatened violence. In 84 per cent of cases the couples were still living together. Before the Court of Appeal ruling, except in Scotland, such husbands could be prosecuted for assault if they used violence but not for rape. The study also found that rapes by husbands outnumbered other rapes by two to one.

It was not immediately clear what kind of sentence might be expected by a husband found guilty of raping his wife. The 'starting point' for rape by a stranger is generally put at about five years, with an increase if the offence was aggravated by violence. On the other hand, a previously settled relationship may be allowed as a ground for mitigation. In some rape cases notoriously light sentences have also been given where the sentencing judge has been of the view that the woman prompted the attack by her own behaviour. In R v R the husband, who had pleaded guilty to attempted rape and assault occasioning actual bodily harm, received a sentence of 3 years imprisonment.

and may be recalled if the authorities deem it necessary.

**party** a person who takes part in legal proceedings. Parties to a civil action may include one or more plaintiffs or defendants. In a criminal trial the parties include the Crown (as prosecutor) and one or more defendants.

**patent** or **letters patent** documents conferring the exclusive right to make, use, and sell an invention for a limited period. Ideas are not eligible; neither is anything not new.

In 1987 the US began issuing patents for new animal forms (new types of livestock and assorted organisms) being created by gene splitting. The payment of $909.5 million by Eastman Kodak to Polaroid 1990 was a record sum for infringement of patent.

**perjury** the offence of deliberately making a false statement on oath (or affirmation) when appearing as a witness in legal proceedings, on a point material to the question at issue. In Britain and the USA it is punishable by a fine, imprisonment, or both.

**perverting the course of justice** the criminal offence of acting in such a way as to prevent justice being done. Examples are tampering with evidence, misleading the police or a court, and threatening witnesses or jurors.

**picketing** gathering of workers and their trade-union representatives to try to persuade others to support them in an industrial dispute. Secondary picketing (picketing somewhere other than one's workplace) has been 'outlawed' since enactment of the Employment Act 1980. This allows for employers or other persons picketed to sue pickets who are not at their own workplace, and who are attempting to persuade other workers to break their contracts.

**plaintiff** a person who brings a civil action in a court of law seeking relief (for example, damages).

**poaching** illegal hunting of game and fish on someone elses property.

**power of attorney** legal authority to act on behalf of another, for a specific transaction, or for a particular period.

**precedent** the common law principle that, in deciding a particular case, judges are bound to follow any applicable principles of law laid down by superior courts in earlier reported cases.

**probate** formal proof of a will. In the UK, if its validity is unquestioned, it is proven in 'common form'; the executor, in the absence of other interested parties, obtains at a probate registry a grant upon their own oath. Otherwise, it must be proved in 'solemn form': its validity established at a probate court (in the Chancery Division of the High Court), those concerned being made parties to the action.

**probation** the placing of offenders under supervision of probation officers in the community, as an alternative to prison.

**procurator fiscal** officer of a Scottish sheriff's court who (combining the role of public prosecutor and coroner) inquires into suspicious deaths and carries out the preliminary questioning of witnesses to crime.

**prosecution** the party by whom criminal proceedings are instituted. In the UK, the prosecution is begun by bringing the accused (defendant) before a magistrate, either by warrant or summons, or by arrest without warrant. Most criminal prosecutions are conducted by the Crown Prosecution Service although other government departments may also prosecute some cases, for example the Department of Inland Revenue. An individual may bring a private prosecution, usually for assault.

**provost** chief magistrate of a Scottish burgh, approximate equivalent of an English mayor.

**proxy** a person authorized to stand in another's place; also the document conferring this right. The term usually refers to voting at meetings, but there may be marriages by proxy.

**public inquiry** in English law, a legal investigation where witnesses are called and evidence is produced in a similar fashion to a court of law. Inquiries may be held as part of legal procedure, or into a matter of public concern.

**Queen's Counsel** (QC) in England, a barrister appointed to senior rank by the Lord Chancellor. When the monarch is a king the term is **King's Counsel (KC)**.

**rape** sexual intercourse without the consent of the subject. Most cases of rape are of women by men. A new ruling in 1991 made rape within marriage an offence; in the first prosecution of such a case a London man was found guilty of raping his wife and jailed for five years.

**receiver** a person appointed by a court to collect and manage the assets of an individual, company, or partnership in serious financial difficulties. In the case of bankruptcy, the assets may be sold and distributed by a receiver to creditors.

**redundancy rights** in English law, the rights of employees to a payment (linked to the length of their employment) if they lose their jobs because they are no longer needed. The statutory right was introduced in 1965, but payments are often made in excess of the statutory scheme.

**remand** the committing of an accused but not convicted person into custody or release on bail pending a court hearing.

**reply, right of** right of a member of the public to respond to a media statement. A statutory right of reply, enforceable by a Press Commission, as exists in many Western European countries, failed to reach the statute book in the UK in 1989. There is no legal provision in the UK that any correction should receive the same prominence as the original statement and legal aid is not available in defamation cases, so that only the wealthy are able to sue. However, the major newspapers signed a Code of Practice in 1989 that promised some public protection.

**reprieve** legal temporary suspension of the execution of a sentence of a criminal court. It is usually associated with the death penalty. It is distinct from a pardon (extinguishing the sentence) and commutation (alteration) of a sentence (for example, from death to life imprisonment).

**rule of law** doctrine that no individual, however powerful, is above the law. The principle had a significant influence on attempts to restrain the arbitrary use of power by rulers and on the growth of legally enforceable human rights in many Western countries. It is often used as a justification for separating legislative from judicial power.

**Scots law** the legal system of Scotland. Owing to its separate development, Scotland has a system differing from the rest of the UK, being based on civil law. Its continued separate existence was guaranteed by the Act of Union with England in 1707.

**settlement out of court** a compromise reached between the parties to a legal dispute. Most civil legal actions are settled out of court, reducing legal costs, and avoiding the uncertainty of the outcome of a trial.

**sheriff** in England and Wales, the crown's chief executive officer in a county for ceremonial purposes; in Scotland, the equivalent of the English county-court judge, but also dealing with criminal cases; and in the USA the popularly elected head law-enforcement officer of a county, combining judicial authority with administrative duties.

**show trial** public and well-reported trials of peo-

EEC LEGISLATION FROM START TO FINISH (DIRECTIVES AND REGULATIONS)

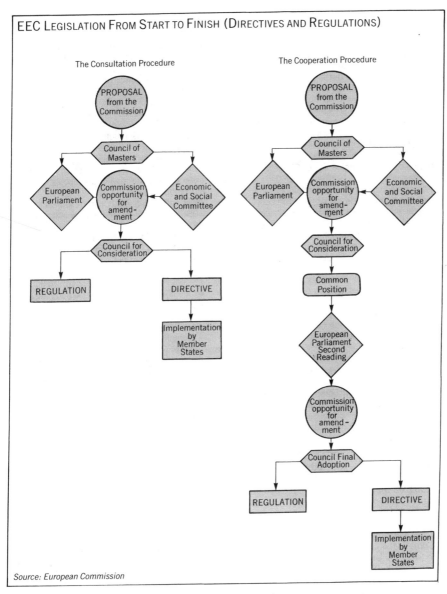

Source: European Commission

ple accused of crimes against the state. In the USSR in the 1930s and 1940s, Stalin carried out show trials against economic saboteurs, Communist Party members, army officers, and even members of the Bolshevik leadership.

**slander** spoken defamatory statement, although if broadcast on radio or television it constitutes libel.

**solicitor** in the UK, a member of one of the two branches of the English legal profession, the other being a barrister. A solicitor is a lawyer who provides all-round legal services (making wills, winding up estates, conveyancing, divorce, and litigation). A solicitor cannot appear at High Court level, but must brief a barrister on behalf of his or her client. Solicitors may become circuit judges and recorders. In the USA the general term is lawyer or attorney.

**subpoena** an order requiring someone who might not otherwise come forward of his or her own volition to give evidence before a court or judicial official at a specific time and place. A witness who fails to comply with a subpoena is in contempt of court.

**summons** a court order officially delivered, requiring someone to appear in court on a certain date.

**tagging, electronic** long-distance monitoring of the movements of people charged with or convicted of a crime, thus enabling them to be

## SOME MAJOR CASES 1990

**Sex discrimination and pensions** Barber v
Guardian Royal Exchange European Court
ruling 1990 that made discrimination on
grounds of sex illegal in the provision of
company pension schemes. This landmark
decision could leave the UK pension industry
facing extra costs of £13 billion a year. Many
company pension schemes followed the state
pension scheme of having a pension age of
65 for men and 60 for women; options are:
raise the pensionable age for women to 65,
have a common pension age of 60, or allow for
flexible retirement from the age of 60.

**Witness to disaster** Hillsborough litigation following a test case brought before the court
in Liverpool in July 1990, individuals who
witness major disasters may be able to recover
damages for psychiatric illness including
post-traumatic stress disorder. Eight of the
claimants had watched the football ground
disaster on tele-
vision, knowing their relatives were present
at the stadium; another watched in a coach
outside as his son died, and a third was sitting
in the stand above the terrace where his two
brothers died. It was the first case where
recovery for nervous shock was extended to
siblings.

Subsequently, the Court of Appeal allowed
the appeal of South Yorkshire police against a
High Court ruling that relatives who watched
the events of the Hillsborough disaster unfold
on television had a legal right to compensation. Recovery for nervous shock was to
remain limited to spouses and parents (or
others in those roles).

**A friend in court?** McKenzie Friend Case (R
v Leicester City Justices ex parte Barrow) at
a time when magistrates' courts throughout
the country were involved in the process of
hundreds of thousands of cases for non-pay-
ment of the poll tax the Divisional Court held
that the 'right' of having a McKenzie friend
(named after this case) to assist in court is
subject to the discretion of the court and
therefore may be forbidden. In this case Mr
and Mrs Barrow were seeking assistance from
a member of a local anti-poll tax group with
experience in this area of the law, as no legal
aid funding was available.

**Dying with dignity** Re J Court of Appeal ruling
1990 that it was not in the interests of a
gravely damaged five-month-old baby (a
ward of court) to put him on a mechanical
ventilator and subject him to all the associated
processes of intensive care, if at some future
time he could not continue breathing unaided.
The baby was therefore to be permitted to die
with dignity from natural causes.

**Right to know** X Ltd v Morgan Grampian Ltd
(Re Goodwin) 1990 case concerning the disclosure of confidential information given to
a journalist which the defendants wanted
in order to identify the source of the leak.
Unlike previous disclosure of source cases, the
leak did not concern any criminal activity or
matter of national security but rather details
of the company's plans for raising additional
working capital. The House of Lords held that
disclosure was necessary in the interests of
justice.

---

detained in their homes rather than in prison.
In the UK, the system was being tested in Nottingham from Aug 1989. The system is in use
in the USA.

**telephone tapping** method of listening in on a
telephone conversation; in the UK and the USA
it is a criminal offence if done without a warrant or the consent of the person concerned.

In 1990 the Home Office carried out an estimated 35,000 telephone taps, and issued 539
warrants.

**tort** a wrongful act for which someone can be
sued for damages in a civil court. It includes
such acts as libel, trespass, injury done to
someone (whether intentionally or by negligence), and inducement to break a contract (although breach of contract itself is not a tort).

In general a tort is distinguished from a
crime in that it affects the interests of an
individual rather than of society at large, but
some crimes can also be torts (for example,
assault).

**treason** act of betrayal, in particular against the
sovereign or the state to which the offender
owes allegiance. Treason is punishable in Britain by death.

**treasure trove** in England, any gold or silver, plate

or bullion found concealed in a house or the
ground, the owner being unknown. Normally,
treasure originally hidden, and not abandoned,
belongs to the crown, but if the treasure was
casually lost or intentionally abandoned, the
first finder is entitled to it against all but the
true owner. Objects buried with no intention
of recovering them, for example in a burial
mound, do not rank as treasure trove, and
belong to the owner of the ground.

**trespass** going on to the land of another without
authority. A landowner has the right to eject a
trespasser by the use of reasonable force and
can sue for any damage caused. A trespasser
who refuses to leave when requested may,
in certain circumstances, be committing a
criminal offence under the Public Order Act
1986 (designed to combat convoys of caravans
trespassing on farm land).

**trial** the determination of an accused person's
innocence or guilt by means of the judicial
examination of the issues of the case in accordance with the law of the land. The two parties
in a trial, the defendant and plaintiff, or their
counsel, put forward their cases and question
the witnesses; on the basis of this evidence the
jury or other tribunal body will decide on the

innocence or guilt of the defendant.

**tribunal** strictly, a court of justice, but used in English law for a body appointed by the government to arbitrate in disputes, or investigate certain matters. Tribunals usually consist of a lawyer as chair, sitting with two lay assessors.

**trust** arrangement whereby a person or group of people holds property for the benefit of others entitled to the beneficial interest.

**verdict** a jury's decision, usually a finding of 'guilty' or 'not guilty'.

**ward of court** in the UK, a child whose guardian is the High Court. Any person may, by issuing proceedings, make the High Court guardian of any child within its jurisdiction. No important step in the child's life can then be taken without the court's leave.

**will** declaration of how a person wishes his or her property to be disposed of after death. It also appoints administrators of the estate (executors) and may contain wishes on other matters, such as place of burial or use of organs for transplant. Wills must comply with formal legal requirements.

**witness** a person who was present at some event (such as an accident, a crime, or the signing of a document) or has relevant special knowledge (such as a medical expert) and can be called on to give evidence in a court of law.

**writ** a document issued by a court requiring performance of certain actions.

# LEGAL AND PENAL INSTITUTIONS

**Bar** to be called to the Bar is to become a barrister. Prospective barristers must complete a course of study in law and be admitted to one of the four Inns of Court before they can be 'called'. The General Council of the Bar and of the Inns of Court (known as the Bar Council) is the professional governing body of the Bar.

**borstal institutions** in the UK, formerly places of detention for offenders aged 15–21. The name was taken from Borstal prison near Rochester, Kent, where the system was first introduced in 1908. From 1983 they were officially known as youth custody centres, and have now been replaced by **young offender institutions**.

**Citizens Advice Bureau** (CAB) UK organization established 1939 to provide information and advice to the public on any subject, such as personal problems, financial, house purchase, or consumer rights. If required, the bureau will act on behalf of citizens, drawing on its own sources of legal and other experts. There are more than 600 bureaux located all over the UK.

**Court of Appeal** UK court comprising two divisions: a Civil Division and a Criminal Division set up under the Criminal Appeals Act 1968. The Court of Appeal consists of 16 Lord Justices of Appeal and a number of ex-officio judges, for example, the Lord Chancellor, the Master of the Rolls, and the President of the Family Division. Usually, three judges sit, but where a case raises new or important issues, up to seven judges may form the court. The Criminal Division of the Court of Appeal has the power to revise sentences or quash a conviction on the grounds that in all the circumstances of the case the verdict is unsafe or unsatisfactory, or that the judgement of the original trial judge was wrong in law, or that there was a material irregularity during the course of the trial.

The Court of Appeal in 1991 had a backlog of appeals by people charged and prosecuted by the West Midlands Serious Crime Squad, which was disbanded due to corruption.

**Court of Protection** in English law, a department of the High Court that deals with the estates of people who are incapable, by reason of mental disorder, of managing their own property and affairs.

**Criminal Injuries Compensation Board** UK board established 1964 to administer financial compensation by the state for victims of crimes of violence. Victims can claim compensation for their injuries, but not for damage to property. The compensation awarded is similar to the amount that would be obtained by a court in damages for personal injury.

**Criminal Investigation Department** (CID) detective branch of the London Metropolitan Police, established 1878 and comprising a force of about 4,000 men and women, recruited entirely from the uniformed police and controlled by an assistant commissioner. Such branches are now also found in the regional police forces.

**Crown Prosecution Service** body established by the Prosecution of Offences Act 1985, responsible for prosecuting all criminal offences in England and Wales. It is headed by the Director of Public Prosecutions (DPP), and brings England and Wales in line with Scotland (which has a procurator fiscal) in having a prosecution service independent of the police.

**European Court of Human Rights** court that hears cases referred from the European Commission of Human Rights, if the commission has failed to negotiate a friendly settlement in a case where individuals' rights have been violated by a member state. The court comprises one judge for every state that is a party to the 1950 convention. Court rulings have forced the Republic of Ireland to drop its constitutional ban on homosexuality, and Germany to cease to exclude political left-and right-wingers from the civil service.

**European Court of Justice** the court of the European Community (EC), which is responsible for interpreting Community law and ruling on breaches by member states and others of such law. It sits in Luxembourg with judges from the member states.

**Inns of Court** four private societies in London, England: Lincoln's Inn, Gray's Inn, Inner Temple, and Middle Temple. All barristers must belong to one of the Inns of Court. The

# PRISON RIOTS AND REFORM

On 1 April 1990 a riot broke out at Strangeways prison, Manchester, one of Europe's largest prisons. The disturbance in which inmates took over the prison, lasted for 25 days. The seige prompted unrest in prisons throughout England and Wales, and 'copycat' riots at Bristol, Cardiff, Dartmoor, Pucklechurch near Bristol, and Glen Parva near Leicester.

The violence at Strangeways caused damage estimated at £20 million and led to the injury of 147 prison officers and 47 prisoners. Throughout the siege prisoners sat on the roof and shouted their demands to the spectators, throwing tiles and other missiles at prison personnel.

Following the disturbances a Court of Appeal Judge, Lord Justice Woolf, was appointed to conduct an enquiry and make recommendations for the overall reform of the prison system. The 600 page document, published in Feb 1991, was widely acclaimed as one of the most significant reports on the Prison Service ever published. Poor conditions and overcrowding in the prisons are cited as being a principle cause which led to the riots. On the day that the riot broke out at Strangeways, the jail which was meant to have a maximum population of 970 inmates was holding 1647 and the conditions inside were described by the judge as being 'insanitary and degrading'. The report underlined the failure of successive governments to fund and manage the prison service adequately.

Prisoners giving evidence also blamed chronic overcrowding and insanitary conditions, complained of long hours of idleness locked in cramped cells, inadequate family visits and censored mail, and lack of independent redress for grievances. Prison officers blamed staff shortages, poor training and lack of leadership. Governors claimed there was a lack of support and assistance from prison department headquarters. The Home Office was criticized for vetoing the plan by Mr Brendan O'Friel, the governor of Strangeways, to storm the jail within 45 hours of the riot's outbreak.

The major recommendations of the Woolf Report are:

—closer cooperation between different parts of the criminal justice system, with judges urged to visit prisons in their area before committing people there;

—creation of a network of community jails, each with a unit of 50–70 prisoners separated from similar units in the same prison;

—separate conditions for remand prisoners and a set maximum period in which prisoners can be held in police cells;

—abolition of the disciplinary powers of the Board of Visitors;

—greater delegation of responsibility to governors and the director-general of the prison service in order to provide more visible leadership;

— better opportunities to maintain family links through more visits and home leave, with prisoners being held in community jails as near to home as possible;

*Inmates on the roof of Manchester's Strangeways prison, April 1990.*

— a clear date to be set for the abolition of slopping out;

— creation of more hostels in the community for mentally ill offenders for whom survival in prison is 'especially difficult'.

— 'contracts' for each prisoner, setting out 'prisoner's expectations and responsibilities'.

On the day of the report's publication Kenneth Baker, the Home Secretary, announced that slopping out in prisons would be abolished by 1994. He also announced that phones for inmates' use would be installed in all prisons, routine censorship ended, and home leave from open prisons doubled. Prisoners would be allowed more visits and families on a low income would be given financial help to visit relatives. A White Paper was promised by July 1991 which would be a 'blueprint' for the prison service in the 21st century.

After the re-opening of Strangeways, prison officers there have lobbied against the policy of 'no cell sharing' advocated by the report. Five former Strangeways prisoners have been charged with the murder of a fellow inmate and others have been charged with offences arising out of the disturbances, including riot and causing grievous bodily harm to prison officers. One prison officer died as an indirect result of the violence.

Meanwhile, the government remained committed to opening 12 new prisons over the next two years as well as refurbishing older prisons, many of which date back to Victorian times. Further reforms were promised by the 1991 Criminal Justice Bill which provided for the contracting out of new remand prisons although not for the privatization of existing prisons.

NUMBER OF PRISONERS HELD—COUNCIL OF EUROPE COUNTRIES (1988)

| Prisoners | Population (000s) | Women (%) | Minors (%) | Foreigners (%) | | |
|---|---|---|---|---|---|---|
| Austria | 5,862 | 7,613 | 4.0 | Age 18: | 1.6 | 10.9 |
| Belgium | 6,450 | 9,862 | 5.3 | | 0.5 | 31.1 |
| Cyprus | 219 | 577 | 5.0 | Age 21: | 18.3 | 38.4 |
| Denmark | 3,469 | 5,101 | — | | — | — |
| Finland | 3,598 | 4,929 | 3.2 | Age 21: | 5.9 | 0.3 |
| France | 46,423 | 57,242 | 4.5 | Age 21: | 12.2 | 25.8 |
| Fed. Rep. of Germany | 52,076 | 61,338 | 4.1 | — | 14.5 | |
| Greece | 4,288 | 9,745 | 4.4 | Age 21: | 6.0 | 22.9 |
| Iceland | 89 | 250 | 3.4 | Age 22: | 12.4 | 1.1 |
| Ireland | 1,953 | 3,551 | 2.6 | Age 21: | 29.3 | 0.9 |
| Italy | 34,675 | 57,409 | 5.0 | Age 18: | 1.4 | 8.9 |
| Luxembourg | 322 | 372 | 5.0 | Age 21: | 5.3 | 41.3 |
| Malta | 221 | 330 | 0.5 | Age 18: | 2.7 | 20.4 |
| Netherlands | 5,827 | 14,567 | 3.6 | Age 23: | 15.3 | 21.2 |
| Norway | 2.041 | 4,217 | — | Age 21: | 6.5 | 11.0 |
| Portugal | 8,181 | 9,857 | 6.5 | Age 21: | 9.6 | 8.8 |
| Spain | 29,244 | 38,712 | 6.8 | Age 21: | 7.7 | 15.1 |
| Sweden | 4,716 | 8,421 | 4.6 | Age 21: | 3.5 | 22.3 |
| Switzerland | 4,679 | 6,401 | 5.6 | Age 18: | 3.8 | 36.0 |
| Turkey | 51,810 | 54,195 | 2.8 | Age 18: | 1.4 | 0.5 |
| UK | 55,457 | 56,919 | 3.4 | Age 18: | 23.7 | 1.3 |
| England and Wales | 48,595 | 50,243 | 3.5 | Age 21: | 23.8 | 1.4 |
| Scotland | 5,076 | 5,112 | 3.4 | Age 21: | 23.2 | 0.2 |
| N Ireland | 1,786 | 1,564 | 1.5 | Age 21: | 23.0 | 1.6 |
| TOTAL | 321,700 | 411,588 | | | | |

Source: Prison Information Bulletin 1/90 Council of Europe

main function of each Inn is the education, government, and protection of its members. Each is under the administration of a body of Benchers (judges and senior barristers).

**International Court of Justice** the main judicial organ of the United Nations, at The Hague, the Netherlands.

**Interpol** (acronym for **Inter**national Criminal **Po**lice Organization) agency founded following the Second International Judicial Police Conference 1923 with its headquarters in Vienna, and reconstituted after World War II with its headquarters in Paris. It has an international criminal register, fingerprint file, and methods index.

**Land Registry, HM** official body set up 1925 to register legal rights to land in England and Wales. There has been a gradual introduction, since 1925, of compulsory registration of land in different areas of the country. This requires the purchaser of land to register details of his or her title and all other rights (such as mortgages and easements) relating to the land. Once registered, the title to the land is guaranteed by the Land Registry, subject to those interests that cannot be registered; this makes the buying and selling of land easier and cheaper. The records are open to public inspection (since Dec 1990).

**Law Commission** in Britain, either of two statutory bodies established 1965 (one for England and Wales and one for Scotland) which consider proposals for law reform and publish their findings. They also keep British law under constant review, systematically developing and reforming it by, for example, the repeal of obsolete and unnecessary enactments.

**law courts** the bodies that adjudicate in legal disputes. Civil and criminal cases are usually dealt with by separate courts. In many countries there is a hierarchy of courts that provide an appeal system.

In England and Wales the court system was reorganized under the Courts Act 1971. The higher courts are: the **House of Lords** (the highest court for the whole of Britain), which deals with both civil and criminal appeals; the **Court of Appeal**, which is divided between criminal and civil appeal courts; the **High Court of Justice** dealing with important civil cases; **crown courts**, which handle criminal cases; and **county courts**, which deal with civil matters. **Magistrates' courts** deal with minor criminal cases and are served by justices of the peace or stipendiary (paid) magistrates; and **juvenile courts** are presided over by specially qualified justices. There are also special courts, such as the Restrictive Practices Court and the Employment Appeal Tribunal.

The courts are organized in six circuits. The towns of each circuit are first-tier (High Court and circuit judges dealing with both criminal and civil cases), second-tier (High Court and circuit judges dealing with criminal cases only), or third-tier (circuit judges dealing with criminal cases only). Cases are allotted according to gravity among High Court and circuit judges and recorders (part-time judges with the same jurisdiction as circuit judges). From 1971, solicitors were allowed for the first time to appear in

# THE BRITISH JUDICIAL SYSTEM

The judicial system in Britain for years enjoyed wide respect throughout the world and became a model for many countries as they achieved full independence from colonial rule. The independence and impartiality of judges, the reliability of the jury system, the integrity of the police forces: all were instanced as examples for less fortunate countries to envy. In the past 20 years or so however, some of this pride in judicial institutions has evaporated as, in a series of miscarriages of justice, their weaknesses have been exposed.

It surely can be no coincidence that this diminution in respect for the machinery of law and order has occurred at a time when terrorist activity, particularly emanating from the divided community of Ireland has increased. The exoneration of the Guildford Four, sentenced in 1975 for bomb attacks, and the Birmingham Six, sentenced in the same year for similar offences, highlighted the deficiencies in the system, but other questionable convictions, such as those of the Maguire Seven and the Tottenham Three, underlined them.

With the release of the Birmingham Six, in March 1991, the home secretary, Kenneth Baker, announced the setting-up of a royal commission, chaired by an eminent academic sociologist and businessman, Lord Runciman of Doxford, to carry out a 'wide ranging review' of the system of criminal justice, including the question of appeals. He told the House of Commons that the commission would examine every aspect of the criminal system from the time a suspect was arrested to arrangements for dealing with alleged miscarriages of justice once normal appeal rights had been exhausted.

The commission would be expected to report within two years.

The appointment of the first royal commission for 12 years indicates the gravity of the problem. It is a marked departure from the approach established by Margaret Thatcher when prime minister. She eschewed commissions and committees of inquiry, believing that they only muddied the waters and fudged the issues. It should be remembered, however, that the setting up of a commission has, historically, been a useful way for a government to convey the impression of prompt action while not having to do anything immediately. Harold Wilson once said that he did not want a commission which would 'take minutes and waste years'. Given the breadth of its range, the commission will, undoubtedly, examine the role of the police but some would argue that this role is sufficiently crucial to justify a completely separate, independent study. In recent years inquiries into police activity have usually consisted of officers from one force looking at another. The last time an independent inquiry was made was nearly 30 years ago, by the Willink royal commission, which reported in 1962. It came to very bland and establishment-orientated conclusions which resulted in little fundamental change. A sharper, more penetrating review might do something to restore public confidence.

Whether or not the Runciman commission enables the British judicial system to regain its lost respect depends on how it goes about its task and on the response of the government in power when it reports. The appointment of a chairman of the calibre of Lord Runciman augurs well but it would be unwise to try to predict its outcome at this early stage.

*The Birmingham Six after their court acquittal Mar 1991.*

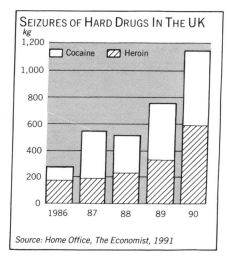

SEIZURES OF HARD DRUGS IN THE UK

kg

- ☐ Cocaine  ▨ Heroin

Source: Home Office, The Economist, 1991

and conduct cases at the level of the crown courts, and solicitors as well as barristers of ten years' standing became eligible for appointment as recorders, who after five years become eligible as circuit judges. In 1989 a Green Paper proposed (1) omitting the Bar's monopoly of higher courts, removing demarcation between barristers and solicitors; (2) cases to be taken on a 'no-win, no-fee' basis (as already happens in Scotland). In the UK 1989 there were 5,500 barristers and 47,000 solicitors.

In Scotland, the supreme civil court is the **Court of Session**, with appeal to the House of Lords; the highest criminal court is the **High Court of Justiciary**, with no appeal to the House of Lords.

**magistrates' court** in England and Wales, a local law court that mainly deals with minor criminal cases, but also decides, in committal proceedings, whether more serious criminal cases should be referred to the crown court. It deals with some civil matters, too, such as licensing certain domestic and matrimonial proceedings, and may include a juvenile court. A magistrates' court consists of between two and seven lay justices of the peace (who are advised on the law by a clerk to the justices), or a single paid lawyer called a stipendiary magistrate.

**Old Bailey** popular name for the Central Criminal Court in London, situated in a street of that name in the City of London, off Ludgate Hill.

**Police Complaints Authority** in the UK, an independent group of a dozen people set up under the Police and Criminal Evidence Act 1984 to supervise the investigation of serious complaints against the police by members of the public.

**prison** place of confinement for those convicted of contravening the laws of the state; most countries claim to aim at rehabilitation. The average number of people in prison in the UK (1990) was 45,500; 1,775 were women

(less than 4%). About 9,400 were on remand (awaiting trial or sentence), and, due to overcrowding in prisons, over 1,000 prisoners were held in police cells. It costs 30 times more per year to keep a prisoner in custody than it would for 100 hours' community service.

Experiments have been made in Britain and elsewhere in 'open prisons' without bars, which included releasing prisoners in the final stages of their sentence to work in ordinary jobs outside the prison, and the provision of aftercare on release. Attempts to deal with the increasing number of young offenders include, from 1982, accommodation in community homes in the case of minor offences, with (in more serious cases) 'short, sharp shock' treatment in detention centres (although the latter was subsequently found to have little effect on reconviction rates).

In 1990 there was widespread rioting in several prisons in Britain, notably the 25-day siege at Strangeways Prison in Manchester; this was the longest ever prison seige in the UK, during which several prisoners died and extensive damage was caused.

**Writers to the Signet** society of Scottish solicitors. Their predecessors were originally clerks in the secretary of state's office entrusted with the preparation of documents requiring the signet, or seal. Scottish solicitors may be members of other societies, such as the Royal Faculty of Procurators in Glasgow.

**Young Offender Institution** in England, institution of detention for young offenders, both juveniles (aged under 17) and young adults (17–21). The period of detention depends both on the seriousness of the offence and on the age and sex of the offender. A number of statutory requirements support the principle that a custodial sentence in a young offender institution should only be used as a last resort for young offenders. The institution was introduced by the Criminal Justice Act 1988.

### Trust in system

*Do you believe or do you not believe that there are cases where people are sent to prison for crimes they didn't commit? If believe: Does this happen a lot or just now and again?*

| | |
|---|---|
| Happens a lot | 13 |
| Just now and again | 65 |
| Don't know how often | 11 |
| Don't believe it happens | 7 |
| Don't know | 4 |

*In general, how satisfied or dissatisfied are you with the way the police in Britain do their job?*

| | |
|---|---|
| Very satisfied | 26 |
| Quite satisfied | 48 |
| Neither satisfied nor dissatisfied | 14 |
| Not very satisfied | 9 |
| Not at all satisfied | 3 |
| Don't know | 0 |

## Police

*Do you think the police should or should not have the power to do the following things?*

| | Should | Should not | Don't know |
|---|---|---|---|
| *Fingerprint everyone in an area where a serious crime has been committed?* | 65 | 31 | 4 |
| *Question suspects before they have been allowed to consult a lawyer?* | 34 | 59 | 7 |
| *Stop and search anyone they think is suspicious?* | 55 | 40 | 4 |
| *Detain suspects for more than 24 hours without charging them?* | 29 | 63 | 9 |
| *Have access to files containing information on citizens who don't have a criminal record?* | 15 | 81 | 4 |
| Use plastic bullets, water canon and teargas to disperse potentially violent demonstrators? | 61 | 33 | 6 |
| *Tap telephones and record private conversations?* | 15 | 78 | 7 |
| *Carry firearms at all times, as in America and some continental countries?* | 22 | 72 | 6 |

*Do you think the police should or should not have the power to do the following things?*

| | Should | Should not | Don't know |
|---|---|---|---|
| *Fingerprint everyone in an area where a serious crime has been committed?* | 65 | 31 | 4 |
| *Question suspects before they have been allowed to consult a lawyer?* | 34 | 59 | 7 |
| *Stop and search anyone they think is suspicious?* | 55 | 40 | 4 |
| *Detain suspects for more than 24 hours without charging them?* | 29 | 63 | 9 |
| *Have access to files containing information on citizens who don't have a criminal record?* | 15 | 81 | 4 |

# PEOPLES AND LANGUAGES

**Abkhazi** a member of a Muslim minority in Georgia, USSR. Abkhazia was a Georgian kingdom from the 4th century, and converted from Christianity to Islam in the 17th century. By the 1980s some 17% of the population were Muslims and two-thirds were of Georgian origin.

**Afrikaans language** an official language (with English) of the Republic of South Africa and Namibia. Spoken mainly by the Afrikaners—descendants of Dutch and other 17th-century colonists—it is a variety of the Dutch language, modified by circumstance and the influence of German, French, and other immigrant as well as local languages. It became a standardized written language about 1875.

**Ainu** aboriginal people of Japan, driven north in the 4th century AD by ancestors of the Japanese. They now number about 25,000, inhabiting Japanese and Soviet territory on Sakhalin, Hokkaido, and the Kuril Islands. Their language has no written form, and is unrelated to any other.

**Algonquin** North American Indians formerly living around the Ottawa River in E Canada. Many now live on reserves in E Ontario, W Québec, and the NE of the USA; others have chosen to live among the general populations of Canada and the USA. A large number of Algonquian languages are spoken by many other native peoples from the Atlantic coast across to the Pacific. They include Cree, Blackfoot, and Cheyenne.

**Amhara** member of an ethnic group forming approximately 25% of the population of Ethiopia; 13,000,000 (1987). The Amhara are traditionally farmers. They speak Amharic, a language of the Semitic branch of the Afro-Asiatic family. Most are members of the Ethiopian Christian Church.

**Annamese** a member of the majority ethnic group in Vietnam, comprising 90% of the population. The Annamese language is distinct from Vietnamese, though it has been influenced by Chinese and has loan words from Khmer. Their religion combines elements of Buddhism, Confucianism, and Taoism, as well as ancestor worship.

**Arab** any of a Semitic people native to the Arabian peninsula, but now settled throughout North Africa and the nations of the Middle East. Arabic is the major Semitic language of the Hamito-Semitic family of W Asia and North Africa, originating among the Arabs of the Arabian peninsula. It is spoken today by about 120 million people in the Middle East and N Africa. Arabic script is written from right to left.

**Armenian** member of the largest ethnic group inhabiting the Soviet republic of Armenia. There are Armenian minorities in the Soviet republic of Azerbaijan, as well as in Turkey and Iran. Christianity was introduced to the ancient Armenian kingdom in the 3rd century. There are 4–5 million speakers of Armenian, which belongs to the Indo-European family of languages.

**Asante** or **Ashanti** person of Asante culture from central Ghana, west of Lake Volta. The Asante language belongs to the Kwa branch of the Niger-Congo family.

**Australian Aborigine** any of the 500 groups of indigenous inhabitants of the continent of Australia, who migrated to this region from S Asia about 40,000 years ago. They were hunters and gatherers, living throughout the continent in small kin-based groups before European settlement. Several hundred different languages developed, the most important being Aranda (Arunta), spoken in central Australia, and Murngin, spoken in Arnhem Land. In recent years there has been a movement for the recognition of Aborigine rights and campaigning against racial discrimination in housing, education, wages, and medical facilities.

**Aymara** member of an American Indian people of Bolivia and Peru, builders of a great culture, who were conquered first by the Incas and then by the Spaniards. Today 1.4 million Aymara farm and herd llamas and alpacas in the highlands; their language, belonging to the Andean-Equatorial language family, survives and their Roman Catholicism incorporates elements of their old beliefs.

**Azerbaijani** or **Azeri** a native of the Azerbaijan region of Iran (population 5,500,000) or the Azerbaijan Soviet republic (population 6,000,000). Azerbaijani is a Turkic language belonging to the Altaic family. 70% of Azerbaijanis are Shi'ite Muslims, 30% are Sunni Muslims.

**Bashkir** a member of the majority ethnic group of the Bashkir Autonomous Soviet Socialist Republic. The Bashkir language belongs to the Turkic branch of the Altaic family, and has about 1,000,000 speakers. The Bashkirs have been Muslims since the 13th century.

**Basque** member of a people who occupy the autonomous Basque region (created 1980) of NE Spain and the adjoining French *département* of Pyrénées-Atlantiques. The Basques are a non-Indo-European people who largely maintained their independence until the 19th century. The Basque language (**Euskara**) is spoken by about 500,000 people around the Bay of Biscay ('the Basque Bay'). It is unrelated to any other language.

**Bengali** person of Bengali culture from Bangladesh and India (W Bengal, Tripura). There are 80–150 million speakers of Bengali, an Indo-Iranian language belonging to the Indo-European family. It is also used by emigrant Bengali and Bangladeshi communities in such countries as the UK and the USA. Bengalis in Bangladesh are predominantly Muslim, whereas those in India are mainly Hindu.

**Bhil** a member of a semi-nomadic people of Dravidian origin, living in NW India

## TRIBAL GROUPS UNDER THREAT

| Country | Tribe | Population | Habitat threat |
|---|---|---|---|
| *ARCTIC* | | | |
| Alaska | Inuit | | |
| Siberia | Eveni | | Industrialization and pollution |
| *AUSTRALASIA* | | | |
| Papua New Guinea | | | |
| *AUSTRALIA* | | | |
| Northern Territory | Oenpelli; Pitjantjatjara; | | |
| | Yakunjatjara; Yirrkala | | Social disintegration |
| Queensland | Arukun; Mapoon and Weipa | | |
| South | Kokatha | | |
| Western | Fringed dwellers; Warmun; | | Social disintegration |
| | Yangngora | | |
| | *Aboriginal population* | 200,000–300,000 | |
| *LATIN AMERICA* | | | |
| Brazil | Apinaye; Atroari | | Demarcation and settlement |
| Vaupes region | | 15,000 | Land security |
| | Barasana | 300 | |
| | Kaingang | | Demarcation and settlement |
| | Kreen Akrore | | |
| | Nambiquara | | |
| | Panare | | |
| Carajas | Parakana | 227 | |
| | Pataxo Ha-Ha-Hai | | Cattle ranching |
| | Satere-Maue | | Oil exploration |
| | Txukarramae | | Demarcation and settlement |
| | Uru-eu-wau-wau | | |
| | Waimiri-Atroari | | Hydro and mining |
| | Yanomani | 21,000 *(1985)* | Mining, etc. |
| | Xavante | | |
| | Xikrin | | |
| *Total number of tribes: 300* | | 120,000 | |
| Chile | Mapuche | 1,000,000 | Government repression |
| Columbia | Barasana | | |
| | Cuiva | | |
| | Maku | | |
| | Sikuani | | Cattle ranching |
| Ecuador | Shuar | | |
| | Waorani | | Oil exploration and missionaries |
| Panama | Guaymi | 80,000 | Land ownership disputes |
| Paraguay | Ache | | |
| | Ayoreo | | Missionary zeal |
| Peru | Amuesha | | Road building and colonization |
| Venezuela | Piaroa | | Cattle ranching |
| *MALAYSIA* (Sarawak) | Penan | | Deforestation |
| *AFRICA* | | | |
| Botswana | Kalahari Bushmen | | |
| Central Africa | Pygmy tribes | 150,000–200,000 | |
| Nigeria | Fulani | | Land erosion |
| Zaire | Efe | | Deforestation |
| *ASIA* | | | |
| Indonesia | | | |
| Tibet | Nomadic tribes | | |
| *USA* | American Indians | | Social destabilization |
| *World population of tribal peoples* | | 200 million | |

*Source: The Times Guide to the Environment 1990*

and numbering about 4,000,000. They are hunter-gatherers and also practise shifting cultivation. The Bhili language belongs to the Indo-European family, as does Gujarati, which is also spoken by the Bhil. Their religion is Hinduism.

**Bihari** a member of a N Indian people, also living in Bangladesh, Nepál, and Pakistan, and numbering over 40,000,000. The Bihari are mainly Muslim. The Bihari language is related to Hindi and has several widely varying dialects. It belongs to the Indic branch of the Indo-European family. Many Bihari were massacred during the formation of Bangladesh, which they opposed.

**Burman** member of the largest ethnic group in Myanmar (formerly Burma). The Burmans, speakers of a Sino-Tibetan language, migrated from the hills of Tibet, settling in the areas around Mandalay by the 11th century AD.

**Bushman** former name for the Kung, an aboriginal people of southern Africa.

**Byelorussian** or **Belorussian** 'White Russian' a native of the Byelorussian Soviet Socialist Republic. Byelorussian, a Balto-Slavic language belonging to the Indo-European family, is spoken by about 10 million people, including some in Poland. It is written in the Cyrillic script. Byelorussian literature dates back to the 11th century AD. Byelorussians are famed for their church architecture.

**Celtic languages** branch of the Indo-European family, divided into two groups: the **Brythonic** or **P-Celtic** (Welsh, Cornish, Breton, and Gaulish) and the **Goidelic** or **Q-Celtic** (Irish, Scottish, and Manx Gaelic). Celtic languages once stretched from the Black Sea to Britain, but have been in decline for centuries, limited to the so-called 'Celtic Fringe' of western Europe.

**Chinese** native to or an inhabitant of China and Taiwan, or a person of Chinese descent. The Chinese make up more than 25% of the world's population, and the Chinese language (Mandarin) is the largest member of the Sino-Tibetan family.

**Chuang** a member of the largest minority group in China, numbering about 15 million. They live in southern China; they build houses on stilts and cultivate rice fields. Their religion includes elements of ancestor worship. The Chuang language belongs to the Tai family.

**Chuvash** a member of the majority ethnic group inhabiting the Chuvash Autonomous Soviet Socialist Republic. The Chuvash have lived in the middle Volga region since the 8th century. The Chuvash language belongs to the Altaic family, though whether it is a member of the Turkic branch or constitutes a branch on its own is not certain.

**Copt** descendant of those ancient Egyptians who adopted Christianity in the 1st century and refused to convert to Islam after the Arab conquest. They now form a small minority (about 5%) of Egypt's population. Coptic is a member of the Hamito-Semitic language family. It is descended from the language of the ancient Egyptians and is the ritual language of the Coptic Christian Church. It is written in the Greek alphabet with some additional characters derived from demotic script.

**creole language** any pidgin language that has ceased to be simply a trade jargon in ports and markets and has become the mother tongue of a particular community. Many creoles have developed into distinct languages with literatures of their own; for example, Jamaican Creole, Haitian Creole, Krio in Sierra Leone, and Tok Pisin, now the official language of Papua New Guinea.

**Dariganga** a Mongolian people numbering only 30,000. Their language is a dialect of Khalka, the official language of Mongolia. In the past, the Dariganga were nomads, and lived by breeding camels for use in the Chinese imperial army. With the rise of the Communist regime in China, they supported the new Mongolian state, and have become sedentary livestock farmers.

**Dinka** a Nilotic minority group in S Sudan. The Dinka, numbering 1–2 million, are primarily cattle herders and inhabit the lands around the river system that flows into the White Nile. Their language belongs to the Nilo-Saharan family. The Dinka's animist beliefs conflict with those of Islam, the official state religion; this has caused clashes between the Dinka and the Sudanese army.

**Dogon** member of the W African Dogon culture from E Mali and NW Burkina Faso. The Dogon number approximately 250,000 and their language belongs to the Voltaic (Gur) branch of the Niger-Congo family.

**Dongxiang** a minority ethnic group living in NW China. The Dongxiang farm in oases in the desert region of Gansu. They are Muslims, in spite of pressure from the state. Their language belongs to the Altaic family.

**Estonian** a member of the largest ethnic group in the Estonian Soviet Socialist Republic. There are 1 million speakers of Estonian, a member of the Finno-Ugric branch of the Uralic family. Most live in Estonia.

**Ewe** a member of a group of people inhabiting Ghana and Togo, and numbering about 25,000,000. The Ewe live by fishing and farming, and practise an animist religion. Their language belongs to the Kwa branch of the Niger-Congo family.

**Fang** a W African people living in the rainforests of Cameroon, Equatorial Guinea, and NW Gabon, numbering about 25,000,000. They live by farming, as well as by hunting and fishing. In the colonial period the Fang were involved in trading, and used coins made of copper and iron. The Fang language belongs to the Bantu branch of the Niger-Congo family.

**Farsi** or **Persian** a language belonging to the Indo-Iranian branch of the Indo-European family, and the official language of Iran (formerly Persia). It is also spoken in Afghanistan, Iraq, and the Tadzhik Soviet Socialist Republic.

**Finno-Ugric** group or family of more than 20

## FEMALE CIRCUMCISION—BARBARISM OR CULTURAL IDENTITY?

In 1980 the Minority Rights Group published a report entitled *Female Circumcision, Excision and Infibulation.* According to the report 74 million women in more than 20 countries had experienced some form of female circumcision. More recent studies have suggested that this custom may be growing and the World Health Organization has estimated that over 80 million women may be affected. Female circumcision is practised across Muslim Africa between Senegal and Somalia, as well as in the United Arab Emirates, Oman, and South Yemen, and among some Muslims in Indonesia and Malaysia. This practice was known in Victorian Britain where women sometimes had the clitoris excised for alleged health reasons. The custom continues among some immigrant communities in western Europe, though it was made illegal in Britain in 1986.

The term 'female circumcision' refers to an operation on women analagous to male circumcision. In the case of boys, however, the penis is left intact whereas in girls the clitoris is often removed. Not only does this deny the girl sexual pleasure in the future, but it may cause great emotional distress and lead to medical problems.

There are three types of female circumcision: *Sunna*, which involves cutting off the hood, and sometimes the tip, of the clitoris; *clitoridectomy*, the excision of the clitoris and removal of parts of the inner and outer labia; *infibulation* (most commonly known in Sudan and Somalia), in which the labia are stitched, after excision of the clitoris, leaving a small hole. Infibulation can cause problems later in life, especially during menstruation and childbirth. An infibulated woman will sometimes be cut open on the night before her marriage, making sexual intercourse very painful. The woman may have to be cut open during childbirth to allow the baby to emerge and in some regions the mother is reinfibulated afterwards.

Female circumcision is usually carried out in the village by an old woman or traditional midwife, and in the majority of cases antiseptics and anaesthetics are not used. Girls of seven or eight are usually circumcised, though the ages can vary from a few days old to puberty. The use of unsterilized implements can give rise to infections and there is a risk that the girl may bleed to death immediately after the operation, particularly if it has been conducted carelessly. Urine and blood retention may be a problem in infibulated girls. In an attempt to combat these problems some countries have made the operation available in hospitals in urban areas.

The communities who practise female circumcision are often unwilling to give up a custom they consider to be important. Uncircumcised women are deemed to be unclean or oversexed and therefore unmarriageable, and mothers insist on having their daughters operated on to prevent them becoming outcasts. Common to many groups who circumcise girls is the belief that each person is born with both male and female elements. In a boy the foreskin represents femininity, whereas in a girl the clitoris represents masculinity; both must be removed to clarify the sex of the child. Some peoples also believe that the clitoris is an aggressive organ that can threaten the male penis and even endanger the baby during childbirth.

The perpetuation of this tradition in Britain is a sensitive issue given the question of self-determination for ethnic communities. The rights of children have to be set against the rights of groups to practise ancient customs. Campaigners against female circumcision, by drawing attention to this practice, risk exposing isolated communities, who already have to contend with racism in their daily lives, to more prejudice. These issues were discussed in a documentary entitled *Female circumcision UK*, which was screened by the BBC in Feb 1991. Louise Panton, the maker of the documentary, argued that attempts to eradicate female circumcision should be conducted sensitively.

languages spoken by some 22 million people in scattered communities from Norway in the west to Siberia in the east and to the Carpathian mountains in the south. Members of the family include Finnish, Lapp, and Hungarian.

**Fon** a people living mainly in Benin, and also in Nigeria, and numbering about 25,000,000. The Fon language belongs to the Kwa branch of the Niger-Congo family. The Fon founded a kingdom which became powerful in the 18th and 19th centuries through the slave trade, with the result that the region became known as the Slave Coast.

**Fulani** member of a W African culture from the southern Sahara and Sahel. Traditionally nomadic pastoralists and traders, Fulani groups are found in Senegal, Guinea, Mali, Burkina Faso, Niger, Nigeria, Chad, and Cameroon. The Fulani language is divided into four dia-

lects and belongs to the W Atlantic branch of the Niger-Congo family; it has over 10,000,000 speakers.

**Galla** or *Oromo* nomadic pastoralists inhabiting S Ethiopia and NW Kenya. Galla is a Hamito-Semitic (Afro-Asiatic) language, and is spoken by about 12,000,000 people.

**Ganda** a member of the Baganda people, the majority ethnic group in Uganda; the Baganda also live in Kenya. Until the 19th century they formed an independent kingdom, the largest in E Africa. It was a British protectorate 1894–1962, and the monarchy was officially overthrown in 1966. Their language, Luganda, belongs to the Niger-Congo language family and has about 3,000,000 speakers.

**Georgian** or *Grazinian* a member of any of a number of related groups which make up the largest ethnic group in the Georgian Soviet Socialist Republic and the surrounding area.

There are 3–4 million speakers of Georgian, a member of the Caucasian language family.

**Germanic languages** branch of the Indo-European language family, divided into *East Germanic* (Gothic, now extinct), *North Germanic* (Danish, Faroese, Icelandic, Norwegian, Swedish), and *West Germanic* (Afrikaans, Dutch, English, Flemish, Frisian, German, Yiddish).

**Gond** member of a heterogeneous people of central India, about half of whom speak unwritten languages belonging to the Dravidian family. The rest speak Indo-European languages. There are over 4 million Gonds, most of whom live in Madhya Pradesh, E Maharashtra, and N Andra Pradesh, although some live in Orissa. Traditionally, many Gonds practised shifting cultivation; agriculture and livestock remain the basis of the economy.

**Guarani** member of a South American Indian people of modern Paraguay, S Brazil, and Bolivia. The Guarani live mainly in reserves; few retain the traditional ways of hunting in the tropical forest, cultivation, and ritual warfare. The Guarani language belongs to the Tupi-Guarani family; it is the most widely spoken language in Paraguay.

**Gujarati** inhabitant of Gujarat on the NW coast of India. The Gujaratis number approximately 30 million and speak their own Indo-European language, Gujarati, which has a long literary tradition. They are predominantly Hindu (90%), with Muslim (8%) and Jain (2%) minorities.

**Hamito-Semitic languages** family of languages spoken throughout the world. It has two main branches, the *Hamitic* languages of N Africa and the *Semitic* languages originating in Syria, Mesopotamia, Palestine, and Arabia, but now found from Morocco in the west to the Persian Gulf in the east.

**Han** the majority ethnic group in China, numbering about 990,000,000. They speak a wide variety of dialects of the same monosyllabic language, a member of the Sino-Tibetan family. Their religion combines Buddhism, Taoism, Confucianism, and ancestor worship.

**Hausa** member of an agricultural Muslim people of NW Nigeria, numbering 9 million. The Hausa language belongs to the Chadic subfamily of the Afro-Asiatic language group. It is used as a trade language throughout W Africa.

**Hindi language** member of the Indo-Iranian branch of the Indo-European language family, the official language of the Republic of India, although resisted as such by the Dravidian-speaking states of the south. Hindi proper is used by some 30% of Indians, in such northern states as Uttar Pradesh and Madhya Pradesh.

**Hmong** member of a SE Asian highland people. They are predominantly hill farmers, rearing pigs and cultivating rice and grain, and many are involved in growing the opium poppy. Estimates of the size of the Hmong population vary between 1.5 million and 5 million, the greatest number being in China. Although traditional beliefs remain important, many have adopted Christianity. Their language belongs to the Sino-Tibetan family. The names *Meo* or *Miao*, sometimes used to refer to the Hmong, are considered derogatory.

**Hui** one of the largest minority ethnic groups in China, numbering about 25,000,000. Members of the Hui live all over China, but are concentrated in the N central region. They have been Muslims since the 10th century, for which they have suffered persecution both before and since the Communist revolution.

**Hutu** the majority ethnic group of both Burundi and Rwanda. The Hutu tend to live as peasant-farmers, while the ruling minority, the Tutsi, are town-dwellers. There is a long history of violent conflict between the two groups. The Hutu language belongs to the Bantu branch of the Niger-Congo family.

**Iban** or *Sea Dayak* a Dayak people of central Borneo. Approximately 250,000 Iban live in the interior uplands of Sarawak, while another 10,000 live in the border area of W Kalimantan. Traditionally the Iban live in long houses divided into separate family units, and practise shifting cuiltivation. Their languages belong to the Austronesian family.

**Ibo** or *Igbo* member of the W African Ibo culture group occupying SE Nigeria and numbering about 18,000,000. Primarily cultivators, they inhabit the richly forested tableland, bounded by the river Niger to the west and the river Cross to the east. They are divided into five main groups, and their languages belong to the Kwa branch of the Niger-Congo family.

**Ifugao** member of an indigenous people of N Luzon in the Philippines, numbering approximately 70,000. In addition to practising shifting cultivation on highland slopes, they build elaborate terraced rice fields. Their language belongs to the Austronesian family.

**Indian languages** traditionally, the languages of the subcontinent of India; since 1947, the languages of the Republic of India. These number some 200, depending on whether a variety is classified as a language or a dialect. They fall into five main groups, the two most widespread of which are the Indo-European languages (mainly in the north) and the Dravidian languages (mainly in the south).

**Indo-European languages** family of languages that includes some of the world's major classical languages (Sanskrit and Pali in India, Zend Avestan in Iran, Greek and Latin in Europe), as well as several of the most widely spoken languages (English worldwide; Spanish in Iberia, Latin America, and elsewhere; and the Hindi group of languages in N India). Indo-European languages were once located only along a geographical band from India through Iran into NW Asia, E Europe, the northern Mediterranean lands, N and W Europe and the British Isles.

**Inuit** a people inhabiting the Arctic coasts of North America, the E islands of the Canadian Arctic, and the ice-free coasts of Greenland. Inuktitut, their language, has about 60,000 speakers; it belongs to the Eskimo-Aleut group.

The Inuit object to the name Eskimos ('eaters of raw meat') given them by the Algonquin Indians.

**Jat** a member of an ethnic group living in Pakistan and N India, and numbering about 11,000,000; they are the largest group in N India. The Jat are predominantly farmers. They speak Punjabi, a language belonging to the Iranian branch of the Indo-European family. They are thought to be related to the Romany people.

**Javanese** a member of the largest ethnic group in the Republic of Indonesia. There are more than fifty million speakers of Javanese, which belongs to the western branch of the Austronesian family. Although the Javanese have a Hindu-Buddhist heritage, they are today predominantly Muslim, practising a branch of Islam known as *Islam Jawa*, which contains many Sufi features.

**Kannada** or *Kanarese* a language spoken in S India, the official state language of Karnataka; also spoken in Tamil Nadu and Maharashtra. There are over 20,000,000 speakers of Kannada, which belongs to the Dravidian family. Written records in Kannada date from the 5th century AD.

**Karen** member of a group of SE Asian peoples, numbering 1.9 million. They live in E Myanmar (formerly Burma), Thailand, and the Irrawaddy delta. Their language belongs to the Thai division of the Sino-Tibetan family. In 1984 the Burmese government began a large-scale military campaign against the Karen National Liberation Army (KNLA), the armed wing of the Karen National Union (KNU).

**Kazakh** or *Kazak* member of a pastoral Kirghiz people of the Kazakh Soviet Socialist Republic. Kazakhs also live in China (Xinjiang, Gansu, and Qinghai), Mongolia, and Afghanistan. There are 5–7 million speakers of Kazakh, a Turkic language belonging to the Altaic family. The Kazakhs are predominantly Sunni Muslim, although pre-Islamic customs have survived. Kazakhs herd horses and make use of camels; they also keep cattle. Traditionally the Kazakhs lived in tents and embarked on seasonal migrations in search of fresh pastures. Collectivized herds were established in the 1920s and 1930s but Soviet economic programmes have had to adapt to local circumstances.

**Khmer** or *Kmer* member of the largest ethnic group in Cambodia, numbering about seven million. Khmer minorities also live in E Thailand and S Vietnam. The Khmer language belongs to the Mon-Khmer family of Austro-Asiatic languages. They live mainly in agricultural and fishing villages under a chief. The Khmers practise Theravāda Buddhism and trace descent through both male and female lines. Traditionally, Khmer society was divided into six groups: the royal family, the Brahmans (who officiated at royal festivals), Buddhist monks, officials, commoners, and slaves.

**Khoikhoi** (formerly *Hottentot*) a people living in Namibia and the Cape Province of South Africa, and numbering about 30,000. Their language is related to San (spoken by the Kung) and belongs to the Khoisan family. Like the Kung, the Khoikhoi once inhabited a wider area, but were driven into the Kalahari Desert by invading Bantu peoples and Dutch colonists in the 18th century. They live as nomadic hunter-gatherers, in family groups, and have animist beliefs.

**Khoisan** the smallest group of languages in Africa. It includes fewer than 50 languages, spoken mainly by the people of the Kalahari Desert (including the Khoikhoi and Kung). Two languages from this group are spoken in Tanzania. The Khoisan languages are known for their click consonants (clicking sounds made with the tongue, which function as consonants).

**Kikuyu** a member of Kenya's dominant ethnic group, numbering about three million. The Kikuyu are primarily cultivators, although many are highly educated and have entered the professions. Their language belongs to the Bantu branch of the Niger-Congo family.

**Kirghiz** a member of a pastoral people numbering approximately 1.5 million. They inhabit the central Asian region bounded by the Hindu Kush, the Himalayas, and the Tian Shan mountains. The Kirghiz are Sunni Muslims, and their Turkic language belongs to the Altaic family. During the winter the Kirghiz live in individual family *yurts* (tents made of felt). In summer they come together in larger settlements of up to 20 yurts. They herd sheep, goats, and yaks, and use Bactrian camels for transporting their possessions.

**Kung** (formerly *Bushman*) a member of a small group of aboriginal peoples of southern Africa, still living to some extent nomadically. They once occupied a large area, but were driven into the Kalahari Desert in the 18th century by Bantu peoples (Sotho and Nguni). Although they were formerly numerous, only some 40,000 now remain. They are traditionally hunters and gatherers, and speak San and other Khoisan languages. Their early art survives in cave paintings.

**Kurd** member of an Iranian people, living mostly in the region called Kurdistan. Although divided among more powerful states, the Kurds have nationalist aspirations; there are some 8 million in Turkey (where they suffer from discriminatory legislation), 5 million in Iran, 4 million in Iraq, 500,000 in Syria, and 100,000 in the USSR. The Kurdish language is a member of the Iranian branch of the Indo-European family and the Kurds are a non-Arab ethnic group. Some 1 million Kurds were made homeless and 25,000 killed as a result of chemical-weapon attacks by Iraq 1984–89, and in 1991 more than 1 million were forced to flee their homes in N Iraq.

The Kurds are predominantly Sunni Muslims, although there are some Shi'ites in Iran. Kurds traditionally owe allegiance to their families, and larger groups are brought together under an agha, or lord. They are predominantly shepherds and farmers, cultivating a wide range of crops and fruit. Kurdish pro-

## DO RACES EXIST?

Both the recent genetic and archaeological evidence seems to indicate the redundancy of thinking of humans in terms of races – all people share, it would appear, a close common ancestry.

According to one school of thought the different human races diverged long ago and developed independently like the parallel candles of a candelabra. Differences in physical appearance, particularly skin colour and stature, could therefore be attributed to the separate evolutionary paths taken by human beings in different environmental conditions. This hypothesis achieved prominence in 1962 with the publication of Carlton Coon's *The Origin of Races*, which is partly derived from earlier studies on race. Coon, a University of Pennsylvania anthropologist, argued that the first modern humans arose in Europe and Asia, though he recognized that the earliest hominids evolved in Africa. On the basis of the information available at the time it was assumed that modern humans did not emerge until around 40,000 years ago when they first appear in the European fossil records. A modified version of this theory—known since the 1980s as the 'candelabra hypothesis'—is still popular among some anthropologists. Milford Wolpoff, for example, a palaeoanthropologist from the University of Michigan, suggested that although the races evolved gradually on distinct lines, there was intermixing. The parallel lines, therefore, are connected by a network of genes flowing between them; the modified candelabra hypothesis is sometimes likened to a trellis.

An opposing thesis—now referred to as the 'Noah's Ark hypothesis'—was debated by the American Anthropological Association in 1987. According to this theory all humans share a common ancestor who lived between 100,000 and 200,000 years ago, and that Africa is the cradle of all humanity. In only 1,000 centuries the descendants of African hunter-gatherers have been transformed into a burgeoning population of some 5 billion people. All these peoples, whatever their cultural or national identity, are biologically the same because—so goes the theory—humankind has not had the time to diverge genetically in any significant way. Despite differences in appearance, human beings are members of a single group who originated recently in one place. There are no grounds, therefore, on which to divide humanity into separate races since the differences are not scientifically meaningful.

The Noah's Ark hypothesis builds on research conducted by Vincent Sarich and Allan Wilson at the University of California, Berkeley, in 1967. By studying the molecular structure of a blood protein in chimpanzees, baboons and humans the scientists showed that baboons and chimpanzees had been evolving separately for 30 million years. In contrast the difference between chimpanzees and humans was much smaller, indicating a relatively recent split around 4–8 million years ago. In the 1980s Rebecca Cann of the University of Hawaii, working in conjunction with Allan Wilson and Mark Stoneking, compared mitochondrial DNA from humans around the world. Mitochondrial DNA was used in this research because it can only be passed on from mothers to their offspring and only changes slightly over time. Scientists have been able to calculate how quickly these changes take place—less than 3% every million years—and can therefore estimate the age of a species. The research team found a variation of half a per cent between all human populations, indicating comparatively recent origins. Furthermore, it was shown that mitochondrial DNA fell into two marginally different categories: one in people of African descent, the other in the rest of humanity. This strongly suggests that African populations are older since they have accumulated slightly more genetic variety than other populations.

The Noah's Ark hypothesis indicates that the ancestors of all non-Africans are descended from people who left Africa some 100,000 years ago, appearing in Java around 60,000 years ago before moving on to Australia. There were other hominids around at the time, such as the Neanderthals, who may have been wiped out by the new arrivals. The new humans may have provided too much competition within the same habitats, perhaps because they were better organized socially. Neanderthals disappeared from Europe around 35,000 years ago, not long after the emergence of *Homo sapiens*. The exact relationship between Neanderthals and other hominids remains unclear and some scientists have suggested that they were the descendants of *Homo erectus*, another hominid that had spread as far as Asia by a million years ago. Wolpoff, however, has argued that a sudden exodus from Africa would have led to a marked discontinuity in the fossil records, which is not the case. According to Wolpoff human evolution took place in different locations over the past one million years and the differences between the races, which are descended from older hominid populations, are significant, though there has been intermixing. Recent research in a cave in Qafzeh in Israel may lend some support to the Noah's Ark hypothesis. Fifteen human skeletons have been excavated and dated to around 90,000 years old, making them the oldest remains of *Homo sapiens* outside Africa. Chris Stringer of the Museum of Natural History in London has suggested that these humans may have been among the earliest people to leave Africa.

fessionals are found in many Middle Eastern cities. (See feature in this section.)

**Lahnda** a language spoken by 15–20 million people in Pakistan and N India. It is closely related to Punjabi and Romany, and belongs to the Indo-Iranian branch of the Indo-European family.

**Latvian** (or **Lett**) a member of the majority ethnic group living in the Latvian Soviet Socialist Republic. The region has been Christian since the 13th century. The Latvian language is also known as **Lettish**; with Lithuanian it is one of the two surviving members of the Baltic branch of the Indo-European family.

**Lithuanian** a member of the majority ethnic group living in the Lithuanian Soviet Socialist Republic, comprising 80% of the population. Through its geographical isolation the Lithuanian language has retained many ancient features of the Indo-European family, and is closely related to Latvian. It acquired a written form in the 16th century, using the Latin alphabet, and is currently spoken by about 3–4 million people.

**Makua** a member of a people living to the N of the Zambezi river in Mozambique. With the Lomwe people, they make up the country's largest ethnic group. The Makua are mainly farmers, living in villages ruled by chiefs. The Makua language belongs to the Niger-Congo family, and has about 5 million speakers.

**Malagasy** inhabitant of or native to Madagascar. Primarily rice farmers, the Malagasy make use of both irrigated fields and swidden (temporary plot) methods. The Malagasy language has about 9 million speakers; it belongs to the Austronesian family and, despite Madagascar's proximity to Africa, contains only a small number of Bantu and Arabic loan words. It seems likely that the earliest settlers came by sea, some 1,500 years ago, from Indonesia.

**Malayalam** a S Indian language, the official language of the state of Kerala. Malayalam is closely related to Tamil, also a member of the Dravidian language family; it is spoken by about 20 million people. Written records in Malayalam date from the 9th century AD.

**Maori** a member of the indigenous Polynesian people of New Zealand, who numbered 294,200 in 1986, about 10% of the total population. Maori is a member of the Polynesian branch of the Malayo-Polynesian language family. Only one-third use the language today, but efforts are being made to strengthen it after a long period of decline and official indifference. The Maoris claim 70% of the country's land; they have secured a ruling that the fishing grounds of the far north belong solely to local Maori people.

**Maratha** or **Mahratta** a people living mainly in Maharashtra, W India. There are about 40 million speakers of Marathi, a language belonging to the Indo-European family. The Maratha are mostly farmers, and practise Hinduism.

**Masai** member of an E African people whose territory is divided between Tanzania and Kenya, and who number about 250,000. They were originally warriors and nomads, breeding humped zebu cattle, but some have adopted a more settled life. Their cooperation is being sought by the Kenyan authorities to help in wildlife conservation. They speak a Nilotic language belonging to the Nilo-Saharan family.

**Mende** a member of a W African people living in the rainforests of central east Sierra Leone and W Liberia. They number approximately 1 million. The Mende are farmers as well as hunter-gatherers, and each of their villages is led by a chief and a group of elders. The Mende language belongs to the Niger-Congo family.

**Moldavian** a member of the majority ethnic group living in the Moldavian Soviet Socialist Republic and making up almost two-thirds of the population; also, an inhabitant of the Romanian province of Moldavia (the two areas were united until 1940). The Moldavian language is a dialect of Romanian, and belongs to the Romance group of the Indo-European family.

**Mon** (or **Talaing**) a member of a minority ethnic group living in Myanmar (Burma) and Thailand. The Mon established kingdoms in the area as early as the 7th century. Much of their culture was absorbed by the Khmer and Thai invaders who conquered them. The Mon language belongs to the Mon-Khmer branch of the Austro-Asiatic family. They are Buddhists, but also retain older animist beliefs.

**Mordvin** a Finnish people inhabiting the middle Volga valley in the USSR. They are known to have lived in the region since the 1st century AD. There are 1 million speakers of Mordvin scattered throughout the USSR, about one-third of whom live in the Mordvinian Soviet Socialist Republic. Mordvin is a Finno-Ugric language belonging to the Uralic family.

**Mossi** a member of the majority ethnic group living in Burkina Faso. Their social structure, based on a monarchy and aristocracy, was established in the 11th century. The Mossi have been prominent traders, using cowrie shells as currency. There are about 4 million speakers of Mossi, a language belonging to the Gur branch of the Niger-Congo family.

**Munda** a member of any one of several groups living in NE and central India, and numbering about 5 million (1983). Their most widely spoken languages are Santali and Mundari, languages of the Munda group, an isolated branch of the Austro-Asiatic family. The Mundas were formerly nomadic hunter-gatherers, but now practise shifting cultivation. They are Hindus, but retain animist beliefs.

**Naga** a member of any of the various peoples who inhabit the highland region near the Indian-Myanmar border; they number approximately 800,000. These peoples do not possess a common name; some of the main groups are Ao, Konyak, Sangtam, Lhota, Sema, Rengma, Chang, and Angami. They live by farming, hunting, and fishing. Their languages belong to the Sino-Tibetan family.

**Nahuatl** a member of any of a group of Mesoamerican Indian peoples (Mexico and Central America), of which the best-known group were the Aztecs. The Nahuatl are the largest ethnic group in Mexico, and their languages, which belong to the Uto-Aztecan (Aztec-Tanoan) family, are spoken by over a million people today.

**Natchez** a member of a North American Indian people of the Mississippi area, one of the Moundbuilder group of peoples. They had a highly developed caste system unusual in North America, headed by a ruler priest (the

'Great Sun'). Members of the highest caste always married members of the lowest caste. The system lasted until the French colonized the area 1731. Only a few Natchez now survive in Oklahoma. Their Muskogean language is extinct.

**Navajo** or **Navaho** (Tena **Navahu** 'large planted field') member of a North American Indian people related to the Apache, and numbering about 200,000, mostly in Arizona. They speak an Athabaskan language, belonging to the Na-Dené family. The Navajo were traditionally cultivators; many now herd sheep and earn an income from tourism, making and selling rugs, blankets, and silver and turquoise jewellery. The Navajo refer to themselves as **Dineh**, 'people'.

**Negrito** a member of any of several groups living on various islands in SE Asia. The Negritos are long-established inhabitants of the region. They include the cave-dwelling Vedda of Sri Lanka, the Andamanese of the Andaman Islands, and the Semang of Malaysia.

**Niger-Congo languages** the largest group of languages in Africa. It includes about 1,000 languages and covers a vast area S of the Sahara desert, from the west coast to the east, and down the east coast as far as South Africa. It is divided into groups and subgroups; the most widely spoken Niger-Congo languages are Swahili (spoken on the E coast), the members of the Bantu group (southern Africa), and Yoruba (Nigeria).

**Nuba** a member of a minority ethnic group living in S Sudan. The Nuba farm terraced fields in the Nuba mountains, to the W of the White Nile. They speak related dialects of Nubian, which belongs to the Chari-Nile family.

**Nyanja** a member of a central African people living mainly in Malawi, and numbering about 400,000 (1984). The Nyanja are predominantly farmers, living in villages under a hereditary monarchy. They speak a Bantu language belonging to the Niger-Congo family.

**Oriya** a member of the majority ethnic group living in the Indian state of Orissa. Oriya is Orissa's official language; it belongs to the Eastern group of the Indo-Iranian branch of the Indo-European family.

**Oromo** a member of a group of E African peoples, especially of S Ethiopia, who speak a Hamito-Semitic (Afro-Asiatic) language.

**Palikur** a group of South American Indians living in N Brazil, and numbering about 1 million (1980). Formerly a warlike people, they once occupied a vast area between the Amazon and Orinoco rivers.

**Pathan** a people of NW Pakistan and Afghanistan, numbering about 14,000,000 (1984). The Pathans comprise distinct groups, some of which live as nomads with herds of goats and camels; while others are farmers. The majority are Sunni Muslims. The Pathans speak Pashto, a member of the Indo-Iranian branch of the Indo-European family. Formerly a constant threat to the British Raj, the Pakistani Pathans are now claiming independence, with

the Afghani Pathans, in their own state of Pakhtoonistan, although this has not yet been recognized.

**pidgin languages** trade jargons, contact languages, or lingua francas arising in ports and markets where people of different linguistic backgrounds meet for commercial and other purposes.

**Potiguara** a group of South American Indians living in NW Brazil, and numbering about 1 million (1983). Their language belongs to the Tupi-Guarani family. Their religion is centred around a shaman, who mediates between the people and the spirit world.

**Punjabi** a member of the majority ethnic group living in the Punjab. Approximately 37,000,000 live in the Pakistan half of Punjab, while another 14,000,000 live on the Indian side of the border. In addition to Sikhs, there are Rajputs in Punjab, some of whom have adopted Islam. The Punjabi language belongs to the Indo-Iranian branch of the Indo-European family. It is considered by some to be a variety of Hindi, by others to be a distinct language.

**Pygmy** (sometimes **Negrillos**) a member of any of several groups of small-statured, dark-skinned peoples of the rainforests of equatorial Africa. They were probably the aboriginal inhabitants of the region, before the arrival of farming peoples from elsewhere. They live nomadically in small groups, as hunter-gatherers; they also trade with other, settled people in the area.

**Quechua** or **Quichua** or **Kechua** a member of the largest group of South American Indians. The Quechua live in the Andean region. Their ancestors included the Inca, who established the Quechua language in the region. Quechua is the second official language of Peru and is widely spoken as a lingua franca in Ecuador, Bolivia, Columbia, Argentina, and Chile; it belongs to the Andean-Equatorial family.

**Romance languages** a branch of Indo-European languages descended from the Latin of the Roman Empire ('popular' or 'vulgar' as opposed to 'classical' Latin). The present-day Romance languages with national status are French, Italian, Portuguese, Romanian, and Spanish.

**Romany** a nomadic people, also called **Gypsy** (a corruption of 'Egyptian', since they were erroneously thought to come from Egypt). They are now believed to have originated in NW India, and live throughout the world. The Romany language, spoken in several different dialects, belongs to the Indic branch of the Indo-European family.

**Russian** a member of the majority ethnic group living in the Russian Soviet Federal Socialist Republic, the largest republic in the Soviet Union. Russians are also often the largest minority in other Soviet republics. Russian is the official language of the Soviet Union, with 130–150 million speakers. Since before the revolution, Russian language and culture have been imposed on the country's minorities; this is to some extent being reversed in the face of growing nationalist feeling in many of the republics. The ancestors of the Russians

**Indo-European Languages**

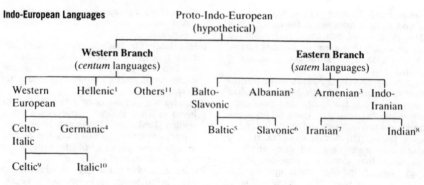

1  Hellenic:        Greek (including *Ancient, *Archaic, *Classical, *Koine, *Byzantine and
                    the modern forms *Demotiki* and *Katharevousa*)
2  Albanian:        Albanian
3  Armenian:        Armenian
4  Germanic:        Afrikaans, *Anglo-Saxon, (Old English), Bavarian, Danish, Dutch/Flemish,
                    English/Scots, Faroese, Frisian, German (Low, High, Swiss, etc), *Gothic,
                    Icelandic, Luxemburgish, *Old Norse, *Old High German, Norwegian,
                    Swedish, Yiddish
5  Baltic:          Latvian, Lithuanian, *Old Prussian
6  Slavonic:        Bulgarian, Byelorussian, Croatian, Czech, Kashubian, Macedonian, Polish,
   (or Slavic)      Pomeranian, Russian, Serbian, Slovak, Slovene, Sorbian, Ukrainian
7  Iranian:         *Avestan (Zend or Zand), *Bactrian, Baluchi, Kurdish, *Median, Ossetic,
                    *Pahlavi, *Parthian, Pashto, Persian (Farsi), Tadzhik
8  Indian:          Assamese, Bengali, Bhili, Bihari, Gujarati, Hindi, Kashmiri, Konkani,
                    Marathi, Oriya, Pahari, *Pali, Punjabi, Rajasthani, *Sanskrit, Sindhi,
                    Sinhalese, Urdu
9  Celtic:          Breton, *Brythonic, *Cornish, Gaelic (Irish, *Manx and Scottish), *Gaulish,
                    *Goidelic, Welsh
10 Italic:          (1) *Latin, *Oscan, *Umbrian
                    (2) Romance: Catalan, French, Gallego (Galician), Italian, Portuguese,
                    Provençal, Romanian (Rumanian), Romansh, Spanish (Castilian)
11 others           *Anatolian (including Hittite), *Tocharian

**The Indo-European languages** An outline diagram of the historical relationships among the
Indo-European languages, followed by lists of languages in each branch of the family tree.
Extinct languages are marked with an asterisk (*).

migrated from central Europe between the 6th
and 8th centuries AD.

**Saami** or **Lapp** a member of a group of
herding people living in N Scandinavia and
the Kola Peninsula, and numbering about
46,000 (1983). Some are nomadic, others
lead a more settled way of life. They live by
herding reindeer, hunting, fishing, and producing handicrafts. Their language belongs
to the Finno-Ugric family. Their religion is
basically animist, but incorporates elements
of Christianity.

**Serbo-Croatian** or **Serbo-Croat** the most widely
spoken language in Yugoslavia. It is a member of the South Slavonic branch of the
Indo-European family. The different dialects
of Serbo-Croatian tend to be written by the
Greek Orthodox Serbs in the Cyrillic script,
and by the Roman Catholic Croats in the Latin
script.

**Shona** member of a Bantu-speaking people of
southern Africa, making up approximately
80% of the population of Zimbabwe. They
also occupy the land between the Save and
Pungure rivers in Mozambique, and smaller
groups are found in South Africa, Botswana,
and Zambia. The Shona are mainly farmers,
living in scattered villages. The Shona language
belongs to the Niger-Congo family.

**Sindhi** a member of the majority ethnic group
living in the Pakistani province of Sind. The
Sindhi language is spoken by about 15 million
people. Since the partition of India and Pakistan 1947, large numbers of Urdu-speaking
refugees have moved into the region from
India, especially into the capital, Karachi.

**Sinhalese** a member of the majority ethnic group
of Sri Lanka (70% of the population). Sinhalese
is the official language of Sri Lanka; it belongs to the Indo-Iranian branch of the Indo-
European family, and is written in a script derived from the Indian Pali form. The Sinhalese

are Buddhists. Since 1971 they have been involved in a violent struggle with the Tamil minority, who are seeking independence.

**Sino-Tibetan languages** a group of languages spoken in SE Asia. This group covers a large area, and includes Chinese and Burmese, both of which have numerous dialects. Some classifications include the Tai group of languages (including Thai and Lao) in the Sino-Tibetan family); other systems place the Tai languages with the Austronesian family.

**Slav** member of an Indo-European people, speaking closely related Slavonic languages. Their ancestors are believed to have included the Sarmatians and Scythians. Moving west from Central Asia, they settled in E and SE Europe during the 2nd and 3rd millennia BC. There are now three groups: Eastern (Russians, Byelorussians, and Ukrainians); Western (Poles, Czechs, Slovaks, and Sorbs or Wends); and Southern (Serbs, Croats, Slovenes, Macedonians, and Bulgars).

**Slavonic languages** or *Slavic languages* branch of the Indo-European language family spoken in central and E Europe, the Balkans, and parts of N Asia. The family comprises the *southern group* (Serbo-Croatian, Slovene, and Macedonian in Yugoslavia, and Bulgarian in Bulgaria); the *western group* (Czech and Slovak in Czechoslovakia, Sorbian in Germany, and Polish and its related dialects); and the *eastern group* (Russian, Ukrainian, and Byelorussian in the USSR).

**Slovene** a member of the Slavic people of Slovenia (NW Yugoslavia), and parts of the Austrian Alpine provinces of Styria and Carinthia. There are 1.5–2 million speakers of Slovene, a language belonging to the South Slavonic branch of the Indo-European family. The Slovenes use the Roman alphabet and the majority belong to the Roman Catholic Church.

**Sotho** a member of a large ethnic group in southern Africa, numbering about 7 million (1987) and living mainly in Botswana, Lesotho, and South Africa. The Sotho are predominantly farmers, living in small village groups. They speak a variety of closely related languages belonging to the Bantu branch of the Niger-Congo family. With English, Sotho is the official language of Lesotho.

**Sundanese** a member of the second largest ethnic group in the Republic of Indonesia. There are more than 20 million speakers of Sundanese, a member of the western branch of the Austronesian family. Like their neighbours, the Javanese, the Sundanese are predominantly Muslim. They are known for their performing arts, especially *jaipongan* dance traditions, and distinctive batik fabrics.

**Swahili** (Arabic *sawahil* 'coasts') a language belonging to the Bantu branch of the Niger-Congo family, widely used in E and central Africa. Swahili originated on the E African coast, as a lingua franca used among traders, and contains many Arabic loan words. It is an official language in Kenya and Tanzania.

The name Swahili is also used for a member of an African people using the language, especially someone living in Zanzibar and adjoining coastal areas of Kenya and Tanzania. The Swahili are not an isolated group, but are part of a mixed coastal society engaged in fishing and trading.

**Tadzhik** or *Tajik* a member of the majority ethnic group living in the Tadzhik Soviet Socialist Republic. The Tadzhiks also live in Afghanistan and parts of Pakistan and W China. The Tadzhiki language belongs to the West Iranian subbranch of the Indo-European family, and is similar to Farsi; it is written in the Cyrillic script. The Tadzhiks have long been associated with neighbouring Turkic peoples and their language contains Altaic loan words. The majority of the Tadzhik people are Sunni Muslims; there is a Shi'ite minority in Afghanistan. In the USSR, the Tadzhiks have, while retaining their cultural identity, adopted skills introduced by the Russians. Today there are both textile and mining industries in Tadzhikistan.

**Tagalog** a member of the majority ethnic group living around Manila on the island of Luzon, in the Philippines, and numbering about 10 million (1988). The Tagalog live by fishing and trading. In its standardized form, known as Pilipino, Tagalog is the official language of the Philipines, and belongs to the Western branch of the Austronesian family. The Tagalogs' religion is a mixture of animism, Christianity, and Islam.

**Tamil** a member of the majority ethnic group living in the Indian state of Tamil Nadu (formerly Madras). Tamils also live in S India, N Sri Lanka, Malaysia, Singapore, and South Africa, totalling 35–55 million worldwide. The 3 million Tamils in Sri Lanka are predominantly Hindu, though some are Muslims, unlike the Sinhalese majority, who are mainly Buddhist. Tamil belongs to the Dravidian family of languages; written records in Tamil date from the 3rd century BC. The Tamil Tigers, most prominent of the various Tamil groupings, are attempting to create a separate homeland in N Sri Lanka through both political and military means.

**Tatar** or *Tartar* a member of a Turkic people, the descendants of the mixed Mongol and Turkic followers of Genghis Khan, called the Golden Horde because of the wealth they gained by plunder. The vast Tatar state was conquered by Russia 1552. The Tatars now live mainly in the Tatar Autonomous Soviet Socialist Republic and Uzbekistan (where they were deported from the Crimea 1944) and SW Siberia, and there are Tatar minorities all over the USSR. There are over 5 million speakers of the Tatar language, which belongs to the Turkic branch of the Altaic family. The Tatar people are mainly Muslim, though some have converted to the Orthodox Church.

**Telugu** a language spoken in SE India. It is the official language of Andhra Pradesh, and is also spoken in Malaysia, giving a total number of speakers of around 50 million. Written records

## THE KURDS

Encouraged by the defeat of the Iraqis in the 1991 Gulf War, Kurdish nationalists rose up against the Ba'athist regime in Baghdad. In spite of the battering received at the hands of the Allies, the Iraqi army was still capable of putting down the revolt. The initial successes were shortlived and by April 2 the Ba'athist regime was sufficiently confident of its control of Iraqi Kurdistan to take journalists into the town of Arbil. Kurdish spokesmen alleged that the Iraqi Republican Guard had massacred civilians in the recaptured towns and refugees, bringing reports of atrocities committed by the Iraqi forces, began to pour across the borders of Iran and Turkey. So began the latest of a series of ill-fated attempts by the Kurds to establish an independent homeland in the Middle East.

The Kurds belong to a distinct ethnic group from the region known as Kurdistan, which is divided between more powerful states. They live in the Taurus Mountains in eastern Anatolia, the Zagros Mountains in W Iran and N Iraq. There are 15–17 million Kurds, the majority of whom live in Turkey (8 million), Iran (5 million), Iraq (4 million) and Syria (500,000). Approximately 100,000 Kurds live in the USSR, mainly in the Armenian Soviet Socialist Republic, and there are Kurdish communities in the Khorasan region (NE Iran) and Lebanon. The Kurds are neither Arabs nor Turks, and their language belongs to the Iranian branch of the Indo-European family. They are predominantly Sunni Muslims, though Sufi traditions

*Kurdish refugees from Iraq, 1991.*

are important, and there are some Shi'ite Kurds in Iran. National dress is still worn in the more mountainous areas, and there is a strong tradition of poetry and music.

The Kurds practice agriculture and cultivate a wide range of crops and fruits. Some shepherds still migrate seasonally from lowland winter pastures to upland summer fields. They may cross national boundaries, making it difficult for governments to control them. Historically the Kurds fought as mercenaries throughout the Middle East and they are known for their military prowess, typified by Saladin (Salah-AD-Din), who was a Kurd. Kurds traditionally owe allegiance to their families and lineages may acknowledge the authority of a sheikh or *aga* (agha). Kurdish professionals, many of whom speak a second language such as Arabic, live in towns both inside and outside Kurdistan.

The early history of the Kurds cannot be traced with any certainty, though Sumerian inscriptions dating from 2,000 BC refer to people who are sometimes said to be the ancestors of the Kurds. The Greek historian Xenophon also mentions Assyrian battles with tribes who may have been Kurdish. The name 'Kurd' is usually dated from the 7th century AD, the time of Islamic conversion. By the 13th century Saladin was leading the united Muslim forces against the Crusaders. Kurdistan eventually came under Ottoman rule and in the 1880s there was a failed attempt to establish an autonomous Kurdish state within the Turkish Empire. The appearance of the first Kurdish newspaper in 1897 marked the rise of Kurdish cultural consciousness. The Treaty of Sèvres 1920 provided a draft scheme for Kurdish independence, though it was never ratified. There were rebellions in 1931–32 and 1944–45 in Iraqi Kurdistan, and in 1946 the Soviets briefly backed the establishment of a Kurdish representative in Iran.

After World War II the Kurds suffered various forms of repression under the governments that control Kurdistan. For example, the Kurds were designated as 'mountain Turks' by the Turkish government, and their language was misrepresented as a dialect of Turkish. Restrictions were also placed on the wearing of Kurdish national dress near to important Turkish administrative centres. The Kurds were also repressed by the shah of Iran and by the successor regime of Ayatollah Khomeini, who put down a Kurdish uprising in 1979–80. In contrast there was slightly more cultural freedom in Iraq and in 1970 the Ba'athist government granted the Kurds a limited degree of autonomy.

This did not last long and, following attempts by the Iraqis to re-locate Kurds from the north to the south, there were revolts in 1977. During the Iran–Iraq War in 1988 the Iraqis are reported to have used cyanide gas at Halabja and other villages. In Nov 1989 the Iraqis created an uninhabited security zone on the Iranian and Turkish frontiers, moving an estimated 100,000–500,000 people.

in Telugu date from the 7th century AD. Telugu belongs to the Dravidian family.

**Thai** a member of the majority ethnic group living in Thailand and N Myanmar (Burma). Thai peoples also live in SW China, Laos, and N Vietnam. They speak Tai languages, all of which belong to the Sino-Tibetan language family. There are over 60 million speakers, the majority of whom live in Thailand. Most Thais are Buddhists, but the traditional belief in spirits, *phi*, remains.

**Tigré** a group of people living in N Ethiopia. The Tigré language is spoken by about 2.5 million people; it belongs to the SE Semitic branch of the Afro-Asiatic family. *Tigrinya* is a closely related language spoken slightly to the south.

**Tswana** a member of the majority ethnic group living in Botswana. The Tswana are divided into four subgroups: the Bakwena, the Bamangwato, the Bangwaketse, and the Batawana. Traditionally they are rural-dwelling farmers, though many now leave their homes to work as migrant labourers in South African industries. The Tswana language belongs to the Bantu branch of the Niger-Congo family.

**Tuareg** Arabic name given to nomadic stock-breeders from the W and central Sahara and Sahel (Algeria, Libya, Mali, Niger, and Burkina Faso). The eight Tuareg groups refer to themselves by their own names. Their language, Tamashek, belongs to the Berber branch of the Afro-Asiatic family and is spoken by 500,000–850,000 people. It is written in a noncursive script known as *tifinagh*, derived from ancient Numidian. Tuareg men wear dark blue robes, turbans, and veils.

**Turkoman** or *Turkman* a member of the majority ethnic group living in the Turkmen Soviet Socialist Republic. They live around the Kara Kum desert, to the E of the Caspian Sea, along the borders of Afghanistan and Iran, and within several republics of the USSR. Traditionally the Turkomen were tent-dwelling pastoral nomads, though the majority are now sedentary farmers, especially in the USSR and Iran. Their language belongs to the Turkic branch of the Altaic family. They are predominantly Sunni Muslims.

**Tutsi** a member of a minority ethnic group living in Rwanda and Burundi. Although fewer in number, they have traditionally been politically dominant over the Hutu majority and the Twa (or Pygmies). The Tutsi are traditionally farmers; they also hold virtually all the positions of importance in Burundi's government and army. They have carried out massacres in response to Hutu rebellions, notably in 1972 and 1988. In Rwanda the balance of power is more even.

**Twa** a member of a minority ethnic group forming 1% of the populations of Burundi and Rwanda. The Twa are the aboriginal inhabitants of the region. They are a pygmoid people, and live as nomadic hunter-gatherers in the forests.

**Uigur** a member of a Turkic people living in NW China and the S Soviet Union; they make up about 80% of the population of the Chinese province of Sinkiang. There are about 5 million speakers of Uigur, a language belonging to the Turkic branch of the Altaic family; it is the official language of the province. The Uigur are known to have lived in the region since the 3rd century AD, and converted to Islam in the 14th century. They have been under Chinese rule since the 17th century. A small number fled to Kazakhstan at that time, and it is from them that the present Soviet minority is descended.

**Ukrainian** a member of the majority ethnic group living in the Ukrainian Soviet Socialist Republic; there are minorities in other parts of the USSR, Poland, Czechoslovakia, and Romania. There are 40–45 million speakers of Ukrainian, a member of the East Slavonic branch of the Indo-European family, closely related to Russian. It is sometimes referred to by Russians as Little Russian, although this is a description that Ukrainians generally do not find appropriate. Ukrainian-speaking communities are also found in Canada and the USA.

**Urdu language** a member of the Indo-Iranian branch of the Indo-European language family, related to Hindi and written not in Devanagari but in Arabic script. Urdu is strongly influenced by Farsi (Persian) and Arabic. It is the official language of Pakistan and a language used by Muslims in India.

**Uzbek** a member of the majority ethnic group (almost 70%) living in the Uzbek Soviet Socialist Republic; minorities live in the Turkmen, Tadzhik, and Kazakh republics, and in Afghanistan. Collectivization of the land was introduced under the Soviet government of the 1930s, though some groups in N Afghanistan are still partly nomadic. There are 10–14 million speakers of the Uzbek language, which belongs to the Turkic branch of the Altaic family. Uzbeks are predominantly Sunni Muslims.

**Vedda** (Sinhalese 'hunter') a member of the aboriginal peoples of Sri Lanka, who occupied the island before the arrival of the Aryans around 550 BC. They live mainly in the central highlands, and many practise shifting cultivation. Formerly cave-dwelling hunter-gatherers, they have now almost died out or merged with the rest of the population. They speak a Sinhalese language, belonging to the Indo-European family.

**Wolof** a member of the majority ethnic group living in Senegal. There is also a Wolof minority in Gambia. The Wolof are predominantly arable farmers, some also raise cattle. Before the French colonized the region in the 19th century, the Wolof were divided into kingdoms; the remnants of this three-tiered social structure comprising aristocracy, artisans, and slaves can still be seen. There are about 2 million speakers of Wolof, a language belonging to the Niger-Congo family. The Wolof are Muslims.

**Xhosa** a member of a Bantu people of southern Africa, living mainly in the Black National State of Transkei. Traditionally, the Xhosa were farmers and pastoralists, with a social structure based on a monarchy. Many are now town-dwellers, and provide much of the unskilled labour in South African mines and factories. Their Bantu language belongs to the Niger-Congo family.

**Yanamamo** or **Yanomamo** (plural **Yanamami**) a member of a semi-nomadic South American Indian people, numbering approximately 15,000, who live in S Venezuela and N Brazil. The Yanamamo language belongs to the Macro-Chibcha family, and is divided into several dialects, although there is a common ritual language. Together with other Amazonian peoples, they have been involved in trying to conserve the rainforest where they live. In Brazil gold prospectors on their territory have spread disease and environmental damage.

**Yao** a member of a people living in S China, N Vietnam, N Laos, Thailand, and Myanmar (Burma), and numbering about 4 million (1984). The Yao are generally hill-dwelling farmers practising shifting cultivation, growing rice, vegetables, and also opium poppies. Some are nomadic. The Yao language may belong to either the Sino-Tibetan or the Thai language family. The Yao incorporate elements of ancestor-worship in their animist religion.

**Yi** a large ethnic minority living in S China; there are also Yi populations in Laos, Thailand, and Vietnam, totalling about 5.5 million (1987). The Yi are farmers, producing both crops and livestock. Their language belongs to the Sino-Tibetan family; their religion is animist.

**Yoruba** a member of the majority ethnic group living in SW Nigeria; there is a Yoruba minority in E Benin. They number approximately 20 million in all, and their language belongs to the Kwa branch of the Niger-Congo family. The Yoruba established powerful city states in the 15th century, known for their advanced culture which includes sculpture, art, and music.

**Zulu** a member of a group of southern African peoples mainly from Natal, South Africa. Their present homeland, Kwazulu, represents the nucleus of the once extensive and militaristic Zulu kingdom. Today many Zulus work in the industrial centres around Johannesburg and Durban. The Zulu language, closely related to Xhosa, belongs to the Bantu branch of the Niger-Congo family.

# GRAMMAR AND USAGE

**adjective** grammatical part of speech for words that describe nouns (for example, *new* and *beautiful*, as in 'a new hat' and 'a beautiful day'). Adjectives generally have three degrees (grades or levels for the description of relationships): the positive degree (*new*, *beautiful*) the comparative degree (*newer*, *more beautiful*), and the superlative degree (*newest*, *most beautiful*).

Some adjectives do not normally need comparative and superlative forms; one person cannot be 'more asleep' than someone else, a lone action is unlikely to be 'the most single-handed action ever seen', and many people dislike the expression 'most unique' or 'almost unique', because something unique is supposed to be the only one that exists. For purposes of emphasis or style these conventions may be set aside ('I don't know who is more unique; they are both remarkable people'). Double comparatives such as 'more bigger' are not grammatical in Standard English, but Shakespeare used a double superlative ('the most unkindest cut of all'). Some adjectives may have both the comparative and superlative forms (*commoner* and *more common*; *commonest* and *most common*), usually shorter words take on the suffixes *-er/-est* but occasionally they may be given the *more/most* forms for emphasis or other reasons ('Which of them is the *most clear?*').

When an adjective comes before a noun it is attributive; when it comes after noun and verb (for example, 'It looks *good*') it is predicative. Some adjectives can only be used predicatively ('The child was asleep', but not 'the asleep child'). The participles of verbs are regularly used adjectivally ('a *sleeping* child', '*boiled* milk'), often in compound forms ('a *quick-acting* medicine', 'a *glass-making* factory'; 'a *hard-boiled* egg', '*well-trained* teachers'). Adjectives are often formed by adding suffixes to nouns (sand: sand*y*; nation: nation*al*).

**adverb** grammatical part of speech for words that modify or describe verbs ('She ran *quickly*'), adjectives ('a *beautifully* clear day'), and adverbs ('They did it *really* well'). Most adverbs are formed from adjectives or past participles by adding *-ly* (*quick: quickly*) or *-ally* (*automatic: automatically*).

Sometimes adverbs are formed by adding *-wise* (*likewise* and *clockwise*, as in 'moving *clockwise*'; in 'a *clockwise* direction', *clockwise* is an adjective). Some adverbs have a distinct form from their partnering adjective; for example, *good/well* ('It was *good* work; they did it *well*'). Others do not derive from adjectives (*very*, in '*very* nice'; *tomorrow*, in 'I'll do it *tomorrow*'); and some are unadapted adjectives (*pretty*, as in 'It's *pretty* good'). Sentence adverbs modify whole sentences or phrases: '*Generally*, it rains a lot here'; '*Usually*, the town is busy at this time of year.' Sometimes there is controversy in such matters. *Hopefully* is universally accepted in sentences like 'He looked at them *hopefully*' (= in a hopeful way), but some people dislike it in '*Hopefully*, we'll see you again next year' (= We hope that we'll see you again next year).

**apostrophe** mark (') used in written English and some other languages. In English it serves primarily to indicate either a missing letter (*mustn't* for *must not*) or number ('*47* for *1947*), or grammatical possession ('*John's* camera', '*women's* dresses'). It is often omitted in proper names (Publishers Association,

Actors Studio, *Collins Dictionary*). Many people otherwise competent in writing have great difficulty with the apostrophe, which has never been stable at any point in its history.

An apostrophe may precede the plural *s* used with numbers and abbreviations (*the 1970's, a group of P.O.W.'s*) but is equally often omitted (*the 1970s, a group of POWs*). For possessives of certain words ending with *s*, usage is split, as between *James's book* and *James' book*. Names and dates used adjectivally are not usually followed by an apostrophe ('a *1950s* car', 'a *Beatles* record'). The use of an apostrophe to help indicate a plural (as in a shopkeeper's *Apple's* and *Tomato's*, followed by their prices) is regarded by many as semiliterate.

**article** grammatical part of speech. There are two articles in English: the *definite article the*, which serves to specify or identify a noun (as in 'This is *the* book I need'), and the *indefinite article a* or (before vowels) *an*, which indicates a single unidentified noun ('They gave me *a* piece of paper and *an* envelope').

Some people use the form 'an' before *h* ('an historic building'); this practice dates from the 17th century, when an initial *h* was often not pronounced (as in '*honour*'), and is nowadays widely considered rather pompous.

**asterisk** starlike punctuation mark ( * ) used to link the asterisked word with a note at the bottom of a page, and to indicate that certain letters are missing from a word (especially a taboo word such as 'f**k').

An asterisk is also used to indicate that a word or usage is nonexistent, for example, 'In English we say three boys and not three *boy'.

**colon** punctuation mark (:) intended to direct the reader's attention forward, usually because what follows explains or develops what has just been written (for example, *The farmer owned the following varieties of dogs: a spaniel, a pointer, a terrier, a border collie, and three mongrels*).

**comma** punctuation mark (,) intended to provide breaks or pauses within a sentence; commas may come at the end of a clause, to set off a phrase, or in lists (for example, *apples, pears, plums, and pineapples*).

Some writers, uncertain where sentences properly end, use a comma instead of a period (or full stop), writing *We saw John last night, it was good to see him again*, rather than *We saw John last night. It was good to see him again*. The meaning is entirely clear in both cases. One solution in such situations is to use a *semicolon* (;), which bridges the gap between the close association of the comma and the sharp separation of the period. For parenthetical commas, see parenthesis.

**conjunction** grammatical part of speech that serves to connect words, phrases, and clauses; for example *and* in 'apples and pears' and *but* in 'we're going but they aren't'.

**exclamation mark** or *exclamation point* punctuation mark (!) used to indicate emphasis or strong emotion ('That's terrible!'). It is appropriate after interjections ('Rats!'), emphatic greetings ('Yo!'), and orders ('Shut up!'), as well as those sentences beginning *How* or *What* that are not questions ('How embarrassing!', 'What a surprise!').

The exclamation mark is most often seen in dialogue. Its use is kept to a minimum in narrative prose and technical writing. Within a quotation an exclamation mark may be placed in square brackets to indicate that the writer or editor is surprised by something. The convention that all sentences in comic books end with an exclamation mark is on the wane.

**grammar** the rules of combining words into phrases, clauses, sentences, and paragraphs. Emphasis on the standardizing impact of print has meant that spoken or colloquial language is often perceived as less grammatical than written language, but all forms of a language, standard or otherwise, have their own grammatical systems of differing complexity. People often acquire several overlapping grammatical systems within one language; for example, one formal system for writing and standard communication and one less formal system for everyday and peer-group communication. Originally 'grammar' was an analytical approach to writing, intended to improve the understanding and the skills of scribes, philosophers, and writers. When compared with Latin, English has been widely regarded as having less grammar or at least a simpler grammar; it would be truer, however, to say that English and Latin have different grammars, each complex in its own way. In linguistics (the contemporary study of language) grammar, or syntax, refers to the arrangement of the elements in a language for the purposes of acceptable communication in speech, writing, and print.

All forms of a language, standard or otherwise, have their grammars or grammatical systems, which children acquire through use; a child may acquire several overlapping systems within one language (especially a nonstandard form for everyday life and a standard form linked with writing, school, and national life). Not even the most comprehensive grammar book (or grammar) of a language like English, French, Arabic, or Japanese completely covers or fixes the implicit grammatical system that people use in their daily lives. The rules and tendencies of natural grammar operate largely in nonconscious ways but can, for many social and professional purposes, be studied and developed for conscious as well as inherent skills.

**hyphen** punctuation mark (-) with two functions: to join words, parts of words, syllables, and so on, for particular purposes; and to mark a word break at the end of a line. Adjectival compounds (see adjective) are hyphenated because they modify the noun jointly rather than separately ('a small-town boy' is a boy from a small town; 'a small town boy' is a small boy from a town). The use of hyphens with adverbs

## WHAT PRICE TRADITIONAL KNOWLEDGE?

Ethnobotanists and anthropologists are becoming increasingly concerned about the use of traditional knowledge by companies in the industrialized world. Natural perfumes, skin creams, insecticides, teas, dyes and fibres are among the products based on the traditional skills of native peoples such as the Amazonian Indians. There is an expanding market for natural products—ranging from food to medicine—and this has stimulated more research by companies into traditional knowledge systems. Some ethnobotanists have estimated that the annual world market from medicines derived from plants discovered by indigenous peoples amounts to US$ 43 billion. Only a tiny proportion of the profits yielded from drugs have reached the indigenous peoples who helped researchers locate them. One of the biggest growth areas in recent years has been in body and hair care products based on plants. Many of these goods were originally devised and used in Third World countries before their commercial potential was realized. The international seed industry also makes use of genetic materials from crops developed by Third World farmers. Plants cultivated by traditional methods are often more drought and disease resistant than crops grown in the industrialized countries.

Some ethnobotanists and anthropologists have argued that the rights of native peoples should be safeguarded and that they should be compensated for their traditional skills. This issue was debated at the first international congress of the International Society for Ethnobiology, held in 1988 in Belem, Brazil. In what has become known as the 'Declaration of Belem' the delegates called for action to protect the intellectual property rights of indigenous peoples. Both the World Intellectual Property Organization and UNESCO have tried to devise conventions to protect aspects of indigenous knowledge. A special symposium on ethical issues relating to anthropological research with native populations was presented at the Society of Applied Anthropology's conference in York, England, in 1990. One of the main exponents

of schemes to protect the intellectual rights of native peoples is Dr Darrell Posey, a well-known ethnobotanist who is Director of the Programme of Ethnobiology, Museu Parense Emilio Goeldi, Belem.

Dr Posey has argued that the contribution made by indigenous peoples is vital for the development of more environmentally sustainable methods of utilizing the earth's resources. For example, only 2% of plant species are regarded by many agronomists as having commercial value; the exploitation, however, of this small proportion is often at the expense of the other 98% of species, many of which face extinction. In contrast, native peoples make use of a wider range of plant species and have, therefore, much to teach the scientific world.

Many scientists oppose the notion of intellectual property rights, arguing that freedom of access to knowledge lies at the heart of scientific endeavour. Doubts about the feasibility of enforcing laws to protect rights in a complex and varied international legal system have also been expressed. In some cases—particularly when the same traditional skills are used by several societies or tribal groups—it may be impossible to establish ownership. Furthermore, in some societies the relevant knowledge may be the preserve of one of the sexes (for example, the women), or belong to certain individuals, such as traditional healers or shamans. In such cases, should only the women or the shamans receive the benefits? It may also prove difficult to find ways of rewarding peoples who do not belong to market-based societies without making them more dependent on the consumer society. Is it realistic to think in terms of paying royalties to peoples who are difficult to contact either through remoteness or nomadic lifestyles? In response, ethnobotanists and anthropologists have argued that native peoples are the custodians of much of the biological diversity of this planet and that they should have the right to decide for themselves whether or not they should enter the market economy. The debate continues.

is redundant unless an identical adjective exists (*well*, *late*, *long*): 'late-blooming plant' but 'brightly blooming plant'.

Phrasal verbs are not hyphenated ('things *turned out* well', 'it *washed up* on the beach') unless used adjectivally ('a well-*turned-out* crowd', 'a *washed-up* athlete'). Nouns formed from phrasal verbs are hyphenated or joined together ('a good *turnout* tonight', 'please do the *washing-up*'). In the use of certain prefixes, modern style is moving towards omitting the hyphen (*noncooperation*).

The hyphenation of compound nouns in English is by no means clear cut; the same person may inadvertently in one article write, for example, *world view*, *worldview* and *world-view*.

Here, conventional hyphenation is a first stage in bringing two words together; if their

close association is then generally agreed, the two words are written or printed as one (*teapot*, as opposed to *tea-pot* or *tea pot*), or are kept apart for visual and aesthetic reasons (*coffee pot* rather than *coffee-pot* or *coffeepot*). Practice does, however, vary greatly.

**inflection** or **inflexion** in grammatical analysis, an ending or other element in a word that indicates its grammatical function (whether plural or singular, masculine or feminine, subject or object, and so on).

In a highly inflected language like Latin, nouns, verbs, and adjectives have many inflectional endings (for example, in the word *amabunt* the base *am* means 'love' and the complex *abunt* indicates the kind of verb, the future tense, indicative mood, active voice, third person, and plurality). English has few inflections: for example, the *s* for plural forms (as in *the books*) and for the third person singular of verbs (as in *He runs*).

**noun** grammatical part of speech that names a person, animal, object, quality, idea, or time. Nouns can refer to objects such as *house, tree* (**concrete nouns**); specific persons and places such as *John Alden*, the *White House* (**proper nouns**); ideas such as *love, anger* (**abstract nouns**). In English many simple words are both noun and verb (*jump, reign, rain*). Adjectives are sometimes used as nouns ('a *local* man', 'one of the *locals*').

A common noun does not begin with a capital letter (*child, cat*), whereas a proper noun does, because it is the name of a particular person, animal, or place (*Jane, Rover, Norfolk*). A concrete noun refers to things that can be sensed (*dog, box*), whereas an abstract noun relates to generalizations abstracted from life as we observe it (*fear, condition, truth*). A **countable noun** can have a plural form (*book: books*), while an **uncountable noun** or mass noun cannot (*dough*). Many English nouns can be used both countably and uncountably (*wine*: 'Have some *wine*; it's one of our best *wines*'). A **collective noun** is singular in form but refers to a group (*flock, group, committee*), and a **compound noun** is made up of two or more nouns (*teapot, baseball team, car-factory strike committee*). A **verbal noun** is formed from a verb as a gerund or otherwise (*build: building*; *regulate: regulation*).

**participle** in grammar, a form of the verb, in English either a **present participle** ending in *-ing* (for example, 'work*ing*' in 'They were work*ing*', 'work*ing* men', and 'a hard-*working* team') or a **past participle** ending in *-ed* in regular verbs (for example, 'train*ed*' in 'They have been *trained* well', '*trained* soldiers', and 'a well-*trained* team').

In irregular verbs the past participle has a special form (for example, drive/*driven*; light/*lit*, burn/*burned, burnt*). The participle is used to open such constructions as '*Coming* down the stairs, she paused and ...' and '*Angered* by the news, he ...'. Such constructions, when not logically formed, may have irritating or ambiguous results. '*Driving* along a country road, a stone broke my windscreen' suggests that stone was driving along the road. This illogical usage is a **misplaced participle**. A **dangling** or **hanging participle** has nothing at all to relate to: 'While *driving* along a country road there was a loud noise under the car.' Such sentences need to be completely re-expressed, except in some well-established usages where the participle can stand alone (for example, '*Taking* all things into consideration, your actions were justified').

**part of speech** the grammatical function of a word, described in the grammatical tradition of the Western world, based on Greek and Latin. The four major parts of speech are the noun, verb, adjective, and adverb; the minor parts of speech vary according to schools of grammatical theory, but include the article, conjunction, preposition, and pronoun.

In languages like Greek and Latin, the part of speech of a word tends to be invariable (usually marked by an ending, or inflection); in English, it is much harder to recognize the function of a word simply by its form. Some English words may have only one function (for example, *and* as a conjunction). Others may have several functions (for example, *fancy*, which is a noun in the phrase 'flights of *fancy*', a verb in '*Fancy* that!', and an adjective in 'a *fancy* hat').

**period** punctuation mark (.). The term 'period' is universally understood in English and is the preferred usage in North America; **full stop** is the preferred term in the UK. The period has two functions: to mark the end of a sentence and to indicate that a word has been abbreviated. It is also used in mathematics to indicate decimals and is then called a **point**.

Such abbreviations as acronyms are unlikely to have periods (NATO rather than N.A.T.O.), and contractions (incorporating the last letter of the word, for example Dr for 'doctor') may or may not have periods. In such contexts as fictional dialogue and advertising, periods sometimes follow incomplete sentences in an effort to represent speech more faithfully or for purposes of emphasis.

**preposition** in grammar, a part of speech coming before a noun or a pronoun to show a location (*in, on*), time (*during*), or some other relationship (for example, figurative relationships in phrases like '*by* heart' or '*on* time').

In the sentence 'Put the book *on* the table', *on* is a preposition governing the noun 'table' and relates the verb 'put' to the phrase 'the table', indicating where the book should go. Some words of English that are often prepositional in function may, however, be used adverbially, as in the sentences, 'He picked the book *up*' and 'He picked *up* the book', in which the ordering is different but the meaning the same. In such cases *up* is called an **adverbial particle** and the form *pick up* is a **phrasal verb**.

**pronoun** in grammar, a part of speech that is used in place of a noun, usually to save repetition of the noun (for example 'The people arrived around nine o'clock. *They* behaved as though we were expecting *them*').

*They, them, he,* and *she* are **personal pronouns** (representing people); *this/these,* and *that/those* are **demonstrative pronouns** (demonstrating or pointing to something: '*this* book and not *that* book'. Words like *that* and *who* can be **relative pronouns** in sentences like 'She said *that* she was coming' and 'Tell me *who* did it' relating one clause to another), and *myself* and *himself* are **reflexive pronouns** (reflecting back to a person, as in 'He did it *himself*').

**punctuation** the system of conventional signs (punctuation marks) and spaces by means of which written and printed language is organized in order to be as readable, clear, and logical as possible.

It contributes to the effective layout of visual language; if a work is not adequately punctuated, there may be problems of ambiguity and unclear association among words. Conventions of punctuation differ from language to language, and there are preferred styles in the punctuation of a language like English. Some people prefer a fuller use of punctuation, while others punctuate lightly; comparably, the use of punctuation will vary according to the kind of passage being produced: a personal letter, a newspaper article, and a technical report are all laid out and punctuated in distinctive ways.

Standard punctuation marks and conventions include the period (full stop or point), comma, colon, semicolon, exclamation mark (or point), question mark, apostrophe, asterisk, hyphen, and parenthesis (including dashes, brackets, and the use of parenthetical commas).

**question mark** punctuation mark (?) used to indicate enquiry or doubt. When indicating enquiry, it is placed at the end of a *direct question* ('Who is coming?') but never at the end of an *indirect question* ('He asked us who was coming'). When indicating doubt, it usually appears between brackets, to show that a writer or editor is puzzled or uncertain about quoted text.

**semicolon** punctuation mark (;) with a function halfway between the separation of sentence from sentence by means of a period, or full stop, and the gentler separation provided by a comma. It also helps separate items in a complex list: 'pens, pencils, and paper; staples, such as rice and beans; tools, various; and rope'.

Rather than the abrupt 'We saw Mark last night. It was good to see him again', and the casual (and often condemned) 'We saw Mark last night, it was good to see him again', the semicolon reflects a link in a two-part statement and is considered good style: *We saw Mark last night; it was good to see him again*. In such cases an alternative is to use a comma followed by *and* or *but*.

**verb** the grammatical part of speech for what someone or something does (*to go*), experiences (*to live*), or is (*to be*). Verbs involve the grammatical categories known as number (singular or plural: 'He *runs*; they *run*'), voice (active or passive: 'She *writes* books; it *is written*'), mood (statements, questions, orders, emphasis, necessity, condition), aspect (completed or continuing action: 'She *danced*; she *was dancing*'), and tense (variation according to time: simple present tense, present progressive tense, simple past tense, and so on). Many verbs are formed from nouns and adjectives by adding affixes (prison: *imprison*; light: *enlighten*; fresh: *freshen up*; pure: *purify*). Some words function as both nouns and verbs (*crack*, *run*), both adjectives and verbs (*clean*; *ready*), and as nouns, adjectives, and verbs (*fancy*). In the sentences 'They *saw* the accident', 'She *is working* today', and 'He *should have been trying to meet* them', the words in italics are verbs (and, in the last case) two verb groups together; these sentences show just how complex the verbs of English can be.

**types of verb**
A **transitive** verb takes a direct object ('He *saw* the house').

An **intransitive** verb has no object ('She *laughed*').

An **auxiliary or helping** verb is used to express tense and/or mood ('He *was* seen'; 'They *may* come').

A **modal** verb or **modal auxiliary** generally shows only mood; common modals are *may/ might*, *will/would*, *can/could*, *shall/should*, *must*.

The **infinitive** of the verb usually includes *to* (*to go*, *to run* and so on), but may be a bare infinitive (for example, after modals, as in 'She may *go*').

A **regular** verb forms tenses in the normal way (*I walk: I walked: I have walked*); irregular verbs do not (*swim: swam: swum; put: put: put*; and so on). Because of their conventional nature, regular verbs are also known as weak verbs, while some irregular verbs are strong verbs with special vowel changes across tenses, as in *swim: swam: swum* and *ride: rode: ridden*.

A **phrasal verb** is a construction in which a particle attaches to a usually single-syllable verb (for example, *put* becoming *put up*, as in 'He put up some money for the project', and *put up with*, as in 'I can't put up with this nonsense any longer').

---

### Languages spoken

---

*Do you speak any language other than English well enough to be able to make sense of a newspaper written in that language? if yes, which language?*

---

| | |
|---|---|
| French | 19 |
| German | 7 |
| Italian | 3 |
| Spanish | 4 |
| Greek | 1 |
| Other | 2 |
| No, none | 75 |

---

# POLITICAL IDEOLOGIES

**absolutism** or *absolute monarchy* system of government in which the ruler or rulers have unlimited power. The principle of an absolute monarch, given a right to rule by God, was extensively used in Europe during the 17th and 18th centuries. Absolute monarchy is contrasted with limited or constitutional monarchy, in which the sovereign's powers are defined or limited.

**anarchism** political belief that society should have no government, laws, police, or other authority, but should be a free association of all its members. It does not mean 'without order'; most theories of anarchism imply an order of a very strict and symmetrical kind, but they maintain that such order can be achieved by cooperation. Anarchism must not be confused with nihilism (a purely negative and destructive activity directed against society); anarchism is essentially a pacifist movement.

**authoritarianism** rule of a country by a dominant elite who repress opponents and the press to maintain their own wealth and power. They are frequently indifferent to activities not affecting their security, and rival power centres, such as trade unions and political parties, are often allowed to exist, although under tight control. An extreme form is totalitarianism.

**collectivism** a position in which the collective (such as the state) has priority over its individual members. It is the opposite of individualism, which is itself a variant of anarchy.

**communism** revolutionary socialism based on the theories of the political philosophers Marx and Engels, emphasizing common ownership of the means of production and a planned economy. The principle held is that each should work according to their capacity and receive according to their needs. Politically, it seeks the overthrow of capitalism through a proletarian revolution. The first communist state was the USSR after the revolution of 1917.

Revolutionary socialist parties and groups united to form communist parties in other countries (in the UK 1920). After World War II, communism was enforced in those countries that came under Soviet occupation. China emerged after 1961 as a rival to the USSR in world communist leadership, and other countries attempted to adapt communism to their own needs.

In the late 1980s there was an expansion of political and economic freedom in Eastern Europe, sparked by the relaxation of strict party orthodoxy in the USSR and the institution of the new policy of *perestroika* ('restructuring') by Mikhail Gorbachev. As a result, the Warsaw Pact countries moved towards the ending of communist rule and its replacement by free elections within more democratic political systems.

**conservatism** approach to government favouring the maintenance of existing institutions and identified with a number of Western political parties, such as the British Conservative, German Christian Democratic, and Australian Liberal parties. It tends to be explicitly nondoctrinaire and pragmatic but generally emphasizes free-enterprise capitalism, minimal government intervention in the economy, rigid law and order, and the importance of national traditions.

**democracy** government by the people, usually through elected representatives. In the modern world, democracy has developed from the American and French revolutions.

In *direct democracy* the whole people meets for the making of laws or the direction of executive officers (for example in Athens in the 5th century BC, and allegedly in modern Libya). Today it is represented mainly by the use of the referendum, as in the UK, France, Switzerland, and certain states of the USA.

The two concepts underlying *liberal democracy* are the right to representative government and the right to enjoy individual freedom. In practice, the principal features of a liberal democratic system include representative institutions based on majority rule, through free elections and a choice of political parties; accountability of the government to the electorate; freedom of expression, assembly, and the individual, guaranteed by an independent judiciary; limitations on the power of government.

It is estimated that approximately a third (1.6 billion) of the world's total population live within political systems founded on liberal democracy. While it is an ideology that has been successfully implemented in all parts of the world, this type of political system tends to flourish best in high-income, 'First World' states (thus, liberal democracies are found in 21 of the world's top 30 countries in terms of per capita income, but in only six of the bottom 50).

*Social democracy* is founded on the belief in the gradual evolution of a democratic socialism within existing political structures. The earliest was the German *Sozialdemokratische Partei* (SPD), today one of the two major German parties, created in 1875. Parties along the lines of the German model were founded in the last two decades of the 19th century in a number of countries including Austria, Belgium, Holland, Hungary, Poland, and Russia. The British Labour Party is in the social democratic tradition.

**egalitarianism** the belief that all citizens in a state should have equal rights and privileges. Interpretations of this can vary, from the notion of equality of opportunity to equality in material welfare and political decision-taking. Some states clearly reject any thought of egalitarianism; most accept the concept of equal opportunities but recognize that people's abilities vary widely. Even those states which claim to be socialist find it necessary to have hierarchical structures in the political, social, and economic spheres. Egalitarianism was one of the principles of the French Revolution.

**fascism** ideology that denies all rights to individuals in their relations with the state; specifically, the totalitarian nationalist movement founded in Italy 1919 by Mussolini and followed by Hitler's Germany 1933.

**imperialism** the policy of extending the power and rule of a government beyond its own boundaries. A country may attempt to dominate others by direct rule or by less obvious means such as control of markets for goods or raw materials. The latter is often called neo-colonialism.

**individualism** a view in which the individual takes precedence over the collective, the opposite of collectivism. The term *possessive individualism* has been applied to the writings of Locke and Bentham, describing society as comprised of individuals interacting through market relations.

**liberalism** political and social theory that favours representative government, freedom of the press, speech, and worship, the abolition of class privileges, the use of state resources to protect the welfare of the individual, and international free trade. It is historically associated with the Liberal Party in the UK and the Democratic Party in the USA.

**Maoism** form of communism based on the ideas and teachings of the Chinese communist leader Mao Zedong. It involves an adaptation of Marxism to suit conditions in China and apportions a much greater role to agriculture and the peasantry in the building of socialism, thus effectively bypassing the capitalist (industrial) stage envisaged by Marx.

**Marxism** philosophical system, developed by the 19th-century German social theorists Marx and Engels, also known as *dialectical materialism*, under which matter gives rise to mind (materialism) and all is subject to change. As applied to history, it supposes that the succession of feudalism, capitalism, socialism, and finally the classless society is inevitable. The stubborn resistance of any existing system to change necessitates its complete overthrow in the *class struggle*—in the case of capitalism, by the proletariat—rather than gradual modification.

**nationalism** a movement that consciously aims to unify a nation, create a state, or liberate it from foreign rule. Nationalist movements became a potent factor in European politics during the 19th century; since 1900 nationalism has become a strong force in Asia and Africa and in the late 1980s revived strongly in E Europe.

**pluralism** in political science, the view that decision-making in contemporary liberal democracies is the outcome of competition among several interest groups in a political system characterized by free elections, representative institutions, and open access to the organs of power. This concept is opposed by corporatism and other approaches that perceive power to be centralized in the state and its principal elites.

**socialism** movement aiming at the establishment of a classless society through the substitution of common for private ownership of the means of production, distribution and exchange. The term is used both to cover all movements with this aim, such as communism and anarchism, and more narrowly for evolutionary socialism or democracy. In general the tendency since 1917 has been for a clear distinction, if not opposition, to exist between parties governed by Marx's revolutionary, 'scientific' socialism and the gradualist, reforming approach of the British Labour Party and Western European Social Democratic Parties.

**Thatcherism** a political outlook associated with Margaret Thatcher but stemming from an individualist view found in Britain's 19th-century Liberal and 20th-century Conservative parties. Thatcherism is an ideology no longer confined to Britain and comprises a belief in the efficacy of market forces, the need for strong central government, and a conviction that self-help is preferable to reliance on the state, combined with a strong element of nationalism.

**theocracy** a political system run by priests, as was once found in Tibet. In practical terms it means a system where religious values determine political decisions. The clearest modern example was Iran during the period when Ayatollah Khomeini was its religious leader, 1979–89. The term was coined by the 1st century AD historian Josephus.

**totalitarianism** government control of all activities within a country, overtly political or otherwise, as in fascist or communist dictatorships. Examples of totalitarian regimes are Italy under Benito Mussolini 1922–45; Germany under Adolph Hitler 1933–45; the USSR under Joseph Stalin from 1930s until his death in 1953; more recently Romania under Nicolae Ceausescu 1974–89.

**Trotskyism** form of Marxism advocated by Leon Trotsky. Its central concept is that of *permanent revolution*. In his view a proletarian revolution, leading to a socialist society, could not be achieved in isolation, so it would be necessary to spark off further revolutions throughout Europe and ultimately worldwide. This was in direct opposition to the Stalinist view that socialism should be built and consolidated within individual countries.

# POLITICAL TERMS

**affirmative action** in the USA, a government-endorsed policy of positive discrimination that favours members of minority ethnic groups and women in such areas as employment and education, designed to counter the effects of long-term discrimination against them. The policy has been controversial, and has prompted lawsuits by white males who have

# OUT WITH THE COLD WAR, IN WITH THE NEW WORLD ORDER?

At the Nov 1990 Paris Conference on Security and Cooperation in Europe (CSCE) four decades of military confrontation between East and West were formally declared at an end. Inaugurating a 'new era of democracy, peace and unity in Europe', a Charter of Paris for a New Europe was adopted by the 34 participating nations. It pledged adherence to the liberal-democratic-pluralist principles of free, fair elections, freedom of thought and expression, respect for private property, and gave encouragement to the development of market economies. The reunion of Europe had clearly been achieved on Western terms.

Concurrently, the leaders of the 16 member states of the NATO and six member states of the Warsaw Pact signed a Treaty on Conventional Armed Forces in Europe (CFE). It agreed upon the imposition of equal, much reduced, ceilings on non-nuclear weapons, and included a joint renunciation of the use of force. Four months later, the Warsaw Pact formally dissolved itself as a military alliance.

The Cold War era, dating from the 1945 Yalta Conference, was over, and the first tentative steps towards what President Bush termed the 'New World Order' were made. Allies at last, the USA and USSR began to cooperate through the United Nations to ensure collective security across the globe, promote progressive values, and help achieve the settlement of outstanding regional conflicts. This dramatic turnaround was made possible by the efforts since 1985 of Soviet leader Mikhail Gorbachev, who, working in tandem with foreign minister Eduard Shevardnadze, launched a thorough review of the USSR's internal and external policies. The conclusion was that competing with NATO in an increasingly high-tech arms race was politically and economically unsustainable. To free resources for the civilian sector, there would have to be progressive retrenchment overseas. The unexpected element within Moscow's 'new thinking' was the rejection of the Brezhnev Doctrine, the idea that socialist states must forever remain so, at gunpoint if necessary. Its

abandonment was heralded by the Feb 1988 announcement of Soviet withdrawal from Afghanistan, and was confirmed by events during the autumn and winter of 1989-90. With the new so-called 'Sinatra Doctrine', the governments and peoples of the USSR's satellite states were allowed to develop in their 'own way'. The consequences were far-reaching: a succession of formerly socialist regimes was rapidly toppled 1989–91 within Eastern Europe and Asia by popular revolutions. In the process, the seemingly fossilized post-World War II political order was dramatically rearranged. Germany was reunited (within NATO), and within the artificial borders of Eastern and Central Europe a succession of regionalist and nationalist conflicts erupted. The Paris CSCE Conference Nov 1990 not only put a formal end to the Cold War era, it started the process of constructing the political-military architecture of a New Europe. Three major new structures and institutions were established: a permanent CSCE secretariat, based in Prague; a Conflict Prevention Centre, based in Vienna; and an Office for Free Elections, based in Warsaw. However, uncertainty surrounded the fate of the military organizations inherited from the Cold War era. By spring 1991 the Warsaw Pact was effectively dissolved and during 1991 most Soviet troops departed from Czechoslovakia, Hungary and Poland, leaving just 360,000 in the eastern Länder of Germany, set to depart by 1994. NATO, however, remains in place and appears unwilling to admit, as associate members, the newly democratized states situated on its front line. A period of readjustment lies ahead. If the fundamental post-1985 changes within the USSR prove irreversible, a longer-term remoulding of Europe's military structures will become necessary, possibly entailing the supersession of NATO by an upgraded Western European Union (WEU), serving as the European Community's defence. Also, following the 1990-91 Gulf Conflict precedent, the United Nations might continue to 'police' the new, less predictable, multipolar world order.

NATO and Warsaw Pact leaders at the Paris Conference on Security and Cooperation in Europe (CSCE), Nov 1990.

## HUMAN RIGHTS UPDATE

**The Universal Declaration of Human Rights** is a charter of civil and political rights drawn up by the United Nations 1948. These rights include the right to life, liberty, education, and equality before the law; to freedom of movement, religion, association, and information; and to a nationality. Under the European Convention of Human Rights 1950, the Council of Europe established the **European Commission of Human Rights** (headquarters in Strasbourg, France), which investigates complaints by states or individuals, and its findings are examined by the **European Court of Human Rights** (established 1959), whose compulsory jurisdiction has been recognized by a number of states, including the UK. In 1988 the European Court condemned as unlawful the UK procedure of holding those suspected of terrorism for up to seven days with no judicial control.

The declaration is not legally binding, and the frequent contraventions worldwide are monitored by organizations such as Amnesty International.

Amnesty International's 1991 report showed that human rights abuses continued and often worsened in 141 countries: in over 100 countries prisoners were tortured or ill-treated; in 29 countries thousands of people disappeared or were executed outside the law; in El Salvador killings by death squads doubled; children disappeared or were shot in Brazil, Guatemala, and Peru. In China, 750 executions by firing squad were the highest number since 1983. Following the Iraqi invasion of Kuwait in Aug 1990, world attention focused on reports of massacre and torture by Saddam Hussein's regime, with other violations receiving less attention from governments and the media—including reports of serious human rights abuses in (amongst other countries) Chad, Colombia, Egypt, El Salvador, Myanmar (Burma), Sudan, Syria, and Turkey.

However, 1990 was a record year for countries abolishing the death penalty—Mozambique, Namibia, the Czech and Slovak Federative Republic, Ireland, Andorra, São Tomé and Príncipe, and Hungary abolished it completely and Nepal abolished it for ordinary offences. There was also a sharp decrease in the use of the death penalty in South Africa.

**Human Rights Day** is 10 Dec, commemorating the adoption of the Universal Declaration of Human Rights by the UN General Assembly.

been denied jobs or education as a result.

Positive discrimination in favour of ethnic-minority construction companies by local government was outlawed in the UK in Jan 1989.

**alliance** agreement between two or more states to come to each other's assistance in the event of war. Alliances were criticized after World War I as having contributed to the outbreak of war but NATO and until 1991 the Warsaw Pact have been major parts of the post-1945 structure of international relations.

**ambassador** officer of the highest rank in the diplomatic service, who represents the head of one sovereign state at the court or capital of another.

**apartheid** the racial-segregation policy of the government of South Africa that began 1948, when it was legislated by the Afrikaner National Party that had gained power; in 1990, apartheid legislation began to be repealed by President de Klerk and a new constitution promised. Also in 1990, Nelson Mandela, the current vice-president of the African National Congress, was finally released.

The term has also been applied to similar movements and other forms of racial separation, for example social or educational, in other parts of the world.

**arms control** attempts to limit the arms race between the superpowers by reaching agreements to restrict the production of certain weapons, as in the Strategic Arms Limitation Talks (SALT) of the 1970s and the Geneva and Helsinki negotiations of the 1980s.

**autonomy** political self-government.

**ballot** the process of voting in an election. In political elections in democracies ballots are usually secret: voters indicate their choice of candidate on a voting slip which is placed in a sealed ballot box. **Ballot rigging** is the fraudulent interference with the voting process or the counting of votes.

**blockade** the cutting-off of a place by hostile forces by land, sea, or air so as to prevent any movement to or fro, in order to compel a surrender without attack. For example, in 1990 a United Nations resolution stated the determination of the member countries to implement a blockade in an attempt to force Iraq, under the leadership of President Saddam Hussein, to withdraw from the invaded territory of Kuwait.

**cabinet** the group of ministers holding a country's highest executive offices who decide government policy. In Britain the cabinet system originated under the Stuarts. Under William III it became customary for the king to select his ministers from the party with a parliamentary majority. The US cabinet, unlike the British, does not initiate legislation, and its members, appointed by the president, must not be members of Congress.

**citizenship** status as a member of a state. In most countries citizenship may be acquired either by birth or by naturalization. The status confers rights such as voting and the protection of the law and also imposes responsibilities such as military service, in some countries.

**civil service** body of administrative staff appointed to carry out the policy of a government. Members of the UK civil service may not take an active part in, and do not change with, the government.

**coalition** association of political groups, usually for some limited or short-term purpose, such as fighting an election or forming a government when one party has failed to secure a majority in a legislature.

**constitution** the fundamental laws of a state, laying down the system of government and defining the relations of the legislature, executive, and judiciary to each other and to the citizens. Since the French Revolution almost all countries (the UK is one exception) have adopted written constitutions; that of the USA (1787) is the oldest.

**council** in local government in England and Wales, a popularly elected local assembly charged with the government of the area within its boundaries. Under the Local Government Act of 1972, there are three types: county councils, district councils, and parish councils.

**coup d'état** or **coup** forcible takeover of the government of a country by elements from within that country, generally carried out by violent or illegal means. It differs from a revolution in typically being carried out by a small group (for example, of army officers or opposition politicians) to install its leader as head of government, rather than being a mass uprising by the people. Recent coups include the overthrow of the socialist government of Chile in 1973 by a right-wing junta, and the military seizure of power in Suriname in Dec 1990.

**détente** (French) a reduction of political tension and the easing of strained relations between nations; for example, the ending of the Cold War 1989–90.

**dictatorship** the term or office of an absolute ruler, overriding the constitution. Although dictatorships were common in Latin America during the 19th century, the only European example during this period was the rule of Napoleon III. The crises following World War I produced many dictatorships, including the regimes of Atatürk and Pilsudski (nationalist); Mussolini, Hitler, Primo de Rivera, Franco, and Salazar (all right-wing); and Stalin (communist).

**diplomacy** process by which states attempt to settle their differences through peaceful means such as negotiation or arbitration.

**dissident** in one-party states, a person intellectually dissenting from the official line. Dissidents have been sent into exile, prison, labour camps, and mental institutions, or deprived of their jobs. In the USSR the number of imprisoned dissidents declined from more than 600 in 1986 to fewer than 100 in 1990, of whom the majority were ethnic nationalists. In China the number of prisoners of conscience increased after the 1989 Tiananmen Square massacre, and in South Africa, despite the release of Nelson Mandela in 1990, numerous political dissidents remained in jail.

**federalism** system of government where two or more separate states unite under a common central government while retaining a considerable degree of local autonomy. A federation should be distinguished from a **confederation**, a looser union of states for mutual assistance.

Switzerland, the USSR, the USA, Canada, Australia, and Malaysia are all examples of federal government, and many supporters of the European Community see it as the forerunner of a federal Europe.

**glasnost** Soviet leader Mikhail Gorbachev's policy of liberalizing various aspects of Soviet life, such as introducing greater freedom of expression and information and opening up relations with Western countries.

Glasnost has involved the lifting of bans on books, plays, and films, the release of political dissidents, the tolerance of religious worship, a reappraisal of Soviet history (destalinization), the encouragement of investigative journalism to uncover political corruption, and the sanctioning of greater candour in the reporting of social problems and disasters (such as Chernobyl).

Under legislation introduced 1990, censorship of mass media was abolished; however, publication of state secrets, calls for the overthrow of the state by force, incitement of national or religious hatred, and state interference in people's private lives were prohibited. Journalists' rights to access were enshrined, and the right of reply instituted. Citizens gained the right to receive information from abroad. But as the political crisis deepened during 1991, censorship began to be reimposed, placing the future of glasnost in doubt.

**high commissioner** representative of one independent Commonwealth country in the capital of another, ranking with ambassador.

**judiciary** in constitutional terms, the system of courts and body of judges in a country. The independence of the judiciary from other branches of the central authority is generally considered to be an essential feature of a democratic political system. This independence is often written into a nation's constitution and is protected from abuse by politicians.

**junta** (Spanish, 'council') the military rulers of a country after an army takeover, as in Turkey in 1980.

**left wing** the progressive, radical, or socialist faction of the political spectrum. The term originated in the French National Assembly 1789, where the nobles sat in the place of honour to the right of the president, and the commons sat to the left. It is also usual to speak of the right, left, and centre, when referring to the different elements composing a single party.

**lobby** individual or pressure group that sets out to influence government action. The lobby is prevalent in the USA, where the term originated in the 1830s from the practice of those wishing to influence state policy waiting for elected representatives in the lobby of the Capitol.

**local government** that part of government dealing mainly with matters concerning the inhabitants of a particular area or town, usually financed at least in part by local taxes. In the USA and UK local government has had com-

## G7

**The Group of Seven** consists of the seven wealthiest nations in the world: the USA, Japan, Germany, France, the UK, Italy, and Canada. Since 1975 the heads of government of these seven countries have met annually at different venues, primarily to discuss economic matters but in recent years have moved more into the political arena.

In July 1991 the seventeenth G7 meeting was held, in London; its proceedings were dominated by the presence (at a post-summit session on the last day) of Soviet leader Mikhail Gorbachev, who was there to address the G7 about his country's economic problems and request assistance from the West in order to achieve the reforms he wanted. He did not receive promises of direct financial aid, but offers of technical and managerial expertise were forthcoming, together with an association with the economic and financial machinery of the West, including the IMF and World Bank.

Perhaps the strongest message to emerge from the 1991 London summit was that G7 is now a solid part of international politics and may well find it necessary to establish some sort of permanent secretariat to ensure that the decisions it takes are followed through and implemented. It seems likely that by 1992, or soon afterwards, the USSR will be admitted into full membership and the Group of Seven will become the Group of Eight.

paratively large powers and responsibilities.

**mandate** in general, any official command; in politics also the right (given by the electors) of an elected government to carry out its programme of policies.

Historically, mandate referred to a territory whose administration was entrusted to Allied states by the League of Nations under the Treaty of Versailles after World War I. Mandated territories were former German and Turkish possessions (including Iraq, Syria, Lebanon, and Palestine). When the United Nations replaced the League of Nations in 1945, mandates that had not achieved independence became known as trust territories.

**manifesto** the published prospectus of a political party, setting out the policies that the party will pursue if elected to govern. When elected to power a party will often claim that the contents of its manifesto constitute a mandate to introduce legislation to bring these policies into effect.

**militia** a body of civilian soldiers, usually with some military training, who are on call in emergencies, distinct from professional soldiers. In Switzerland, the militia is the national defence force, and every able-bodied man is liable for service in it. In the UK the **Territorial Army** and in the USA the **National Guard** have supplanted earlier voluntary militias.

**nationalization** policy of bringing a country's essential services and industries under public ownership. It was pursued, for example,

by the UK Labour government 1945–51. In recent years the trend towards nationalization has slowed and in many countries (the UK, France, and Japan) reversed (privatization). Assets in the hands of foreign governments or companies may also be nationalized; for example, Iran's oil industry, the Suez Canal, and US-owned fruit plantations in Guatemala, all in the 1950s.

**parliament** the legislative body of a country. The world's oldest parliament is the Icelandic Althing from about 930. The UK parliament is usually dated from 1265. The Supreme Soviet of the USSR, with 1,500 members, may be the world's largest legislature.

In the UK, Parliament is the supreme legislature, comprising the House of Commons and the House of Lords. The origins of parliament are in the 13th century, but its powers were not established until the late 17th century. The powers of the Lords were curtailed 1911, and the duration of parliaments was fixed at five years, but any parliament may extend its own life, as happened during both world wars. It meets in the Palace of Westminster, London.

**perestroika** in Soviet politics, the wide-ranging economic and political reforms initiated during Mikhail Gorbachev's leadership of the Soviet state.

The term was first proposed at the 26th Party Congress in 1979 and actively promoted by Gorbachev from 1985. Originally, in the economic sphere, perestroika was conceived as involving the 'switching onto a track of intensive development' by automation and improved labour efficiency. It has evolved to attend increasingly to market indicators and incentives ('market socialism') and a gradual dismantlement of the Stalinist central-planning system, with decision-taking authority being devolved to self-financing enterprises.

**president** usual title of the head of state in a republic; the power of the office may range from the equivalent of a constitutional monarch to the actual head of the government.

**pressure group** or **interest group** or **lobby** group that puts pressure on governments or parties to ensure laws and treatment favourable to its own interest. Pressure groups have played an increasingly prominent role in contemporary Western democracies. In general they fall into two types: groups concerned with a single issue, such as nuclear disarmament, and groups attempting to promote their own interest, such as oil producers.

**prime minister** or **premier** head of a parliamentary government, usually the leader of the largest party.

In some countries, such as Australia, a distinction is drawn between the prime minister of the whole country and the premier of an individual state. In countries with an executive president, the prime minister is of lesser standing, whereas in those with dual executives, such as France, power is shared with the president.

**privatization** reconversion of nationalized services and industries to private ownership, as under the Conservative governments in the UK after 1953, especially the Thatcher government 1979–90, and in France since 1986.

**propaganda** the systematic spreading (propagation) of information or disinformation, usually to promote a religious or political doctrine with the intention of instilling particular attitudes or responses.

**purge** the removal (for example from a political party) of suspected opponents or persons regarded as undesirable. In 1934 the Nazis carried out a purge of their party and a number of party leaders were executed for an alleged plot against Hitler. During the 1930s purges were conducted in the USSR under Joseph Stalin, carried out by the secret police against political opponents, communist party members, minorities, civil servants, and large sections of the armed forces' officer corps. Some 10 million people were executed or deported to labour camps from 1934 to 1938. Later purges include communist purges in Hungary 1949, Czechoslovakia 1951, and China 1955.

**radical** anyone with opinions more extreme than the main current of a country's major political party or parties. It is more often applied to those with left-wing opinions.

**rainbow coalition** or **rainbow alliance** from the mid-1980s, a loose, left-of-centre grouping of disparate elements, encompassing sections of society that are traditionally politically underrepresented, such as nonwhite ethnic groups. Its aims include promoting minority rights and equal opportunities.

**referendum** procedure whereby a decision on proposed legislation is referred to the electorate for settlement by direct vote of all the people.

It is most frequently employed in Switzerland, the first country to use it, but has also been used in Australia, New Zealand, Québec, and certain states of the USA. It was used in the UK for the first time 1975 on the issue of membership of the European Community. Critics argue that referenda undermine parliamentary authority, but they do allow the elector to participate directly in decision-making. A similar device is the **recall**, whereby voters are given the opportunity of demanding the dismissal from office of officials.

**refugee** a person fleeing from oppressive or dangerous conditions—such as political, religious, or military persecution—to a foreign country. They come from every race and religion, and few areas of the world have been spared the tragedy of refugees. Their numbers grow every year: in 1970 they numbered 2.5 million; in 1985, 10 million; in 1987, 12 million; in 1990, 15 million; in June 1991, 17 million, most of them women and children.

Refugees are the responsibility of the United Nations High Commission for Refugees (UNHCR), which was created by the UN General Assembly in 1945. Originally set up for a period of three years, as the numbers of refugees grew, its mandate has been repeatedly

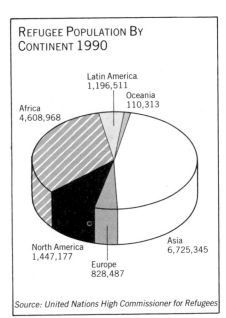

REFUGEE POPULATION BY CONTINENT 1990

Latin America 1,196,511
Oceania 110,313
Africa 4,608,968
North America 1,447,177
Europe 828,487
Asia 6,725,345

Source: United Nations High Commissioner for Refugees

renewed. Its funds come chiefly from government contributions, and its main functions are to protect refugees, to find durable solutions for them, and to provide them with the necessary assistance until solutions can be found.

**right wing** the more conservative or reactionary section of a political party or spectrum. It originated in the French National Assembly 1789, where the nobles sat in the place of honour on the president's right, whereas the commons were on his left (hence left wing).

**sanction** economic or military measure taken by a state or number of states to enforce international law. Examples of the recent use of sanctions are the attempted economic boycott of Rhodesia, after its unilateral declaration of independence 1965, by the United Nations; the call for measures against South Africa on human-rights grounds by the United Nations and other organizations from 1985; the economic boycott of Iraq (1990) in protest over its invasion of Kuwait, following resolutions passed by the United Nations.

**secretary of state** in the UK, a title held by a number of ministers, for example, the secretary of state for foreign and commonwealth affairs. In the USA the secretary of state deals with foreign affairs.

**shuttle diplomacy** form of international diplomacy prominent in the 1970s where an independent mediator would travel between belligerent parties in order to try and achieve a compromise solution.

In 1990–91 it was practised by US Secretary of State, James Baker, in the period leading up to, and following, the Gulf War.

**sovereignty** absolute authority within a given territory. The possession of sovereignty is taken to be the distinguishing feature of the state, as against other forms of community. The term

# GERMAN UNIFICATION: WHO WILL BEAR THE COST?

On 3 Oct 1990, one year after the massive, euphoric 'people power' demonstrations that toppled the senile socialist autocracy of the misnamed German Democratic Republic (GDR), political unification of the divided Germanies was at last achieved. In the process, a new European superstate was forged. Overnight, through uniting 62 million westerners (Wessis) with 16.4 million easterners (Ossis), this new, enlarged Federal Republic (FRG) became the world's twelfth most populous nation, possessing its third greatest economy. Political unification proved to be a remarkably smooth and swift affair. Or, in business parlance, it constituted a friendly takeover, with the West German constitution being maintained, and East Germany's pre-1949 Länder (states) being re-established as integral parts of the new federation. All-German political parties were formed, inevitably dominated by professional democratic politicians drawn from the West, as was the cabinet. Economic and social unification was to be a more protracted and perilous process. Currency union took effect July 1990, and demographic fusion had begun even earlier, when half a million Ossi economic refugees engulfed the western Länder during 1989 and early 1990. However, full economic convergence was more challenging. On the one side lay the old FRG, the economic powerhouse of Western Europe, one of the world's richest states, and renowned for its industrial efficiency. On the other side lay the GDR, which, although the most successful East European socialist state, had a legacy of a top-heavy, centralized and nationalized economic structure, appalling levels of pollution, and qualitatively inferior standards of living. The voters of the East enthusiastically supported the right-of-centre Christian Democrats (CDU) in 1990 elections, attracted by Chancellor Kohl's promise that the immediate embrace of capitalism would bring about improved living standards. However, as

1991 progressed, the true economic and social cost of unification became brutally clear. Initially, during the summer and autumn of 1990, easterners, with their former Ostmark savings now converted into Deutschmarks, went on a spending spree for long-denied, high-quality, western-produced consumer items. However, as low productivity eastern enterprises were more fully exposed to open competition with the developed world, a mass of bankruptcies ensued. By mid-March 1991, unemployment in the eastern Länder exceeded 30%, compared with 7% in the west, and is predicted to top 50% by the year's end.

Resentful of their comparatively low living standards and their treatment as colonized 'second class citizens' by arrogant, well-heeled Wessi tourists and businesspeople, easterners reacted bitterly. In late March 1991 huge anti-Kohl demonstrations were held in Leipzig, Dresden, Berlin, and other eastern cities and there was a worrying increase in strikes, petty crime, plant occupations, public violence, suicides and open racial disharmony. Unification also had deleterious effects on the western Länder. Chancellor Kohl's pre-election pledges were not substantiated as help for the eastern Länder resulted in tax increases, a growth in the federal deficit, and rises in interest rates and inflation. The Federal Republic, previously a model of stability, was faced with marches on Bonn by the jobless Ossis and witch-hunts for members of the former GDR secret police (Stasi).

Sanguine observers anticipated integration's 'teething troubles' would last for only two or three years before a new 'economic miracle' got underway. Less optimistic pundits warned that the eastern Länder were likely to remain underdeveloped for decades, breeding an intense sense of injustice. Whether the full assimilation is brief or long, the cost will, inevitably, be high and likely to have a profound effect.

*East German workers begin to demolish the Berlin Wall near the Brandenburg Gate, Feb 1990.*

## US-Soviet Summits

| year | heads of government | venue | results |
|------|---------------------|-------|---------|
| 1972 | Nixon and Brezhnev | Moscow | SALT I accord (Strategic Arms Limitation Talks) limited the rate of nuclear-arms buildup. Treaty on anti-ballistic missiles. |
| 1974 | Ford and Brezhnev | Vladivostok | No substantive results. |
| 1979 | Carter and Brezhnev | Vienna | SALT II accord. |
| 1985 | Reagan and Gorbachev | Geneva | No substantive results; signs of détente. |
| 1986 | Reagan and Gorbachev | Reykjavik | Dramatic offer of arms reductions by Gorbachev but disagreement on Strategic Defense Initiative by Reagan. |
| 1987 | Reagan and Gorbachev | Washington | Intermediate Nuclear Forces (INF) Treaty signed. |
| 1988 | Reagan and Gorbachev | Moscow | INF Treaty ratified. |
| 1989 | Bush and Gorbachev | Malta | No substantive results. |
| 1990 | Bush and Gorbachev | Washington | Strategic Arms Reduction Talks agreement outlined. |
| 1991 | Bush and Gorbachev | Moscow | Strategic Arms Reduction Treaty signed. |

has an internal aspect, in that it refers to the ultimate source of authority within a state, such as a parliament or monarch, and an external aspect, where it denotes the independence of the state from any outside authority. In the latter sense, the preservation of national sovereignty is a major factor in the UK conservative government's opposition to certain aspects of EC plans for European integration (such as a single currency and a single foreign policy).

**state** territory that forms its own domestic and foreign policy, acting through laws that are typically decided by a government and carried out, by force if necessary, by agents of that government. It can be argued that growth of regional international bodies such as the European Community means that states no longer enjoy absolute sovereignty.

**summit** or **summit conference** meeting of heads of government to discuss common interests, especially meetings between leaders of the USA and the USSR. The term was first used during World War II, and the Yalta Conference and Potsdam Conference 1945 were summits that did much to determine the political structure of the postwar world. Later summits have been of varying importance, partly as public-relations exercises.

**terrorism** systematic violence in the furtherance of political aims, often by small guerrilla groups, such as the Fatah Revolutionary Council led by Abu Nidal, a splinter group that split from the Palestine Liberation Organization in 1973.

**trade union** organization of employed workers formed to undertake collective bargaining with employers and to try to achieve improved working conditions for its members. Attitudes of government to unions and of unions to management vary greatly from country to country. Probably the most effective trade-union system is that of Sweden, and the most internationally known is the Polish Solidarity.

The **Trades Union Congress** in the UK is a voluntary organization of trade unions, founded in 1868. Delegates of affiliated unions meet annually to consider matters affecting their members. In 1991 there were 78 affiliated unions, with an aggregate membership of 10.4 million. Its headquarters are in London.

**unilateralism** support for **unilateral nuclear disarmament**: scrapping a country's nuclear weapons without waiting for other countries to agree to do so at the same time.

**veto** (Latin 'I forbid') exercise by a sovereign, branch of legislature, or other political power, of the right to prevent the enactment or operation of a law, or the taking of some course of action.

**vote** expression of opinion by ballot, show of hands, or other means. In systems that employ direct vote, the plebiscite and referendum are fundamental mechanisms. In parliamentary elections the results can be calculated in a number of ways. The main electoral systems are:

*simple plurality* or *first past the post*, with single-member constituencies (USA, UK, India, Canada);

*absolute majority*, achieved for example by the *alternative vote*, where the voter, in single-member constituencies, chooses a candidate by marking preferences (Australia), or by the *second ballot*, where, if a clear decision is not reached immediately, a second ballot is held (France, Egypt);

*proportional representation*, achieved for example by the *party list* system (Israel, most countries of Western Europe, and several in South America), the *additional member* system (Germany), the *single transferable vote* (Ireland and Malta), and the *limited vote* (Japan).

All British subjects over 18, except peers, the insane, and felons, are entitled to vote in UK local government and parliamentary elections. A register is prepared annually, and since 1872 voting has been by secret ballot. The voting system is by a simple majority in single-member constituencies.

Voter registration and turnout in the USA remains the lowest in the industrialized world. In 1988, 37% of potential voters failed to register and barely 50% bothered to vote in the presidential election, so that George Bush became president with the support of only 27% of the people.

**welfare state** political system under which the state (rather than the individual or the private sector) has responsibility for the welfare

# THE ANTI-GORBACHEV COUP—HARBINGER OF A SECOND RUSSIAN REVOLUTION

1990–91 had been a year of some highs, but mostly lows, for the USSR president, Mikhail Gorbachev. Still immensely respected abroad, Gorbachev had become increasingly unpopular at home. His reform programme had failed to deliver the 'economic goods', with Soviet GNP declining by 6% during 1990 and set to fall by a catastrophic 16% during 1991. Meanwhile, his initiatives of *glasnost* and *demokratizatsiya* had fanned nationalist and anti-communist unrest to such an extent that the Union appeared imperilled.

By the spring of 1991, with his public approval rating in single figures and anxious to restore order and save the Union, President Gorbachev had forged a tactical alliance with conservative elements within the Communist Party (CPSU), military, and KGB. He had already sanctioned the appointment of Gennady Yanayev and Valentin Pavlov, both cautious apparatchiks, as vice president and prime minister, and the hardline Boris Pugo as Interior Minister. With the despatch in Jan 1991 of Black Beret special forces into Lithuania and Latvia, the postponement of the proposed Feb 1991 summit with US President Bush, the imposition of fresh curbs on state television and radio, and the amassing of greater presidential executive and decree powers, it appeared that the Soviet 'reform experiment' had been finally halted. As both the former foreign minister Eduard Shevardnadze and the Russian federation (RSFSR) president Boris Yeltsin had warned, a renewed dictatorship seemed imminent.

Once more, however, Gorbachev confounded the soothsayers of doom, and forged, in April 1991, a new centre-left reformist alliance with Yeltsin and the leaders of nine other republics, entering into a political and economic 'stabilization pact' and promising, under the terms of a new Union Treaty, further democratization and decentralization. Also, on 30-31 July 1991 a superpower summit was held successfully in Moscow, with a Strategic Arms Reduction Treaty (START) signed.

Gorbachev's renewed commitment to reform so vexed conservatives that on 18 June 1991 Prime Minister Pavlov headed an attempted 'constitutional coup', demanding that the Soviet parliament greatly increase his executive powers at the president's expense. This move was thwarted by Gorbachev, who on 4 Aug 1991 left Moscow for a two-week family holiday in the Crimea. But on 16 Aug, Alexander Yakovlev—a long-time liberal ally who had been forced out of the CPSU—warned that in Gorbachev's absence a 'Stalinist coup' was being hatched, and even provided Gorbachev with some of the plotters' names.

Despite this forewarning, the anti-Gorbachev coup, launched in the early hours of 19 Aug, still came as a dramatic shock to the Soviet people and international community. Instituted by an eight-man junta, which included the Pavlov-plot 'Gang of Four', and headed by the colourless Yanayev, it took place the day before the new Union Treaty was due to be signed in Moscow. Clearly, it represented a last-ditch effort by the CPSU 'old guard' to recentralize political and economic authority within the Union.

But within hours of the coup there were indications that it lacked the requisite efficiency, ruthlessness, and cohesion, and that—faced with a Soviet people roused from its traditional passivity—it might be overturned. Although Gorbachev was confined in the Crimea (allegedly 'ill'), Boris Yeltsin remained at large, taking refuge with supporters in the barricaded Russian Parliament building. Furthermore, although the junta had established control over the USSR's airwaves and presses, it had been unable to block incoming foreign television and radio broadcasts; inexplicably, it had also failed to cut off telecommunication and fax links between the Russian Parliament building and other republics and international leaders.

Courageously and charismatically, Yeltsin—accorded external support by President Bush and internal backing from Leningrad's democratic mayor Anatoly Sobchak, nationalists in the Baltics and western Ukraine, and the coalminers of the Kuzbass—set about organizing popular and constitutional resistance. Between 19-21 Aug, wavering elements within the army and KGB were won over. Meanwhile, divisions emerged within the conspirators' ranks, with senior generals refusing to order their troops to fire on unarmed civilians. A 'Tiananmen solution' had been rejected. Instead, on Wednesday 21 Aug, unable to wrest control of the Russian Parliament building, the *putsch* quickly disintegrated. Kept informed of events through the BBC's World Service, President Gorbachev was released from dacha detention and returned quietly to Moscow early on Thursday morning. The 'Gang of Eight', excepting Pugo who had committed suicide, was arrested, along with its accomplices.

The largely inept coup lasted just 61 hours. However, so immense were its repercussions that a second Russian revolution was effectively ushered in, entailing the collapse of communism and the rupturing of the Union. As noted on 26 Aug by the chastened Gorbachev, when he addressed the Supreme Soviet, the USSR to which he had returned was 'a different country'. The CPSU, having forfeited its legitimacy, was dissolved, with the much-weakened Gorbachev remaining in office as a non-party President. Byelorussia and the Ukraine joined the Baltics, Armenia, Georgia, and Moldova in declaring full independence, while Yeltsin, now the country's dominant figure, began to aggrandize authority, securing the appointment of supporters to key positions in the new Union government and claiming charge of the armed forces. Clearly, the *putsch* had disastrously backfired on the 'adventurists', serving rather as a spur for the processes of reform and decentralization.

## Ten Largest Unions 1991

| | trade union | membership |
|---|---|---|
| 1 | Transport & General Workers (TGW) | 1,233,891 |
| 2 | General Municipal Boilermakers (GMB) | 921,000 |
| 3 | National and Local Government Officers Association (NALGO) | 744,453 |
| 4 | Amalgamated Engineering Union (AEU) | 702,228 |
| 5 | Manufacturing Science Finance (MSF) | 653,000 |
| 6 | National Union of Public Employees (NUPE) | 578,992 |
| 7 | Union of Shop, Distributive and Allied Workers (USDAW) | 361,789 |
| 8 | Union of Construction, Allied Trades & Technicians (UCATT) | 207,232 |
| 9 | Confederation of Health Services Employees (COHSE) | 203,311 |
| 10 | Union of Communication Workers (UCW) | 201,200 |

## Ten Smallest Unions 1991

| | | |
|---|---|---|
| 1 | Sheffield Wool Shear Workers Union | 17 |
| 2 | Society of Shuttlemakers | 29 |
| 3 | Military and Orchestral Music Instrument-Makers Trade Society | 42 |
| 4 | Scottish Union of Power-loom Overlookers | 70 |
| 5 | Card Setting Machine Tenters' Association | 88 |
| 6 | Amalgamated Association of Beamers, Twisters and Drawers (Hand and Machine) | 403 |
| 7 | Engineering and Fastener Trade Union | 430 |
| 8 | Yorkshire Association of Power-loom Overlookers | 519 |
| 9 | General Union of Associations of Loom Overlookers | 680 |
| 10 | Northern Carpets Trade Union | 770 |

*Source:* TUC

of its citizens. Services such as unemployment and sickness benefits, family allowances and incomes supplements, pensions, medical care, and education may be provided and financed through state insurance schemes and taxation.

Internationally, the aim of creating a welfare state has been adopted in several countries, particularly in Scandinavia, but, again, often more as an ideal than a reality. The welfare state concept was built into the political structures of communist states, led by the Soviet Union, but even here economic realities have tempered its practical implementation.

# UK CENTRAL GOVERNMENT

Central government in the UK is currently based on 16 major departments of state, each headed by a minister who is a member of the cabinet, and 16 minor or subdepartments.

**Major departments**

Ministry of Agriculture, Fisheries and Food
Ministry of Defence
Department of Education and Science
Department of Employment
Department of Energy
Department of the Environment
Foreign and Commonwealth Office
Department of Health
Home Office
Northern Ireland Office
Scottish Office
Department of Social Security
Department of Trade and Industry
Department of Transport
Treasury
Welsh Office

The Treasury is the one department with two cabinet representatives, the chancellor of the Exchequer and the chief secretary to the Treasury, and, since the prime minister is formally also First Lord of the Treasury, it can be argued that the cabinet representation is threefold.

**Minor departments**

Board of Inland Revenue
Central Office of Information
Department of National Savings
Export Credits Guarantee Department
H M Customs and Excise Department
Her Majesty's Household
Her Majesty's Stationery Office
Law Officers' Department
Lord Advocate's Department
Lord Chancellor's Department*
Office of Arts and Libraries
Office of the Minister for the Civil Service
Overseas Development Administration
Parliamentary Counsel's Office
Paymaster General's Office
Privy Council Office*
* *Direct representation in the cabinet.*

**Non-departmental cabinet members**

Apart from the prime minister, there are three members of the cabinet without specific departmental responsibilities: Lord President of the Council, who is Leader of the House of Commons; Lord Privy Seal, who is Leader of the House of Lords; and Chancellor of the Duchy of Lancaster, who is chair of the Conservative Party.

**Ministerial gradings**

The top-ranking ministers are members of the cabinet. Most cabinet ministers heading departments are now styled secretary of state. The exceptions are the minister of Agriculture, Fisheries and Food, the Lord Chancellor, and the chancellor of the Exchequer. The other ministers, in descending order of rank, are:

*minister of state* (who may sometimes be of cabinet rank) (may sometimes be styled minister of state and sometimes minister).

*undersecretary of state* (may sometimes be styled minister).

*parliamentary undersecretary* (in the case of Agriculture, Fisheries and Food, and the Treasury, styled parliamentary secretary).

When the minister heading a major department is styled secretary of state, junior ministers in that department are styled parliamentary undersecretaries. In other cases they are styled parliamentary secretaries.

## Civil-service gradings

The three most senior grades in the home civil service, found in all major departments, are: permanent secretary; deputy secretary; undersecretary.

## Typical structure of a department

All departments have specific, distinctive features but most conform to the following pattern: political head: secretary of state, supported by one or more ministers of state and junior ministers; nonpolitical head: permanent secretary, supported by administrative, executive, and clerical staff.

## Major departments

### Ministry of Agriculture, Fisheries and Food
*established*1955, through combination of existing agriculture, fisheries, and food ministries
*responsibilities* agriculture, horticulture, fisheries, and food policies
*ministerial team* minister, one minister of state, two parliamentary secretaries
*head* John Selwyn Gummer
*permanent staff* 10,400
*administrative headquarters* Whitehall Place, London SW1.

### Ministry of Defence
*established* 1964, when Admiralty, War Office, and Air Defence were brought together in one ministry
*responsibilities* national defence, including overall control of the Royal Navy, Army, and Royal Air Force, and arms procurement
*ministerial team* secretary of state, two ministers of state, two parliamentary undersecretaries
*head* Tom King
*permanent staff* 98,000, including Royal Ordnance factories
*administrative headquarters* Whitehall, London SW1.

### Department of Education and Science
*established* 1944, as the Ministry of Education
*responsibilities* education and scientific research policies

*ministerial team* secretary of state, one minister of state, two parliamentary undersecretaries
*head* Kenneth Clarke
*permanent staff* 2,600
*administrative headquarters* York Road, London SE1.

### Department of Employment
*established* 1970 in its present form. The original Ministry of Labour was formed in 1917
*responsibilities* employment and training policies
*ministerial team* secretary of state, one minister of state, two parliamentary undersecretaries
*head* Michael Howard
*permanent staff* 53,700
*administrative headquarters* Tothill Street, London SW1.

### Department of Energy
*established* 1974 in its present form. Ministry of Fuel and Power was formed in 1942
*responsibilities* energy policies, including nuclear, coal, electricity, oil, and gas
*ministerial team* secretary of state, one minister of state, one parliamentary undersecretary
*head* John Wakeham
*permanent staff* 1,300
*administrative headquarters* Palace Street, London SW1.

### Department of the Environment
*established* 1970, bringing together ministries of Housing and Local Government, Transport, and Building and Works. Transport returned to an independent status in 1975
*responsibilities* housing, construction, local government, sport and recreation policies, and preservation of the environment
*ministerial team* secretary of state, four ministers of state, three parliamentary undersecretaries
*head* Michael Heseltine
*permanent staff* 19,400
*administrative headquarters* Marsham Street, London SW1.

### Foreign and Commonwealth Office
*established* 1782, as the Foreign Office
*responsibilities* conduct of foreign policy, representation of British interests abroad, relations with other members of the Commonwealth, overseas aid policy and administration
*ministerial team* secretary of state, one minister of cabinet rank (responsible for overseas aid administration), three ministers of state, one parliamentary undersecretary
*head* Douglas Hurd
*permanent staff* 8,300
*administrative headquarters* Downing Street, London SW1.

### Department of Health
*established* 1988, following the division of the Department of Health and Social Security into two separate departments. Ministry of Health formed in 1919
*responsibilities* operation of the national health service and overall policies on health
*ministerial team* secretary of state, one minister

of state, two parliamentary undersecretaries
*head* William Waldegrave
*permanent staff* 11,400, excluding NHS staff
*administrative headquarters* Whitehall,
London SW1.
**Home Office**
*established* 1782
*responsibilities* administration of justice, pe-
nal system (including the prison and probation
services), police, fire, civil defence, licensing
(including marriage, liquor, theatres, and cinemas), radio and television broadcasting, im-
migration and nationality policies
*ministerial team* secretary of state, three ministers of state, one parliamentary undersecretary
*head* Kenneth Baker
*permanent staff* 45,000
*administrative headquarters* Queen Anne's
Gate, London SW1.
**Northern Ireland Office**
*established* 1972
*responsibilities* direct government of Northern Ireland, including administration of security, law and order, and economic, industrial,
and social policies
*ministerial team* secretary of state, one minister
of state, four parliamentary undersecretaries
*head* Peter Brooke
*permanent staff* 29,500
*administrative headquarters* Whitehall, London SW1, and Belfast.
**Scottish Office**
*established* 1707 England, 1938 Scotland
*responsibilities* administration for Scotland of
policies on agriculture and fisheries, education, industrial development, law and order,
and health
*ministerial team* secretary of state, two
ministers of state, two parliamentary undersecretaries
*head* Ian Lang
*permanent staff* 13,000
*administrative headquarters* Whitehall, London SW1, and Edinburgh.
**Department of Social Security**
*established* 1988, after being part of the Department of Health and Social Security
*responsibilities* administration of social-
service policies, including pensions, unemployment, income support, and disability benefits
*ministerial team* secretary of state, one minister
of state, two parliamentary undersecretaries
*head* Tony Newton
*permanent staff* 78,000
*administrative headquarters* Whitehall, London SW1.
**Department of Trade and Industry**
*established* 1970, bringing together the Board
of Trade, founded in 1786, and the Ministry of
Technology, formed in 1964
*responsibilities* administration of policies on
international trade, industry, competition, industrial research and assistance to exporters
*ministerial team* secretary of state, two ministers
of state, two parliamentary undersecretaries

*head* Peter Lilley
*permanent staff* 12,500
*administrative headquarters* Marsham Street,
London SW1.
**Department of Transport**
*established* 1975, in its present form
*responsibilities* land, sea, and air transport
policies, including sponsorship of British Rail,
and construction and maintenance of motor-
ways and trunk roads
*ministerial team* secretary of state, one minister
of state, two parliamentary undersecretaries
*head* Malcolm Rifkind
*permanent staff* 16,000
*administrative headquarters* Victoria Street,
London SW1.
**Treasury**
*established* 1612
*responsibilities* control of public expenditure,
national economic policy, including monetary
and fiscal measures, efficiency in the public
sector, international finance, and oversight of
the financial system
*ministerial team* chancellor of the Exchequer,
chief secretary (of cabinet rank), three ministers of state rank (paymaster general, financial
secretary, and economic secretary), one parliamentary secretary
*chancellor* Norman Lamont
*chief secretary* David Mellor
*permanent staff* 3,200
*administrative headquarters* Parliament
Street, London SW1.
**Welsh Office**
*established* 1951
*responsibilities* administration for Wales of
policies on agriculture, education, health
and social services, local government, planning, sport, and tourism. It is also responsible for promoting the Welsh language and
culture
*ministerial team* secretary of state, one
minister of state, one parliamentary undersecretary
*head* David Hunt
*permanent staff* 2,300
*administrative headquarters* Whitehall, London SW1, and Cardiff.

**Minor departments**

**Board of Inland Revenue**
*parent department* Treasury
*responsibilities* collection of central government taxes, other than VAT and customs and
excise duties, throughout the UK.
**Cabinet Office**
*parent department* Cabinet
*responsibilities* services the cabinet and all its
committees and subcommittees; it organizes
meetings, prepares and distributes agendas
and cabinet papers, including minutes; decides, with the prime minister, which issues
should go to the full cabinet and which to one
of its committees or subcommittees.
**Central Office of Information** (COI)
*parent department* Treasury
*responsibilities* operation of government in-

formation services.

**Customs and Excise Department**
*parent department* Treasury
*responsibilities* collection of customs and excise duties, including VAT.

**Department of National Savings**
*parent department* Treasury
*responsibilities* management of government savings schemes.

**Exports Credits Guarantee Department**
*parent department* Department of Trade and Industry
*responsibilities* management of government scheme to underwrite finance for exporters.

**Her Majesty's Household**
*parent department* Lord Chamberlain
*responsibilities* management of the affairs of the royal household.

**Her Majesty's Stationery Office** (HMSO)
*parent department* Treasury
*responsibilities* production and sale of government publications.

**Law Officers' Department**
*parent department* freestanding, under Attorney General
*responsibilities* legal advice to the government and representation of the Crown in court.

**Lord Advocate's Department**
*parent department* freestanding
*responsibilities* administration of law in Scotland.

**Lord Chancellor's Department**
*parent department* freestanding, under Lord Chancellor
*responsibilities* administration of civil law in England and Wales, including the appointment of the judiciary in lower courts and advice on appointments in the higher courts. The Lord Chancellor also presides over sittings in the House of Lords.

**Office of Arts and Libraries**
*parent department* Privy Council Office, under Lord President of the Council
*responsibilities* promotion of the arts.

**Office of the Minister for the Civil Service**
*parent department* prime minister
*responsibilities* management of the home civil service.

**Overseas Development Administration** (ODA)
*parent department* Foreign and Commonwealth Office
*responsibilities* administration of development assistance to overseas countries.

**Parliamentary Counsel's Office**
*parent department* freestanding
*responsibilities* drafting of parliamentary legislation.

**Paymaster General's Office**
*parent department* Treasury
*responsibilities* administration of payment of government financial liabilities.

**Privy Council Office**
*parent department* freestanding, under Lord President of the Council
*responsibilities* a miscellany of duties, including management of the civil service and promotion of the arts.

### European Community

*Here is a list of things that the European Community is urging Britain to do at the moment. Could you tell me in each case whether you think this is something Britain should do, or*

|  | Should | Should not | Don't know |
|---|---|---|---|
| a) Agree to European standards for the cleanliness of our beaches? | | | |
| | 95 | 3 | 2 |
| b) Make it possible for citizens of any European Community country to travel to any other without needing a passport? | | | |
| | 56 | 38 | 6 |
| c) The creation in the next few years of a single European Currency, involving the disappearance of the pound sterling, the French franc and so on? | | | |
| | 33 | 53 | 13 |
| d) Adopt a programme to promote the teaching of other European languages in schools throughout the Community? | | | |
| | 86 | 10 | 4 |
| e) Agree to the abolition of all frontier controls between Community countries? | | | |
| | 44 | 42 | 13 |

# RELIGIOUS TRADITIONS

**BCE/CE** before the common era (BCE) and common era (CE) are abbreviations used in this section to replace, respectively, before Christ (BC) and anno Domini (AD).

**African religions** there is a wide variety of belief and practice in African religion. Most indigenous African religions are basically polytheistic (believing in a number of gods), but there is often a concept of one High God, generally a creator who has withdrawn from interaction with the world. There are also many spirits, which are present in all natural objects: water is seen as a particularly powerful force. Dead ancestors are very important in African religions, and are consulted before major undertakings. If offended, they can cause natural disasters and sterility, so they must be placated with offerings. In society, healers are highly regarded, as they deal with supernatural powers, as do diviners, but the most powerful human figure is the chief-king, who is surrounded by prohibitions because he is so dangerous: he is the life of the tribe incarnate, though because of this he may be required to sacrifice himself to preserve the health of his people.

**Australian aboriginal religion** the creation story of the Australian Aborigines is recorded in the *Dreamtime* stories. These reveal how giant human and other animals sprang from the earth, sea, and sky and criss-crossed the empty continent of Australia on a journey known as Dreamtime. At the end of their journey they returned into the earth where it is believed their spirits still exist. The places where they travelled or sank back into the land became mountain ranges, rocks, and sites full of sacred meaning.

Every sacred site has its own Dreamtime story that is part of the sacred law and must be re-enacted at certain times of the year in order to maintain the life of the land and the Dreamtime. Each Australian Aborigine has their own particular Dreamtime Ancestor although they are related to many other ancestors through kinship. When hunting, Aborigines are careful never to trap, maim, or kill the animals who are associated with their kinship ancestors.

**Buddhism** one of the great world religions, which originated in India about 500 BC. It derives from the teaching of Buddha, who is regarded as one of a series of such enlightened beings; there are no gods. The chief doctrine is that of **karma**, good or evil deeds meeting an appropriate reward or punishment either in this life or (through reincarnation) a long succession of lives. The main divisions in Buddhism are **Theravāda** (or Hīnayāna) in SE Asia and **Mahāyāna** in N Asia; **Lamaism** in Tibet and **Zen** in Japan are among the many Mahāyāna sects. Its symbol is the lotus. There are approximately 300 million (1990) Buddhists worldwide.

*scriptures* The only complete canon of the Buddhist scriptures is that of the Sinhalese (Sri Lanka) Buddhists, in Pāli, but other schools have essentially the same canon in Sanskrit. The scriptures, known as *pitakas* (baskets), date from the 2nd to 6th centuries CE. There are three divisions: **vinaya** (discipline), listing offences and rules of life; the sūtras (discourse) or **dharma** (doctrine), the exposition of Buddhism by Buddha and his disciples; and **abhidharma** (further doctrine), later discussions on doctrine.

*beliefs* The self is not regarded as permanent, as it is subject to change and decay. It it attachment to the things that are essentially impermanent that cause delusion, suffering, greed, and aversion, the origin of karma, and they in turn create further karma and the sense of self is reinforced. Actions which incline towards selflessness are called 'skilful karma' and they are on the path leading to enlightenment. In the **Four Noble Truths** the Buddha acknowledged the existence and source of suffering, and showed the way of deliverance from it through the **Eightfold Path**. The aim of following the Eightfold Path is to break the chain of karma and achieve dissociation from the body by attaining **nirvana** ('blowing out')—the eradication of all desires, either in annihilation or by absorption of the self in the infinite. Supreme reverence is accorded to the historical Buddha (Śākyamuni, or, when referred to by his clan name, Gautama), who is seen as one in a long and ongoing line of Buddhas, the next one (Maitreya) being due *c.* CE 3000.

*divisions:* **Theravāda Buddhism**, the School of the Elders, also known as **Hīnayāna** or Lesser Vehicle, prevails in SE Asia (Sri Lanka, Thailand, and Burma), and emphasizes the mendicant, meditative life as the way to break the cycle of **samsāra**, or death and rebirth. Its three alternative goals are *arahat*: one who has gained insight into the true nature of things; *Paccekabuddha*, an enlightened one who lives alone and does not teach; and fully awakened *Buddha*. Its scriptures are written in *Pāli*, an Indo-Aryan language with its roots in N India. In India itself Buddhism had virtually died out by the 13th century, and was replaced by Hinduism. However, it has 5 million devotees

## LEADING ORGANIZED RELIGIONS OF THE WORLD (1990)

| Religion | Followers |
| --- | --- |
| Christianity | 1,382,000,000 |
| Islam | 819,000,000 |
| Hinduism | 653,000,000 |
| Buddhism | 300,000,000 |
| Judaism | 18,000,000 |
| Sikhism | 16,500,000 |
| Confucianism | 5,750,000 |
| Baha'ism | 4,500,000 |
| Jainism | 4,000,000 |
| Shintoism | 3,200,000 |

*Source: Icorec.*

in the 20th century and is still growing. *Mahāyāna*, or Greater Vehicle arose at the beginning of the Christian era. This tradition emphasized the eternal, formless principle of the Buddha as the essence of all things. It exhorts the individual not merely to attain personal nirvana, but to become a trainee Buddha, or *bodhisattva*, and so save others; this meant the faithful could be brought to enlightenment by a bodhisattva without following the austerities of Theravāda, and the cults of various Buddhas and bodhisattvas arose. Mahāyāna Buddhism also emphasises *shunyata*, or the experiential understanding of the emptiness of all things, even Buddhist doctrine.

Mahāyāna Buddhism prevails in N Asia (China, Korea, Japan, and Tibet). In the 6th century CE Mahāyāna spread to China with the teachings of Bodhidharma and formed Ch'an, which became established in Japan from the 12th century as *Zen Buddhism*. Zen emphasises silent meditation with sudden interruptions from a master to encourage awakening of the mind. Japan also has the lay organization *Sōka Gakkai* (Value Creation Society), founded 1930, which equates absolute faith with immediate material benefit; by the 1980s it was followed by more than 7 million households.

Esoteric, Tantric, or Diamond Buddhism became popular in Tibet and Japan, and holds that enlightenment is already within the disciple and with the proper guidance (that is privately passed on by a master), can be realized.

**Christianity** world religion derived from the teaching of Jesus in the first third of the 1st century, with a present-day membership of about 1 billion. It is divided into different groups or denominations which differ in some areas of belief and practice. Its main divisions are the Roman Catholic, Eastern Orthodox, and Protestant churches. There are approximately 1,382 million (1990) Christian believers worldwide.

*beliefs* Christianity is based on the belief that the man Jesus, born about 2,000 years ago, is 'the Christ', the Son of God, and that his death and resurrection broke down the barrier that human sinfulness put between humanity and God. Christians believe in one God with three aspects or persons: God the Father, God the Son (Jesus), and God the Holy Spirit, who is the power of God working in the world. Christians believe in God the Creator, who came to Earth as Jesus, was crucified, resurrected three days after his death, appeared to his disciples, and then ascended into heaven.

Christians believe that Jesus is alive and present in the world as the Holy Spirit. The main commandments are to love God and to love one's neighbour as oneself, which, if followed successfully, lead to an afterlife in heaven.

*divisions:* **Orthodox Church** or **Eastern Orthodox Church** or **Greek Orthodox Church** a federation of self-governing Christian churches mainly found in E and SE Europe, the USSR, and parts of Asia. The centre of worship is the Eucharist. There is a married clergy, except for bishops; the Immaculate Conception is not accepted. The highest rank in the church is that of Ecumenical Patriarch, or Bishop of Istanbul. There are approximately 135 million (1990) adherents.

The church's teaching is based on the Bible, and the Nicene Creed (as modified by the Council of Constantinople 381) is the only confession of faith used. The celebration of the Eucharist has changed little since the 6th century. The ritual is elaborate, and accompanied by singing in which both men and women take part, but no instrumental music is used. Besides the seven sacraments, the prayer book contains many other services for daily life. During the marriage service, the bride and groom are crowned.

Its adherents include Greeks, Russians, Romanians, Serbians, Bulgarians, Georgians, and Albanians. In the last 200 years the Orthodox Church has spread into China, Korea, Japan, and the USA, as well as among the people of Siberia and central Asia. Some of the churches were founded by the apostles and their disciples; all conduct services in their own languages and follow their own customs and traditions, but are in full communion with one another. There are many monasteries, for example Mount Athos in Greece, which has flourished since the 10th century. The senior church of Eastern Christendom is that of Constantinople (Istanbul).

*Protestantism* one of the main divisions of Christianity, which emerged from Roman Catholicism at the Reformation. The chief denominations are the Anglican Communion (Episcopalian in the USA), Baptists, Lutherans, Methodists, Pentecostals, and Presbyterians, with a total membership of about 327 million (1990).

Protestantism takes its name from the protest of Luther and his supporters at the Diet of Spires 1529 against the decision to reaffirm the edict of the Diet of Worms against the Reformation. The first conscious statement of Protestantism as a distinct movement was the Confession of Augsbury 1530. The chief characteristics of original Protestantism are the acceptance of the Bible as the only source of truth, the universal priesthood of all believers, and forgiveness of sins solely through faith in Jesus Christ. The Protestant church minimises the liturgical aspects of Christianity and emphasizes the preaching and hearing of the word of God before sacramental faith and practice. The many interpretations of doctrine and practice are reflected in the various denominations. The ecumenical movement of the 20th century has unsuccessfully attempted to reunite various Protestant denominations and, to some extent, the Protestant churches and the Catholic church. During the last 20 years there has been a worldwide upsurge in Christianity taking place largely outside the established church.

*Roman Catholicism* one of the main divi-

# THE RUSSIAN ORTHODOX CHURCH: FORGING A NEW IDENTITY

At the turn of the century, the Russian Orthodox monastery of St Panteleimon, on the Holy Mountain of Athos in Greece, had over 3,000 Russian monks. Today, a handful of Russian monks live in the echoing vastness of the monastery. It might seem at first as if Russian Orthodoxy were dying. But nothing could be further from the truth. If the Greek Government would drop their xenophobic policy of refusing Russians the right to come to Mt Athos, the monastery would soon reach 3,000 and could probably double in size and still not meet the need.

The fact is that the Russian Orthodox Church after 70 years of persecution, is now experiencing a renewal and revival. The Russian Orthodox Church has stood up against the communist ideology and forces of the Soviet Union. In the early days of the Revolution, it saw thousands of its priests killed and even its Patriarch murdered. Under Stalin, thousands more were killed. When the war with Hitler broke out, Stalin realized the power of the Church to mobilize people and relations improved. After the War, and particularly in the 1950s and '60s, thousands of churches were closed or demolished and the Church was severely hampered. Yet it was in the Church that many critics found both refuge and inspiration. This has earned the respect of many within Russian society—believers and non-believers alike. The State continues to return hundreds of confiscated churches and is restoring some of its rights, is asking for its help in teaching a moral code in schools and is generally guiding the country. Under the leadership of the new Patriarch of Moscow, Alexi, elected in 1990, the Church is responding cautiously to these changes, and is trying to ensure it is not overstretched. Its experience of the last 70 years is a powerful reminder of the fluidity of life in Russia.

The Church is experiencing a revival in numbers, both in those wishing to be ordained and in the general spiritual desires and interest of millions of ordinary people. In a world of turmoil, the Church's authority and spiritual wisdom is eagerly sought. But this brings tension between those who wish to go faster than the leadership. There are other problems too. Many people feel some of the old bishops and certain clergy are spies of the Party or are so deeply compromised in their past as to have lost spiritual authority.

The breakaway Russian Church in the USA, the Orthodox Church of America (OCA), has long disputed the right of the present leadership to their position and has stirred the pot by sending 'missionaries' to bring certain parishes into their way of thinking.

The Church leadership is also worried by certain other trends within the Church. Part of the revival is extremely fundamentalist and fused to the deep Russian interest in apocalyptic thinking. When Chernobyl took place in 1986, the Church was asked by the State to issue a formal statement saying that this was not the start of the End of the World—for the name Chernobyl means Dark Star, one of the fearful signs in the Book of Revelation which heralds the end of the World. Even more disturbing is the use of religion—especially Russian Orthodoxy—by some extreme Russian nationalist groups. Their linking of the Church with racist and violent nationalism is something the leadership has tried to be very firm about refuting.

The revival in spiritual interest and the fact that most Russians still look to their Church to meet their spiritual yearnings means the Church is returning to its old position. The figures for baptisms, weddings and funerals are all much higher than those of five years ago. Perhaps more importantly, young people are coming to the Church in increasing numbers—looking for some guidance in a society where the old rules have broken down.

All these problems and possibilities face the newly emerging Church. They are both signs of the changing times and strains from a troubled past. How the Church faces up to them will decide not just the future of the Church, but to a very great extent, the future of Russia itself.

*A gathering of Russian Orthodox priests.*

sions of the Christian religion, separate from the Eastern Orthodox Church from 1054, and headed by the pope. For history and beliefs, see Christianity. Membership is about 920 million worldwide (1990), concentrated in S Europe, Latin America, and the Philippines.

The Protestant churches separated from the Catholic with the Reformation in the 16th century, to which the Counter-Reformation was a response. An attempt to update Catholic doctrines in the late 19th century was condemned by Pope Pius X in 1907, and more recent moves have been rejected by John Paul II.

*doctrine* The focus of liturgical life is the Mass or Eucharist, and attendance is obligatory on Sundays and Feasts of Obligation such as Christmas or Easter. The Roman Catholic differs from the other Christian churches in that it acknowledges the supreme jurisdiction of the pope, infallible when he speaks *ex cathedra* ('from the throne'); in the doctrine of the Immaculate Conception (which states that the Virgin Mary, the mother of Jesus, was conceived without the original sin with which all other human beings are born); and in according a special place to the Virgin Mary.

*organization* Since the Second Vatican Council 1962–66, major changes have taken place. They include the use of vernacular or everyday language instead of Latin in the liturgy, and increased freedom amongst the religious and lay orders. The pope has an episcopal synod of 200 bishops elected by local hierarchies to collaborate in the government of the church. The priesthood is celibate and there is a strong emphasis on the monastic orders.

**Confucianism** the body of beliefs and practices that are based on the Chinese classics and supported by the authority of the philosopher Confucius (Kong Zi). The origin of things is seen in the union of **yin** and **yang**, the passive and active principles. Human relationships follow the patriarchal pattern. For more than 2,000 years Chinese political government, social organization, and individual conduct was shaped by Confucian principles. In 1912, Confucian philosophy, as a basis for government, was dropped by the state. There are approximately 5.75 million Confucian believers (1990) worldwide.

The writings on which Confucianism is based include the ideas of a group of traditional books edited by Confucius, as well as his own works, such as the *Analects*, and those of some of his pupils. The *I Ching* is included among the Confucianist texts.

*doctrine* Until 1912 the emperor of China was regarded as the father of his people, appointed by heaven to rule. The Superior Man was the ideal human and filial piety was the chief virtue. Accompanying a high morality was a kind of ancestor worship.

*practices* Under the emperor, sacrifices were offered to heaven and earth, the heavenly bodies, the imperial ancestors, various nature gods, and Confucius himself. These were abolished at the Revolution in 1912, but ancestor worship (better expressed as reverence and remembrance) remained a regular practice in the home.

Under communism Confucianism continued. The defence minister Lin Biao was associated with the religion, and although the communist leader Mao Zedong undertook an anti-Confucius campaign 1974–76, this was not pursued by the succeeding regime.

**Hinduism** religion originating in N India about 4,000 years ago, which is superficially and in some of its forms polytheistic, but has a concept of the supreme spirit, Brahman, above the many divine manifestations. These include the triad of chief gods (the Trimurti): Brahma, Vishnu, and Siva (creator, preserver, and destroyer). Central to Hinduism are the beliefs in reincarnation and karma; the oldest scriptures are the *Vedas*. Temple worship is almost universally observed and there are many festivals.

There are over 653 million (1990) Hindus worldwide. Women are not regarded as the equals of men but should be treated with kindness and respect. Muslim influence in N India led to the veiling of women and the restriction of their movements from about the end of the 12th century.

*roots* Hindu beliefs originated in the Indus Valley civilization dating from about 4,500 years ago. Much of the tradition that is now associated with Hinduism stems from the ritual and religion of the Aryans who invaded N India about 3,000 years ago.

*scriptures* The *Veda* collection of hymns, compiled by the Aryans, was followed by the philosophical *Upanishads*, centring on the doctrine of Brahman, and the epics *Rāmāyana* and *Mahābhārata* (which includes the *Bhagavad-Gītā*), all from before the Christian era.

*beliefs* Hindu belief and ritual can vary greatly even between neighbouring villages. Some deities achieve widespread popularity such as Krishna, Hanuman, Lakshmi, and Durga; others, more localized and specialized, are referred to particularly in times of sickness or need. Some deities manifest themselves in different incarnations or avatars such as Rama or Krishna: both avatars of the god Vishnu.

Underlying this multi-faceted worship is the creative strength of Brahman, the Supreme Being. Hindus believe that all living things are part of Brahman: they are sparks of atman or divine life that transmute from one body to another, sometimes descending into the form of a plant or an insect, sometimes the body of a human. This is all according to its karma or past actions which are the cause of its sufferings or joy as it rises and falls in *samsara* (the endless cycle of birth and death). Humans have the opportunity, through knowledge and devotion, to break the karmic chain and achieve final liberation or moksha. The atman is then free to return to Brahman. The creative force of the universe is recognized in the god Brahma, once he has brought the cosmos into being it is sustained by Vishnu

## RELIGIOUS UNREST IN INDIA: UNHOLY WAR?

The word 'Hindu' appeared in the English language in the 19th century. Persian Muslims and their descendants, who ruled India for close to eight hundred years, used it to name the people who lived beside the river Indus. It never occurred to Hindus that they were Hindus until invading rulers told them so. In their own Sanskrit language, the sub-continent is called Bharat, and there is no single generic term for their religious practice, because they have never seen it as separate from their existence, any more than the air they breathe. Ironically, the name given them by Muslims and Christians simply means 'people of India', 'Hinduism'.

Indeed, because the people of India are a tolerant people, religions brought in from outside—often less tolerant ones—have flourished among them even at the expense of their own. It was partially as a result of tensions between Hindus and Muslims that the Sikh religion grew up around Guru Nanak (1469-1538) in an effort to find common ground. In the 17th century, in the face of increasing persecution, Sikhs fought to protect their Hindu brothers and sisters from the Mogul rulers. The Sikh leader Guru Gobind Singh won back from Emperor Aurangzeb the sacred birthplace of Rama in Ayodhya. Here a Rama temple had stood since ancient times until the infamous Babur demolished it in 1528 and replaced it with a mosque—the Babri Masjid. Later a Hindu temple was built just outside the mosque gates

*A protest in Kashmir against Muslim violence.*

and became the subject of constant feud. After his humiliating defeat by Gobind Singh, Aurangzeb returned and destroyed this second Hindu temple, and is said to have slaughtered ten thousand Hindu devotees in the process.

It is recorded that in 1857 local Hindus and Muslims formed a pact to fight the British in which a settlement was reached to return the site for ever to the Hindus. Unfortunately, the British defeated the alliance and the agreement was never executed. In 1949 a statue of Lord Rama appeared inside the by then abandoned mosque and since that time Hindu priests have been allowed to maintain worship before the deity of Rama, although the ruins of the mosque have been closed to the public by court decree pending a solution to the dispute.

It is this dispute that erupted in 1989 when it became the focus of a national campaign to gain recognition for Hindu rights, orchestrated by the Visva Hindu Parishad, a leading international Hindu organization. The VHP vowed to build a Hindu temple alongside the mosque and held a foundation-laying ceremony. At first the government supported them but then, in the face of Muslim protest, they banned the temple construction. This led to over two hundred thousand Hindu pilgrims marching on Ayodhya to demand the right to build their temple, with bricks gathered from half the villages of India. In a bloody confrontation armed police prevented them from reaching the holy site and over a hundred Hindus were shot dead.

Since this showdown there has been an uneasy truce, but there are some hopes that an agreement may still be reached. There are pacifists on both sides. Homi Taleyarkhan, a liberal Muslim leader, has called for 'a solution to the problem arising from the dispute, turning Ayodhya from an area of hostility to a model of hospitality of faiths, meaning respect for all religions.' Mahant Nitya Gopaldas, vice-president of the Committee to Liberate the Birthplace of Rama, said, 'The sadhus (Hindu religious leaders) do not want any violence, therefore the temple construction has been put off for the time being.'

However, it is an open question as to how long the day of reckoning can be delayed. There is growing discontent among Hindus, who complain of being second-class citizens in their own land. There is also the legacy of history: it is said that the Moguls destroyed over 60,000 Hindu temples in North India during the 16th and 17th centuries. Many fear that if Hindus succeed in Ayodhya, other sites will come up for repossession and there is no knowing where it will end. What we are witnessing is a slow awakening of the reaction to a thousand years of religious and cultural suppression.

Hinduism has no significant tradition of religious persecution; it has always believed in a multiplicity of forms of God and paths of worship; it upholds the ideal of non-violence even to the point of vegetarianism. The world has little to fear from a revitalized Hinduism.

and then annihilated by the god Shiva, only to be created once more by Brahma. Vishnu and Shiva are, respectively, the forces of light and darkness, preservation and destruction, with Brahma as the balancing force that enables the existence and interaction of life. The cosmos is seen as both real and an illusion (*maya*), since its reality is not lasting; the cosmos is itself personified as the goddess Maya.

*practice* Hinduism has a complex of rites and ceremonies performed within the framework of the *jati* or caste system under the supervision of the Brahman priests and teachers. In India, caste is traditionally derived from the four classes of early Hindu society: brahmans (priests), kshatriyas (nobles and warriors), vaisyas (traders and cultivators), and sudras (servants). A fifth class, the untouchables, regarded as polluting in its origins, remained (and still largely remains) on the edge of Hindu society. The Indian Constituent Assembly 1947 made discrimination against the Scheduled Castes or Depressed Classes illegal, but strong prejudice continues.

*Western influence* The International Society for Krishna Consciousness (ISKON), the western organization of the Hare Krishna movement, was introduced to the west by Swami Prabhupada (1896–1977). Members are expected to lead ascetic lives. It is based on devotion to Krishna which includes study of the *Bhagavad-Gita*, temple and home ritual, and the chanting of the name Hare (saviour) Krishna. Members are expected to avoid meat, eggs, alcohol, tea, coffee, drugs, and gambling. Sexual relationships should be for procreation within the bonds of marriage.

**Islam** religion founded in the Arabian peninsula in the early 7th century CE. It emphasizes the oneness of God, his omnipotence, benificence, and inscrutability. The sacred book is the **Koran** or **Quran** of the prophet Muhammad, the Prophet or Messenger of Allah. There are two main Muslim sects: **Sunni** and **Shi'ite**. Other schools include **Sufism**, a mystical movement originating in the 8th century. There are over 819 million Muslims (1990) worldwide.

*beliefs* The fundamental beliefs of Islam are contained in the Adhan: 'I bear witness that there is no God but Allah and Muhammad is the Prophet of Allah.' Creation, Fall of Adam, angels and jinns, heaven and hell, Day of Judgment, God's predestination of good and evil, and the succession of scriptures revealed to the prophets, including Moses and Jesus, but of which the perfect, final form is the **Koran**, divided into 114 **suras** or chapters, said to have been divinely revealed to Muhammad; the original is said to be preserved beside the throne of Allah in heaven.

*Islamic law* Islam embodies a secular law (the **Shari'a** or 'Highway'), which is clarified for Shi'ites by reference to their own version of the **sunna**, 'practice' of the Prophet as transmitted by his companions and embodied in the Hadith; the Sunni sect also take into account **ijma'**, the endorsement by universal consent

of practices and beliefs among the faithful. For the Sufi, the **Sharia**, is the starting point on the 'Sufi Path' to self-enlightenment. A **mufti** is a legal expert who guides the courts in their interpretation. (In Turkey until the establishment of the republic 1924 the mufti had supreme spiritual authority.)

*organization* There is no organized church or priesthood, although Muhammad's descendants (the Hashim family) and popularly recognized holy men, mullahs, and ayatollahs are accorded respect.

*observances* The Shari'a includes the observances known as the 'Five Pillars of the Faith' which are binding on all adult male believers. The observances include: *shahada* or profession of the faith; *salat* or worship five times a day facing the holy city of Mecca (the call to prayer is given by a muezzin, usually from the minaret or tower of a mosque); *zakat* or obligatory almsgiving; *saum* or fasting sunrise to sunset through Ramadan (ninth month of the year, which varies with the calendar); and the *hajj* or pilgrimage to Mecca at least once in a lifetime.

*history* Islam began as a militant and missionary religion, and between 711 and 1492 spread east into India, west over N Africa, then north across Gibraltar into the Iberian peninsula. During the Middle Ages, Islamic scholars preserved ancient Greco-Roman learning, while the Dark Ages prevailed in Christian Europe. Islam was seen as an enemy of Christianity by European countries during the Crusades, and Christian states united against a Muslim nation as late as the Battle of Lepanto 1571. Driven from Europe, Islam remained established in N Africa and the Middle East.

Islam is a major force in the Arab world and is a focus for nationalism among the peoples of Soviet Central Asia. It is also a significant factor in Pakistan, Indonesia, Malaysia, and parts of Africa. It is the second largest religion in the UK. Since World War II there has been a resurgence of fundamentalist Islam (often passionately opposed to the ideas of the West) in Iran, Libya, Afghanistan, and elsewhere. In the UK 1987 the manifesto *The Muslim Voice* demanded rights for Muslim views on education (such as single-sex teaching) and on the avoidance of dancing, mixed bathing, and sex education.

*divisions: Shi'ite* or **Shiah** member of a sect of Islam who believe that Ali was Muhammad's first true successor. The term Shi'ite originally referred to shi'a ('the partisans') of Ali. They are doctrinally opposed to the Sunni Muslims. They developed their own law differing only in minor directions, such as inheritance and the status of women. Holy men have greater authority in the Shi'ite sect than in the Sunni sect. They are prominent in Iran, the Lebanon, and Indo-Pakistan, and are also found in Iraq and Bahrain. In the aftermath of the Gulf War 1991, many thousands of Shi'ites in Iraq were forced to take refuge in the marshes of S Iraq, after unsuccessfully rebelling against

Saddam Hussein. Shi'ite sacred shrines were desecrated and atrocities committed by the armed forces on civilians. There are approximately 129 million Shi'ites (1990) worldwide.

Breakaway sub-sects include the *Alawite* sect, to which the ruling party in Syria belongs; the *Ismaili* sect, with the Aga Khan IV (1936–   ) as its spiritual head; and the Baha'i religion founded from a Muslim splinter group.

**Sufism** a mystical movement of Islam which originated in the 8th century. Sufis believe that deep intuition is the only real guide to knowledge. The movement has a strong strain of asceticism. The name derives from the *suf*, a rough woollen robe worn as an indication of disregard for material things. There are a number of groups or brotherhoods within Sufism, each with its own method of meditative practice, one of which is the whirling dance of the dervishes.

**Sunni** a member of the larger of the two main sects of Islam. Sunni Muslims believe that the first three caliphs were all legitimate successors of the prophet Muhammad, and that guidance on belief and life should come from the Koran and the Hadith, and from the Shari'a, not from a human authority or spiritual leader. Imams in Sunni Islam are educated lay teachers of the faith and prayer leaders. The name derives from the *Sunna*, Arabic 'code of behaviour', the body of traditional law evolved from the teaching and acts of Muhammad. There are approximately 690 million (1990) Sunni Muslims worldwide.

**Jainism** ancient Indian religion, sometimes regarded as an offshoot of Hinduism. Jains believe that non-injury to living beings is the highest religion, and their code of ethics is based on sympathy and compassion for all forms of life. They also believe in karma. In Jainism there is no deity and, like Buddhism, it is a monastic, ascetic religion. There are two main sects: the Digambaras and the Swetambaras. Jainism practises the most extreme form of non-violence (*ahimsā*) of all Indian sects, and influenced the philosophy of Mahātmā Gāndhī. Jains number approximately 4 million (1990); there are Jain communities throughout the world but the majority live in India.

Jainism's sacred books record the teachings of Mahavira (*c.* 540–468 BCE), the last in a line of 24 great masters called Tirthankaras (or *jinas*, 'those who overcome'). Mahavira was born in Vessali (now Bihar), E India. He became an ascetic at the age of 30, achieved enlightenment at 42, and preached for 30 years.

During the 3rd century BCE two divisions arose regarding the extent of austerities. The Digambaras ('sky-clad') believe that enlightenment can only occur when all possessions have been given up, including clothes, and that it can only be achieved when a soul is born into a human male body. Monks of this sect go naked on the final stages of their spiritual path. The Swetambaras ('white-clad') believe that both human sexes can achieve enlightenment and that nakedness is not a prerequisite.

**Judaism** the religion of the ancient Hebrews and their descendents the Jews, based, according to the Old Testament, on a covenant between God and Abraham about 2000 BCE, and the renewal of the covenant with Moses about 1200 BCE. It rests on the concept of one eternal invisible God, whose will is revealed in the *Torah* and who has a special relationship with the Jewish people. The Torah comprises the first five books of the Bible (the Pentateuch), which contains the history, laws, and guide to life for correct behaviour. Besides those living in Israel, there are large Jewish populations today in the USA, USSR, the UK and Commonwealth nations, and in Jewish communities throughout the world. There are approximately 18 million Jews (1990), with about 9 million in the Americas, 5 million in Europe, and 4 million in Asia, Africa, and the Pacific.

*scriptures* The *Talmud* combines the *Mishna*, rabbinical commentary on the law handed down orally from CE 70 and put in writing about 200, and the *Gemara*, legal discussions in the schools of Palestine and Babylon from the 3rd and 4th centuries. The *Haggadah* is a part of the Talmud dealing with stories of heroes. The *Midrash* is a collection of commentaries on the scriptures written 400–1200, mainly in Palestine. Along with the *Torah* they are regarded as authoritative sources of Jewish ritual, worship, and practice.

*observances* The *synagogue* (in US non-Orthodox usage *temple*) is the local building for congregational worship (originally simply the place where the Torah was read and expounded); its characteristic feature is the Ark, the enclosure where the Torah scrolls are kept. *Rabbis* are ordained teachers schooled in the Jewish law and ritual who act as spiritual leaders and pastors of their communities; some devote themselves to study. Religious practices include: circumcision, daily services in Hebrew, observance of the *Sabbath* (sunset on Friday to sunset Saturday) as a day of rest, and, among Orthodox Jews, strict dietary laws. High Holy days include *Rosh Hashanah* marking the Jewish New Year (first new moon after the autumn equinox) and, a week later, the religious fast *Yom Kippur* (Day of Atonement). Other holidays are celebrated throughout the year to commemorate various events of Biblical history.

*history* In the late Middle Ages when Europe and Western Asia were divided into Christian and Islamic countries, the Jewish people also found itself divided into two main groups. Jews in central and eastern Europe, namely in Germany and Poland, were called *Ashkenazi*. Sefardic Jews can trace their tradition back to the Mediterranean countries, particularly Spain and Portugal under Muslim rule. When they were expelled in 1492 they settled in north Africa, the Levant, the Far East and northern Europe. The two traditions differ in a number of ritual and cultural ways but their theology and basic Jewish practice is the same. The Hassidic sects of eastern Europe and some north African and Oriental countries also differ from other groups in their rites but they, too, maintain the concept of divine authority. *divisions* In the 19th and early 20th centuries there was a move by some Jewish groups away from traditional or orthodox observances. This trend gave rise to a number of groups within Judaism. **Orthodox Jews**, who form the majority, assert the supreme authority of the Torah, adhere to all the traditions of Judaism, including the strict dietary laws and the segregation of women in the synagogue. **Reform Judaism** rejects the idea that Jews are the chosen people, has a liberal interpretation of the dietary laws, and takes a critical attitude towards the Torah. **Conservative Judaism** is a compromise between Orthodox and Reform in its acceptance of the traditional law, making some allowances for modern conditions, although its services and ceremonies are closer to Orthodox than to Reform. **Liberal Judaism**, or **Reconstructionism**, goes further than Reform in attempting to adapt Judaism to the needs of the modern world and to interpret the Torah in the light of current scholarship. In all the groups except Orthodox, women are not segregated in the synagogue, and there are female rabbis in both Reform and Liberal Judaism. In the 20th century many people who call themselves Jews prefer to identify Judaism with a historical and cultural tradition rather than with strict religious observance, and a contemporary debate (complicated by the history of non-Jewish attitudes towards Jews) centres on the question of how to define a Jew. As in other religions, fundamentalist movements have emerged, for example, Gush Emunim.

**North American indigenous religions** these form a wide variety, but have some features in common, especially a belief that everything in nature is alive and contains powerful forces which can be helpful or harmful to humans. If the forces are to be helpful, they must be treated with respect, and so hunting and other activities require ritual and preparation. Certain people are believed to be in contact with or possessed by the spirit world and so to have special powers; but each individual can also seek power and vision through ordeals and fasting.

**Shinto** the indigenous religion of Japan. It combines an empathetic oneness with natural forces and loyalty to the reigning dynasty as descendants of the Sun goddess, Amaterasu-Omikami. Traditional Shinto followers stressed obedience and devotion to the emperor, and an aggressive nationalistic aspect was developed by the Meiji rulers. Today Shinto has discarded these aspects. There are about 3.2 million (1990) adherents worldwide.

Shinto is the Chinese transliteration of the Japanese **Kami-no-Michi**. Shinto ceremonies appeal to the Kami, the mysterious forces of nature manifest in topographical features such as mountains, trees, stones, springs, and caves. Shinto focuses on purity, devotion, and

sincerity; aberrations can be cleansed through purification rituals. In addition, purification procedures make the worshipper presentable and acceptable when making requests before the Kami.

Shinto's holiest shrine is at Ise, near Kyoto, where in the temple of the Sun Goddess is preserved the mirror that she is supposed to have given to Jimmu, the first emperor, in the 7th century BCE. Sectarian Shinto consists of 130 sects; the sects are officially recognized but not state-supported (as was state Shinto until its disestablishment after World War II and Emperor Hirohito's disavowal of his divinity 1946).

There is no Shinto philosophical literature although there are texts on mythologies, ceremonial and administrative procedures, religious laws, and chronicles of ruling families and temple construction.

**Sikhism** religion professed by 14 million Indians, living mainly in the Punjab. Sikhism was founded by Nanak (1469–c. 1539). Sikhs believe in a single God who is the immortal creator of the universe and who has never been incarnate in any form, and in the equality of all human beings; Sikhism is strongly opposed to caste divisions. There are approximately 16.5 million (1990) adherents worldwide.

Their holy book is the *Guru Granth Sahib*. Guru Gobind Singh (1666–1708) instituted the Khanda-di-Pahul, the Baptism of the Sword, and established the *Khalsa* ('pure'), the company of the faithful. The Khalsa wear the five Ks: *kes*, long hair; *kangha*, a comb; *kirpan*, a sword; *kachh*, short trousers; and *kara*, a steel bracelet. Sikh men take the last name 'Singh' ('lion') and women 'Kaur' ('princess').

*beliefs* Human beings can make themselves ready to find God by prayer and meditation but can achieve closeness to God only as a result of God's *nadar* (grace). Sikhs believe in reincarnation and that the ten human gurus were teachers through whom the spirit of Guru Nanak was passed on to live today in the *Guru Granth Sahib* and the Khalsa.

*practice* Sikhs do not have a specific holy day, but hold their main services on the day of rest of the country in which they are living. Daily prayer is important in Sikhism, and the gurdwara (the Sikh place for worship) functions as a social as well as religious centre; it contains a kitchen, the *langar*, where all, male and female, Sikh and non-Sikh, may eat together as equals. Sikh women take the same role as men in religious observances, for example, in reading from the *Guru Granth Sahib* at the gurdwara. Festivals in honour of the ten human gurus include a complete reading of the *Guru Granth Sahib*; Sikhs also celebrate at the time of some of the major Hindu festivals, but their emphasis is on aspects of Sikh belief and the example of the gurus. Sikhs avoid the use of all nonmedicinal drugs and, in particular, tobacco.

*history* On Nanak's death he was followed as guru by a succession of leaders who converted the Sikhs (the word means 'disciple') into a military confraternity which established itself as a political power. Gobind Singh was assassinated by a Muslim 1708, and since then the *Guru Granth Sahib* has taken the place of a leader.

Upon the partition of India many Sikhs migrated from W to E Punjab, and in 1966 the efforts of Sant Fateh Singh (c. 1911–72) led to the creation of a Sikh state within India by partition of the Punjab. However, the Akali separatist movement agitates for a completely independent Sikh state, Khalistan, and a revival of fundamentalist belief and was headed from 1978 by Sant Jarnail Singh Bhindranwale (1947–84), killed in the siege of the Golden Temple, Amritsar. In retaliation for this, the Indian prime minister Indira Gandhi was assassinated in Oct of the same year by her Sikh bodyguards. Heavy rioting followed, in which 1,000 Sikhs were killed. Mrs Gandhi's successor, Rajiv Gandhi, reached an agreement for the election of a popular government in the Punjab and for state representatives to the Indian parliament with the moderate Sikh leader Sant Harchand Singh Longowal, who was himself killed 1985 by Sikh extremists.

**South American indigenous religions** religious beliefs and practice are diverse and since early Indian contact with whites there has been some reconciliation between Christian and local belief, and also the emergence of new religious movements. Many of the local religions have the concept of a supreme religious force or god, but this force is often so remote or great that it is not worshipped directly. There are many powerful spirits, including souls of the ancestors, that inhabit and influence the natural environment and the lives of humans. To maintain harmony with the forest, rivers, or animals these spirits are respected and frequently associated with creation myths or as the harbingers of fortune or suffering, and they are not hunted, for example, the anaconda snake amongst the Sarema people of the Amazonian rainforest.

**Taoism** Chinese philosophical system, traditionally founded by the Chinese philosopher Lao Zi 6th century BCE. He is also attributed authorship of the scriptures, *Tao Te Ching*, which were apparently compiled later in the 3rd century BCE. The 'tao' or 'way' denotes the hidden principle of the universe, and less stress is laid on good deeds than on harmonious interaction with the environment, which automatically ensures right behaviour. The second major work is that of Zhuangzi (c. 389–286 BCE), *The Way of Zhuangzi*. The magical side of Taoism is illustrated by the *I Ching* or *Book of Changes*, a book of divination. There are approximately 190 million (1990) Taoists worldwide.

*beliefs* The universe is believed to be kept in balance by the opposing forces of yin and yang that operate in dynamic tension between themselves. Yin is female and watery: the force in the moon and rain which reached its peak in the winter; yang is masculine and solid: the

force in the sun and earth which reaches its peak in the summer. The interaction of yin and yang is believed to shape all life.

This magical, ritualistic aspect of Taoism developed from the 2nd century CE and was largely responsible for its popular growth; it stresses physical immortality, and this was attempted by means ranging from dietary regulation and fasting to alchemy. By the 3rd century, worship of gods had begun to appear, including that of the stove god Tsao Chun. From the 4th century, rivalry between Taoists and Mahāyāna Buddhists was strong in China, leading to persecution of one religion by the other; this was resolved by mutual assimilation, and Taoism developed monastic communities similar to those of the Buddhists.

Taoist texts record the tradition of mental and physical discipline, and methods to use in healing, exorcism, and the quest for immortality.

**Zoroastrianism** pre-Islamic Persian religion founded by the Persian prophet Zarathustra or Zoroaster (Greek), and still practised by the Parsees in India. The *Zendavesta* are the sacred scriptures of the faith. The theology is dualistic, **Ahura Mazda** or **Ormuzd** (the good God) being perpetually in conflict with **Ahriman** (the evil God), but the former is assured of eventual victory. There are approximately 150,000 (1990) adherents worldwide.

*beliefs* Humanity has been given free will to choose between the two powers, thus rendering believers responsible for their fate after death in heaven or hell. Moral and physical purity is central to all aspects of Zoroastrianism *yasna* or worship: since life and work are part of worship, there should be purity of action. Fire is considered sacred, and Ahura Mazda believed to be present when the ritual flame is worshipped at home or in the temple. It is believed that there will be a second universal judgement at *Frashokereti*, a time when the dead will be raised and the world cleansed of unnatural impurity.

The Parsee community in Bombay is now the main centre of Zoroastrianism, but since conversion is generally considered impossible, the numbers in India have been steadily decreasing at the rate of 10% per decade since 1947. Parsee groups, mainly in Delhi and outside India, have been pushing for the acceptance of converts, but the concern of the majority in Bombay is that their religious and cultural heritage will be lost.

# RELIGIOUS MOVEMENTS

**Baha'i** movement founded in 19th-century Persia by a Muslim splinter group, the Babis. It evolved into the Baha'i religion under the leadership of Baha'ullah. His message in essence was that all great religious leaders are manifestations of the unknowable God and all scriptures are sacred. There is no priesthood: all Baha'is are expected to teach, and to work towards world unification. There are about 4.5 million (1990) Baha'is worldwide.

**Jehovah's Witness** member of a religious organization originating in the USA 1872 under Charles Taze Russell (1852–1916). Jehovah's Witnesses attach great importance to Christ's Second Coming, which Russell predicted would occur 1914, and which Witnesses still believe is imminent. All Witnesses are expected to take part in house-to-house preaching; there are no clergy. There are approximately 6.75 million (1990) adherents worldwide.

**Mormon** or *Latter-day Saint* member of a Christian sect, the *Church of Jesus Christ of Latter-day Saints*, founded at Fayette, New York, in 1830 by Joseph Smith. According to Smith, Mormon was an ancient prophet in North America whose *Book of Mormon*, of which Smith claimed divine revelation, is accepted by Mormons as part of the Christian scriptures. In the 19th century the faction led by Brigham Young was polygamous. It is a missionary church with headquarters in Utah and a worldwide membership of about 5 million.

**Rajneesh meditation** meditation based on the teachings of the Indian Shree Rajneesh (born Chaadra Mohan Jain), established in the early 1970s. Until 1989 he called himself *Bhagwan* (Hindi 'God'). His followers, who number about half a million worldwide, regard themselves as Sannyas, or Hindu ascetics; they wear orange robes and carry a string of prayer beads. They are not expected to observe any specific prohibitions but to be guided by their instincts.

**Rastafarianism** religion originating in the West Indies, based on the ideas of Marcus Garvey, who called on black people to return to Africa and set up a black-governed country there. When Haile Selassie (*Ras Tafari*, 'Lion of Judah') was crowned emperor of Ethiopia 1930, this was seen as a fulfilment of prophecy and Rastafarians acknowledged him as the Messiah, the incarnation of God (*Jah*). The use of ganja (marijuana) is a sacrament. There are no churches. There were about one million Rastafarians by 1990.

**Scientology** (Latin *scire* 'to know' and Greek *logos* 'branch of learning') an 'applied religious philosophy' based on dianetics, founded in California in 1954 by L Ron Hubbard as the *Church of Scientology*. Through a form of psychotherapy it claims to 'increase man's spiritual awareness', but its methods of recruiting and retaining converts have met criticism. Its headquarters from 1959 have been in Sussex, England.

**Seventh Day Adventist** often called an *Adventist* member of the Protestant religious sect of the same name. It originated in the USA in the fervent expectation of Christ's Second Coming, or advent, that swept across New York State following William Miller's prophecy that Christ would return on 22 Oct, 1844. When this failed to come to pass, a number of Millerites, as his followers were called, reinterpreted his prophetic speculations and continued to maintain that the millennium was imminent. Adventists observe Saturday as the Sabbath and emphasize healing, temperance, and diet; many are vegetarians. The sect has about 500,000 members in the USA.

**transcendental meditation** (TM) technique of focusing the mind, based in part on Hindu meditation. Meditators are given a *mantra* (a special word or phrase) to repeat over and over to themselves; such meditation is believed to benefit the practitioner by relieving stress and inducing a feeling of well-being and relaxation. It was introduced to the West by Maharishi Mahesh Yogi and popularized by the Beatles in the late 1960s.

**Unification Church** or *Moonies* church founded in Korea 1954 by the Reverend Sun Myung Moon. The theology unites Christian and Taoist ideas and is based on Moon's book *Divine Principle*, which teaches that the original purpose of creation was to set up a perfect family, in a perfect relationship with God. The church has met with criticism over its recruiting methods and use of finances. The number of members (often called 'moonies') is about 200,000 worldwide.

**Unitarianism** a Christian denomination that rejects the orthodox doctrine of the Trinity and gives a preeminent position to Jesus as a religious teacher, while denying his deity. Unitarians believe in individual conscience and reason as a guide to right action, rejecting the doctrines of original sin, the atonement, and eternal punishment. There are approximately 750,000 adherents (1990) worldwide.

# RITES OF PASSAGES

Most religions mark certain important stages in a person's life, such as birth, initiation, marriage, and death, by special ceremonies or rites of passage. These rituals provide a way of publicly recognizing a change of status; they are also a time for the whole community to reaffirm its faith.

**Birth rites** Birth is often a time of rejoicing, but it is also a time of new responsibility. The rituals associated with birth mark the child's entrance into a new community and the adult's commitment to that child.

*Hindu birth rites* begin with the choice of a suitable day for conception, and continue through pregnancy; the mother-to-be must avoid certain foods and recite verses from the Hindu holy books. When the baby is born, there are a number of further ceremonies including naming the child, the calculation of a horoscope, and the inscription of the word 'aum' (the elemental sound of the universe) in honey on the child's tongue. The last of these ceremonies, the shaving of the child's hair, may take place up to two years after the birth.

## THE MAJOR FAITHS: COMING TOGETHER OR AS FAR APART AS EVER?

The Gulf War of 1991 highlighted the use of the name of God in war and thus raised issues of the role of the concept of the Just War. Both sides claimed that God was on their side. President Bush called upon Dr Billy Graham to be with him during the hours of decision prior to the actual offensive, and the US military leaders assured their troops that God was with them. On the Iraqi side, Saddam Hussein called for a Jihad—a Holy War—against the USA and its allies and likewise claimed that God was with him and his troops. All three of the faiths involved—Islam, Christianity and Judaism—have strong views on warfare. In Islam the idea of the Holy War dates back to the time of the Prophet Muhammad who declared that war against infidels and for the faith was not only justifiable, it may actually be necessary. However, the Jihad also lays down very strict rules for the conduct of such a war.

In Christianity, the idea of the Just War arose during the 11th to 12th centuries as a balance to the almost constant warfare in Europe. The Church laid down conditions in which warfare could be justified—thus outlawing all other forms. For war to be considered just, it must be a lesser evil than allowing the situation to continue; must be capable of being won swiftly and must not harm the innocent.

Judaism has a wide range of views on warfare, from pacifism through to religious warfare to defend the faith.

The Gulf crisis made it imperative for religious leaders to say where they stood, not just on the issue of this war, but on the issue of modern warfare per se. Only two major religious figures came out clearly against this war and any other war. The Pope and the Dalai Lama. Of these, the Pope's statement was both the most forceful and in some ways the most surprising. For the Pope rejected the validity of any claim that modern warfare could be considered capable of being a Just War. The cost in civilian lives ruled that out of court according to the Pope.

Other religious leaders found themselves either foretelling that this war was the start of the end of days—this was a refrain echoed in the US evangelical camps—or claiming that this was indeed a Just War. Thus the Archbishop of Canterbury defended the use of British forces on the grounds that it was a Just War, and the leading Iraqi and Jordanian imams also claimed that it was a Just War or Holy War—but on behalf of the Iraqi forces. In Israel, the voices were more muted and Judaism found itself in the difficult position of remaining neutral while Scud missiles fell on the cities.

The environmental destruction which the war unleashed put into stark relief a growing area of concern for all religion—ecology. In 1986 the World Wide Fund for Nature International had called together leaders of the five main religions—Buddhism, Christianity, Hinduism, Islam and Judaism—in Assisi, Italy, to discuss ways in which the main faiths could further the concerns of ecology. From that meeting arose the Network on Conservation and Religion. By 1991 three other faiths, the Baha'is, Sikhs and Jains had officially joined this network, to work on ecological issues. In his address to the world on New Year's Day 1990, the Pope had made ecology his key concern. The World Council of Churches, meeting for its once every eight years General Assembly in Canberra, Feb 1991 likewise focused on ecology as a primary issue for the Churches. Meanwhile, the head of the Orthodox Churches, the Patriarch of Constantinople created a new feast day to celebrate creation and urged all Orthodox Christians to become involved with ecology.

The Jains, overcoming divisions going back two thousand years, united to develop a programme on ecology for their holy sites and for India in general, while in 1991 the Hindu temples of Vrindavan—Krishna's holy city—were working on major ecological programmes for their environment.

While the faiths appear to be as divided about and by the issue of war as ever, they do seem to have found some degree of unity of purpose in the idea of being just to the environment.

*Saddam Hussein at prayer in a Kurdish mosque in Arbil.*

Hindus believe that these ceremonies will help the child towards a better rebirth.

**Sikh birth rites** Sikhs believe that the first words which a child should hear are those of the Mool Mantra, the beginning of the Sikh holy book, and so, as soon as the baby is born, it is washed and the words of the Mool Mantra whispered into its ear. A few weeks later the child is taken to the gurdwara, the Sikh place of worship, to be named. The initial of the name is chosen by opening the *Guru Granth Sahib* at random and choosing the first letter of the hymn on the left hand page.

**Muslim birth rites** the first words which a Muslim baby will hear are those of the call to prayer, which is used to call Muslims to the mosque or place of worship each day; these words, which contain the basic beliefs of Islam, are whispered into its ears. Seven days later, the child is named. This ceremony involves the shaving of the baby's head. If the child is a boy, he will also be circumcised at this time, to recall Abraham and his son Ismail.

**Jewish birth rites** the surgical operation of *circumcision* consists of the removal of a small part of the foreskin. All Jewish boys must be circumcised on the eighth day after birth, as long as health permits. During circumcision a prayer is said which recalls the covenant or agreement God made with Abraham and the ceremony marks the boy's entry into this covenant. If the child is a girl, her name is announced in the synagogue (the Jewish place of worship) by the father on the first Sabbath after her birth.

**Christian birth rites** universal in the Christian Church from its beginning has been the religious initiation rite of **baptism** (Greek 'to dip'), involving immersion in or sprinkling with water. In the baptismal ceremony, sponsors or godparents make vows on behalf of the child which are renewed by the child at confirmation. Baptism was originally administered to adults by immersion, and infant baptism has been common only since the 6th century. In some of the Protestant churches, adults are still baptized by immersion in a pool of water. The immersion symbolizes death and new life.

**Chinese birth rites** Chinese babies are not named until the first month after birth; then the Full Month ceremony is held, with special foods, including red eggs which are symbols of luck and new life. The name given to the baby is a nickname designed to convince any malevolent spirits that the child is not worth stealing.

**Initiation rites** Initiation is a passage into full membership of a group, whether religious or social. It gives the individual both rights and responsibilities.

**Sikh initiation rites** the tenth guru of Sikhism, Guru Gobind Singh, set up a brotherhood of dedicated Sikhs, the Khalsa; any sufficiently mature and dedicated Sikh may apply to join the Khalsa. The ceremony is conducted by five members of the Khalsa in the presence of the *Guru Granth Sahib*, the Sikh holy book; it involves special prayers, the sharing of karah

parshad (a sweet mixture) to symbolize the equality of Sikhs, and the drinking and sprinkling of amrit (sugar and water). Those initiated in the Khalsa should always wear five things known as the Five K's: uncut hair; a steel bracelet; a short sword; a comb and *kaccha*, a type of shorts.

**Jewish initiation** is marked by the **bar mitzvah** (Hebrew 'son of the commandment'), initiation of a boy at the age of 14 into the adult Jewish community; less common is the bat mitzvah for girls. In the synagogue, the boy says a special bar mitzvah prayer promising to keep God's commandments, and accept responsibility for his actions before God; he then reads a passage from the Torah in the synagogue on the Sabbath. After this, he is regarded as a full member of the congregation.

**Christian initation** is marked by **confirmation**, a rite by which a previously baptized person is admitted to full membership of the Christian Church. It consists in the laying on of hands by a bishop, in order that the confirmed person may receive the gift of the Holy Spirit, the third aspect of the Trinity. Among Anglicans, the rite is deferred until the child is able to comprehend the fundamental beliefs of Christian doctrine.

**Marriage rites** Marriage involves not only a change in status for the two people concerned, but also a new set of relationships for their families and the probability of children. In many cultures the choice of marriage partner is made by the parents, though the participants usually have some say in the matter.

**Hindu marriage rites** Hindu weddings may take place at the bride's home, or in a temple. The bride usually wears a red sari, and her hands and feet are painted with patterns in henna, an orange dye. Offerings are made before a sacred fire and prayers said; the bride and groom take seven steps around the fire, which symbolize food, strength, wealth, good fortune, children, the seasons, and everlasting friendship.

**Sikh wedding rites** a Sikh wedding may be held anywhere, as long as the *Guru Granth Sahib* is present. During the ceremony, the couple show their assent to the marriage by bowing to the holy book. The couple walk together round the *Guru Granth Sahib* four times as a hymn written by the fourth Guru is sung: this hymn contains all the basic teachings of Sikhism.

**Jewish wedding rites** the ceremony usually takes place in the synagogue, the place of worship. The bride and groom, with their parents, stand under a canopy or chupah. Blessings are recited by the rabbi, the religious leader, and the groom gives the bride a ring. The couple are now legally married and the *ketubah* or marriage contract, is read out. At the end of the ceremony the groom steps on and shatters a glass as a reminder, amidst the happiness, of the destruction of the Temple at Jerusalem.

**Christian marriage rites** Christian marriages are usually celebrated at the place of worship (church or chapel). The groom is accompanied by a helper, or best man, while the bride is escorted by her father, who officially 'gives' her to her new husband, and by attendants (bridesmaids). The couple make promises to love, honour and care for each other and exchange rings.

***Muslim marriage rites*** Muslim weddings may take place in the bride's home or in the place of worship, the mosque. The bride and groom are normally in separate rooms throughout the short ceremony. There is often a reading from the Koran, and a talk on the duties of marriage. The couple must consent to the marriage three times, and rings are exchanged.

***Chinese wedding rites*** in Chinese weddings, the concept of yin and yang, the two complementary forces which make up the universe, plays a prominent part; among their other attributes yin is seen as female and yang as male. There is a series of rituals leading up to the wedding, including the giving of gifts, an exchange of horoscopes (a prediction of a person's fortune) and a payment to the bride's family. The ceremony itself involves offerings and prayers to the bridegroom's ancestors and the household gods.

**Death rites** Death rites fulfil three main purposes: to comfort and strengthen the dying person, to comfort those left behind, and to ensure the best possible outcome for the deceased person in the next world or next birth. In several religions, such as Sikhism, Judaism, and Islam, people are encouraged to speak a declaration of faith before death, and Sikhs and Muslims read from their holy books to the dying person. Some religions discourage mourning, because they feel that death should not be regarded as a tragedy for the individual, especially after a long life, while others such as Judaism, set time aside for the family to grieve. There are many ways in which religions try to help the deceased in the afterlife. The Chinese offer practical help: since the afterlife may have resemblances to this life, replicas of useful goods, cars, washing machines, and money, are burnt at the funeral for the use of the deceased who will, with the other ancestors, now watch over the family.

# HOLY BOOKS

Many religions have a book or books which are regarded as holy or as providing especial wisdom. These books are treated with great reverence and copies may be kept in a place particularly set aside or have specific ceremonies associated with them. Such books are sometimes referred to as scriptures.

**Buddhist** Buddhist literature is divided into two groups, the teachings and discourses of the Buddha himself, and the teachings of saints, sages, and scholars. Since Buddhism was transmitted by word of mouth for about five hundred years after the death of the Buddha, it is difficult to say which of these writings contain the original word of the Buddha and which are later additions. One of the fundamental differences between the Hinayana and Mahayana schools is the attribution of the Buddha's word to the various texts. The Buddha's words are assembled in the ***Tipitaka*** or ***Tripitaka*** (three baskets) containing sutra (discourses), vinaya (rules of discipline), abhidharma (further knowledge). Important texts in this group include the commentaries on the Buddha's word by Buddhagosa in the Theravada tradition and Nagarjuna and Asanga in the early Indian Mahayana tradition.

**Chinese** Since Chinese religion is a mixture of Buddhism, Confucianism and Taoism, the Chinese generally respect the writings of all three. The main text of Taoism is the Tao Te Ching, attributed to the traditional founder of Taoism, Lao Tzu, although its date and authorship are obscure. Confucianism's main writings are those of Confucius himself, especially the Analects or 'selected sayings'. Confucius is traditionally the author of the Five Classics: ***Su Ching, Shi Ching, Li Chi, I Ching***, and the annals of ***Lu***.

Buddhist literature that emerged from China developed a practical approach that appealed to the Chinese sense of balance and the preference for direct, intuitive practice is reflected in the Ch'an school with such writing as Seng Chao's *On the Immutability of Phenomena*; and Tu Shun's *Meditation upon the Dharmadhadhatu*.

**Christian** The Christian ***Bible*** (Greek *ta biblia* 'the books') consists of the ***Old Testament***, the first five books of the Hebrew Bible, and the ***New Testament***, originally written in Greek, containing the Gospels, Acts of the Apostles, Letters and Revelation. It is believed that the books of the New Testament were written within a hundred years of the death of Christ, and from the 4th century were recognized by the Christian church as canonical. Early church history is recorded in the ***Acts of the Apostles***, the life of Jesus Christ in the four ***Gospels***, the epistles are the letters of St Paul and other Christian leaders to fellow Christians, and the New Testament closes with the ***Book of Revelation*** which records St John's vision of the end of time and Christ's second coming.

**Hindu** ***Veda*** (Sanskrit, divine knowledge). The most sacred of the Hindu scriptures, hymns written in an old form of Sanskrit; the oldest may date from 1500 or 2000 BCE. The four main collections are: the Rigveda (hymns and praises); Yajurveda (prayers and sacrificial formulae); Sâmaveda (hymns); and Atharvaveda, (spells, charms, and chants).

***Ramayana*** Hindu epic of 24,000 stanzas written in Sanskrit. It was assembled in its received form between the 1st century BCE and 1st century CE. The story reveals how Rama, an incarnation of the god Vishnu, and his friend Hanuman (the monkey chieftain) strive to recover Rama's wife, Sita, abducted by the

## EQUAL RITES?: WOMEN AND THE CHURCH

The status of women in the major faiths is very difficult to reconcile with contemporary views on the role of women in society.

In recent years the treatment of women has come under considerable attack. To begin with it was feminist writers and groups who saw in the patriarchal nature and language of the faiths a powerful vehicle for the subjugation of women. These voices were soon joined by women within the faiths who began to question traditional roles, language and status. For example: In Buddhism, debate is taking place on the role of women and in particular on the validity and role of the nuns. This is most pronounced amongst Western Buddhists, but writers and thinkers in countries such as Thailand are also questioning the older models and raising issues such as whether the low status of women in Buddhism has led to the sort of prostitution now so rampant in Thailand.

In Judaism, the Reform Synagogues have women rabbis, but the new Chief Rabbi of Great Britain has stated publicly that he sees no need to change the situation in all Orthodox synagogues, where men and women sit segregated and women are not able to become rabbis. The debate continues.

It is in Christianity that the most striking changes have taken place. Over the last few decades, many Protestant churches have started to ordain women priests—thus breaking one of the strongest, visible signs of male dominance. Many churches have tried to rid their writings of sexist language. The changes have often been controversial. But not all churches have moved this way. The Orthodox Churches will not yet consider the ordination of women and see it as being unacceptable that other churches have changed the centuries old pattern. Despite considerable internal pressure, the leadership of the Roman Catholic Church refuses to discuss women as priests. But the most painful example of the difficulty this new consciousness brings is undoubtably the Church of England.

The first modern women priests were Anglicans, ordained in China during the war. Many Anglican churches around the world now have women priests—even bishops. Yet the Mother Church in England has spent over 20 years dithering. In the early 1970s it agreed that there were no theological, biblical or pastoral reasons why women should not be ordained—but not just yet! Since that time a vigorous campaign has been mounted against women being ordained, by the right-wing and Anglo-Catholic sections of the Church. This debate has dragged on for nearly 20 years. In 1991 the parishes and diocesan synods of the Church were asked for their views. In 1992, the Synod will vote on whether to ordain women to the full priesthood—women can already carry out all priestly functions except consecrate the Eucharist. If the vote goes for women, then some priests have threatened to leave the Church of England and form a continuing Church of England. This was done in the USA after women priests were authorized in the late 1970's. If it goes against women, then many women will leave the Church. 1992 will be a tough year for the Church of England.

Another debate has been opened up in the last year by, amongst others, the theologian Daphne Hampson. She has questioned whether it is possible for Christianity to be reformed away from a patriarchal faith. Her conclusion, that it cannot, and that therefore women should explore their spirituality away from the Church has caused many women in the churches to look even more deeply into the question of their identity as women and their identity as Christians.

There is no question that the now widely accepted equality of status for women means that not just Christianity will have to undergo this sort of questioning. What sorts of changes this will lead to in our understanding of both the Divine and of men and women, is only just beginning to be glimpsed.

*Barbara Harris, first female bishop of the Episcopal Church, was consecrated in Boston, USA Feb 1989.*

demon king Ravana. It upholds the Hindu ideal of a relationship between a man and woman.

**Mahābhārata** Sanskrit ('great poem of the Bharatas') Hindu epic of 90,000 stanzas probably written between the 2nd century BCE and the end of the 1st century CE. With the *Rāmāyana*, it forms the two great epics of Hindu literature. The story is set on the Upper Ganges plain and deals with the fortunes of two rival families, the Kauravas and the Pandavas. It reveals the ethical values of ancient Hindu society and individual responsibility in particular. The central and most popular part is the *Bhagavad-Gītā* or *Song of the Blessed One*, a religious and philosophical poem delivered by Krishna to the hero Arjuna. The *Bhagavad Gītā* is regarded as one of the essential Hindu religious texts.

**Jain** The Swetabaras' canon is the **Siddhanta** assembled in the 5th century CE which includes accounts of the monastic discipline and teachings of Mahavira. The Digambaras' canon is made of two early Pakrit texts (Indian vernacular language) supplemented by commentaries from later scholars. There is also a large body of literature, dating from the 8th century CE, including narratives, commentaries, and cosmologies on existing texts. This later material is generally accepted by both Jain groups.

**Jewish** The **Torah** contains the first five books of the Hebrew Bible and it is given absolute religious authority by orthodox Jews. As well as referring to the first five books of Moses the **Torah** is sometimes used as a term for the whole Hebrew Bible. The First Five Books of Moses contain 613 laws covering social and religious customs, and histories of the early patriarchs

of the Jewish nation. The Hebrew Bible contains two further sections, the Prophets, and the Writings.

The Oral Law, traditionally revealed to Moses on Mount Sinai alongside the Written Law, is codified in the Mishna which was compiled after the destruction of the Temple CE 70. Further debates and interpretations by rabbis on the Torah's law and guidance are recorded in the Gemara and Midrash. The combined texts of the Mishna, Gemara, and Midrash, together with later rabbinical commentaries, are recorded in the **Talmud** the main compilation of traditional Jewish thought.

**Muslim Koran** more properly, Quran, though both are transliterations; the sacred book of Islam. Written in the purest Arabic, it contains 114 suras or chapters, and is stated to have been divinely revealed to the prophet Muhammad from Allah through the angel Jibra'el; the original is supposed to be preserved beside the throne of Allah in heaven.

**Sikh** The Sikh holy book is the *Guru Granth Sahib*, also known as the *Adi Granth* or 'first book'. It is a collection of hymns by the Sikh gurus or teachers, as well as by Muslim and Hindu writers, which was compiled largely by the fifth guru, Guru Arjan, and completed by the tenth guru, Guru Gobind Singh. On the death of the tenth guru, the *Guru Granth Sahib* took over the role of teacher and leader of the Sikhs. Guidance is sought by opening the holy book at random and reading verses. Any copy of the *Guru Granth Sahib* must have a special room to itself; people entering the room must cover their heads and remove their shoes. All copies of the holy book are idential, having 1,430 pages, and written in Gurmukhi, the written form of Punjabi.

# RELIGIOUS FIGURES

**Abraham** *c.*2300 BCE. In the Old Testament, founder of the Jewish nation. Jehovah promised him heirs and land for his people in Canaan (Israel), renamed him Abraham ('father of many nations') and tested his faith by a command (later retracted) to sacrifice his son Isaac. Jehovah's promise to Abraham was fulfilled when the descendants of Abraham's grandson, Jacob, were led out of Egypt by Moses.

**Abu Bakr** or **Abu-Bekr** 573–634. 'Father of the virgin', name used by Abd-el-Ka'aba from about 618 when the prophet Muhammad married his daughter Ayesha. He was a close adviser to Muhammad in the period 622–32. On the prophet's death, he became the first caliph adding Mesopotamia to the Muslim world and instigating expansion into Iraq and Syria.

**Ali** *c.* 598–660. 4th caliph of Islam. He was born in Mecca, the son of Abu Talib, uncle to the prophet Muhammad, who gave him his daughter Fatima in marriage. On Muhammad's death

## Religious Festivals

| Date | Festival | Religion | Commemorating |
|------|----------|----------|---------------|
| 6 Jan | Epiphany | Western Christian | coming of the Magi |
| 6–7 Jan | Christmas | Orthodox Christian | birth of Jesus |
| 18–19 Jan | Epiphany | Orthodox Christian | coming of the Magi |
| Jan–Feb | New Year | Chinese | Return of Kitchen god to heaven |
| Feb–Mar | Shrove Tuesday | Christian | day before Lent |
| | Ash Wednesday | Christian | first day of Lent |
| | Purim | Jewish | story of Esther |
| | Mahashivaratri | Hindu | Siva |
| Mar–Apr | Palm Sunday | Western Christian | Jesus's entry into Jerusalem |
| | Good Friday | Western Christian | crucifixion of Jesus |
| | Easter Sunday | Western Christian | resurrection of Jesus |
| | Passover | Jewish | escape from slavery in Egypt |
| | Holi | Hindu | Krishna |
| | Holi Mohalla | Sikh | (coincides with Holi) |
| | Rama Naumi | Hindu | birth of Rama |
| | Ching Ming | Chinese | remembrance of the dead |
| 13 Apr | Baisakhi | Sikh | founding of the Kalsa |
| Apr–May | Easter | Orthodox Christian | death and resurrection of Jesus |
| | Lailut ul Isra wal Mi'raj | Muslim | Prophet Muhammad's journey Jerusalem and then up to Heaven |
| | Lailat ul-Bara'h | Muslim | forgiveness before Ramadan |
| May–Jun | Shavuot | Jewish | giving of ten Comandments to Moses |
| | Lailat ul-Qadr | Muslim | revelation of the Qur'an to Muhammad |
| | Eid ul-Fitr | Muslim | end of Ramadan |
| | Pentecost (Whitsun) | | Christian Jesus's followers receiving the Holy Spirit |
| | Wesak | Buddhist | day of Buddha's birth, enlightenment and death |
| | Martyrdom of Guru Arjan | Sikh | death of fifth guru of Sikhism |
| June | Dragon Boat Festival | Chinese | Chinese martyr |
| Jul | Dhammacakka | Buddhist | preaching of Buddha's first sermon |
| | Eid ul-Adha | Muslim | Ibrahim's willingness to sacrifice his son |
| Aug | Raksha Bandhan | Hindu | family |
| Aug–Sept | Janmashtami | Hindu | birthday of Khrishna |
| Sept | Moon Festival | Chinese | Chinese hero |
| Sept–Oct | Rosh Hashana | Jewish | start of Jewish New Year |
| | Yom Kippur | Jewish | day of atonement |
| | Succot | Jewish | Israelites' time in the wilderness |
| Oct | Dusshera | Hindu | goddess Devi |
| Oct–Nov | Divali | Hindu | goddess Lakshmi |
| | Divali | Sikh | release of Guru Hargobind from prison |
| Nov | Guru Nanak's Birthday | Sikh | founder of Sikhism |
| 1 Nov | All Saint's Day | Christian | deceased Christian saints and holy people |
| 2 Nov | All Soul's Day | Christian | Christian deceased |
| | Bodhi Day | Buddhist (Mahāyāna) | Buddha's enlightenment |
| Dec | Hanukkah | Jewish | recapture of Temple of Jerusalem |
| | Winter Festival | Chinese | time of feasting |
| 25 Dec | Christmas | Western Christian | birth of Christ |
| Dec–Jan | Birthday of Guru Gobind Sind | Sikh | last (tenth) human guru of Sikhism |
| | Martyrdom of Guru Tegh Bahadur | Sikh | ninth guru of Sikhism |

632, Ali had a claim to succeed him, but this was not conceded until 656. After a stormy reign, he was assassinated. Around Ali's name the controversy has raged between the Sunni and the Shi'ites, the former denying his right to the caliphate and the latter supporting it.

**Asoka** c.273–238 BCE. Indian emperor, and Buddhist convert from Hinduism. He issued edicts, carved on pillars and rock faces throughout his dominions, promoting wise government and the cultivation of moral virtues according to Buddhist teachings. Many still survive, and are amongst the oldest deciphered texts in India. In Patna there are the remains of a hall built by him.

**Augustine, St** first archbishop of Canterbury, England. He was sent from Rome to convert England to Christianity by Pope Gregory I. He landed at Ebbsfleet in Kent 597, and soon after baptized Ethelbert, King of Kent, along with many of his subjects. He was consecrated bishop of the English at Arles in the same year, and appointed archbishop 601, establishing his see at Canterbury. Feast day 26 May.

**Bodhidharma** 6th century CE. Indian Buddhist and teacher. He entered China from S India about 520, and was the founder of the Ch'an school (Zen is the Japanese derivation). Ch'an focuses on contemplation leading to intuitive meditation, a direct pointing to and stilling of the human mind. In the 20th century, Zen has attracted many followers in the west.

**Buddha** 'enlightened one', title of Prince *Gautama Siddhārtha* c.563–483 BCE. Religious leader, founder of Buddhism, born at Lumbini in Nepál. At the age of 29, he left his wife and son and a life of luxury, to escape from the material burdens of existence. After six years of austerity he realized that asceticism, like overindulgence, was futile, and chose the middle way of meditation. He became enlightened under a bo or bodhi tree in Bihar, India. He began teaching at Varanasi, and founded the Sangha, an order of monks. He spent the rest of his life travelling around N India, and died at Kusinagara in Uttar Pradesh.

**Confucius** Latinized form of *K'ung Tzu*, 'Kong the master' 551–479 BCE. Chinese sage whose name is given to Confucianism. He devoted his life to relieving suffering among the poor through governmental and administrative reform. His emphasis on tradition and ethics attracted a growing number of pupils during his lifetime. *The Analects of Confucius*, a compilation of his teachings, was published after his death. Within three hundred years of the death of Confucius his teaching was adopted by the Chinese state, and remained so until 1912.

**Ghazzali, al-** 1058–1111. Muslim philosopher and one of the most celebrated Sufis (Muslim mystics). He was responsible for easing the conflict between the Sufi and the Ulema, a body of Muslim religious and legal scholars.

**Gobind Singh** 1666–1708. Indian religious leader, the tenth and last guru (teacher) of Sikhism, 1675–1708, and founder of the Sikh brotherhood known as the Khalsa. On his death, the Sikh holy book, the *Guru Granth Sahib*, replaced the line of human gurus as the teacher and guide of the Sikh community.

**Jesus** c.4 BCE–CE 29 or 30. Hebrew preacher on whose teachings Christianity was founded. According to the accounts of his life in the four Gospels, he was born in Bethlehem, Palestine, son of God and the Virgin Mary, and brought up by Mary and her husband Joseph as a carpenter in Nazareth. After adult baptism, he gathered 12 disciples, but his preaching antagonized the Roman authorities and he was executed by crucifixion. Three days later there came reports of his resurrection and, later, his ascension to heaven.

**Lao Zi** or Lao Tzu c.604–531 BCE. Chinese philosopher, commonly regarded as the founder of Taoism, with its emphasis on the Tao, the inevitable and harmonious way of the universe. Nothing certain is known of his life, and he is variously said to have lived in the 6th or the

4th century BCE. The *Tao Tê Ching*, the Taoist scripture, is attributed to him but apparently dates from the 3rd century BCE.

**Luther** Martin 1483–1546. German Christian reformer, a founder of Protestantism. While he was a priest at the University of Wittenberg, he wrote an attack on the sale of indulgences (remissions of punishment for sin) in 95 theses which he nailed to a church door 1517, in defiance of papal condemnation. The Holy Roman Emperor Charles V summoned him to the Diet of Worms 1521, where he refused to retract his objections. Originally intending reform, his protest led to schism, with the emergence, following the Augsburg Confession 1530, of a new Protestant Church. Luther is regarded as the instigator of the Protestant revolution, and Lutheranism is now the major religion of many north-European countries including Germany, Sweden, and Denmark.

**Mahavira** c.540–468 BCE. Indian teacher and scholar. He was born into the warrior-king caste in Vessili (now Bihar). He became an ascetic at 30, achieved enlightenment at 42, and preached for 30 years. He was last in a line of 24 Jain masters called *Tirthankaras* or jinas ('those who overcome').

**Maimonides** Moses (Moses Ben Maimon) 1135–1204. Jewish rabbi and philosopher, born in Córdoba, Spain. Known as one of the greatest Hebrew scholars, he attempted to reconcile faith and reason. He was author of the *Thirteen Principles of Faith*.

**Moses** c. 13th century BCE. Hebrew lawgiver and judge who led the Israelites out of Egypt to the promised land of Canaan. On Mount Sinai he claimed to have received from Jehovah the oral and written Law, including the *Ten Commandments* engraved on tablets of stone. The first five books of the Old Testament—in Judaism, the *Torah*—are ascribed to him.

**Muhammad** or *Mohammed, Mahomet* c. 570–632. Prophet of Islam, born in Mecca on the Arabian peninsula. He began his prophetic mission c. 610 CE when it is believed he began to receive the revelations of the *Koran*, revealed to him by God (it was later written down by his followers), through the angel Jibra'el. He fled from persecution to the town now known as Medina in 622: the flight, *Hegira*, marks the beginning of the Islamic era.

**Nanak** 1469–c. 1539. Indian guru and founder of Sikhism, a religion based on the unity of God and the equality of all human beings. He was strongly opposed to caste divisions. He was the first of ten human gurus in the Sikh faith.

**Paul, St** c.3–c.AD 68. Christian missionary and martyr; in the New Testament, one of the apostles and author of 13 epistles. He is said to have been converted by a vision on the road to Damascus. His emblems are a sword and a book; feast day 29 June.

**Shankara** 799–833. Hindu philosopher who wrote commentaries on some of the major Hindu scriptures, as well as hymns and essays on religious ideas. Shankara was responsible for the final form of the Advaita

Vedanta school of Hindu philosophy, which teaches that Brahman, the supreme being, is all that exists in the universe, everything else is illusion. Shankara was fiercely opposed to Buddhism and may have influenced its decline in India.

**Zoroaster** or **Zarathushtra** 6th century or 16th century BCE. Persian prophet and religious teacher, founder of Zoroastrianism. Zoroaster believed that he had seen God, Ahura Mazda, in a vision. His first vision came at the age of 30 and, after initial rejection and violent attack, he converted King Vishtaspa. Subsequently, his teachings spread rapidly, becoming the official religion of the kingdom. Zoroastrianism was a dualistic theology: the god of absolute purity and goodness, Ahura Mazda, being opposed by the twin spirit of violence and death, Angra Mainyu. According to tradition, Zoroaster was murdered at the age of 70 while praying at the altar.

# HOLY PLACES

The concept of *pilgrimage*, a journey to sacred places inspired by religious devotion, is common to many religions. For Hindus the holy places include Benares and the purifying Ganges; for Buddhists, Bodhgaya, the site of the Buddha's enlightenment, the Tooth of the Buddha in Sri Lanka, and numerous temples and sacred mountains throughout China and south-east Asia; for the ancient Greeks the shrines at Delphi, Ephesus, among others; for the Jews, the Western Wall at Jerusalem; and for Muslims, Mecca. Among Christians, pilgrimages were common by the second century, and as a direct result of the established necessity of making pilgrimages there arose the numerous hospices catering for pilgrims, the religious orders of knighthood, and the Crusades. The great centres of Christian pilgrimages have been, or are, Jerusalem, Rome, the tomb of St James of Compostella in Spain, the shrine of Becket at Canterbury, and the holy places at La Salette and Lourdes in France.

**Amritsar** city in the Punjab, India, founded 1577. It is the religious centre of the Sikhs and contains the Golden Temple and Guru Nanak University 1969, named after the first Sikh Guru.

**Jerusalem** ancient city of Palestine, which is a holy place for Jews, Christians and Muslims. It was divided in 1948 between the new republic of Israel and Jordan. In 1950 the western New City was proclaimed as the Israeli capital, and following the Israeli capture of the eastern Old City in 1967 from the Jordanians, it was affirmed in 1980 that the united city was the country's capital, but the United Nations does not recognize the claim.

*history* by 1400 BCE Jerusalem was ruled by a king subject to Egypt, but c. 1000 BCE David, the second king of Israel, made it the capital of a united Jewish kingdom. It was captured by Nebuchadnezzar 586 BCE, who deported its population. Later conquerors include Alexander the Great and Pompey (63 BCE), and it was under Roman rule that Jesus Christ was executed. In 70 CE a Jewish revolt led to its complete destruction by Titus. It was first conquered by Islam in 637; was captured by Crusaders, Christians who were fighting the Muslims in Israel, 1099, and recaptured by Saladin 1187, to remain under almost unbroken Islamic rule until the British occupation of Palestine in 1917.

Notable buildings include the Church of the Holy Sepulchre (built 335), and the mosque of the Dome of the Rock. The latter was built on the site of Solomon's Temple, and the Western ('wailing') Wall, held sacred by Jews, is part of the walled platform on which the Temple once stood.

**Temple** the centre of Jewish national worship at Jerusalem. Three temples occupied the site: Solomon's Temple, which was destroyed by Nebuchadnezzar; Zerubbabel's Temple, built after the return from Babylon; and Herod's Temple, which was destroyed by the Romans in 70 CE. The Mosque of Omar occupies the site. The Wailing Wall is the surviving part of the western wall of the platform of the enclosure of the Temple of Herod, so-called by tourists because of the chanting style of the Jews in their prayers there. Under Jordanian rule Jews had no access to the place, but Israel took this part of the city in the 1967 campaign.

**Mecca** city of Saudi Arabia, the holiest city of the Muslim world, where the Prophet was born. It stands in the desert, in a valley about 72 km/45 mi east of Jidda, its port on the Red Sea, with which it is linked by an asphalted road, and long before the time of Muhammad was a commercial centre, caravan junction, and place of pilgrimage. In the centre of Mecca is the Great Mosque, in whose courtyard is the Kaaba; it also contains the well Zam-Zam, associated by tradition with Ishmael, the son of Abraham, and his mother Hagar, and the Maqām Ibrāhīm, a holy stone believed to bear the imprint of Abraham's foot.

*kaaba* the oblong building in the quadrangle of the Great Mosque at Mecca into the north-east corner of which is built the black stone declared by Muhammad to have been given to Abraham by Gabriel, and devoutly revered by Muslim pilgrims. The name means chamber.

**Medina** city in Saudi Arabia, about 355 km/220 mi north of Mecca. To Muslims it is a holy city second only to Mecca, since Muhammad lived here for many years after he fled from Mecca, and died here. The Mosque of the Prophet is believed to contain Muhammad's tomb, and those of the caliphs or Muslim leaders Abu Bakr, Omar, and Fatima, Muhammad's daughter.

**Varanasi** or **Benares** Indian city on the sacred Ganges river in Uttar Pradesh. It is holy to Hindus with a 5 km/3 mi frontage of stairways (ghats), leading up from the river to innumerable streets, temples, and the 1,500 golden shrines. The ritual of purification is practised daily by thousands of devout Hindus, who bathe from the ghats in the sacred river. At the burning ghats, the ashes, following cremation, are scattered on the river, a ritual followed to ensure a favourable reincarnation.

# FESTIVALS

**Buddhist festivals**
*Wesak* the day of the Buddha's birth, enlightenment and death. A large act of worship is held and gifts given to monks; captive animals may be freed.
*Dhammacakka* celebrates the preaching of the Buddha's first sermon. Visits are made to monasteries and gifts are given to the monks.
*Bodhi Day* Mahayana Buddhist celebration of the Buddha's enlightenment.
**Chinese festivals**
*New Year* time when the Kitchen God, whose picture is in every home, returns to heaven to report on the family's behaviour during the year. There are elaborate lion dances and fireworks, and vegetarian feasts are eaten.
*Ching Ming* a time for visiting ancestral tombs, making offerings and remembering the dead.
*Dragon Boat Festival* celebrates the story of a brave official who persuaded a harsh emperor to relent over his crippling taxation of the people by drowning himself. Races are held between boats carved to resemble dragons, in memory of the boat chase to save the official's body from being eaten by dragons and demons.
*Moon Festival* commemorates the story of a brave woman who defied her husband, a wicked king, to stop him obtaining immortality, and was carried off by the gods to live on the moon. The festival is held at the harvest full moon and the moon is greeted with incense, lanterns and feasting.
*Winter Festival* time of feasting to build up strength for the winter ahead.
**Christian festivals**
*Epiphany* annual festival (6 Jan) of the Christian Church, celebrating the coming of the Magi or wise men to Bethlehem with gifts for the infant Christ, and symbolizing the manifestation of Christ to the world. It is the twelfth day after Christmas, and marks the end of the Christmas festivities. In many countries the night before, called *Twelfth Night*, is marked by the giving of gifts.
*Shrove Tuesday* the day before Ash Wednesday. The name comes from the Anglo-Saxon *scrifan*, to shrive, and in former times it was the time for confession before Lent. Another name for it is Pancake Tuesday; the pancakes are a survival of merry-making in anticipation of Lenten abstinence.
*Ash Wednesday* first day of Lent, the period in the Christian calendar leading up to Easter; in the Catholic Church the foreheads of the congregation are marked with a cross in ash, as a sign of penitence.
*Lent* in the Christian Church, the forty days' period of fasting which precedes Easter, beginning on Ash Wednesday, but omitting Sundays.
*Palm Sunday* the Sunday before Easter, and first day of Holy Week; so-called to commemorate Christ's entry into Jerusalem, when the crowd strewed palm leaves in his path.
*Good Friday* (probably a corruption of God's Friday). In the Christian Church, the Friday before Easter, which is kept in memory of the Crucifixion (the death of Jesus).
*Easter* feast of the Christian Church, commemorating the Resurrection of Christ. It usually falls around the time of the Jewish Passover since Christ's crucifixion coincided with the time of this festival. The English name derives from Eostre, Anglo-Saxon goddess of spring, who was honoured in Apr. Eggs are given at this time as a symbol of new life.
*Whitsun* celebrates the filling of the followers of Jesus with the Holy Spirit, which Christians believe to be the third aspect of God, after Jesus had returned to heaven. As the disciples went out and told everyone about Jesus, so at Whitsun many Christians go on processions around the parish boundaries.
*Advent* the time leading up to Christmas; a time of preparation for Christians.
*Christmas* day on which the birth of Christ is celebrated by Christians. Although the actual birth date is unknown, the choice of a date near the winter solstice owned much to missionary desire to facilitate conversion of pagans, for example in Britain 25 Dec had been kept as a festival long before the introduction of Christianity. Many of its customs also have a non-Christian origin.
**Hindu festivals**
*Mahashivaratri* Festival of Siva, who is celebrated as lord of the dance, dancing on the demon of ignorance.
*Holi* a harvest time festival in honour of Krishna, when bonfires are lit; people throw coloured water at each other and play games and tricks as a reminder of Krishna's mischievous behaviour.
*Rama Naumi* celebration of the Birth of Rama. An eight-day fast during which the *Rāmāyana* is recited; the fast is broken on the ninth day with fruit and nuts, and offerings are made to Rama.
*Raksha Bandhan* a family festival in which sisters present their brothers with a bracelet of thread to protect them from harm, in return for which the brothers promise to look after their sisters.
*Janmashtami* celebration of the birthday of Krishna. Children act out stories of Krishna, and a statue of the young Krishna is used in the celebrations.
*Dusshera* a festival (also known as Durga Puja) which lasts ten days; the great goddess Devi is worshipped in her many forms.
*Divali* a new year festival which honours

Lakshmi, goddess of fortune. Lights are lit in every window.

## Jewish festivals

**Purim** celebrates the story of Esther, a Jewish woman who risked her life to save her people from treacherous slaughter. The story is read from a scroll in the synagogue, and the congregation boo and hiss when the villain's name is read out. It is a time for noisy parties and merriment.

**Passover** (Pesach) festival which commemorates the escape from slavery in Egypt. A special meal, the seder meal, is eaten and the story of how the Jews were saved by God from this bondage is told.

**Shavuot** or **Pentecost** commemorates the giving of the ten commandments to Moses.

**Rosh Hashanah** the two-day festival at the start of the Jewish New Year (first new moon after the autumn equinox), a time for repentence and forgiveness. This reflective period is brought to a close nine days later at Yom Kippur. Rosh Hashanah begins on the first day of the month of Tishri (Sept–Oct), the seventh month of the Jewish year.

**Yom Kippur (Day of Atonement)** day of Jewish religious fast held on the tenth day of Tishri. Final forgiveness is sought for past deeds and the Kol Nidrei is sung in the synagogue to end the old vows of the past year and to prepare for the demands of the coming year. The festival ends with the blowing of the shofar, the ram's horn.

**Succot** the feast of Tabernacles (tents), a reminder of the time the Israelites spent wandering in the wilderness. Temporary homes of branches are built at the synagogue and sometimes at home.

**Hanukkah** celebrates the recapture and rededication of the Temple of Jerusalem by Judah Maccabee in 165 BCE. The festival lasts eight days; each day, a new candle is lit on a special candlestick or menorah.

## Muslim festivals

The Muslim calendar is lunar, and correspondences with the Western calendar cannot be given; festivals fall 11–12 days earlier each year.

**Lailat ul-Isra Wal Mi'raj** celebrates Muhammad's night journey by horse to Jerusalem and up to heaven.

**Lailat ul-Barah** the night of forgiveness; a time to prepare for Ramadan.

**Ramadan** the ninth month of the Muslim year, throughout which a strict fast is observed during the hours of daylight.

**Lailat ul-Qadr** commemorates the night the Koran was first revealed to Muhammad.

**Eid ul-Fitr** the end of the fast of Ramadan. Gifts are given to charity, new clothes are worn and sweets are given.

**Eid ul-Adha** celebrates the faith of the prophet Abraham, who was prepared to sacrifice his son Ismail when Allah asked him to. Lamb is eaten and shared with the poor, as a reminder of the sheep which Allah provided as a sacrifice instead of Ismail.

**Day of Hirja** commemorates the journey of Muhammad from Mecca to Medina.

## Sikh festivals

**Hola Mohalla** a three-day festival held at the time of the Hindu festival Holi. Sporting competitions and other tests of skill take place.

**Baisakhi** originally a harvest festival, it now celebrates the founding of the Khalsa, the Sikh brotherhood, and commemorates those Sikhs killed by British troops in Amritsar on Baisakhi, 1919.

**Martyrdom of Guru Arjan** commemorates the death of the fifth guru, Guru Arjan, who built the Golden Temple at Amritsar and compiled the main part of the Sikh holy book.

**Divali** celebrates the release from prison of the sixth guru, Guru Hargobind, who also managed to secure the release of 51 Hindu princes who were imprisoned with him.

**Guru Nanak's birthday** celebrates the birth of the founder of the first guru of Sikhism.

**Martyrdom of Guru Tegh Bahadur** the ninth guru, martyred for the faith.

**Birthday of Guru Gobind Singh** The tenth and last human guru of Sikhism, and the founder of the Khalsa.

## Religious beliefs

*Which, if any, of the following do you believe in?*

|  | Yes | No | Don't know |
| --- | --- | --- | --- |
| a) The devil | 26 | 65 | 9 |
| b) Hell | 24 | 65 | 11 |
| c) Heaven | 55 | 34 | 11 |
| d) God | 64 | 24 | 12 |
| e) Reincarnation | 27 | 56 | 17 |

*Would you say you are very religious, somewhat religious or not religious at all?*

| Very religious | 7 |
| --- | --- |
| Somewhat religious | 49 |
| Not religious | 42 |
| Don't know | 1 |

*Irrespective of your own religious beliefs, would you like your children to be brought up within a framework of religious teaching at school, or not?*

| Yes | 57 |
| --- | --- |
| No | 10 |
| Don't know | 5 |
| No children | 29 |

*Do you believe the morality of society would or would not suffer if most people abandoned religious belief?*

| Would | 71 |
| --- | --- |
| Would not | 18 |
| Don't know | 11 |

# TRANSPORT

**air transport** people first took to the air in balloons and began powered flight in airships, but the history of flying is dominated by the aeroplane. The aeroplane is a development of the model glider, first flown by George Cayley in 1804. It was not until the invention of the petrol engine that powered flight become feasible. The Wright brothers in the USA first achieved success, when they flew their biplane *Flyer* on 17 Dec 1903. In Europe, France led in aeroplane design (Voisin brothers) and Louis Blériot brought aviation much publicity by crossing the Channel in 1909. The first powered flight in the UK was made by S F Cody in 1908. In 1912 Sopwith and Bristol both built small biplanes.

The stimulus of World War I (1914–18) and the rapid development of the petrol engine led to increased power, and speeds rose to 320 kph/200 mph. Streamlining the body of planes became imperative: the body, wings, and exposed parts were reshaped to reduce drag. Eventually the biplane was superseded by the internally braced monoplane structure—for example, the Hawker Hurricane and Supermarine Spitfire fighters and the Avro Lancaster and Boeing Flying Fortress bombers of World War II (1939–45).

The German Heinkel 178, built 1939, ushered in a new era in aviation. It was the first jet plane, driven, not as all planes before it with a propeller, but by a jet of hot gases. The first British jet aircraft, the Gloster E.28/39, flew from Cranwell, Lincolnshire, on 15 May 1941, powered by a jet engine invented by Frank Whittle. Twin-jet Meteor fighters were in use by the end of the war. The rapid development of the jet plane led to enormous increases in power and speed until air-compressability effects were felt near the speed of sound, which at first seemed to be a flight speed limit (the sound barrier). To exceed supersonic speed, mere streamlining of the aircraft body became insufficient: wings were swept back, engines buried in wings and tail units, and bodies were even eliminated in all-wing delta designs.

In the 1950s the first jet airliners, such as the Comet, were introduced. Today jet planes dominate aviation, although many light planes still use piston engines and propellers. The late 1960s saw the introduction of the jumbo jet, and in 1976 the Anglo-French Concorde, which makes a transatlantic crossing in under three hours, came into commercial service.

During the 1950s and 1960s research was done on V/STOL (vertical and/or short take-off) aircraft. The British Harrier jet fighter has been the only VTOL aircraft to achieve commercial success, but STOL technology has fed into subsequent generations of aircraft. The 1960s and 1970s also saw the development of variable geometry ('swing-wing') aircraft, whose wings can be swept back in flight to achieve higher speeds. In the 1980s much progress has been made in 'fly-by-wire' aircraft with computer-aided controls.

International partnerships have developed both civilian and military aircraft. The Panavia Tornado is a joint project of British, German and Italian aircraft companies. It is an advanced swing-wing craft of multiple roles—interception, strike, ground support, and reconnaissance. The Airbus is a wide-bodied airliner built jointly by companies

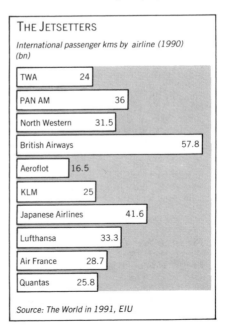

INTERNATIONAL AIRPORT TRAFFIC

Passengers (m, 1989)

| Airport | Passengers |
| --- | --- |
| Paris CDG | 20.3 |
| Hong Kong | 16.2 |
| Amsterdam | 15.3 |
| New York JFK | 30.3 |
| Tokyo | 17.6 |
| London Gatwick | 21.2 |
| Frankfurt | 26.0 |
| London Heathrow | 39.7 |

*Source: The World in 1991, EIU*

THE JETSETTERS

International passenger kms by airline (1990) (bn)

| Airline | |
| --- | --- |
| TWA | 24 |
| PAN AM | 36 |
| North Western | 31.5 |
| British Airways | 57.8 |
| Aeroflot | 16.5 |
| KLM | 25 |
| Japanese Airlines | 41.6 |
| Lufthansa | 33.3 |
| Air France | 28.7 |
| Quantas | 25.8 |

*Source: The World in 1991, EIU*

from France, Germany, the UK, the Netherlands, and Spain.

**aeroplane** heavier-than-air craft supported in flight by fixed wings: it may be unpowered (a glider) or powered, when it is propelled by the thrust of a jet engine or propeller. It must be designed aerodynamically, since streamlining ensures maximum flight efficiency. The shape of a plane depends on its use and operating speed—aircraft operating at well below the speed of sound need not be as streamlined as supersonic aircraft.

Efficient streamlining prevents the formation of shock waves over the body surface and wings, which would cause instability and power loss. The wing of an aeroplane has the cross-sectional shape of an aerofoil, being broad and curved at the front, flat underneath, curved on top, and tapered to a sharp point at the rear. The wings are so shaped that air passing above them is speeded up, reducing pressure below atmospheric pressure, while that above is slowed. This results in a force acting vertically upwards, called lift, which counters the aircraft's weight. In level flight, lift equals weight. The wings develop sufficient lift to support the plane when they move quickly through the air. The thrust that causes propulsion comes from the reaction to the air stream accelerated backwards by the propeller or the gases shooting backwards from the jet exhaust. In flight the engine thrust must overcome the air resistance, or drag. Drag depends on frontal area (large in the case of an airliner; small in the case of a fighter plane) and shape (drag coefficient); in level flight, drag equals thrust. The drag is reduced by streamlining the plane, resulting in higher speed and reduced fuel consumption for a given power. Less fuel need be carried for a given distance of travel, so a larger payload (cargo or passengers) can be carried.

Planes are constructed using light but strong aluminium alloys such as duralumin (with copper, magnesium, and so on). For supersonic planes special stainless steel and titanium may be used in areas subjected to high heat loads. The structure of the plane, or the airframe (wings, fuselage, and so on) consists of a surface skin of alloy sheets supported at intervals by struts known as ribs and stringers.

The structure is bonded together by riveting or by powerful adhesives such as epoxy resins. In certain critical areas, which have to withstand very high stresses (such as the wing roots), body panels are machined from solid metal for extra strength.

*Fastest aeroplane*—the Lockheed SR-71, holder of the world air-speed record of 3,529 kph/2,193 mph (over Mach 3.3).

*Fastest airliner*—Concorde, which can cruise at up to Mach 2.2 (2,333 kph/1,450 mph).

*Largest airliner*—Boeing 747, with a wingspan of 59.6 m/195.7 ft and a length of 70.7 m/231.8 ft.

*Largest volume aeroplane*—the Guppy-201, with a usable volume of 1,104 cu m/39,000 cu ft.

**airship** a power-driven balloon. All airships have streamlined envelopes or hulls, which contain the inflation gas, and are either non-rigid, semi-rigid, or rigid. Count Ferdinand von Zeppelin (1838–1917) pioneered the rigid type, named after him, and used for bombing raids on the UK in World War I. The destruction by fire of the British R101 in 1930 halted airship building in Britain, but the Germans continued and built the 248 m/812 ft long *Hindenburg*. However, this airship exploded at Lakehurst, New Jersey 1937, marking the effective end of airship travel. The early airships were vulnerable because they used hydrogen for inflation. It is the lightest gas, but highly flammable. After World War II, interest grew in airships using the nonflammable gas helium. They cause minimum noise, can lift enormous loads, and are economical on fuel. Britain's Airship Industries received large orders in 1987 from the US Navy for airships to be used for coastguard patrols, and the Advanced Airship Corporation on the Isle of Man was reported in 1989 to be constructing the fastest passenger airship ever built (80 knots), powered by twin-propeller turbine engines.

**balloon** bag or envelope of impermeable fabric that rises from the ground when filled with a gas lighter than the surrounding air. In 1783, the first successful human ascent was piloted by Pilâtre de Rozier in Paris, in a hot-air balloon designed by the Montgolfier brothers. During the French Revolution balloons were used for observation; in World War II they were used to defend London against low-flying aircraft. Balloons continue in use for sport, and as an economical means of meteorological, infrared, gamma-ray, and ultraviolet observation. The first transatlantic crossing by balloon (from Presque Isle, Maine to Miserey, France) was made 11–17 Aug 1978 by a US team.

**helicopter** an aircraft that achieves both lift and propulsion by means of a rotary wing, or rotor, on top of the fuselage. It can take off and land vertically, move in any direction, or remain stationary in the air. Igor Sikorsky built the first practical single rotor craft, in the USA 1939. The rotor of a helicopter has two or more blades, which are of aerofoil cross-section, like an aeroplane's wings. Lift and propulsion are achieved by angling the blades as they rotate. A single-rotor helicopter must also have a small tail rotor to counter the tendency of the body to spin in the opposite direction to the main rotor. Twin-rotor helicopters, like the Boeing Chinook, have their rotors turning in opposite directions, and this prevents the body from spinning.

Helicopters are now widely used in passenger service, rescue missions on land and sea, police pursuits and traffic control, firefighting, and agriculture. In war they carry troops and equipment into difficult terrain, make aerial reconnaissance and attacks, and carry wounded to aid stations. Helicopters are increasingly being associated with naval aircraft carriers, as many as 30 helicopters being used on larger

AIR TRANSPORT: CHRONOLOGY

| | |
|---|---|
| 1783 | First human flight, by Jean F Pilâtre de Rozier and the Marquis d'Arlandes, in Paris, using a hot-air balloon made by Joseph and Etienne Montgolfier; first ascent in a hydrogen-filled balloon by Jacques Charles and M N Robert in Paris. |
| 1785 | Jean-Pierre Blanchard and John J Jeffries made the first balloon crossing of the English Channel. |
| 1804 | George Cayley flew the first true aeroplane, a model glider 1.5 m/5 ft long. |
| 1852 | Henri Giffard flew the first steam-powered airship over Paris. |
| 1891–96 | Otto Lilienthal piloted a glider in flight. |
| 1903 | First powered and controlled flight of a heavier-than-air machine by Orville Wright, at Kitty Hawk, North Carolina, USA. |
| 1909 | Louis Bleriot flew across the English Channel in 36 minutes. |
| 1919 | First flight across the Atlantic by Albert C Read, using a flying boat; first non-stop flight across the Atlantic by John William Alcock and Arthur Whitten Brown in 16 hours 27 minutes; first complete flight from the UK to Australia by Ross Smith and Keith Smith. |
| 1923 | Juan de la Cieva flew the first autogyro with a rotating wing. |
| 1927 | Charles Lindbergh made the first solo nonstop flight across the Atlantic. |
| 1928 | First trans-Pacific flight, from San Francisco to Brisbane, by Charles Kinsford Smith and C T P Ulm. |
| 1930 | Frank Whittle patented the jet engine; Amy Johnson became the first woman to fly solo from England to Australia. |
| 1937 | The first fully pressurized aircraft, the Lockheed XC-35, came into service. |
| 1939 | Erich Warsitz flew the first jet aeroplane, in Germany; Igor Sikorsky designed the first modern helicopter, with a large main rotor and a smaller tail rotor. |
| 1947 | A rocket-powered plane, the Bell X-1, was the first aircraft to fly faster than the speed of sound. |
| 1949 | The de Havilland Comet, the first jet airliner, entered service; James Gallagher made the first nonstop round-the-world flight, in a Boeing Superfortress. |
| 1953 | The first vertical takeoff aircraft, the Rolls-Royce 'Flying Bedstead', was tested. |
| 1968 | The world's first supersonic airliner, the Soviet TU-144, flew for the first time. |
| 1969 | First flight of the BAC/Aérospatiale supersonic airliner Concorde. |
| 1970 | The Boeing 747 jumbo jet entered service, carrying 500 passengers. |
| 1976 | A Lockheed SR-17A, piloted by Eldon W Joersz and George T Morgan, set the world air-speed record of 3,529.56 kph/2,193.167 mph over Beale Air Force Base, California, USA. |
| 1978 | US team made the first transatlantic crossing by balloon, in the helium-filled *Double Eagle II*. |
| 1979 | First crossing of the English Channel by a human-powered aircraft, *Gossamer Albatross*, piloted by Bryan Allen. |
| 1981 | The solar-powered *Solar Challenger* flew across the English Channel, from Paris to Kent, taking 5 hours for the 262 km/162.8 mi journey. |
| 1986 | Dick Rutan and Jeana Yeager made the first nonstop flight around the world without refuelling, piloting *Voyager*, which completed the flight in 9 days 3 minutes 44 seconds. |
| 1987 | Richard Branson and Per Lindstard made the first transatlantic crossing by hot-air balloon, *Virgin Atlantic Challenger*, the largest ever flown. |
| 1988 | *Daedelus*, a human-powered craft piloted by Kanellos Kanellopoulos, flew 118 m/74 mi across the Aegean Sea. |

carriers, in combination with V/STOL aircraft, such as Harriers. The helicopter may possess depth charges and homing torpedoes guided to submarine or surface targets beyond the carrier's attack range. It may also use dunking sonar to find targets beyond the carrier's own radar horizon.

**jet propulsion** a method of propulsion in which an object is propelled in one direction by a jet, or stream of gases, moving in the other. This follows from Newton's celebrated third law of motion 'to every action, there is an equal and opposite reaction'. The most widespread application of the jet principle is in the jet engine, the commonest kind of aero-engine.

The jet engine is a type of gas turbine. Air, after passing through a forward-facing intake, is compressed by a compressor, or fan, and fed into a combustion chamber. Fuel (usually kerosene) is sprayed in and ignited. The hot gas produced expands rapidly rearwards, spinning a turbine that drives the compressor before being finally ejected from a rearward-facing tail pipe, at very high speed. Reaction to the jet of gases streaming backwards produces a propulsive thrust forwards, which acts on the aircraft through its engine-mountings, not from any pushing of the hot gas stream against the static air.

**rocket** a projectile driven by the reaction of gases produced by a fast-burning fuel. Unlike the jet

## RIDING A SUNBEAM: SOLAR-POWERED CARS

In 1990 the World Solar Challenge, a race across Australia for solar-powered cars, was won by a Swiss car, the Spirit of Biel-Bienne. 26 cars set off from Darwin in the Northern territory on 11 November. Six days later the Spirit of Biel-Bienne entered Adelaide in South Australia after a journey of 3,007 km/1,868 mi across the barren terrain of central Australia. The territory covered seems an ideal testing ground for solar cars; the intense Australian sun is about 1 kW per square metre, enough for the cars to reach speeds of over 100 kph/62 mph. However, freak storms, lightning, thick cloud, and heavy rain plagued the contestants. One car, entered by a Danish team, was lifted off the ground by a miniature tornado, hurled 30 m/100 ft, and damaged beyond repair. In spite of these difficulties the Spirit of Biel-Bienne averaged 65 kph/40 mph.

The Spirit of Biel-Bienne's win was largely due to its innovative solar cells, developed by Martin Green of the University of New South Wales in Sydney. The cells are made from single crystals of silicon, which have been etched with a laser into a pattern of hills and valleys. This means that the surface area is increased and the cells catch more sunlight. The prototype cells cost $160,000 and have an efficiency of 18%; the mass-produced cells, planned for manufacture in Australia, Spain, and Germany, will be much cheaper.

This contrasts markedly with the cells used by the winner of the first race in 1987, General Motors' SunRaycer. Sunraycer used gallium arsenide cells, again with an efficiency of about 18%, but reportedly costing around £600,000. The car took about the same time as the Biel-Bienne to complete the race, illustrating that progress has been made on costs and fabricating techniques but not on performance. Indeed, there seems to be a theoretical limit, close to present performance, for solar cells. For this reason, a spokesman for General Motors has said, 'These are not the cars of the future'.

The future probably lies with battery-powered cars, with solar arrays to recharge the batteries while they are parked in the sun. Paradoxically, the least efficient of the cells used in the World Solar Challenge may be the most promising in this context. The Southern Cross car, entered by the Semiconductor Energy Laboratory of Japan, in conjunction with Mazda, uses cells that are half as efficient as those in most other vehicles. They develop 0.6 kW of power, compared with the more-usual 1.4 kW. The exciting thing about these cells is that they are made from amorphous silicon, in which the atoms are arranged randomly, rather than crystals, in which the atoms are regularly arranged. Cells made from this form of silicon are cheaper, thinner, and can be moulded to curved shapes—for example, to match car bodywork.

Amorphous-silicon cells have already been used in a solar-powered plane, the Sun Seeker, built by Eric Raymond in California. The single-seater plane has the top surfaces of its wings covered with 700 cells, which generate 300 watts of electricity. This charges the nickel-cadmium batteries, which in turn drive the 2.4-metre propeller. The mass production of cheap cells such as these could transform the fortunes of solar-power technology.

*The Spirit of Biel-Bienne, winner of the 1990 World Solar challenge.*

RAIL TRANSPORT: CHRONOLOGY

| | |
|---|---|
| 1500s | Tramways—wooden tracks along which trolleys ran—were in use in mines. |
| 1804 | Richard Trevithick built the first steam locomotive and ran it on a track at the Pen-y-darren ironworks in South Wales. |
| 1825 | British engineer George Stephenson built the first public railway to carry steam trains — the Stockton and Darlington line. |
| 1829 | Stephenson designed his locomotive *Rocket*, which trounced its rivals at the Rainhill trials. |
| 1830 | Stephenson completed the Liverpool and Manchester Railway, the first steam passenger line; the first US-built locomotive, *Best Friend of Charleston*, went into service on the South Carolina Railroad. |
| 1835 | Germany pioneered steam railways in Europe, using *Der Adler*, a locomotive built by Stephenson. |
| 1863 | Robert Fairlie, a Scot, patented a locomotive with pivoting driving bogies, allowing tight curves in the track (this was later applied in the Garratt locomotives); London opened the world's first underground railway, powered by steam. |
| 1869 | The first US transcontinental railway was completed at Promontory, Utah, when the Union Pacific and the Central Pacific railroads met; George Westinghouse of the USA invented the compressed-air brake. |
| 1879 | Werner von Siemens demonstrated an electric train in Germany; Volk's Electric Railway along the Brighton seafront was the world's first public electric railway. |
| 1883 | Charles Lartique built the first monorail, in Ireland. |
| 1885 | The trans-Canada continental railway was completed, from Montreal in the east to Port Moody, British Columbia, in the west. |
| 1890 | The first electric underground railway opened in London. |
| 1901 | The world's most successful monorail, the Wuppertal Schwebebahn, went into service. |
| 1912 | The first diesel locomotive took to the rails in Germany. |
| 1938 | The British steam locomotive *Mallard* set a steam-rail speed record of 201 kph/125 mph. |
| 1941 | Swiss Federal Railways introduced a gas-turbine locomotive. |
| 1964 | Japan National Railways inaugurated the 512 km/320 mi New Tokaido line between Osaka and Tokyo, on which run the 210 kph/130 mph 'bullet' trains. |
| 1973 | British Rail's High Speed Train (HST) set a diesel rail speed record of 22 kph/143 mph. |
| 1979 | Japan National Railways' maglev test vehicle ML-500 attained a speed of 517 kph/321 mph. |
| 1981 | France's TGV superfast trains began operation between Paris and Lyons, regularly attaining a peak speed of 270 kph/168 mph. |
| 1987 | British Rail set a new diesel-traction speed record of 238.9 kph/148.5 mph, on a test run between Darlington and York; France and the UK began work on the Channel Tunnel, a railway link connecting the two countries, running beneath the English Channel. |
| 1988 | The West German Intercity Experimental train reached 405 kph/252 mph on test run between Würzburg amd Fulda. |
| 1990 | A new rail-speed record of 515 kph/320 mph was established by a French TGV train, on a stretch of line between Tours and Paris. |
| 1991 | British and French twin tunnels meet 23 km/14 mi out to sea to form the Channel Tunnel. |

engine, which is also a reaction engine, the rocket engine carries its own oxygen supply to burn its fuel and is totally independent of any surrounding atmosphere. As rockets are the only form of propulsion available that can function in a vacuum, they are essential to the exploration of outer space. Multistage rockets have to be used for this, consisting of a number of rockets joined together. For warfare, rocket heads carry an explosive device.

**rail transport** is by means of a system of parallel tracks, laid upon the ground, upon which vehicles can travel. Tracks to carry goods waggons were in use at collieries in the 18th century, but the first practical public passenger service

was that between Stockton and Darlington in 1825, under the power of Stephenson's engine 'Locomotion'. A railway boom ensued, and railways were the major form of land transport for passengers and goods until after World War II when the private car, coach services, internal air services, and road haulage door-to-door, destroyed their monopoly. In the UK the railways (known as British Rail from 1965) were nationalized in 1948, and the network increasingly shrank. In the USA and Canada railways made the 19th-century exploitation of the central and western territories possible, and in the USA underpinned the victory of the north in the Civil War, the 'Railway War'. In

# EUROPE'S HIGH-SPEED RAIL NETWORK: WHERE HAVE WE GOT TO?

On 1 December 1990, Britain was physically united with the European continent for the first time since the sea rose and filled the English Channel at the end of the last ice age. About 23 km/14 mi out to sea, British and French engineers broke through the last section of rock separating the two ends of the Channel Tunnel. The tunnel is due for completion in 1993, and will have two 'running' tunnels, which will carry trains between France and England, and a third 'service' tunnel, which will be used for maintenance work and emergency access.

The tunnel is part of an ambitious plan to update and extend Europe's rail network. By 2020 a high-speed rail network will connect most of the capitals and major cities of Europe. Trains will race along the new tracks at speeds approaching 322 kph/200 mph. The journey from Frankfurt to Berlin will take two hours, compared with the present four hours. Brussels will become a suburb of Paris, a mere 1 hour 20 minutes away. The London-to-Paris journey will take 2 hours 30 minutes, assuming a high-speed link is built across Kent.

Few governments have failed to be impressed by the success of the French Train à Grande Vitesse (TGV). Since it began operating in 1981, it has carried more than 110 million passengers between Paris and Lyons, at average speeds of 26 kph/167 mph. The French state-owned railway organization, SNCF, has continued to expand its high-speed network. TGV trains now reach 299 kph/186 mph between Paris and Le Mans. A third TGV line is under construction linking Paris with the Channel Tunnel, Brussels, and Cologne. Over the next 20 years, SNCF plans to create a vast network of 3,400 km/2,100 mi, including a link between Paris, Strasbourg, and Germany.

Italy has the only other operational high-speed train. Called the Pendolino, it is a tilting train like the ill-fated British Advanced Passenger Train, which failed to get into service due to technical problems. The Pendolino reaches speeds of 241 kph/150 mph between Turin and Rome. It is planned to extend the route to Venice and Naples, and to develop a 306 kph/190 mph train, the ETR500.

Spurred on by the French and Italian successes, other countries are developing high-speed rail networks. Germany is spending £7 billion on its ICE (InterCity Experimental) high-speed train, a heavier version of the TGV. The ICE took the world rail-speed record in 1988 with a run at 407 kph/252 mph, but the record was regained in 1990 by the TGV with a speed of 515 kph/320 mph. Spain is spending £10 billion to update its rail system, starting with a high-speed link between Madrid and Seville. The Netherlands, Belgium, and Denmark have similar projects on hand.

Naturally, there are technical problems to be overcome: the TGV, ICE, and Pendolino were not designed to be compatible with each other's national networks; signalling is different in each country; and the voltages and track widths vary. The Transmanche supertrain, which will operate through the Channel Tunnel, is to be equipped with three different electrical systems in order to allow it to be used with the French, Belgian, and British supplies. The first moves towards making the different technologies compatible began in 1989 with a test run of the ICE over French rails. The test was successful and the ICE, with its heavier loads, was able to run without damaging the French lines.

The European Community is forcing the pace of development, recognizing that good railways are essential to the development of Europe, whose road and air links are becoming increasingly congested. The French, Germans, Dutch, and Belgians have agreed a set of lines to be completed by 1998. Most of these links will be built with government subsidies, or state-owned railway companies will be allowed to borrow at advantageous rates. The British government, however, has so far refused to finance high-speed links.

*The Transmanche Supertrain, which will operate through the Channel Tunnel.*

## DEATHS CAUSED BY TRAFFIC ACCIDENTS (1990) PER 100,000 POPULATION

| | Male | Female |
|---|---|---|
| Canada | 22.1 | 9.1 |
| USA | 28.4 | 11.0 |
| Germany | 18.3 | 6.9 |
| UK | 14.0 | 5.7 |
| Japan | 15.2 | 5.3 |
| Hungary | 24.3 | 8.0 |
| Italy | 24.9 | 7.3 |
| Mexico | 30.0 | 8.0 |
| Australia | 26.6 | 10.7 |
| Israel | 13.8 | 5.7 |
| Switzerland | 22.8 | 7.2 |

Source: The World in 1991

countries with less developed road systems and large areas of difficult terrain, the railway is still important, as in India, China, South America, and the USSR. Electrification, or the use of diesel electric engines, has superseded the steam engine in most countries, and there has been some revival in the popularity of the train for longer distance 'inter-city' services.

**monorail** a railway that runs on a single (mono) rail. It was invented in 1882 to carry light loads, and when run by electricity was called a *telpher*. The most successful monorail, the Wuppertal Schwebebahn, has been running in Germany since 1901. It is a suspension monorail, where the passenger cars hang from an arm fixed to a trolley that runs along the rail. Today most monorails are of the straddle type, where the passenger cars run on top of the rail. They are used to transport passengers between terminals at some airports—as at Birmingham, where the monorail works on the *maglev* (magnetic levitation) principle.

**tramway** a transport system for use in cities, by which wheeled vehicles run along parallel rails. It originated in collieries in the 18th century. The earliest passenger system was established in 1832, in New York, and by the 1860s horse-drawn trams plied in London and Liverpool. Trams are now powered either by electric conductor rails below ground, or conductor arms connected to overhead wires, but their use on public roads is very limited because of their lack of manoeuvrability. Greater flexibility is achieved with the *trolleybus*, similarly powered by conductor arms overhead but without tracks. In the 1980s both trams and trolleybuses were being revived in some areas. Both vehicles have the advantage of being nonpolluting to the local environment.

**road transport** specially constructed, reinforced tracks became necessary with the invention of wheeled vehicles in about 3000 BC and most ancient civilizations had some form of road network. The Romans developed engineering techniques that were not equalled for another 1,400 years. Until the late 18th century most European roads were haphazardly maintained, making winter travel difficult. In the UK the turnpike system of collecting tolls created some improvement. The

Scottish engineers Thomas Telford and John McAdam introduced sophisticated construction methods in the early 19th century. Recent developments have included durable surface compounds and machinery for rapid ground preparation.

**bicycle** a pedal-driven two-wheeled vehicle. It consists of a metal frame mounted on two large wire-spoked wheels, with handlebars in front and a seat between the front and back wheels. The first pedal-bicycle was invented by Kirkpatrick Macmillan, a Scot, in about 1840, pneumatic tyres being added from 1846, and by 1888 these had been improved by J B Dunlop to boost the cycling craze of the turn of the century. Design changes were then minor until the small-wheeled Moulton bicycle appeared after World War II. The bicycle is an energy-efficient, nonpolluting form of transport and is used throughout the world.

**car** a small self-propelled vehicle able to be run and be steered on normal roads. Most are four-wheeled and have water-cooled, piston-type internal-combustion engines fuelled by petrol or diesel.

Although it is recorded that in 1479 one Gilles de Dom was paid 25 livres by the treasurer of Antwerp, for supplying such a vehicle, the forerunner of the automobile is generally agreed to be Nicolas-Joseph Cugnot's cumbrous steam carriage 1769, still preserved in Paris. Another Parisian, Étienne Lenoir, made the first gas engine in 1860, and in 1885 Benz built and ran the first petrol-driven motor car. Panhard 1890 (front radiator, engine under the bonnet, sliding-pinion gearbox, wooden ladder-chassis) and Mercédès 1901 (honeycomb radiator, in-line four-cylinder engine, gate-change gearbox, pressed-steel chassis) set the pattern for the modern car.

A typical modern medium-sized saloon car has a semi-monocoque construction in which

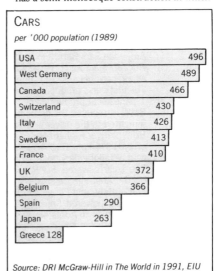

## CARS

*per '000 population (1989)*

| | |
|---|---|
| USA | 496 |
| West Germany | 489 |
| Canada | 466 |
| Switzerland | 430 |
| Italy | 426 |
| Sweden | 413 |
| France | 410 |
| UK | 372 |
| Belgium | 366 |
| Spain | 290 |
| Japan | 263 |
| Greece | 128 |

Source: DRI McGraw-Hill in The World in 1991, EIU

---

CAR: CHRONOLOGY

| | |
|---|---|
| 1769 | Nicholas-Joseph Cugnot in France built a steam tractor. |
| 1860 | Jean Etienne Lenoir built a gas-fuelled internal-combustion engine. |
| 1831 | The British government passed the 'Red Flag' Act, requiring a man to precede a 'horseless carriage' with a red flag. |
| 1876 | Nikolaus August Otto improved the gas engine, making it a practical power source. |
| 1885 | Gottlieb Daimler developed a successful lightweight petrol engine and fitted it to a bicycle to create the prototype of the modern motorbike; Karl Benz fitted his lightweight petrol engine to a three-wheeled carriage to pioneer the motor car. |
| 1886 | Gottlieb Daimler fitted his engine to a four-wheeled carriage to produce a four-wheeled motor car. |
| 1891 | René Panhard and Emile Levassor established the modern design of cars by putting the engine in front. |
| 1896 | Frederick Lanchester introduced epicyclic gearing, which foreshadowed automatic transmission. |
| 1901 | The first Mercedes took to the roads. It was the direct ancestor of the modern car; Ransome Olds in the USA introduced mass production on an assembly line. |
| 1906 | Rolls-Royce introduced the legendary Silver Ghost, which established their reputation for superlatively engineered cars. |
| 1908 | Henry Ford used assembly-line production to manufacture his famous Model T, nicknamed the Tin Lizzie because lightweight steel sheets were used for the body, which looked 'tinny'. |
| 1911 | Cadillac introduced the electric starter and dynamo lighting. |
| 1913 | Ford introduced the moving conveyor belt to the assembly line, further accelerating production of the Model T. |
| 1920 | Duesenberg began fitting four-wheel hydraulic brakes. |
| 1922 | The Lancia Lambda featured unitary (all-in-one) construction and independent front suspension. |
| 1928 | Cadillac introduced the synchromesh gearbox, greatly facilitating gear changing. |
| 1934 | Citroën pioneered front-wheel drive in their 2CV model. |
| 1936 | Fiat introduced their baby car, the Topolino, 500 cc. |
| 1938 | Germany produced their 'people's car', the Volkswagen 'beetle'. |
| 1948 | Jaguar launched the XK120 sports car; Michelin introduced the radial-ply tyre; Goodrich produced the tubeless tyre. |
| 1950 | Dunlop announced the disc brake. |
| 1951 | Buick and Chrysler in the USA introduced power steering. |
| 1952 | Rover's gas-turbine car set a speed record of 243 kph/152 mph. |
| 1954 | Bosch introduced fuel-injection for cars. |
| 1955 | Citroën produced the advanced DS-19 'shark-front' car with hydropneumatic suspension. |
| 1957 | Felix Wankel built his first rotary petrol engine. |
| 1959 | BMC (now Rover) introduced the Issigonis-designed Mini, with front-wheel drive, transverse engine, and independent rubber suspension. |
| 1966 | California introduced legislation regarding air pollution by cars. |
| 1972 | Dunlop introduced safety tyres, which sealed themselves after a burst. |
| 1979 | American Sam Barrett exceeded the speed of sound in the rocket-engined *Budweiser Rocket*, reaching 1,190.377 kph/739.666 mph, a speed not officially recognized as a record because of timing difficulties. |
| 1980 | The first mass-produced car with four-wheel drive, the Audi Quattro, was introduced; Japanese car production overtook that of the USA. |
| 1981 | BMW introduced the on-board computer, which monitored engine performance and indicated to the driver when a service was required. |
| 1983 | British driver Richard Noble set an official speed record in the jet-engined *Thrust 2* of 1,019.4 kph/ 633.468 mph; Austin Rover introduced the Maestro, the first car with a 'talking dashboard' that alerted the driver to problems. |
| 1987 | The solar-powered *SunRaycer* travelled 3,000 km/1,864 mi from Darwin to Adelaide, Australia, in six days. |
| 1990 | Fiat of Italy, and Peugeot of France launched electric passenger cars on the market; the solar-powered *Spirit of Biel-Bienne* won a 3,000 km/1,864 mi race, travelling from Darwin to Adelaide, Australia in six days. |

---

the body panels, suitably reinforced, support the road loads through independent front and rear sprung suspension, with seats located within the wheelbase for comfort. It is usually powered by a petrol engine using a carburettor to mix petrol and air for feeding to the engine cylinders (typically four or six). The engine is usually water cooled. From the engine, power is transmitted through a clutch to a four-or five-speed gearbox and thence, in a

## CARS OF THE FUTURE: TRENDS IN THE AUTOMOBILE INDUSTRY

The 1991 Barcelona Motor Show witnessed the rebirth of the two-stroke engine as a power source for automobiles. Although the two-stroke has long been popular for powering motorcycles, lawn mowers, and outboard motor boats, its use in automobiles has declined. Saab abandoned the two-stroke over a decade ago; the unloved Wartburg lasted only until Germany unified. Now, however, a new fuel-injection system has transformed the noisy, smoky and inefficient engine into a compact power source, 10% more powerful and 20% more economical than the equivalent six-cylinder four-stroke engine. The two-stroke Ford Ghia Zag in the Barcelona Show shows the way forward. General Motors, Chrysler, Fiat, Jaguar, Peugeot, Renault, Volvo, Volkswagen, and the big Japanese firms, are all engaged in two-stroke research.

New engines, new fuels, more aerodynamic styling, and smarter electronics—these are the trends today. Alternative fuels reduce air pollution. Better styling boosts efficiency by reducing drag. Electronics inside the automobile optimizes engine performance; on-board digitized maps navigate around traffic jams, saving fuel and time.

Concern over air pollution has spurred the search for cleaner-burning fuels. There are long-standing research programs on methanol, ethanol, natural gas, hydrogen, and electricity. Methanol—wood alcohol—seems to be the front runner. It burns more cleanly than petrol, yielding about one-tenth the hydrocarbon emissions. It can be made from coal or natural gas, both abundant fuels. However, conventional cars need to be adapted to run on methanol. The engine must be made corrosion resistant, and the fuel tank must be larger because methanol provides 40% less energy per gallon than petrol. Ethanol shares many of the features of methanol, and experience in Brazil, which began using ethanol produced from sugar cane in 1975, has been generally positive. Hydrogen, the only truly clean-burning

fuel, poses problems because it is difficult to store.

Electric cars have promised much, but even enthusiasts admit that there will only be limited applications. The problem lies in the batteries. The General Motors two-seater prototype electric car, the Impact, uses lead-acid batteries that give a range of about 190 km/120 mi at 88 kph/55 mph, close to the car's top speed. The batteries, which costs around $1,500, take six hours to recharge and have to be replaced every 32,000 km/20,000 mi. A new type of battery developed in Japan in 1990 may save the electric car. The new battery is a form of capacitor, which stores electricity as static charge rather than in chemical form. Weight for weight, its capacity is 20 times larger than that of a lead-acid battery. It is cheap, and can be charged quickly, in about 30 seconds, at lower voltages than conventional batteries.

Electronic systems currently make up about 6% of a car's value; by the year 2000, experts think that proportion will climb to 20%. Antilock brakes and active suspensions will be under computer control, and there will be an assortment of systems providing information on road conditions and optimum routes. The most sophisticated of these IVHS (intelligent vehicle/highway systems) are in use in Japan. All Japanese systems are based on a digitized map stored on a compact disc. A small computer converts the information to a colour map at a scale selected by the driver. Various systems are used to keep track of the car's position. Toyota uses a solid-state compass to determine direction, and sensors on the car's wheels to measure distance travelled. Mazda uses signals from the US navigation satellites, as well as compass and wheel sensors. All these systems suffer from the accumulation of small errors over a period, but this problem will be solved in the mid 1990s when about 180,000 radio locator beacons are installed along Japan's major highways.

*General Motors' prototype electric car, The Impact.*

FASTEST SCHEDULED PASSENGER TRAIN RUNS (1990)

| Country | Train | From | To | miles | min. | mph |
|---------|-------|------|-----|-------|------|-----|
| France | TGV trains | Paris | Macon | 225.7 | 100 | 135.4 |
| Japan | Yamabiko trains | Morica | Sendi | 106.3 | 50 | 127.6 |
| Great Britain | High Speed Trains | Swindon | Reading | 41.5 | 23 | 108.3 |
| West Germany | Intercity trains | Celle | Velzen | 32.5 | 19 | 102.6 |
| USA | 20 Metroliner | Baltimore | Wilmington | 68.4 | 43 | 95.0 |
| Italy | IC501 | Milan | Bologna | 135.8 | 86 | 94.7 |
| USA | Express Metroliner | Metropark | Washington | 201.0 | 129 | 93.5 |
| USA | Express Metroliner | New York | New Carrollton | 216.0 | 143 | 90.8 |
| Soviet Union | High Speed Train | Leningrad | Moscow | 403.6 | 270 | 89.7 |
| Sweden | Seven trains | Skvode | Hallsberg | 70.8 | 48 | 88.5 |

Source: The World Almanac and Book of Facts 1991

front-engine rear-drive car, through a drive (propeller) shaft to a differential gear, which drives the rear wheels. In a front-engine front-wheel drive car, clutch, gearbox, and final drive are incorporated with the engine unit. An increasing number of high-performance cars are being offered with four-wheel drive. This gives vastly superior roadholding in wet and icy conditions.

**internal-combustion engine** a heat engine in which fuel is burned inside the engine, contrasting with an external-combustion engine (such as the steam engine) in which fuel is burned in a separate unit. The petrol and diesel engines are both internal-combustion engines. They are reciprocating piston engines in which pistons move up and down in cylinders to effect the engine operating cycle. This may be a four-stroke cycle or a two-stroke cycle. Gas turbines and jet and rocket engines are sometimes also considered to be internal-combustion engines because they burn their fuel inside their combustion chambers.

**motorcycle** or **motorbike** a two-wheeled vehicle propelled by a petrol engine. Daimler created the first motorcycle when he installed his lightweight petrol engine in a bicycle frame in 1885. The first really successful two-wheel design was devised by Michael and Eugene Werner in France 1901. They adopted the classic motorcycle layout with the engine low down between the wheels. Harley Davidson in the USA and Triumph in the UK began manufacture 1903. Road races like the Isle of Man TT (Tourist Trophy), established in 1907, helped improve motorcycle design and it soon evolved into more or less its present form. Today Japanese motorcycles, such as Honda, Suzuki, Yamaha, and Kawasaki, dominate the world market. They make a wide variety of machines, from mopeds (lightweights with pedal assistance) to streamlined superbikes capable of speeds up to 250 kph/160 mph.

**sea transport** people have travelled on and across the seas, for various purposes, throughout history. The Greeks and Phoenicians built wooden ships, propelled by oar or sail, to transport themselves and their goods across the sea. The Romans and Carthaginians built war galleys equipped with rams and several tiers of oars. The oak ships of the Vikings were designed for rough seas, and propelled by oar and sail. The Crusader fleet of Richard the Lionheart was largely of sail. By 1840 iron had largely replaced wood, but fast-sailing clippers survived, built with wooden planks on iron frames. The USA and the UK experimented with steam propulsion as the 19th century opened. The paddle-wheel-propelled *Comet* appeared 1812, the Canadian *Royal William* crossed the Atlantic 1833, and the English *Great Western* steamed from Bristol to New York 1838. Pettit Smith first used the screw propeller in the *Archimedes* 1839, and after 1850 the paddle-wheel became largely obsolete, its use being confined to the inland waterways, particularly the great American rivers. The introduction of the internal-combustion engine and turbine completed the revolution in propulsion until the advent of nuclear-powered vessels after World War II, chiefly submarines. More recently hovercraft and wave-piercing catamarans (vessels with a long pointed main hull and two outriggers) have been developed for specialized purposes, particularly as short-distance ferries—for example, the catamarans introduced 1991 by Hoverspeed cross the English Channel from Dover to Calais in 35 min, cruising at a speed of 35 knots (84.5 kph/52.5 mph). Sailing ships in automated form for cargo purposes, and maglev (magnetic-levitation) ships, are in development.

**Largest ship**—the oil tanker *Seawise Giant*, which is 458 m/1,505 ft long, with a beam of 69 m/226 ft. Of 564,739 tonnes/555,816 tons deadweight, it was launched in 1979.

**Largest passenger liner**—the *Queen Elizabeth*, 83,673 gross tonnes/82,351 tons, 314 m/1,031 ft long with a beam of 36 m/118 ft. Launched in 1940, it was gutted by fire in 1972.

**Longest passenger liner**—the *Norway*, launched in 1961 as the *France*. It weighs 70,202 tonnes/69,093 tons, and measures 316 m/1,035 ft long.

**hovercraft** a vehicle that rides on a cushion of high-pressure air, free from all contact with the surface beneath, invented by British engineer Christopher Cockerell 1959. Hovercraft need a smooth terrain when operating overland, and are best adapted to use on lakes, sheltered coastal waters, river estuaries and swamps. They are useful in places where harbours have not been established. Large hovercraft (SR-N4) operate a swift car-ferry service

SEA TRANSPORT CHRONOLOGY

**BC**

| | |
|---|---|
| **8000–7000** | Reed boats developed in Mesopotamia and Egypt; dug-out canoes used in NW Europe. |
| **4000–3000** | Egyptians used single-masted square-rigged ships on Nile. |
| **1200** | Phoenicians built keeled boats with hulls of wooden planks. |
| **1st century BC** | Chinese invented the rudder. |
| **AD 200** | Chinese built ships with several masts. |
| **200–300** | Arabs and Romans developed fore-and-aft rigging that allowed boats to sail across the direction of wind. |
| **800–900** | Square-rigged Viking longboats crossed the North Sea to Britain, the Faroe Islands, and Iceland. |
| **1090** | Chinese invented the magnetic compass. |
| **1400–1500** | Three-masted ships developed in western Europe, stimulating voyages of exploration. |
| **1620** | Dutch engineer Cornelius Drebbel invented the submarine. |
| **1776** | US engineer David Bushnell built a handpowered submarine, *Turtle*, with buoyancy tanks. |
| **1777** | The first boat with an iron hull built in Yorkshire, England. |
| **1783** | French engineer Jouffroy d'Abbans built the first paddle-driven steam boat. |
| **1802** | Scottish engineer William Symington launched the first stern paddle-wheel steamer *Charlotte Dundas*. |
| **1836** | The screw propeller was patented, by Francis Pettit Smith in the UK. |
| **1838** | British engineer Isambard Kingdom Brunel's *Great Western*, the first steamship built for crossing the Atlantic, sailed from Bristol to New York in 15 days. |
| **1845** | *Great Britain*, also built by Isambard Kingdom Brunel, became the first propeller-driven iron ship to cross the Atlantic. |
| **1845** | The first clipper ship, *Rainbow*, was launched in the USA. |
| **1863** | *Plongeur*, the first submarine powered by an air-driven engine was launched in France. |
| **1866** | The British clippers *Taeping* and *Ariel* sailed, laden with tea, from China to London in 99 days. |
| **1886** | German engineer Gottlieb Daimler built the first boat powered by an internal-combustion engine. |
| **1897** | English engineer Charles Parson fitted a steam turbine to *Turbinia*, making it the fastest boat of the time. |
| **1900** | Irish-American John Philip Holland designed the first modern submarine *Holland VI*, fitted with an electric motor for underwater sailing and an internal-combustion engine for surface travel; E Forlanini of Italy built the first hydrofoil. |
| **1902** | The French ship *Petit-Pierre* became the first boat to be powered by a diesel engine. |
| **1955** | The first nuclear-powered submarine, *Nautilus*, was built; the hovercraft was patented by British inventor Christopher Cockerell. |
| **1959** | The first nuclear-powered ship, the Soviet ice-breaker *Lenin*, was commissioned; the US *Savannah* became the first nuclear-powered merchant (passenger and cargo) ship. |
| **1980** | Launch of the first wind-assisted commercial ship for half a century, the Japanese tanker *Shin-Aitoku-Maru*. |
| **1983** | German engineer Ortwin Fries invented a hinged ship designed to bend into a V-shape in order to scoop up oil spillages in its jaws. |
| **1989** | *Gentry Eagle* set a record for the fastest crossing of the Atlantic by a power vessel, taking 2 days, 14 hours, and 7 minutes. |
| **1990** | *Hoverspeed Great Britain*, a wave-piercing catamaran, crossed the Atlantic in 3 days, 7 hours, and 52 minutes, setting a record for the fastest crossing by a passenger vessel. |

across the English Channel, taking only about 35 minutes between Dover and Calais.

**hydrofoil boat** a boat whose hull rises out of the water when it travels at speed. The boat gets its lift from a set of hydrofoils, underwater wings that develop lift in the water in much the same way that an aeroplane wing develops lift in the air.

**jetfoil** an advanced type of hydrofoil boat built by Boeing, propelled by water jets. It features horizontal, fully submerged hydrofoils fore and aft, and has a sophisticated computerized control system to maintain its stability in all waters. Jetfoils have been in service worldwide since 1975. A jetfoil service currently operates between Dover and Ostend, with a passage time of 1 hr 40 min.

**submarine** an underwater ship, especially a warship. The first underwater boat was constructed for King James I of England by the Dutch scientist Cornelius van Drebbel 1620. A century and a half later, David Bushness in the USA designed a submarine called *Turtle* for attacking British ships. In both world wars submarines, from the oceangoing to the midget type, played a vital role. The conventional submarine of this period was driven by diesel engine on the surface and by battery-powered electric motors underwater. The diesel engine also drove a generator that produced electricity to charge the batteries.

In 1955 the USA launched the first nuclear-powered submarine, *Nautilus*. The US nuclear submarine *Ohio*, USA, in service from 1981, is 170 m/560 ft long and carries 24 Trident missiles, each with 12 independently targetable nuclear warheads. The nuclear warheads on US submarines have a range that is being extended to 11,000 km/6.750 mi. Operating depth is usually up to 300 m/1,000 ft, and nuclear power speeds of 30 knots (i.e. 55 kph/34 mph) are reached. As in all nuclear submarines, propulsion is by steam turbine driving a propellor. The steam is raised using the heat given off by the nuclear reactor.

## Public transport

*Here are some things people say about using public transport at the moment. Could you tell me which you personally agree with and which you disagree with?*

|  | Agree | Dis-agree | Don't know |
|---|---|---|---|
| The general standards of service are improving | 29 | 57 | 14 |
| The standard of time-keeping is high | 23 | 60 | 17 |
| Crowding is getting worse | 67 | 18 | 14 |
| The staff on the buses, railways and so on are more helpful than they used to be | 27 | 50 | 23 |
| On the whole, public transport provides good value for money | 45 | 41 | 14 |
| Trains, buses and so on are gradually becoming more comfortable | 50 | 37 | 13 |

*Is having a car an absolute necessity or could you and your family get along without one if you had to? (All car drivers)*

| Absolute necessity | 58 |
|---|---|
| Could get along | 41 |
| Don't know | 0 |

*I am going to read out a number of the reasons*

*people feel they need to have a car. Could you tell me which ones apply to you? (All 'absolute necessity')*

| In order to get to work | 57 |
|---|---|
| Because there is no public transport available | 19 |
| Because the available public transport is not adequate | 40 |
| Because I (or a member of my family) need the car for work | 48 |
| Disabled | 4 |
| Convenient for holidays etc | 8 |
| Anything else | 7 |

*Here are some things people say about using public transport at the moment. Could you tell me which you personally agree with and which you disagree with?*

|  | Agree | Dis-agree | Don't know |
|---|---|---|---|
| The general standards of service are improving | 29 | 57 | 14 |
| The standard of time-keeping is high | 23 | 60 | 17 |
| Crowding is getting worse | 67 | 18 | 14 |
| The staff on the buses, railways and so on are more helpful than they used to be | 27 | 50 | 23 |
| On the whole, public transport provides good value for money | 45 | 41 | 14 |
| Trains, buses and so on are gradually becoming more comfortable | 50 | 37 | 13 |

*Which of these possible solutions would you yourself prefer to see adopted? (All 'very/fairly serious')*

| Building more roads | 33 |
|---|---|
| Taxing people more highly to discourage people from driving | 7 |
| Making cars more expensive to buy | 4 |
| Subsidising public transport so that people would use buses and trains more instead of their cars | 69 |
| Rationing the use of cars so that each car could only be driven a limited number of miles each year | 7 |
| Don't know, none of these | 9 |

# MILITARY TERMS

**ABM** abbreviation for *anti-ballistic missile* (see *nuclear warfare* in this section).

**air force** a nation's fighting aircraft and the organization that maintains them.
*history* The emergence of the aeroplane at first brought only limited recognition of its potential value as a means of waging war. Like the balloon, used since the American Civil War, it was considered a way of extending the vision of ground forces. A unified air force was established in the UK 1918, Italy 1923, France 1928, Germany 1935 (after repudiating the arms limitations of the Versailles treaty), and the USA 1947 (it began as the Aeronautical Division of the Army Signal Corps in 1907, and evolved into the Army's Air Service Division by 1918; by 1926 it was the Air Corps and in World War II the Army Air Force). The main specialized groupings formed during World War I—such as *combat, bombing, reconnaissance,* and *transport*—were adapted and modified in World War II; activity was extended, with self-contained tactical air forces to meet the needs of ground commanders in the main theatres of land operations and for the attack on and defence of shipping over narrow seas.

During the period 1945–60 the piston engine was superseded by the jet engine, which propelled aircraft at supersonic speeds; extremely precise electronic guidance systems made both missiles and aircraft equally reliable delivery systems; and flights of much longer duration became possible with air-to-air refuelling. The US Strategic Air Command's bombers can patrol 24 hours a day armed with thermonuclear weapons. It was briefly anticipated that the pilot might become redundant, but the continuation of conventional warfare and the evolution of tactical nuclear weapons have led in the 1970s and 1980s to the development of advanced combat aircraft able to fly supersonically beneath an enemy's radar on strike and reconnaissance missions, as well as so-called stealth aircraft that cannot be detected by radar.

**Allied Mobile Force** (AMF) permanent multinational military force established 1960 to move immediately to any NATO country under threat of attack. Its headquarters are in Heidelberg, Germany.

**Allies, the** in World War I, the 23 countries allied against the Central Powers (Germany, Austria-Hungary, Turkey and Bulgaria), including France, Italy, Russia, Great Britain and Commonwealth, and, in the latter part of the war, the USA; and in World War II, the 49 countries allied against the Axis powers (Germany, Italy and Japan), including France, Great Britain and Commonwealth, the USA, and the USSR. In the 1991 Gulf War, there were 28 countries in the Allied coalition.

**Armistice Day** anniversary of the armistice signed 11 Nov 1918, ending World War I.

**armour** body protection worn in battle. Body armour is depicted in Greek and Roman art. Chain mail was developed in the Middle Ages but the craft of the armourer in Europe reached its height in design in the 15th century, when knights were completely encased in plate armour that still allowed freedom of movement. Medieval Japanese armour was articulated, made of iron, gilded metal, leather, and silk. Contemporary bulletproof vests and riot gear are forms of armour. The term is used in a modern context to refer to a mechanized armoured vehicle, such as a tank.

**arms trade** the sale of arms from a manufacturing country to another nation. Nearly 50% of the world's arms exports end up in the Middle East, and most of the rest in Third World countries. Iraq, for instance, was armed in the years leading up to the 1991 Gulf War mainly by the USSR but also by France, Brazil, and South Africa.

The proportion of global arms spending accounted for by Third World countries was 24% in the late 1980s (up from 6% in 1965). Arms exports are known in the trade as 'arms transfers'.

In the UK, the Defence Export Services, a department of the Ministry of Defence, is responsible for British arms exports. Its annual budget is about £10 million.

**army** organized military force for fighting on land. A national army is used to further a political policy by force either within the state or on the territory of another state. Most countries have a national army, maintained at the expense of the state, raised either by conscription (compulsory military service) or voluntarily (paid professionals). Private armies may be employed by individuals and groups. As a result of the ending of the Cold War, the US, Soviet and European armies are undergoing substantial cuts between 1991 and 1995. The UK army will be cut from 155,000 to 116,000.

**artillery** collective term for military firearms too heavy to be carried. Artillery can be mounted on ships or aeroplanes and includes cannons and missile launchers.

**ASAT** acronym for *antisatellite weapon.*

**AWACS** acronym for *Airborne Warning and Control System.* The system incorporates a long-range surveillance and detection radar mounted on a Boeing E-3 sentry aircraft. The system was used with great success in the 1991 Gulf War.

**battalion** or *unit* the basic personnel unit in the military system, usually consisting of four or five companies and about 500–600 soldiers. A battalion is commanded by a lieutenant colonel. Several battalions form a brigade.

**battleship** class of large warships with the biggest guns and heaviest armour. In 1991, four US battleships were in active service.

**biological warfare** use of living organisms, or of infectious material derived from them, to bring about death or disease in humans, animals, or plants. It was condemned by the Geneva

## THE WORLD'S LEADING ARMS EXPORTERS(*US$m)

|  | 1985 | 1989 |
|---|---|---|
| USSR | 12,796 | 11,652 |
| USA | 8,800 | 10,755 |
| France | 3,970 | 2,732 |
| UK | 1,699 | 1,620 |
| China | 1,088 | 779 |
| FR Germany | 1,025 | 780 |
| Czechoslovakia | 497 | 546 |
| Italy | 646 | 149 |
| Sweden | 163 | 323 |
| Netherlands | 88 | 631 |

Source: SIPRI Yearbook 1990
* at constant 1985 prices

Convention 1925, to which the United Nations has urged all states to adhere. Nevertheless research in this area continues; the Biological Weapons Convention permits research for defence purposes but does not define how this differs from offensive weapons development. In 1990 the US Department of Defense allocated $60 million to research, develop and test defence systems. Advances in genetic engineering make the development of new varieties of potentially offensive biological weapons more likely. At least ten countries have this capability.

**bomb** container filled with explosive or chemical material and generally used in warfare. There are also incendiary bombs and nuclear bombs and missiles (see nuclear warfare). Any object designed to cause damage by explosion can be called a bomb (car bombs, letter bombs). Initially dropped from aeroplanes (from World War I), bombs were in World War II also launched by rocket (V1, V2). The 1960s saw the development of missiles that could be launched from aircraft, land sites, or submarines. Although high explosive is increasingly delivered by means of missiles, free fall and so-called 'smart' or laser-guided munitions are still widely used.

The rapid development of *laser guidance systems* in the 1970s meant that precise destruction of small but vital targets could be more effectively achieved with standard 450 kg/1,000 lb high-explosive bombs. The laser beam may be directed at the target by the army from the ground, but additional flexibility is gained by coupling ground-directed beams with those of guidance carried in high-performance aircraft accompanying the bombers, for example, the Laser Ranging Marker Target System (LRMTS). These systems' effectiveness was demonstrated during the Gulf War of 1991.

**brigade** military formation consisting of a minimum of two battalions, but more usually three or more, as well as supporting arms. There are typically about 5,000 soldiers in a brigade, which is commanded by a brigadier. Two or more brigades form a division.

**carrier warfare** naval warfare involving aircraft carriers. Carrier warfare was conducted during World War II in the battle of the Coral Sea May 1942, which stopped the Japanese advance in the South Pacific, and in the battle of Midway Islands June 1942, which weakened the Japanese navy through the loss of four aircraft carriers. The US Navy deployed six aircraft carriers during the Gulf War 1991.

**Central Command** US military strike force consisting of units from the army, navy, and air force, which operates in the Middle East and North Africa. Its headquarters are in Fort McDill, Florida. It was established 1979, following the Iranian hostage crisis and the Soviet invasion of Afghanistan, and was known as the Rapid Deployment Force until 1983. It commanded coalition forces in the Gulf War 1991.

**chemical warfare** use in war of gaseous, liquid, or solid substances intended to have a toxic or lethal effect on humans, animals, or plants. Together with biological warfare, it was banned 1925 by the Geneva Convention, although this has not always been observed. In 1989, when the 149-nation Conference on Chemical Weapons unanimously voted to outlaw chemical weapons, the total US stockpile was estimated at 30,000 tonnes and the Soviet stockpile variously at 30,000 and 300,000 tonnes.

In a deal with the USA, the USSR offered to eliminate its stocks; the USA began replacing its stocks with new 'binary' nerve- gas weapons. In 1990 President Bush offered to destroy all US chemical weapons if the convention to outlaw them were ratified in 1992. Some 20 nations currently hold chemical weapons, including Iraq, Iran, Israel, Syria, Libya, South Africa, and China.

**civil defence** or *civil protection* organized activities by the civilian population of a state to mitigate the effects of enemy attack on them. The threat of nuclear weapons in the post-World War II period led to the building of fallout shelters in the USA, the USSR, and elsewhere. China has networks of tunnels in the cities that are meant to enable the population to escape nuclear fallout and reach the countryside, but which do not protect against the actual blast. Sweden and Switzerland have highly developed civil-defence systems.

A new structure of 'Home Defence' was introduced in the early 1980s in Britain, in which the voluntary services, local authorities, the Home Service Force, and the Territorial Army would cooperate. Regulations came into force in 1983 compelling local authorities to take part in civil-defence exercises. Councils have to provide blast-proof bunkers and communication links, train staff, and take part in the exercises. In July 1991 it was announced that much of the Home Defence infrastructure would be severely cut back since the Cold War had ended.

**COIN** acronym for *counter insurgency*, the suppression by a state's armed forces of uprisings against the state. Also called internal security (IS) operations of counter-revolutionary warfare (CRW). The British army has been engaged in COIN operations in Northern Ireland

since 1969.
**commando** member of a specially trained, highly mobile military unit. The term originated in South Africa in the 19th century, where it referred to Boer military reprisal raids against Africans and, in the South African Wars, against the British. Commando units have often carried out operations behind enemy lines.
**company** in the army, a subunit of a battalion. It consists of about 120 soldiers, and is commanded by a major in the British army, a captain or major in the US army. Four or five companies make a battalion.
**corps** a military formation consisting of 2–5 divisions. Its strength is between 50,000 and 120,000 men. All branches of the army are represented. A corps is commanded by a lieutenant general or, in the USA, a three-star general. Two or more corps form an army group.
**deception** in warfare, the use of dummies, decoys, and electronics to trick the enemy into believing in and preparing to defend against armies that do not exist.
   The Allied ground offensive in the 1991 Gulf War was launched 160 km/100 mi west of where the Iraqi army was led to believe it would take place—a deception technique which completely wrong-footed the Iraqi forces.
**Delta Force** US antiguerrilla force, based at Fort Bragg, North Carolina, and modelled on the British Special Air Service.
**destroyer** small, fast warship designed for antisubmarine work. They played a critical role in the convoy system in World War II. Modern destroyers often carry guided missiles and displace 3,700–5,650 tonnes.
**disarmament** the reduction of a country's weapons of war. Most disarmament talks since World War II have been concerned with nuclear-arms verification, but biological, chemical, and conventional weapons have also come under discussion at the United Nations and in other forums.
**division** military formation consisting of two or more brigades. A major general at divisional headquarters commands the brigades and also additional artillery, engineers, attack helicopters, and other logistic support. There are 10,000 or more soldiers in a division. Two or more divisions form a corps.
**early warning** in war, advance notice of incoming attack, often associated with nuclear attack. There are early-warning radar systems in the UK (Fylingdales), Alaska, and Greenland. *Airborne early warning* (AEW) is provided by sentry planes; NATO has such a system.
   The most efficient AEW system, which NATO uses, is the Boeing Sentry AWACS (airborne warning and control system), capable of covering a wide area. Carrier battle groups also need AEW. During the 1982 Falklands War the British Royal Navy was not equipped with adequate over-the-horizon surveillance capability, and some ships were hit and sunk by Exocet surface-to-surface missiles.
**explosive** any material capable of a sudden release

of energy and the rapid formation of a large volume of gas, leading when compressed to the development of a high-pressure wave (blast). Examples include gelignite, dynamite, nitroglycerin, nitrobenzene, TNT (trinitrotoluene), and RDX (Research Department Explosive).
**fallout** harmful radioactive material released into the atmosphere in the debris of a nuclear explosion and descending to the surface. Such material can enter the food chain.
**field marshal** the highest rank in many European armies. A British field marshal is equivalent to a US general.
**firearm** weapon from which projectiles are discharged by the combustion of an explosive. Firearms are generally divided into two main sections: *artillery* (ordnance or cannon), with a bore greater than 2.54 cm/1 in, and *small arms*, with a bore of less than 2.54 cm/1 in. Although gunpowder was known in Europe 60 years previously, the invention of guns dates from 1300–25, and is attributed to Berthold Schwartz, a German monk.
**flag** piece of cloth used as an emblem or symbol for nationalistic, religious, or military displays, or as a means of signalling. Flags have been used since ancient times.
**frigate** warship, an escort vessel smaller than a destroyer. Before 1975 the term referred to a warship larger than a destroyer but smaller than a light cruiser. In the 18th and 19th centuries a frigate was a small, fast sailing warship.
**general** senior military rank, the ascending grades being major general, lieutenant general, and general. The US rank of general of the army is equivalent to the British field marshal.
**guerrilla** irregular soldier fighting in a small unofficial unit, typically against an established or occupying power, and engaging in sabotage, ambush, and the like, rather than pitched battles against an opposing army. Guerrilla tactics have been used both by resistance armies in wartime (for example, the Vietnam War) and in peacetime by national liberation groups and militant political extremists (for example the PLO; Tamil Tigers).
   Political activists who resort to violence, particularly *urban guerrillas*, tend to be called 'freedom fighters' by those who support their cause, 'terrorists' by those who oppose it.
   Efforts by governments to put a stop to their activities have had only sporadic success. The Council of Europe has set up the European Convention on the Suppression of Terrorism, to which many governments are signatories. In the UK the Prevention of Terrorism Act 1984 is aimed particularly at the IRA. The Institute for the Study of Terrorism was founded in London 1986.
**Gurkha** a people living in the mountains of Nepál, whose young men have been recruited since 1815 for the British and Indian armies. There are currently five battalions of Gurkhas in the British Army (though the cuts of July 1991 will probably reduce these to two), though there

# MILITARY INTELLIGENCE: DOES IT SAVE LIVES?

The Gulf War was a war by appointment. The UN deadline of 15 Jan 1991 had been fixed since Resolution 678 was passed in Nov 1990. This facilitated a sustained gathering of intelligence over a period of months that ensured meticulous planning. Information on targets throughout Iraq was gathered from a number of sources: satellite surveillance, special forces, remotely piloted vehicles, high level reconnaissance aircraft, the Airborne Warning and Command System (AWACS) and the Joint Surveillance and Target Acquisition and Reconnaissance System (JSTARS) as well as so-called human intelligence (HUMINT) gathered before the outbreak of hostilities by released hostages, agents, refugees and returning diplomats. With all the intelligence gathering assets in place that any military commander could possibly have wanted and a deadline to work to, it was possible to plan strategic and tactical air and land operations in every detail. This is a luxury that is unlikely to be provided in a similar conflict in the future and certainly one that cannot be assumed.

In the weeks before the ground offensive the allies manufactured a grand charade using airpower, offensive patrolling, artillery bombardment, troop deployments and bogus radio traffic to suggest that the main allied thrust was going to be across the Saudi-Kuwait border supported by an amphibious landing in the northern Gulf. All the while an envelopment on a grand scale 100 miles to the west was being planned. And when it took place it achieved total surprise. It was followed by a degree of speed and mobility that proved to be beyond the comprehension of the Iraqi military mind. Massive armoured forces cut through southern Iraq to within 150 miles of Baghdad in hours. With their air forces neutralized and their command, control and communications ($C^3$) system crippled, the Iraqis were blind and deaf. If proof was needed it was demonstrated yet again the advantages of the offensive on the modern battlefield. Maginot Lines can be outflanked, enveloped, avoided and encircled. Even if none of these options are available, the attacker can achieve a total superiority by concentrating his forces and breaking through at a point of his own choosing with overwhelming force. But all this assumes a highly developed $C^3$ system. Once again the Gulf War demonstrated that neither a superiority in force levels or state of the art hardware necessarily in themselves guarantee military success. It is the intelligent application and coordination of these resources which produces effective results. Thus the edge which coalition forces enjoyed in Surveillance and Target Acquisition (STA) equipment was crucial. Coalition commanders were able to 'read the battle' and dispose of their forces more efficiently. Since targets were acquired more precisely, fire could be brought to bear more accurately. It is not so much the *weight* of the fire that is important as its *accuracy*. Conversely the Iraqi army was capable—at least in theory—of producing an enormous weight of fire relatively

inaccurately so that perhaps 90% of the rounds fired would not cause significant damage. Had chemical weapons been employed it is likely that would have been similarly ineffective due to a lack of accurate target data. In the case of NATO armies, on the other hand, targets can be acquired accurately by a variety of means including AWACS, Satellites, Forward Looking Infra Red (FLIR), Sideways Looking Airborne Radar (SLAR), Synthetic Aperture Radar (SAR), Infra Red Line Scan (IRLS), Sound Ranging, Remotely Piloted Vehicles (RPVS), low level photoreconnaissance aircraft and special forces.

In the Falklands War, Argentinian artillery outnumbered the British by a factor of approximately 5–1, but British fire was greatly more effective because it was efficiently directed and coordinated. The Gulf War confirmed beyond doubt the continued need for substantial investment in the STA area. Equally important is continued investment in $C^3$ systems. On the other hand an ability to degrade the enemy's $C^3$ system with a significant Electronic Counter Measures (ECM) capability is also a war-winning factor. In this area, perhaps in particular, the Gulf War provided a false lesson. A more sophisticated opponent would not only have been better equipped to withstand the ECM onslaught but would also have posed a significant ECM threat to coalition forces.

Finally, the Gulf War demonstrated that—despite its inherent weaknesses—coalition warfare can work. In future, it is unlikely that nations will be able to project significant force unilaterally. Role specialization and equipment standardization become even more relevant in such a context.

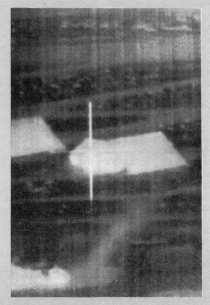

*French Jaguar attacking a target in Kuwait.*

are many more in the Indian Army.

**home service force** (HSF) military unit established in the UK 1982, linked to the Territorial Army and recruited from volunteers of ages 18–60 with previous army (TA or Regular) experience. It was introduced to guard key points and installations likely to be the target of enemy 'special forces' and saboteurs, so releasing other units for mobile defence roles.

**ICBM** abbreviation for *intercontinental ballistic missile* (see nuclear warfare in this section).

**Luftwaffe** German air force. In World War I and, as reorganized by the Nazi leader Goering 1933, in World War II, it also covered anti-aircraft defence and the launching of the flying bombs V1, V2.

**manoeuvre** in warfare, to move around the battlefield so as to gain an advantage over the enemy. It implies rapid movement, shock action, and surprise. Bold manoeuvre warfare can be synonymous with blitzkrieg or a swift military campaign. An example of manoeuvre warfare was the wide-ranging encirclement of the Iraqi army by coalition forces in the 1991 Gulf War.

**marines** fighting force that operates both on land and at sea. The *US Marine Corps* (1775) is constituted as an arm of the US Navy. It is made up of infantry and air support units trained and equipped for amphibious landings under fire. The *Royal Marines* founded by Charles II 1664 is the British equivalent, numbering approximately 7,000 (1991), and is part of the Royal Navy.

**mercenary** soldier hired by the army of another country or by a private army. Mercenary military service originated in the 14th century, when cash payment on a regular basis was the only means of guaranteeing soldiers' loyalty. In the 20th century mercenaries have been common in wars and guerrilla activity in Asia, Africa, and Latin America.

Article 47 of the 1977 Additional Protocols to the Geneva Convention stipulates that 'a mercenary shall not have the right to be a combatant or a prisoner of war' but leaves a party to the Protocols the freedom to grant such status if so wished.

**minesweeper** small naval vessel for locating and destroying mines at sea. A typical minesweeper weighs about 725 tonnes, and is built of reinforced plastic (immune to magnetic and acoustic mines). Remote-controlled miniature submarines may be used to lay charges next to the mines and destroy them.

**mobilization** the preparation of armed forces (land, sea, air) for active service.

**MRBM** abbreviation for *medium-range ballistic missile* such as the French M-5 ballistic missile.

**navy** fleet of ships, usually a nation's warships, and the organization to maintain them. The USSR has one of the world's largest merchant fleets, and the world's largest fishing, hydrographic, and oceanographic fleets, in which all ships have intelligence-gathering equipment. In the early 1990s, the UK had a force of small carriers, destroyers, frigates, and submarines.

In the light of the 1991 Armed Forces reductions, the Royal Navy will be reduced from approximately 50 to 40 destroyers and frigates, and the submarine fleet will be reduced by 50%.

**NBC** abbreviation for nuclear, biological and chemical warfare, a term used to describe the form of warfare fought with weapons of mass destruction. The only case of nuclear warfare to date was the dropping of two nuclear weapons on Hiroshima and Nagasaki by the US Air Force in 1945, with the purpose of forcing Japan to surrender in World War II. Biological warfare is a weapon that is difficult to use in the field of battle but which could be used as a strategic weapon to poison water supplies or cause epidemics. Chemical weapons were first used during World War I in the form of mustard gas, and they have been used since in Vietnam, Afghanistan, and during the Iran–Iraq war by the Iraquis.

**North Atlantic Treaty Organization** (NATO) association set up 1949 to provide for the collective defence of the major W European and North American states against the perceived threat from the USSR. Its chief body is the Council of Foreign Ministers (who have representatives in permanent session), and there is an international secretariat in Brussels, Belgium, and also the Military Committee consisting of the Chiefs of Staff. The military headquarters SHAPE (Supreme Headquarters Allied Powers, Europe) is in Chièvres, near Mons, Belgium. In 1990, after a meeting in London, NATO declared that nuclear weapons were 'weapons of last resort' rather than 'flexible response', and offered to withdraw all nuclear artillery shells from Europe if the USSR did the same. With the ending of the Cold War and the changed relationship between the superpowers, the role of NATO is under reassessment, as is that of its counterpart the Warsaw Pact.

**nuclear warfare** war involving the use of nuclear weapons. Nuclear-weapons research began in Britain 1940, but was transferred to the USA after it entered World War II. The research programme, known as the Manhattan Project, was directed by J Robert Oppenheimer. The first atom bomb relied on the use of a chemical explosion to trigger a chain reaction. The first test explosion was at Alamogordo, New Mexico, 16 July 1945; the first use in war was by the USA against Japan 6 Aug 1945 at Hiroshima and three days later at Nagasaki. The worldwide total of nuclear weapons in 1990 was about 50,000, and the number of countries possessing nuclear weapons stood officially at five—USA, USSR, UK, France, and China—although some other nations were thought either to have a usable stockpile of these weapons (Israel) or the ability to produce them quickly (Brazil, India, Pakistan, South Africa).

*atom bomb* The original weapon relied on use of a chemical explosion to trigger a chain reaction.

*hydrogen bomb* A much more powerful weapon

than the atom bomb, it relies on the release of thermonuclear energy by the condensation of hydrogen nuclei to helium nuclei (as happens in the Sun). The first detonation was at Eniwetok Atoll, Pacific Ocean, 1952 by the USA.

**neutron bomb** or enhanced radiation weapon (ERW) It is a very small hydrogen bomb that has relatively high radiation but relatively low blast, designed to kill (in up to six days) by a brief neutron radiation that leaves buildings and weaponry intact.

**nuclear methods of attack** now include aircraft bombs, missiles (long- or short-range, surface to surface, air to surface, and surface to air), depth charges, and high-powered landmines ('atomic demolition munitions' to destroy bridges and roads. The major subjects of Soviet–US negotiation are:

**intercontinental ballistic missiles** (ICBMs), which have from 1968 been equipped with clusters of warheads (which can be directed to individual targets) and are known as multiple independently targetable re-entry vehicles (MIRVs). The 1980s US-designed MX (Peacekeeper) carries up to ten warheads in each missile. In 1989, the UK agreed to purchase submarine-launched Trident missiles from the USA. Each warhead has eight independently targetable re-entry vehicles (each nuclear-armed) with a range of about 6,400 km/4,000 mi to eight separate targets within about 240 km/150 mi of the central aiming point. The Trident system was scheduled to enter service within the Royal Navy in the mid-1990s.

**nuclear methods of defence** include:

**antiballistic missile** (ABM) Earth-based systems with two types of missile, one short-range with high acceleration, and one comparatively long-range for interception above the atmosphere.

**Strategic Defense Initiative** (announced by the USA 1983 to be operative from 2000; popularly known as the 'Star Wars' programme). The danger of nuclear weapons increases with the number of nations possessing them (USA 1945, USSR 1949, UK 1952, France 1960, China 1964), and nuclear-arms verification has been complicated by the ban on above-ground testing. Testing grounds include Lop Nor (China); Mururoa Atoll in the S Pacific (France); Nevada Desert, Amchitka Islands in the Aleutians (USA); Semipalatinsk in central Asia, Novaya Zemlya Islands in the Arctic (USSR).

**platoon** in the army, the smallest infantry unit. It contains 30–40 soldiers and is commanded by a lieutenant or second lieutenant. There are three or four platoons in a company.

**prisoner of war** (POW) person captured in war, who has fallen into the hands of, or surrendered to, an opponent. Such captives may be held in prisoner-of-war camps. The treatment of POWs is governed by the Geneva Convention.

**Rapid Reaction Force** or **(RRF)** any military unit that is maintained at a high state of readiness to react to an emergency. Specifically it is the corps-sized unit, the formation of which was announced by NATO in May 1991 to meet threats anywhere in its area of responsibility.

**reconnaissance** the gathering of information about a military objective. This can be carried out by a reconnaissance (or 'recce') patrol, or by using a small, fast-moving recce vehicle or an aircraft configured for the recce role, or a remotely piloted vehicle (RPV). The SAS (Special Air Service) carried out invaluable reconnaissance work in the 1991 Gulf War. Less precise information was provided by satellites.

**Red Army** former name of the army of the USSR. It developed from the Red Guards, volunteers who carried out the Bolshevik revolution, and received its name because it fought under the red flag. It was officially renamed the **Soviet Army** 1946. The Chinese revolutionary army was also called the Red Army.

**regiment** military formation equivalent to a battalion in parts of the British army, and to a brigade in the armies of many countries, including the USSR. In the British infantry, a regiment may encompass more than one battalion, and soldiers belong to the same regiment throughout their career.

**Royal Air Force** (RAF) the air force of Britain. The RAF was formed 1918 by the merger of the Royal Naval Air Service and the Royal Flying Corps. It numbers approximately 85,000 (1991), with some 48 front line squadrons of aircraft out of approximately 600 aircraft. The 1991 defence cuts will reduce this by 15 squadrons.

**Royal British Legion** full name of the British Legion, a nonpolitical body promoting the welfare of war veterans and their dependants.

**Royal Marines** British military force trained for amphibious warfare. See marine.

**services, armed** the air, sea, and land forces of a country; also called the armed forces.

**SHAPE** abbreviation for **Supreme Headquarters Allied Powers Europe**, situated near Mons, Belgium, and the headquarters of NATO's Supreme Allied Commander Europe (SACEUR).

**SLBM** abbreviation for **submarine-launched ballistic missile**.

**Special Air Service** (SAS) specialist British regiment recruited from regiments throughout the army. It has served in Malaysia, Oman, Yemen, the Falklands, Northern Ireland, and during the 1991 Gulf War, as well as against international terrorists, as in the siege of the Iranian embassy in London 1980.

**Strategic Defense Initiative** (SDI) also called **Star Wars** attempt by the USA to develop a defence system, using advanced laser and particle-beam technology (and based in part outside the Earth's atmosphere) against incoming nuclear missiles. It was announced by President Reagan in March 1983, and the research had by 1990 cost over $16.5 billion. In 1988, the joint Chiefs of Staff announced that they expected to be able to intercept no more than 30% of incoming missiles.

## NUCLEAR, BIOLOGICAL, AND CHEMICAL WARFARE

Nuclear, biological, and chemical (NBC) warfare, although each are distinct forms of war, are usually referred to in the composite form. NBC weapons are all weapons of mass extermination and they each require total protection for the body against any contact with radioactive dust, biological agents or chemicals.

It is the conventional wisdom that security in the nuclear age has depended upon the establishment of a relatively stable deterrence system between the USA and the USSR, and the restriction of the development of any other such systems other than those of Great Britain, France and China. But also forming a part of the overall security relationship are the Non-Proliferation Treaty (NPT) which limits the further spread of nuclear arsenals and the Anti-Ballistic Missile (ABM) Treaty which confirms parity between the two superpowers in this commodity. With these two fundamental treaties in place it is argued that a whole network of arms control mechanisms can be developed which can further assist in restricting and reducing weapons of mass destruction. The multilateral NPT became effective 1970 and today there are 139 signatures. The Treaty has to be renewed after 25 years of operation in 1995. A new regime will have to recognize that control by restriction is not enough. As more states gain the capability to produce nuclear weapons, the aim must be to persuade them that production is unnecessary, for example by the enhancement of both bilateral agreements

*Protective clothing for NBC warfare.*

as well as regional security arrangements—such as for example nuclear free zones—or even just preventing open declarations of capability so as to moderate the response may be the best that can be done. Perhaps 35–40 states have the technological capability to make nuclear weapons, but it is nations such as Iraq, North Korea, India or Pakistan in unstable regions of the world that are the main source of worry. The control of chemical weapons is equally worrisome. The prohibition of chemical weapons was set out in the multilateral Geneva Protocol of 1925 which remains the only international legal mechanism for the control of chemical weapons. There are at present 112 parties to the Protocol.

In 1989 the UN Conference on Disarmament drew up a draft convention on chemical weapons (CCW) which looks like forming the basis for a new international agreement on CW. Proliferation continues, although the USA and USSR agree on the need for a convention. Chemical warfare, however, is a reality with which modern armies have to contend. Iraq used chemical weapons during the 1980–88 Iran-Iraq War and inflicted massive casualties on largely unprotected Iranian Revolutionary Guards, although it chose not to use chemical warfare during the 1991 Gulf War.

Chemical agents are compounds which can be used offensively to cause casualties and to disrupt the defence, or defensively to create contaminated areas difficult for the enemy to cross or occupy. For these reasons a whole range of agents have been developed, some of which are more lethal than others and some of which are more persistent than others.

They are relatively simple to manufacture. Any country with a chemical industry can manufacture them, although their storage and maintenance present problems. Chemical stockpiles deteriorate, unstable compounds break down and the handling and security of such deadly compounds present serious problems to even a major power. It is for these reasons that the development of so called 'binary' chemical weapons in the USA is so significant. The principle upon which these weapons is based is that two individually harmless compounds are combined into a deadly chemical agent only in the shell or bomb within which they are housed and then only when the projectile is armed or fired. This greatly reduces storage problems.

The use of biological weapons was also originally prohibited by the 1925 Geneva Protocol. The additional Biological Weapons Convention (BWC) of 1972 was widely claimed to be the only significant post World War II disarmament achievement until the International Nuclear Forces Treaty was signed.

Controls on the proliferation of NBC weapons are in place. However, they are not entirely comprehensive nor can they always be verified. The only way forward is to use existing agreements and work to improve them. Renegade states such as North Korea may yet be brought within the fold.

Israel, Japan, and the UK are among the nations assisting in SDI research and development. In 1987 Gorbachev acknowledged that the USSR was developing a similar defence system. The SDI programme was subsequently scaled down dramatically, and it is unlikely that the original concept will ever be deployed.

**tank** armoured fighting vehicle that runs on tracks and is fitted with weapons systems capable of defeating other tanks and destroying life and property. The term was originally a code name for the first effective tracked and armoured fighting vehicle, invented by the British soldier and scholar Ernest Swinton, and used in the battle of the Somme 1916.

A tank consists of a body or hull of thick steel, on which are mounted machine guns and a larger gun. The hull contains the crew (usually consisting of a commander, driver, and one or two soldiers), engine, radio, fuel tanks, and ammunition. The tank travels on caterpillar tracks that enable it to cross rough ground and debris. It is known today as an MBT (main battle tank).

**Territorial Army** British force of volunteer soldiers, created from volunteer regiments (incorporated 1872) as the **Territorial Force** 1908. It was raised and administered by county associations, and intended primarily for home defence. It was renamed Territorial Army 1922. Merged with the Regular Army in World War II, it was revived 1947, and replaced by a smaller, more highly trained Territorial and Army Volunteer Reserve, again renamed Territorial Army 1979.

**war** act of force, usually on behalf of the state, intended to compel a declared enemy to obey the will of the other. The aim is to render the opponent incapable of further resistance by destroying its capability and will to bear arms in pursuit of its own aims. War is therefore a continuation of politics carried on with violent and destructive means, as an instrument of policy.

The estimated figure for loss of life in Third World wars since 1945 is 17 million. War is generally divided into **strategy**, the planning and conduct of a war, and **tactics**, the deployment of forces in battle.

Types of war include:

**guerrilla war** the waging of low-level conflict by irregular forces against an occupying army or against the rear of an enemy force. Examples include Mao Zedong's campaign against the Nationalist Chinese and T E Lawrence's Arab revolt against the Turks;

**low-intensity conflict** US term for its interventions in the Third World (stepped up in the 1980s), ranging from drug-running to funding and training guerrillas, and fought with political, economic, and cultural weapons as well as by military means;

**civil war** the waging of war by opposing parties, or members of different regions, within a state. The American Civil War 1861–65, the

English Civil War of the 17th century, and the Spanish Civil War 1936–39 are notable examples;

**limited war** the concept that a war may be limited in both geographical extent and levels of force exerted and have aims that stop short of achieving the destruction of the enemy. The Korean War 1950–53 falls within this category;

**total war** the waging of war against both combatants and noncombatants, taking the view that no distinction should be made between them. The Spanish Civil War marked the beginning of this type of warfare, in which bombing from the air included both civilian and military targets;

**absolute war** the view that there should be no limitations, such as law, compassion, or prudence, in the application of force, the sole aim being to achieve the complete annihilation of one's opponent. Such a concept contradicts the notion, formulated by Clausewitz, of war as an instrument of political dialogue since it implies that no dialogue is actually intended. It has been claimed that nuclear warfare would assume such proportions and would be in accordance with the doctrine of mutually assured destruction (MAD).

**warship** fighting ship armed and crewed for war. The supremacy of the battleship at the beginning of the 20th century was rivalled during World War I by the development of submarine attack, and was rendered obsolescent in World War II with the advent of long-range air attack. Today the largest and most important surface warships are the aircraft carriers.

**aircraft carriers** The large-scale aircraft carrier was temporarily out of favour, as too vulnerable, until the resumption of building, especially by the USSR, in the late 1970s and 1980s. The *Carl Vinson* USA 1982 weighs 81,600 tonnes.

Some countries, such as the UK, have opted for **mini-carriers** with vertical takeoff aircraft and long-range helicopters. Mini-carriers evolved in the early 1970s and have been advocated by US military reformers.

**submarines** The first nuclear-powered submarine was the US *Nautilus* 1955; the first Polaris was the *George Washington* 1960. Submarines fall into two classes: the specially designed, almost silent **attack submarine**, intended to release its fast torpedoes and missiles at comparatively close range, and the **ballistic-missile submarine** with guided missiles of such long range that the submarine itself is virtually undetectable to the enemy. For the USA these submarines form one leg of the strategic 'triad' of land-based missiles, crewed bombers, and submarine-launched missiles.

**battleships** The US Navy has recommissioned and modernized several World War II battleships for shore bombardment and force projection purposes. These were used with great effect during the 1991 Gulf War.

**withdrawal** in a military action, an orderly

movement of forces in a rearward direction in order to occupy more favourable ground. It is voluntary and controlled, unlike a retreat.

**women's services** the organized military use of women on a large scale, a 20th-century development. First, women replaced men in factories, on farms, and in noncombat tasks during wartime; they are now found in combat units in many countries, including the USA, Cuba, the UK, the USSR, and Israel.

# TREATIES AND CONFERENCES

**Georgetown, Declaration of** call in 1972, at a conference in Guyana of nonaligned countries, for a multipolar system to replace the two world power blocs, and for the Mediterranean Sea and Indian Ocean to be neutral.

**Helsinki Conference** international conference 1975 at which 35 countries, including the USSR and the USA, attempted to reach agreement on cooperation in security, economics, science, technology, and human rights.

**INF** abbreviation for *intermediate nuclear forces*, as in the Intermediate Nuclear Forces Treaty.

**Intermediate Nuclear Forces Treaty** agreement signed 8 Dec 1987 between the USA and the USSR to eliminate all ground-based nuclear missiles in Europe that were capable of hitting only European targets (including European Russia). It reduced the countries' nuclear arsenals by some 2,000 (4% of the total). The treaty included provisions for each country to inspect the other's bases. A total of 1,269 weapons (945 Soviet, 234 US) was destroyed in the first year of the treaty.

**Paris, Treaty of** any of various peace treaties signed in Paris.

**SALT** abbreviation for *Strategic Arms Limitation Talks*, a series of US–Soviet negotiations 1969–79.

**START** abbreviation for *Strategic Arms Reduction Talks*.

**Strategic Arms Limitation Talks** (SALT) series of US–Soviet discussions aimed at reducing the rate of nuclear-arms build-up. The talks, delayed by the Soviet invasion of Czechoslovakia 1968, began in 1969 between the US President Lyndon Johnson and the

Soviet leader Brezhnev. Neither the SALT I accord (effective 1972–77) nor SALT II called for reductions in nuclear weaponry, merely a limit on the expansion of these forces. SALT II was mainly negotiated by US President Ford before 1976 and signed by Soviet leader Brezhnev and President Carter in Vienna in 1979. It was never fully ratified because of the Soviet occupation of Afghanistan, although the terms of the accord were respected by both sides until President Reagan exceeded its limitations during his second term 1985–89. SALT talks were superseded by START (Strategic Arms Reduction Talks) negotiations under Reagan, and the first significant reductions began under Soviet President Gorbachev.

**Strategic Arms Reduction Talks** (START) phase in US–Soviet peace discussions. START began with talks in Geneva 1983, leading to the signing of the Intermediate Nuclear Forces (INF) treaty 1987. In 1989 proposals for reductions in strategic nuclear weapons systems were added to the agenda. In July 1991 Presidents Bush and Gorbachev agreed in principle to sign a START treaty Aug 1991 cutting strategic nuclear warheads (land based ballistic missiles, sea launched ballistic missiles, and strategic bombers) by approximately one third to 6,000 for the USSR, and 7,000 for the USA.

**Versailles, Treaty of** peace treaty after World War I between the Allies and Germany, signed 28 June 1919. It established the League of Nations. Germany surrendered Alsace-Lorraine to France, and large areas in the east to Poland, and made smaller cessions to Czechoslovakia, Lithuania, Belgium, and Denmark. The Rhineland was demilitarized, German rearmament was restricted, and Germany agreed to pay reparations for war damage. The treaty was never ratified by the USA, which made a separate peace with Germany and Austria 1921.

**Western European Union** (WEU) organization established 1955 as a consultative forum for military issues among the W European governments: Belgium, France, Holland, Italy, Luxembourg, the UK, West Germany, and (from 1988) Spain and Portugal.

**Yalta Conference** in 1945, a meeting at which the Allied leaders Churchill (UK), Roosevelt (USA), and Stalin (USSR) completed plans for the defeat of Germany in World War II and the foundation of the United Nations. It took place in Yalta, a Soviet holiday resort in the Crimea.

---

TREATIES OF PARIS

| | |
|---|---|
| **1919–20** | The conference preparing the Treaty of Versailles at the end of World War I was held in Paris. |
| **1946** | After World War II the peace treaties between the Allies and Italy, Romania, Hungary, Bulgaria, and Finland. |
| **1951** | Treaty signed by France, West Germany, Italy, Belgium, Netherlands and Luxemburg, embodying the Schuman Plan to set up a single coal and steel authority. |
| **1973** | Ending US participation in the Vietnam War. |

# WARS AND LEADERS

**Alamein, El, Battles of** in World War II, two decisive battles in the western desert, N Egypt. In the *First Battle of El Alamein* 1–27 Jul 1942 the British 8th Army under Auchinleck held the German and Italian forces under Rommel. In the *Second Battle of El Alamein* 23 Oct–4 Nov 1942 Montgomery defeated Rommel.

**Arab-Israeli Wars** a series of wars between Israel and various Arab states in the Middle East since the founding of the state of Israel 1948.

*First Arab-Israeli War* 14 Oct 1948–13 Jan/24 Mar 1949. As soon as the independent state of Israel had been proclaimed by the Jews in Palestine, it was invaded by combined Arab forces. The Israelis defeated them and went on to annex territory until they controlled 75% of what had been Palestine under British mandate.

*Second Arab-Israeli War* or *Suez War* 29 Oct–4 Nov 1956. After Egypt had taken control of the Suez Canal and blockaded the Straits of Tiran, Israel, with British and French support, invaded and captured Sinai and the Gaza Strip, from which it withdrew under heavy US pressure after the entry of a UN force.

*Third Arab-Israeli War* 5–10 June 1967, the *Six Day War*. It resulted in the Israeli capture of the Golan Heights from Syria; the E half of Jerusalem and the West Bank from Jordan; and, in the south, the Gaza Strip and Sinai Peninsula as far as the Suez Canal.

*Fourth Arab-Israeli War* 2–22/24 Oct 1973, the *'October War'* or *Yom Kippur War*, so called because the Israeli forces were taken by surprise on the Day of Atonement. It started with the recrossing of the Suez Canal by Egyptian forces who made initial gains, as did the Syrians in the Golan Heights area. However, the Israelis stabilized the position in both cases.

*Fifth Arab-Israeli War* From 1978 the presence of Palestinian guerrillas in Lebanon led to Arab raids on Israel and Israeli retaliatory incursions, but on 6 June 1982 Israel launched a full-scale invasion. By 14 June Beirut was encircled, and Palestine Liberation Organization (PLO) and Syrian forces were evacuated (mainly to Syria) 21–31 Aug, but in Feb 1985 there was a unilateral Israeli withdrawal from the country without any gain for losses incurred. Israel maintains a 'security zone' in S Lebanon and supports the South Lebanese Army militia as a buffer against Palestinian guerrilla incursions.

**Arnhem, Battle of** in World War II, airborne operation by the Allies, 17–26 Sept 1944, to secure a bridgehead over the Rhine, thereby opening the way for a thrust towards the Ruhr and a possible early end to the war. It was only partially successful, with 7,600 casualties. Arnhem is a city in the Netherlands, on the Rhine SE of Utrecht; population (1988) 297,000. It produces salt, chemicals, and pharmaceuticals.

**Arras, Battle of** battle of World War I, April–May 1917. It was an effective but costly British attack on German forces in support of a French offensive, which was only partially successful, on the Siegfried Line. British casualties totalled 84,000 as compared to 75,000 German casualties.

**Atlantic, Battle of the** continuous battle fought in the Atlantic Ocean throughout World War II (1939–45) by the sea and air forces of the Allies and Germany, to control the supply routes to Britain. The number of U-boats destroyed by the Allies during the war was nearly 800. At least 2,200 convoys of 75,000 merchant ships crossed the Atlantic, protected by US naval forces. Before the US entry into the war 1941, destroyers were supplied to the British under the Lend-Lease Act 1941.

**Bataan** peninsula in Luzon, the Philippines, which was defended against the Japanese in World War II by US and Filipino troops under General MacArthur 1 Jan–9 Apr 1942. MacArthur was evacuated, but some 67,000 Allied prisoners died on the *Bataan Death March* to camps in the interior.

**Bradley** Omar Nelson 1893–1981. US general in World War II. In 1943 he commanded the 2nd US Corps in their victories in Tunisia and Sicily, leading to the surrender of 250,000 Axis troops, and in 1944 led the US troops in the invasion of France. His command, as the 12th Army Group, grew to 1.3 million troops, the largest US force ever assembled.

**Britain, Battle of** World War II air battle between German and British air forces over Britain lasting 10 Jul–31 Oct 1940.

At the outset the Germans had the advantage because they had seized airfields in the Netherlands, Belgium, and France, which were basically safe from attack and from which SE England was within easy range. On 1 Aug 1940 the Luftwaffe had about 4,500 aircraft of all kinds, compared to about 3,000 for the RAF. The Battle of Britain had been intended as a preliminary to the German invasion plan *Seelöwe* (Sea Lion), which Hitler indefinitely postponed 17 Sept and abandoned 10 Oct, choosing instead to invade the USSR.

**Bulge, Battle of the** or *Ardennes offensive* in World War II, Hitler's plan, code-named 'Watch on the Rhine', for a breakthrough by his field marshal Rundstedt aimed at the US line in Ardennes 16 Dec 1944–28 Jan 1945. There were 77,000 Allied casualties and 130,000 German, including Hitler's last powerful reserve, his Panzer elite. Although US troops were encircled for some weeks at Bastogne, the German counteroffensive failed.

**Caporetto** former name of Kobarid, Yugoslavia (see entry).

**Cassino** town in S Italy, 80 km/50 mi NW of Naples; at the foot of Monte Cassino; population (1981) 31,139. It was the scene of heavy fighting during World War II in 1944, when most of the town was destroyed. It was rebuilt 1.5 km/1 mi to the N. The abbey on the summit of Monte Cassino, founded by St Benedict in 529, was rebuilt in 1956.

**Clausewitz** Karl von 1780–1831. Prussian officer and writer on war, born near Magdeburg. His book *Vom Kriege/On War* 1833, translated into English 1873, gave a new philosophical foundation to the art of war and put forward a concept of strategy that was influential until World War I.

**D-day** 6 June 1944, the day of the Allied invasion of Normandy under the command of General Eisenhower, with the aim of liberating Western Europe from German occupation. The Anglo-American invasion fleet landed on the Normandy beaches on the stretch of coast between the Orne River and St Marcouf. Artificial harbours known as 'Mulberries' were constructed and towed across the Channel so that equipment and armaments could be unloaded on to the beaches. After overcoming fierce resistance the Allies broke through the German defences; Paris was liberated on 25 Aug, and Brussels on 2 Sept.

**de Gaulle** Charles André Joseph Marie 1890–1970. French general and first president of the Fifth Republic 1959–69. He organized the Free French troops fighting the Nazis 1940–44, was head of the provisional French government 1944–46, and leader of his own Gaullist party. In 1958 the national assembly asked him to form a government during France's economic recovery and to solve the crisis in Algeria. He became president at the end of 1958, having changed the constitution to provide for a presidential system, and served until 1969.

**Desert Storm, Operation** codename of the military action to eject the Iraqi army from Kuwait in 1991. The build-up phase was codenamed *Operation Desert Shield* and lasted from Aug 1990, when Kuwait was first invaded by Iraq, to Jan 1991 when Operation Desert Storm was unleashed, starting the Gulf War. Desert Storm ended with the defeat of the Iraqi army in the Kuwaiti theatre of operations in late Feb 1991.

**Dönitz** Karl 1891–1980. German admiral, originator of the wolf-pack submarine technique, which sank 15 million tonnes of Allied shipping in World War II. He succeeded Hitler in 1945, capitulated, and was imprisoned 1946–56.

**Dunkirk** (French *Dunkerque*) seaport on the N coast of France, in Nord *département*, on the Strait of Dover; population (1983) 83,760, conurbation 196,000.

It was close to the front line during much of World War I, and in World War II, 337,131 Allied troops (including about 110,000 French) were evacuated from the beaches as German forces approached.

**Falklands War** 1982 war between Argentina and the UK. Some 30,000 Argentine troops invaded and occupied the British colony/dependency of the Falklands in the South Atlantic, renamed them Las Malvinas and declared them a sovereign part of Argentina. A British task force of about 15,000 soldiers, sailors, and airmen was assembled over a period of months and

an amphibious landing took place on 20 May at San Carlos Bay in the Sound between East and West Falkland. Shortly thereafter British troops marched on Port Stanley and Darwin. Finally, on 12 June, British troops launched a surprise attack on Argentine positions outside Port Stanley, capturing 400 troops and isolating the town. Two days later all Argentine forces on the island surrendered. The most significant event of the war at sea was the sinking of the Argentine cruiser *Belgrano*, by the British nuclear attack submarine HMS *Conqueror* when some 300 Argentines lost their lives. There were approximately 250 UK casualties, and 1,500 Argentine casualties during the hostilities. The war cost £1.6 billion.

**Fuchs** Klaus (Emil Julius) 1911–1988. German spy who worked on atom-bomb research in the UK in World War II. He was imprisoned 1950–59 for passing information to the USSR and resettled in East Germany.

**Fuller** John Frederick Charles 1878–1966. British major general and military theorist who propounded the concept of armoured warfare which, when interpreted by the Germans, became *blitzkrieg* in 1940.

**Gallipoli** port in European Turkey, giving its name to the peninsula (ancient name *Chersonesus*) on which it stands. In World War I, at the instigation of Winston Churchill, an unsuccessful attempt was made Feb 1915–Jan 1916 by Allied troops to force their way through the Dardanelles and link up with Russia. The campaign was fought mainly by Australian and New Zealand (ANZAC) forces, who suffered heavy losses. An estimated 36,000 Commonwealth troops died during the nine-month campaign.

**Galtieri** Leopoldo 1926– . Argentinian general, leading member of the right-wing military junta that ordered the seizure 1982 of the Falkland Islands (Malvinas), a British colony in the SW Atlantic claimed by Argentina. He and his fellow junta members were tried for abuse of human rights and court-martialled for their conduct of the war; he was sentenced to 12 years in prison in 1986.

**Georgetown, Declaration of** call in 1972, at a conference in Guyana of nonaligned countries, for a multipolar system to replace the two world power blocs, and for the Mediterranean Sea and Indian Ocean to be neutral.

**Gulf War** 16 Jan–28 Feb 1991 war between Iraq and a coalition of 28 nations led by the USA. The invasion and annexation of Kuwait by Iraq on 2 Aug 1990 provoked a build-up of US troops in Saudi Arabia, eventually totalling over 500,000. The UK subsequently deployed 42,000 troops, France 15,000, Egypt 20,000, and other nations smaller contingents. An air offensive lasting six weeks, in which 'smart' weapons came of age, destroyed perhaps one-third of Iraqi equipment and inflicted massive casualties. A 100-hour ground war followed, which effectively destroyed the remnants of the 500,000-strong Iraqi army in or near Kuwait. The cost of the war is estimated to be $60–70

## SMART WEAPONS: HOW EFFECTIVE ARE THEY?

The 1991 Gulf War was notable for the remarkable success of so-called 'smart' weaponry, that is missiles or bombs that have the capability of homing in on a point target with great accuracy. The Tomahawk land attack missile (TLAM) was a spectacular success in Operation Desert Storm. A distinctive feature of TLAM is its guidance system which allows it to determine where it is at regular intervals. The missiles are fitted with inertial guidance, but such systems tend to lose accuracy as the missile flies. To detect errors when flying over land, the Tomahawk relies on a technique called TERCOM (terrain contour matching). Its computer carries maps of the local terrain as seen by radar altimeter, one map for every 150 km/95 mi or so. At appropriate times, the computer studies the terrain that the missile's altimeter is seeing, compares the readings to those of an appropriate map, and thus determines the missile's position. This updates the inertial guidance, which can keep the course until the next position check.

The resulting accuracy can be quite high. In an early test, a Tomahawk launched from a submarine off the California coast flew 483 km/300 mi to a test range in Nevada and sailed into its target, a banner stretched between two poles. Such accuracy, however, depends on the availability of terrain maps, which are made by aircraft. What's more, a cruise missile cannot readily use the TERCOM technique to cross an extensive stretch of ocean and hit a land target.

But the Navstar navigational system will overcome these problems. Navstar, which is just coming into use, relies on a global network of navigational satellites. It can be used either as a complement to TERCOM or as a substitute for it. In the latter case, it eliminates the need for digitized terrain maps, which may be difficult for a Third World government to obtain. Navstar operates at all altitudes, over sea as well as land, and in all weather. In tests it has enabled missiles to determine their positions to within 12 m/39 ft.

Laser guidance allows even higher accuracy. In this technique, a laser operator, who can be far from the missile launcher, shines a laser on to the target. An optical system in the missile sees the spot and directs the weapon accordingly. Laser guidance was the basis of the 'smart bombs' of the Vietnam War, with which the US Air Force succeeded in knocking out heavily defended North Vietnamese bridges that had withstood earlier attacks. In land warfare, their counterpart is the Copperhead, a rocket fired from a 155 mm howitzer. It can knock out a tank at ranges exceeding 16 km/10 mi, which is far beyond the reach of tank-mounted cannon.

Laser guidance has shown its usefulness in the Persian Gulf War. A dramatic example was the destruction of the Ministry of Air Defence in Baghdad. That building had a thick roof and was located in a part of the city where fear of civilian casualties might have discouraged attack. But an Air Force 'smart bomb', probably using laser guidance, flew into an air shaft and blew it up. Even with only TERCOM and without lasers, the Tomahawk has also been a mainstay of the war with Iraq. It has been fired by the hundreds and reportedly has shown an accuracy in aim of 8 m/25 ft. One newspaper correspondent reported seeing a missile fly past his hotel window clearly following the main road. Smart weapons played a leading role in the allied victory in the Gulf War. They were not always effective, for instance when a laser-guided bomb failed to enter the 'basket' (i.e. the area of influence of the laser marker) and thus did not track on to the target, or on other occasions the control surfaces of laser guided weapons locked causing them to veer away from the target. But in the majority of cases they were remarkably successful. But how much smarter can smart weapons get? Western powers and the USA in particular has long relied on its technological edge to offset its adversaries' strength in numbers. That strategy will continue. For instance, in the USA McDonnell Douglas and General Dynamics are well along the road towards developing an advanced Stealth cruise missile. In December 1990 McDonnell Douglas also flew the prototype of a new family of 'stand-off' smart bombs for the US Navy that can be launched from a distance from low-flying attack planes, soar to high altitudes, seek out the target and then dive down and destroy it. Smart weapons came of age in the Gulf War and undoubtedly are here to stay. Not only are they highly effective but they are also cost effective and they have the added attraction that they save civilian lives thus winning the propaganda war as well as the shooting war.

View from Stealth F-117 bomber shows precision bombing as the cross-hairs centre on door of missile storage hanger.

billion. By mid-May 1991 $54.5 billion was pledged by the Japanese, Germans, and Saudi Arabians, of which $36 billion has been received.

**Hiroshima** industrial city and port on the S coast of Honshu, Japan, destroyed by the first wartime use of an atomic bomb 6 Aug 1945. The city has largely been rebuilt since the war; population (1987) 1,034,000.

Towards the end of World War II the city was utterly devastated by the US atom bomb. More than 10 sq km/4 sq mi was obliterated, with very heavy damage outside that area. Casualties totalled at least 137,000 out of a population of 343,000: 78,150 were found dead, others died later.

**Iwo Jima** largest of the Japanese Volcano Islands in the W Pacific Ocean, 1,222 km/760 mi S of Tokyo; area 21 sq km/8 sq mi. Annexed by Japan 1891, it was captured by the USA 1945 after fierce fighting. It was returned to Japan 1968.

**Jutland, Battle of** naval battle of World War I, fought between England and Germany on 31 May 1916, off the W coast of Jutland. Its outcome was indecisive, but the German fleet remained in port for the rest of the war.

**Khe Sanh** in the Vietnam War, US Marine outpost near the Laotian border and just south of the demilitarized zone between North and South Vietnam. Garrisoned by 4,000 Marines, it was attacked unsuccessfully by 20,000 North Vietnamese troops 21 Jan–7 Apr 1968.

**Kobarid** formerly *Caporetto* village on the Isonzo river, in Slovenia, NW Yugoslavia. Originally in Hungary, it was in Italy from 1918, and in 1947 became Kobarid. During World War I, German-Austrian troops defeated Italian forces there 1917.

**Liddell Hart** Basil 1895–1970. British military strategist. He was an exponent of mechanized warfare, and his ideas were adopted in Germany 1935 in creating the 1st Panzer Division, combining motorized infantry and tanks. From 1937 he advised the UK War Office on army reorganization.

**Marne, Battles of the** in World War I, two unsuccessful German offensives: *First Battle* 6–9 Sept 1914, von Moltke's advance was halted by the British Expeditionary Force and the French under Foch; *Second Battle* 15 July–4 Aug 1918, Ludendorff's advance was defeated by British, French, and US troops under the French general Pétain, and German morale crumbled.

**Mons** (Flemish *Bergen*) industrial city (coalmining, textiles, sugar) and capital of the province of Hainaut, Belgium; population (1985) 90,500. The military headquarters of NATO is at nearby Chièvres-Casteau.

**Montgomery** Bernard Law, 1st Viscount Montgomery of Alamein 1887–1976. British field marshal. In World War II he commanded the 8th Army in N Africa in the Second Battle of El Alamein 1942. As commander of British troops in N Europe from 1944, he received the German surrender on 1945.

**Okinawa** largest of the Japanese Ryukyu Islands

in the W Pacific; area 2,250 sq km/869 sq mi; population (1986) 1,190,000. It was captured by the USA in the *Battle of Okinawa* 1 Apr–21 June 1945, with 47,000 US casualties (12,000 dead) and 60,000 Japanese (only a few hundred survived as prisoners); the island was returned to Japan 1972.

**Passchendaele** village in W Flanders, Belgium, near Ypres. The Passchendaele ridge before Ypres was the object of a costly and unsuccessful British offensive in World War I, between July and Nov 1917; British casualties numbered nearly 400,000.

**Patton** George (Smith) 1885–1945. US general in World War II, known as 'Blood and Guts'. He commanded the 2nd Armoured Division 1940, and in 1942 led the Western Task Force that landed at Casablanca, Morocco. After commanding the 7th Army, he led the 3rd Army across France and into Germany, and in 1945 took over the 15th Army.

**Pearl Harbor** an inlet of the Pacific Ocean where the US naval base is situated in Hawaii on Oahu Island. It was the scene of a Japanese surprise air attack on 7 Dec 1941, that brought the US into World War II. It took place while Japanese envoys were holding so-called peace talks in Washington. The local commanders Admiral Kummel and Lieutenant General Short were relieved of their posts and held responsible for the fact that the base, despite warnings, was totally unprepared at the time of the attack. About 3,300 US military personnel were killed, 4 battleships were lost, and a large part of the US Pacific fleet was destroyed or damaged. The Japanese, angered by US embargoes of oil and other war materiel and convinced that US entry into the war was inevitable, opted to strike a major blow in hopes of forcing US concessions. Instead, it galvanized public opinion and raised anti-Japanese sentiment to a fever pitch, with war declared thereafter.

**Rommel** Erwin 1891–1944. German field marshal. He served in World War I, and in World War II he played an important part in the invasions of central Europe and France. He was commander of the N African offensive from 1941 (when he was nicknamed 'Desert Fox') until defeated in the Battles of El Alamein. He was commander in chief for a short time against the Allies in Europe 1944 but (as a sympathizer with the Stauffenberg plot against Hitler) was forced to commit suicide.

**Russo-Japanese War** war between Russia and Japan 1904–05, which arose from conflicting ambitions in Korea and Manchuria, specifically, the Russian occupation of Port Arthur (modern Lüda) 1896 and of the Amur province 1900. Japan successfully besieged Port Arthur May 1904–Jan 1905, took Mukden 29 Feb–10 Mar, and on 27 May defeated the Russian Baltic fleet, which had sailed halfway around the world to Tsushima Strait. A peace was signed in Portsmouth, New Hampshire, USA, 23 Aug 1905. Russia surrendered its lease on Port Arthur, ceded S Sakhalin to Japan, evacuated

Manchuria, and recognized Japan's interests in Korea.

**Schwarzkopf** H Norman 1934– . US general in the Gulf War. A considered, calculating approach belies his 'Stormin' Norman' image. A graduate from the military academy of West Point, he obtained a masters degree in guided missile engineering. He became an infantryman and later a paratrooper. He was a battalion commander during the Vietnam War, earning two Purple Hearts and three Silver Stars for his two tours of service there. As Supreme Commander of the Allied Forces in the Gulf, he planned and executed a blitzkrieg campaign, termed 'Desert Storm' which sustained remarkably few casualties, whilst crushing the enemy. His diplomatic skills were extended to the full in maintaining a 28-member Arab–Western anti-Iraqi military coalition. With victory secured, he emerged in March 1991 with a national approval rating in excess of 90%

**Sevastopol** or **Sebastopol** port, resort, and fortress in the Crimea, Ukraine Republic, USSR; population (1987) 350,000. It is the base of the Soviet Black Sea fleet and also has shipyards and a wine-making industry. Founded by Catherine II 1784, it was successfully besieged by the English and French in the Crimean War (Oct 1854–Sept 1855), and in World War II by the Germans (Nov 1941–July 1942), but was retaken by the Soviets 1944.

**Sinai** Egyptian peninsula, at the head of the Red Sea; area 65,000 sq km/25,000 sq mi. Resources include oil, natural gas, manganese, and coal; irrigation water from the river Nile is carried under the Suez Canal.

Sinai was occupied by Israel 1967–82. After the Battle of Sinai 1973, Israel began a gradual withdrawal from the area, under the disengagement agreement 1975, and the Camp David peace treaty 1979 and restored the whole of Sinai to Egyptian control by Apr 1982.

**Sino-Japanese Wars** wars waged by Japan against China to expand to the mainland.

*First Sino-Japanese War* 1894–95. Under the treaty of Shimonoseki, Japan secured the 'independence' of Korea, cession of Taiwan and the nearby Pescadores Islands, and the Liaodong peninsula (for a naval base). France, Germany, and Russia pressured Japan into returning the last-named, which Russia occupied 1896 to establish Port Arthur (now Lüda); this led to the Russo-Japanese War 1904–05.

*Second Sino–Japanese War* 1931–45. The Japanese occupied Manchuria, turning it into the puppet state of Manchukuo; they also attacked Shanghai and moved into NE China. In 1941 the Japanese attacked Pearl Harbor, leading to the extension of lend-lease aid to China and US entry into war against Japan and its allies. In Sep 1945, the Chinese received the Japanese surrender at Nanjing, after the Allies had concluded World War II.

**Somme** river in N France, on which Amiens and Abbeville stand; length 240 km/150 mi. It rises in Aisne *département* and flows W through Somme *département* to the English Channel.

**Stalingrad** former name (1925–61) of the Soviet city of Volgograd.

**Tirpitz** Alfred von 1849–1930. German admiral. As secretary for the navy 1897–1916, he created the German navy and planned the World War I U-boat campaign.

**Tonkin Gulf Incident** clash that triggered US entry into the Vietnam War in Aug 1964. Two US destroyers (USS *C Turner Joy* and USS *Maddox*) reported that they were fired on by North Vietnamese torpedo boats. It is unclear whether hostile shots were actually fired, but the reported attack was taken as a pretext for retaliatory air raids against North Vietnam. On 7 Aug the US Congress passed the **Tonkin Resolution**, which allowed President Johnson 'to take all necessary steps, including the use of armed forces' to help SEATO (South-East Asia Treaty Organization) members 'defend their freedom'. This resolution formed the basis for the considerable increase in US military involvement in the Vietnam War; it was repealed 1970.

**Verdun** fortress town in NE France on the Meuse. During World War I it became the symbol of French resistance, withstanding a German onslaught in 1916.

**Vietnam War** 1954–75. War between communist North Vietnam and US-backed South Vietnam. 200,000 South Vietnamese soldiers, 1 million North Vietnamese soldiers, and 500,000 civilians were killed. 56,555 US soldiers were killed 1961–75, a fifth of them by their own troops. The war destroyed 50% of the country's forest cover and 20% of agricultural land. Cambodia, a neutral neighbour, was bombed by the US 1969–75, with 1 million killed or wounded.

**Volgograd** formerly (until 1925) *Tsaritsyn*, and (1925–61) *Stalingrad* industrial city in SW USSR, on the river Volga; population (1987) 988,000. Its successful defence 1942–43 against Germany was a major turning point for the Allied forces in World War II. The German 6th Army under field marshal Friedrich Paulus, captured Stalingrad 1943, but was forced to surrender to the Soviets under marshal Georgi Zhukov. After intense fighting, the Germans lost 70,000 men.

**World War I** 1914–18. War between the Central European Powers (Germany, Austria-Hungary, and allies) on one side and the Triple Entente (Britain and the British Empire, France, and Russia) and their allies, including the USA (which entered 1917), on the other side. An estimated 10 million lives were lost and twice that number were wounded.

**World War II** 1939–45. war between Germany, Italy, and Japan (the Axis powers) on one side, and Britain, the Commonwealth, France, the USA, the USSR, and China (the Allied powers) on the other. An estimated 55 million lives were lost, 20 million of them citizens of the USSR.

**Ypres** (Flemish *Ieper*) Belgian town in W Flanders, 40 km/25 mi S of Ostend, a site of three major battles 1914–17 fought in World War I. In Oct–Nov 1914 the Germans launched an assault on British defensive positions and captured the Messines Ridge, but failed to take Ypres. In Apr–May 1915, the Germans launched a renewed attack using poison gas and chlorine (the first recorded use in war), in an unsuccessful attempt to break the British line. In July–Nov 1917 (known also as Passchendaele), an allied offensive, including British, Canadian, and Australian troops, was launched under British commander-in-chief Douglas Haig, in an attempt to capture ports on the Belgian coast held by Germans. The long and bitter battle, fought in appalling conditions of driving rain and waterlogged ground, achieved an advance of only 8 km/5 mi of territory that was of no strategic significance. The allied attack cost over 300,000 casualties.

**Zhukov** Georgi Konstantinovich 1896–1974. Marshal of the USSR in World War II and minister of defence 1955–57. As chief of staff from 1941, he defended Moscow 1941, counterattacked at Stalingrad in 1942, organized the relief of Leningrad 1943, and led the offensive from the Ukraine Mar 1944 which ended in the fall of Berlin. He subsequently commanded the Soviet occupation forces in Germany.

# WEAPONS AND EQUIPMENT

**aircraft carrier** sea-going base for military aircraft. After World War II the cost and vulnerability of such large vessels were thought to have outweighed their advantages. However, by 1980 the desire to have a means of destroying enemy aircraft beyond the range of a ship's own weapons, especially on convoy duty, led to a widespread revival of aircraft carriers of 20,000–30,000 tonnes. Aircraft carriers are equipped with combinations of fixed-wing aircraft, helicopters, missile launchers, and anti-aircraft guns.

**armoured personnel carrier** (APC) wheeled or tracked military vehicle designed to transport up to ten people. Armoured to withstand small-arms fire and shell splinters, it is used on battlefields.

**assault ship** naval vessel designed to land and support troops and vehicles under hostile conditions.

**bayonet** short sword attached to the muzzle of a firearm. The new British Army rifle, the SA-80, is fitted with a bayonet; its predecessor, the SLR, was similarly equipped and used, with its bayonet, during the 1982 Falklands conflict.

**binary weapon** in chemical warfare, weapon consisting of two substances that in isolation are harmless but when mixed together form a poisonous nerve gas. They are loaded into the delivery system separately and combine after launch.

**enhanced radiation weapon** another name for the neutron bomb.

**fuel-air explosive** warhead containing a highly flammable petroleum and oxygen mixture; when released over a target, this mixes with the oxygen in the atmosphere and produces a vapour which, when ignited, causes a blast approximately five times more powerful than conventional high explosives. Fuel-air explosives were used by the US Air Force in the 1991 Gulf War to flatten Iraqi defensive positions.

**Harrier** the only truly successful vertical takeoff and landing fixed-wing aircraft, often called the *jump jet*. Built in Britain, it made its first flight 1966. It has a single jet engine and a set of swivelling nozzles. These deflect the jet exhaust vertically downwards for takeoff and landing, and to the rear for normal flight. Designed to fly from confined spaces with minimal ground support, it refuels in midair.

**incendiary bomb** a bomb containing inflammable matter. Usually dropped by aircraft, incendiary bombs were used in World War I, and were a major weapon in attacks on cities in World War II. To hinder firefighters, delayed-action high-explosive bombs were usually dropped with them. In the Vietnam War, the USA used napalm in incendiary bombs.

**machine gun** rapid-firing automatic gun. The forerunner of the modern machine gun was the Gatling, perfected in the USA in 1860 and used in the Civil War. The Maxim of 1884 was recoil-operated, but some later types have been gas-operated (Bren) or recoil assisted by gas (some versions of the Browning). The *submachine-gun*, exploited by Chicago gangsters in the 1920s, was widely used in World War II; for instance, the Thompson, often called the Tommy gun.

**mechanized infantry combat vehicle** (MICV) tracked military vehicle designed to fight as part of an armoured battle group; that is, with tanks. It is armed with a quick-firing cannon and one or more machine guns. MICVs have replaced armoured personnel carriers.

**mine** explosive charge on land or sea, or in the atmosphere, designed to be detonated by contact, vibration (for example from an enemy engine), magnetic influence, or a timing device. Countermeasures include metal detectors (useless for plastic types), specially equipped helicopters, and (at sea) minesweepers.

**missile** rocket-propelled weapon, which may be nuclear-armed. Modern missiles are classified according to range into *intercontinental ballistic missiles* (ICBMs, capable of reaching targets over 5,500 km/3,400 mi), *intermediate-range* (1,100 km/680 mi–2,750 km/1,700mi), and *short-range* (under 1,100 km/680 mi) missiles. They are also categorized as *surface to surface*, *surface to air*, *air to air*, or *air to surface*.

A *ballistic missile* is one whose trajectory is governed by gravity once the power is shut off. The first long-range ballistic missile used in warfare was the V2 launched by Germany against Britain in World War II. Outside the industrialized countries, 22 states had active ballistic-missile programmes by 1989, and

GULF WAR CHRONOLOGY

| | |
|---|---|
| **2 Aug 1990** | Iraqi troops invaded Kuwait and rapidly seized control. |
| **7 Aug 1990** | The USA sent troops and planes to Saudi Arabia. |
| **14 Sept 1990** | Iraqi troops raided several Western diplomatic missions in Kuwait City. Tom King, UK Defence Secretary, announced the dispatch of the 'Desert Rats'—the 7th Armoured Brigade—to the Gulf. |
| **15 Sept 1990** | France began to send troops to Saudi Arabia. |
| **8 Nov 1990** | The USA announced plans to increase its armed forces in the Gulf Region to 400,000. |
| **19 Nov 1990** | Iraq announced that it would add 250,000 troops to bolster its 430,000 strong army. |
| **22 Nov 1990** | Britain announced that it would send 15,000 more troops to the Gulf. |
| **29 Nov 1990** | The United Nations Security Council authorized the use of force against Iraq if it did not withdraw totally from Kuwait by 15 Jan 1991. |
| **8–13 Dec 1990** | Most of the 2,000 western hostages held in Iraq and Kuwait were released. |
| **9 Jan 1991** | US secretary of state James Baker and Iraqi foreign minister Tariq Aziz failed to reach agreement over the Gulf crisis. |
| **13 Jan 1991** | United Nations General Secretary Pérez de Cuéllar failed to make progress towards peace in Baghdad. |
| **16 Jan 1991** | A US-led international force launched air and missile attacks (in Operation 'Desert Storm') on Iraq and Iraqi occupied Kuwait, within 17 hours of the United Nations' deadline for Iraqi withdrawal. |
| **17 Jan 1991** | More than 1,000 Allied air sorties took place in the first 14 hours of battle. The US launched 100 Tomahawk cruise missiles from ships in the Persian Gulf. Iraq responded by firing eight Scud missiles into Israel, and one into Saudi Arabia. More than 100,000 German antiwar protesters marched through Germany. |
| **19 Jan 1991** | USA sent Patriot antimissile missiles to Israel after another Scud attack. Several thousand US antiwar protesters marched through Washington DC and San Francisco. |
| **24 Jan 1991** | More than 15,000 Allied air sorties flown, with 23 aircraft lost. |
| **25 Jan 1991** | Iraq deliberately created an oil spill in the Persian Gulf which grew to be among the largest, most ecologically destructive on record. |
| **29 January 1991** | Iraq began its first major ground offensive into Saudi Arabia. |
| **2 Feb 1991** | An antiwar protest of 40,000 people was held in London. |
| **18 Feb 1991** | Soviet President Gorbachev met Iraqi Foreign Minister Tariq Aziz and presented a Soviet peace proposal. |
| **19 Feb 1991** | An Iranian newspaper reported Iraqi war casualties at more than 20,000 dead, and 60,000 wounded. |
| **21 Feb 1991** | The USSR announced that Iraq agreed to a proposal for withdrawal from Kuwait. |
| **22 Feb 1991** | In the wake of the Soviet-Iraqi peace initiative, President Bush set a noon 23 Feb deadline for Iraq to commence a large-scale withdrawal from Kuwait, or face a ground assault from the Allied forces. |
| **23 Feb 1991** | The deadline was not met, and the Allied ground offensive on Iraq began. |
| **24 Feb 1991** | Large numbers of Iraqi soldiers surrendered. |
| **25 Feb 1991** | Baghdad announced orders for Iraqi soldiers to withdraw from Kuwait. |
| **26 Feb 1991** | Kuwaiti resistance leaders claimed control over Kuwait City. Approximately 600 Kuwaiti oil wells were reported ablaze. |
| **27 Feb 1991** | US Army VII Corps engaged the Iraqi Republican Guard in a major tank battle. President Bush announced at 9.00 pm that Kuwait was liberated, and that the Allies would cease fire. |
| **28 Feb 1991** | Iraq announced a cease-fire. Total allied combat fatalities were 141. Estimates of Iraqi troops and civilians killed and wounded ranged up to 100,000. |
| **2 March 1991** | The United Nations Security Council set out the terms for a formal end to hostilities. |
| **4 March 1991** | Kuwait's crown prince and premier Sheik Saad al- Abdallah Al Sabah returned to his newly liberated country. |
| **5 March 1991** | Iraq freed the last of 45 Allied prisoners of war. |
| **7–8 March 1991** | Iraq freed about 1,200 Kuwaiti prisoners of war, the first of some 2,000. |
| **6 April 1991** | The Iraqi government accepted the cease-fire terms of the United Nations, bringing a formal end to the Gulf War. The USA spent $61.1 billion fighting the Gulf War, including $43.1 billion contributed by the Allies. |

17 had deployed these weapons: Afghanistan, Argentina, Brazil, Cuba, Egypt, India, Iran, Iraq, Israel, North Korea, South Korea, Libya, Pakistan, Saudi Arabia, South Africa, Syria, and Taiwan. Non-nuclear short-range missiles were used during the Iran–Iraq War 1980–88 against Iraqi cities.

A **cruise missile** is in effect a pilotless, computer-guided aircraft. They can be sealaunched from submarines or surface ships, or launched from the air or the ground. In the Falklands conflict 1982, small, conventionally armed sea-skimming missiles were used (the French Exocet) against British ships by the Argentine forces, and similar small missiles have been used against aircraft and ships elsewhere.

Battlefield missiles used in the 1991 Gulf War include anti-tank missiles and short-range attack missiles. NATO announced in 1990 that it was phasing out ground-launched nuclear battlefield missiles, and these are being replaced by types of tactical air-to-surface missile (TASM), also with nuclear warheads.

**mortar** method of projecting a bomb via a high trajectory at a target up to 6–7 km/3–4 mi away. A mortar bomb is stabilized in flight by means of tail fins. The high trajectory results in a high angle of attack and makes mortar more suitable than artillery for use in built-up areas or mountains; mortars are not, however, as accurate. Artillery also differs in firing a projectile through a rifled barrel, thus creating greater muzzle velocity.

**napalm** fuel used in flamethrowers and incendiary bombs. Produced from jellied petrol, it is a mixture of *na*phthenic and *palm*itic acids. Napalm causes extensive burns because it sticks to the skin even when aflame. It was widely used by the US Army during the Vietnam War.

**Patriot** a ground-to-air medium-range missile system used in the air defence role. It has high-altitude coverage, electronic jamming capability, and excellent mobility. It was tested in battle against SCUD missiles fired by the Iraqis in the 1991 Gulf War.

**periscope** optical instrument designed for observation from a concealed position such as from a submerged submarine. In its basic form it consists of a tube with parallel mirrors at each end, inclined at 45° to its axis. The periscope attained prominence in naval and military operations of World War I.

## THE WORLD'S LEADING TANKS

| | Country of manufacture |
|---|---|
| M1 Al Abrams | USA |
| Challenger 2 | UK |
| Leopard 2 | Germany |
| Challenger 1 | UK |
| Le Clerc | France |
| T-80 | USSR |
| T-72 | USSR |
| Merkava | Israel |
| Vickers Main Battle Tank | UK |
| AMX 30 | France |

**remotely piloted vehicle** (RPV) crewless miniaircraft used for military surveillance and to select targets in battle. RPVs barely show up on radar, so they can fly over a battlefield without being shot down, and they are equipped to transmit TV images to an operator on the ground.

RPVs were used by Israeli forces in 1982 in Lebanon and by the Allies in the 1991 Gulf War. The US system is called Aquila and the British system Phoenix.

**rifle** firearm that has spiral grooves (rifling) in its barrel. When a bullet is fired, the rifling makes it spin, thereby improving accuracy. Rifles were first introduced in the late 18th century.

**Scud** surface-to-surface missile designed and produced in the USSR, which can be armed with a nuclear, chemical, or conventional warhead. The **Scud-B**, deployed on a mobile launcher, was the version most commonly used by the Iraqi army in the Gulf War 1991. It is a relatively inaccurate weapon.

**Semtex** plastic explosive, manufactured in Czechoslovakia. It is safe to handle (it can only be ignited by a detonator), and difficult to trace, since it has no smell. It has been used by extremist groups in the Middle East and by the IRA in Northern Ireland.

0.5 kg of Semtex is thought to have been the cause of an explosion that destroyed a Pan-American Boeing 747 in flight over Lockerbie, Scotland, in Dec 1988, killing 270 people.

**small arms** one of the two main divisions of firearms, guns that can be carried by hand. The first small arms were portable handguns in use in the late 14th century, supported on the ground and ignited by hand. Today's

## THE WORLD'S TOP FIGHTING AIRCRAFT

| | Main Role | Country of Manufacture |
|---|---|---|
| F-117A Stealth Bomber | bomber | USA |
| F-16 | fighter/reconnaissance | USA |
| Tornado GR1 | strike | UK/Germany/Italy |
| F-111 | bomber | USA |
| F-15 | fighter/attack | USA |
| A-10 Thunderbolt | close support | USA |
| Harrier | close support/fighter | UK/USA |
| Jaguar | support/strike | UK |
| F-14 Tomcat | interceptor/fighter | USA |
| Mig-29 Fulcrum | fighter/attack | USSR |

small arms range from breech-loading single shot rifles and shotguns to sophisticated automatic and semiautomatic weapons. In 1980, there were 11,522 deaths in the USA caused by hand-held guns; in the UK, there were 8.

**smart weapons** programmable missiles which can be guided to their target by either laser technology, TV homing technology, or TERCOM (terrain contour matching). A smart bomb or missile relies on its pinpoint accuracy to destroy a target rather than the size of its warhead. Examples include: the cruise missile (Tomahawk) , laser-guided artillery shells (Copperhead), laser-guided bombs and short-range TV guided missiles such as SLAM. Smart weapons were first used on the battlefield in the Gulf War, but only 3% of all the bombs dropped or missiles fired were 'smart'. Of that 3%, it is estimated that 50–70% of those fired hit their targets, which is a high accuracy rate.

**stealth technology** methods used to make an aircraft as invisible as possible, primarily to radar detection but also to detection by visual means and heat sensors. This is achieved by a combination of aircraft-design elements: smoothing off all radar-reflecting sharp edges; covering the aircraft with radar-absorbent materials; fitting engine coverings that hide the exhaust and heat signatures of the aircraft; and other, secret technologies.

The US F-117A stealth fighter-bomber was used successfully during the 1991 Gulf War to attack targets in Baghdad competely undetected. The B-2 bomber, a larger, projected stealth aircraft, may be too expensive to put into production.

**TASM** abbreviation for *tactical air-to-surface missile*, a missile with a range of under 500 km/300 mi and a nuclear warhead. TASMs are being developed independently by the USA and France to replace the surface-to-surface missiles being phased out by NATO from 1990.

**torpedo** self-propelled underwater missile, invented 1866 by British engineer Robert Whitehead. Modern torpedoes are homing missiles; some resemble mines in that they lie on the seabed until activated by the acoustic signal of a passing ship. A television camera enables them to be remotely controlled, and in the final stage of attack they lock on to the radar or sonar signals of the target ship.

**U-2** a US military reconnaissance aeroplane, used in secret flights over the USSR from 1956 to photograph military installations. In 1960 a U-2 was shot down over the USSR and the pilot, Gary Powers, was captured and imprisoned. He was exchanged for a US-held Soviet agent two years later.

**U-boat** German submarine. The title was used in both world wars.

**vertical takeoff and landing craft** (VTOL) aircraft that can take off and land vertically. Helicopters, airships, and balloons can do this, as can a few fixed-wing aeroplanes.

---

### Patriotism

*If there were another war, would you be willing to fight for your country?*

| | |
|---|---|
| Yes | 51 |
| Depends on circumstances | 14 |
| No | 32 |
| Don't know | 3 |

*Would you say you would support this country even if it did something you strongly disagree with?*

| | |
|---|---|
| Yes, would support | 40 |
| No, would not support | 47 |
| Don't know | 13 |

*Do you think Britons have more or less pride in our country than they did, say, five years ago?*

| | |
|---|---|
| More | 11 |
| Less | 62 |
| Same | 24 |
| Don't know | 3 |

# ECONOMICS AND BUSINESS

# TERMS

**accountancy** financial management of businesses and other organizations, from balance sheets to policy decisions.

**added value** or **value added** the sales revenue from selling a firm's products less the cost of the materials or purchases used in those products. It is an increasingly used indicator of relative efficiency within and between firms, although in the latter case open to distortion where mark-up varies between standard and premium-priced segments of a market.

**alpha share** a share in any of the companies most commonly traded—that is, the larger companies.

**amortization** the ending of a debt by paying it off gradually, over a period of time. The term is used to describe either the paying off of a cash debt or the accounting procedure by which the value of an asset is progressively reduced (depreciated) over a number of years.

**annual general meeting** (AGM) yearly meeting of the shareholders of a company or the members of an organization, at which business including consideration of the annual report and accounts, the election of officers, and the appointment of auditors is normally carried out. UK company law requires an AGM to be called by the board of directors.

**annual percentage rate** (APR) the charge (including interest) for granting consumer credit, expressed as an equivalent once-a-year percentage figure of the amount of the credit granted. In the UK, lenders are legally required to state the APR when advertising loans.

**arbitrageur** a person who buys securities (such as currency or commodities) in one country or market for immediate resale in another market, to take advantage of different prices. Arbitrage became widespread during the 1970s and 1980s with the increasing deregulation of financial markets.

**articles of association** in the UK, the rules governing the relationship between a registered company, its members (shareholders), and its directors. The articles of association are deposited with the registrar of companies. In the USA they are called *by-laws*.

**asset** the land or property of a company or individual, payments due from bills, investments, and anything else owned that can be turned into cash. On a company's balance sheet, total assets must be equal to liabilities (money and services owed).

**asset stripping** sale, or exploitation by other means, of assets of a business often taken over for the purpose. The parts of the business may be potentially more valuable separately than together. Asset stripping is a major force for the more efficient use of assets.

**audit** the official inspection of a company's accounts by a qualified accountant as required each year by law to ensure that the company balance sheet reflects the true state of its affairs.

**balance sheet** a statement of the financial position of a company or individual on a specific date, showing both assets and liabilities.

**bankruptcy** the process by which the property of a person (in legal terms, an individual or corporation) unable to pay debts is taken away under a court order and divided fairly among the person's creditors, after preferential payments such as taxes and wages. Proceedings may be instituted either by the debtor (voluntary bankruptcy) or by any creditor for a substantial sum (involuntary bankruptcy). Until discharged, a bankrupt is severely restricted in financial activities.

**barter** the exchange of goods or services without the use of money.

**base lending rate** the rate of interest to which most bank lending is linked, the actual rate depending on the status of the borrower. A prestigious company might command a rate only 1% above base rate while an individual would be charged several points above.

**bear** a speculator who sells stocks or shares on the stock exchange expecting a fall in the price in order to buy them back at a profit, the opposite of a bull. In a bear market, prices fall, and bears prosper.

**beta share** a share traded less actively on the stock exchange than an alpha share.

**bill of exchange** a form of commercial credit instrument, or IOU, used in international trade. In Britain, a bill of exchange is defined by the Bills of Exchange Act 1882 as an unconditional order in writing addressed by one person to another, signed by the person giving it, requiring the person to whom it is addressed to pay on demand or at a fixed or determinable future time a certain sum in money to or to the order of a specified person, or to the bearer. US practice is governed by the Uniform Negotiable Instruments Law, drafted on the same lines as the British, and accepted by all states by 1927.

**bill of lading** document giving proof of particular goods having been loaded on a ship. The person to whom the goods are being sent normally needs to show the bill of lading in order to obtain the release of the goods. For air freight, there is an *air waybill*.

**blue chip** a stock that is considered strong and reliable in terms of the dividend yield and capital value. Blue chip companies are favoured by stock market investors more interested in security than risk taking.

**bond** a security issued by a government, local authority, company, bank, or other institution on fixed interest. Usually a long-term security, a bond may be irredeemable, secured or unsecured. Property bonds are non-fixed securities with the yield fixed to property investment. See also Eurobond.

**brand leader** branded product that has the largest share of the market for all products of that type.

**broker** intermediary who arranges the sale of

BIG US BANKRUPTCIES, 1991 PRICES - LIABILITIES $BN

| | Date | Actual | 1991 prices |
|---|---|---|---|
| Texaco | 1987 | 21.6 | 25.8 |
| Penn Central | 1970 | 3.3 | 11.4 |
| Campeau | 1990 | 9.9 | 10.5 |
| Lomas Financial | 1989 | 6.1 | 6.6 |
| Continential Air | 1990 | 6.2 | 6.2 |
| LTV | 1986 | 4.7 | 5.8 |
| Southmark | 1989 | 4.0 | 4.3 |
| Eastern Air Lines | 1989 | 3.2 | 3.5 |
| Southland | 1990 | 3.4 | 3.4 |
| Drexel Burnham Lambert | 1990 | 3.0 | 3.2 |
| Wickes | 1982 | 2.0 | 2.8 |
| Itel | 1981 | 1.7 | 2.6 |
| W T Grant | 1975 | 1.0 | 2.5 |
| Pan Am | 1991 | 2.4 | 2.4 |
| Hills Department Stores | 1991 | 2.3 | 2.3 |
| Interco | 1991 | 2.2 | 2.2 |
| Global Marine | 1986 | 1.8 | 2.2 |
| Baldwin-United | 1983 | 1.6 | 2.1 |
| Laventhal & Horwath | 1990 | 2.0 | 2.0 |
| PS New Hampshire | 1988 | 1.7 | 2.0 |

Note: excludes banks
*Source: The Economist*

financial products (shares, insurance, mortgages, and so on) to the public for a commission or brokerage fee.

**bull** a speculator who buys stocks or shares on the stock exchange expecting a rise in the price in order to sell them later at a profit, the opposite of a bear. In a bull market, prices rise and bulls profit.

**Business Expansion Scheme** UK government scheme, launched 1981, offering tax relief to encourage private investment in high-risk ventures, later extended to forms of investment in property.

**call** a demand for money, usually instalments of part-paid securities.

**capital expenditure** spending on fixed assets such as plant and equipment, trade investments, or the purchase of other businesses.

**capital flight** transfer of funds from a particular national economy or out of a particular currency in anticipation of less attractive investment conditions.

**cartel** (German *Kartell*, a group) firms that remain independent but which enter into agreement to set mutually acceptable prices for their products. A cartel may restrict output or raise prices in order to prevent entrants to the market and increase member profits.

**cash flow** the input of cash required to cover all expenses of a business, whether revenue or capital. Alternatively, the actual or prospective balance between the various outgoing and incoming movements, which is designated negative or positive according to whether outflow or inflow is greater.

**commodity** something produced for sale. Commodities may be consumer goods, such as radios, or producer goods, such as copper bars. *Commodity markets* deal in raw or semi-raw materials that are amenable to grading and that can be stored for considerable periods

without deterioration.

**company** a number of people grouped together as a business enterprise. Types of company include public limited companies, partnerships, joint ventures, sole proprietorships, and branches of foreign companies. Most companies are private limited companies and, unlike public companies, cannot offer their shares to the general public.

**Confederation of British Industry** (CBI) UK organization of employers, established 1965, combining the former Federation of British Industries (founded 1916), British Employers' Confederation, and National Association of British Manufacturers.

**convertible loan stock** stock or bond (paying a fixed interest) that may be converted into a stated number of shares at a specific date.

**corporate strategy** the way an organization intends to meet its objectives. This may be set out in a document of its principles, its situation, and the environment in which it expects to operate.

**cost-benefit analysis** technique used in making business decisions that tries to take into account factors that are difficult to quantify and therefore might be overlooked.

**critical path analysis** procedure used in the management of complex business projects, which indicates the project's minimum duration and those subprojects critical to reduction in execution time, by identifying the duration and the relationship between them.

**cumulative preference share** preference share whose entitlement to dividend is carried forward to a subsequent year whenever a dividend is not paid.

**current asset** or *circulating* or *floating asset* any asset of a business that could be turned into cash in a limited period of time, generally less than a year. Current assets include stocks,

THE *FINANCIAL TIMES* EUROPEAN TOP 20
COMPANIES, 1989 $BN

| | turnover | pre-tax profits |
|---|---|---|
| Royal Dutch/Shell | 89.3 | 12.7 |
| IRI | 54.5 | n.a. |
| British Petroleum | 50.7 | 4.3 |
| Daimler-Benz | 45.4 | 5.7 |
| Fiat | 42.1 | 4.3 |
| Volkswagen | 38.8 | 1.8 |
| Unilever | 36.8 | 3.1 |
| Siemens | 36.3* | 1.7 |
| Nestlé | 33.7 | 2.7 |
| Deutsche Bundespost | 33.5 | n.a. |
| BAT Industries | 31.0 | 3.5 |
| Renault | 30.8 | n.a. |
| Philips | 30.2 | 0.7 |
| ENI | 30.1 | n.a. |
| Veba | 29.2 | 1.6 |
| BASF | 28.3 | 2.6 |
| Hoechst | 27.3 | 2.5 |
| Peugeot | 27.0 | 2.9 |
| Elf Aquitaine | 26.5 | 2.1 |
| Electricité de France | 25.8 | n.a. |

\* Year ending 30th Sept 1989
*Source: Financial Times*

accounts receivable or billings, short-term investments, and cash.

**current liability** any debt of a business that falls due within one year. Current liabilities include creditors (including employees), bank overdrafts, and interest.

**current ratio** in a company, the ratio of current assets to current liabilities. It is a general indication of the adequacy of an organization's working capital and its ability to meet day-to-day calls upon it.

**debenture** loan raised by a company using its assets as security for repayment.

**decision theory** mathematical technique for analysing decision-making problems, especially over unpredictable factors, seeking to minimize error; it includes game theory, risk analysis, and utility theory.

**deferred share** a share that typically warrants a dividend only after a specified dividend has been paid on the ordinary shares; it may, however, be entitled to a dividend on all the profits after that point.

**depreciation** a fall in value of an asset (such as factory machinery) resulting from age, wear and tear, or other circumstances. It is a factor in assessing company profit.

**diversification** a corporate strategy of entering distinctly new products or markets as opposed to simply adding to an existing product range. A company may diversify in order to spread its risks or because its original area of operation is becoming less profitable.

**dividend** the amount of money that company directors decide should be taken out of profits for distribution to shareholders. It is usually declared as a percentage or fixed amount per share. Most companies pay dividends once or twice a year.

**economies of scale** increase in production capacity at a financial cost that is more than compensated for by the greater volume of output. In a dress factory, for example, a reduction in the unit cost may be possible only by the addition of new machinery, which would be worthwhile only if the volume of dresses produced were increased and there were sufficient market demand for them.

**electronic funds transfer at point of sale** (EFTPOS) the transfer of funds from one bank account to another by electronic means. For example, a bank customer inserts a plastic card in a point-of-sale computer terminal in a supermarket, and telephone lines are used to make an automatic debit from the customer's bank account to settle the bill.

**end-use certificate** in shipping, a document intended to assure authorities of the eventual application (generally also the final customer and destination) of a particular actual or intended shipment. End-use certificates are needed in cases where there are political controls on exports.

**equity** a company's assets, less its liabilities, which are the property of the owner or shareholders. Popularly, equities are stocks and shares which, unlike debentures and preference shares, do not pay interest at fixed rates but pay dividends based on the company's performance. The value of equities tends to rise over the long term, but in the short term they are a risk investment because of fluctuating values.

**Eurobond** a bond underwritten by an international syndicate and sold in countries other than the country of the currency in which the issue is denominated. They provide longer-term financing than is possible with loans in Eurodollars.

**executive director** company director who is also an employee of the company.

**experience curve** the observed effect of improved performance of individuals and organizations as experience of a repeated task increases.

**factoring** lending money to a company on the security of their accounts receivable; this is often done of the basis of collecting those accounts. Factoring also means acting as a commission agent for the sale of goods.

**Financial Times indices** scales for measuring aspects of the stock market, published by the *Financial Times* of London. They are: FT ordinary, FT- SE 100, FT-Actuaries All Share, FT Government Securities, FT Fixed Interest, FT-SE Eurotrack 200, FT-Actuaries World Index and Indices of National and Regional Markets.

**franchise** the right given by a manufacturer to a distributor to market the manufacturer's product.

**future** a contract to buy or sell a specific quantity of a particular commodity or currency (or even a purely notional sum, such as the value of a particular stock index) at a particular date in the future. There is usually no physical exchange between buyer and seller. It is only the

## THE INTERNATIONAL STOCK EXCHANGE

The purpose of the International Stock Exchange of the United Kingdom and Republic of Ireland Ltd (ISE) is to be a marketplace for the trading of securities. Its headquarters are in London and there are other centres in Belfast, Birmingham, Dublin, Glasgow, and Manchester. It is one of the largest in the world in terms of the number of securities listed (over 7,000) and their variety. There are some 5,100 individual members and about 400 member firms. These operate in a central marketplace, trading in UK and overseas company shares (or equities) and UK government stocks (also known as gilts), as well as other investment vehicles such as fixed-interest loans, and traded options on equities and indices.

The Stock Exchange's market function is vital in helping companies to raise new money. This involves not only the facility of providing for new flotations but also the means of reselling shares, since, without this, investors would be less willing to commit their resources in the first place. Both are vital for ensuring adequate funds for expansion of companies and, through them, expansion of the economy.

For a company entering the market for the first time, two Stock Exchange markets are available: the Official List and the Unlisted Securities Market (USM). The former exists for well-established companies, which must operate within strict guidelines with regard, for example, to their reporting of financial information. The latter has less rigorous entry requirements and was established in 1980 to trade in the shares of newer and generally smaller companies.

The year 1986 saw the most significant changes in the 200-year history of the ISE. In March of that year banks, insurance companies, and overseas securities houses were allowed to become members of the Exchange and to buy existing member firms. On 27 Oct, three major reforms, popularly known as the Big Bang, took place. These were:

—the abolition of fixed scales of minimum commission charged by dealers; commissions then became negotiable

—the abolition of the distinction between brokers and jobbers. Dealers are now permitted to trade in securities on their own account as principals or 'market makers', as well as on behalf of clients as their agents

—the implementation of a computer-screen-based dealing system called Stock Exchange Automatic Quotations (SEAQ), which displays quotes from competing market makers as well as trade reports on UK and international securities.

Following the introduction of SEAQ, the buying and selling of securities takes place in the firms' own dealing rooms. The traditional face-to-face dealing on the floor of the Stock Exchange ceased.

In 1990 the Stock Exchange rules were changed in conformity with European Community (EC) directives on listing information. To ensure that shares in British companies may be quoted on the same basis as those traded in other EC countries, the ISE has reduced the minimum trading record requirement from five years to three, with a minimum of 25% of shares held by the public. At the same time the trading record requirement for the USM was reduced from three to two years with a minimum of 10% of the shares in public hands.

Many of the changes made over the last five years have been aimed at maintaining the leading position that the London-based Stock Exchange holds by comparison with those overseas. With so much mutual influence between the leading exchanges of the USA, Japan, and Europe, and the growing strength of those based elsewhere in the EC, especially Frankfurt, the rewards and challenges associated with maintaining its standing will be considerable.

---

difference between the ground value and the market value that changes hands. The *futures market* trades in financial futures (for example, LIFFE, the London International Financial Futures Exchange).

**gearing, financial** the relationship between fixed-interest debt and shareholders' equity used to finance a company. The additional profit made by borrowing at fixed interest and earning a greater return on those funds than the interest payable accrues to the shareholders. A high proportion of fixed-interest funding, known as 'high gearing', can leave the firm more vulnerable in poorer trading conditions.

**GmbH** abbreviation for *Gesellschaft mit beschrankter Haftung* (German 'limited liability company').

**golden share** share, often with overriding voting powers, issued by governments to control privatized companies.

**greenmail** payment made by a target company to

avoid a bid; for example, buying back a stake in its own shares (where permitted) from a potential predator at an inflated price.

**grey market** dealing in shares using methods that are legal but perhaps officially frowned upon—for example, before issue and flotation.

**gross** of a particular figure or price, calculated before the deduction of specific items such as commission, discounts, interest, and taxes. The opposite is net.

**inflation accounting** a method of accounting that allows for the changing purchasing power of money due to inflation.

**insider trading** or *insider dealing* illegal use of privileged information in dealing on the stock exchanges, for example when a company takeover bid is imminent. Insider trading is in theory detected by the *Securities and Exchange Commission* (SEC) in the USA, and by the *Securities and Investment Board* (SIB) in the UK. Neither agency, however, has any legal powers other than public disclosure and do not bring prosecution themselves.

**insolvent** unable to pay debts.

**investment trust** public company that makes investments in other companies on behalf of its shareholders. It may issue shares to raise capital and issue fixed-interest securities.

**issued capital** the nominal value of those shares in a company that have been allotted. The issued capital is equivalent to the amount invested, provided the issue has not been at a premium price.

**joint venture** an undertaking in which an individual or legal entity of one company or country forms a company with those of another, with risks being shared.

**junk bond** derogatory term for a security, officially rated as 'below investment grade'. It is issued in order to raise capital quickly, typically to finance a takeover to be paid for by the sale of assets once the company is acquired. Junk bonds have a high yield, but are a high-risk investment.

**just-in-time** (JIT) production management practice requiring that incoming supplies arrive at the time when they are needed by the customer, most typically in a manufacturer's assembly operations. JIT requires considerable cooperation between supplier and customer, but can reduce expenses and improve efficiency.

**key-results analysis** management procedure involving the identification of performance components critical to a particular process or event, the necessary level of performance required from them, and the methods of monitoring to be used.

**learning curve** graphical representation of the improvement in performance of a person executing a new task.

**leveraged buyout** the purchase of a controlling proportion of the shares of a company by its own management, financed almost exclusively by borrowing. It is so called because the ratio of a company's long-term debt to its equity (capital assets) is known as its 'leverage'.

**lien** in law, the right to retain goods owned by another until the owner has satisfied a claim against him by the person in possession of the goods. For example, the goods may have been provided as security for a debt.

**limited company** or **joint stock company** the usual type of company formation in the UK. It has its origins in the trading companies that began to proliferate in the 16th century. The capital of a limited company is divided into small units, and profits are distributed according to shareholding.

**liquidation** the termination of a company by converting all its assets into money to pay off its liabilities.

**management buyout** purchase of control of a company by its management, generally with debt funding, making it a leveraged buyout.

**market capitalization** the market value of a company, based on the market price of all its issued securities—a price that would be unlikely to

apply, however, if a bid were actually made for control of them.

**market maker** in the UK, a stockbroker entitled to deal directly on the stock exchange. The role was created in Oct 1986, when the jobber (intermediary) disappeared from the stock exchange. Market makers trade in the dual capacity of broker and jobber.

**market segment** portion of a market characterized by such similarity of customers, their requirements and/or buying behaviour that those who sell the products or services bought by these customers can aim their marketing effort specifically at this segment.

**memorandum of association** document that defines the purpose of a company and the amount and different classes of share capital. In the UK, the memorandum is drawn up on formation of the company, together with the articles of association.

**merger** the linking of two or more companies, either by creating a new organization by consolidating the original companies or by absorption by one of the others. Unlike a takeover, which is not always a voluntary fusion of the parties, a merger is the result of an agreement.

**minority interest** an item in the consolidated accounts of a holding company that represents the value of any shares in its subsidiaries that it does not itself own.

**multinational corporation** company or enterprise operating in several countries, usually defined as one that has 25% or more of its output capacity located outside its country of origin.

**net** of a particular figure or price, calculated after the deduction of specific items such as commission, discounts, interest, and taxes. The opposite is gross.

**net assets** either the total assets of a company less its current liabilities (that is, the capital employed) or the total assets less current liabilities, debt capital, long-term loans and provisions, which would form the amount available to ordinary shareholders if the company were to be wound up.

**net worth** the total assets of a company less its total liabilities, equivalent to the interest of the ordinary shareholders in the company.

**nonexecutive director** member of the board of a company who is not an employee of the company. A nonexecutive director can provide a wider perspective to the outlook of the board, but may be limited by not having access to informal sources of information.

**nonvoting share** ordinary share in a company that is without entitlement to vote at shareholders' meetings. Shares are often distinguished as A-shares (voting) and B-shares (nonvoting).

**option** a contract giving the owner the right (as opposed to the obligation, as with futures contracts) to buy or sell a specific quantity of a particular commodity or currency at a future date and at an agreed price, in return for a premium. The buyer or seller can decide not to exercise the option if it would prove disadvantageous.

## BIG US MERGERS, 1991 PRICES - VALUE $BN

| Acquirer | Target | Date | Actual | 1991 prices |
|---|---|---|---|---|
| KKR | RJR Nabisco | 1989 | 24.7 | 27.0 |
| US Steel | 11 firms | 1901 | 1.4 | 22.1 |
| Chevron | Gulf | 1984 | 13.3 | 17.3 |
| Philip Morris | Kraft | 1988 | 12.6 | 14.1 |
| Bristol-Myers | Squibb | 1989 | 12.5 | 13.4 |
| Time Warner | Warner Communications | 1990 | 12.6 | 13.4 |
| Texaco | Getty Oil | 1984 | 10.1 | 13.3 |
| Du Pont | Conoco | 1981 | 6.9 | 10.0 |
| British Petroleum | Standard Oil | 1987 | 7.6 | 9.0 |
| Beecham Group | SmithKline Beckman | 1989 | 8.3 | 9.0 |
| US Steel | Marathon Oil | 1982 | 6.2 | 8.8 |
| KKR | Beatrice | 1986 | 6.3 | 7.8 |
| Dow Chemical | Marion Laboratories | 1989 | 7.1 | 7.6 |
| General Electric | RCA | 1986 | 6.1 | 7.6 |
| American Tobacco | 7 firms | 1903 | 0.5 | 7.5 |
| Campeau | Federated Department Stores | 1988 | 6.5 | 7.4 |
| Mobil | Superior Oil | 1984 | 5.7 | 7.4 |
| Royal Dutch/Shell | Shell Oil | 1985 | 5.7 | 7.1 |
| Philip Morris | General Foods | 1985 | 5.6 | 7.0 |
| Atlantic-Richfield | Sinclair Oil | 1969 | 1.9 | 6.8 |

Source: The Economist

**overhead** fixed costs in a business that do not vary in the short term. These might include property rental, heating and lighting, insurance, and administration costs.

**poison pill** a tactic to avoid hostile takeover by making the target unattractive. For example, a company may give a certain class of shareholders the right to have their shares redeemed at a very good price in the event of the company being taken over, thus involving the potential predator in considerable extra cost.

**preference share** a share in a company with rights in various ways superior to those of ordinary shares; for example, priority to a fixed dividend and priority over ordinary shares in the event of the company being wound up.

**premium price** difference between the current market price of a security and its issue price (where the current price is the greater).

**price/earnings ratio** or *p/e ratio* a company's share price divided by its earnings per share after tax.

**prime rate** the rate charged by commercial banks to their best customers. It is the base rate on which other rates are calculated according to the risk involved. Only borrowers who have the highest credit rating qualify for the prime rate.

**profit-sharing scheme** in a company, arrangements for some or all the employees to receive cash or shares on a basis generally related to the performance of the company.

**put option** the right to sell a specific number of shares at a specific price on or before a specific date.

**rate of return** the income from an investment expressed as a percentage of the cost of that investment.

**receiver** a person appointed by a court to collect and manage the assets of an individual, company, or partnership in serious financial difficulties. In the case of bankruptcy, the assets may be sold and distributed by a receiver to creditors.

**redeemable preference share** in finance, a share in a company that the company has a right to buy back at a specific price.

**reverse takeover** a takeover where a company sells itself to another to avoid being itself the target of a purchase by an unwelcome predator.

**rights issue** new shares offered to existing shareholders to raise new capital. Shareholders receive a discount on the market price while the company benefits from not having the costs of a re-launch of the new issue.

**risk capital** or *venture capital* finance provided by venture capital companies, individuals, and merchant banks for medium or long-term business ventures that are not their own and in which there is a strong element of risk.

**scrip issue** or *subscription certificate* a free issue of new shares to existing shareholders based on their holdings. It does not involve the raising of new capital as in a rights issue.

**Securities and Exchange Commission** (SEC) official US agency created in 1934 to ensure full disclosure to the investing public and protection against malpractice in the securities (stocks and shares) and financial markets (such as insider trading).

**Securities and Investment Board** official UK body with the overall responsibility for policing financial dealings in the City of London. Introduced in 1987 following the deregulation process of the so-called Big Bang, it acts as an umbrella organization to such self-regulating bodies as the Stock Exchange.

**sequestrator** person or organization appointed by a court of law to control the assets of another person or organization within the jurisdiction of that court.

**stag** a subscriber for new share issues who expects to profit from a premium price on early trading in the shares.

**Standard and Poor's Stock Price Index** or *S & P 500* index of the US stock market covering 500 stocks broken down into sectors.

**stock exchange** institution for the buying and selling of stocks and shares (securities).

**stocks and shares** investment holdings (securities) in private or public undertakings. Although distinctions have become blurred, in the UK stock usually means fixed-interest securities (such as those issued by central and local government), while shares represent a stake in the ownership of a trading company which, if they are ordinary shares, yield to the owner dividends reflecting the success of the company. In the USA the term stock generally signifies what in the UK are ordinary shares.

**SWOT analysis** breakdown of an organization into its *s*trengths and *w*eaknesses (the internal analysis), with an assessment of the *o*pportunities open to it and the *t*hreats confronting it. SWOT analysis is commonly used in marketing and strategic studies.

**takeover** the acquisition by one company of a sufficient number of shares in another company to have effective control of that company – usually 51%, although a controlling stake may be as little as 30%. Takeovers may be agreed or contested; methods employed include the dawn raid, and methods of avoiding an unwelcome takeover include reverse takeover, poison pills or inviting a white knight to make a takeover bid.

**TESSA** (acronym for *ta*x-*e*xempt *s*pecial *s*avings *a*ccount) UK scheme, introduced 1991, to encourage longer-term savings by making interest tax-free on deposits of up to 9,000 over five years.

**unit trust** a company that invests its clients' funds in other companies. The units it issues represent holdings of shares, which means unit shareholders have a wider spread of capital than if they bought shares on the stock market.

**venture capital** or *risk capital* money put up by investors such as merchant banks to fund a new company or expansion of an established company. The organization providing the money receives a share of the company's equity and seeks to make a profit by rapid growth in the value of its stake, as a result of expansion by the start-up company or 'venture'.

**white knight** a company invited by the target of a takeover bid to make a rival bid. The company invited to bid is usually one that is already on good terms with the target company.

**yield** the annual percentage return from an investment; on ordinary shares it is the dividend expressed as a percentage.

**zero-based budgeting** management technique requiring that no resources for a new period of a programme are approved and/or released unless their justification can be demonstrated against alternative options.

# NEWS

### ACQUISITIONS, BIDS, BUYOUTS, AND MERGERS

**Aquascutum and DAKS go east**

Poor prospects due to the recession and a generous cash offer of £65 million secured DAKS for Sankyo Seiko, hitherto its distributor in Japan. The expected injection of additional funds should enable DAKS to be marketed more widely on an international basis. In 1990 another quality London garment business, Aquascutum, had been purchased by Renown, Sankyo's leading competitor in Japan.

**Burmah acquire Foseco**

In Dec 1990 Burmah Castrol won a bitter takeover battle for the speciality metallurgical chemicals and abrasives manufacturer Foseco. The price of £259 million involved Burmah raising its gearing from nil to almost 60%. Orderly disposals are intended, but falling interest rates will assist.

**Closure of the Bank of Commerce and Credit International**

BCCI's closure was ordered by the Bank of England on 5 July 1991 following allegations of fraud and corruption. The ruler and government of the emirate of Abu Dhabi, who control 77% of the bank's shares, launched an initiative to restructure the bank and, on 30 July, pledged over £50 million in order to safeguard 75% of each UK depositor's money (up to a maximum of £5,000).

**Fujitsu in the UK**

Illustrating the widespread Japanese move into Europe and the increasing globalization of their operations, Fujitsu, a major Japanese technology group, in July 1990 purchased 80% of ICL, STC's computer subsidiary, for £743 million. Its European identity is to be maintained with

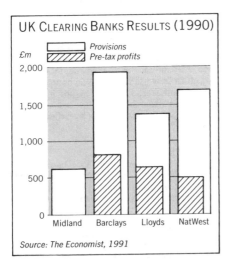

UK CLEARING BANKS RESULTS (1990)

£m — Provisions / Pre-tax profits

2,000

1,500

1,000

500

0

Midland   Barclays   Lloyds   NatWest

Source: The Economist, 1991

## WHO'S BUYING LONDON——JAN 90–MAR 91

| West End | | City | |
|---|---|---|---|
| Source | | Source | |
| UK | 19.5 | Japan | 43.0 |
| Scandinavia | 15.5 | UK | 27.0 |
| Japan | 13.0 | Scandinavia | 10.5 |
| Netherlands | 7.5 | US | 5.0 |
| Middle East | 7.5 | France | 4.0 |
| Other Europe | 7.0 | Other Europe | 3.0 |
| France | 6.0 | Netherlands | 2.5 |
| US | 2.0 | Middle East | 2.0 |
| Other | 22.0 | Other | 3.0 |
| Total ( m) | 1,298 | Total ( m) | 2,106 |

Source: The Banker

the aim of a 25% public flotation within five years. In March 1991 Fujitsu also bought 74.9% of Fulcrum Communications, BT's last manufacturing operation, and has since announced plans for an integrated-circuit plant in Durham.

### Grattans Mail Order bought by Germans
Operating losses of £41 million forced Next to sell Grattans to the leading German mail-order company Otto Versand. The price of £165 million was achieved because of the interest shown by rivals Sears. Next Directory was not part of the deal, suggesting an eventual return by Next to the market segment from which their growth started.

### Matsushita buys MCA
Dec 1990 saw Matsushita Electrical Industries complete the largest takeover so far by a Japanese company in the USA. MCA (Music Corporation of America), a major films, music, and leisure group, was purchased for $6.1 billion.

### Sky TV takes over British Satellite Broadcasting
With over £1.7 billion being invested before cash flow was likely to be positive, BSB losses reported at £7 million a week, and substantial write-offs at Sky by Rupert Murdoch's News International, analysts now say that the risk to shareholders is not so much financial as political in the longer term—the possibility exists that a future government may alter taxation legislation. Otherwise, analysts believe that vast profits are likely before the end of the century.

### Smiths and Boots merge their DIY operations
Fears of saturation in the late 1980s in the £4.5-billion DIY superstore market were aroused after Boots bought Ward White for £900 million with their subsidiary Payless thought to be £400 million of the total. It came as no surprise that W H Smith's Do It All and Payless then merged into a new company called Do It All, although clearly the cost of creating a common branding will be high. Boots has not sold FADS despite offers of over £80 million.

### STC goes to Northern Telecom
In Nov 1990 Northern Telecom of Canada secured acceptance by STC, a UK telecommunications-equipment manufacturer, of its cash offer of £1.9 billion. Nortel already owned 27% of STC and aims to improve its access to British Telecom and other European customers. STC, which sold its ICL subsidiary to Fujitsu in July 1990, recognized its need for association or alliance to address the problems confronting the world's smaller telecommunications manufacturers.

### Volkswagen lands Skoda
After a fierce fight with Renault (in partnership with Volvo), VW succeeded in purchasing 70% of the equity in the Czech car-maker Skoda for 9.5 billion Deutschmarks and went on to launch a major capital investment plan of DM 25 billion to finance developments in China, Germany, Spain, Portugal, and Czechoslovakia. Skoda were advised by British accountants Price Waterhouse. VW are number four worldwide in car manufacturing.

## PROGRESS AND ENTERPRISE

### Airbus in profit
With deliveries in 1990 of $4.6 billion, Airbus Industries, a consortium of Aérospatiale of France, MBB of Germany, British Aerospace, and Casa of Spain, achieved its first operating profit—of $120 million. Deliveries next year are anticipated to approach $7 billion. The low dollar value does not trouble the consortium itself but significantly reduces the return to the partners measured in their national currencies.

### Body Shop
Anita Roddick's natural cosmetics manufacturer, retailer, and franchiser rode the generally depressed conditions in the high street with interim profit to Nov 1990 up to £7.9 million, due largely to a 62% growth overseas, 25% growth through overseas outlets operating throughout the period. The Body Shop then had 360 outlets, mostly franchises, in 37 countries, of which 154 were in the UK.

### British Airways
BA caught the eye in March 1991 with its imaginative draw for 50,000 airline tickets, promoted with £50 million, as a response to the 20% downturn in world airline traffic brought about by the Gulf War. Plans for tie-ups in Europe include a partnership for a low-cost airline in Germany and the revamping of an earlier possible deal with Sabena.

### Canary Wharf
The steel structure of Britain's tallest building (250 m/800 ft high, 60 m/200 ft more than the Nat West tower) and Europe's largest commercial development was completed in Nov 1990. The depressed financial services industry has been slower to move into the completed parts than expected. By spring 1991 occupancy of the first two phases had barely reached 50%. Delays on the Docklands Light Railway have not helped.

## THE RISE AND RISE OF THE BUSINESS SCHOOL

Business schools have boomed in the UK and Europe in the late 1980s and early 1990s. A pecking order of business schools has developed, with the London, Manchester, and Warwick University Business Schools in the UK, and INSEAD (Institut Européen d'Administration des Affaires), Paris, and Lyon in France competing fiercely for top place.

The emphasis of training has changed from highly theoretical studies to skill-based courses, examining principles such as leadership, motivation, team building, and information technology. In the UK, the Management Charter Initiative (MCI) has focused attention on the need to train managers to become more effective in the workplace, and has led to the establishment of business schools with undergraduate, postgraduate, and post-experience programmes in a number of universities and polytechnics.

Throughout Europe, there has been a rapid growth in the provision of Master of Business Administration (MBA) courses, along the lines of those set up earlier in the USA. The MBA is a top-level business qualification course that is becoming increasingly recognized as a requirement for appointment to senior managerial positions. Typically, the course covers all the major business functions, such as marketing, finance, personnel, and production, as well as information technology, economics, law, and behavioural science. Increasingly, these courses take an international focus and some involve time spent in more than one country as part of the programme.

As well as qualification courses such as the MBA, business schools also provide a range of short courses. These may be tailored to meet the needs of particular client organizations or they may be aimed at managers holding particular types of jobs. Some business schools are attempting to link in-company courses to qualification courses by credit-rating them. In the UK, the Credit Accumulation and Transfer Scheme (CATS) enables qualifications to be gained by building up credits from accredited modules. This scheme is being developed on a European-wide basis, but there is a long way to go before a common set of procedures is developed. As yet, the MBA is the only management qualification to gain international acceptability.

Some leading business schools are offering open-learning management courses to reach a wider market. The Open University has been the leader in this field but some other providers—universities such as Warwick and Strathclyde, and polytechnics such as Oxford and Kingston—have also developed successful schemes. Some are available internationally; Oxford Polytechnic's open-learning course has been launched in Hungary, and over 500 Hungarian managers have enrolled on the programme.

Business schools are becoming increasingly popular with students who require a vocationally relevant qualification; it is to be hoped that the entry of more and more suppliers into the market does not reduce standards.

### How Corporations Rank The Top Business Schools

| 1989 Wall Street Journal survey of US schools | 1989 Expression (American Express) survey of schools worldwide |
|---|---|
| 1 Northwestern (Kellogg) | 1 Manchester Bus. School |
| 2 Pennsylvania (Wharton) | 2 INSEAD |
| 3 Harvard | 3 LBS |
| 4 Columbia | 4 Harvard |
| 5 Chicago | 5 Cranfield |
| 6 Michigan (Ann Arbor) | 6 Stanford |
| 7 Indiana | 7 Henley |
| 8 Virginia (Colgate Darden) | 8 Warwick |
| 9 Stanford | 9 Pennsylvania (Wharton) |
| 10 Duke (Fuqua) | 10 Bradford |

*Source: Accountancy Age, June 1991*

**Channel Tunnel breakthrough**
After financial uncertainties prompted by higher estimates to completion, the final tranche of funding was satisfactorily arranged in Feb 1991. The tunnel is on schedule for opening in June 1993. The debates about the route of the fast rail link to London and safety of operations continue.

**Export Credit Guarantee Department (ECGD)**
The UK government's efforts to privatize ECGD, which provides British exporters with insurance against commercial and political risks of default by foreign customers, did not proceed smoothly. British insurance companies gradually withdrew

until by early 1991 only insurers from Italy and the Netherlands remained in the contest. This looked set to put British exporters in the position of competing with foreign firms backed by their own governments' guarantees, while themselves depending on foreign commercial insurance. A rethink looks to be on the cards.

**GEC Alsthom**
The imaginative joint venture between Alcatel Alsthom of France and the British GEC in regard to their activities in power engineering and transportation equipment revealed its longer-term priorities at a press conference in Jan 1991. Despite recent acquisitions in Europe, in

particular control of Fiat's railway equipment subsidiary, it sees its main opportunities around the Pacific rim. The interesting contrast of organizational cultures between the two parents was acknowledged.

## Guinness Peat Aviation
GPA, based in Ireland and the world's largest aircraft-leasing company, reported contracted lease revenues up 66% (US $5 billion to $8.3 billion) in the year to March 1991. Profits were not expected to match, having grown only 9% in the nine months to Dec 1990. The size of their fleet rose by 66 to 306 aircraft in the year.

## Honda in the UK
With an engine plant already operating in Swindon and car assembly there due to commence in late 1992, Honda's plans for the European market are coming to fruition. Swindon plans to produce 100,000 vehicles a year from 1995/96 and 200,000 engines. Output will be shared equally with Rover, in which Honda has a 20% holding. Rover owns 20% of Honda's UK manufacturing subsidiary, controlled by Honda Motors Europe. Honda and Nissan epitomize the excellent future prospects for UK car manufacture; at the same time the threat to indigenous European production— except, perhaps, for components.

## Kobe Steel sets up in the UK
In 1986, Kobe Steel decided to diversify from its traditional involvement in steelmaking and machinery into advanced materials, in particular polymers and composites. As part of the globalization of all its operations and acknowledging the originality of Western scientists, Kobe has set up a research centre at the Surrey Research Park in addition to facilities it has in Japan and the USA.

## Nissan in the UK
In Dec 1990, Nissan Corporation announced its decision to separate from its hitherto sole UK distributor of 21 years' standing, Nissan UK, a privately owned company controlled by Octav Botnar. Despite bitter recriminations and threats of legal action, Nissan aims within one year to set up a dealer network alternative to the 386-strong coverage controlled by Botnar's company.

## Nokia grows on the European stage
Nokia, Finland's second largest quoted corporation, confirmed its position as one of the most dynamic newcomers on the European scene with acquisition in Feb 1991 of Technophone of the UK, lifting it into being the second largest cellular telephone manufacturer in the world after the Japanese NEC. Acquisitions through the 1980s had turned Nokia into the third largest TV manufacturer in Europe after Thomson and Philips.

## Racal
Imaginative restructuring continues. The telecommunications subsidiary notable for its successful Vodaphone cellular radio operation had been partly demerged in 1988. In Nov 1990, Racal announced the intention to complete that process, floating off its Racal Chubb security subsidiary and organizing a management buyout for the balance—in which there is a high proportion of military activities. Precautions against a hostile bid were assumed to be the motive.

## Tesco
The highly successful rights issue in Jan 1991, yielding £572 million, and a rise in profits excluding property of 28% to £417 million were two of the factors leading to Ian McLaurin becoming Britain's highest-paid director. He is now paid £1.48 million a year.

# TROUBLES

## Allied Lyons
The loss of £150 million on currency dealings wiped £300 million off the market capitalization and led to the departures of the chair and chief executive and of the finance director. A takeover bid is possible for a company still to announce a strategy in response to the 1989 Monopolies and Mergers Commission Report.

## Bank of New England
By providing $750 million working capital and guaranteeing deposits, the US Federal Deposit Insurance Corporation rescued the 15th largest bank in the USA while a buyer is sought. Depending on the price, the BNE could be attractive to a Midwest or West Coast bank seeking to establish itself on the East Coast. Concern remains that BNE's difficulties may indicate wider problems in the US banking industry.

## Bond Corporation
Efforts were made to keep the Bond Corporation afloat after it announced record losses for Australia of A$2.5 billion (US $1.92 billion) for the year to July 1990. Alan Bond himself resigned in Sept and a scheme of a debt for equity swap likely to yield investors perhaps 25 cents in the dollar went on month after month. Meanwhile Alan Bond and the corporation and various of its subsidiaries were receiving critical attention from the Australian courts and the Australian stock exchange.

## British and Commonwealth
The financial-services group failed in June 1990, four months after the collapse of its computer-leasing subsidiary Atlantic Computers. Subsidiaries for which sell-off, break-up, or flotation were being considered include EXCO International, the world's largest money broker; Oppenheimer Management Corporation, US mutual-fund managers; B & C Merchant Bank; Provincial Bank; Stock Beech, a Bristol-based stock broker; Hampton and Sons, estate agents.

## CASH RICH UK COMPANIES

| | £m |
|---|---|
| Glaxo | 1,600 |
| GEC | 974* |
| Hanson | 550 |
| British Steel | 453 |
| Reuters | 235 |
| Rolls-Royce | 200 |
| Smiths Ind | 115 |
| Charter Consol | 110 |
| Carlton Comm | 100 |

### Coloroll

A creation of the 1980s, Coloroll expanded fast through debt-funded acquisitions largely into carpets, ceramics, and wall coverings. Vulnerable on account of high gearing, it went into receivership in June 1990 with debts of £400 million. After 1,100 initial redundancies, a succession of household-name subsidiaries, including Denby and Edinburgh Crystal, were sold, also Kosset Carpets and Staffordshire Tableware, which went to management buyouts.

### Daimler Benz

With 90% of profit still derived from Mercedes, the financial year 1990 provided further evidence that diversification is not yet bringing direct benefits. AEG has still to return a profit and Deutsche Aerospace, formerly MBB, Dornier, and MTU saw orders fall 43%. Debis Financial Services fared better and may link with Mitsubishi in the future.

### International Leisure Group

The recession and the Gulf War immeasurably damaged the British travel industry in 1990/91, but the biggest surprise came with the collapse of the largest operator after Thompson: Air Europe and its parent ILG Group. Competitors, including Dan Air, themselves subject to some speculation at the time, moved quickly to apply for the vacant routes. Thomson, Airtours, and Owners Abroad were all said to be reporting increased sales after the collapse.

### John Fairfax Group

The well-known Australian group went into receivership in Dec 1990 with debts of A$1.7 billion. Australian law permits receivers to attempt to trade a company out of difficulty and this remains a possibility. British media organizations are understood to be interested.

### Levitt Group

The Levitt financial-services group went into liquidation in Dec 1990 with first indications of losses of up to £40 million; 18,000 investors were affected, some of whom may benefit from the Investors' Protection Scheme. At the same time, the group's founder, Roger Levitt, was charged with the theft of £665,000 from two clients.

### Marks and Spencer

The doyen of British retail style and performance acknowledged its susceptibility to economic pressures when its profit growth in the year 1990/91 was only 2% to £615.5 million, and 850 staff redundancies were announced.

### Midland Bank

With bad debts of £700 million, the dividend halved, and the collapse of the proposed merger with Hong Kong and Shanghai Bank, Chair Kit McMahon left in March to be replaced by Peter Walters, formerly of British Petroleum. Some 1,800 jobs have been shed and more are likely: a takeover bid looks increasingly probable.

### PanAm

Operations continue under US bankruptcy provisions, Chapter 11. Boeing and General Electric watch anxiously, having lost heavily when Eastern Airlines folded. With their Heathrow routes sold to United, PanAm aim to continue to fly transatlantic from Gatwick and perhaps seek a merger in the longer term.

### Polly Peck

Since the collapse in the autumn of 1990 of the electronics-to-fruit conglomerate built up by Asil Nadir, its Turkish Cypriot chair, efforts have continued to achieve its reconstruction and survival. Total debts amount to around £1.15 billion, of which it is believed that £650 million may not be repaid. Meanwhile the charges against Nadir on 18 counts of theft and false accounting continue concerning amounts of over £20 million.

### Record Japanese bankruptcy

Nanatomi, a Japanese resort developer, sought the protection of the courts in Jan 1991 with debts of 300 billion yen (£1.15 billion). Its problems are understood to have arisen from the weakening of the inflated Japanese property markets and from speculation in the shares of other companies. The bankruptcy is the third largest in Japanese history.

### Wallenberg

The high cost of defending Saab-Scania from local greenmailer Sven Olof Johansson indicates that as Sweden's capital market is liberalized, the Wallenberg empire must choose which of the companies it controls it can afford to keep. Alfa-Laval was sold to the Swiss Tetra Pak and it is thought that Saab Auto, Scandia Insurance, and Astra Pharmaceuticals may follow.

## MAJOR RESTRUCTURING

### Harrods

Despite their continued investment and sales growth reported at 25%, the background of criticism and complaint directed at the al-Fayed connection was unabated. Robin Leigh-Pemberton, governor of the Bank of England, declined to reveal much to the House of Commons Select Committee about Harrods Bank Ltd. The substance and grounds for government inaction over the reported criticisms in the Department of Trade and Industry report on the al-Fayed takeover was felt still to leave significant questions unanswered—especially as seen by Tiny Rowlands, chair of the Lonrho Group.

**Laura Ashley**
The painful reordering of Laura Ashley's affairs precipitated by the retail slump continued. Six plants in the UK and Ireland are being closed and 85% of its garment production is being moved overseas. Financial controls and operational efficiencies have been improved. The Penhaligon perfumery business has been sold and in Nov 1990, a 15% investment in Laura Ashley was made by Aeon, the Japanese retailer that is its partner in Japan.

**Philips**
With sales on a plateau and profits tumbling to a loss of £1.2 billion in 1990, Jan Timmer, the new president of Philips, the Dutch electronics group, acted decisively by instituting a major restructuring involving the loss of 45,000 jobs (20% of the workforce) and a thorough re-examination of the group's entire product portfolio.

**Rover and British Aerospace**
The purchase of Rover Group from the UK government in July 1988 and the role of the deal's architect, Lord Young, re-entered the headlines in Feb 1991 with a report from the Trade and Industry Committee of the House of Commons. For two and a half years the committee had studied the case, grilling witnesses and finally arguing over its report. It concluded that the deal could well have been the best solution for the government, but was highly critical of the way in which information on it had been withheld or only partially reported. Meanwhile, the European Commission had demanded repayment by British Aerospace of £44 million of the sweeteners received from the government, with the possibility of a further £40 million.

**Saatchi and Saatchi**
The long-awaited financial rescue package for the troubled advertising agency was finally agreed in Feb 1991 after representations from Lord Rothschild, who owned 20% of the preference stock. Shares had fallen from 275p in 1990 to a low of 15p in early 1991. Saatchi was subsequently reinstated as the agency for the Conservative Party in the run-up to the next election.

---

**Trust**

---

*Who do you trust most to tell the truth?*
*And which next? (Includes first mention)*

|  | Most | Top two |
|---|---|---|
| Doctor | 42 | 68 |
| Priest | 27 | 45 |
| Solicitor | 10 | 25 |
| Teacher | 4 | 12 |
| Scientist | 2 | 6 |
| Journalist | 0 | 0 |
| Military top brass | 0 | 0 |
| Politician | 0 | 1 |
| Trade union leader | 0 | 2 |
| None of these | 6 | 9 |
| Don't know | 2 | 1 |

---

# INSTITUTIONS AND ORGANIZATIONS

**Arab Common Market** organization founded 1965, providing for the abolition of customs duties on agricultural products, and reductions on other items, between the member states: Egypt, Iraq, Jordan, and Syria.

**Arab Monetary Fund** (AMF) money reserve established 1976 by 20 Arab states plus the Palestine Liberation Organization to provide a mechanism for promoting greater stability in exchange rates and to coordinate Arab economic and monetary policies. It operates mainly by regulating petrodollars within the Arab community to make member countries less dependent on the West for the handling of their surplus money. The fund's headquarters are in Abu Dhabi in the United Arab Emirates.

**Asian Development Bank** (ADB) a bank founded 1966 to stimulate growth in Asia and the Far East by administering direct loans and technical assistance. Members include 30 countries within the region and 14 countries of W Europe and North America. The headquarters are in Manila, Philippines.

**Bank for International Settlements** (BIS) organization whose function is to promote co-operation between central banks and to facilitate international financial settlements, including transactions in European Currency Units (ECUs). Central banks of the main trading states are members, each providing a director to the board, which meets at least ten times a year. BIS was founded 1930, originally to coordinate war reparations, and is based in Basel, Switzerland.

**Bank of England** UK central bank founded by Act of Parliament in 1694. It was entrusted with the note issue in 1844 and nationalized in 1946. It is banker to the clearing banks and the UK government. As the government's bank, it manages and arranges the financing of the public-sector borrowing requirement and the national debt, implements monetary policy and exchange-rate policy through intervention in foreign-exchange markets, and supervises the UK banking system.

**Central American Common Market** ODECA (*Organización de Estados Centro-americanos*) economic alliance established in 1960 by El Salvador, Guatemala, Honduras (seceded 1970), and Nicaragua; Costa Rica joined in 1962. Its headquarters are in San Salvador.

**Colombo Plan** plan for cooperative economic development in S and SE Asia, established 1951. The member countries meet annually to discuss economic and development plans such as irrigation, hydroelectric schemes, and technical training. The plan has no central fund but technical assistance and financing of development projects are arranged through individual governments or the International Bank for Re-

construction and Development.

**Comecon** (*Council for Mutual Economic Assistance*, or CMEA) economic organization established 1949 and prompted by the Marshall Plan, linking the USSR with Bulgaria, Czechoslovakia, Hungary, Poland, Romania, East Germany (from 1950), Mongolia (from 1962), Cuba (from 1972), and Vietnam (from 1978), with Yugoslavia as an associated member. Albania also belonged 1949–61.

The secretariat is based in Moscow and regular annual meetings are held in the member countries. It was agreed in 1987 that official relations should be established with the European Community, and a free-market approach to trading was adopted 1990. In Jan 1991 it was agreed that Comecon should be effectively disbanded and replaced by a new body, the Organization for International Economic Co-operation (OIEC), probably to be based in Budapest. The OIEC would act as a 'clearing house' for mutual East European trade and to co-ordinate East European policy towards the European Community. From Jan 1991, trade between Comecon members was switched from the transferable rouble to a hard currency basis, with adverse consequences for East European importers of Soviet oil and gas.

**European Free Trade Association** (EFTA) organization established 1960 and as of 1988 consisting of Austria, Finland, Iceland, Norway, Sweden, and Switzerland. There are no import duties between members. Of the origi-

WORLD'S TOP 20 COMPANIES*

*By market capitalization, May 1991*

| | £bn | 0 | 20 | 40 | 60 | 80 | 100 | 120 |
|---|---|---|---|---|---|---|---|---|
| NTT* | | | | | | | | |
| Exxon | | | | | | | | |
| Royal Dutch/Shell | | | | | | | | |
| Philip Morris | | | | | | | | |
| General Electric | | | | | | | | |
| IBM | | | | | | | | |
| Wal-Mart Stores | | | | | | | | |
| Toyota Motor | | | | | | | | |
| Merck | | | | | | | | |
| AT&T | | | | | | | | |
| Bristol-Myers Squibb | | | | | | | | |
| British Telecom | | | | | | | | |
| Tokyo Electric Power | | | | | | | | |
| Coca-Cola | | | | | | | | |
| BP | | | | | | | | |
| Johnston & Johnston | | | | | | | | |
| Nomura Securities | | | | | | | | |
| Du Pont de Nemours | | | | | | | | |
| Procter & Gamble | | | | | | | | |
| Hitachi | | | | | | | | |

*Nippon Telegraph and Telephone*

Source: The Economist

## ECONOMIC AND MONETARY UNION IN EUROPE

The entry of the UK into the Exchange Rate Mechanism (ERM), of the European Monetary System (EMS) in October 1990 threw the whole issue of Economic and Monetary Union (EMU) in Europe into the spotlight, with concerns expressed about economic sovereignty. Stage I of the Delors Plan for EMU has already been accepted by all members of the EC, who are supposed to be taking steps to implement the three main aspects of Delors Stage I. These are the creation of the Single European Market by the end of 1992, membership of the ERM by all member countries, and improvements in the co-ordination of economic policies of EC members.

'1992' has become the popular name for the programme of measures for the completion of the Single European Market published in 1985 and due to be completed by the end of 1992. The aim of the programme is seen as eliminating non-tariff barriers to trade within the EC, including frontier controls, differing technical standards and regulations, state subsidies to industry and agriculture, the exclusion of non-domestic producers from government purchasing contracts, and differing tax rates. The EC Commission suggests that there would be reductions in costs as a result of the expanded market and greater competition. The removal of barriers to trade is likely to benefit a significant proportion of consumers and efficient producers, but damage less efficient producers. In order to offset the possible damaging social effects, a 'Social Charter' has been proposed, including worker participation in industry and minimum wages, though many of its features have been opposed by the UK Government.

The EMS is seen as an essential part of the development of EMU, and a possible precursor of a single European currency. There are three essential elements to the EMS: The European Currency Unit (ECU), the ERM and the European Monetary Co-operation Fund (the EMCF). The ECU is a 'basket' of European Community (EC) currencies, and each member country's currency is given a weight in the ECU according to its share in EC GDP (Gross Domestic Product) and trade. The Deutschmark has the largest weight in the ECU at 30 per cent, which means that 30 per cent of the movement in the ECU is due to movement in the Deutschmark. The countries participating in the ERM (now all EC members except Greece and Portugal) agree to keep their currencies within a narrow band of fluctuation either side of a central rate with the ECU and with each indi-

vidual ERM currency, using central bank and EMCF reserves. Sterling's central rate with the Deutschmark is £1 = DM2.95. In May 1991, Sterling was within two pfennigs of its central DM rate. Sterling's central rates against all the ERM currencies are shown in the table.

Most of the ERM currencies are allowed a maximum fluctuation of 4.5% (approximately 2.25 per cent either side of the central rates). Sterling and the peseta are allowed a maximum of 12 per cent. However, in practice, the fact that divergence against the ECU and each individual currency is taken into account means that a currency is likely to reach its effective limit against other currencies before it has reached its full limit. For example, if sterling falls against the deutschmark, and the deutschmark rises against the ECU, then sterling will reach its DM limit before its ECU limit.

The main focus of dispute between the UK and other EC governments has been the creation of a single European monetary policy (Delors Stage II) and the creation of a single European Currency (Delors Stage III). In June 1990, the British Government proposed the 'hard' ECU plan, in order to avoid what it saw as the imposition of a single currency. The ECU would be 'hard' in the sense that it would not be allowed to depreciate against any member currency. It would circulate alongside national currencies, and would be managed by a new institution, the European Monetary Fund. Most EC countries are opposed to the 'hard' ECU plan, although some transitional arrangements from national currencies to a single currency are likely to be needed. In May 1990 Jacques Delors proposed to allow Britain to leave the final decision to adopt the ECU to 'a future House of Commons'. This is likely to result in the British Government signing the treaty for a single European Currency at the end of 1991. The earliest date for the introduction of the single currency is likely to be in 1997.

### Sterling Central Rates in the ERM

| | |
|---|---|
| Belgian/Luxembourg franc | 60.8451 |
| Danish krone | 11.2526 |
| Deutschmark | 2.95000 |
| Peseta | 191.750 |
| French franc | 9.89389 |
| Irish punt | 1.10118 |
| Lira | 2207.25 |
| Dutch florin | 3.32389 |
| ECU | 1.43492 |

nal members, Britain and Denmark left (1972) to join the European Community, as subsequently did Portugal (1985).

**European Monetary System** (EMS) attempt by the European Community to bring financial cooperation and monetary stability to Europe. It was established 1979 in the wake of the 1974 oil crisis, which brought growing economic disruption to European economies because of floating exchange rates. Central to the EMS is the *Exchange Rate Mechanism* (ERM), a voluntary system of semi-fixed exchange rates based on the European Currency Unit (ECU).

The UK entered the ERM in Oct 1990. In 1990 and 1991, Sterling's central rate with the ECU within the ERM was £1=1.43ECU. There are also central rates with other ERM currencies; Sterling's central rate with the

ECONOMIC GROWTH IN THE G7 COUNTRIES -
AVERAGE ANNUAL GROWTH RATE (% OF GDP)

|  | 1965–80 | 1980–88 |
|---|---|---|
| United Kingdom | 2.4 | 2.8 |
| Italy* | 4.3 | 2.2 |
| France* | 4.0 | 1.8 |
| Canada | 5.1 | 3.3 |
| Germany, Fed. Rep.* | 3.3 | 1.8 |
| United States | 2.7 | 3.3 |
| Japan* | 6.5 | 3.9 |

*GDP and its componets are at purchaser values.
Source: World Development Report 1990

Deutschmark was £1=DM2.95 in 1990 and 1991.

**Federal Reserve System** ('Fed') US central banking system and note-issue authority, established 1913 to regulate the country's credit and monetary affairs. The Fed consists of the 12 federal reserve banks and their 25 branches and other facilities throughout the country; it is headed by a board of governors in Washington, appointed by the US president with Senate approval.

**General Agreement on Tariffs and Trade** (GATT) organization within the United Nations founded 1948 with the aim of encouraging free trade between nations through low tariffs, abolitions of quotas, and curbs on subsidies.

The latest round of GATT talks began in Sept 1986 in Uruguay. This, known as the Uruguay round, ended with talks in Geneva in 1990, at which the USA opposed EC restrictions on agricultural imports, but wanted to maintain restrictions on textile imports into the USA.

**International Monetary Fund** (IMF) specialized agency of the United Nations, headquarters Washington DC, established under the 1944 Bretton Woods agreement and operational since 1947. It seeks to promote international monetary cooperation and the growth of world trade, and to smooth multilateral payment arrangements among member states. IMF stand-by loans are available to members in balance of payments difficulties (the amount being governed by the member's quota), usually on the basis of acceptance of instruction on stipulated corrective measures.

The Fund also operates other drawing facilities, including several designed to provide preferential credit to developing countries with liquidity problems. Having previously operated in US dollars linked to gold, the IMF has used since 1972 the special drawing right (SDR) as its standard unit of account, valued in terms of a weighted 'basket' of major currencies. Since the 1971 Smithsonian agreement permitting wider fluctuations from specified currency parities, IMF rules have been progressively adapted to the increasing prevalence of fully floating exchange rates.

**LIFFE** acronym for *London International Financial Futures Exchange*, one of the exchanges in London where futures contracts are traded. Established in 1982, it provides a worldwide exchange for futures dealers and investors, and began options trading in 1985. All transactions pass through a clearing house which serves as a financially independent guarantor and regulator of the exchange; the Bank of England also supervises the exchange. LIFFE was a forerunner of the Big Bang in bringing US-style 'open-house' dealing (as opposed to telephone dealing) to the UK.

**Monopolies and Mergers Commission** (MMC) UK government body re-established in 1973 under the Fair Trading Act and, since 1980, embracing the Competition Act. Its role is to investigate and report when there is a risk of creating a monopoly following a company merger or takeover, or when a newspaper or newspaper assets are transferred. It also investigates companies, nationalized industries, or local authorities that are suspected of operating in a noncompetitive way. The US equivalent is the *Federal Trade Commission* (FTC).

**Organization for Economic Cooperation and Development** (OECD) Paris-based international organization of 24 industrialized countries, which coordinates member states' economic policy strategies. The OECD's subsidiary bodies include the International Energy Agency 1974, set up in the face of a world oil crisis.

It superseded the Organization for European Economic Cooperation (established 1948 to promote European recovery under the Marshall Plan) 1961, when the USA and Canada became members and its scope was extended to include development aid. The OECD members are: Australia, Austria, Belgium, Canada, Denmark, Finland, France, Germany, Greece, Iceland, Ireland, Italy, Japan, Luxembourg, Netherlands, New Zealand, Norway, Portugal, Spain, Sweden, Switzerland, Turkey, UK, and USA.

**Organization of the Petroleum Exporting Countries** (OPEC) body established 1960 to coordinate price and supply policies of oil-producing states, and also to improve the position of Third World states by forcing Western states to open their markets to the resultant products. Its concerted action in raising prices in the 1970s triggered worldwide recession but also lessened demand so that its influence was reduced by the mid-1980s. OPEC members are: Algeria, Ecuador, Gabon, Indonesia, Iran, Iraq, Kuwait, Libya, Nigeria, Qatar, Saudi Arabia, United Arab Emirates, and Venezuela.

OPEC's importance in the world market was reflected in its ability to implement oil price increases from $3 a barrel in 1973 to $30 a barrel in 1980. In the 1980s, OPEC's dominant position was undermined by reduced demand for oil in industrialized countries, increased non-OPEC oil supplies, and production of alternative energy. These factors contributed to the dramatic fall in world oil prices to $10 a barrel in July 1986 from $28 at the beginning of the year. OPEC's efforts to stabilize oil prices through mandatory reduced production have been resisted by various members.

**Securities and Exchange Commission** (SEC) US

INFLATION: INTERNATIONAL COMPARISONS
AVERAGE ANNUAL PERCENTAGE RATE

|  | 1965–80 | 1980–88 |
| --- | --- | --- |
| Algeria | 10.5 | 4.4 |
| Argentina | 78.2 | 290.5 |
| Spain | 12.3 | 10.1 |
| UK | 11.1 | 5.7 |
| France | 8.4 | 7.1 |
| Germany, Fed. Rep. | 5.2 | 2.8 |
| USA | 6.5 | 4.0 |
| Japan | 7.7 | 1.3 |

Source: OECD Main Economic Indicators

federal agency created in 1934 to ensure full disclosure to the investing public and protection against malpractice in the securities (stocks and shares) and financial markets (such as insider trading).

**Securities and Investment Board** UK body with overall responsibility for policing financial dealings in the City of London. Introduced in 1987 following the deregulation process of the so-called Big Bang, it acts as an umbrella organization to such self-regulating bodies as the Stock Exchange.

**World Bank** popular name for the *International Bank for Reconstruction and Development*, established 1945 under the 1944 Bretton Woods agreement, which also created the International Monetary Fund. The World Bank is a specialized agency of the United Nations that borrows in the commercial market and lends on commercial terms. The *International Development Association* is an arm of the World Bank.

The World Bank now earns almost as much money from interest and loan repayments as it hands out in new loans every year. Over 60% of the bank's loans goes to suppliers outside the borrower countries for such things as consultancy services, oil, and machinery. Control of the bank is vested in a board of executives representing national governments, whose votes are apportioned according to the amount they have funded the bank. Thus the USA has nearly 20% of the vote and always appoints the board's president.

In 1989 the World Bank made a net transfer of $42.9 billion to developing countries.

# TERMS

**aid, development** money given or lent on concessional terms to developing countries or spent on maintaining agencies for this purpose. In the late 1980s official aid from governments of richer nations amounted to $45–60 billion annually whereas voluntary organizations in the West received about $2.4 billion a year for the Third World. The World Bank is the largest dispenser of aid. All industrialized United Nations (UN) member countries devote a proportion of their gross national product to aid, ranging from 0.20% of GNP (Ireland) to 1.10% (Norway) (1988 figures). Each country spends more than half this contribution on direct bilateral assistance to countries with which it has historical or military links or hopes to encourage trade. The rest goes to international organizations such as UN and World Bank agencies, which distribute aid multilaterally.

The UK development-aid budget in 1988 was 0.32% of GNP, with India and Kenya among the principal beneficiaries. The European Development Fund (an arm of the European Community) and the International Development Association (an arm of the World Bank) receive approximately 5% and 8% respectively of the UK development-aid budget. The Overseas Development Administration is the department of the Foreign Office that handles bilateral aid.

The combined overseas development aid of all EC member countries is less than the sum ($20 billion) the EC spends every year on storing surplus food produced by European farmers.

In 1988, the US development-aid budget was 0.21% of GNP, with Israel and Egypt among the principal beneficiaries; Turkey, Pakistan, and the Philippines are also major beneficiaries. The United States Agency for International Development (USAID) is the State Department body responsible for bilateral aid. The USA is the largest contributor to, and thus the most powerful member of, the International Development Association.

**annual percentage rate** (APR) rate of interest on credit sales or borrowing that reflects the fact that the proportion of the amount outstanding paid in interest rises as the repayments are made. It is usually approximately double the flat rate of interest, or simple interest.

**balance of payments** a tabular account of a country's debit and credit transactions with other countries. Items are divided into the *current account*, which includes both visible trade (imports and exports) and invisible trade (such as transport, tourism, interest, and dividends), and the *capital account*, which includes investment in and out of the country, international grants, and loans. Deficits or surpluses on these accounts are brought into balance by buying and selling reserves of foreign currencies.

A *balance of payments crisis* arises when a country's current account deteriorates because the cost of imports exceeds income from exports. In developing countries persistent trade deficits often result in heavy government borrowing overseas, which in turn leads to a debt crisis.

**bank** financial institution that uses funds deposited with it to lend money to companies or individuals, and which also provides financial services to its customers.

A *central bank* (in the UK, the Bank of England) issues currency for the government, in order to provide cash for circulation and ex-

UK INFLATION (1985–1991)

*Prices*

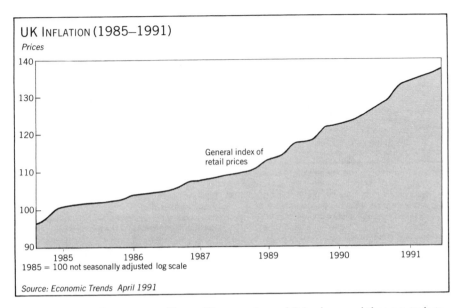

1985 = 100 not seasonally adjusted  log scale

*Source: Economic Trends  April 1991*

change. In terms of assets, seven of the world's top ten banks were Japanese in 1988.

**Big Bang** popular term for the major changes instituted in late 1986 to the organization and practices of the City of London as Britain's financial centre, ensuring that London retained its place as a leading world financial centre. Facilitated in part by computerization and on-line communications, the changes included the liberalization of the London Stock Exchange. This involved merging the functions of jobber (dealer in stocks and shares) and broker (who mediates between the jobber and the public), introducing negotiated commission rates, and allowing foreign banks and financial companies to own British brokers/jobbers, or themselves to join the London Stock Exchange.

**capital** accumulated or inherited wealth held in the form of assets (such as stocks and shares, property, and bank deposits). In stricter terms, capital is defined as the stock of goods used in the production of other goods, and may be **fixed capital** (such as buildings, plant, and machinery) that is durable, or **circulating capital** (raw materials and components) that is used up quickly.

**collective bargaining** the process whereby management, representing an employer, and a trade union, representing employees, agree to negotiate jointly terms and conditions of employment. Agreements can be company-based or industry-wide.

**comparative advantage** law of international trade first elaborated by David Ricardo showing that trade becomes advantageous if the cost of production of particular items differs between one country and another.

At a simple level, if wine is cheaper to produce in country A than in country B, and the reverse is true of cheese, A can specialize in

wine and B in cheese and they can trade to mutual benefit.

**consumption** the purchase of goods and services for final use, as opposed to spending by firms on capital goods, known as capital formation.

**cost of living** the cost of goods and services needed for an average standard of living. In Britain the cost-of-living index was introduced 1914 and based on the expenditure of a working-class family of man, woman, and three children; the standard is 100. Known from 1947 as the Retail Price Index (RPI), it is revised to allow for inflation.

Supplementary to the RPI are the Consumer's Expenditure Deflator (formerly Consumer Price Index) and the Tax and Price Index (TPI), introduced in 1979. Comprehensive indexation has been advocated as a means of controlling inflation by linking all forms of income (such as wages and investment), contractual debts and tax scales, to the RPI. Index-linked savings schemes were introduced in the UK in 1975.

**credit** means by which goods or services are obtained without immediate payment, usually by agreeing to pay interest. The three main forms are **consumer credit** (usually extended to individuals by retailers), **bank credit** (such as overdrafts or personal loans) and **trade credit** (common in the commercial world both within countries and internationally). Consumer credit is increasingly used to pay for goods. In the USA in 1989 it amounted to $711.8 billion, with about 18.5% of disposable income expended on hire-purchase and credit-card payments.

In the UK in 1990, new credit advanced to consumers amounted to approximately £40 billion.

**crowding out** a hypothetical situation in which an increase in government expenditure results

## THE UK RECESSION

The recession has been the subject of much political and economic debate, which has included the exact nature of a 'recession'. The standard economists' definition of a recession is a continuous fall in the output measure of Gross Domestic Product (GDP) over two quarters. Essentially, this means that a recession occurs when the production of all goods and services in the economy falls for six months or more. One of the reasons for the intense political debate about whether or not the UK was in a recession at the end of 1990 was that is cannot be definitively stated that a recession has occurred until the six-month fall in output has been experienced and recorded. Recently released official statistics show that GDP fell in the third and fourth quarters of 1990, and in the first quarter of 1991. The 1990–91 recession is the third recession in the last 20 years with the last two occurring between 1973 and 1975, and between 1979 and 1981.

A recession is part of the fluctuations in economic activity known as the trade cycle. The table shows that Economic Growth (measured as the change in GDP from one year to the next) was rising significantly from 1986 to 1988. As the economy reaches its peak, it becomes more and more difficult for increases in supply to match increases in demand, and prices increase at a faster rate, i.e. inflation rises. The increase in inflation then contributes to the subsequent slowdown in economic activity. This process can be seen at work with inflation rising with economic growth from 3.4% in 1986 to 9.5% in 1990, with particularly high levels of inflation in 1989 and 1990 slowing down economic growth.

The slowdown in economic growth in the UK since 1989 can partly be explained by a slowdown in world economic activity, but it has been more severe than in other countries. This is to some extent the result of high interest rates designed to dampen down demand and hence reduce inflation. Bank base rates in-

creased from 8.5 to 13% cent in 1988, and to 15% in 1989. It was only with the UK's entry into the ERM in September 1990 that the government felt able to reduce interest rates without a damaging fall in the pound, and since then further cuts have been made as the recession reflects the depressed state of demand. In May 1991, base rates remain relatively high at 12 per cent. The Chancellor of the Exchequer, Norman Lamont, made the Government's priorities clear when he said, 'Rising unemployment and the recession have been the price we've had to pay to get inflation down ... that is a price well worth paying.' The belief behind these words is that reductions in inflation make the economy more competitive in the long term. However, the severity of the recession has also brought with it a 20% cut in manufacturing investment over the past year. In contrast to the previous recession which was concentrated most heavily in the manufacturing sector, the 1990–91 recession has spread to the service sector and the regions associated with it. While the South East remains the most prosperous region in terms of output and employment, it suffered the sharpest rise in unemployment in the last quarter of 1990. As the table shows, the recession is likely to continue for most of 1991, with output forecast to have fallen by 1% over the whole of the year.

It seems likely that output will begin to rise at the end of 1991 or the beginning of 1992, though it will be some time before economic growth returns to anything like the OECD average, which is 3.5% at the time of writing.

**Economic Growth in the UK**

| | |
|---|---|
| 1986 | 3.2% |
| 1987 | 4.4% |
| 1988 | 4.5% |
| 1989 | 2.1% |
| 1990 | 1.0% |
| 1991 | −1.0% |
| (forecast) | |

in a fall in private-sector investment, either because it causes inflation or a rise in interest rates (as a result of increased government borrowing) or because it reduces the efficiency of production as a result of government intervention. Crowding out has been used in recent years as a justification of supply-side economics such as the privatization of state-owned industries and services.

**currency** the type of money in use in a country, for example the US dollar, the UK pound sterling, the German Deutschmark and the Japanese yen.

**debt crisis** any situation in which an individual, company, or country owes more to others than it can repay or pay interest on; more specifically, the massive indebtedness of many Third World countries that became acute in the 1980s, threatening the stability of the international banking system as many debtor coun-

tries became unable to service their debts.

**depreciation** decline of a currency's value in relation to other currencies. Depreciation also describes the fall in value of an asset (such as factory machinery) resulting from age, wear and tear, or other circumstances. It is an important factor in assessing company profit.

**deregulation** action to abolish or reduce state controls and supervision over private economic activities, as with the deregulation of the US airline industry 1978. Its purpose is to improve competitiveness. In Britain the major changes in the City of London 1986 (the Big Bang) were in part deregulation.

**devaluation** lowering of the official value of a currency against other currencies, so that exports become cheaper and imports more expensive. Used when a country is badly in deficit in its balance of trade, it results in the goods the country produces being cheaper abroad, so

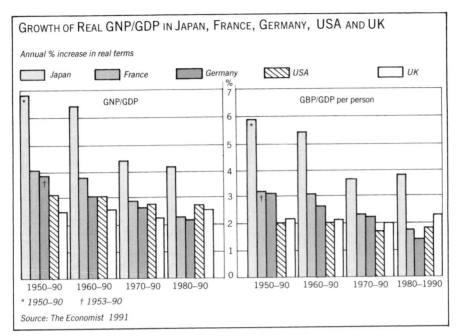

GROWTH OF REAL GNP/GDP IN JAPAN, FRANCE, GERMANY, USA AND UK

Annual % increase in real terms

Japan · France · Germany · USA · UK

GNP/GDP

GBP/GDP per person

1950–90   1960–90   1970–90   1980–90      1950–90   1960–90   1970–90   1980–1990

\* 1950–90   † 1953–90

Source: *The Economist* 1991

that the economy is stimulated by increased foreign demand.

The increased cost of imported food, raw materials, and manufactured goods as a consequence of devaluation may, however, stimulate an acceleration in inflation, especially when commodities are rising in price because of increased world demand. **Revaluation** is the opposite process.

Devaluations of important currencies upset the balance of the world's money markets and encourage speculation. Significant devaluations include that of the German mark in the 1920s and Britain's devaluation of sterling in the 1960s. To promote greater stability, many countries have allowed the value of their currencies to 'float', that is, to fluctuate in value.

**disinvestment** the withdrawal of investments in a country for political reasons. The term is also used to describe non-replacement of stock as it wears out.

It is generally applied to the removal of funds from South Africa in the 1970s and 1980s by such multinational companies as General Motors and to the withdrawal of private investment funds (by universities, pension funds, and other organizations) from portfolios doing business in South Africa. Disinvestment may be motivated by fear of loss of business in the home market caused by adverse publicity or by fear of loss of foreign resources if the local government changes.

**Dow Jones Index** (*Dow Jones Industrial 30 Share Index*) scale for measuring the average share price and percentage change of 30 major US industrial companies.

**economic growth** the rate of growth of output of all goods and services in an economy, usually

measured as the percentage increase in gross domestic product or gross national product from one year to the next. It is regarded as an indicator of the rate of increase or decrease (if economic growth is negative) in the standard of living.

**electronic funds transfer** (EFT) method of transferring funds automatically from one account to another by electronic means, for example *electronic funds transfer at point of sale* (EFTPOS), which provides for the automatic transfer of money from buyer to seller at the time of sale. In the UK the system is not yet widely used (Barclay's Connect card is the only vehicle widely promoted for the purpose).

**exchange rate** the price at which one currency is bought or sold in terms of other currencies, gold, or accounting units such as the special drawing right (SDR) of the International Monetary Fund. Exchange rates may be fixed by international agreement or by government policy; or they may be wholly or partly allowed to 'float' (that is, find their own level) in world currency markets, as with most major currencies since the 1970s.

**export** goods or service produced in one country and sold to another. Exports may be visible (goods physically exported) or invisible (services provided in the exporting country but paid for by residents of another country).

**Financial Times Index** (FT Index) an indicator measuring the daily movement of 30 major industrial share prices on the London Stock Exchange (1935 = 100), issued by the UK *Financial Times* newspaper. Other FT indices cover government securities, fixed-interest securities, goldmine shares, and Stock Exchange activity.

UNEMPLOYMENT - INTERNATIONAL
COMPARISON *(1990)

| | % |
|---|---|
| Sweden | 1.5 |
| Japan | 2.1 |
| Finland | 3.4 |
| Portugal | 4.6 |
| Germany | 5.1 |
| Norway | 5.2 |
| United States | 5.4 |
| Major seven | 5.6 |
| OECD average | 6.1 |
| United Kingdom | 6.9 |
| Australia | 6.9 |
| Netherlands | 7.5 |
| New Zealand | 7.7 |
| Belgium | 7.9 |
| Canada | 8.1 |
| OECD–Europe | 8.1 |
| EC average | 8.4 |
| France | 9.0 |
| Italy | 9.9 |
| Ireland | 14.0 |
| Spain | 15.9 |

* standardized rates
Source: OECD Main Economic Indicators

**fiscal policy** that part of government policy devoted to achieving the desired level of revenue, notably through taxation, and deciding the priorities and purposes governing expenditure.

**gilt-edged securities** stocks and shares issued and guaranteed by the British government to raise funds and traded on the Stock Exchange. A relatively risk-free investment, gilts bear fixed interest and are usually redeemable on a specified date. According to the redemption date, they are described as short (up to five years), medium, or long (15 years or more).

**gross domestic product** (GDP) the value of the output of all goods and services produced within a nation's borders, normally given as a total for the year. It thus includes the production of foreign-owned firms within the country, but excludes the income of domestically owned firms located abroad.

Since output is derived from expenditure on goods and services by firms, consumers, and government net of imports; and income (in the form of wages, salaries, interest, rent, and profits) is derived from the production of goods and services, GDP can be measured either by the sum of total output or expenditure or incomes. However, in practice there is usually a slight discrepancy between the three because of the highly complex calculations involved. GDP fluctuates in relation to the trade cycle and standard of living.

In the UK, the percentage increase in GDP from one year to the next is the standard measure of economic growth.

**gross national product** (GNP) the most commonly used measurement of the wealth of a country. GNP is defined as the total value of all goods and services produced by firms owned by the country concerned. It is measured as the gross domestic product plus income from abroad, minus income earned during the same period by foreign investors within the country. The national income of a country is the GNP minus whatever sum of money needs to be set aside to replace ageing capital stock.

**hyperinflation** rapid and uncontrolled inflation, or increases in prices, usually associated with political and/or social instability (as in Germany in the 1920s and Latin America in the 1970s and 1980s).

**import** product or service that one country purchases from another for domestic consumption, or for processing and re-exporting (Hong Kong, for example, is heavily dependent on imports for its export business). Imports may be visible (goods) or invisible (services). If an importing country does not have a counterbalancing value of exports, it may experience balance-of-payments difficulties and accordingly consider restricting imports by some form of protectionism (such as an import tariff or imposing import quotas).

**incomes policy** government-initiated exercise to curb inflation by restraining rises in incomes, on either a voluntary or a compulsory basis; often linked with action to control prices, in which case it becomes a prices and incomes policy.

In Britain incomes policies have been applied at different times since the 1950s, with limited success. An alternative to incomes policy, employed by the post-1979 Conservative government in Britain, is monetary policy, which attempts to manage the economy by controlling the quantity of money in circulation (money supply).

**income tax** a direct tax levied on personal income, mainly wages and salaries, but which may include the value of receipts other than in cash. It is one of the main instruments for achieving a government's income redistribution objectives. In contrast, *indirect taxes* are duties payable whenever a specific product is purchased; examples include VAT and customs duties.

Most countries impose income taxes on company (corporation) profits and on individuals (personal), although the rates and systems differ widely from country to country. In the case of companies in particular, income tax returns are prepared by an accountant, who will take advantage of the various exemptions, deductions, and allowances available. Personal income taxes are usually progressive so that the poorest members of society pay little or no tax, while the rich make much larger contributions.

**inflation** a rise in the general level of prices. The many causes include *cost-push inflation* that occurred in 1974 as a result of the world price increase in oil, thus increasing production costs. *Demand-pull inflation* results when overall demand exceeds supply. Suppressed inflation occurs in controlled economies and is reflected in rationing, shortages, and black market prices. Deflation, a fall in the general level of prices, is the reverse of inflation.

**interest** a sum of money paid by a borrower to a lender in return for the loan, usually expressed as a percentage per annum.

**Simple interest** is interest calculated as a straight percentage of the amount loaned or invested. In **compound interest**, the interest earned over a period of time (for example, per annum) is added to the investment, so that at the end of the next period interest is paid on that total.

**investment** the purchase of any asset with the potential to yield future financial benefit to the purchaser (such as a house, a work of art, stocks and shares, or even a private education).

**laissez faire** theory that the state should not intervene in economic affairs, except to break up a monopoly.

The 20th century has seen an increasing degree of state intervention to promote social benefits, which after World War II in Europe was extended into the field of nationalization of leading industries and services. However, from the 1970s *laissez-faire* policies were again pursued in the UK and the USA.

**market forces** the forces of demand (a want backed by the ability to pay) and supply (the willingness and ability to supply).

Some economists argue that resources are allocated most efficiently when producers are able to respond to consumer demand without intervention from 'distortions' such as governments and trade unions, and that profits and competition betwen firms and individuals provide sufficient incentives to produce efficiently (monetarism). Critics of this view suggest that market forces alone may not be efficient because they fail to consider social costs and benefits, and may also fail to provide for the needs of the less well-off, since private firms aiming to make a profit respond to the ability to pay.

**monetarism** economic policy, advocated by the economist Milton Friedman and the Chicago school of economists, that proposes control of a country's money supply to keep it in step with the country's ability to produce goods, with the aim of curbing inflation. Cutting government spending is advocated, and the long-term aim is to return as much of the economy as possible to the private sector, allegedly in the interests of efficiency.

Central banks—in the USA, the Federal Reserve Bank—use the discount rate and other tools to restrict or expand the supply of money to the economy. Unemployment may result from some efforts to withdraw government 'safety nets,' but monetarists claim it is less than eventually occurs if the more interventionist methods of Keynesian economics are adopted. Monetarist policies were widely adopted in the 1980s in response to the inflation problems caused by spiraling oil prices in 1979.

Additionally, credit is restricted by high interest rates, and industry is not cushioned against internal market forces or overseas competition (with the aim of preventing 'overmanning', 'restrictive' union practices, and 'excessive' wage demands).

**monetary policy** economic policy aimed at controlling the amount of money in circulation, usually through controlling the level of lending or credit. Increasing interest rates is an example of a contractionary monetary policy, which aims to reduce inflation by reducing the rate of growth of spending in the economy.

**money** any common medium of exchange acceptable in payment for goods or services or for the settlement of debts. Money is usually coinage (invented by the Chinese in the second millennium BC) and paper notes (used by the Chinese from about AD 800). Recent developments such as the cheque and credit card fulfil many of the traditional functions of money.

**money supply** the quantity of money in circulation in an economy at any given time. It can include notes, coins, and clearing-bank and other deposits used for everyday payments. Changes in the quantity of lending are a major determinant of changes in the money supply. One of the main principles of monetarism is that increases in the money supply in excess of the rate of economic growth are the major cause of inflation.

In the UK there are several definitions of money supply. M0 was defined as notes and coins in circulation, together with the operational balance of clearing banks with the Bank of England. The M1 definition encompasses M0 plus current account deposits; M2, now rarely used, covers the M1 items plus deposit accounts; M3 covers M2 items plus all other deposits held by UK citizens and companies in the UK banking sector. In May 1987 the Bank of England introduced new terms including M4 (M3 plus building society deposits) and M5 (M4 plus Treasury bills and local authority deposits).

**monopoly** the domination of a market for a particular product or service by a single company, which can therefore restrict competition and keep prices high. In practice, a company can be said to have a monopoly when it controls a significant proportion of the market (technically an oligopoly).

In the UK, monopoly was originally a royal grant of the sole right to manufacture or sell a certain article. The Fair Trading Act of 1973 defines a monopoly supplier as one having 'a quarter of the market', and the Monopolies and Mergers Commission controls any attempt to reach this position; in the USA 'antitrust laws' are similarly used. In communist systems the state itself has the overall monopoly; in capitalist ones some services such as transport or electricity supply may be state monopolies, but in the UK the Competition Act of 1980 covers both private monopolies and possible abuses in the public sector. A **monopsony** is a situation in which there is only one buyer, for example, most governments are the only legal purchasers of military equipment inside

UK UNEMPLOYMENT 1971–1989

| | Workforce in employment (m) | Unemployed (000's) |
|---|---|---|
| 1971 | 25,229 | 731,4 |
| 1972 | 25,288 | 852.4 |
| 1973 | 25,633 | 622.5 |
| 1974 | 25,676 | 599.3 |
| 1975 | 25,894 | 902.8 |
| 1976 | 26,110 | 1,298.9 |
| 1977 | 26,224 | 1,413.6 |
| 1978 | 26,358 | 1,410.5 |
| 1979 | 26,627 | 1,312.1 |
| 1980 | 26,839 | 1,611.2 |
| 1981 | 26,741 | 2,481.8 |
| 1982 | 26,677 | 2,904.1 |
| 1983 | 26,610 | 3,127.4 |
| 1984 | 27,265 | 3,158.3 |
| 1985 | 27,714 | 3,281.4 |
| 1986 | 27,791 | 3,312.4 |
| 1987 | 27,979 | 2,993.0 |
| 1988 | 28,260 | 2,425.7 |
| 1989 | 28,504 | 1,841.3 |

Source: Economic Trends 1991, Annual Supplement

their countries.

**multiplier** the theoretical concept, formulated by John Maynard Keynes, of the effect on national income or employment of an adjustment in overall demand. For example, investment by a company in a new plant will stimulate new income and expenditure, which will in turn generate new investment, and so on, so that the actual increase in national income may be several times greater than the original investment.

**national debt** debt incurred by the central government of a country to its own people and institutions and also to overseas creditors. If it does not wish to raise taxes to finance its activities, a government can borrow from the public by means of selling interest-bearing bonds, for example, or from abroad. Traditionally, a major cause of incurring national debt was the cost of war but in recent decades governments have borrowed heavily in order to finance development or nationalization, to

MAIN INDUSTRIES IN BRITAIN PRIVATIZED SINCE 1979:

British Telecom
British Gas Corporation
British National Oil Corporation
British Airways
British Airports Authority
British Aerospace
British Shipbuilders
British Steel
British Transport Docks Board
National Freight Company
Electricity Supply
Enterprise Oil
Jaguar
National Freight Company
Rover Group
Water Supply

support an ailing currency, or to avoid raising taxation.

On 31 March 1991 the UK national debt was approximately £80 billion. This represented a fall in the national debt since 1988, but was a short-term trend, as a budget deficit of £8 billion was forecast for 1991–92, rising to £12 billion in the following year.

**national insurance** in the UK, state social security scheme which provides child allowances, maternity benefits, and payments to the unemployed, sick, and retired, and also covers medical treatment. It is paid for by weekly contributions from employees and employers.

**newly industrialized country** (NIC) country that has in recent decades experienced a breakthrough into manufacturing and rapid export-led economic growth. The prime examples are Taiwan, Hong Kong, Singapore, and South Korea. Their economic development during the 1970s and 1980s was partly due to a rapid increase of manufactured goods in their exports.

**oligopoly** a situation in which a few companies control the major part of a particular market and concert their actions to perpetuate such control. This may include an agreement to fix prices (a cartel).

**poll tax** tax levied on every individual, without reference to his or her income or property. Being simple to administer, it was among the earliest sorts of tax (introduced in England 1377), but because of its indiscriminate nature (it is a regressive tax, in that it falls proportionately more heavily on poorer people) it has often proved unpopular.

**privatization** the policy or process of selling or transferring state-owned or public assets and services (nationalized industries) to private investors. Privatization of services takes place by the contracting out to private firms of the rendering of services previously supplied by public authorities. The proponents of privatization argue for the public benefit from its theoretically greater efficiency in a competitive market, and the release of resources for more appropriate use by government. Those against privatization believe that it removes a country's assets from all the people to a minority, whereas public utilities such as gas and water become private monopolies, and that a profit-making state-owned company raises revenue for the government.

In many cases the trend towards privatization was prompted by dissatisfaction with the high level of subsidies being given to often inefficient state enterprise. The term 'privatization' is used even when the state retains a majority share of an enterprise.

The policy has been pursued by the post-1979 Conservative administration in Britain, and by recent governments in France, Japan (Nippon Telegraph and Telephone Corporation 1985, Japan Railways 1987, Japan Air Lines 1987), Italy, and elsewhere. By 1988 the practice had spread worldwide with communist countries such as China and Cuba selling off

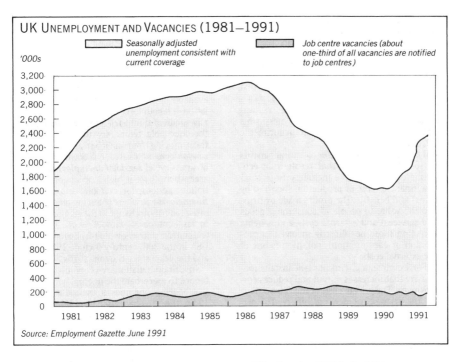

UK UNEMPLOYMENT AND VACANCIES (1981–1991)

Seasonally adjusted unemployment consistent with current coverage

Job centre vacancies (about one-third of all vacancies are notified to job centres)

'000s

Source: Employment Gazette June 1991

housing to private tenants.

**productivity** the output produced by a given quantity of labour, usually measured as output per person employed in the firm, industry, sector, or economy concerned. Productivity is determined by the quality and quantity of the fixed capital used by labour, and the effort of the workers concerned. The level of productivity is a major determinant of cost-efficiency: higher productivity tends to reduce average costs of production. Increases in productivity in a whole economy are a major determinant of economic growth.

It is important to distinguish between the rate of growth of productivity and the level of productivity, since at lower levels of productivity, higher rates of productivity growth may be achieved.

**profit-sharing** system whereby an employer pays the workers a fixed share of the company's profits. It originated in France in the early 19th century and was widely practised for a time within the cooperative movement.

**public-sector borrowing requirement** (PSBR) amount of money needed by a government to cover any deficit in financing its own activities, including loans to local authorities and public corporations, and also the funds raised by local authorities and public corporations from other sources.

The PSBR is financed chiefly by sales of debt to the public outside the banking system (gilt-edged securities, national savings, and local-authority stocks and bonds), by external transactions with other countries, and by borrowing from the banking system. In the

UK, after the 1986 budget this measure was changed to the *Public Sector Financial Deficit (PSFD)*, which is net of the asset sales due to privatization thought to distort the PSBR.

**public-sector debt repayment** (PSDR) the amount left over when government expenditure (public spending) is subtracted from government receipts. This occurs only when government spending is less than government receipts. A PSDR enables a government to repay some of the national debt.

**quantity theory of money** economic theory claiming that an increase in the amount of money in circulation causes a proportionate increase in prices.

The theory dates from the 17th century and was elaborated by the US economist Irving Fisher (1867–1947). Supported and developed by Milton Friedman, it forms the theoretical basis of monetarism.

**recession** a fall in business activity lasting more than a few months, causing stagnation in a country's output. A serious recession is called a *slump*.

**reserve currency** a country's holding of internationally acceptable means of payment (major foreign currencies or gold); central banks also hold the ultimate reserve of money for their domestic banking sector. On the asset side of company balance sheets, undistributed profits are listed as reserves.

**retail price index** (RPI) indicator of variations in the cost of living, superseded in the USA by the consumer price index.

**savings** unspent income, after deduction of tax. In economics a distinction is made between investment, involving the purchase of capital goods, such as buying a house, and saving (where capital goods are not directly purchased, for example, buying shares).

**Say's law** the 'law of markets' formulated by Jean-Baptiste Say (1767–1832) to the effect that supply creates its own demand and that resources can never be under-used. Widely accepted by classical economists, the 'law' was regarded as erroneous by J M Keynes in his analysis of the depression in Britain during the 1920s and 1930s.

**social costs and benefits** the costs and benefits to society as a whole that result from economic decisions. These include private costs (the financial cost of production incurred by firms) and benefits (the profits made by firms and the value to people of consuming goods and services) and external costs and benefits (affecting those not directly involved in production or consumption); pollution is one of the external costs.

For example, a chemical plant installs machinery that increases output and reduces employment. The private costs of the extra output are the price of the new machinery. The private benefits are the increases in the chemical firm's profits and in consumption. The external costs include the effects of any increased pollution as a result of the increased output, and the effects of increased unemployment, such as higher expenditure on unemployment benefits. The external benefits include any improvements in technology that other firms can benefit from.

**stagflation** economic condition (experienced in Europe in the 1970s) in which rapid inflation is accompanied by stagnating, even declining, output and by increasing unemployment. Its cause is often sharp increases in costs of raw materials and/or labour.

**stock exchange** institution for the buying and selling of stocks and shares (securities). The world's largest stock exchanges are London, New York (Wall Street), and Tokyo. The former division on the London Stock Exchange between brokers (who bought shares from jobbers to sell to the public) and jobbers (who sold them only to brokers on commission, the 'jobbers' turn') was abolished in 1986.

**trade cycle** or **business cycle** period of time that includes a peak and trough of economic activity, as measured by a country's national income. In Keynesian economics (those of the economist John Maynard Keynes), one of the main roles of the government is to smooth out the peaks and troughs of the trade cycle by intervening in the economy, thus minimizing 'overheating' and 'stagnation'. This is accomplished by regulating interest rates and government spending to maintain a proper balance of economic activity.

**Treasury bill** in Britain, borrowing by the government in the form of a promissory note to repay the bearer 91 days from the date of issue; such bills represent a flexible and relatively cheap way for the government to borrow money for immediate needs.

**unemployment** lack of paid employment. The unemployed are usually defined as those out of work who are available for and actively seeking work. Unemployment is measured either as a total or as a percentage of those who are available for work, known as the working population or labour force. Unemployment is generally subdivided into *frictional unemployment*, the inevitable temporary unemployment of those moving from one job to another; *cyclical unemployment*, caused by a downswing in the business cycle; *seasonal unemployment*, in an area where there is high demand only during holiday periods, for example; and *structural unemployment*, where changing technology or other long-term change in the economy results in large numbers without work. Periods of widespread unemployment in Europe and the USA in the 20th century include 1929–1930s, and the years since the mid-1970s.

In Britain deflationary economic measures tended to exacerbate the unemployment trend that began in the mid-1970s, and in the mid-1980s the rate had risen to 14% (although the basis on which it is calculated has in recent years been changed several times and many commentators argue that the real rate is higher). Since Sept 1988 it has been measured as the total or percentage of the working population unemployed and claiming benefit. This only includes people aged 18 or over, since the under-18s are assumed to be in full-time education or training. As the British economy experienced significant economic growth between 1986 and 1989, the rate of unemployment fell to a low of 5.6% in April 1990 (using the post-1988 definition) but rose again during the 1990–91 recession, standing at 7.6% in April 1991.

Many Third World countries suffer from severe unemployment and underemployment; the problem is exacerbated by rapid growth of population and lack of skills. In industrialized countries unemployment has been a phenomenon since the mid-1970s, when the rise in world oil prices caused a downturn in economic activity, and greater use of high technology improved output without creating more jobs. The average unemployment rate in industrialized countries (the members of the Organization for Economic Cooperation and Development) rose to 11% in 1987 compared with only 3% in 1970, with some countries, such as Spain and Ireland, suffering around 20%. In the USA the unemployment rate was 5.4% in 1990. In China, nearly a quarter of the urban labour force is unemployed.

**unlisted securities markets** markets for shares of companies not included in the official list for the main market of the stock exchange. These lower-tier markets where unlisted shares are traded are less stringently regulated and provide an important intermediate step to the main markets.

# THE ARTS

# HISTORY

**architecture** the art of designing structures. The term covers design of the visual appearance of structures; their internal arrangements of space; selection of external and internal building materials; design or selection of natural and artificial lighting systems, as well as mechanical, electrical, and plumbing systems; and design or selection of decorations and furnishings. Architectural style may emerge from evolution of techniques and styles particular to a culture in a given time period with or without identifiable individuals as architects or may be attributed to specific individuals or groups of architects working together on a project.

*early architecture* little remains of the earliest forms of architecture, but archaeologists have examined remains of prehistoric sites and documented Stone Age villages of wooden post buildings with above-ground construction of organic materials such as mud or wattle and daub from the Upper Paleolithic, Mesolithic, and Neolithic periods in Asia, the Middle East, Europe, and the Americas. More extensive remains of stone-built structures have given clues to later Neolithic farming communities as well as habitations, storehouses, and religious and civic structures of early civilizations. The best documented are those of ancient Egypt, where exhaustive work in the 19th and 20th centuries revealed much about ordinary buildings, the monumental structures such as the pyramid tombs near modern Cairo, and the temple and tomb complexes concentrated at Luxor and Thebes.

*Classical* this architecture evolved its basic forms in Greece between the 16th and 2nd centuries BC. Its hallmark characteristic is its post-and-lintel construction of temples and public structures, classified into the Doric, Ionic, and Corinthian orders, defined by simple, scrolled, and acanthus-leaf capitals for support columns, respectively. The Romans copied and expanded on Greek Classical forms, notably introducing bricks and concrete and inventing the vault, arch, and dome for public buildings and aqueducts.

*Byzantine* this architecture developed primarily in the E Roman Empire from the 4th century, with its centre at Byzantium (later named Constantinople, currently known as Istanbul). Its most notable feature was construction of churches, some very large, based on the Greek cross plan (Hagia Sophia, Istanbul; St Mark's, Venice), with formalized painted and mosaic decoration.

*Islamic* this architecture developed from the 8th century, when the Islamic religion spread from its centre in the Middle East W to Spain and E to China and parts of the Philippine Islands. Notable features are the development of the tower with dome and the pointed arch. Islamic architecture, particularly through Spanish examples such as the Great Mosque at Córdoba and the Alhambra in Granada, profoundly influenced Christian church architecture – for example, by adoption of the pointed arch into the Gothic arch.

*Romanesque* this architecture in W European Christianity developed from the 8th to the 12th centuries. It is marked by churches with massive walls for structural integrity, rounded arches, small windows, and resulting dark volumes of interior space. In England this style is generally referred to as Norman architecture (Durham Cathedral). The style enjoyed a renewal of interest in Europe and the USA in the late 19th and early 20th centuries.

*Gothic* this architecture emerged out of Romanesque, since the pointed arch and flying buttress made it possible to change from thick supporting walls to lighter curtain walls with extensive expansion of window areas (and stained-glass artwork) and resulting increases in interior light. Gothic architecture was developed particularly in France from the 12th to 16th centuries. The style is divided into Early Gothic (Sens Cathedral), High Gothic (Chartres Cathedral), and Late or Flamboyant Gothic. In England the corresponding divisions are Early English (Salisbury Cathedral), Decorated (Wells Cathedral), and Perpendicular (Kings College Chapel, Cambridge). Gothic was also developed extensively in Germany and neighbouring countries and in Italy.

*Renaissance* this architecture of 15th- and 16th-century Europe saw the rebirth of Classical form and motifs in the Italian Neo-Classical movement. A major source of inspiration was the work of the 1st-century BC Roman engineer Vitruvius for Palladio, Alberti, Brunelleschi, Bramante, and Michelangelo, the major Renaissance architects. The Palladian style was extensively used later in England by Inigo Jones and the Classical idiom by Christopher Wren. Classical or Neo-Classical style and its elements have been popular in the USA from the 18th century, as evident in much of the civic and commercial architecture since the time of the early republic (the US Capitol and Supreme Court buildings in Washington; many state capitols).

*Baroque* European architecture of the 17th and 18th centuries elaborated on Classical models with exuberant and extravagant decoration. In large-scale public buildings, the style is best seen in the innovative work of Giovanni Bernini and Francesco Borromini in Italy and later by John Vanbrugh, Nicholas Hawksmoor, and Christopher Wren in England. There were numerous practitioners in France and the German-speaking countries; Vienna is rich in Baroque work.

*Rococo* this architecture extends the Baroque style with an even greater extravagance of design motifs, using a new lightness of detail and naturalistic elements, such as shells, flowers, and trees.

**Neo-Classical** European architecture of the 18th and 19th centuries again focused on the more severe Classical idiom (inspired by archaeological finds), producing, for example, the large-scale rebuilding of London by Robert Adam and John Nash and later of Paris by Georges Haussman.

**Neo-Gothic** the later part of the 19th century saw a Gothic revival, most evident in churches and public buildings (Houses of Parliament, London, Charles Barry).

**Art Nouveau** was a new movement arising at the end of the 19th century, characterized by sinuous, flowing shapes, informal room plans, and particular attention to interior as well as architectural design. The style is best seen in England in the work of Charles Rennie Mackintosh (Glasgow Art School), in Paris at the entrances to the Metro and in Spain by that of Antonio Gaudí.

**Modernism** an increasing emphasis on rationalism and reduction of ornament led to Modernism (also known as Functionalism or International Style) in the 1930s. Seeking to exclude everything that did not have a purpose, the latest technological advances in glass, steel, and concrete were used to full advantage. Major architects included Frank Lloyd Wright, Mies van der Rohe, Le Corbusier, and Alvar Aalto.

**Town planning** also emerged as a discipline in its own right and whole new cities were planned, such as Le Corbusier's Chandigarh in India and Brasilia in Brazil.

**Brutalism** architectural style of the 1950s and 1960s that evolved from the work of Le Corbusier and Mies van der Rohe. It stressed functionalism and honesty to materials; steel and concrete were favoured. In the UK the style was developed by Alison and Peter Smithson.

**Neo-Vernacular** by the 1970s a reversion from this movement showed itself in a renewed enthusiasm for vernacular architecture (traditional local styles), to be seen in the work of, for instance, the British firm Darbourne and Darke.

**Post-Modernism** in the 1980s a Post-Modernist movement emerged, which split into two camps: **high tech**, represented in Britain by architects such as Norman Foster, Richard Rogers, and James Stirling (Hong Kong and Shanghai Bank, Hong Kong, Lloyd's, London, *Staatsgalerie Stuttgart* respectively); and architects using elements from the architecture of previous times, either following certain tenets of the Classical orders – Neo-Classicism yet again – such as Quinlan Terry, or using such elements at whim, such as Michael Graves.

**Deconstruction** a style that fragments forms and space by taking the usual building elements of floors, walls, and ceilings and sliding them apart to create a sense of disorientation and movement. Its proponents include Zaha Hadid (1950– ) in the UK, Frank Gehry (1929– )

and Peter Eisenman (1932– ) in the USA, and Co-op Himmelbau in Austria.

# BIOGRAPHIES

**Aalto** Alvar 1898–1976. Finnish architect and designer. One of Finland's first Modernists, his architectural style was unique, characterized by asymmetry, curved walls, and contrast of natural materials. His buildings include the Hall of Residence at the Massachusetts Institute of Technology, Cambridge, Massachusetts 1947–49; Technical High School, Otaniemi 1962–65; and Finlandia Hall, Helsinki 1972. He invented a new form of laminated bent plywood furniture in 1932 and won many design awards for household and industrial items.

**Adam** family of Scottish architects and designers. **William Adam** (1689–1748) was the leading Scottish architect of his day, and his son **Robert Adam** (1728–1792) is considered one of the greatest British architects of the late 18th century, who transformed the prevailing Palladian fashion in architecture to a Neo-Classical style. He designed interiors for many great country houses and earned a considerable reputation as a furniture designer.

**Alberti** Leon Battista 1404–1472. Italian Renaissance architect and theorist who recognized the principles of Classical architecture and their modification for Renaissance practice in *On Architecture* 1452.

**Archigram** London-based group of English architects in the 1960s including Peter Cook (1936– ), Dennis Crompton (1935– ), and Mike Webb (1937– ). Their work was experimental and polemical; architecture was to be technological and flexible.

**Barry** Charles 1795–1860. English architect of the Neo-Gothic Houses of Parliament at Westminster, London, 1840–60, in collaboration with Pugin.

**Berlage** Hendrikus 1856–1934. Dutch architect of the Amsterdam Stock Exchange 1897–1903, whose individualist style marked a move away from 19th-century historicism and towards Dutch Expressionism.

**Bernini** Giovanni Lorenzo 1598–1680. Italian sculptor, architect, and painter, a leading figure in the development of the Baroque style. His work in Rome includes the colonnaded piazza in front of St Peter's Basilica (1656), fountains (as in the Piazza Navona), and papal monuments. His sculpture includes *The Ecstasy of St Theresa* 1645–52 (Sta Maria della Vittoria, Rome) and numerous portrait busts.

**Borromini** Francesco 1599–1667. Italian Baroque architect, one of the two most important (with Bernini) in 17th-century Rome. Whereas Bernini designed in a florid, expansive style, his pupil Borromini developed a highly idiosyncratic and austere use of the classical language of architecture. The churches of San

Carlo alle Quattro Fontane and San Ivo in Rome demonstrate his revolutionary disregard for convention.

**Bramante** Donato *c.* 1444–1514. Italian Renaissance architect and artist. He spent the first part of his life mostly in Milan where he built the Tempietto of San Pietro, Rome *c.* 1502. Inspired by Classical designs, he was employed by Pope Julius II in rebuilding part of the Vatican and St Peter's in Rome. His work exercised a profound effect upon the development of Renaissance architecture in Italy.

**Breuer** Marcel 1902–1981. Hungarian-born architect and designer, who studied and taught at the Bauhaus school in Germany. His tubular steel chair 1925 was the first of its kind. He moved to England, then to the USA, where he was in partnership with Walter Gropius 1937–40. His buildings show an affinity with natural materials; the best known is the Bijenkorf, Rotterdam (with Elzas) 1953.

**Brunelleschi** Filippo 1377–1446. Italian Renaissance architect. One of the earliest and greatest Renaissance architects, he pioneered the scientific use of perspective. He was responsible for the construction of the dome of Florence Cathedral (completed 1438), a feat deemed impossible by many of his contemporaries.

**Burlington** Richard Boyle, 3rd Earl of 1694- -1753. English architectural patron and architect; one of the premier exponents of the Palladian style in Britain. His buildings, such as Chiswick House in London (1725–29), are characterized by absolute adherence to the Classical rules. His major protégé was William Kent.

**Butterfield** William 1814–1900. English architect. His work is Gothic Revival characterized by vigorous, aggressive forms and multicoloured striped and patterned brickwork, as in the church of All Saints, Margaret Street, London, and Keble College, Oxford.

**Chambers** William 1726–1796. English architect and popularizer of Chinese influence (for example, the pagoda in Kew Gardens, London) and designer of Somerset House, London.

**Coates** Nigel 1949– . English architect. While teaching at the Architectural Association in London in the early 1980s, Coates and a group of students founded NATO (*N*arrative *A*rchitecture *To*day) and produced an influential series of manifestoes and drawings on the theme of the imaginative regeneration of derelict areas of London.

**Eyck** Aldo van 1918– . Dutch architect with a strong commitment to social architecture. His works include an Orphans' Home 1957–60 and a refugee for single mothers, Mothers' House 1978, both in Amsterdam.

**Farrell** Terry 1938– . English architect working in a Post-Modern idiom, largely for corporate clients seeking an alternative to the rigours of High Tech or Modernist office blocks. His Embankment Place scheme 1991 sits theatrically on the north bank of the Thames

in London and has been likened to a giant jukebox.

**Foster** Norman 1935– . English architect of the High Tech school. His works include the Willis Faber office, Ipswich, 1978, the Sainsbury Centre for Visual Arts at the University of East Anglia 1979, the headquarters of the Hongkong and Shanghai Bank, Hong Kong, 1986, and Stansted Airport, Essex, 1991.

**Fuller** (Richard) Buckminster 1895–1983. US architect and engineer. In 1947 he invented the lightweight *geodesic dome*, a half-sphere of triangular components independent of buttress or vault. It combined the maximum strength with the minimum structure. Within 30 years over 50,000 had been built.

**Gaudí** Antonio 1852–1926. Spanish architect distinguished for his flamboyant Art Nouveau style. He designed both domestic and industrial buildings. His spectacular Church of the Holy Family, Barcelona, begun 1883, is still under construction.

**Gehry** Frank 1929– . US architect, based in Los Angeles. His architecture approaches abstract art in its use of collage and montage techniques.

**Gibbs** James 1682–1754. Scottish Neo-Classical architect whose works include St Martin-in-the-Fields, London 1722–26, Radcliffe Camera, Oxford 1737–49, and Bank Hall, Warrington, Cheshire 1750.

**Gilbert** Cass 1859–1934. US architect, major developer of the skyscraper. His most notable work is the Woolworth Building, New York 1913, the highest building in America (265 m/ 868 ft) when built and famous for its use of Gothic decorative detail. He was also architect of the US Supreme Court building in Washington DC, the Minnesota state capitol in St Paul, and the US Customs House in New York City.

**Gropius** Walter Adolf 1883–1969. German architect who lived in the USA from 1937. A founder-director of the Bauhaus school in Weimar 1919–28, he was an advocate of team architecture and artistic standards in industrial production. He was an early proponent of the international modern style defined by glass curtain walls, cubic blocks, and unsupported corners. His works include the Fagus-Werke (a shoe factory in Prussia), the Model Factory at the 1914 Werkbund exhibition in Cologne, and the Harvard Graduate Center 1949–50.

**Hardouin-Mansart** 1646–1708. French architect to Louis XIV from 1675. He designed the lavish Baroque extensions to the palace of Versailles (from 1678) and Grand Trianon. Other works include the Invalides Chapel in Paris 1680–91, the Place de Vendôme, and the Place des Victoires, in Paris.

**Haussmann** Georges Eugène, Baron Haussmann 1809–1891. French administrator who re-planned medieval Paris 1853–70 with wide boulevards and parks. The cost of his scheme and his authoritarianism caused opposition, and he was made to resign.

**Hawksmoor** Nicholas 1661–1736. English archi-

# CANARY WHARF – THE ONCE AND FUTURE CITY?

In 1989, 15 million gallons of concrete were poured into the foundations of the Canary Wharf development and a controversy was cemented. It touched on several issues: architecture, town planning, and the new business methods of the 1980s. Owned by the Canadian development company Olympia & York, Canary Wharf was designed on a huge scale, to be built in five phases over a period of 7–10 years. The site, at the northern end of the Isle of Dogs in London's Docklands, covered 71 acres. At its centre rose the Canary Wharf Tower, designed by the US-based architect Cesar Pelli to be the tallest in Britain at the time of construction in 1990 (at 244 m/800 ft), and claimed by the developers to be London's first true skyscraper, the bold marker of a new economic future. Many of the individual buildings are designed in a style comparable to American civic architecture—large buildings in steel and glass with masonry cladding, ranged around green circuses and squares. Courts along the waterfront, a fountain, works of art, and gardens decorate the public spaces. Among the many architects involved, the most notable were Pelli, I M Pei (architect of the glass pyramid at the Louvre in Paris), and the Italian Aldo Rossi, winner of the 1990 Pritzker Prize, who had not yet built in this country.

For developers, a huge advantage of the Docklands site was that full planning permission was not required, the area being a special enterprise zone under the aegis of the LDDC (London Docklands Development Corporation). Unlike the equally controversial development of the Spitalfields site in London's East End, which went to a public enquiry, there was little external intervention in the site planning or the appearance of Canary Wharf. This was also in sharp contrast to the proposed development of London's Kings Cross goods yards, where the developers had to answer to local community and conservation groups, in pursuit of the requisite planning permissions. Canary Wharf was, by contrast, in a derelict area, ringed by poor communities which were less vocal in their opposition to the scheme. It is obvious, therefore, why developers were attracted to the Docklands site, with its simplified planning procedures and freedom from commissions, committees, and pressure groups.

It is less obvious, however, that this is good for architecture, for the site, or for the local communities. Even the developers of Canary Wharf have since castigated Docklands as an urban failure. In a 1991 report, they argued that in the rush to develop the area commercially, hospitals, schools, colleges and artistic and sporting facilities had all been neglected, and that little sense of place or community had been achieved. The Docklands free-for-all, as it developed in the late 1980s, may be seen as a triumph of venture capitalism, or, alternatively, as a failure to implement the kind of town planning rules or zoning laws which have contain urban degeneration elsewhere helped.

At Canary Wharf a total of 10 million sq ft of new office space was planned to be created by the end of the century. But already, in the 1990s, recession has replaced the building boom of the 1980s and there is a glut of office space on the market. In the public mind, Canary Wharf and the rapid expansion of Docklands came to be associated with the fat years of Thatcherism, personified by that archetypal hate-figure, the Yuppie. In the leaner '90s it remains to be seen whether the completed project will become a dinosaur of the Thatcher era, looming over the eastern fringes of the city, or whether the developers can still pull off a success comparable to their World Financial Center in New York.

*Canary Wharf, London's Docklands.*

tect, assistant to Christopher Wren in designing London churches and St Paul's Cathedral; joint architect with Vanbrugh of Castle Howard and Blenheim Palace. His genius is displayed in a quirky and uncompromising style incorporating elements from both Gothic and Classical sources.

**Howard** Ebenezer 1850–1928. English town planner and founder of the ideal of the garden city, through his book *Tomorrow* 1898 (republished as *Garden Cities of Tomorrow* 1902).

**Isozaki** Arata 1931– . Japanese architect. One of Kenzo Tange's team 1954–63, his Post-Modernist works include Ochanomizu Square, Tokyo (retaining the existing facades), and buildings for the 1992 Barcelona Olympics.

**Jencks** Charles 1939– . US architectural theorist and furniture designer. He coined the term 'Post-Modern Architecture' and wrote *The Language of Post-Modern Architecture* 1984.

**Johnson** Philip (Cortelyou) 1906– . US architect who coined the term 'international style'. Originally designing in the style of Mies van der Rohe, he later became an exponent of Post-Modernism. He designed the giant AT&T building in New York 1978, a pink skyscraper with a Chippendale-style cabinet top.

**Jones** Inigo 1573–c. 1652. English architect. Born in London, he studied in Italy and was influenced by the works of Palladio. He was employed by James I to design scenery for Ben Jonson's masques. In 1619 he designed his English Renaissance masterpiece, the banqueting room at Whitehall, London.

**Kahn** Louis 1901–1974. US architect, born in Estonia. He developed a classically romantic style, in which functional 'servant' areas, such as stairwells and air ducts, featured prominently, often as tower-like structures surrounding the main living and working, or 'served', areas. His projects are characterized by an imaginative use of concrete and brick and include the Salk Institute for Biological Studies, La Jolla, California, and the British Art Center at Yale University.

**Lasdun** Denys 1914– . English architect. He designed the Royal College of Surgeons in Regent's Park, London 1960–64, some of the buildings at the University of East Anglia, Norwich, and the National Theatre 1976–77 on London's South Bank.

**Le Corbusier** Assumed name of Charles-Édouard Jeanneret 1887–1965. Swiss architect. His functionalist approach to town planning in industrial society was based on the interrelationship between machine forms and the techniques of modern architecture. His concept, *La Ville Radieuse*, developed in Marseille, France (1945–50) and Chandigarh, India, placed buildings and open spaces with related functions in a circular formation, with buildings based on standard-sized units mathematically calculated according to the proportions of the human figure.

**Ledoux** Claude-Nicolas 1736–1806. French

Neo-Classical architect, stylistically comparable to E-L Boullée in his use of austere, geometric forms, exemplified in his toll houses for Paris; for instance, the Barrière de la Villette in the Place de Stalingrad.

**Lethaby** William Richard 1857–1931. English architect. An assistant to Richard Norman Shaw, he embraced the principles of William Morris and Philip Webb in the Arts and Crafts movement, and was cofounder and first director of the Central School of Arts and Crafts from 1894. He wrote a collection of essays entitled *Form in Civilization* 1922.

**Lutyens** Edwin Landseer 1869–1944. English architect. His designs ranged from picturesque to Renaissance style country houses and ultimately evolved into a Classical style as in the Cenotaph, London, and the Viceroy's House, New Delhi.

**Mackintosh** Charles Rennie 1868–1928. Scottish architect, designer, and painter, whose chief work includes the Glasgow School of Art 1896, various Glasgow tea rooms 1897–c. 1911, and Hill House, Helensburgh, 1902–03. His early work is Art Nouveau; he subsequently developed a unique style, both rational and expressive.

**Mansart** Jules Hardouin 1646–1708. see Hardouin-Mansart, Jules.

**Meier** Richard 1934– . US architect whose white designs spring from the poetic modernism of the Le Corbusier villas of the 1920s. His abstract style is at its most mature in the Museum für Kunsthandwerk (Museum of Arts and Crafts), Frankfurt, West Germany, which was completed 1984.

**Mendelsohn** Erich 1887–1953. German Expressionist architect who designed the Einstein Tower, Potsdam, 1919–20. His later work fused Modernist and Expressionist styles; in Britain he built the de la Warr Pavilion 1935–36 in Bexhill-on-Sea, East Sussex. In 1941 he settled in the USA, where he built the Maimonides Hospital, San Francisco, 1946–50.

**Michelangelo** Buonarroti 1475–1564. Italian sculptor, painter, architect, and poet, active in his native Florence and in Rome. His giant talent dominated the High Renaissance. Michelangelo became the architect and sculptor of the Medici funerary chapel 1520–34 in San Lorenzo, he also designed San Lorenzo's library. In his last years he took over the completion of St Peter's basilica, Rome, and designed its great dome. Michelangelo had a lasting influence, with the Mannerist school of architecture copying his decorative details and motifs.

**Mies van der Rohe** Ludwig 1886–1969. German architect who practised in the USA from 1937. He succeeded Gropius as director of the Bauhaus 1929–33. He became professor at the Illinois Technical Institute 1938–58, for which he designed new buildings on characteristically functional lines from 1941. He also designed the bronze-and-glass Seagram building in New York City 1956–59 and numerous apartment blocks. He designed the National Gallery,

Berlin 1963–68.

**Moore** Charles 1925– . US architect with an eclectic approach to design. He was an early exponent of Post-Modernism in, for example, his students' housing for Kresage College, University of California at Santa Cruz, 1972--74, and the Piazza d'Italia in New Orleans, 1979.

**Nash** John 1752–1835. English architect. He laid out Regent's Park, London, and its approaches. Between 1813 and 1820 he planned Regent Street (later rebuilt), repaired and enlarged Buckingham Palace (for which he designed Marble Arch), and rebuilt Brighton Pavilion in flamboyant oriental style.

**Nervi** Pier Luigi 1891–1979. Italian architect who used soft steel mesh within concrete to give it flowing form. For example, the Turin exhibition hall 1949; the UNESCO building in Paris 1952; and the cathedral at New Norcia, near Perth, Australia 1960.

**Neutra** Richard Joseph 1892–1970. Austrian-born architect, who became a US citizen 1929. His works, often in impressive landscape settings, include Lovell Health House, Los Angeles (1929), and Mathematics Park, Princeton, New Jersey.

**Niemeyer** Oscar 1907– . Brazilian architect, joint designer of the United Nations headquarters in New York, and of many buildings in Brasília.

**Olbrich** Joseph Maria 1867–1908. Viennese architect who worked under Otto Wagner and was opposed to the overornamentation of Art Nouveau. His major buildings, however, remain Art Nouveau in spirit: the Vienna Sezession 1897–98, the Hochzeitsturm 1907, and the Tietz department store in Düsseldorf, Germany.

**Palladio** Andrea 1518–1580. Italian Renaissance architect noted for his harmonious and balanced Classical structures. He designed numerous country houses in and around Vicenza, Italy, making use of Roman Classical forms, symmetry, and proportion. He also designed churches in Venice and published his studies of Classical form in several illustrated books. His ideas were revived in England in the early 17th century by Inigo Jones and in the 18th century by Lord Burlington and later by architects in Italy, Holland, Germany, Russia, and the US.

**Paxton** Joseph 1801–1865. English architect, garden superintendent to the Duke of Devonshire from 1826 and designer of the Great Exhibition building 1851 (Crystal Palace), revolutionary in its structural use of glass and iron.

**Piranesi** Giambattista 1720–1778. Italian architect, most significant for his powerful etchings of Roman antiquities and as a theorist of architecture, advocating imaginative use of Roman models. Only one of his designs was built, Sta Maria del Priorato, Rome.

**Pugin** Augustus Welby Northmore 1812–1852. English architect, collaborator with Barry in the detailed design of the Houses of Parliament.

He did much to revive Gothic architecture in England.

**Rogers** Richard 1933– . English architect. His works include the Centre Pompidou in Paris 1977 (jointly with Renzo Piano) and the Lloyd's building in London 1986.

**Rossi** Aldo 1931– . Italian architect and theorist. Rossi is strongly influenced by rationalist thought and Neo-Classicism. His works include the Gallaratese II apartment complex in Milan, 1970; the Modena cemetery, 1973, and the Teatro del Mondo/Floating Theatre in Venice, 1979. He won the Pritzker prize 1990.

**Saarinen** Eero 1910–1961. Finnish-born US architect distinguished for a wide range of innovative modern designs using a variety of creative shapes for buildings. His works include the US embassy, London, the TWA terminal, New York, and Dulles Airport, Washington DC. He collaborated on a number of projects with his father, Eliel Saarinen.

**Saarinen** Eliel 1873–1950. Finnish architect and town planner, founder of the Finnish Romantic school. In 1923 he emigrated to the USA, where he contributed to US skyscraper design by his work in Chicago, and later turned to functionalism.

**Sant'Elia** Antonio 1888–1916. Italian architect. His drawings convey a Futurist vision of a metropolis with skyscrapers, traffic lanes, and streamlined factories.

**Schinkel** Karl Friedrich 1781–1841. Prussian Neo-Classical architect. Major works include the Old Museum, Berlin, 1823–30, the Nikolaikirche in Potsdam 1830–37, and the Roman Bath 1833 in the park of Potsdam.

**Scott** (George) Gilbert 1811–1878. English architect. As the leading practical architect in the mid-19th-century Gothic revival in England, Scott was responsible for the building or restoration of many public buildings, including the Albert Memorial, the Foreign Office, and St Pancras Station, all in London.

**Serlio** Sebastiano 1475–1554. Italian architect and painter, author of *L'Architettura* 1537–51, which set down practical rules for the use of the Classical orders, and was used by architects of the Neo-Classical style throughout Europe.

**Shaw** (Richard) Norman 1831–1912. English architect. He was the leader of the trend away from Gothic and Tudor styles back to Georgian lines. His buildings include Swan House, Chelsea, 1876.

**Sinan** 1489–1588. Ottoman architect, chief architect from 1538 to Suleiman the Magnificent. Among the hundreds of buildings he designed are the Suleimaniye in Istanbul, a mosque complex, and the Topkapi Saray, palace of the sultan (now a museum).

**Smirke** Robert 1780–1867. English Classical architect, designer of the British Museum, London (1823–47).

**Smithson** Alison (1928– ) and Peter (1923– ) English architects, teachers, and theorists, best known for their development in the 1950s and 1960s of the style known as Brutalism, for example in Hunstanton School, Norfolk, 1954; the Economist Building, London, 1964; and Robin Hood Gardens, London, 1968–72.

**Soane** John 1753–1837. English architect, whose individual Neo-Classical designs anticipated contemporary taste. He designed his own house in Lincoln's Inn Fields, London, now the Soane Museum. Little remains of his extensive work at the Bank of England, London.

**Speer** Albert 1905–1981. German architect and minister in the Nazi government during World War II. Commissioned by Hitler, Speer, like his counterparts in Fascist Italy, chose an overblown Classicism to glorify the state, as, for example, in his plan for the Berlin and Nuremberg Party Congress Grounds 1934.

**Stirling** James 1926– . English architect, associated with collegiate and museum architecture. His works include the engineering building at Leicester University, and the Clore Gallery (the extension to house the Turner collection) at the Tate Gallery, London, opened in 1987.

**Sullivan** Louis Henry 1856–1924. US architect who worked in Chicago and designed early skyscrapers such as the Wainwright Building, St Louis, 1890 and the Guaranty Building, Buffalo, 1894. He was influential in the anti-ornament movement. Frank Lloyd Wright was his pupil.

**Tange** Kenzo 1913– . Japanese architect. His works include the National Gymnasium, Tokyo, for the 1964 Olympics, and the city of Abuja, planned to replace Lagos as the capital of Nigeria.

**Terry** (John) Quinlan 1937– . English Neo-Classical architect. His work includes country houses, for example Merks Hall, Great Dunmow, Essex, 1982, and the larger-scale Richmond, London, riverside project, commissioned 1984.

**Vanbrugh** John 1664–1726. English Baroque architect and dramatist. He designed Blenheim Palace, Oxfordshire, and Castle Howard, Yorkshire, and wrote the comic dramas *The Relapse* 1696 and *The Provok'd Wife* 1697.

**van Eyck** Aldo Dutch architect; see Eyck, Aldo van.

**Venturi** Robert 1925– . US architect. He pioneered Post-Modernism through his books, *Complexity and Contradiction in Architecture* 1967 and *Learning from Las Vegas* 1972. In 1986 he was commissioned to design an extension to the National Gallery, London.

**Vitruvius** (Marcus Vitruvius Pollio) 1st century BC. Roman architect, whose ten-volume interpretation of Roman architecture *De architectura* influenced Alberti and Palladio.

**Voysey** Charles Francis Annesley 1857–1941. English architect and designer. He designed country houses which were characteristically asymmetrical with massive buttresses, long sloping roofs, and rough-cast walls. He also designed textiles and wallpaper.

**Wagner** Otto 1841–1918. Viennese architect. Initially designing in the Art Nouveau style, for example Vienna Stadtbahn 1894–97, he later rejected ornament for rationalism, as in the Post Office Savings Bank, Vienna, 1904–06. He influenced Viennese architects such as Josef Hoffmann, Adolf Loos, and Joseph Olbrich.

**Waterhouse** Alfred 1830–1905. English architect. He was a leading exponent of Victorian Neo-Gothic using, typically, multicoloured tiles and bricks. His works include the Natural History Museum in London 1868.

**Webb** Philip (Speakman) 1831–1915. English architect. He mostly designed private houses, including the Red House, Bexley Heath, Sussex, for William Morris, and was one of the leading figures, with Richard Norman Shaw and C F A Voysey, in the revival of domestic English architecture in the late 19th century.

**Wren** Christopher 1632–1723. English architect, designer of St Paul's Cathedral, London, built 1675–1710; many London churches including St Bride's, Fleet Street, and St Mary-le-Bow, Cheapside; the Royal Exchange; Marlborough House; and the Sheldonian Theatre, Oxford.

**Wright** Frank Lloyd 1869–1959. US architect, who, as a student of Louis Sullivan 1888–93, rejected Neo-Classicist styles for 'organic architecture' in which buildings reflected their natural surroundings. Among his buildings are the Robie house 1909 in Chicago; his Spring Green home, Wisconsin, Taliesin East 1925; Falling Water, near Pittsburgh, Pennsylvania, 1936, a house built straddling a waterfall; the Johnson Wax Company Administration building, Racine, Wisconsin, 1938, and the company's Laboratory Tower 1949; the high-rise Price Company Tower, Bartlesville, Oklahoma, 1953; and the Guggenheim Museum, New York, 1959.

# TERMS

**adobe** building constructed of sun-dried mud bricks commonly found in Spain, Latin America, and New Mexico.

**arch** curved structure of masonry that supports the weight of material over an open space, as in a bridge or doorway. It orginally consisted of several wedge-shaped stones supported by their mutual pressure. The term is also applied to any curved structure that is an arch in form only.

**atrium** an inner, open courtyard. Originally the central court or main room of an ancient Roman house, open to the sky, often with a shallow pool to catch water.

**bailey** open space or court of a stone-built castle.

**basilica** type of Roman public building; a large roofed hall flanked by columns, generally with an aisle on each side, used for judicial or other public business. The earliest known basilica, at Pompeii, dates from the 2nd century BC. This architectural form was adopted by the early Christians for their churches.

**brick** common building material, rectangular in shape, made of clay that has been fired in a

# THE VENTURI EXTENSION TO THE NATIONAL GALLERY – CAUSE CELÈBRE?

The story of the extension to the National Gallery in London's Trafalgar Square, at least part of which should be sub-titled the Prince and the Architects, starts in 1982, nine years before the completed building opened to the public. The Trustees had planned an extension to house the Italian Renaissance collection which was to include offices to fund the gallery space. The Secretary of State for the Environment insisted on an open competition to choose the architects. Seven were shortlisted and the competition advisers listed the top three in 1982, but there was no consensus about which was the outright winner. Opinion was divided and the Secretary of State and his advisers broke the impasse by suggesting the Trustees choose not a design but an architect, who would then be asked to redesign his scheme. Accordingly, the British firm Ahrends, Burton & Koralek (ABK) were selected and given a new brief. Some of the unsuccessful competitors were angry that the goal posts had been moved. Critics said the muddle typified the English establishment's attitude towards art. The prestigious new gallery for some of the nation's – and the world's – greatest pictures was to be produced by an unhappy coalition of property developers, architects and academics. ABK produced, through consultation with the Gallery staff, a scheme which was what was required, at least as regards the internal layout. However, the modifications destroyed many of the virtues of the original scheme. In addition, the building was designed in a modernist style, with flat roofs, a tall tower and a gridded façade. Even before the scheme reached the planners many members of the architectural establishment had attacked it. 'Back to the drawing board please' asked Charles Jencks; 'a catastrophe for British culture if it goes ahead' said Leon Krier. Enter the Prince. Making his first foray into the debate about public architecture, the Prince of Wales memorably described the proposed scheme as resembling 'a monstrous carbuncle on the face of a well-loved friend'. The debate raged and feelings ran high. The Prince went on to make further pronouncements on the parlous state of modern architecture. In 1987 *Blueprint* magazine argued in an editorial that his assumption of the role of supreme arbiter of architectural taste represented the largest expansion of the royal prerogative in a century, and that he exercised the authority of 'an absolutist Habsburg'. Yet the Prince did seem to speak for 'ordinary' people; he was able to articulate the point of view of the man on the Clapham omnibus and, if he was to be believed, that seasoned traveller preferred Neo-Classical architecture. In such a climate the tide turned against the proposed National Gallery scheme and the developers dropped out. The day was saved by the offer of funding for the new gallery by the Sainsbury family. Freed from the need to fund the project from office

development, the trustees gratefully accepted and invited a number of new architects to submit proposals. The brief did not use the word 'postmodern' but the trustees made it clear that the new design should be 'sympathetic'. The architect selected, the American Robert Venturi, was a theorist and teacher who had been in the vanguard of the move against the Modern Movement. He was known for his statement 'Main Street is almost all right'. In other words, a degree of diversity enlivens public spaces. They do not require rigid planning or strict rules; jokes are allowed.

Inside and outside need not be in the same style. Venturi took the Neo-Classical features of the existing National Gallery, designed by William Wilkins in 1832–8, and reapplied them jokily in his extension, borrowing, breaking up and rearranging classical motifs such as pilasters, and inserting polychromatic Egyptian columns in the Portland stone façade. The inconsistency that Venturi argued for in his writings was exemplified in many features of the building. It is worth noting that Venturi, alone of all the architects, submitted a written proposal, and won the competition without a single drawing.

In 1990 there was a competition for an extension to Dulwich Picture Gallery, completed in 1814 by Sir John Soane who is often regarded as the founding father of gallery design. The controversial prize-winning entry, by Zetek, O'Neill & Grasby, was uncompromisingly modernist. However, the modest proposal at Dulwich paradoxically highlighted 'self-effacement' as an architectural virtue in the design of art galleries. Architecture should take a back seat in the display of paintings, it was said. Others argued that sites of national importance in Central London deserved strong architectural statements to stand as a monument to their time.

*The National Gallery Sainsbury Wing, Trafalgar Square, London*

kiln. Bricks are made by kneading a mixture of crushed clay and other materials into a stiff mud and extruding it into a ribbon. The ribbon is cut into individual bricks, which are fired at a temperature of up to about 1,000°C/ 1,800°F. Bricks may alternatively be pressed into shape in moulds.

**buttress** reinforcement in brick or masonry, built against a wall to give it strength. A *flying buttress* is an arc transmitting the force of the wall to be supported to an outer buttress, common in Gothic architecture.

**cantilever** beam or structure that is fixed at one end only, though it may be supported at some point along its length; for example, a diving board. The cantilever principle, widely used in construction engineering, eliminates the need for a second main support at the free end of the beam, allowing for more elegant structures and reducing the amount of materials required. Many large-span bridges have been built on the cantilever principle.

**caryatid** building support or pillar in the shape of a woman, the name deriving from the Karyatides who were priestesses at the temple of Artemis at Karyai; a male figure is a *telamon* or *atlas*.

**castle** the private fortress of a king or noble during the Middle Ages. At first a building on a mound surrounded by a wooden fence, this was later copied in stone. The earliest castles in Britain were built following the Norman Conquest, and the art of castle building reached a peak in Europe during the 13th century. By the 15th century, the need for castles for domestic defence had largely disappeared, and the advent of gunpowder had made them largely useless against attack.

**cement** any bonding agent used to unite particles in a single mass or to cause one surface to adhere to another. *Portland cement* is a powder obtained from burning together a mixture of lime (or chalk) and clay, and when mixed with water and sand or gravel, turns into mortar or concrete. In geology, a chemically precipitated material such as carbonate that occupies the interstices of clastic rocks is called cement.

**château** term originally applied to a French medieval castle, but now used to describe a country house or important residence in France. The château was first used as a domestic building in the late 15th century; by the reign of Louis XIII (1610–43) fortifications such as moats and keeps were no longer used for defensive purposes, but merely as decorative features. The Loire valley contains some fine examples of châteaux.

**cladding** thin layer of external covering on a building; for example, tiles, wood, stone, concrete.

**cloister** a covered walk within a convent or monastery, often opening onto a courtyard.

**colonnade** row of columns supporting arches or an entablature.

**column** a structure, round or polygonal in plan, erected vertically as a support for some part of a building. Cretan paintings reveal the existence of wooden columns in Aegean architecture,

about 1500 BC. The Hittites, Assyrians, and Egyptians also used wooden columns, and they are a feature of the monumental architecture of China and Japan. In Classical architecture there are five principal types of column; see *order*.

**community architecture** movement enabling people to work directly with architects in the design and building of their own homes and neighbourhoods. It is an approach strongly encouraged by the Prince of Wales.

**concrete** building material composed of cement, stone, sand, and water. It has been used since Roman and Egyptian times. During the 20th century, it has been increasingly employed as an economical alternative to materials such as brick and wood.

**conservation, architectural** attempts to maintain the character of buildings and historical areas. In England this is subject to a growing body of legislation that has designated more listed buildings. There are now over 6,000 conservation areas throughout England alone.

**Corinthian** in Classical architecture, one of the five types of column; see *order*.

**curtain wall** in buildings, a light-weight wall of glass or aluminium that is not load-bearing and is hung from a metal frame rather than built up from the ground like a brick wall. Curtain walls are typically used in high-rise blocks.

**Doric** in Classical architecture, one of the five types of column; see *order*.

**garden city** a town built in a rural area and designed to combine town and country advantages, with its own industries, controlled developments, private and public gardens, and cultural centre. The idea was proposed by Ebenezer Howard (1850–1928) who, in 1899 founded the Garden City Association, which established the first garden city, Letchworth (in Hertfordshire).

**gargoyle** spout projecting from the roof gutter of a building with the purpose of directing water away from the wall. The term is usually applied to the ornamental forms found in Gothic architecture; these were carved in stone in the form of fantastic animals, angels, or human heads.

**green belt** area surrounding a large city, officially designated not to be built on but preserved as open space (for agricultural and recreational use).

**ha-ha** in landscape gardening, a sunken boundary wall permitting an unobstructed view beyond a garden; a device much used by Capability Brown in the 18th century.

**Ionic** in Classical architecture, one of the five types of column; see *order*.

**keep** or *dungeon* or *donjon* the main tower of a castle, containing enough accommodation to serve as living-quarters under siege conditions.

**listed building** a building officially recognized as having historical or architectural interest and therefore legally protected from alteration or demolition. In England the listing is drawn up by the Secretary of State for the Environment under the advice of the English Heritage organization, which provides various resources for architectural conservation.

**mezzanine** architectural term for a storey with a lower ceiling placed between two main storeys, usually between the ground and first floors of a building.

**minaret** slender turret or tower attached to a Muslim mosque or to buildings designed in that style. It has one or more balconies, from which the *muezzin* calls the people to prayer five times a day.

**misericord** or *miserere* in church architecture, a projection on the underside of a hinged seat of the choir stalls, used as a rest for a priest when standing during long services. Misericords are often decorated with carvings.

**module** in construction, a standard or unit that governs the form of the rest: for example, Japanese room sizes are traditionally governed by multiples of standard tatami floor mats; today prefabricated buildings are mass-produced in a similar way. The components of a spacecraft are designed in coordination; for example, for the Apollo Moon landings the craft comprised a command module (for working, eating, sleeping), service module (electricity generators, oxygen supplies, manoeuvring rocket), and lunar module (to land and return the astronauts).

**obelisk** tall, tapering column of stone, much used in ancient Egyptian as well as Roman architecture.

**order** in Classical architecture, the column (including capital, shaft, and base) and the entablature, considered as an architectural whole. The five orders are Doric, Ionic, Corinthian, Tuscan, and Composite.

**pantheon** originally a temple for worshipping all the gods, such as that in ancient Rome, rebuilt by Hadrian and still used as a church. In more recent times, it is a building where famous people are buried (Panthéon, Paris).

**pediment** the triangular part crowning the fronts of buildings in classic styles. The pediment was a distinctive feature of Greek temples.

**peristyle** range of columns surrounding a building or open courtyard.

**piano nobile** the main floor of a house, containing the main reception room.

**portico** porch with a pediment and columns.

**prestressed concrete** reinforced concrete in which ducts enclose mechanically tensioned steel cables. This allows the most efficient use of the tensile strength of steel with the compressive strength of concrete.

**pylon** steel lattice tower that supports high-tension electrical cables. In ancient Egyptian architecture, a pylon is one of a pair of inward-sloping towers that flank an entrance.

**pyramid** four-sided building with triangular sides used in ancient Egypt to enclose a royal tomb; for example, the Great Pyramid of Khufu/Cheops at Giza, near Cairo; 230 m/ 755 ft square and 147 m/481 ft high. In Babylon and Assyria broadly stepped pyramids (ziggurats) were used as the base for a shrine to

architectural orders

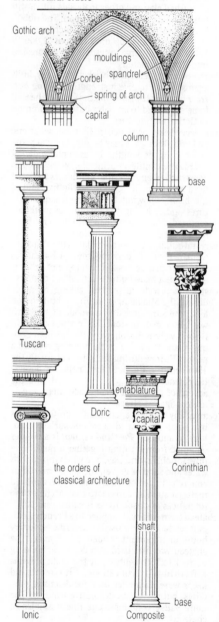

the orders of classical architecture

a god: the Tower of Babel was probably one of these.

**RIBA** abbreviation for *Royal Institute of British Architects*.

**satellite town** new town planned and built to serve a particular local industry, or as a dormitory or overspill town for people who work in a nearby metropolis. New towns in Britain include Port Sunlight near Birkenhead (Cheshire), built to house workers at Lever

Brothers soap factories. More recent examples include Welwyn Garden City (1948), Cumbernauld (1955), and Milton Keynes (1967).

**sick building syndrome** malaise diagnosed in the early 1980s among office workers and thought to be caused by such pollutants as formaldehyde (from furniture and insulating materials), benzene (from paint), and the solvent trichloroethylene, concentrated in air-conditioned buildings. Symptoms include headache, sore throat, tiredness, colds, and flu. Studies have found that it can cause a 40% drop in productivity and a 30% rise in absenteeism.

**skyscraper** building so tall that it appears to 'scrape the sky', developed 1868 in New York, USA, where land prices were high and the geology adapted to such methods of construction. Skyscrapers are now found in cities throughout the world. The world's tallest free-standing structure is the CN (Canadian National) Tower, Toronto, 555 m/1,821 ft.

**town planning** the design of buildings or groups of buildings in a physical and social context, concentrating on the relationship between various buildings and their environment, as well as on their uses. See also garden city; new town.

**Tuscan** in Classical architecture, one of the five types of column; see **order**.

**urban renewal** the adaptation of existing buildings in towns and cities to meet changes in economic, social, and environmental requirements, rather than demolishing them.

**vault** arched ceiling or roof built mainly of stone or bricks.

**vernacular** the domestic or peasant building tradition of different localities, not designed by trained architects; for example, thatched cottages in England, stone in Scotland, adobe huts in Mexico, wooden buildings in the Nordic countries.

### New buildings

*When new buildings are being designed, what do you think the architect or designer has most in mind—the overall look of the building or how it will be used by the people in it?*

| | |
|---|---|
| Overall look | 52 |
| Its uses | 37 |
| Don't know | 13 |

# HISTORY OF WESTERN ART

In the visual arts of Western civilization, painting and sculpture have been the dominant forms for many centuries. This has not always been the case in other cultures. Islamic art, for example, is one of ornament, as artists were forbidden to portray living creatures. In some cultures masks, tattoos, pottery, and metalwork have been the main forms of visual art. In the recent past technology has made new art forms possible, such as photography and cinema, and today electronic media—computer graphics, computer-aided animation and 'painting', and other imaging techniques—have led to entirely new ways of creating and presenting visual images.

## ANCIENT ART

**prehistoric art** 25,000–1000 BC. The history of the fine arts, painting and sculpture, begins about 21,000 BC in the Paleolithic, or Old Stone Age. Vivid, lifelike images of animals and humans have been found incised, painted or sculpted on the walls deep inside the caves where our ancestors sheltered, mostly in Spain and in southwestern France, but also in Portugal, Sicily, and Russia. The images of reindeer, mammoth, horses and bison are most common, varying from very small to almost lifesize. It is thought that they served as part of a 'magic' ritual to ensure a successful hunt. Paintings such as those at the caves of *Lascaux* in France show great skill in drawing, with vigorous and sweepingly graceful outlines. Stone Age people also used flint tools to carve small figurines in bone, horn, or stone. The most famous of these is the so-called *Venus of Willendorf*, a limestone statuette 11 cm/4.5 in high, found in lower Austria and dating from about 21,000 BC. Her exaggeratedly bulbous form makes clear her magic significance as a fertility figure.

**art of early civilizations** 14,000–300 BC. Architecture became the new art form when people began to settle in communities as farmers rather than as hunters. They decorated their buildings with sculpture, imposing a sense of pattern and order on them, although Stonehenge in Britain (1800–1400 BC) had not achieved this sophistication. In Europe, *Celtic art* ornamented tombs, crosses, metalwork and pottery with stylized animal and plant forms in swirling curvilinear patterns. Pottery had reached Europe from the Near East where it began as early as 5500 BC in Mesopotamia, where sign pictures also grew into cuneiform (wedge-shaped) writing. The Near and Middle East produced many highly developed urban civilizations, including the **Sumerian** (4000 BC), and the **Persian** (550 BC). In these cultures, sculptures and reliefs of people, gods, and animals decorated palaces, temples, and tombs telling stories or praising their gods and rulers. A fine example is the grand stairway of the *Persian royal palace*, Persepolis, from 518–516 BC. Outstanding examples of precious metalwork, glassware, and pottery also survive, of which there are splendid collections in the British Museum and the Louvre.

**Egyptian art** 3000–200 BC. The *Great Sphinx at Giza* (2680–2565 BC), a gigantic human-headed lion carved from an outcropping of natural rock, is the supreme example of Egyptian sculpture. 56 m/185 ft long and 19 m/63 ft high, it was meant to guard for eternity the god-king's pyramid tomb nearby. Most Egyptian art is funerary, largely consisting of sculptured relief panels painted in bright, lifelike colours covering the walls of tombs and temples. They depend on strong, simple outlines, the main aim being clarity: to portray the dead in their idealized prime, their servants and families, and the objects, animals, foods and activities they enjoyed in life, so that these could be magically transported into the afterworld to be enjoyed forever.

Human forms are composed almost diagrammatically to show the whole of a person, face and legs in profile, upper torso in front view, hips three-quarters and with the eye magnified. If anything needed further description a hieroglyphic label would be added. Statues, whether of wood or stone, were also generally painted. They retain a strong cubic sense of the block from which they were hewn, with the figures facing straight ahead, the arms in a single unit with the body. The serene vision of eternity found in all Egyptian art is epitomized in the beautiful portrait head of *Queen Nefertiti* in the Staatlich Museum, Berlin, dating from about 1360 BC.

**art of Aegean civilizations** 2800–100 BC. The **Minoan** and **Mycenean** civilizations flourished in the area of the Aegean Sea from about 2800 BC. Based on the island of Crete, Minoan society was pleasure-loving and open, and its major monument, the new *palace at Knossos* 1700 BC, was decorated with cheerful frescoes of scenes from daily life, plants, birds, and leaping fish and dolphins. Their pottery was painted in the same fresh, spontaneous style with plant and animal motifs curving to suit the form of the vases. In 1400 BC they were conquered by the Myceneans from the Peloponnese, whose art reflected their more warlike society. Instead of airy palaces, they constructed fortified citadels such as Mycenae itself, which was entered through the *Lion Gate* 1330 BC, named for the remarkable monumental sculpture that adorns it. In the nearby Cyclades Islands a unique art form emerged about 2800 BC: the small marble *Cycladic figures* much admired today, which represent the Great Mother Goddess in such streamlined simplicity that her face is simply an elongated oval with a triangular nose.

Many of the ideas and art forms of these early sea-faring civilizations were to be adapted by the Greeks who came from Central Asia between 2000–1000 BC to establish their own splendid culture that was to dominate Western taste and thought for many centuries.

## CLASSICAL ART

**Greek art** 1000–400 BC. Greek temples are almost sculptures in themselves, designed not to be entered but to be looked at. The sculptured reliefs which decorated them, such as the *Elgin Marbles* (now in the British Museum) which came from the Parthenon in Athens, show perfectly the Greek artistic ideal: the human form at its most beautiful.

The major periods of Greek art can be divided into the Archaic (late 8th century–480 BC), Classical (480–323 BC), and Hellenistic (323–27 BC). No large-scale painting survives, although colour was very important, and even the white marble sculptures we admire today were originally brightly painted.

In the **Archaic** period the statues of naked standing men (*kouroi*) and draped females (*korai*) show an Egyptian influence in their rigid frontality. By about 500 BC the figure was allowed to relax its weight onto one leg and immediately seemed to come alive. The archaic smile which gave these early figures a certain cheerful sameness vanished in the **Classical** period when expressions assumed a dignified serenity. Further movement was introduced in new poses such as in Myron's bronze *Diskobolus/The Discus Thrower* 460–50 BC, and in the rhythmic Parthenon reliefs of men and horses supervised by Phidias. Artists were no longer anonymous and among sculptors whose work is known are **Praxiteles**, **Scopas**, **Lysippus**, and **Polykleitos**, whose *Doryphoros/The Spear Carrier* 450–440 BC was of such harmony and poise that it set a standard for beautiful proportions which is still in use today. Praxiteles introduced the female nude into the sculptural repertory with the graceful *Aphrodite of Knidos, c.* 350 BC. It was easier to express movement in bronze, hollow-cast by the lost wax method, but few bronze sculptures survive and many are known only through Roman copies in marble.

The **Hellenistic** period, when the Greek Empire under Alexander the Great spread to Egypt and beyond Iraq, produced such sculptures as the *Winged Victory of Samothrace* with its dramatic drapery, the expressive *Dying Gaul* and the tortured *Laocoon*, which explored the effects of movement and of deeply-felt emotion.

*Vase painting* is the one form of Greek painting which has survived the centuries. Good, even great, artists worked as both potters and painters until the 5th century BC and the works they signed were exported throughout the Empire. Made in several standard shapes and sizes, the pottery served as functional containers for wine, water, and oil. The first decoration took the form of simple lines and circles, from which the *'Geometric style'* emerged near Athens in the 10th century BC. It consisted of precisely drawn patterns, the most charac-

teristic being the key meander. Gradually the bands of decoration multiplied and the human figure, geometrically stylized, was added.

About 700 BC the potters of Corinth invented the **black figure** technique in which the unglazed red clay was painted in black with mythological scenes, gods and battles in a narrative frieze. About 530 BC Athenian potters reversed the process and developed the more sophisticated **red figure** pottery, which allowed for more detailed and elaborate painting of the figures in red against a black background. This grew increasingly naturalistic, with lively scenes of daily life. The finest examples date from the mid-6th century to mid-5th century BC at Athens. Later painters tried to follow major art trends and represent spatial depth, dissipating the unique quality of their fine linear technique.

The ancient Greeks excelled in carving gems and cameos, and in jewellery and metalwork. They also invented the pictorial mosaic and from the 5th century BC onwards floors were paved with coloured pebbles depicting mythological subjects. Later, specially cut cubes of stone and glass called *tesserae* were used, and Greek craftsmen working for the Romans reproduced famous paintings such as that of *Alexander at the Battle of Issus* from Pompeii, giving us some idea of these lost masterpieces.

**Roman art** 753 BC–AD 410. During the 8th century BC the Etruscans appeared as the first native Italian civilization, north and west of the river Tiber. Their art shows influences of archaic Greece and the Near East. Their coffins (*sarcophagi*), carved with reliefs and topped with portraits of the dead, reclining on one elbow as if at an eternal banquet, were to influence the later Romans and early Christians.

Under Julius Caesar's successor Augustus (27 BC–AD 14) the Roman Empire was established. Art and architecture played an important role in unifying the European nations under Roman rule. The Romans greatly admired Greek art and became the first collectors, importing vast quantities of marbles and bronzes, and even Greek craftsmen to make copies. Realistic portrait sculpture was an important original development by the Romans. A cult of heroes began and in public places official statues were erected of generals, rulers and philosophers. The portrait bust developed as a new art form from about 75 BC; these were serious, factual portraits of a rugged race of patriarchs to whose wisdom and authority their subject nations should reasonably submit.

*Narrative relief sculpture* also flourished in Rome, again linked to the need to commemorate publicly the glorious victories of their heroes. These appeared on monumental altars, triumphal arches and giant columns such as *Trajan's Column* AD 106–113 which records his historic battles like a strip cartoon, winding its way around the column for 200 m/656 ft. Strict realism in portraiture gave way to a certain amount of Greek-style idealization in the ing church portals, on capitals and corbels, it translated manuscript illuminations into stone, combining naturalistic elements from the antique Roman style with the fantastic, poetical, and pattern-loving Celtic and Germanic tradition. Imaginary beasts, monsters, saints, and sinners mingle with humour and innocence in an enchanted world of biblical themes. Fine examples remain in Burgundy and southwest France, extending down into Spain on the pilgrimage route to Santiago de Compostela.

Gothic during the late 12th and 13th centuries European cities began to raise great cathedrals, and sculptural decoration became more monumental. The cathedrals of Chartres and Reims in France had such extensive sculptural programmes that many artists came from far afield to work and learn there. A new interest in the natural world is shown in such examples as the strikingly life-like founder figures of Naumberg Cathedral, East Germany, (c. 1245) or in the naturalistic foliage on the capitals at Southwell in England.

With the increased height of the cathedrals, stained glass windows became their new glory. Chartres, where an entire set of stained glass is preserved, awesomely illustrates the magical effect of coloured light seemingly suspended within its dark interior. Both windows and sculpture, by depicting the lives of the saints and texts from the bible, gave the faithful an encyclopedic view of the Christian history of the world.

Art patronage, although still mainly concerned with religious imagery, now burgeoned in the many small courts of Europe and under this influence art became more stylized, delicate and refined. Even the Virgin Mary was portrayed as an elegant young queen. In her most characteristic pose, holding the Christ child in her arms, her weight shifts gracefully onto one hip causing her body to form an S-curve and her drapery to fall into elegant folds. This figure stance, the 'Gothic sway', became a hallmark of the period. Court patronage produced exquisite small ivories, precious goldsmith's work, devotional books illustrated with miniatures, and tapestries which warmed cold castle walls, depicting romantic tales or the joys of springtime.

In Italy, the monumentality of the antique Roman past subdued the spread of northern Gothic ideas. A type of Gothic Classicism was developed by the sculptors Nicola and Giovanni Pisano (working 1258–1314) whose four great pulpits carved in relief (at Siena, Pistoia, and two at Pisa) show the influence of antique sarcophagi but also that of French Gothic in the dramatic expressiveness of their figures.

An innovative group of painters brought the art of fresco painting, always important in Italy, to a new height. Giotto's cycle of the lives of Mary and Christ in the Arena Chapel, Padua (c. 1300) set a new standard for figural naturalism, seen as proto-Renaissance, and in the Town Hall of Siena Ambrogio Lorenzetti

illustrated the effects of Good and Bad Government (1337) in panoramic townscapes and landscapes.

Panel painting, in jewel-like colours on a gold background, developed from Byzantine models, and the Sienese painter Duccio's Maestá for the High Altar of Siena Cathedral (1308–11) achieved a peak of expressive power of line and colour. Simone Martini developed this into courtly refinement in both frescoes (for example Assisi, Siena) and panel paintings, and became a major influence on the International Gothic style which in the years around 1400 achieved the perfect mix of French courtliness and the Italian command of form, together with a delight in the observed details of nature. A magnificent example of this moment in art can be seen in the miniatures painted for the devotional book, the Très Riches Heures du Duc de Berry, by the Flemish Limbourg brothers in about 1415.

## THE ITALIAN RENAISSANCE

Florence the rebirth or 'Renaissance' of Classical art and learning began in Florence in the early 15th century. The self-made men of Florence, merchants and bankers, saw themselves as direct descendants of the great men of ancient Rome and, led by the Medici family, vied with each other in patronage of all the arts, building palaces and churches filled with sculptured and painted monuments to themselves. In this new age of humanism, people—and the aesthetic delights of the world they lived in—were suddenly important.

The most far-reaching artistic innovation of the period, which was one of continual discovery and rediscovery, was that of scientific perspective by Filippo Brunelleschi 1377–1446, the architect who later built the dome of Florence Cathedral. Perspective allowed artists to create an authentic three-dimensional space, correctly sized to the figures within their paintings. Masaccio 1401–28 used this new style to superb effect in his frescoes in the Brancacci Chapel, Santa Maria del Carmine, in which the apostles look like Roman gods. The sculptor Donatello c. 1386–1466 used perspective in his relief sculptures. His bronze statues like the youthful David 1430–2, the first free-standing nude since antiquity, or his equestrian statue of the mercenary General Gattamelata (Padua, 1443) look back to Classical prototypes but have the alert liveliness of all early Renaissance art. In his later work, such as his wood-carving of the aged Mary Magdalene 1445, he sought dramatic expression through distortion, even ugliness. His only real rival was the goldsmith and bronze sculptor Lorenzo Ghiberti 1378–1455, who only gradually adapted his graceful International Gothic style to Renaissance ideals in such works as the gilt-bronze Baptistery doors which Michelangelo called 'The Gates of Paradise'.

Paolo Uccello's (1397–1475) decorative

## TEN HIGHEST PRICES EVER PAID FOR WORKS OF ART AT AUCTION

| Artist | Title of work | Auction house/date of sale | Auction price $m |
|---|---|---|---|
| Van Gogh | Portrait of Dr Gachet | Christie's, May 1990 | 82.5 |
| Renoir | Au Moulin de la Galette | Sotheby's, May 1990 | 78.1 |
| Van Gogh | Irises | Sotheby's, Nov 1987 | 53.9 |
| Picasso | Les Noces de Pierette | Binoche et Godeau, Nov 1989 | 51.9 |
| Picasso | Self portrait—Yo Picasso | Sotheby's, May 1989 | 47.8 |
| Picasso | Au Lapine Agile | Sotheby's, Nov 1989 | 40.7 |
| Van Gogh | Sunflowers | Christie's, Mar 1987 | 40.3 |
| Picasso | Acrobate et Jeune Arlequin | Christie's, May 1989 | 38.9 |
| Pontormo | Portrait of Duke Cosimo I de Medici | Christie's, Nov 1988 | 35.2 |
| Manet | Rue Mosnier decorated with flags | Christie's, Nov 1989 | 26.4 |

Source: Cultural Trends 1990

propaganda statues of the emperors, befitting their semi-divine status. Gods and allegorical figures feature with Rome's heroes on such narrative relief sculptures as those on Augustus's giant altar to peace, the *Ara Pacis* 13–9 BC.

Very little **Roman painting** has survived, and much of what is is due to the volcanic eruption of Mount Vesuvius in AD 79 which buried the southern Italian seaside towns of Pompeii and Herculaneum under ash, thus preserving the lively and impressionistic wall paintings (frescoes) which decorated the holiday villas of an art-loving elite. Favourite motifs were illusionistic and still-life. A type of interior decoration known as **Grotesque**, rediscovered in Rome during the Renaissance, combined swirling plant motifs, strange animals and tiny fanciful scenes. Grotesque was much used in later decorative schemes whenever it was fashionable to quote the Classical period.

The art of **mosaic** was universally popular throughout the Roman Empire. It was introduced from Greece and used for floors as well as walls and vaults, in *trompe l'oeil* effects, geometric patterns and scenes from daily life and mythology.

## MEDIEVAL ART

**early Christian and Byzantine art** AD 330–1453. In 312 the Emperor Constantine was converted to Christianity and made it one of the official religions of the Roman State. Churches were built, and artistic traditions adapted to the portrayal of the new Christian saints and symbols. Roman burial chests *(sarcophagi)* were adopted by the Christians and their imagery of pagan myths gradually changed into biblical themes.

**Byzantine style** developed in the East in Constantinople which in 330 became the headquarters of the Roman Empire, and an Eastern Christian tradition was maintained there until 1453 when Constantinople was conquered by the Turks. The use of mosaic came to be associated with both Byzantine art and early Christian church decoration in the West. Ravenna became the Western imperial capital in the 5th century, and the ecclesiastical buildings there, built in the 5th and 6th centuries, are a glorious tribute to the art of mosaic, presenting powerful religious images on walls and vaults in brilliant, glittering colour. Byzantine art moved away from the natural portrayal of people and became highly stylized, symbolizing the divine. Ornament became flattened into intricate lacework patterns. Oriental, highly decorative, and unchanging, the Byzantine style can be seen in the icons—often thought to be capable of working miracles—which have remained for centuries the main religious art of Greece and Russia.

**art of the Dark Ages** AD 400–800. The 400 years between the fall of the Roman Empire and the establishment of Charlemagne's new Holy Roman Empire in 800 are traditionally known as the Dark Ages, and the art of that period as belonging to the **Migration Period**. Through a time of turmoil and invasion, with the northern 'barbarians' overrunning the old Mediterranean civilizations, the Christian church maintained its stability and the interchange of artistic traditions fostered creativity.

The art of the migrant peoples consisted mainly of portable objects, articles of personal use or adornment. They excelled in metalwork and jewellery, often in gold with garnet or enamel inlays and ornamented with highly stylized, animal-based interlace patterns. This type of ornament was translated into manuscript illumination such as the decorated pages of the *Lindisfarne Gospel* (in the British Museum) which dates from the 7th century, or the 8th century *Book of Kells* (in Trinity College, Dublin). With Charlemagne's Christian Empire modelled on that of ancient Rome, a cultural renaissance ensued, drawing its inspiration from the late Classical artistic traditions the early Christians. At Charlemagne's capital, Aachen, the human figure was reintroduced into art and continuous narrative was rediscovered in the *Tours Bibles* produced there. They in turn influenced the sculptured reliefs on the bronze doors at St Michael's Church, Hildesheim in Germany, dating from 1015, the first doors cast in one piece in the West since Roman times.

**art of the Middle Ages** AD 800–1300. Under the unifying force of the Latin Church, a new civilization spread across Europe which during the 10th century produced a style in art called **Romanesque**, and, in England, **Norman**. Chiefly evident in relief sculpture surround-

# TO RESTORE OR NOT TO RESTORE—WHAT IS A WORK OF ART?

At the end of the October of 1512, Michelangelo Buonarotti put the final touches to the Sistine Chapel ceiling. It had taken him four years of immense physical discomfort working in a medium, fresco, of which he had very little experience. Nevertheless, it came to be regarded as one of the greatest masterpieces of Western civilisation.

Nearly 500 years later, the Vatican authorities decided that the ceiling was due for comprehensive cleaning and restoration. Previous restorers through the centuries had attempted to brighten the surface by applying varnishes made from animal glues. But these too had eventually darkened and, worse still, had recently started to blister and fall away, in some places taking the painted surface with them.

The new team of restorers, led by Gianluigi Colalucci, took ten years to complete their task, which was fully unveiled to the public in 1990. What they revealed was a spectacular transformation from darkness into light, dull muted tones had become brilliant even garish colours—results that have divided critical opinion.

The art historical arguments centre around Michelangelo's technical ability in the art of fresco, a difficult and complicated medium. In its purest form, *buon fresco*, the artist paints directly onto a layer of freshly applied wet plaster, *intonaco*. As it dries, the water-based paint is bound into the plaster and the colours visibly lighten. The difficulty lies in attempting to match the colours when starting a new section of plaster the following day. Any failure to do this can be remedied by overpainting the combined sections when dry, *a secco*, in order to harmonize them. Did Michelangelo apply any such *a secco* finishing touches? The Vatican experts think not but many disagree.

Of equal concern are the scientific arguments about the solvent, AB57, used in the restoration. This substance was developed by the Vatican Museum specifically for fresco. It is applied in the form of a gel but in some cases leaving it on for too long has resulted in the paint itself being removed. It is also feared that, if moisture levels build up, the presence of the solvent in the fresco fabric could cause corrosion and salt formation. Added to this, the removal of the varnishes has made the fresco surface even more vulnerable to modern pollution.

One positive outcome of this controversy is the extent to which it has publicized the mysteriously inconsistent 'science' of conservation, an activity usually carried out behind closed doors in laboratory-type conditions. In this case, the entire process was filmed by Nippon Television, who sponsored the restoration in exchange for the right to reproduce the work for a limited period. Was the sponsor's desire for good, clear pictures an added pressure on the conservation team? Is such a desire symptomatic of an age hungry for ever more attention-grabbing images? Is the Sistine Chapel just the latest victim of a temporary aesthetic fashion, a masterpiece mugged by the vagaries of taste?

Such a conclusion might seem an insult to the care and hard work of the Vatican team but even within Italy there has been a variety of responses to the cleaned ceiling. Recently the Professor of Conservation Studies at Milan University described it as an 'impoverished version of Michelangelo's work'. The arguments will resurface, especially when work begins on the Chapel's 'Last Judgement' (AB57 is not to be used) but what remains incontrovertible is that once you have taken too much off a picture there is no way you can put it back.

*Fresco in the Sistine Chapel, Rome before (left) and after (right) its restoration.*

## NOTABLE FAKES AND FORGERIES RECENTLY BROUGHT TO LIGHT

**Madonna with Cat** A Madonna attributed to Leonardo da Vinci, acclaimed by many critics and historians as an authentic, historically important masterpiece, was painted in the 1930s as a joke. The work of Cesare Turbino, a Turin artist, the *Madonna with Cat* was shown at an exhibition of Leonardo's art in Milan in 1939. Declared a miraculously rediscovered lost masterpiece, the painting disappeared after the exhibition, and it was assumed that it had been sold into a private collection. In fact, it remained hanging on the painter's wall until his death 50 years later.

**Dali prints** After a four-year investigation into a racket involving fake Salvador Dali prints that netted an estimated $100 million (£50 million), and a five-month trial in Hawaii, the massive art fraud appears to have been brought to an end. However, because of inevitable fears in the market and the lack of a full *catalogue raisonné* (descriptive catalogue) for works after 1949, most prints from that date onwards, whether authentic or not, have been rendered worthless.

**'fake factory'** Scotland Yard's art and antique squad unmasked what was said to be the largest international fake factory for years. Faked Noël Coward paintings, coins, and automobile memorabilia worth £1.5 million

were produced and eased quietly into the market during 1987 and 1988.

**Possible fakes and forgeries under investigation**

**Rembrandt** During the past 25 years a group of Dutch Rembrandt buffs have worked through the painter's oeuvre, attributing dozens to less famous members of his studio. Each time this is done, millions are wiped off a painting's value. By mid-1991, 40 works had thus been struck down. Included among these was the self-portrait in the Wallace Collection in London.

**the Getty kouros** The authenticity of a Greek statue owned by the Getty Museum (reputedly bought for $6 million) continues to be questioned by experts. While the *kouros* (standing man) awaits the final verdict, away from the public's view, a battle is being waged between laboratory scientists and those adhering to traditional methodologies of authentication.

**van Gogh** Doubt has been cast by the Dutch-born art historian Dr Walter Feilchenfeldt on the authenticity of three van Gogh self-portraits currently hanging in Oslo, New York, and Connecticut. The results of the investigation will be published by the van Gogh Museum, Amsterdam.

---

paintings reflect an obsessive interest in mathematical perspective. **Fra Angelico** c. 1400–55 used delicate colours and a simple style to express his religious feeling. Andrea **Del Castagno**'s style was fiercely linear. The antithesis of his violent suffering figures are Piero **della Francesca**'s strangely silent ones. Solidly rounded in pale light, immobile within perfect perspective spaces, they express an enigmatic timelessness. His mastery of geometry, proportion, form, and colour is breathtakingly evident in his frescoes of *The Legend of the True Cross* in San Francesco in Arezzo 1452–66.

Many sculptors produced public statues, grandiose tombs, Roman-style portrait busts and innumerable versions of the Madonna and Child. The Florentines enjoyed seeing themselves in religious paintings and they appear in crowd scenes in many magnificent frescoes in the churches of their city, such as those by Domenico del **Ghirlandaio**. He was the most popular painter in Florence in the latter part of the 15th century, respected for his honesty, which is epitomized in his portrait of *An Old Man with a Child* c. 1480 in the Louvre. His contemporaries included **Pollaiuolo**, whose interest centres on the nude in action; **Verrocchio**, famous for the equestrian statue of Bartolomeo Colleoni in Venice 1481–96; and **Botticelli** 1445–1510, whose poetic, gracefully linear paintings of Madonnas and mythological subjects such as *The Birth of Venus* 1482 show the Florentine ideal of female beauty. Almost

every art work produced included some reference to antiquity, either in form or content. **Leonardo da Vinci** 1452–1519. Through his genius, the art of the early 16th century became the **High Renaissance**, attaining a grandeur that appealed particularly to the popes, who now became the leading art patrons in their attempt to build the 'New Rome'. Leonardo's enquiring scientific mind led him to investigate every aspect of the natural world from anatomy to aerodynamics. His notebooks and drawings remain his finest legacy, but his experiments also revolutionized painting style. Instead of a white background, he used a dark one to allow the overlying colour a more three-dimensional existence. He invented 'aerial perspective' whereby the misty atmosphere (*sfumato*) blurs and changes the colours of the landscape as it dissolves into the distance. His principle of grouping figures within an imaginary pyramid, linked by their gestures and emotions, became a High Renaissance compositional rule. His *Madonna of the Rocks* (Louvre) exemplifies all these ideas.

**Michelangelo** Buonarroti 1475–1564. His giant talent dominated the High Renaissance and led his contemporaries to label him 'Divine'. No other artist could escape his influence. He said of his stone carvings, such as the monumental *David* in Florence (1501–4) that he was simply revealing the figure hidden within the block. His massive figure style was translated into paint in the *Sistine Chapel frescoes* (Vatican,

Rome) covering the ceiling with human figures, mostly nude, all grandly Classical, telling the Old Testament story from Genesis to the Deluge (1508–11) and finishing on the altar wall with a titanic *Last Judgement* 1541.

**Raphael** (Raffaello Sanzio) 1483–1520. He quickly mastered the innovations of Leonardo and Michelangelo and in 1509 was commissioned to fresco the *Stanza della Segnature* in the Vatican, where his classicist *School of Athens* is his masterpiece. Immensely prolific and popular, he combined both delicacy and grandeur in his work.

**Mannerism** Giulio **Romano**, Raphael's principal follower, exaggerated his style into an individual one of his own, heralding the next major art movement, Mannerism. This flouted the 'rules' of Renaissance order and harmony by striving for idiosyncratic, sometimes alarming, effects. The Florentine Andrea **del Sarto** 1486–1531 and his assistants **Pontormo** and Rosso **Fiorentino** each pursued self-consciously mannered styles, as did Giorgio **Vasari**, who is chiefly remembered for his book *The Lives of the Most Excellent Architects, Painters and Sculptors* 1550, in which he coined the term 'Mannerist' and laid down the chronology of the history of art which is still in use today. Mannerism appealed particularly to courtly patrons and it became increasingly effete. The Medici, now grand dukes, employed such artists as the sculptor Benvenuto **Cellini** (1500–71), as famous for his racy autobiography as for the gilt salt cellar he made for the King of France; Agnolo **Bronzino**, whose patrician portraits display a stony hauteur; and Giovanni **Bologna**, whose elegant small bronze statuettes were widely reproduced.

**Venice** the Venetian Renaissance was slow in coming because of the city's traditional links with the East. Two non-Venetians were influential: Antonello **da Messina** (c. 1430–79), who in 1475 brought to Venice the new Flemish technique of oil painting, and Andrea **Mantegna** (c. 1431–1506), an archaeologically-minded painter whose figures looked like antique sculptures. Giovanni **Bellini** (c. 1430–1516) specialized in devotional pictures of the Madonna, but his sensitive appreciation of light and colour introduced that element of sensuality to Venetian talent which later made **Titian** (Tiziano Vecellio) (1487–1576) the preferred painter of Emperor Charles V and his son Philip II of Spain. His fellow-painter **Giorgione** (c. 1478–1510) died young, leaving only a few securely attributed works, but who nevertheless made an innovative mark with his small, intimate, easel paintings and a new treatment of figures in a landscape. **Veronese** (c. 1528–88) and Jacopo **Tintoretto** (1518–94) worked on a much larger scale, Veronese excelling in sumptuous *trompe l'oeil* interior decorations and Tintoretto in dramatic religious paintings, spectacularly lit and composed with daring foreshortening. His paintings for the Venetian Scuola di San Rocco 1566–88

foreshadow, in their exciting exuberance, the next major movement, the *Baroque*.

## THE 15TH AND 16TH CENTURIES

Northern European artists took their inspiration from Gothic sources, but shared with the Italians an insatiable interest in realistic portrayals of themselves and their world.

**Netherlands** one of the first examples of the new *humanism* was the work of Claus **Sluter** (c. 1380–1406). His mourning figures on the tomb of Philip the Bold, Duke of Burgundy, their faces hidden by the hoods of their robes, are poignantly mute but solidly real people.

In Flanders where the patrons were wealthy merchants, Robert **Campin** (1378–1444) put his *Madonna and Child before a Firescreen* (1420–30, National Gallery, London) into an ordinary living room and through its open window showed a Flemish town. Mary's halo is replaced by the circular firescreen behind her, an example of disguised symbolism, making the supernatural seem real.

Among Campin's followers, all marvellous draughtsmen, was Jan **van Eyck** (d.1441) whose strength lay in his detailed analysis of the beauty of the world around him. His innovative recipe for oil painting makes his colours glow like precious jewels. In his *Arnolfini Wedding* (1434, National Gallery, London) the bride and groom appear in a domestic interior crammed with disguised symbols, in a kind of pictorial marriage certificate. Flemish realism reached Italy with the Portinari Altarpiece, an *Adoration of the Shepherds* by Hugo **van der Goes** (d. 1481). Commissioned by the Medici agent in Bruges, it was sent to Florence where it had a considerable effect on Italian artists. The quietly contemplative portraits of Hans **Memlinc** (d. 1481) sum up the achievement of 15th-century Netherlands painters.

Individual styles proliferated in the 16th century. Hieronymus **Bosch** (c. 1450–1516) painted nightmarish scenes filled with diminutive human figures caught in a surrealist demonic world. Pieter **Bruegel** the Elder (1525/30–69) treated biblical subjects as contemporary events, viewing with compassion a miserable humanity. In his paintings of the seasons 1565 he brilliantly evokes both winter's icy silence and the golden warmth of summer.

**Germany** the giant among German artists was Albrecht **Dürer** (1471–1528). His intellectual powers put him in line with the great Italian masters and their influence introduced a new solidity of form into his basically Gothic style. Particularly important as a graphic artist, he was widely influential through woodcuts and engravings. Mathias **Grünewald** (c. 1460–1528), a tragic visionary, used colour symbolically in the *Isenheim Altar* (1512–15, Colmar), painted for hospital patients to see the crucified Christ, covered with festering wounds, sharing their suffering. Lucas **Cranach** the Elder (1473–1538) painted self-conscious courtly nudes, and Albrecht **Altdorfer** (c.1489–1538) painted landscapes in which tiny human figures are dwarfed by nature's immensity.

**Spain** Philip II did not care for the work of **El Greco** (1541–1614), the painter who really established Spain as an artistic centre. Trained in Venice, and particularly influenced by Tintoretto, he developed his hallucinatory style in Toledo, where his patrons were ecclesiastics and the intelligentsia. In his *Burial of Count Orgaz* 1586 the flame-like figures and unearthly colours blend mystic vision and reality.

**England** Renaissance ideas arrived with the German Hans **Holbein** the Younger (1497–1543), who was by 1536 court painter to Henry VIII. His piercing portraits of the king and his wives, and his delicate portrait drawings, give a superb pictorial record of the Tudor court. The court of Elizabeth I comes to life for us through the art of the miniature. Nicholas **Hilliard** (c. 1547–1619) developed an unparalleled technique, delicate, refined and often lyrically poetic as in his *Young Man amid Roses* (c. 1590, Victoria and Albert Museum, London).

**France** Jean **Fouquet** (c. 1420–81) painted miniatures as well as altarpieces in which Italian influences take tangible shape. Jean **Clouet** (d. 1541) and his son François (d. 1572) were court painters to King Francis I. Jean's portrait of the king splendidly expresses the king's concern with elegance and decoration, and François' half-nude portrait of Diane de Poitiers, *The Lady in Her Bath*, is a piece of refined eroticism. His style reflects Italian Mannerist ideas as developed by the so-called *School of Fontainebleau* founded by Giovanni Battista **Rosso** (also called Rosso Fiorentino) and Francesco **Primaticcio** who came to decorate the royal hunting lodge in the 1530s. They devised a unique type of stucco decoration combining figures in high relief with decorative swags, cartouches and strapwork. These Mannerist motifs were copied all over northern Europe, where they were called 'Renaissance'.

## THE 17TH CENTURY

**Italy** in Rome, the Counter-Reformation of the Catholic church against Protestantism launched an exciting, emotionally appealing new style, the *Baroque*. The sculptor and architect Gianlorenzo **Bernini** (1598–1680) was its principal exponent, revitalizing Rome with his exuberantly dramatic masterpieces. His *Ecstasy of St Teresa* at Santa Maria della Vittoria is a theatrical set-piece in which supernatural light pours from a hidden window to illuminate the rapturous saint, whose body seems to shudder as an angel prepares to pierce her heart with the arrow of divine love.

Large-scale illusionistic fresco painting transformed ceilings into heavens, thronged with flying saints and angels. A spectacular example is Pietro **da Cortona**'s colossal *Allegory of Divine Providence* 1629–37 in the Barberini Palace, glorifying the pope and his family.

Hundreds of figures are drawn upwards toward God's golden light, aswarm with bees, the Barberini family emblem.

Balancing this flamboyant artistic stream were the *Classicists*, who even in religious commissions looked back to the concepts of harmony and order of antiquity. Annibale **Carracci** (1560–1609) in the years around 1600 decorated Cardinal Farnese's gallery of antique sculpture in the Farnese Palace, turning the walls and ceiling into a *trompe l'oeil* classical picture gallery. He also introduced the landscape as a new category of art with his *Flight into Egypt* 1603, which has as its real subject an idealized vision of the classical Roman countryside, harmonious and calm.

Among Carracci's assistants who became famous in their own right were the consistently classicizing **Domenichino** (1581–1641) and Guido **Reni** (1575–1642) who often succumbed to popular taste with emotive paintings of repentant sinners rolling tearful eyes toward heaven.

The work of Michelangelo Merisi da **Caravaggio** (1573–1619) introduced something totally different and unique, a harsh realism in which ordinary folk with dirty feet appear as saints and apostles, lit by a raking spotlight as if God's piercing eye had picked them out from the surrounding blackness of sin. One of his most striking followers was Georges **de la Tour** (1593–1652), a French artist whose simplified figures assume a spiritual purity, modelled by God's light in the form of a single candle shining in the darkness.

**France** art was used to establish the splendour of Louis XIV's centralized authority and divine kingship. Although grandiose in the extreme, the decorative schemes, portraits, and history paintings produced by the members of the new artists' Academy (formed 1648) were based on Classical rules, rigidly controlled by Charles **Lebrun** (1619–90), who was appointed First Painter to the King in 1662. He was the first Director of the Academy and of the Gobelins Manufactory, which employed its members to produce the art, tapestries, and furnishings for Louis's new Palace of Versailles.

The two major French artists of the century lived in Rome, escaping the constricting grip of the Academy. Claude **Lorrain** (1600–82) was the first painter to specialize entirely in landscapes, reducing the story-telling elements to small foreground figures. The romantic suggestiveness of the Classical past appealed to him, and he created an enchanting idyllic world, luminous and poetic. The intellectual Nicolas **Poussin** (1594–1665) composed his classical landscapes with mathematical precision but his people remained important, noble and heroic. Not even his religious works escape the pervasive influence of antiquity. In his *Last Supper* (1647, Edinburgh) Christ and the disciples lounge on couches as if at a Roman banquet.

**Spain** as in Rome, art in Spain aimed to excite Counter-Reformation zeal. José **Ribera**

## RECENT ART THEFTS

### Thefts from museums

Eleven uninsured paintings (including a rare **Vermeer**) estimated at $200 million (£125 million) were stolen from the Isabella Stewart Gardner Museum in Boston in the spring of 1990. The paintings still remain untraced.

A number of **van Goghs** were stolen from Dutch museums between 1989 and 1991. In 1989, a ransom was demanded in exchange for three stolen van Gogh paintings. The ransom was not paid. Three paintings stolen in early 1991 were retrieved two days after their theft. On 14 April 1991 two thieves broke into the Van Gogh Museum in Amsterdam and stole 20 paintings. The paintings, worth an estimated $200 million, were recovered less than an hour later by police who found them in a car near a railway station.

A 17th-century **Japanese statuette**, valued at £100,000, was stolen from the British Museum in March 1990. It disappeared some time between 9:30 and 10 am when the museum opened, and it has not yet been found.

In 1990, the French museum authorities produced a list of art stolen during the last decade from their premises. It revealed that 200 works had disappeared from 50 institutions, either through daylight robbery or by more clandestine operations from inside. Among those listed are the well-known thefts of **La Nain's** *Game of Cards* (stolen during an exhibition), **Monet's** *Le Soleil Levant* (taken during a raid on the Marmottan Museum), and a **Renoir** portrait (cut from its frame in the Louvre by a visitor in July 1990).

In Dec 1990, the French Central Office for the Repression of Thefts of Artwork found the nine paintings stolen in the daylight robbery in 1985 from the Marmottan Museum in Paris. Included among the stolen paintings were two **Renoirs** and several **Monets**, one of them the extremely famous and valuable canvas *Impression: Sunrise* that gave Impressionism its name. The paintings were found in an empty flat in Corsica.

### Thefts from galleries and private collections, London 1990

**12 April: Henry Moore** prints of unknown value were stolen when thieves entered the second-floor window of Harlech Fine Arts Holdings of Dover Street, central London.
**May:** Art treasures worth £2 million were stolen from Roberto Memmo's private collection in a house in Mayfair. According to Scotland Yard, the robbery bore the hallmarks of a professional robbery commissioned by an art collector or dealer. The haul included an oil painting on wood by the Florentine Mannerist **Bronzino**, said to be worth at least £500,000.
**2 May:** £200,000 worth of **Galle** and **Daum** French glass was stolen from the French Glass House, Kensington, when staff were tied up by the thieves.
**14 June:** Four Dutch 17th-century paintings, including a £225,000 landscape by Salomon **van Ruysdael**, were stolen from Van Haeften's London gallery by burglars using scaffolding at the rear of the building for their entry.
**18 June:** A painting called *Peasant Festival*

by the Dutch artist **Savary** was stolen from the Entwhistle Gallery in Bond Street. The painting, valued at £350,000, was recovered by the police.
**22–24 July:** £250,000 worth of oil paintings were stolen from a private flat on Sloane Street while the owner was abroad.
**29 July:** Scaffolding was used to smash the window of the Trinity Gallery in Albemarle Street, where £200,000 worth of modern Irish paintings, including *Landscape* by William **Scott**, were stolen.
**16 Sept:** Three paintings worth an estimated £6 million were stolen from Lincoln's Inn. Police believe that the works, two by **Gainsborough** and one by **Reynolds**, were stolen to order.
**10 Nov:** A **Turner** painting worth £1 million and a work by the 18th-century Venetian master Michele **Marieschi** (estimated value £250,000) were stolen from a Chelsea flat. The burglars bluffed their way in, attacked the owner, and cut the paintings from their frames.

---

(1591–1652) carried a Caravaggesque style to brutal extremes to shock people into identifying with the sufferings inherent in Christian history. Francisco **Zurbarán** (1598–1664) expressed religious feeling in the opposite way, with solemn, silent monks and saints lost in a private world of meditation. Bartolomé Estebán **Murillo** (1617–82) painted sentimental *Holy Families* and sugar-sweet *Madonnas* fluently, cheerfully, and with a feather-light touch and lovely colours.

Diego Rodriguez de Silva **Velazquez** (1599–

1660) was the giant of Spanish painting, reflecting many aspects of the 17th-century Spanish world. By 1623 he was court painter to Philip IV in Madrid, where he was influenced by Philip's collection of 16th century Venetian paintings. The most fascinating of his lifelike portraits of the Spanish court is *Las Meninas/The Ladies-in-Waiting* 1655 (Prado, Madrid), a complex group portrait which includes Velazquez himself at his easel, and the king and queen as pale reflections in a mirror.

**Netherlands** Peter Paul **Rubens** (1577–1640)

brought the sensual exuberance of the Italian Baroque to the Netherlands. A many-sided genius, artist, scholar and diplomat, he used his powerful pictorial imagination to create, with an army of assistants, innumerable religious and allegorical paintings for the churches and palaces of Catholic Europe. His largest commission was the cycle of 21 enormous canvases allegorizing the life of Marie de Medici, Queen of France (Louvre, Paris). His sheer delight in life can be seen in his magnificent colours, opulent nudes, and expansive landscapes.

Rubens' Grand Baroque style did not suit the Protestant merchants of the new Dutch Republic, who wanted small paintings reflecting their own lives and interests. Among the artists who responded to this demand, the towering genius was **Rembrandt** van Rijn (1606–69), all of whose paintings hint at some inner drama. In his portraits and biblical scenes he saw light as a spiritual mystery which momentarily allows his characters to loom out of the surrounding shadows. His self-portraits (nearly 100 in number) touchingly trace the drama of his own passage through life and even the large group portrait, *The Night Watch* 1642, becomes a suspense story. A master draughtsman and printmaker, over 1,000 of his drawings survive.

The greatest of the straightforward portraitists was Frans **Hals**, whose free brushstrokes caught fleeting moments brilliantly in such paintings as the so-called *Laughing Cavalier* 1624 (Wallace Collection, London).

*Genre pictures*, scenes of daily life, merrymakers and peasants—often uncouth, comic, or satirical—were the speciality of such painters as Jan **Steen** (1626–79), in whose anecdotal scenes of traditional festivals or slovenly households the pleasures of drink, gluttony, and wantonness hold sway.

During the 1650s genre painters took a different view of their society. Instead of depicting boisterous low-life, painters like Pieter de **Hooch** (1629–84) chose scenes of domestic virtue, well-ordered households where families live in harmony in quiet sunlit rooms. Jan **Vermeer** (1632–75) was the greatest master of these scenes of peaceful prosperity, arranging domestic interiors as if they were abstract forms and enclosing his characters within an enamelled world of pearly light. *A Young Woman Standing at a Virginal* (National Gallery, London) is a superb example of the small group of paintings he produced, each one a masterpiece.

The Dutch specialities of seascape and landscape made giant strides during the century, based on low horizons with emphasis on a great expanse of sky. Experts in this were Aelbert **Cuyp** (1620–91) who bathed his views in a golden light, and Jacob van **Ruisdael** (1638/9–1709), who painted in many moods, responding to the shifting patterns of light and shade in nature.

*Still-life* painting also burgeoned: fruit, flowers, fish, banquets, breakfasts, groaning boards of every kind, in which the artist displayed skill in painting inanimate objects, often with a hidden religious significance.

**England** Charles I had employed Rubens to paint the ceiling of the Banqueting House at Whitehall 1629–30. Rubens's assistant Anthony **van Dyck** became Court Painter in 1632 and created magnificent portraits of the aristocracy, cool and elegant in shimmering silks. The German Peter **Lely** succeeded him under the Restoration to depict a society that exudes an air of well-fed decadence. By contrast, the English-born Samuel **Cooper** (1609–72), painter to the Parliamentarians and most famous for his portraits of Oliver Cromwell ('warts and all'), was a miniaturist whose serious, objective portraits raised the status of his art to that of oil painting.

## THE 18TH CENTURY

**France** the beginning of the 18th century saw the start of a frivolous new style in art, the *Rococo*. Jean-Antoine **Watteau** (1684–1721) devised for his aristocratic patrons a *Fête Gallante*, a type of painting in which amorous couples in poetic landscapes contemplate the transience of life and love.

The more overtly sensual work of François **Boucher** (1703–70), First Painter to Louis XV, included voluptuous scenes of naked gods and goddesses. Painting at the same time, but completely against the mainstream, was Jean-Baptiste-Siméon **Chardin** (1699–1779), whose still-lifes and genre scenes have a masterful dignity. Jean-Honoré **Fragonard** (1732–1806) continued with the Rococo theme under Louis XVI, light-heartedly reflecting the licentiousness of courtly life. But all this changed with the Revolution and in 1789 Neo-Classicism became the dominant style under the Republic. Its artistic dictator, Jacques-Louis **David** (1748–1825) in his *Death of Marat* turned a political murder into a classical tragedy. Later, under Napoleon's Empire, David painted heroic portraits and scenes celebrating its glory.

**Italy** Antonio **Canova** (1757–1822), the sculptor, also exalted Napoleon and his family in classicizing portraits, and the vogue for this style dominated most English and European sculpture right through the Victorian era. Rococo illusionistic fresco-painting in Italy was the special province of Giovanni-Battista **Tiepolo** (1696–1770), a Venetian who decorated palaces and churches there and elsewhere in Europe. His painted ceilings became vast, airy regions whose delicate colour shadings made the sky seem endless.

The *vedutisti* (view-painters) produced souvenir views for young English gentlemen making the Grand Tour to complete their education with first-hand viewing of Renaissance and Classical art. In Venice, Francesco **Guardi** (1712–93) painted atmospheric visions of the floating city, pulsating with life. The views of (Giovanni) Antonio **Canaletto** (1697–1768),

## Major Western Artists

| period | painters | sculptors |
|---|---|---|
| classical | | Myron 5th century BC |
| | | Phidias 5th century BC |
| | | Polykleitos 5th century BC |
| | | Praxiteles 4th century BC |
| | | Lysippus 4th century BC |
| medieval | Limbourg brothers | Nicola and |
| | early 15th century | Giovanni Pisano working |
| | | c. 1258–1314 |
| | Duccio c. 1255/60–c. 1318 | Claus Sluter c. 1380–1406 |
| | Giotto c. 1266–1337 | |
| | Lorenzetti 1306–1345 | |
| Italian Renaissance | Masaccio 1401–1428 | Ghiberti 1378– 1455 |
| | Leonardo da Vinci 1425–1519 | Donatello 1386–1466 |
| | Bellini c. 1430–1516 | Michaelangelo 1475–1564 |
| | Mantegna c. 1431–1506 | |
| | Raphael 1483–1520 | |
| | Titian 1487–1576 | |
| Mannerism | Rosso Fiorentino 1494–1540 | Cellini 1500–1571 |
| | Pontormo 1494–1556 | Giambologna 1529–1608 |
| | Giulio Romano 1499–1546 | |
| | Bronzino 1503–1572 | |
| | Vasari 1511–1574 | |
| 15th and 16th centuries | van Eyck died 1441 | |
| outside Italy | Bosch 1450–1516 | |
| | Dürer 1471–1528 | |
| | Brueghel 1525/30–1569 | |
| | Holbein 1497–1543 | |
| | El Greco 1541–1614 | |
| 17th century | Carracci 1560–1609 | Bernini 1598–1680 |
| | Caravaggio 1573–1619 | |
| | Rubens 1577–1640 | |
| | Poussin 1594–1665 | |
| | Velázquez 1599–1660 | |
| | Claude 1600–1682 | |
| | Rembrandt 1606–1669 | |
| 18th century | Watteau 1684–1721 | Canova 1757–1822 |
| | Tiepolo 1696–1770 | |
| | Gainsborough 1727–1788 | |
| | Goya 1746–1828 | |
| | David 1748–1825 | |
| 19th century | Friedrich 1774–1840 | Rodin 1840–1917 |
| | Turner 1775–1851 | |
| | Ingres 1780–1867 | |
| | Delacroix 1798–1863 | |
| | Courbet 1819–1877 | |
| | Manet 1832–1883 | |
| | Monet 1840–1926 | |
| | Cézanne 1839–1906 | |
| | van Gogh 1853–1890 | |
| 20th century | Kandinsky 1866–1944 | Brancusi 1876–1957 |
| | Matisse 1869–1954 | Giacometti 1901–1966 |
| | Mondrian 1872–1944 | Moore 1898–1986 |
| | Picasso 1881–1973 | Smith, David 1906–1965 |
| | Malevich 1878–1935 | Kepworth 1903–1975 |
| | Duchamp 1887–1968 | Calder, Alexander 1898–1976 |
| | Pollock 1912–1956 | Gabo 1890–1977 |
| | Warhol 1928–1987 | |
| | Bacon 1910– | |
| | Braque 1882–1963 | |
| | Klee 1879–1940 | |
| | Rothko 1903–1970 | |

though faithfully observed, are static in comparison.

In Rome, Giovanni Battista **Piranesi** (1720–78) produced etchings inspired by his feelings for the evocative quality of ruins. His most original work, however, was a series which turned the ruins into images of terrifying imaginary prisons, fantasies of architectural madness.

**Spain** produced one artist of enormous talent and versatility, Francisco de **Goya** y Lucientes (1746–1828), whose work expresses a wide range of feeling and emotion and explores a variety of themes. Court Painter to Charles IV and later to Joseph Bonaparte under the French occupation of Spain, his portraits were acutely perceptive, his war scenes savagely dramatic, his religious paintings believable and his strange late fantasies powerfully imaginative. He is often seen as the source of 20th century art.

**England** produced a memorable group of fine artists, each expressing the varied interests of the age. Joseph **Wright** of Derby (1734–97), scientifically-minded, painted such scenes as *Experiment with an Air Pump* 1768. George **Stubbs** (1724–1806) specialized in horse paintings, based on painstaking scientific investigation. Joshua **Reynolds** (1723–92), first President of the Royal Academy (founded 1768) wanted to introduce the European Grand Manner into English painting with history paintings on exalted themes of heroism, but the demand was for portraits; his were confident but lacking in spontaneity, based more on theory than on inspiration.

Thomas **Gainsborough** (1727–88) was also a popular portraitist, although he would have preferred to paint landscapes and made much of them in the backgrounds of his pictures. William **Hogarth** (1697–1764) is best known through engravings of his satirical series of paintings, such as *The Rake's Progress*.

Reacting against the academic theorizing of Reynolds, the poet William **Blake** (1757–1827) illustrated his writings with mystical visions, and the imaginative Henry **Fuseli** (1741–1825) plumbed the depths of his subconscious for grotesque and fantastic dream images in such paintings as *The Nightmare*.

## THE 19TH CENTURY

**France** vast historical, religious, and mythological pictures were no longer greatly in demand, and after the fall of Napoleon in 1814 French artists trained in the Academic Grand Manner had to seek new dramatic themes. They looked to the world around them; Theodore **Géricault** (1791–1824) found his subject in the gruesome sufferings of the survivors of a recent shipwreck, which he portrayed in his huge *Raft of the Medusa* (1816, Louvre, Paris). His desire to express and evoke emotion put Géricault among the **Romantics**, whose art sought to speak passionately to the heart in contrast to the **Classicists** who appealed to the intellect. These two opposing approaches dominated much of the art of the century.

Eugène **Delacroix** (1798–1863) became the best-known Romantic painter. His *Massacre of Chios* (1824, Louvre) shows Greeks enslaved by wild Turkish horsemen, a contemporary atrocity. Admired as a colourist, he used a technique of divided brushwork—adjacent brush marks of contrasting colour which the eye mixes as it scans—that anticipates the Impressionists. He learned this from seeing Constable's *Hay Wain* when it was exhibited in Paris in 1824.

By contrast, the brushwork is invisible in the enamelled paintings of Jean-Auguste-Dominique **Ingres** (1780–1867), the leading exponent of French Neo-Classicism. Drawing was the foundation of his style, emphasizing line and control at the expense of colour and expression.

Gustave **Courbet** (1819–77), reacting against both Classicists and Romantics, set out to establish a new **Realism**, based solely on direct observation of the things around him. His *Burial at Ornans* 1850 showed ordinary working people gathered round a village grave, and shocked the Establishment art world with its 'vulgarity' and 'coarseness'. Another Realist was Honoré **Daumier** (1808–79) whose lithographs of the 1830s dissected Parisian society with a surgeon's scalpel.

Throughout Europe, 19th-century artists found their ideal subject matter in the landscape. In France, Jean-Baptiste-Camille **Corot** (1796–1875) made it acceptable by recomposing his open-air studies into a harmonious, classical whole, although a romantic mood pervades his later misty confections. Theodore **Rousseau** (1812–67) led a group of artists who in 1844 sought refuge from the Industrial Revolution in the woods of Barbizon near Paris. Their close observation of nature produced a new awareness of its changing moods. Jean-François **Millet** (1814–75) also settled at Barbizon but his romantic landscapes, such as *The Angelus* (1857–9, Louvre), introduce idealized peasants who manage to commune with nature while toiling to wrest from it their daily bread.

**Germany** a different, more melancholy Romantic sensibility invaded the landscapes of a small group of painters working in Germany. Seeking to express the mystery of God in nature and people's oneness with it, the evocative paintings of Caspar David **Friedrich** (1774–1840) usually include a small poetic figure contemplating distant mountain peaks or moonlit seashores.

**England** the two greatest artists of the century were landscapists—Joseph Mallord William **Turner** (1775–1851) and John **Constable** (1776–1837), both finding inspiration in the thriving English watercolour school. Turner was the master painter of English Romanticism. Not concerned with the human figure, it was always through nature itself that he could express human feeling, as in the poignant last voyage of the ship *The Fighting Téméraire*

# ART COLLECTIONS: A HISTORY OF LOOT AND PLUNDER?

Much of the history of the West's greatest art collections is the history of loot and plunder. Napoleon set the precedent, filling the Louvre with treasures stolen from those countries he had conquered. These included the four bronze horses from San Marco in Venice which had previously been taken from Constantinople by the Venetians in 1202. With Napoleon's final defeat in 1815, the horses were returned along with most—but not all—of his other booty.

It was in gratitude to the British for driving Napoleon's troops out of Egypt (then part of the Turkish Empire) that the Turks permitted Lord Elgin to take whatever he wanted from the already dilapidated Parthenon in Athens. The fact that the Turks were an occupying power seems not to have mattered very much but when the Greeks gained their independence in 1833 they wanted the so-called Elgin Marbles back. Now, 158 years later, the British Museum is still adamant that they should not be returned. They argue that the sculptures were legitimately acquired and are anyway far better off in London than in Athens. What the Museum also cannot countenance is the loss of one of its greatest attractions and the precedent this would set for the return of other nationally significant treasures.

Whatever the Greeks' moral claim to ownership, there is little doubt about the Museum's legal title to the sculptures. Even so, many museum purchases take place, usually unwittingly, against an often murky background. The annual turnover in the sale of illegally acquired artworks is in the region of $1 billion. If an object passes through a sufficient number of hands it is often very difficult for the original owners to retrieve it. According to Interpol only one object in ten is recovered. In 1989, the Cypriot government successfully sued for the return

*A centaur attacking a lapith tribesman—detail from the Parthenon sculptures (British Museum.)*

of four 6th-century Byzantine mosaics which had been taken from a church in Kanakria some years after the Turkish invasion in 1974. An Indianapolis dealer, Peg Goldberg, had purchased them in Switzerland for just over $1 million and was offering them for $20 million when the Getty Museum alerted the Cypriots. The judge ruled against her, saying that she had failed to conduct a reasonable inquiry into whether 'the seller had the capacity to convey property rights'.

It is unusual for museums to return an object to its place of origin unless their claim to title is under threat. Recently the Australian National Gallery returned the Paracas burial mantle to Peru. They were under no legal obligation to do so even though it had been shown that the textile was stolen from the National Museum of Peru in 1973. Around the same time the Peruvians were less successful at retrieving other pre-Columbian artefacts in the USA where a judge decided that their claim to title was unproven. Australia's act of goodwill is partially due to their recent acceptance of the 1970 Unesco Convention on the Means of Prohibiting and Preventing the Illicit Import and Export and Transfer of Ownership of Cultural Property. 68 countries are now cooperating in an attempt to halt what has been called an 'epidemic' of cultural theft. The UK is not one of them, possibly because the Elgin Marbles' return to Athens is high on the Convention's agenda.

The recent revelations of hoards of paintings and treasures taken from Germany by the Red Army at the end of the World War II is likely to prove something of a test case for the 1990 Soviet-Germany treaty. Clause 16 specifies the return of 'missing or illegally deported treasures of art on the two sides' respective territories'. German museums and galleries are busy drawing up lists of items such as the gold jewellery excavated from the site of Troy by Schliemann in 1873, paintings from Frederick the Great's Palace at Sans Soucis, and millions of books and manuscripts, including Hitler's own personal library, thought to be rotting away just outside Moscow.

The Soviets had always denied the existence of their war booty and the occasional return of objects, such as the Pergamon Altar back to East Berlin in 1957, was controversial. It was argued that keeping it was some form of reparation for the appalling acts of pillage perpetrated by the Nazis. Although the Germans failed to enter Leningrad, the surrounding Tsarist palaces were almost completely destroyed after their contents had been systematically removed. It has been estimated that out of 41,000 objects in the Kiev Museum of Ukrainian Art, the Nazis removed all but 1,400. Few of these have ever been traced and any exchange is likely to be extremely one-sided, particularly when one considers that many paintings still hanging in German museums are works confiscated for Hitler which have never been returned to their original owners.

(1839, Tate Gallery, London). His increasing obsession with light and its deep emotional significance turned his late pictures into misty abstract visions. Reputedly his dying words were 'The sun is God'.

Constable too was fascinated with the effects of light. He made innumerable painted sketches of the changing windy sky and in his *Hay Wain* of 1821 used white marks like snowflakes to express the way light gave the landscape its freshness and sparkle.

Although primarily interested in romantic literary or biblical themes, the **Pre-Raphaelites** led by Dante Gabriel **Rossetti** (1828–82) in the 1840s and 1850s took a detailed look at nature, in their claim to a realistic vision; from this influence the medievalist designer-artist William **Morris** (1834–96) developed his stylized patterns of leaves and flowers for fabrics and wallpapers.

The opposition to the Pre-Raphaelites was led by two Establishment artists, Frederic, Lord **Leighton** (1830–96) and Lawrence **Alma-Tadema** (1836–1912), whose equally romantic view pretended to Classicism by centring on pseudo-genre scenes of daily life in ancient Greece and Rome. This pleased their educated patrons enough to earn knighthoods for them both.

**Impressionism** in the second half of the century France took an innovative look at nature. A direct precursor was Edouard **Manet** (1832–83), who carried on Courbet's scientific spirit of realism, making the eye the sole judge of reality. Stylistically, he gave up modelling forms in volume in favour of *suggesting* them by juxtaposed colours and gradations of tones, and, like Courbet, the subject matter of his pictures was always modern life. His *Déjeuner sur l'herbe/Luncheon on the Grass* (Louvre) updated a Renaissance prototype to 1862.

The Impressionists delighted in painting real life but the scenes and objects they painted became increasingly less important than the way they were affected by the ever-changing play of light. Evolving in the 1860s, the Impressionist group painted out of doors, capturing the immediacy and freshness of light on rippling water or on moving leaves. To catch these fleeting moments they broke up the forms they painted into fragments of pure colour laid side by side directly on the canvas, rather than mixing them on a palette. The members of the group were Alfred **Sisley** (1839–99), Camille **Pissarro** (1831–1903), Claude **Monet** (1840–1926) whose *Impression, Sunrise* of 1872 (Musée Marmottan, Paris) gave the movement its name, Pierre-Auguste **Renoir** (1841–1919), and Edgar **Degas** (1834–1917). By the late 1870s they had each gone on to pursue individual interests, and the acceptance of a common purpose had had its day. Sisley and Pissarro continued painting landscapes, but Renoir became more interested in the female nude and Degas in 'snapshot' studies of dancers and jockeys. Degas hardly ever painted landscapes but instead concentrated on the

spectacle of the racetrack and the ballet in oddly angled compositions influenced by snapshot photography. Monet remained obsessed with the optical effects of light on colour and carried his original fragmented technique to the final extreme in series of paintings such as those of the façade of Rouen Cathedral 1894 or his famous water lilies, showing the changing colour effects at different times of day. With these variations on a theme the actual subject did not matter at all, and in this he anticipated the abstract art of the 20th century.

**Post-Impressionism** other artists of the same generation who used the innovations of the Impressionists as a basis for developing their own styles are called the Post-Impressionists. They include Paul **Cézanne** (1839–1906), who infused something more permanent into their spontaneous vision by using geometrical shapes to form a solid scaffolding for his pictorial compositions; and Georges **Seurat** (1859–91), who achieved greater structure in his landscapes through the technique of *pointillism* (also known as Neo-Impressionism) which turns the Impressionist's separate brush-strokes into minute points of pure colour. The eye then mixes these for itself. Green grass, for instance, is made up of closely packed points of blue and yellow. In this painstaking method any idea of spontaneity vanishes, and the effect is stable and serene.

Henri de **Toulouse-Lautrec** (1864–1901) portrayed the low-life of Parisian bars and music halls without sentiment or judgement. Like Degas, he recorded contemporary life in informal poses from odd angles and his bold, colourful posters show the influence of Japanese colour prints.

The great Dutch individualist Vincent **van Gogh** (1853–90) longed to give visible form to every emotion and used violent rhythmic brushwork and brilliant unnatural colours to express his inner passions, even in something as simple as a pot of sunflowers. Paul **Gauguin** (1848–1903) also went beyond the Impressionists' notion of reality, seeking a more direct experience of life in the magical rites of so-called primitive peoples in his colourful works from the South Seas.

**Symbolism** was a movement initiated by poets as a reaction to materialist values, and their 1886 Manifesto sought to re-establish the imagination in art. Their most admired painter was Gustave **Moreau** (1826–98) whose paintings of biblical and mythological subjects contain psychological overtones expressed through exotic settings, strange colours and eerie light. Odilon **Redon** (1840–1916) translated dreams into bizarre and striking visual images. In the paintings of the Norwegian Edvard **Munch** (1863–1944), a particularly northern sense of fear and alienation is given extreme expression in such painings as *The Scream* (1893).

**The Nabis** (from Hebrew 'prophet') were followers of Gauguin who used simple forms and flat colours as he did for emotional effect, in a new style called *synthetisme*. Among the Nabis, Pierre **Bonnard** (1867–1947) and Edouard **Vuillard** (1868–1940) were less concerned with mystical ideas and found that with contemporary domestic interiors they could develop their interest in sumptuously coloured and patterned surfaces. Their work was dubbed *intimisme*.

**sculpture** the work of the Parisian Auguste **Rodin** (1840–1917) shows an extraordinary technical facility and a deep understanding of the human form. A romantic realist who infused his forms with passion, such famous sculptures as *The Thinker* and *The Kiss* were originally designed for a never-completed giant set of bronze doors, *The Gates of Hell*, with themes taken from Dante's *Divine Comedy*. The Musée Rodin in Paris houses many examples of his work and their preparatory drawings.

## THE 20TH CENTURY

The 20th century has been an age of experimentation, with the boundaries of art being continually stretched by a succession of avant-garde movements. The anti-naturalism of the Symbolists and the Post-Impressionists, which attempted to reveal the essential reality behind the mere appearance of things, was continued in the first decade by Picasso, Matisse, and other artists before finally developing into complete abstraction.

**Fauvism**, a short-lived movement, began in France around 1905 and ended just three years later. The painters were nicknamed *Les Fauves* ('wild beasts') because of the extreme brilliance of the colours, which were often applied in jarring combinations to heighten the emotional impact. Henri **Matisse** (1869–1954), the major figure of the movement, spent his life refining this expressive use of pure colour partially influenced by the pattern-making of North African decorative art. André **Derain** (1880–1954) at this time enlarged the brushstrokes of Neo-Impressionism to produce a vibrant mosaic of colour, whereas Maurice **de Vlaminck** (1876–1958) was more influenced by the violent intensity of van Gogh. Georges **Rouault** (1871–1958), though associated with the group, employed more sombre colours enclosed by thick dark outlines reminiscent of stained glass.

**Cubism** was invented by Pablo **Picasso** (1881–1973) and the former Fauvist Georges **Braque** (1882–1963).

By fragmenting the objects they depicted, then reconstructing them as a series of almost geometric facets that overlap and interlock with each other, they attempted to explode the harmonious and unified perspective of the Renaissance. In its place is an image of multiple viewpoints seen simultaneously. Initially the work grew out of Picasso's fascination with African sculpture as in his *Les Demoiselles d'Avignon* (1907, Museum of Modern Art, New York). The influence of Cézanne can also be found in the simplification of forms and the

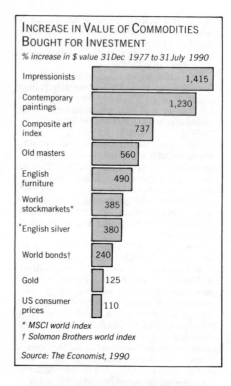

INCREASE IN VALUE OF COMMODITIES BOUGHT FOR INVESTMENT

*% increase in $ value 31 Dec 1977 to 31 July 1990*

| | |
|---|---|
| Impressionists | 1,415 |
| Contemporary paintings | 1,230 |
| Composite art index | 737 |
| Old masters | 560 |
| English furniture | 490 |
| World stockmarkets* | 385 |
| *English silver | 380 |
| World bonds† | 240 |
| Gold | 125 |
| US consumer prices | 110 |

\* MSCI world index
† Solomon Brothers world index

Source: The Economist, 1990

ambiguity of the picture space. Emotion and narrative were avoided, colours were muted, and anti-illusionistic devices such as stencilled writing and collage were introduced. The two artists worked closely together from 1907 to 1914 but neither believed in theorizing about their work. This was done by later followers Juan Gris, Albert Gleizes, Jean Metzinger, Fernand Léger, and Robert **Delaunay**, the last named forming his own, more sensual and poetic variant of Cubism known as *Orphism*.

**Futurism** The Italian poet Filippo **Marinetti** (1876–1944) published the *Futurist Manifesto* in 1909, which demanded a new art to celebrate the age of the machine. He called for the destruction of the museums and eulogized the modern world and the 'beauty of speed and energy'. The most talented of the artists inspired by his ideas was the painter and sculptor Umberto **Boccioni** (1882–1916), who wrote his own *Technical Manifesto of Painting* the following year. But it was not until a trip to Paris and contact with Cubism that the Futurist artists managed to create a sufficiently dynamic style to match their rhetoric. Giacomo **Balla** (1871–1958) produced the painting *Dog on a Leash* which attempted to convey sequential movement in the manner of the photographers Muybridge and Marey. Gino **Severini** painted a topsy-turvy landscape as if seen from the moving window of a *Suburban Train Arriving at Paris* 1915 (Tate Gallery, London). Boccioni's sculpture *Unique Forms of Continuity in Space* 1913 (Tate Gallery) shows

FIVE HIGHEST PRICES PAID FOR WORKS BY LIVING ARTISTS AT AUCTION (1988–90)

| | Artist | Title of work | Auction house/Year of sale | Auction price $m |
|---|---|---|---|---|
| 1 | de Kooning | *Interchange** | Sotheby's, 1989 | 20.68 |
| 2 | Johns | *False Start* | Sotheby's, 1988 | 17.05 |
| 3 | de Kooning | *July* | Christie's, 1990 | 8.8 |
| 4 | Lichtenstein | *Torpedo Los!* | Christie's, 1990 | 6.8 |
| 5 | Lichtenstein | *Kiss II* | Christie's, 1990 | 6.05 |

*\* holds record price for a work by a living artist.*

the dynamic interaction between a striding figure and its surrounding space.

**Expressionism** Germany was the scene of two successive Expressionist groups. In 1905 a group of artists in Dresden, with obvious parallels to the Fauves, founded *Die Brücke* ('the bridge'). Led by Ernst Ludwig **Kirchner** (1880–1938), they sought to express their 'inner convictions ... with spontaneity and sincerity'. This raw subjectivity is best seen in Kirchner's vivid scenes of the Berlin streets and in the prints of Karl **Schmidt-Rotluff** (1884–1976). The woodcut was a favourite medium of the group because of its primitive simplicity. In Munich *Der Blaue Reiter* ('the blue rider') group was set up in 1911 by Wassily **Kandinsky** (1866–1944). Influenced by the spiritual ideas of the Theosophists, Kandinsky believed that precise emotional and spiritual ideas could be conveyed by form and colour. He evolved a highly subjective style which finally became purely abstract. His colleague Franc **Marc** (1880–1916), partially inspired by Orphism, produced pantheistic celebrations of nature in which animals, particularly horses, dominate.

**Suprematism** After working in a manner that fused Cubism and Futurism with Russian folk styles, Kasimir **Malevich** (1878–1935) developed an abstract language of simple geometrical forms which he called Suprematism. In 1913, he painted a black square on a white ground as a rejection of 'ordinary objective life'. A white square on a white ground represented the ultimate in spiritual enlightenment, uniting the viewer with the infinite.

**Constructivism** was another Russian movement that also employed a nonobjective visual language, but in the service of the Revolution rather than the spiritual. *Beat the Whites with the Red Wedge* 1919 by El **Lissitsky** (1890–1941) (a student of Malevich) has an easily understandable and overtly political message. Vladimir **Tatlin** (1885–1953) designed a *Monument to the Third International* as a vast, skeletal, rotating tower, symbolic of technical endeavour and aspiration – it was never built. Naum **Gabo** (1890–1977) was less political than Tatlin but as important in pioneering the new 'constructed' architectural sculpture that employed materials like plastic to reveal the structural logic of the form. Stalin denounced these artists as bourgeois formalists and instead favoured a highly academic, official style known as Socialist Realism.

**Neo-Plasticism** Dutch painter Piet **Mondrian** (1872–1944), like Malevich, tried to express the 'truths of the universe' through pure aesthetics. Using primary colours, black, white, and grey, he painted parallel horizontal lines that intersected vertical ones. The perfection described by the parallel lines, the right-angle intersections, and the rectangles of pure colour were meant to mirror the ultimate perfection of the universe. In 1917 he headed a group called *De Stijl* ('the style') which included Theo **van Doesburg** (1883–1931) and the furniture designer Gerrit **Rietveld** (1888–1964). Like the Constructivists, with whom they had links, they believed in the artist as 'designer' with responsibilities to enhance every aspect of modern life by their work.

Many of the ideas of these seemingly disparate Modern groups were propagated at the **Bauhaus**, an influential German school of art and design, where several major artists, including Kandinsky, taught.

**Dada**, so called for its infantile associations, was considerably less positive and utopian in its aims. Born at the Cabaret Voltaire, Zürich, Switzerland, in 1916, it was an anarchic series of gestures that aimed to shock by undermining the sanctity of art with all its rules and values. Tristan **Tzara** 'created' poems by tearing out words from newspapers, then drawing them out of a hat. Similarly, Hans **Arp** (1887–1966) made collages by randomly dropping pieces of paper, then fixing them where they landed. Chance was more valid than choice. At the same time in New York, Marcel **Duchamp** (1887–1968) exhibited 'ready-made' art works: a snow shovel bought in a hardware store, a bicycle wheel mounted on a stool, a urinal.

**Surrealism** succeeded Dada. In 1922 the French writer André **Breton** made it a coherent and organized group, precisely what Dada rejected. Freud's investigations into the unconscious were an inspiration, as were the strange empty townscapes of the Italian painter Giorgio **de Chirico** (1888–1978). Some Surrealist artists, like André **Masson** (1896– ) and Joan **Miro** (1893–1983), attempted to connect with the unconscious through automatic drawing. Others, like Salvador **Dali** (1904–1989) and René **Magritte** (1898–1967), used a more realistic style to create an imagery of dreams. In both cases, thought and creativity were liberated by the absence of reason. Even Picasso was regarded as a Surrealist by Breton and certainly his work of the late 1920s and the 1930s explored the destructive human impulses. This is most dramatically seen in *Guernica* 1936 (Prado, Madrid), in which his horrified reaction to the German Luftwaffe's bombing of a Basque town during the Spanish Civil War has the quality of an epic nightmare.

The impact of Surrealism was widespread. In Britain the landscapes of Paul **Nash** (1889–1946) became even more haunted and mysterious. The Swiss painter Paul **Klee** painted quirky semiabstract pictures and Marc **Chagall** (1881–1955) evoked the memories of his Jewish-Russian childhood. Both artists delved into the imagination for their visions in a way that paralleled Surrealism.

**Abstract Expressionism** Many European artists moved to the USA in the years around World War II. New York became the centre of world art and Abstract Expressionism its first major movement. Influenced by Mondrian as well as by Surrealism, US avant-garde painting divided into two groups: the Gesture painters (or Action painters) and the Colour Field painters. Jackson **Pollock** (1912–1956) led the Gesture painters. By putting his canvas on the floor and swirling paint on it, he created a complex web of multicoloured trails which spectators could retrace with their eyes, thereby reliving the artist's dynamic act of creation. The Colour Field painter Mark **Rothko** 1903–1970 filled large canvases with shimmering blocks of solid colour, the contemplation of which offered the spectator a transcendent experience.

**Pop art** was to some extent a reaction against the anguished soul-searching of Abstract Expressionism as well as being a celebration of consumerism and popular culture. Pop artists plundered the mass media, employing the imagery of advertising, comic strips, and the movies. Jasper **Johns** (1930–  ) gave us paintings of targets and the American flag in endless permutations. Andy **Warhol** (1928–1987), through the medium of the screen print, transformed celebrities and events, from Marilyn Monroe to the electric chair, into contemporary icons. Roy **Lichtenstein** (1923–  ), in paintings like *Whaam!* 1963 (Tate Gallery, London) presents a comic-strip moment in a wittily depersonalized parody of its original style. In the UK, artists like Richard **Hamilton** and Eduoardo **Paolozzi** had a similar disregard for the division between high and low culture. In Paolozzi's case this meant using almost any material that came to hand, making his collages and sculptures almost archaeological concentrates of the late 20th century.

**Op art** The paintings of Victor **Vasarely** (1908–  ) and Bridget **Riley** (1931–  ) use abstraction to create optical illusions, confusing the spectator's eye with coloured lines and dots that appear to jump, blend, and waver.

In sculpture the influence of Rodin dominated the early years of the century. Matisse, **Bourdelle**, and the Cubist sculptors extended Rodin's liberated attitude to the human form as a complex and dynamic surface. The raw directness of African sculpture affected the work

of Jacob **Epstein**, Henri **Gaudier-Brzeska**, and **Modigliani**, while in Germany Ernst **Barlach** derived similar inspiration from late Gothic sculpture. Constantin **Brancusi** (1876–1957) in his carvings gradually refined and simplified his work into pure, almost abstract forms, like the ovoid *Prometheus* of 1911. Henry **Moore** (1898–1957) created a more rugged reduction of the human form which reflects the full and flowing contours of nature. At the other extreme, the elongated and emaciated figures of Alberto **Giacometti** (1901–1966) emit a sense of spiritual and existential isolation. Both Dada and Cubist collage encouraged a more varied and untraditional choice and use of materials, evident in the work of the Russian Constructivists. In the 1930s Picasso and Julio **Gonzalez** (1876–1972) made highly linear 'drawings in space' by welding sheets and strips of metal together. This direction was pursued in a more dramatic and monumental way by David **Smith** (1906–1965) and his fellow American Alexander **Calder** (1898–1976), who invented mobiles, flat shapes attached in patterns to rods that hang from the ceiling and move gently in the air. More recently Jean **Tinguely** (1925–  ) has employed electricity to create movement in his elaborate, whimsical machine constructions.

**contemporary trends** Since the freethinking 1960s, a bewildering number of new trends and movements have appeared, many of which stress the intellectual and material processes behind an art work's creation.

*Minimalism* reacted to the promiscuity of Pop art by reducing the art object to a bare and essential purity, devoid of any exterior reference or meaning. *Equivalent VIII* 1966 by Carl **Andre**, two layers of bricks laid on the floor, caused great controversy when purchased by the Tate Gallery, London.

*Super Realism* or *Photo Realism* imitates reality through exact, illusionistic copies of colour photographs in the work of Richard **Estes** and waxworklike sculptures in the work of Duane **Hanson**. Meaning and intention are obscured by the clinical detachment of the execution and the banality of the subject matter.

*Conceptualism* Here the actual art object is challenged and sometimes replaced by the ideas behind it. Documentation in the form of statements and photographs may be presented on gallery walls.

*Performance art* is the staging of events by artists. It may be theatrical but it differs from theatre in its emphasis on visual complexity rather than on a text. In *Body art* the artist uses his or her own body as a vehicle for often confrontational ideas.

*Land art* or *Earth art* involves the direct interaction of the artist with the environment. It is usually ephemeral and so preserved only in documentation. **Christo** (1935–  ) has wrapped up part of the Australian coastline 1979, erected a curtain in a Colorado valley 1981, and a long running fence across California 1986. Richard **Long** maps and photographs his landscape journeys, displaying them in galleries with works made from natural materials collected en route.

Although these developments undermined the conventional notion of the art work as permanent and unique, traditional forms like figurative oil painting have, even so, continued to thrive since World War II, albeit in increasingly extreme manifestations. In the work of the painter Francis **Bacon** (1910– ), scenes of horror and brutality are presented as the typical condition of modern humans. Since the 1970s, other painters, the so-called *Neo-Expressionists* or *Bad painters*, like Julian Schnabel, Anselm Kiefer, Georg Baselitz, and Francesco Clemente, have created an equally direct and lurid visual language in order to explore issues of personal and national history and mythology.

# EASTERN ART

**Islamic art** is one of ornament, for under the Muslim religion artists could not usurp the divine right of creation by portraying living creatures. Intricate, interlacing patterns based on geometry, Arabic calligraphy, and stylized plant motifs (including the swirling 'Arabesque') swarm over surfaces, structured by a rigid sense of symmetry. Lustreware pottery, ceramic tiles, and carpets were primary art forms. In Islamic Persia miniature painting illustrating literary or historical scenes, often in a lovingly detailed Paradise Garden setting, flourished during the Safavid period (1502–1736) and after 1526 under the Moghul Empire in India.

**Chinese art** manifested itself in pottery as early as 4000 BC, and its porcelains and jade and ivory carvings, are major art forms. Painting was influenced by calligraphy; the ideographic script, which used the same brush, ink, and paper, called for the same dexterity, and produced the same spontaneous impression. Whether as hanging scrolls or hand-scrolls that unrolled to provide a continuous picture, paintings on silk and paper included calligraphy, often a poem. Traditional subjects were a bamboo branch, sprig of blossom, or snowy mountain landscape. Seen from a birds-eye view, the space within a landscape was as meaningful as the subject.

**Indian art** influenced all of South-East Asia. From Buddha's death (485 BC) it centred on the religion which revered him as 'The Incarnation of the Truth'. Images of the Buddha followed a symbolic pattern: his plumpness signified well-being, his posture relaxation, his expression tranquillity. Hinduism also flourished and both Buddhist and Hindu temples were covered in high-relief sculpture. By the 13th century Hinduism became the major religion. The figures of its many exotic deities are rounded and sensuous, their poses based on religious dance movements. Eroticism enters with exuberantly amorous couples symbolizing the unity of the divine. Miniature painting, beginning in the 11th century, reached its peak under the Moghuls (16th–17th centuries).

**Japanese art** mastered all the Chinese and Buddhist traditions, adding its own interest in surface texture, bright colours, and dramatic compositions. Its most original contribution to world art was the *ukiyo-e* colour print. Originating in genre paintings of 16th–17th century theatre scenes, actors, and geishas, it developed into the woodcut, and after 1740 the true colour print, while its subject matter expanded beyond the amusements of daily life to include flowers, birds, animals, and landscapes. Their brilliant combination of flat decorative colour and expressive pattern influenced 19th-century European art. Masters included Utamaro (1753–1806) and Hokusai (1760–1849). Distinguished artists also worked in miniature sculpture, producing tiny carved *netsuke* figures, later widely collected in the West.

# THE GREATEST ART FORGERS OF THE 20TH CENTURY

**Dossena**, Alceo 1878–1937 To this day referred to as the 'king of forgers', Italian Alceo Dossena was able to assimilate and evoke a wide range of period and personal styles, never actually copying but successfully suggesting work ranging from ancient Greek to Renaissance. Once established in a Roman studio, Dossena was employed by two unscrupulous dealers and their contacts to execute sculpture according to their orders for a piece 'in the manner of' this or that master. When Dossena eventually understood that he had been badly exploited and underpaid (he had been robbed of millions), he revealed himself to the public through court action against his dealers. A vast body of work scattered throughout Europe and the USA was then identified as Dossena's. After a short period of celebrity, his reputation declined and he died a pauper, condemned for having been an unwitting forger.

**van Meegeren** Henricus Antonius 1889–1947 The Dutch van Meegeren had embarked on his career as a forger by 1923, when a Frans Hals forgery of his was bought and later denounced as a fake. He is best known for the series of fake 'Vermeers' and 'de Hooghs' he produced between 1937 and 1943, many of which were eagerly bought up by the Dutch government and museums. Much to his chagrin, the leading Nazi Hermann Goering succeeded in buying one of his forgeries, *Christ and the Adulteress*, in 1942. After the end of the German occupation of the Netherlands in 1945, van Meegeren was arrested on the charge of collaboration with the Nazi government through the sale of what was considered a Dutch national treasure. Confronted with this serious charge, he confessed to his 'Vermeer' forgeries and was charged instead with fraud. Having caused the embarrassment of the nation's art historians, museum directors and curators, restorers and technical experts, as well as some of the most prominent dealers and collectors, van Meegeren, who had becomer a national hero of sorts, was sentenced to one year's imprisonment, but died before serving his sentence.

**de Hory** Elmyr 20th century In a secret studio on the Mediterranean island of Ibiza, the Hungarian de Hory created forgeries of paintings and drawings by practically every modern artist of any economic repute. At first, de Hory faked and sold works to many European and US galleries and even a few museums, almost always on the pretext of having financial reasons to part with family treasures. Between 1961 and 1967, however, under the guidance of his two dealers, de Hory apparently forged some $60 million worth of paintings and drawings which were sold to millionaires, art dealers, and museums. Some $250,000 worth of 'Derains', 'Dufys', and 'Modiglianis' were acquired by the Japanese National Museum of Modern Art in Tokyo. According to his biographer and fellow forger, during this period de Hory produced perhaps 1,000 items, 75–90% of which remain in collections or museums, unrecognized or undisclosed as fakes. Because of the threat to the reputations of his victims posed by publicity, de Hory has never been prosecuted for forgery.

**Keating** Tom 1917–1984 The English painter Keating was probably the most prolific and versatile art forger to be exposed in Britain

this century. According to his own account, between the 1950s and 1970s he produced some 2,000 fakes of about a hundred different artists, including Samuel Palmer. He claimed that his outright forgery was a form of protest against the exploitation of artists by dealers. The uncovering of Keating's forgeries began in March 1976, and by Aug of that year he made a general confession at a press conference. His revelations caused a sensation in the country and consternation in the London art market, turning him into a popular hero. He was arrested in 1977, but all charges were later dropped because of his poor health. A posthumous sale of his work brought in £274,000—about seven times the estimate.

**'Maestro del Ricciolo'** (Master of the Curl) Numerous forgeries of Old Master drawings by this skilful perpetrator infested the art market during the late 1980s. His productions are mostly drawn imitations of the 18th-century Venetians Antonio Canaletto (1697–1768) and Francesco Guardi (1712–1793). These fakes are invariably drawn on old paper, often with a prominent watermark.

### Art ownership

*A millionaire recently said that he wished to be buried with some of his priceless works of art. Some people say that they belong to him, he's paid for them, so he can do what he likes with them. Others say that we cannot let such unique works of art disappear from view in this way. Which of these two views comes closest to your own?*

| | |
|---|---|
| He can do what he likes | 45 |
| Cannot let them disappear | 49 |
| Don't know | 5 |

# GREAT WRITERS

**Abú Nuwás** Hasan ibn Háni 762–c. 815. Arab poet celebrated for the freedom, eroticism and ironic lightness of touch he brought to traditional forms.

**Andersen** Hans Christian 1805–1875. Danish writer. His fairy tales such as 'The Ugly Duckling', 'The Emperor's New Clothes', and 'The Snow Queen', gained him international fame and have been translated into many languages.

**Ariosto** Ludovico 1474–1533. Italian poet, born in Reggio. He wrote Latin poems and comedies along Classical lines, including the poem *Orlando Furioso* 1516, 1532, an epic treatment of the *Roland* story, and considered to be the perfect poetic expression of the Italian Renaissance.

**Machado de Assis** Joaquim Maria 1839–1908. Brazilian writer and poet. He is regarded as the greatest Brazilian novelist. His sceptical, ironic wit is well displayed in his 30 volumes of novels and short stories, including *Epitaph for a Small Winner* 1880 and *Dom Casmurro* 1900.

**Asturias** Miguel Ángel 1899–1974. Guatemalan author and diplomat. He published poetry, Guatemalan legends, and novels, such as *El Señor Presidente/The President* 1946, *Men of Corn* 1949, and *Strong Wind* 1950, attacking Latin-American dictatorships and 'Yankee imperialism'. Nobel Prize for Literature 1967.

**Atwood** Margaret (Eleanor) 1939– . Canadian novelist, short-story writer, and poet. Her novels, which often treat feminist themes with wit and irony, include *The Edible Woman* 1969, *Life Before Man* 1979, *Bodily Harm* 1981, *The Handmaid's Tale* 1986, and *Cat's Eye* 1989.

**Austen** Jane 1775–1817. English novelist whose books are set within the confines of middle-class provincial society, and show her skill at drawing characters and situations with delicate irony. Her principal works are *Sense and Sensibility* 1811 (like its successors, published anonymously), *Pride and Prejudice* 1813, *Mansfield Park* 1814, *Emma* 1816, *Persuasion* 1818, and *Northanger Abbey* 1818. She died at Winchester and is buried in the cathedral.

**Baldwin** James 1924–1987. US writer, born in New York City, who portrayed the condition of black Americans in contemporary society. His works include the novels *Go Tell It on the Mountain* 1953, *Another Country* 1962, and *Just Above My Head* 1979; the play *The Amen Corner* 1955; and the autobiographical essays *Notes of a Native Son* 1955 and *The Fire Next Time* 1963. He was active in the civil rights movement.

**Balzac** Honoré de 1799–1850. French novelist. His first success was *Les Chouans/The Chouans* and *La Physiologie du mariage/The Physiology of Marriage* 1829, inspired by Scott. This was the beginning of the long series of novels *La Comédie humaine/The*

*Human Comedy* (planned as 143 volumes, of which 80 were completed), depicting vice and folly in contemporary French society. He also wrote the Rabelaisian *Contes drolatiques/Ribald Tales* 1833.

**Bashō** Pen name of Matsuo Munefusa 1644–1694. Japanese poet who was a master of the *haiku*, a 17-syllable poetic form with lines of 5, 7, and 5 syllables, which he infused with subtle allusiveness and made the accepted form of poetic expression in Japan. His most famous work is *Oku-no-hosomichi/The Narrow Road to the Deep North* 1694, an account of a visit to northern Japan, which consists of haikus interspersed with prose passages.

**Baudelaire** Charles Pierre 1821–1867. French poet, whose work combined rhythmical and musical perfection with a morbid romanticism and eroticism, finding beauty in decadence and evil. His first book of verse, *Les Fleurs du mal/Flowers of Evil* 1857, was condemned by the censor as endangering public morals, but was enormously influential, paving the way for Arthur Rimbaud, Paul Verlaine, and the symbolist school.

**Bellow** Saul 1915– . Canadian-born US novelist of Russian descent, whose finely styled works and skilled characterizations of life, especially contemporary Jewish-American life, won him the Nobel Prize for Literature 1976. His works usually portray an individual's frustrating relationship with the ongoing events of an indifferent society, and include the picaresque *The Adventures of Augie March* 1953, the philosophically speculative *Herzog* 1964, *Humboldt's Gift* 1975, *The Dean's December* 1982, and *The Bellarosa Connection* 1989.

**Blake** William 1757–1827. English poet, painter, and mystic, a leading figure in the Romantic period. His visionary, symbolic poems include *Songs of Innocence* 1789 and *Songs of Experience* 1794. He engraved the text and illustrations for his works and hand-coloured them, mostly in watercolour. He also illustrated works by John Milton and William Shakespeare.

**Boccaccio** Giovanni 1313–1375. Italian poet, chiefly known for the collection of tales called the *Decameron* 1348–53. The bawdiness and exuberance of this work, as well as its narrative skill and characterization, made the work enormously popular and influential, inspiring Chaucer, Shakespeare, Dryden, and Keats among many others.

**Böll** Heinrich 1917–1985. West German novelist. A radical Catholic and anti-Nazi, he attacked Germany's political past and the materialism of its contemporary society. His many publications include poems, short stories, and novels which satirize German society, for example *Billard um Halbzehn/Billiards at Half-Past Nine* 1959 and *Gruppenbild mit Dame/Group Portrait with Lady* 1971. Nobel Prize for Literature 1972.

**Borges** Jorge Luis 1899–1986. Argentinian poet and short-story writer. In 1961 he became director of the National Library, Buenos Aires,

## MOST POPULAR TYPES OF BOOKS BOUGHT

| Women | | Men | |
| --- | --- | --- | --- |
| | *Type* | | *Type* |
| 1 | Romance/Love stories | 1 | Crime/thrillers |
| 2 | Cookery books | 2 | Specialist reference/text books |
| 3 | Puzzle/quiz books | 3 | Car repair manuals |
| 4 | Crime/thrillers | 4 | War/adventure stories |
| 5 | Gardening/plants | 5 | Road atlas |
| 6 | Food/drink | 6 | Sports/games books |
| 7 | Historical novels | 7 | Local street guides |
| 8 | Road atlas | 8 | Cookery books |
| 9 | Diet/health/beauty | 9 | Sports/games instruction books |
| 10 | 20th century novels | 10 | Science fiction |

*Source: Lifestyle Pocket Book 1991, NTC Publications Ltd*

and was professor of English literature at the university there. He is known for his fantastic and paradoxical work *Ficciones/Fictions* 1944.

**Brontë** family of English writers, including the three sisters **Charlotte** (1816–55), **Emily Jane** (1818–48) and **Anne** (1820–49), and their brother **Patrick Branwell** (1817–48). Their most enduring works are Charlotte Brontë's *Jane Eyre* 1847 and Emily Brontë's *Wuthering Heights* 1847. Later works include Anne's *The Tenant of Wildfell Hall* 1848 and Charlotte's *Shirley* 1849 and *Villette* 1853.

**Burns** Robert 1759–1796. Scottish poet who used the Scots dialect at a time when it was not considered suitably 'elevated' for literature. Burns's first volume, *Poems, Chiefly in the Scottish Dialect*, appeared in 1786. In addition to his poetry Burns wrote or adapted many songs, including 'Auld Lang Syne'.

**Byron** George Gordon, 6th Baron Byron 1788–1824. English poet who became the symbol of Romanticism and political liberalism throughout Europe in the 19th century. His reputation was established with the first two cantos of *Childe Harold* 1812. Later works include *The Prisoner of Chillon* 1816, *Beppo* 1818, *Mazeppa* 1819, and, most notably, *Don Juan* 1819–24. He left England in 1816, spending most of his later life in Italy. In 1823 he sailed for Greece to further the Greek struggle for independence, but died of fever at Missolonghi.

**Camoëns** or **Camões**, Luís Vaz de 1524–1580. Portuguese poet and soldier. He went on various military expeditions, and was shipwrecked in 1558. His poem, *Os Lusiades/The Lusiads*, published 1572, tells the story of the explorer Vasco da Gama and incorporates much Portuguese history; it has become the country's national epic. His posthumously published lyric poetry is also now valued.

**Camus** Albert 1913–1960. Algerian-born French writer. A journalist in France, he was active in the Resistance during World War II. His novels, which owe much to existentialism, include *L'Etranger/The Outsider* 1942, *La Peste/The*

*Plague* 1948, and *L'Homme Révolté/The Rebel* 1952. He was awarded the Nobel Prize for Literature 1957.

**Cao Chan** or **Ts'ao Chan** 1719–1763. Chinese novelist. His tragic love story *Hung Lou Meng/The Dream of the Red Chamber* published 1792, involves the downfall of a Manchu family and is semi-autobiographical.

**Carroll** Lewis. Pen name of Charles Lutwidge Dodgson 1832–1898. English mathematician and writer of children's books, including the classics *Alice's Adventures in Wonderland* 1865 and its sequel *Through the Looking Glass* 1872. He also published mathematics books under his own name.

**Cervantes Saavedra**, Miguel de 1547–1616. Spanish novelist, playwright, and poet, whose masterpiece, *Don Quixote* (in full *El ingenioso hidalgo Don Quixote de la Mancha*) was published 1605. In 1613, his *Novelas Ejemplares/Exemplary Novels* appeared, followed by *Viaje del Parnaso/The Voyage to Parnassus* 1614. A spurious second part of *Don Quixote* prompted Cervantes to bring out his own second part in 1615, often considered superior to the first in construction and characterization.

**Chaucer** Geoffrey *c.* 1340–1400. English poet, the greatest and most influential English poet of the Middle Ages. In his masterpiece, *The Canterbury Tales* (*c.* 1387), a collection of tales told by pilgrims on their way to the shrine of Thomas à Becket, he showed his genius for metre and characterization. His other work includes the French-influenced *Romance of the Rose* and an adaptation of Boccaccio's *Troilus and Criseyde*. The great popularity of his work assured the dominance of the southern English dialect in literature.

**Conrad** Joseph 1857–1924. English novelist of Polish parentage, born Teodor Jozef Konrad Korzeniowski in the Ukraine. His novels include *Almayer's Folly* 1895, *Lord Jim* 1900, *Heart of Darkness* 1902, *Nostromo* 1904, *The Secret Agent* 1907, and *Under Western Eyes* 1911. His works vividly evoke the mysteries of sea life and exotic foreign settings and explore the psychological isolation of the 'outsider'.

**Dante Alighieri** 1265–1321. Italian poet. His masterpiece *La Divina Commedia/The Divine Comedy* 1307–21, the greatest poem of the Middle Ages, is an epic account in three parts of his journey through Hell, Purgatory, and Paradise, during which he is guided part of the way by the poet Virgil; on a metaphorical level the journey is also one of Dante's own spiritual development. Other works include the philosophical prose treatise *Convivio/The Banquet* 1306–08, the first major work of its kind to be written in Italian rather than Latin; *Monarchia/On World Government* 1310–13, expounding his political theories; *De vulgari eloquentia/Concerning the Vulgar Tongue* 1304–06, an original Latin work on Italian, its dialects, and kindred languages; and *Canzoniere/Lyrics*, containing his scattered lyrics.

**Darío** Rubén. Pen name of Félix Rubén García Sarmiento 1867–1916. Nicaraguan poet. His first major work *Azul/Azure* 1888, a collection of prose and verse influenced by French Symbolism, created a sensation. He went on to establish *modernismo*, the Spanish-American modernist literary movement, distinguished by an idiosyncratic and deliberately frivolous style that broke away from the prevailing Spanish provincialism and adapted French poetic models. His vitality and eclecticism influenced every poet writing in Spanish after him, both in the New World and in Spain.

**Defoe** Daniel 1660–1731. English novelist and journalist. His best-known work, *Robinson Crusoe* 1719, was greatly influential in the development of the novel. An active pamphleteer and political critic, he was imprisoned 1702–04 following publication of the ironic *The Shortest Way With Dissenters*. Fictional works include *Moll Flanders* 1722 and *A Journal of the Plague Year* 1724. Altogether he produced over 500 books, pamphlets, and journals.

**Dickens** Charles 1812–1870. English novelist, popular for his memorable characters and his portrayal of the social evils of Victorian England. In 1836 he published the first number of the *Pickwick Papers*, followed by *Oliver Twist* 1838, the first of his 'reforming' novels; *Nicholas Nickleby* 1839; *Barnaby Rudge* 1840; *The Old Curiosity Shop* 1841; and *David Copperfield* 1849. Among his later books are *Hard Times* 1854; *Little Dorritt* 1857; *A Tale of Two Cities* 1859 and *Great Expectations* 1861.

**Donne** John 1571–1631. English metaphysical poet whose work is characterized by subtle imagery and figurative language. In 1615 Donne took orders in the Church of England and as dean of St Paul's Cathedral, London, was noted for his sermons. His poetry includes the sonnets 'Batter my heart, three person'd God' and 'Death be not proud', elegies, and satires.

**Dos Passos** John 1896–1970. US author. He made his reputation with the war novels *One Man's Initiation* 1919 and *Three Soldiers* 1921. His major work is the trilogy *U.S.A.* 1930–36, which gives a panoramic view of US life through the device of placing fictitious characters against the setting of real newspaper headlines and contemporary events.

**Dostoievsky** Fyodor Mikhailovich 1821–1881. Russian novelist. Remarkable for their profound psychological insight, Dostoievsky's novels have greatly influenced Russian writers, and since the beginning of the 20th century have been increasingly influential abroad. In 1849 he was sentenced to four years' hard labour in Siberia, followed by army service, for printing socialist propaganda. *The House of the Dead* 1861 recalls his prison experiences, followed by his major works *Crime and Punishment* 1866, *The Idiot* 1868–69, and *The Brothers Karamazov* 1880.

**Duras** Marguerite 1914– . French writer. Her works include short stories (*Des Journées entières dans les arbres*), plays (*La Musica*), film scripts (*Hiroshima mon amour* 1960),

**Approximately how many books have you bought in the last 12 months?**

| | |
|---|---|
| None | 37% |
| Up to 5 | 25% |
| 6 - 9 | 9% |
| 10 - 15 | 14% |
| 16 - 19 | 0% |
| 20 - 25 | 5% |
| 26 - 29 | 0% |
| 30 - 35 | 2% |
| 36 - 39 | 0% |
| 40 or more | 0% |
| average number of books bought | 5.4% |

and novels such as *Le Vice-Consul* 1966, evoking an existentialist world from the setting of Calcutta, and *Emily L.* 1989. *La vie matérielle* (published in France 1987) appeared in England as *Practicalities* 1990. Her autobiographical novel, *La Douleur*, is set in Paris in 1945.

**Eliot** George. Pen name of Mary Ann Evans 1819–1880. English novelist who portrayed Victorian society, including its intellectual hypocrisy, with realism and irony. In 1857 she published the story 'Amos Barton', the first of the *Scenes of Clerical Life*. This was followed by the novels *Adam Bede* 1859, *The Mill on the Floss* 1860, and *Silas Marner* 1861. *Middlemarch* 1872 is now considered one of the greatest novels of the 19th century. Her final book *Daniel Deronda* 1876 was concerned with anti-Semitism. She also wrote poetry.

**Eliot** T(homas) S(tearns) 1888–1965. US poet, playwright, and critic who lived in London from 1915. His first volume of poetry, *Prufrock and Other Observations* 1917, introduced new verse forms and rhythms, and expressed the disillusionment of the generation affected by World War I; further collections include *The Waste Land* 1922, which established his central position in modern poetry; *The Hollow Men* 1925, and *Old Possum's Book of Practical Cats* 1939. *Four Quartets* 1943 revealed his religious vision. His plays include *Murder in the Cathedral* 1935 and *The Cocktail Party* 1949. He was also an influential literary critic, and helped to re-assess the importance of Donne. He was awarded the Nobel Prize for Literature in 1948.

**Faulkner** William 1897–1962. US novelist who wrote in an experimental stream-of-consciousness style. His works include *The Sound and the Fury* 1929, dealing with a Southern US family in decline; *As I Lay Dying* 1930; *Light in August* 1932, a study of segregation; *The Unvanquished* 1938, stories of the Civil War; and *The Hamlet* 1940, *The Town* 1957, and *The Mansion* 1959, a trilogy covering the rise of the materialist Snopes family. He was awarded the Nobel Prize for Literature in 1949.

**Fielding** Henry 1707–1754. English novelist whose narrative power influenced the form and technique of the novel and helped to make it the most popular form of literature in England. In 1742 he parodied Richardson's novel *Pamela*

## THE BIG ENGLISH-LANGUAGE PUBLISHERS

| | Owner | Worldwide sales ($m) | Consumer Imprints |
|---|---|---|---|
| 1 | News Corporation (Australia) | 1,417 | Harper & Row, Scott, Foresman, (US), Harper Collins, Grafton (UK) |
| 2 | Paramount Communications (US) | 1,300 | Simon & Schuster (US, UK) |
| 3 | Hachette (France) | 1,089 | Grolier (US) |
| 4 | Reed (UK) | 925 | Octopus, Heinemann, Secker & Warburg, Methuen (UK) |
| 5 | Pearson (UK) | 905 | Viking, Penguin (US, UK), New American Library (US), Hamish Hamilton, Michael Joseph (UK) |
| 6 | Harcourt Brace Jovanovich (US) | 879 | [academic and professional books] |
| 7 | Bertelsmann (West Germany) | 843 | Bantam, Doubleday, Dell (US), Transworld (UK) |
| 8 | Reader's Digest (US) | 843 | [book series] |
| 9 | Time Warner (US) | 843 | Little Brown (US) |
| 10 | Times Mirror (US) | 650 | [professional books] |
| 11 | Random House (US) | 630 | Crown, Alfred Knopf (US), Century Hutchinson, Chatto & Windus, Bodley Head, Jonathan Cape (UK) |
| 12 | Maxwell Communications Corporation (UK) | 593 | Macmillan (US), Macdonald, Sphere (UK) |

*Source: The Economist 1990*

in his *Joseph Andrews*, which was followed by *Jonathan Wild the Great* 1743; his masterpiece *Tom Jones* 1749, which he described as a 'comic epic in prose'; and *Amelia* 1751.

**Firdawsi** Mansûr Abu'l-Qâsim *c.* 935–*c.* 1020. Persian poet, the greatest epic poet of Persia. His *Shahnama/The Book of Kings* relates the history of Persia in 60,000 verses, and included the legend of Sohrab and Rustum, in which the father unknowingly kills the son in battle.

**Fitzgerald** F(rancis) Scott (Key) 1896–1940. US novelist and short-story writer. His early autobiographical novel *This Side of Paradise* 1920 made him known in the postwar society of the East Coast, and *The Great Gatsby* 1925 epitomizes the Jazz Age.

**Flaubert** Gustave 1821–1880. French novelist, one of the greatest of the 19th century. His masterpiece, noted for its psychological realism, is *Madame Bovary* 1857. He entered Paris literary circles 1840, but in 1846 moved to Rouen, where he remained for the rest of his life. *Salammbô* 1862 earned him the Legion of Honour 1866, and was followed by *L'Education sentimentale/Sentimental Education* 1869, and *La Tentation de Saint Antoine/The Temptation of St Anthony* 1874. Flaubert also wrote the short stories *Trois contes/Three Tales* 1877.

**García Márquez** Gabriel 1928– . Colombian novelist. His sweeping novel *Cien años de soledad/One Hundred Years of Solitude* 1967 (which tells the story of a family over a period of six generations) is an example of magic realism, a technique used to heighten the intensity of realistic portrayal of social and political issues by introducing grotesque or fanciful material. His other books include *El amor en los tiempos del cólera/Love in the Time of Cholera* 1985. Nobel Prize for Literature 1982.

**Gide** André 1869–1951. French novelist, born in Paris. His work is largely autobiographical and concerned with the dual themes of self-fulfilment and renunciation. It includes *L'Immoraliste/The Immoralist* 1902, *La Porte étroite/Strait Is the Gate* 1909, *Les Caves du Vatican/The Vatican Cellars* 1914, and *Les Faux-monnayeurs/The Counterfeiters* 1926; and an almost lifelong *Journal*. Nobel Prize for Literature 1947.

**Goethe** Johann Wolfgang von 1749–1832. German poet, novelist, and dramatist, generally considered the founder of modern German literature, and leader of the Romantic *Sturm und Drang* movement. His works include the autobiographical *Die Leiden des Jungen Werthers/The Sorrows of the Young Werther* 1774 and *Faust* 1808, his masterpiece. A visit to Italy 1786–88 inspired the classical dramas *Iphigenie auf Tauris/Iphigenia in Tauris* 1787 and *Tasso* 1790.

**Gogol** Nikolai Vasilyevich 1809–1852. Russian writer. His first success was a collection of stories, *Evenings on a Farm near Dikanka* 1831–32, followed by *Mirgorod* 1835. Later works include *Arabesques* 1835, the comedy play *The Inspector General* 1836, and the picaresque novel *Dead Souls* 1842, which satirizes Russian provincial society.

**Grass** Günter 1927– . German writer. Born in Danzig, he studied at the art academies of Düsseldorf and Berlin, worked as a writer and sculptor (first in Paris and later in Berlin), and in 1958 won the coveted 'Group 47' prize. The grotesque humour and socialist feeling of his novels *Die Blechtrommel/The Tin Drum* 1959 and *Der Butt/The Flounder* 1977 are also characteristic of many of his poems.

**Greene** (Henry) Graham 1904–1991. English writer, whose novels of guilt, despair, and penitence, include *The Man Within* 1929, *Brighton Rock* 1938, *The Power and the Glory* 1940, *The Heart of the Matter* 1948, *The Third Man* 1950, *The Honorary Consul* 1973, *Monsignor Quixote* 1982, and *The Captain and the Enemy* 1988.

**Hâfiz** Shams al-Din Muhammad *c.* 1326–1390. Persian lyric poet, who was born in Shiraz and taught in a Dervish college there. His *Diwan*, a collection of short odes, extols the pleasures of life and satirizes his fellow Dervishes.

**Which of these books do you have in your home at the moment?**

| type of book | today | 1959 |
|---|---|---|
| cookery book | 87% | 80% |
| encyclopedia | 66% | 50% |
| atlas | 77% | 51% |
| the Bible | 79% | 84% |
| first aid book | 52% | 58% |
| dictionary | 91% | 75% |
| book on child care | 29% | 24% |
| book on Shakespeare's plays | 30% | 28% |
| none of these | 2% | 3% |

Source:Gallup

**Hardy** Thomas 1840–1928. English novelist and poet. His novels, set in rural 'Wessex' (his native West Country), portray intense human relationships played out in a harshly indifferent natural world. They include *Far From the Madding Crowd* 1874, *The Return of the Native* 1878, *The Mayor of Casterbridge* 1886, *The Woodlanders* 1887, *Tess of the D'Urbervilles* 1891, and *Jude the Obscure* 1895. The latter, portraying social attitudes towards education, marriage, divorce, and suicide, aroused great antagonism, which reinforced his decision to confine himself to verse. His poetry includes the *Wessex Poems* 1898, and several volumes of lyrics.

**Heine** Heinrich 1797–1856. German romantic poet and journalist, who wrote *Reisebilder* 1826 and *Buch der Lieder/Book of Songs* 1827. From 1831 he lived mainly in Paris, working as a correspondent for German newspapers. Schubert and Schumann set many of his lyrics to music.

**Hemingway** Ernest 1898–1961. US writer. War, bullfighting, and fishing were used symbolically in his writings to represent honour, dignity, and primitivism—prominent themes in his short stories and novels, which included *A Farewell to Arms* 1929, *For Whom the Bell Tolls* 1940, and *The Old Man and the Sea* 1952. His deceptively simple writing styles attracted many imitators. He received the Nobel Prize for Literature in 1954.

**Homer** lived *c.* 8th century BC. Legendary Greek epic poet. According to tradition he was a blind minstrel and the author of the *Iliad* and the *Odyssey*, which are probably based on much older stories, passed on orally, concerning war with Troy in the 12th century BC.

**Horace** 65–8 BC. Roman lyric poet and satirist. He became a leading poet under the patronage of Emperor Augustus. His works include *Satires* 35–30 BC; the four books of *Odes* about 25–24 BC; *Epistles*, a series of verse letters; and a critical work, *Ars poetica*.

**Hugo** Victor (Marie) 1802–1885. French poet, novelist, and dramatist. The *Odes et poésies diverses* appeared 1822, and his verse play *Hernani* 1830 established him as the leader of French Romanticism. More volumes of verse followed between his series of dramatic novels,

which included *The Hunchback of Notre Dame* 1831 and *Les Misérables* 1862.

**Huxley** Aldous (Leonard) 1894–1963. English writer. The satirical disillusionment of his first novel, *Crome Yellow* 1921, continued throughout *Antic Hay* 1923, *Those Barren Leaves* 1925, *Point Counter Point* 1928, and *Brave New World* 1932, in which human beings are mass produced in the laboratory under the control of the omnipotent state.

**Iqbāl** Muhammad 1875–1938. Islamic poet and thinker. His literary works, in Urdu and Persian, were mostly verse in the classical style, suitable for public recitation. He sought through his writings to arouse Muslims to take their place in the modern world.

**Ishiguro** Kazuo 1954– . Japanese-born British novelist. His novel *An Artist of the Floating World* won the 1986 Whitbread Prize, and *The Remains of the Day* won the 1989 Booker Prize.

**James** Henry 1843–1916. US novelist, who lived in Europe from 1875 and became a naturalized British subject 1915. His novels deal with the impact of sophisticated European culture on the innocent American. They include *The Portrait of a Lady* 1881, *Washington Square* 1881, *The Bostonians* 1886, *The Ambassadors* 1903, and *The Golden Bowl* 1904. He also wrote more than a hundred shorter works of fiction, notably the supernatural tale *The Turn of the Screw* 1898.

**Johnson** Samuel, known as 'Dr Johnson', 1709–1784. English lexicographer, author, and critic, also a brilliant conversationalist and the dominant figure in 18th-century London literary society. His *Dictionary*, published 1755, remained authoritative for over a century, and is still remarkable for the vigour of its definitions. In 1764 he founded the 'Literary Club', whose members included Joshua Reynolds, Edmund Burke, Oliver Goldsmith, David Garrick, and James Boswell, Johnson's biographer.

**Joyce** James (Augustine Aloysius) 1882–1941. Irish writer, born in Dublin, who revolutionized the form of the English novel with his 'stream of consciousness' technique. His works include *Dubliners* 1914 (short stories), *Portrait of the Artist as a Young Man* 1916, *Ulysses* 1922, and *Finnegan's Wake* 1939.

**Kafka** Franz 1883–1924. Czech novelist, born in Prague, who wrote in German. His three unfinished allegorical novels *Der Prozess/The Trial* 1925, *Der Schloss/The Castle* 1926, and *Amerika/America* 1927 were posthumously published despite his instructions that they should be destroyed. His short stories include 'Die Verwandlung/The Metamorphosis' 1915, in which a man turns into a huge insect.

**Kālidāsa** lived 5th century AD. Indian epic poet and dramatist. His works, in Sanskrit, include the classic drama *Sakuntala*, the love story of King Dushyanta and the nymph Sakuntala.

**Keats** John 1795–1821. English poet, a leading figure of the Romantic movement. He published his first volume of poetry 1817; this was followed by *Endymion, Isabella,* and *Hyperion* 1818, 'The Eve of St Agnes', his odes 'To Autumn', 'On a Grecian Urn', and 'To a Nightingale', and 'Lamia' 1819. His final volume of poems appeared in 1820.

**Kerouac** Jack 1923–1969. US novelist who named and epitomized the Beat Generation of the 1950s. His books, all autobiographical, include *On the Road* 1957, *Big Sur* 1963, and *Desolation Angel* 1965.

**Kipling** (Joseph) Rudyard 1865–1936. English writer, born in India. His stories for children include the *Jungle Books* 1894–1895, *Stalky and Co* 1899, and the *Just So Stories* 1902. Other works include the novel *Kim* 1901, the short story 'His Gift', poetry, and the unfinished autobiography *Something of Myself* 1937. In his heyday he enjoyed enormous popularity, and although subsequently denigrated for alleged 'jingoist imperialism', his work is increasingly valued for its complex characterization and subtle moral viewpoints. Nobel Prize for Literature 1907.

**La Fontaine** Jean de 1621–1695. French poet. He was born at Château-Thierry, and from 1656 lived largely in Paris, the friend of Molière, Jean Racine, and Nicolas Boileau. His works include *Fables* 1668–94 and *Contes* 1665–74, a series of witty and bawdy tales in verse.

**Lawrence** D(avid) H(erbert) 1885–1930. English writer whose work expresses his belief in emotion and the sexual impulse as creative and true to human nature. His novels include *Sons and Lovers* 1913, *The Rainbow* 1915, *Women in Love* 1921, and *Lady Chatterley's Lover* 1928 (the latter was banned as obscene in the UK until 1960). Lawrence also wrote short stories (for example 'The Woman Who Rode Away') and poetry.

**Leopardi** Giacomo, Count Leopardi 1798–1837. Italian romantic poet. The first collection of his uniquely pessimistic poems, *I Versi/Verses,* appeared in 1824, and was followed by his philosophical *Operette morali/Minor Moral Works* 1827, in prose, and *I Canti/Lyrics* 1831.

**Levi** Primo 1919–1987. Italian novelist. He joined the anti-Fascist resistance during World War II, was captured, and sent to the concentration camp at Auschwitz. He wrote of these experiences in *Se questo è un uomo/If This Is a Man* 1947.

**Lewis** (Harry) Sinclair 1885–1951. US novelist. He made a reputation with satirical novels: *Main Street* 1920, depicting American small-town life; *Babbitt* 1922, the story of a real-estate dealer of the Midwest caught in the conventions of his milieu; *Arrowsmith* 1925, a study of the pettiness in medical science; and *Elmer Gantry* 1927, a satiric portrayal of evangelical religion. *Dodsworth*, a gentler novel of a US industrialist, was published 1929. He was the first American to be awarded the Nobel Prize for Literature 1930.

**Li Po** 705–762. Chinese poet. He used traditional literary forms, but his exuberance, the boldness of his imagination, and the intensity of his feeling have won him recognition as perhaps the greatest of all Chinese poets. Although he was mostly concerned with higher themes, he is also remembered for his celebratory verses on drinking.

**London** Jack (John Griffith) 1876–1916. US novelist, author of the adventure stories *The Call of the Wild* 1903, *The Sea Wolf* 1904, and *White Fang* 1906.

**Lorca** Federico García 1898–1936. Spanish poet and playwright, born in Granada. *Romancero gitano/Gipsy Ballad-book* 1928 shows the influence of the Andalusian songs of the area. In 1929–30 Lorca visited New York, and his experiences are reflected in *Poeta en Nueva York/Poet in New York* 1940. His poems include *Lament,* written for the bullfighter Mejías. He was shot by the Falangists during the Spanish Civil War.

**Machado de Assis** Joaquim Maria 1839–1908. Brazilian writer and poet. He is regarded as the greatest Brazilian novelist. His sceptical, ironic wit is well displayed in his 30 volumes of novels and short stories, including *Epitaph for a Small Winner* 1880 and *Dom Casmurro* 1900.

**Mann** Thomas 1875–1955. German novelist and critic, concerned with the theme of the artist's relation to society. His first novel was *Buddenbrooks* 1901, which, followed by *Der Zauberberg/The Magic Mountain* 1924, led to a Nobel Prize for Literature 1929. Later works include *Dr Faustus* 1947 and *Die Bekenntnisse des Hochstaplers Felix Krull/Confessions of Felix Krull* 1954. Notable among his works of short fiction is *Der Tod in Venedig/Death in Venice* 1913.

**Manzoni** Alessandro, Count Manzoni 1785–1873. Italian poet and novelist, author of the historical romance, *I promessi sposi/The Betrothed* 1825–27, set in Spanish-occupied Milan during the 17th century. Verdi's *Requiem* commemorates him.

**Maupassant** Guy de 1850–1893. French author who established a reputation with the short story 'Boule de Suif/Ball of Fat' 1880 and wrote some 300 short stories in all. His novels include *Une Vie/A Woman's Life* 1883 and *Bel-Ami* 1885. He was encouraged as a writer by Gustave Flaubert.

**Melville** Herman 1819–1891. US writer, whose *Moby-Dick* 1851 was inspired by his whaling experiences in the South Seas. These experiences were also the basis for earlier fiction, such as *Typee* 1846 and *Omoo* 1847. He published several volumes of verse, as well as short stories (*The Piazza Tales* 1856). *Billy Budd* was completed just before his death and published 1924. Although most of his works were unappreciated during his lifetime, today he is one of the most highly regarded of US authors.

**Milton** John 1608–1674. English poet. His early poems include the pastoral *L'allegro* and *Il penseroso* 1632, the masque *Comus* 1633, and the elegy *Lycidas* 1637. His middle years were devoted to the Puritan cause and pamphleteering, including one advocating divorce, and another (*Areopagitica*) freedom of the

## Prix Goncourt for fiction (French)

| | |
|---|---|
| 1980 | Yves Navarre *Le Jardin d'acclimation* |
| 1981 | Lucien Bodard *Anne Marie* |
| 1982 | Dominique Fernandez *Dans la Main de l'ange* |
| 1983 | Frederick Tristan *Les Égares* |
| 1984 | Marguerite Duras *L'Amant* |
| 1985 | Yann Queffelec *Les Noces barbares* |
| 1986 | Michel Host *Valet de Nuit* |
| 1987 | Tahir Ben Jelloun *La Nuit Sacrée* |
| 1988 | Erik Orsenna *L'Exposition Coloniale* |
| 1989 | Jean Vautrin *Un Grand Pas Vers le Bon Dieu* |
| 1990 | Jean Rouault *Les Champs d'Honneur* |

## Pulitzer Prize for Fiction (American)

| | |
|---|---|
| 1980 | Norman Mailer *The Executioner's Song* |
| 1981 | John Kennedy Toole *A Confederacy of Dunces* |
| 1982 | John Updike *Rabbit is Rich* |
| 1983 | Alice Walker *The Color Purple* |
| 1984 | William Kennedy *Ironweed* |
| 1985 | Alison Lurie *Foreign Affairs* |
| 1986 | Larry McMurtry *Lonesome Dove* |
| 1987 | Peter Taylor *A Summer to Memphis* |
| 1988 | Toni Morrison *Beloved* |
| 1989 | Anne Tyler *Breathing Lessons* |
| 1990 | Oscar Hijelos *The Mambo Kings Play Songs of Love* |

## Booker Prize for Fiction (British)

| | |
|---|---|
| 1980 | William Golding *Rites of Passage* |
| 1981 | Salman Rushdie *Midnight's Children* |
| 1982 | Thomas Keneally *Schindler's Ark* |
| 1983 | J M Coetzee *Life and Times of Michael K* |
| 1984 | Anita Brookner *Hotel du Lac* |
| 1985 | Keri Hulme *The Bone People* |
| 1986 | Kingsley Amis *The Old Devils* |
| 1987 | Penelope Lively *Moon Tiger* |
| 1988 | Peter Carey *Oscar and Lucinda* |
| 1989 | Kazuo Ishiguro *Remains of the Day* |
| 1990 | A S Byatt *Possession* |

## Nobel Prize for Literature (International)

| | |
|---|---|
| 1980 | Czeslaw Milosz (Polish-American) |
| 1981 | Elias Canetti (Bulgarian-British) |
| 1982 | Gabriel García Márquez (Columbian-Mexican) |
| 1983 | William Golding (British) |
| 1984 | Jaroslav Seifert (Czechoslovakian) |
| 1985 | Claude Simon (French) |
| 1986 | Wole Soyinka (Nigerian) |
| 1987 | Joseph Brodsky (Soviet) |
| 1988 | Naguib Mahfouz (Egyptian) |
| 1989 | Camilo Jose Cela (Spanish) |
| 1990 | Octavio Paz (Mexican) |

**Nabokov** Vladimir 1899–1977. US writer who left his native Russia 1917 and began writing in English in the 1940s. His most widely known book is *Lolita* 1955, the story of the middle-aged Humbert Humbert's infatuation with a precocious child of 12. His other books include *Laughter in the Dark* 1938, *The Real Life of Sebastian Knight* 1945, *Pnin* 1957, and his memoirs *Speak, Memory* 1947.

**Naipaul** V(idiadhar) S(urajprasad) 1932– . British writer, born in Trinidad of Hindu parents. His novels include *A House for Mr Biswas* 1961, *The Mimic Men* 1967, *A Bend in the River* 1979, and *Finding the Centre* 1984. His brother **Shiva(dhar) Naipaul** (1940–85) was also a novelist (*Fireflies* 1970) and journalist.

**Neruda** Pablo. Pen name of Neftalí Ricardo Reyes y Basualto 1904–1973. Chilean poet and diplomat. His work includes lyrics and the epic poem of the American continent *Canto General* 1950. He served as consul and ambassador to many countries. Nobel Prize for Literature 1971.

**Orwell** George. Pen name of Eric Arthur Blair 1903–1950. English author. His books include the satire *Animal Farm* 1945, which included such sayings as 'All animals are equal, but some are more equal than others', and the prophetic *Nineteen Eighty-Four* 1949, portraying the dangers of excessive state control over the individual. Other works include *Down and Out in Paris and London* 1933 and *Homage to Catalonia* 1938.

**Ovid** (Publius Ovidius Naso) 43 BC–AD 17. Roman poet. His poetry deals mainly with the themes of love (*Amores* 20 BC, *Ars amatoria* 1 BC,

press. From 1649 he was (Latin) secretary to the Council of State, his assistants (as his sight failed) including Andrew Marvell. The masterpieces of his old age are his epic poems on biblical themes, *Paradise Lost* 1667, *Paradise Regained* 1677, and the classic drama *Samson Agonistes* 1677.

**Mishima** Yukio 1925–1970. Japanese novelist whose work often deals with sexual desire and perversion, as in *Confessions of a Mask* 1949 and *The Temple of the Golden Pavilion* 1956. He committed hara-kiri (ritual suicide) as a protest against what he saw as the corruption of the nation and the loss of the samurai warrior tradition.

**Montaigne** Michel Eyquem de 1533–1592. French writer, regarded as the creator of the essay form. In 1580 he published the first two volumes of his *Essais*, the third volume appeared in 1588. Montaigne deals with all aspects of life from an urbanely sceptical viewpoint. Through the translation by John Florio in 1603, he influenced Shakespeare and other English writers.

**Musil** Robert 1880–1942. Austrian novelist, author of the unfinished *Der Mann ohne Eigenschaften/The Man without Qualities* (three volumes, 1930–43). Its hero shares the author's background of philosophical study and scientific and military training, and is preoccupied with the problems of the self viewed from a mystic but agnostic viewpoint.

mythology (*Metamorphoses* AD 2), and exile (*Tristia* AD 9–12).

**Pasternak** Boris Leonidovich 1890–1960. Russian poet and novelist. His novel *Dr Zhivago* 1957 was banned in the USSR as a 'hostile act', and followed by a Nobel prize (which he declined). *Dr Zhivago* has since been unbanned and Pasternak posthumously rehabilitated.

**Paz** Octavio 1914– . Mexican poet and essayist. His works reflect many influences, including Marxism, surrealism, and Aztec mythology. His celebrated poem *Piedra del sol/Sun Stone* 1957 uses contrasting images, centring upon the Aztec Calendar Stone (representing the Aztec universe), to symbolize the loneliness of individuals and their search for union with others. Nobel Prize for Literature 1990.

**Perrault** Charles 1628–1703. French author of the fairy tales *Contes de ma mère l'oye/Mother Goose's Fairy Tales* 1697, which include 'Sleeping Beauty', 'Little Red Riding Hood', 'Blue Beard', 'Puss in Boots', and 'Cinderella'.

**Pessoa** Fernando 1888–1935. Portuguese poet. Born in Lisbon, he was brought up in South Africa and was bilingual in English and Portuguese. His verse is considered to be the finest written in Portuguese this century. He wrote under three assumed names, which he called 'heteronyms'—Alvaro de Campos, Ricardo Reis, and Alberto Caeiro—for each of which he invented a biography.

**Petrarch** (Italian **Petrarca**) Francesco 1304–1374. Italian poet, born in Arezzo, a devotee of the Classical tradition. His *Il Canzoniere* is composed of sonnets in praise of his idealized love 'Laura', whom he first saw 1327 (she was a married woman and refused to become his mistress). His 14-line sonnets, in a form which was given the name Petrarchan, were influential for centuries.

**Poe** Edgar Allan 1809–1849. US writer and poet. His short stories are renowned for their horrific atmosphere (as in *The Fall of the House of Usher* 1839) and acute reasoning (for example, *The Gold Bug* 1843 and *The Murders in the Rue Morgue* 1841, in which the investigators Legrand and Dupin anticipate Arthur Conan Doyle's Sherlock Holmes). His most famous poem is 'The Raven' 1844.

**Pope** Alexander 1688–1744. English poet and satirist. He established his reputation with the precocious *Pastorals* 1709 and *Essay on Criticism* 1711, which were followed by a parody of the heroic epic *The Rape of the Lock* 1712–14 and 'Eloisa to Abelard' 1717. Other works include a highly Neo-Classical translation of Homer's *Iliad* and *Odyssey* 1715–26.

**Pound** Ezra 1885–1972. US poet who lived in London from 1908. His *Personae* and *Exultations* 1909 established the principles of the Imagist movement. His largest work was the series of *Cantos* 1925–1969 (intended to number 100), which attempted a massive reappraisal of history.

**Proust** Marcel 1871–1922. French novelist and critic. His immense autobiographical work *À la recherche du temps perdu/Remembrance of Things Past* 1913–27, consisting of a series of novels, is the expression of his childhood memories coaxed from his subconscious; it is also a precise reflection of life in provincial France at the end of the 19th century.

**Pushkin** Aleksandr 1799–1837. Russian poet and writer. He was exiled 1820 for his political verse and in 1824 was in trouble for his atheistic opinions. He wrote ballads such as *The Gypsies* 1827, and the novel in verse *Eugene Onegin* 1823–31. Other works include the tragic drama *Boris Godunov* 1825, and the prose pieces *The Captain's Daughter* 1836 and *The Queen of Spades* 1834. Pushkin's range was wide, and his willingness to experiment freed later Russian writers from many of the archaic conventions of the literature of his time.

**Pynchon** Thomas 1937– . US novelist who created a bizarre, labyrinthine world in his books, the first of which was *V* 1963. *Gravity's Rainbow* 1973 represents a major achievement in 20th-century literature, with its fantastic imagery and esoteric language, drawn from mathematics and science.

**Rabelais** François 1495–1553. French satirist, monk, and physician, whose name has become synonymous with bawdy humour. He was educated in the Renaissance humanist tradition and was the author of satirical allegories, including *La Vie inestimable de Gargantua/The Inestimable Life of Gargantua* 1535 and *Faits et dits héroïques du grand Pantagruel/Deeds and Sayings of the Great Pantagruel* 1533, about two giants (father and son) Gargantua and Pantagruel.

**Richardson** Samuel 1689–1761. English novelist, one of the founders of the modern novel. *Pamela* 1740–41, written in the form of a series of letters and containing much dramatic conversation, was sensationally popular all across Europe, and was followed by *Clarissa* 1747–48 and *Sir Charles Grandison* 1753–54.

**Rilke** Rainer Maria 1875–1926. Austrian writer, born in Prague. His prose works include the semi-autobiographical *Die Aufzeichnungen des Malte Laurids Brigge/Notebook of Malte Laurids Brigge* 1910, and his poetical works include *Die Sonnette an Orpheus/Sonnets to Orpheus* 1923 and *Duisener Elegien/Duino Elegies* 1923. His verse is characterized by a form of mystic pantheism that seeks to achieve a state of ecstasy in which existence can be apprehended as a whole.

**Rimbaud** (Jean Nicolas) Arthur 1854–1891. French Symbolist poet. His verse was chiefly written before the age of 20, notably *Les Illuminations* published 1886. From 1871 he lived with Verlaine.

**Rousseau** Jean-Jacques 1712–1778. French social philosopher and writer, born in Geneva, Switzerland. *Discourses on the Origins of Inequality* 1754 made his name: he denounced civilized society and postulated the paradox of the superiority of the 'noble savage'. *Social Contract* 1762 emphasized the rights of the people over those of the government, and stated that a government could be legitimately overthrown if it failed to express the general will of the people. It was a significant influence on the French Revolution. In the novel *Emile* 1762 he outlined a new theory of education, based on natural development and the power of example, to elicit the unspoiled nature and abilities of children. *Confessions*, published posthumously 1782, was a frank account of his occasionally immoral life and was a founding work of autobiography.

**Salinger** J(erome) D(avid) 1919– . US writer, author of the classic novel of mid-20th-century adolescence *The Catcher in the Rye* 1951. He also wrote short stories about a Jewish family named Glass, including *Franny and Zooey* 1961.

**Sartre** Jean-Paul 1905–1980. French author and philosopher, a leading proponent of existentialism in postwar philosophy. He published his first novel, *La Nausée/Nausea*, 1937, followed by the trilogy *Les Chemins de la Liberté/Roads to Freedom* 1944–45 and many plays, including *Huis Clos/In Camera* 1944.

**Scott** Walter 1771–1832. Scottish novelist and poet. His first works were translations of German ballads, followed by poems such as 'The Lady of the Lake' 1810 and 'Lord of the Isles' 1815. He gained a European reputation for his historical novels such as *Heart of Midlothian* 1818, *Ivanhoe* 1819, and *The Fair Maid of Perth* 1828. His last years were marked by frantic writing to pay off his debts, after the bankruptcy of his publishing company in 1826.

**Shakespeare** William 1564–1616. English dramatist and poet, the greatest English playwright; he also wrote numerous sonnets. (See *Theatre* for more.)

**Shelley** Percy Bysshe 1792–1822. English lyric poet, a leading figure in the Romantic movement. Expelled from Oxford university for atheism, he fought all his life against religion and for political freedom. This is reflected in his early poems such as *Queen Mab* 1813. He later wrote tragedies including *The Cenci* 1818, lyric dramas such as *Prometheus Unbound* 1820, and lyrical poems such as 'Ode to the West Wind'. He drowned while sailing in Italy.

**Singer** Isaac Bashevis 1904–1991. Polish-born US novelist and short-story writer. His works, written in Yiddish, then translated into English, often portray traditional Jewish life in Poland and the USA, and the loneliness of old age. They include *Gimpel the Fool* 1957, *The Slave* 1960, *Shosha* 1978, *Old Love* 1979, *Lost in America* 1981, *The Image and Other Stories* 1985, and *The Death of Methuselah* 1988. He has also written plays and books for children. In 1978 he was awarded the Nobel Prize for Literature.

**Solzhenitsyn** Alexander (Isayevich) 1918– . Soviet novelist, a US citizen from 1974. After military service, he was in prison and exile 1945–57 for anti-Stalinist comments. Much of his writing is semi-autobiographical and highly critical of the system, including *One Day in the Life of Ivan Denisovich* 1962 which deals with the labour camps under Stalin, and

*The Gulag Archipelago* 1973, an exposé of the whole Soviet labour camp network. This led to his expulsion from the USSR 1974.

**Soyinka** Wole 1934– . Nigerian author who was a political prisoner in Nigeria 1967–69. His works include the play *The Lion and the Jewel* 1963; his prison memoirs *The Man Died* 1972; *Aké, The Years of Childhood* 1982, an autobiography, and *Isara*, a fictionalized memoir 1989. He was the first African to receive the Nobel Prize for Literature, in 1986.

**Spenser** Edmund *c.* 1552–1599. English poet, who has been called the 'poet's poet' because of his rich imagery and command of versification. He is known for his moral allegory *The Faerie Queene*, of which six books survive (three published 1590 and three 1596). Other books include *The Shepheard's Calendar* 1579, *Astrophel* 1586, the love sonnets *Amoretti* and the *Epithalamion* 1595.

**Steinbeck** John (Ernst) 1902–1968. US novelist. His realist novels, such as *In Dubious Battle* 1936, *Of Mice and Men* 1937, and *The Grapes of Wrath* 1939 (Pulitzer prize 1940), portray agricultural life in his native California, where migrant farm labourers from the Oklahoma dust bowl struggled to survive. He received the Nobel Prize for Literature in 1962.

**Stendhal** pen name of Marie Henri Beyle 1783–1842. French novelist. His novels *Le Rouge et le noir/The Red and the Black* 1830 and *La Chartreuse de Parme/The Charterhouse of Parme* 1839 were pioneering works in their treatment of disguise and hypocrisy; a review of the latter by Balzac in 1840 furthered Stendhal's reputation.

**Sterne** Laurence 1713–1768. Irish writer, creator of the comic anti-hero Tristram Shandy. *The Life and Opinions of Tristram Shandy, Gent* 1760–67, an eccentrically whimsical and bawdy novel, foreshadowed many of the techniques and devices of 20th-century novelists, including James Joyce. His other works include *A Sentimental Journey through France and Italy* 1768.

**Stevenson** Robert Louis 1850–1894. Scottish novelist and poet, author of the adventure novel *Treasure Island* 1883. Later works included the novels *Kidnapped* 1886, *The Master of Ballantrae* 1889, *Dr Jekyll and Mr Hyde* 1886, and the anthology *A Child's Garden of Verses* 1885.

**Swift** Jonathan 1667–1745. Irish satirist and Anglican cleric, author of *Gulliver's Travels* 1726, an allegory describing travel to lands inhabited by giants, miniature people, and intelligent horses. Other works include *The Tale of a Tub* 1704, attacking corruption in religion and learning; contributions to the Tory paper *The Examiner*, of which he was editor 1710–11; the satirical *A Modest Proposal* 1729, which suggested that children of the poor should be eaten; and many essays and pamphlets.

**Tagore** Rabindranath 1861–1941. Bengali Indian writer, born in Calcutta, who translated into

English his own verse *Gitanjali* ('song offerings') 1912 and his verse play *Chitra* 1896. Nobel Prize for Literature 1913.

**Tennyson** Alfred, 1st Baron Tennyson 1809–1892. English poet, poet laureate 1850–96, whose verse has a majestic, musical quality. His works include 'The Lady of Shalott', 'The Lotus Eaters', 'Ulysses', 'Break, Break, Break', 'The Charge of the Light Brigade'; the longer narratives *Locksley Hall* 1832 and *Maud* 1855; the elegy *In Memoriam* 1850; and a long series of poems on the Arthurian legends *The Idylls of the King* 1857–85.

**Thackeray** William Makepeace 1811–1863. English novelist and essayist, born in Calcutta, India. He was a regular contributor to *Fraser's Magazine* and *Punch*. *Vanity Fair* 1847–48 was his first novel, followed by *Pendennis* 1848, *Henry Esmond* 1852 (and its sequel *The Virginians* 1857–59), and *The Newcomes* 1853–55, in which Thackeray's tendency to sentimentality is most marked.

**Tolstoy** Leo Nikolaievich 1828–1910. Russian novelist who wrote *Tales from Sebastopol* 1856, *War and Peace* 1863–69, and *Anna Karenina* 1873–77. From 1880 Tolstoy underwent a profound spiritual crisis and took up various moral positions, including passive resistance to evil, rejection of authority (religious or civil) and private ownership, and a return to basic mystical Christianity. He was excommunicated by the Orthodox Church, and his later works were banned.

**Turgenev** Ivan Sergeievich 1818–1883. Russian writer, notable for poetic realism, pessimism, and skill in characterization. His works include the play *A Month in the Country* 1849, and the novels *A Nest of Gentlefolk* 1858, *Fathers and Sons* 1862, and *Virgin Soil* 1877. His series *A Sportsman's Sketches* 1852 criticized serfdom.

**Twain** Mark. Pen name of Samuel Langhorne Clemens 1835–1910. US writer. He established his reputation with the comic masterpiece *The Innocents Abroad* 1869 and two classic American novels, in dialect, *The Adventures of Tom Sawyer* 1876 and *The Adventures of Huckleberry Finn* 1885. He also wrote satire, as in *A Connecticut Yankee at King Arthur's Court* 1889.

**Verlaine** Paul 1844–1896. French lyric poet who was influenced by the poets Baudelaire and Rimbaud. His volumes of verse include *Poèmes saturniens/Saturnine Poems* 1866, *Fêtes galantes/Amorous Entertainments* 1869 and *Romances sans paroles/Songs without Words* 1874. In 1873 he was imprisoned for attempting to shoot Rimbaud. His later works reflect his attempts to lead a reformed life. He was acknowledged as leader of the Symbolist poets.

**Villon** François 1431–c. 1465. French poet who used satiric humour, pathos, and lyric power in works written in *argot* (slang) of the time. Very little of his work survives, but it includes the *Ballade des dames du temps jadis/Ballad of the Ladies of Former Times*, *Petit Testament* 1456, and *Grand Testament* 1461.

**Virgil** (Publius Vergilius Maro) 70–19 BC. Roman poet who wrote the *Eclogues* 37 BC, a series of pastoral poems; the *Georgics* 30 B, four books on the art of farming; and his epic masterpiece, the *Aeneid*.

**Voltaire** Pen name of François-Marie Arouet 1694–1778. French writer who believed in deism, and devoted himself to tolerance, justice, and humanity. He was threatened with arrest for *Lettres philosophiques sur les anglais/Philosophical Letters on the English* 1733 (essays in favour of English ways, thought, and political practice) and had to take refuge. Other writings include *Le Siècle de Louis XIV/The Age of Louis XIV* 1751; *Candide* 1759, a parody on Leibniz's 'best of all possible worlds'; and *Dictionnaire philosophique* 1764.

**Walker** Alice 1944– . US poet, novelist, critic, and essay writer. She was active in the US civil-rights movement in the 1960s and, as a black woman, wrote about the double burden of racist and sexist oppression that such women bear. Her novel *The Color Purple* 1983 (film, 1985) won the Pulitzer Prize.

**Wharton** Edith (born Jones) 1862–1937. US novelist. Her work, known for its subtlety and form and influenced by her friend Henry James, was mostly set in New York society. It includes *The House of Mirth* 1905, which made her reputation; the grim, uncharacteristic novel of New England *Ethan Frome* 1911; *The Custom of the Country* 1913, and *The Age of Innocence* 1920.

**Whitman** Walt(er) 1819–1892. US poet who published *Leaves of Grass* 1855, which contains the symbolic 'Song of Myself'. It used unconventional free verse (with no rhyme or regular rhythm) and scandalized the public by its frank celebration of sexuality.

**Woolf** Virginia (née Virginia Stephen) 1882–1941. English novelist and critic. Her first novel, *The Voyage Out* 1915, explored the tensions experienced by women who want marriage and a career. In *Mrs Dalloway* 1925 she perfected her 'stream of consciousness' technique. Among her later books are *To the Lighthouse* 1927, *Orlando* 1928, and *The Years* 1937, which considers the importance of economic independence for women.

**Wordsworth** William 1770–1850. English Romantic poet. In 1797 he moved with his sister Dorothy to Somerset to be near Samuel Taylor Coleridge, collaborating with him on *Lyrical Ballads* 1798 (which included 'Tintern Abbey'). From 1799 he lived in the Lake District, and later works include *Poems* 1807 (including 'Intimations of Immortality') and *The Prelude* (written by 1805, published 1850). He was appointed poet laureate in 1843.

**Yeats** W(illiam) (B)utler 1865–1939. Irish poet. He was a leader of the Celtic revival and a founder of the Abbey Theatre in Dublin. His early work was romantic and lyrical, as in the poem 'The Lake Isle of Innisfree' and plays *The Countess Cathleen* 1892 and *The Land of Heart's Desire* 1894. His later books of poetry include *The Wild Swans at Coole* 1917 and

*The Winding Stair* 1929. He was a senator of the Irish Free State 1922–28. Nobel Prize for Literature 1923.

**Zola** Émile Edouard Charles Antoine 1840–1902. French novelist and social reformer. With *La Fortune des Rougon/The Fortune of the Rougons* 1867 he began a series of some 20 naturalistic novels, portraying the fortunes of a French family under the Second Empire. They include *Le Ventre de Paris/The Underbelly of Paris* 1873, *Nana* 1880, and *La Débâcle/The Debacle* 1892. In 1898 he published *J'accuse/I Accuse*, a pamphlet indicting the persecutors of Alfred Dreyfus, for which he was prosecuted for libel but later pardoned.

# CINEMA

Hollywood's pre-eminence in the bygone studio era rested not on its being able to produce a *Magnificent Ambersons* once a decade but on being able to produce a *Magnificent Obsession* every other week. The staple genres—weepies, war films, westerns, sundry others—provided, however undistinguished were many individual examples, the basis for an infinite variety of permutations.

In more recent times, though, this situation has vanished. The chances of a new Orson Welles emerging have seemed hardly less remote than those of prising popular filmmaking free from the stranglehold of obeisance to the teenagers who over the past two decades (and the situation is that of a vicious circle) have dominated the mass movie audience. At least since *Star Wars* the popular cinema seems prevailingly to have comprised exercises in special effects, interspersed with crime thrillers which are little more

### Awards for Best Film from Four Top Festivals

*Cannes Film Festival*
*Palme d'Or for Best Film*
| | |
|---|---|
| 1985 | *When Father Was Away on Business* (Yug) |
| 1986 | *The Mission* (UK) |
| 1987 | *Under the Sun of Satan* (Fr) |
| 1988 | *Pelle the Conqueror* (Den) |
| 1989 | *Sex, Lies and Videotape* (USA) |
| 1990 | *Wild at Heart* (USA) |
| 1991 | *Barton Fink* (USA) |

*Venice Film Festival*
*Golden Lion for Best Film*
| | |
|---|---|
| 1985 | *Sans toit ni loi aka Vagabonde* (Fr) |
| 1986 | *Le Rayon Vert* (Fr) |
| 1987 | *Au Revoir les Enfants* (Fr) |
| 1988 | *La Leggenda del Santo Bevitore (The Legend of the Holy Drinker)* (It) |
| 1989 | *Beiqing Chengshi (City of Sadness)* (Taiwan) |
| 1990 | *Rosencrantz and Guildenstern are Dead* (UK) |

*Berlin Film Festival*
*Golden Bear for Best Film*
| | |
|---|---|
| 1985 | *Wetherby* (UK); *Die Frau und der Fremde* (FRG) |
| 1986 | *Stammheim* (FRG) |
| 1987 | *The Theme* (USSR) |
| 1988 | *Red Shorghum* (China) |
| 1989 | *Rain Man* (USA) |
| 1990 | *Skylarks on a String* (Czech); *Music Box* (USA) |
| 1991 | *La Casa del Sorriso (House of Smiles)* (It) |

*British Academy of Film and Television Arts (BAFTA)*
*Best Film Awards*
| | |
|---|---|
| 1985 | *The Killing Fields* (UK) |
| 1986 | *The Purple Rose of Cairo* (USA) |
| 1987 | *A Room with a View* (UK) |
| 1988 | *Jean de Florette* (Fr) |
| 1989 | *The Last Emperor* (USA) |
| 1990 | *Dead Poets Society* (USA) |
| 1991 | *Goodfellas* (USA) |

### Number of Feature Films Produced (Including Co-productions)

| | 1985 | 1986 | 1987 | 1988 | 1989 |
|---|---|---|---|---|---|
| UK | 55 | 39 | 51 | 56 | 38 |
| France | 151 | 134 | 133 | 137 | – |
| West Germany | 64 | 60 | 65 | 57 | – |
| Italy | 89 | 114 | 116 | 124 | 117 |
| Japan | 319 | 311 | 286 | 265 | 255 |
| Spain | 76 | 60 | 69 | 63 | 47 |

*Source: British Film Institute*

### Country of Origin of Films Shown in the UK (1989–1990)

| Country | Number |
|---|---|
| USA | 154 |
| UK | 52 |
| Western Europe | 35 |
| Eastern Europe | 6 |
| Australia | 10 |
| Others | 19 |
| TOTAL | 276 |

*Source: British Film Institute*

than pretexts to smash up cars and property, or comedies which frequently resemble the same scenarios bereft of any (or much) loss of life.

It is not, of course, the case that intelligent entertainments—films like *Wall Street*, which engage with contemporary life in dynamic form—are not made, but simply that they have increasingly come to be seen as exceptions to the rule. And certainly when the annual Academy Awards come round, and it is necessary to focus attention on some example of responsible popular filmmaking, it has lately, as likely as not,

**Kevin Kostner in** *Dances with wolves*

## Box Office Hits Worldwide (1990)

| Country | Film | Company | Receipts/Admissions |
|---|---|---|---|
| Australia | Pretty Woman (USA) | Touchstone | A$26,098,946 |
| Belgium | Dead Poets Society (USA) | Warner | Bfr 41,140,495 |
| Brazil | Lua De Cristal (Brazil) | Art-Columbia | 4,000,000 admissions |
| France | Dead Poets Society (USA) | Warner | Ffr 95,211,054 |
| Italy | Indiana Jones and the Last Crusade (USA) | UIP | $15,621,000 |
| Japan | Back to the Future II (USA) | UIP | 5,530,000,000 Yen |
| Spain | Dead Poets Society (USA) | Warner | 2,282,222 admissions |
| UK | Ghost (USA) | UIP | £17,269,748 |
| USA | Ghost (USA) | Paramount | $197,954,919 |
| USSR | Crocodile Dundee II (Australia) | | 47,400,000 admissions |

Source: Screen International Film & TV Yearbook 1991

## Top Ten Films of 1990, UK

| | Film | Company | Receipts (£) |
|---|---|---|---|
| 1 | Ghost (USA) | UIP | 17,269,748 |
| 2 | Pretty Woman (USA) | Warner | 11,990,862 |
| 3 | Look Who's Talking (USA) | Columbia/Tri-Star | 10,117,000 |
| 4 | Honey, I Shrunk The Kids (USA) | Warner | 9,395,091 |
| 5 | Total Recall (USA) | Guild | 8,508,181 |
| 6 | Ghostbusters II (USA) | Columbia/Tri-Star | 8,301,000 |
| 7 | Back To The Future: Part III (USA) | UIP | 7,996,334 |
| 8 | Gremlins 2: The New Batch (USA) | Warner | 7,419,354 |
| 9 | Back To The Future: Part II (USA) | UIP | 7,252,133 |
| 10 | When Harry Met Sally (USA) | Palace | 7,000,000 |

Source: Screen International Film & TV Yearbook 1991

## Top Ten Films of 1990, USA

| | Film | Company | Receipts (US$) |
|---|---|---|---|
| 1 | Ghost (USA) | Paramount | 197,954,919 |
| 2 | Pretty Woman (USA) | Buena Vista | 178,406,268 |
| 3 | Teenage Mutant Ninja Turtles (USA) | New Line | 135,265,915 |
| 4 | The Hunt For Red October (USA) | Paramount | 120,709,868 |
| 5 | Total Recall (USA) | Tri-Star | 118,572,502 |
| 6 | Die Hard II: Die Harder (USA) | 20th Fox | 115,194,879 |
| 7 | Driving Miss Daisy (USA) | Warner Bros. | 106,593,296 |
| 8 | Dick Tracy (USA) | Buena Vista | 103,738,726 |
| 9 | Back To The Future: Part III (USA) | Universal | 87,530,497 |
| 10 | The War Of The Roses (USA) | 20th Fox | 86,048,505 |

Source: Screen International Film & TV Yearbook 1991

been found necessary to look abroad, to *Gandhi* or *The Last Emperor*—films which did not, in fact, draw in any sizeable share of the American audience.

Not this year, however, when the accolade was bestowed upon *Dances With Wolves*, a film ostensibly of that most American, if latterly all but defunct of genres, the western, and one which had already met with huge box-office approval. But then, this past year has not, commercially speaking, been consonant with recent trends. Shakespearean tragedy has even been made into the stuff of popular success in the shape of Franco Zeffirelli's film of *Hamlet*, which transplanted Mel Gibson, hitherto a leading man of action movies, to the realms of the classics. Gibson, who made a respectable showing in the role, judiciously pointed out that Shakespeare's hero was not only given to introspection but was also responsible for killing a large number of people.

The biggest box-office grosses were rung up by *Home Alone*, *Ghost*, and *Pretty Woman*: all were comedies, made on a modest physical scale and on relatively modest budgets ($18m in the case

of the first and third, $27m for *Ghost*). The first centres on a child, the other two on romantic attachments; all are sentimentally affirmative. So too is another surprise success, the comedy drama *Driving Miss Daisy* (made for only $8m and thus, in terms of ratio of production costs to gross receipts, the year's most profitable picture). And while *Dances With Wolves* ends elegiacally, the film's appeal seems to be predicated upon its conjuring up of a romantic, not to say romanticized, vision of proto-environmentalist harmony.

For reasons that have nothing to do with art and everything to do with balance sheets—given that North American cinema admissions last year declined by nearly 7% and that demographics have rendered the teenage share of the market somewhat less significant—executive perceptions have been changing. According to Jeffrey Katzenburg, chairman of the Disney corporation, 'we should look long and hard at the blockbuster business, and then get out of it.' It is perhaps revealing that all the 'major' companies passed up the chance to produce either *Driving Miss Daisy* or *Dances With Wolves*, and that *Home*

## CINEMA: CHRONOLOGY

| | |
|---|---|
| 1826–34 | Various machines invented to show moving images: the stroboscope, zoetrope, and thaumatrope. |
| 1872 | Eadweard Muybridge demonstrated movement of horses' legs by using 24 cameras. |
| 1877 | Invention of Praxinoscope; developed as a projector of successive images on screen in 1879 in France. |
| 1878–95 | Marey, a French physiologist, developed various types of camera for recording human and animal movements. |
| 1887 | Augustin le Prince produced the first series of images on a perforated film; Thomas Edison, having developed the phonograph, took the first steps in developing a motion-picture recording and reproducing device to accompany recorded sound. |
| 1888 | William Friese-Greene showed the first celluloid film and patented a movie camera. |
| 1889 | Edison invented 35mm film. |
| 1890–94 | Edison, using perforated film, developed his Kinetograph camera and Kinetoscope individual viewer; developed commercially in New York, London, and Paris. |
| 1895 | The Lumière brothers, Auguste (1862–1954) and Louis (1864–1948), projected, to a paying audience, a film of an oncoming train arriving at a station. Some of the audience fled in terror. |
| 1896 | Pathé introduced the Berliner gramophone, using discs in synchronization with film. Lack of amplification, however, made the performances ineffective. |
| 1899 | Edison tried to improve amplification by using banks of phonographs. |
| 1900 | Attempts to synchronize film and disc were made by Gaumont in France and Goldschmidt in Germany, leading later to the Vitaphone system of the USA. |
| 1902 | Georges Méliès (1861–1938) made *Le Voyage dans la Lune/A Trip to the Moon.* |
| 1903 | The first Western was made in the USA: *The Great Train Robbery* by Edwin S Porter. |
| 1906 | The earliest colour film (Kinemacolor) was patented in Britain by George Albert Smith. |
| 1908–11 | In France, Emile Cohl experimented with film animation. |
| 1910 | With the influence of US Studios, film actors and actresses began to be recognized as international stars. |
| 1912 | In Britain, Eugene Lauste designed experimental 'sound on film' systems. |
| 1914–18 | Full newsreel coverage of World War I. |
| 1915 | *The Birth of a Nation*, D W Griffith's epic on the American Civil War, was released in the USA. |
| 1917 | 35mm was officially adopted as the standard format for motion picture film by the Society of Motion Picture Engineers of America. |
| 1918–19 | A sound system called Tri-Ergon was developed in Germany, which led to sound being recorded on film photographically. The photography of sound was also developed by Lee De Forrest in his Phonofilm system. |
| 1923 | First sound film (as Phonofilm) demonstrated. |
| 1926 | *Don Juan*, a silent film with a synchronized music score, was released. |
| 1927 | Release of the first major sound film, *The Jazz Singer*, consisting of some songs and a few moments of dialogue, by Warner Brothers, New York City. The first Academy Awards (Oscars). |
| 1928 | Walt Disney released his first Mickey Mouse cartoon, *Steamboat Willie*. The first all-talking film, *Lights of New York*, was released. |
| 1930 | *The Big Trail*, a Western filmed and shown in 70mm rather than the standard 35mm format, was released. 70mm is still used, but usually only for big-budget epics such as *Lawrence of Arabia*. |
| 1932 | Technicolor (three-colour) process introduced and used for a Walt Disney cartoon film. |
| 1935 | *Becky Sharp*, the first film in three-colour Technicolor (a process now abandoned), was released. |
| 1937 | Walt Disney released the first feature-length (82 minutes) cartoon, *Snow White and the Seven Dwarfs*. |
| 1939 | *Gone With the Wind*, regarded as one of Hollywood's greatest achievements, was released. |
| 1952 | Cinerama, a wide-screen presentation using three cameras and three projectors, was introduced in New York. |
| 1953 | Commercial 3-D (three-dimensional) cinema and wide-screen CinemaScope were launched in the USA. CinemaScope used a single camera and projector to produce a wide-screen effect by using an anamorphic lens. The cameras were clumsy and the audiences disliked wearing the obligatory glasses. The new wide-screen cinema was accompanied by the introduction of Stereographic sound, which eventually became standard. |

---

CINEMA: CHRONOLOGY: Cont.

| | |
|---|---|
| **1959** | The first film in Smell-O-Vision, *The Scent of Mystery,* was released. The process did not catch on. |
| **1970** | Most major films were released in Dolby stereo. |
| **1981** | Designated 'the Year of Colour Film' by director Martin Scorsese in a campaign to draw attention to, and arrest, the deterioration of colour film shot since 1950 on unstable Eastman Kodak stock. |
| **1982** | One of the first and most effective attempts at feature-length, computer-generated animation was *Tron,* Walt Disney's $20-million bid to break into the booming fantasy market. 3-D made a brief comeback; some of the films released that used the process, such as *Jaws 3-D* and *Friday the 13th Part 3,* were commercial successes, but the revival was short-lived. |
| **1987** | US House Judiciary Committee petitioned by leading Hollywood filmmakers to protect their work from electronic 'colorization', the new process by which black-and-white films were tinted for television transmission. |

---

*Alone,* eventually made by Fox, had previously been turned down by Warners.

But even if blockbusters are a dying breed, their influence will not simply disappear; nor, necessarily should it be permitted to do so. It is true that, of the runners-up in last year's box-office stakes, *Die Hard 2* is only a mindlessly lurid shocker, bereft even of the high-octane technique which distinguished its predecessor. But the other, *Total Recall* (budget $60m) is in many respects an astonishing achievement, pushing both graphic violence and effects of optical and technological legerdemain to virtually unparalleled extremes. It is also a work of great narrative complexity, with roots, given its themes of amnesia and conspiracy, in the noir thrillers of the 1940s.

Moreover, it is revealing to compare the film with *Dances With Wolves.* Respectively set in the middle of the next century and the middle of the last, the one begins with its protagonist awakening from a nightmare to confront another waking one, while the other starts with its hero on the operating table and then miraculously arising to begin a new life (though it could also figuratively be read as the wish-fulfilling fantasy of a delirious mind).

Both films tap in, via their respective generic conventions, to concern with the suppression of individuality and the ruination of the environment; and it is precisely the distancing afforded by those conventions which render such concerns imaginatively involving (just as the glamourized fantastication of *Pretty Woman* may tell us more than a documentary about changing sexual attitudes).

*Wolves,* though, is 'respectable' where *Recall* is not; but then *Casablanca* was not regarded as all that respectable in its day. Perhaps we should not judge—or write the obituary of post-studio era Hollywood—too quickly.

**What people watch**

*Stars/genres thought to be IN*

| | |
|---|---|
| Clint Eastwood films | 47 |
| Going to the cinema | 44 |
| John Wayne films | 42 |
| Marilyn Monroe films | 37 |
| Humphrey Bogart films | 36 |
| James Bond films | 34 |
| Charlie Chaplin films | 33 |
| Humphrey Bogart | 23 |
| Watching 'blue' movies | 23 |

## ACADEMY AWARDS: RECENT WINNERS

**1971** Best Picture: *The French Connection*; Best Director: William Friedkin *The French Connection*; Best Actor: Gene Hackman *The French Connection*; Best Actress: Jane Fonda *Klute*

**1972** Best Picture: *The Godfather*; Best Director: Bob Fosse *Cabaret*; Best Actor: Marlon Brando *The Godfather*; Best Actress: Liza Minnelli *Cabaret*

**1973** Best Picture: *The Sting*; Best Director: George Roy Hill *The Sting*; Best Actor: Jack Lemmon *Save the Tiger*; Best Actress: Glenda Jackson *A Touch of Class*

**1974** Best Picture: *The Godfather II*; Best Director: Francis Ford Coppola *The Godfather II*; Best Actor: Art Carney *Harry and Tonto*; Best Actress: Ellen Burstyn *Alice Doesn't Live Here Anymore*

**1975** Best Picture: *One Flew Over the Cuckoo's Nest*; Best Director: Milos Forman *One Flew Over the Cuckoo's Nest*; Best Actor: Jack Nicholson *One Flew Over the Cuckoo's Nest*; Best Actress: Louise Fletcher *One Flew Over the Cuckoo's Nest*

**1976** Best Picture: *Rocky*; Best Director: John G Avildsen *Rocky*; Best Actor: Peter Finch *Network*; Best Actress: Faye Dunaway *Network*

**1977** Best Picture: *Annie Hall*; Best Director: Woody Allen *Annie Hall*; Best Actor: Richard Dreyfuss *The Goodbye Girl*; Best Actress: Diane Keaton *Annie Hall*

**1978** Best Picture: *The Deer Hunter*; Best Director: Michael Cimino *The Deer Hunter*; Best Actor: Jon Voight *Coming Home*; Best Actress: Jane Fonda *Coming Home*

**1979** Best Picture: *Kramer vs Kramer*; Best Director: Robert Benton *Kramer vs Kramer*; Best Actor: Dustin Hoffman *Kramer vs Kramer*; Best Actress: Sally Field *Norma Rae*

**1980** Best Picture: *Ordinary People*; Best Director: Robert Redford *Ordinary People*; Best Actor: Robert De Niro *Raging Bull*; Best Actress: Sissy Spacek *Coal Miner's Daughter*

**1981** Best Picture: *Chariots of Fire*; Best Director: Warren Beatty *Reds*; Best Actor: Henry Fonda *On Golden Pond*; Best Actress: Katharine Hepburn *On Golden Pond*

**1982** Best Picture: *Gandhi*; Best Director: Richard Attenborough *Gandhi*; Best Actor: Ben Kingsley *Gandhi*; Best Actress: Meryl Streep *Sophie's Choice*

**1983** Best Picture: *Terms of Endearment*; Best Director: James L Brooks *Terms of Endearment*; Best Actor: Robert Duvall *Tender Mercies*; Best Actress: Shirley MacLaine *Terms of Endearment*

**1984** Best Picture: *Amadeus*; Best Director: Milos Forman *Amadeus*; Best Actor: F Murray Abraham *Amadeus*; Best Actress: Sally Field *Places in the Heart*

**1985** Best Picture: *Out of Africa*; Best Director: Sidney Pollack *Out of Africa*; Best Actor: William Hurt *Kiss of the Spiderwoman*; Best Actress: Geraldine Page *The Trip to Bountiful*

**1986** Best Picture: *Platoon*; Best Director: Oliver Stone *Platoon*; Best Actor: Paul Newman *The Color of Money*; Best Actress: Marlee Matlin *Children of a Lesser God*

**1987** Best Picture: *The Last Emperor*; Best Director: Bernardo Bertolucci *The Last Emperor*; Best Actor: Michael Douglas *Wall Street*; Best Actress: Cher *Moonstruck*

**1988** Best Picture: *Rain Man*; Best Director: Barry Levinson *Rain Man*; Best Actor: Dustin Hoffman *Rain Man*; Best Actress: Jodie Foster *The Accused*

**1989** Best Picture: *My Left Foot*; Best Director: Oliver Stone *Born on the 4th of July*; Best Actor: Daniel Day-Lewis *My Left Foot*; Best Actress: Jessica Tandy *Driving Miss Daisy*

**1990** Best Picture: *Dances with Wolves*; Best Director: Kevin Costner *Dances with Wolves*; Best Actor: Jeremy Irons *Reversal of Fortune*; Best Actress: Kathy Bates *Misery*

# MODERN DANCE

Modern dance is a 20th-century dance idiom that evolved in opposition to ballet by those seeking a freer and more immediate means of dance expression. In the USA, Martha Graham and Merce Cunningham were leading exponents of modern dance.

It was pioneered by American women seeking individual freedom and release from Victorian restrictions. Isadora Duncan and Loie Fuller worked mainly in Europe, but it is from Ruth St Denis, who founded the Denishawn School in Los Angeles 1915 with her partner Ted Shawn, that the first generation of modern dance proper—Martha Graham, Doris Humphrey, and Charles Weidman—emerged.

Doris Humphrey opened a school and performing group in New York 1928. The Humphrey-Weidman technique was based on the kinetic theory of *fall and recovery*. Humphrey's most famous protégé was José Limón.

Martha Graham's distinctive technique is based on **contraction and release**. From her company and School of Contemporary Dance, opened 1927 in New York, a long line of dancers and choreographers continues to

## THE WORLD OF DANCE: LOST FOR LEADERSHIP?

The loss of Martha Graham, grande dame of modern dance, and the universally loved English ballerina, Margot Fonteyn, brings sharply into focus the end of an era in dance.

The earlier deaths of George Balanchine, Lucia Chase, Anthony Tudor, and Frederick Ashton has left the dance world seriously depleted of leaders with vision. This comes at a time, when following the 'dance explosion' of the 60s and 70s dance has been hit doubly by the recession of the 80s and early 90s. Rising costs, funding cuts, and loss of tax incentives in the private sector have all contributed to the current climate where smaller companies have opted for mergers, as in the case of Murray Louis and Alwyn Nikolai, and larger ones have split their base of operations, for example the Cincinnati/New Orleans Ballet. Increasingly as major companies face huge deficits, often in the millions, the administration of financial affairs has taken precedence over artistic direction.

Major companies faced with finding a suitable successor to follow in the footsteps of the founder director have often turned to former principal dancers as a solution. The record has, however, been a poor one when trying to mix artistry with financial acumen. Take the example of American Ballet Theater. Established in 1940 as a full-scale company in the European 'Opera House' style, it has always presented a roster of glamourous guest celebrities in a repertory of both the standard classics, and works by new, especially American, choreographers. The Company's long-term success and survival have been largely due to the drive and devotion of Lucia Chase, co-founder, lifelong director, and often financial saviour.

In 1980 the board hired Mikhail Baryshnikov in the belief that his box-office appeal and celebrity status could provde the right formula, even though he had no experience as a director. He brought in Kenneth MacMillan from the Royal Ballet and Twyla Tharp. Fresh from a season at the New York City Ballet, he sought to introduce some of that company's traditions with less success. His decision to appoint a former businessman, Charles France, as personal assistant constructed a seemingly impenetrable barrier between him and the dancers which led to increasingly rancorous pay and rehearsal disputes. Added to this was the friction caused by Baryshnikov's refusal to take part in many aspects of the company's affairs.

The New York City Ballet is a company which faces a different problem. Backed initially by Lincoln Kirstein, George Balanchine forged a company and dancers in his own inimitable neo-classical style. Balanchine-trained dancers with their distinctive technical virtuosity, speed and brilliance can be singled out anywhere. The enormous repertory is built up entirely of works by himself and his Associate Choreographer, Jerome Robbins. When the executors appointed Robbins and former principal dancer Peter Martins as joint Ballet Masters they must have felt all was in good hands. But Robbins left with Martins in sole charge. He is steadily replacing the Balanchine/Robbins repertory with works of his own, but these have yet to attain the stature of his predecessors.

In the UK too there have been changes. The Sadler Wells Theatre ballet has moved from its homebase in London to Birmingham and made the successful transformation into the Birmingham Royal Ballet.

London Festival Ballet has changed its name to English National Ballet, a curiously anonymous sounding choice. 'English Festival Ballet' would have been more appropriate and given a sense of continuity with the company's history. The appointment of Lady Pamela Harlech to the board may bring it greater stability. The newly-appointed artistic director, Hungarian-born Ivan Nagy, brings valuable experience both as a dancer and a director. During his five years with the Santiago Ballet he completely rebuilt the company, raising the standards, bringing in dancers from all over the world, and enlarging the repertory. In 1986 he directed the Cincinnati/New Orleans Ballet, a dual venture with two boards and two companies in two different cities. Unlike Baryshnikov, Nagy is no longer involved in a performing or choreographic career and can devote his full attention to the needs of the company. This is the guide to the future, and let us hope we have passed the intermediate stage in the development of dance companies.

## MODERN DANCE: CHRONOLOGY

| | |
|---|---|
| 1900 | At the Paris World Fair, a special theatre was built for Loie Fuller to accommodate her dances involving original lighting effects, diaphanous scarves and costumes, and mechanical effects. |
| 1900–02 | Isadora Duncan triumphed in London, Paris, Budapest, Vienna, Munich, Berlin. Much admired by Fokine and Diaghilev, she abandoned corsets, dancing barefoot in a simple, flowing Greek tunic; a great contribution to dance was her insistence on using great music. |
| 1915 | Denishawn School founded in Los Angeles by Ruth St Denis and her husband and partner Ted Shawn. The first platform for Modern Dance in America, Graham, Humphrey and Weidman all began their careers at Denishawn. |
| 1927 | Martha Graham opened her School of Contemporary Dance in New York City evolving and teaching the (now world-famous) Graham Technique based on 'contraction and release', and forming her company. |
| 1928 | Doris Humphrey and Charles Weidman open the Humphrey–Weidman School, teaching their method based on the principles of 'fall and recovery'. |
| 1930 | *Lamentations* premiered in New York City: Graham solo using whole body to express inner emotion without reliance on narrative or mime. |
| 1931 | *The Shakers*, premiered New York City; choreographed by Humphrey, it dramatically illustrates her use of 'fall and recovery' technique. |
| 1932 | Ted Shawn opened his Summer theatre at 'Jacob's Pillow', Mass. forming the all-male troupe Ted Shawn and His Men, which did much to raise the status of male dancers, touring the US. |
| 1936 | Hanya Holm, former student of Mary Weidman in Germany, opened her studio in New York City. |
| 1941 | The first Jacob's Pillow Dance Festival established with Ted Shawn as director. Ted Shawn Theater built. |
| 1944 | Graham's most memorable work, *Appalachian Spring* premiered in New York City with a specially commissioned score by Aaron Copland; Graham danced The Bride and Erick Hawkins, (whom she married earlier that year) The Husbandman. |
| 1947 | The José Limón Dance Company formed; an immediate success. |
| 1952 | Merce Cunningham formed his own company appointing composer, and longterm collaborator, John Cage as musical director. Steps and directions were selected by chance, eliminating the role of choreographer. |
| 1954 | Paul Taylor Dance Company formed. A former Cunningham and Graham dancer, Taylor's generous, free and athletic style of choreography—in works ranging from witty and lyrical to bleak satire—often used atypical dancers. |
| 1955 | Premiére of Anna Sokolow's *Rooms* in New York City. Her works stress social commitment and concerns. |
| 1958 | Alvin Ailey American Dance Theater (later A City Center Dance Theater) formed, New York City. A multi-racial company, Ailey's works depict life in urban and rural Black America. |
| 1960 | *Revelations*, Ailey's 'signature-piece' premiered in New York City, set to traditional spirituals and Gospel music. |
| 1962 | Judson Dance Theater, a collective of choreographers exploring Cunningham's theories (at his Judson St. Studio) went further, abandoning formal dance technique and concentrating on every-day movement: the leading names were Trisha Brown, Lucinda Childs, Steve Paxton, Yvonne Rainer, and later, Laura Dean and Kei Takei. |
| 1966 | Norman Morrice returned to Ballet Rambert after two years in New York City studying with Graham, and the company shifted to Modern Dance, abandoning the classics. |
| 1967 | Robert Cohan, former longterm Graham dancer, invited to England to direct the newly formed London Contemporary Dance Theatre. |
| 1968 | Lar Lubovitch Dance Company formed in New York City. Collaborating with minimalist composers Steve Reich and Philip Glass he evolved a parallel form of choreography. |
| 1969 | 'The Place' opened in London, new home for London Contemporary Dance Theatre providing its own theatre, and studios for the School. |
| 1971 | Twyla Tharp's *Eight Jelly Rolls* premiered in New York City, to the New Orleans piano music of Jelly Roll Morton. Hiding serious technique behind free-style carefree movement and off-beat humour she was immediately popular. |
| 1980 | Mark Morris debut in his own works at the Merce Cunningham Studio, New York City. |
| 1981 | First showing Kei Takei's *Light*, an 11-hour work in 15 parts. |
| 1987 | Rambert Dance Company became the new name for Ballet Rambert. |
| 1990 | *Maple Leaf Rag*, Martha Graham's final work, premiered in New York City. |

## Avant-Garde Dance Repertory

| date | title | choreographer | place |
|------|-------|---------------|-------|
| 1969 | Moving Earth | Kei Takei | New York |
| 1970 | Walking on the Wall | Trisha Brown | New York |
| 1971 | Education of the Girlchild | Meredith Monk | New York |
| 1978 | Café Müller | Pina Bausch | Essen |
| 1986 | The Watteau Duet | Karole Armitage | New York |
| 1988 | I Am Curious Orange | Michael Clark | Amsterdam |

emerge. Among them, Erick Hawkins, Merce Cunningham, Glenn Tetley, Paul Taylor, and Dan Waggoner have each evolved his own style.

In the UK, the London Contemporary Dance Theatre and school was set up 1967 by Robert Cohan, a long-time Graham dancer. It is the only European institute authorized to teach Graham Technique. Richard Alston, Siobhan Davies, and Robert North studied, performed, and choreographed there.

In Germany, the originators of a modernist movement known as Central European dance were Jacques Dalcroze and Rudolph Laban. The leading exponents, Mary Wigman, Harald Kreutzberg, and Kurt Joss, had some influence on modern dance through their visits to the USA and through Hanya Holm, a former Wigman dancer who settled and taught in New York, and with whom Alwyn Nikolais was originally associated.

# AVANT-GARDE DANCE

Avant-garde dance is an experimental form of dance that rejects the conventions of modern dance. It is often performed in informal

## Modern Dance Repertory

| Date | Dance | Composer | Choreographer | Place |
|------|-------|----------|---------------|-------|
| 1906 | Radha | Delibes | Ruth St Denis | Los Angeles |
| 1930 | The Shakers | Lawrence | Doris Humphrey | New York City |
| 1931 | Primitive Mysteries | Horst | Martha Graham | New York City |
| 1935 | Kinetic Molpai | Meeker | Ted Shawn | Los Angeles |
| 1937 | Trend | Varèse | Hanya Holm | Bennington College, NY |
| 1944 | Appalachian Spring | Copland | Martha Graham | New York City |
| 1949 | The Moor's Pavane | Purcell | José Limón | Connecticut College, CT |
| 1955 | Rooms | Hopkins | Anna Sokolow | New York City |
| 1958 | Clytemnestra | El-Dabh | Martha Graham | New York City |
| 1958 | Blues Suite | Trad/Blues | Alvin Ailey | New York City |
| 1958 | Summerspace | Feldman | Merce Cunningham | Connecticut College, CT |
| 1960 | Acrobats of God | Surinach | Martha Graham | New York City |
| 1960 | Revelations | Trad/Spirituals | Alvin Ailey | New York City |
| 1960 | 8 Clear Places | Dlugozewski | Erick Hawkins | New York City |
| 1962 | Aureole | Hayden | Paul Taylor | New York City |
| 1967 | Harbinger | Prokofiev | Eliot Feld | New York City |
| 1969 | Moving Earth | | Kei Takei | New York City |
| 1969 | Transitions | Webern | John Butler | Cologne |
| 1970 | Walking On The Wall | | Trisha Brown | New York City |
| 1971 | Education Of The Girlchild | Meredith Monk | Meredith Monk | New York City |
| 1971 | Eight Jelly Rolls | Jelly Roll Morton | Twyla Tharp | New York City |
| 1972 | The Lark Ascending | Vaughn Williams | Alvin Ailey | New York City |
| 1973 | Deuce Coupe | Beach Boys | Twyla Tharp | New York City |
| 1974 | Troy Game | Downes/Batacuda | Robert North | London |
| 1975 | Esplanade | J S Bach | Paul Taylor | New York City |
| 1976 | Push Comes To Shove | Hayden/Jos Lamb | Twyla Tharp | New York City |
| 1977 | Marimba | Steve Reich | Lar Lubovitch | New York City |
| 1978 | Café Müller | | Pina Bausch | Essen |
| 1978 | North Star | Philip Glass | Lar Lubovitch | New York City |
| 1980 | Bell High | Maxwell Davies | Richard Alston | London |
| 1983 | Midsummer | Tippet | Richard Alston | London |
| 1986 | The Watteau Duet | | Karole Armitage | New York City |
| 1988 | I Am Curious Orange | | Michael Clark | Amsterdam |
| 1988 | Space | Steve Reich | Laura Dean | New York City |
| 1988 | Drink To Me Only With Thine Eyes | Virgil Thompson | Mark Morris | New York City |
| 1990 | Maple Leaf Rag | Scott Joplin | Martha Graham | New York City |

## THE BALLET REPERTORY

| date | ballet | composer | choreographer | place |
|------|--------|----------|---------------|-------|
| 1670 | Le Bourgeois Gentil homme | Lully | Beauchamp | Chambord |
| 1761 | Don Juan | Gluck | Angiolini | Vienna |
| 1778 | Les Petits Riens | Mozart | Noverre | Paris |
| 1828 | La Fille Mal Gardée | Hérold | Aumer | Paris |
| 1832 | La Sylphide | Schneitzhoeffer | F. Taglioni | Paris |
| 1841 | Giselle | Adam | Coralli/Perrot | Paris |
| 1844 | La Esmeralda | Pugni | Perrot | London |
| 1869 | Don Quixote | Minkus | M. Petipa | Moscow |
| 1877 | La Bayadère | Minkus | M. Petipa | St Petersburg |
| 1877 | Swan Lake | Tchaikovsky | Reisinger | Moscow |
| 1890 | The Sleeping Beauty | Tchaikovsky | M. Petipa | St Petersburg |
| 1892 | Nutcracker | Tchaikovsky | M. Petipa/Ivanov | St Petersburg |
| 1898 | Raymonda | Glazunov | M.Petipa | St Petersburg |
| 1905 | The Dying Swan | Saint-Saëns | Fokine | St Petersburg |
| 1907 | Les Sylphides | Chopin | Fokine | St Petersburg |
| 1910 | Le Carnaval | Schumann | Fokine | St Petersburg |
| 1910 | The Firebird | Stravinsky | Fokine | Paris |
| 1911 | Petrushka | Stravinsky | Fokine | Paris |
| 1911 | Le Spectre de la Rose | Weber | Fokine | Monte Carlo |
| 1912 | L'Après-midi d'un Faune | Debussy | Nijinsky | Paris |
| 1912 | Daphnis and Chloë | Ravel | Fokine | Paris |
| 1913 | Jeux | Debussy | Nijinsky | Paris |
| 1913 | The Rite of Spring | Stravinsky | Nijinsky | Paris |
| 1915 | El Amor Brujo | Falla | Imperio | Madrid |
| 1923 | Les Noces | Stravinsky | Nijinska | Paris |
| 1924 | Les Biches | Poulenc | Nijinska | Monte Carlo |
| 1928 | Le Baiser de la Fée | Tchaikovsky | Nijinska | Paris |
| 1928 | Bolero | Ravel | Nijinska | Paris |
| 1929 | The Prodigal Son | Prokofiev | Balanchine | Paris |
| 1931 | Bacchus and Ariadne | Roussel | Lifar | Paris |
| 1931 | Job | Vaughan Williams | de Valois | London |
| 1934 | Serenade | Tchaikovsky | Balanchine | New York |
| 1937 | Les Patineurs | Meyerbeer/Lambert | Ashton | London |
| 1938 | Billy the Kid | Copland | Loring | Chicago |
| 1938 | Romeo and Juliet | Prokofiev | Psota | Brno, Moravia |
| 1942 | The Miraculous Mandarin | Bartók | Milloss | Milan |
| 1942 | Rodeo | Copland | de Mille | New York |
| 1942 | Gayaneh | Khachaturian | Anisimova | Molotov-Perm |
| 1944 | Appalachian Spring | Copland | Graham | Washington |
| 1944 | Fancy Free | Bernstein | Robbins | New York |
| 1945 | Cinderella | Prokofiev | Zakharov | Moscow |
| 1949 | Carmen | Bizet | Petit | London |
| 1953 | Afternoon of a Faun | Debussy | Robbins | New York |
| 1956 | Spartacus | Khachaturian | Jacobson | Leningrad |
| 1957 | Agon | Stravinsky | Balanchine | New York |
| 1959 | Episodes | Webern | Balanchine | New York |
| 1962 | A Midsummer Night's Dream | Mendelssohn | Balanchine | New York |
| 1964 | The Dream | Mendelssohn/Lanchbery | Ashton | London |
| 1965 | The Song of the Earth | Mahler | MacMillan | Stuttgart |
| 1967 | Anastasia | Martinu | MacMillan | New York |
| 1968 | Enigma Variations | Elgar | Ashton | London |
| 1969 | Dancers at a Gathering | Chopin | Robbins | New York |
| 1969 | The Taming of the Shrew | Stolze/Scarlatti | Cranko | Stuttgart |
| 1972 | Duo Concertante | Stravinsky | Balanchine | New York |
| 1974 | Elite Syncopations | Joplin, etc | MacMillan | London |
| 1976 | A Month in the Country | Chopin/Lanchbery | Ashton | London |
| 1978 | Mayerling | Liszt/Lanchbery | MacMillan | London |
| 1978 | Symphony of Psalms | Stravinsky | Kylian | Scheveningen |
| 1980 | Gloria | Poulenc | MacMillan | London |
| 1980 | Rhapsody | Rachmaninov | Ashton | London |

spaces—museums, rooftops, even scaling walls. Dance that is today avant-garde usually enters mainstream dance eventually in some form.

In the USA, avant-garde dance stemmed mainly from Merce Cunningham in New York and the exploration of his ideas by musician Robert Dunn in a series of choreographer's workshops which eventually became the Judson Dance Theater. While retaining technique and rhythm, Cunningham deleted the role of choreographer, giving dancers a new freedom. Steps and directions were random choices arrived at by lottery or a tossed coin, and he rejected both dramatic and romantic content, concentrating on form. The Judson collective went further, denying even the necessity for technique and concentrating on the use of everyday movement—walking, spinning, jumping. Karole Armitage, Trisha Brown, Lucinda Childs, and Steve Paxton, followed by Laura Dean and Keitakei, are the leading names in this movement.

In the UK, Rosemary Butcher and Michael Clark (both of whom worked with Post-Modernists in New York) are the leading avant-garde names. Clark's work often involves the use of zany props and outrageous costumes.

In Essen, Germany, Pina Bausch with her Wuppertal Tanztheater (dance theatre) is the most compelling influence in European dance since Diaghilev. Her works, often several hours long, blend elements of dance, music, dialogue, gesture, psychology, comedy, and stark fear, and may be performed on floors covered with churned earth, rose petals, or water.

### Dancing

*Can you dance?*

|  |  |
|---|---|
| Yes | 48 |
| Yes, but not very well | 20 |
| No | 32 |

*Have you ever paid for dancing lessons?*

|  |  |
|---|---|
| Yes | 25 |
| No | 75 |

# THE NEWSPAPER BARONS

**Beaverbrook** (William) Max(well) Aitken, 1st Baron Beaverbrook 1879–1964. British financier, newspaper proprietor, and politician, born in Canada. He bought a majority interest in the *Daily Express* 1919 (which he turned into the most widely-read newspaper in the world), founded the *Sunday Express* 1921, and bought the London *Evening Standard* 1929. He served in Lloyd George's World War I cabinet and Churchill's World War II cabinet.

Beaverbrook became a stockbroker 1907 and by 1910 had become a cement millionaire. He went to England 1910, where he entered parliament as a Conservative and became Andrew Bonar Law's private secretary. Beaverbrook became Britain's first minister of information 1918, and became minister of supply 1941–42, an office which he filled with characteristic drive and success. He wrote *Politicians and the War* 1928–32, *Men and Power* 1956, and *The Decline and Fall of Lloyd George* 1963.

**Black** Conrad (Moffat) 1940– . Canadian industrialist and newspaper publisher, chair since 1985 and chief executive since 1990 of the Daily Telegraph plc, which also owns the *Sunday Telegraph* and the weekly *Spectator* magazine.

Black, who owned 20 Canadian newspapers, bought more than 50% of the ailing *Daily Telegraph* for ˙4.5 million. Modern management methods and a revived *Daily Telegraph* under former war correspondent Max Hastings soon made the company highly profitable, although the *Sunday Telegraph* still had to struggle in the overcrowded Sunday market. Black, an erudite, scholarly figure and a staunch Thatcherite, had political views that seemed to the right of Hastings, but they arrived at a working arrangement after some initial difficulty.

**Hearst** William Randolph 1863–1951. US newspaper publisher, celebrated for his introduction of banner headlines, lavish illustration, and the sensationalist approach known as 'yellow journalism'. He began with his father's paper, the San Francisco *Examiner* 1887. He then bought the New York *Journal* 1895, tripled its circulation, and by 1925 owned 25 newspapers in 17 cities. A campaigner in numerous controversies, and a strong isolationist, he was the model for Citizen Kane in the 1941 film of that name by Orson Welles.

**Maxwell** (Ian) Robert 1923– . Czech-born English newspaper proprietor and publisher with worldwide interests. In the UK the national newspapers he owns are, from 1984, the *Daily Mirror*, *Sunday Mirror*, and *The People*, and in 1990 he launched the weekly *European*. His British papers all support the Labour Party.

After a controversial career in magazine publishing and printing and many failed attempts

CIRCULATION TRENDS IN UK NEWSPAPERS 1984–1990 (m)

| | 1984 | 1985 | 1986 | 1987 | 1988 | 1989 | 1990 | change 90/84 |
|---|---|---|---|---|---|---|---|---|
| *National dailies* | | | | | | | | |
| Daily Express | 2,002 | 1,902 | 1,729 | 1,690 | 1,637 | 1,575 | 1,574 | -21.4 |
| Daily Mail | 1,864 | 1,815 | 1,732 | 1,810 | 1,759 | 1,723 | 1,689 | -9.4 |
| Mirror | 3,494 | 3,033 | 3,139 | 3,128 | 3,157 | 3,092 | 3,106 | -11.1 |
| The Star | 1,633 | 1,455 | 1,278 | 1,137 | 967 | 891 | 915 | -44.0 |
| The Sun | 4,084 | 4,125 | 4,050 | 4,219 | 4,017 | 3,896 | | -4.6 |
| Today | - | - | 307 | 340 | 548 | 589 | 561 | - |
| *Total Populars* | 13,077 | 12,330 | 12,235 | 12,150 | 12,287 | 11,887 | 11,741 | -10.2 |
| The Daily Telegraph | 1,235 | 1,202 | 1,132 | 1,169 | 1,127 | 1,103 | 1,081 | -12.5 |
| Financial Times (UK) | 172 | 181 | 193 | 222 | 206 | 202 | 191 | 11.0 |
| The Guardian | 472 | 487 | 507 | 460 | 438 | 431 | 427 | -9.5 |
| The Independent | - | - | 303 | 361 | 387 | 412 | 412 | - |
| The Times | 457 | 478 | 467 | 447 | 436 | 428 | 426 | -6.8 |
| *Total Qualities* | 2,336 | 2,348 | 2,602 | 2,659 | 2,594 | 2,576 | 2,538 | 8.6 |
| *National Sundays* | | | | | | | | |
| The Mail on Sunday | 1,607 | 1,631 | 1,601 | 1,854 | 1,919 | 1,892 | 1,896 | 18.0 |
| News of the World | 4,698 | 5,103 | 4,954 | 5,096 | 5,360 | 5,186 | 5,046 | 7.4 |
| Sunday Express | 2,542 | 2,449 | 2,181 | 2,228 | 2,033 | 1,854 | 1,696 | -33.3 |
| Sunday Mirror | 3,489 | 3,009 | 3,046 | 2,894 | 2,953 | 2,926 | 2,902 | -16.8 |
| Sunday Sport | - | - | - | - | 551 | 477 | 427 | - |
| The People | 3,253 | 2,962 | 2,983 | 2,856 | 2,743 | 2,642 | 2,577 | -20.8 |
| *Total Populars* | 15,589 | 15,154 | 14,765 | 14,928 | 15,559 | 14,977 | 14,544 | -6.7 |
| The Observer | 744 | 736 | 769 | 764 | 722 | 639 | 559 | -24.9 |
| Sunday Telegraph | 713 | 686 | 686 | 739 | 693 | 633 | 590 | -17.3 |
| Sunday Times | 1,260 | 1,251 | 1,147 | 1,250 | 1,315 | 1,248 | 1,176 | -6.7 |
| Independent on Sunday | - | - | - | - | - | - | 352 | - |
| *Total Qualities* | 2,717 | 2,673 | 2,602 | 2,753 | 2,730 | 2,520 | 2,677 | -1.5 |

*Source: The Media Pocket Book 1991, NTC Publications Ltd.*

# WHATEVER HAPPENED TO THE PRESS COUNCIL?

From 1953 until 1990 the Press Council was virtually the only channel through which a complaint could be made about the conduct of newspapers, short of a writ for libel (where legal aid is not allowed and costs can run into tens of thousands). The first Royal Commission on the Press, reporting in 1949, had recommended establishment of a General Council of the Press with some lay members and a lay chairman, which was to derive its authority from the industry itself, and not have a statutory basis. Newspaper publishers held prolonged discussions designed to limit the Council to minimal functions; the proposal was getting nowhere until in 1952 an MP introduced a bill to establish a statutory Council. Within a year a voluntary Press Council was established with 15 editorial and 10 management nominees. Its principal objectives were (a) to preserve the established freedom of the Press, and (b) to maintain the character of the British press in accordance with the highest professional and commercial standards. It proved quite ineffective.

A second Royal Commission on the Press, chaired by Lord Shawcross, reporting in 1962, criticized the failure of the industry to appoint any lay members to the Council and urged the threat of statutory action if nothing was done. Again the industry responded rapidly. In 1964 five lay members and a lay chairman (Lord Devlin) were added to 20 professional members and the name was changed to the Press Council. At this stage the Council was perhaps seen more as a robust guardian of press freedom than a safeguard of individual rights.

A third Royal Commission, chaired by Oliver McGregor, reported in 1977 and again criticized the Council as ineffective, saying that it 'had so far failed to persuade the knowl-edgeable public that it deals satisfactorily with complaints against newspapers'. McGregor's recommendations suggested that the Council should be better staffed and better funded; that it should initiate more complaints itself; that it should draw up a code of conduct; and that it should take a stronger line on inaccuracy and bias.

This time the Council adjusted its membership to give parity between lay members and professionals (bringing the total to 37), but rejected any idea of a code of conduct. Funding remained low. Criticism of the council began to mount. Some of the chairmen were too legalistic in their approach. Procedures were extremely cumbersome leading to excessive delays in handling complaints. Although the Council's report on the behaviour of the press in chasing stories and harassing individuals during the Yorkshire Ripper case was trenchant and effective, a growing number of adjudications were treated with scorn. Louis Blom-Cooper QC, appointed chairman in 1989, set about reforming the Council with bustling energy but became unpopular with some publishers.

Meanwhile mounting public concern about cases of outrageous invasion of privacy—such as attempts to pry into the hospital where the popular TV presenter Russell Harty lay dying, and the hounding of Princess Anne's former maid after the theft of some letters from her household, combined with the £1 million libel on Elton John over a rent boy's false allegations—led to bills being introduced in the House of Commons, one to promote privacy and the other to afford the right of reply.

To meet this criticism the Conservative Government appointed a committee, chaired by David Calcutt QC, to inquire into privacy and related matters, notably 'to improve recourse against the press for the individual citizen'. The committee, which included two journalists (one of whom was appointed editor of *The Times* while the committee was sitting), recommended that the press should be given one final chance to prove that a voluntary system of regulation could work and to this end that the Press Council should be superseded by a Press Complaints Commission. The Commission was to be smaller, better funded, and its members should be independent and of high calibre. Its role was more defined; it no longer included the task of upholding press freedom.

The newspaper publishers, under the vigorous chairmanship of Frank Rogers, acted swiftly. Funding of about £1.5m a year (50% more than that available to the Press Council) was speedily secured; McGregor, now a peer, was appointed chairman; and a sub-committee chaired by the editor of *The News of the World* produced a new Code of Practice which was accepted by editors of the national newspapers.

The Commission began operations on New Year's Day 1991. The jury is still out on its performance, but clamour for statutory action against the press has died away, for a time . . .

*Mr Kenneth Morgan, OBE, Director of the Press Complaints Commission, London.*

## Women's General Interest Magazines, 1991

| Title | | |
|---|---|---|
| Annabel | DC Thomson & Co | Monthly |
| Bella | Bauer | Weekly |
| Best | Grüner & Jahr | Weekly |
| Chat | IPC Women's Magazines Group | Weekly |
| Company | National Magazine Company Ltd | Monthly |
| Cosmopolitan | National Magazine Company Ltd | Monthly |
| Elle | Hachette Magazines Ltd | Monthly |
| Essentials | IPC Women's Magazines Group | Monthly |
| Family Circle | IPC Women's Magazines Group | Monthly |
| Good Housekeeping | National Magazine Company Ltd | Monthly |
| Harpers & Queen | National Magazine Company Ltd | Monthly |
| Hello | Hello Ltd | Weekly |
| Living | IPC Women's Magazines Group | Monthly |
| Looks | EMAP Metro | Monthly |
| Marie Claire | European Magazines Ltd | Monthly |
| Me | IPC Women's Magazines Group | Weekly |
| More! | EMAP Metro | Fortnightly |
| My Weekly | DC Thomson & Co | Weekly |
| New Woman | Murdoch Magazines (UK) Ltd | Monthly |
| 19 | Holborn Publishing Group (IPC) | Monthly |
| Options | Southbank Publications | Monthly |
| People's Friend | DC Thomson & Co | Weekly |
| Prima | Grüner & Jahr | Monthly |
| She | National Magazine Company Ltd | Monthly |
| Take a Break | Bauer | Weekly |
| Tatler | Tatler Publishing Company Ltd (Condé Nast) | Monthly |
| The Lady | The Lady | Weekly |
| True Romances | Argus | Monthly |
| True Stories | Argus | Monthly |
| Vogue | Condé Nash | Monthly |
| Woman | IPC Women's Magazines Group | Weekly |
| Woman and Home | IPC Women's Magazines Group | Monthly |
| Woman's Journal | Southbank Publications | Monthly |
| Woman's Own | IPC Women's Magazines Group | Weekly |
| Woman's Realm | IPC Women's Magazines Group | Weekly |
| Woman's Story | Argus | Monthly |
| Woman's Weekly | IPC Women's Magazines Group | Weekly |

Source: Mintel Market Intelligence

to buy a newspaper, he finally bought the Mirror Group in 1984 from Reed International. Ruthlessly pruning costs and introducing run-of-paper (ROP) colour well ahead of Rupert Murdoch, his major rival, he transformed the Mirror Group into a highly profitable concern. He also made investments in European and Israeli media companies.

Changing direction in 1991, he acquired the loss-making New York *Daily News*, which was on the verge of closure after a bitter labour dispute. To reduce debts by £200 million he then floated off 49% of the Mirror Group, retaining 51%.

Maxwell was a Labour member of Parliament 1964–70 and his newspapers are firm Labour supporters, although privately he admired much that Margaret Thatcher accomplished. In 1990 he launched the *European*, a weekly newspaper that at first failed to make an immediate impact and was in effect relaunched under a new editor as a more popular newspaper in 1991.

**Murdoch** (Keith) Rupert 1931– . Australian-born US media magnate with diverse interests

in the USA, the UK, Australia, and other countries. A dynamic figure, Murdoch is conversant with all aspects of newspaper production, and has made frequent editorial interventions in his largely right-wing papers. His UK newspapers, controlled by News International (NI), a wholly owned subsidiary of the Australian-based News Corporation, are the top-selling *Sun* and *News of the World*, the faltering tabloid *Today*, the highly profitable *Sunday Times*, and the loss-making *Times*. News International also owns 50% of the satellite company Sky Television. In the USA his companies own *TV Guide*, several TV stations, and a major share in Fox films.

The sleaze and intrusion that characterized Murdoch's tabloid journalism provoked strong criticism and have been toned down. As a result of the worldwide advertising recession and heavy initial losses on satellite TV, Murdoch faced financial difficulty 1991 in servicing bank loans which totalled more than $7 billion: he sold most of his US magazines while putting his British magazines on the market. Murdoch has shown increased interest in films and is currently based in Hollywood. He became a US

# INVASION OF OVERSEAS MAGAZINES: HAVEN'T WE GOT ENOUGH OF OUR OWN?

Magazines originating overseas have enjoyed a healthy readership in Britain for decades. The two US news magazines *Time* and *Newsweek* have long been familiar on British newsstands, and the fashion magazine *Vogue*, although launched by an American, at one time fell into the hands of a British newspaper publisher, Lord Camrose. *Cosmopolitan*, the US magazine that highlighted the pleasures of 'sex for the single girl', crossed the Atlantic at the beginning of the 1970s. Even so, the 1980s were remarkable for the sheer number of foreign magazines launched in the UK.

In 1986 a wave of what became known as 'panzer publishing' began. That year the German publishing colossus Grüner & Jahr launched *Prima*, a monthly magazine addressing the practical side of housekeeping. Containing recipes, inset paper patterns as complicated as navigational charts, and hints about health, gardening, pets, and much else, *Prima* was an immediate success and was soon selling a million plus, aided by competitive pricing and heavy promotion. That was followed by *Best*, a weekly from the same firm, which also went back to the basics of journalism for women whose reading attention span had apparently been shortened by overexposure to television.

Another German publisher, H Bauer, launched *Bella* along these same lines in 1987. Common to all these German publications was a willingness on the part of the publishers to spend heavily and, if necessary, wait years for breakeven, so long as they won a major share of the women's market. Advertising content was minimal; everything was sacrificed to success in the battle for readers.

The British firm IPC, which had previously enjoyed a virtual monopoly in mass-market women's magazines with such long- established titles as *Woman's Weekly*, *Woman's Own*, and *Woman*, suddenly found the going very tough, but soon rallied and launched some new titles of its own, such as the weeklies *Me* and *Chat* and the monthly *Essentials*. By the last six months of 1990, the Grüner & Jahr titles had fallen back, but Bauer's *Bella* was still at the top with the same company's *Take a Break* not far behind. Circulations were as follows (ABC figures unless otherwise stated):

| | | |
|---|---|---|
| *Bella* | 1,191,189 | (publisher's audit) |
| *Woman's Weekly* | 1,067,382 | |
| *Take a Break* | 924,634 | (publisher's audit) |
| *Woman's Own* | 830,086 | |
| *Woman* | 805,511 | |
| *Me* | 733,412 | |
| *Best* | 679,349 | |
| *Prima* | 673,871 | |

Publishers from other countries caught the mood. From France came *Marie Claire* and *Elle*, two fashion magazines to compete with *Vogue*.

From the USA Rupert Murdoch brought over *New Woman*, a magazine about relationships for the woman 'who knows what she wants'; this was followed in 1990 by *Mirabella*, a monthly for the slightly older woman. From Spain emerged perhaps the most innovative magazine of all: *Hello!*, a colour illustrated weekly that gave only the benign and acceptable side of life, particularly the home lives of the famous. And readers loved its absence of sleaze. From modest beginnings *Hello!* was selling 346,540 copies a week at the end of 1990, an increase of 44% over the year.

The invasion from overseas did not take place without casualties. *W*, a fashion news magazine from the USA, quickly folded. Murdoch, beset with financial problems mainly stemming from his involvement with satellite television, closed *Mirabella*, which had fallen far short of its circulation targets, and made known his willingness to sell the British version of *New Woman*. (The US version was also sold.) Other foreign publishers shouldered heavy losses in the hope that the market would turn.

In publishing there is always a new wrinkle and in 1991 Condé Nast found it: they staged a British launch for *Vanity Fair*, a trendy, ultrasophisticated monthly edited with extraordinary flair by the gifted British-born Tina Brown. The innovation was that the editorial text was identical with that published in the USA—only the ads were British. Since the magazine already had a cult following in the UK, the aim of swelling British sales from 20,000 to 50,000 seemed well within reach. But at what price? Would British advertising pay for the extra cost of British printing? The experiment continued.

*Some of the top-selling women's magazines*

citizen in 1985.

**Northcliffe** Alfred Charles William Harmsworth, 1st Viscount Northcliffe 1865–1922. English newspaper proprietor, born in Dublin. Founding the *Daily Mail* 1896, he revolutionized popular journalism, and with the *Daily Mirror* 1903 originated the picture paper. In 1908 he also obtained control of *The Times*. His brother **Harold Sidney Harmsworth, 1st Viscount Rothermere** (1868–1940), was associated with him in many of his newspapers.

**Preston** Peter (John) 1938– . English editor and newspaper executive, editor of the moderate left-wing daily *Guardian* since 1975. Preston can be an inspired writer and is a shrewd judge of journalism. Since 1988 he has also been chair of Guardian Newspapers Ltd owned by the Scott Trust set up to safeguard the newspaper by descendants of C P Scott, owner and editor of the *Manchester Guardian*, who wrote in 1926: 'Comment is free but facts are sacred.'

Despite some mistakes, Preston has presided over a paper of consistently high editorial quality, which in mid-1991 was selling in excess of *The Times* and the *Independent*. Perhaps his biggest error was so to handle a confidential document provided by Sarah Tisdall, a junior civil servant, that she was successfully prosecuted and imprisoned. A new modular make-up, introduced 1988 on the advice of an outside designer, was also criticized.

Politically the paper generally supports Labour but its columnists are allowed a free hand. Hugo Young, who also chairs the Scott Trust, is an outstanding political columnist. The paper campaigns strongly against interference with press freedom at home or abroad.

**Rothermere** Vere (Harold Esmond Harmsworth), 3rd Viscount 1925– . English newspaper proprietor. As chair of Associated Newspapers he controls the *Daily Mail* (founded by his great-uncle Lord Northcliffe, the creative genius of popular journalism in Britain) as well as a string of regional newspapers. In 1982 he launched the *Mail on Sunday*. Facing a very expensive disaster, he switched editors within weeks of the launch and ultimately secured a triumph.

Two of his boldest moves involved newspaper closures. In 1971, allowed by his father Esmond, a highly ineffective publisher, to take control of the newspapers, Rothermere closed the *Daily Sketch* and successfully transformed the *Mail* into a tabloid, with David English as the editor. In 1977, he closed the London *Evening News* with heavy loss of jobs, but obtained a half-share of the more successful *Evening Standard*, obtaining the remaining half in 1985.

Lord Rothermere, an engaging and amused observer of the publishing scene, is expected eventually to hand over control to his son, thus retaining family control over four generations.

**Stevens of Ludgate** David (Robert), Lord 1936– . British financier and newspaper publisher. He succeeded to the chair of United Newspapers, a major provincial newspaper and magazine group based in the north of England,

in 1981. He secured Express Newspapers (the *Daily Express, Sunday Express, Daily Star,* and a few provincial newspapers such as the *Falmouth Packet*) in 1985.

As a newspaper publisher, Stevens showed an uncertain touch: in an effort to revive the *Star*, he entered into an unsuccessful short-lived partnership with David Sullivan, publisher of the weekly tabloid *Sunday Sport*. Neither advertisers nor readers liked the change. He then personally appointed an inexperienced executive from the *Sunday Times* as editor of the *Sunday Express*, who failed to halt the paper's long decline. John Junor, columnist and former editor of the *Sunday Express* resigned, and went over to its major rival: the *Mail on Sunday*. However, the appointment of Nick Lloyd as editor of the *Daily Express*, was more successful. In 1991 Lloyd's wife Eve Pollard, who had been editing the *Sunday Mirror* with some flair, was appointed editor of the *Sunday Express*.

**Whittam-Smith** Andreas 1937– . English journalist and editor, founder of the *Independent* 1986. Whittam-Smith was editor of the *Daily Telegraph*, before launching the *Independent*. After an initial decline in sales, its circulation moved steadily upwards to challenge *The Times*.

The launch of the *Independent* was made at an opportune time: many of Rupert Murdoch's journalists were disenchanted by the forced move to Wapping and transferred to the new newspaper; demand for advertising was also strong. The paper's independent and idiosyncratic outlook appealed to readers and advertisers. However, with the country moving into recession, the 1990 launch of the *Independent on Sunday* was less successful: although circulation targets were hit, lack of advertising produced losses of £500,000 a month. Further funds were raised by selling 15% shareholdings to two European newspapers.

# CARTOONS AND CREATORS

**Asterix** comic strip character created by French cartoonist Albert Uderzo. Asterix, the belligerent, wing-helmeted hero originally appeared in France 1959 as 'Asterix le Gaulois/Asterix the Gaul, and rapidly achieved popularity. Asterix made his comic debut in the UK in 1965 as Beric the Bold, aided and abetted by his rotund henchman, Chief Caradoc.

**Batman** comic strip character created by US cartoonist Bob Kane, Batman first appeared as The Bat-Man 1939. Characterized by his black bat-like mask and cape, Batman's alter-ego is millionaire playboy Bruce Wayne. His youthful aide, former circus performer Dick Grayson, is known as Robin the boy wonder. Together they travel in their 'batmobile' and combat the criminal activities of (among others) the Joker, the Penguin, the Riddler, and the Catwoman.

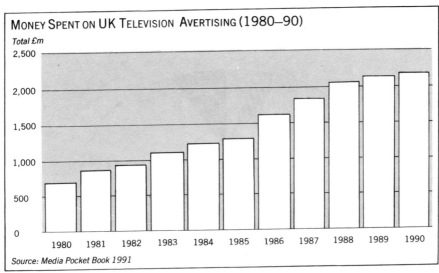

MONEY SPENT ON UK TELEVISION AVERTISING (1980–90)

Total £m

Source: Media Pocket Book 1991

*Batman* appeared in the cinema 1943, 1949, and more recently 1989. He also starred in a television series in the 1960s.

**Betty Boop** comic strip character created by Grim Natwick for Max Fleischer's 'Talkartoons' 1915. Betty Boop was characterized by her short curly black hair, black mini dress and wide-eyed appeal, and was supposedly based on the original boop-a-doop singer, Helen Kane. She was popular throughout the 1920s and 1930s, and the cartoons in which she appeared usually made comments on social follies of the time. Her film debut was in *Dizzy Dishes* 1930.

**Bugs Bunny** cartoon character initially created by US cartoonist Bob Clampett for *Porky's Hare Hunt* 1938. The long-eared, carrot-crunching rabbit with goofy incisors, and familiar catchphrase 'Eh, what's up, Doc?' starred again in *A Wild Hare* 1940. By 1962 he had appeared in 159 films, and won an Academy Award for *Knighty Knight Bugs* 1958.

**comic book** publication in strip-cartoon form. Comic books are usually aimed at children, although in Japan, Latin America, and Europe millions of adults read them. Artistically sophisticated adult comics and **graphic novels** are produced in the USA and several European countries, notably France. Comic books developed from comic strips in newspapers or, like those of Walt Disney, as spinoffs from animated cartoon films.

**comic strip** or **strip cartoon** sequence of several frames of drawings in cartoon style. Strips, which may work independently or form instalments of a serial, are usually humorous or satirical in content. Longer stories in comic-strip form are published separately as comic books. Some have been made into animated films.

**Day** Clarence (Shepard, Jr) 1874–1935. US cartoonist and author. His autobiographical memoir *Life with Father* 1935 became a national bestseller, a long-running Broadway play from 1939, and a popular feature film 1947. Day's sequels to that work, *Life with Mother* 1937 and *Father and I* 1940, were published after his death.

**Dick Tracy** comic strip character created by US cartoonist Chester Gould 1931. The strong-jawed detective battles against the ruthless criminal underworld against such characters as Flattop, Pruneface, Itchy, and the Stooge, with the help of his pea-brained crew of law-enforcers: Helmlock Holmes, Jo Jitsu, Go Go Gomez. Dick Tracy became a television series in the 1950s. The film *Dick Tracy* 1990 starred US pop star Madonna, and US actor Warren Beatty.

MOST POPULAR VIDEO RENTAL FILMS

| | Title | Director | Year made |
|---|---|---|---|
| 1 | E.T. The Extra-Terrestrial | S Spielberg | 1982 |
| 2 | Star Wars | G Lucas | 1977 |
| 3 | Return Of The Jedi | R Marquand | 1983 |
| 4 | Batman | T Burton | 1989 |
| 5 | The Empire Strikes Back | I Kershner | 1980 |
| 6 | Ghostbusters | I Reitman | 1984 |
| 7 | Jaws | S Spielberg | 1975 |
| 8 | Raiders Of The Lost Ark | S Spielberg | 1981 |
| 9 | Indiana Jones And The Last Crusade | S Spielberg | 1989 |
| 10 | Indiana Jones And The Temple Of Doom | S Spielberg | 1984 |

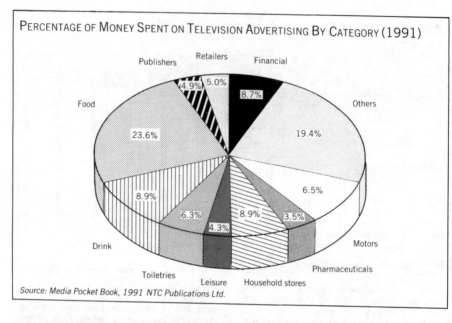

PERCENTAGE OF MONEY SPENT ON TELEVISION ADVERTISING BY CATEGORY (1991)

Publishers — Retailers — Financial
4.9% — 5.0% — 8.7%
Food — 23.6%
Others — 19.4%
6.5%
8.9%
6.3% — 8.9% — 3.5%
4.3%
Drink
Motors
Toiletries
Leisure — Household stores
Pharmaceuticals

Source: Media Pocket Book, 1991 NTC Publications Ltd.

**Disney** Walt (Walter Elias) 1901–1966. US filmmaker who became a pioneer of family entertainment. He and his brother established an animation studio in Hollywood in 1923, and his first Mickey Mouse animated cartoon (*Plane Crazy*) appeared in black and white 1928. *Steamboat Willie* 1928 was his first Mickey Mouse cartoon in colour. He developed the 'Silly Symphony,' a type of cartoon based on the close association of music with the visual image, such as *Fantasia* 1940. His many feature-length cartoons include *Snow White and the Seven Dwarfs* 1938 (his first), *Pinocchio* 1939, *Dumbo* 1941, *Bambi* 1942, *Cinderella* 1950, *Alice in Wonderland* 1952, and *Peter Pan* 1953. Published materials such as books, magazines, comic books, and records accompanied his films and helped to popularize his animated characters worldwide.

**Donald Duck** cartoon character created by US animator Walt Disney. The belligerent, sailor-suited duck first appeared in a supporting role for the 'Silly Symphony' short of *The Wise Little Hen* 1934. He rapidly gained popularity and achieved star billing, for the first time in *Donald and Pluto* 1936. From 1936 he appeared in a weekly US newspaper strip. He won an Academy Award with *Der Fuhrer's Face* 1942.

**Felix the Cat** cartoon character created by Australian cartoonist Pat Sullivan 1919, Felix was the first international superstar in cartoon films. Felix, a perky and indestructible black cat first appeared in *Feline Follies* 1919. Between 1925 and 1929 he appeared in 78 films, and appeared in Sullivan's final film *The Last Life* 1929. 'Felix Kept on Walking' was the signature tune especially created for him in the mid-1920s. Felix was the first cartoon character to make the crossing from screen

to comic strip, appearing in his own newspaper strip 1923. He made a comeback in *Felix the Cat and the Goose that Laid the Golden Egg* 1936, and reappeared again in a television series beginning 1960, complete with a magic bag giving him special powers. Stories depicted the scheming Professor and his bulldog assistant, Rock Bottom, trying to steal the bag.

**Flash Gordon** comic strip character created by US cartoonist Alex Raymond 1934. Flash, a Yale graduate and astronaut, with female companion Dale Arden starred in outer space adventures. He travelled in Dr Zarkov's home-made rocketship to thwart evil warlock, Ming the Merciless, emperor of the planet Mongo. His exploits were featured in three Hollywood serials featuring US actor Buster Crabbe, the first of which *Flash Gordon* appeared 1936, followed by *Flash Gordon's Trip to Mars* 1938, and *Flash Gordon Conquers the Universe* 1940.

**Fleischer** Max 1889–1972. Austrian-born US cartoonist. With his younger brother, Dave (1894–1972) as director, Fleischer animated and produced cartoons from 1917. His first major series was *Out of the Inkwell* 1918 starring Koko the Clown. He created the acclaimed and long-running cartoon characters Betty Boop and Popeye. His feature films include *Gulliver's Travels* 1939 and *Superman* 1941.

**Flintstones, the** cartoon comedy series appearing on television created by US animators William Hanna and Joseph Barbera 1960. It featured Stone Age caveman Fred Flintstone and his half-wit neighbour Barney Rubble, together with their wives Wilma and Betty living in the town of Bedrock. Fred's cry of 'Yabba dabba do!' as he tried out a new invention with Barney, became his catchphrase. It was the first cartoon series to move to the prime-

## HOURS SPENT WATCHING TELEVISION (1990)

| | hours per day | hours per year |
|---|---|---|
| BBC1 and 2 | 1.38 | 47.6 |
| ITV and C4 | 1.48 | 52.4 |
| All stations | 3.26 | 100.00 |

Source: BARB

time viewing slot of Friday night.

**Giles** Carl Ronald 1916– . British cartoonist for the *Daily* and *Sunday Express* from 1943, noted for his creation of a family with a formidable 'Grandma'.

**Lancaster** Osbert 1908–1986. English cartoonist and writer. In 1939 he began producing daily 'pocket cartoons' for the *Daily Express*, in which he satirized current social mores through such characters as Maudie Littlehampton.

**Low** David 1891–1963. New Zealand-born British political cartoonist, creator (in newspapers such as the London *Evening Standard*) of Colonel Blimp, the TUC carthorse, and others.

**Mickey Mouse** cartoon character created by US animator Walt Disney, characterized by his black disc-shaped ears, red-buttoned pants, and white gloves. He made his film debut in *Plane Crazy* 1928, and starred in the first synchronized sound cartoon *Steamboat Willie* 1928. Mickey's own comic, *Mickey Mouse Weekly* started 1936 and ran 920 issues. He went on to make feature film appearances in *Fantasia* 1940 (as the 'Sorcerer's Apprentice'), *Fun and Fancy Free* 1947, and *The Simple Things* 1953.

**Pink Panther** cartoon character created by David de Partie and Friz Freleng for the opening credits of Blake Edwards's film *The Pink Panther* 1964. The laconic but mute pink panther appeared in *Pink Phink* 1964 for which he won an Academy Award. The Pink Panther then went on to appear in a number of sequels about the accident-prone detective Inspector Clouseau, played by English actor Peter Sellers, including *A Shot in the Dark* 1964, and *The Return of the Pink Panther* 1975.

**Popeye** comic strip character created by US cartoonist Elzie Crisler Segar 1929. Popeye made his first appearance in *Thimble Theatre* as a feisty, pipe-smoking, spinach-eating sailor, whose motto was 'I yam what I yam!' He made his first film appearance in *Popeye the Sailor* 1933. By 1957, he had starred in over 200 cartoons, including *Popeye the Sailor Meets Sinbad the Sailor* 1936. Lanky-legged, button-nosed Olive Oyl, his girlfriend, and adventurous baby boy Swee'pea made later appearances, and a film version by US director Robert Altman appeared in the 1980s.

**Rupert Bear** comic strip character created by English cartoonist Mary Tourtel 1920. Rupert Bear, in his scarf, jumper and trousers was the star of the longest-lived children's strip in the UK, making his debut as 'The Little Lost Bear' in the *Daily Express*. Rupert's adventures in the village of Nutwood, together with his friends Bill Badger, Algy Pug, and Edward Trunk, were

continued by Alfred Bestall after Tourtel's retirement 1935.

**Schulz** Charles Monroe 1922– . US cartoonist. His idea for the 'Peanuts' cartoon strip was accepted by United Features Syndicate 1950 and has appeared in more than 2,000 newspapers worldwide. As the characters Snoopy, Charlie Brown, Lucy, and Linus became famous throughout the country, Schulz further promoted them through merchandise lines and television specials. In 1967 a musical based on the 'Peanuts' characters, *You're a Good Man, Charlie Brown*, played on Broadway. The film, *A Boy Named Charlie Brown* followed in 1968, with the philosophizing beagle starring in *Snoopy Comes Home* 1972.

**Spiderman** comic strip character created by US cartoonist Stan Lee 1952. Bitten by a radioactive spider, Spiderman has the ability to climb walls, dangle from ceilings, and spin webs – all useful skills in tackling underground criminals. Spiderman's alter-ego is shy college student Peter Parker, a reporter for the New York *Daily Bugle*. He first appeared in the British comic *Pow* 1967, and made television appearances in the 1960s and 1970s.

**Sullivan** Pat(rick) 1887–1933. Australian-born US cartoonist of the silent cartoon film period. His first series featured his own newspaper strip hero *Sammie Johnson* 1916. He created the first cartoon hero to achieve world fame: *Felix the Cat* 1920.

**Superman** comic strip character created 1938 in the USA by writer Jerome Siegel and artist Joseph Shuster. Mild-mannered Clark Kent, reporter for the *Daily Planet* could transform himself into Superman, able to leap tall buildings in a single bound when trouble reared its head, his only weakness being kryptonite, which nullifies his superhuman powers. He first starred in the film *Superman* 1941, and featured in several films, television, and other media. In the German philosopher Nietzsche's work, his ideal future human being was the *Übermensch*, or Superman.

**Tintin** comic strip character created by Belgian artist Hergé (Georges Remi). Tintin the 12-year-old boy reporter, together with his dog Snowy, starred in many mysterious adventures, first appearing in *Tintin in the land of the Soviets* 1929–30.

**Tom and Jerry** cartoon twosome featuring mean-minded cat Tom and mischievous mouse Jerry, with Butch the Bulldog appearing as a subsidiary character. They were created by US animators William Hanna and Joseph Barbera. They made their film debut in *Puss Gets the Boot* 1939, and appeared in *Yankee Doodle Mouse* 1943, and *Johann Mouse* 1952, all of which won Academy Awards. The typically violent scenarios (with Tom regularly succumbing to seemingly fatal accidents) attracted criticism, but the humour, and happy resolution of most of the cartoons ensured their popularity. They made their cinema debut in *Pet Peeves* 1954, and appeared in a total of 154 short cartoons.

**Viz** adult comic, founded by English editor Chris

Donald 1979. Advertised as Britain's rudest comic, it includes such controversial characters as Sid the Sexist, the Flat Slags, and the Topless Skateboard Nuns. By 1991 it was selling more than a million copies to a largely male readership.

**Yogi Bear** cartoon character created for television by US animators William Hanna and Joseph Barbera. The shrewd, smiling Yogi, together with his accomplice Boo-Boo (a cautious cub) steal picnic baskets from tourists and generally create mischief for Mr Ranger in Jellystone Park. Yogi Bear made his US comicbook debut in 1959, and appeared in his first feature length film *Hey There It's Yogi Bear* 1964.

# TELEVISION

**British Broadcasting Corporation** (BBC) the UK state-owned broadcasting network. It operates television and national and local radio stations, and is financed solely by the sale of television viewing licences. It is not allowed to carry advertisements. Overseas radio broadcasts (World Service) have a government subsidy.

**IBA** abbreviation for *Independent Broadcasting Authority*, former name of the Independent Television Commission, UK regulatory body for commercial television and radio.

**Independent Television Commission** (ITC) (formerly the *Independent Broadcasting Authority*) the UK corporate body established by legislation to provide commercially funded television (ITV from 1955) and local radio (ILR from 1973) services. During the 1980s, this role was expanded to include the setting-up of Channel 4 (launched 1982) and the provision of services broadcast directly by satellite into homes (DBS). Government proposals in 1988 recommended replacing the IBA and the Cable Authority (body established 1984 to develop cable TV services) with an Independent Television Commission to oversee all commercial TV services. Commercial radio, to include three new national services, would be overseen by a separate new radio authority.

## Newspapers

*Do you think that the controls on what newspapers may or may not print, are too tight, not tight enough or are about right?*

|  | Today | Mar 1988 |
| --- | --- | --- |
| Too tight | 12 | 17 |
| Not tight enough | 41 | 34 |
| About right | 40 | 43 |
| Don't know | 6 | 6 |

*Do you think that the newspapers have enough access to the way the government works, not enough access or too much access?*

|  | Today | Mar 1988 |
| --- | --- | --- |
| Enough | 30 | 31 |
| Not enough | 49 | 48 |
| Too much | 8 | 8 |
| Don't know | 13 | 13 |

# GREAT COMPOSERS

**Bach** Johann Sebastian 1685–1750. German composer. His appointments included positions at the courts of Weimar and Anhalt-Köthen, and from 1723 until his death, he was musical director at St Thomas's choir school in Leipzig. Bach was a master of counterpoint (combining different forms of an original melody), and his music epitomizes the Baroque polyphonic style. His orchestral music includes the six *Brandenburg Concertos*, other concertos for keyboard instrument and violin, and four orchestral suites. Bach's keyboard music, for clavier and organ, his fugues, and his choral music are of equal importance. He also wrote chamber music and songs.

**Bartók** Béla 1881–1945. Hungarian composer. Regarded as a child prodigy, he studied music at the Budapest Conservatory, later working with Hungarian composer Zoltán Kodály in recording and transcribing local folk music for a government project. This led him to develop a personal musical language combining folk elements with mathematical concepts of tone and rhythmic proportion. His large output includes six string quartets, a ballet *The Miraculous Mandarin* 1919, which was banned because of its subject matter (it was set in a brothel), concertos, an opera, and graded teaching pieces for piano. He died in the USA, having fled from Hungary in 1940.

**Beethoven** Ludwig van 1770–1827. German composer and pianist, whose mastery of musical expression in every genre made him the dominant influence on 19th-century music. Beethoven's repertoire includes concert overtures; the opera *Fidelio*; five piano concertos and two for violin (one unfinished); 32 piano sonatas, including the *Moonlight* and *Appassionata*; 17 string quartets; the *Mass in D* (*Missa solemnis*); and nine symphonies, as well as many youthful works. He usually played his own piano pieces and conducted his orchestral works until he was hampered by deafness 1801; nevertheless he continued to compose.

**Berg** Alban 1885–1935. Austrian composer. He studied under Schoenberg and was associated with him as one of the leaders of the serial, or 12-tone, school of composition. His output includes orchestral, chamber, and vocal music as well as two operas, *Wozzeck* 1925, a grim story of working-class life, and the unfinished *Lulu* 1929–35.

**Berlioz** (Louis) Hector 1803–1869. French Romantic composer and the founder of modern orchestration. Much of his music was inspired by drama and literature and has a theatrical quality. He wrote symphonic works, such as *Symphonie fantastique* and *Roméo et Juliette*; dramatic cantatas including *La Damnation de Faust* and *L'Enfance du Christ*; sacred music; and three operas, *Béatrice et Bénédict*, *Benvenuto Cellini*, and *Les Troyens*.

**Brahms** Johannes 1833–1897. German composer, pianist, and conductor. Considered one of the greatest composers of symphonic music and of songs, his works include four symphonies; lieder (songs); concertos for piano and for violin; chamber music; sonatas; and the choral *A German Requiem* 1868. He performed and conducted his own works.

**Britten** (Edward) Benjamin, 1913–1976. English composer. He often wrote for the individual voice; for example, the role in the opera *Peter Grimes* 1945, based on verses by Crabbe, was created for English tenor Peter Pears. Among his many works are the *Young Person's Guide to the Orchestra* 1946; the chamber opera *The Rape of Lucretia* 1946; *Billy Budd* 1951; *A Midsummer Night's Dream* 1960; and *Death in Venice* 1973.

**Bruckner** (Joseph) Anton 1824–1896. Austrian Romantic composer. He was cathedral organist at Linz 1856–68, and from 1868 he was professor at the Vienna Conservatoire. His works include many choral pieces and 11 symphonies, the last unfinished. His compositions were influenced by Richard Wagner and Beethoven.

**Chopin** Frédéric (François) 1810–1849. Polish composer and pianist. He made his debut as a pianist at the age of eight. As a performer, Chopin revolutionized the technique of pianoforte-playing, turning the hands outwards and favouring a light, responsive touch. His compositions for piano, which include two concertos and other works with orchestra, are characterized by great volatility of mood and rhythmic fluidity.

**Debussy** (Achille-) Claude 1862–1918. French composer. He broke with the dominant tradition of German Romanticism and introduced new qualities of melody and harmony based on the whole-tone scale, evoking oriental music. He is considered to be the originator of musical Impressionism. His work includes *Prélude à l'après-midi d'un faune* 1894 and the opera *Pelléas et Mélisande* 1902.

**Dvořák** Antonin (Leopold) 1841–1904. Czech composer. International recognition came with his series of Slavonic Dances 1877–86, and he was director of the National Conservatory, New York, 1892–95. Works such as his *New World Symphony* 1893 reflect his interest in American folk themes, including black and

## Top 10 Full-Price Classical Albums – 1990

| 1 | *In concert* | Carreras/Domingo/Pavarotti |
|---|---|---|
| 2 | *Essential Pavarotti* | Luciano Pavarotti |
| 3 | *Vivaldi Four Seasons* | Nigel Kennedy/ECO |
| 4 | *Mendelssohn/Bruch/ Schubert* | Nigel Kennedy/ECO |
| 5 | *Bernstein in Berlin* | Leonard Bernstein |
| 6 | *Essential Domingo* | Placido Domingo |
| 7 | *Elgar Cello Concerto* | Du Pré/Baker/LSO |
| 8 | *Songs of Inspiration* | Kiri Te Kanawa |
| 9 | *Opera Extravaganza* | Luis Cobos |
| 10 | *Holst The Planets* | von Karajan/BPO |

## CLASSICAL MUSIC USING UNUSUAL INSTRUMENTS

| | |
|---|---|
| accordion | Gerhard Nonet, *Metamorphoses* |
| antique cymbals | Debussy, *L'Après-midi d'un faune* |
| anvils | Wagner, *Das Rheingold*; Verdi, *Il Trovatore*; Varèse, *Ionisation* |
| basset horn (tenor clarinet) | Mozart, *Masonic Funeral Music*; Stockhausen, *Donnerstag aus LICHT* |
| bass tuba | Vaughan Williams, *Concerto in F minor* |
| bell plates | Boulez, *Rituel in Memoriam Maderna* |
| brake drums | John Cage, *First Construction in Metal* |
| castanets | Manuel de Falla, *The Three-Cornered Hat*; Ravel, *Alborada del Gracioso* |
| celesta | Tchaikovsky, *Nutcracker Suite*; Bartók, *Music for Strings, Percussion and Celesta* |
| cimbalom | Kodály, *Háry János*; Stravinsky, *Renard* |
| cowbell | Richard Strauss, *Alpen Symphony*; Mahler, Symphonies No 6 and 7 |
| electric guitar | Martin, *Trois Poèmes de Villon* |
| flexatone | Schoenberg, *Variations Opus 31 for Orchestra* |
| glass armonica | Mozart, Beethoven (attributed) |
| guero | Stravinsky, *Rite of Spring* |
| harmonium | Schoenberg, *Herzgewächse*; Saint-Saëns, *L'Assassination du Duc de Guise* |
| heckelphone (baritone oboe) | Richard Strauss, *Salome* |
| Japanese tuned bowls (*rin*) | Stockhausen, *Inori* |
| Jew's harp | Albrechtsberger, concerto |
| lion roar (cord or friction drum) | Varèse, *Ionisation* |
| marimbula | H W Henze, *El Cimarrón* |
| mouth organ | Vaughan Williams, *Romanza in D flat*; concertos by Benjamin, Darius Milhaud |
| musical saw | George Crumb, *Ancient Voices of Children* |
| musical top | Stockhausen, *Zodiac* |
| musical toys (trumpet, drum, rattle, cuckoo, bird warbler, and so on) | Leopold Mozart, 'Toy' Symphony |
| ondes Martenot | Messiaen, *Turangalîla Symphony* |
| panpipes | Mozart, *The Magic Flute* |
| prepared piano | John Cage, *Sonatas and Interludes*; Ravel, *L'Enfant et les Sortilèges* |
| piano roll | Stravinsky, *Les Noces* 1917; Conlon Nancarrow |
| ratchet | Beethoven, *Wellington's Victory*; Schoenberg, *Gurrelieder* |
| sarrusaphone (contrabass oboe) | Stravinsky, *Threni* |
| saxophone | Richard Strauss, *'Domestic' Symphony*; Webern, *Quartet Opus 22* |
| slapstick (whip) | Britten, *The Burning Fiery Furnace* |
| Swanee whistle | Ravel, *L'Enfant et les sortilèges* |

Native American. He wrote nine symphonies; tone poems; operas; including *Rusalka* 1901; large-scale choral works; the *Carnival* and other overtures; violin and cello concertos; chamber music; piano pieces; and songs. His Romantic music extends the classical tradition of Beethoven and Brahms and displays the influence of Czech folk music.

**Elgar** Edward (William) 1857–1934. English composer. His *Enigma Variations* appeared 1899, and although his celebrated choral work, the oratorio setting of Newman's *The Dream of Gerontius*, was initially a failure, it was well received at Düsseldorf in 1902. Many of his earlier works were then performed, including the *Pomp and Circumstance* marches.

**Franck** César Auguste 1822–1890. Belgian composer. His music, mainly religious and Romantic in style, includes the Symphony in D minor 1866–68, *Symphonic Variations* 1885 for piano and orchestra, the Violin Sonata 1886, the oratorio *Les Béatitudes/The Beatitudes* 1879, and many organ pieces.

**Grieg** Edvard Hagerup 1843–1907. Norwegian composer. Much of his music is small scale, particularly his songs, dances, sonatas, and piano works. Among his orchestral works are the *Piano Concerto* 1869 and the incidental music for Ibsen's *Peer Gynt* 1876.

**Handel** Georg Frideric 1685–1759. German composer, who became a British subject 1726. His first opera, *Almira*, was performed in Hamburg 1705. In 1710 he was appointed Kapellmeister to the elector of Hanover (the future George I of England). In 1712 he settled in England, where he established his popularity with works such as the *Water Music* 1717 (written for George I). His great choral works include the *Messiah* 1742 and the later oratorios *Samson* 1743, *Belshazzar* 1745, *Judas Maccabaeus* 1747, and *Jephtha* 1752.

**Haydn** Franz Joseph 1732–1809. Austrian composer. A teacher of Mozart and Beethoven, he was a major exponent of the classical sonata form in his numerous chamber and orchestral works (he wrote more than 100 symphonies). He also composed choral music, including the oratorios *The Creation* 1798 and *The Seasons* 1801. He was the first great master of the string quartet.

**Janáček** Leoš 1854–1928. Czech composer. He became director of the Conservatoire at Brno

## GREAT COMPOSERS

| | | | |
|---|---|---|---|
| Giovanni Palestrina | c.1525–1594 | Italian | motets, masses |
| Claudio Monteverdi | 1567–1643 | Italian | operas, vocal music |
| Henry Purcell | 1659–1695 | English | vocal music, operas |
| Antonio Vivaldi | 1678–1741 | Italian | concertos, chamber music |
| Georg Friedrich Handel | 1685–1759 | German | oratorios, operas, orchestra |
| Johann Sebastian Bach | 1685–1750 | German | keyboard choral music, concertos |
| Joseph Haydn | 1732–1809 | Austrian | symphonies, oratorios, chamber music |
| Wolfgang Mozart | 1756–1791 | Austrian | symphonies, operas, chamber music |
| Ludwig van Beethoven | 1770–1827 | German | symphonies, chamber music |
| Carl Maria von Weber | 1786–1826 | German | operas, concertos |
| Gioacchino Rossini | 1792–1868 | Italian | operas |
| Franz Schubert | 1797–1828 | Austrian | songs, symphonies, chamber music |
| Hector Berlioz | 1803–1869 | French | operas, symphonies |
| Felix Mendelssohn | 1809–1847 | German | symphonies, concertos |
| Frederik Chopin | 1810–1849 | Polish | piano music |
| Robert Schumann | 1810–1856 | German | piano, vocal music, concertos |
| Franz Liszt | 1811–1886 | Hungarian | piano, orchestral music |
| Richard Wagner | 1813–1883 | German | operas |
| Giuseppe Verdi | 1813–1901 | Italian | operas |
| César Franck | 1822–1890 | Belgian | symphony, organ works |
| Bedrich Smetana | 1824–1884 | Czech | symphonies, operas |
| Anton Bruckner | 1824–1896 | Austrian | symphonies |
| Johann Strauss II | 1825–1899 | Austrian | waltzes, operettas |
| Johannes Brahms | 1833–1897 | German | symphonies, concertos |
| Camille Saint Saëns | 1835–1921 | French | symphonies, concertos, operas |
| Modest Mussorgsky | 1839–1881 | Russian | operas, orchestral music |
| Peter Tchaikovsky | 1840–1893 | Russian | ballet music, symphonies |
| Antonin Dvořák | 1841–1904 | Czech | symphonies, operas |
| Edvard Grieg | 1843–1907 | Norwegian | concertos, orchestra music |
| Nikolai Rimsky-Korsakov | 1844–1908 | Russian | operas, orchestral music |
| Leos Janáček | 1854–1928 | Czech, | operas, chamber music |
| Edward Elgar | 1857–1934 | English | orchestral music |
| Giacomo Puccini | 1858–1924 | Italian | operas |
| Gustav Mahler | 1860–1911 | Czech | symphonies |
| Claude Debussy | 1862–1918 | French | operas, orchestral music |
| Richard Strauss | 1864–1949 | German | operas, orchestral music |
| Carl Nielsen | 1865–1931 | Danish | symphonies |
| Jean Sibelius | 1865–1957 | Finnish | symphonies, orchestral music |
| Sergei Rachmaninov | 1873–1943 | Russian | symphonies, concertos |
| Arnold Schoenberg | 1874–1951 | Austrian | operas, orchestral, and chamber music |
| Maurice Ravel | 1875–1937 | French | piano, chamber music |
| Béla Bartók | 1881–1945 | Hungarian | operas, concertos |
| Igor Stravinsky | 1882–1971 | Russian | ballets, operas |
| Anton Webern | 1883–1945 | Austrian | chamber, vocal music |
| Alban Berg | 1885–1935 | Austrian | operas, chamber music |
| Sergei Prokofiev | 1891–1953 | Russian | symphonies, ballets |
| George Gershwin | 1898–1937 | American | musicals, operas |
| Dmitri Shostakovich | 1906–1975 | Russian | piano music |
| Oliver Messiaen | 1908– | French | piano, organ, orchestral music |
| Benjamin Britten | 1913–1976 | English | vocal music, opera |
| Karlheinz Stockhausen | 1928– | German | electronic, vocal music |

in 1919 and professor at the Prague Conservatoire in 1920. His music, highly original and influenced by Moravian folk music, includes arrangements of folk songs, operas (*Jenufa* 1904, *The Cunning Little Vixen* 1924), and the choral *Glagolitic Mass* 1927.

**Liszt** Franz 1811–1886. Hungarian composer and pianist. An outstanding virtuoso of the piano, he was an established concert artist by the age of 12. His expressive, romantic, and frequently chromatic works include piano music (*Transcendental Studies* 1851), symphonies, piano concertos, and organ music. Much of his music

is programmatic; he also originated the symphonic poem.

**Mahler** Gustav 1860–1911. Austrian composer and conductor. His ten symphonies, the moving *Das Lied von der Erde/Song of the Earth* 1909, and his song cycles display a synthesis of Romanticism and new uses of chromatic harmonies and musical forms.

**Mendelssohn (-Bartholdy)** (Jakob Ludwig) Felix 1809–1847. German composer, also a pianist and conductor. As a child he composed and performed with his own orchestra and as an adult was helpful to Schumann's career.

## MAJOR OPERAS AND THEIR FIRST PERFORMANCES

| Date | Opera | Composer | Librettist | Place |
|---|---|---|---|---|
| 1607 | Orfeo | Monteverdi | Striggio | Mantua |
| 1642 | The Coronation of Poppea | Monteverdi | Busenello | Venice |
| 1689 | Dido and Aeneas | Purcell | Tate | London |
| 1724 | Julius Caesar in Egypt | Handel | Haym | London |
| 1762 | Orpheus and Eurydice | Gluck | Calzabigi | Vienna |
| 1786 | The Marriage of Figaro | Mozart | Da Ponte | Vienna |
| 1787 | Don Giovanni | Mozart | Da Ponte | Prague |
| 1790 | Così fan tutte | Mozart | Da Ponte | Vienna |
| 1791 | The Magic Flute | Mozart | Schikaneder | Vienna |
| 1805 | Fidelio | Beethoven | Sonnleithner | Vienna |
| 1816 | The Barber of Seville | Rossini | Sterbini | Rome |
| 1821 | Der Freischütz | Weber | Kind | Berlin |
| 1831 | Norma | Bellini | Romani | Milan |
| 1835 | Lucia di Lammermoor | Donizetti | Cammarano | Naples |
| 1836 | Les Huguenots | Meyerbeer | Scribe | Paris |
| 1842 | Russlan and Ludmilla | Glinka | Shirkov/Bakhturin | St Petersburg |
| 1850 | Lohengrin | Wagner | Wagner | Weimar |
| 1851 | Rigoletto | Verdi | Piave | Venice |
| 1853 | Il Trovatore | Verdi | Cammarano | Rome |
| 1853 | La Traviata | Verdi | Piave | Venice |
| 1859 | Faust | Gounod | Barbier/Carré | Paris |
| 1865 | Tristan and Isolde | Wagner | Wagner | Munich |
| 1866 | The Bartered Bride | Smetana | Sabina | Prague |
| 1868 | Die Meistersinger | Wagner | Wagner | Munich |
| 1871 | Aida | Verdi | Ghislanzoni | Cairo |
| 1874 | Boris Godunov | Mussorgsky | Mussorgsky | St Petersburg |
| 1874 | Die Fledermaus | Johann Strauss II | Haffner/Genée | Vienna |
| 1875 | Carmen | Bizet | Meilhac/Halévy | Paris |
| 1876 | The Ring of the Nibelung | Wagner | Wagner | Bayreuth |
| 1879 | Eugene Onegin | Tchaikovsky | Tchaikovsky/Shilovsky | Moscow |
| 1881 | The Tales of Hoffman | Offenbach | Barbier | Paris |
| 1882 | Parsifal | Wagner | Wagner | Bayreuth |
| 1885 | The Mikado | Sullivan | Gilbert | London |
| 1887 | Otello | Verdi | Boito | Milan |
| 1890 | Cavalleria Rusticana | Mascagni | Menasci/Targioni-Tozzetti | Rome |
| 1890 | Prince Igor | Borodin | Borodin | St Petersburg |
| 1892 | Pagliacci | Leoncavallo | Leocavallo | Milan |
| 1892 | Werther | Massenet | Blau/Milliet/Hartmann | Vienna |
| 1896 | La Bohème | Puccini | Giacosa/Illica | Turin |
| 1900 | Tosca | Puccini | Giacosa/Illica | Rome |
| 1902 | Pelléas et Mélisande | Debussy | Maeterlinck | Paris |
| 1904 | Jenufa | Janáček | Janáček | Brno |
| 1904 | Madame Butterfly | Puccini | Giacosa/Illica | Milan |
| 1905 | Salome | Richard Strauss | Wilde/Lachmann | Dresden |
| 1909 | The Golden Cockerel | Rimsky-Korsakov | Byelsky | Moscow |
| 1911 | Der Rosenkavalier | Richard Strauss | Hofmannsthal | Dresden |
| 1918 | Duke Bluebeard's Castle | Bartók | Balázs | Budapest |
| 1925 | Wozzeck | Berg | Berg | Berlin |
| 1935 | Porgy and Bess | Gershwin | Ira Gershwin/Heyward | Boston |
| 1937 | Lulu | Berg | Berg | Zürich |
| 1945 | Peter Grimes | Britten | Slater | London |
| 1946 | War and Peace | Prokofiev | Prokiev/Mendelson | Leningrad |
| 1951 | The Rake's Progress | Stravinsky | Auden/Kallman | Venice |
| 1978 | Paradise Lost | Penderecki | Fry | Chicago |
| 1986 | The Mask of Orpheus | Birtwistle | Zinovieff | London |

Among his best-known works are *A Midsummer Night's Dream* 1827; the *Fingal's Cave* overture 1832; and five symphonies, which include the Reformation 1830, the Italian 1833, and the Scottish 1842. He was instrumental in promoting the revival of interest in J S Bach's music.

**Messiaen** Olivier 1908– . French composer and organist. His music is mystical in character, vividly coloured, and incorporates transcriptions of birdsong. Among his works are the *Quartet for the End of Time* 1941, the large-scale *Turangalila Symphony* 1949, and solo organ and piano pieces. His theories of melody, harmony, and rhythm, drawing on medieval and oriental music, have inspired contemporary composers such as Pierre Boulez and Stockhausen.

**Monteverdi** Claudio (Giovanni Antonio) 1567–1643. Italian composer. His pioneering early operas include *Orfeo* 1607 and *The Coronation of Poppea* 1642. He also wrote madrigals, motets, and sacred music, notably the *Vespers* 1610.

**Mozart** Wolfgang Amadeus 1756–1791. Austrian composer and performer who showed astonishing precocity as a child and was an adult virtuoso. He was trained by his father, **Leopold Mozart** (1719–1787). From an early age he composed prolifically, his works including 27 piano concertos, 23 string quartets, 35 violin sonatas, and more than 50 symphonies. His operas include *Idomeneo* 1781, *Le Nozze di Figaro/The Marriage of Figaro* 1786, *Don Giovanni* 1787, *Così fan tutte/Thus Do All Women* 1790, and *Die Zauberflöte/The Magic Flute* 1791. Strongly influenced by Haydn, Mozart's music marks the height of the Classical age in its purity of melody and form.

**Mussorgsky** Modest Petrovich 1839–1881. Russian composer, who was largely self-taught. His opera *Boris Godunov* was completed in 1869, although not produced in St Petersburg until 1874. Some of his works were 'revised' by Rimsky-Korsakov, and only recently has their harsh original beauty been recognized.

**Nielsen** Carl (August) 1865–1931. Danish composer. His works show a progressive tonality, as in his opera *Saul and David* 1902 and six symphonies.

**Palestrina** Giovanni Pierluigi da 1525–1594. Italian composer of secular and sacred choral music. Apart from motets and madrigals, he also wrote 105 masses, including *Missa Papae Marcelli*.

**Prokofiev** Sergey (Sergeyevich) 1891–1953. Soviet composer. His music includes operas such as *The Love of Three Oranges* 1921; ballets for Russian ballet manager Sergei Diaghilev, including *Romeo and Juliet* 1935; seven symphonies including the *Classical Symphony* 1916–17; music for films; piano and violin concertos; songs and cantatas (for example, that composed for the 30th anniversary of the October Revolution); and *Peter and the Wolf* 1936.

**Puccini** Giacomo (Antonio Domenico Michele Secondo Maria) 1858–1924. Italian opera composer whose music shows a strong gift for melody and dramatic effect. His realist works include *Manon Lescaut* 1893, *La Bohème* 1896, *Tosca* 1900, *Madame Butterfly* 1904, and the unfinished *Turandot* 1926.

**Purcell** Henry 1659–1695. English Baroque composer. His work can be highly expressive, for example, the opera *Dido and Aeneas* 1689 and music for Dryden's *King Arthur* 1691 and for *The Fairy Queen* 1692. He wrote more than 500 works, ranging from secular operas and incidental music for plays to cantatas and church music.

**Rachmaninov** Sergei (Vasilevich) 1873–1943. Russian composer, conductor, and pianist.

After the 1917 Revolution he lived in the USA. His dramatically emotional Romantic music has a strong melodic basis and includes operas, such as *Francesca da Rimini* 1906, three symphonies, four piano concertos, piano pieces, and songs. Among his other works are the *Prelude in C Sharp Minor* 1882 for piano and *Rhapsody on a Theme of Paganini* 1934 for piano and orchestra.

**Ravel** (Joseph) Maurice 1875–1937. French composer. His work is characterized by its sensuousness, unresolved dissonances, and 'tone colour'. Examples are the piano pieces *Pavane pour une infante défunte* 1899 and *Jeux d'eau* 1901, and the ballets *Daphnis et Chloë* 1912 and *Boléro* 1928.

**Rimsky-Korsakov** Nikolay Andreyevich 1844–1908. Russian composer. He used Russian folk idiom and rhythms in his Romantic compositions and published a text on orchestration. His operas include *The Maid of Pskov* 1873, *The Snow Maiden* 1882, *Mozart and Salieri* 1898, and *The Golden Cockerel* 1907, a satirical attack on despotism that was banned until 1909.

**Rossini** Gioachino (Antonio) 1792–1868. Italian composer. His first success was the opera *Tancredi* 1813. In 1816 his 'opera buffa' *Il barbiere di Siviglia/The Barber of Seville* was produced in Rome. During his fertile composition period 1815–23 he produced 20 operas, and created (with Gaetano Donizetti and Vincenzo Bellini) the 19th-century Italian operatic style. After *Guillaume Tell/William Tell* 1829 he gave up writing opera and his later years were spent in Bologna and Paris.

**Saint-Saëns** (Charles) Camille 1835–1921. French composer, pianist, and organist. Among his many lyrical Romantic pieces are concertos, the symphonic poem *Danse macabre* 1875, the opera *Samson et Dalila* 1877, and the orchestral *Carnaval des animaux/Carnival of the Animals* 1886.

**Schoenberg** Arnold (Franz Walter) 1874–1951. Austro-Hungarian composer, a US citizen from 1941. After Romantic early works such as *Verklärte Nacht/Transfigured Night* 1899 and the *Gurrelieder/Songs of Gurra* 1900–11, he experimented with atonality (absence of key), producing works such as *Pierrot Lunaire* 1912 for chamber ensemble and voice, before developing the 12-tone system of musical composition. This was further developed by his pupils Alban Berg and Anton Webern.

**Schubert** Franz (Peter) 1797–1828. Austrian composer. He was only 31 when he died, but his musical output was prodigious. His ten symphonies include the incomplete eighth in B minor (the 'Unfinished') and the 'Great' in C major. He wrote chamber and piano music, including the 'Trout Quintet', and over 600 lieder (songs) combining the Romantic expression of emotion with pure melody. They include the cycles *Die schöne Müllerin/The Beautiful Maid of the Mill* 1823 and *Die Winterreise/The Winter Journey* 1827.

**Schumann** Robert Alexander 1810–1856. German composer. His Romantic songs and short

## FAMOUS NAMES AND NICKNAMES IN MUSIC

| Nickname and famous names | Title and description | Composer |
|---|---|---|
| ABEGG Variations | Theme and Variations Opus I | Schumann |
| Academic Festival Overture | Opus 80 | Brahms |
| Acceleration Waltz | Opus 234 | Johann Strauss II |
| Air on a G String | from Suite No 3 in D Major | J S Bach |
| Airplane Sonata | for piano | Anthiel |
| And did those feet | setting of Blake's poem 'Jerusalem' | Parry |
| Appassionata Sonata | No 23 in F Minor Opus 57 | Beethoven |
| Archduke Trio | No 7 in B Flat Major Opus 97 | Beethoven |
| Blue Danube, (Beautiful) | waltz | Johann Strauss II |
| Boléro | for orchestra | Ravel |
| Carnival of the Animals | zoological fantasy for orchestra | Saint-Saëns |
| Choral Symphony | No 9 in D minor Opus 125 | Beethoven |
| Claire de Lune | No 3 from Suite Bergamasque for piano | Debussy |
| Clock Symphony | No 101 in D Minor | Haydn |
| Coffee Cantata | No 211 | J S Bach |
| Colonel Bogey | march | Alford |
| Coronation Concerto | for piano No 26 in D major | Mozart |
| The Creation | oratorio | Haydn |
| Death and the Maiden | Quartet No 14 in D minor | Schubert |
| Death and Transfiguration | tone poem Opus 28 | R Strauss |
| Density 21.5 | for (platinum) flute | Varèse |
| Devil's Trill | sonata | Tartini |
| Dissonant Quartet | No 19 in C Minor | Mozart |
| Dumky Trio | No 4 in E minor Opus 90 | Dvořák |
| Egmont Overture | Opus 84 | Beethoven |
| The '1812' Overture | Opus 49 | Tchaikovsky |
| Emperor Concerto | for piano No 5 in E flat major Opus 73 | Beethoven |
| Emperor Quartet | Opus 76 No 3 in C major | Haydn |
| Emperor Waltz | | Johann Strauss II |
| Eroica Symphony | No 3 in E flat major Opus 55 | Beethoven |
| Farewell Symphony | No 45 in F sharp minor | Haydn |
| Fingal's Cave Overture | | Mendelssohn |
| Finlandia | symphonic poem Opus 26 No 7 | Sibelius |
| Flight of the Bumble-Bee | from the opera The Tale of the Tsar Sultan | Rimsky-Korsakov |
| The '48' | Preludes and Fugues (The Well-tempered Clavier) | J S Bach |
| Four Seasons | four concertos presenting the seasons | Vivaldi |
| Für Elise/For Elise | No 25 in A Minor of 25 Bagatelles for piano Opus 33 | Beethoven |
| Goldberg Variations | for clavier | J S Bach |
| Golden Sonata | from Sonatas in Four Parts | Purcell |
| Great C Major Symphony | No 9 | Schubert |
| Hallelujah Chorus | from the oratorio The Messiah | Handel |
| Hammerklavier Sonata | No 29 in B flat Opus 106 | Beethoven |
| Ionisation | for percussion ensemble | Varèse |
| Iron Foundry | character piece for orchestra | Mossolov |
| Italian Concerto | for solo harsichord | J S Bach |
| Italian Symphony | No 4 in A major Opus 90 | Mendelssohn |
| Jesu Joy of Man's Desiring | aria from Cantata No 147 | J S Bach |
| Jupiter Symphony | No 41 in C Major | Mozart |
| Land of Hope and Glory | setting of the Pomp and Circumstance March Opus 39 No 1 | Elgar |
| The Lark Ascending | Romance for violin and orchestra | Vaughan Williams |
| Liberty Bell | march | Sousa |
| London Symphony | No 104 | Haydn |
| Mack the Knife | song from The Threepenny Opera | Weill |
| Minute Waltz | Opus 64 No 1 in D flat minor for piano | Chopin |
| Moonlight Sonata | No 14 in C sharp minor for piano | Beethoven |
| New World Symphony | (From The New World) No 9 in E minor opus 95 | Dvořák |
| Nessun' Dorma/None shall sleep | 1990 World Cup Song aria from Act 3 of Turandot opera | Puccini |
| Nutcracker Suite | from the ballet The Nutcracker | Tchaikovsky |

piano pieces show simplicity combined with an ability to portray mood and emotion. Among his compositions are four symphonies, a violin concerto, a piano concerto, sonatas, and song cycles, such as *Dichterliebe/Poet's Love* 1840. Mendelssohn championed many of his works.

**Shostakovich** Dmitry (Dmitriyevich) 1906–1975. Soviet composer. His music is tonal, expressive, and sometimes highly dramatic; it has not always been to official Soviet taste. He wrote 15 symphonies, chamber music, ballets, and operas, the latter including *Lady Macbeth of Mtsensk* 1934, which was suppressed as 'too divorced from the proletariat', but revived as *Katerina Izmaylova* 1963.

**Sibelius** Jean (Christian) 1865–1957. Finnish composer. His works include nationalistic symphonic poems such as *En Saga* 1893 and *Finlandia* 1900, a violin concerto 1904, and seven symphonies.

**Smetana** Bedřich 1824–1884. Czech composer, whose music has a distinct national character, as in for example the operas *The Bartered Bride* 1866, *Dalibor* 1868, and the symphonic suite *My Country* 1875–80. He conducted the National Theatre of Prague 1866–74.

**Stockhausen** Karlheinz 1928– . German composer of avant-garde music, who has continued to explore new musical sounds and compositional techniques since the 1950s. His major works include *Gesang der Jünglinge* 1956 and *Kontakte* 1960 (electronic music); *Klavierstücke I–XIV* 1952–85; *Momente* 1961–64, *Mikrophonie I* 1964, and *Sirius* 1977. Since 1977 all his works have been part of *Licht*, a cycle of seven musical ceremonies intended for performance on the evenings of a week. He has completed *Donnerstag* 1980, *Samstag* 1984, and *Montag* 1988.

**Strauss** Johann (Baptist) 1825–1899. Austrian conductor and composer, the son of Johann Strauss (1804–49). In 1872 he gave up conducting and wrote operettas, such as *Die Fledermaus* 1874, and numerous waltzes, such as *The Blue Danube* and *Tales from the Vienna Woods*, which gained him the title 'The Waltz King'.

**Strauss** Richard (Georg) 1864–1949. German composer and conductor. He followed the German Romantic tradition but had a strongly personal style, characterized by his bold, colourful orchestration. He first wrote tone poems such as *Don Juan* 1889, *Till Eulenspiegel's Merry Pranks* 1895, and *Also sprach Zarathustra* 1896. He then moved on to opera with *Salome* 1905, and *Elektra* 1909, both of which have elements of polytonality. He reverted to a more traditional style with *Der Rosenkavalier* 1911.

**Stravinsky** Igor 1882–1971. Russian composer, later of French (1934) and US (1945) nationality. He studied under Rimsky-Korsakov and wrote the music for the Diaghilev ballets *The Firebird* 1910, *Petrushka* 1911, and *The Rite of Spring* 1913 (controversial at the time for their unorthodox rhythms and harmonies). His versatile work ranges from his Neo-Classical ballet *Pulcinella* 1920, to the choral-orchestral *Sym-*

*phony of Psalms* 1930. He later made use of serial techniques in works such as the *Canticum Sacrum* 1955 and the ballet *Agon* 1953–57.

**Tchaikovsky** Pyotr Il'yich 1840–1893. Russian composer. His strong sense of melody, personal expression, and brilliant orchestration are clear throughout his many Romantic works, which include six symphonies, three piano concertos and a violin concerto, operas (for example, *Eugene Onegin* 1879), ballets (for example *The Nutcracker* 1892), orchestral fantasies (for example *Romeo and Juliet* 1870), and chamber and vocal music.

**Varèse** Edgard 1885–1965. French composer, who settled in New York 1916 where he founded the New Symphony Orchestra 1919 to further the cause of modern music. His work is experimental and often dissonant, combining electronic sounds with orchestral instruments, and includes *Hyperprism* 1923, *Intégrales* 1931, and *Poème Electronique* 1958.

**Verdi** Giuseppe (Fortunino Francesco) 1813–1901. Italian opera composer of the Romantic period who took his native operatic style to new heights of dramatic expression. In 1842 he wrote the opera *Nabucco*, followed by *Ernani* 1844 and *Rigoletto* 1851. Other works include *Il Trovatore* and *La Traviata* both 1853, *Aïda* 1871, and the masterpieces of his old age, *Otello* 1887 and *Falstaff* 1893. His *Requiem* 1874 commemorates Alessandro Manzoni.

**Vivaldi** Antonio (Lucio) 1678–1741. Italian Baroque composer, violinist, and conductor. He wrote 23 symphonies, 75 sonatas, over 400 concertos, including the *Four Seasons* (about 1725) for violin and orchestra, over 40 operas, and much sacred music. His work was largely neglected until the 1930s.

**Wagner** Richard 1813–1883. Greman opera composer. He revolutionized the 19th-century conception of opera, envisaging it as a wholly new art form in which musical, poetic, and scenic elements should be unified through such devices as the *leitmotif*. His operas include *Tannhäuser* 1845, *Lohengrin* 1850, and *Tristan und Isolde* 1865. In 1872 he founded the Festival Theatre in Bayreuth; his masterpiece *Der Ring des Nibelungen/The Ring of the Nibelung*, a sequence of four operas, was first performed there in 1876. His last work, *Parsifal*, was produced in 1882.

# POPULAR MUSIC

**Armstrong** Louis ('Satchmo') 1901–1971. US jazz cornet and trumpet player and singer, born in New Orleans. His Chicago recordings in the 1920s with the Hot Five and Hot Seven brought him recognition for his warm and pure trumpet tone, his skill at improvisation, and his quirky, gravelly voice. From the 1930s he also appeared in films.

**Beach Boys, the** US pop group formed 1961.

They began as exponents of vocal-harmony surf music with Chuck Berry guitar riffs (their hits include 'Surfin' USA' 1963 and 'Help Me, Rhonda' 1965) but the compositions, arrangements, and production by Brian Wilson (1942– ) became highly complex under the influence of psychedelic rock, peaking with 'Good Vibrations' 1966. Wilson spent most of the next 20 years in retirement but returned with a solo album 1988.

**Beatles, the** English pop group 1960–70. The members, all born in Liverpool, were John Lennon (1940–80, rhythm guitar, vocals), Paul McCartney (1942– , bass, vocals), George Harrison (1943– , lead guitar, vocals), and Ringo Starr (formerly Richard Starkey, 1940– , drums). Using songs written largely by Lennon and McCartney, the Beatles dominated rock music and pop culture in the 1960s.

**beat music** pop music that evolved in the UK in the early 1960s, known in its purest form as Mersey beat, and as British Invasion in the USA. The beat groups characteristically had a simple, guitar-dominated line-up, vocal harmonies, and catchy tunes. They included the Beatles (1960–70), the Hollies (1962– ), and the Zombies (1962–67).

**bebop** or **bop** hot jazz style, rhythmically complex, virtuosic, and highly improvisational, developed in New York 1945–55 by Charlie Parker, Dizzy Gillespie, Thelonius Monk, and other black musicians disaffected with dance bands and racism and determined to create music that would be too difficult for white people to play.

**Berry** Chuck (Charles Edward) 1926– . US rock-and-roll singer, prolific songwriter, and guitarist. His characteristic guitar riffs became staples of rock music, and his humorous storytelling lyrics were also emulated. He had a string of hits in the 1950s and 1960s beginning with 'Maybellene' 1955 and enjoyed a resurgence of popularity in the 1980s.

**bhangra** pop music evolved in the UK in the late 1970s from traditional Punjabi music, combining electronic instruments and ethnic drums.

**big-band jazz** swing music created in the late 1930s and 1940s by bands of 13 or more players, such as those of Duke Ellington and Benny Goodman. Big-band jazz relied on fixed arrangements rather than improvisation.

**blues** African-American music that originated in the rural South in the late 19th century, characterized by a 12-bar construction and often melancholy lyrics. Blues guitar and vocal styles have played a vital part in the development of jazz and pop music in general.

*1920s–1930s* The *rural* or *delta blues* was usually performed solo with guitar or harmonica, by artists such as Robert Johnson (1911–1938) and Bukka White (1906–1977), but the earliest recorded style, *classic blues*, by musicians such as W C Handy (1873–1958) and Bessie Smith (1894–1937), was sung with a small band.

*1940s–1950s Urban blues*, using electric amplification, emerged in the northern cities, chiefly Chicago. As exemplified by Howlin' Wolf (adopted name of Chester Burnett, 1910–1976), Muddy Waters (adopted name of McKinley Morganfield, 1915–1983), and John Lee Hooker (1917– ), urban blues became *rhythm and blues*.

*1960s* The jazz-influenced guitar style of B B King (1925– ) inspired many musicians of the **British blues boom**, including Eric Clapton (1945– ).

*1980s* The 'blues *noir*' of Robert Cray (1953– ) found a wide audience.

**boogie-woogie** jazz played on the piano, using a repeated motif for the left hand. It was common in the USA from around 1900 to the 1950s. Boogie-woogie players included Pinetop Smith (1904–1929), Meade 'Lux' Lewis (1905–1964), and Jimmy Yancey (1898–1951). Rock-and-roll pianists like Jerry Lee Lewis adopted the style.

**Bowie** David. Stage name of David Jones 1947– . British pop singer, songwriter, and actor. He became a glam-rock star with the release of the album *The Rise and Fall of Ziggy Stardust and the Spiders from Mars* 1972, and collaborated in the mid-1970s with the electronic virtuoso Brian Eno (1948– ) and Iggy Pop. He has also acted in plays and films, including Nicolas Roeg's *The Man Who Fell to Earth* 1976.

**Byrds, the** US pioneering folk-rock group 1964–73. Emulated for their 12-string guitar sound, as on the hits 'Mr Tambourine Man' (a 1965 version of Bob Dylan's song) and 'Eight Miles High' 1966, they moved towards country rock in the late 1960s.

**Cajun** member of a French-speaking community of Louisiana, USA, descended from French-Canadians who, in the 18th century, were driven there from Nova Scotia (then known as Acadia, from which the name Cajun comes). *Cajun music* has a lively rhythm and features steel guitar, fiddle, and accordion.

**calypso** West Indian satirical ballad with a syncopated beat. Calypso is a traditional song form of Trinidad, a feature of its annual carnival, with roots in W African praise singing. It was first popularized in the USA by Harry Belafonte (1927– ) in 1956. Mighty Sparrow (1935– ) is Trinidad's best-known calypso singer.

**Charles** Ray 1930– . US singer, songwriter, and pianist, whose first hits were 'I've Got A Woman' 1955, 'What'd I Say' 1959, and 'Georgia on My Mind' 1960. He has recorded gospel, blues, rock, soul, country, and rhythm and blues.

**Clapton** Eric 1945– . English blues and rock guitarist, singer, and composer, member of the Yardbirds 1963–65 and Cream 1966–68. Originally a blues purist, then one of the pioneers of heavy rock with Cream and on the album *Layla* 1970 (released under the name of Derek and the Dominos), he later adopted a more laid-back style in his solo career, as on *Journeyman* 1989.

**Coleman** Ornette 1930– . US alto saxophonist and jazz composer. In the late 1950s he rejected the established structural principles of jazz for free avant-garde improvisation. He has worked with small and large groups, ethnic musicians of different traditions, and symphony orchestras.

**Coltrane** John (William) 1926–1967. US jazz saxophonist who first came to prominence in 1955 with the Miles Davis quintet, later playing with Thelonious Monk 1957. He was a powerful and individual artist, whose performances featured much experimentation. His 1960s quartet was highly regarded for its innovations in melody and harmony.

**Costello** Elvis. Stage name of Declan McManus 1954– . English rock singer, songwriter, and guitarist, whose intricate yet impassioned lyrics made him one of Britain's foremost songwriters. The great stylistic range of his work was evident from his 1977 debut *My Aim Is True*. His backing group 1978–86 was the Attractions.

**country and western** or **country music** popular music of the white US South and West; it evolved from the folk music of the English, Irish, and Scottish settlers and has a strong blues influence. Characteristic instruments are slide guitar, mandolin, and fiddle. Lyrics typically extol family values and traditional sex roles, and often have a strong narrative element. Country music encompasses a variety of regional styles, and ranges from mournful ballads to fast and intricate dance music.

*1920s* Jimmie Rodgers (1897–1933) wrote a series of 'Blue Yodel' songs that made him the first country-music recording star.

*1930s* Nashville, Tennessee, became a centre for the country-music industry, with the Grand Ole Opry a showcase for performers. The Carter Family arranged and recorded hundreds of traditional songs. Hollywood invented the singing cowboy.

*1940s* Hank Williams (1923–1953) emerged as the most significant singer and songwriter; *western swing* spread from Texas.

*1950s* The *honky-tonk* sound; Kentucky *bluegrass*; ballad singers included Jim Reeves (1923–1964) and Patsy Cline (1932–1963).

*1960s* Songs of the Bakersfield, California, school, dominated by Buck Owens (1929– ) and Merle Haggard (1937– ), contrasted with lush Nashville productions of singers such as George Jones (1931– ) and Tammy Wynette (1942– ).

*1970s* Dolly Parton (1946– ) and Emmylou Harris (1947– ); the Austin, Texas, *outlaws* Willie Nelson (1933– ) and Waylon Jennings (1937– ); *country rock* pioneered by Gram Parsons (1946–1973).

*1980s* Neotraditionalist *new country* represented by Randy Travis (1963– ), Dwight Yoakam (1957– ), and Nanci Griffith (1954– ).

**Crosby** Bing (Harry Lillis) 1904–1977. US film actor and singer who achieved world success with his distinctive style of crooning in such songs as 'Pennies from Heaven' 1936 (featured in a film of the same name) and 'White Christmas' 1942. He won an acting Oscar for *Going My*

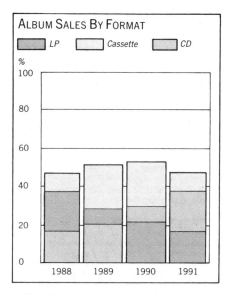

**ALBUM SALES BY FORMAT**

LP    Cassette    CD

*Way* 1944, and made a series of film comedies with Dorothy Lamour and Bob Hope, the last being *Road to Hong Kong* 1962.

**Davis** Miles (Dewey, Jr) 1926– . US jazz trumpeter, composer, and bandleader. He recorded bebop with Charlie Parker 1945, pioneered cool jazz in the 1950s and jazz-rock fusion beginning in the late 1960s. His significant albums include *Birth of the Cool* 1957 (recorded 1949 and 1950), *Sketches of Spain* 1959, and *Bitches' Brew* 1970.

**Dixieland jazz** jazz style that originated in New Orleans, USA, in the early 20th century, dominated by cornet, trombone, and clarinet. The trumpeter Louis Armstrong emerged from this style. The *trad jazz* movement in the UK in the 1940s–50s was a Dixieland revival.

**Doors, the** US psychedelic rock group formed 1965 in Los Angeles by Jim Morrison (1943–1971, vocals), Ray Manzarek (1935– , keyboards), Robby Krieger (1946– , guitar), and John Densmore (1944– , drums). Their first hit was 'Light My Fire' from their debut album *The Doors* 1967. They were noted for Morrison's poetic lyrics and flamboyant performance.

**Dylan** Bob. Adopted name of Robert Allen Zimmerman 1941– . US singer and songwriter whose increasingly obscure lyrics provided catchphrases for a generation and influenced innumerable songwriters. He began in the folk-music tradition but from 1965 worked in an individualistic rock style, as on the albums *Highway 61 Revisited* 1965 and *Blonde on Blonde* 1966.

**Ellington** Duke (Edward Kennedy) 1899–1974. US pianist who had an outstanding career as a composer and arranger of jazz. He wrote numerous pieces for his own jazz orchestra, accentuating the strengths of individual virtuoso instrumentalists, and became one of the leading figures in jazz over a 55-year

## IS YOUR CD OBSOLETE?

The history of home sound reproduction progressed, for most of the century, in an orderly fashion: from wax cylinders to vinyl records in the earliest days, from 78 rpm to 33⅓ during the early 1950s, from mono to stereo gradually in the 1960s. Tape cassettes from 1963 did not drive out the vinyl record but extended the market with the proliferation of car and personal stereos. The introduction of compact discs in 1982 necessitated another considerable outlay on equipment by the consumer, and started a debate about the respective merits of analogue and digital sound that still continues. Now, hot on the heels of CD, we are confronted with the initials DAT and DCC.

**Can we keep up? Should we keep up?**
*Digital audio tape* (DAT) cassettes are about half the size of standard cassettes and can carry two hours of sound on each side. Like CDs, they are digitally recorded: the sound signal is sampled by a microchip at the rate of 48,000 times per second, magnetically stored, and reproduced in short pulses of current. DAT machines are constructed like video cassette recorders (though they use metal audio tape), with a movable playback head, the tape winding in a spiral around a rotating drum. The tape can also carry additional information; for example, you can programme it to skip a particular track and repeat another. DAT players/recorders were developed in 1987 but not marketed in the UK until 1989, and even then there was no prerecorded product to go with them. The music business has been hostile to DAT because of fears that bootleggers would take illegal advantage of its ability to make perfect copies of CDs; even ordinary home taping still frightens the industry, although its detrimental effect on record sales has not been proved. (Recordable CDs are not commercially available.) A system has now been internationally agreed whereby it is not possible to make more than one copy of any CD or prerecorded DAT. While waiting for the prerecorded cassettes, though, DAT has found a niche where its manufacturers did not foresee it: in recording studios, where they have proved ideal for making master tapes.

DCC stands for *digital compact cassette*. It is roughly the same size as an ordinary cassette and, though you cannot play it on a normal tape recorder, you *can* play your old tapes on a DCC machine. Known as 'backwards compatibility', it is a consequence of the DCC player having a stationary playback and recording head similar to that in standard tape decks. This makes DCC machines cheaper than DAT to manufacture and the tapes (DCC uses chrome video tape) are also more easily mass-produced, because they can be copied at 64 times the playing speed, whereas DAT has to be copied in real time. The playing time for a DCC is 90 minutes, and like DAT they are copy-protected and can be individually programmed for playing order. The cassette boxes are built more ruggedly than standard ones, and the tape is less sensitive to heat and moisture, which will give DCC an advantage for use in cars. An extra feature of some DCC decks is a liquid-crystal digital-display screen, which can show track titles and any other information encoded on the tape. DCC machines are expected to be in the shops in 1992, with some 500 prerecorded tapes to go with them.

When LPs were first introduced in the USA 1948, EMI took four years to release them in the UK because it was felt that they would never catch on. Now we may be facing the death of the vinyl record, or at least its relegation to specialist shops, as has already happened in Japan. In 1989 CDs overtook vinyl in sales in the UK (41.7 million to 37.9 million) and in 1990 50 million CDs were sold, compared to 24 million vinyl LPs, but also 74 million cassettes. Worldwide cassettes are the biggest sellers: in 1990 more than 1 billion prerecorded audiocassettes were sold, plus another 1.5 billion blank tapes, and 200 million tape players compared to 20 million CD players.

The news in 1991 of the impending arrival of Digalog, a way of mass-producing conventional cassettes to give them a far clearer sound than previously possible, may therefore give pause to those who are torn between DAT and DCC.

---

span. Some of his most popular compositions include 'Mood Indigo', 'Sophisticated Lady', 'Solitude', and 'Black and Tan Fantasy'. He was one of the founders of big-band jazz.

**Fitzgerald** Ella 1918– . US jazz singer, recognized as one of the finest, most lyrical voices in jazz, both in solo work and with big bands. She is celebrated for her smooth interpretations of Gershwin and Cole Porter songs.

**funk** dance music of black US origin, relying on heavy percussion in polyrhythmic patterns. Leading exponents include James Brown (1928–  ) and George Clinton (1940–  ).

**Gershwin** George 1898–1937. US composer who wrote both 'serious' music, such as the tone poem *Rhapsody in Blue* 1924 and *An American in Paris* 1928, and popular musicals and songs, many with lyrics by his brother *Ira Gershwin*

(1896–1983), including 'I Got Rhythm', ''S Wonderful', and 'Embraceable You'. His opera *Porgy and Bess*, an ambitious work that incorporated jazz rhythms and popular song styles in an operatic format, was his masterpiece.

**Gillespie** Dizzy (John Birks) 1917–  . US jazz trumpeter who, with Charlie Parker, was the chief creator and exponent of the bebop style.

**Goodman** Benny (Benjamin David) 1909–1986. US clarinetist, nicknamed the 'King of Swing' for the new jazz idiom he introduced with arranger Fletcher Henderson (1897–1952). Leader of his own swing band 1934–40, and again later, he is associated with numbers such as 'Blue Skies' and 'Let's Dance'.

**gospel music** vocal music developed in the 1920s in the black Baptist churches of the US South from spirituals, which were 18th- and 19th-century hymns joined to the old African pentatonic (five-note) scale. Outstanding among the early gospel singers was Mahalia Jackson (1911–1972), but from the 1930s to the mid-1950s male harmony groups predominated, among them the Dixie Hummingbirds, the Swan Silvertones, and the Five Blind Boys of Mississippi.

**Guthrie** Woody (Woodrow Wilson) 1912–1967. US folk singer and songwriter whose left-wing protest songs, 'dustbowl ballads', and 'talking blues' influenced, among others, Bob Dylan; they include 'Deportees', 'Hard Travelin'', and 'This Land Is Your Land'.

**Hammer, MC** Stage name of Stanley Kirk Burrell 1963– . US rap vocalist and songwriter. His pop-oriented rap style and exuberant dancing gave him a wide appeal, especially in the video-based market, and his second LP, *Please Hammer Don't Hurt 'Em* 1990, sold 13 million copies in one year.

**hardcore** strident rock music that evolved from punk. It entails playing (guitars and drums) as fast as possible with loud, angry shouting. Tracks lasting only five seconds consisting of a loud 'Aaarrgh!' encapsulate the form. *Thrash metal* and *death metal* are very similar but developed from heavy metal. *Artcore* uses noise for artistic as well as shock effect.

**Hawkins** Coleman (Randolph) 1904–1969. US virtuoso tenor saxophonist. He was, until 1934, a soloist in the swing band led by Fletcher Henderson (1898–1952), and was an influential figure in bringing the jazz saxophone to prominence as a solo instrument.

**heavy metal** a style of rock characterized by loudness, sex-and-violence imagery, and guitar solos. Heavy metal developed out of the hard rock of the late 1960s and early 1970s, was performed by such groups as Led Zeppelin and Deep Purple, and enjoyed a resurgence in the late 1980s. Bands include Van Halen (formed 1974), Def Leppard (formed 1977), and Guns 'n' Roses (formed 1987).

**Hendrix** Jimi (James Marshall) 1942–1970. US rock guitarist, songwriter, and singer, legendary for his virtuoso experimental technique and flamboyance. *Are You Experienced?* 1967 was his first album. He greatly expanded the vocabulary of the electric guitar and influenced both rock and jazz musicians.

**hip-hop** popular music originating in New York in the early 1980s. It uses scratching (a percussive effect obtained by manually rotating a vinyl record) and heavily accented electronic drums behind a rap vocal. The term 'hip-hop' also comprises break dancing and graffiti.

**Holiday** Billie. Stage name of Eleanora Gough McKay 1915–1959. US jazz singer, also known as 'Lady Day'. She made her debut in Harlem clubs and became known for her emotionally charged delivery and idiosyncratic phrasing; she brought a blues feel to performances with swing bands. Songs she made her own include 'Strange Fruit' and 'I Cover the Waterfront'.

**Holly** Buddy. Stage name of Charles Hardin Holley 1936–1959. US rock-and-roll singer,

guitarist, and songwriter, born in Lubbock, Texas. Holly had a distinctive, hiccuping vocal style and was an early experimenter with recording techniques. Many of his hits with his band, the Crickets, such as 'That'll Be the Day' 1957, 'Peggy Sue' 1957, and 'Maybe Baby' 1958, have become classics. He died in a plane crash.

**house music** dance music of the 1980s originating in the inner-city clubs of Chicago, USA, combining funk with European high-tech pop, and using dub, digital sampling, and cross-fading. *Acid house* has minimal vocals and melody, instead surrounding the mechanically emphasized 4/4 beat with found noises, stripped-down synthesizer riffs, and a wandering bass line. Other variants include *hip-house*, with rap elements, and *acid jazz*.

**indie** or *independent* in music, a record label that is neither owned nor distributed by one of the large conglomerates ('majors') that dominate the industry. Without a corporate bureaucratic structure, the independent labels are often quicker to respond to new trends and more idealistic in their aims. What has become loosely known as *indie music* therefore tends to be experimental, amateurish, or at the cutting edge of street fashion.

**Jackson** Michael 1958– . US rock singer and songwriter whose videos and live performances are meticulously choreographed. He began his career as the youngest member of the *Jackson Five*, but soon surpassed his brothers in popularity as a solo performer. His first solo hit was 'Got to Be There' 1971; his worldwide popularity peaked with the albums *Thriller* 1982 (which sold 41 million copies, a world record) and *Bad* 1987.

**jazz** polyphonic, syncopated music characterized by solo virtuosic improvisation, which developed in the USA at the turn of the 20th century. It had its roots in black American and other popular music and evolved various distinct vocal and instrumental forms.

*1880–1900* Originated chiefly in New Orleans from ragtime.

*1920s* During Prohibition, the centre of jazz moved to Chicago (Louis Armstrong, Bix Beiderbecke) and St Louis. By the end of the decade the focus had shifted to New York City (Art Tatum, Fletcher Henderson).

*1930s* The *swing* bands used call-and-response arrangements with improvised solos (Paul Whiteman, Benny Goodman).

*1940s* swing grew into the *big band* era with jazz composed as well as arranged (Glenn Miller, Duke Ellington); rise of *West Coast* jazz (Stan Kenton) and rhythmically complex, highly improvisational *bebop* (Charlie Parker, Dizzy Gillespie, Thelonius Monk).

*1950s* Jazz had ceased to be dance music; *cool jazz* (Stan Getz, Miles Davis, Lionel Hampton, Modern Jazz Quartet) developed in reaction to the insistent, 'hot' bebop and *hard bop*.

*1960s* *Free-form* or *free jazz* (Ornette Coleman, John Coltrane).

***1970s Jazz rock*** (US group Weather Report, formed 1970; British guitarist John McLaughlin, 1942– ); jazz funk (US saxophonist Grover Washington Jr, 1943– ); more eclectic free jazz (US pianist Keith Jarrett, 1945– ).

***1980s*** Resurgence of tradition (US trumpeter Wynton Marsalis, 1962– ; British saxophonist Courtney Pine, 1965– ) and avant-garde (US chamber-music Kronos Quartet, formed 1978; anarchic UK group Loose Tubes, formed 1983).

**karaoke** amateur singing in public to prerecorded backing tapes. Karaoke originated in Japan and spread to other parts of the world in the 1980s. In Japan, karaoke machines—jukeboxes of backing tracks to well-known popular songs, usually with a microphone attached—have been installed not only in bars but also in taxis.

**Lennon** John 1940–1980. UK rock singer, songwriter, and guitarist. While still a member of the Beatles, he collaborated intermittently with his wife ***Yoko Ono*** (1933– ). 'Give Peace a Chance', a hit 1969, became an anthem of the peace movement. His solo work alternated between the confessional and the political, as on ***Imagine*** 1971. He was shot dead by a fan.

**Madonna** stage name of Madonna Louise Ciccone 1958– . US pop singer and actress who presents herself on stage and in videos with exaggerated sexuality and Catholic trappings. Her first hit was 'Like a Virgin' 1984; others include 'Material Girl' 1985 and 'Like a Prayer' 1989. Her films include ***Desperately Seeking Susan*** 1985 and ***Dick Tracy*** 1990.

**Marley** Bob (Robert Nesta) 1945–1981. Jamaican reggae singer, a Rastafarian whose songs, many of which were topical and political, popularized reggae worldwide in the 1970s. One of his greatest hit songs is 'No Woman No Cry'; his albums include ***Natty Dread*** 1975 and ***Exodus*** 1977.

**Miller** Glenn 1904–1944. US trombonist and, as bandleader, exponent of the big-band swing sound from 1938. He composed his signature tune 'Moonlight Serenade' (a hit 1939). Miller became leader of the US Army Air Force Band in Europe 1942, made broadcasts to troops throughout the world during World War II, and disappeared without trace on a flight between England and France.

## TOP 10 ALBUMS—1990

| | | |
|---|---|---|
| 1 | *But Seriously* | Phil Collins |
| 2 | *The Immaculate Collection* | Madonna |
| 3 | *In Concert* | Carreras/Domingo/ Pavarotti |
| 4 | *Very Best Of* | Elton John |
| 5 | *Soul Provider* | Michael Bolton |
| 6 | *Essential Pavarotti* | Luciano Pavarotti |
| 7 | *Only Yesterday* | Carpenters |
| 8 | *Now 18* | Various |
| 9 | *Sleeping With The Past* | Elton John |
| 10 | *Serious Hits...Live* | Phil Collins |

## TOP 10 CD ALBUMS OF ALL TIME

| | | |
|---|---|---|
| 1 | *But Seriously* | Phil Collins |
| 2 | *Very Best Of* | Elton John |
| 3 | *The Immaculate Collection* | Madonna |
| 4 | *Serious Hits...Live* | Phil Collins |
| 5 | *A New Flame* | Simply Red |
| 6 | *Foreign Affair* | Tina Turner |
| 7 | *The Road To Hell* | Chris Rea |
| 8 | *Listen Without Prejudice* | George Michael |
| 9 | *Money For Nothing* | Dire Straits |
| 10 | *Greatest Hits* | Eurythmics |

**Mingus** Charles 1922–1979. US jazz bassist and composer. His experimentation with atonality and dissonant effects opened the way for the new style of free collective jazz improvisation of the 1960s.

**Monk** Thelonious (Sphere) 1917–1982. US jazz pianist and composer who took part in the development of bebop. He had a highly idiosyncratic style, but numbers such as 'Round Midnight' and 'Blue Monk' have become standards.

**Morrison** Van (George Ivan) 1945– . Northern Irish singer and songwriter whose jazz-inflected Celtic soul style was already in evidence on ***Astral Weeks*** 1968 and has been highly influential. Among other albums are ***Tupelo Honey*** 1971, ***Veedon Fleece*** 1974, and ***Avalon Sunset*** 1989.

**New Age** instrumental or ambient music of the 1980s, often semi-acoustic or electronic; less insistent than rock.

**New Wave** in pop music, a style that evolved parallel to punk in the second half of the 1970s. It shared the urban aggressive spirit of punk but was musically and lyrically more sophisticated; examples are the early work of Elvis Costello and Talking Heads.

**Parker** Charlie (Charles Christopher 'Bird', 'Yardbird') 1920–1955. US alto saxophonist and jazz composer, associated with the trumpeter Dizzy Gillespie in developing the bebop style. His mastery of improvisation inspired performers on all jazz instruments.

**pop music** short for ***popular music***, umbrella term for contemporary music not classifiable as jazz or classical. Pop became distinct from folk music with the advent of sound-recording techniques, and has incorporated blues, country and western, and music-hall elements; electronic amplification and other technological innovations have played a large part in the creation of new styles. The traditional format is a song of roughly three minutes with verse, chorus, and middle eight bars.

***1910s*** The singer Al Jolson was one of the first recording stars. Ragtime was still popular.

***1920s*** In the USA Paul Whiteman and his orchestra played danceable jazz, the country singer Jimmie Rodgers (1897–1933) reached a new record-buying public, the blues was burgeoning; in the UK popular singers included Al Bowlly (1899–1941, born in Mozambique).

**1930s** Crooner Bing Crosby and vocal groups such as the Andrews Sisters were the alternatives to swing bands.

**1940s** *rhythm and blues* evolved in the USA while Frank Sinatra was a teen idol and Glenn Miller played dance music; the UK preferred singers such as Vera Lynn.

**1950s** In the USA *doo-wop* (a vocal group style based on *a cappella* street-corner singing) preceded *rockabilly* and the rise of *rock and roll* (Elvis Presley, Chuck Berry). British pop records were often cover versions of US originals.

**1960s** The Beatles and the *Mersey beat* transcended UK borders, followed by the Rolling Stones, *hard rock* (the Who, Led Zeppelin), *art rock* (Genesis, Yes). In the USA *surf music* (group harmony vocals or fast, loud, guitar-based instrumentals) preceded *Motown*, *folk rock* (the Byrds, Bob Dylan), and *blues rock* (Jimi Hendrix, Janis Joplin). *Psychedelic rock* evolved from 1966 on both sides of the Atlantic (the Doors, Pink Floyd, Jefferson Airplane).

**1970s** The first half of the decade produced *glitter rock* (David Bowie), *heavy metal*, and *disco* (dance music with a very emphatic, mechanical beat); in the UK also *pub rock* (a return to basics, focusing on live performance); *reggae* spread from Jamaica. From 1976 *punk* was ascendant; the US term *New Wave* encompassed bands not entirely within the punk idiom (Talking Heads, Elvis Costello).

**1980s** Punk continued as *hardcore* or mutated into *gothic*; dance music developed regional US variants: *hip-hop* (New York), *go-go* (Washington DC), and *house* (Chicago). Live audiences grew, leading to anthemic *stadium rock* (U2, Bruce Springsteen) and increasingly elaborate stage performances (Michael Jackson, Prince, Madonna). An interest in *world music* sparked new fusions.

**1990s** *Rap* and heavy metal predominated in the USA at the start of the decade; on the UK *indie* scene, dance music (Happy Mondays, Inspiral Carpets) and a new wave of guitar groups (Ride, Lush) drew on the psychedelic era.

**Porter** Cole (Albert) 1892–1964. US composer and lyricist, mainly of musical comedies. His witty, sophisticated songs like 'Let's Do It' 1928, 'I Get a Kick Out of You' 1934, and 'Don't Fence Me In' 1944 have been widely recorded and admired. His shows, many of which were made into films, include *The Gay Divorcee* 1932 and *Kiss Me Kate* 1948.

**Presley** Elvis (Aaron) 1935–1977. US singer and guitarist, the most influential performer of the rock-and-roll era. With his recordings for Sun Records in Memphis, Tennessee, 1954–55 and early hits such as 'Heartbreak Hotel' 1956, 'Hound Dog' 1956, and 'Love Me Tender' 1956, he created an individual vocal style, influenced by Southern blues, gospel music, country music, and rhythm and blues.

**Prince** stage name of Prince Rogers Nelson 1960– . US pop musician who composes, arranges, and produces his own records and often plays all the instruments. His albums, including *1999* 1982 and *Purple Rain* 1984, contain elements of rock, funk, and jazz.

**psychedelic rock** or *acid rock* pop music that usually involves advanced electronic equipment for both light and sound. The free-form improvisations and light shows that appeared about 1966, attempting to suggest or improve on mind-altering drug experiences, had by the 1980s evolved into stadium performances with lasers and other special effects. Bands included the Doors, Pink Floyd, and Jefferson Airplane.

**punk** movement of disaffected youth of the late 1970s, manifesting itself in fashions and music designed to shock or intimidate. *Punk rock* began in the UK and stressed aggressive performance within a three-chord, three-minute format, as exemplified by the Sex Pistols.

**ragtime** syncopated music ('ragged time') in 2/4 rhythm, usually played on piano. It developed in the USA among black musicians in the late 19th century; it was influenced by folk tradition, minstrel shows, and marching bands, and later was incorporated into jazz. Scott Joplin was a leading writer of ragtime pieces, called 'rags'.

**raï** Algerian pop music developed in the 1970s from the Bedouin song form *melhoun*, using synthesizers and electronic drums.

**rap music** rapid, rhythmic chant over a prerecorded repetitive backing track. Rap emerged in New York 1979 as part of the hip-hop culture, although the macho, swaggering lyrics that initially predominated have roots in ritual boasts and insults. Different styles were flourishing by the 1990s: jazz rap, funk rap, reggae rap, and so on.

**Reed** Lou 1942– . US rock singer and songwriter, member (1965–70) of the New York avant-garde group *the Velvet Underground*, perhaps the most influential band of the period. His solo work deals largely with urban alienation and angst, and includes the albums *Berlin* 1973, *Street Hassle* 1978, and *New York* 1989.

**reggae** predominant form of West Indian popular music of the 1970s and 1980s, characterized by a heavily accented offbeat and a thick bass line. The lyrics often refer to Rastafarianism. Musicians include Bob Marley, Lee 'Scratch' Perry (1940– , performer and producer), and the group Black Uhuru (1974– ). Reggae is also played in the UK, South Africa, and elsewhere.

## Top 10 Singles Artists of 1990

| | |
|---|---|
| 1 | New Kids on the Block |
| 2 | Righteous Brothers |
| 3 | Madonna |
| 4 | SNAP |
| 5 | Sinead O'Connor |
| 6 | Adamski |
| 7 | Elton John |
| 8 | Kylie Minogue |
| 9 | Beats International |
| 10 | Vanilla Ice |

## THE TEN HIGHEST SELLING LPS OF ALL TIME

| | | |
|---|---|---|
| 1 | Dire Straits | *Brothers in Arms* |
| 2 | The Beatles | *Sergeant Pepper's Lonely Hearts Club Band* |
| 3 | Michael Jackson | *Thriller* |
| 4 | Abba | *Greatest Hits* |
| 5 | Simon & Garfunkel | *Bridge Over Troubled Water* |
| 6 | Fleetwood Mac | *Rumours* |
| 7 | Pink Floyd | *Dark Side of the Moon* |
| 8 | Queen | *Greatest Hits* |
| 9 | Michael Jackson | *Bad* |
| 10 | Phil Collins | *No Jacket Required* |

**remix** in pop music, the studio practice of reassembling a recording from all or some of its individual components, often with the addition of new elements. Issuing a recording in several different remixes ensures additional sales to collectors and increases airplay; remixes can be geared specifically to radio, dance clubs, and so on. The practice accompanied the rise of the 12-inch single in the 1980s. Some record producers specialize in remixing. In 1987 Madonna became the first artist in the USA to release an album consisting entirely of remixes (*You Can Dance*).

**rhythm and blues** (R & B) US popular music of the 1940s–60s, which drew on swing and jump-jazz rhythms and blues vocals and was a progenitor of rock and roll. It diversified into soul, funk, and other styles. R & B artists include Bo Diddley (1928–  ), Jackie Wilson (1934–84), and Etta James (*c.* 1938–  ).

**Robinson** Smokey (William) 1940–  . US singer, songwriter, and record producer, associated with Motown records from its conception. He was lead singer of the Miracles 1957–72 (hits include 'Shop Around' 1961, 'The Tears of a Clown' 1970) and his solo hits include 'Cruisin'' 1979 and 'Being With You' 1981. His light tenor voice and wordplay characterize his work.

**rock and roll** pop music born of a fusion of rhythm and blues and country and western and based on electric guitar and drums. In the mid-1950s, with the advent of Elvis Presley, it became the heartbeat of teenage rebellion in the West and also had considerable impact on other parts of the world. It found perhaps its purest form in late-1950s *rockabilly*; the blanket term 'rock' later came to comprise a multitude of styles.

**Rolling Stones, the** British band formed 1962, once notorious as the 'bad boys' of rock. Original members were Mick Jagger (1943–  ), Keith Richards (1943–  ), Brian Jones (1942–1969), Bill Wyman (1936–  ), Charlie Watts (1941–  ), and the pianist Ian Stewart (1938–1985). A rock-and-roll institution, the Rolling Stones were still performing and recording in the 1990s.

**salsa** Latin big-band dance music popularized by Puerto Ricans in New York City in the 1980s and by, among others, the Panamanian singer Rubén Blades (1948–  ).

**Simon** Paul 1942–  . US pop singer and songwriter. In a folk-rock duo with Art Garfunkel (1942–  ), he had such hits as 'Mrs Robinson' 1968 and 'Bridge Over Troubled Water' 1970. Simon's solo work includes the critically acclaimed album *Graceland* 1986, for which he drew on Cajun and African music.

**Sinatra** Frank (Francis Albert) 1915–  . US singer and film actor. Celebrated for his phrasing and emotion, especially on love ballads, he is particularly associated with the song 'My Way'. His films from 1941 include *From Here to Eternity* 1953 (Academy Award) and *Guys and Dolls* 1955.

**Smiths, the** English four-piece rock group (1982–87) from Manchester. Their songs, with lyrics by singer Morrissey (1959–  ) and tunes by guitarist Johnny Marr (1964–  ), drew on diverse sources such as rockabilly, Mersey beat, and the Byrds, with confessional humour and images of urban desolation. They were Britain's main cult band in the 1980s.

**soca** Latin Caribbean music, a mixture of *sou*l and *ca*lypso.

**Sondheim** Stephen (Joshua) 1930–  . US composer and lyricist. He wrote the lyrics of Leonard Bernstein's *West Side Story* 1957 and composed witty and sophisticated musicals, including *A Little Night Music* 1973, *Pacific Overtures* 1976, *Sweeney Todd* 1979, *Into the Woods* 1987, and *Sunday in the Park with George* 1989.

**soul music** emotionally intense style of rhythm and blues sung by, among others, Sam Cooke (1931–1964), Aretha Franklin (1942–  ), and Al Green (1946–  ). A synthesis of blues, gospel music, and jazz, it emerged in the 1950s. By the late 1980s, it had become associated with bland bedroom ballads.

**Spector** Phil 1940–  . US record producer,

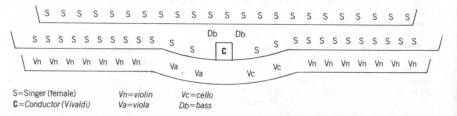

S=Singer (female)    *Vn*=violin    *Vc*=cello
**C**=Conductor (Vivaldi)    *Va*=viola    *Db*=bass

Orchestra: Vivaldi's arrangement of a female choir and string orchestra. The three tiers are approximately 5 ft/1.5m, 10 ft/3m, 15 ft/4.5m above floor level. The conductor stands on the second tier.

known for the 'wall of sound', created using a large orchestra, distinguishing his work in the early 1960s with vocal groups such as the Crystals and the Ronettes. He withdrew into semi-retirement in 1966 but his influence can still be heard.

**Springsteen** Bruce 1949– . US rock singer, songwriter, and guitarist, born in New Jersey. His music combines melodies in traditional rock idiom and reflective lyrics about working-class life on albums such as *Born to Run* 1975 and *Born in the USA* 1984.

**steel band** musical ensemble common in the West Indies, consisting mostly of percussion instruments made from oil drums that give a sweet, metallic ringing tone.

**Supremes, the** US vocal group, pioneers of the Motown sound, formed 1959 in Detroit. Beginning in 1962, the group was a trio comprising, initially, Diana Ross (1944– ), Mary Wilson (1944– ), and Florence Ballard (1943–1976). The most successful female group of the 1960s, they had a string of pop hits beginning with 'Where Did Our Love Go?' 1964 and 'Baby Love' 1964. Diana Ross left to pursue a solo career 1969.

**swing music** jazz style popular in the 1930s–40s. A big-band sound with a simple harmonic base of varying tempo from the rhythm section (percussion, guitar, piano), harmonic brass and woodwind sections (sometimes strings), and superimposed solo melodic line from, for example, trumpet, clarinet, or saxophone. Exponents included Benny Goodman, Duke Ellington, and Glenn Miller, who introduced jazz to a mass white audience.

**syncopation** the deliberate upsetting of rhythm by shifting the accent to a beat that is normally unaccented.

**U2** Irish rock group formed 1977 by singer Bono Vox (born Paul Hewson, 1960– ), guitarist Dave 'The Edge' Evans (1961– ), bassist Adam Clayton (1960– ), and drummer Larry Mullen (1961– ). Committed Christians, they play socially concerned rock, and their albums include *The Unforgettable Fire* 1984, *The Joshua Tree* 1987, and the soundtrack from their documentary film *Rattle and Hum* 1988.

**world music** or **roots music** any music whose regional character has not been lost in the melting pot of the pop industry. Examples are W African *mbalax*, E African *soukous*, S African *mbaqanga*, French Antillean *zouk*, Javanese gamelan, Latin American salsa and lambada, Cajun music, European folk music, and rural blues, as well as combinations of these (flamenco guitar and kora; dub polka).

**Young** Neil 1945– . Canadian rock guitarist, singer, and songwriter, in the USA from 1966. His high, plaintive voice and loud, abrasive guitar make his work instantly recognizable despite abrupt changes of style throughout his career. *Rust Never Sleeps* 1979 and *Ragged Glory* 1990 (both with the group Crazy Horse) are among his best work.

**zydeco** dance music originating in Louisiana,

USA, similar to Cajun but more heavily influenced by blues and West Indian music.

## MUSICAL TERMS

**acoustics** in general, the experimental and theoretical science of sound and its transmission; in particular, that branch of the science that has to do with the phenomena of sound in a particular space such as a room or theatre.

**alto** (1) low-register female voice, also called *contralto*; (2) high adult male voice, also known as counter tenor; (3) (French) viola.

**anthem** a short, usually elaborate, religious choral composition, sometimes accompanied by the organ; also a song of loyalty and devotion.

**aria** solo vocal piece in an opera or oratorio, often in three sections, the third repeating the first after a contrasting central section.

**atonality** music in which there is an apparent absence of key; often associated with an expressionist style.

**bagatelle** a short character piece, often for piano.

**bar** a modular unit of rhythm, shown in notation by vertical 'barring' of the musical continuum into sections of usually constant duration and rhythmic content. The alternative term is 'measure'.

**baritone** lower-range male voice between bass and tenor.

**bass** (1) lowest range of male voice; (2) lower regions of musical pitch; (3) a double bass.

**bel canto** an 18th-century Italian style of singing with emphasis on perfect technique and beautiful tone. The style reached its peak in the operas of Rossini, Donizetti, and Bellini.

**cadence** termination of a musical line or phrase, expressed rhythmically and harmonically.

**cadenza** an unaccompanied bravura passage (requiring elaborate, virtuoso execution) in the style of an improvisation for the soloist during a concerto.

**canon** an echo form for two or more parts repeating and following a leading melody at regular time intervals to achieve a harmonious effect. It is often found in classical music, for example Vivaldi and J S Bach.

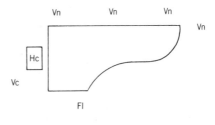

Hc=harpsichord    Fl=flute
Vc=cello          Vn=violin

*Orchestra: Frederick the Great gives a concert, c. 1760. He plays solo flute. All players face inward.*

## Some Musical Expressions

| | | | |
|---|---|---|---|
| accelerando | gradually faster | presto, prestissimo | at speed, at high speed |
| adagio, adagietto | easy-going | quasi | sort of, rather |
| agitato | agitated | ripieno | the accompanying ensemble |
| alla breve | four beat as two to the bar | ritardando | gradually coming to a stop |
| allargando | spreading out in tempo | ritenuto | pulling back |
| allegro, allegretto | with lightness of action | ritornello | refrain |
| andante, andantino | with movement | rubato | borrowed (time) |
| brio, con | with spirit | secco | with a dry tone |
| calando | winding down, slower and softer | segno | cue sign |
| cantabile | singing | segue | follow on |
| capo (da) | from the top (beginning) | sempre | always |
| concerto | the solo (group): cf ripieno | sforzata, sforzando | with a force tone |
| crescendo | gradually louder | smorzando | smothering, stifling the tone |
| deciso | firmly | sotto voce | in an undertone |
| diminuendo | gradually softer | spiccato | bounced (of the bow off the string) |
| divisi a 2, 3, etc. | divided in 2, 3, etc. parts | staccato, -issimo | short, very short |
| dolce, dolcissimo | soft and sweetly | subito | sudden, suddenly |
| doloroso | mournfully | Takt | (German) beat, metre, bar (measure) |
| espressivo | with expression | tema | theme |
| flatterzunge | (German) fluttertongue | tenuto | holding back |
| fuoco, con | with fire | tessitura | range of instrument or voice |
| giocoso | with fun | tranquillo | calmly |
| grave | with gravity | tanto | so much |
| largo, larghetto | expansively | troppo | too much |
| legato | smoothly | via | remove (e.g. mute) |
| lento | slowly | veloce | at speed |
| l'istesso (tempo) | the same (tempo) | vivo, vivace | with life |
| loco | in (its usual) place | voce, voci | voice, voices |
| lungo, lunga | long | volante | as though flying |
| misterioso | mysteriously | wieder | (German) again |
| molto | much, very | Zeitmass | (German) tempo |
| pesante | weightily | zingaresca | gipsy |
| poco, pochissimo | a little, very little | zu 2 | (German) 1. for 2 players; 2. in 2 parts |
| portamento | lifting (note to note) | | |

**cantata** an extended work for voices, from the Italian, meaning 'sung', as opposed to sonata ('sounded') for instruments. A cantata can be sacred or secular, sometimes uses solo voices, and usually has orchestral accompaniment. The first printed collection of sacred cantata texts dates from 1670.

**capriccio** a short instrumental piece, often humorous or whimsical in character.

**chamber music** music suitable for performance in a small room or chamber, rather than in the concert hall, and usually written for instrumental combinations, played with one instrument to a part, as in the string quartet.

**classical** music written in the late 17th and 18th centuries; Western music of any period that does not belong to the folk or popular traditions.

**clef** the symbol used to indicate the pitch of the lines of the staff in musical notation.

**coda** a concluding section of a movement added to indicate finality.

**coloratura** a rapid ornamental vocal passage with runs and trills. A *coloratura soprano* is a light, high voice suited to such music.

**concerto** composition, usually in three movements, for solo instrument (or instruments) and orchestra. It developed during the 18th century from the *concerto grosso* form for string orchestra, in which a group of solo instruments is contrasted with a full orchestra.

**contralto** a low-registered female voice; also called an *alto*.

**counterpoint** the art of combining different forms of an original melody with apparent freedom and yet to harmonious effect. Palestrina and J S Bach were masters of counterpoint.

**diatonic** a scale consisting of the seven notes of any major or minor key.

**encore** (French 'again') an unprogrammed extra item, usually short and well-known, played at the end of a concert to please an enthusiastic audience.

**étude** a musical exercise designed to develop technique.

**finale** the last movement or section of a composition, by implication resolute in character.

**fret** an inlaid ridge of ivory or metal, or of circlets of nylon, marking positions in the fingerboard of a plucked or bowed string instrument indicating changes of pitch.

**fugue** a contrapuntal form (with two or more melodies) for a number of parts or 'voices', which enter successively in imitation of each other. It was raised to a high art by J S Bach.

**gamelan** Indonesian orchestra employing tuned gongs, xylophones, metallophones (with bars of metal), cymbals, drums, flutes, and fiddles, the music of which has inspired such Western composers as Debussy, Colin McPhee, John

Cage, Benjamin Britten, and Philip Glass.

**Gregorian chant** any of a body of plainsong choral chants associated with Pope Gregory the Great (540–604), which became standard in the Roman Catholic Church.

**harmonics** a series of partial vibrations that combine to form a musical tone. The number and relative prominence of harmonics produced determines an instrument's tone colour (timbre). An oboe is rich in harmonics, the flute has few. Harmonics conform to successive divisions of the sounding air column or string: their pitches are harmonious.

**impromptu** a short instrumental piece that suggests spontaneity. Composers of piano impromptus include Schubert and Chopin.

**intermezzo** a short orchestral interlude often used between the acts of an opera to denote the passage of time; by extension, a short piece for an instrument to be played between other more substantial works.

**key** the diatonic scale around which a piece of music is written; for example, a passage in the key of C major will mainly use the notes of the C major scale. The term is also used for the lever activated by a keyboard player, such as a piano key.

**libretto** the text of an opera or other dramatic vocal work, or the scenario of a ballet.

**madrigal** a form of secular song in four or five parts, usually sung without instrumental accompaniment. It originated in 14th-century Italy. Madrigal composers include Andrea Gabrieli, Claudio Monteverdi, Thomas Morley, and Orlando Gibbons.

**melody** a sequence of notes forming a theme or tune.

**metre** accentuation pattern characteristic of a musical line; the regularity underlying musical rhythm.

**mezzo-soprano** female singing voice halfway between soprano and contralto.

**middle C** the C in mid-keyboard, so-called because it also marks the meeting-point of bass and treble clefs in keyboard notation.

**minuet** European courtly dance of the 17th century, later used with the trio as the third movement in a Classical symphony.

**modulation** movement from one key to another.

**movement** a section of a large work, such as a symphony, which is often complete in itself.

**Muzak** proprietary name for 'piped music' recorded to strict psychological criteria for transmission in a variety of work environments in order to improve occupier or customer morale.

**nocturne** a lyrical, dreamy piece, often for piano, introduced by John Field (1782–1837) and adopted by Chopin.

**opera** dramatic musical work in which singing takes the place of speech. In opera the music accompanying the action has paramount importance, although dancing and spectacular staging may also play their parts. Opera originated in late 16th-century Florence when the musical declamation, lyrical monologues, and choruses of Classical Greek drama were reproduced in current forms.

**operetta** a short amusing musical play, which may use spoken dialogue.

**opus** a term, used with a figure, to indicate the numbering of a composer's works, usually in chronological order.

**oratorio** musical setting of religious texts, scored for orchestra, chorus, and solo voices, on a scale more dramatic and larger than that of a cantata.

**orchestration** the scoring of a composition for orchestra; the choice of instruments of a score expanded for orchestra (often by another

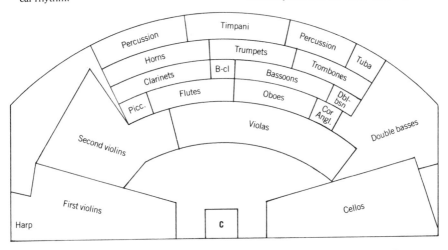

Picc. = Piccolo     Dbl-bsn = Double bassoon     Bcl = Bass clarinet     Cor Angl. = Cor Anglais
C = conductor

*Orchestra: Setting most usual today. It is unbalanced — the bass instruments tend to the right, treble instruments to the left.*

hand). A work may be written for piano, and then transferred to an orchestral score.

**overture** a piece of instrumental music, usually preceding an opera. There are also overtures to suites and plays, ballets, and 'concert' overtures, such as Elgar's *Cockaigne* and John Ireland's descriptive *London Overture*.

**prelude** a composition intended as the preface to further music, to set a mood for a stage work, as in Wagner's *Lohengrin*; as used by Chopin, a short piano work.

**requiem** in the Roman Catholic church, a mass for the dead. Musical settings include those by Palestrina, Mozart, Berlioz, and Verdi.

**rhapsody** instrumental fantasia, often based on folk melodies, such as Lizst's *Hungarian Rhapsodies* 1853–54.

**rhythm** the patterning of music in movement; a recurring unit of long and short time values.

**rondo** or *rondeau* form of instrumental music in which the principal section returns like a refrain. Rondo form is often used for the last movement of a sonata or concerto.

**scale** a sequence of pitches that establishes a key, and in some respects the character of a composition. A scale is defined by its starting note and may be *major* or *minor* depending on the order of intervals. A *chromatic* scale is the full range of 12 notes: it has no key because there is no fixed starting point. A *whole-tone* scale is a six-note scale and is also indeterminate in key: only two are possible. A *diatonic* scale has seven notes, a *pentatonic* scale has five.

**scherzo** a lively piece, usually in rapid triple (3/4) time; often used for the third movement of a symphony, sonata, or quartet.

**serenade** a musical piece for chamber orchestra or wind instruments in several movements, originally intended for evening entertainment, such as Mozart's *Eine kleine Nachtmusik/A Little Night Music*.

**sonata** a piece of instrumental music written for a soloist or a small ensemble and consisting of a series of related movements.

**soprano** the highest range of the female voice.

**suite** formerly a grouping of old dance forms; later the term came to be used to describe a set of instrumental pieces, sometimes assembled from a stage work, such as Tchaikovsky's *Nutcracker Suite* 1891–92.

**symphonic poem** a term originated by Liszt for his 13 one-movement orchestral works that interpret a story from literature or history, also used by many other composers. Richard Strauss preferred the title *tone poem*.

**symphony** a musical composition for orchestra, traditionally in four separate but closely related movements. It developed from the smaller sonata form, the Italian overture, and the dance suite of the 18th century.

**syncopation** the deliberate upsetting of rhythm by shifting the accent to a beat that is normally unaccented.

**tempo** the speed at which a piece is played.

**tenor** the highest range of adult male voice when not using falsetto (a male voice singing in the female register).

**timbre** the tone colour of an instrument.

**tonality** the observance of a key structure; that is, the recognition of the importance of a tonic or key note and of the diatonic scale built upon it.

**vibrato** a slight but rapid fluctuation of intensity in voice or instrument.

---

### Elvis Presley

*In the past few years, there have been a lot of rumours and stories about whether or not Elvis Presley is really dead. Do you think there is any possibility that these rumours are true and that Elvis Presly is still alive, or don't you think so?*

| | |
|---|---|
| Yes | 8 |
| No | 81 |
| Don't know | 10 |

# KEY NAMES

**Adams** Ansel 1902–1984. US photographer best known for his printed images of dramatic landscapes and organic forms of the American West. He was associated with the zone system of exposure estimation.

Adams worked to establish photography as a fine art. He founded the first museum collection of photography, at New York City's Museum of Modern Art 1937.

**Atget** Eugène 1857–1927. French photographer. He took up photography at the age of 40, and for 30 years documented urban Paris, leaving some 10,000 photos.

**Avedon** Richard 1923– . US photographer. A fashion photographer with *Harper's Bazaar* magazine in New York in the mid-1940s, he later became one of the highest-paid commercial photographers.

**Bailey** David 1938– . English fashion photographer, chiefly associated with *Vogue* magazine from the 1960s. He has published several books of his work, exhibited widely, and also made films.

**Beaton** Cecil 1904–1980. English portrait and fashion photographer, designer, illustrator, diarist, and conversationalist. He produced portrait studies and also designed scenery and costumes for ballets, and sets for plays and films.

**Bourke-White** Margaret 1906–1971. US photographer. As an editor of *Fortune* magazine 1929–33, she travelled extensively in the USSR, publishing several collections of photographs. Later, with her husband, the writer Erskine Caldwell, she published photo collections of American and European subjects. On the staff of *Life* magazine from 1936, she covered combat in World War II and documented India's postwar struggle for independence.

**Brady** Matthew B *c.* 1823–1896. US photographer. Famed for his skill in photographic portraiture, he published *The Gallery of Illustrious Americans* 1850. With the outbreak of the US Civil War 1861, Brady and his staff became the foremost photographers of battle scenes and military life. Although his war photos were widely reproduced, Brady later suffered a series of financial reverses and died in poverty.

**Brandt** Bill 1904–1983 English photographer. He studied with Man Ray in Paris in 1929; during the 1930s he made a series of social records contrasting the lives of the rich and the poor, and during World War II documented conditions in London in the Blitz. His outstanding creative work was his treatment of the nude, published in *Perspective of Nudes* 1966 and *Shadows of Light* 1966.

**Brassaï** Adopted name of Gyula Halesz 1899–1986. French photographer of Hungarian origin. From the early 1930s on he documented, mainly by flash, the nightlife of Paris, before turning to more abstract work.

**Cameron** Julia Margaret 1815–1879. English photographer. She made lively, revealing portraits of the Victorian intelligentsia using a large camera, five-minute exposures, and wet plates. Her subjects included Charles Darwin and Alfred Tennyson.

**Cartier-Bresson** Henri 1908– . French photographer, one of the greatest photographic artists. His documentary work was shot in black and white, using a small format camera. His work is remarkable for its tightly structured composition and his ability to capture the decisive moment.

**Daguerre** Louis Jacques Mande 1789–1851. French pioneer of photography. Together with Niépce, he is credited with the invention of photography (though others were reaching the same point simultaneously). In 1838 he invented the daguerreotype, a single image process, superseded ten years later by Talbot's negative/positive process.

**Evans** Walker 1903–1975. US photographer best known for his documentary photographs of people in the rural American South during the Great Depression of the 1930s. Many of his photographs appeared in James Agee's book *Let Us Now Praise Famous Men* 1941. Throughout his career, he devoted much attention to photographing architecture. He also produced a renowned series of photographs of people in the New York City subways.

**Fenton** Roger 1819–1869. English photographer. The world's first war photographer, he went to the Crimea 1855; he also founded the Royal Photographic Society in London.

**Hill** David Octavius 1802–1870. Scottish photographer who, in collaboration with Robert Adamson (1821–1848), made extensive use of the calotype process in their large collection of

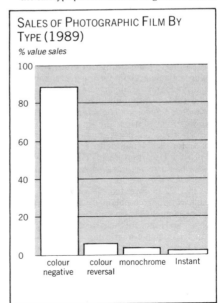

SALES OF PHOTOGRAPHIC FILM BY TYPE (1989)

*% value sales*

portraits taken in Edinburgh 1843–48.

**Hine** Lewis 1874–1940. US photographer. His dramatic photographs of child labour conditions in American factories at the beginning of the 20th century led to changes in state and local labour laws.

Hine began to document social conditions by photographing the immigrants arriving at New York's Ellis Island 1904–08, as well as their tenement homes and the sweatshops in which they worked. His publication of those photos 1908 is considered the first 'photo story'. In later years, Hine photographed various government projects and the construction of the Empire State Building, published 1930 in his *Men at Work*.

**Hosking** Eric (John) 1909–1990. English wildlife photographer best known for his documentation of British birds, especially owls. Beginning at the age of eight and still photographing in Africa at 80, he covered all aspects of bird life and illustrated thousands of books.

**Kertész** André 1894–1986. Hungarian-born US photographer. A master of the 35-mm format camera, he recorded his immediate environment with wit and style. He lived in Paris 1925–36, where he befriended and photographed many avant-garde artists and writers, and in New York City 1936–86, where he did commercial photography for major US magazines as well as creative photography.

**Land** Edwin Herbert 1909–1991. US inventor of the Polaroid Land camera 1947, which developed the film in one minute inside the camera and produced an 'instant' photograph. Land established the Polaroid Corporation 1937–80. His research also led to a process for 3-D pictures, 'instant' colour film, 'instant' motion pictures, and a new theory of colour perception, the 'retinex' theory 1977.

**Lange** Dorothea 1895–1965. US photographer. After establishing a private studio in San Francisco, she was hired in 1935 by the federal Farm Security Administration to document the westward migration of farm families from the Dust Bowl of the southern-central USA. She won national acclaim for the gritty realism of her photographs, which were widely exhibited and subsequently published as *An American Exodus: A Record of Human Erosion* 1939.

**Man Ray** adopted name of Emmanuel Rudnitsky 1890–1977. US photographer, painter, and sculptor, active mainly in France; associated with the Dada movement. His pictures often showed Surrealist images like the photograph *Le Violon d'Ingres* 1924.

In 1922 he invented the **rayograph**, a black and white image obtained without a camera by placing objects on sensitized photographic paper and exposing them to light; he also used the technique of solarization (partly reversing the tones on a photograph). His photographs include portraits of many artists and writers.

**Mapplethorpe** Robert 1946–1989. US art photographer known for his use of racial and homoerotic imagery chiefly in fine platinum prints. He developed a style of polished el-

egance in his gallery art works.

**McCullin** Donald 1935– . British war photographer. He began as a freelance photojournalist for Sunday newspapers and went on to cover hostilities in the Congo, Vietnam, Cambodia, Biafra, India, Pakistan, and Northern Ireland. He has published several books of his work and held many exhibitions.

**Moholy-Nagy** Laszlo 1895–1946. US photographer, born in Hungary. He lived in Germany 1923–29, where he was a member of the Bauhaus school, and fled from the Nazis in 1935. Through the publication of his illuminating theories and practical experiments, he had great influence on 20th-century photography and design.

**Muybridge** Eadweard. Adopted name of Edward James Muggeridge 1830–1904. English-born US photographer. He made a series of animal locomotion photographs in the USA in the 1870s and proved that, when a horse trots, there are times when all its feet are off the ground. He also explored motion in birds and humans, publishing the results in *Animal Locomotion* 1899.

**Nadar** adopted name of Gaspard-Félix Tournachon 1820–1910. French portrait photographer and caricaturist. He took the first aerial photographs (from a balloon 1858) and was the first to take flash photographs (using magnesium bulbs).

**Namuth** Hans 1915–1990. German-born US photographer who specialized in portraits and documentary work. He began as a photojournalist in Europe in the 1930s and opened a portrait studio in New York in 1950. His work includes documentation of the Guatemalan Mam Indians (published as *Los Todos Santeros*

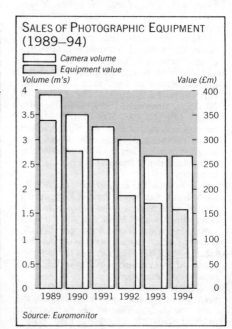

SALES OF PHOTOGRAPHIC EQUIPMENT
(1989–94)

▢ *Camera volume*
▢ *Equipment value*

*Source: Euromonitor*

---

PHOTOGRAPHY CHRONOLOGY

| | |
|---|---|
| 1515 | Leonardo da Vinci described the camera obscura. |
| 1750 | The Italian painter Canaletto used a camera obscura as an aid to his painting in Venice. |
| 1790 | Thomas Wedgwood in England made photograms—placing objects on leather, sensitized using silver nitrate. |
| 1826 | Nicephore Niépce (1765–1833), a French doctor, produced the world's first photograph from nature on pewter plates with a camera obscura and an eight-hour exposure. |
| 1835 | Niépce and Louis Daguerre produced the first Daguerreotype camera photograph. |
| 1839 | Daguerre was awarded an annuity by the French government and his process given to the world. The term 'photography' was coined by English astronomer John Herschel. |
| 1840 | Invention of Petzval lens, which reduced exposure time by 90%. |
| 1841 | Fox Talbot's Calotype process was patented—the first multi-copy method of photography using a negative/positive process, sensitized with silver iodide. |
| 1844 | Fox Talbot published the first photographic book, *The Pencil of Nature*. |
| 1845 | Hill and Adamson began to use Calotypes for portraits in Edinburgh. |
| 1851 | Fox Talbot used a one-thousandth of a second exposure to demonstrate high-speed photography. Invention of the wet-collodion-on-glass process and the waxed-paper negative. Photographs displayed at the Great Exhibition in London. |
| 1852 | The London Society of Arts exhibited 779 photographs. |
| 1855 | Roger Fenton made documentary photographs of the Crimean war from a specially constructed caravan with portable darkroom. |
| 1859 | Nadar in Paris made photographs underground using battery powered arc lights. |
| 1860 | Queen Victoria was photographed by Mayall. Abraham Lincoln was photographed by Matthew Brady for political campaigning. |
| 1861 | Single-lens reflex plate camera patented by Thomas Sutton. Principles of three-colour photography demonstrated by J C Maxwell. |
| 1862 | Nadar took aerial photographs over Paris. |
| 1870 | Julia Margaret Cameron used long lenses for her distinctive portraits. |
| 1871 | Gelatine-silver bromide developed. |
| 1878 | In the USA Eadweard Muybridge analyzed the movements of animals through sequential photographs, using a series of cameras. |
| 1879 | Photogravure process invented. |
| 1880 | A silver bromide emulsion was fixed with hypo. Photographs were first reproduced in newspapers in New York using the half-tone engraving process. The first twin-lens reflex camera was produced in London. |
| 1880 | Gelatine-silver chloride paper introduced. |
| 1884 | George Eastman produced flexible negative film. |
| 1889 | Eastman Company in the USA produced the Kodak No 1 camera and roll film, facilitating universal, hand-held snapshots. |
| 1891 | First telephoto lens. Interference process of colour photography developed by French doctor Gabriel Lippmann. |
| 1897 | First issue of Alfred Stieglitz's *Camera Notes* in the USA. |
| 1902 | In Germany Deckel invented a prototype leaf shutter and Zeiss introduced the Tessar lens. |
| 1904 | The autochrome colour process was patented by the Lumière brothers. |
| 1905 | Stieglitz opened the gallery '291' in New York promoting photography. Lewis Hine used photography to expose the exploitation of children in American factories, causing protective laws to be passed. |
| 1907 | The autochrome process began to be factory-produced. |
| 1914 | Oskar Barnack designed a prototype Leica camera for Leitz in Germany. |
| 1924 | Leitz launched the first 35mm camera, the Leica, delayed because of World War I. It became very popular with photojournalists because it was quiet, small, dependable, and had a range of lenses and accessories. |
| 1929 | Rolleiflex produced a twin-lens reflex camera in Germany. |
| 1935 | In the USA, Mannes and Godowsky invented Kodachrome transparency film, which produced sharp images and rich colour quality. Electronic flash was invented in the USA. |
| 1936 | *Life* magazine, significant for its photojournalism, was first published in the USA. |
| 1938 | *Picture Post* magazine was introduced in the UK. |
| 1940 | Multigrade enlarging paper by Ilford was made available in the UK. |
| 1942 | Kodacolor negative film introduced. |
| 1945 | The zone system of exposure estimation published in the book *Exposure Record* by Ansel Adams. |

## PHOTOGRAPHY CHRONOLOGY (cont.)

| | |
|---|---|
| 1947 | Polaroid black and white instant process film invented by Dr Edwin Land, who set up the Polaroid corporation in Boston, Massachusetts. Principles of holography demonstrated in England by Dennis Gabor. |
| 1955 | Kodak introduced Tri-X, a black and white 200 ASA film. |
| 1959 | The zoom lens invented in Germany by Voigtlander. |
| 1960 | Laser invented in the USA, making holography possible. Polacolor, a self-processing colour film, introduced by Polaroid, using a 60-second colour film and dye diffusion technique. |
| 1963 | Cibachrome, paper and chemicals for printing directly from transparencies, was made available by Ciba-Geigy of Switzerland; one of the most permanent processes. |
| 1966 | International Center of Photography established in New York. |
| 1969 | Photographs taken on the Moon by US astronauts. |
| 1970 | Charge-coupled device invented at Bell Laboratories in New Jersey, USA, to record very faint images (for example in astronomy). *Rencontres Internationales de la Photographie*, annual summer festival of photography with workshops founded in Arles, France. |
| 1971 | Opening of the Photographers' Gallery, London, and the Photo Archive of the Biblioteque Nationale, Paris. |
| 1972 | SX70 system, a single-lens reflex camera with instant prints, produced by Polaroid. |
| 1975 | Center for Creative Photography established at the University of Arizona. |
| 1980 | Ansel Adams sold an original print, *Moonrise: Hernandez*, for $45,000, a record price, in the USA. *Voyager 1* sent photographs of Saturn back to Earth across space. |
| 1983 | National Museum of Photography, Film and Television opened in Bradford, England. |
| 1985 | Minolta Corporation in Japan introduced the Minolta 7000—the world's first body-integral autofocus single-lens reflex camera. |
| 1988 | Electronic camera, which stores pictures on magnetic disc instead of on film, introduced in Japan. |
| 1990 | Kodak introduced PhotoCD which converts 35mm camera pictures (on film) into digital form and stores them on compact disc (CD) for viewing on TV. |

1989) and of US artists from the 1950s (published as *Artists 1950–1981*). He also carried out assignments for magazines.

**Parkinson** Norman (adopted name of Ronald William Parkinson Smith) 1913–1990. English fashion and portrait photographer who caught the essential glamour of each decade from the 1930s to the 1980s. Chiefly associated with the magazines *Vogue* and *Queen*, he was best known for his colour work, and from the late 1960s took many official portraits of the UK royal family.

**Penn** Irving 1917– . US fashion, advertising, portrait, editorial, and fine art photographer. In 1948 he took the first of many journeys to Africa and the Far East, resulting in a series of portrait photographs of local people, avoiding sophisticated technique. He was associated for many years with *Vogue* magazine in the USA.

**Siskind** Aaron 1903–1991. US art photographer who began as a documentary photographer and in 1940 made a radical change towards a poetic exploration of forms and planes, inspired by the Abstract Expressionist painters.

**Steichen** Edward 1897–1973. Luxembourg-born US photographer, who with Alfred Stieglitz helped to establish photography as an art form. His style evolved during his career from painterly impressionism to realism.

During World War I he helped to develop aerial photography, and in World War II he directed US naval-combat photography. He turned to fashion and advertising 1923–38,

working mainly for *Vogue* and *Vanity Fair* magazines. He was in charge of the Museum of Modern Art's photography collection 1947–62, where in 1955 he organized the renowned 'Family of Man' exhibition.

**Stieglitz** Alfred 1864–1946. US photographer. After forming the Photo Secession group in 1903, he began the magazine *Camera Work*. Through exhibitions at his gallery '291' in New York he helped to establish photography as an art form. His works include 'Winter, Fifth Avenue' 1893 and 'Steerage' 1907. In 1924 he married the painter Georgia O'Keeffe, who was the model in many of his photographs.

**Strand** Paul 1890–1976. US photographer who used large-format cameras for his strong, clear, close-up photographs of natural objects.

**Talbot** William Henry Fox 1800–1877. English pioneer of photography. He invented the paper-based calotype process, the first negative/positive method. Talbot made photograms several years before Daguerre's invention was announced.

**Weston** Edward 1886–1958. US photographer. A founding member of the 'f/64' group (after the smallest lens opening), a school of photography advocating sharp definition. He is noted for the technical mastery, composition, and clarity in his California landscapes, clouds, gourds, cacti, and nude studies.

In his photography, Weston aimed for realism. He never used artificial light and seldom enlarged, cropped, or retouched his negatives.

His aesthetic principles dominated American photography for many years.

**Wolcott** Marion Post 1910–1990. US documentary photographer best known for her work for the Farm Security Administration (with Walker Evans and Dorothea Lange), showing the conditions of poor farmers in the late 1930s in Kentucky and the deep South.

# TERMS

**aperture** an opening in the camera that allows light to pass through the lens to strike the film. Controlled by shutter speed and the iris diaphragm, it can be set mechanically or electronically at various diameters.

**ASA** a numbering system for rating the speed of films, devised by the American Standards Association. It has now been superseded by *ISO*, the International Standards Organization.

**camera** optical device used in photography for recording on film still or, in the case of a movie or video camera, moving images. There are small-, medium-, and large-format cameras; the format refers to the size of recorded image and the dimensions of the print obtained.

The simplest camera is a light-proof box with, at one end, a lens in front of a hole of variable size. The size of the hole is termed the aperture, and it can be changed by adjusting the diaphragm, or disc. At the opposite side of the camera is the light-sensitive film. A shutter situated between the lens and the film stops light reaching the film until a picture is taken, at which point an upsidedown image of the scene in front of the camera is formed on the film. The image is not visible until the film is treated by developing and fixing.

A simple camera has a fixed shutter speed and aperture, chosen so that on a sunny day the correct amount of light is admitted. More complex cameras allow the shutter speed and aperture to be adjusted; most have a built-in exposure meter to help choose the correct combination of shutter speed and aperture for the ambient conditions and subject matter. The most versatile camera is the single lens reflex (SLR) which allows the lens to be removed and special lenses attached.

**Cibachrome** a process of printing directly from transparencies. Distinguished by rich, saturated colours, it can be home-processed and the colours are highly resistant to fading. It was introduced 1963.

**daguerreotype** a single-image process using mercury vapour and an iodine-sensitized silvered plate; discovered by Daguerre in 1838.

**developing** the process that produces a visible image on exposed photographic film.

Developing involves treating the exposed film with a chemical developer, a reducing agent that changes the light-altered silver salts in the film into dark metallic silver. The developed image is made permanent with a fixer,

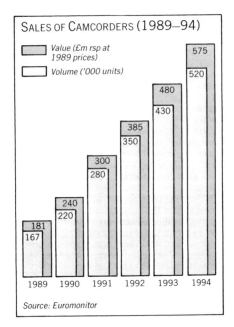

SALES OF CAMCORDERS (1989–94)

Value (£m rsp at 1989 prices)

Volume ('000 units)

| 1989 | 1990 | 1991 | 1992 | 1993 | 1994 |
|------|------|------|------|------|------|
| 181  | 240  | 300  | 385  | 480  | 575  |
| 167  | 220  | 280  | 350  | 430  | 520  |

Source: Euromonitor

which dissolves away any silver salts which were not affected by light. The developed image is a negative, or reverse image: darkest where the strongest light hit the film, lightest where the least light fell. To produce a positive image, the negative is itself photographed, and the development process reverses the shading, producing the final print.

**dye-transfer print** a print made by a relatively permanent colour process that uses red, yellow, and blue separation negatives printed together.

**f-number** measure of the relative aperture of a telescope or camera lens; it indicates the light-gathering power of the lens. Each successive *f* number represents a halving of exposure speed.

**focus** the distance that a lens must be moved in order to obtain a sharp image on the light-sensitive film at the back of the camera. The lens is moved away from the film to focus the image of closer objects. The focusing distance is often marked on a scale around the lens; however, many cameras now have an automatic focusing (*autofocus*) mechanism that uses an electric motor to move the lens.

**hypo** a term for sodium thiosulphate, discovered 1819 by John Herschel, and used as a fixative for photographic images since 1837.

**ISO** a numbering system for rating the speed of films, devised by the International Standards Organization.

**lens** a piece of glass (or other transparent material) with two polished surfaces—one concave or convex, and the other plane, concave, or convex—that converges or diverges rays of light and forms optical images. It is an essential component of cameras, microscopes, telescopes, and almost all optical instruments.

A *telephoto lens* is of longer focal length than normal and takes a very narrow view and gives a large image through a combination of telescopic and ordinary photographic lenses. A *wide-angle lens* is of shorter focal length than normal, taking in a wider angle of view. A *zoom lens*, by variation of focal length, allows speedy transition from long shots to close-ups.

**negative/positive** a reverse image, which when printed is again reversed, restoring the original scene. It was invented by Talbot about 1834.

**photography** process for reproducing images on sensitized materials by various forms of radiant energy, including visible light, ultraviolet, infrared, X-rays, atomic radiations and electron beams.

The most familiar photographic process depends upon the fact that certain silver compounds (called halides) are sensitive to light. A photographic film is coated with these compounds and, in a camera, is exposed to light. An image, or picture, of the scene before the camera is formed on the film because the silver halides become activated (light-altered) where light falls but not where light does not fall. The image is made visible by the process of developing, made permanent by fixing, and, finally, is usually printed on paper. Motion-picture photography uses a camera which exposes a roll of film to a rapid succession of views which, when developed, are projected in rapid succession to provide a moving image.

**rangefinder** instrument for determining the range or distance of an object from the observer; used to focus a camera or to sight a gun accurately. A *rangefinder camera* has a rotating mirror or prism that alters the image seen through the viewfinder, which is quite separate from the lens and coupled to the focusing mechanism.

**reflex camera** camera that uses a mirror and prisms to reflect light passing through the lens into the viewfinder, showing the photographer the exact scene that is being shot. When the shutter button is released the mirror springs out of the way, allowing light to reach the film. The most common type is the single-lens reflex (SLR) camera. The twin-lens reflex (TLR) camera has two lenses: one has a mirror for viewing, the other is used for exposing the film.

**SLR** abbreviation for *single-lens reflex*, a type of camera in which the image can be seen through the lens before a picture is taken. A small mirror directs light entering the lens to the viewfinder. When a picture is taken the mirror moves rapidly aside to allow the light to reach the film. The SLR allows different lenses, such as close-up or zoom lenses, to be used as the photographer can see exactly what is being focused on.

**TLR camera** twin-lens reflex camera that has a viewing lens of the same angle of view and focal length mounted above and parallel to the taking lens.

**transparency** a picture on slide film. This captures the original in a positive image (direct reversal) and can be used for projection or printing on positive-to-positive print material, for example by the Cibachrome or Kodak R-type process. Slide film is usually colour but can be obtained in black and white.

**zone system** a system of exposure estimation invented by Ansel Adams that groups infinite tonal gradations into ten zones, zone 0 being black and zone 10 white. An f-stop change in exposure is required from zone to zone.

---

### Happy snaps

*Some people like to have their photographs taken, some people don't mind and some people dislike it. What would you say about having your photograph taken?*

| | |
|---|---|
| Like a lot | 4 |
| Like a little | 5 |
| Don't mind | 50 |
| Dislike a little | 19 |
| Dislike a lot | 23 |

*Do you carry a photograph of your husband/wife or children in your wallet/handbag, or do you have one at work?*

| | |
|---|---|
| Yes, wallet/handbag | 27 |
| Yes, at work | 4 |
| No, neither | 53 |
| Not applicable | 16 |

# GENRES

**Absurd, Theatre of the** avant-garde drama originating with a group of playwrights in the 1950s and 1960s, including Beckett, Ionesco, Genet, and Pinter. Their work expressed the belief that in a godless universe, human existence has no meaning or purpose and therefore all communication breaks down. Logical construction and argument gives way to irrational and illogical speech and to its ultimate conclusion, silence. The plays emerge as dramatized poetic images of the human predicament.

**burlesque** in the 17th and 18th centuries, a form of satirical comedy parodying a particular play or dramatic genre. For example, John Gay's *The Beggar's Opera* 1728 is a burlesque of 18th century opera, and Sheridan's *The Critic* 1779 satirizes the sentimentality in the drama of this time. In the USA, the term was used for a sex-and-comedy show, consisting of a variety of acts, including acrobats, chorus, and comedy numbers. During the 1920s the striptease was introduced to counteract the growing popularity of the cinema, and Gypsy Rose Lee became its most famous artiste. Burlesque was frequently banned in the USA.

**circus** an entertainment, often held in a large tent ('big top'), involving acrobats, clowns, and sometimes performing animals. In 1897, the US showman P T Barnum created the 'Greatest Show on Earth', which included a circus, menagerie, and 'freaks', all transported in 100 rail cars. From the 1970s there was increasing protest against the inclusion of animal acts.

**comedy** in the simplest terms, a drama with a happy ending, as opposed to tragedy. The comic tradition developed in Ancient Greece, in the farcical satires of Aristophanes. The Vices and Devil of the medieval morality plays developed into the stock comic characters of the Renaissance Comedy of Humours with such notable villains as Jonson's Mosca in *Volpone*. The timeless comedies of Shakespeare and Molière were followed in England during the 17th century by the witty and often licentious comedy of manners of Restoration writers such as Etherege, Wycherley, and Congreve. Sentimental comedy dominated most of the 19th century, though little of it is remembered in the late 20th century, which prefers the realistic tradition of Shaw and the elegant social comedies of Wilde. The polished comedies of Coward and Rattigan from the 1920s to the 1940s were eclipsed during the late 1950s and 60s by a trend towards satire and a more cynical humour as seen in the works of Joe Orton and Peter Nichols. From the 1970s the dark comedies of Alan Ayckbourn have dominated the English stage.

**commedia dell'arte** popular form of Italian improvised drama in the 16th and 17th centuries, performed by trained troupes of actors and involving stock characters and situations. It exerted considerable influence on writers such as Molière and on the genres of pantomime, harlequinade, and the Punch and Judy show. It laid the foundation for the mime tradition, particularly in France.

**Cruelty, Theatre of** performance that aims to shock the audience into an awareness of basic, primitive human nature, through the release of feelings usually repressed by conventional behaviour. The spectators should suffer a change through their shared experience with the actors. The theory was first advanced by Antonin Artaud in his book *Le Théâtre et son double* 1938 and adopted by a number of writers and directors.

**farce** broad form of comedy involving stereotyped characters in complex, often improbable situations frequently revolving around extramarital relationships (hence the term 'bedroom farce'). The farce usually depicts a world where order has collapsed into anarchy. Representatives of authority are powerless to control a spiralling momentum of madness. Originating from the physical knockabout comedy of Greek satyr plays and the broad humour developed from medieval religious drama, the farce was developed and perfected during the 19th century by Labiche and Feydeau in France, and Pinero in England. In modern times two notable English series have been the Aldwych farces of Ben Travers in the 1920s and 1930s and the Whitehall farces produced by Brian Rix during the 1950s and 1960s.

**fringe theatre** plays that are anti-establishment or experimental, and performed in informal venues, in contrast to mainstream commercial theatre. In the UK, the term originated in the 1960s from the activities held on the 'fringe' of the Edinburgh Festival. The US equivalent is off-off-Broadway (off-Broadway is mainstream theatre that is not on Broadway).

**kabuki** drama originating in late 16th-century Japan, drawing on the more aristocratic Nō tradition, and incorporating acting, dance, and evocative vocal and/or instrumental music used to enhance dramatic situations. Plays are long, episodic, and based mainly on legendary themes; content is secondary to the display of elaborate costumes, staging, and virtuoso ability of the actors, who are all male.

**masque** spectacular and essentially aristocratic entertainment with a fantastic or mythological theme in which music, dance, and extravagant costumes and scenic design figured larger than the plot. Originating in Italy, it reached its height of popularity at the English court between 1600 and 1640, with the collaboration of Ben Jonson as writer and Inigo Jones as stage designer. The masque had great influence on the development of ballet and opera, and the elaborate frame in which it was performed developed into the proscenium arch.

**melodrama** a play with romantic and sensational plot elements, often unsubtly acted. Originally it meant a play accompanied by music. The early melodramas used extravagant theatrical effects to heighten violent emotions, and

THEATRE CHRONOLOGY

| | |
|---|---|
| c 3200 BC | Beginnings of Egyptian religious drama, essentially ritualistic. |
| c 600 | Choral performances (dithyrambs) in honour of Dionysus form beginnings of Greek tragedy, according to Aristotle. |
| c 534 BC | First festival of tragedy held in Athens and won by Thespis. |
| 500–300 BC | Great age of Greek drama, which included tragedy, comedy, and satyr plays (grotesque farce). |
| 468 BC | Sophocles' first victory at Athens festival. His use of a third actor altered the course of the tragic form. |
| 458 BC | Aeschylus' *Oresteia* first performed. |
| c 425–388 BC | Comedies of Aristophanes, including *The Birds* 414, *Lysistrata* 411, and *The Frogs* 405. In tragedy the importance of the chorus diminished under Euripedes, author of *The Bacchae* 405. |
| c 350 BC | Menander's 'New Comedy' of social manners developed. |
| c 330 BC | Aristotle's *Poetics* analysed the nature of tragedy. Theatre of Dionysus in Athens built. |
| c 240–AD 500 | Emergence of Roman drama, adapted from Greek originals under Plautus, Terence and Seneca. All were to have great influence on Elizabethan writers. |
| c AD 375 | Kâlidâsa's *Sakuntalâ marked the height of Sanskrit drama in India.* |
| c 970 | Earliest example of Christian liturgical drama, written by Ethelwold, bishop of Winchester |
| 1210 | Priests were forbidden to appear on public stage. This led to secularization of drama in the vernacular. |
| c 1250–1500 | European mystery (or miracle) plays flourished, first in the churches, later in market places, and performed in England by town guilds. |
| c 1375 | Nōor Noh drama developed in Japan. |
| c 1495 | *Everyman*, the best known of all the morality plays, first performed. |
| 1500–1600 | Italian commedia dell'arte troupes performed popular, improvised comedies; they were to have a large influence on Molière and on English Harlequinade and Pantomime. |
| c 1551 | Nicholas Udall's *Ralph Roister Doister* written, the first English comedy. |
| c 1576 | First English playhouse, The Theatre, built by James Burbage in Shoreditch, London. |
| 1587 | Marlowe's *Tamburlaine the Great* marked an important advance in the use of blank verse and the beginning of the great age of Elizabethan and Jacobean drama in England. |
| c 1589 | Kyd's *Spanish Tragedy*—the first of the 'revenge' tragedies. |
| 1594 | Lord Chamberlain's Men formed; a theatre company to which Shakespeare was attached as actor and writer from 1595. |
| 1599 | The Globe Theatre built on Bankside, Southwark, London. |
| c 1590–1612 | Shakespeare's greatest plays, including *Hamlet* and *King Lear*, were written. |
| 1604 | Inigo Jones designed *The Masque of Blackness* for James I, written by Ben Jonson. Masques were the height of fashion at the English court around this time. |
| 1613 | The Globe Theatre burned down (rebuilt 1614; demolished 1644). |
| 1614 | Lope de Vega's *Fuenteovejuna/The Sheep Wall* marked Spanish renaissance in drama. |
| 1637 | Corneille's *Le Cid* established classical tragedy in France. |
| 1642 | Act of Parliament closed all English theatres. |
| 1660 | With the restoration of Charles II to the English throne, dramatic performances recommenced. The first professional actress appeared as Desdemona in Shakespeare's *Othello*. |
| 1664 | Molière's *Tartuffe* was banned for three years by religious factions. |
| 1667 | Racine's first success, *Andromaque*. |
| 1680 | Comédie-Française formed by Louis XIV. |
| 1700 | Congreve, the greatest exponent of Restoration comedy, wrote *The Way of the World*. |
| 1716 | First known American theatre built in Williamsburg. |
| 1728 | Gay's *The Beggar's Opera* first performed. |
| 1737 | Stage Licensing Act required all plays to be licensed and approved by the Lord Chamberlain before performance in Britain. |
| 1747 | Garrick became manager of Drury Lane Theatre, London. |
| 1767–8 | In Germany, Lessing's *Minna von Barnhelm* and publication of *Hamburgische Dramaturgie*. |

THEATRE CHRONOLOGY: CONT.

| | |
|---|---|
| 1773 | In England, Goldsmith's *She Stoops to Conquer* and Sheridan's *The Rivals* 1775 established the 'comedy of manners'. Goethe's *Götz von Berlichingen* is the first 'Sturm und Drang' play (literally storm and stress); this German Romantic movement, depicting extravagant emotions, was influential throughout Europe at this time and led to the rise of English melodrama. |
| 1775 | Sarah Siddons, English tragedy actress, made her debut at the Drury Lane Theatre. |
| 1781 | Schiller's *Die Raüber/The Robbers* |
| 1784 | Beaumarchais' *Le Mariage de Figaro* , (written 1778) finally performed after difficulties with censorship because of its alleged revolutionary tendencies. |
| 1802 | Holcroft's *A Tale of Mystery* marked the rise of melodrama in England. |
| 1814 | Edmund Kean's London debut as Shylock in Shakespeare's *The Merchant of Venice*. |
| 1815 | Gas lighting installed at Covent Garden, London. |
| 1830 | Hugo's *Hernani* caused riots in Paris. His work marked the beginning of a new Romantic drama, changing the course of French theatre. |
| 1836 | Gogol's *The Government Inspector*—a social satire—initially passed the Russian censors. |
| 1838 | Debut of the French tragic actress Rachel at the Comédie-Française. |
| 1843 | The Theatres Act further strengthened the powers of the Lord Chamberlain to censor plays. |
| 1869 | Sarah Bernhardt's first success, in *Le Passant* in Paris. |
| 1878 | Henry Irving became actor-manager of the Lyceum with Ellen Terry as leading lady. |
| 1879 | Ibsen's *A Doll's House*—an example of Ibsen's hugely influential plays, which marked the beginning of realism in European theatre. |
| 1888 | Strindberg's *Miss Julie*. |
| 1893 | Shaw wrote *Mrs Warren's Profession* (banned until 1902 because it deals with prostitution). Shaw's works bring the new realistic drama to Britain and introduce social and political issues as subjects for the theatre. |
| 1895 | Wilde's *The Importance of Being Earnest*. |
| 1896 | The first performance of Chekhov's *The Seagull* failed. |
| 1899 | Abbey Theatre, Dublin, founded by W B Yeats and Lady Gregory, marked the beginning of an Irish dramatic revival. |
| 1904 | Chekhov's *The Cherry Orchard* . Founding of Royal Academy of Dramatic Art (RADA) to train young actors, by Beerbohm Tree in London. |
| 1904–07 | Granville Barker and J E Vedrenne were managers of the Royal Court Theatre and directed works by Shaw, Yeats, Ibsen, and Galsworthy. |
| 1919 | Theatre Guild founded in US to perform less commercial new plays. |
| 1923 | Shaw's *St Joan*. O'Casey's first play, *The Shadow of a Gunman*. |
| 1925 | Coward's *Hay Fever* . Travers' *A Cuckoo in the Nest*, the first of the Aldwych farces. |
| 1928 | Brecht's *Die Dreigroschenoper/The Threepenny Opera* with score by Kurt Weill. In the USA, Jerome Kern's *Show Boat* with Paul Robeson, one example of the success of musical comedies. Others by Cole Porter, Irving Berlin, and George Gershwin became popular. |
| 1930 | Gielgud's first performance as Hamlet. |
| 1935 | T S Eliot's *Murder in the Cathedral*. |
| 1943 | The first of the musicals, *Oklahoma!*, opened. |
| 1947 | First Edinburgh Festival with fringe theatre events. Tennessee Williams's *A Streetcar Named Desire*. |
| 1953 | Arthur Miller's *The Crucible* opened during the period of witch-hunting of communists in USA under McCarthy. *Waiting for Godot* by Beckett exemplified the Theatre of the Absurd. |
| 1956 | English Stage Company formed at the Royal Court Theatre to provide a platform for new dramatists. Osborne's *Look Back in Anger* included in its first season. |
| 1957 | Bernstein's *West Side Story* opened in New York. |
| 1960 | Pinter's *The Caretaker*. |
| 1961 | Royal Shakespeare Company formed under directorship of Peter Hall, based at Stratford and the Aldwych, London. |
| 1963–4 | National Theatre Company formed at the Old Vic under the directorship of Laurence Olivier. |
| 1965 | Edward Bond's *Saved* initially banned by the Lord Chamberlain. |
| 1967 | Stoppard's *Rosencrantz and Guildenstern are Dead*. Success in USA of *Hair* - first of the 'rock' musicals. |
| 1968 | Abolition of theatre censorship in UK. |
| 1970 | Peter Brook's production of *A Midsummer Night's Dream*. |

| THEATRE CHRONOLOGY: CONT. | |
|---|---|
| 1976 | National Theatre opened a new theatre complex on the South Bank, London. |
| 1980 | Howard Brenton's *The Romans in Britain* led to a private prosecution of the director for obscenity. |
| 1982 | Royal Shakespeare Company opened at the Barbican Centre, London. |
| 1982–83 | Trevor Nunn's production *Nicholas Nickleby* won Tony award, marking its success in UK and USA. |
| 1986 | *The Phantom of the Opera* opened in London, the latest in a series of successful Lloyd Webber musicals. |
| 1987 | The Theatre Museum opened in Covent Garden, London. Planning permission granted for the building of a replica of the Globe Theatre on the original site. |
| 1989 | Remains of the Rose Theatre, where Shakespeare's plays were first performed, were discovered at Southwark, South London. |
| 1990 | The Royal Shakespeare Company suspended its work at the Barbican Centre, London for six months, pleading lack of funds. |
| 1991 | Agatha Christie's *The Mousetrap* entered its 39th year, the longest-running play in the world. |

overblown characters, often emphasizing one trait at the expense of others. By the end of the 19th century, melodrama had become a popular genre of stage play.

**mime** a type of acting in which meaning is conveyed by precise gestures, movements of the whole body, and facial expressions. It is an essential element in the training of actors. Mime has developed as a form of theatre, particularly in France, where Marcel Marceau and Jean Louis Barrault have continued the traditions established in the 19th century by Deburau and the practices of the commedia dell'arte in Italy. In ancient Greece, mime was a crude, realistic comedy with dialogue and exaggerated gesture.

**morality play** didactic medieval verse drama, which differs from the mystery play in that it dramatizes Everyman's journey from birth to death rather than the events of the Bible. Human characters are replaced by personified virtues and vices, the limited humorous elements being provided by the Devil. Morality plays exerted an influence on the course of Elizabethan drama.

**music hall** light entertainment, in which singers, dancers, comedians, and acrobats perform in 'turns', and presided over by a flamboyant master of ceremonies. It reached its heyday in the late 19th century, by which time special ornate theatres had been built in most English towns to accommodate what had originally been barroom entertainment. Famous music hall performers included Albert Chevalier, Marie Lloyd, Harry Lauder, and George Formby. Many had their special character trademark, such as Vesta Tilley's immaculate masculine outfit as Burlington Bertie. With the introduction of radio and television, music hall declined but has had something of a revival in the informal entertainment of the pub–the place of its origin. The US equivalent is known as 'vaudeville'.

**musical** 20th-century form of theatre, combining elements of song, dance, and the spoken word, often characterized by lavish staging and large casts. It developed from the operettas and musical comedies of the 19th century.

The **operetta** is a light-hearted entertainment with extensive musical content: Jaques Offenbach, Johann Strauss, Franz Lehár, and Gilbert and Sullivan all composed operettas. The **musical comedy** is an anglicization of the French *opéra bouffe*, of which the first was *A Gaiety Girl* 1893, mounted by George Edwardes (1852–1915) at the Gaiety Theatre, London. Typical of the 1920s were *The Student Prince* 1924 and *The Desert Song* 1926 by Sigmund Romberg. The genre reached a more sophisticated expression in the USA during the 1930s and 1940s with the work of George Gershwin, Cole Porter, Irving Berlin, and Jerome Kern. The word 'comedy' was dropped and the era of the 'musical' arrived in 1943 with *Oklahoma!* by Rodgers and Hammerstein II. Plot and character were now given more serious attention. Two great successes of the mid-1950s were Lerner and Loewe's *My Fair Lady* 1956 (based on Shaw's *Pygmalion*) and Bernstein's *West Side Story* 1957 (based on Shakespeare's *Romeo and Juliet*). Sandy Wilson's *The Boy Friend* 1953 revived the British musical and was followed by hits such as Lionel Bart's *Oliver!* 1960. Musicals began to branch into religious and political themes with *Oh What a Lovely War!* 1963, produced by Joan Littlewood and Charles Chiltern, and the Andrew Lloyd Webber musicals *Jesus Christ Superstar* 1970 and *Evita* 1978. In the 1980s 19th-century melodrama was popular, for example *Phantom of the Opera* 1986 and *Les Misérables* 1987. In recent years the American musical has declined in output owing to high production costs. Nevertheless, Stephen Sondheim has written and composed an outstanding number of musicals of originality, wit, and beauty in staging and score. These include *Sunday in the Park with George* 1989 and *Into the Woods* 1990.

**mystery play** or **miracle play** medieval religious drama based on stories from the Bible. Mystery plays were performed around the time of church festivals, reaching their height in Europe during the 15th and 16th centuries. A whole cycle running from the Creation to the Last Judgement was performed in separate scenes on mobile wagons by various town

## Recent Award Winners

American Theatre Wing Antoinette Perry (Tony) Awards, 1985–1991 (Best play, best musical, and best revival production)

| | |
|---|---|
| 1985 | *Biloxi Blues Big River, Joe Egg* |
| 1986 | *I'm Not Rappaport, The Mystery of Edwin Drood, Sweet Charity* |
| 1987 | *Fences, Les Miserables, All My Sons* |
| 1988 | *M. Butterfly, The Phantom of the Opera, Anything Goes* |
| 1989 | *The Heidi Chronicles, Jerome Robbins' Broadway, Our Town* |
| 1990 | *The Grapes of Wrath, City of Angels, Gypsy* |
| 1991 | *Lost in Yonkers, The Will Rogers Follies, Fiddler on the Roof* |

The Laurence Olivier Awards, presented by The Society of West End Theatre (best play, best musical, and best comedy)

| | |
|---|---|
| 1985 | *Red Noses, Me and My Girl, A Chorus of Disapproval* |
| 1986 | *Les Liaisons Dangereuses, The Phantom of the Opera, When We Are Married* |
| 1987 | *Serious Money, Follies, Three Men on a Horse* |
| 1988 | *Our Country's Good, Candide, Shirley Valentine* |
| 1989/90 | *Racing Demon, Return to the Forbidden Planet, Single Spies* |
| 1991 | *Dancing at Lughnasa, Sunday in the Park with George, Out of Order* |

Evening Standard Drama Awards (best play, best musical, and best comedy)

| | |
|---|---|
| 1985 | *Pravda, Are You Lonesome Tonight?, A Chorus of Disapproval* |
| 1986 | *Les Liaisons Dangereuses, The Phantom of the Opera, A Month of Sundays* |
| 1987 | *A Small Family Business, Follies, Serious Money* |
| 1988 | *Aristocrats, award for best musical was not presented, Lettice and Lovage* |
| 1989 | *Ghetto, Miss Saigon, Henceforward* |
| 1990 | *Shadowlands, Into the Woods, Man of the Moment* and *Jeffrey Bernard is Unwell* (joint award) |

guilds. Four English cycles survive: those of Chester, Coventry, Wakefield (or Townley). Versions are still performed, notably the York cycle at York. The German equivalent of the mystery play, the *Mysterienspiel*, survives today as the *Passion Play* . It is essentially concerned with the Crucifixion of Christ and the most famous takes place every ten years at Oberammergau.

**Nó** or **Noh** classical, aristocratic Japanese drama, which developed from the 14th to the 16th centuries, and is still performed. It is based on a narrative of impermanence. The pine tree that always decorates the rear panel of the stage is a symbol of constancy against which all themes of impermanence are played. There is a reper-

tory of some 250 pieces, of which five, one from each of the several classes devoted to different subjects, may be put on in a performance lasting a whole day. Dance, mime, music, and chanting develop the mythical or historical themes. All the actors are men, some of whom wear masks and elaborate costumes; scenery is limited. Nó influenced kabuki drama.

**pageant** originally the wagon on which medieval plays were performed; the term was later applied to the street procession of songs, dances, and historical tableaux that became fashionable during the 1920s, and which exists today in forms such as the Lord Mayor's Show in London. Related to the pageant is the open-air entertainment *son et lumière*, in which the history of the venue is performed in a series of episodes accompanied by sound and projected lighting effects.

**pantomime** in the British theatre, a traditional Christmas entertainment with its origins in the harlequin spectacles of the 18th century and burlesque of the 19th century, which gave rise to the tradition of the principal boy being played by an actress and the dame by an actor. The harlequin's role diminished altogether as themes developed on folktales such as *The Sleeping Beauty* and *Cinderella*, and with the introduction of additional material such as popular songs, topical comedy, and audience participation. The term 'pantomime' was also applied to Roman dumbshows performed by a masked actor, to 18th-century ballets with mythical themes, and, in 19th-century France, to the wordless Pierrot plays from which modern mime developed.

**puppet theatre** drama acted by puppets manipulated by usually unseen operators. By the 16th and 17th centuries refined versions of the travelling puppet shows became popular with the aristocracy, and puppets were extensively used as vehicles for caricature and satire until the 19th century. There has been a revival of interest in the 20th century, partly stimulated by the influence of the *jōruri* tradition in Japan, with its large, intricate puppets, and by leading exponents of rod puppets such as Obraztsov and his Moscow Puppet Theatre, and most recently by Fluck and Law, whose satirical *Spitting Image* puppets, caricaturing public figures, have appeared on British television.

**revue** stage presentation involving short satirical and topical items in the form of songs, sketches, and monologues; it originated in the late 19th century. The first revue in the UK seems to have been *Under the Clock* 1893 by Seymour Hicks and Charles Brookfield. The 1920s revues were spectacular entertainments, but the 'intimate revue' became increasingly popular, employing writers such as Noel Coward. During the 1960s the satirical revue took off with the Cambridge Footlights' production *Beyond the Fringe* 1961, firmly establishing the revue tradition among the young and at fringe theatrical events.

**tragedy** in general, a play dealing with a serious theme, traditionally one in which the leading character meets disaster either as a result of personal failings or circumstances beyond his or her control. In classical tragedy the protagonist is faced with an impossible choice. This Greek view of tragedy, expressed in the work of Aeschylus, Sophocles, and Euripides, and later defined by Aristotle, has been predominant in the western tradition. In the 20th century tragedies in the narrow Greek sense of dealing with exalted personages in an elevated manner has virtually died out. Tragedy has been replaced by dramas with 'tragic' implications or overtones, as in the work of Ibsen, O'Neill, Tennessee Williams, Pinter, and Osborne, for example, or by the hybrid tragicomedy.

# GREAT DRAMATISTS

**Aeschylus** c 525–456 BC. Greek dramatist, widely regarded as the founder of European tragedy. By the introduction of a second actor he made true dialogue and dramatic action possible. Aeschylus wrote some 90 plays between 499 and 458, of which seven survive. These are *The Suppliant Women*, performed about 490; *The Persians* 472; *Seven Against Thebes* 467; *Prometheus Bound*, about 460; and the *Oresteia* trilogy 458, dealing with the curse on the house of Atreus.

**Anouilh** Jean 1910–1987. French playwright whose plays dramatize his concerns with the contrasts between innocence and experience, poverty in a world of riches, and the role of memory. His plays include *Antigone* 1943, *L'Invitation au château/Ring Round the Moon* 1947, *La Répétition ou l'amour puni/The Rehearsal* 1950, and *Becket* 1959, about Thomas Becket and Henry II.

**Aristophanes** c 445–385 BC. Greek comedic dramatist. Of his 11 extant plays, the early comedies are remarkable for the violent satire with which he ridiculed the democratic war leaders. He also satirized contemporary issues such as the new learning of Socrates in *The Clouds* 423 and the power of women in *Lysistrata* 411. The chorus plays a prominent role, frequently giving the play its title, as in *The Birds* 414, *The Wasps* 422, and *The Frogs* 405.

**Ashcroft** Peggy 1907–1991. English actress. Her many leading roles included Desdemona in *Othello* (with Paul Robeson), Juliet in *Romeo and Juliet* 1935 (with Laurence Olivier and John Gielgud), Hedda Gabler 1954, and appearances in the television play *Caught on a Train* 1980 (BAFTA award), the series *The Jewel in the Crown* 1984 and the film *A Passage to India* 1985.

**Ayckbourn** Alan 1939– . English dramatist, and director of the Stephen Joseph Theatre in the Round, Scarborough, from 1959. His prolific output, characterized by comic dialogue and experiments in dramatic structure, includes the trilogy *The Norman Conquests* 1974, in which each play presents the events of a single weekend from a different vantage point; *A Woman in Mind* 1986; *Henceforward* 1987; and *Man of the Moment* 1988.

**Beckett** Samuel 1906–1990. Irish novelist and dramatist who wrote in French and English. His *En attendant Godot/Waiting for Godot* 1953, in which two tramps wait endlessly for the enigmatic 'Godot', brought the Theatre of the Absurd to public attention, portraying the 'absurdity' of the human condition in an irrational universe. This predicament is explored to further extremes in *Fin de Partie/Endgame* 1957 and *Happy Days* 1961. Nobel Prize for Literature 1969.

**Bond** Edward 1935– . English dramatist. His work often makes use of historical settings to expose modern injustices. Bond's early plays aroused controversy because of the savagery of some of his imagery—for example, the brutal stoning of a baby by bored youths in *Saved* 1965. Other works include *Early Morning* 1968, the last play to be banned in the

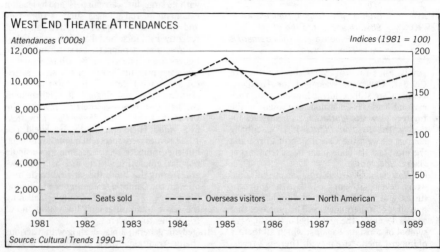

WEST END THEATRE ATTENDANCES

Attendances ('000s)                                    Indices (1981 = 100)

Seats sold ——— Overseas visitors ------ North American —·—·—

Source: Cultural Trends 1990–1

UK by the Lord Chamberlain; *Lear* 1972, a reworking of Shakespeare's play; *Bingo* 1973, an account of Shakespeare's last days; and *The War Plays* 1985.

**Branagh** Kenneth 1960– . English actor and director. He founded, with David Parfitt, the Renaissance Theatre Company 1987, was a notable Hamlet and Touchstone in 1988, and in 1989 directed and starred in a film of Shakespeare's *Henry V*.

**Brecht** Bertolt 1898–1956. German dramatist and poet who aimed to destroy the 'suspension of disbelief' usual in the theatre and to express Marxist ideas. His work includes *Die Dreigoschenoper/The Threepenny Opera* 1928 (an adaptation of John Gay's *The Beggar's Opera*, with music by Kurt Weill); *Mutter Courage/Mother Courage* 1941, set during the Thirty Years' War; *and Der kaukasische Kreidekreis/The Caucasian Chalk Circle* 1949. In 1949 he established the Berliner Ensemble theatre group in East Germany.

**Brook** Peter (Stephen Paul) 1925– . English director. His experimental work with the Royal Shakespeare Company included a production of *A Midsummer Night's Dream* 1970, set in a white gymnasium and combining elements of circus and commedia dell'arte. In 1970 he established Le Centre International de Créations Théâtrales (International Centre for Theatre Research) in Paris. His later productions with the Théâtre Bouffes du Nord transcend Western theatre conventions and include *The Conference of the Birds* 1973, based on a Persian story; *The Ik* 1975, and *The Mahabarata* 1985/88, a cycle of three plays lasting ten hours, based on the Hindu epic.

**Chekhov** Anton Pavlovich 1860–1904. Russian dramatist and writer. His plays concentrate on the creation of atmosphere and the delineation of internal development, rather than external action. His first play, *Ivanov* 1887, was a failure, as was *The Seagull* 1896 until revived by Stanislavsky 1898 at the Moscow Arts Theatre, for which Chekhov went on to write his major plays *Uncle Vanya* 1899, *The Three Sisters* 1901, and *The Cherry Orchard* 1904.

**Churchill** Caryl 1938– . English playwright, whose predominantly radical and feminist works include *Top Girls* 1982, a study of the hazards encountered by 'career' women throughout history; *Serious Money* 1987, which satirized the world of the brash young brokers of the City of London; and *Mad Forest* 1990, set in Romania during the overthrow of the Ceauşescu regime.

**Congreve** William 1670–1729. English dramatist and poet. His first success was the comedy *The Old Bachelor* 1693, followed by *The Double Dealer* 1694, *Love for Love* 1695, the tragedy *The Mourning Bride* 1697, and *The Way of the World* 1700. His plays, which satirize the social affectations of the time, are characterized by elegant wit and wordplay.

**Corneille** Pierre 1606–1684. French dramatist. His many tragedies, such as *Oedipe* 1659, glorify the strength of will governed by reason, and established the French classical dramatic tradition for the next two centuries. His first play, *Mélite*, was performed 1629, followed by others that gained him a brief period of favour with Cardinal Richelieu. *Le Cid* 1636 was attacked by the Academicians, although it received public acclaim. Later plays were based on Aristotle's unities of time, place, and action.

**Coward** Noël 1899–1973. English playwright, actor, producer, director, and composer, who epitomized the witty and sophisticated man of the theatre. From his first success with *The Young Idea* 1923, he wrote and appeared in plays and comedies on both sides of the Atlantic such as *Hay Fever* 1925, *Private Lives* 1930 with Gertrude Lawrence, *Design for Living* 1933, and *Blithe Spirit* 1941.

**Craig** Edward Gordon 1872–1966. English director and stage designer. His innovations and theories on stage design and lighting effects, expounded in *On the Art of the Theatre* 1911, had a profound influence on stage production in Europe and the USA.

**Dench** Judi (Judith Olivia) 1934– . English actress who made her professional debut as Ophelia in *Hamlet* 1957 with the Old Vic Company. Her Shakespearean roles include Portia in *Twelfth Night*, Lady Macbeth, and Cleopatra. She is also a versatile comedy actress and has appeared in musicals, notably as Sally Bowles in *Cabaret* 1968.

**Donellan** Declan 1953– . British theatre director, cofounder of **Cheek by Jowl** theatre company 1981, and associate director of the National Theatre from 1989. His irreverent and audacious productions include many classics, such as Racine's *Andromaque* 1985, Corneille's *Le Cid* 1987, and Ibsen's *Peer Gynt* 1990.

**Euripides** c 484–407 BC. Greek dramatist whose plays dealt with social issues and the emotions and reactions of ordinary people rather than with the deities and grandiose themes of his contemporaries. He wrote more than 80 plays, of which 18 survive, including *Alcestis* 438, *Medea* 431, *Andromache* 426, *The Trojan Women* 415, *Electra* 413, *Iphigenia in Tauris* 413, and *The Bacchae* 405 BC. His influence on later drama was probably greater than that of either of the other two great tragedians, Aeschylus and Sophocles.

**Eyre** Richard (Charles Hastings) 1943– . English stage and film director who succeeded Peter Hall as artistic director of the National Theatre, London, 1988. His productions include *Guys and Dolls* 1982, *Bartholomew Fair* 1988, *Hamlet* 1989, and *Richard III* 1990, set in 1930s Britain.

**Fo** Dario 1926– . Italian playwright. His plays are predominantly political satires combining black humour with slapstick. They include *Morte accidentale di un anarchico/Accidental Death of an Anarchist* 1970, and *Non si paga non si paga/Can't Pay? Won't Pay!* 1975/1981.

**Garrick** David 1717–79. English actor and theatre manager. From 1747 he became joint licensee of the Drury Lane theatre with his own company, and instituted a number of significant theatrical conventions, including concealed stage lighting, banishing spectators from the stage, and naturalistic painted backdrops. Garrick was also responsible for changing the acting style of his time, by replacing the traditional declamatory delivery with a naturalness of manner.

**Genet** Jean 1910–1986. French dramatist, novelist, and poet, an exponent of the Theatre of Cruelty. His turbulent life and early years spent in prison are reflected in his drama, characterized by ritual, role-play, and illusion, in which his characters come to act out their bizarre and violent fantasies. His plays include *Les bonnes/The Maids* 1947, *Le balcon/The Balcony* 1957, and two plays dealing with the Algerian situation: *Les nègres/The Blacks* 1959, and *Les paravents/The Screens* 1961.

**Gielgud** John 1904– . English actor and director, renowned as one of the greatest Shakespearean actors of his time. He made his debut at the Old Vic in 1921, and his numerous stage appearances range from works by Chekhov and Sheridan to those of Alan Bennett, Harold Pinter, and David Storey.

**Goethe** Johann Wolfgang von 1749–1832. German poet and dramatist. His play *Götz von Berlichingen* 1773, inspired by the work of Shakespeare, became the cornerstone of the Romantic *Sturm und Drang* ('storm and stress') movement. His masterpiece, the poetic play *Faust*, was published in two parts: Part I in 1808, Part II posthumously in 1833. Its length and sheer scale present enormous staging difficulties; producers have often resorted to using *Urfaust*, an earlier draft, not discovered until 1886.

**Granville-Barker** Harley 1877–1946. English theatre director and author. He was director and manager with J E Vedrenne at the Royal Court Theatre, London, 1904–18, producing plays by Shaw, Yeats, Ibsen, Galsworthy, and Masefield. Granville- Barker's plays include *Waste* 1907, *The Voysey Inheritance* 1905, and *The Madras House* 1910. His series of *Prefaces to Shakespeare* 1927–47 influenced the staging of Shakespeare for many years.

**Hall** Peter (Reginald Frederick) 1930– . English theatre, opera, and film director. He was director of the Royal Shakespeare Theatre at Stratford 1960–68 and developed the Royal Shakespeare Company 1968–73 until appointed director of the National Theatre 1973–88, succeeding Laurence Olivier. His productions include *Waiting for Godot* 1955, *The Wars of the Roses* 1963, *The Homecoming* stage 1967 and film 1973, and *The Oresteia* 1981. In 1988 he founded the Peter Hall Company, which opened with Tennessee Williams' *Orpheus Descending*.

**Ibsen** Henrik 1828–1906. Norwegian dramatist whose work, characterized by its poetic realism, revolutionized European theatre. His two great verse dramas, *Brand* 1866 and *Peer Gynt* 1867, were followed by realistic plays dealing with social issues, including *Pillars of Society* 1877, *A Doll's House* 1879, *Ghosts* 1881, *An Enemy of the People* 1882, *The Wild Duck* 1884, *Rosmersholm* 1886, *The Lady from the Sea* 1888 and *Hedda Gabler* 1890. His later plays, moving towards symbolism, include *Little Eyolf* 1894 and *When We Dead Awaken* 1899.

**Ionesco** Eugène 1912– . Romanian-born French dramatist, a leading exponent of the Theatre of the Absurd. Most of his plays are in one act and express his concern with the futility of language as a means of communication. These include *La Cantatrice chauve/The Bald Prima Donna* 1950 and *La Leçon/The Lesson* 1951. Later full-length plays include *Rhinocéros* 1959 and *Le Roi se meurt/Exit the King* 1962.

**Irving** Henry. Stage name of John Brodribb 1838–1905. English actor and manager. He established his reputation from 1871, chiefly at the Lyceum Theatre in London, where he became manager 1878. He staged a series of successful Shakespearean productions there, including *Romeo and Juliet* 1882, with himself and Ellen Terry playing the leading roles. He was the first actor to be knighted, in 1895.

**Jonson** Ben 1572–1637. English dramatist, poet, and critic. *Every Man in His Humour* 1598 established the English 'comedy of humours', in which each character embodies a 'humour', or vice, such as greed, lust, or avarice. His first extant tragedy is *Sejanus* 1603, which included Shakespeare as a member of the original cast. The plays of his middle years include *Volpone, or the Fox* 1606, *The Alchemist* 1610, and *Bartholomew Fair* 1614.

**Leigh** Mike 1943– . English playwright and filmmaker, noted for his sharp social satires. He directs his own plays, which evolve through improvisation before they are scripted; they include the comedies *Goose Pimples* 1981 and *Home Sweet Home* 1982. Leigh's work for television includes *Nuts in May* 1976 and *Abigail's Party* 1977; his films *High Hopes* 1989 and *Life Is Sweet* 1991.

**Lorca** Federico García 1898–1936. Spanish poet and dramatist. His plays include the three powerful and intense 'Spanish Earth' tragedies *Bodas de sangre/Blood Wedding* 1933, a savage story of feuding families; *Yerma* 1934; and *La Casa de Bernarda Alba/The House of Bernarda Alba* 1936. He was killed by fascist Falangists in the Spanish Civil War.

**McKellen** Ian Murray 1939– . English actor acclaimed as the leading Shakespearean player of his generation. His major stage roles include Macbeth 1977; Max in Martin Sherman's *Bent* 1979; Platonov in Chekhov's *Wild Honey* 1986, Iago in *Othello* 1989, and Richard III 1990. His films include *Priest of Love* 1982 and *Plenty* 1985.

**Mamet** David 1947– . US playwright. His plays, with their vivid, freewheeling language and sense of ordinary US life, include *American Buffalo* 1977, *Sexual Perversity in Chicago* 1978, *Glengarry Glen Ross* 1984, and *Speed-*

*the-Plow* 1987.

**Marlowe** Christopher 1564–93. English poet and dramatist, a contemporary of Shakespeare, and a strong influence on the course of Elizabethan drama. His work includes the blank-verse plays *Tamburlaine the Great* about 1587, *The Jew of Malta* about 1590, and *Edward II* and *The Tragical History of Doctor Faustus* both about 1592. He was murdered in a Deptford tavern, allegedly in a dispute over the bill, but it may have been a political killing.

**Miller** Arthur 1915– . American playwright. His plays deal with family relationships and contemporary American values, and include *All My Sons* 1947, a condemnation of war profiteering; *Death of a Salesman* 1949; *The Crucible* 1953, based on the Salem witch trials of the 17th century but reflecting the communist witch-hunts of Senator Joe McCarthy in the 1950s; and *After the Fall* 1964, in which the character of Maggie is allegedly based on the actress Marilyn Monroe, to whom Miller was married 1956–61. His prolific output still continues: *Danger: Memory!* appeared in 1987.

**Molière** pen name of Jean-Baptiste Poquelin 1622–1673. French comic dramatist and actor who founded and acted in the Illustre-Théâtre in Paris from 1643. After failure and prison he formed a successful touring company and returned to Paris in 1658. He established his reputation with *Les Précieuses ridicules/The Affected Wives* 1660. This was followed by his great satiric masterpieces, which include: *L'Ecole des femmes/The School for Wives* 1662; *Le Tartuffe/Tartuffe* 1664, banned until 1669 for attacking the hypocrisy of the clergy; *Le Misanthrope/The Misanthrope* 1666; *L'Avare/The Miser* 1668; *Le Bourgeois gentilhomme/The Would-be Gentleman* 1670; and *Le Malade imaginaire/The Hypochondriac* 1673.

**O'Casey** Sean. Adopted name of John Casey 1884–1964. Irish dramatist. His early plays are tragicomedies, blending realism with symbolism and poetic with vernacular speech: *The Shadow of a Gunman* 1922, *Juno and the Paycock* 1925, and *The Plough and the Stars* 1926. Later plays include *Red Roses for Me* 1946 and *The Drums of Father Ned* 1960.

**Olivier** Laurence Kerr, Baron Olivier 1907–1989. English actor and director. He established his reputation at the Old Vic, particularly in *Hamlet* 1937. His other major stage roles include Henry V, Richard III, and Archie Rice in John Osborne's *The Entertainer*, which were all filmed. He was director of the Chichester Festival Theatre from 1961–65 and first director of the National Theatre Company 1962–73. He was one of the finest English actors in the history of the theatre.

**O'Neill** Eugene Gladstone 1888–1953. US dramatist. His first full-length play, *Beyond the Horizon* 1920, won a Pulitzer Prize. His best plays are characterized by a down-to-earth quality even when he is experimenting with expressionism, symbolism, or stream of consciousness, and include *The Emperor Jones* 1921, *Desire under the Elms* 1924, *Mourning Becomes Electra* 1931 (a version of Aeschylus' *Oresteia*) and *The Iceman Cometh* 1946. His masterpiece, *Long Day's Journey into Night*, written in 1941, was first performed posthumously in 1956. He was awarded a Nobel Prize for Literature 1936.

**Orton** Joe 1933–1967. English dramatist in whose black comedies surreal and violent action takes place in genteel and unlikely settings. Plays include *Entertaining Mr Sloane* 1964, *Loot* 1966, and *What the Butler Saw* 1968. He was murdered by his lover Kenneth Halliwell.

**Osborne** John (James) 1929– . English dramatist. He was one of the first Angry Young Men (anti- establishment writers of the 1950s) of British theatre with his debut play, *Look Back in Anger* 1956. Other plays include *The Entertainer* 1957, *Luther* 1960, and *Watch It Come Down* 1976.

**Pinero** Arthur Wing 1855–1934. English dramatist. A leading exponent of the 'well-made' play, he enjoyed great contemporary success with his farces *The Magistrate* 1885, *Dandy Dick* 1886, and *The Cabinet Minister* 1890. A departure to more substantial social drama came with *The Second Mrs Tanqueray* 1893, and the comedies *Trelawny of the 'Wells'* 1898 and *The Gay Lord Quex* 1899.

**Pinter** Harold 1930– . English dramatist and director. Many of his plays are ambiguous comedies on the theme of the breakdown of communication, broadly in the tradition of the Theatre of the Absurd. They include *The Birthday Party* 1958; *The Caretaker* 1960; *The Homecoming* 1965; and a series of one-act plays, *The Lover* 1963, *Silence* and *Landscape* 1969, and *No Man's Land* 1975. His plays entered the political arena with *Mountain Language* 1988.

**Pirandello** Luigi 1867–1936. Italian dramatist and novelist. His plays revolve around the themes of the futility of human endeavour and the impossibility of defining reality, and include *Sei personaggi in cerca d'autore/Six Characters in Search of an Author* 1921 and *Enrico Quarto/Henry IV* 1922. Nobel Prize for Literature 1934.

**Racine** Jean 1639–99. French dramatist and exponent of the classical tragedy in French drama. His subjects came from Greek mythology and he observed the rules of classical Greek drama. Most of his tragedies have women in the title role—for example, *Andromaque* 1667, *Iphigénie* 1674, and *Phèdre* 1677. After the contemporary failure of *Phèdre*, he gave up writing for the secular stage, but was persuaded by Madame de Maintenon, the second wife of Louis XIV, to write two religious dramas, *Esther* 1689 and *Athalie* 1691, which achieved posthumous success.

**Reinhardt** Max. Stage name of Max Goldmann 1873–1943. Austrian actor, director, and manager whose Expressionist style was predominant in German theatre and film during the 1920s and 1930s. He excelled in lavish spectacles—for example, *Oedipus Rex* in Munich

1910 and *The Miracle* at Olympia, London, 1911, which are remembered for his control of huge crowds on stage, and use of new lighting techniques and stage devices. Reinhardt also directed small-scale intimate dramas in the smaller Berlin theatres and founded the Salzburg Festival in 1917.

**Sartre** Jean-Paul 1905–80. French writer and philosopher. A founder of existentialism, he expressed its tenets in his plays, which include *Les Mouches/The Flies* 1943, a retelling of the Orestes myth, and *Huis-clos/In Camera* 1944, in which three characters are confined in a hell of their own making. In 1951 his most ambitious, but less theatrically successful, play *Le Diable et le Bon Dieu* was written, followed by *Nekrassov* 1955 and *Les Séquestrés d'Altona/The Condemned of Altona* 1959. He refused the Nobel Prize for Literature in 1964.

**Schiller** Johann Christoph Friedrich von 1759 –1805. German dramatist, poet, and historian. He was a leading exponent of the *Sturm und Drang* ('storm and stress') movement. His first play *Die Räuber/The Robbers* 1782 was an immediate success, particularly with the young. This was followed by *Kabale und Liebe/Love and Intrigue* 1784 and a romantic historical tragedy, *Don Carlos* 1789. His later works include the historical trilogy *Wallenstein* 1798–9, and the classical dramas *Maria Stuart* 1800, *Die Jungfrau von Orleans/The Maid of Orleans* 1801, and *Wilhelm Tell* 1804.

**Shakespeare** William 1564–1616. English playwright and poet. Established in London by 1589 as an actor and a playwright, he was England's unrivalled dramatist until his death, and is considered the greatest English dramatist. His plays, written in blank verse, can be broadly divided into **lyric plays**, including *Romeo and Juliet* and *A Midsummer Night's Dream*; **comedies**, including *The Comedy of Errors*, *As You Like It*, *Much Ado About Nothing*, and *Measure For Measure*; **historical plays**, such as *Henry VI* (in three parts), *Richard III*, and *Henry IV* (in two parts), which often showed cynical political wisdom; and **tragedies**, such as *Hamlet*, *Macbeth*, and *King Lear*.

For the first 200 years after his death, Shakespeare's plays were frequently performed in cut or revised form (Nahun Tate's *King Lear* was given a happy ending), and it was not until the 19th century, with the critical assessments of Coleridge and Hazlitt, that the original texts were restored. Since then the plays have been consistently performed throughout the world, and have exerted an immeasurable influence on the history of the theatre.

**Shaw** George Bernard 1856–1950. Irish dramatist and critic. A prolific writer, he allied himself with a new and essentially political and polemical movement in the theatre, aiming in his work to engage the audience's social conscience and intellect as well as its emotions. His plays include *Mrs Warren's Profession* (1893, but banned until 1902 because it dealt with prostitution), *Arms and the Man* 1894, *Candida* 1895, the epic *Man and Superman*

1905, *Major Barbara* 1905, *Pygmalion* 1913 (adapted as the musical *My Fair Lady*), *Heartbreak House* 1920, and *St Joan* 1923. Nobel Prize for Literature 1925.

**Shepard** Sam 1943– . US dramatist and actor. His work combines colloquial American dialogue with striking visual imagery, and includes *The Tooth of Crime* 1972 and *Buried Child* 1978, for which he won the Pulitzer Prize. *Seduced* 1979 is based on the life of the recluse Howard Hughes. He has acted in a number of films, including *The Right Stuff* 1983, *Fool for Love* 1986, based on his play of the same name, and *Steel Magnolias* 1989.

**Sheridan** Richard Brinsley 1751–1816. Irish dramatist and theatre manager. His plays were masterpieces of the 'comedy of manners'—a more refined version of the earlier and coarser Restoration dramas, and include *The Rivals* 1775, celebrated for the character of Mrs Malaprop; *The School for Scandal* 1777; and *The Critic* 1779. Sheridan was manager of the Drury Lane Theatre from 1776, and became a member of parliament 1780.

**Simon** (Marvin) Neil 1927– . US playwright. His stage plays include the wryly comic *Barefoot in the Park* 1963, *The Odd Couple* 1965, and *The Sunshine Boys* 1972, and the more serious, autobiographical trilogy *Brighton Beach Memoirs* 1983, *Biloxi Blues* 1985, and *Broadway Bound* 1986. He has also written screenplays and co-written musicals.

**Sophocles** 496–406. Greek dramatist who, with Aeschylus and Euripides, is one of the three great tragedians. He modified the form of tragedy by introducing a third actor, developing stage scenery, and reducing the chorus to a lyrical device emphasising changes of mood rather than directly affecting the action. Sophocles wrote over 100 plays, of which seven tragedies and a large fragment of a satyr play (a tragedy treated in a grotesquely comic fashion) survive. These include *Ajax* about 450, *Antigone* about 441, *Oedipus Rex* about 425, *Electra* about 409, and *Oedipus at Colonus* about 406.

**Stanislavsky** Konstantin Sergeivich 1863–1938. Russian actor, director, and teacher of acting. He was a cofounder of the Moscow Art Theatre 1898 and achieved his greatest success as a director with his productions of Chekhov and Gorky. He rejected the declamatory style of acting in favour of a more realistic approach concentrating on the psychological development of character. He described his techniques in *My Life in Art* 1924, *An Actor Prepares* 1926, and other works, which had great influence on acting in Europe and the USA.

**Stoppard** Tom 1937– . Czechoslovak-born British playwright, whose works use wit and wordplay to explore logical and philosophical ideas. He wrote *Rosencrantz and Guildenstern are Dead* 1967 (the film of which he directed 1989). This was followed by comedies including *The Real Inspector Hound* 1968, *Jumpers* 1972, *Travesties* 1974, *Dirty Linen* 1976, *The Real Thing* 1982, and *Hapgood* 1988.

**Strindberg** August 1849–1912. Swedish dramatist and novelist. His plays, influential in the development of dramatic technique, are in a variety of styles including historical plays, symbolic dramas (the two-part *Dödsdansen/The Dance of Death* 1901), and 'chamber plays', such as *Spoksonaten/The Ghost [Spook] Sonata* 1907. *Fadern/ The Father* 1887 and *Fröken Julie/Miss Julie* 1888 are both powerful studies of human frailty and hostility between the sexes.

**Synge** J(ohn) M(illington) 1871–1909. Irish playwright, a leading figure in the Irish dramatic revival of the early 20th century. His six plays show a poetic ear for the speech patterns of the Aran Islands and West Ireland. They include *In the Shadow of the Glen* 1903, *Riders to the Sea* 1904, and *The Playboy of the Western World* 1907, which caused riots at the Abbey Theatre, Dublin, when first performed.

**Vega, Lope Felix de (Carpio)** 1562–1635. Spanish dramatist and poet, one of the founders of modern Spanish drama. He wrote over 1,500 plays (of which 426 are still in existence), mostly tragicomedies. He set out his views on drama in *Arte nuevo de hacer comedias/The New Art of Writing Plays* 1609, in which he adopts a practical approach while reaffirming the classical form. *Fuenteovejuna/The Sheep Wall* 1614 has been acclaimed in this century as the first proletarian drama.

**Warner** Deborah 1959– . English theatre director who founded the Kick Theatre company 1980. Discarding period costume and furnished sets, she adopted an uncluttered approach to the classics, including productions of many Shakespeare plays and Sophocles' *Electra*.

**Webster** John c 1580–1634. English dramatist who ranks after Shakespeare as the greatest tragedian of his time and is the Jacobean whose works are most frequently revived today. His two great plays *The White Devil* about 1612 and *The Duchess of Malfi* 1613/14 are dark, violent tragedies obsessed with death and decay, and infused with poetic brilliance.

**Wilde** Oscar (Fingal O'Flahertie Wills) 1854–1900. Irish writer. In the theatre he is best known for his elegant, stylish comedies with witty dialogue, such as *Lady Windermere's Fan* 1892, *A Woman of No Importance* 1893, *An Ideal Husband* 1895, and his most consistently successful play, *The Importance of Being Earnest* 1895. The drama *Salome* 1893, based on the biblical character, was written in French; considered scandalous by the British censor, it was first performed in Paris 1896 with the actress Sarah Bernhardt in the title role.

**Williams** Tennessee. Pen name of Thomas Lanier Williams 1911–1983. US playwright, an exponent of psychological realism with a marked interest in the visual elements of the theatre and a mastery of language. His plays, usually set in the Deep South against a background of decadence and degradation, include *The Glass Menagerie* 1945, *A Streetcar Named Desire* 1947, and *Cat on a Hot Tin Roof* 1955.

### Actors

*Who do you think are the better actors and actresses—people who appear:*

| | |
|---|---|
| Mainly in the theatre | 48 |
| Mainly in cinema films | 20 |
| Mainly on television | 18 |
| Don't know | 15 |

# SCIENCE AND TECHNOLOGY

# TERMS AND TECHNIQUES

**absolute dating** methods that determine age in calendar years by reference to a fixed time scale. Also called chronometric dating, it usually incorporates a measure of uncertainty, expressed as a standard deviation.

**accelerator mass spectrometry** (AMS) a new radiocarbon dating method that determines the actual number of carbon-14 atoms in a sample rather than the small numbers of carbon-14 atoms that decay radioactively during the measurement time of the conventional method. This method requires only a tiny sample, and its measurement time is only about one hour (as opposed to days for radiocarbon dating), but it is expensive.

**aerial photography** (or aerial archaeology) technique for taking photographs from a high level, particularly useful in distinguishing surface features (such as crop marks, soil marks, shadow marks) not clearly visible from ground level and which indicate the presence of ancient features; for example, crops will show differences in growth and colour if they are growing over a buried wall foundation or other stone feature.

**aerial reconnaissance** techniques used in the recording and interpretation of archaeological sites from the air, and also useful in discovering new sites. *Thermal prospection* (also called thermography) is an expensive remote-sensing method that uses heat sensors in aircraft which scan the varying temperatures of remains below ground. Images produced from LANDSAT satellites have been used to discover ancient sites and landscapes (in particular Mayan sites in Mesoamerica); SLAR (sideways looking aerial radar) from NASA aircraft has also been used to reveal ancient sites and field systems.

**anthropology** the study of humanity's physical characteristics and culture, generally divided into the three subdisciplines of physical (biological) anthropology, social (cultural) anthropology, and archaeology.

**archaeology** the study of the human past through the systematic recovery and analysis of material remains. Its aims are to recover, describe and classify this material, to describe the form and behaviour of past societies, and to understand the reasons for this behaviour. A truly interdisciplinary subject, it has borrowed many of its major theoretical and methodological concepts and approaches from history and anthropology.

*methods* Principal activities include preliminary field (or site) surveys, excavation (where necessary), and the classification, dating, and interpretation of finds. Related disciplines that have been useful in archaeological reconstruction include stratigraphy (the study of geological strata), dendrochronology (the establishment of chronological sequences through the study of tree rings), palaeobotany (the study of ancient pollens, seeds, and grains), epigraphy (the study of inscriptions), and numismatics (the study of coins). Since 1958 radiocarbon dating has been used and refined to establish the age of archaeological strata and associated materials.

**archaeomagnetic dating** dating technique based on the palaeomagnetism of archaeological materials such as baked clay structures (hearths, kilns, ovens). When originally heated, their magnetic particles realigned with the Earth's magnetic field at the time, and since that field changes over time, local and regional chronologies of field-direction can be built up and independently dated. In England for example such curves have been established for the last 2000 years, allowing for any sample to be dated within that span to within approximately 50 years.

**archaeozoology** (or zooarchaeology) a branch of archaeology involving the analysis of animal remains for information on physiology and ecology; for the interpretation of these remains in association with artifacts and people; and for data on subsistence, dietary and butchering patterns, animal domestication, and palaeoenvironment.

**artifact** any movable object that has been used, modified, or manufactured by humans, such as a tool, weapon or vessel.

**assemblage** a collection of artifacts occurring together at a particular time and place that can be considered a single analytic unit. Frequently repeated assemblages that represent a broad range of human activity are termed an archaeological culture.

**atomic absorption spectrometry** a technique used to determine quantitatively the chemical composition of artifactual metals, minerals, and rocks, in order to identify raw material sources, to relate artifacts of the same material, or to trace trade routes. A sample of the material is atomized in a flame, and its light intensity measured. The method is slow and destructive.

**attribute** a characteristic element of a particular archaeological culture or group; or a specific element of an individual artifact, such as the rim of a pot or the base of a projectile point, or a type of decoration, raw material, or colour.

**auger** a tool used to collect sediment and soil samples below ground without hand excavation, or to determine the depth and type of archaeological deposits. The auger may be hand- or machine-powered.

**bosing** a subsurface detection technique for locating buried pits or ditches, carried out by striking the surface of the ground with a heavy wooden mallet; a duller sound is produced over any disturbance.

**Bronze Age** stage of prehistory and early history when bronze became the first metal worked extensively and used for tools and weapons. The second 'age' in the three-age system, it

## ARCHAEOLOGY: CHRONOLOGY

| | |
|---|---|
| 14th–16th centuries | The Renaissance revived interest in classical Greek and Roman art and architecture, including ruins and buried art and artefacts. |
| 1748 | The buried Roman city of Pompeii was discovered under ash from Vesuvius. |
| 1784 | Thomas Jefferson dug an Indian burial mound on the Rivanna River in Virginia and wrote a report on his finds. |
| 1790 | John Frere identified Old Stone Age (Palaeolithic) tools together with large extinct animals. |
| 1822 | Champollion deciphered Egyptian hieroglyphics. |
| 1836 | C J Thomsen devised the Stone, Bronze, and Iron Age classification. |
| 1840s | A H Layard excavated the Assyrian capital of Nineveh. |
| 1868 | Great Zimbabwe ruins in E Africa first seen by Europeans. |
| 1871 | Heinrich Schliemann began excavations at Troy. |
| 1879 | Ice Age paintings were first discovered at Altamira, Spain. |
| 1880s | A H Pitt-Rivers set new standards in meticulous excavation, recording, and typological studies, based on the principles of stratigraphy. |
| 1891 | W M F Petrie began excavating Akhetaton in Egypt. |
| 1899–1935 | A J Evans excavated Minoan Knossos in Crete. |
| 1900–44 | Max Uhle began the systematic study of the civilizations of Peru. |
| 1911 | The Inca city of Machu Picchu discovered by Hiram Bingham in the Andes. |
| 1911–12 | Piltdown skull 'discovered'; proved a fake 1949. |
| 1914–18 | Osbert Crawford developed the technique of aerial survey of sites. |
| 1922 | Tutankhamen's tomb in Egypt opened by Howard Carter. |
| 1926 | A kill site in Folsom, New Mexico, was found with human-made spearpoints in association with ancient bison. |
| 1935 | Dendrochronology (dating events in the distant past by counting tree rings) developed by Andrew E Douglass; useful where preserved timbers are present. |
| 1939 | Anglo-Saxon ship-burial treasure found at Sutton Hoo, England. |
| 1940 | Lascaux, the most spectacular decorated cave of the Ice Age, discovered by four boys in the Dordogne, France. |
| 1947 | The first of the Dead Sea Scrolls discovered. |
| 1948 | *Proconsul* prehistoric ape discovered by Mary Leakey in Kenya; several early hominid fossils found by Louis Leakey in Olduvai Gorge 1950s–1970s. |
| 1953 | Michael Ventris deciphered Minoan Linear B. |
| 1960s | Radiocarbon and thermoluminescence measurement developed as aids for dating remains. |
| 1961 | Swedish warship *Wasa* raised at Stockholm. |
| 1963 | W B Emery pioneered rescue archaeology at Abu Simbel before the site was flooded by the Aswan Dam. |
| 1974 | Tomb of Shi Huangdi discovered in China. |
| 1975 | Hominid nicknamed 'Lucy', c. 3 million years old, discovered at Hadar, Ethiopia. |
| 1976 | Footprints of hominids, c. 3.8 million years old, found in hardened mud at Laetoli, Tanzania. |
| 1978 | Tomb attributed to Philip II of Macedon (Alexander the Great's father) discovered in Greece. |
| 1979 | The Aztec capital Tenochtitlán excavated beneath a zone of Mexico City. |
| 1982 | The English king Henry VIII's warship *Mary Rose* of 1545 was raised and studied with new techniques in underwater archaeology. |
| 1985 | The tomb of Maya, Tutankhamen's treasurer, discovered at Saqqara, Egypt. |
| 1988 | Turin Shroud established as of medieval date by radiocarbon dating. |
| 1989 | Remains of Globe and Rose Theatres discovered in London, where many of Shakespeare's plays were originally performed. |

developed out of the Stone Age, preceded the Iron Age, and may be dated 5000–1200 BC in the Middle East and about 2200–500 BC in Europe. Mining and metalworking were the first specialized industries, and the invention of the wheel during this time revolutionized transport. Agricultural productivity (which began during the Neolithic period, about 10,000 BC), and hence the size of the population that could be supported, was transformed by the ox-drawn plough. Recent discoveries in Thailand suggest that the Far East, rather than the Middle East, was the cradle of the Bronze Age.

**cognitive archaeology** the study of past ways of thought from material remains, and of the meanings evoked by the symbolic nature of material culture.

**computerized axial tomography** (CAT) a technique for looking inside bodies or mummies without disturbing them. X-ray scans made at intervals produce a series of cross-sectional 'slices' that the computer can reformat to create images from any angle.

**context** an artifact's context may refer to its matrix (the sediment or material surrounding it), its provenance (its 3-dimensional position within that matrix), and its association with other artifacts in the matrix.

**contract archaeology** archaeological survey and/ or excavation, today increasingly required by state legislation, most often in advance of highway construction or urban development.

**core** solid cylinder of sediment or soil collected with a coring device and used to evaluate the geological context and stratigraphy of archaeological material or to obtain palaeobotanical samples; a stone blank from which flakes or blades are removed.

**cross-dating** method of demonstrating contemporaneity of two cultural groups by establishing links between them, for example the presence of objects of both groups in one another's archaeological contexts.

**cultural anthropology** (social anthropology) a subdiscipline of anthropology that analyzes human culture and society, the non-biological and behavioural aspects of humanity. Two principal branches are ethnography (the study at first hand of living cultures) and ethnology (the comparison of cultures using ethnographic evidence).

**cultural resource management** (CRM) the legally mandated protection of archaeological sites located on public lands in the USA that are threatened by destruction through development.

**dendrochronology** dating technique that uses tree-ring sequences to date timbers and other logs from archaeological structures and sites. This technique is based on the principle that every year trees add a ring of growth, and by counting these rings their age can be determined. An unbroken series of rings can be built up and extended back for centuries by 'overlapping' identical sequences preserved on modern and ancient timbers; subsequently, any piece of wood found in the area can have its rings checked against the master sequence and its precise age established. 'Floating' chronologies, which do not extend to the present day, have been built up in many regions worldwide and allow for relative dating between structures and sites.

In North America, sequences of tree rings extending back over 8,000 years have been obtained by using cores from the bristle-cone pine (*Pinus aristata*), which can live for over 4,000 years. Such sequences have proved very useful for calibrating, or correcting, radiocarbon dates, which were found to have serious discrepancies due to a differences in the atmosphere's carbon-14 content over time.

**diffusion** the spread of ideas, objects or cultural traits from one culture or society to another, rather than their independent invention; for example a diffusionist school of thought held that Egypt was the source of metallurgy and megalithic building, whereas it is now accepted that these traits arose independently in different areas.

**dowsing** unconventional and controversial method for locating subsurface features by holding out a twig, rod, or pendulum and waiting for it to move. Although used at times in archaeology, it is not taken seriously by most archaeologists.

**electrolysis** a cleaning process in archaeological conservation, especially of material from underwater archaeology, involving immersing the object in a chemical solution, and passing a weak current between it and a surrounding metal grill. Corrosive salts move slowly from the object (cathode) to the grill (anode), leaving the artifact clean.

**electron spin resonance** (ESR) is a nondestructive dating method applicable to teeth, bone, heat-treated flint, ceramics, sediments and stalagmitic concretions.

It enables electrons, displaced by natural radiation and then trapped in the structure, to be measured; their number indicate the age of the specimen.

**environmental archaeology** a subfield of archaeology aimed at identifying processes, factors and conditions of past biological and physical environmental systems and how they relate to cultural systems. It is an eminently interdisciplinary field, where archaeologists and natural scientists combine to reconstruct the human uses of plants and animals and how societies adapted to changing environmental conditions.

**eolith** naturally shaped or fractured stone found in Lower Pleistocene deposits and once believed by some archaeologists to be the oldest known artifact type, dating to the pre-Palaeolithic era. They are now recognized as not humanly made.

**ethnoarchaeology** the study of human behaviour, and of the material culture of living societies, in order to see how materials enter the archaeological record, and hence to provide hypotheses explaining the production, use, and disposal patterns of ancient material culture.

**ethnography** the description and analysis of individual contemporary cultures, using anthropological techniques like participant observation (where the anthropologist lives in the society being studied) and a reliance on informants. Ethnography has provided many data of use to the archaeologist as analogies.

**ethnology** the use of ethnographic data in a comparative analysis to understand how cultures work and why they change, with a view to deriving general principles about human society.

**excavation** the systematic recovery of archaeological data through the exposure of buried sites and artifacts. Excavation is destructive, and is therefore accompanied by a comprehensive recording of all material found and its three-dimensional locations (its context). As much material and information as possible must be recovered from any 'dig'. A full record of all the techniques employed in the excavation itself must also be made, so that future archaeologists will be able to evaluate the results of the work accurately.

## Chronological Chart Showing Major Cultural Developments Worldwide

| Years AD/BC | North Europe | Mediterranean | Near East | Egypt and Africa |
|---|---|---|---|---|
| 1,500 | | | | Great Zimbabwe |
| 1,000 | Medieval states | BYZANTINE EMPIRE | | |
| 500 | | | ISLAM | |
| AD | ROMAN EMPIRE | ROMAN EMPIRE | | Towns (Africa) AXUM |
| BC | | | | |
| 500 | IRON AGE | CLASSICAL GREECE | PERSIA BABYLON | LATE PERIOD |
| 1,000 | | | ASSYRIA | NEW KINGDOM |
| 1,500 | | Iron | HITITES | MIDDLE KINGDOM |
| | | MYCENAE | Iron | |
| 2,000 | BRONZE AGE (Stonehenge) | MINOAN | | OLD KINGDOM (Pyramids) |
| 2,500 | | | SUMER | EARLY DYNASTIC |
| 3,000 | | | Writing | |
| 3,500 | | | Cities | Towns (Egypt) |
| | | | Wheeled vehicles | |
| 4,000 | | | | |
| 4,500 | Megaliths | Copper (Balkans) | | |
| 5,000 | Farming, pottery | | | |
| 5,500 | | | Irrigation | |
| 6,000 | | | | |
| 6,500 | | Farming, pottery | Copper | Cattle (North Africa) |
| 7,000 | | | Pottery | Pottery (Sudan) |
| 7,500 | | | Wheat, rye etc | |
| 8,000 | | | | |
| 8,500 | | | | |
| 9,000 | | | Sheep | |
| 9,500 | | | | |
| 10,000 | | | | |

*Information supplied by Paul Bahn*

Besides being destructive, excavation is also costly. For both these reasons, it should be used only as a last resort. It can be partial, in which only a sample of the site is investigated, or total. Samples are chosen either by informed guesswork, in which case excavators investigate those areas they feel will be most productive, or statistically, in which case the sample is drawn using various statistical techniques, so as to ensure that it is representative. An important goal of excavation is a full understanding of a site's stratigraphy, that is the vertical layering of a site. These layers or levels can be defined naturally (e.g. soil changes), culturally (e.g.

different occupation levels), or arbitrarily (e.g. 10 cm/4 in levels). Excavation can also be done horizontally, to uncover larger areas of a particular layer to reveal the spatial relationships between artifacts and features in that layer. Known as open-area excavation, this is used especially where single-period deposits lie close to the surface and the time dimension is represented by lateral movement rather than by the placing of one building on top of the preceding one.

Most excavators employ a flexible combination of vertical and horizontal digging to adapt to the nature of their site and the questions they are seeking to answer.

| India | East Asia and Pacific | North America | Meso-America | South America | Years AD/BC |
|---|---|---|---|---|---|
| | | | | INCA | 1,500 |
| | | | AZTEC | | |
| | | Cahokia | | | 1,000 |
| | New Zealand | Chaco | "TOLTEC" | CHIMU | |
| | settled | HOPEWELL | | | 500 |
| | States (Japan) | | MAYA | | |
| | | PUEBLOS | | | AB |
| | Great Wall | | TEOTIHUACAN | MOCHE | |
| MAURYAN | (China) | | | | BC |
| | Cast iron | | | | |
| Iron | (China) | | | | 500 |
| | | | | | |
| | Lapita | Maize | | CHAVIN | 1,000 |
| | (Polynesia) | (Southwest) | OLMEC | | |
| | SHANG (China) | | | | 1,500 |
| | | | | | |
| | | | | | 2,000 |
| INDUS | | | | | |
| | Walled villages | | | | 2,500 |
| | (China) | | | Temple-mounds | |
| | | | | | 3,000 |
| | | | | Maize, llama | |
| | | | | cotton | 3,500 |
| | | | | | |
| | | | | | 4,000 |
| | | | | | |
| | | | | | 4,500 |
| | | | | | |
| | | | | | 5,000 |
| | Rice-millet | | Maize | | |
| | (China) | | | Manioc | 5,500 |
| | | | | Pottery | |
| | | | | (Amazonia) | 6,000 |
| | | | Beans, squash, | Beans, squash | |
| | | | peppers | peppers | 6,500 |
| Farming | Gardens | | | | |
| | (New Guinea) | | | | 7,000 |
| | | | | | |
| | | | | | 7,500 |
| | | | | | |
| | | | | | 8,000 |
| | | | | | |
| | | | | | 8,500 |
| | | | | | |
| | | | | | 9,000 |
| | | | | | |
| | | | | | 9,500 |
| | Pottery (Japan) | | | | |
| | | | | | 10,000 |

**experimental archaeology** the controlled replication of ancient technologies and behaviour in order to provide hypotheses that can be tested by actual archaeological data. Experiments can range in size from the reproduction of ancient tools in order to learn about their processes of manufacture and use, and their effectiveness, to the construction of whole villages and ancient subsistence practices in long-term experiments.

**feature** a non-portable element of a site, such as a hearth, wall, post-hole, or activity area.

**field survey** the examination of the surface of the earth for evidence of archaeological remains, without recourse to excavation. Surveys can be carried out unsystematically, where **field walking** takes place over areas suspected of having archaeological material, and the location of any finds or surface features encountered is plotted; or systematically, where the area is divided into a grid and a sample of its sectors are walked, making the survey more representative of the whole and hence more accurate.

**fission-track dating** dating method based on the natural and spontaneous nuclear fission of uranium-238 and its physical product, linear atomic displacements (tracks) created along the trajectory of released energized fission fragments. Knowing the rate of fission (a constant), the uranium content of the material and the number of fission tracks by counting, the age of the material can be determined. The method is most widely used to date volcanic deposits adjacent to archaeological material.

**geomagnetic reversal** a periodic reversal in the Earth's magnetic field (where magnetic north becomes south, and vice versa), occurring most recently c. 700,000 years ago. A sequence of such reversals stretching back millions of years has been built up with the aid of potassium-argon dating. Finding part of the sequence in the rocks of early hominid sites in Africa provides a useful method of checking other dating methods.

**grid system** an excavation technique that divides a site into squares to facilitate the recording of excavated objects and features. The practice includes both the vertical and horizontal dimensions by retaining intact baulks (standing sections) of earth between the excavated squares of the grid so that different layers can be traced and correlated across the site of the vertical profiles.

**hoard** a deliberately buried group of valuables or prized possessions, often in times of conflict or war, which were never reclaimed. Coins, objects in precious metals, and scrap metal are the most common objects found in hoards. In July 1991 the largest hoard found in Britain was discovered, consisting of 7,000 15th-century coins; it was declared treasure trove.

**infra-red absorption spectrometry** physical technique used to determine mineralogy or chemical composition of artifacts and organic substances, particularly amber. A sample is bombarded by infra-red radiation which causes the atoms in it to vibrate at frequencies characteristic of the atom species present. That part of the radiation spectrum vibrating at the same frequencies as absorbed by the amount of transmitted radiation at each wavelength is detected, forming the basis for identification. The method is useful for detecting ambers from different sources.

**Iron Age** the developmental stage of human technology when weapons and tools were made from iron. Iron was produced in Thailand by about 1600 BC but was considered inferior in strength to bronze until about 1000 when metallurgical techniques improved and the alloy steel was produced by adding carbon during the smelting process. In Europe it begins around 1100 BC, and early Iron Age cultures are represented by the Villanovans in Italy and Hallstatt and La Tène in central and western Europe; it is also the time when Celtic art flourished. The end of the period overlaps with the expansion of imperial Rome around the 1st Century BC, but beyond the borders of the Empire it is generally taken to end much later, around the 4th–6th centuries AD.

**isotopic analysis** the analysis of ratios of the principal isotopes preserved in human bone in order to reconstruct ancient diet, based on the principle that different food categories (e.g. marine resources) leave specific chemical signatures in the body.

### How Long Did it Take to Construct a Prehistoric Monument?

| Late Neolithic | labour hours |
|---|---|
| Stonehenge | 30,000,000 |
| Henge | 1,000,000 |
| | |
| *Early Neolithic* | |
| Causewayed Camp | 100,000 |
| Long Barrow | 10,000 |

Long Barrow: a burial mound, usually for collective inhumations; in some parts of Britain they comprised earth or chalk over a wooden mortuary structure; in others they included large stones, or megaliths.

Causewayed Camp: an enclosure with one or more circuits of ditch interrupted by numerous causeways. Unsuitable for defence, they were probably tribal meeting places or ritual centres.

Henge: a ritual enclosure, usually circular, comprising a bank and internal ditch, with one or two opposing entrances. Substantial timber buildings stood inside, and occasionally a stone circle.

*(Source: Paul Bahn)*

**landscape archaeology** the study of human occupation and activities on landscapes, in particular the patterning of settlements and sites within that broad perspective through time.

**magnetometer** device for measuring the intensity of the earth's magnetic field; distortions in this field occur when archaeological structures such as kilns and hearths are present, or pits and ditches. The technique allows for such features to be located without disturbing the ground, and for excavation to be focussed on the likeliest area.

**material culture** the physical, humanly-made remains of past societies (tools, buildings, etc.) which constitute the major source of evidence for archaeology.

**medieval archaeology** the archaeological study of the medieval period in Europe; in America and Australia the equivalent is *historical archaeology*, where it is directed at the colonial and post-colonial periods.

**Mesolithic** the Middle Stone Age developmental stage of human technology and of prehistory, following the Palaeolithic and preceeding the Neolithic. While the environment changed with the withdrawal of the Pleistocene ice sheets around 10,000 years ago, the old Palaeolithic hunting and gathering way of life continued during the Mesolithic; changes in the tool assemblages however reflect adaptations to environmental changes, with the flint industries of this period characterized by microliths (very small flint tools) in great number. With the introduction of farming and stock-rearing the Mesolithic gave way to the Neolithic (occurring in Britain around 4000 BC).

**metal detector** electronic device for detecting metal on or beneath the surface of the ground. It is used to survey areas for buried metallic objects, occasionally by archaeologists. However, their indiscriminate use by 'treasure hunters' led to their banning on recognized archaeological

## PICTURING THE PAST: COMPUTER GRAPHICS IN ARCHAEOLOGY

From surveying techniques to on-site recording to statistical analysis in the lab, computers have long played a vital part in archaeological research. Increasingly, though, it is in the application of computer graphics that the most innovative developments are taking place, and as archaeologists find themselves faced with decreased resources and funding, the use of automation techniques—particularly for labour-intensive tasks such as drawing site plans—becomes increasingly important.

In the vanguard of computer graphics (cg) applications to archaeology is computer-aided design (CAD). In the Department of Classical Archaeology at the University of Pennsylvania, AutoCAD is used to map and reconstruct architectural features discovered in excavations at Corinth. The program allows for the 3-D rendering and projection of ancient structures, and for them to be viewed from any angle, perspective, and elevation. At Oxford University, archaeologists studying a cg-generated model of a Roman temple could simulate a walk through the temple precinct and note the psychological effects of the architecture on the viewer according to where one stood in the precinct. Similar to the interactive world of virtual reality, computer graphics offers the viewer a 3-D image which alters in response to the (simulated) altered position or perspective of the viewer.

At the Department of Urban Archaeology at the Museum of London, topographic and architectural information from over 50 sites has been entered into the computer graphics system (using digitized Ordnance Survey maps for the City as the base), along with information on the dating of each feature. From this the computer can construct 'snapshots' of that area of London at different times within the Roman period, allowing for detailed and accurate maps to be drawn up. Ultimately, the system will allow for the complete cartographic coverage of ancient London, and serve as the graphics database for a Geographical Information System (GIS) for the archaeology of London. To assist in the reconstruction of complex composite site plans from 'single context plans' (that is, drawings representing each archaeological context, which can then be assembled into phase plans), a program called Hindsight was developed by Bryan Alvey (Cultural Heritage Information Consultants, London). Written in AutoCAD's AUTOLISP language and in C, it allows input of single context plans using a digitizer attached to a microcomputer; it can then reconstruct phase or period composite plans of any part, or all, of the site, and then output them at any scale (to a plotter or similar output device). In the creation of a composite plan, the system refers all the time to a matrix of stratigraphic relationships, enabling it to create a 3-D model that shows in one drawing both the phase plans and (with the depth dimension representing time) their sequence of deposition. Additionally, the use of colour in Hindsight allows for certain categories—such as ceramics, soil type, environmental material—to be shown for any context (for example, the frequency of Roman pottery in a particular phase).

Imaging techniques such as CAT and MRI (computerized axial tomography and magnetic resonance imaging) are also proving valuable aids to archaeology and anthropology. Using MRI on 7000-year-old skulls retrieved from a pond site in Florida revealed intact brain tissue, from which scientists were able to extract and analyze much of the original DNA material. An unidentifiable piece of organic material recovered from the same site was examined by means of a video-enhanced microscope, and through digitizing and enlarging the image it was revealed that the material was a piece of finely-woven cloth, the most complex sample of fabric of such an early date discovered in the Americas. A closer look through a scanning electron microscope showed that the fabric was in fact composed of palm fronds which were chewed and pulled through the weaver's teeth.

As computer graphics for the microcomputer becomes more affordable, it will become a standard tool in archaeological research. More sophisticated techniques (such as solid modelling) which allow for the 3-D rendering and rotation of objects will not only 'flesh out' schematic drawings but also allow for the immediate classification of artifacts; so, for example, once the attributes of a pottery fragment are recorded the program can identify and classify that fragment, reconstruct it into a whole pot, and provide additional information (its frequency in different strata, dating, typological development, etc.) retrieved from the artifact database. While the immediate benefits of the new technologies lie mainly in the automation of repetitive drawing tasks, the possibilities for new and imaginative applications extend to all areas of archaeology, not least in the teaching and presentation of the subject, where the visual organization of data can make all the difference between not understanding a very specialized language and making immediate sense out of, say, the results of an excavation or the lifespan of an artifact.

---

sites in some countries; in Britain the law forbids the use of metal detectors on 'scheduled' (that is nationally important) sites.

**metallographic examination** a method of analyzing the manufacturing techniques of metal artifacts. A cross-sectional slice of an artifact is polished, etched to highlight internal structures, and examined under a metallurgical microscope. The reflected light of the microscope enhances uneven surfaces revealing grain size, shape and boundaries, inclusions, fabric, defects, and other detail.

**microwear analysis** (or *usewear analysis*) the examination of the surface and working edge of an artifact for signs of use (such as damage or residue), often by means of a high-powered microscope. The technique is principally used

COMPARATIVE SURVIVAL RATES FOR MATERIAL IN WET AND ORDINARY
DRYLAND SITES

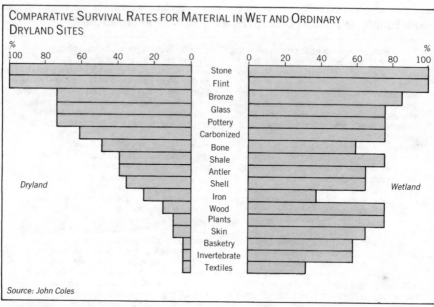

Source: John Coles

in the study of stone tools, which suffer diagnostic damage or polishing when used to cut, saw, or pierce other materials.

**Neolithic** last period of the Stone Age, characterized by settled communities based on agriculture and the domestication of animals, and identified by sophisticated, finely honed stone tools, and ceramic wares. The earliest neolithic communities appeared about 9000 BC in southwest Asia, followed by Egypt, India, and China. In Europe farming began in about 6500 BC in the Balkans and Aegean, spreading north and east. Sometimes called the Neolithic Revolution, the period marks the most important single development of humanity as it brought with it sedentarism, which in turn encouraged population growth and greater specialization.

**neutron activation analysis** (NAA) a physical technique of chemical analysis used to determine the composition of a wide range of materials found in archaeological contexts. A specimen is bombarded with neutrons which interact with nuclei in the sample to form radioactive isotopes that emit gamma rays as they decay. The energy spectrum of the emitted rays is detected with a counter and constituent elements and concentrations are identified by the characteristic energy spectrum of emitted rays and its intensity.

**New Archaeology** a development in the 1960s aimed at making archaeology more scientific, now more often referred to as Processual Archaeology. It proposed that archaeology should openly state its assumptions and use specific scientific procedures. Some adherents of New Archaeology believed that laws of human behaviour were obtainable by using the correct methodologies.

**optical emission spectrometry** (OES) a physical technique used to identify trace elements in

stone and metal artifacts and ceramics that may aid in identifying the source of that material. A sample is bombarded with a laser beam or other energy source, exciting the atoms; as the atoms relax they emit light of a wavelength characteristic of the constituent atoms. The wavelength spectrum and intensity are analyzed for the type and concentrations of constituent elements present.

**palaeobotany** (archaeobotany) the recovery and identification of plant remains from archaeological contexts, and their use in the reconstruction of past environments and economies.

**Palaeolithic** earliest stage of human technology and development of the Stone Age, beginning with the emergence of hominids and the production of the earliest stone tools (approximately 3 million years ago), and lasting till the retreat of the ice sheets about 10,000 years ago. Its subdivisions are the Lower Palaeolithic, in which the earliest hominids appear (*Australopithecus* and *Homo erectus*); the Middle Palaeolithic, the Age of the Neanderthals; and the Upper Palaeolithic, marked by the appearance of *Homo sapiens* and the remarkable cave art of western Europe (for example the caves at Lascaux). The final stage also saw the colonization of the New World and Australia.

**phosphate analysis** a technique of taking soil samples at regular intervals from the surface of a site and its surroundings to identify, through chemical analysis of phosphorus concentrations in the soil, human settlements and activity and burial areas within sites. Excrement and bone are relatively high in phosphorus content, so human activity and remains tend to produce comparatively large concentrations of phosphates.

**physical anthropology** (biological anthropology) a subdiscipline of anthropology that studies human biological or physical characteristics and how they evolved.

**pollen analysis** (palynology) the study of fossil and living pollen and spores, utilized in palaeoenvironmental and palaeoclimatic reconstruction, in identifying natural and humanly induced vegetation changes, and in developing relative chronologies.

Since different genera (and sometimes species) of pollen have distinct characteristics of size, shape, and markings on the coat, the study of these pollen grains can reveal information on the dominant flora, and thus the climate, of a particular period. Pollen grains are extremely resistant and therefore well-preserved in rocks and particularly abundant in peat.

**potassium-argon dating** an isotopic dating method based on the radioactive decay of potassium-40 to the stable isotope argon-40. The method is used primarily to date volcanic layers in stratigraphic sequences with archaeological deposits, and the palaeomagnetic reversal timescale. Ages are based on the known half-life of 40K, and the ratio of 40K/40Ar. The method is routinely applied from about 100,000 to 30 million years ago.

**prehistory** the period of human history for which there is no contemporary documentary evidence; it constitutes the longest segment of the human past, and is the major object of study of archaeology. Prehistory and history can overlap in time—for example, prehistoric Iron Age cultures existed at the same time as the historic Roman culture; and in our own age, 'prehistoric' societies have existed contemporaneously with modern ones, for example the Kung Bushmen or the Australian aborigines.

**protohistory** period following prehistory but prior to the appearance of history as documented in written records.

**radiocarbon dating** a radiometric dating technique used for determining the age of carbon-bearing materials including wood and plant remains, bone, peat, and shell. It is based on the radioactive decay of the carbon-14 isotope in the sample to nitrogen, with the release of (beta) particles that is initiated when an organism dies and ceases to exchange carbon-14 with the atmosphere. After death the carbon-14 content is a function of time and is determined by counting (beta) particles with either a proportional gas or a liquid scintillation counter for a period of time.

The method yields reliable ages back to c. 30,000 years, but its results require correction since the atmospheric production rate of carbon-14 has not been constant through time. Radiocarbon dates from tree rings showed that material before 1000 BC had been exposed to greater concentrations of carbon-14. Now radiocarbon dates are calibrated against calendar dates obtained from tree rings, or, for earlier periods, against uranium/thorium dates obtained from coral. A new advance, AMS (accelerator mass spectrometry) requires only tiny samples of the material being dated, and counts the atoms of carbon-14 directly, disregarding their decay.

**relative dating** dating methods that measure differences in age utilizing an ordinal scale, for example, they include sequencing of events or objects relative to one another but without linkage to ages in calendar years.

**remote sensing** general term for reconnaissance and surface survey techniques that provide information without disturbing subsurface archaeological deposits.

**rescue archaeology** (or *salvage archaeology*) the branch of archaeology that deals with the impact of contemporary construction and other developments on archaeological sites, and the various laws enacted to mitigate the threat. It involves the location and recording (usually by rapid excavation) of archaeological sites in advance of their destruction.

**resistivity survey** a geophysical survey method used to locate buried features and structures with a resistivity meter. An electrical current is passed through the soil between electrodes and the resistance (normally a consequence of moisture content) is recorded. In this way buried features can be detected through their differential retention of groundwater (so, for example, a stone feature will show greater resistance than the soil around it, and a damp pit will show less).

**seriation** a relative dating technique that organizes artifacts temporally, according to their relative popularity. Evolutionary seriation is based on changes that represent essentially technological improvements, while stylistic seriation is based on gradual changes in the frequencies of stylistic attributes, so that the greater the similarity in style, the closer in age artifacts are to each other.

**site** any location where there is evidence for past human behaviour. A site can be as small as an isolated find, which is either a single artifact or a small number of artifacts, or as

---

## A BRONZE AGE IDOL?

A 'golden calf' was unearthed near the Israeli port city of Ashkelon by Harvard University archaeologists in 1990. Believed to be an object of worship dating from the second milennium BC, it was recovered almost intact; it measures about 11 cm/4.5 in long and 10.8 cm/4.25 in tall, and is made of bronze and other metals. In about 1550 BC the temple in which it was housed was destroyed, during a conquest of Ashkelon. In the *Bible*, golden calves similar in form but much larger are mentioned in the story of Aaron during the Exodus, in ancient Jerusalem's rivalry with northern, calf-worshipping Hebrew king Jeroboam, and in other accounts from the Old Testament.

large as an ancient city. Sites are classified according to function: major types include domestic/habitation sites, kill sites, processing/butchering sites.

**site catchment analysis** (SCA) the definition of the site catchment, the total area from which the site's contents have been derived (i.e. the full inventory of its artifactual and non-artifactual remains, and their sources), and an assessment of the catchment's economic potential.

**site exploitation territory** (SET) the territory surrounding a site that was habitually exploited by the site's inhabitants. Territories are normally seen as having a radius of one hour walking distance for farmers, and a two-hour distance for hunter-gatherers.

**sondage** a deep test-pit, employed to investigate a site's stratigraphy prior to carrying out larger-scale excavation.

**spectrographic analysis** technique used to analyze the component elements in a compound, based on the principle that light given off upon volatization breaks up into a distinctive pattern when split into a spectrum by a prism. By analyzing the pattern of lines in the spectrum the composition of elements present in a compound can be determined. The technique has been especially useful in metal analysis, but is also applied to pottery, obsidian, and glass.

**step-trenching** excavation technique used on very deep sites such as Near Eastern 'tells' (mounds) where a large area opened at the top gradually narrows as the dig descends in a series of large steps.

**Stone Age** the developmental stage of humans in prehistory before the use of metals, when tools and weapons were made of stone (especially flint), wood, bone, and antler. The Stone Age is subdivided into the Old or Palaeolithic, the Middle or Mesolithic, and the New or Neolithic. The people of the Old Stone Age were hunters, whereas the Neolithic people took the first steps in agriculture, the domestication of animals, weaving, and pottery.

**stratigraphy** the study of the formation, composition, sequence, and correlation of stratified sediment, soils and rocks. Stratigraphy is the principal means by which the context of archaeological deposits is evaluated, chronologies are constructed, and events are sequenced. It is invaluable for interpreting the sequence of deposition of the site and thereby the relative ages of artifacts, features and other phenomena in the site.

**thermoluminescence**(TL) is used to date fired archaeological material such as pottery and burned flint tools. When the material was originally fired, any electrons trapped in it by radiation escaped, emitting light known as thermoluminescence, and thereby setting the TL clock to zero. By measuring the amount of TL emitted when the material is reheated, and knowing its radioactive content, one can calculate the lapse of time since the original firing.

**thin-section analysis** technique using a sample chip—ground down to a paper thin sheet and

---

**Heritage**

*How strongly do you agree or disagree with the following statements?*

*a) In Britain, we don't attach sufficient importance to preserving the richness of our historical sites and architectural heritage*

*b) I would pay to visit more historical sites if they weren't so dull and took more trouble to make a visit more interesting and entertaining?*

| | Today | | Mar 1989 | |
| --- | --- | --- | --- | --- |
| | (a) | (b) | (a) | (b) |
| Agree strongly | 22 | 13 | 12 | 5 |
| Agree | 44 | 42 | 46 | 38 |
| Neither agree nor disagree | 13 | 16 | 17 | 20 |
| Disagree | 19 | 23 | 23 | 34 |
| Disagree strongly | 2 | 6 | 2 | 3 |

---

mounted on a glass slide—that is utilized in petrological analysis of the mineralogical composition of ceramics, stone artifacts and soils.

**Three Age System** scheme first formulated by Christian Thomsen (1788–1865) between 1816–19 to divide prehistory into a Stone Age, Bronze Age, and Iron Age. Subsequently, the Stone Age was subdivided into the Old and the New (the Palaeolithic and Neolithic); the Middle (Mesolithic) Stone Age was added later, as well as the Copper Age (inserted between the New Stone Age and Bronze Age). While providing a valuable and valid classification system for prehistoric material, it did not provide dates but only a sequence of developmental stages, which, furthermore, were not necessarily followed in that order by different societies.

**trace element analysis** the study (e.g. by neutron activation analysis or X-ray fluorescence) of elements that occur naturally in minor amounts in minerals in soil and sediment. Trace elements can be identified by various analyses and may serve as 'fingerprints' for some artifact raw material sources.

**typology** the systematic organization of artifacts into types on the basis of their shared attributes. The two objectives are classification, i.e. grouping objects according to their shape, leading to a type series; and, through the comparison of different types, to discover how these types relate to each other. The latter process can lead to seriation, which demonstrates the *development* of a type of artifact (the development may be related to function, technological advance, fashion, etc.). Such information requires an independent dating source for at least several examples in the series in order to establish the rate of change.

**underwater reconnaissance** geophysical methods of underwater survey including the proton magnetometer, towed behind a survey vessel to detect iron and steel objects that distort the earth's magnetic field; side-scan sonar, that transmits sound waves in a fan-shaped beam to produce a graphic image of subsurface features on the sea-bed; and a sub-bottom profiler that emits sound pulses that bounce back from features and objects buried under the sea-floor.

**X-ray diffraction analysis** a physical technique used to identify the mineralogy of material such as ceramics, stone, sediments and weathering products on metals. The sample is ground to powder, and exposed to X-rays at various angles; the diffraction patterns produced are compared with reference standards for identification.

**X-ray fluorescence spectrometry** (XRF) a physical technique used to determine the major and trace elements in the chemical composition of materials such as ceramics, obsidian and glass that may help in identifying the material source. The sample is bombarded with X-rays, and the wavelengths of the released energy, or fluorescent X-rays, are detected and measured. Different elements have unique wavelengths, while their concentrations can be estimated from the intensity of the released X-rays.

# SPACE EXPLORATION

**Ames Research Center** NASA installation at Mountain View, California, for research into aeronautics and life sciences. Ames has managed the Pioneer series of planetary probes and is involved in the search for extraterrestrial life.

**Apollo project** US space project to land a person on the Moon, achieved 20 July 1969, when Neil Armstrong was the first to set foot there. He was accompanied on the Moon's surface by Col Edwin E Aldrin Jr; Michael Collins remained in the orbiting command module.

**Apollo-Soyuz test project** joint US-Soviet space mission in which an Apollo and a Soyuz craft docked while in orbit around the Earth on 17 July 1975. The craft remained attached for two days and crew members were able to move from one craft to the other through an airlock attached to the nose of the Apollo. The mission was designed to test rescue procedures as well as having political significance.

**Ariane** series of launch vehicles built by the European Space Agency (first flight 1979). The launch site is at Kourou in French Guiana. Ariane is a three-stage rocket using liquid fuels. Small solid-fuel and liquid-fuel boosters can be attached to its first stage to increase carrying power.

**Ariel** series of six UK satellites launched by the US 1962–79, the most significant of which was Ariel 5, 1974, which made a pioneering survey of the sky at X-ray wavelengths.

**astronaut** a person making flights into space; the Soviet term is *cosmonaut*.

**astronautics** the science of space travel.

**astronomy** the science of the celestial bodies: the Sun, the Moon, and the planets; the stars and galaxies; and all other objects in the universe. It is concerned with their positions, motions, distances, and physical conditions, and with their origins and evolution. Astronomy thus divides into fields such as astrophysics, celestial mechanics, and cosmology.

**Baikonur** the main Soviet launch site for spacecraft, located at Tyuratam, near the Aral Sea.

**Cape Canaveral** promontory on the Atlantic coast of Florida, USA, 367 km/228 mi N of Miami, used as a rocket launch site by NASA.

**Cassini** a joint space probe of NASA and the European Space Agency to the planet Saturn. Cassini is scheduled to be launched in Nov 1995 and will go into orbit around Saturn in Dec 2003, dropping off a sub-probe, Huygens, to land on Saturn's largest moon, Titan.

**communications satellite** a relay station in space for sending telephone, television, telex, and other messages around the world. Messages are sent to and from the satellites via ground stations. Most communications satellites are in geostationary orbit, appearing to hang fixed over one point on the Earth's surface.

**Cosmos** name used since the early 1960s for nearly all Soviet artificial satellites. Over 2,100 Cosmos satellites had been launched by Jan 1991.

**Delta rocket** a US rocket used to launch many scientific and communications satellites since 1960, based on the Thor ballistic missile. Several increasingly powerful versions were produced as satellites became larger and heavier. Solid-fuel boosters were attached to the first stage to increase lifting power.

**Edwards Air Force Base** military USAF centre in California, situated on a dry lake bed, often used as a landing site by the Space Shuttle.

**Energia** the most powerful Soviet space rocket, first launched 15 May 1987. The Energia booster is used to launch the Soviet Space Shuttle and is capable, with the use of strap-on boosters, of launching payloads of up to 190 tonnes/195 tons into Earth orbit.

**European Space Agency** (ESA) an organization of European countries (Austria, Belgium, Denmark, France, Germany, Ireland, Italy, the Netherlands, Norway, Spain, Sweden, Switzerland, and the UK) that engages in space research and technology. It was founded 1975, with headquarters in Paris.

**Explorer** a series of US scientific satellites. *Explorer 1*, launched Jan 1958, was the first US satellite in orbit and discovered the Van Allen radiation belts around the Earth.

*Galileo* spacecraft launched from the space shuttle *Atlantis* in Oct 1989, on a six-year journey to Jupiter. It flew past Venus in Feb 1990 and was scheduled to fly twice past the Earth (Dec 1990 and Dec 1992), using the gravitational fields of these planets to accelerate it towards its final destination.

**Gemini project** US space programme (1965–66) in which astronauts practised rendezvous and docking of spacecraft, and working outside their spacecraft, in preparation for the Apollo Moon landings.

**geostationary orbit** the circular path 35,900 km/22,300 mi above the Earth's equator on which a satellite takes 24 hours, moving from west to east, to complete an orbit, thus appearing to hang stationary over one place on the Earth's surface. Geostationary orbits are particularly used for communications satellites and weather satellites. They were first thought of by the author Arthur C Clarke. A *geosynchronous orbit* lies at the same distance from Earth but is inclined to the equator.

*Giotto* space probe built by the European Space Agency to study Halley's comet. Launched by an Ariane rocket in July 1985, *Giotto* passed within 600 km/375 mi of the comet's nucleus on 13 March 1986. On 2 July 1990 it flew 23,000 km/14,000 mi from Earth, which diverted its path to encounter another comet, Grigg-Skjellerup, on 10 July 1992.

**Goddard Space Flight Center** NASA installation at Greenbelt, Maryland, responsible for the operation of NASA's unmanned scientific satellites, including the Hubble Space Telescope. It is also home of the National Space Science Data centre, a repository of data collected by

## ASTRONOMY: CHRONOLOGY

| | |
|---|---|
| **2300 BC** | Chinese astronomers made their earliest observations. |
| **2000** | Babylonian priests made their first observational records. |
| **1900** | Stonehenge was constructed: first phase. |
| **365** | The Chinese observed the satellites of Jupiter with the naked eye. |
| **3rd cent. BC** | Aristarchus argued that the Sun is the centre of the solar system. |
| **2nd cent.AD** | Ptolemy's complicated Earth-centred system was promulgated, which dominated the astronomy of the Middle Ages. |
| **1543** | Copernicus revived the ideas of Aristarchus in *De Revolutionibus*. |
| **1608** | Lippershey invented the telescope, which was first used by Galileo 1609. |
| **1609** | Kepler's first two laws of planetary motion were published (the third appeared 1619). |
| **1632** | Leiden established the world's first official observatory. |
| **1633** | Galileo's theories were condemned by the Inquisition. |
| **1675** | The Royal Greenwich Observatory was founded in England. |
| **1687** | Newton's *Principia* was published, including his 'law of universal gravitation'. |
| **1718** | Halley predicted the return of the comet named after him, observed 1758: its last return was 1986. |
| **1781** | Herschel discovered Uranus and recognized stellar systems beyond our Galaxy. |
| **1796** | Laplace elaborated his theory of the origin of the solar system. |
| **1801** | Piazzi discovered the first asteroid, Ceres. |
| **1814** | Fraunhofer first studied absorption lines in the solar spectrum. |
| **1846** | Neptune was identified by Galle, following predictions by Adams and Leverrier. |
| **1859** | Kirchhoff explained dark lines in the sun's spectrum. |
| **1887** | The earliest photographic star charts were produced. |
| **1889** | E E Barnard took the first photographs of the Milky Way. |
| **1908** | Fragment of comet fell at Tunguska, Siberia. |
| **1920** | Eddington began the study of interstellar matter. |
| **1923** | Hubble proved that the galaxies are systems independent of the Milky Way, and by 1930 had confirmed the concept of an expanding universe. |
| **1930** | The planet Pluto was discovered by Clyde Tombaugh at the Lowell Observatory, Arizona, USA. |
| **1931** | Jansky founded radioastronomy. |
| **1945** | Radar contact with the Moon was established by Z Bay of Hungary and the US Army Signal Corps Laboratory. |
| **1948** | The 5-m Hale reflector telescope was installed at Mount Palomar, California, USA. |
| **1955** | The Jodrell Bank telescope dish in England was completed. |
| **1957** | The first Sputnik satellite (USSR) opened the age of space observation. |
| **1962** | The first X-ray source was discovered in Scorpius. |
| **1963** | The first quasar was discovered. |
| **1967** | The first pulsar was discovered by Jocelyn Bell and Antony Hewish. |
| **1969** | The first crewed Moon landing was made by US astronauts. |
| **1976** | A 6-m reflector telescope was installed at Mount Semirodniki (USSR). |
| **1977** | Uranus was discovered to have rings. |
| **1977** | The spacecraft *Voyager 1* and *2* were launched, passing Jupiter and Saturn 1979–81. |
| **1978** | The spacecraft *Pioneer Venus 1* and *2* reached Venus. |
| **1978** | A satellite of Pluto, Charon, was discovered by James Christy of the US Naval Observatory. |
| **1986** | Halley's comet returned. *Voyager 2* flew by Uranus. |
| **1987** | Bright supernova visible to the naked eye for the first time since 1604. |
| **1989** | *Voyager 2* flew by Neptune. |

satellites.

**Hipparcos** acronym for the **high precision parallax collecting satellite** launched by the European Space Agency in Aug 1989. Named after the Greek astronomer Hipparchus, it is the world's first astrometry satellite designed to provide precise positions and apparent motions of stars. The accuracy of these measurements from space will be far greater than from ground-based telescopes.

**Hubble Space Telescope** (HST) telescope placed into orbit around the Earth, at an altitude of 610 km/380 mi, by the Space Shuttle *Dis-* covery in April 1990. It has a main mirror 2.4 m/94 in wide, which suffers from spherical aberration and so cannot be focused properly. Yet, because it is above the atmosphere, the HST outperforms ground-based telescopes. Computer techniques are being used to improve the images from the telescope until the arrival of a maintenance mission to install corrective optics.

**Intelsat** International Telecommunications Satellite Organization, established 1964 to operate a worldwide system of communications satellites. More than 100 countries are members of

Intelsat, with headquarters in Washington DC. Intelsat satellites are stationed in geostationary orbit (maintaining their positions relative to the Earth) over the Atlantic, Pacific, and Indian Oceans. The first Intelsat satellite was *Early Bird*, launched 1965.

**IRAS** the Infrared Astronomy Satellite, a joint US/UK/Dutch satellite, launched 1983, surveyed the sky at infrared wavelengths, studying areas of star formation, distant galaxies, possible embryo planetary systems around other stars, and discovering five new comets in our own solar system.

**Jet Propulsion Laboratory** NASA installation at Pasadena, California, operated by the California Institute of Technology. It is the command centre for NASA's deep space probes such as the Voyager, Magellan, and Galileo missions, with which it communicates via the Deep Space Network of radio telescopes at Goldstone, California; Madrid, Spain; and Canberra, Australia.

**Johnson Space Center** NASA installation at Houston, Texas, home of mission control for manned space missions. It is the main centre for the selection and training of astronauts.

**Kennedy Space Center** the NASA launch site on Merritt Island, near Cape Canaveral, Florida, used for Apollo and space-shuttle launches.

**Kourou** second-largest town of French Guiana, NW of Cayenne, site of the Guiana Space Centre of the European Space Agency. Situated near the equator, it is an ideal site for launches of satellites into geostationary orbit.

**Landsat** a series of satellites used for monitoring Earth resources. The first was launched 1972.

**Magellan** a NASA space probe to Venus, launched in May 1989, went into orbit around Venus in Aug 1990 to make a detailed map of the planet by radar. It revealed volcanoes, meteorite craters, and fold mountains on the planet's surface.

**Mariner spacecraft** series of US space probes that explored the planets Mercury, Venus, and Mars 1962–75.

**Marshall Space Flight Center** NASA installation at Huntsville, Alabama, where the Saturn series of rockets and the Space Shuttle engines were developed. It also manages various payloads for the Space Shuttle, including the Spacelab space station.

*Mir* Soviet space station, the core of which was launched 20 Feb 1986. *Mir* is intended to be a permanently occupied space station.

**Moon probe** crewless spacecraft used to investigate the Moon. Early probes flew past the Moon or crash-landed on it, but later ones achieved soft landings or went into orbit. Soviet probes included the Luna series. US probes (Ranger, Surveyor, Lunar Orbiter) prepared the way for the Apollo crewed flights.

**NASA** National Aeronautics and Space Administration, the US government agency, founded 1958, for spaceflight and aeronautical research. Its headquarters are in Washington DC and its main installation is at the Kennedy Space Center.

**Pioneer probes** a series of US solar-system space probes 1958–78. The probes *Pioneer 4–9* went into solar orbit to monitor the Sun's activity during the 1960s and early 1970s. *Pioneer 5*, launched 1960, was the first of a series to study the solar wind between the planets. *Pioneer 10*, launched Mar 1972, was the first probe to reach Jupiter (Dec 1973) and to leave the solar system 1983. *Pioneer 11*, launched April 1973, passed Jupiter Dec 1974, and was the first probe to reach Saturn (Sept 1979), before also leaving the solar system. *Pioneer 10* and *11* carry plaques containing messages from Earth in case they are found by other civilizations among the stars. Pioneer Venus probes were launched May and Aug 1978. One orbited Venus, and the other dropped three probes onto the surface. In early 1990 *Pioneer 10* was 7.1 billion km from the Sun.

**Plesetsk** rocket-launching site 170 km/105 mi S of Archangel, USSR. From here the USSR has launched artificial satellites since 1966, mostly military.

**Proton rocket** Soviet space rocket introduced 1965, used to launch heavy satellites, space probes, and the *Salyut* and *Mir* space stations.

**Redstone rocket** short-range US military missile, modified for use as a space launcher. Redstone rockets launched the first two Mercury flights. A modified Redstone, *Juno 1*, launched the first US satellite, *Explorer 1*, in 1958.

**rocket** projectile driven by the reaction of gases produced by a fast-burning fuel. Unlike jet engines, which are also reaction engines, modern rockets carry their own oxygen supply to burn their fuel and are totally independent of any surrounding atmosphere. As rockets are the only form of propulsion available that can function in a vacuum, they are essential to exploration in outer space. Multistage rockets have to be used, consisting of a number of rockets joined together.

**ROSAT** joint US/German/UK satellite launched 1990 to study cosmic sources of X-rays and extremely short ultraviolet wavelengths, named after Wilhelm Röntgen, the discoverer of X-rays.

**Salyut** series of seven space stations launched by the USSR 1971–82. *Salyut* was cylindrical in shape, 15 m/50 ft long, and weighed 19 tonnes. It housed two or three cosmonauts at a time, for missions lasting up to eight months.

**satellite** any small body that orbits a larger one, either natural or artificial. Natural satellites that orbit planets are called moons. The first *artificial satellite*, *Sputnik 1*, was launched into orbit around the Earth by the USSR 1957. Artificial satellites are used for scientific purposes, communications, weather forecasting, and military applications. The largest artificial satellites can be seen by the naked eye.

**Saturn rocket** family of large US rockets, developed by Wernher von Braun for the Apollo project. The two-stage Saturn IB was used for launching Apollo spacecraft into orbit around the Earth. The three-stage Saturn V sent Apollo spacecraft to the Moon, and launched the

## GRAVITY ASSIST—FREE RIDE TO THE PLANETS

As space probes have become bigger and heavier, so rockets needed to launch them have become more powerful. However, space scientists have been able to speed spacecraft up and change their course without need for rockets at all, by using the gravity of the planets.

The trick, called gravity assist, has some strange consequences. In 1990, a probe to study the Sun, *Ulysses*, started on its journey by heading out towards Jupiter, while another probe, *Galileo*—whose destination really is Jupiter—first flew past Venus and then the Earth. A third probe, *Giotto*, veteran of the encounter with Halley's Comet in 1986, received a new lease of life in 1990 when it, too, swung past the Earth, emerging on a new course to visit a second comet.

Using gravity assist to reach the outer planets was first studied in detail in 1965 at NASA's Jet Propulsion Laboratory by a graduate student, Gary Flandro. He found that, thanks to a fortunate alignment of Jupiter, Saturn, Uranus and Neptune in the 1980s, all four planets could be visited by one spacecraft. Each planet in turn would 'slingshot' the craft to its next destination. Flandro's vision became the astounding odyssey of *Voyager 2*, launched 1977, which reached Neptune 1989. Without gravity assist, it would not have got there until around 2017.

How does gravity assist work? Firstly, a planet's gravity bends the trajectory of a passing space probe, in the same way that you would be swung around if you grabbed hold of a post as you ran past it. The crucial difference, though, is that the planet is itself on the move, orbiting the Sun, so the probe picks up additional speed from the planet as it passes. At first sight, gravity assist might seem to amount to a free source of energy. Not quite. In speeding up the space probe, the planet itself is slowed down—but by such an infinitesimal amount that the difference could never be measured.

In 1990 the Earth was used for the first time in a gravity assist manoeuvre by two space probes. First to pass by was *Giotto*, the European probe that plunged through the head of Halley's Comet in March 1986, photographing its 'dirty snowball' nucleus. Radio contact was re-established with *Giotto* in Feb 1990 and a small manoeuvre by its on-

board thrusters ensured that it passed 23,000 km/14,300 miles on 2 July 1990, exactly five years after launch. It was diverted onto a new and larger orbit that will intercept Comet Grigg-Skjellerup on 10 July 1992.

To have accomplished this with a rocket would have required over 50 times more fuel than remained on board. To the Earth, the price was a slowing of its movement in orbit by 1mm every 100 million years. *Giotto's* camera is no longer working, but other instruments will sample the comet to compare it with Halley's.

NASA's *Galileo* space probe to Jupiter was a double victim of the Space Shuttle explosion in 1986. Its launch was delayed, and the safety-conscious NASA decreed that the rocket intended to boost it away from Earth, a liquid-fuelled Centaur, was too dangerous to carry in the Shuttle's cargo bay. Instead, *Galileo* would have to make do with a safer upper stage that lacked the power to reach Jupiter. The answer to this conundrum was a six-year flight path that involved three gravity assists, one from Venus and two from Earth.

*Galileo* was eventually launched by the Space Shuttle *Atlantis* in October 1989 on a course that first took it past Venus in Feb 1990. Here it was swung back on a path that took it a mere 960 km/590 miles above the Earth on 8 December 1990, picking up 26,000 kph/16,000 mph in speed. Another Earth flyby in December 1992 will finally fling *Galileo* towards Jupiter, which it will reach in late 1995. As a result of these flybys, when the Sun swells up into a red giant billions of years into the future the Earth will fall into the Sun about ten minutes earlier than would otherwise have been the case.

Jupiter itself will be used in 1992 for the heftiest gravity assist of all, throwing a probe called *Ulysses* at right angles to the plane of the Earth's orbit to give us our first-ever view of the poles of the Sun. No launch vehicle is powerful enough to do this on its own.

*Ulysses*, built by the European Space Agency, was launched by the Space Shuttle *Discovery* in Oct 1990. It will fly over the northern hemisphere of Jupiter in Feb 1992, whereupon its path will be swung sharply downwards so that it loops first under the south pole of the Sun in 1994 and then over the North Pole a year later in a mission lasting five years.

*Skylab* space station. The liftoff thrust of a Saturn V was 3,500 tonnes. After Apollo and *Skylab*, the Saturn rockets were retired in favour of the Space Shuttle.

**Skylab** US space station, launched 14 May 1973, made from the adapted upper stage of a Saturn V rocket. At 75 tonnes, it was the heaviest object ever put into space, and was 25.6 m/84 ft long. *Skylab* contained a workshop for carrying out experiments in weightlessness, an observatory for monitoring the Sun, and cameras for photographing the Earth's surface.

**Soyuz** continuing series of Soviet spacecraft, capable of carrying up to three cosmonauts.

Soyuz spacecraft consist of three parts: a rear section containing engines; the central crew compartment; and a forward compartment that gives additional room for working and living space. They are now used for ferrying crews up to space stations, though they were originally used for independent space flight.

**Spacelab** a small space station built by the European Space Agency, carried in the cargo bay of the Space Shuttle, in which it remains throughout each flight, returning to Earth with the Shuttle. Spacelab consists of a pressurized module in which astronauts can work, and a series of **pallets**, open to the vacuum of

---

## STRANDED IN SPACE?

Two Soviet cosmonauts hit the headlines in 1990 when they nearly locked themselves out of the *Mir* space station while examining damage to their *Soyuz* ferry craft that could have left them trapped in orbit. Anatoli Solovyov and Aleksandr Balandin had been launched to *Mir* in February aboard *Soyuz TM-9*. During the launch, insulating blankets that protect the *Soyuz* from extremes of heat and cold in orbit ripped loose. There was a danger that the re-entry heat shield underneath could have been damaged, and the loose blankets could have blocked the view of the navigation devices that line the ship for re-entry. If so, a rescue mission would have been necessary.

Ground controllers sent up repair equipment in an unmanned module that docked with the space station in June, along with instructions on carrying out the repair. On 17 July Solovyov and Balandin carefully worked their way along the outside of *Mir* to reach the damaged *Soyuz*. Unable to reattach the loose blankets, they instead simply folded them out of the way,

having ascertained that there was no other damage to *Soyuz* that would prevent a safe return to Earth.

But when the two men tried to get back into the *Mir* space station they were faced with an unpleasant surprise—the outer hatch of the airlock refused to close. With the air in their spacesuits running low, there was no time to investigate the problem. They were forced to leave the outer door open and move on into the next compartment of *Mir*. By the time they were safely inside, they had spent over seven hours in their space suits, a Soviet record.

Nine days later they made a second spacewalk to examine the stuck hatch. They found that a hinge had been damaged when the hatch was opened. Ground controllers later blamed the cosmonauts for opening it before the airlock was fully depressurized. After removing a sliver of broken metal, they closed the hatch success-fully. A subsequent crew replaced the hinge after Solovyov and Balandin returned to Earth 9 Aug.

---

space, on which equipment is mounted.

**space probe** any instrumented object sent beyond Earth to collect data from other parts of the solar system and from deep space. The first probe was the Soviet *Lunik 1*, which flew past the Moon 1959. The first successful planetary probe was the US *Mariner 2*, which flew past Venus 1962, using transfer orbit. The first space probe to leave the solar system was *Pioneer 10* 1983. Space probes include *Giotto*, the Moon probes, and the Mariner, Pioneer, Viking, and Voyager series. Japan launched its first space probe in Feb 1990.

**space shuttle** reusable crewed spacecraft. The first was launched 12 April 1981 by the USA. It was developed by NASA to reduce the cost of using space for commercial, scientific, and military purposes. After leaving its payload in space, the space-shuttle orbiter can be flown back to Earth to land on a runway, and is then available for reuse.

**space sickness** or *space adaptation syndrome* a feeling of nausea, sometimes accompanied by vomiting, experienced by about 40% of all astronauts during their first few days in space. It is akin to travel sickness, and is thought to be caused by confusion of the body's balancing mechanism, located in the inner ear, by weightlessness. The sensation passes after a few days as the body adapts.

**space station** any large structure designed for human occupation in space for extended periods of time. Space stations are used for carrying out astronomical observations and surveys of Earth, as well as for biological studies and the processing of materials in weightlessness. The first space station was *Salyut 1*, and the USA has launched *Skylab*. NASA plans to build a larger space station, to be called *Freedom*, in orbit during the 1990s,

in cooperation with other countries, including the European Space Agency, which is building a module called *Columbus*, and Japan, also building a module.

**space suit** a protective suit worn by astronauts and cosmonauts in space. It provides an insulated, air-conditioned cocoon in which people can live and work for hours at a time while outside the spacecraft. Inside the suit is a cooling garment that keeps the body at a comfortable temperature even during vigorous work. The suit provides air to breathe, and removes exhaled carbon dioxide and moisture. The suit's outer layers insulate the occupant from the extremes of hot and cold in space ($-150°C/-240°F$ in the shade to $+180°C/350°F$ in sunlight), and from the impact of small meteorites. Some space suits have a jet-propelled backpack, which the wearer can use to move about.

**Sputnik** a series of ten Soviet Earth-orbiting satellites. *Sputnik 1* was the first artificial satellite, launched 4 Oct 1957. It weighed 84 kg/185 lb, with a 58 cm/23 in diameter, and carried only a simple radio transmitter which allowed scientists to track it as it orbited Earth. It burned up in the atmosphere 92 days later. Sputniks were superseded in the early 1960s by the Cosmos series.

*Telstar* US communications satellite, launched 10 July 1962, which relayed the first live television transmissions between the USA and Europe. *Telstar* orbited the Earth in 158 minutes, and so had to be tracked by ground stations, unlike the geostationary satellites of today.

**Titan rocket** family of US space rockets, developed from the Titan intercontinental missile. Two-stage Titan rockets launched the Gemini crewed missions. More powerful Titans, with

## Space Diary — Main Launches May 1990–May 1991

| Launch date | Flight | Remarks |
| --- | --- | --- |
| **1990** 31 May | Kristall | 20-tonne technology module launched to *Mir*. Contains docking port for Soviet space shuttle |
| 1 June | ROSAT | X-ray and ultraviolet astronomy satellite launched from Cape Canaveral by Delta II rocket |
| 25 July | CRRES | Combined Release and Radiation Effects Satellite launched from Cape Canaveral by Atlas I rocket. Released clouds of barium and lithium vapour in January 1991 to study Earth's magnetic field |
| 1 August | Soyuz TM-10 | Gennady Manakov and Gennady Strekalov launched to *Mir* space station to replace Anatoli Solovyov and Aleksandr Balandin |
| 6 October | STS 41 | Space Shuttle *Discovery* launched Ulysses space probe. *Crew*: Richard Richards, Robert Cabana, William Shepherd, Bruce Melnick, Thomas Akers. Landed Edwards Air Force Base 10 October |
| 15 November | STS 38 | Space Shuttle *Atlantis* launched spy satellite. *Crew*:Richard Covey, Frank Culbertson, Robert Springer, Carl Meade, Charles 'Sam' Gemar. Landed Kennedy Space Center 20 November |
| 2 December | STS 35 | Space Shuttle *Columbia* launched Astro-1 ultraviolet observatory and Broad Band X-ray Telescope. *Crew*: Vance Brand, Guy Gardner, Mike Lounge, Jeff Hoffman, Robert Parker, Ronald Parise, Samuel Durrance. Landed Edwards Air Force Base 11 December |
| 2 December | Soyuz TM-11 | Japanese TV journalist Toyohiro Akiyama launched with Viktor Afanasyev and Musa Manarov to Mir space station. Akiyama landed 10 December with Gennady Manakov and Gennady Strekalov |
| **1991** 5 April | STS 37 | Space Shuttle *Atlantis* launched Gamma Ray Observatory to survey the sky at Gamma Ray wavelengths. *Crew*: Steven Nagel, Kenneth Cameron, Linda Godwin, Jerry Ross, Jay Apt. Apt and Ross made the first US spacewalks for 5 years |
| 28 April | STS 39 | Space Shuttle *Discovery* landed on Dept of Defense mission to help develop 'Star Wars' sensors for identifying missiles in space. *Crew*: Michael Coats, Blaine Hammond, Gregory Harbaugh, Donald McMonagle, Guion Bluford, Charles Veach, Richard Hieb. Landed Kennedy Space Center 6 May |
| 18 May | Soyuz TM-12 | British astronaut Helen Sharman launched with Anatoli Artsebarsky and Sergei Krikalek to *Mir* space station. Sharman landed on 26 May in Soyuz TM-11 with Viktor Afanasyev and Musa Manarov. Manarov now holds record for longest time spent in space, 541 days, having also spent a year aboard *Mir* in 1988. |

additional stages and strap-on boosters, were used to launch spy satellites and space probes, including Viking and Voyager.

**Tyuratam** site of the Baikonur Cosmodrome, USSR.

**Ulysses** joint NASA/ESA probe to study the Sun's poles, launched 1990 by the Space Shuttle *Discovery*. The gravity of Jupiter will swing it onto a path that loops it first under the Sun's south pole and then over the north pole to study the Sun and solar wind at latitudes not observable from the Earth.

**Vanguard** an early series of US Earth-orbiting satellites and their associated rocket launcher. *Vanguard 1* was the second US satellite, launched 17 March 1958 by the three-stage Vanguard rocket. Tracking of its orbit revealed that Earth is slightly pear-shaped. The series ended Sept 1959 with *Vanguard 3*.

**Viking probes** two US space probes to Mars, each one consisting of an orbiter and a lander. They were launched 20 Aug and 9 Sept 1975. They transmitted colour pictures, and analysed the soil. No definite signs of life were found.

**Voskhod** Soviet spacecraft used in the mid-1960s; it was modified from the single-seat Vostok, and was the first spacecraft capable of carrying two or three cosmonauts. During *Voskhod 2*'s flight 1965, Alexei Leonov made the first space walk.

**Vostok** the first Soviet spacecraft, used 1961–63. Vostok was a metal sphere 2.3 m/7.5 ft in diameter, capable of carrying one cosmonaut. It made flights lasting up to five days. *Vostok 1* carried the first person into space, Yuri Gagarin.

**Voyager probes** two US space probes, originally Mariners. *Voyager 1*, launched 5 Sept 1977, passed Jupiter March 1979, and reached Saturn Nov 1980. *Voyager 2* was launched earlier, 20 Aug 1977, on a slower trajectory that took it past Jupiter July 1979, Saturn Aug 1981, Uranus Jan 1986, and Neptune Aug 1989. Like the Pioneer probes, the Voyagers are on their way out of the solar system. Their tasks now include helping scientists to locate

## WHAT SHALL WE CALL THE FEATURES OF VENUS?

Magellan, NASA's latest space probe to Venus, went into orbit around the planet in Aug 1990 and began to map its surface by radar. Unbroken clouds permanently mask the surface of Venus from telescopes on Earth, but radio waves can penetrate them. Venus has been mapped previously by US and Soviet probes, as well as by radar from Earth, but Magellan's survey is ten times more detailed, showing details as small as 120 m/400 ft across.

Magellan scans Venus in strips as it orbits from pole to pole. Despite some early interruptions in communications, Magellan's pictures began to reveal folded mountains, volcanic vents, outpourings of lava, and large meteorite craters on the surface.

Venus is similar in size to the Earth but has evolved totally differently, suffering catastrophic global warming that has left it with hellish conditions—surface temperature 470°C/878°F, atmospheric pressure 90 times that at Earth's sea level, and clouds of sulphuric acid. Needless to say there is no water on Venus today, but if it existed in the past then river beds and shorelines might still be visible—although none were apparent in the early images. It seems that the surface of Venus has been extensively reworked by geological activity, erasing signs of Venus's early evolution.

Other questions Magellan is intended to answer is whether the volcanoes on the planet are still active and whether the planet's crust is broken into shifting plates like that of Earth. Magellan takes over eight months to map Venus once, and over a lifetime of five years it should map the planet eight times in all. These scans can be compared for signs of surface changes. Magellan's success, though, has presented the mapmakers with a new problem—what to name all the new features being revealed. The International Astronomical Union, astronomy's governing body, has decreed Venus to be a feminist planet, and the major features have already been named after mythological females including Aphrodite, Ishtar and Lakshmi. Now the Astronomical Union is turning to smaller features and will eventually require thousands of names. Living persons are excluded, but among those proposed are Gertrude Stein, Virginia Woolf, Rachel Carson, Margaret Mead, and Mary, Queen of Scots.

---

the position of the heliopause, the boundary at which the influence of the Sun gives way to the forces exerted by other stars. Both *Voyagers* carry specially coded long-playing records called 'Sounds of Earth' for the enlightenment of any other civilizations that might find them.

**weightlessness** condition in which there is no gravitational force acting on a body, either because gravitational force is cancelled out by equal and opposite acceleration, or because the body is so far outside a planet's gravitational field that no force is exerted upon it.

# THE SOLAR SYSTEM

**Apollo asteroid** member of a group of asteroids whose orbits cross that of the Earth. They are named after the first of their kind, Apollo, discovered 1932 and then lost until 1973. Apollo asteroids are so small and faint that they are difficult to see except when close to Earth (Apollo is about 2 km/1.2 mi across).

**asteroid** or *minor planet* any of many thousands of small bodies, composed of rock and iron, that orbit the Sun. Most lie in a belt between the orbits of Mars and Jupiter, and are thought to be fragments left over from the formation of the solar system. About 100,000 may exist, but their total mass is only a few hundredths the mass of the Moon.

**aurora** coloured light in the night sky near the Earth's magnetic poles, called *aurora borealis*, 'northern lights', in the northern hemisphere and *aurora australis* in the southern hemisphere. An aurora is usually in the form of a luminous arch followed by folded bands and rays, usually green but often showing shades of blue and red, and sometimes yellow or white. Auroras are caused at heights of over 100 km/60 mi by a fast stream of charged particles from solar flares and low-density 'holes' in the Sun's corona. These are guided by the Earth's magnetic field towards the north and south magnetic poles, where they enter the upper atmosphere and bombard the gases in the atmosphere, causing them to emit visible light.

**Baily's beads** bright spots of sunlight seen around the edge of the Moon for a few seconds immediately before and after a total eclipse of the Sun, caused by sunlight shining between mountains at the Moon's edge. Sometimes one bead is much brighter than the others, producing the so-called *diamond ring* effect. The effect was described 1836 by the English astronomer Francis Baily (1774–1844), a wealthy stockbroker who retired in 1825 to devote himself to astronomy.

**Callisto** second largest moon of Jupiter, 4,800 km/3,000 mi in diameter, orbiting every 16.7 days at a distance of 1.9 million km/1.2 million mi from the planet. Its surface is covered with large craters.

**Ceres** the largest asteroid, 940 km/584 mi in diameter, and the first to be discovered (by Giuseppe Piazzi 1801). Ceres is a rock that orbits the Sun every 4.6 years at an average distance of 414 million km/257 million mi. Its mass is about one-seventieth (0.014) of that of the Moon.

**Chiron** unusual solar-system object orbiting between Saturn and Uranus, discovered 1977 by US astronomer Charles T Kowal (1940– ). Initially classified as an asteroid, it is now believed to be a giant cometary nucleus about 200 km/120 mi across, composed of ice with a dark crust of carbon dust.

**chromosphere** a layer of mostly hydrogen gas about 10,000 km/6,000 mi deep above the visible surface of the Sun (the photosphere). It appears pinkish-red during eclipses of the Sun.

**comet** small, icy body orbiting the Sun, usually on a highly elliptical path. A comet consists of a central nucleus a few kilometres across, often likened to a dirty snowball because it consists mostly of ice mixed with dust. As the comet approaches the Sun the nucleus heats up, releasing gas and dust which form a tenuous coma, up to 100,000 km/60,000 mi wide, around the nucleus. Gas and dust stream away from the coma to form one or more tails, which may extend for millions of kilometres.

**corona** a faint halo of hot (about 2,000,000°C/3,600,000°F) and tenuous gas around the Sun, which boils from the surface. It is visible at solar eclipses or through a **coronagraph**, an instrument that blocks light from the Sun's brilliant disc. Gas flows away from the corona to form the solar wind.

**crater** a hollow in the ground caused by the impact of a meteorite, asteroid or comet. The Moon and inner planets, as well as many of the moons of the outer planets, are heavily cratered by impacts. Over 100 features on Earth up to 140 km/87 mi in diameter are believed to be the results of meteorite impact, although some are so eroded that they no longer look like craters. The most famous meteorite crater on Earth is the Barringer crater in Arizona, 1.2 km/0.75 mi in diameter, formed in prehistoric times by an iron meteorite weighing perhaps 100,000 tons.

**crescent** the curved shape of the Moon when it appears less than half-illuminated.

**Deimos** one of the two moons of Mars. It is irregularly shaped, 15 × 12 × 11 km/9 × 7.5 × 7 mi orbits at a height of 24,000 km/15,000 mi every 1.26 days, and is not as heavily cratered as the other moon, Phobos. Deimos was discovered 1877 by US astronomer Asaph Hall (1829–1907), and is thought to be an asteroid captured by Mars' gravity.

**Earth** the third planet from the Sun. It is almost spherical, flattened slightly at the poles, and is composed of three concentric layers: the core, the mantle, and the crust. 70% of the surface (including the north and south polar icecaps) is covered with water. The Earth is surrounded by a life-supporting atmosphere and is the only planet on which life is known to exist.

*mean distance from the Sun* 149,500,000 km/92,860,000 mi

*equatorial diameter* 12,756 km/7,923 mi

*circumference* 40,070 km/24,900 mi

*rotation period* 23 hr 56 min 4.1 sec

*year* (complete orbit, or sidereal period) 365 days 5 hr 48 min 46 sec. Earth's average speed around the Sun is 30 kps/18.5 mps; the plane

of its orbit is inclined to its equatorial plane at an angle of 23.5°, the reason for the changing seasons

*atmosphere* nitrogen 78.09%; oxygen 20.95%; argon 0.93%; carbon dioxide 0.03%; and less than 0.0001% neon, helium, krypton, hydrogen, xenon, ozone, radon

*surface* land surface 150,000,000 sq km/57,500,000 sq mi (greatest height above sea level 8,872 m/29,118 ft Mount Everest); water surface 361,000,000 sq km/139,400,000 sq mi (greatest depth 11,034 m/36,201 ft Mariana Trench in the Pacific). The interior is thought to be an inner core about 2,600 km/1,600 mi in diameter, of solid iron and nickel; an outer core about 2,250 km/1,400 mi thick, of molten iron and nickel; and a mantle of mostly solid rock about 2,900 km/1,800 mi thick, separated by the Mohorovičić discontinuity from the Earth's crust. The crust and the topmost layer of the mantle form about 12 major moving plates, some of which carry the continents. The plates are in constant, slow motion, called tectonic drift

*satellite* the Moon

*age* 4.6 billion years. The Earth was formed with the rest of the Solar System by consolidation of interstellar dust. Life began about 3.5 billion years ago.

**eclipse** the passage of an astronomical body through the shadow of another. The term is usually used for solar and lunar eclipses, which may be either partial or total, but also, for example, for eclipses by Jupiter of its satellites. An eclipse of a star by a body in the solar system is called an occultation.

**Encke's comet** the comet with the shortest known orbital period, 3.3 years. It is named after German mathematician and astronomer Johann Franz Encke (1791–1865) who in 1819 calculated the orbit from earlier sightings.

**Eros** an asteroid, discovered 1898, that can pass 22 million km/14 million mi from the Earth, as in 1975. Eros was the first asteroid to be discovered that has an orbit coming within that of Mars. It is elongated, measures about 36 × 12 km/22 × 7 mi, rotates around its shortest axis every 5.3 hours, and orbits the Sun every 1.8 years.

**Europa** the fourth largest moon of the planet Jupiter, diameter 3,140 km/1,950 mi, orbiting 671,000 km/417,000 mi from the planet every 3.55 days. It is covered by ice and crisscrossed by thousands of thin cracks, each some 50,000 km/30,000 mi long.

**flare, solar** a brilliant eruption on the Sun above a sunspot, thought to be caused by release of magnetic energy. Flares reach maximum brightness within a few minutes, then fade away over about an hour. They eject a burst of atomic particles into space at up to 1,000 kps/600 mps. When these particles reach Earth they can cause radio blackouts, disruptions of the Earth's magnetic field, and auroras.

**Ganymede** the largest moon of the planet Jupiter, and the largest moon in the solar system, 5,260 km/3,270 mi in diameter (larger than

ECLIPSES 1992

| Date | Time of max. eclipse (UT) | Type of eclipse | Maximum duration (solar eclipses) and main area of visibility |
| --- | --- | --- | --- |
| January 4 | 23h 6m | Sun annular | Duration 11 min 41 sec. Pacific. |
| June 15 | 04h 57m | Moon partial | North and South America. |
| June 30 | 12h 11m | Sun total | Duration 5 min 21 sec. South Atlantic. |
| December 9 | 23h 44m | Moon total | Africa, Europe. |
| December 24 | 00h 32m | Sun partial | Northern Pacific. |

the planet Mercury). It orbits Jupiter every 7.2 days at a distance of 1.1 million km/ 700,000 mi. Its surface is a mixture of cratered and grooved terrain.

**Halley's comet** a comet that orbits the Sun about every 76 years, named after Edmond Halley, who calculated its orbit. It is the brightest and most conspicuous of the periodic comets. Recorded sightings go back over 2,000 years. It travels around the Sun in the opposite direction to the planets. Its orbit is inclined at almost 20° to the main plane of the solar system and ranges between the orbits of Venus and Neptune. It will next reappear 2061.

**heliosphere** region of space through which the solar wind flows outwards from the Sun. The *heliopause* is the boundary of this region, believed to lie about 100 astronomical units from the Sun, where the flow of the solar wind merges with the interstellar gas.

**Icarus** an Apollo asteroid 1.5 km/1 mi in diameter, discovered 1949. It orbits the Sun every 409 days at a distance of 28 million–186 million km/28 million–300 million mi (0.19–2.0 astronomical units). It was the first asteroid known to approach the Sun closer than does the planet Mercury. In 1968 it passed 6 million km/4 million mi from the Earth.

**inferior planet** a planet (Mercury or Venus) whose orbit lies within that of the Earth, best observed when at its greatest elongation from the Sun, either at eastern elongation in the evening (setting after the Sun) or at western elongation in the morning (rising before the Sun).

**interplanetary matter** gas and dust thinly spread through the solar system. The gas flows outwards from the Sun as the solar wind. Fine dust lies in the plane of the solar system, scattering sunlight to cause the zodiacal light. Swarms of dust shed by comets enter the Earth's atmosphere to cause meteor showers.

**Io** the third largest moon of the planet Jupiter, 3,630 km/2,260 mi in diameter, orbiting in 1.77 days at a distance of 422,000 km/ 262,000 mi. It is the most volcanically active body in the solar system, covered by hundreds of vents that erupt not lava but sulphur, giving Io an orange-coloured surface.

**Jupiter** the fifth planet from the Sun, and the largest in the solar system (equatorial diameter 142,800 km/88,700 mi), with a mass more than twice that of all the other planets combined, 318 times that of the Earth's. It takes

11.86 years to orbit the Sun, at an average distance of 778 million km/484 million mi, and has at least 16 moons. It is largely composed of hydrogen and helium, liquefied by pressure in its interior, and probably with a rocky core larger than the Earth. Its main feature is the Great Red Spot, a cloud of rising gases, revolving anticlockwise, 14,000 km/8,500 mi wide and some 30,000 km/20,000 mi long.

**Lagrangian points** the five locations in space where the centrifugal and gravitational forces of two bodies neutralize each other; a third, less massive body located at any one of these points will be held in equilibrium with respect to the other two. Three of the points, L1–L3, lie on a line joining the two large bodies. The other two points, L4 and L5, which are the most stable, lie on either side of this line. Their existence was predicted 1772 by Joseph Louis Lagrange.

**magnetosphere** the volume of space, surrounding a planet, controlled by the planet's magnetic field, and acting as a magnetic 'shell'. The Earth's extends 64,000 km/40,000 mi towards the Sun, but many times this distance on the side away from the Sun.

**mare** (plural *maria*) dark lowland plain on the Moon. The name comes from Latin 'sea', because these areas were once wrongly thought to be water.

**Mars** the fourth planet from the Sun, average distance 227.9 million km/141.6 million mi. It revolves around the Sun in 687 Earth days, and has a rotation period of 24 hr 37 min. It is much smaller than Venus or Earth, with diameter 6,780 km/4,210 mi, and mass 0.11 that of Earth. Mars is slightly pear-shaped, with a low, level northern hemisphere, which is comparatively uncratered and geologically 'young', and a heavily cratered 'ancient' southern hemisphere.

**Mercury** the closest planet to the Sun, at an average distance of 58 million km/36 million mi. Its diameter is 4,880 km/3,030 mi, its mass 0.056 that of Earth. Mercury orbits the Sun every 88 days, and spins on its axis every 59 days. On its sunward side the surface temperature reaches over 400°C/752°F, but on the 'night' side it falls to –170°C/–274°F. Mercury has an atmosphere with minute traces of argon and helium. In 1974 the US space probe *Mariner 10* discovered that its surface is cratered by meteorite impacts. Mercury has no moons.

**meteor** a flash of light in the sky, popularly known as a *shooting* or *falling star*, caused by a particle of dust, a *meteoroid*, entering the atmosphere at speeds up to 70 kps/45 mps and burning up by friction at a height of around 100 km/60 mi. On any clear night, several *sporadic* meteors can be seen each hour.

**meteorite** a piece of rock or metal from space that reaches the surface of the Earth, Moon, or other body. Most meteorites are thought to be fragments from asteroids, although some may be pieces from the heads of comets. Most are stony, although some are made of iron and a few have a mixed rock-iron composition. Meteorites provide evidence for the nature of the solar system and may be similar to the Earth's core and mantle, neither of which can be observed directly.

**moon** any natural satellite that orbits a planet. Mercury and Venus are the only planets in the solar system that do not have moons.

**Moon** the natural satellite of Earth, 3,476 km/2,160 mi in diameter, with a mass 0.012 (approximately one-eightieth) that of Earth. Its surface gravity is only 0.16 (one-sixth) that of Earth. Its average distance from Earth is 384,404 km/238,857 mi, and it orbits in a west-to-east direction every 27.32 days (the *sidereal month*). It spins on its axis with one side permanently turned towards Earth. The Moon has no atmosphere or water. Much of our information about the Moon is derived from photographs and measurements taken by US and Soviet Moon probes; from geological samples brought back by US Apollo astronauts and by Soviet Luna probes; and from experiments set up by the US astronauts 1969–72.

**Neptune** the eighth planet in average distance from the Sun. Neptune orbits the Sun every 164.8 years at an average distance of 4.497 billion km/2.794 billion mi. It is a giant gas (hydrogen, helium, methane) planet, with a diameter of 48,600 km/30,200 mi and a mass 17.2 times that of Earth. Its rotation period is 16 hours 7 minutes. The methane in its atmosphere absorbs red light and gives the planet a blue colouring. It is believed to have a central rocky core covered by a layer of ice. Neptune has eight known moons.

**occultation** the temporary obscuring of a star by a body in the solar system. Occultations are used to provide information about changes in an orbit, and the structure of objects in space, such as radio sources.

**Oort cloud** spherical cloud of comets beyond Pluto, extending out to about 100,000 astronomical units (1.5 light years) from the Sun. The gravitational effect of passing stars and the rest of our Galaxy disturbs comets from the cloud so that they fall in towards the Sun on highly elongated orbits, becoming visible from Earth. As many as 10 trillion comets may reside in the Oort cloud, named after Jan Oort who postulated it in 1950.

**Phobos** one of the two moons of Mars, discovered 1877 by the US astronomer Asaph Hall (1829–1907). It is an irregularly shaped lump of rock, cratered by meteorite impacts. Phobos is 27 × 22 × 19 km/17 × 13 × 12 mi across, and orbits Mars every 0.32 days at a distance of 9,400 km/5,840 mi from the planet's centre. It is thought to be an asteroid captured by Mars' gravity.

**photosphere** the visible surface of the Sun, which emits light and heat. About 300 km/200 mi deep, it consists of incandescent gas at a temperature of 5,800K (5,530°C/9,980°F).

**planet** a large celestial body in orbit around a star, composed of rock, metal, or gas. There are nine planets in the solar system: Mercury, Venus, Earth, Mars, Jupiter, Saturn, Uranus, Neptune, and Pluto.

**Pluto** the smallest and, usually, outermost planet of the solar system. The existence of Pluto was predicted by calculation by Percival Lowell and the planet was located by Clyde Tombaugh 1930. It orbits the Sun every 248.5 years at an average distance of 5.9 billion km/3.6 billion mi. Its highly elliptical orbit occasionally takes it within the orbit of Neptune, such as 1979–99. Pluto has a diameter of about 2,300 km/1,400 mi, and a mass about 0.002 that of Earth. It is of low density, composed of rock and ice, with frozen methane on its surface and a thin atmosphere.

**prominence** bright cloud of gas projecting from the Sun into space 100,000 km/60,000 mi or more. *Quiescent prominences* last for months, and are held in place by magnetic fields in the Sun's corona. *Surge prominences* shoot gas into space at speeds of 1,000 kps/600 mps. *Loop prominences* are gases falling back to the Sun's surface after a solar flare.

**satellite** any small body that orbits a larger one, either natural or artificial. Natural satellites that orbit planets are called moons. The first

## LARGEST PLANETARY SATELLITES

| planet | satellite | diameter in km | mean distance from centre of primary in km | orbital period in days | reciprocal mass (planet = 1) |
|--------|-----------|----------------|--------------------------------------------|------------------------|------------------------------|
| Jupiter | Ganymede | 5,262 | 1,070,000 | 7.16 | 12,800 |
| Saturn | Titan | 5,150 | 1,221,800 | 15.95 | 4,200 |
| Jupiter | Callisto | 4,800 | 1,883,000 | 16.69 | 17,700 |
| Jupiter | Io | 3,630 | 421,600 | 1.77 | 21,400 |
| Earth | Moon | 3,476 | 384,400 | 27.32 | 81.3 |
| Jupiter | Europa | 3,138 | 670,900 | 3.55 | 39,700 |
| Neptune | Triton | 2,700 | 354,300 | 5.88 | 770 |

*artificial satellite*, *Sputnik 1*, was launched into orbit around the Earth by the USSR 1957. Artificial satellites are used for scientific purposes, communications, weather forecasting, and military applications. The largest artificial satellites can be seen by the naked eye.

**Saturn** the second largest planet in the solar system, sixth from the Sun, and encircled by bright and easily visible equatorial rings. Viewed through a telescope it is ochre. Saturn orbits the Sun every 29.46 years at an average distance of 1,427,000,000 km/ 886,700,000 mi. Its equatorial diameter is 120,000 km/75,000 mi, but its polar diameter is 12,000 km/7,450 mi smaller, a result of its fast rotation and low density, the lowest of any planet. Saturn spins on its axis every 10 hours 14 minutes at its equator, slowing to 10 hours 40 minutes at high latitudes. Its mass is 95 times that of Earth, and its magnetic field 1,000 times stronger. Saturn is believed to have a small core of rock and iron, encased in ice and topped by a deep layer of liquid hydrogen. There are over 20 known moons, its largest being Titan. The rings visible from Earth begin about 14,000 km/9,000 mi from the planet's cloudtops and extend out to about 76,000 km/47,000 mi. Made of small chunks of ice and rock (averaging 1 m/3 ft across), they are 275,000 km/170,000 mi rim to rim, but only 100 m/300 ft thick. The Voyager probes showed that the rings actually consist of thousands of closely spaced ringlets, looking like the grooves in a gramophone record.

**solar system** the Sun and all the bodies orbiting it: the nine planets (Mercury, Venus, Earth, Mars, Jupiter, Saturn, Uranus, Neptune, and Pluto), their moons, the asteroids, and the comets. It is thought to have formed from a cloud of gas and dust in space about 4.6 billion years ago. The Sun contains 99% of the mass of the solar system. The edge of the solar system is not clearly defined, marked only by the limit of the Sun's gravitational influence, which extends about 1.5 light years, almost halfway to the nearest star, Alpha Centauri, 4.3 light years away.

**solar wind** a stream of atomic particles, mostly protons and electrons, from the Sun's corona, flowing outwards at speeds of between 300 kps/ 200 mps and 1,000 kps/600 mps.

**spicules, solar** short-lived jets of hot gas in the upper chromosphere of the Sun. Spiky in appearance, they move at high velocities along lines of magnetic force to which they owe their shapes, and last for a few minutes each. Spicules appear to disperse material into the corona.

**Sun** the star at the centre of the solar system. Its diameter is 1,392,000 km/ 865,000 mi; its temperature at the surface is about 5,800K (5,530°C/9,980°F), and at the centre 15,000,000K (15,000,000°C/ 27,000,000°F). It is composed of about 70% hydrogen and 30% helium, with other elements making up less than 1%. The Sun's energy is generated by nuclear fusion reactions that turn hydrogen into helium at its centre. It is about 4.7 billion years old, with a predicted lifetime of 10 billion years.

**sunspot** a dark patch on the surface of the Sun, actually an area of cooler gas, thought to be caused by strong magnetic fields that block the outward flow of heat to the Sun's surface. Sunspots consist of a dark central *umbra*, about 4,000K (3,700°C/6,700°F), and a lighter surrounding *penumbra*, about 5,500K (5,200°C/9,400°F). They last from several days to over a month, ranging in size from 2,000 km/1,250 mi to groups stretching for over 100,000 km/62,000 mi. The number of sunspots visible at a given time varies from none to over 100 in a cycle averaging 11 years.

**superior planet** planet that is farther away from the Sun than the Earth: that is, Mars, Jupiter, Saturn, Uranus, Neptune, and Pluto.

**tektite** small, rounded glassy stone, found in certain regions of the Earth, such as Australasia. They are probably the scattered drops of molten rock thrown out by the impact of a large meteorite.

**Titan** largest moon of the planet Saturn, with a diameter of 5,150 km/3,200 mi and a mean distance from Saturn of 1,222,000 km/ 759,000 mi. It was discovered 1655 by Christiaan Huygens, and is the second largest moon in the solar system (Ganymede, of Jupiter, is larger).

**Uranus** the seventh planet from the Sun, discovered by William Herschel 1781. It is twice as far out as the sixth planet, Saturn. Uranus has a diameter of 50,800 km/31,600 mi and a mass 14.5 times that of Earth. It orbits the Sun in 84 years at an average distance of 2,870 million km/1,783 million mi. The spin axis of Uranus is tilted at 98°, so that one pole points towards the Sun, giving extreme seasons. It has 15 moons, and in 1977 was discovered to have thin rings around its equator.

**Venus** the second planet from the Sun. It orbits the Sun every 225 days at an average distance of 108.2 million km/67.2 million mi and can approach the Earth to within 38 million km/ 24 million mi, closer than any other planet. Its diameter is 12,100 km/7,500 mi and its mass is 0.82 that of Earth. Venus rotates on its axis more slowly than any other planet, once every 243 days and from east to west, the opposite direction to the other planets (except Uranus). Venus is shrouded by clouds of sulphuric acid droplets that sweep across the planet from east to west every four days. The atmosphere is almost entirely carbon dioxide, which traps the Sun's heat by the greenhouse effect and raises the planet's surface temperature to 480°C/900°F, with an atmospheric pressure 90 times that at Earth's surface.

**zodiacal light** a cone-shaped light sometimes seen extending from the Sun along the ecliptic, visible after sunset or before sunrise. It is due to thinly spread dust particles in the central plane of the solar system. It is very faint, and requires a dark, clear sky to be seen.

# TECHNICAL TERMS

**aberration of starlight** the apparent displacement of a star from its true position, due to the combined effects of the speed of light and the speed of the Earth in orbit around the Sun (about 30 kps/18.5 mps).

**albedo** the fraction of the incoming light reflected by a body such as a planet. A body with a high albedo, near 1, is very bright, while a body with a low albedo, near 0, is dark. The Moon has an average albedo of 0.12, Venus 0.65, Earth 0.37.

**aphelion** the point at which an object, travelling in an elliptical orbit around the Sun, is at its furthest from the Sun.

**apogee** the point at which an object, travelling in an elliptical orbit around the Earth, is at its furthest from the Earth.

**arc minute, arc second** units for measuring small angles, used in geometry, surveying, map-making, and astronomy. An arc minute is one-sixtieth of a degree, and an arc second one-sixtieth of an arc minute. Small distances in the sky, as between two close stars or the apparent width of a planet's disc, are expressed in minutes and seconds of arc.

**astronomical unit** unit (symbol AU) equal to the mean distance of the Earth from the Sun: 149,597,870 km/92,955,800 mi. It is used to describe planetary distances. Light travels this distance in approximately 8.3 minutes.

**calendar** the division of the year into months, weeks, and days and the method of ordering the years. From year one, an assumed date of the birth of Jesus, dates are calculated backwards (BC 'before Christ', or BCE 'before common era') and forwards (AD, Latin, *anno domini* 'in the year of the Lord' or CE 'common era'). The *lunar month* (period between one new moon and the next) naturally averages 29.5 days, but the Western calendar uses for convenience a *calendar month* with a complete number of days, 30 or 31 (Feb has 28). For adjustments, since there are slightly fewer than six extra hours a year left over, they are added to Feb as a 29th day every fourth year (*leap year*), century years being excepted unless they are divisible by 400. For example 1896 was a leap year; 1900 was not.

**celestial mechanics** the branch of astronomy that deals with the calculation of the orbits of celestial bodies, their gravitational attractions (such as those that produce Earth's tides), and also the orbits of artificial satellites and space probes. It is based on the laws of motion and gravity laid down by Newton.

**celestial sphere** imaginary sphere surrounding the Earth, on which the celestial bodies seem to lie. The positions of bodies such as stars, planets and galaxies are specified by their coordinates on the celestial sphere. The equivalents of latitude and longitude on the celestial sphere are called declination and right ascension (which is measured in hours from 0 to 24). The **celestial poles** lie directly above the Earth's poles, and the **celestial equator** lies over the Earth's equator. The celestial sphere appears to rotate once around the Earth each day, actually a result of the rotation of the Earth on its axis.

**conjunction** the alignment of two celestial bodies as seen from Earth. A superior planet (or other object) is in conjunction when it lies behind the Sun. An inferior planet (or other object) comes to **inferior conjunction** when it passes between the Earth and the Sun; it is at **superior conjunction** when it passes behind the Sun. **Planetary conjunction** takes place when a planet is closely aligned with another celestial object, such as the Moon, a star, or another planet.

**cosmology** the study of the structure of the universe. Modern cosmology began in the 1920s with the discovery that the universe is expanding, which suggested that it began in an explosion, the Big Bang. An alternative view, the steady-state theory, claimed that the universe has no origin, but is expanding because new matter is being continually created.

**day** the time taken for the Earth to rotate once on its axis. The **solar day** is the time that the Earth takes to rotate once relative to the Sun. It is divided into 24 hours, and is the basis of our civil day. The **sidereal day** is the time that the Earth takes to rotate once relative to the stars. It is 3 minutes 56 seconds shorter than the solar day, because the Sun's position against the background of stars as seen from Earth changes as the Earth orbits it.

**declination** the coordinate on the celestial sphere (imaginary sphere surrounding the Earth) that corresponds to latitude on the Earth's surface. Declination runs from $0°$ at the celestial equator to $90°$ at the north and south celestial poles.

**ecliptic** the path, against the background of stars, that the Sun appears to follow each year as the Earth orbits the Sun. It can be thought of as the plane of the Earth's orbit projected on to the celestial sphere (imaginary sphere around the Earth).

**elongation** the angular distance between the Sun and a planet or other solar-system object. This angle is $0°$ at conjunction, $90°$ at quadrature, and $180°$ at opposition.

**equinox** the points in spring and autumn at which the Sun's path, the ecliptic, crosses the celestial equator, so that the day and night are of approximately equal length. The **vernal equinox** occurs about 21 March and the **autumnal equinox**, 23 Sept.

**escape velocity** minimum velocity with which an object must be projected for it to escape from the gravitational pull of a planetary body. In the case of the Earth, the escape velocity 11.2 kps/6.9 mps; the Moon 2.4 kps/1.5 mps; Mars 5 kps/3.1 mps; and Jupiter 59.6 kps/37 mps.

**exobiology** the study of life forms that may possibly exist elsewhere in the universe, and of the effects of extraterrestrial environments on Earth organisms.

**geostationary orbit** the circular path 35,900 km/ 22,300 mi above the Earth's equator on which a satellite takes 24 hours, moving from west to east, to complete an orbit, thus appearing to hang stationary over one place on the Earth's surface. Geostationary orbits are particularly used for communications satellites and weather satellites. They were first thought of by the author Arthur C Clarke. A *geosynchronous orbit* lies at the same distance from Earth but is inclined to the equator.

**gravitational lens** the bending of light by a gravitational field, predicted by Einstein's general theory of relativity. The effect was first detected in 1917 when the light from stars was found to be bent as it passed the totally eclipsed Sun. More remarkable is the splitting of light from distant quasars into two or more images by intervening galaxies. In 1979 the first double image of a quasar produced by gravitational lensing was discovered and a quadruple image of another quasar was later found.

**gravity** the force of attraction that arises between objects by virtue of their masses. On Earth, gravity is the force of attraction between any object in the Earth's gravitational field and the Earth itself.

**Greenwich Mean Time** (GMT) local time on the zero line of longitude (the **Greenwich meridian**), which passes through the Old Royal Observatory at Greenwich, London. It was replaced 1972 by coordinated universal time (UTC).

**Hertzsprung-Russell diagram** a graph on which the surface temperatures of stars are plotted against their luminosities. Most stars, including the Sun, fall into a narrow band called the *main sequence*. When a star grows old it moves from the main sequence to the upper right part of the graph, into the area of the giants and supergiants. At the end of its life, as the star shrinks to become a white dwarf, it moves again, to the bottom left area. It is named after the Dane Ejnar Hertzsprung and the American Henry Norris Russell, who independently devised it in the years 1911–13.

**Hubble's constant** a measure of the rate at which the universe is expanding, named after Edwin Hubble. Observations suggest that galaxies are moving apart at a rate of 50–100 kps/30–60 mps for every million parsecs of distance. This means that the universe, which began at one point according to the Big Bang theory, is between 10 billion and 20 billion years old.

**Hubble's law** the law that relates a galaxy's distance from us to its speed of recession as the universe expands, announced in 1929 by Edwin Hubble. He found that galaxies are moving apart at speeds that increase in direct proportion to their distance apart. The rate of expansion is known as Hubble's constant.

**inclination** the angle between the ecliptic and the plane of the orbit of a planet, asteroid, or comet. In the case of satellites orbiting a planet, it is the angle between the plane of

orbit of the satellite and the equator of the planet.

**light year** the distance travelled by a beam of light in a vacuum in one year, approximately 9.46 trillion (million million) km/5.88 trillion miles.

**magnitude** measure of the brightness of a star or other celestial object. The larger the number denoting the magnitude, the fainter the object. Zero or first magnitude indicates some of the brightest stars. Still brighter are those of negative magnitude, such as Sirius, whose magnitude is –1.46. *Apparent magnitude* is the brightness of an object as seen from Earth, *absolute magnitude* the brightness at a standard distance of 10 parsecs (32.6 light years).

**month** unit of time based on the motion of the Moon around the Earth. The time from one new or full Moon to the next (the *synodic* or *lunar month*) is 29.53 days. The time for the Moon to complete one orbit around the Earth relative to the stars (the *sidereal month*) is 27.32 days. The *solar month* equals 30.44 days, and is exactly one-twelfth of the solar or tropical year, the time taken for the Earth to orbit the Sun. The *calendar month* is a human invention, devised to fit the calendar year.

**nadir** the point on the celestial sphere vertically below the observer and hence diametrically opposite the *zenith*.

**nutation** a slight 'nodding' of the Earth in space, caused by the varying gravitational pulls of the Sun and Moon. Nutation changes the angle of the Earth's axial tilt (average 23.5°) by about 9 seconds of arc to either side of its mean position, a complete cycle taking just over 18.5 years.

**opposition** the moment at which a body in the solar system lies opposite the Sun in the sky as seen from the Earth and crosses the meridian at about midnight.

**orbit** the path of one body in space around another, such as the orbit of Earth around the Sun, or the Moon around Earth. When the two bodies are similar in mass, as in a double star, both bodies move around their common centre of mass. The movement of objects in orbit follows Kepler's laws, which apply to artificial satellites as well as to natural bodies.

**parallax** the change in the apparent position of an object against its background when viewed from two different positions. Nearby stars show a shift owing to parallax when viewed from different positions on the Earth's orbit around the Sun. A star's parallax is used to deduce its distance.

**parsec** a unit (symbol pc) used for distances to stars and galaxies. One parsec is equal to 3.2616 light years, $2.063 \times 10^5$ astronomical units, and $3.086 \times 10^{13}$ km.

**perigee** the point at which an object, travelling in an elliptical orbit around the Earth, is at its closest to the Earth.

**perihelion** the point at which an object, travelling in an elliptical orbit around the Sun, is at its closest to the Sun.

**phase** the apparent shape of the Moon or a planet

when all or part of its illuminated hemisphere is facing Earth. The Moon undergoes a full cycle of phases from new (when between Earth and the Sun) through first quarter (when at 90° eastern elongation from the Sun), full (when opposite the Sun), and last quarter (when at 90° western elongation from the Sun). The inferior planets can also undergo a full cycle of phases, as can an asteroid passing inside the Earth's orbit.

**precession** a slow wobble of the Earth on its axis, like that of a spinning top. The gravitational pulls of the Sun and Moon on the Earth's equatorial bulge cause the Earth's axis to trace out a circle on the sky every 25,800 years. The position of the celestial poles is constantly changing owing to precession, as are the positions of the equinoxes (the points at which the celestial equator intersects the Sun's path around the sky). The *precession of the equinoxes* means that there is a gradual westward drift in the ecliptic—the path that the Sun appears to follow—and in the coordinates of objects on the celestial sphere; this is why the dates of the astrological signs of the zodiac no longer correspond to the times of year when the Sun actually passes through the constellations. For example, the Sun passes through Leo from mid-Aug to mid-Sept, but the astrological dates for Leo are between about 23 July and 22 Aug.

**proper motion** the gradual change in the position of a star that results from its motion in orbit around our Galaxy, the Milky Way. Proper motions are slight and undetectable to the naked eye, but can be accurately measured on telescopic photographs taken many years apart. Barnard's Star is the star with the largest proper motion, 10.3 arc seconds per year.

**red shift** the lengthening of the wavelengths of light from an object as a result of the object's motion away from us. It is an example of the Doppler effect. The red shift in light from galaxies is evidence that the universe is expanding.

**right ascension** the coordinate on the celestial sphere that corresponds to longitude on the surface of the Earth. It is measured in hours, minutes, and seconds eastwards from the point where the Sun's path, the ecliptic, intersects the celestial equator; this point is called the *vernal equinox*.

**sidereal period** the orbital period of a planet around the Sun, or a moon around a planet, with reference to a background star. The sidereal period of a planet is in effect its 'year'. A synodic period is a full circle as seen from Earth.

**singularity** the point at the centre of a black hole at which it is predicted that the infinite gravitational forces will compress the infalling mass of the collapsing star to infinite density. It is a point in space-time at which the known laws of physics break down. Also, it is thought, in the Big Bang theory of the origin of the universe, to be the point from which the expansion of the universe began.

**solstice** either of the points at which the Sun is farthest north or south of the celestial equator each year. The *summer solstice*, when the Sun is farthest north, occurs around 21 June; the *winter solstice* around 22 Dec.

**speckle interferometry** technique whereby large telescopes can achieve high resolution of astronomical objects despite the adverse effects of the atmosphere through which light from the object under study must pass. It involves the taking of large numbers of images, each under high magnification and with short exposure times. The pictures are then combined to form the final picture. The technique was introduced by the French astronomer Antoine Labeyrie 1970.

**synodic period** the time taken for a planet or moon to return to the same position in its orbit as seen from the Earth; that is, from one opposition to the next. It differs from the sidereal period because the Earth is moving in orbit around the Sun.

**transfer orbit** elliptical path followed by a spacecraft moving from one orbit to another, designed to save fuel although at the expense of a longer journey time.

**transit** the passage of a smaller object across the visible disc of a larger one. Transits of the inferior planets occur when they pass directly between the Earth and Sun, and are seen as tiny dark spots against the Sun's disc.

**universal time** (UT) another name for Greenwich Mean Time. It is based on the rotation of the Earth, which is not quite constant. Since 1972, UT has been replaced by *coordinated universal time* (UTC), which is based on uniform atomic time.

**year** a unit of time measurement, based on the orbital period of the Earth around the Sun.

**zenith** the uppermost point of the celestial horizon, immediately above the observer; the nadir is below, diametrically opposite.

**zodiac** the zone of the heavens containing the paths of the Sun, Moon, and planets. When this was devised by the ancient Greeks, only five planets were known, making the zodiac about 16° wide. The stars in it are grouped into 12 signs (constellations), each 30° in extent: Aries, Taurus, Gemini, Cancer, Leo, Virgo, Libra, Scorpius, Sagittarius, Capricornus, Aquarius, and Pisces. Because of the precession of the equinoxes, the current constellations do not cover the same areas of sky as the zodiacal signs of the same name.

# STARS, GALAXIES, AND THE UNIVERSE

**Algol** or *Beta Persei* an eclipsing binary, a pair of rotating stars in the constellation Perseus, one of which eclipses the other every 69 hours, causing its brightness to drop by two thirds.

**Alpha Centauri** or *Rigil Kent* the brightest star

---

### THE PAYING CUSTOMER IN SPACE

Japanese TV reporter Toyohiro Akiyama became the first fare-paying passenger in space in Dec 1990 when he flew up to the Soviet *Mir* space station for a week with cosmonauts Viktor Afanasyev and Musa Manarov. The trip, for which Akiyama's employers, Tokyo Broadcasting System, paid a reported $12 million, is part of a new Soviet move towards increased commercialization of their space programme, which includes carrying advertising on the launch rocket.

Akiyama, 48, chief foreign news editor at Tokyo Broadcasting, had been in training for over a year, but turned out to have little of the right stuff once in orbit. He spent most of the first few days feeling space sick and complaining about the effects of weightlessness. An 80-a-day smoker, he had given up cigarettes and beer before the flight but in space soon found himself craving for a puff.

His launch was transmitted live to viewers in Japan and he sent daily reports from orbit. At first he described himself as feeling like 'a pregnant woman suffering morning sickness' and was unable to eat much. 'All this has made me realize what gravity does to the human body,' he said. Akiyama took with him six Japanese tree frogs, which seemed to have considerably less difficulty than he did in adapting to weightlessness. Looking down on Japan he said his heart filled with joy, but he expressed concern about a haze of pollution visible over Japan and the USA.

By chance, Akiyama was launched on the same day, 2 Dec, as the Space Shuttle *Columbia* with the Astro-1 observatory. For a week there were 12 people in space simultaneously, an all-time record—seven aboard *Columbia*, two already in *Mir* plus Akiyama and his two companions. At one stage *Columbia* passed 50 km/30 mi from *Mir* and the Shuttle astronauts were able to see it through binoculars.

Akiyama returned to Earth on 10 Dec, accompanied by the two cosmonauts who had been aboard *Mir* since August. 'I feel like I don't have any legs,' he said as he struggled to readjust to the pull of gravity. 'I've come back to Earth full of desires.' He itemized eating, smoking, and a beer.

---

in the constellation Centaurus and the third brightest star in the sky. It is actually a triple star (see binary star); the two brighter stars orbit each other every 80 years, and the third, Proxima Centauri is the closest star to the Sun, 4.2 light years away, 0.1 light years closer than the other two.

**Andromeda galaxy** galaxy 2.2 million light years away from Earth in the constellation Andromeda, and the most distant object visible to the naked eye. It is the largest member of the Local Group of galaxies. Like the Milky Way, it is a spiral orbited by several companion galaxies but contains about twice as many stars. It is about 200,000 light years across.

**Barnard's star** second closest star to the Sun, six light years away in the constellation Ophiuchus. It is a faint red dwarf of 10th magnitude, visible only through a telescope. It is named after the US astronomer Edward E Barnard (1857–1923), who discovered in 1916 that it has the fastest proper motion of any star, crossing 1 degree of sky every 350 years.

**Big Bang** the hypothetical 'explosive' event that marked the origin of the universe as we know it. At the time of the Big Bang, the entire universe was squeezed into a hot, superdense state. The Big Bang explosion threw this compacted material outwards, producing the expanding universe. The cause of the Big Bang is unknown; observations of the current rate of expansion of the universe suggest that it took place about 15 billion years ago.

**binary star** a pair of stars moving in orbit around their common centre of mass. Observations show that most stars are binary, or even multiple – for example, the nearest star system to the Sun, Alpha Centauri.

**black hole** object in space whose gravity is so great that nothing can escape from it, not even light. Thought to form when massive stars shrink at the ends of their lives, a black hole sucks in more matter, including other stars, from the space around it. Matter that falls into a black hole is squeezed to infinite density at the centre of the hole. Black holes can be detected because gas falling towards them becomes so hot that it emits X-rays.

**brown dwarf** hypothetical object less massive than a star, but heavier than a planet. Brown dwarfs would not have enough mass to ignite nuclear reactions at their centres, but would shine by heat released during their contraction from a gas cloud. Because of the difficulty of detection, no brown dwarfs have been spotted with certainty, but some astronomers believe that vast numbers of them may exist throughout the Galaxy.

**Cepheid variable** yellow supergiant star that varies regularly in brightness every few days or weeks as a result of pulsations. The time that a Cepheid variable takes to pulsate is directly related to its average brightness; the longer the pulsation period, the brighter the star.

**constellation** one of the 88 areas into which the sky is divided for the purposes of identifying and naming celestial objects. The first constellations were simple, arbitrary patterns of stars in which early civilizations visualized gods, sacred beasts, and mythical heroes.

**cosmic background radiation** the electromagnetic radiation, also known as the 3° radiation, left over from the original formation of the universe in the Big Bang around 15 billion years ago. It corresponds to an overall background temperature of 3K

(–270°C/–454°F), or 3°C/37°F above absolute zero.

**Crab nebula** cloud of gas 6,000 light years from Earth, in the constellation Taurus. It is the remains of a star that exploded as a supernova (observed as a brilliant point of light on Earth 1054). At its centre is a pulsar that flashes 30 times a second. The name comes from its crablike shape.

**double star** two stars that appear close together. Most double stars attract each other due to gravity, and orbit each other, forming a genuine binary star, but other double stars are at different distances from Earth, and lie in the same line of sight only by chance. Through a telescope both types of double star will look the same.

**eclipsing binary** a binary (double) star in which the two stars periodically pass in front of each other as seen from Earth.

**galaxy** a congregation of millions or billions of stars, held together by gravity. *Spiral galaxies*, such as the Milky Way, are flattened in shape, with a central bulge of old stars surrounded by a disc of younger stars, arranged in spiral arms like a Catherine wheel. *Barred spirals* are spiral galaxies that have a straight bar of stars across their centre, from the ends of which the spiral arms emerge. The arms of spiral galaxies contain gas and dust from which new stars are still forming. *Elliptical galaxies* contain old stars and very little gas. They include the most massive galaxies known, containing a trillion stars. At least some elliptical galaxies are thought to be formed by mergers between spiral galaxies. There are also irregular galaxies. Most galaxies occur in clusters, containing anything from a few to thousands of members.

**globular cluster** spherical or near-spherical star cluster from approximately 10,000 to millions of stars. More than a hundred globular clusters are distributed in a spherical halo around our Galaxy. They consist of old stars, formed early in our Galaxy's history. Globular clusters are also found around other galaxies.

**interstellar molecules** over 50 different types of molecules existing in gas clouds in our Galaxy. Most have been detected by their radio emissions, but some have been found by the absorption lines they produce in the spectra of starlight. The most complex molecules, many of them based on carbon, are found in the dense clouds where stars are forming. They may be significant for the origin of life elsewhere in space.

**Local Group** a cluster of about 30 galaxies that includes our own, the Milky Way. Like other groups of galaxies, the Local Group is held together by the gravitational attraction among its members, and does not expand with the expanding universe. Its two largest galaxies are the Milky Way and the Andromeda galaxy; most of the others are small and faint.

**Magellanic Clouds** in astronomy, the two galaxies nearest to our own Galaxy. They are irregularly shaped, and appear as detached parts of the Milky Way, in the southern constellations Dorado and Tucana.

**Milky Way** faint band of light crossing the night sky, consisting of stars in the plane of our Galaxy. The name Milky Way is often used for the Galaxy itself. It is a spiral galaxy, about 100,000 light years in diameter, containing at least 100 billion stars. The Sun is in one of its spiral arms, about 25,000 light years from the centre.

**Mira** or **Omicron Ceti** the brightest long-period pulsating variable star, located in the constellation Cetus. Mira was the first star discovered to vary periodically in brightness.

**nebula** a cloud of gas and dust in space. Nebulae are the birthplaces of stars. An *emission nebula*, such as the Orion nebula, glows brightly because its gas is energized by stars that have formed within it. In a *reflection nebula*, starlight reflects off grains of dust in the nebula, such as surrounds the stars of the Pleiades cluster. A *dark nebula* is a dense cloud, composed of molecular hydrogen, which partially or completely absorbs light behind it. Examples include the Coalsack nebula in Crux and the Horsehead nebula in Orion. Some nebulae are produced by gas thrown off from dying stars.

**neutron star** a very small, 'superdense' star composed mostly of neutrons. They are thought to form when massive stars explode as supernovae, during which the protons and electrons of the star's atoms merge, due to intense gravitational collapse, to make neutrons. A neutron star may have the mass of up to three Suns, compressed into a globe only 20 km/12 mi in diameter. If its mass is any greater, its gravity will be so strong that it will shrink even further to become a black hole. Being so small, neutron stars can spin very quickly. The rapidly 'flashing' radio stars called pulsars are believed to be neutron stars. The 'flashing' is caused by a rotating beam of radio energy similar in behaviour to a lighthouse beam of light.

**nova** (plural *novae*) a faint star that suddenly erupts in brightness by 10,000 times or more. Novae are believed to occur in close double star systems, where gas from one star flows to a companion white dwarf. The gas ignites, and is thrown off in an explosion at speeds of 1,500 kps/930 mps or more. Unlike a supernova, the star is not completely disrupted by the outburst.

**Olbers' paradox** a question put forward 1826 by Heinrich Olbers, who asked: If the universe is infinite in extent and filled with stars, why is the sky dark at night? The answer is that the stars do not live infinitely long, so there is not enough starlight to fill the universe. A wrong answer, frequently given, is that the expansion of the universe weakens the starlight.

**Orion nebula** a luminous cloud of gas and dust 1,500 light years away, in the constellation Orion, from which stars are forming. It is about 15 light years in diameter, and contains enough gas to make a cluster of thousands of stars. At the nebula's centre is a group of hot young stars, called the **Trapezium**, which make the surrounding gas glow. The nebula is visible to the naked eye as a misty patch below the belt of Orion.

**oscillating universe** a theory that states that the gravitational attraction of the mass within the universe will eventually slow down and stop the expansion of the universe. The outward motions of the galaxies will then be reversed, eventually resulting in a 'Big Crunch' where all the matter in the universe would be contracted into a small volume of high density. This could undergo a further Big Bang, thereby creating another expansion phase. The theory suggests that the universe would alternately expand and collapse through alternate Big Bangs and Big Crunches.

**planetary nebula** a shell of gas thrown off by a star at the end of its life. Planetary nebulae have nothing to do with planets. They were named by William Herschel, who thought their rounded shape resembled the disc of a planet. After a star such as the Sun has expanded to become a red giant, its outer layers are ejected into space to form a planetary nebula, leaving the core as a white dwarf at the centre.

**Polaris** or **Pole Star** or **North Star** the bright star closest to the north celestial pole, and the brightest star in the constellation Ursa Minor. Its position is indicated by the 'pointers' in Ursa Major. Polaris is a yellow supergiant about 500 light years away.

**Proxima Centauri** the closest star to the Sun, 4.2 light years away. It is a faint red dwarf, visible only with a telescope, and is a member of the Alpha Centauri triple-star system.

**pulsar** celestial source that emits pulses of energy at regular intervals, ranging from a few seconds to a few thousandths of a second. They were discovered 1967, and are thought to be rapidly rotating neutron stars, which flash at radio and other wavelengths as they spin. Over 400 radio pulsars are known in our Galaxy, although a million or so may exist.

**quasar** (from **quas**i-stell**ar** object or QSO) a class of celestial objects far beyond our Galaxy, discovered 1964–65. Quasars appear star-like, but each emits more energy than 100 giant galaxies. They are thought to be at the centre of distant galaxies, their brilliance emanating from the stars and gas falling towards an immense black hole at their nucleus. Quasar light shows a large red shift, indicating that they are very young and the most distant extragalactic objects known, the furthest lying over 10 billion light years away. Some quasars emit radio waves, which is how they were first identified 1963, but most are radio-quiet. About 3,000 are now known in a compact region of space, hence the suggestion that they spiral towards a massive black hole.

**radio galaxy** galaxy that is a strong source of electromagnetic waves of radio wavelengths. All galaxies, including our own, emit some radio waves, but radio galaxies are up to a million times more powerful.

**red dwarf** any star that is cool, faint, and small (about one-tenth the mass and diameter of the Sun). They burn slowly, and have estimated lifetimes of 100 billion years. Red dwarfs may be the most abundant type of star, but are difficult to see because they are so faint. Two of the closest stars to the Sun, Proxima Centauri and Barnard's Star, are red dwarfs.

**red giant** any large bright star with a cool surface. It is thought to represent a late stage in the evolution of a star like the Sun, as it runs out of hydrogen fuel at its centre. Red giants have diameters between 10 and 100 times that of the Sun. They are very bright because they are so large, although their surface temperature is lower than that of the Sun, about 2,000–3,000K (1,700°C/3,000°F–2,700°C/5,000°F).

**Seyfert galaxy** a type of galaxy whose small, bright centre is caused by hot gas moving at high speed around a massive central object, possibly a black hole. Almost all Seyferts are spiral galaxies. They seem to be closely related to quasars, but are about 100 times fainter. They are named after their discoverer Carl Seyfert (1911–60).

**star** luminous globe of gas, producing its own heat and light by nuclear reactions. Stars are born from nebulae, and consist mostly of hydrogen and helium gases. Surface temperatures range from 2,000°C/3,600°F to above 30,000°C/54,000°F, and the corresponding colours range from red to blue-white. The brightest stars have masses 100 times that of the Sun, and emit as much light as millions of suns; they live for less than a million years before exploding as supernovae. The faintest stars are the red dwarfs, less than one-thousandth the brightness of the Sun.

**star cluster** group of related stars, usually held together by gravity. Members of a star cluster are thought to form together from one large cloud of gas in space. **Open clusters** such as the Pleiades contain from a dozen to many hundreds of young stars, loosely scattered over several light years. **Globular clusters** are larger and much more densely packed, containing perhaps 100,000 old stars.

**steady-state theory** theory that the universe appears the same wherever (and whenever) viewed. This seems to be refuted by the existence of cosmic background radiation, however.

**supernova** the explosive death of a star, which temporarily attains a brightness of 100 million Suns or more, so that it can shine as brilliantly as a small galaxy for a few days or weeks.

**universe** all of space and its contents, the study of which is called cosmology. The universe is thought to be between 10 billion and 20 billion years old, and is mostly empty space, dotted with galaxies for as far as telescopes can see. The most distant detected galaxies and quasars lie 10 billion light years or more from Earth, and are moving farther apart as the universe expands. Several theories attempt to explain how the universe came into being and

## ASTRONOMERS ROYAL

| | |
|---|---|
| John Flamsteed | 1675–1719 |
| Edmond Halley | 1720–1742 |
| James Bradley | 1742–1762 |
| Nathaniel Bliss | 1762–1764 |
| Nevil Maskelyne | 1765–1811 |
| John Pond | 1811–1835 |
| Goerge Airy | 1835–1881 |
| William Christie | 1881–1910 |
| Frank Dyson | 1910–1933 |
| Harold Spencer Jones | 1933–1955 |
| Richard Woolley | 1956–1971 |
| Martin Ryle | 1972–1982 |
| F Graham Smith | 1982–1990 |
| Arnold Wolfendale | 1991– |

evolved, for example, the Big Bang theory of an expanding universe originating in a single explosive event, and the contradictory steady-state theory.

**variable star** a star whose brightness changes, either regularly or irregularly, over a period ranging from a few hours to months or even years. The Cepheid variables regularly expand and contract in size every few days or weeks.

**white dwarf** a small, hot star, the last stage in the life of a star such as the Sun. White dwarfs have a mass similar to that of the Sun, but only 1% of the Sun's diameter, similar in size to the Earth. Most have surface temperatures of 8,000°C/14,400°F or more, hotter than the Sun. Yet, being so small, their overall luminosities may be less than 1% of that of the Sun.

# TELESCOPES AND OBSERVATORIES

**Algonquin Radio Observatory** site in Ontario, Canada, of the 46 m/150 ft radio telescope of the National Research Council of Canada, opened 1966.

**Arecibo** site in Puerto Rico of the world's largest single-dish radio telescope, 305 m/1,000 ft in diameter. It is built in a natural hollow, and uses the rotation of the Earth to scan the sky. It has been used both for radar work on the planets and for conventional radio astronomy, and is operated by Cornell University, USA.

**astrolabe** ancient navigational instrument, forerunner of the sextant. Astrolabes usually consisted of a flat disc with a sighting rod that could be pivoted to point at the Sun or bright stars. From the altitude of the Sun or star above the horizon, the local time could be estimated.

**astrophotography** the use of photography in astronomical research. The first successful photograph of a celestial object was the daguerreotype plate of the Moon taken by John W Draper (1811–1882) of the USA in March 1840. The first photograph of a star, Vega, was taken by US astronomer William C Bond (1789–1859) in 1850.

**Australia Telescope** an array of radio telescopes at three locations in Australia, operated by the Commonwealth Scientific and Industrial Research Organization (CSIRO). Six 22-m/72-ft dishes in a line 6 km/10 mi long at Culgoora, New South Wales, form the so-called Compact Array which can be used in combination with another 22–m dish at Siding Spring, NSW, and the 64-m/210-ft radio telescope at Parkes, NSW.

**charge-coupled device** (CCD) device for forming images electronically, using a layer of silicon that releases electrons when struck by incoming light. The electrons are stored in pixels and read off into a computer at the end of the exposure. CCDs have now almost entirely replaced photographic film for applications such as astrophotography where extreme sensitivity to light is paramount.

**David Dunlap Observatory** Canadian observatory at Richmond Hill, Ontario, operated by the University of Toronto, with a 1.88-m/74-in reflector, the largest optical telescope in Canada, opened 1935.

**Dominion Astrophysical Observatory** Canadian observatory near Victoria, British Columbia, the site of a 1.85-m/73-in reflector opened 1918, operated by the National Research Council of Canada. The associated Dominion Radio Astrophysical Observatory at Penticton, BC, operates a 26-m/84-ft radio dish and an aperture synthesis radio telescope.

**Effelsberg** site near Bonn, Germany, of the world's largest fully steerable radio telescope, the 100-m/328-ft radio dish of the Max Planck Institute for Radio Astronomy, opened 1971.

**European Southern Observatory** observatory operated jointly by Belgium, Denmark, France, Germany, Italy, the Netherlands, Sweden and Switzerland with headquarters near Munich. Its telescopes, located at La Silla, Chile, include a 3.6-m/142-in reflector opened 1976 and the 3.58-m/141-in New Technology Telescope opened 1990. By 1988 work began on the Very Large Telescope, consisting of four 8-m/315-in reflectors mounted independently but capable of working in combination.

**Jodrell Bank** site in Cheshire, England, of the Nuffield Radio Astronomy Laboratories of the University of Manchester. Its largest instrument is the 76 m/250 ft radio dish (the Lovell Telescope), completed 1957 and modified 1970. A 38 m × 25 m/125 ft × 82 ft elliptical radio dish was introduced 1964, capable of working at shorter wavelengths. These radio telescopes are used in conjunction with six smaller dishes up to 230 km/143 mi apart in an array called MERLIN (*m*ulti-*e*lement *r*adio- *l*inked *i*nterferometer *n*etwork) to produce detailed maps of radio sources.

**Kitt Peak National Observatory** observatory in the Quinlan Mountains near Tucson, Arizona, operated by AURA (Association of Universities for Research into Astronomy). Its main telescopes are the 4-m/158-in Mayall reflector, opened 1973, and the McMath Solar Telescope, opened 1962, the world's largest of its type.

---

## NEW ASTRONOMER ROYAL APPOINTED

Arnold Wolfendale, 63, was appointed Astronomer Royal on 2 Jan 1991. He is the 14th person to hold the office, and succeeds Sir Francis Graham Smith who retired in Sept 1990.

Professor Wolfendale has been professor of physics at the University of Durham since 1965 and has specialized in the study of cosmic rays, the fast-moving atomic particles that are believed to be emitted by supernova explosions and violent events within galaxies and quasars. Since 1988 he has been chairman of the scientific board that spends government money on astronomy and planetary science research. He was President of the Royal Astronomical Society from 1981

to 1983.

The post of Astronomer Royal was created in 1765 by King Charles II and was a title originally awarded to the Director of the Royal Observatory at Greenwich. In 1971 the two posts were made separate and since then the title has been purely honorary with no official duties nor any reimbursement attached. However, the Astronomer Royal is expected to speak on behalf of British astronomy, and on his appointment Professor Wolfendale pledged himself to fight government funding cuts that are threatening plans for a new large telescope and several other projects. Professor Wolfendale's appointment runs until 1994.

---

Among numerous other telescopes on the site is a 2.3-m/90-in reflector owned by the Steward Observatory of the University of Arizona.

**Las Campanas Observatory** site in Chile of the 2.5-m/100-in Du Pont telescope of the Carnegie Institution of Washington, opened 1977.

**Lick Observatory** observatory of the University of California and Mount Hamilton, California. Its main instruments are the 3.04-m/120-in Shane reflector, opened 1959, and a 91-cm/36-in refractor, opened 1888, the second-largest refractor in the world.

**Lowell Observatory** founded by Percival Lowell at Flagstaff, Arizona, with a 61-cm/24-in refractor opened in 1896. The observatory now operates other telescopes at a nearby site on Anderson Mesa including the 1.83-m/72-in Perkins reflector of Ohio State and Ohio Wesleyan Universities.

**Mauna Kea** astronomical observatory in Hawaii, USA, built on a dormant volcano at 4,200 m/13,784 ft above sea level. Because of its elevation high above clouds, atmospheric moisture, and artificial lighting, Mauna Kea is ideal for infrared astronomy. The first telescope on the site was installed 1970.

**Mcdonald Observatory** the observatory of the University of Texas on Mount Locke, Texas, site of a 2.72-m/107-in reflector opened 1969 and a 2.08-m/82-in reflector opened 1939.

**Mills Cross** a type of radio telescope consisting of two rows of aerials at right angles to each other, invented 1953 by the Australian radio astronomer Bernard Mills (1920–    ). The cross-shape produces a narrow beam useful for pinpointing the positions of radio sources.

**Mount Wilson** site near Los Angeles of the 2.5-m/100-in Hooker telescope opened 1917 with which Edwin Hubble discovered the expansion of the Universe, closed in 1985 when the Carnegie Institution withdrew its support. Two solar telescopes in towers 18.3 m/60 ft and 45.7 m/150 ft tall, and a 1.5-m/60-in reflector opened 1908, still operate there.

**Mullard Radio Astronomy Observatory** the radio observatory of the University of Cambridge, England. Its main instrument is the

Ryle Telescope, eight dishes 12.8 m/42 ft wide in a line of 5 km/3 mi long, opened 1972.

**Multiple Mirror Telescope** unique telescope on Mount Hopkins, Arizona, opened 1979, consisting of six 1.83-m/72-in mirrors mounted in a hexagon, the light-collecting area of which equals that of a single mirror 4.5 m/176 in diameter. It is planned to replace the six mirrors with a single mirror 6.5 m/256 in wide.

**observatory** a site or facility for observation of natural phenomena. The modern observatory dates from the invention of the telescope. Most early observatories were near towns, but with the advent of big telescopes, clear skies with little background light, and hence high, remote sites, became essential. The most powerful optical telescopes covering the sky are at Mauna Kea; Mount Palomar; Kitt Peak, Arizona; La Palma, Canary Islands; Cerro Tololo and La Silla, Chile; Siding Spring, Australia; and Mount Semirodniki, Caucasus, USSR. Radio astronomy observatories include Jodrell Bank; the Mullard, Cambridge, England; Arecibo; Effelsberg, Germany; and Parkes. Observatories are also carried on aircraft or sent into orbit as satellites, in space stations, and on the Space Shuttle. The Hubble Space Telescope was launched into orbit in April 1990. The Very Large Telescope is under construction by the European Southern Observatory (ESO) in the mountains of N Chile and is expected to be in operation by 1997.

**Palomar, Mount** the location, since 1948, of an observatory, 80 km/50 mi NE of San Diego, California, USA. It has a 5 m/200 in diameter reflector called the Hale.

**Parkes** the site in New South Wales of the Australian National Radio Astronomy Observatory, featuring a radio telescope of 64 m/210 ft aperture, run by the Commonwealth Scientific and Industrial Research Organization.

**planetarium** complex optical projection device by means of which the motions of stars and planets are reproduced on a domed ceiling representing the sky.

**radio telescope** instrument for detecting radio waves from the universe. Radio telescopes usually consist of a metal bowl that collects and focuses radio waves the way a concave mirror collects and focuses light waves. Other radio telescopes are shaped like long troughs, and some consist of simple rod-shaped aerials. Radio telescopes are much larger than optical telescopes, because the wavelengths they are detecting are much longer than the wavelength of light. A large dish such as that at Jodrell Bank, England, can see the radio sky less clearly than a small optical telescope sees the visible sky. The largest single dish is 305 m/1,000 ft across, at Arecibo, Puerto Rico.

**Royal Greenwich Observatory** the national astronomical observatory of the UK, founded 1675 at Greenwich, SE London, England, to provide navigational information for sailors. After World War II it was moved to Herstmonceux Castle, Sussex; in 1990 it was transferred to Cambridge. It also operates telescopes on La Palma in the Canary Islands, including the 4.2-m/165-in William Herschel Telescope, commissioned 1987.

**Siding Spring Mountain** peak 400 km/250 mi NW of Sydney, site of the UK Schmidt Telescope, opened 1973, and the 3.9-m/154-in *Anglo-Australian Telescope*, opened 1975, which was the first big telescope to be fully computer-controlled. It is one of the most powerful telescopes in the southern hemisphere.

**South African Astronomical Observatory** national observatory of South Africa at Sutherland, founded in 1973 after the merger of the Royal Observatory, Cape Town, and the Republic Observatory, Johannesburg, and operated by the Council for Scientific and Industrial Research of South Africa. Its main telescope is a 1.88-m/74-in reflector formerly at the Radcliffe Observatory, Pretoria.

**sundial** instrument measuring time by means of a shadow cast by the Sun. Almost completely superseded by the proliferation of clocks, it survives ornamentally in gardens. The dial is marked with the hours at graduated distances, and a style or gnomon (parallel to Earth's axis and pointing to the north) casts the shadow.

**telescope** device for collecting and focusing light and other forms of electromagnetic radiation. A telescope produces a magnified image, which makes the object seem nearer, and it shows objects fainter than can be seen by the eye alone. A telescope with a large aperture, or opening, can distinguish finer detail and fainter objects than one with a small aperture. The *refracting telescope* uses lenses, and the *reflecting telescope* uses mirrors. A third type, the *catadioptric telescope*, with a combination of lenses and mirrors, is used increasingly.

**US Naval Observatory** US government observatory in Washington, DC, which provides the nation's time service and publishes almanacs for navigators, surveyors, and astronomers. It contains a 66-cm/26-in refracting telescope opened 1873. A 1.55-m/61-in reflector for measuring positions of celestial objects was opened 1964 at Flagstaff, Arizona.

**Very Large Array** (VLA) the largest and most complex single-site radio telescope in the world. It is located on the Plains of San Augustine, 80 km/50 mi west of Socorro, New Mexico. It consists of 27 dish antennae, each 25 m/82 ft in diameter, arranged along three equally spaced arms forming a Y-shaped array. Two of the arms are 21 km/13 mi long, and the third, to the north, is 19 km/11.8 mi long. The dishes are mounted on railway tracks enabling the configuration and size of the array to be altered as required.

**Yerkes Observatory** astronomical centre in Wisconsin, USA, founded by George Hale in 1897. It houses the world's largest refracting optical telescope, with a lens of diameter 102 cm/40 in.

**Zelenchukskaya** site of the world's largest single-mirror optical telescope, with a mirror 6 m/236 in diameter, in the Caucasus Mountains of Russia. At the same site is the RATAN 600 radio telescope, consisting of radio reflectors in a circle 600 m/2,000 ft diameter. Both instruments are operated by the USSR Academy of Sciences.

## Outer space

*If you had the chance in your lifetime to travel into outer space, would you do so or not?*

|  | Today | Jun 1986 |
|---|---|---|
| Yes | 44 | 31 |
| No | 55 | 64 |
| Don't know | 2 | 5 |

*Have you ever seen anything you thought was a UFO?*

| | |
|---|---|
| Yes, seen | 13 |
| No | 82 |
| Never heard of | 4 |

# CLASSIFICATION

**analytical chemistry** branch of chemistry that deals with the determination of the chemical composition of substances. *Qualitative analysis* determines the identities of the substances in a given sample; *quantitative analysis* determines how much of a particular substance is present.

**biochemistry** science concerned with the chemistry of living organisms: the structure and reactions of proteins (such as enzymes), nucleic acids, carbohydrates, and lipids.

**inorganic chemistry** the branch of chemistry dealing with the chemical properties of the elements and their compounds, excluding the more complex covalent compounds of carbon, which are considered in organic chemistry.

**organic chemistry** branch of chemistry that deals with carbon compounds. Organic compounds form the chemical basis of life and are more abundant than inorganic compounds. The basis of organic chemistry is the ability of carbon to form long chains of atoms, branching chains, rings, and other complex structures. In a typical organic compound, each carbon atom forms bonds covalently with each of its neighbouring carbon atoms in a chain or ring, and additionally with other atoms, commonly hydrogen, oxygen, nitrogen, or sulphur. Compounds containing only carbon and hydrogen are known as *hydrocarbons*.

**physical chemistry** branch of chemistry concerned with examining the relationships between the chemical compositions of substances and the physical properties that they display. Most chemical reactions exhibit some physical phenomenon (change of state, temperature, pressure, or volume, or the use or production of electricity), and the measurement and study of such phenomena has led to many chemical theories and laws.

**ammonia** $NH_3$ colourless pungent-smelling gas, lighter than air and very soluble in water. It is made on an industrial scale by the Haber process, and used mainly to produce nitrogenous fertilizers, some explosives, and nitric acid.

# INORGANIC CHEMISTRY

**carbon** nonmetallic element, symbol C, atomic number 6, relative atomic mass 12.011. It is one of the most widely distributed elements, both inorganically and organically, and occurs in combination with other elements in all plants and animals.

The atoms of carbon can link with one another in rings or chains, giving rise to innumerable complex compounds. It occurs in nature (1) in the pure state in the crystalline forms of graphite and diamond; (2) as calcium carbonate ($CaCO_3$) in carbonaceous rocks such as chalk and limestone; (3) as carbon dioxide ($CO_2$) in the atmosphere; and (4) as hydrocarbons in the fossil fuels petroleum, coal, and natural gas. Noncrystalline forms of pure carbon include charcoal and coal. When added to steel, carbon forms a wide range of alloys. In its elemental form, it is widely used as a moderator in nuclear reactors; as colloidal graphite it is a good lubricant, which, when deposited on a surface in a vacuum, obviates photoelectric and secondary emission of electrons. The radioactive isotope C-14 (half-life 5,730 years) is widely used in archaeological dating and as a tracer in biological research.

**gold** heavy, precious, yellow, metallic element; symbol Au, atomic number 79, relative atomic mass 197.0. It is unaffected by temperature changes and is highly resistant to acids. For manufacture, gold is alloyed with another strengthening metal, its purity being measured in carats on a scale of 24. In 1990 the three leading gold-producing countries were: South Africa, 605.4 tonnes; USA, 295 tonnes; and USSR, 260 tonnes. In 1989 gold deposits were found in Greenland with an estimated yield of 12 tonnes per year.

**halogen** any of a group of five nonmetallic elements with similar chemical bonding properties: fluorine, chlorine, bromine, iodine, and astatine. They form a linked group in the periodic table of the elements, descending from fluorine, the most reactive, to astatine, the least reactive. They combine directly with most metals to form salts, such as common salt (NaCl). Each halogen has seven electrons in its valence shell, which accounts for the chemical similarities displayed by the group.

**hydrochloric acid** HCl solution of hydrogen chloride (a colourless, acidic gas) in water. The concentrated acid is about 35% hydrogen chloride and is corrosive. The acid is a typical strong, monobasic acid forming only one series of salts, the chlorides. It has many industrial uses, including recovery of zinc from galvanized scrap iron and the production of chlorine. It is also produced in the stomachs of animals for the purposes of digestion.

**hydrogen** colourless, odourless, gaseous, nonmetallic element, symbol H, atomic number 1, relative atomic mass 1.00797. It is the lightest of all the elements and occurs on Earth chiefly in combination with oxygen as water. Hydrogen is the most abundant element in the universe, where it accounts for 93% of the total number of atoms and 76% of the total mass. It is a component of most stars, including the Sun, whose heat and light are produced through the nuclear-fusion process that converts hydrogen into helium. When subjected to a pressure 500,000 times greater than that of the Earth's atmosphere, hydrogen becomes a solid with metallic properties. Its industrial uses include the hardening of oils and fats by hydrogenation.

**metal** any of a class of chemical elements with certain chemical characteristics and physical

---

BIOCHEMISTRY: CHRONOLOGY

| | |
|---|---|
| c.1830 | Johannes Müller discovered proteins. |
| 1833 | Anselme Payen and J F Persoz first isolated an enzyme. |
| 1862 | Haemoglobin was first crystallized. |
| 1869 | The genetic material DNA (deoxyribonucleic acid) was discovered by Friedrich Mieschler. |
| 1899 | Emil Fischer postulated the 'lock-and-key' hypothesis to explain the specificity of enzyme action. |
| 1913 | Leonor Michaelis and M L Menten developed a mathematical equation describing the rate of enzyme-catalyzed reactions. |
| 1915 | The hormone thyroxine was first isolated from thyroid-gland tissue. |
| 1920 | The chromosome theory of heredity was postulated by Thomas Hunt Morgan; growth hormone was discovered by Herbert McLean Evans and J A Long. |
| 1921 | Insulin was first isolated from the pancreas by Frederick Grant Banting and Charles Best. |
| 1926 | Insulin was obtained in pure crystalline form. |
| 1927 | Thyroxine was first synthesized. |
| 1928 | Alexander Fleming discovered penicillin. |
| 1931 | Paul Karrer deduced the structure of retinol (vitamin A); vitamin D compounds were obtained in crystalline form by Adolf Windaus and Askew, independently of each other. |
| 1932 | Charles Glen King isolated ascorbic acid (vitamin C). |
| 1933 | Tadeusz Reichstein synthesized ascorbic acid. |
| 1935 | Richard Kuhn and Karrer established the structure of riboflavin (vitamin $B_2$). |
| 1936 | Robert Williams established the structure of thiamine (vitamin $B_1$); biotin was isolated by Kogl and Tonnis. |
| 1937 | Niacin was isolated and identified by Conrad Arnold Elvehjem. |
| 1938 | Pyridoxine (vitamin $B_6$) was isolated in pure crystalline form. |
| 1939 | The structure of pyridoxine was determined by Kuhn. |
| 1940 | Hans Krebs proposed the citric acid (Krebs) cycle; Hickman isolated retinol in pure crystalline form; Williams established the structure of pantothenic acid; biotin was identified by Albert Szent-Györgyi, Vincent Du Vigneaud, and co-workers. |
| 1941 | Penicillin was isolated and characterized by Howard Florey and Ernst Chain. |
| 1943 | The role of DNA in genetic inheritance was first demonstrated by Oswald Avery, Colin MacLeod, and Maclyn McCarty. |
| 1950 | The basic components of DNA were established by Erwin Chargaff; the alpha-helix structure of proteins was established by Linus Pauling and R B Corey. |
| 1953 | James Watson and Francis Crick determined the molecular structure of DNA. |
| 1956 | Mahlon Hoagland and Paul Zamecnik discovered transfer RNA (ribonucleic acid); mechanisms for the biosynthesis of RNA and DNA were discovered by Arthur Kornberg and Severo Ochoa. |
| 1957 | Interferon was discovered by Alick Isaacs and Jean Lindemann. |
| 1958 | The structure of RNA was determined. |
| 1960 | Messenger RNA was discovered by Sydney Brenner and François Jacob. |
| 1961 | Marshall Warren Nirenberg and Ochoa determined the chemical nature of the genetic code. |
| 1965 | Insulin was first synthesized. |
| 1966 | The immobilization of enzymes was achieved by Chibata. |
| 1968 | Brain hormones were discovered by Roger Guillemin and Andrew Victor Schally. |
| 1975 | J Hughes and Hans Walter Kosterlitz discovered encephalins. |
| 1976 | Guillemin discovered endorphins. |
| 1977 | Baxter isolated the genetic code for human growth hormone. |
| 1978 | Human insulin was first produced by genetic engineering. |
| 1979 | The biosynthetic production of human growth hormone was announced by Howard Goodman and J Baxter of the University of California, and by D V Goeddel and Seeburg of Genentech. |
| 1982 | Louis Chedid and Michael Sela developed the first synthesized vaccine. |
| 1983 | The first commercially available product of genetic engineering (Humulin) was launched. |
| 1985 | Alec Jeffreys devised genetic fingerprinting. |
| 1990 | Jean-Marie Lehn, Ulrich Koert, and Margaret M Harding at Louis Pasteur University, France reported the synthesis of a new class of compounds, called nucleohelicates, that mimic the double helical structure of DNA, turned inside out. |

properties; they are good conductors of heat and electricity; opaque but reflect light well; malleable, which enables them to be cold-worked and rolled into sheets; and ductile, which permits them to be drawn into thin wires. Metallic elements comprise about 75% of the 109 elements shown in the periodic table of the elements. They form alloys with each other, bases with the hydroxyl radical (OH), and replace the hydrogen in an acid to form a salt. The majority are found in nature in the combined form only, as compounds or mineral ores; about 16 of them also occur in the elemental form, as native metals. Their chemical properties are largely determined by the extent to which their atoms can lose one or more electrons and form positive ions (cations). They have been put to many uses, both structural and decorative, since prehistoric times, and the Copper Age, Bronze Age, and Iron Age are named after the metal that formed the technological base for that stage of human evolution.

**nitrate** any salt of nitric acid, containing the $NO_3^-$ ion. Nitrates of various kinds are used in explosives, in the chemical industry, in curing meat, and as inorganic fertilizers. They are the most water-soluble salts known.

**nitric acid** or *aqua fortis* $HNO_3$ fuming acid obtained by the oxidation of ammonia or the action of sulphuric acid on potassium nitrate. It is a highly corrosive acid, dissolving most metals, and a strong oxidizing agent. It is used in the nitration and esterification of organic substances, and in the making of sulphuric acid, nitrates, explosives, plastics, and dyes.

**nitrogen** colourless, odourless, tasteless, gaseous, nonmetallic element, symbol N, atomic number 7, relative atomic mass 14.0067. It forms almost 80% of the Earth's atmosphere by volume and is a constituent of all plant and animal tissues (in proteins and nucleic acids). Nitrogen is obtained for industrial use by the liquefaction and fractional distillation of air. It is used in the Haber process to make ammonia, $NH_3$, and to provide an inert atmosphere for certain chemical reactions. Its compounds are used in the manufacture of foods, drugs, fertilizers, dyes, and explosives.

**nonmetal** one of a set of elements (around 20 in total) with certain physical and chemical properties opposite to those of metals. Nonmetals accept electrons, and are sometimes called electronegative elements.

**oxygen** colourless, odourless, tasteless, nonmetallic, gaseous element, symbol O, atomic number 8, relative atomic mass 15.9994. It is the most abundant element in the Earth's crust (almost 50% by mass), forms about 21% by volume of the atmosphere, and is present in combined form in water, carbon dioxide, silicon dioxide (quartz), iron ore, calcium carbonate (limestone), and many other substances. Life on Earth evolved using oxygen, which is a by-product of photosynthesis and the basis for respiration in plants and animals. Oxygen is obtained for industrial use

by the fractional distillation of liquid air, by the electrolysis of water, or by heating manganese(IV) oxide with potassium chlorate. It is essential for combustion, and is used with ethyne (acetylene) in high-temperature oxy-acetylene welding and cutting torches. Ozone is an allotrope of oxygen.

**phosphate** salt or ester of phosphoric acid. Phosphates are used as fertilizers, and are required for the development of healthy root systems. They are involved in many biochemical processes, often as part of complex molecules, such as adenosine triphosphate (ATP).

**rust** reddish-brown oxide of iron formed by the action of moisture and oxygen on the metal. It consists mainly of hydrated iron(III) oxide ($Fe_2O_3.H_2O$) and iron(III) hydroxide ($Fe(OH)_3$).

**silicon** brittle, nonmetallic element, symbol Si, atomic number 14, relative atomic mass 28.086. It is the second most abundant element (after oxygen) in the Earth's crust and occurs in amorphous and crystalline forms. In nature it is found only in combination with other elements, chiefly with oxygen in silica (silicon dioxide, $SiO_2$) and the silicates. These form the mineral quartz, which makes up most sands, gravels, and beaches.

**silver** white, lustrous, extremely malleable and ductile, metallic element, symbol Ag (from Latin *argentum*), atomic number 47, relative atomic mass 107.868.

It occurs in nature in ores and as a free metal; the chief ores are sulphides, from which the metal is extracted by smelting with lead. It is one of the best metallic conductors of both heat and electricity; its most useful compounds are the chloride and bromide, which darken on exposure to light and are the basis of photographic emulsions.

**sulphur** brittle, pale-yellow, nonmetallic element, symbol S, atomic number 16, relative atomic mass 32.064. It occurs in three allotropic forms: two crystalline (called rhombic and monoclinic, following the arrangements of the atoms within the crystals) and one amorphous. It burns in air with a blue flame and a stifling odour. Insoluble in water but soluble in carbon disulphide, it is a good electrical insulator. Sulphur is widely used in the manufacture of sulphuric acid (used to treat phosphate rock to make fertilizers) and in making paper, matches, gunpowder and fireworks, in vulcanizing rubber, and in medicines and insecticides.

**sulphuric acid** or *oil of vitriol* $H_2SO_4$ a dense, viscous, colourless liquid that is extremely corrosive. It gives out heat when added to water and can cause severe burns. Sulphuric acid is used extensively in the chemical industry, in the refining of petrol, and in the manufacture of fertilizers, detergents, explosives, and dyes. It forms the acid component of car batteries.

**transuranic element** or *transuranium element* chemical element with an atomic number of 93 or more—that is, with a greater number of protons in the nucleus than has uranium. All transuranic elements are radioactive. Neptunium and plutonium are found in nature; the others are synthesized in nuclear reactions.

# ORGANIC CHEMISTRY

**alcohol** any member of a group of organic chemical compounds characterized by the presence of one or more aliphatic OH (hydroxyl) groups in the molecule, and which form esters with acids. The main uses of alcohols are as solvents for gums, resins, lacquers, and varnishes; in the making of dyes; for essential oils in perfumery; and for medical substances in pharmacy. Alcohol (ethanol) is produced naturally in the fermentation process and is consumed as part of alcoholic beverages.

**aldehyde** any of a group of organic chemical compounds prepared by oxidation of primary alcohols, so that the OH (hydroxyl) group loses its hydrogen to give an oxygen joined by a double bond to a carbon atom (the aldehyde group, with the formula CHO).

**aliphatic compound** organic chemical compound in which the bonding electrons are localized within the vicinity of the bonded atoms. Its carbon atoms are joined in straight chains, as in hexane ($C_6H_{14}$), or in branched chains, as in 2-methylpentane ($CH_3CH(CH_3)CH_2CH_2CH_3$). Cyclic compounds that do not have delocalized electrons

are also aliphatic, as in the alicyclic compound cyclohexane ($C_6H_{12}$) or the heterocyclic piperidine ($C_5H_{11}N$). Compare aromatic compound.

**alkane** member of a group of hydrocarbons having the general formula $C_nH_{2n+2}$, commonly known as *paraffins*. Lighter alkanes, such as methane, ethane, propane, and butane, are colourless gases; heavier ones are liquids or solids. In nature they are found in natural gas and petroleum. As alkanes contain only single covalent bonds, they are said to be saturated.

**alkene** member of a group of hydrocarbons having the general formula $C_nH_{2n}$, formerly known as olefins. Lighter alkenes, such as ethene and propene, are gases, obtained from the cracking of oil fractions. Alkenes are unsaturated compounds, characterized by one or more double bonds between adjacent carbon atoms. They react by addition, and many useful compounds, such as poly(ethene), are made from them.

**alkyne** member of a group of hydrocarbons with the general formula $C_nH_{2n-2}$, formerly known as the acetylenes. They are unsaturated compounds, characterized by one or more triple bonds between adjacent carbon atoms. Lighter alkynes, such as ethyne, are gases; heavier ones are liquids or solids.

**amine** any of a class of organic chemical compounds in which one or more of the hydrogen atoms of ammonia have been replaced by other groups of atoms.

**amino acid** water-soluble organic molecule, mainly composed of carbon, oxygen, hydrogen, and nitrogen, containing both a basic

## PLASTIC

Any of the stable synthetic materials that are fluid at some stage in their manufacture, when they can be shaped, and that later set to rigid or semi-rigid solids. Plastics today are chiefly derived from petroleum. Most are polymers, made up of long chains of molecules.

Processed by extrusion, injection-moulding, vacuum-forming and compression, plastics emerge in consistencies ranging from hard and inflexible to soft and rubbery. They replace an increasing number of natural substances, being lightweight, easy to clean, durable, and capable of being rendered very strong—for example, by the addition of carbon fibres—for building aircraft and other engineering projects.

*Thermoplastics* soften when warmed, then re-harden as they cool. Examples of thermoplastics include polystyrene, a clear plastic used in kitchen utensils or (when expanded into a 'foam' by gas injection) in insulation and ceiling tiles; polyethylene or polythene, used for containers and wrapping; and polyvinyl chloride (PVC), used for drainpipes, floor tiles, audio discs, shoes, and handbags.

*Thermosets* remain rigid once set, and do not soften when warmed. They include bakelite, used in electrical insulation and telephone receivers; epoxy resins, used in paints and varnishes, to laminate wood, and as adhesives; polyesters, used in synthetic textile fibres and,

with fibreglass reinforcement, in car bodies and boat hulls; and polyurethane, prepared in liquid form as a paint or varnish, and in foam form for upholstery and in lining materials (where it may be a fire hazard). One group of plastics, the silicones, are chemically inert, have good electrical properties, and repel water. Silicones find use in silicone rubber, paints, electrical insulation materials, laminates, waterproofing for walls, stain-resistant textiles, and cosmetics.

*Shape-memory polymers* are plastics that can be crumpled or flattened and will resume their original shape when heated. They include transpolyisoprene and polynorbornene. The initial shape is determined by heating the polymer to over 35° C and pouring it into a metal mould. The shape can be altered with boiling water and the substance solidifies again when its temperature falls below 35°C.

*Biodegradable plastics* are increasingly in demand: Biopol was developed in 1990. Soil microorganisms are used to build the plastic in their cells from carbon dioxide and water (it constitutes 80% of their cell tissue). The unused parts of the microorganism are dissolved away by heating in water. The discarded plastic can be placed in landfill sites where it breaks back down into carbon dioxide and water. It costs three to five times as much as ordinary plastics to produce.

amine group ($NH_2$) and an acidic carboxyl (COOH) group. When two or more amino acids are joined together, they are known as peptides; proteins are made up of interacting polypeptides (peptide chains consisting of more than three amino acids) and are folded or twisted in characteristic shapes.

**aromatic compound** organic chemical compound in which some of the bonding electrons are delocalized (shared amongst several atoms within the molecule and not localized in the vicinity of the atoms involved in bonding). The commonest aromatic compounds have ring structures, the atoms comprising the ring being either all carbon or containing one or more different atoms (usually nitrogen, sulphur, or oxygen). Typical examples are benzene ($C_6H_6$) and pyridine ($C_6H_5N$).

**ester** organic compound formed by the reaction between an alcohol and an acid, with the elimination of water. Unlike salts, esters are covalent compounds.

**ethanoic acid** common name *acetic acid* $CH_3CO_2H$ one of the simplest fatty acids (a series of organic acids). In the pure state it is a colourless liquid with an unpleasant pungent odour; it solidifies to an icelike mass of crystals at 16.7°C/62.4°F, and hence is often called glacial ethanoic acid. Vinegar contains 5% or more ethanoic acid, produced by fermentation.

**ether** any of a series of organic chemical compounds having an oxygen atom linking the carbon atoms of two hydrocarbon radical goups (general formula R-O-R]); also the common name for ethoxyethane $C_2H_5OC_2H_5$ (also called diethyl ether). Ethoxyethane is a colourless, volatile, inflammable liquid, slightly soluble in water, miscible with ethanol. It is prepared by treatment of ethanol with excess concentrated sulphuric acid at 140°C/284°F. It is used as an anaesthetic by vapour inhalation and as an external cleansing agent before surgical operations. It is also used as a solvent, and in the extraction of oils, fats, waxes, resins, and alkaloids.

**fatty acid** or *carboxylic acid* organic compound consisting of a hydrocarbon chain, up to 24 carbon atoms long, with a carboxyl group (–COOH) at one end.

**functional group** a small number of atoms in an arrangement that determines the chemical properties of the group and of the molecule to which it is attached (for example, the carboxyl group COOH, or the amine group $NH_2$). Organic compounds can be considered as structural skeletons, with a high carbon content, with functional groups attached.

**homologous series** a series of organic chemicals with similar chemical properties whose members differ by a constant relative molecular mass.

**hydrocarbon** any of a class of chemical compounds containing only hydrogen and carbon (for example, the alkanes and alkenes). Hydrocarbons are obtained industrially principally from petroleum and coal tar.

**isomer** chemical compound having the same molecular composition and mass as another, but with different physical or chemical properties owing to the different structural arrangement of its constituent atoms. For example, the organic compounds butane ($CH_3(CH_2)CH_3$) and methyl propane ($CH_3CH(CH_3)CH_3$) are isomers, each possessing four carbon atoms and ten hydrogen atoms but differing in the way that these are arranged with respect to each other.

**ketone** member of the group of organic compounds containing the carbonyl group (C=O) bonded to two atoms of carbon (instead of one carbon and one hydrogen as in aldehydes). Ketones are liquids or low-melting-point solids, slightly soluble in water.

**lipid** any of a large number of esters of fatty acids, commonly formed by the reaction of a fatty acid with glycerol. They are soluble in alcohol but not in water. Lipids are the chief constituents of plant and animal waxes, fats, and oils.

**phenol** member of a group of aromatic chemical compounds with weakly acidic properties, which are characterized by a hydroxyl (OH) group attached directly to an aromatic ring. The simplest of the phenols, derived from benzene, is also known as phenol and has the formula $C_6H_5OH$. It is sometimes called *carbolic acid* and can be extracted from coal tar. Pure phenol consists of colourless, needle-shaped crystals, which take up moisture from the atmosphere. It has a strong and characteristic smell and was once used as an antiseptic. It is, however, toxic by absorption through the skin.

**polyester** synthetic resin formed by the condensation of polyhydric alcohols (alcohols containing more than one hydroxyl group) with dibasic acids (acids containing two replaceable hydrogen atoms). Polyesters are thermosetting plastics, used in making synthetic fibres, such as Dacron and Terylene, and constructional plastics. With glass fibre added as reinforcement, polyesters are used in car bodies and boat hulls.

**polymer** compound made up of a large, long-chain or branching matrix composed of many repeated simple units (*monomers*). There are many polymers, both natural (cellulose, chitin, lignin) and synthetic (polyethylene and nylon, types of plastic). Synthetic polymers belong to two groups: thermosoftening and thermosetting.

**polyunsaturate** type of fat or oil containing a high proportion of triglyceride molecules whose fatty-acid chains contain several double bonds. By contrast, the fatty-acid chains of the triglycerides in saturated fats (such as lard) contain only single bonds. Polyunsaturated fats are generally considered healthier for human nutrition than are saturated fats, and are widely used in margarines and cooking oils.

**saturated compound** organic compound, such as

TRANSURANIC ELEMENTS

| atomic number | name | symbol | year of discovery | source of first preparation identified | isotope | half life of first isotope identified |
|---|---|---|---|---|---|---|
| actinide series | | | | | | |
| 93 | neptunium | Np | 1940 | irradiation of uranium-238 with neutrons | Np-239 | 2.35 days |
| 94 | plutonium | Pu | 1941 | Bombardment of uranium-238 with deuterons | Pu-238 | 86.4 years |
| 95 | americium | Am | 1944 | irradiation of plutonium-239 with neutrons | Am-241 | 458 years |
| 96 | curium | Cm | 1944 | bombardment of plutonium-239 with helium nuclei | Cm-242 | 162.5 days |
| 97 | berkelium | Bk | 1949 | bombardment of americium-241 with helium nuclei | Bk-243 | 4.5 hours |
| 98 | californium | Cf | 1950 | bombardment of curium-242 with helium nuclei | Cf-245 | 44 minutes |
| 99 | einsteinium | Es | 1952 | irradiation of uranium-238 with neutrons in first thermonuclear explosion | Es-253 | 20 days |
| 100 | fermium | Fm | 1953 | irradiation of uranium-238 with neutrons in first thermonuclear explosion | Fm-235 | 16 hours |
| 101 | mendelevium | Md | 1955 | bombardment of einsteinium-253 with helium nuclei | Md-256 | 1.5 hours |
| 102 | nobelium | No | 1958 | bombardment of curium-246 with carbon nuclei | No-255 | 3 seconds |
| 103 | lawrencium | Lr | 1961 | bombardment of californium-252 with boron nuclei | Lr-257 | 8 seconds |
| super-heavy elements | | | | | | |
| 104 | unnilquadium* (also called rutherfordium or kurchatovium) | Unq | 1969 | bombardment of californium-249 with carbon-12 nuclei | U4–257 | 4 seconds |
| 105 | unnilpentium* (also called hahnium or nielsbohrium) | Unp | 1970 | bombardment of californium-249 with nitrogen-15 nuclei | U5–260 | 1.6 seconds |
| 106 | unnilhexium* | Unh | 1974 | bombardment of californium-249 with oxygen-18 nuclei | U6–263 | 0.9 seconds |
| 107 | unnilseptium* | Uns | 1977 | bombardment of bismuth-209 with nuclei of chromium-54 | U7 | 2 milliseconds |
| 108 | unniloctium* | Uno | 1984 | bombardment of lead-208 | U8–265 | a few milliseconds |
| 109 | unnilennium* | Une | 1982 | bombardment of bismuth-209 | U9 | 5 milliseconds |

*Names for elements 104–109 are as proposed by the International Union for Pure and Applied Chemistry in

propane, that contains only single covalent bonds. Saturated organic compounds can only undergo further reaction by substitution reactions, as in the production of chloropropane from propane.

**unsaturated compound** chemical compound in which two adjacent atoms are bonded by a double or triple covalent bond.

# STRUCTURE

**atom** the smallest unit of matter that can take part in a chemical reaction, and which cannot be broken down chemically into anything simpler. An atom is made up of protons and neutrons in a central nucleus surrounded by electrons. The atoms of the various elements differ in atomic number, relative atomic mass, and chemical behaviour. There are 109 different types of atom, corresponding with the 109 known elements as listed in the periodic table of the elements.

**atomic number** or *proton number* the number (symbol $Z$) of protons in the nucleus of an atom. It is equal to the positive charge on the nucleus. In a neutral atom, it is also equal to the number of electrons surrounding the nucleus. The 109 elements are arranged in the periodic table of the elements according to their atomic number.

**bond** the result of the forces of attraction that hold together atoms of an element or elements to form a molecule. The principal types

## DISCOVERY OF THE ELEMENTS

| Date | Element (symbol) | Discoverer |
|---|---|---|
| prehistoric knowledge | antimony (Sb) | |
| | arsenic (As) | |
| | bismuth (Bi) | |
| | carbon (C) | |
| | copper (Cu) | |
| | gold (Au) | |
| | iron (Fe) | |
| | lead (Pb) | |
| | mercury (Hg) | |
| | silver (Ag) | |
| | sulphur (S) | |
| | tin (Sn) | |
| | zinc (Zn) | |
| 1557 | platinum (Pt) | Julius Scaliger |
| 1669 | phosphorus (P) | Hennig Brand |
| 1735 | cobalt (Co) | Georg Brandt |
| 1751 | nickel (Ni) | Axel Cronstedt |
| 1755 | magnesium (Mg) | Joseph Black (isolated by Humphry Davy 1808) |
| 1766 | hydrogen (H) | Henry Cavendish |
| 1771 | fluorine (F) | Karl Scheele (isolated by Henri Moissan 1886) |
| 1772 | nitrogen (N) | Daniel Rutherford |
| 1774 | chlorine (Cl) | Scheele |
| | manganese (Mn) | Johann Gottlieb Gahn |
| | oxygen (O) | Joseph Priestley and Karl Scheele, independently of each other |
| 1778 | molybdenum (Mo) | detected by Karl Scheele (isolated by Peter Jacob Hjelm 1782) |
| 1782 | tellurium (Te) | Franz Müller |
| 1783 | tungsten (W) | Juan José Elhuyar and Fausto Elhuyar |
| 1789 | uranium (U) | Martin Klaproth (isolated by Eugène Péligot 1841) |
| | zirconium (Zr) | Klaproth |
| 1790 | titanium (Ti) | William Gregor |
| 1794 | yttrium (Y) | Johan Gadolin |
| 1797 | chromium (Cr) | Louis-Nicolas Vauquelin |
| 1798 | beryllium (Be) | Vauquelin (isolated by Friedrich Wöhler and Antoine-Alexandre-Brutus Bussy 1828) |
| 1801 | vanadium (V) | Andrés del Rio (disputed), or Nils Sefström 1830 |
| | niobium (Nb) | Charles Hatchett |
| 1802 | tantalum (Ta) | Anders Ekeberg |
| 1803 | cerium (Ce) | Jöns Berzelius and Wilhelm Hisinger, and independently by Klaproth |
| | iridium (Ir) | Smithson Tennant |
| | osmium (Os) | Tennant |
| | palladium (Pd) | William Wollaston |
| | rhodium (Rh) | Wollaston |
| 1807 | potassium (K) | Humphry Davy |
| | sodium (Na) | Davy |
| 1808 | barium (Ba) | Davy |
| | boron (B) | Davy, and independently by Joseph Gay-Lussac and Louis-Jacques Thénard |
| | calcium (Ca) | Davy |
| | strontium (Sr) | Davy |
| 1811 | iodine (I) | Bernard Courtois |
| 1817 | cadmium (Cd) | Friedrich Strohmeyer |
| | lithium (Li) | Johan Arfwedson |
| | selenium (Se) | Jöns Berzelius |
| 1823 | silicon (Si) | Berzelius |
| 1824 | aluminium (Al) | Hans Oersted (also attributed to Friedrich Wöhler 1827) |
| 1826 | bromine (Br) | Antoine-Jérôme Balard |
| 1827 | ruthenium (Ru) | G W Osann (isolated by Karl Klaus 1844) |
| 1828 | thorium (Th) | Berzelius |
| 1839 | lanthanum (La) | Carl Mosander |
| 1842 | erbium (Er) | Mosander |
| 1843 | terbium (Tb) | Mosander |
| 1860 | caesium (Cs) | Robert Bunsen and Gustav Kirchoff |
| 1861 | rubidium (Rb) | Bunsen and Kirchoff |
| | thallium (Tl) | William Crookes (isolated by Crookes and Lamy, independently of each other 1862) |
| 1863 | indium (In) | Ferdinand Reich and Hieronymus Richter |
| 1868 | helium (He) | Pierre Janssen |
| 1875 | gallium (Ga) | Paul Lecoq de Boisbaudran |
| 1876 | scandium (Sc) | Lars Nilson |
| 1878 | ytterbium (Yb) | Jean Charles de Marignac |
| 1879 | holmium (Ho) | Per Cleve |
| | samarium (Sm) | Lecoq de Boisbaudran |
| | thulium (Tm) | Cleve |
| 1885 | neodymium (Nd) | Carl von Welsbach |
| | praseodymium (Pr) | von Welsbach |
| 1886 | dysprosium (Dy) | Lecoq de Boisbaudran |
| | gadolinium (Gd) | Lecoq de Boisbaudran |
| | germanium (Ge) | Clemens Winkler |
| 1894 | argon (Ar) | John Rayleigh and William Ramsay |
| 1898 | krypton (Kr) | Ramsay and Morris Travers |
| | neon (Ne) | Ramsay and Travers |
| | polonium (Po) | Marie and Pierre Curie |
| | radium (Ra) | Marie Curie |
| | xenon (Xe) | Ramsay and Travers |
| 1899 | actinium (Ac) | André Debierne |
| 1900 | radon (Rn) | Friedrich Dorn |
| 1901 | europium (Eu) | Eugène Demarçay |
| 1907 | lutetium (Lu) | Georges Urbain and von Welsbach, independently of each other |
| 1913 | protactinium (Pa) | Kasimir Fajans and O Göhring |
| | hafnium (Hf) | Dirk Coster and Georg von Hevesy |
| 1925 | rhenium (Re) | Walter Noddack, Ida Tacke, and Otto Berg |
| 1937 | technetium (Tc) | Carlo Perrier and Emilio Segrè |
| 1939 | francium (Fr) | Marguérite Perey |

## DISCOVERY OF THE ELEMENTS Cont.

| | | |
|---|---|---|
| 1940 | astatine (At) | Dale R Corson, K R MacKenzie, and Segrè |
| | neptunium (Np) | Edwin M McMillan and Philip Abelson |
| | plutonium (Pu) | Glenn T Seaborg, McMillan, Joseph W Kennedy, and Arthur C Wahl |
| 1944 | americium (Am) | Seaborg, Ralph A James, Leon O Morgan, and Albert Ghiorso |
| | curium (Cm) | Seaborg, James, and Ghiorso |
| 1945 | promethium (Pm) | J A Marinsky, Lawrence E Glendenin, and Charles D Coryell |
| 1949 | berkelium (Bk) | Seaborg, Stanley G Thompson, and Ghiorso |
| 1950 | californium (Cf) | Seaborg, Thompson, Kenneth Street Jr, and Ghiorso |
| 1952 | einsteinium (Es) | Ghiorso and co-workers |
| | fermium (Fm) | Ghiorso and co-workers |
| 1955 | mendelevium (Md) | Ghiorso, Bernard G Harvey, Gregory R Choppin, Thompson, and Seaborg |
| 1958 | nobelium (No) | Ghiorso, Torbjørn Sikkeland, J R Walton, and Seaborg |
| 1961 | lawrencium (Lr) | Ghiorso, Sikkeland, Almon E Larsh, and Robert M Latimer |
| 1964 | unnilquadium (Unq) | claimed by Soviet scientist Georgii Flerov and co-workers (disputed by US workers) |
| 1967 | unnilpentium (Unp) | claimed by Flerov and co-workers (disputed by US workers) |
| 1969 | unnilquadium (Unq) | claimed by US scientist Albert Ghiorso and co-workers (disputed by Soviet workers) |
| 1970 | unnilpentium (Unp) | claimed by Ghiorso and co-workers (disputed by Soviet workers) |
| 1974 | unnilhexium (Unh) | claimed by Flerov and co-workers, and, independently, by Ghiorso and co-workers |
| 1976 | unnilseptium (Uns) | Flerov and Yuri Oganessian (confirmed by German scientist Peter Armbruster and co-workers) |
| 1982 | unnilennium (Une) | Armbruster and co-workers |
| 1984 | unniloctium (Uno) | Armbruster and co-workers |

of bonding are ionic, covalent, metallic, and intermolecular (such as hydrogen bonding).

**compound** chemical substance made up of two or more elements bonded together, so that they cannot be separated by physical means. Compounds are held together by ionic or covalent bonds.

**covalent bond** chemical bond in which the two combining atoms share a pair of electrons. It is often represented by a single line drawn between the two atoms. Covalently bonded substances include hydrogen ($H_2$), water ($H_2O$), and most organic substances.

**electron** stable, negatively charged elementary particle, a constituent of all atoms and the basic particle of electricity. A beam of electrons will undergo diffraction (scattering), and produce interference patterns, in the same way as electromagnetic waves such as light; hence they may also be regarded as waves.

**electronegativity** the ease with which an atom can attract electrons to itself. Electronegative elements attract electrons, so forming negative ions.

**element** substance that cannot be split chemically into simpler substances. The atoms of a particular element all have the same number of protons in their nuclei (their atomic number). Elements are classified in the periodic table. Of the 109 known elements, 95 are known to occur in nature (those with atomic numbers 1–95). Those from 96 to 109 do not occur in nature and are synthesized only, produced in particle accelerators. Eighty-one of the elements are stable; all the others, which include atomic numbers 43, 61, and from 84 up, are radioactive.

**formula** a representation of a molecule, radical, or ion, in which the component chemical elements are represented by their symbols. An *empirical formula* indicates the simplest ratio of the elements in a compound, without indicating how many of them there are or how they are combined. A *molecular formula* gives the number of each type of element present in one molecule. A *structural formula* shows the relative positions of the atoms and the bonds between them. For example, for ethanoic acid, the empirical formula is $CH_2O$, the molecular formula is $C_2H_4O_2$, and the structural formula is $CH_3COOH$.

**ion** an atom, or group of atoms, which is either positively charged (*cation*) or negatively charged (*anion*), as a result of the loss or gain of electrons during chemical reactions or exposure to certain forms of radiation.

**ionic bond** or *electrovalent bond* bond produced when atoms of one element donate electrons to another element that accepts the electrons, forming positively and negatively charged ions respectively. The electrostatic attraction between the oppositely charged ions constitutes the bond.

**isotope** one of two or more atoms that have the same atomic number (same number of protons), but which contain a different number

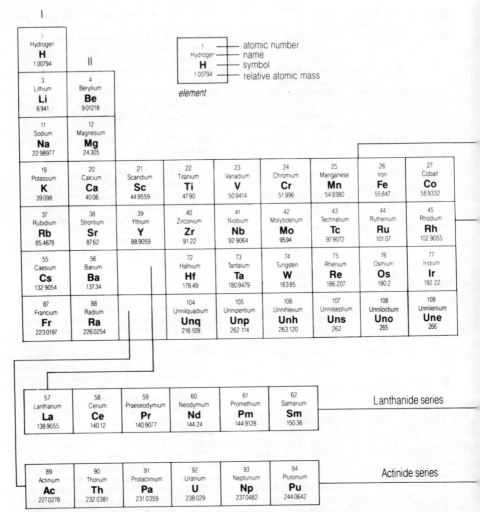

| Group | | | | | | | | | |
|---|---|---|---|---|---|---|---|---|---|
| **I** | **II** | | | | | | | | |
| 1<br>Hydrogen<br>**H**<br>1.00794 | | | | | | | | | |
| 3<br>Lithium<br>**Li**<br>6.941 | 4<br>Beryllium<br>**Be**<br>9.01218 | | | | | | | | |
| 11<br>Sodium<br>**Na**<br>22.98977 | 12<br>Magnesium<br>**Mg**<br>24.305 | | | | | | | | |
| 19<br>Potassium<br>**K**<br>39.098 | 20<br>Calcium<br>**Ca**<br>40.06 | 21<br>Scandium<br>**Sc**<br>44.9559 | 22<br>Titanium<br>**Ti**<br>47.90 | 23<br>Vanadium<br>**V**<br>50.9414 | 24<br>Chromium<br>**Cr**<br>51.996 | 25<br>Manganese<br>**Mn**<br>54.9380 | 26<br>Iron<br>**Fe**<br>55.847 | 27<br>Cobalt<br>**Co**<br>58.9332 | |
| 37<br>Rubidium<br>**Rb**<br>85.4678 | 38<br>Strontium<br>**Sr**<br>87.62 | 39<br>Yttrium<br>**Y**<br>88.9059 | 40<br>Zirconium<br>**Zr**<br>91.22 | 41<br>Niobium<br>**Nb**<br>92.9064 | 42<br>Molybdenum<br>**Mo**<br>95.94 | 43<br>Technetium<br>**Tc**<br>97.9072 | 44<br>Ruthenium<br>**Ru**<br>101.07 | 45<br>Rhodium<br>**Rh**<br>102.9055 | |
| 55<br>Caesium<br>**Cs**<br>132.9054 | 56<br>Barium<br>**Ba**<br>137.34 | | 72<br>Hafnium<br>**Hf**<br>178.49 | 73<br>Tantalum<br>**Ta**<br>180.9479 | 74<br>Tungsten<br>**W**<br>183.85 | 75<br>Rhenium<br>**Re**<br>186.207 | 76<br>Osmium<br>**Os**<br>190.2 | 77<br>Iridium<br>**Ir**<br>192.22 | |
| 87<br>Francium<br>**Fr**<br>223.0197 | 88<br>Radium<br>**Ra**<br>226.0254 | | 104<br>Unniiquadium<br>**Unq**<br>216.109 | 105<br>Unnipentium<br>**Unp**<br>262.114 | 106<br>Unnihexium<br>**Unh**<br>263.120 | 107<br>Unnilseptium<br>**Uns**<br>262 | 108<br>Unniloctium<br>**Uno**<br>265 | 109<br>Unnilenium<br>**Une**<br>266 | |

element: atomic number — name — symbol — relative atomic mass (1 Hydrogen **H** 1.00794)

**Lanthanide series**

| 57<br>Lanthanum<br>**La**<br>138.9055 | 58<br>Cerium<br>**Ce**<br>140.12 | 59<br>Praeseodymium<br>**Pr**<br>140.9077 | 60<br>Neodymium<br>**Nd**<br>144.24 | 61<br>Promethium<br>**Pm**<br>144.9128 | 62<br>Samarium<br>**Sm**<br>150.36 |
|---|---|---|---|---|---|

**Actinide series**

| 89<br>Actinium<br>**Ac**<br>227.0278 | 90<br>Thorium<br>**Th**<br>232.0381 | 91<br>Protactinium<br>**Pa**<br>231.0359 | 92<br>Uranium<br>**U**<br>238.029 | 93<br>Neptunium<br>**Np**<br>237.0482 | 94<br>Plutonium<br>**Pu**<br>244.0642 |
|---|---|---|---|---|---|

of neutrons, thus differing in their atomic masses.

They may be stable or radioactive, naturally occurring or synthesized. The term was coined by English chemist Frederick Soddy, pioneer researcher in atomic disintegration.

**lone pair** a pair of electrons in the outermost shell of an atom that are not used in bonding. In certain circumstances, they will allow the atom to bond with atoms, ions, or molecules (such as boron trifluoride, $BF_3$) that are deficient in electrons, forming coordinate covalent (dative) bonds in which they provide both of the bonding electrons.

**molecule** the smallest unit of an element or compound that can exist and still retain the characteristics of the element or compound. A molecule of an element consists of one or more like atoms; a molecule of a compound consists of two or more different atoms bonded together. They vary in size and complexity from the hydrogen molecule ($H_2$) to the large macromolecules of proteins. They are held together by ionic bonds, in which the atoms gain or lose electrons to form ions, or covalent bonds, where electrons from each atom are shared in a new molecular orbital.

**neutron** one of the three chief subatomic particles (the others being the proton and the electron). Neutrons have about the same mass as protons but no electric charge, and occur in the nuclei of all atoms except hydrogen. They contribute to the mass of atoms but do not affect their chemistry, which depends on the proton or electron numbers. For instance, isotopes of a single element (with different masses) differ only in the number of neutrons in their nuclei and have identical chemical properties.

**periodic table of the elements** in chemistry, a table setting out the classification of the elements following the statement by Russian chemist Dmitri Mendeleyev 1869 that 'the properties of elements are in periodic depend-

**periodic tables of the elements**

| | | | | | | 0 |
|---|---|---|---|---|---|---|
| | | | | | | 2<br>Helium<br>**He**<br>4.00260 |
| | III | IV | V | VI | VII | |
| | 5<br>Boron<br>**B**<br>10.81 | 6<br>Carbon<br>**C**<br>12.011 | 7<br>Nitrogen<br>**N**<br>14.0067 | 8<br>Oxygen<br>**O**<br>15.9994 | 9<br>Fluorine<br>**F**<br>18.99840 | 10<br>Neon<br>**Ne**<br>20.179 |
| | 13<br>Aluminium<br>**Al**<br>26.98154 | 14<br>Silicon<br>**Si**<br>28.086 | 15<br>Phosphorus<br>**P**<br>30.97376P | 16<br>Sulphur<br>**S**<br>32.06 | 17<br>Chlorine<br>**Cl**<br>35.453 | 18<br>Argon<br>**Ar**<br>39.948 |

| 28<br>Nickel<br>**Ni**<br>58.70 | 29<br>Copper<br>**Cu**<br>63.546 | 30<br>Zinc<br>**Zn**<br>65.38 | 31<br>Gallium<br>**Ga**<br>69.72 | 32<br>Germanium<br>**Ge**<br>72.59 | 33<br>Arsenic<br>**As**<br>74.9216 | 34<br>Selenium<br>**Se**<br>78.96 | 35<br>Bromine<br>**Br**<br>79.904 | 36<br>Krypton<br>**Kr**<br>83.80 |
|---|---|---|---|---|---|---|---|---|
| 46<br>Palladium<br>**Pd**<br>106.4 | 47<br>Silver<br>**Ag**<br>107.868 | 48<br>Cadmium<br>**Cd**<br>112.40 | 49<br>Indium<br>**In**<br>114.82 | 50<br>Tin<br>**Sn**<br>118.69 | 51<br>Antimony<br>**Sb**<br>121.75 | 52<br>Tellurium<br>**Te**<br>127.75 | 53<br>Iodine<br>**I**<br>126.9045 | 54<br>Xenon<br>**Xe**<br>131.30 |
| 78<br>Platinum<br>**Pt**<br>195.09 | 79<br>Gold<br>**Au**<br>196.9665 | 80<br>Mercury<br>**Hg**<br>200.59 | 81<br>Thallium<br>**Tl**<br>204.37 | 82<br>Lead<br>**Pb**<br>207.37 | 83<br>Bismuth<br>**Bi**<br>207.2 | 84<br>Polonium<br>**Po**<br>210 | 85<br>Astatine<br>**At**<br>211 | 86<br>Radon<br>**Rn**<br>222.0176 |

| 63<br>Europium<br>**Eu**<br>151.96 | 64<br>Gadolinium<br>**Gd**<br>157.25 | 65<br>Terbium<br>**Tb**<br>158.9254 | 66<br>Dysprosium<br>**Dy**<br>162.50 | 67<br>Holmium<br>**Ho**<br>164.9304 | 68<br>Erbium<br>**Er**<br>167.26 | 69<br>Thulium<br>**Tm**<br>168.9342 | 70<br>Ytterbium<br>**Yb**<br>173.04 | 71<br>Lutetium<br>**Lu**<br>174.97 |
|---|---|---|---|---|---|---|---|---|

| 95<br>Americium<br>**Am**<br>243.0614 | 96<br>Curium<br>**Cm**<br>247.0703 | 97<br>Berkelium<br>**Bk**<br>247.0703 | 98<br>Californium<br>**Cf**<br>251.0786 | 99<br>Einsteinium<br>**Es**<br>252.0828 | 100<br>Fermium<br>**Fm**<br>257.0951 | 101<br>Mendelevium<br>**Md**<br>258.0986 | 102<br>Nobelium<br>**No**<br>259.1009 | 103<br>Lawrencium<br>**Lr**<br>260.1054 |
|---|---|---|---|---|---|---|---|---|

ence upon their atomic weight'. (Today elements are classified by their atomic number rather than by their relative atomic mass.) The properties of the elements are a direct consequence of the electronic (and nuclear) structure of their atoms. Striking similarities exist between the chemical properties of the elements in each of the table's vertical columns (called *groups*), which are numbered I–VII and then 0 (from left to right) to reflect the number of electrons in the outermost unfilled shell and hence the maximum valency. A gradation of properties may be traced along the horizontal rows (called *periods*). Metallic character increases across a period from right to left, and down a group. A large block of elements, between groups II and III, contains the transition elements, characterized by displaying more than one valency state.

**proton** (Greek 'first') positively charged subatomic particle, a fundamental constituent of any atomic nucleus. Its lifespan is effectively infinite.

**relative atomic mass** the mass of an atom. It depends on the number of protons and neutrons in the atom, the electrons having negligible mass. It is calculated relative to one-twelfth the mass of an atom of carbon-12. If more than one isotope of the element is present, the relative atomic mass is calculated by taking an average that takes account of the relative proportions of each isotope, resulting in values that are not whole numbers. The term *atomic weight*, although commonly used, is strictly speaking incorrect.

**valency** the measure of an element's ability to combine with other elements, expressed as the number of atoms of hydrogen (or any other standard univalent element) capable of uniting with (or replacing) its atoms. The number of electrons in the outermost shell of the atom dictates the combining ability of an element.

### Isomer

butane $CH_3(CH_2)_2CH_3$

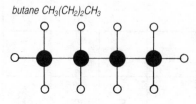

methyl propane $CH_3CH(CH_3)CH_3$

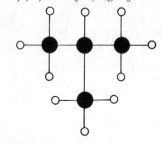

○ hydrogen atom

● carbon atom

— covalent bond

# REACTIVITY

**acid** compound that, in solution in an ionizing solvent (usually water), gives rise to hydrogen ions ($H^+$ or protons). In modern chemistry, acids are defined as substances that are proton donors and accept electrons from a base to form ionic bonds. Acids react with bases to form salts, and they act as solvents. Strong acids are corrosive; dilute acids have a sour or sharp taste, although in some organic acids this may be partially masked by other flavour characteristics. Acids are classified as monobasic, dibasic, tribasic, and so forth, according to the number of hydrogen atoms, replaceable by bases, in a molecule.

**activation energy** the energy required in order to start a chemical reaction.

**alkali** chemical compound classed as a base that is soluble in water. Alkalis neutralize acids and are soapy to the touch.

**base** a substance that accepts protons, such as the hydroxide ion ($OH^-$ and ammonia ($NH_3$). Bases react with acids to give a salt. Those that dissolve in water are called alkalis.

**catalyst** substance that alters the speed of, or makes possible, a chemical or biochemical reaction but remains unchanged at the end of the reaction. Enzymes are natural biochemical catalysts. In practice most catalysts are used to speed up reactions.

**chain reaction** a mechanism that produces a succession of reactions, usually involving free radicals, where the products of one stage are

the reactants of the next. A chain reaction is characterized by the continual generation of reactive substances.

**chemical equation** method of indicating the reactants and products of a chemical reaction by using chemical symbols and formulae. A chemical equation gives two basic pieces of information: (1) the reactants (on the left-hand side) and products (right-hand side); and (2) the reacting proportions (stoichiometry)—that is, how many units of each reactant and product are involved. The equation must balance; that is, the total number of atoms of a particular element on the left-hand side must be the same as the number of atoms of that element on the right-hand side.

**chemical equilibrium** condition in which the products of a reversible chemical reaction are formed at the same rate at which they decompose back into the reactants, so that the concentration of each reactant and product remains constant.

**decomposition** the process whereby a chemical compound is reduced to its component substances. In biology, it is the destruction of dead organisms either by chemical reduction or by the action of decomposers.

**dissociation** the process whereby a single compound splits into two or more smaller products, which may be capable of recombining to form the reactant.

**energy of reaction** energy released or absorbed during a chemical reaction, also called *enthalpy of reaction* or *heat of reaction*.

**enzyme** biological catalyst produced in cells, and capable of speeding up the chemical reactions necessary for life. Enzymes are not themselves destroyed by this process. They are large, complex proteins, and are highly specific, each chemical reaction requiring its own particular enzyme. Digestive enzymes include amylases (which digest starch), lipases (which digest fats), and proteases (which digest protein). Other enzymes play a part in the conversion of food energy into ATP; the manufacture of all the molecular components of the body; the replication of DNA when a cell divides; the production of hormones; and the control of movement of substances into and out of cells.

**free radical** an atom or molecule that has an unpaired electron and is therefore highly reactive. Most free radicals are very short-lived. If free radicals are produced in living organisms they can be very damaging.

**ion exchange** process whereby an ion in one compound is replaced by a different ion, of the same charge, from another compound. It is the basis of a type of chromatography in which the components of a mixture of ions in solution are separated according to the ease with which they will replace the ions on the polymer matrix through which they flow. Ion-exchange resins are used to soften water by exchanging the dissolved ions responsible for the water's hardness with others that do not have this effect.

**neutralization** a process occurring when the excess acid (or excess base) in a substance is reacted with added base (or added acid) so that the resulting substance is neither acidic nor basic.

**oxidation** the loss of electrons, gain of oxygen, or loss of hydrogen by an atom, ion, or molecule during a chemical reaction.

**rate of reaction** the speed at which a chemical reaction proceeds. It is usually expressed in terms of the concentration (usually in moles per litre) of a reactant consumed, or product formed, in unit time; so the units would be moles per litre per second (mol $l^{-1}$ $s^{-1}$). The rate of a reaction may be affected by the concentration of the reactants, the temperature of the reactants, and the presence of a catalyst. If the reaction is entirely in the gas state, pressure affects the rate, and, for solids, the particle size.

**reaction** the coming together of two or more atoms, ions or molecules with the result that a chemical change takes place. The nature of the reaction is portrayed by a chemical equation.

**reactivity series** chemical series produced by arranging the metals in order of their ease of reaction with reagents such as oxygen, water, and acids. This arrangement aids the understanding of the properties of metals, helps to explain differences between them, and enables predictions to be made about a metal's behaviour, based on a knowledge of its position or properties.

**redox reaction** chemical change where one reactant is reduced and the other reactant oxidized. The reaction can only occur if both reactants are present and each changes simultaneously. For example, hydrogen reduces copper(II) oxide to copper while it is itself oxidized to water. The corrosion of iron and the reactions taking place in electric and electolytic cells are just a few instances of redox reactions.

**reduction** the gain of electrons, loss of oxygen, or gain of hydrogen by an atom, ion, or molecule during a chemical reaction.

**salt** any compound formed from an acid and a base through the replacement of all or part of the hydrogen in the acid by a metal or electropositive radical. *Common salt* is sodium chloride.

**strength of acids and bases** the ability of acids and bases to dissociate in solution with water, and hence to produce a low or high pH respectively.

# PROPERTIES

**boiling point** for any given liquid, the temperature at which any further application of heat will convert the liquid to vapour. The temperature remains at this point until all the liquid has vapourized. It is invariable under similar conditions of pressure—for example, the boiling point of water under standard atmospheric pressure is 100°C/212°F. The lower the pressure, the lower the boiling point and vice versa.

**buffer** mixture of chemical compounds chosen to maintain a steady pH.

**colloid** substance composed of extremely small particles of one material (the dispersed phase) evenly and stably distributed in another material (the continuous phase). The size of the dispersed particles (1–1,000 nanometres/0.000039–0.039 in across) is less than that of particles in suspension but greater than that of molecules in true solution. Colloids involving gases include *aerosols* (dispersions of liquid or solid particles in a gas, as in fog or smoke) and *foams* (dispersions of gases in liquids). Those involving liquids include *emulsions* (in which both the dispersed and the continuous phases are liquids) and *sols* (solid particles dispersed in a liquid). Sols in which both phases contribute to a molecular three-dimensional network have a jellylike form and are known as *gels*; gelatine, starch 'solution', and silica gel are common examples.

**diffusion** the spontaneous and random movement of molecules or particles in a fluid (gas or liquid) from a region in which they are at a high concentration to a region in which they are at a low concentration, until a uniform concentration is achieved throughout. No mechanical mixing or stirring is involved. For instance, if a drop of ink is added to water, its molecules will diffuse until their colour becomes evenly distributed throughout.

**dipole** the uneven distribution of magnetic or electrical characteristics within a molecule or substance so that it behaves as though it possesses two equal but opposite poles or charges, a finite distance apart. The uneven distribution of electrons within a molecule composed of atoms of different electronegativities may result in an apparent concentration of electrons towards one end of the molecule and a deficiency towards the other, so that it forms a dipole consisting of apparently separated positive and negative charges. A bar magnet behaves as though its magnetism were concentrated in separate north and south magnetic poles because of the uneven distribution of its magnetic field.

**emulsion** colloid consisting of a stable dispersion of a liquid in another liquid—for example, oil and water in some cosmetic lotions.

**freezing point** for any given liquid, the temperature at which any further removal of heat will convert the liquid into the solid state. The temperature remains at this point until all the liquid has solidified. It is invariable under similar conditions of pressure—for example, the freezing point of water under standard atmospheric pressure is 0°C/32°F.

**immiscible** term describing liquids that will not mix with each other, such as oil and water. When two immiscible liquids are shaken together, a turbid mixture is produced. This normally forms separate layers on being left to stand.

**mixture** a substance containing two or more compounds that still retain their separate physical and chemical properties. There is no chemical bonding between them and they can be separated from each other by physical means (compare compound).

**pH** scale for measuring acidity or alkalinity. A pH of 7.0 indicates neutrality, below 7 is acid, while above 7 is alkaline.

**precipitation** the formation of a suspension of solid, insoluble particles in a liquid as a result of a reaction within the liquid between two or more soluble substances. If the particles settle, they form a *precipitate*; if the particles are very small and remain in suspension, they form a *colloidal precipitate*.

**radioactivity** spontaneous alteration of the nuclei of radioactive atoms, accompanied by the emission of radiation. It is the property exhibited by the radioactive isotopes of stable elements and all isotopes of radioactive elements.

**solute** substance that is dissolved in another substance.

**solution** two or more substances mixed to form a single, homogeneous phase. One of the substances is the *solvent* and the others (*solutes*) are said to be dissolved in it.

**solvent** substance, usually a liquid, that will dissolve another substance. Although the commonest solvent is water, in popular use the term refers to low-boiling-point organic liquids, which are harmful if used in a confined space. They can give rise to respiratory problems, liver damage, and neurological complaints.

**sublimation** the conversion of a solid to vapour without passing through the liquid phase.

# CHEMICALS WE USE

**acesulfame-K** non-carbohydrate sweetener that is up to 300 times as sweet as sugar. It is used in soft drinks, desserts, and puddings.

**additive** chemical added to a substance for technological advantage. Examples are the anti-knock agents used in petroleum fuels and the fungicides added to wallpaper pastes. In food technology, an additive is any natural or artificial chemical that is added to a processed food in order to prolong its shelf life, alter its colour or flavour, or improve its nutritional value.

Many chemical food additives are used and they are subject to regulation, since individuals may be affected by constant exposure even to traces of certain additives and may suffer side effects ranging from headaches and hyperactivity to cancer. Within the EC, approved additives are given an official E number.

**aspartame** non-carbohydrate sweetener used in foods under the tradename Nutrasweet. It is about 200 times as sweet as sugar and, unlike saccharine, has no aftertaste.

**caramel** complex mixture of substances produced by heating sugars, without charring, until they turn brown. Caramel is used as colouring and flavouring in foods. Its production in the manufacture of sugar confection gives rise to a toffee-like sweet of the same name.

**carbohydrate** chemical compound composed of carbon, hydrogen, and oxygen, with the basic formula $C_m(H_2O)_n$, and related compounds with the same basic structure but modified functional groups. The simplest carbohydrates are sugars (*monosaccharides*, such as glucose and fructose, and *disaccharides*, such as sucrose), which are soluble compounds, some with a sweet taste. When these basic sugar units are joined together in long chains or branching structures they form *polysaccharides*, such as starch and glycogen, which often serve as food stores in living organisms.

**cyclamate** derivative of cyclohexysulphamic acid, formerly used as an artificial sweetener.

**dough** mixture consisting primarily of flour, water, and yeast, which is used in the manufacture of bread. The preparation of dough involves thorough kneading and standing in a warm place to 'prove' (increase in volume) so that the enzymes in the dough can break down the starch from the flour into smaller sugar molecules, which are then fermented by the yeast. This releases carbon dioxide, which causes the dough to rise.

**drug** any of a range of chemicals voluntarily or involuntarily introduced into the bodies of humans and animals in order to enhance or suppress a biological function. Most drugs in use are medicines (pharmaceuticals), used to prevent or treat diseases, or to relieve their symptoms; they include antibiotics, cytotoxic drugs, immunosuppressives, sedatives, and pain-relievers (analgesics).

**fat** naturally occurring, soft, greasy substance that forms a rich source and store of energy in animals and plants. It consists chiefly of triglycerides (lipids containing three fatty acid molecules linked to a molecule of glycerol) and phospholipids, but also contains fat-soluble vitamins, minerals, and other substances in small amounts. Animal fat contains cholesterol, which is believed to be a major contributor to heart disease in humans.

**fluoridation** addition of small amounts of fluoride salts to drinking water by certain water authorities to help prevent tooth decay. Experiments in Britain, the USA, and elsewhere have indicated that a concentration of fluoride of 1 part per million in tap water retards the decay of teeth in children by more than 50%.

**fructose** $C_6H_{12}O_6$ a sugar that occurs naturally in honey, the nectar of flowers, and many sweet fruits; it is commercially prepared from glucose. Fructose is a monosaccharide, whereas the more familar cane or beet sugar is a disaccharide, made up of two monosaccharide units: fructose and glucose. It is sweeter than cane sugar.

**glucose** or *grape-sugar* $C_6H_{12}O_6$ monosaccharide sugar present in the blood, and found also in honey and fruit juices. It is a source of

## ELEMENTARY MY DEAR MENDELEYEV

While alchemists were trying to convert base metals to gold, real progress was achieved by the interpretaion of natural phenomena. It was the appreciation of the differences between natural ores that led to the discoveries of new elements. Several attempts were made to relate the properties of known elements in a way which would highlight similarities and differences between them. The culmination of this in 1869 was the Periodic Table of Mendeleyev. As well as grouping similar elements together, it indicated gaps where as yet unknown elements might be placed.

As each new element was discovered, its discoverer named it. The main problem seems to have been who is entitled to claim 'ownership' of the discovery. Should it be the first person to identify its existence, the person who first isolates it from nature as a relatively pure compound, or perhaps as the element itself? Perhaps the honour should go to the person who demonstrates from examination of its properties that it is in fact a new element. Examination of history shows that no single criterion of ownership has been applied universally.

Beryllium was discovered as its oxide by Vauquelin in beryl and in emeralds in 1798 but the metal itself was not isolated until thirty years later, by Wohler and Bussy working independently of each other. Cerium was similarly discovered in combined form in 1803 by Klaproth and also by Berzelius and Hisinger. It was left to Hillebrand and Norton in 1875 to prepare the metal itself.

Mosander isolated the ore 'yttria' in 1842 and separated it into three different substances. The fraction containing erbium was later shown to contain no fewer than five different oxides, only one of which was the oxide of erbium. The oxide was not isolated in pure form until 1905, by Urbain and James. It was not until 1934 that Klemm and Bommer first produced erbium metal in a reasonably pure state.

There are many such stories but the most unfortunate person was del Rio. He discovered vanadium in 1801 but was persuaded by a French chemist that it was nothing more than impure chromium. Consequently, the discovery is often attributed to Sefstrom, who rediscovered it in 1820. It was not obtained in rea-

sonably pure form until 1867, by Roscoe, and purity in the region of 99.3 to 99.8% was not achieved until 1927.

In recent years many newly discovered elements have been radioactive, survive for very short periods of time and isolated, if at all, in minuscule quantities. Recognition of their existence has relied on interpretation of short-lived properties. The traditional chemist of years ago would have difficulty relating to a study of elements that don't occur naturally, aren't available in sufficent quantities to see, handle and examine and aren't around for more than a few seconds, or even less. Yet it is due to discoveries of these elements that a sub-set of elements, tranactinides, was perceived. The position of transient, artificial elements within a conceptual organization may appear to be rather academic yet it does change scientific perceptions of what might yet be found, or made. It is now predicted that a further range of elements may be round the corner.

In principle, the ownership of artificial elements should be easier to determine than for natural ones. However, it is more difficult to identify the short-lived atoms and even more difficult to persuade your competitors of your triumphs. There is currently dispute between the scientists of Dubna, USSR, and Berkeley, USA, over the discovery of elements 104 and 105. In 1964 the Russians bombarded plutonium-242 with neon-22 and claimed to have detected element isotope 260 of element with half-life 0.15 second. The Americans claim to be unable to repeat this experiment but have produced isotopes 257, 258 and 259 by bombarding californium-249 with carbon-12 and carbon-13 (1969). Half-lives are respectively 4–5 seconds, 0.01 second and 3–4 seconds. A similar story exists for element 105, with each group using different reactions. Elements 104 and 105 have therefore more than a single name. Element 104 is kurchatovium (USSR) and rutherfordium (USA). Element 105 is hahnium (USA), the Russians not giving it a name. To simplify matters the International Union of Pure and Applied Chemistry (IUPAC) has suggested temporary names of unnilquadium and unnilpentium but these are not necessarily universally accepted.

energy for the body, being produced from other sugars and starches to form the 'energy currency' of many biochemical reactions also involving ATP.

**hard water**  water that does not lather easily with soap, and produces 'fur' or 'scale' in kettles. It is caused by the presence of certain salts of calcium and magnesium. *Temporary hardness* is caused by the presence of dissolved hydrogencarbonates (bicarbonates); when the water is boiled, they are converted to insoluble carbonates that precipitate as 'scale'. *Permanent hardness* is caused by sulphates and silicates, which are not affected by boiling.

**lactic acid**  or *2-hydroxypropanoic acid* $CH_3$-$CHOHCOOH$ organic acid, a colourless, almost odourless liquid, produced by certain bacteria during fermentation and by active muscle cells when they are exercised hard and are experiencing oxygen debt. It occurs in yoghurt, buttermilk, sour cream, poor wine, and certain plant extracts, and is used in food preservation and in the preparation of pharmaceuticals.

**monosodium glutamate**  (MSG) $NaC_5H_8NO_4$ a white, crystalline powder, the sodium salt of glutamic acid (an amino acid). It is used to enhance the flavour of many packaged and 'fast foods', and in Chinese cooking. Ill ef-

**Ph**

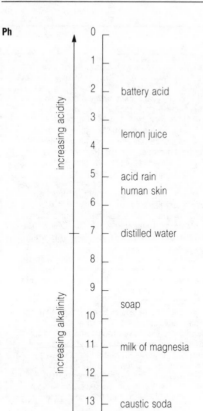

increasing acidity

increasing alkalinity

| | |
|---|---|
| 0 | |
| 1 | |
| 2 | battery acid |
| 3 | |
| 4 | lemon juice |
| 5 | acid rain |
| | human skin |
| 6 | |
| 7 | distilled water |
| 8 | |
| 9 | |
| 10 | soap |
| 11 | milk of magnesia |
| 12 | |
| 13 | caustic soda |
| 14 | |

fects, such as dizziness and heart palpitations, may arise from its overconsumption, and some people are very sensitive to it, even in small amounts. MSG is prepared commercially from vegetable protein, such as sugar beet pulp.

**oil** inflammable substance, usually insoluble in water, and chiefly composed of carbon and hydrogen. Oils may be solids (fats and waxes) or liquids. The three main types are: *essential oils*, obtained from plants; *fixed oils*, obtained from animals and plants; and *mineral oils*, obtained chiefly from the refining of petroleum. Eight of the 14 top-earning companies in the USA in 1990 (led by Exxon with $7 billion in sales) are in the global petroleum industry.

**plaster of Paris** form of calcium sulphate, obtained from gypsum; it is mixed with water for making casts and moulds.

**protein** complex, biologically important substance composed of amino acids joined by peptide bonds. Other types of bond, such as sulphur–sulphur bonds, hydrogen bonds, and cation bridges between acid sites, are responsible for creating the protein's characteristic three-dimensional structure, which may be fibrous, globular, or pleated.

**saccharin** or *ortho-sulpho benzimide* $C_7H_5NO_3S$

sweet, white, crystalline solid derived from coal tar and substituted for sugar. Since 1977 it has been regarded as potentially carcinogenic. Its use is not universally permitted and it has been largely replaced by other sweetening agents.

**salt, common** or *sodium chloride* NaCl white crystalline solid, found dissolved in sea water and as rock salt (halite) in large deposits and salt domes. Common salt is used extensively in the food industry as a preservative and for flavouring, and in the chemical industry in the making of chlorine and sodium. While common salt is an essential part of our diet, some medical experts believe that excess salt can lead to high blood pressure and increased risk of heart attacks.

**starch** widely distributed, high-molecular-mass carbohydrate, produced by plants as a food store; main dietary sources are cereals, legumes, and tubers, including potatoes. It consists of varying proportions of two glucose polymers (polysaccharides): straight-chain (amylose) and branched (amylopectin) molecules.

**steroid** any of a group of cyclic, unsaturated alcohols (lipids without fatty acid components), which, like sterols, have a complex molecular structure consisting of four carbon rings. Steroids include the sex hormones, such as testosterone, the corticosteroid hormones produced by the adrenal gland, bile acids, and cholesterol. The term is commonly used to refer to anabolic steroids, a class of hormones used in medicine and, usually illicitly, in sport to stimulate tissue growth.

**sucrose** or *cane sugar* or *beet sugar* $C_{12}H_{22}O_{10}$ a sugar found in the pith of sugar cane and in sugar beets. It is popularly known as sugar. Sucrose is a disaccharide sugar, each of its molecules being made up of two simple sugar (monosaccharide) units: glucose and fructose.

**sulphur dioxide** $SO_2$ pungent gas produced by burning sulphur in air or oxygen. It is widely used for disinfecting food vessels and equipment, and as a preservative in some food products. It occurs in industrial flue gases and is a major cause of acid rain.

**thaumatin** naturally occurring, non-carbohydrate sweetener derived from the bacterium *Thaumatococcus danielli*. Its sweetness is not sensed as quickly as that of other sweeteners, and it is not as widely used in the food industry.

**water** $H_2O$ liquid without colour, taste, or odour. It is an oxide of hydrogen. Water begins to freeze solid at 0°C or 32°F, and to boil at 100°C or 212°F. When liquid, it is virtually incompressible; frozen, it expands by $\frac{1}{11}$ of its volume. At 39.2F/4°C, one cubic centimetre of water has a mass of one gram, its maximum density, forming the unit of specific gravity. It has the highest known specific heat, and acts as an efficient solvent, particularly when hot. Most of the world's water is in the sea; less than 0.01% is fresh water.

# HARMFUL CHEMICALS

**arsenic** brittle, greyish-white, weakly metallic element, symbol As, atomic number 33, relative atomic mass 74.92. It occurs in many ores and occasionally in its elemental state, and is widely distributed, being present in minute quantities in the soil, the sea, and the human body. In larger quantities, it is poisonous, accumulating in the body and causing vomiting, diarrhoea, tingling and possibly numbness in the limbs, and collapse. The chief source of arsenic compounds is as a by-product from metallurgical processes.

**carbon monoxide** CO colourless, odourless gas formed when carbon is oxidized in a limited supply of air. It is a poisonous constituent of car exhaust fumes, forming a stable com-

---

## CFCs AND AFTER

CFCs are a class of compounds that have been tailor-made for use primarily as aerosol expellants, refrigerants and in plastic foams, specifically because they are chemically unreactive and therefore thought to be harmless.

They are saturated compounds containing three elements only—chlorine, fluorine, and carbon. Industrial terminology is coded but can readily be deciphered. A typical example is CFC113. The first digit is one fewer than the number of carbon atoms; the second one more than the number of hydrogen atoms and the third is the number of fluorine atoms present in a molecule. The number of chlorine atoms present is the number necessary to satisfy valency requirements. For example, CFC113 is C2F3Cl3. Trichlorofluoromethane (CFCl3) should be CFC011 but the initial zero is dropped to give CFC11.

Paradoxically, it is the unreactivity of CFCs under normal circumstances that makes them such an environmental hazard. Over a period of time, so far of the order of 50 years, they have steadily drifted unchanged into the upper atmosphere, where they are a double hazard. They are estimated to make up 17% of greenhouse gases and also play a significant part in the depletion of the ozone layer some 20 km above the Earth's surface. These two effects are different and unrelated.

The greenhouse effect is so named as a parallel to the heat generated in a greenhouse. Infrared radiation cannot penetrate most substances, or at least does so only partially. Only a small fraction of heat accumulated or produced within a greenhouse can escape through the glass. A largely impervious shield of gases 8–16 km above the Earth's surface similarly traps heat.

The role of CFCs in the depletion of the ozone layer is totally different. Although under normal circumstances they are highly stable molecules, exposure to the intense ultra-violet radiation in the upper atmosphere where they have been accumulating results in the splitting of the molecules into highly reactive free radicals, including chlorine radicals. It is accepted that the exposure of ozone molecules ($O_3$) to ultra-violet also results in the generation of the free radical of monatomic oxygen (O) and the normal diatomic oxygen atom ($O_2$). These may then recombine to regenerate ozone as the free radicals cannot exist alone. Some may unite with similar radicals to form oxygen molecules. Additionally, diatomic oxygen molecules may be split by ultra-violet to produce monatomic oxygen radicals. Under normal circumstances, these processes of splitting and reforming are occurring all the time. There are known to be seasonal variations in the ozone layer, but over a long period of time there is an equilibrium established—that is, until the chlorine radical, and other culprits associated with other types of compounds, came on the scene. This mops up the monatomic oxygen atom, first to give a ClO radical, which pairs off to give the peroxide $Cl_2O_2$. Further absorbed radiation degrades this back to diatomic oxygen and chlorine radicals, which can mop up yet more oxygen. The net result is a shift in the ozone–oxygen equilibrium towards increased levels of oxygen, and depletion of ozone. The two main concerns are that chlorine is regenerated and not decayed and that the full influence of existing CFCs is still unknown as relatively recent emissions have not yet reached the danger zone.

Clearly CFCs must be replaced, but international policy seems to be a phasing-out rather than an immediate ban. Replacement molecules are already on the stocks. These are similar types of molecules but some or all chlorine atoms have been replaced with hydrogen. They are named hydrofluorocarbons (HFCs) and hydrochlorofluorocarbons (HCFCs), respectively. The introduction of hydrogen into the molecule makes it less stable so that it decomposes before it can reach the danger zone. The codenames are deciphered in identical fashion to those for CFCs. The nomenclature gives no indication of the way atoms are arranged in the molecule so a further suffix may be added. CHF2CHF2 is HFC134 and CF3CH2F is HFC134a.

HFC134a is a substitute for CFC12 as a refrigerant. HFC123 substitutes CFC11 in plastic foam. Most replacements for CFCs are greenhouse gases. They don't contribute to ozone depletion but it is possible that atmospheric decay at lower altitudes may generate a new problem. Professor Banks of UMIST, Manchester has proposed possible pathways that, if correct, would result in more acid rain and the liberation of trifluoroethanoic acid into the atmosphere. Any hazards associated with this are at present unpredictable. No doubt influenced by the considerable element of competitiveness, industry seems to have rushed into a commitment that may take us from the frying pan into the fire. Can we afford to wait and see?

---

## NOBEL PRIZE FOR CHEMISTRY

*prizewinners*

| | |
|---|---|
| 1951 | Edwin M McMillan (USA) and Glenn T Seaborg (USA): chemistry of transuranic elements |
| 1952 | Archer Martin (UK) and Richard Synge (UK): invention of partition chromatography |
| 1953 | Hermann Staudinger (Germany): discoveries in macromolecular chemistry |
| 1954 | Linus Pauling (USA): nature of chemical bonds, especially in complex substances |
| 1955 | Vincent Du Vigneaud (USA): investigations into biochemically important sulphur compounds, and the first synthesis of a polypeptide hormone |
| 1956 | Cyril Hinshelwood (UK) and Nikoly Semenov (USSR): mechanism of chemical reactions |
| 1957 | Alexander Todd (UK): nucleotides and nucleotide coenzymes |
| 1958 | Frederick Sanger (UK): structure of proteins, especially insulin |
| 1959 | Jaroslav Heyrovský (Czechoslovakia): polarographic methods of chemical analysis |
| 1960 | Willard Libby (USA): radiocarbon dating in archaeology, geology, and geography |
| 1961 | Melvin Calvin (USA): assimilation of carbon dioxide by plants |
| 1962 | Max Perutz (UK) and John Kendrew (UK): structures of globular proteins |
| 1963 | Karl Ziegler (Germany) and Giulio Natta (Italy): chemistry and technology of high polymers |
| 1964 | Dorothy Crowfoot Hodgkin (UK): crystallographic determination of the structures of biochemical compounds, notably penicillin and cyanocobalamin (vitamin $B_{12}$) |
| 1965 | Robert Woodward (USA): organic synthesis |
| 1966 | Robert Mulliken (USA): molecular orbital theory of chemical bonds and structures |
| 1967 | Manfred Eigen (Germany), Ronald Norrish (UK), and George Porter (UK): investigation of rapid chemical reactions by means of very short pulses of energy |
| 1968 | Lars Onsager (USA): discovery of reciprocal relations, fundamental for the thermodynamics of irreversible processes |
| 1969 | Derek Barton (UK) and Odd Hassel (Norway): concept and applications of conformation |
| 1970 | Luis Federico Leloir (Argentina): discovery of sugar nucleotides and their role in carbohydrate biosynthesis |
| 1971 | Gerhard Herzberg (Germany): electronic structure and geometry of molecules, particularly free radicals |
| 1972 | Christian B Anfinsen (USA), Stanford Moore (USA), and William H Stein (USA): amino-acid structure and biological activity of the enzyme ribonuclease |
| 1973 | Ernst Fischer (Germany) and Geoffrey Wilkinson (UK): chemistry of organometallic sandwich compounds |
| 1974 | Paul J Flory (USA): physical chemistry of macromolecules |
| 1975 | John Cornforth (Australia): stereochemistry of enzyme- catalysed reactions. Vladimir Prelog (Yugoslavia): stereochemistry of organic molecules and their reactions |
| 1976 | William N Lipscomb (USA): structure and chemical bonding of boranes (compounds of boron and hydrogen) |
| 1977 | Ilya Prigogine (USSR): themodynamics of irreversible and dissipative processes |
| 1978 | Peter Mitchell (UK): biological energy transfer and chemiosmotic theory |
| 1979 | Herbert C Brown (USA) and Georg Wittig (Germany): use of boron and phosphorus compounds, respectively, in organic syntheses |
| 1980 | Paul Berg (USA): biochemistry of nucleic acids, especialy recombinant-DNA. Walter Gilbert (USA) and Frederick Sanger (UK): base sequences in nucleic acids |
| 1981 | Kenichi Fukui (Japan) and Roald Hoffmann (USA): theories concerning chemical reactions |
| 1982 | Aaron Klug (UK): crystallographic electron microscopy: structure of biologically important nucleic-acid–protein complexes |
| 1983 | Henry Taube (USA): electron-transfer reactions in inorganic chemical reactions |
| 1984 | Bruce Merrifield (USA): chemical syntheses on a solid matrix |
| 1985 | Herbert A Hauptman (USA) and Jerome Karle (USA): methods of determining crystal structures |
| 1986 | Dudley R Herschbach (USA), Yuan T Lee (USA), and John C Polanyi (Canada): dynamics of chemical elementary processes |
| 1987 | Donald J Cram (USA), Jean-Marie Lehn (France), and Charles J Pedersen (USA): molecules with highly selective structure-specific interactions |
| 1988 | Johann Deisenhofer (Germany), Robert Huber (Germany), and Hartmut Michel (Germany): three-dimensional structure of the reaction centre of photosynthesis |
| 1989 | Sydney Altman (USA) and Thomas Cech (USA): discovery of catalytic function of RNA |
| 1990 | Elias James Corey (USA): new methods of synthesizing chemical compounds |

pound with haemoglobin in the blood, thus preventing the haemoglobin from transporting oxygen to the body tissues.

**DDT** abbreviation for *dichloro-diphenyl-tri-chloroethane* $(ClC_6H_4)_2CHCCl_3$ insecticide discovered in 1939 by Swiss chemist Paul Müller. It is useful in the control of insects that spread malaria, but resistant strains develop. DDT is highly toxic and persists in the environment and in living tissue. Its use is now banned in most countries.

**dioxin** any of a family of over 200 organic chemicals, all of which are heterocyclic hydrocarbons. The term is commonly applied, however, to only one member of the family, 2,3,7,8-tetrachlorodibenzodioxin (2,3,7,8- TCDD), a highly toxic chemical that occurred as an impurity in a defoliant (Agent Orange) used in the Vietnam War, and in the weedkiller 2,4,5-T. It has been associated with a disfiguring skin complaint (chloracne), birth defects, miscarriages, and cancer.

**halon** organic chemical compound containing one or two carbon atoms, together with bromine and other halogens. The most commonly used are halon 1211 (bromochlorodifluoromethane) and halon 1301 (bromotrifluoromethane). The halons are gases and are widely used in fire extinguishers. As destroyers of the ozone layer, they are up to ten times more effective than chlorofluorocarbons (CFCs), to which they are chemically related.

**lead** heavy, soft, malleable, grey, metallic element, symbol Pb (from Latin *plumbum*), atomic number 82, relative atomic mass 207.19. It is used in making batteries, glass, ceramics, and alloys such as pewter and solder. Lead is a cumulative poison, causing abdominal pain, anaemia, and nerve or brain damage. The addition of lead tetraethyl, $Pb(C_2H_5)_4$, to leaded petrol to improve the performance of car engines has resulted in atmospheric pollution by lead compounds, which can lead to impaired learning ability in children exposed to this pollution over long periods of time. This has prompted a gradual shift to the use of unleaded petrol.

**mercury** or *quicksilver* heavy, silver-grey, metallic element, symbol Hg (from Latin *hydrargyrum*), atomic number 80, relative atomic mass 200.59. It is a dense, mobile liquid with a low melting point ($-38.87°C/-37.96°F$). Industrial uses include the making of chemicals, mercury-vapour lamps, power-control switches, batteries, barometers, and thermometers. An amalgam (alloy) of mercury and silver is used in dentistry for filling cavities in teeth. Mercury and its compounds are cumulative poisons that can contaminate the food chain, and cause intestinal disturbance, kidney and brain damage, and birth defects in humans. Eating fish and shellfish caught from seas in which mercury wastes have been dumped is the major cause of

**Hazard labels**

harmful/irritant

toxic

radioactive

explosive

flammable

corrosive

oxidizing/supports fire

poisoning.

**nicotine** $C_{10}H_{14}N_2$ an alkaloid (nitrogenous compound) obtained from the dried leaves of the tobacco plant *Nicotiana tabacum* and used as an insecticide. It is the component of cigarette smoke that causes physical addiction. A colourless oil, soluble in water, it turns brown on exposure to the air.

**ozone** $O_3$ highly reactive pale-blue gas with a penetrating odour. Ozone is an allotrope of oxygen, made up of three atoms of oxygen. It is formed when the molecule of the stable form of oxygen ($O_2$) is split by ultraviolet radiation or electrical discharge. It forms a layer in the upper atmosphere, which protects life on Earth from ultraviolet rays, a cause of skin cancer. At lower atmospheric levels it is an air pollutant and contributes to the greenhouse effect.

**radon** colourless, odourless, gaseous, radioactive, nonmetallic element, symbol Rn, atomic number 86, relative atomic mass 222. It is formed by the radioactive decay of radium in rocks and soil. In certain areas, such as Devon, Cornwall, and SE Scotland, the gas forms a natural hazard, seeping upwards into houses and increasing the probability of the inhabitants contracting lung cancer.

## INDUSTRIAL CHEMICAL PROCESSES

| | |
|---|---|
| **c.1100** | Alcohol was first distilled. |
| **1746** | John Roebuck invented the lead-chamber process for the manufacture of sulphuric acid. |
| **1790** | Nicolas Leblanc developed a process for making sodium carbonate from sodium chloride (common salt). |
| **1827** | John Walker invented phosphorus matches. |
| **1831** | Peregrine Phillips developed the contact process for the production of sulphuric acid; it was first used on an industrial scale 1875. |
| **1834** | Justus von Liebig developed melamine. |
| **1835** | Tetrachloroethene (vinyl chloride) was first prepared. |
| **1850** | Ammonia was first produced from coal gas. |
| **1855** | A technique was patented for the production of cellulose nitrate (nitrocellulose) fibres, the first artificial fibres. |
| **1856** | Henry Bessemer developed the Bessemer converter for the production of steel. |
| **1857** | William Henry Perkin set up the first synthetic-dye factory. |
| **1861** | Ernest Solvay patented a method for the production of sodium carbonate from sodium chloride and ammonia; the first production plant was established 1863. |
| **1862** | Alexander Parkes produced the first known synthetic plastic (Parkesine, or xylonite) from cellulose nitrate, vegetable oils, and camphor; it was the forerunner of celluloid. |
| **1864** | William Siemens and Pierre Emile Martin developed the Siemens–Martin process (open-hearth method) for the production of steel. |
| **1868** | Henry Deacon invented the Deacon process for the production of chlorine by the catalytic oxidation of hydrogen chloride. |
| **1869** | Celluloid was first produced from cellulose nitrate and camphor. |
| **1880** | The first laboratory preparation of polyacrylic substances. |
| **1886** | Charles M Hall and Paul-Louis-Toussaint Héroult developed, independently of each other, a method for producing aluminium by the electrolysis of aluminium oxide. |
| **1891** | Rayon was invented. Herman Frasch patented the Frasch process for the recovery of sulphur from underground deposits. Lindemann produced the first epoxy resins. |
| **1894** | Carl Kellner and Hamilton Castner developed, independently of each other, a method for the production of sodium hydroxide by the electrolysis of brine. |
| **1895** | The Thermit reaction for the reduction of metallic oxides to their molten metals was developed by Johann Goldschmidt. |
| **1902** | Friedrich Wilhelm Ostwald patented a process for the production of nitric acid by the catalytic oxidation of ammonia. |
| **1908** | Fritz Haber invented the Haber process for the production of ammonia from nitrogen and hydrogen. Heike Kamerlingh-Onnes prepared liquid helium. |
| **1909** | The first totally synthetic plastic (Bakelite) was produced by Leo Baekeland. |
| **1912** | I Ostromislensky patented the use of plasticizers in the manufacture of plastic, rendering the product (PVC) mouldable. |
| **1913** | The thermal cracking of petroleum was established. |
| **1919** | Elwood Haynes patented non-rusting stainless steel. |
| **1927** | The commercial production of polyacrylic polymers began. |
| **1930** | Freons were first prepared and used in refrigeration plants. William Chalmers produced the polymer of methyl methacrylate (later marketed as Perspex). |
| **1933** | E W Fawcett and R O Gibson first produced polyethylene. |
| **1935** | The catalytic cracking of petroleum was introduced. Triacetate film (used as base for photographic film) was developed. |
| **1937** | Wallace Carothers invented nylon; polyurethanes were first produced. |
| **1938** | Roy Plunkett first produced polytetrafluoroethene (PTFE, marketed as Teflon). |
| **1943** | The industrial production of silicones was initiated. |
| **1941** | J R Whinfield invented Terylene. |
| **1955** | Artificial diamonds were first produced. |
| **1959** | The Du Pont company developed Lycra. |
| **1963** | Leslie Phillips and co-workers at the Royal Aircraft Establishment, Farnborough invented carbon fibre. |
| **1980** | Japanese company Nippon Oil patented the use of methyl-tert-butyl ether (MTBE) as a lead-free antiknock additive to petrol. |
| **1984** | About 2,500 people died in Bhopal, central India when poisonous methyl isocyanate gas escaped from a chemical plant owned by US company Union Carbide. |
| **1990** | ICI began production of the hydrofluorocarbon Klea 134a, a substitute for CFCs in refrigerators and air-conditioning systems. |

# ARTEFACTS AND PROCESSES

**adhesive** substance that sticks two surfaces together. Natural adhesives (glues) include gelatin in its crude industrial form (made from bones, hide fragments, and fish offal) and vegetable gums. Synthetic adhesives include thermoplastic and thermosetting resins, which are often stronger than the substances they join; mixtures of epoxy resin and hardener that set by chemical reaction; and elastomeric (stretching) adhesives for flexible joints. Superglues are fast-setting adhesives used in very small quantities.

**alloy** metal blended with some other metallic or nonmetallic substance to give it special qualities, such as resistance to corrosion, greater hardness, or tensile strength. Useful alloys include bronze, brass, cupronickel, duralumin, German silver, gunmetal, pewter, solder, steel, and stainless steel. The most recent alloys include the superplastics: alloys that can stretch 100% at specific temperatures, permitting, for example, their injection into moulds as easily as plastic.

**anode** the positive electrode of an electrolytic cell, towards which negative particles (anions), usually in solution, are attracted.

**battery** any energy-storage device allowing release of electricity on demand. It is made up of one or more electrical cells.

**brewing** the making of beer, ale, or other alcoholic beverage from malt and barley by steeping (mashing), boiling, and fermenting. Mashing the barley releases its sugars. Yeast is then added, which contains the enzymes needed to convert the sugars into ethanol (alcohol) and carbon dioxide. Hops are added to give a bitter taste.

**cathode** the negative electrode of an electrolytic cell, towards which positive particles (cations), usually in solution, are attracted.

**chromatography** technique used for separating the components of a mixture. This is brought about by means of two immiscible substances, one of which (the *mobile phase*) transports the sample mixture through the other (the stationary phase). The mobile phase may be a gas or a liquid; the stationary phase may be a liquid or a solid, and may be in a column, on paper, or in a thin layer on a glass or plastic support. The components of the mixture are adsorbed or impeded by the stationary phase to different extents and therefore become separated.

**cracking** reaction where a large alkane molecule is broken down by heat into a smaller alkane and a small alkene molecule. The reaction is carried out at a high temperature (600°C or higher) and often in the presence of a catalyst. It is the main method of preparation of alkenes and is also used to manufacture

petrol from the higher-boiling-point fractions obtained from the fractional distillation (fractionation) of crude oil.

**detergent** surface-active cleansing agent. The common detergents are made from hydrocarbons and sulphuric acid, and their long-chain molecules have a type of structure similar to that of soap molecules: a salt group at one end attached to a long hydrocarbon 'tail'. They have the advantage over soap in that they do not produce scum by forming insoluble salts with the calcium and magnesium ions present in hard water.

**distillation** technique used to purify liquids or to separate mixtures of liquids possessing different boiling points.

**fermentation** the breakdown of sugars by bacteria and yeasts using a method of respiration without oxygen (anaerobic). Fermentation processes have long been utilized in baking bread, making beer and wine, and producing cheese, yoghurt, soy sauce, and many other foodstuffs.

**indicator** chemical compound that changes its structure and colour in response to its environment. The commonest chemical indicators detect changes in pH (for example, litmus), or in the oxidation state of a system (redox indicators).

**litmus** dye obtained from various lichens and used in chemistry as an indicator to test the acidic or alkaline nature of aqueous solutions; it turns red in the presence of acid, and blue in the presence of alkali.

**soap** a mixture of the sodium salts of various fatty acids: palmitic, stearic, and oleic acid. It is made by the action of sodium hydroxide (caustic soda) or potassium hydroxide (caustic potash) on fats of animal or vegetable origin. Soap makes grease and dirt disperse in water in a similar manner to a detergent.

**universal indicator** a mixture of pH indicators, used to gauge the acidity or alkalinity of a solution. Each component changes colour at a different pH value, and so the indicator is capable of displaying a range of colours, according to the pH of the test solution, from red (at pH1) to purple (at pH13).

---

**Chemical formulae**

*Hera are a few common chemical formulae you might come across in everyday life. Do you know what they are otherwise known as? For example, what is H2O?*

| | |
|---|---|
| Correct - Water | 79 |
| Other answers | 3 |
| Don't know | 18 |
| And CO2? | |
| Correct - Carbon dioxide | 47 |
| Other answers | 17 |
| Don't know | 36 |

---

# HOW COMPUTERS WORK

Despite their impressive capabilities, computers are really only able to perform the simplest of tasks: adding or multiplying two numbers together; determining whether one number is higher than another; and so on. It is their ability to perform these tasks extremely quickly and in a predefined sequence that gives them their apparent power.

At the heart of the computer is a *CPU* (central processing unit). The CPU is built around an *arithmetic and logic unit* (ALU) which performs all the basic computations. It includes a set of registers that provide limited storage for immediate data and results. The whole thing is coordinated by an internal *clock*.

The CPU is supported by *memory*. This is used to store large amounts of data, as well as programs (instructions). There are two main types of memory. *Internal memory* is readily available to the CPU. It can be accessed very quickly, but its contents are lost when the power is removed. *External memory* is used for longer-term storage. It is usually in the form of a physical device such as a tape or disc. These generally provide a higher capacity than internal memory, but are considerably slower. The CPU cannot access external memory directly, so data has to be transferred to internal memory before it can be used.

The CPU communicates with external devices by means of a *bus*. This carries data between the various types of memory, and also to and from the *ports*, to which peripherals such as keyboards, screens, and printers are attached.

## Programming

Computers have no intelligence of their own. They work by carrying out the detailed instructions provided by a programmer. The programmer's job is to break down the required task into a series of simple steps.

Programs are written in a *programming language*, designed for the convenience of the programmer. They are then translated into *machine code*, which the computer can execute. The translation is itself done by the computer, using a special program called a *compiler* (which performs the translation before the program is run) or an *interpreter* (which translates each part of the program as it is being executed).

## Types of computer

There are four main classes of computer, corresponding roughly to memory capacity and processing speed. *Microcomputers* (also called *personal computers* or *PCs*) are the smallest and least expensive. They are widely used in the home, in schools, and in businesses of all sizes. *Minicomputers* are generally larger, and are found in universities and larger companies. They often support up to a hundred simultaneous users. *Mainframes* support many hundreds of simultaneous users and have very large storage capacities. They are found in large organizations such as banks and government departments. *Supercomputers* are the most powerful of all. There are few of them in the world, and they are used for specialized scientific tasks such as nuclear research and weather forecasting.

Computers are also classified by *generation*. The first generation of computers was developed in the 1940s and 1950s, and made from valves and wire circuits. Second-generation computers, emerging in the early 1960s, incorporated transistors and printed circuits. The third generation, from the late 1960s to the present, used integrated circuits. Fourth-generation computers are the most commonly used today, and are based on microprocessors and large-scale integrations. Finally, a fifth generation is emerging, using very large-scale integration (VLSI) and parallel processors.

# COMPUTER HARDWARE

**disc** the commonest type of external storage, used for storing large volumes of data. A magnetic disc is rotated at high speed in a disc-drive unit as a read/write (playback or record) head passes over its surfaces to 'read' the magnetic variations that encode the data. *Floppy discs* are the least expensive type. They typically hold between 360 kilobytes and 1.4 megabytes, and are small and light enough to be sent through the post. *Hard discs* are much faster and have higher capacities, sometimes hundreds of megabytes. They are permanently housed in a sealed case. Recently, optical *compact discs* have emerged as an alternative to magnetic discs. They use a laser beam to read data encoded as tiny pits on the disc's surface. They have enormous capacities (sometimes over a billion bytes) but cannot always be written directly by the computer.

**graphics tablet** or *bit pad* input device in which

| THE WORLD'S TOP COMPUTER MAKERS | | |
|---|---|---|
| | Computer sales 1989, $ bn | Net liquid assets latest, $ bn |
| IBM | 57.3 | 14.2 |
| Digital Equipment | 12.9 | 4.3 |
| Fujitsu | 12.3 | 2.7 |
| NEC | 11.5 | 2.1 |
| Unisys | 9.3 | 1.5 |
| Hitachi | 9.3 | 15.6 |
| Hewlett-Packard | 8.2 | 2.0 |
| Groupe Bull | 6.5 | 0.7 |
| Apple Computer | 5.4 | 1.4 |
| NCR | 5.2 | 0.9 |
| Olivetti | 4.9 | 5.9 |
| Siemens | 4.7 | 23.6 |
| Toshiba | 4.6 | 5.1 |
| Compaq | 2.9 | 0.7 |
| Matsushita | 2.8 | 15.1 |
| Source: The Economist | | |

## JAPAN TAKES TO FUZZY LOGIC

Fuzzy is now a key marketing word in Japan, where firms are starting to exploit 'fuzzy logic' control circuitry in computerized products. Matsushita, National, Mitsubishi, Sanyo, Sharp, Sony, and others are breaking sales records with fuzzy video cameras, vacuum cleaners, TV sets, toasters, fridges, microwave ovens, air conditioners and other consumer goods.

A fuzzy TV set can increase picture brightness as the room gets darker, and turn up the sound when people sit farther from the set. Sony's XBR can even adjust colour quality by comparing the broadcast picture with a set of 40 'perfect' pictures held in memory.

Matsushita's Aisaigo Day Fuzzy vacuum cleaner (Aisaigo means 'beloved wife') has sensors. It knows when it moves from carpet to parquet and varies the suction to suit. Matsushita also sells a fuzzy washing machine with sensors. It considers the type and amount of washing, detergent and dirt before selecting from hundreds of different wash cycles. Most people find it hard to choose from 10 options on old-fashioned electronic machines, but fuzzy logic copes easily with 600. The same firm's Panasonic NV-S1 video camcorder reduces the 'jitter' from camera-shake by storing images and analysing them. It detects tiny shifts due to unsteady hands and uses an earlier image to smooth out the picture.

Fuzzy logic is a term coined 1965 by Lotfi Zadeh, of the University of California at Berkeley, although the core concepts go back to the work of a Polish mathematician, Jan Lukasiewicz, in the 1920s.

Zadeh was dealing with concepts that cannot be precisely defined in mathematical terms, such as height and beautiful. A 6ft male may be tall or short, depending on whether he is shopping in a Malaysian street market or playing for a US basketball team. Age is another indeterminate concept. A computer program might classify people as young if they are 29.99 years old and middle-aged when they become 30. Real life doesn't have the neat divisions of binary (yes/no, black/white) computer logic.

Fuzzy logic allows objects to be members of contradictory sets. There is only a greater probability that something belongs to one set rather than another. Thus a glass of water may have an 80% chance of being described as hot, depending on room temperature, and whether you're going to wash in it or make tea with it.

Fuzzy logic captured the Japanese imagination in 1988 with the opening of an underground railway in Sendai, 200 miles north of Tokyo. The driverless trains are controlled by a predictive fuzzy-logic-based expert system developed by Seiji Yasunobu at Hitachi. This gives such a smooth ride that strap-hanging is, apparently, a thing of the past.

Toshiba's voice-controlled lift system has a fuzzy prediction and control program which works out how long people have been waiting, and favours those who have been stuck for a minute or more. With eight lifts, the average waiting time is 10 to 15 % less; the number of times you wait more than a minute is cut by 30 to 40%.

Mitsubishi's Beaver Warp Inverter Air Conditioner maintains constant air temperatures using 50 fuzzy rules instead of arbitrary thresholds. By avoiding the rapid on-off cycles produced by simple thermostatic controls, it uses 24% less energy than traditional systems. And, of course, it knows it should warm or cool the air quicker when people are about than if the room is empty.

The Japanese think fuzzy logic is a core technology for the 21st century. In 1988 the Ministry of International Trade and Industry set up the Laboratory for International Fuzzy Engineering (LIFE), with $70 million to fund five years' research. LIFE's 50 members include many leading Japanese firms such as Fujitsu, Honda, IBM Japan, Mazda, NEC, Nippon Steel, Sony, and Toshiba. The value of Japan's fuzzy logic research and development has been estimated at $500 million a year.

Many US mathematicians scoffed at Zadeh's theories, saying fuzzy concepts could be represented using conventional maths. Only a few took his ideas seriously. These included scientists at AT&T's Bell Labs who, in 1985, demonstrated the first micro-processor designed to handle fuzzy logic.

The situation is not without precedent. Western manufacturers ignored the earlier work of US mathematician W. Edwards Deming, on statistical quality control. The Japanese used his ideas to become the world's leading producers of consumer goods—as Deming predicted they would. Applying Zadeh's ideas could have equally dramatic effects.

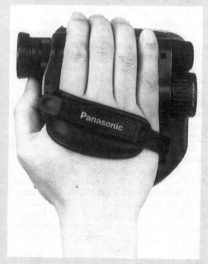

*Fuzzy logic is responsible for reducing camera-shake in Panasonic's camcorder.*

| | Sales (m) | % |
|---|---|---|
| IBM | 495.9 | 27.2 |
| Compaq | 451.5 | 24.8 |
| Apple | 140.5 | 7.7 |
| Toshiba | 123.0 | 6.7 |
| Tandon | 84.9 | 4.7 |
| Apricot | 65.3 | 3.6 |
| Amstrad | 49.4 | 2.7 |
| Victor | 45.9 | 2.5 |
| Olivetti | 44.2 | 2.4 |
| Tulip | 34.6 | 1.9 |
| ICL | 32.5 | 1.8 |
| Epson | 24.9 | 1.4 |
| Arche | 15.1 | 0.8 |
| Commodore | 14.9 | 0.8 |
| Opus | 11.5 | 0.6 |
| Tandy | 5.3 | 0.3 |
| Others | 183.0 | 10.0 |
| *Total* | *1,822.6* | *100.0* |

\* 12 months to September *Source: EIV Retail Business No 399*

a stylus or cursor is moved by hand over a flat surface. The computer can keep track of the position of the stylus, so enabling the operator to input drawings or diagrams.

**joystick** an input device that signals to a computer the direction and extent of displacement of a hand-held lever. It is similar to the joystick used to control the flight of an aircraft.

**keyboard** the commonest input device, used by the operator to input data and instructions into the computer. It resembles a typewriter keyboard but with additional keys. Most keyboards have a separate numeric keypad (like a calculator) as well as special keys for controlling the cursor and performing predefined functions (such as calling up a help screen).

**light pen** an input device resembling an ordinary pen, used to indicate locations on a computer screen. With certain computer-aided design (CAD) programs, the light pen can be used to instruct the computer to change the shape, size, position, and colours of sections of a screen image.

**memory** the part of the system used to store data and programs. *RAM* (random-access memory) is the type most commonly used for internal memory. It is made of a collection of integrated circuits (chips). It can be both read from and written to by the computer, but its contents are lost when the power is removed. By contrast, *ROM* (read-only memory) cannot be altered by the computer, and its contents are retained when the machine is switched off. It is used to hold data and programs that will rarely or never need altering, such as the computer's operating system. External memory devices include discs and magnetic tape.

**modem** (*mo*dulator-*dem*odulator) device that enables computers to send and receive data over a telephone line. It converts digital signals to analogue and back again.

**mouse** input device used to control a pointer on the screen. Moving the mouse across a desktop causes corresponding movement of the pointer. In this way, the operator can manipulate objects on the screen and make menu selections.

**plotter** output device for drawing pictures, diagrams, and plans. Flatbed plotters move a pen across the paper while roller plotters roll the paper past the pen as it moves from side to side.

**printer** device for producing printed copies of text and graphics. Types include *dot matrix*, which uses patterns of dots to create characters and images, the quality of which varies with the number of 'pins' in the print head (9-pin is low quality, 24-pin is much higher); *laser*, which produces very high-quality text and graphics but is more expensive to operate; and *ink-jet*, which produces a quality approaching that of the laser printer.

**screen** or *monitor* output device on which the computer displays information for the benefit of the operator. The commonest type is the *cathode-ray tube* (CRT), which is similar to a television screen. Portable computers often use *liquid crystal display* (LCD) screens. These are harder to read than CRTs, but require less power, making them suitable for battery operation.

**touch screen** an input device allowing the user to communicate with the computer by touching a display screen with a finger. In this way, the user can point to a required menu option or item of data. Touch screens are used less widely than other pointing devices such as the joystick or mouse.

**VDU** (visual display unit) single device incorporating a keyboard and screen. They are frequently used with mainframes and minicomputers, but less so with personal computers.

# USES OF COMPUTERS

**artificial intelligence** (AI) the creation of computer programs that can perform actions comparable with those of an intelligent human. Current AI research covers areas such as planning (for robot behaviour), language understanding, pattern recognition, and knowledge representation.

**CAD (computer-aided design)** the use of computers for creating and editing design drawings. CAD is widely used in architecture, electronics, and engineering; for example, in the motor industry, where it is used to assist in designing cars.

**CAL (computer-assisted learning)** the use of computers in education and training, where the computer displays instructional material to a student and asks questions about the information given. The student's answers determine the sequence of the lessons.

**CAM (computer-aided manufacture)** the use of computers to control production processes—in

**Computer hardware**

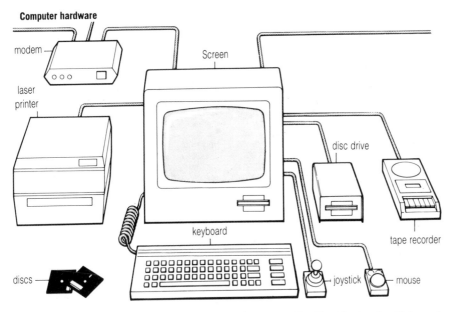

particular, machine tools and robots.

**computer game** or **video game** a computer-controlled game in which the computer (usually) opposes the human player. Computer games typically employ fast, animated graphics and synthesized sound.

**computer graphics** the use of computers to display and manipulate information in pictorial form. The output may be as simple as a pie chart, or as complex as an animated sequence in a science-fiction film, or a seemingly three-dimensional engineering blueprint. Input may be achieved by drawing with a mouse or stylus on a graphics tablet, or by drawing directly on to the screen with a light pen. Computer graphics are increasingly used in computer-aided design (CAD), and to generate models and simulations in engineering, meteorology, medicine and surgery, and other fields of science.

**databases and record-keeping systems** many computer applications involve some form of structured data storage, or database. For example, an accounting system might be built around a database containing details of customers and suppliers. In larger computers, the database is organized in such a way that it is available to any program that needs it, without the programs needing to be aware of how the data are actually stored. The term database is also sometimes used for simple record-keeping systems, such as mailing lists, in which there are facilities for searching, sorting, and producing reports.

**desktop publishing (DTP)** small-scale typesetting and page make-up. DTP programs can produce originals, containing text and graphics, with text set in different typefaces and sizes. The pages can be previewed on the screen before final printing on a laser printer.

**electronic mail** or **E-mail** system in which people use computers to send messages to each other. Messages are stored in 'mailboxes' in a computer until the recipient is ready to read them. There are several large public systems, such as British Telecom's Dialcom, which have many thousands of subscribers.

**expert system** program for giving advice, such as diagnosing an illness or interpreting the law, based on knowledge derived from a human expert.

**point-of-sale system** system that records purchases in shops, typically operating through computerized cash registers. Point-of-sale systems are often used for the automatic updating of stock figures, and for transferring money from the shopper's bank account to the shop's.

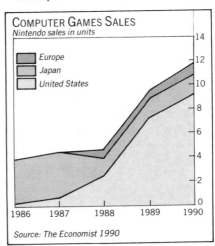

COMPUTER GAMES SALES
Nintendo sales in units

Source: The Economist 1990

## VIRTUAL REALITY—A WORLD OF DIFFERENCE

Virtual reality (VR) is all about creating and experiencing imaginary worlds that are constructed inside computers. This world is sometimes known as Cyberspace, a term popularized by the 'cyberpunk' novels of science-fiction writer William Gibson. It depends on new technology, but the idea is as old as entertainment.

Anyone who becomes 'lost in a book' has mentally entered an imaginary, fictional world created by the words of the author. The theatre and cinema similarly fabricate 'virtual worlds' where we suspend our disbelief. VR is just the latest step down a very long road. Where it differs from earlier approaches is that it offers unprecedented interaction. Instead of merely reading the words or watching the action on the stage, you become part of it.

The pioneering work in the VR business was done by those who developed realistic flight simulators for pilot training, and the 'head up displays' that provided fighter pilots with information by projecting it on to the visors of their helmets. Such developments consumed vast military budgets. Today's VR practitioners are generally more interested in creating imaginary worlds or alternate realities.

VR systems typically include a head-set or helmet, position detectors, and some sort of control device. Computer-generated stereo images are supplied to small TV sets mounted inside the VR helmet, which has thick correcting lenses to make the view appear to be at infinity. If you turn to your left, for example, this is detected by magnetic position sensors, and the computer generates the appropriate view. This is just computer graphics. Computer-generated sounds can be added if the helmet includes a pair of earphones. A control device allows the user to move around inside the virtual world. If the VR world is, say, a flight simulation, this might be a simple joystick. More sophisticated control is provided by a data glove, which has

fibre-optic cables running up and down the backs of the fingers. This can feed gestures back to the computer. For example, snapping your fingers might summon up a menu from which you could select alternatives, such as switching to a different virtual world. Virtual worlds are, at the moment, primitive and confusing, and moving within them is difficult. But what is now primitive was, ten years ago, impossible, and in another ten years VR may be extremely sophisticated. High-definition images may even be written directly on the retina of the eye using microlasers.

Virtual reality has many uses and even more potential. It can enable people to 'walk around' inside a proposed new building while it is still on the drawing board. It lets scientists fly over the surface of Mars. Using computer networks, people can meet and talk in virtual reality even if they are physically far from one another. Chemists can enter a virtual world and construct new molecules by picking up atoms and sticking them together. Some commercial games arcades have already opened, where people can sit inside a VR machine and fly high-speed fighters in combat or drive battle tanks. Virtual reality can also be used to convert vast quantities of business data into instantly comprehensible form. It should be much easier to spot stock shortages by flying through a virtual warehouse than by reading columns of numbers.

Nowadays almost everything in the Western world is planned, designed, listed, stored or traded as computer data at some stage in its life. US writer John Barlow provides a telling example to doubting Thomases: 'Cyberspace is where your money is right now,' he says. 'It's just bytes, sloshing around in the datasphere.' Making the 'datasphere' inhabitable is what virtual reality might ultimately be about.

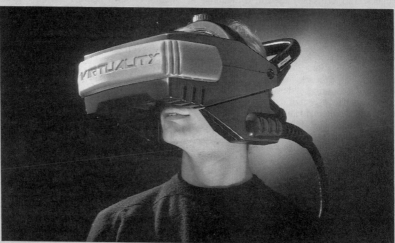

*The virtual reality helmet allows its wearer to enter an imaginary world.*

# CLIENT-SERVER COMPUTING: THE FUTURE IS OPEN SYSTEMS

The next decade in computing will see changes just as dramatic as the last one, if not more so. In 1980, before the launch of the IBM PC, few people were aware that microcomputers were going to sweep the world, selling in tens of millions. Today, another dramatic change is beginning. It is a change that is turning the traditional world of computing upside down. It is the move to open systems and client/server computing.

Old-style computing was centralized, hierarchical and proprietary. The mainframe was at the centre, with minicomputers added to provide departmental computing, and—later—PCs to provide personal computing. The mainframe was the master and other machines were slaves. Most computers were incompatible with one another, even if they were all made by the same company.

New-style computing is open, distributed, and has only two levels—clients and servers—instead of three or more. It is based on multi-vendor peer-to-peer networks where every system has to be able to communicate with others. Client workstations are the ones people use, while servers provide services.

Client workstations can include almost any type of microcomputer or engineering workstation, intelligent terminals, and devices such as cash machines (automated tellers) and computer-controlled traffic lights. Servers can include any computer that runs a multi-tasking operating system, and general-purpose computers including minis and mainframes. However, servers will quickly become dedicated machines—print servers, file servers, communications servers, and so on. A specialized machine will almost always do the job better and cheaper than a general-purpose model.

The idea is that any workstation should be able to request a job and have it done by an appropriate machine. If this is accepted, the old master–slave relationship is overturned. Servers are servants: large computers exist to serve small ones.

The change to client/server systems is not simply technical, but cultural and financial. Centralized, hierarchical systems grew up when computing was a back-office activity, designed to make tasks such as payroll, stock control and invoicing more efficient. Now the focus has moved to the use of computer power as a front-office activity for gaining a competitive edge by giving the customer a better service. Information must be delivered at the point of sale—to the cash machine, the till, the travel agent's counter, the betting shop, or to the insurance agent with a laptop PC—for processing. In the 1980s, salespeople made phone calls because there wasn't time to send a letter. In the 1990s, they have to have the data on-line, right now, because there isn't time to make a phone call. Customers don't want to wait.

Distributed networks are needed to put the computer power where it is needed. Luckily these may be cheaper to install and are cheaper to run than centralized systems: partly this is because they often make use of the 'economies of small' provided by microprocessors, which offer better price/performance ratios than traditional systems, and partly because staff, software maintenance, and communications costs are lower.

Open systems are a requirement because no company, and no computer user, is an island. Once, companies could manage with proprietary computers because no one else was bothered about their stock control system. But already, large firms are starting to send out orders and receive payments on-line using EDI (electronic data interchange) networks. Communications with government and the European Community will follow.

Since suppliers, customers, and governments inevitably have different types of computer, the only choice is for everyone to follow an internationally agreed set of standards. These standards are being developed via the International Standards Organization (ISO) under the banner of OSI, or open systems interconnection. Governments and large firms are already major backers of OSI. Small firms will have to follow or see their business disappear.

All-pervasive data networks have so far been mainly the stuff of science fiction, some of it utopian and some of it distinctly unpleasant. Building these networks is going to be as significant as the building of road, rail and telephone networks were to previous generations. The process is well under way. The only curious thing is that so few people are aware of it, or bothered about it.

---

**simulation** the representation of real-life situations in a computer program. For example, the program might simulate traffic flow to assist planners to decide the effect of changes to road layouts.

**speech recognition** techniques whereby a computer can understand ordinary speech. Spoken words are divided into 'frames', each lasting about one-thirtieth of a second, which are converted to a wave form. These are then compared with a series of stored frames to determine the most likely word. Research into speech recognition started in 1938, but the technology became sufficiently developed for commercial applications only in the late 1980s.

**spreadsheet** program that mimics a sheet of ruled paper, divided into columns and rows. The user enters values in the sheet, then instructs the program to perform some operation on them, such as totalling a column or finding the average of a series of numbers. Highly complex numerical analyses can be built up from these simple steps. Spreadsheets are widely used for bookkeeping, forecasting, financial control, analysing results of experiments, and so on.

---

### COMPUTER FRAUD IN THE UK

Computer fraud accounted for a total of £133,556 stolen from six government departments between 1986 and 1990, according to a report from the National Audit Office. Although the evidence of fraud and abuse is small, the risks are high, with transactions totalling more than £300 billion being processed on government computers each year. Despite some degree of progress over the past few years there remains much to be done to improve the government's computer security procedures. The weakest link in the computer security chain is the people who use the system.

Statistics for financial fraud in general increased to £434 million from Jan to Oct 1990 (only £86 million of this was money obtained, the rest attempted). A large chunk of this was clearly computer-related, if not strictly computer crime. The UK government's Audit Commission put computer fraud at £2.56 million in its last (1987) report. But the report is voluntary and the UK clearing banks have not responded to attempts to get them to take part in three-yearly surveys. As banks in the UK (and Europe generally) do not have to report computer crime to the police to claim on their insurance and are under no legal requirement to report computer crimes per se to their regulators, computer crime figures are notoriously unreliable.

---

**word processing** the use of a program that allows the operator to type text into the computer memory, and then to retrieve it, alter it, and manipulate it in various ways before finally printing it on paper. Word processing is often used to speed up the typing of successive drafts of a long document and for creating large numbers of personalized letters. Many word processors include facilities for checking spellings, looking up synonyms, and adding graphics to the text.

# TERMS

**ASCII** (acronym from *A*merican *s*tandard *c*ode for *i*nformation *i*nterchange ) a coding system in which numbers (between 0 and 127) are assigned to letters, digits, and punctuation symbols. For example, 45 represents a hyphen and 65 a capital A. The first 32 codes are used for control functions, such as carriage return and backspace. Strictly speaking, ASCII is a seven-bit code, but an eighth bit (binary digit) is often used to provide parity or to allow for extra characters. The system is widely used for the storage of text and for the transmission of data between computers. Although computers work in binary code, ASCII numbers

are usually quoted as decimal or hexadecimal numbers.

**binary number system** or *binary number code* system of numbers to base two, using combinations of the digits 1 and 0. Binary numbers play a key role in digital computers, in which they form the basis of the internal coding of information, the values of bits (short for 'binary digits') being represented as on/off (1 and 0) states of switches and high/low voltages in circuits.

**bit** the smallest unit of information; a binary digit or place in a binary number. A byte contains 8 bits.

**boot** or *bootstrap* the process of starting up the computer. Most computers have a small, built-in program whose only job is to load a slightly larger program, usually from a disc, which in turn loads the main operating system.

**buffer** part of the memory used to hold data while it is waiting to be used. For example, a program might store data in a printer buffer until the printer is ready to print it.

**byte** a basic unit of storage of information. A byte contains 8 bits and can hold either a single character (letter, digit, or punctuation symbol) or a number between 0 and 255. Not all computers use bytes, although the unit is widely used in microcomputers.

**chip** alternative term for *integrated circuit*, a complete electronic circuit on a slice of silicon (or other semiconductor) crystal only a few millimetres square.

**client-server architecture** a system in which the mechanics of storing data are separated from the programs that use the data. For example, the 'server' might be a central database, typically located on a large computer that is reserved for this purpose. The 'client' would be an ordinary program that requests data from the server as needed.

**data** facts, figures, and symbols stored in computers. The term is often used to mean raw, unprocessed facts, as distinct from information, to which a meaning or interpretation has been applied.

**data compression** techniques for reducing the amount of storage needed for a given amount of data. They include word tokenization (in which frequently used words are stored as shorter codes), variable bit lengths (in which common characters are represented by fewer bits than less common ones), and run-length encoding (in which a repeated value is stored once along with a count).

**DOS** (acronym from *d*isc *o*perating *s*ystem) an operating system specifically designed for use with disc storage; also used as an alternative name for a particular operating system, MS-DOS.

**function** a small part of a program that supplies a specific value; for example, the square root of a specified number, or the current date. Most programming languages incorporate a number of built-in functions; some allow programmers to write their own. A function may have one or more arguments (the values on which the

## NUMBER SYSTEMS

| Binary<br>(base 2) | Octal<br>(base 8) | Decimal<br>(base 10) | Hexadecimal<br>(base 16) |
|---|---|---|---|
| 0 | 0 | 0 | 0 |
| 1 | 1 | 1 | 1 |
| 10 | 2 | 2 | 2 |
| 11 | 3 | 3 | 3 |
| 100 | 4 | 4 | 4 |
| 101 | 5 | 5 | 5 |
| 110 | 6 | 6 | 6 |
| 111 | 7 | 7 | 7 |
| 1000 | 10 | 8 | 8 |
| 1001 | 11 | 9 | 9 |
| 1010 | 12 | 10 | A |
| 1011 | 13 | 11 | B |
| 1100 | 14 | 12 | C |
| 1101 | 15 | 13 | D |
| 1110 | 16 | 14 | E |
| 1111 | 17 | 15 | F |
| 10000 | 20 | 16 | 10 |
| 1111111 | 377 | 255 | FF |
| 11111010001 | 3721 | 2001 | 7D1 |

function operates). A **function key** on a keyboard is one which, when pressed, performs a designated task, such as ending a program.

**gigabyte** a unit of memory equal to 1,024 megabytes. It is also used, less precisely, to mean 1,000 million bytes.

**hacking** unauthorized access to a computer, either for fun or for malicious or fraudulent purposes. Hackers generally use microcomputers and telephone lines to obtain access.

**hardware** the mechanical, electrical, and electronic components of a computer system, as opposed to the various programs, which constitute software.

**hexadecimal number system** number system to the base 16. In hex (as it is commonly known) the decimal numbers 0–15 are represented by the characters 0, 1, 2, 3, 4, 5, 6, 7, 8, 9, A, B, C, D, E, F. Hexadecimal numbers are easy to convert to the computer's internal binary code and are more compact than binary numbers.

**hypertext** system for viewing information (both text and pictures) on a computer's screen in such a way that related items of information can easily be reached. For example, the program might display a map of a country; if the user points (with a mouse) to a particular city, the program displays information about that city.

**integrated circuit** or **chip** a miniaturized electronic circuit produced on a single crystal, or chip, of a semiconducting material such as silicon. It may contain more than a million transistors, resistors, and capacitors and yet measure only 5 mm/0.2 in square and 1 mm/0.04 in thick. The IC is encapsulated within a plastic or ceramic case, and linked via gold wires to metal pins with which it is connected to a printed circuit board and the other components that make up electronic

devices such as computers and calculators.

**interface** the point of contact between two programs or pieces of equipment. The term is most often used for the physical connection between the computer and a peripheral device. For example, a printer interface is the cabling and circuitry used to transfer data from the computer to the printer and to compensate for differences in speed and coding systems.

**kilobyte** (KB) a unit of memory equal to 1,024 bytes.

**laptop computer** portable microcomputer, small enough to be used on the operator's lap. It consists of a single unit, incorporating a keyboard, floppy disc or hard disc drives, and a screen. The screen often forms a lid that folds back in use. It uses a liquid crystal or gas plasma display, rather than the bulkier and heavier cathode ray tubes found in most VDUs. A typical laptop computer measures about 360 mm × 380 mm × 100 mm, and weighs 3–7 kg.

**macro** in programming, a new command created by combining a number of existing ones. For example, if the language has separate commands for obtaining data from the keyboard and for displaying data on the screen, the programmer might create a macro that performs both these tasks with one command. A **macro key** is a key on the keyboard that combines the effects of several individual key presses.

**megabyte** a unit of memory equal to 1,024 kilobytes. It is also used, less precisely, to mean 1 million bytes.

**microprocessor** a computer's central processing unit (CPU) contained on a single integrated circuit. The appearance of the first microprocessors in 1971 heralded the introduction of the microcomputer. The microprocessor has led to a dramatic fall in the size and cost of

---

### POLL ON COMPUTER HACKING

*Has your company got a policy on computer security?*
Yes 73      No 21      Don't know 6

*And do you have a policy for the protection of your data against computer hackers?*
Yes 70      No 27      Don't know 3

*Do you believe computer hacking could happen to your own company?*
Yes 65      No 34      Don't know 1

*Do you intend to take any further steps towards obtaining greater protection from computer hackers?*
Yes 49      No 51      Don't know —

UK companies are still alarmingly complacent about the dangers of dependence on computer technology, according to the results of a Gallup survey. For example, most respondents acknowledge 'hacking' (unauthorized access to computer systems) as a significant threat, yet almost a third of managers questioned admitted that they had no clear defence policy against hackers. Six per cent said they did not know whether their companies operated a security policy.

---

COMPUTING: CHRONOLOGY

| | |
|---|---|
| 1614 | Scottish mathematician John Napier invented logarithms. |
| 1625 | William Oughtred (1575–1660) invented the slide rule. |
| 1623 | Wilhelm Schickard (1592–1635) invented the mechanical calculating machine. |
| 1645 | Blaise Pascal produced a calculator. |
| 1672–74 | Gottfried Wilhelm Leibniz built his first calculator, the Stepped Reckoner. |
| 1801 | Joseph-Marie Jacquard developed an automatic loom controlled by punched cards. |
| 1820 | First mass-produced calculator, the Arithmometer, invented by Charles Thomas de Colmar (1785–1870). |
| 1822 | Charles Babbage developed the difference engine, a device for calculating the values of logarithms and trigometric functions. |
| 1830s | Babbage created the first design for the analytical engine, a calculating machine capable of being driven by an external program. |
| 1890 | Herman Hollerith developed the punched-card ruler for the USA census. |
| 1936 | Alan Turing published the mathematical theory of computing. |
| 1938 | Konrad Zuse constructed the first binary calculator, using Boolean algebra. |
| 1939 | J V Atanasoff of Iowa State University became the first to use electronic means for mechanizing arithmetical operations. |
| 1943 | The Colossus electronic code-breaker was developed by Alan Turing and his team at Bletchley Park, England; the first electronic program-controlled calculator, the Harvard University Mark I (or Automatic Sequence-Controlled Calculator), was completed. |
| 1945 | ENIAC (electronic numerator, integrator, analyser and computer) was completed at the University of Pennsylvania. |
| 1948 | The first stored-program computer, the Manchester University (England) Mark I, was developed. |
| 1951 | Ferranti Mark I, the first commercially produced computer, was launched; Whirlwind, the first real-time computer, was built for the USA air-defence system; transistors began to be developed. |
| 1952 | EDVAC (electronic discrete variable computer) was completed at the Institute for Advanced Study, Princeton, USA (by John Von Neumann and others). |
| 1953 | Magnetic-core memory was developed. |
| 1957 | FORTRAN, the first high-level computer language, was developed by IBM. |
| 1958 | The first integrated circuit was produced. |
| 1963 | PDP-8, the first minicomputer, was built by Digital Equipment (DEC); the first electronic calculator was developed by the Bell Punch Company. |
| 1964 | IBM System/360, the first compatible family of computers, was launched. |
| 1965 | The first supercomputer, the Control Data CD6600, was developed. |
| 1971 | The first microprocessor, the Intel 4004, was introduced. |
| 1974 | CLIP-4, the first computer with a parallel architecture, was developed. |
| 1975 | The first personal computer, Altair 8800, was produced. |
| 1981 | The Xerox Start system, the first WIMP (windows, icons, menus and pointing devices) system, was developed . |
| 1985 | The Inmos T414 Transputer, the first 'off-the-shelf' RISC microprocessor for building parallel computers, was launched. |
| 1988 | The first optical microchip, which uses light instead of electricity, was developed. |
| 1989 | Wafer-scale silicon memory chips, able to store 200 million characters, were launched. |
| 1990 | Microsoft releases Windows 3, a windowing environment for PCs. |

---

computers and to the introduction of dedicated computers in washing machines, cars, and so on.

**MS-DOS** (abbreviation of *Microsoft Disc Operating System*) operating system produced by the Microsoft Corporation, widely used on microcomputers with 16- bit microprocessors. A version called PC-DOS is sold by IBM specifically for their range of personal computers. MS-DOS and PC-DOS are usually referred to

---

WORLDWIDE PORTABLE COMPUTER SALES

*Units in 000s*

| | 1989 | 1990 | 1991 | 1992 | 1993 | 1994 |
|---|---|---|---|---|---|---|
| US | 833 | 1,053 | 1,367 | 1,690 | 1,985 | 2,200 |
| W Europe | 480 | 650 | 950 | 1,250 | 1,550 | 1850 |
| Japan | 480 | 890 | 1,300 | 1,731 | 2,288 | 3,109 |
| Rest | 222 | 300 | 386 | 481 | 578 | 699 |
| *Total* | *2,015* | *2,892* | *4,003* | *5,152* | *6,401* | *7,858* |

Source: Financial Times

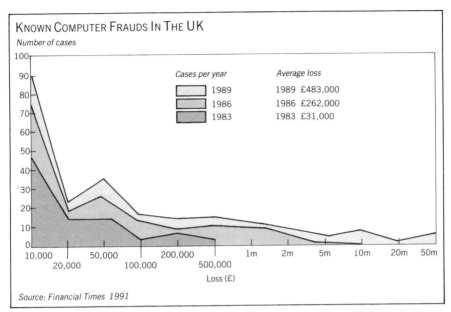

KNOWN COMPUTER FRAUDS IN THE UK

*Number of cases*

| Cases per year | Average loss |
|---|---|
| 1989 | 1989 £483,000 |
| 1986 | 1986 £262,000 |
| 1983 | 1983 £31,000 |

Loss (£)

*Source: Financial Times 1991*

as DOS. MS-DOS first appeared in the early 1980s, and was based on an earlier system for computers with 8-bit microprocessors, CP/M.

**multitasking** or **multiprogramming** a system in which one processor appears to run several different programs (or different parts of the same program) at the same time. All the programs are held in memory together and each is allowed to run for a certain period, for example while other programs are waiting for a peripheral device to work or for input from an operator. The ability to multitask depends on the operating system rather than the type of computer.

**neural network** artificial network of processors that attempts to mimic the structure of neurons in the human brain. Neural networks may be electronic, optical, or simulated by computer software. The chief characteristic of neural networks is their ability to sum up large amounts of imprecise data and decide whether they match a pattern or not. Networks of this type may be used in developing robot vision, matching fingerprints, and analysing fluctuations in stock-market prices. However, it is thought unlikely by scientists that such networks will ever be able accurately to imitate the human brain, which is very much more complicated; it contains around 10 billion neurons, whereas current artificial networks contain only a hundred or so.

**operating system** (OS) a program that controls the basic operation of a computer. A typical OS controls the peripheral devices, organizes the filing system, provides a means of communicating with the operator, and runs other programs.

**parity** the state of a number, being either even or odd. In computing, a parity bit is sometimes added to numbers to help ensure accuracy.

The bit is chosen so that the total number of 1s, including the extra bit, is always of the same parity.

**pixel** (contraction of 'picture element') a single dot on a computer screen. All screen images are made up of a collection of pixels, with each pixel being either off (dark) or on (illuminated, possibly in colour). The number of pixels available determines the screen's resolution. Typical resolutions of microcomputer screens vary from 320 × 200 pixels to 640 × 480 pixels, but screens with over 1,000 pixels are now quite common for graphic (pictorial) displays.

**procedure** a small part of a computer program, which performs a specific task, such as clearing the screen or sorting a file. In some programming languages there is an overlap between procedures, functions, and subroutines. Careful use of procedures is an element of structured programming. A *procedural language*, such as BASIC, is one in which the programmer describes a task in terms of how it is to be done, as opposed to a *declarative language*, such as PROLOG, in which it is described in terms of the required result.

**protocol** an agreed set of standards for the transfer of data between different devices. They cover transmission speed, format of data, and the signals required to synchronize the transfer.

**RISC** (acronym from *r*educed *i*nstruction-*s*et *c*omputer) a processor on a single integrated circuit, or chip, that is faster and more powerful than others in common use today. By reducing the range of operations the processor can carry out, the chips are able to optimize those operations to execute more quickly. Computers based on RISC chips became commercially available in the late 1980s, but are less widespread than traditional processors.

**software** a collection of programs and procedures

## PROGRAMMING LANGUAGES

| Language | Main Uses | Description |
| --- | --- | --- |
| assembler languages | jobs needing detailed control of the hardware, fast execution, and small program sizes | fast and efficient but require considerable effort and skill |
| BASIC (*b*eginner's *a*ll-purpose *s*ymbolic *i*nstruction *c*ode) | in education and the home, and among nonprofessional programmers, such as engineers | easy to learn; early versions lacked the features of other languages |
| C | systems programming; general programming | fast and efficient; widely used as a general-purpose language; popular among professional programmers |
| COBOL (*com*mon *b*usiness-*o*riented *l*anguage) | business programming | strongly oriented towards commercial work; easy to learn but very verbose; widely used on mainframes |
| FORTRAN (*for*mula *tran*slation) | scientific and computational work | based on mathematical formulae; popular among engineers, scientists, and mathematicians |
| LISP (*list* *p*rocessing) | artificial intelligence | symbolic language with a reputation for being hard to learn; popular in the academic and research communities |
| Modula-2 | systems and real-time programming; general programming | highly structured; intended to replace Pascal for 'real-world' applications |
| OBERON | general programming | small, compact language incorporating many of the features of PASCAL and Modula-2 |
| PASCAL (*program appliqué à la selection et la compilation automatique de la litterature*) | general-purpose language | highly structured; widely used for teaching programming in universities |
| PROLOG (*pro*gramming in *log*ic) | artificial intelligence | symbolic-logic programming system, originally intended for theorem solving but now used more generally in artificial intelligence |

for making a computer perform a specific task, as opposed to the machine and circuitry itself, known as hardware. Software is created by programmers and either distributed on a suitable medium, such as the floppy disc, or built into the computer in the form of firmware. Examples of software include operating systems, compilers, and application programs, such as payrolls. No computer can function without some form of software.

**Unix** operating system designed for minicomputers but becoming increasingly popular on large microcomputers, workstations, and supercomputers. It was developed by Bell Laboratories in the late 1960s, and is closely related to the programming language C. Its wide range of functions and flexibility have made it widely used by universities and in commercial software.

**virtual memory** a technique whereby a portion of external memory is used as an extension of internal memory. The contents of an area of RAM are stored on, say, a hard disc while they are not needed, and brought back into main memory when required. The process, known as paging or segmentation, is hidden from the programmer, to whom the computer's internal memory appears larger than it really is.

**virtual reality** advanced form of computer simulation, in which a participant has the illusion of being part of an artificial environment. The participant views the environment through two tiny 3-D television screens built into a visor. Sensors detect movements of the head

or body, causing the apparent viewing position to change. The technology is still under development.

**virus** a piece of software that can replicate itself and transfer itself from one computer to another, without the user being aware of it. Some viruses are relatively harmless, but others can damage or destroy data. They are written by anonymous programmers, often maliciously, and are spread along telephone lines or on floppy discs. Many are very difficult to eradicate.

**word** a unit of storage. The size of a word varies from one computer to another. In a popular microcomputer, it is 16 bits or 2 bytes; on many mainframes it is 32 bits.

**WYSIWYG** (acronym from *w*hat *y*ou *s*ee *i*s *w*hat *y*ou *g*et) a program that attempts to display on the screen a faithful representation of the final printed output. For example, a WYSIWYG word processor would show actual line widths, page breaks, and the sizes and styles of type.

# THE INTERIOR OF THE EARTH

**asthenosphere** a division of the Earth's structure lying beneath the lithosphere, at a depth of approximately 70 km/45 mi to 260 km/160 mi. It is thought to be the soft, partially molten layer of the mantle on which the rigid plates of the Earth's surface move to produce the motions of plate tectonics.

**bed** a single sedimentary rock unit with a distinct set of physical characteristics or contained fossils, readily distinguishable from those of beds above and below. Well-defined partings called *bedding planes* separate successive beds or strata.

**continent** any one of the large land masses of Earth, as distinct from ocean. They are Asia, Africa, North America, South America, Europe, Australia, and Antarctica. Continents are constantly moving and evolving a process known as Plate Tectonics. A continent does not end at the coastline; its boundary is the edge of the shallow continental shelf (part of the continental crust, made of sial), which may extend several hundred miles or kilometres out to sea.

**core** the innermost part of the structure of Earth. It is divided into an inner core, the upper boundary of which is 1,700 km/1,060 mi from the centre, and an outer core, 1,820 km/1,130 mi thick. Both parts are thought to consist of iron-nickel alloy, with the inner core being solid and the outer core being liquid. The temperature may be 3,000°C/5,400°F.

**craton** or *shield* the core of a continent, a vast tract of highly deformed metamorphic rock around which the continent has been built. Intense mountain-building periods shook these shield areas in Precambrian times before stable conditions set in.

**crust** the outermost part of the structure of Earth, consisting of two distinct parts, the oceanic crust and the continental crust. The *oceanic* crust is on average about 10 km/6.2 mi thick and consists mostly of basaltic types of rock. By contrast, the *continental* crust is primarily granitic in composition and more complex in its structure. Because of the movements of plate tectonics, the oceanic crust is in no place older than about 200 million years. However, parts of the continental crust are over three billion years old.

**diagenesis** or *lithification* the physical and chemical changes by which a sediment becomes a sedimentary rock. The main processes involved include compaction of the grains, and the cementing of the grains together by the growth of new minerals deposited by percolating groundwater.

**earthquake** shaking or convulsion of the Earth's surface, the scientific study of which is called seismology. Earthquakes result from a build-up of stresses within rocks until strained to fracturing point. Most occur along faults (fractures or breaks) in the Earth's crust. Plate tectonic movements generate the major proportion of all earthquakes; as two plates move past each other, they can become jammed and deformed, and earthquakes occur when they spring free. Most earthquakes happen under the sea. Their force is measured on the Richter scale.

**epicentre** the point on the Earth's surface immediately above the seismic focus of an earthquake. Most damage usually takes place at an earthquake's epicentre. The term sometimes refers to a point directly above or below a nuclear explosion ('at ground zero').

**fault** a fracture in the Earth's crust along which the two sides have moved as a result of differing strains in the adjacent rock bodies. Displacement of rock masses horizontally or vertically along a fault may be microscopic, or it may be massive, causing major earthquakes.

**fold** a bend in rock beds. If the bend is arched up in the middle it is called an *anticline*; if it sags downwards in the middle it is called a *syncline*. The line along which a bed of rock folds is called its axis. The axial plane is the plane joining the axes of successive beds.

**geochemistry** the science of chemistry as it applies to geology. It deals with the relative and absolute abundances of the chemical elements and their isotopes in the Earth, and also with the chemical changes that accompany geologic processes.

**geophysics** branch of geology using physics to study the Earth's surface, interior, and atmosphere. Studies also include winds, weather, tides, earthquakes, volcanoes, and their effects.

**geothermal energy** energy produced by the use of natural steam, subterranean hot water, and hot dry rock for heating and electricity generation. Hot water is pumped to the surface and converted to steam or run through a heat exchanger; or dry steam is directed through turbines to produce electricity.

**geyser** a natural spring that intermittently dis-

**continent**

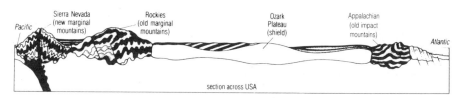

section across USA

# EARTHQUAKES: ADVANCES IN PROTECTION AND PREDICITON

1990 saw a number of earthquakes around the world, including the devastating Iranian earthquakes in June which measured 7.7 on the Richter scale and cost 50,000 lives. Earthquakes are caused by movement along faults, and so they are more frequent in regions that are known to have a great deal of fault activity — particularly areas close to the boundaries of the Earth's tectonic plates. Iran lies on the boundary between the Arabian and the Asian plates and so such an earthquake was not surprising. Other earthquakes, however, occurred in regions not known for earthquake activity, such as Missouri in the USA on 26 Sept and the Welsh Borderlands and Sheffield in the UK on 2 April and 8 Feb respectively. Research conducted at the US Geological Survey's National Earthquake Information Center in Colorado, and the US Geological Survey Seismic Observatory in Virginia suggests that a big earthquake occurring in an area not traditionally prone to earthquakes could cause much more damage than one in the more earthquake-susceptible regions such as California. Historical statistics show that a big earthquake in the central and eastern part of the continent is about two-thirds as likely as one in California over the next 30 years. East of the Rockies the continental rocks are old

*A National Center for Earthquake Engineering Research investigator at the State University of New York at Buffalo, monitors performance of a structure subjected to earthquake vibrations on the university's 'shake table'. The three-storey steel-frame structure is equipped with active tendon controls which give the model human-like ability to counter earthquake forces.*

and strong. They transmit shock waves much more efficiently. Should an earthquake disrupt them the effect will be felt over a much larger area than in the shattered faulted rocks of the west. Besides that, buildings of the east tend not to be designed with possible earthquake damage in mind. A tall building whips back and forth with the vibration of an earthquake. If the dimensions of the building are such that the speed of the whipping action happens to be 'tuned' to the vibration of the earthquake, then the whipping builds up and the building collapses. The earthquake vibration depends largely on the nature of the surface on which the foundations are set, and so nowadays the vibration characteristics of the underlying soil are taken into account before a building is designed. A design feature that is under investigation by the University of California's Earthquake Engineering Research Center in San Francisco is that of 'base isolation'. The theory is that the building is separated from its foundations by bearings or rubber joints that absorb much of the earthquake shock before it reaches the building itself. Another idea, being pursued by the National Center for Earthquake Research at the State University of New York, involves encasing the building with wire mesh covered with cement. This would prevent the wall components, like bricks or blocks, from sliding sideways in relation to one another during the shaking.

More highly technological techniques are being tried out in Japan. These involve computerized sets of sensors in the basement that analyze the earthquake's vibration and instantaneously transmit the results to pistons and counterweights throughout the building. These continually adjust the building's loading and reduce the stresses in the structure.

The science of earthquake proofing is developing swiftly, but that of earthquake prediction less so. One development is the discovery, by Stanford University, that very low frequency radio waves passing through rocks change their amplitude a few hours before an earthquake. This may be due to electrical currents generated by pressure in the rocks, or it may be related to the opening of microscopic cracks as the rocks begin to fail. Possibly related to this is the discovery by Japanese researchers that electromagnetic radiation is emitted by rocks immediately prior to an earthquake. Up to now this has not been useful, as there was no way to tell the difference between this radiation and that produced by the Earth's ionosphere or by industry. Two researchers, Takahashi and Fijinawa, have managed to distinguish the horizontal electrical fields generated by ionospheric radiation from the vertical fields produced by the rocks, and have eliminated the artificial interference by siting their instruments far from cities and industry. Since their installation in March 1989 the instruments have recorded changes in radiation several hours before earthquakes on 5, 9 and 13 July 1990.

## MAJOR 20TH-CENTURY EARTHQUAKES

| date | place | magnitude (Richter scale) | approximate number of deaths |
|------|-------|-----------|-------------|
| 1906 | San Francisco, USA | 8.3 | 3,000 |
| 1908 | Messina, Italy | 7.5 | 83,000 |
| 1915 | Avezzano, Italy | 7.5 | 29,980 |
| 1920 | Gansu, China | 8.6 | 100,000 |
| 1923 | Tokyo, Japan | 8.3 | 99,330 |
| 1927 | Nan-Shan, China | 8.3 | 200,000 |
| 1932 | Gansu, China | 7.6 | 70,000 |
| 1935 | Quetta, India | 7.5 | 30,000 |
| 1939 | Erzincan, Turkey | 7.9 | 30,000 |
| 1939 | Chillan, Chile | 8.3 | 28,000 |
| 1948 | USSR | 7.3 | 110,000 |
| 1970 | N Peru | 7.7 | 66,794 |
| 1976 | Tangshan, China | 8.2 | 242,000 |
| 1978 | NE Iran | 7.7 | 25,000 |
| 1980 | El Asnam, Algeria | 7.3 | 20,000 |
| 1988 | Armenia, USSR | 6.9 | 25,000 |
| 1990 | NW Iran | 7.7 | 50,000 |

charges an explosive column of steam and hot water into the air.

**intrusion** mass of igneous rock that has formed by 'injection' of molten rock, or magma, into existing cracks beneath the surface of the Earth, as distinct from a volcanic rock mass which has erupted from the surface. Intrusion features include vertical cylindrical structures such as stocks and necks, sheet structures such as dykes that cut across the strata and sills that push between them, and laccoliths, which are blisters that push up the overlying rock.

**lava** molten material that erupts from a volcano and cools to form extrusive igneous rock. A lava high in silica is viscous and sticky and does not flow far, wheras low-silica lava can flow for long distances.

**lithosphere** the topmost layer of the Earth's structure, forming the jigsaw of plates that take part in the movements of plate tectonics. The lithosphere comprises the crust and a portion of the upper mantle. It is regarded as being rigid and moves about on the semi-molten asthenosphere. The lithosphere is about 75 km/ 47 mi thick.

**magma** molten material beneath the Earth's surface from which igneous rocks are formed. Lava is magma that has reached the surface, losing some of its components on the way.

**mantle** the intermediate zone of the Earth between the crust and the core. It is thought to consist of silicate minerals such as olivine and spinel.

**Mercalli scale** a scale used to measure the intensity of an earthquake. It differs from the Richter scale, which measures *magnitude*. It is named after the Italian seismologist Giuseppe Mercalli (1850–1914).

**metamorphism** geological term referring to the changes in rocks of the Earth's crust caused by increasing pressure and temperature. The resulting rocks are metamorphic rocks. All metamorphic changes take place in solid rocks. If the rocks melt and then harden, they become igneous rocks.

**Mohorovičić discontinuity** also *Moho* or *M-discontinuity* boundary that separates the Earth's crust and mantle, marked by a rapid increase in the speed of earthquake waves. It follows the variations in the thickness of the crust and is found approximately 32 km/20 mi below the continents and about 10 km/6 mi below the oceans. It is named after the Yugoslav geophysicist Andrija Mohorovičić (1857–1936) who suspected its presence after analysing seismic waves from the Kulpa Valley earthquake 1909.

**petrology** branch of geology that deals with the study of rocks, their mineral compositions, and their origins.

**Richter scale** a scale based on measurement of seismic waves, used to determine the magnitude of an earthquake at the epicentre. The magnitude of an earthquake differs from the intensity, measured by the Mercalli scale, which is subjective and varies from place to place for the same earthquake.

**sial** in geochemistry and geophysics, term denoting the substance of the Earth's continental crust, as distinct from the sima of the ocean crust. The name is derived from *si*lica and *al*umina, its two main chemical constituents.

**sima** in geochemistry and geophysics, term denoting the substance of the Earth's oceanic crust, as distinct from the sial of the continental crust. The name is derived from *si*lica and *ma*gnesia, its two main chemical constituents.

**volcano** vent in the Earth's crust from which molten rock, lava, ashes, and gases are ejected. Usually it is cone-shaped with a pitlike opening at the top called the crater. Some volcanoes, for example Stromboli and Vesuvius in Italy, eject the material with explosive violence; others, for example on Hawaii, are quiet and the lava simply rises into the crater and flows over the rim.

# THE SURFACE OF THE EARTH

**abyssal zone** dark ocean area 2,000–6,000 m/ 6,500–19,500 ft deep; temperature 4°C/ 39°F. Three-quarters of the area of the deep ocean floor lies in the abyssal zone. It is too far from the surface for photosynthesis to take place. Some fish and crustaceans living there are blind or have their own light sources. The region above is the bathyal zone; the region below, the hadyal zone.

**alluvial deposit** a layer of broken rocky matter, or sediment, formed from material that has been carried in suspension by a river or stream and dropped as the velocity of the current changes. River plains and deltas are made entirely of alluvial deposits, but smaller pockets can be found in the beds of upland torrents.

**Antarctic Circle** an imaginary line that encircles the South Pole at latitude 66° 32] S. The line encompasses the continent of Antarctica and

**fold**

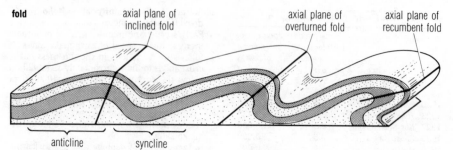

axial plane of
inclined fold

axial plane of
overturned fold

axial plane of
recumbent fold

anticline          syncline

the Antarctic Ocean.

**anticline** a fold in the rocks of the Earth's crust in which the layers or beds bulge upwards to form an arch (seldom preserved intact).

**aquifer** any rock formation containing water that can be extracted by a well. The rock of an aquifer must be porous and permeable (full of interconnected holes) so that it can absorb water.

**archipelago** a group of islands, or an area of sea containing a group of islands. The islands of an archipelago are usually volcanic in origin, and they sometimes represent the tops of peaks in areas around continental margins flooded by the sea.

**Arctic Circle** an imaginary line that encircles the North Pole at latitude 66° 32ⵏ N. Within this line there is at least one day in the summer during which the sun never sets, and at least one day in the winter during which the sun never rises.

**artesian well** a well in which water rises from its aquifer under natural pressure. Such a well may be drilled into an aquifer that is confined by impermeable beds both above and below. If the water table (the top of the region of water saturation) in that aquifer is above the level of the well head, hydrostatic pressure will force the water to the surface.

**badlands** a barren landscape cut by erosion into a maze of ravines, pinnacles, gullies and sharp-edged ridges. South Dakota and Nebraska, USA, are examples.

**caldera** a very large basin-shaped crater. Calderas are found at the tops of volcanoes, where the original peak has collapsed into an empty chamber beneath. The basin, many times larger than the original volcanic vent, may be flooded, producing a crater lake, or the flat floor may contain a number of small volcanic cones, produced by volcanic activity after the collapse.

**crater** a bowl-shaped topographic feature, usually round and with steep sides. Craters are formed by explosive events such as the eruption of a volcano or by the impact of a meteorite. A caldera is a much larger feature.

**delta** a roughly fanlike tract of land at a river's mouth, formed by deposited silt or sediment. Familiar examples of large deltas are those of the Mississippi, Ganges and Brahmaputra, Rhône, Po, Danube, and Nile; the shape of the Nile delta is like the Greek letter Δ, and thus gave rise to the name.

**desert** area without sufficient rainfall and, consequently, vegetation to support human life. Scientifically, this term includes the ice areas of the polar regions. Almost 33% of Earth's land surface is desert, and this proportion is increasing.

**dune** a mound or ridge of wind-drifted sand. Loose sand is blown and bounced along by the wind, up the windward side of a dune. The sand particles then fall to rest on the lee side, while more are blown up from the windward side. In this way a dune moves gradually downwind.

**equator** the *terrestrial equator* is the great circle whose plane is perpendicular to the Earth's axis (the line joining the poles). Its length is 40,092 km/24,901.8 mi, divided into 360 degrees of longitude. The *celestial equator* is the circle in which the plane of the Earth's equator intersects the celestial sphere.

**erosion** the processes whereby the rocks and soil of the Earth's surface are loosened, worn away, and transported (weathering does not involve transportation). There are two types, chemical and physical. *Chemical erosion* involves the alteration of the mineral component of the rock, by means of rainwater or the substances dissolved in it, and its subsequent movement. *Physical erosion* involves the breakdown and transportation of exposed rocks by physical forces. In practice the two work together.

**fjord** or *fiord* narrow sea inlet enclosed by high cliffs. Fjords are found in Norway and elsewhere. *Fiordland* is the deeply indented SW coast of South Island, New Zealand; one of the most beautiful inlets is Milford Sound.

**flood plain** the area bordering a stream or river over which water spreads in time of flood. When stream discharge exceeds channel capacity, water rises over the channel banks and floods the adjacent low-lying lands. A river flood plain can be regarded as part of its natural domain, statistically certain to be claimed by the river at repeated intervals. By plotting floods that have occurred and extrapolating from that data we can speak of ten-year floods, 100-year floods, 500-year floods, and so forth, based on the statistical probability of flooding across certain parts of the flood plain.

**glacier** a body of ice, originating in mountains in snowfields above the snowline, which traverses land surfaces (glacier flow). It moves slowly down a valley or depression, and is constantly replenished from its source. The scenery produced by the erosive action of glaciers is characteristic and includes U-shaped valleys, corries, arêtes, and various features formed by the deposition of moraine (rocky debris).

**ground water** the water formed underground in porous rock strata and soils and issuing as springs and streams. The ground-water table (or water table) is the boundary between two zones of rock or soil. Below the water table the pores are completely filled with water (called the saturated zone); above the water table is an unsaturated zone. Sandy or other kinds of beds that are filled with ground water are called aquifers. Most ground water near the surface moves slowly through the ground while the water table stays in the same place. The depth of the water table reflects the balance between the rate of infiltration, called recharge, and the rate of discharge at springs or rivers or pumped water wells. The force of gravity makes underground water run 'downhill' underground just as it does above the surface. The greater the slope and the permeability, the greater the speed. Velocities vary from 100 cm/40 in per day to 0.5 cm/0.2 in.

**International Date Line** (IDL) a modification of the 180th meridian that marks the difference in time between E and W. The date is put forward a day when crossing the line going W, and back a day when going E. The IDL was chosen at the International Meridian Conference in 1884.

**island** an area of land surrounded entirely by water. Australia is classed as a continent rather than an island, because of its size.

**landslide** a sudden downward movement of a mass of soil or rocks from a cliff or steep slope. Landslides happen when a slope becomes unstable, usually because the base has been undercut or certain boundaries of materials within the mass have become wet and slippery.

**latitude and longitude** angular distances defining position on the globe. *Latitude* (abbreviation lat.) is the angular distance of any point from the equator, measured N or S along the Earth's curved surface, equalling the angle between the respective horizontal planes. It is measured in degrees, minutes, and seconds, each minute equalling one nautical mile (1.85 km/1.15 mi) in length. *Longitude* (abbreviation long.) is the angle between the terrestrial meridian through a place, and a standard meridian now taken at Greenwich, England. At the equator one degree of longitude measures approximately 113 km/70 mi.

**meander** a loop-shaped curve in a river flowing across flat country. As a river flows, any curve in its course is accentuated by the current. The current is fastest on the outside of the curve where it cuts into the bank; on the curve's inside the current is slow and deposits any transported material. In this way the river changes its course across the floodplain.

**meridian** half a great circle drawn on the Earth's surface passing through both poles and thus through all places with the same longitude. Terrestrial longitudes are usually measured from the Greenwich Meridian.

**moraine** rocky debris or till carried along and deposited by a glacier. Material eroded from the side of a glaciated valley and carried along the glacier's edge is called lateral moraine; that worn from the valley floor and carried along the base of the glacier is called ground moraine. Rubble dropped at the foot of a melting glacier is called terminal moraine.

**peat** fibrous organic substance found in bogs and

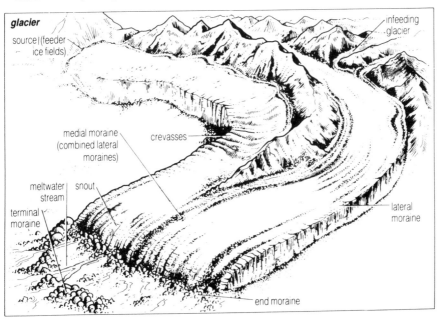

glacier
source (feeder ice fields)
infeeding glacier
medial moraine (combined lateral moraines)
crevasses
meltwater stream
snout
terminal moraine
lateral moraine
end moraine

### latitude and magnitude

*Point X lies on longitude 60°W*

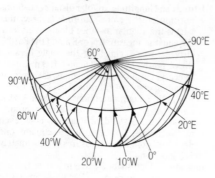

*Point X lies on latitude 20°S*

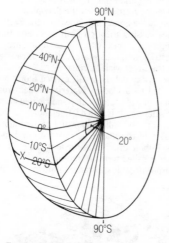

*Together longitude 60°W latitude 20°S places point X on a precise position on the globe.*

formed by the incomplete decomposition of plants such as sphagnum moss. The USSR, Canada, Finland, Ireland, and other places have large deposits, which have been dried and used as fuel from ancient times. Peat can also be used as a soil additive.

**permafrost** condition in which a deep layer of soil does not thaw out during the summer but remains at below 0°C/32°F for at least two years, despite thawing of the soil above. It is claimed that 26% of the world's land surface is permafrost.

**plateau** elevated area of fairly flat land, or a mountainous region in which the peaks are at the same height. An *intermontane plateau* is one surrounded by mountains. A *piedmont plateau* is one that lies between the mountains and low-lying land. A *continental plateau* rises abruptly from low-lying lands or the sea.

**poles** geographic north and south points of the axis about which the Earth rotates. The magnetic poles are the points towards which a freely suspended magnetic needle will point; however, they vary continually.

**rift valley** valley formed by the subsidence of a block of the Earth's crust between two or more parallel faults. Rift valleys are steep-sided and form where the crust is being pulled apart, as at ocean ridges, or in the Great Rift Valley of E Africa.

**sand** loose grains of rock, sized 0.02–2.00 mm/ 0.0008–0.0800 in in diameter, consisting chiefly of quartz, but owing their varying colour to mixtures of other minerals. It is used in cement-making, as an abrasive, in glass-making, and for other purposes.

**scarp and dip** the two slopes formed when a sedimentary bed outcrops as a landscape feature. The scarp is the slope that cuts across the bedding plane; the dip is the opposite slope which follows the bedding plane. The scarp is usually steep, while the dip is a gentle slope.

**sediment** any loose material that has 'settled' – deposited from suspension in water, ice, or air, generally as the water current or wind speed decreases. Typical sediments are, in order of increasing coarseness, clay, mud, silt, sand, gravel, pebbles, cobbles, and boulders.

**soil** loose covering of broken rocky material and decaying organic matter overlying the bedrock of the Earth's surface. Various types of soil develop under different conditions: deep soils form in warm wet climates and in valleys; shallow soils form in cool dry areas and on slopes. *Pedology*, the study of soil, is significant because of the relative importance of different soil types to agriculture.

**stalactite and stalagmite** cave structures formed by the deposition of calcite dissolved in ground water. *Stalactites* grow downwards from the roofs or walls and can be icicle-shaped, straw-shaped, curtain-shaped, or formed as terraces. *Stalagmites* grow upwards from the cave floor and can be conical, fir-cone-shaped, or resemble a stack of saucers. Growing stalactites and stalagmites may meet to form a continuous column from floor to ceiling.

**syncline** geological term for a fold in the rocks of the Earth's crust in which the layers or beds dip inwards, thus forming a trough-like structure with a sag in the middle. The opposite structure, with the beds arching upwards, is an anticline.

**topography** the surface shape and aspect of the land, and its study. Topography deals with relief and contours, the distribution of mountains and valleys, the patterns of rivers, and all other features, natural and artificial, that produce the landscape.

**tropics** the area between the tropics of Cancer and Capricorn, defined by the parallels of latitude approximately 23°30| N and S of the equator. They are the limits of the area of Earth's surface in which the Sun can be directly overhead.

**water table** level of ground below which the rocks

## CROP CIRCLES: MESSAGES FROM THE UNKNOWN OR HOAX?

No one knows for certain what causes crop circles. These large, circular areas of swirling, flattened grain have appeared in Britain's fields with increasing frequency every summer since 1980. During the summer of 1990, over 1,000 formations, most of them in the Southeast of England, were reported by researchers ('cereologists') at the Centre for Crop Circle Studies in Petersfield, Hampshire. The first crop circles reported were simple circles. Then circles appeared in pairs, then triplets, quadruplets, and quintuplets. Then came circles with single rings around them, then double rings. There have been circles with smaller satellites and circles with a so-called 'swastika pattern', in which the direction of the swirling grain changes in each quarter-circle. 1990's most impressive formation appeared in Alton Barnes, Wiltshire in July, and consisted of large circles, small circles, rings, and rectangles.

Crop circles could have been tailor-made for the media. Their swirling patterns of flattened grain look wonderful in pictures and on television, and they tend to appear during the slow season for news stories. The Alton Barnes formation was picked up as the front cover photograph of Led Zeppelin's 1990 LP. A programme in the BBC's 1989 series of *Country File* showed an effective way to make a crop circle: an army team of about 4–5 people linked arms and shuffled their feet carefully, turning around a stationary central person. Despite this graphic demonstration, many persist in believing that the circles must have some less prosaic explanation. Most of the research into crop circles has been conducted by dedicated amateurs rather than professional scientists. The exception to this is physicist Terence Meaden, founder of the Tornado and Storm Research Organisation in Bradford-on-Avon, Wiltshire. Meaden theorizes that the circles are caused by ionized stationary whirlwinds that generate an electromagnetic field he calls a 'plasma vortex'. Meaden believes the plasma vortex theory can also explain some UFO sightings. Generally speaking, while Meaden has struggled to adapt his theory to the ever-increasing complexity of crop formations, most find it hard to accept that a whirlwind, however electromagnetically charged, could make squares. The most attention-getting theory is that of amateur UK researchers Colin Andrews and Pat Delgado (respectively, a council employee and a retired inventor) who believe that whatever is producing the circles must be intelligent—aliens, perhaps, or the earth itself, trying to communicate with us. Reinforcement for this theory comes from witnesses who claim to have seen mysterious lights in the sky at night in areas where circle formations were found the next day.

Cereologists using dowsing techniques to study the circles claim to have found a relationship between the circles and ley lines (there is no scientific evidence that the latter exist), and claim that dowsing detects fields of mysterious energy in the circles. But dowsing itself—that

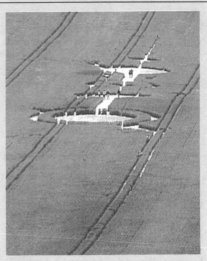

*Crop circles in a cornfield.*

is, using a forked stick or other similar device to detect water, oil, gold, or electromagnetic fields—is a questionable method of researching these phenomena: there is no scientific evidence that it works. One peculiarity about crop circles is that until very recently they were unknown outside the UK, even in places like the USA, where there are many large fields of grain. In 1990, after *Omni* magazine published an article about the UK circles, crop circles began appearing in the USA. This is, as the Southampton-based Wessex Skeptics group has pointed out, consistent with the theory that the circles are made by people—pranksters or farmers' clubs—as is the continually increasing complexity and number of the formations. Each year through the 1980s has seen increasing media coverage and each year has seen more crop circles: advertising apparently works. A few people have confessed publicly to having made crop circles which were accepted as 'genuine' by cereologists. 1990 saw a complex monitoring project, 'Operation Blackbird', mounted by Andrews and Delgado in conjunction with the BBC. Andrews and Delgado were triumphant when a large, new formation appeared in a field in Wiltshire they had monitored overnight. Their triumph was short-lived, however: on entering the circles, they found a Ouija board and a wooden cross at the centre of each. These circles were unquestionably hoaxes. Looking at crop circle photographs, it's easy to understand the sense of wonder researchers feel—the circles are genuinely awesome, artistic, and magnificent. But the human race has created many wonders in its history: the Parthenon, computers, the Pyramids, the Sphinx, Stonehenge, automobiles, the *Mona Lisa*. Compared to these things, crop circles are easy to make. Why should we look for a more exotic explanation for them?

Beaufort Scale

| number and description | features | air speed mi per hr | m per sec |
|---|---|---|---|
| 0 calm | smoke rises vertically; water smooth | less than 1 | less than 0.3 |
| 1 light air | smoke shows wind direction; water ruffled | 1–3 | 0.3–1.5 |
| 2 slight breeze | leaves rustle; wind felt on face | 4–7 | 1.6–3.3 |
| 3 gentle breeze | loose paper blows around | 8–12 | 3.4–5.4 |
| 4 moderate breeze | branches sway | 13–18 | 5.5–7.9 |
| 5 fresh breeze | small trees sway, leaves blown off | 19–24 | 8.0–10.7 |
| 6 strong breeze | whistling in telephone wires; sea spray from waves | 25–31 | 10.8–13.8 |
| 7 moderate gale | large trees sway | 32–38 | 13.9–17.1 |
| 8 fresh gale | twigs break from trees | 39–46 | 17.2–20.7 |
| 9 strong gale | branches break from trees | 47–54 | 20.8–24.4 |
| 10 whole gale | trees uprooted, weak buildings collapse | 55–63 | 24.5–28.4 |
| 11 storm | widespread damage | 64–72 | 28.5–32.6 |
| 12 hurricane | widespread structural damage | 73–82 | above 32.7 |

are saturated with water. Thus above the water table water will drain downwards, and where the water table cuts the surface of the ground, a spring results. The water table usually follows surface contours, and it varies with rainfall. In many irrigated areas the water table is lowering because of the extracted water. That below N China, for example, is sinking at a rate of 1 m/ 3 ft a year.

**weathering** process by which exposed rocks are broken down by the action of rain, frost, wind, and other elements of the weather. Two types of weathering are recognized: physical and chemical. They usually occur together.

# ATMOSPHERE AND OCEAN

**barometer** instrument that measures atmospheric pressure as an indication of weather. Most often used are the *mercury barometer* and the *aneroid barometer*.

**bathyal zone** the upper part of the ocean, which lies on the Continental shelf at a depth of between 200 m/656 ft and 2,000 m/6,561 ft.

**beach** strip of land bordering the sea, normally consisting of boulders and pebbles on exposed coasts or sand on sheltered coasts. It is usually defined by the high- and low-water marks.

**Beaufort scale** system of recording wind velocity, devised in 1806 by Francis Beaufort. It is a numerical scale ranging from 0 to 17, calm being indicated by 0 and a hurricane by 12; 13–17 indicate degrees of hurricane force.

**climate** weather conditions at a particular place over a period of time. Climate encompasses all the meteorological elements and the factors that influence them. The primary factors that determine the variations of climate over the surface of the Earth are: (a) the effect of latitude and the tilt of the Earth's axis to the plane of the orbit about the Sun (66.5°); (b) the large-scale movements of different wind belts over the Earth's surface; (c) the temperature difference between land and sea; (d) contours of the ground; and (e) location of

the area in relation to ocean currents. Catastrophic variations to climate may be caused by the impact of another planetary body, or by clouds resulting from volcanic activity. The most important local or global meteorological changes brought about by human activity are those linked with ozone depleters and the greenhouse effect.

**cloud** water vapour condensed into minute water particles that float in masses in the atmosphere. Clouds, like fogs or mists, which occur at lower levels, are formed by the cooling of air charged with water vapour, which generally condenses around tiny dust particles.

**Coriolis effect** a result of the deflective force of the Earth's west to east rotation. Winds, ocean currents, and aircraft are deflected to the right of their direction of travel in the Northern hemisphere and to the left in the Southern hemisphere.

**current** the flow of a body of water or air moving in a definite direction. There are three basic types of oceanic currents: *drift currents* are broad and slow-moving; *stream currents* are narrow and swift-moving; and *upwelling currents* bring cold, nutrient-rich water from the ocean bottom.

**doldrums** area of low atmospheric pressure along the equator, largely applied to oceans at the convergence of the NE and SE trade winds. To some extent the area affected moves N and S with seasonal changes.

**drought** period of prolonged dry weather. The area of the world subject to serious droughts, such as the Sahara, is increasing because of destruction of forests, overgrazing, and poor agricultural practices.

**estuary** river mouth widening into the sea, where fresh water mixes with salt water and tidal effects are felt.

**exosphere** the uppermost layer of the atmosphere. It is an ill-defined zone above the thermosphere, beginning at about 700 km/435 mi and fading off into the vacuum of space. The gases are extremely thin, with hydrogen as the main constituent.

**fog** cloud that collects at the surface of the Earth, composed of water vapour that has condensed

## WEATHERING

*physical weathering*

| | |
|---|---|
| temperature changes | weakening rocks by expansion and contraction |
| frost | wedging rocks apart by the expansion of water on freezing |
| rain | making loose slopes unstable |
| wind | wearing away rocks by sandblasting, and moving sand dunes along |
| unloading | the loosening of rock layers by release of pressure after the erosion and removal of those layers above |

*chemical weathering*

| | |
|---|---|
| carbonation | the breakdown of calcite by reaction with carbonic acid in rainwater |
| hydrolysis | the breakdown of feldspar into china clay by reaction with carbonic acid in rainwater |
| oxidation | the breakdown of iron-rich minerals due to rusting |
| hydration | the expansion of certain minerals due to the uptake of water |

*gravity*

| | |
|---|---|
| soil creep | the slow downslope movement of surface material |
| landslide | the rapid downward movement of solid material |
| avalanche | scouring by ice, snow, and accumulated debris |

*rivers*

| | |
|---|---|
| abrasion | wearing away stream beds and banks by trundling boulders along |
| corrasion | the wear on the boulders themselves as they are carried along |

*glaciers*

| | |
|---|---|
| deepening | of valleys by the weight of ice |
| scouring | of rock surfaces by embedded rocky debris |

*sea*

| | |
|---|---|
| hydraulic effect | expansion of air pockets in rocks and cliffs by constant hammering by waves |
| abrasion | see *Rivers* above |
| corrosion | see *Rivers* above |

on particles of dust in the atmosphere. Cloud and fog are both caused by the air temperature falling below dew point. The thickness of fog depends on the number of water particles it contains. Usually, fog is formed by the meeting of two currents of air, one cooler than the other, or by warm air flowing over a cold surface. Sea fogs commonly occur where warm and cold currents meet and the air above them mixes.

**front** the interface between two air masses of different temperature or humidity. A **cold front** marks the line of advance of a cold air mass from below, as it displaces a warm air mass; a **warm front** marks the advance of a warm air mass pushing a cold one forward.

**frost** condition of the weather when the air temperature is below freezing, 0°C/32°F. Water in the atmosphere is deposited as ice crystals on the ground or exposed objects. As cold air is heavier than warm, ground frost is more common than hoar frost, which is formed by

**rift valley**

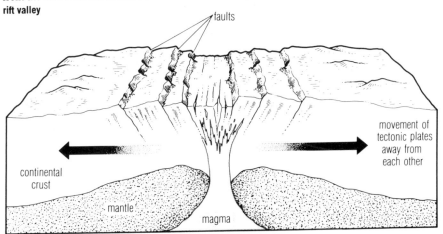

**Cloud**

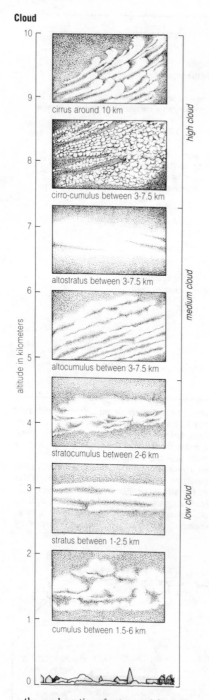

cirrus around 10 km

cirro-cumulus between 3-7.5 km

altostratus between 3-7.5 km

altocumulus between 3-7.5 km

stratocumulus between 2-6 km

stratus between 1-2.5 km

cumulus between 1.5-6 km

high cloud

medium cloud

low cloud

altitude in kilometers

## GREENHOUSE GASES: THE OFFENDERS

| | | Tonnes per capita |
|---|---|---|
| 1 | Lao People's Democratic Republic | 10.0 |
| 2 | Qatar | 8.8 |
| 3 | United Arab Emirates | 5.8 |
| 4 | Bahrain | 4.9 |
| 5 | Canada | 4.5 |
| 6 | Luxembourg | 4.3 |
| 7 | Brazil | 4.3 |
| 8 | Côte d'Ivoire | 4.2 |
| 9 | USA | 4.2 |
| 10 | Kuwait | 4.1 |
| 11 | Australia | 3.9 |
| 12 | German Democratic Republic | 3.7 |
| 13 | Oman | 3.5 |
| 14 | Saudi Arabia | 3.3 |
| 15 | New Zealand | 3.2 |
| 16 | Netherlands | 2.9 |
| 17 | Denmark | 2.8 |
| 18 | Costa Rica | 2.8 |
| 19 | Singapore | 2.7 |
| 20 | UK | 2.7 |
| 21 | Germany, Federal Republic | 2.7 |
| 22 | Finland | 2.6 |
| 23 | Ireland | 2.5 |
| 24 | Belgium | 2.5 |
| 25 | USSR | 2.5 |

*Source: World Resources 1990–91*

the air. The result is a rise in the Earth's temperature; in a garden greenhouse, the glass walls have the same effect. The main greenhouse gases are carbon dioxide, methane, and chlorofluorocarbons. Fossil-fuel consumption and forest fires are the main causes of carbon dioxide buildup; methane is a byproduct of agriculture (rice, cattle, sheep). Water vapour is another greenhouse gas. The United Nations Environment Programme estimates an increase in average world temperatures of 1.5°C/2.7°F with a consequent rise of 20 cm/7.7 in in sea level by 2025. (See feature in this section.)

**gyre** the circular surface rotation of ocean water in each major sea (a type of current). Gyres are large and permanent, and occupy the N and S halves of the three major oceans. Their movements are dictated by the prevailing winds and the Coriolis effect. Gyres move clockwise in the northern hemisphere and anticlockwise in the southern hemisphere.

**hail** precipitation in the form of pellets of ice (hailstones). It is caused by the circulation of moisture in strong convection currents, usually within cumulonimbus clouds.

**hurricane** revolving storm in tropical regions, called **typhoon** in the N Pacific. It originates between 5° and 20° N or S of the equator, when the surface temperature of the ocean is above 27°C/80°F. A central calm area, called the eye, is surrounded by inwardly spiralling winds (anticlockwise in the N hemisphere) of up to 320 kph/200 mph. A hurricane is accompanied by lightning and torrential rain, and can cause extensive damage. In meteorology, a hurricane is a wind of force 12 or more on

the condensation of water particles in the same way that dew collects.

**greenhouse effect** in the Earth's atmosphere, the trapping of solar radiation, which, absorbed by the Earth and re-emitted from the surface, is prevented from escaping by various gases in

## GLOBAL WARMING: THE GROWING FEARS

In the mid-1970s it was believed that a new ice age was coming. Statistical analyses of ancient weather records and glacier extents suggested that the climates were cooling. Then, in the mid-1980s a possible 'nuclear winter' was discussed. This postulated a severe cooling of the world's climates by the palls of smoke and dust blasted into the atmosphere as a result of nuclear warfare. All this shows a great public and scientific awareness of the possibilities of climatic change – a very understandable concern about an essential part of our environment. Nowadays the emphasis is on the possibility of 'greenhouse effect'.

The concept is quite simple. Plants, to live, use the sun's energy to extract carbon from the carbon dioxide gas of the atmosphere. Fossil fuels are based on carbon derived from living things that took many millions of years to collect. We are now burning all this carbon away to use the energy locked up in it. As a side effect we are returning to the atmosphere in a few decades all the carbon dioxide broken down over those millions of years. Thus the composition of the atmosphere is changing. As well as carbon dioxide there are increased proportions of methane and CFCs. All these allow sunlight to pass through to the Earth's surface. Heat re-radiated by the Earth's surface, however, consists largely of infrared rays which are trapped by these gases, and the air temperature close to the ground increases. If this is allowed to continue the result would be a worldwide change in climatic zones and vegetation zones, drought in many of the world's most significant crop-growing areas, climatic instability brought about by the contrast between the cold ice caps and increasing temperatures elsewhere, and a rise in sea level due to melting ice.

This is borne out by climatic observation. 1983 had higher average world temperatures than ever before recorded. This record was broken in 1987, and again in 1988. The hot years coincided with the El Niño effect—a temporary reversal of currents in the Pacific Ocean which usually results in a short-lived increase in global temperatures. However world average temperatures in 1990 were the highest yet, and did not coincide with an El Niño event. This increase is attributed to the greenhouse gases.

The Intergovernmental Panel on Climate Change working from the Stockholm Environment Institute published some alarming figures in Oct 1990. Natural ecosystems could only cope with a rise of 1°C at a rate of change of 0.1°C per year. Coral reefs and wetlands could only survive with a sea level rise of less than 2 centimetres per decade. Human society could only cope with a rise of 2°C at a rate of 0.2°C per year and an overall sea level rise of 20 centimetres. These figures could be reached by the 2030s.

The Second World Climate Conference was held in Geneva between 31 Oct and 9 Nov 1990 to try to obtain an international consensus on what to do about this. Scientists from 130 nations proposed that specific targets be set for the reduction of industrial carbon dioxide by the end of the century. For example, the European Community's ministers for environment wanted the emissions of carbon dioxide to be stabilized at 1990 levels by the year 2000. The German government made its own decision to cut its carbon dioxide emissions by between 25% and 30% by 2005. However no formal international agreement was reached. The United States, in particular, saw carbon dioxide as being only part of the problem and wanted to see an agreement that encompassed the other greenhouse gases as well.

On the other hand there is a significant body of scientific opinion that believes that the threat is overemphasized. The Marshall Institute in Washington DC states that the recent rise in temperatures can be put down to natural variations in sunlight. It has also been stated that the temperature increases have been noted only in urban environments where local pollution, and reflection of heat from concrete buildings and roadways distort the readings. A 10-year study by NASA and the University of Alabama reported in 1990 that readings from satellites launched between 1979 and 1988 found no evidence of warming in the upper atmosphere.

More climatic interference was instigated in March 1991, when retreating Iraqi forces set fire to Kuwait's 500 or so oil wells. The resulting pall of smoke renewed fears of the 'nuclear winter' and a disruption of the monsoon climate of the entire Indian Ocean area.

In fact, to date the initial fears have not been realized and the effects have been local ones, even though soot particles have been found as far away as Japan.

the Beaufort scale.

The most intense hurricane recorded in the Caribbean/Atlantic sector was Hurricane Gilbert in 1988, with sustained winds of 280 kph/175 mph and gusts of over 320 kph/200 mph.

**isobar** a line drawn on maps and weather charts linking all places with the same atmospheric pressure (usually measured in millibars). When used in weather forecasting, the distance between the isobars is an indication of the barometric gradient.

**jet stream** a narrow band of very fast wind (velocities of over 150 kph/95 mph) found at altitudes of 10–16 km/6–10 mi in the upper troposphere or lower stratosphere. Jet streams usually occur about the latitudes of the Westerlies (35°–60°).

**lagoon** coastal body of shallow salt water, usually with limited access to the sea. The term is normally used to describe the shallow sea area cut off by a coral reef or barrier islands.

**magnetic storm** a sudden disturbance affecting the Earth's magnetic field, causing anomalies in radio transmissions and magnetic compasses. It is probably caused by sunspot activity.

**Mediterranean climate** climate characterized by hot dry summers and warm wet winters. Mediterranean zones are situated in either hemisphere on the western side of continents, between latitudes of 30° and 60°.

**mesosphere** layer in the Earth's atmosphere above the stratosphere and below the thermosphere. It lies between about 50 km/31 mi and 80 km/50 mi above the ground.

**meteorology** the scientific observation and study of the atmosphere, so that weather can be accurately forecasted. Data from meteorological stations and weather satellites is collated by computer at central agencies such as the Meteorological Office in Bracknell, near London, and a forecast and weather maps based on current readings are issued at regular intervals.

**monsoon** a wind system that dominates the climate of a wide region, with seasonal reversals of direction; in particular, the wind in S Asia that blows towards the sea in winter and towards the land in summer, bringing heavy rain. The monsoon may cause destructive flooding all over India and SE Asia from April to Sept. Thousands of people are rendered homeless each year. The Guinea monsoon is a southwesterly wind that blows in W Africa from April to Sept, throughout the rainy season.

**ocean ridge** topographical feature of the seabed indicating the presence of a constructive plate margin produced by the rise of magma to the surface. It can rise thousands of metres above the surrounding abyssal plain.

**ocean trench** topographical feature of the seabed indicating the presence of a destructive plate margin (produced by the movements of plate tectonics). The subduction or dragging downward of one plate of the lithosphere beneath

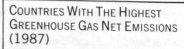

### COUNTRIES WITH THE HIGHEST GREENHOUSE GAS NET EMISSIONS (1987)

Carbon dioxide equivalents
(bn metric tons of carbon)

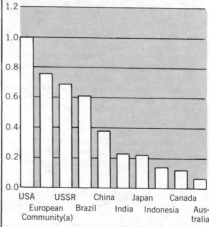

**Note:** a. The European Community comprises 12 countries: Belgium, Denmark, France, Federal Republic of Germany, Greece, Ireland, Italy, Luxembourg, the Netherlands, Portugal, Spain, United Kingdom.

Source: World Resources 1990–91,
The World Resources Institute with UNEP & UNDP

another means that the ocean floor is pulled down.

**ooze** sediment of fine texture consisting mainly of organic matter found on the ocean floor at depths greater than 2,000 m/6,600 ft. Several kinds of ooze exist, each named after its constituents.

**rain** technically termed *precipitation* separate

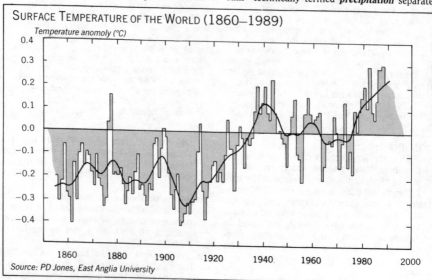

### SURFACE TEMPERATURE OF THE WORLD (1860–1989)

Temperature anomoly (°C)

Source: PD Jones, East Anglia University

## Some Environmental Monitoring Programmes Using Satellite Remote Sensing

| Programme | Agency | Status | Objectives |
|---|---|---|---|
| POES: Polar-orbiting Operational Environment Satellites | NOAA | Operational since 1970 | Weather observations |
| METEOSAT: Meteorology Satellite | ESA | Operational since 1977 | Weather observations |
| LANDSAT: Land Remote Sensing Satellite | EOSAT | Operational since 1972 | Vegetation, crop and land-use inventory |
| LAGEOS-1: Laser Geodynamics Satellite-1 | NASA | Operational since 1976 | Geodynamics, gravity field |
| SPOT-1: Système Probatoire d'Observation de la Terre-1 | France | Operational since 1986 | Land use, earth resources |
| IRS: Indian Remote Sensing Satellite (e.g. Rohini-2) | India | Operational since 1981 | Earth resources |
| MOS-1: Marine Observation Satellite-1 | NASDA (Japan) | Operational since 1987 | State of sea surface and atmosphere |
| LAGEOS-2: Laser Geodynamics Satellite-2 | NASA-PSN (Italy) | Operational since 1988 | Geodynamics, gravity field |
| ERS-1: Earth Remote Sensing Satellite-1 | ESA | Launch 1990 | Imaging of oceans, ice fields, land areas |
| N-ROSS: Navy Remote Sensing System | US Navy | Launch 1991 | Ocean topography, surface winds, ice extent |
| JERS-1: Japan Earth Remote Sensing Satellite-1 | NASDA (Japan) | Launch 1991 | Earth resources |
| TOPEX/POSEIDON: Ocean Topography Experiment | NASA-CNES (France) | Start 1987, Launch 1991 | Ocean surface topography |
| RADARSAT: Canadian Radar Satellite | Canada | Start 1986, Launch 1991 | Studies of Arctic ice, ocean studies, earth resources |
| GRM: Geopotential Research Mission | NASA | Start 1989, Launch 1992 | Measure global geoid and magnetic field |
| EOS: Earth Observing System/ Polar-Orbiting Platforms | NASA | Start 1989, Launch 1994 | Long-term global earth observations |
| European Polar Orbiting Platform (Columbus) | ESA | Planned | Long term comprehensive research, operational and commercial earth observations |
| Rainfall mission | NASA | Start 1991, Launch 1994 | Tropical precipitation measurements |
| REPRESENTATIVE SPACE SHUTTLE INSTRUMENTS | | | |
| ATMOS: Atmospheric Trace Molecules Observed by Spectroscopy | NASA | Current | Atmospheric chemical composition |
| ACR: Active Cavity Radiometer | NASA | Current | Solar energy output |
| SUSIM: Solar Ultraviolet Spectral Irradiance Monitor | NASA | Current | Ultraviolet solar observations |
| MAPS: Measurement of Air Pollution from Shuttle | NASA | Current/in development | Tropospheric carbon monoxide |
| INDIVIDUAL INSTRUMENTS FOR LONG-TERM GLOBAL OBSERVATIONS | | | |
| Total Ozone Monitor | NASA | Planned | Monitor global ozone |
| Laser Ranger: | NASA | Planned | Continental motions |
| Scanning Radar Altimeter | NASA | Planned | Continental topography |

CNES Centre National d'Études Spatiales (France); EOSAT The EOSAT Company; ESA European Space Agency; NASDA Japan Space Agency; NOAA National Oceanic and Atmospheric Administration (USA); NSF National Science Foundation (USA); PSN Piano Spaziale Nazionale (Italian National Space Plan); USGS United States Geological Survey
*Source: UNEP Environmental Data Report 89/90*

GEOLOGICAL TIME CHART

| eon | era | period | epoch | millions of years ago | life forms |
|---|---|---|---|---|---|
| Phanerozoic | Cenozoic | Quaternary | Holocene | 0.01 | |
| | | | Pleistocene | 1.8 | humans appear |
| | | Tertiary | Pliocene | 5 | |
| | | | Miocene | 25 | |
| | | | Oligocene | 38 | |
| | | | Eocene | 55 | |
| | | | Palaeocene | 65 | mammals flourish |
| | Mesozoic | Cretaceous | | 144 | heyday of dinosaurs |
| | | Jurassic | | 213 | first birds |
| | | Triassic | | 248 | first mammals and dinosaurs |
| | Palaeozoic | Permian | | 286 | reptiles expand |
| | | Carboniferous | | 360 | first reptiles |
| | | Devonian | | 408 | first amphibians |
| | | Silurian | | 438 | first land plants |
| | | Ordovician | | 505 | first fish |
| | | Cambrian | | 590 | first fossils |
| | Precambrian | Proterozoic | | 2500 | earliest living things |
| | | Archaean | | 4600 | |

wind speeds of 160–480 kph/100–300 mph, destroying everything in their path. They are common in the central USA and Australia.

**trade wind** prevailing wind that blows towards the equator from the northeast and southeast. Trade winds are caused by hot air rising at the equator and the consequent movement of air from north and south to take its place. The winds are deflected towards the west because of the Earth's west-to-east rotation. The unpredictable calms known as the doldrums lie at their convergence.

**troposphere** lower part of the Earth's atmosphere extending about 10.5 km/6.5 mi from the Earth's surface, in which temperature decreases with height to about −60°C/−76°F except in local layers of temperature inversion. The *tropopause* is the upper boundary of the troposphere above which the temperature increases slowly with height within the atmosphere.

**tsunami** (Japanese 'harbour wave') giant wave generated by an undersea earthquake or other disturbance. In the open ocean it may take the form of several successive waves, travelling at tens of kilometres per hour but with an amplitude (height) of approximately a metre. In the coastal shallows, tsunamis slow down and build up, producing towering waves that can sweep inland and cause great loss of life and property.

**weather** the day-to-day variation of climatic and atmospheric conditions at any one place, or the state of these conditions at a place at any one time. Such conditions include humidity, precipitation, temperature, cloud cover, visibility, and wind. To a meteorologist the term 'weather' is limited to the state of the sky, precipitation, and visibility as affected by fog or mist.

**Westerlies** prevailing winds from the W that oc-

cur in both hemispheres between latitudes of about 35° and 60°. Unlike the trade winds, they are very variable and produce stormy weather.

**wind** lateral movement of the Earth's atmosphere from high- to low-pressure areas. Although modified by features such as land and water, there is a basic worldwide system of trade winds, Westerlies, monsoons, and others.

# THE DEVELOPING EARTH

**Archaean** or *Archaeozoic* the earliest period of geological time; the first part of the Precambrian era, from the formation of Earth up to about 2,500 million years ago. It is a time when no life existed, and with every new discovery of ancient life its upper boundary is being pushed further back.

**Cambrian** period of geological time 590–505 million years ago; the first period of the Palaeozoic era. All invertebrate animal life appeared, and marine algae was widespread. The earliest fossils with hard shells, such as trilobites, date from this period.

**Carboniferous** period of geological time 360–286 million years ago, the fifth period of the Palaeozoic era. In the USA it is regarded as two periods: the Mississippian (lower) and the Pennsylvanian (upper). Typical of the lower-Carboniferous rocks are shallow-water limestones, while upper-Carboniferous rocks have delta deposits with coal (hence the name). Amphibians were abundant, and reptiles evolved.

**continental drift** theory proposed by the German meteorologist Alfred Wegener in 1915 that, about 200 million years ago, Earth consisted of a single large continent (Pangaea) that sub-

## WARM POLES: FOSSIL EVIDENCE OF PAST CLIMATES

The wilderness continent of Antarctica, and the chill ice-bound wastes of the Arctic are perhaps the most hostile environments on this planet. Yet it was not always thus. Coal has been mined on Spitzbergen in the Arctic ocean since 1906, suggesting that there were once lush conditions thereabouts. Finds at both ends of the Earth during the last few years are giving us details of the ancient climatic picture.

A small dinosaur was discovered near Melbourne in Australia in 1989. On the face of it this does not seem too surprising considering the present-day climates and latitudes of that continent. However, in early Cretaceous times 130 million years ago, that part of Australia lay at latitude 80° South—a latitude that is today deep in the Antarctic continent. In 1987 fossils of late Cretaceous dinosaurs were found in Alaska at a site that would have had a latitude of 80° North in those times. It seemed unlikely that such animals could survive the conditions that exist so close to the poles, and so it was suggested that in times gone past the Earth's axis was more vertical than it is now. This would mean that there would not have been the continuous daylight in the summer and continuous darkness in the winter, and the seasons would not have been so marked or so extreme. Antarctic fossils suggest otherwise. In Cretaceous times the Antarctic Peninsula consisted of a series of volcanic islands that lay at about the latitude in which they now lie. They were heavily forested, with rainforests of monkeypuzzle and beech trees with an undergrowth of ferns. Such forests are now found in southern South America and New Zealand. Hot silica-rich water from the volcanoes petrified the wood to such fine detail that the annual growth rings can be studied. These show a pronounced seasonal variation of growth indicating that the seasons were as extreme as they are now. In the Canadian Arctic, Ellesmere Island and Axel Heiberg Island have fossil forests of Eocene age—about 50 million years old. These also grew at the high latitude of about 80° North. The trees were mostly swamp cypress and redwood, showing swampy conditions. Animal remains found with them include alligators, tortoises and hippopotamus-like mammals—10° from the North Pole! Again the suggestion was made that the Earth's axis was less steeply tilted than it is at the moment, but again that was disproved by the presence of pronounced tree rings that show a marked seasonal growth. Anyway, such an arrangement would mean that the sun would have been always too low in the sky to produce the intensity of sunlight needed for forest growth.

It is evident from all these finds that the climates of the polar reaches were much milder than they are at present. A possible reason, suggested by Pennsylvania State University, may have been the position of the continents. In the Cretaceous and Eocene times there was a seaway that circled the world near the equator—North America was separate from South America, and Africa and India were separated from Asia by a sea called the Tethys. The constant equatorial current produced here would have sent eddies of warm water towards the poles and the climate everywhere would have been milder.

Eocene deep-sea sediments studied by the University of Michigan and that of Rhode Island show only fine dust particles, suggesting a lack of strong winds, and thus an overall mild climate. Another suggestion, from the Geological Survey of Canada, is that volcanic carbon dioxide released by activity associated with the moving continents produced a greenhouse effect. More up-to-date fossil forests, only about 4 million years old, have been found in the Vestfold Hills of eastern Antarctica about 70° South. These indicate that the climate was at least 10° warmer then. Even more recent forests, 2–3 million years old—Pliocene in age—lie in the Transantarctic Mountains only 5° from the South Pole, and also in regions of northern Canada now covered by cold tundra. Climates were warmer right up to the beginning of the Ice Age. The sea levels were about 35 metres higher than today. The US Geological Survey initiated a research programme called PRISM—Pliocene Research Interpretation and Synoptic Mapping—in 1990. The USSR is cooperating in the project, as are scientists from Iceland, the UK and Japan. Their findings should have a bearing on our knowledge of the changing climates of today.

**tsunami** (Japanese 'harbour wave') giant wave generated by an undersea earthquake or other disturbance. In the open ocean it may take the form of several successive waves, travelling at tens of kilometres per hour but with an amplitude (height) of approximately a metre. In the coastal shallows, tsunamis slow down and build up, producing towering waves that can sweep inland and cause great loss of life and property.

**weather** the day-to-day variation of climatic and atmospheric conditions at any one place, or the state of these conditions at a place at any one time. Such conditions include humidity, precipitation, temperature, cloud cover, visibility, and wind. To a meteorologist the term 'weather' is limited to the state of the sky, precipitation, and visibility as affected by fog or mist.

**Westerlies** prevailing winds from the W that occur in both hemispheres between latitudes of about 35° and 60°. Unlike the trade winds, they are very variable and produce stormy weather.

**wind** lateral movement of the Earth's atmosphere from high- to low-pressure areas. Although modified by features such as land and water, there is a basic worldwide system of trade winds, Westerlies, monsoons, and others.

# THE DEVELOPING EARTH

**Archaean** or *Archaeozoic* the earliest period of geological time; the first part of the Precambrian era, from the formation of Earth up to about 2,500 million years ago. It is a time when no life existed, and with every new discovery of ancient life its upper boundary is being pushed further back.

**Cambrian** period of geological time 590–505 million years ago; the first period of the Palaeozoic era. All invertebrate animal life appeared, and marine algae was widespread. The earliest fossils with hard shells, such as trilobites, date from this period.

**Carboniferous** period of geological time 360–286 million years ago, the fifth period of the Palaeozoic era. In the USA it is regarded as two periods: the Mississippian (lower) and the Pennsylvanian (upper). Typical of the lower-Carboniferous rocks are shallow-water limestones, while upper-Carboniferous rocks have delta deposits with coal (hence the name). Amphibians were abundant, and reptiles evolved.

**continental drift** theory proposed by the German meteorologist Alfred Wegener in 1915 that, about 200 million years ago, Earth consisted of a single large continent (Pangaea) that subsequently broke apart to form the continents known today. Such vast continental movements could not be satisfactorily explained until the study of plate tectonics in the 1960s.

**Cretaceous** period of geological time 144–65 million years ago. It is the last period of the Mesozoic era, during which angiosperm (seed-bearing) plants evolved, and dinosaurs and other reptiles reached a peak before almost complete extinction at the end of the period. Chalk is a typical rock type of the second half of the period.

**dating** the science of determining the age of geological structures, rocks, and fossils, and placing them in the context of geological time.

**Devonian** period of geological time 408–360 million years ago, the fourth period of the Palaeozoic era. Many desert sandstones from North America and Europe date from this time. The first land plants flourished in the Devonian period, corals were abundant in the seas, amphibians evolved from air-breathing fish, and

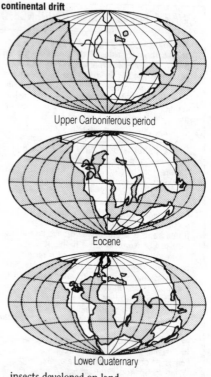

continental drift

Upper Carboniferous period

Eocene

Lower Quaternary

insects developed on land.

**epoch** a subdivision of a geologic period in the geologic time scale. Epochs are sometimes given their own names (such as the Paleocene, Eocene, Oligocene, Miocene, and Pliocene epochs comprising the Tertiary period), or they are referred to as the late, early, or middle portions of a given period (as the Late Cretaceous or the Middle Triassic epoch).

**era** any of the major divisions of geologic time, each including several periods, but smaller than an eon. The currently recognized eras all fall within the Phanerozoic eon—or the vast span of time, starting about 590 million years ago, when fossils are found to become abundant. The eras in ascending order are the Palaeozoic, Mesozoic, and Cenozoic. We are living in the Recent epoch of the Quaternary period of the Cenozoic era.

**geological time** time scale embracing the history of the Earth from its physical origin to the present day. Geological time is divided into eras (Precambrian, Palaeozoic, Mesozoic, Cenozoic), which in turn are divided into periods, epochs, ages, and finally chrons.

**Gondwanaland** or *Gondwana* land mass, including the continents of South America, Africa, Australia, and Antarctica, that formed the southern half of Pangaea, the 'supercontinent' or world continent that existed between 250 and 200 million years ago. The northern half was Laurasia. The baobab tree of Africa and Australia is a relic of Gondwanaland.

**Holocene** epoch of geological time that began

## MAJOR ICE AGES

| name | date (years ago) |
| --- | --- |
| Pleistocene | 1.7 million–10,000 |
| Permo-Carboniferous | 330–250 million |
| Ordovician | 440–430 million |
| Verangian | 615–570 million |
| Sturtian | 820–770 million |
| Gnejso | 940–880 million |
| Huronian | 2,700–1,800 million |

10,000 years ago, the second epoch of the Quaternary period. The glaciers retreated, the climate became warmer, and humans developed significantly.

**Iapetus Ocean** or **Proto-Atlantic** sea that existed in early Palaeozoic times between the continent that was to become Europe and that which was to become North America. The continents moved together in the late Palaeozoic, obliterating the ocean. When they moved apart once more, they formed the Atlantic.

**ice age** any period of glaciation occurring in the Earth's history, but particularly that in the Pleistocene epoch, immediately preceding historic times. On the North American continent, glaciers reached as far south as the Great Lakes, and an ice sheet spread over N Europe, leaving its remains as far south as Switzerland. There were several glacial advances separated by interglacial stages during which the ice melted and temperatures were higher than today.

**K-T boundary** geologists' shorthand for the boundary between the rocks of the Cretaceous and the Tertiary periods. It marks the extinction of the dinosaurs and in many places reveals a layer of iridium, possibly deposited by a meteorite that may have caused the extinction by its impact.

**Laurasia** former land mass or supercontinent, formed by the fusion of North America, Greenland, Europe, and Asia. It made up the northern half of Pangaea, the 'world continent' that is thought to have existed between 250 and 200 million years ago. The southern half was Gondwanaland.

**mass extinction** an event that produced the extinction of many species at about the same time. One notable example is the boundary between the Cretaceous and Tertiary periods (known as the K-T boundary) that saw the extinction of the dinosaurs and other big reptiles, and many of the marine invertebrates as well. Mass extinctions have taken place several times during Earth's history. The Age of Man may eventually be regarded as another.

**Mesozoic** era of geological time 248–65 million years ago, consisting of the Triassic, Jurassic, and Cretaceous periods. At the beginning of the era, the continents were joined together as Pangaea, dinosaurs and other giant reptiles dominated the sea and air; and ferns, horsetails, and cycads thrived in a warm climate worldwide. By the end of the Mesozoic era, the continents had begun to assume their present positions, flowering plants were dominant and many of the large reptiles and marine fauna were becoming extinct.

**Ordovician** period of geological time 505–438 million years ago; the second period of the Palaeozoic era. Animal life was confined to the sea: reef-building algae and the first jawless fish are characteristic.

**palaeomagnetism** the science of the reconstruction of the Earth's ancient magnetic field and the former positions of the continents from the evidence of **remanent magnetization** in ancient rocks; that is, traces left by the Earth's magnetic field in igneous rocks before they cool. Palaeomagnetism shows that the Earth's magnetic field has reversed itself—the magnetic north pole becoming the magnetic south pole, and vice versa—at approximate half-million-year intervals, with shorter reversal periods in between the major spans.

**palaeontology** the study of ancient life that encompasses the structure of ancient organisms and their environment, evolution, and ecology, as revealed by their fossils.

**Palaeozoic** era of geological time 590–248 million years ago. It comprises the Cambrian, Ordovician, Silurian, Devonian, Carboniferous, and Permian periods. The Cambrian, Ordovician, and Silurian constitute the Lower Palaeozoic; the Devonian, Carboniferous, and Permian make up the Upper Palaeozoic. The era includes the evolution of hard-shelled multicellular life forms in the sea; the invasion of land by plants and animals; and the evolution of fish, amphibians, and early reptiles. The earliest identifiable fossils date from this era. The climate was mostly warm with short ice ages. The continents were very different from the present ones but, towards the end of the era, all were joined together as a single world continent called Pangaea.

**Pangaea** or **Pangea** world continent, named by Alfred Wegener, that existed between 250 and 200 million years ago, made up of all the continental masses. It may be regarded as a combination of Laurasia in the north and Gondwanaland in the south, the rest of Earth being covered by the Panthalassa ocean.

**Panthalassa** ocean that covered the surface of the Earth not occupied by the world continent Pangaea between 250 and 200 million years ago.

**Permian** period of geological time 286–248 million years ago, the last period of the Palaeozoic era. Its end was marked by a significant change in marine life, including the extinction of many corals and trilobites. Deserts were widespread, and terrestrial amphibians and mammal-like reptiles flourished. Cone-bearing plants (gymnosperms) came to prominence.

**Phanerozoic** eon in Earth history, consisting of the most recent 590 million years. It comprises the Palaeozoic, Mesozoic, and Cenozoic eras. The vast majority of fossils come from this eon, owing to the evolution of hard shells and internal skeletons. The name means 'interval of well-displayed life'.

**plate tectonics** concept that attributes continental drift and seafloor spreading to the continual formation and destruction of the outermost layer of the Earth. This layer is seen as consisting of major and minor plates, curved to the planet's spherical shape and with a jigsaw fit to one another. Convection currents within the Earth's mantle produce upwellings of new material along joint lines at the surface, forming ridges (for example the Mid-Atlantic Ridge). The new material extends the plates, and these move away from the ridges. Where two plates collide, one overrides the other and the lower is absorbed back into the mantle. These 'subduction zones' occur in the ocean trenches.

**Precambrian** the time from the formation of Earth (4.6 billion years ago) up to 590 million years ago. Its boundary with the succeeding Cambrian period marks the time when animals first developed hard outer parts (exoskeletons) and so left abundant fossil remains. It comprises about 85% of geological time and is divided into two periods: the Archaean and the Proterozoic.

**Proterozoic** period of geological time, 2.5 billion to 590 million years ago, the second division of the Precambrian era. It is defined as the time of simple life, since many rocks dating from this eon show traces of biological activity, and some contain the fossils of bacteria and algae.

**Quaternary** period of geological time that began 1.8 million years ago and is still in process. It is divided into the Pleistocene and Holocene epochs.

**seafloor spreading** growth of the ocean crust outwards (sideways) from mid-ocean ridges. The concept of seafloor spreading has been combined with that of continental drift and incorporated into plate tectonics.

**stratigraphy** branch of geology that deals with the sequence of formation of sedimentary rock layers and the conditions under which they were formed. Its basis was developed by William Smith (1769–1839), a British canal engineer.

**stromatolite** mound produced in shallow water by mats of algae that trap mud particles. Another mat grows on the trapped mud layer and this traps another layer of mud and so on. The stromatolite grows to heights of a metre or so. They are uncommon today but their fossils are among the earliest evidence for living things—over 2,000 million years old.

**tectonics** the study of the movements of rocks on the Earth's surface. On a small scale tectonics involves the formation of folds and faults, but on a large scale plate tectonics deals with the movement of the Earth's surface as a whole.

**Tertiary** period of geological time 65–1.8 million years ago, divided into five epochs: Palaeocene, Eocene, Oligocene, Miocene, and Pliocene. During the Tertiary, mammals took over all the ecological niches left vacant by the extinction of the dinosaurs, and became the prevalent land animals. The continents took on their present positions, and climatic and vegetation zones as we know them became established. Within the geological time column the Tertiary follows the Cretaceous period and is succeeded by the Quaternary period.

**Triassic** period of geological time 248–213 million years ago, the first period of the Mesozoic era. The continents were fused together to form the world continent Pangaea. Triassic sediments contain remains of early dinosaurs and other reptiles now extinct. By late Triassic times, the first mammals had evolved.

# TERMS

The chief direct sources of energy are oil, coal, wood, and natural gas, and indirectly, electricity produced by the use of such fuels or derived from water power or nuclear fission. Increasing costs and the prospect of exhaustion of coal, oil and gas resources, led in the 1980s to consideration of alternative sources. These included solar power, which provides completely 'clean' energy; wind and wave power; tidal power, which like geothermal power, is geographically limited in application; utilization of organic waste, such as chicken manure; photosynthetic power, produced by the use of simple, fast-reproducing plants as fuel; and nuclear power, by fusion rather than fission.

**biofuel** any solid, liquid, or gaseous fuel produced from organic (once living) matter, either directly from plants or indirectly from industrial, commercial, domestic, or agricultural wastes. There are three main avenues for the development of biofuels: combustion of dry organic wastes (such as refuse, industrial and agricultural wastes, straw, wood, and peat); digestion of wet wastes in the absence of oxygen (anaerobic digestion) to produce biogas (containing up to 60% methane), or fermentation of sugar cane or corn to produce alcohol; and energy forestry (producing fast-growing wood for fuel).

**electricity generation and supply** electricity is the most useful and most convenient form of energy there is. It can readily be converted into heat and light, and used to power machines. Because electricity flows readily through wires, it can be made, or generated, in one place and distributed to anywhere it is needed. Electricity is generated at power stations, where a suitable energy source is made to drive turbines that spin the electricity generators. The generators produce alternating current (AC), and the producing units are generally called turboalternators. The main energy sources for electricity generation are coal, oil, water power (hydroelectricity), natural gas, and nuclear power, with limited contributions from wind power, tidal power, and geothermal power. Nuclear fuel provides the cheapest form of electricity generation in Britain, but environmental considerations may limit its future development.

Electricity is generated at power stations at a voltage of about 25,000 volts, which is not a suitable voltage for long-distance transmission. For minimal power loss transmission must take place at very high voltage—up to 400,000 volts or more. The generated voltage is therefore increased, or stepped-up, by a transformer. The resulting high voltage electricity is then fed into the main arteries of the grid system. This is an interconnected network of power stations and distribution centres covering a large area, sometimes (as in the UK) countrywide, even (as in Europe) from country to country. After transmission to a local substation, the line voltage is reduced by a step-down transformer and distributed by consumers.

**fossil fuel** fuel, such as coal, oil, or natural gas, formed from the fossilized remains of plants that lived hundreds of millions of years ago. Fossil fuels are a nonrenewable resource and will eventually run out. Extraction of coal causes considerable environmental pollution, and burning coal contributes to problems of acid rain and the greenhouse effect.

**geothermal energy** either subterranean hot water pumped to the surface and converted to steam or run through a heat exchanger, or dry steam from an underground source, directed through turbines to produce electricity. The 'hot dry rock' system pumps cold water into fractured rocks deep underground and then extracts the heated water.

**heat pump** machine, run by electricity, that cools the interior of a building by removing heat from the interior air and pumping it out or, conversely, heats the inside by extracting energy from the exterior atmosphere, or from a hot-water source, and pumping it in. A heat pump may transfer more than twice as much energy, in the form of heat, as is needed to run it.

**heat storage** means of storing heat for later release. It is usually achieved by using materials that undergo phase changes at ordinary temperatures—for example, sodium pyrophosphate, which freezes at 7°C. This salt is used to store off-peak heat in the home, being liquefied by cheap heat during the night, and then freezing, if the temperature falls below 7°C, to give off heat during the day. Other developments include the use of plastic crystals that change their structure, rather than melt, when heated. These can be incorporated in clothing or curtains.

**hydroelectric power** electricity generated by water power. In a typical hydroelectric-power (HEP) scheme water stored in a reservoir, often created by damming a river, is piped into water turbines, coupled to electricity generators. In pumped-storage plants water flowing through the turbines is recycled. A tidal-power station is a HEP plant that exploits the rise and fall of the tides. Today about one-fifth of the world's electricity comes from hydroelectric power. Such plants have a prodigious generating capacity. The Grand Coulee plant in Washington State, USA, has a power output of some 10,000 megawatts. The Itaipu power station on the Parana

## OIL CONSUMPTION (1989)

| | (m of barrels) |
|---|---|
| US | 6,323.6 |
| Japan | 1,818.1 |
| West Germany | 831.5 |
| Italy | 708.1 |
| France | 677.4 |
| Canada | 643.1 |
| UK | 634.0 |

*Source: The World Almanac & Book of Facts 1991*

## ENERGY FUTURE: WEIGHING THE ALTERNATIVES

Nothing happens without energy. As the world's population burgeons, it demands ever more energy to support industrial expansion and accommodate its need for motorized transport. From 1900 to 1990 global energy consumption increased more than 15-fold; it is expected to increase by another 50–60% by 2010.

At present, the fossil fuels—coal, oil, and natural gas—provide about 78% of the world's energy, with renewables (such as hydroelectric and biomass sources) contributing 18%, and nuclear stations providing most of the rest. One problem is immediately apparent: fossil fuels will not last forever. At the present rate of consumption, the world's known oil reserves will only last about 40 years, its gas reserves will last about 60 years, and its coal reserves will last about 250 years. The consumption of fossil fuels also threatens the global environment. Sulphurous and nitrous gases given off by coal- and oil-burning power stations cause acid rain, and each year the burning of fossil fuels causes 5 billion tonnes/4.9 billion tons of carbon dioxide to be pumped into the atmosphere, intensifying the greenhouse effect and, it is predicted, disturbing the Earth's climate.

Clearly there is a pressing need to restrict the consumption of fossil fuels. But is this possible? It seems likely that the world population will reach 7 billion by 2010 and industrialization will by then have doubled. At present, the citizens of developing countries use much less fuel than do people in developed countries. In Nepál, for example, the average person uses only one-thousandth as much fuel as a person in the USA. But as developing countries seek to improve the living conditions of their expanding populations, their need for energy increases. During the period 1980–85, the population of the developing countries grew by 11%, but their energy consumption grew by 22%.

There are two main ways in which the situation might be resolved, and a sustainable energy economy established. Firstly, new non-polluting sources of energy must be developed and, secondly, all energy must be used more efficiently.

There are opportunities for developing the established energy sources. Of the fossil fuels, natural gas burns most cleanly, and some analysts feel that natural gas burnt in turbines similar to jet engines offers the best choice for electricity generation. Even coal, which is a dirty fuel, can be burnt cleanly and with greater efficiency using fluidized bed technology, in which burning coal is suspended in a stream

of air. However, these technologies still release carbon dioxide into the atmosphere.

Carbon-free energy is produced by nuclear reactors. But high costs and public anxiety about safety have caused reservations about investment in nuclear power. More advanced reactor design could restore confidence: work is in progress on a new generation of 'passively stable' designs that need no external control, and on safety systems that prevent run-away power build-ups.

The possibilities for renewable energy sources may be more limited than was once thought. The British government, when reviewing new energy sources, classified only four technologies as 'economically attractive' for the UK. The technologies thought most hopeful were passive solar design (the design of buildings so that they absorb and retain as much of the Sun's heat as possible), combustion of dry wastes, digestion of wastes (mainly in landfill rubbish dumps) to produce methane gas, and some small-scale hydroelectric schemes. Technologies classified as 'promising but uncertain' included wind energy on land, tidal energy, shoreline wave energy, and geothermal hot-dry-rock sources. The UK officially abandoned hot-dry-rock research in early 1991. Classified as 'long shot' for the UK were active solar heating, offshore wind energy, offshore wave energy, and geothermal aquifers. In other countries, special circumstances, such as high sunshine in desert areas, may allow more rapid development of particular technologies than in the UK.

Greater efficiency is the best hope of buying time until new sources are developed. There are opportunities for energy efficiency in the design of buildings—for example, 'superinsulated' houses in Sweden and the Netherlands require 89% less heat than normal, and installing low-emissivity windows (windows that radiate little heat) saves significant energy in office blocks. New condensing furnaces can reduce energy demand by nearly 30% because they extract heat from their exhaust gases, rather than waste it. The production of electricity can be made more efficient by co-generation—the combined production of heat and electricity—in which the heat remaining in the steam after it has passed through the electricity generator is used for other industrial processes. Existing techniques could be used to increase fuel economy in cars—up to 23 km per litre/65 mi per gallon. Government policies, especially in the developed countries, are needed to speed the adoption of these technologies.

river (Brazil/Paraguay) has a potential capacity of 12,000 megawatts.

**natural gas** mixture of flammable gases found in the Earth's crust (often in association with petroleum), now one of the world's three main fossil fuels (with coal and oil). Natural gas is a mixture of hydrocarbons, chiefly methane, with ethane, butane, and propane.

**nuclear energy** energy from the inner core or nucleus of atoms, as opposed to energy released in chemical processes such as burning.

*nuclear fission* as in an atom bomb, is achieved by allowing a neutron to strike the nucleus of an atom of uranium-235, which then splits apart to release perhaps two to three other

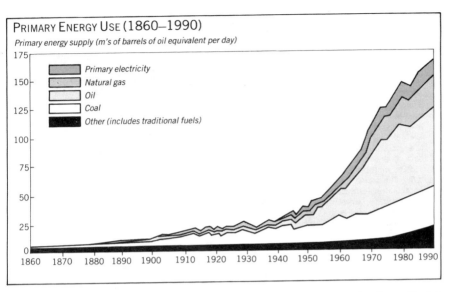

PRIMARY ENERGY USE (1860–1990)
Primary energy supply (m's of barrels of oil equivalent per day)

- Primary electricity
- Natural gas
- Oil
- Coal
- Other (includes traditional fuels)

neutrons. If the material is pure uranium-235, a chain reaction is set up when these neutrons in turn strike other nuclei. This happens with great rapidity, resulting in the tremendous burst of energy associated with the atom bomb. However, the process can be controlled by absorbing excess neutrons in 'control rods' (which may be made of steel alloyed with boron), and slowing down the speed of those neutrons allowed to act. This is what happens inside a nuclear power plant.
**nuclear fusion** is the release of thermonuclear energy by the combination of hydrogen nuclei to form helium nuclei. It is the process that takes place in a hydrogen bomb and, as a continuing reaction, in the Sun and other stars. Attempts to harness it for commercial power production have so far not succeeded.
**reactors** there are various types of (fission) reactor in use. In a gas-cooled reactor, a circulating gas under pressure (such as carbon dioxide) removes heat from the core of the reactor, which usually contains natural uranium and has neutron-absorbing control rods made of boron. The Calder Hall reactor is of this type. An advanced gas-cooled reactor (AGR) generally has enriched uranium oxide as its fuel. A water-cooled reactor, such as the steam-generating heavy-water reactor at Winfrith, Dorset, has water circulating through the hot core. The water is converted to steam, which drives turbo-alternators for generating electricity. In a pressurized water reactor (PWR) the coolant consists of a sealed system of pressurized heavy water (deuterium oxide), which heats ordinary water to form steam in heat exchangers. The spent fuel from either type of reactor contains some plutonium, which can be extracted and used as fuel for the so-called fast breeder reactor (such as the one at Dounreay, Scotland). This produces more plutonium than it consumes (hence its name)

by converting uranium placed as a blanket round the main core. The usual coolant is liquid sodium, a substance that is difficult to handle. A major danger with any type of reactor is the possibility of meltdown, which can result in the release of radioactive material. Problems can also arise over the processing of nuclear fuel and disposal of nuclear waste.
**nuclear accidents** the most serious have been:
**April 1986** at Chernobyl (USSR): a leak from a non-pressurized boiling-water reactor, one of the largest in the Soviet Union, caused by overheating. The resulting clouds of radioactive isotopes were traced as far away as Sweden. Vast tracts of land and hundreds of people were contaminated.
**1979** at Three Mile Island, Harrisburg, USA: a pressurized water reactor leaked radioactive matter as a result of a combination of mechanical and electrical failure, as well as operator error.
**1957** at Windscale (now Sellafield), England: fire destroyed the core of a reactor, releasing large quantities of radioactive fumes into the atmosphere.
**nuclear waste** is produced in three forms:
**gas** usually in small enough quantity to be released into the atmosphere;
**solid** irradiated fuel-element cans and other equipment. When of low activity, this is packaged for sea disposal (for example, at a site 450 km/300 mi off Land's End), but this is controversial. High-activity waste may be combustible (plutonium being recovered from the incinerator), or may be buried, the latter being another source of controversy;
**liquid** high-activity liquid wastes pose the greatest problems of all. Storage has been proposed in salt mines, granite formations, or 'clay basins'; or on or under the seabed. However, no container can be guaranteed (as international

## UPDATE ON ALTERNATIVE SOURCES OF ENERGY

If we could exploit only a small fraction of the energy that reaches Earth from the Sun, our energy problems would be over. The energy that falls on the Earth each year is more than 12,000 times the world's annual energy consumption. The sunshine falling on the USA's roads alone each year is equivalent to twice the energy of all the coal and oil burnt in the entire world during that year. This energy is not easy to exploit, but several solar-energy technologies have advanced during recent years. During the 1990s, wind power, solar thermal (heating) systems, and biomass sources are likely to become important in some parts of the world.

The world's largest wind farm—a collection of wind turbines—is in California at Altamont Pass. This site has 7,500 turbines, producing about 85% of the world's wind energy. The development of the Altamont Pass farm was stimulated by favourable tax incentives. These incentives have now ceased but the California wind-power industry still thrives. Thanks to gradual improvement of the turbines and better general management, the cost of wind-generated electricity has dropped to seven cents a unit, compared to a cost of five cents a unit for electricity from a coal-fired station.

Across the Atlantic, the European Community has estimated that there is potential for about 400,000 big wind turbines in Europe, capable of producing three times Europe's present energy needs. In the UK in 1990, the VAWT 850, one of the largest wind turbines in Europe, was opened at Carmarthen Bay, South Wales. Supporters of renewable energy welcomed the new turbine, but complained of the UK's slow progress in harnessing wind energy. Government subsidies were held to be too low, and the Non-Fossil Fuel Obligation—the amount of energy that the newly-privatized electricity-distribution companies must by law obtain from non-fossil sources—was said to be too small, compared with countries such as Denmark, where there are more than 3,000 turbines.

California also leads the world in solar thermal electricity generation. The LUZ Corporation has built a solar thermal plant in the Mojave Desert that generates 275 million watts (275 MW). By 1994, the system will have expanded by another 300 MW. The LUZ plant uses parabolic mirrors to focus sunlight on oil-carrying pipes. The oil is heated as it circulates through the pipe and is used to produce steam to drive turbine generators.

An alternative system uses sun-tracking mirrors that focus sunlight onto a central receiver. During the 1970s, a number of plants were built using this technology, including a 10 MW plant called Solar One at Daggett, California, and a 5 MW unit at Almeria, Spain. The major project of this type at present is the European Phoebus Project, which is planning to build a 30 MW plant in Jordan.

Biomass is material, such as wood, that is created by plants during photosynthesis. Solar energy is stored within it. The simplest way of releasing this energy is to burn the plant

*The VAWT 850 wind turbine at Carmarthen Bay, Wales.*

material for fuel. Biomass has a number of attractive features. It is readily available in most regions and, unlike fossil fuels, does not increase the overall carbon dioxide content of the atmosphere when burnt (the carbon dioxide released by burning is exactly balanced by the carbon dioxide absorbed during the growth of the fuel material).

The most efficient use of biomass is found in situations where there are large amounts of plant residues available from industrial processes, such as in the sugar cane or alcohol industries. The residues are converted into gas by heating them with air and steam, and the gas produced burnt in a turbine. Alternatively, alcohol may be produced by fermentation of biomass-derived sugars. This process is used on a large scale in Brazil to produce motor fuel.

The photovoltaic, or solar, cell produces electricity directly from sunlight. Solar cells are used extensively in calculators and to generate power in space satellites, and their cost is dropping rapidly, from $60 per unit in 1970 to 25 cents per unit in 1990. This is still about five times the cost of conventional electricity, but is sufficiently low to encourage further research. In the USA, a variety of systems are being tested, once again in California, by the Pacific Gas and Electric Company. In Japan, photovoltaic systems powerful enough for domestic use are connected to the grid. In Germany, several installations are being tested, the largest of which is expected eventually to produce 1 MW.

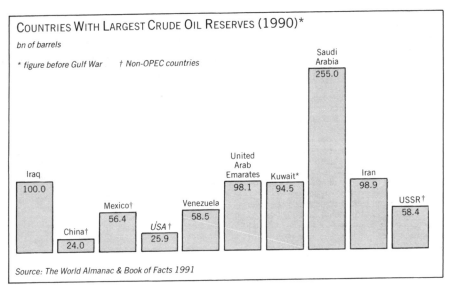

COUNTRIES WITH LARGEST CRUDE OIL RESERVES (1990)*

bn of barrels

\* figure before Gulf War    † Non-OPEC countries

Saudi Arabia 255.0

Iraq 100.0

China† 24.0

Mexico† 56.4

USA† 25.9

Venezuela 58.5

United Arab Emarates 98.1

Kuwait* 94.5

Iran 98.9

USSR† 58.4

Source: The World Almanac & Book of Facts 1991

authorities require) against decay, volcanic action, and so on, for 100,000 years. The most promising of the proposed methods involves the vitrification of liquid waste into solid glass cylinders, which might then be placed in titanium-cobalt alloy containers and deposited on other planets. If these containers were stored beneath the sea they would start to corrode after 1,000 years, and would dissolve within the following 1,000 years.

**petroleum** or **crude oil** natural mineral oil, a thick greenish-brown flammable liquid found underground in permeable rocks, and consisting of hydrocarbons mixed with oxygen, sulphur, nitrogen, and other elements in varying proportions. The products derived from petroleum include the fossil fuels oil and petrol (gasoline). Eight of the 14 top-earning companies in the USA in 1990 (led by Exxon with $7 billion in sales) are in the global petroleum industry.

Petroleum is thought to be derived from ancient organic material that has been converted by, first, bacterial action, then heat and pressure. The exploitation of oilfields began with the first commercial well in Pennsylvania 1859. The USA led in production until the 1960s, when the Middle East outproduced other areas, their immense reserves leading to a worldwide dependence on cheap oil for transport and industry. In 1961 the Organization of the Petroleum Exporting Countries (OPEC) was established to avoid exploitation of member countries; after OPEC's price rises in 1973, the International Energy Agency (IEA) was established 1974 to protect the interests of oil-consuming countries. New technologies were introduced to pump oil from offshore and from the Arctic (the Alaska pipeline) in an effort to avoid a monopoly by OPEC.

The burning of petroleum fuel is one cause of air pollution. The transport of oil can lead to major catastrophes—for example, the *Torrey Canyon* tanker lost off SW England 1967, which led to an agreement by the international oil companies 1968 to pay compensation for massive shore pollution. The 1989 oil spill in Alaska from the *Exxon Valdez* damaged the area's fragile environment, despite clean-up efforts.

**renewable resource** natural resource that is replaced by natural processes in a reasonable amount of time. Soil, water, forests, plants, and animals are all renewable resources as long as they are properly conserved. Solar, wind, wave, and geothermal energies are based on renewable resources.

**solar energy** energy derived from the Sun's radiation. A solar furnace, such as that built in 1970 at Odeillo in the French Pyrenees, has thousands of mirrors to focus the Sun's rays; it produces uncontaminated, intensive heat for industrial and scientific or experimental purposes. Other solar heaters produce less energy and may have industrial or domestic uses. They usually consist of a black (heat-absorbing) panel containing pipes through which air or water is circulated, either by thermal convection or by a pump. Solar energy may also be harnessed indirectly using solar cells, made up of panels of semiconductor material (usually silicon) that generate electricity when illuminated by sunlight. Because of their high cost and low-power output, solar cells have found few applications outside space probes and artificial satellites.

**tidal power station** hydroelectric power plant that uses the 'head' of water created by the rise and fall of the ocean tides to spin the water turbines. An example is at St Malo, France.

**turbine** an engine in which steam, water or gas is made to spin a rotating shaft. Turbines are among the most powerful machines. Steam turbines are used to drive ships' propellers

## NUCLEAR POWER: WHERE ARE WE NOW?

Nuclear power has been getting a bad press lately. Public anxiety about the safety of nuclear plants grew after the 1986 accident at Chernobyl. In 1990, further ammunition was handed to the anti-nuclear lobby in the UK during the government's privatization of the electricity industry. Financial arguments seemed to show that nuclear electricity was much more expensive than non-nuclear electricity. However, it is worth noting that most countries find nuclear electricity cheaper than that from fossil fuel. Pricing in the UK is largely the result of abnormally-high rates of return, short pay-back times, and financial-safety factors.

Despite the lack of confidence in the economics of the industry (mainly in the UK and USA), the capacity of the world's nuclear stations grew in 1990. The 424 nuclear-power plants operating throughout the world at the end of 1990 were capable of producing 324 million units of electricity, compared with 318 million units the year before. Ten reactors started operation in 1990; twelve reactors closed down. 83 reactors were being constructed.

Most reactors under construction are light-water thermal reactors. These reactors use ordinary water to slow the neutrons in the power-producing core to low or 'thermal' temperatures. Slow neutrons split the atoms of the uranium fuel, to release energy, more efficiently. The next generation of thermal reactors, which will play a major role in electricity generation through to the end of the 21st century, are being designed so that they do not require external safety systems to stabilize them in an emergency. The Swedish PIUS (Process Inherent Ultimate Safety) reactor is typical. Its energy-

generating core, primary cooling circuit, and steam generator are immersed in a large pool of cold water (containing dissolved boron) in a prestressed-concrete pressure vessel. In normal operation, pressure developed by the cooling pump keeps the borated water from entering the core. But if the cooling system were to be disturbed, this water would flood the core. The boron would absorb the neutrons and the core would automatically shut down.

In the early decades of the next century, fast reactors will be employed alongside the thermal reactors. Fast reactors extract 60 times more power from natural uranium than thermal reactors, and their use should allow world resources of uranium to meet electricity requirements for the next 1,000 years. In Europe, the UK and France have led the development of these reactors through the operation of their experimental reactors—Phenix in SW France and the Prototype Fast Reactor (PFR) at Dounreay in Scotland. It is now generally agreed that the technology is ready for commercial exploitation, and a design organisation has been set up to produce the European Fast Reactor (EFR). Construction of the EFR is due to start in 1997 and operation by 2005. Commercial deployment of fast breeders will probably start in around 2020, when many of the existing thermal reactors will need replacing.

Fusion reactors—in which hydrogen nuclei are forced together to release energy—are a longterm option. They have attractive features: an unlimited supply of fuel (hydrogen from seawater), less dangerous waste products, and inherent safety. Experiments at Princeton, USA, in 1990 have demonstrated the feasibility of a fusion process in which the fuel, or plasma, heated to 400 million=C, generates 50,000 watts of power. The Joint European Torus (JET) at the Culham laboratory, NW England, has also had success. It has produced plasma at temperatures of 250 million=C for more than one second, which would be equivalent to a power of 12 million watts (12 MW) if deuterium and tritium fuel were used. Tritium will be introduced into JET in 1994, and it is then expected to produce a net energy output.

If these developments are to be applied commercially, the nuclear industry must not only meet the vast technical challenges presented, it must also convince the public and governments of the value and safety of nuclear energy.

### PROBABLE TIMETABLE FOR THE DEPLOYMENT OF NUCLEAR POWER

| | |
|---|---|
| * up to 2030: | introduction of inherently safe light-water thermal reactors |
| * 2020 to 2030: | first commercial exploitation of fast reactors |
| * 2030 to 2100: | electricity generated by both thermal and fast reactors; demonstration of fusion power generation |
| * 2100 to 2300: | widespread electricity generation by fast reactors; first commercial exploitation of fusion power |

and the generators in power stations; water turbines spin the generators in hydroelectric power plants; and gas turbines, in the guise of jet engines, power most aircraft, and drive machines in industry. The high-temperature, high-pressure steam for steam turbines is raised in boilers heated by furnaces burning coal, oil or gas, or by nuclear energy. A steam turbine consists of a shaft, or rotor, which rotates inside a fixed casing

(stator). The rotor carries 'wheels' consisting of blades, or vanes. The stator has vanes set between the vanes of the rotor, which direct the steam through the rotor vanes at the optimum angle.

**water mill** machine that harnesses the energy in flowing water to produce mechanical power, typically for milling (grinding) grain. Water from a stream is directed against the paddles of a water wheel to make it turn. Simple gearing transfers this motion to the millstones. The modern equivalent of the water wheel is the water turbine, used in hydroelectric power plants.

**wave power** power obtained by harnessing the energy of water waves. Various schemes have been advanced since 1973, when oil prices rose dramatically and an energy shortage threatened. In 1974 English engineer Stephen Salter developed the duck—a floating boom whose segments nod up and down with the waves. The nodding motion can be used to drive pumps and spin generators. Another device, developed in Japan, uses an oscillating water column to harness wave power.

**windmill** a mill with sails or vanes that, by the action of wind upon them, drive machinery for grinding corn, pumping water, and so on. Windmills were used in the East in ancient times, and in Europe they were first used in Germany and the Netherlands in the 12th century. The main types of early windmill are the *post mill*, which is turned round a post when the direction of the wind changes, and the *tower mill*, which has a revolving turret on top. It usually has a device (fantail) that keeps the sails pointing into the wind. In the USA a light type of windmill with steel sails supported on a long steel girder shaft was introduced for use on farms. The energy crisis has led to modern experiments with wind turbines, designed to use wind power on a major scale. They usually have a propeller-type rotor mounted on a tall shell tower. The turbine drives a generator for producing electricity.

**wind turbine** windmill of advanced aerodynamic design connected to an electricity generator and used in wind-power installations. Wind turbines can be either large propeller-type rotors mounted on a tall tower, or flexible metal strips fixed to a vertical axle at top and bottom. The world's largest wind turbine is on Hawaii, in the Pacific Ocean. It has two blades 50 m/164 ft long on top of a tower 20 storeys high.

## Nuclear energy

*What would you do if a nuclear power station were to be built in your area?*

| | |
|---|---|
| Would agree to its being built | 9 |
| Would not oppose though would feel anxious about it | 22 |
| Would oppose | 60 |
| Would not feel anything | 5 |
| Don't know | 4 |

*Nuclear power stations produce waste that will remain radioactive for centuries, but this can be buried at sea or deep underground. Do you think this is a risk worth taking or not?*

| | |
|---|---|
| Worth taking | 26 |
| Not worth taking | 66 |
| Don't know | 9 |

*And which do you believe are the main disadvantages of using nuclear power stations to generate electricity?*

| | |
|---|---|
| Risk of catastrophic failure | 58 |
| Dangerous to health | 56 |
| Pollutes the environment | 41 |
| Looks ugly, spoils the landscape | 28 |
| Cannot be near towns and villages | 26 |
| Much local disruption during building | 15 |
| Takes up a lot of land | 14 |
| Produces expensive electricity | 11 |
| Unreliable, not always working | 10 |
| Noisy | 7 |
| Other | 2 |
| None | 3 |
| Don't know | 8 |

# THE NATURAL WORLD

**carbon cycle** the sequence by which carbon circulates and is recycled through the natural world. The carbon element from carbon dioxide, released into the atmosphere by living things as a result of respiration, is taken up by plants during photosynthesis and converted into carbohydrates; the oxygen component is released back into the atmosphere. The simplest link in the carbon cycle, however, occurs when an animal eats a plant and carbon is transferred from, say, a leaf cell to the animal body. Today, the carbon cycle is in danger of being disrupted by the increased consumption and burning of fossil fuels, and the burning of large tracts of tropical forests, as a result of which levels of carbon dioxide are building up in the atmosphere and probably contributing to the greenhouse effect.

**climate** weather conditions at a particular place over a period of time. Climate encompasses all the meteorological elements and the factors that influence them. The primary factors that determine the variations of climate over the surface of the Earth are: (a) the effect of latitude and the tilt of the Earth's axis to the plane of the orbit about the Sun (66.5°); (b) the large-scale movements of different wind belts over the Earth's surface; (c) the temperature difference between land and sea; (d) contours of the ground; and (e) location of the area in relation to ocean currents. Catastrophic variations to climate may be caused by the impact of another planetary body, or by clouds resulting from volcanic activity.

The most important local or global meterological changes brought about by human activity are those linked with ozone depleters and the greenhouse effect.

**deforestation** the destruction of forest for timber, fuelwood, charcoal burning, and clearing for agriculture and extractive industries such as mining, without planting new trees to replace those lost (reafforestation) or working on a cycle that allows the natural forest to regenerate. Deforestation causes fertile soil to be blown away or washed into rivers, leading to soil erosion, drought, flooding, and loss of wildlife.

Deforestation is taking place in both tropical rainforests and temperate forests.(See feature in this section.)

**desertification** the creation of deserts by changes in climate, or by human-aided processes such as overgrazing, destruction of forest belts, and exhaustion of the soil by too intensive cultivation without restoration of fertility; all usually prompted by the pressures of expanding populations. The process can be reversed by special planting (marram grass, trees) and by the use of water-absorbent plastic grains (a polymer absorbent of 40 times its own weight of water), which, added to the sand, enable crops to be grown. About 135 million people are directly affected by desertification, mainly in Africa, the Indian subcontinent, and South America.

**firewood** the principal fuel for some 1.5 billion people, mainly in the Third World. In principle a renewable energy source, firewood is being cut far faster than the trees can regenerate in many areas of Africa and Asia, leading to deforestation. (In Mali, for example, wood provides 97% of total energy consumption, and deforestation is running at an estimated 9,000 hectares a year.) The heat efficiency of firewood can be increased by use of stoves, but many people cannot afford to buy these.

**fossil fuel** fuel, such as coal, oil, and natural gas, formed from the fossilized remains of plants that lived hundreds of millions of years ago. Fossil fuels are a nonrenewable resource and will eventually run out. Extraction of coal causes considerable environmental pollution, and burning coal contributes to problems of acid rain and the greenhouse effect.

**habitat** the localized environment in which an organism lives, and which provides for all (or almost all) of its needs. The diversity of habitats found within the Earth's ecosystem is enormous, and they are changing all the time. Many can be considered inorganic or physical, for example the Arctic ice cap, a cave, or a cliff face. Others are more complex, for instance a woodland or a forest floor. Some habitats are so precise that they are called **microhabitats**, such as the area under a stone where a particular type of insect lives. Most habitats provide a home for many species.

**hedge** or **hedgerow** row of closely planted shrubs or low trees, generally acting as a land division and windbreak. Hedges also serve as a source of food and as a refuge for wildlife, and provide a habitat not unlike the understorey of a natural forest.

**mangrove** any of several shrubs and trees, especially of the mangrove family Rhizophoraceae,

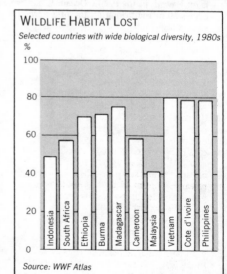

WILDLIFE HABITAT LOST

*Selected countries with wide biological diversity, 1980s*
%

Indonesia | South Africa | Ethiopia | Burma | Madagascar | Cameroon | Malaysia | Vietnam | Cote d' Ivoire | Philippines

Source: WWF Atlas

found in the muddy swamps of tropical coasts and estuaries. By sending down aerial roots from their branches, they rapidly form close-growing mangrove thickets. Their timber is impervious to water and resists marine worms.

**national park** land set aside and conserved for public enjoyment. The first was Yellowstone National Park, USA, established 1872. National parks include not only the most scenic places, but also places distinguished for their historic, prehistoric, or scientific interest, or for their superior recreational assets. They range from areas the size of small countries to pockets of just a few hectares.

There are ten national parks in England and Wales; they are run by National Park Authorities and are financed by national government (75%) and local government (25%).

**nature reserve** area set aside to protect a habitat and the wildlife that lives within it, with only restricted admission for the public. A nature reserve often provides a sanctuary for rare species. The world's largest is Etosha Reserve, Namibia, with an area of 99,520 sq km/ 38,415 sq mi.

**niche** in ecology, the 'place' occupied by a species in its habitat, including all chemical, physical, and biological components, such as what it eats, the time of day at which the species feeds, temperature, moisture, the parts of the habitat that it uses (for example, trees or open grassland), the way it reproduces, and how it behaves. It is believed that no two species can occupy exactly the same niche, because they would be in direct competition for the same resources at every stage of their life cycle.

**nonrenewable resource** natural resource, such as coal or oil, that takes thousands or millions of years to form naturally and can therefore not be replaced once it is consumed. The main energy sources used by humans are nonrenewable resources.

**oceanography** the study of the oceans, their origin, composition, structure, history, and wildlife (seabirds, fish, plankton, and other organisms). It involves the study of water movements—currents, waves, and tides—and the chemical and physical properties of the seawater. It deals with the origin and topography of the ocean floor—ocean trenches and ridges formed by plate tectonics, and continental shelves from the submerged portions of the continents. Much oceanography uses computer simulations to plot the possible movements of the waters, and many studies are carried out by remote sensing.

The World Ocean Circulation Experiment, begun 1990 and set to last seven years, involves researchers from 44 countries examining the physics of the ocean and its role in the climate of the Earth. It is based at Southampton University, England.

**overfishing** fishing at rates that exceed the sustained-yield cropping of fish species, resulting in a net population decline. For example, in the North Atlantic, herring has been fished to the verge of extinction and the cod and had-

## WORLDWIDE PROTECTION OF NATURAL AREAS

|  | All protected areas | |
|---|---|---|
|  | Number | Area (ha) |
| World | 5,289 | 529,081,551 |
| Africa | 521 | 101,875,251 |
| Asia | 1,126 | 61,367,197 |
| Europe | 1,347 | 31,326,547 |
| North and Central America | 890 | 193,908,695 |
| South America | 453 | 80,123,051 |
| USSR | 171 | 20,773,379 |
| Oceania | 774 | 39,499,579 |

*Source: World Resources 1990-91*

dock populations are severely depleted. In the Third World, use of huge factory ships, often by Western fisheries, has depleted stocks for local people who cannot obtain protein in any other way.

**rainforest** dense forest found on or near the equator where the climate is hot and wet. Over half the tropical rainforests are in Central and South America, the rest in SE Asia and Africa. Although covering approximately 8% of the Earth's land surface, they make up about 50% of all growing wood on the planet, and harbour at least 40% of the Earth's species (plants and animals). Rainforests are being destroyed at an increasing rate as their valuable timber is harvested and land cleared for agriculture, causing problems of deforestation, soil erosion, and flooding. By 1990 50% of the world's rainforest had been removed. If clearance continues at the present rate, all of the world's primary (undisturbed) rainforest will disappear or be damaged within the next 30 years.

Rainforests can be divided into several kinds: tropical, montane, upper montane or cloud, mangrove, and subtropical. They are characterized by a great diversity of species, usually of tall broad-leafed evergreen trees, with many climbing vines and ferns, some of which are a main source of raw materials for medicines. Rainforests are some of the most complex and diverse ecosystems on the planet and help to regulate global weather patterns. When deforestation occurs, the microclimate of the mature forest disappears; soil erosion and flooding become major problems since rainforests protect the shallow tropical soils.

Clearing of the rainforests may lead to a global warming of the atmosphere, and contribute to the greenhouse effect. Deforestation also causes the salt level in the ground to rise to the surface, making the land unsuitable for farming or ranching.

**renewable resource** a natural resource that is replaced by natural processes in a reasonable amount of time. Soil, water, forests, plants, and animals are all renewable resources as long as they are properly conserved. Solar, wind, wave, and geothermal energies are based on renewable resources.

## TROPICAL MARINE AREAS UNDER THREAT

**Mangroves**

| | |
|---|---|
| Niger River delta, Nigeria | Exploited for timber, fuel, fodder and urban expansion. |
| Kenya and Tanzania | Cleared for fuelwood, building materials and tourist resorts. |
| Indus River mouth, Pakistan | Over-exploitation for fuel, fodder and building material. |
| Sundarbans, India and Bangladesh | Over-exploitation for fuel, fodder, timber and fishponds. |
| Malaysia and Gulf of Thailand | Destruction for fish and shellfish ponds and agricultural land. |
| Philippines | Destruction for timber, tannin, fuelwood and fish and shellfish ponds. |
| Indonesia | Massive destruction for logging and woodchip industries, fish and shellfish ponds and for building materials and fuelwood. |
| Queensland, Australia | Town and tourist development. |
| US south coast, Texas to Florida | Over-development of coastline for urban expansion, resorts, housing estates. Also used as rubbish dumps. |
| Panama | Cleared for fish and shrimp ponds. |
| Ecuador | Cleared for fish and shrimp ponds. |
| Caribbean | All mangrove stands disturbed. Main threats: tourism and coastal land development. |

**Seagrasses**

| | |
|---|---|
| East Africa | Under threat from heavy sedimentation of shallow coastal waters caused by erosion of agricultural lands. |
| Southeast Asia | Under threat from loss of mangroves, coastal development, urban expansion and bucket dredging for tin. |
| Caribbean and Gulf of Mexico | Under threat from dredge and fill operations, loss of mangroves, coastal development for tourism, oil production. |

**Coral reefs**

| | |
|---|---|
| East Africa | Coral mining for building materials, blast fishing, tourist trade and sedimentation. |
| The Gulf | Oil and industrial pollution, sedimentation. |
| Thailand and Malaysia | Tourist resorts, bucket dredging for tin, over-fishing. |
| Philippines | Blast fishing, coral mining, collection for tourist trade and use of poisons. |
| Southern Japan — Ryukyu Archipelago | Destroyed by coastal development and sedimentation. |
| Indonesia | Destroyed by blast fishing, coral mining, tourist trade and coastal development. |
| South Pacific | Tourism, sedimentation from coastal development. |
| Wider Caribbean | Collection for tourist trade, coastal development, mangrove destruction/ sedimentation and damage by boat anchors. |

Source: World Wildlife Fund

**slash and burn** simple agricultural method whereby natural vegetation is cut and burned, and the clearing then farmed for a few years until the soil loses its fertility, whereupon farmers move on and leave the area to regrow. Although this is possible with a small, widely dispersed population, it becomes unsustainable with more people and is now a form of deforestation.

**soil erosion** the wearing away and redistribution of the Earth's soil layer. It is caused by the action of water, wind, and ice, and also by improper methods of agriculture. If unchecked, soil erosion results in the formation of deserts. It has been estimated that 20% of the world's cultivated topsoil was lost between 1950 and 1990.

If the rate of erosion exceeds the rate of soil formation (from rock), then the land will decline and eventually become infertile. The removal of forests or other vegetation often leads to serious soil erosion, because plant roots bind soil, and without them the soil is free to wash or blow away, as in the American dust bowl. The effect is worse on hillsides, and there has been devastating loss of soil where forests have been cleared from mountainsides, as in Madagscar. Improved agricultural practices are needed to combat soil erosion. Wind-

breaks, such as hedges or strips planted with coarse grass, are valuable. Organic farming can reduce soil erosion by as much as 75%.

**sustained-yield cropping** the removal of surplus individuals from a population of organisms so that the population maintains a constant size. This usually requires selective removal of animals of all ages and both sexes to ensure a balanced population structure. Taking too many individuals can result in a population decline, as in overfishing.

**water** Water covers 70% of the Earth's surface; less than 0.01% is fresh water. It occurs as standing (oceans, lakes) and running (rivers, streams) water, and in the form of rain and vapour, and supports all forms of life on Earth.

Water supply in sparsely populated regions usually comes from underground water rising to the surface in natural springs, supplemented by pumps and wells. Urban sources are deep artesian wells, rivers, and reservoirs, usually formed from enlarged lakes or dammed and flooded valleys, from which water is conveyed by pipes, conduits, and aqueducts to filter beds. As water seeps through layers of shingle, gravel, and sand, harmful organisms are removed and the water is then distributed by pumping or gravitation through mains and pipes. Often other substances are added

# DEFORESTATION—A DISASTER IN THE MAKING

The statistics of tropical-rainforest destruction are emotive and frightening: an area the size of Wales destroyed every month; a football pitch a second ... In reality, despite countless research projects and satellite imagery, we still have an incomplete picture of what is happening. One thing that everyone agrees on is that tropical rainforests are being burned, felled, and degraded at a rate that will make them a rarity in a few years' time, if current trends continue.

'Tropical rainforest' is a general term describing the lush, highly diverse forests found in an irregular belt around the equator. The largest concentrations are in Latin America, W Africa, SE Asia, and Australasia, with smaller areas in S India, parts of E Africa, and Central America. Despite making up only one-third of the world's forests, tropical rainforests contain four-fifths of the vegetation and half the world's species of plants and animals. In the dark, humid understorey, nutrients are recycled extremely fast and most are locked in living material, so that the ground below contains far less humus than in a temperate forest.

Now the forests are being rapidly destroyed. Loggers and miners move into forest regions, building roads and towns, and degrading or destroying the forest. Landless peasants follow along the dirt tracks, desperate for somewhere to farm. Sometimes the government gives them a helping hand, such as the disastrous transmigration programme in Indonesia, where thousands of people were moved into forest regions on the island of Kalimantan, in settlement projects that have mainly failed. Ranchers in the Amazon burned an area of forest the size of France in 1989, to create cattle pasture that lasts for only a few years before reverting to useless scrub. Some 200 million people still rely primarily on wood fuel, and charcoal burning is a major cause of destruction in countries such as India.

Tropical forests once covered 16 million sq km/6 million sq mi. If current trends continue, just a few fragments will remain in most areas within 50 years. Thailand, Vietnam, and the Philippines have all lost around 80% of their forests, the Ivory Coast at least 90%, Central America over 80%. Other countries still contain vast forests but are destroying them at an accelerated rate. The Amazon forest of Brazil, which is larger than the whole of Western Europe, looks set to be halved within 20 years. The issue reached new levels of international concern at the beginning of the 1990s, when clear links were drawn between forest destruction and global changes in weather patterns, including the greenhouse effect, especially when forests are burned.

Deforestation alters weather patterns and can lead to drought. On the other hand, monsoon rains in deforested areas cause serious soil erosion, leading to flooding and siltation further downstream. Some of the vast hydroelectric projects developed throughout the Third World have estimated lifetimes of only 10 or 20 years because of siltation of the reservoirs due to forest loss.

The scale of the disaster has prompted international efforts to halt or reverse the process. Unfortunately, so far there have been more words than action. An Oct 1990 meeting of the International Tropical Timber Organization, set up to regulate the timber trade, failed to halt the logging of Malaysia's Sabah and Sarawak states, which has already halved the forest and will reduce it to one-fifth by 2010 at current logging rates. In Jan 1991, a South Korean company agreed plans to log one-tenth of Guyana's forests, one of the few relatively untouched tropical forest areas left in the world. The Tropical Forest Action Plan, an initiative of the United Nations Food and Agriculture Organization and nongovernmental organizations, has done little to halt overcutting.

But there are a few small signs of hope. An international certification scheme is being set up to identify tropical timber from forests and plantations managed sustainably. Awareness of the problem is now global. Money from the international community is starting to become available for conservation work, management, training, and education. These changes could offer hope for forests in the future, but we still do not know if they will act fast enough.

## ANNUAL DEFORESTATION (1980s)

| | Extent (000s ha) | % total forest |
|---|---|---|
| LATIN AMERICA | 12,473 | 1.45 |
| Belize | 9 | 0.7 |
| Costa Rica | 124 | 6.9 |
| El Salvador | 5 | 3.2 |
| Guatemala | 90 | 2.0 |
| Honduras | 90 | 2.3 |
| Mexico | 615 | 1.3 |
| Nicaragua | 121 | 2.7 |
| Panama | 36 | 0.9 |
| *Central America (totals)* | *1,090* | *1.6* |
| Argentina | NA | NA |
| Bolivia | 117 | 0.2 |
| Brazil | 9,050 | 1.8 |
| Chile | 50 | 0.7 |
| Colombia | 890 | 1.7 |
| Ecuador | 340 | 2.3 |
| Guyana | 3 | 0.0 |
| Paraguay | 212 | 1.1 |
| Peru | 270 | 0.4 |
| Suriname | 3 | 0.0 |
| Uruguay | NA | NA |
| Venezuela | 245 | 0.7 |
| *South America (totals)* | *11,180* | *1.3* |
| AFRICA | 245 | 0.7 |
| ASIA | 4,500 | 0.9 |

*Source: World Resources 1990–91*

to the water, such as chlorine and fluorine; aluminium sulphate is the most widely used chemical in water treatment. In towns, besides industrial demands, domestic and municipal (road washing, sewage) needs account for about 1354l/30 gal per head each day. In coastal desert areas, such as the Arabian peninsula, desalination plants remove salt from sea water. The Earth's waters, both fresh and saline, have been polluted by industrial and domestic chemicals, many of which are toxic and others radioactive.

The British water industry was privatized 1989, and the European Commission announced its intention to take the UK to court for failing to meet EC drinking-water standards on nitrate and pesticide levels.

**wilderness** area of uncultivated and uninhabited land, which is usually located some distance from towns and cities. In the USA wilderness areas are specially designated by Congress and protected by federal agencies.

**wildlife trade** international trade in live plants and animals, and in wildlife products such as skins, horns, shells, and feathers. The trade has made some species virtually extinct, and whole ecosystems (for example, coral reefs) are threatened. Wildlife trade is to some extent regulated by CITES.

Species almost eradicated by trade in their products include many of the largest whales, crocodiles, marine turtles, and some wild cats. Until recently, some 2 million snake skins were exported from India every year. Populations of black rhino and African elephant have collapsed because of hunting for their tusks (ivory), and poaching remains a problem in cases where trade is prohibited.

# ENVIRONMENTAL POLLUTANTS

**acid rain** acidic rainfall, thought to be caused principally by the release into the atmosphere of sulphur dioxide ($SO_2$) and oxides of nitrogen. Sulphur dioxide is formed from the burning of fossil fuels such as coal that contain high quantities of sulphur, and nitrogen oxides are contributed from industrial activities and car exhaust fumes.

Acid rain is linked with damage to and death of forests and lake organisms in Scandinavia, Europe, and eastern North America. It also results in damage to buildings and statues.

**aerosol** particles of liquid or solid suspended in a gas. Fog is a common natural example. Aerosol cans, which contain pressurized gas mixed with a propellant, are used to spray liquid in the form of tiny drops of such products as scents and cleaners. Until recently, most aerosols used chlorofluorocarbons (CFCs) as propellants. However, these were found to cause destruction of the ozone layer in the

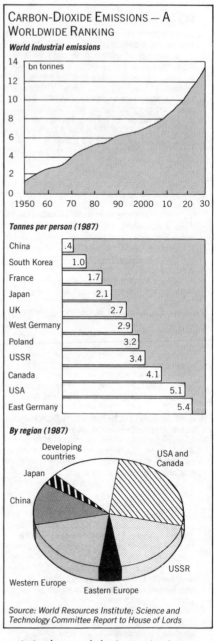

CARBON-DIOXIDE EMISSIONS — A WORLDWIDE RANKING

*World Industrial emissions*

*Tonnes per person (1987)*

| | |
|---|---|
| China | .4 |
| South Korea | 1.0 |
| France | 1.7 |
| Japan | 2.1 |
| UK | 2.7 |
| West Germany | 2.9 |
| Poland | 3.2 |
| USSR | 3.4 |
| Canada | 4.1 |
| USA | 5.1 |
| East Germany | 5.4 |

*By region (1987)*

Developing countries; USA and Canada; Japan; China; Western Europe; Eastern Europe; USSR

Source: World Resources Institute; Science and Technology Committee Report to House of Lords

stratosphere, and the international community has agreed to phase out their use. Most so-called 'ozone-friendly' aerosols also use ozone-depleting chemicals, although they are not as destructive as CFCs. Some of the products sprayed, such as pesticides, can be directly toxic to humans.

**air pollution** contamination of the atmosphere caused by the discharge, accidental or deliberate, of a wide range of toxic substances. Often the amount of the released substance is relatively high in a certain locality, so the harmful effects are more noticeable. The cost of preventing any discharge of pollutants into the air is prohibitive, so attempts are more usually made to reduce gradually the amount of discharge and to disperse this as quickly as possible by using a very tall chimney, or by intermittent release.

**carbon dioxide** $CO_2$ colourless gas, slightly soluble in water and denser than air, produced by living things during the processes of respiration and the decay of organic matter; its increasing density is contributing to global warming (see greenhouse effect in this section).

Britain has 1% of the world's population, yet it produces 3% of $CO_2$ emissions; the USA has 5% of the world's population and produces 25% of $CO_2$ emissions.

**chlorofluorocarbon** (CFC) synthetic chemical, which is odourless, nontoxic, nonflammable, and chemically inert. CFCs are used as propellants in aerosol cans, refrigerants in refrigerators and air conditioners, and in the manufacture of foam boxes for take-away food cartons. They are partly responsible for the destruction of the ozone layer. In June 1990 representatives of 93 nations, including the UK and the USA, agreed to phase out production of CFCs and various other ozone-depleting chemicals by the end of the 20th century.

When CFCs are released into the atmosphere, they drift up slowly into the stratosphere, where, under the influence of ultraviolet radiation from the Sun, they break down into chlorine atoms which destroy the ozone layer and allow harmful radiation from the Sun to reach the Earth's surface. CFCs can remain in the atmosphere for more than 100 years. (See feature in Chemistry.)

**dioxin** any of a family of over 200 organic chemicals, of which 2,3,7,8-tetrachlorodibenzodioxin (2,3,7,8-TCDD) is the most widespread. A highly toxic chemical, it has been associated with a disfiguring skin complaint (chloracne), birth defects, miscarriages, and cancer.

Disasters involving accidental release of large amounts of dioxin into the environment have occurred at Seveso in Italy and Times Beach in Missouri, USA. Small amounts of dioxins are released by the burning of a wide range of chlorinated materials (treated wood, exhaust fumes from fuels treated with chlorinated additives, and plastics). The discovery of dioxin contamination in food and mothers' breast milk has led the EC to decrease significantly dioxin emissions from incinerators.

UK government figures released 1989 showed dioxin levels 100 times higher than guidelines it has set for environmental dioxin in breast milk, suggesting dioxin contamination is more widespread than previously thought.

**eutrophication** the excessive enrichment of rivers, lakes, and shallow sea areas, primarily by nitrate fertilizers, washed from the soil by rain, and by phosphates from fertilizers and detergents in municipal sewage. These encourage the growth of algae and bacteria which use up the oxygen in the water, thereby making it uninhabitable for fishes and other animal life.

**global warming** projected imminent climate change attributed to the greenhouse effect.

**greenhouse effect** in the Earth's atmosphere, the trapping of solar radiation, which, absorbed by the Earth and re-emitted from the surface, is prevented from escaping by various gases in the air. The result is a rise in the Earth's temperature; in a garden greenhouse, the glass walls have the same effect. The main greenhouse gases are carbon dioxide, methane, and chlorofluorocarbons. Fossil-fuel consumption and forest fires are the main causes of carbon dioxide buildup; methane is a byproduct of agriculture (rice, cattle, sheep). Water vapour is another greenhouse gas. United Nations Environment Programme estimates an increase in average world temperatures of 1.5°C/2.7°F with a consequent rise of 20 cm/7.7 in in sea level by 2025.

The concentration of carbon dioxide in the atmosphere is estimated to have risen by 25% since the Industrial Revolution, and 10% since 1950; the rate of increase is now 0.5% a year. Chlorofluorocarbon levels are rising by 5% a year, and nitrous oxide levels by 0.4% a year, resulting in a global warming effect of 0.5% since 1900, and a rise of about 0.1°C a year in the temperature of the world's oceans during the 1980s. Arctic ice was 6–7 m/20–23 ft thick in 1976 and had reduced to 4–5 m/13–17 ft by 1987.

Low-lying areas and entire countries are threatened by flooding, and crops will be affected by the change in climate.

Dubbed the 'greenhouse effect' by Swedish scientist Svante Arrhenius, it was first predicted in 1827 by French mathematician Joseph Fourier (1768–1830).

A computer model from the British Meteorological Office predicts a warming of 2.7°C for a doubling of carbon dioxide.(See feature in Earth Science.)

**leaching** process by which substances are washed out of the soil. Fertilizers leached out of the soil find their way into rivers and cause water pollution. In tropical areas, leaching of the soil after deforestation removes scarce nutrients and leads to a dramatic loss of soil fertility.

**mercury** heavy, silver-grey, metallic element, symbol Hg. Mercury is a cumulative poison that can contaminate the food chain, and cause intestinal disturbance, kidney and brain damage, and birth defects in humans. The discharge into the sea of organic mercury compounds such as dimethylmercury is the major cause of mercury poisoning in the latter half of the twentieth century. Between 1953 and 1975, 684 people in the Japanese fishing village of Minamata were poisoned (115 fatally) by organic mercury wastes that had been dumped into the bay and had accumulated in the bodies of fish and shellfish.

**nitrate** any salt of nitric acid, containing the

$NO_3^-$ ion. Nitrates in the soil, whether naturally occurring or from inorganic or organic fertilizers, can be used by plants to make proteins and nucleic acids. Being soluble in water, nitrates are leached out by rain into streams and reservoirs. High levels are now found in drinking water in arable areas. These may be harmful to newborn babies, and it is possible that they contribute to stomach cancer, although the evidence for this is unproven. The UK current standard is 100 milligrams per litre, double the EC limits to be implemented by 1993.

**oil spill** oil released by damage to or discharge from a tanker or oil installation. An oil spill kills all shore life, clogging up the feathers of birds and suffocating other creatures. At sea toxic chemicals leach into the water below, poisoning sea life. Mixed with dust, the oil forms globules that sink to the seabed, poisoning sea life there as well.

In March 1989 the *Exxon Valdez* spilled oil in Alaska's Prince William Sound, covering 12,400 sq km/4,800 sq mi and killing at least 34,000 sea birds, 10,000 sea otters, and up to 16 whales. The world's largest oil spill was in the Gulf in Jan 1991, the result of deliberate action on the part of the Iraquis during the Gulf War.

**ozone** $O_3$ highly reactive pale-blue gas with a penetrating odour. It forms a layer in the upper atmosphere, which protects life on Earth from ultraviolet rays, a cause of skin cancer. At lower atmospheric levels it is an air pollutant and contributes to the greenhouse effect. At ground level, ozone can cause asthma attacks, stunted growth in plants, and corrosion of certain materials. It is produced by the action of sunlight on car exhaust fumes, and is a major air pollutant in hot summers.

A continent-sized hole has formed over Antarctica as a result of damage to the ozone layer caused in part by chlorofluorocarbons (CFCs). In 1989 ozone depletion was 50% over the Antarctic compared with 3% over the Arctic. However, ozone depletion over the polar regions is the most dramatic manifestation of a general global effect. At ground level, ozone is so dangerous that the US Environment Protection Agency recommends people should not be exposed for more than one hour a day to ozone levels of 120 parts per billion (ppb), while the World Health Organization recommends a lower 76–100 ppb. It is known that even at levels of 60 ppb ozone causes respiratory problems, and may cause the yields of some crops to fall. In the USA, the annual economic loss due to ozone has been estimated at $5.4 billion.

**ozone depleter** any chemical that destroys the ozone in the stratosphere. Most ozone depleters are chemically stable compounds containing chlorine or bromine, which remain unchanged for long enough to drift up to the upper atmosphere. The best known are chlorofluorocarbons (CFCs), but many other ozone depleters are known, including halons, used in some fire extinguishers; methyl chloroform and carbon tetrachloride, both solvents; some CFC substitutes; and the pesticide methyl bromide.

**packaging** material, usually of metal, paper, or plastic, used to protect products, make them easier to display, and as a form of advertising. Packaging is in part responsible for the magnitude of the waste problem globally, and environmentalists have targeted packaging materials as being wasteful of energy and resources.

**pesticide** any chemical used in farming, gardening, and indoors to combat pests. Pesticides are of three main types: *insecticides* (to kill insects), *fungicides* (to kill fungal diseases), and *herbicides* (to kill plants, mainly those considered weeds). The safest pesticides are those made from plants, such as the insecticides pyrethrum and derris. Pesticides cause a number of pollution problems through spray drift on to surrounding areas, direct contamination of users or the public, and as residues on food. The aid organization Oxfam estimates that pesticides cause about 10,000 deaths worldwide every year.

More potent are synthetic products, such as chlorinated hydrocarbons. These products, including DDT and dieldrin, are highly toxic to wildlife and human beings, so their use is now restricted by law in some areas and is declining. Safer pesticides such as malathion are based on organic phosphorus compounds, but they still

## MAJOR OIL SPILLS

| year | place | source | quantity tonnes | litres |
|---|---|---|---|---|
| 1967 | off Cornwall, England | Torrey Canyon | 107,100 | |
| 1968 | off South Africa | World Glory | | 51,194,000 |
| 1972 | Gulf of Oman | Sea Star | 103,500 | |
| 1977 | North Sea | Ekofisk oil field | | 31,040,000 |
| 1978 | off France | Amoco Cadiz | 200,000 | |
| 1979 | Gulf of Mexico | Itox 1 oil well | 540,000 | |
| 1979 | off Trinidad and Tobago | Atlantic Empress and Aegean Captain | 270,000 | |
| 1983 | Persian Gulf | Nowruz oil field | 540,000 | |
| 1983 | off South Africa | Castillo de Beliver | 225,000 | |
| 1989 | off Alaska | Exxon Valdez | | 40,504,000 |
| 1991 | The Gulf | oil wells in Kuwait and Iraq | | |

## OIL SPILL IN THE GULF

Over the last 25 years, there has been a steady increase in the frequency and severity of serious accidents from oil spills at sea. Disasters have become known by the names of stricken ships and oil platforms: the *Torrey Canyon* off the Cornish coast, the *Amoco Cadiz* in the Persian Gulf, and, most recently, the *Exxon Valdez* in Alaska, which spread oil along almost 4,000 km/2,500 mi of ecologically fragile coastline and killed tens of thousands of seabirds.

Less obvious, but probably even more serious, is the steady oil pollution from tank washings in ships, flaring at oilfields, and leakage in the distribution system. Risks are certainly increased by carelessness and such semilegal practices as washing out the tanks of oil tankers while they are at sea. But deliberate pollution entered the picture only with the Gulf War in January 1991. As the US Air Force began its bombardment of Baghdad, the Iraqi president, Saddam Hussein, carried out his threat to cause unprecedented pollution damage by ordering the release of massive amounts of oil into the environment.

First, the Iraqis began deliberately pumping oil into the Gulf from land and offshore facilities in Kuwait. More oil was released after the US bombing raids, and a slick also started from Khafji in Saudi Arabia after a missile hit. At least 1.5 million barrels of oil were lost. Three huge slicks drifted down the Gulf, killing sea and wading birds, and threatening marine turtles and members of the already endangered population of dugong, or sea cow, a large marine mammal.

Oil kills in a number of ways. It contains poisonous chemicals that dissolve in water and kill plankton, the drifting shoals of tiny plants and animals that form the basis of the food chain. Shrimps and fish also die. Oil coats the body surface of larger animals, destroying their temperature regulation; birds' feathers lose their waxy coating and the birds become waterlogged and die of cold. They may also be poisoned as they try to clean oil off feathers. Some die of starvation because they can no longer see through the water to catch fish. Once it has sunk to the seabed, the oil also kills coral and seaweeds by smothering them.

The marine slicks alone would have been one of the worst oil disasters in history. But as the Iraqi troops retreated, they set fire to almost 600 oil wells, mainly by detonating mines set months previously. The result was the largest fire in history, with 3–6 million barrels of oil going up in flames every day, covering up to 8,000 sq km/3,000 sq mi in a dense pall of smoke. Soot from the Gulf was measured as far away as Kashmir in N India. To make matters worse, about 80 wells not on fire were badly damaged in the war, and gushing oil out on the desert sands.

Capping all the burning wells will take months, if not years. There are three main methods. If the control valve is intact, fire

*An oil-soaked cormorant sits on the beach near the Saudi Arabian-Kuwait border, unable to walk or swim.*

fighters in special suits can approach the wells directly, hidden behind metal shields and moving under a curtain of cooling water, and close the valves manually. But if the control valve is damaged, the capping is trickier. One option is to extinguish the fire by a controlled explosion, which uses up all the oxygen in the area; once this occurs, a new wellhead is installed to stop the oil flow, although this is a highly dangerous operation. Alternatively, a new borehole has to be drilled into the reservoir, and a mixture of oil and mud pumped down to block the flow of oil and gas to the surface. Once this is completed, the well can be plugged from the top.

Although the Gulf War caused an environmental catastrophe, the complete ecological destruction that some biologists feared does no longer seem likely. Thousands of seabirds have been killed in the Gulf, but the highly threatened populations of turtles and dugongs do not appear to have suffered serious losses.

The impact of air pollution will inevitably be more serious and longer lasting, in the form of acid rain, crop damage, and health effects, but we have been spared the worldwide ecological catastrophe predicted by the environmental adviser to King Hussein of Jordan. One thing is clear, however. Threats to cause massive pollution are now part of the modern weaponry of war, and must be taken into account by strategists and ecologists from now on.

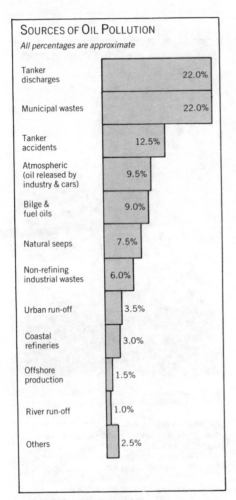

## SOURCES OF OIL POLLUTION

*All percentages are approximate*

| | |
|---|---|
| Tanker discharges | 22.0% |
| Municipal wastes | 22.0% |
| Tanker accidents | 12.5% |
| Atmospheric (oil released by industry & cars) | 9.5% |
| Bilge & fuel oils | 9.0% |
| Natural seeps | 7.5% |
| Non-refining industrial wastes | 6.0% |
| Urban run-off | 3.5% |
| Coastal refineries | 3.0% |
| Offshore production | 1.5% |
| River run-off | 1.0% |
| Others | 2.5% |

present hazards to health.

Pesticides were used to deforest SE Asia during the Vietnam War, causing death and destruction to the area's ecology and lasting health and agricultural problems.

There are around 4,000 cases of acute pesticide poisoning a year in the UK. In 1985, 400 different chemicals were approved in the UK for use as pesticides.

**pollution** the harmful effect on the environment of by-products of human activity, principally industrial and agricultural processes—for example noise, smoke, car emissions, chemical effluents in seas and rivers, pesticides, sewage, and household waste. Pollution contributes to the greenhouse effect.

Pollution control involves higher production costs for the industries concerned, but failure to implement adequate controls will result in further irreversible environmental damage and an increase in the incidence of diseases such as cancer.

In the UK 1987 air pollution caused by carbon monoxide emission from road transport was measured at 5.26 million tonnes. In Feb 1990 the UK had failed to apply 21 European Community Laws on air and water pollution and faced prosecution before the European Court of Justice on 31 of the 160 EC directives in force.

The existence of 1,300 toxic waste tips in the UK in 1990 posed a considerable threat of increased water pollution.

**slurry** form of manure composed mainly of liquids. Slurry is collected and stored on many farms, especially when large numbers of animals are kept in factory units. When slurry tanks are accidentally or deliberately breached, large amounts can spill into rivers, killing fish and causing eutrophication.

**Waldsterben** (German 'forest death') tree dieback (disease where first the young shoots die, then the larger branches) related to air pollution, common throughout the industrialized world. It appears to be caused by a mixture of pollutants, and the precise chemical mix varies between locations, but it includes acid rain, ozone, sulphur dioxide, and nitrogen oxides.

*Waldsterben* was first noticed in the Black Forest of Germany during the late 1970s, and is spreading to many Third World countries, such as China. Despite initial hopes that Britain's trees had not been damaged, research has now shown them to be among the most badly affected in Europe.

**waste** materials that are no longer needed and are discarded. Examples are household waste, industrial waste (which often contains toxic chemicals), medical waste (which may contain organisms that cause disease), and nuclear waste (which is radioactive). By recycling, some waste materials can be reclaimed for further use.

There has been a tendency to increase the amount of waste generated per person in industrialized countries, particularly through the growth in disposable consumer products, creating a 'throwaway society'. In the USA, 40 tonnes of solid waste is generated annually per person. In Britain, the average person throws away about ten times their own body weight in household refuse each year.

**water pollution** any addition to fresh or sea water that disrupts biological processes or causes a health hazard. Common pollutants include nitrate, pesticides, and sewage, though a huge range of industrial contaminants also enter water—legally, accidentally, and through illegal dumping.

**weedkiller** or *herbicide* chemical that kills some or all plants. Selective herbicides are effective with cereal crops because they kill all broad-leaved plants without affecting grasslike leaves. Those that kill all plants include sodium chlorate and paraquat. The widespread use of weedkillers in agriculture has led to a dramatic increase in crop yield but also to pollution of soil and water supplies and killing birds and small animals, as well as creating a health hazard for humans.

# ENVIRONMENTAL ISSUES

**biodegradable** capable of being broken down by living organisms, principally bacteria and fungi. Biodegradable substances, such as food and sewage, can therefore be rendered harmless by natural processes. The process of decay leads to compaction and liquefaction, and to the release of nutrients that are then recycled by the ecosystem. Nonbiodegradable substances, such as glass, heavy metals, and most types of plastic, present major problems of disposal.

**catalytic converter** device for reducing toxic emissions from the internal-combustion engine. It converts harmful exhaust products to relatively harmless ones by passing exhaust gases over a mixture of catalysts. *Oxidation catalysts* convert hydrocarbons into carbon dioxide and water; *three-way catalysts* convert oxides of nitrogen back into nitrogen. Catalytic converters are standard in the USA, where a 90% reduction in pollution from cars was achieved without loss of engine performance or fuel economy.

**compost** organic material decomposed by bacteria under controlled conditions to make a nutrient-rich natural fertilizer for use in gardening or farming. A well-made compost heap reaches a high temperature during the composting process, killing most weed seeds that might be present.

**ecology** the study of the relationship among organisms and the environments in which they live, including all living and nonliving components. The term was coined by the biologist Ernst Haeckel 1866.

Ecology may be concerned with individual organisms (for example, behavioural ecology, feeding strategies), with populations (for example, population dynamics), or with entire communities (for example, competition between species for access to resources in an ecosystem, or predator–prey relationships). A knowledge of ecology is essential in addressing many environmental problems, such as the consequences of pollution.

**energy conservation** methods of reducing energy use through insulation, increasing energy efficiency, and changes in patterns of use. Profligate energy use by industrialized countries contributes greatly to air pollution and the greenhouse effect when it draws on nonrenewable energy sources.

The average annual decrease in energy consumption in relation to gross national product 1973–87 was 1.2% in France, 2% in the UK, 2.1% in the USA, and 2.8% in Japan.

**green audit** inspection of a company's accounts to assess the total environmental impact of its activities or of a particular product or process.

For example, a green audit of a manufactured product looks at the impact of production (including energy use and the extraction of raw materials used in manufacture), use (which may cause pollution and other hazards), and disposal (potential for recycling, and whether waste causes pollution). Companies are increasingly using green audits to find ways of reducing their environmental impact.

**insulation** process or material that prevents or reduces the flow of electricity, heat or sound from one place to another. *Thermal* or *heat insulation* makes use of insulating materials such as fibreglass to reduce the loss of heat through the roof and walls of buildings. The U-value of a material is a measure of its ability to conduct heat—a material chosen as an insulator should therefore have a low U-value.

**nuclear safety** the use of nuclear energy has given rise to concern over safety. Anxiety has been heightened by accidents such as at Windscale (UK), Three Mile Island (USA) and Chernobyl (USSR). There has also been mounting concern about the production and disposal of nuclear waste, the toxic by-products of the nuclear energy industry. Burial on land or at sea raises problems of safety, environmental pollution, and security. Nuclear waste may have an active life of several thousand years and there are no guarantees of the safety of the various methods of disposal. Nuclear safety is still a controversial subject. In 1990 a scientific study revealed an increased risk of leukemia in children whose fathers had worked at Sellafield between 1950 and 1985. Sellafield (UK) is the world's greatest discharger of radioactive waste.

**organic farming** farming without the use of synthetic fertilizers (such as nitrates and phosphates) or pesticides (herbicides, insecticides ,and fungicides) or other agrochemicals (such as hormones, growth stimulants, or fruit regulators). (For more, see Food and Agriculture.)

**polluter pays principle** the idea that whoever causes pollution is responsible for the cost of repairing any damage. The principle is accepted in British law but has in practice often been ignored; for example, farmers causing the death of fish through slurry pollution have not been fined the full costs of restocking the river.

**recycling** processing of industrial and household waste (such as paper, glass, and some metals and plastics) so that it can be reused, thus saving expenditure on scarce raw materials, slowing down the depletion of nonrenewable resources, and helping to reduce pollution.

Producing steel from scrap reduces energy

SOURCES OF MARINE POLLUTION

| Source | All potential pollutants (%) |
|---|---|
| Land-based discharges | 44.0 |
| Atmospheric inputs | 33.0 |
| Marine transport | 12.0 |
| Dumping | 10.0 |
| Oil exploration/production | 1.0 |

*Source: The Times Guide to the Environment 1990*

---

## BioSphere2

In the Arizona desert, the largest ecological test project ever—a 'planet in a bottle'—got underway in May 1991.

Under a glass dome, several different habitats were recreated, and representatives of nearly 4,000 species, including eight humans, were sealed in the biosphere for two years from spring 1991 to see how effectively recycling of air, water, and waste can work in an enclosed environment, and whether a stable ecosystem can be created (ultimately BS2 is a prototype space colony).

BS2 is in fact not the second in a series: Earth itself is regarded as BioSphere 1. Experiments with biospheres that hold only relatively simple life forms have been carried out for decades, and a 21-day trial period in 1989 that included humans preceded the construction of BS2. The sealed area covers a total of 3.5 acres. Habitats represented in it are tropical rainforest, salt marsh, desert, coral reef, and savanna, as well as a section for intensive agriculture. The people within will be entirely self-sufficient, except for electricity: solar panels to provide energy for cooling, heating, pumping, and lighting would have been too expensive, so there is a 3.7-megawatt power station on the outside. The biospherians also have a computer link with the outside world.

The cost of setting up and maintaining the project has been estimated at $100 million, some of which will be covered by paying visitors, who can view the inhabitants through the geodesic glass dome. It is run by a private company, Space Biospheres Ventures, with funding from an ecology-minded oil millionaire, Edward P Bass (1945– ), and other investors who expect to find commercial applications for the techniques that are developed in the course of the project. The US space agency, NASA, is also monitoring BS2, hoping to acquire knowledge that can be utilized in building a base on Mars.

---

consumption by 65%, air pollution by 85%, water pollution by 76%, and eliminates mining wastes. Making recycled paper cuts energy use by 25%–60%, air pollution by 74%, and water pollution by 35%. Recycling aluminium cuts energy use by 95%; recycling glass, by 33%.

**reuse** multiple use of a product (often forms of packaging), by returning it to the manufacturer or processor each time. Many such returnable items are sold with a deposit which is reimbursed if the item is returned. Reuse is usually more energy- and resource-efficient than recycling unless there are large transport or cleaning costs.

**sewage disposal** the disposal of human excreta and other waterborne waste products from houses, streets, and factories. Conveyed through sewers to sewage works, sewage has to undergo a series of treatments to be acceptable for discharge into rivers or

the sea, according to various local laws and ordinances.

In the industrialized countries of the West, most industries are responsible for disposing of their own wastes. Government agencies establish industrial waste-disposal standards. In most countries, sewage systems for residential areas are the responsibility of local authorities. The solid waste (sludge) may be spread over fields as a fertilizer or, in a few countries, dumped at sea.

Raw sewage, or sewage that has not been treated properly, is one serious source of water pollution and a cause of eutrophication. A significant proportion of bathing beaches in densely populated regions have unacceptably high bacterial content, largely as a result of untreated sewage being discharged into rivers and the sea.

The use of raw sewage as a fertilizer (long practised in China) has the drawback that disease-causing microorganisms can survive in the soil and be transferred to people or animals by consumption of subsequent crops. Sewage sludge is safer, but may contain dangerous levels of heavy metals and other industrial contaminants.

In 1987, Britain dumped more than 4,700 tonnes/4,626 tons of sewage sludge into the North Sea, and 4,200 tonnes/4,134 tons into the Irish Sea and other coastal areas. Also dumped in British coastal waters, other than the Irish Sea, were 6,462 tonnes/6,360 tons of zinc, 2,887 tonnes/2,841 tons of lead, 1,306 tonnes/1,285 tons of chromium, and 8 tonnes/7.8 tons of arsenic. Dumped into the Irish Sea were 916 tonnes/902 tons of zinc, 297 tonnes/298 tons of lead, 200 tonnes/197 tons of chromium, and 1 tonne/0.98 tons of arsenic.

**waste disposal** methods used for getting rid of waste material. Methods of waste disposal vary according to the materials in the waste and include incineration, burial at designated sites, and dumping at sea. Organic waste can be treated and reused as fertilizer (see sewage disposal). Nuclear and toxic waste is usually buried or dumped at sea, which, while addressing the short-term disposal problem, creates a potential toxic 'time bomb' with long-term consequences for marine life.

Waste disposal is an ever-increasing problem. Environmental groups, such as Greenpeace and Friends of the Earth, are campaigning for more recycling, a change in life style so that less waste (from consumer packaging to nuclear materials) is produced, and for safer methods of disposal.

The industrial waste dumped every year by the UK in the North Sea includes 550,000 tonnes/541,310 tons of fly ash from coal-fired power stations. The British government agreed in 1989 to stop North Sea dumping from 1993, but dumping in the heavily polluted Irish Sea will continue. Industrial pollution is responsible for serious ecological damage, including an epidemic that killed hundreds of seals in 1989.

TEN WAYS TO REDUCE DAMAGE TO THE ENVIRONMENT

1. Minimize use of your car, and travel by bike, bus or train instead.
2. Avoid aerosols where possible, and if you do use them, only choose those clearly marked 'ozone friendly'.
3. Do not buy tropical hardwood products, unless they are certified as coming from sustainably managed forests by an independent body.
4. Select the most energy-efficient electrical appliances you can find.
5. Save energy by draught-stripping and insulating your home.
6. Recycle waste paper, bottles, and aluminium cans, and compost all vegetable and garden waste.
7. Choose recycled paper products wherever possible.
8. Save water by having a shower instead of a bath, installing a dual flush toilet, and using a water butt for the garden.
9. Always buy organically grown food where it is available.
10. Avoid overconsumption.

# WORKING TOWARDS A BETTER ENVIRONMENT

**CITES** abbreviation for *Convention on International Trade in Endangered Species*, an international convention founded in 1973 (under the auspices of the International Union for the Conservation of Nature) to regulate the trade in endangered species of animals and plants; it is signed by 81 countries. When voluntary codes such as CITES fail to stem the trade in particular species, national and international bans sometimes come into effect (for example those operated by the European Community on most whale products).

**Council for the Protection of Rural England** countryside conservation group with a brief that extends from planning controls to energy policy. A central organization campaigns on national issues and 42 local groups lobby on regional matters. The *Council for the Protection of Rural Wales* is the Welsh equivalent.

**Earth Summit** official name of the United Nations Conference on Environment and Development scheduled to take place in Rio de Janeiro, Brazil during 1992. The conference is planned to set the agenda for international efforts in environmental protection until the end of the century and beyond.

**Environmentally Sensitive Area** (ESA) scheme introduced by the UK Ministry of Agriculture 1984, as a result of EC legislation, to protect some of the most beautiful areas of the British countryside from the loss and damage caused by agricultural change. The first areas to be designated ESAs are in the Pennine Dales, the North Peak District, the Norfolk Broads, the Breckland, the Suffolk River Valleys, the Test Valley, the South Downs, the Somerset Levels and Moors, West Penwith, Cornwall, the Shropshire Borders, the Cambrian Mountains, and the Lleyn Peninsula.

In these ESAs farmers are encouraged to use traditional methods to preserve the value of the land as a wildlife habitat. A farmer who joins the scheme agrees to manage the land in this way for at least five years. In return for this agreement, the Ministry of Agriculture pays the farmer a sum that reflects the financial losses incurred as a result of reconciling conservation with commercial farming. Environmentally Sensitive Areas now amount to some 110,495 hectares, or 1% of England's farmland.

**Environmental Protection Agency** US agency set up 1970 to control water and air quality, industrial and commercial wastes, pesticides, noise, and radiation. In its own words, it aims to protect 'the country from being degraded, and its health threatened, by a multitude of human activities initiated without regard to long-ranging effects upon the life-supporting properties, the economic uses, and the recreational value of air, land, and water'.

**Friends of the Earth** (FoE or FOE) environmental pressure group, established in the UK 1971, that aims to protect the environment and to promote rational and sustainable use of the Earth's resources. It campaigns on issues such as acid rain; air, sea, river, and land pollution; recycling; disposal of toxic wastes; nuclear power and renewable energy; the destruction of rainforests; pesticides; and agriculture. FoE has branches in 30 countries.

**Gaia hypothesis** theory that the Earth's living and nonliving systems form an inseparable whole that is regulated and kept adapted for life by living organisms themselves. The planet therefore functions as a single organism, or a giant cell. Since life and environment are so closely linked, there is a need for humans to understand and maintain the physical environment and living things around them. The Gaia hypothesis was elaborated by James Lovelock in the 1970s.

**Green Party** political party aiming to 'preserve the planet and its people', based on the premise that incessant economic growth is unsustainable. The leaderless party structure reflects a general commitment to decentralization. Green parties sprang up in W Europe in the 1970s and in E Europe from 1988. Parties in different countries are linked to one another but unaffiliated to any pressure group. They had a number of parliamentary seats in 1989: Austria 8, Belgium 11, Finland 4, Italy 20, Luxembourg 2, Republic of Ireland 1, Sweden 20, Switzerland 9, West Germany 42; and 24 members of the European Parliament (Belgium 3, France 9, Italy 3, Portugal 1, West Germany 8).

**Greenpeace** international environmental pressure group, founded 1971, with a policy of

## THE SIZE OF THE PROBLEM

| | Total waste kg per head per year | Recycled* % | Trends in recycling |
|---|---|---|---|
| **Paper** | | | |
| W. Europe | 170–180 | 40–45 (range 20–65) | Sharply upward in 1970s–1980s, levelling now, falling in Italy and UK. |
| Japan | 170 | 50 | 39% in 1975, 49% in 1985, level since |
| USA | 270 | 25 | Up from 19% in 1975 |
| **Aluminium** | | | |
| W. Europe | 18–20 | 30 | Level since 1984 |
| Japan | 22 | 40 | Level since 1986 |
| USA | 10 | 32 | Up from 9% in 1975 |
| **Glass** | | | |
| W. Europe | 25 | 30 (range 8–63) | Upward in 1980s, levelling off |
| Japan | 7 | 55 | Upward since 1980 |
| USA | 50 | 12 | Up from 3% in 1975 |
| **Plastic** | | | |
| W. Europe | 17 | 5† | Consumption and recycling rates rising rapidly |
| Japan | 25 | 0 | – |
| USA | 55 | 1 | – |

\* Does not include incineration
† not post-consumer, mostly collected
*Source: OECD; US Environmental Protection Agency*

nonviolent direct action backed by scientific research. During a protest against French atmospheric nuclear testing in the S Pacific 1985, its ship *Rainbow Warrior* was sunk by French intelligence agents, killing a crew member.

**Henry Doubleday Research Association** gardening group founded by Lawrence Hills to investigate organic growing techniques. It runs the *National Centre for Organic Gardening*, a 22-acre demonstration site, at Ryton on Dunsmore near Coventry, England. The association is named after the man who first imported Russian comfrey, a popular green manuring crop.

**International Union for the Conservation of Nature** (IUCN) an organization established by the United Nations to promote the conservation of wildlife and habitats as part of the national policies of member states. It has formulated guidelines and established research programmes (such as the International Biological Programme, IBP), and set up advisory bodies (such as Survival Services Commission, SSC). In 1980 it launched the *World Conservation Strategy* to highlight particular problems, designating a small number of areas as *World Heritage Sites* to ensure their survival as unspoilt habitats (for example, Yosemite National Park in the USA, and the Simen Mountains in Ethiopia).

**Montréal Protocol** international agreement, signed 1987, to reduce production of ozone-depleting chemicals (see ozone depleters in Enviromental Pollutants section) by 35% by 1999 and thus protect the ozone layer. The protocol (under the Vienna Convention for the Protection of the Ozone Layer) was scheduled for review in 1992. The green movement criticized the agreement as inadequate, arguing

that an 85% reduction in ozone depleters would be necessary just to stabilize the ozone layer at 1987 levels.

**National Rivers Authority** UK environmental agency launched Sept 1989. It is responsible for managing water resources, investigating pollution controls, and taking over flood controls and land drainage from the former ten regional water authorities of England and Wales.

**National Trust** British trust founded 1895 for the preservation of land and buildings of historic interest or beauty, incorporated by Act of Parliament 1907. It is the largest private landowner in Britain. The National Trust for Scotland was established 1931.

**Natural Environment Research Council** (NERC) UK organization established by royal charter 1965 to undertake and support research in the earth sciences, to give advice both on exploiting natural resources and on protecting the environment, and to support education and training of scientists in these fields of study. Research areas include geothermal energy, industrial pollution, waste disposal, satellite surveying, acid rain, biotechnology, atmospheric circulation, and climate. Research is carried out principally within the UK but also in Antarctica and in many developing countries. It comprises 13 research bodies.

**Nature Conservancy Council** (NCC) UK government agency established by Act of Parliament 1973 (Nature Conservancy created by royal charter 1949). It is responsible for designating and managing national nature reserves and other conservation areas, advising government ministers on policies, providing advice and information, and commissioning or undertaking relevant scientific research.

**Radioactive Incident Monitoring Network** (RIMNET) monitoring network located at 46

## DEBT-FOR-NATURE SWAPS

During the 1980s, many countries in the Third World built up staggering debts with private and international banks, and with aid lenders, in the industrialized North. This was by no means entirely the fault of Third World governments. They were pressed to borrow large sums by Western institutions, and then trapped by a catastrophic change in interest rates, caused by the boom in the US dollar and some European currencies. By the end of the decade, the total debt from South to North had reached a trillion dollars, and interest payments were crippling national economies.

The debt crisis, as it became known, has a direct effect on the environment. Countries desperately trying to service their debts, by making regular interest payments, were forced to increase production to levels that were incompatible with good environmental practice. Forests were felled to provide timber, or to clear land for growing cash crops for export. Industries were pushed into maximum production with scant regard for any pollution this created.

Debt-for-nature swaps are an attempt by environment groups in the North to help reduce the debt problem of countries in the South, while promoting conservation. They are agreements under which debts are effectively written off, with a cash payment, in exchange for a commitment by the debtor country to undertake projects for environmental protection.

To date, most debt-for-nature swaps have concentrated on setting aside areas of land, and especially tropical rainforest, for protection. They have involved private conservation foundations in the North. The first swap took place in 1987, when the US environmental group Conservation International bought $650,000 worth of Bolivia's national debt from Citicorp International at a discounted price of $100,000.

The debt was then swapped for an undertaking by the Bolivian government to set aside 9 million hectares/22,239,000 acres of Amazon forest adjacent to the existing Beni Biosphere Reserve, and establish a $250,000 trust in local currency to finance the administration of the new reserve.

Since then, a number of other debt-for-nature swaps have been carried out, notably by the World Wide Fund for Nature. Participating countries include the Philippines, Costa Rica, and Ecuador.

In theory, this is a way of tackling two problems at once: relieving the debt burden and promoting conservation in the South. However, debt-for-nature swaps have attracted considerable criticism.

Some people, especially within the debtor countries, see them as a form of neocolonialism. They argue that the debts were created more by economic conditions in the North, the strategy of Western governments and financial institutions, and in some cases a minority of inept or corrupt officials in the South. If that is so, there is no justification for using debts to force debtor countries into long-term commitments that they may be unwilling or unable to fulfil.

Another, more pragmatic objection centres on the workability of such schemes. Many 'reserves' established in the South have not been protected in practice, so, although they sound good, the forests are still felled and the wildlife destroyed. It will be extremely difficult for a small, independent conservation organization in, say, the USA to ensure that 'their' area of land remains adequately protected, especially after a few changes of government.

Indeed, one of the concerns about some of the existing swaps is that land set aside has included the homes of indigenous tribal people, who were not consulted about the new status of their traditional territory, and certainly had nothing whatsoever to do with incurring the debt in the first place. Supporters of the system, on the other hand, claim that a well-structured debt-for-nature swap can provide an invaluable resource for environmental groups working in the South, and is also a vital holding operation until better long-term strategies for management are developed.

But debt for nature is not just a North-South issue. In June 1991 the head of the Polish government's debt conversion team furthered discussions with the 17 lender nations in the Paris Club about the country's debt to them. The Paris Club agreed to reduce Poland's debt by 50% with individual members free to reduce another 10% if they wished. The 10%, if all members agreed, would add up to £1.8bn and would be paid by Poland into an environmental fund over an 18-year period.

In 1991, a new twist was added to the debate when the first debt-for-nature swap was discussed in the North. California is negotiating to buy 1,200 hectares/2,965 acres of ancient redwood forest in return for paying off some of the debts of its owner, Pacific Lumber. If successful, this might well ease some of the tensions surrounding North–South transactions of this type. However, debt for nature is no substitute for properly funded long-term management policies for forests and other areas, which must be developed by the government of the country concerned, rather than imposed by outside agencies.

(to be raised to about 90) Meteorological Office sites throughout the UK. It feeds into a central computer, and was installed in 1989 to record contamination levels from nuclear incidents such as the Chernobyl disaster.

**Single European Act** 1986 update of the Treaty of Rome (signed in 1957) that provides a legal basis for action by the European Community in matters relating to the environment. The Act requires that environmental protection shall be a part of all other Community policies. Also, it allows for agreement by a qualified majority on some legislation, whereas before such decisions had to be unanimous.

**site of special scientific interest** (SSSI) area designated as being of particular environmental interest by one of the regional bodies of the UK government's Nature Conservancy Council. Numbers fluctuate, but there were over 5,000 SSSIs in 1991, covering about 6% of Britain. Although SSSIs enjoy some legal protection, this does not in practice always prevent damage or destruction; during 1989, for example, 44 SSSIs were so badly damaged that they were no longer worth protecting.

**Soil Association** the foremost UK organization promoting organic agriculture as a healthier alternative for consumers and producers. Established in 1946, its objectives are to research, develop, and promote sustainable relationships between the soil, plants, animals, people, and the biosphere, with the goal of producing healthier food and improving the environment. It also sets the Standards for Organic Agriculture; administers and monitors the Symbol Scheme (the Symbol is a quality mark for organically grown food); researches and publishes findings on organic issues; lobbies the government for changes in agriculture; and promotes educational programmes for the general public on organic farming.

**World Wide Fund for Nature** (WWF, formerly the *World Wildlife Fund*) international organization established 1961 to raise funds for conservation by public appeal. Its headquarters are in Gland, Switzerland. Projects include conservation of particular species, for example, the tiger and giant panda, and special areas, such as the Simen Mountains, Ethiopia.

---

**Environmental issues**

---

*In a general election would a party's policies towards environmental issues influence your vote, a lot, a little, or not at all?*

---

| | |
|---|---|
| A lot | 39 |
| A little | 38 |
| Not at all | 19 |
| Don't know | 4 |

---

*Do you agree or disagree with the following statement: Protecting the environment is so important that requirements and standards cannot be too high and continuing environmental improvements must be made regardless of cost.*

---

| | |
|---|---|
| Agree | 83 |
| Disagree | 10 |
| Don't know | 7 |

---

*Think about the people who are actively involved in groups that are concerned about environmental issues. Do you think most of these people are reasonable people, or are most of them extremists?*

---

| | |
|---|---|
| Reasonable | 68 |
| Extremists | 18 |
| Depends | 9 |
| Don't know | 5 |

---

# FOOD AND DRINK

**beer** alcoholic drink made from fermented malt (germinating barley or other grain) and water, flavoured with hops. It contains between 1% and 6% alcohol. The medieval distinction between beer (containing hops) and *ale* (without hops) has now fallen into disuse and beer has come to be used strictly as a generic term including ale, stout, and lager. *Stout* is a sweet, dark beer, fermented at the top of the brewing vessel and strongly flavoured with roasted grain; *lager* is a light beer, bottom fermented and matured over a longer period.

**biscuit** a small, flat, brittle cake of baked dough. The basic components of biscuit dough are weak flour and fat. Other ingredients such as eggs, sugar, nuts, chocolate, dried fruit, and spices may be added to vary the flavour and texture. Originally made from slices of unleavened bread baked until hard and dry, biscuits could be stored for several years, and were a useful, though dull, source of carbohydrate on long sea voyages and military campaigns. The first biscuit factory opened in Carlisle, northern England, in 1815. The UK is Europe's largest producer and consumer of factory-made biscuits.

**bread** food baked from a dough of flour, liquid (water or milk) and salt. Many other ingredients may be added to vary the flavour or texture. The dough may be leavened (raised, usually by the action of yeast) or unleavened. Bread has been a staple of human diet in many civilizations as long as agriculture has been practised. Potato, banana, and cassava bread are among some local varieties, but most breads are made from cereals such as wheat, barley, rye, and oats, which form elastic proteins called glutens when mixed with water. Traditionally bread has been made from whole grains, which were ground into a rough meal. White bread was developed by the end of the 19th century by roller-milling, which removed the wheat germ and produced a fine flour to satisfy fashionable consumer demand. In modern manufacturing processes, fermentation is speeded up using ascorbic acid (vitamin C) and potassium bromide, with fast-acting flour improvers. Today, some of the nutrients removed in the processing of bread are synthetically replaced.

**bulghur wheat** or *bulgar* or *burghul* cracked wholewheat, made by cooking the grains, then drying and cracking them. It is widely eaten in the Middle East. Coarser bulghur may be cooked in the same way as rice; more finely ground bulghur is mixed with minced meat to make a paste that may be eaten as a dip with salad, or shaped and stuffed before being grilled or fried.

**butter** solid yellowish fat made by churning cream. It is usually salted. In the UK, butter typically consists of about 82% fat,

0.4% protein, and up to 16% water; it contains 1,300 micrograms of vitamin A per 100 g/3.5 oz in summer, and 500 micrograms per 100 g/3.5 oz in winter.

**cake** a baked food item made from a mixture of weak flour, sugar, eggs, and fat (usually butter or margarine). Other ingredients such as nuts, chocolate, and fresh or dried fruits can be added, and pastry is sometimes used as a base. Cakes may be eaten to celebrate occasions such as birthdays or weddings, and a specific type of cake is often associated with a particular event—for example, heavy fruit cakes covered with marzipan and icing that are traditionally eaten at Christmas. Easter cakes include the fruited simnel cake and the pyramid-shaped Russian *pashka*, made from sweetened curd cheese and filled with dried fruit and nuts. The UK is Europe's biggest producer of factory-made cakes.

**cereal, breakfast** food prepared from the seeds of cereal crops. Breakfast cereals fall into two groups: those that require cooking (oats, cooked in milk to make porridge); and ready-to-eat cereals. The second group accounts for the major share of the market; it includes refined and sweetened varieties as well as whole cereals such as muesli. Whole cereals are more nutritious and provide more fibre than the refined cereals, which often have vitamins and flavourings added to replace those lost in the refining process.

**cheese** food made from the curds (solids) of soured milk from cows, sheep, or goats, separated from the whey (liquid), then salted, put into moulds, and pressed into firm blocks. Cheese is ripened with bacteria or surface fungi, and kept for a time to mature before being eaten.

*Soft cheeses* may be ripe or unripe, and include the low-fat cottage cheese, fromage frais, and quark, and the high-fat soft cheeses such as Bel Paese, Camembert, and Neufchâtel.

*Semi-hard cheeses* are ripened by bacteria (Munster) or by bacteria and surface fungi (Port-Salut, St Paulin, and Gouda); they may also have penicillin moulds injected into them (Roquefort, Gorgonzola, Blue Stilton, and Wensleydale).

*Hard cheeses* are ripened by bacteria, for example Cheddar, Cheshire, and Caciocavallo; some have large holes in them (Emmental and Gruyère).

*Very hard cheeses*, such as Parmesan and Spalen, are made with skimmed milk.

*Processed cheese* is made with dried skimmed milk powder and additives.

*Whey cheese* is made by heat coagulation of the proteins from whey; examples are Mysost and Primost.

In France (from 1980) cheese has the same *appellation contrôlée* status as wine if it is made only in a special defined area—for example, Cantal and Roquefort are *appellation contrôlée* cheeses, but not Camembert and Brie, which are made in more than one region.

## COMPOSITION OF CHEESES

| cheese | fat (%) | protein (%) | calcium (mg/100g) | salt (mg/100g) | (Kcal/100g) |
|---|---|---|---|---|---|
| Cheddar | 32.2 | 25 | 750 | 700 | 398 |
| Roquefort | 31.5 | 21.5 | 315 | – | 368 |
| Camembert | minimum 26.0 | 17.5 | 105 | – | 299 |
| Emmental | 28.0 | 27.5 | 925 | 710 | 370 |
| processed | 28.0 | 25 | 850 | 1,150 | 360 |
| cottage | 0.3 | 17 | 90 | 290 | 86 |

**cider** a fermented drink made from the juice of the apple; in the USA the term cider usually refers to unfermented (non-alcoholic) apple juice. Cider has been made for more than 2,000 years, and for many centuries has been a popular drink in France and England, which are now its main centres of production.

A similar drink, *perry*, is made from the fermented juice of sour pears. It is produced commercially in France, Germany, and SW England.

**cocoa and chocolate** food products made from the cacao (or cocoa) bean, fruit of a tropical tree *Theobroma cacao*, native to Central America but now cultivated mainly in W Africa. Chocolate as a drink was introduced to Europe from the New World by the Spanish in the 16th century; solid chocolate was first produced in the late 18th century.

Preparation takes place in the importing country and consists chiefly of roasting, winnowing, and grinding the nib (the edible portion of the bean) to form a thick paste consisting of cocoa solids and fat (cocoa butter). If *cocoa* for drinking is required, a proportion of the cocoa butter is removed by hydraulic pressure and the remaining cocoa is reduced by further grinding and sieving to a fine powder. *Plain chocolate* is made by removing some of the cocoa butter and adding a little sugar. It is dark and has a slightly bitter flavour. *Milk chocolate* is a sweeter variety, made by adding condensed or powdered milk and a larger amount of sugar. In the UK cheaper vegetable fats are widely substituted for milk and it need contain only 20% cocoa solids. *White chocolate* contains cocoa butter but no cocoa solids, and is flavoured with sugar and vanilla.

**coffee** beverage made by infusing the roasted and ground beanlike seeds of evergreen shrubs of the genus *Coffea*. It contains a stimulant, caffeine. Coffee drinking began in Arab regions in the 14th century but did not become common in Europe until 300 years later, when the first coffee houses were opened in Vienna, and soon after in Paris and London. The world's largest producers of coffee are Brazil, Colombia, and the Ivory Coast; others include Indonesia (Java), Ethiopia, India, Hawaii, and Jamaica.

The flavour of coffee beans depends on the variety grown, the location of the plantation, and the manner in which the beans were processed—for example, *Arabica* beans, grown at high altitudes, are considered finer than the cheaper *Robusta* and *Liberian* varieties.

Manufacturers, therefore, blend beans from a number of sources in order to achieve a consistent product.

**cream** the part of milk that has the highest fat content; it can be separated by centrifugation or gravity (if milk is left to stand, the upper layer will be cream, the lower layer skimmed milk). If cream is to be whipped successfully, it must contain at least 30% fat. In the UK, *single cream* has a fat content of 18%; the thicker *double cream* has a fat content of 48%. *Clotted cream* is made by scalding double cream and skimming off the yellow crust produced. It should contain 55% fat and 4% protein.

**egg** the shell-covered egg of a domestic chicken, duck, or goose, or of a game bird such as quail. It is a highly nutritious food: the albumin, or egg white, of a chicken's egg is 10% protein; the yolk is 33% fat and 15% protein, and contains vitamins A, B, and D. The yolk also contains cholesterol, a fatty substance associated with heart disease in humans.

Eggs have many uses in cooking. They can be used for thickening sauces, binding and coating crumbly foods, and for raising batters and cakes; whisked egg white gives a foamy texture to soufflés and desserts; and yolk acts as an emulsifier, keeping oil in suspension in mixtures such as mayonnaise.

**fish** the flesh or roe (eggs) of freshwater or saltwater fish. The nutritional composition of fish is similar to that of meat, although the fat content is generally lower and most of the fat takes the form of polyunsaturated oil. Oily fish have a fat content of 8–20%, and include salmon, mackerel, and herring. White fish such as cod, haddock, and whiting contain only 0.4–4% fat. Fish are good sources of vitamin B and iodine, and extracts from the livers of fatty fish are used commercially as sources of vitamins A and D.

**flour** foodstuff made by grinding starchy vegetable materials, usually cereal grains, into a fine powder. Flour may also be made from root vegetables such as potato and cassava, and from pulses such as soya beans and chick peas. The most commonly used cereal flour is *wheat flour*. It may contain varying proportions of bran (husk) and wheatgerm (embryo), ranging from 100% wholemeal flour to refined white flour, which has less than 75% of the whole grain. *Granary flour* contains malted flakes of wheat. The properties of flour depend on the strain of wheat used. Bread requires strong ('hard') flour with a high gluten content (gluten is a protein that enables the dough to stretch during rising).

---

## FOOD HYGIENE: DO WE TAKE ENOUGH CARE?

The number of incidents of food poisoning is continuing to rise in the UK. Reported cases over the Northern health region have increased from 600 a year in 1982 to 4,000 in 1990. The number of cases rose by 49% in the Trent region over the same period. According to Donald Acheson, the Chief Medical Officer, these increases cannot just be due to greater public awareness, because the number of cases reported by East Anglia and Mersey is half that reported by Yorkshire.

Food that is freshly prepared and eaten in the home is becoming an increasingly rare phenomenon. It has been replaced in this country by snacking and eating from high-street fast-food outlets. Food is chosen with little attention to quality. We now have less control than ever over the quality of the food that we eat; the standards of hygiene by which the food is kept and prepared are no longer under our individual control.

In 1990 the British government passed the Food Safety Act, covering commercial cooks, storage of food, and producers and sellers of food. Producers and sellers now have to make sure that food is not just safe in the short term but also in the long term. Food handlers need to be trained as they are in Italy and Germany. (In Germany they are also tested for intestinal parasites and other diseases before they can handle food.) Public health is to be protected by the new law-enforcement officers required by every local authority. Whether the new Act is strong enough to reduce the rising numbers of food poisoning cases will depend on the regulations that follow. Further changes in the industry will certainly be necessary after 1992, when the UK becomes bound by European Community regulations.

Abattoir practices and the levels of contamination in poultry are particular areas of concern. *Salmonella* poisoning became a household word in 1988 when the junior health minister Edwina Currie declared that most eggs were contaminated with the bacterium. The ensuing media attention resulted in a much greater public awareness of *salmonella*, although another bacterium *Campylobacter* is believed to be responsible for more cases of food and water poisoning. It is found in contaminated poultry, unpasteurized milk, and water, and may also be picked up from pets. *Listeria, Clostridium botulinium*, and *Staphylococcus aureas* are other bacteria that have aroused public concern.

The causes of the increase in food poisoning are many, according to the Richmond Committee, set up after the *Salmonella* scandal of 1988 and 1989. New technologies such as cook-chill, changing lifestyles that demand more convenience foods and a long shelf life, and the growth of international travel have all contributed to the problem.

The risk of contracting food poisoning can be reduced by using a few simple precautions. The sell-by and eat-by dates of packaged foods, and the star ratings of frozen foods should be noted and complied with. Foods cannot be kept indefinitely even in freezers, as freezing does not kill bacteria and moulds but merely prevents their growing. The operating temperatures of our freezers, refrigerators, and ovens should be checked regularly. Cooked and raw foods should be stored separately in order to prevent cross-contamination, and attention should be given to personal hygiene and to the cleanliness of utensils and surfaces. We depend on the food industry to follow the recent guidelines set down by the government, and ensure that hygiene standards are kept through the food chain, from the farm to the factory to the shop, and on to us, the buyer. From then on, it is our responsibility to store, prepare, and cook the foods safely.

---

**Durum flour** also has a high gluten content, and is used for pasta. Cakes and biscuits are made from weak ('soft') flour containing less gluten. Much of the flour available now is bleached to whiten it; bleaching also destroys some of its vitamin content, so synthetic vitamins are added to replace them.

**fruit** in botany, the ripened ovary of a flower, including the seeds that it encloses; in popular terms, a fruit is any sweet, fleshy plant item, such as an orange, strawberry, or rhubarb stalk. The latter definition excludes many true botanical fruits such as tomatoes, cucumbers, and wheat grains. When eaten, fruits provide energy, fibre, vitamins, minerals, and enzymes, but little protein.

Broadly, fruits are divided into three agricultural categories on the basis of the climate in which they grow. **Temperate fruits** require a cold season for satisfactory growth. In order of abundance, these include, apples, pears, plums, peaches, apricots, cherries, and soft fruits, such as raspberries and strawberries. **Subtropical fruits** require warm conditions but can survive light frosts; they include oranges and other citrus fruits, dates, pomegranates, and avocados. **Tropical fruits** cannot tolerate temperatures that drop close to freezing point; they include bananas, mangoes, pineapples, papayas, and litchis. Technical advances in storage and transport have made tropical fruits available to consumers in temperate areas, and fresh temperate fruits available all year in major markets.

**fruit juice** juice extracted from fruits, either by pressing (citrus fruits), or by spinning at high speeds in a centrifuge (other fruits). Although fruit juice provides no fibre, its nutritional value is close to that of the whole fruit. The most widely used juices are orange, apple, grapefruit, pineapple, and tomato. Most fruit juices are transported in concentrated form, and are diluted and pasteurized before being packaged. Concentrated juices may be used as sweeteners in cooking.

**herb** any plant with a distinctive smell or taste, used in flavouring food, in medicine, or in perfumery. Most herbs are temperate plants; they include bay, thyme, borage, mint, chives, and tarragon. Their leaves and stems release aromatic oils on being crushed, chopped, or heated, and may be used fresh, dried, or freeze-dried.

**honey** sweet syrup produced by honey bees from the nectar of flowers. It is stored in honeycombs and made in excess of their needs as food for the winter. Honey comprises various sugars, mainly fructose and glucose, with enzymes, colouring matter, acids, and pollen grains. It has antibacterial properties and was widely used in ancient Egypt, Greece, and Rome as a wound salve.

**ice cream** rich, creamy, frozen confectionery, made commercially from the early 20th century from various milk products, sugar, and fruit and nut flavourings, usually with additives to improve keeping qualities and ease of serving. In the UK, the sale is permitted of ice cream made with 'non-milk' animal or vegetable fat. Water ices and sorbets are frozen fruit juices and do not contain milk or cream. Sherbet is a frozen dessert of watered fruit juice, egg white, and sugar, like an ice, but with gelatin and milk added.

**lard** the melted and clarified edible fat of pigs. It can be heated to very high temperatures without burning.

**liqueur** alcoholic liquor made by infusing flavouring substances (fruits, herbs, spices) in alcohol. For example, crème de cassis is an infusion of blackcurrants in rum, and maraschino is an infusion of cherries in brandy. Specific recipes are closely guarded commercial secrets. Originally liqueurs were used as medicines and are still thought of as aids to digestion.

**margarine** butter substitute made from animal fats and/or vegetable oils. The French chemist Hippolyte Mège-Mouries invented margarine in 1889. Today, margarines are usually made with vegetable oils, such as soy, corn (maize), or sunflower oil, giving a product low in saturated fats, and fortified with vitamins A and D.

**meat** flesh of animals taken as food; in Western countries, it is chiefly provided by the muscle tissue of domesticated cattle (beef and veal),

sheep (lamb and mutton), pigs (pork), and poultry. Beef, lamb, and mutton are termed *red meats*; poultry, pork, and veal are termed *white meats*. Meat has a high protein content and is a good source of B-vitamins and iron; its fat tends to have a high proportion of saturated fatty acids. Major exporters include Argentina, Australia, New Zealand, Canada, the USA, and Denmark (chiefly bacon). The practice of cooking meat is at least 600,000 years old. More than 40% of the world's grain is now fed to animals intended for meat consumption. *Game* is meat obtained from wild animals and birds, such as deer, hare, grouse, pheasant, and wild duck. It has a stronger flavour than that of farm-reared animals, and is thought to be less easy to digest. Before being cooked, therefore, it is stored suspended ('hung') in a cool place to make it more tender. At one time, game was hung until it was almost rotten ('high'), but it is now stored for a shorter period (2–8 days). *Offal* comprises the edible internal organs of an animal, and also its head, feet, tail, tongue, and bone marrow. It is generally cheaper than other meats.

*Meat substitutes* include textured vegetable protein (TVP), usually made from soya beans, and Quorn (developed by Rank Hovis McDougall), which is made from mycoprotein, a tiny relative of mushrooms that grows prolifically in culture. Both are rich in protein and low in fat.

**milk** the secretion of the mammary glands of female mammals, with which they suckle their young (during lactation). Over 85% is water, the remainder comprising protein, fat, lactose (a sugar), calcium, phosphorus, iron, and vitamins. The milk of cows, goats, and sheep is often consumed by humans, but only Western societies drink milk after infancy; for people in most of the world, milk causes flatulence and diarrhoea. Milk composition varies among species; human milk contains less protein and more lactose than that of cows. *Skimmed milk* is what remains when the cream has been separated from milk. It is readily dried. *Semi-skimmed milk* is milk from which just over half of the cream has been removed. *Evaporated milk* is milk reduced by heat until it reaches about half its volume. *Condensed milk* is concentrated to about a third of its original volume with added sugar.

## COMPOSITION OF MILKS

| source | protein (g/100ml) | fat (g/100 ml) | carbohydrate (g/100ml) | energy (Kcal/100 ml) |
|---|---|---|---|---|
| cow | 3.5 | 3.5 | 5.0 | 65 |
| buffalo | 4.3 | 7.5 | 4.5 | 105 |
| camel | 3.7 | 4.2 | 4.0 | 70 |
| ewe | 6.5 | 7.0 | 5.0 | 110 |
| goat | 3.7 | 5.0 | 4.5 | 75 |
| mare | 1.3 | 1.2 | 5.5 | 30 |
| reindeer | 10.5 | 22.5 | 2.5 | 250 |
| human | 1.1 | 6.2 | 7.5 | 70 |

**mineral water** water with mineral constituents gathered from the rocks with which it comes in contact, and bottled at source. Some mineral waters are naturally sparkling; others are artificially carbonated with carbon dioxide under pressure. Fears about the quality of tap water in many areas of the UK contributed to the greatly increased sales of mineral water from the 1980s.

The most widely sold mineral water in the UK is Perrier, from the French village of Vergèze in W Provence. It is naturally carbonated, but the gas is removed at source and then used to recarbonate the water during bottling. In 1990 minute traces of benzene, a cancer-causing chemical, were found in samples of Perrier, and 160 million bottles were recalled. Production was resumed once charcoal filters at the bottling plant had been replaced.

**mushroom** the fruiting body of certain fungi, consisting of an upright stem and a spore-producing cap with radiating gills on the undersurface. Most species are inedible or even poisonous. Cultivated edible mushrooms are usually species of the genus *Agaricus*. Edible wild, or field, mushrooms include the cep *Boletus edulis*, the chanterelle *Cantharellus cibarius*, and the horn of plenty *Cratellus cornicupoides*, all woodland species; and the horse mushroom *Agaricus arvensis* and shaggy ink cap *Coprinus comatus*, found in grassland. The most prized mushrooms are truffles (various species of *Tuber*), which fruit underground, and morels (species of *Morchella*).

**mustard** a strong-tasting condiment made from the whole, crushed, or ground seeds of the black, brown, or white mustard plants. Its main use is as an accompaniment for meat, though it can also be used in sauces and dressings, and with fish. English mustard is made from finely ground black and white mustard seed mixed with turmeric. French Dijon mustard contains black and brown mustard seed, verjuice (the juice of unripe grapes), oil, and white wine. Other varieties are made with vinegar, and may be flavoured with herbs or garlic.

**nut** in botany, a dry, single-seeded fruit; commonly, an edible seed or fruit with a woody shell, such as a coconut, almond, walnut, peanut (groundnut), Brazil nut, or hazel nut. The edible parts of most nuts provide a concentrated, nutritious food, containing vitamins, minerals, and enzymes, about 50% fat, and 10–20% protein, although a few, such as chestnuts, are high in carbohydrates and have only a moderate protein content of 5%. Nuts also provide edible oils.

**oil, cooking** a fat that is liquid at room temperature, extracted from the seeds or fruits of certain plants and used for frying, salad dressings, and sauces and condiments such as mayonnaise and mustard. Plants used for cooking oil include sunflower, olive, maize (corn), soya, peanut, and rape. Vegetable oil is a blend of more than one type of oil. Most

oils are hot pressed and refined, a process that leaves them without smell or flavour. Cold-pressed, unrefined oils keep their flavour. Oils are generally low in cholesterol and contain a high proportion of polyunsaturated or monounsaturated fatty acids, although all except soya and corn oil become saturated when heated.

**pasta** food made from a dough of durum-wheat flour or semolina, water, and, sometimes, egg, and cooked in boiling water. It is usually served with a sauce. Pasta is creamy-yellow in colour, but may be coloured green with spinach, or red with tomato. It is available either fresh or dried, and comes in a wide variety of shapes: in narrow strands (spaghetti, vermicelli), flat or in ribbons (lasagne, tagliatelle, fettucine), shell-shaped (conchiglie, lumache), butterfly-shaped (farfalle), tubular (cannelloni, macaroni, penne), and twisted (fusilli). Some varieties are sold ready stuffed with a meat, cheese, herb, or vegetable filling (ravioli, agnolotti, tortellini).

**pastry** a baked dough made from flour, fat, water, and salt. It makes a useful base or container for soft, moist fillings, and is widely used for tarts, pies, quiches, and pasties. Richer pastries may include eggs, yeast, or sugar. Types include: short pastry, flaked pastries, suet crust, filo, choux. *Puff pastry* is made with a higher proportion of fat. Its preparation involves repeated folding, which, with the fat, makes it flaky.

**pepper** hot, aromatic spice derived from the berry of the climbing plant *Piper nigrum*, native to the E Indies. The dried berries (corns) may be crushed or ground to release their flavour, or may be used whole. Green peppercorns are berries that have been harvested while unripe, and dried or canned; black peppercorns are unripe berries that have been left to darken and shrivel in the Sun; and white peppercorns are dried ripe berries that have had their outer husks removed. Black peppercorns are hotter but less aromatic than white peppercorns. The mild pink peppercorns that became fashionable in the 1980s are the fruits of a different plant, a member of the poison ivy family.

**potato** the tuberous root of the perennial plant *Solanum tuberosum*, native to the Andes of South America. One of the most versatile of foods, the potato is cultivated in many varieties, particularly in temperate regions. It is a good source of carbohydate, fibre, and vitamin C, and also contains some protein, phosphates, and iron. The unrelated *sweet potato*, native to tropical America, has a sweet, orange or yellow flesh, and is rich in vitamin A.

Potato varieties can be grouped according to when their tubers mature: *new* or *early potatoes* are gathered in the spring and summer, are generally small and waxy, and are suitable for boiling in their skins and canning; the larger *maincrop potatoes* are lifted in the autumn, are more floury in texture,

### AVERAGE DAILY ENERGY REQUIREMENTS (KCAL/DAY)

|  | Light activity | Moderate activity | Heavy activity |
| --- | --- | --- | --- |
| Men | 2,015 | 2,314 | 2,730 |
| Women | 2,496 | 2,624 | 2,912 |

and are suitable for mashing and baking, and for commercial processing into products such as frozen chips, crisps and snacks, and potato flour.

**pulse** dried seed, such as a pea, bean, or lentil, gathered from the pod of a leguminous plant. Pulses provide a concentrated source of vegetable protein, and make a vital contribution to the diet in countries where meat is scarce, and among vegetarians.

*Soya beans* are the major temperate protein crop in the West; most are used for oil production or for animal feed. In Asia, most are processed into soya milk and tofu (beancurd). *Miso* is soya beans fermented with cereal grains, water, and salt, used in soups and sauces; soya sauce is beans fermented with salt; *tamari* is similar to soya sauce but stronger, having been matured for up to two years. *Peanuts* (groundnuts), which are not true nuts but pulses grown in underground pods, dominate pulse production in the tropical world. They yield a valuable oil and form the basis for numerous processed foods, such as peanut butter. Canned *baked beans* are usually a variety of haricot bean.

**rice** grain of *Oryza sativa*, the principal cereal of the wet regions of the tropics, but grown also in the Po valley of Italy, and in the USA in Louisiana, the Carolinas, and California. Boiled or ground into flour, it forms the staple food of one-third of the world population. It is rich in carbohydrate and contains 8–9% protein. Brown rice (rice that has not been husked) has valuable B-vitamins that are lost in husking, or polishing. Most of the rice eaten in the world is, however, sold in polished form.

**salt, common** or *sodium chloride* NaCl white crystalline solid, found dissolved in sea water and as rock salt (halite) in large deposits and salt domes. It is used extensively in the food industry as a preservative and for flavouring. While common salt is an essential part of our diet, some medical experts believe that excess salt can lead to high blood pressure and increased risk of heart attacks.

**sauce** a liquid used in cooking or served with food to add to its flavour. Sauces may be thick or thin, hot or cold, sweet or savoury. There are sauces suitable for serving with almost any dish, ranging from the simplest vinaigrette, a cold mixture of oil, vinegar, and seasonings, to cooked sauces containing cream, wine, egg yolks, or herbs.

**shellfish** common name for any aquatic invertebrate with a shell, including both molluscs and crustaceans. Many species are eaten, including oyster, scallop, crab, lobster, shrimp, mussel, and clam. Shellfish are high in protein and minerals. They do not keep well, and should only be used if known to be fresh. They become tough if overcooked; some are eaten raw.

**soft drink** a non-alcoholic drink, usually sweetened. Soft drinks may be carbonated (made fizzy by the introduction of carbon dioxide under pressure), as in lemonade, ginger ale, and tonic water. Many fruit-flavoured drinks contain no fruit, consisting only of water, sugar or artificial sweetener, and synthetic flavourings. In the UK, undiluted fruit squash must contain stipulated amounts of fruit or of fruit juice. In 1990, the British public drank 4.1 billion litres of soft drinks, at a cost of £5 billion. Coca-Cola and Schweppes is the largest soft-drink company in the UK, with 40% of the market.

**spice** any aromatic vegetable substance used as a condiment and for flavouring food. Spices are mostly obtained from tropical plants, and include pepper, nutmeg, ginger, and cinnamon. They have little food value but increase the appetite and may facilitate digestion.

**spirit** strong alcoholic liquor, distilled from the fruit, seeds, roots, or stems of certain plants. Fruit-based spirits include Calvados (apples), and brandy (grapes); grain-based spirits include whisky (malted barley, with other grains sometimes added), gin (barley, maize, or rye), sake (rice); others include rum (sugar cane), and tequila (agave). Spirits are usually matured for several years before use; they may be drunk on their own, diluted, or iced. Sake, from Japan, is heated before serving.

**stock** liquid used as a base for soups, stews, or sauces. *White stock* is made from poultry or veal, and vegetables boiled together in water. *Brown stock* is made from red meat or bones, and vegetables, browned in fat before being boiled in water.

**sugar** a sweet, soluble crystalline carbohydrate, such as sucrose, glucose, fructose, maltose, and lactose. It is easily digested and forms a major source of energy. The term is popularly used to refer only to sucrose, the type most commonly used in cooking and in the food industry as a sweetener and (in high concentrations) preservative. A high consumption of sucrose is associated with tooth decay and

### RELATIVE SWEETNESS OF ARTIFICIAL SWEETENERS

| Artificial sweetener | Relative sweetness (sucrose = 1.0) |
| --- | --- |
| thaumatin | 3,000 |
| saccharin | 300 |
| aspartame | 200 |
| acesulfame-K | 150 |
| cyclamate | 30 |

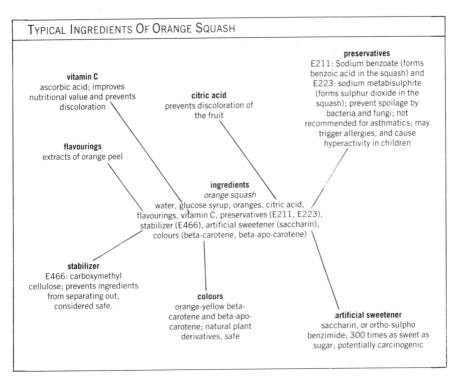

TYPICAL INGREDIENTS OF ORANGE SQUASH

**vitamin C**
ascorbic acid; improves nutritional value and prevents discoloration

**flavourings**
extracts of orange peel

**citric acid**
prevents discoloration of the fruit

**preservatives**
E211: Sodium benzoate (forms benzoic acid in the squash) and E223: sodium metabisulphite (forms sulphur dioxide in the squash); prevent spoilage by bacteria and fungi; not recommended for asthmatics; may trigger allergies, and cause hyperactivity in children

**ingredients**
*orange squash*
water, glucose syrup, oranges, citric acid, flavourings, vitamin C, preservatives (E211, E223), stabilizer (E466), artificial sweetener (saccharin), colours (beta-carotene, beta-apo-carotene)

**stabilizer**
E466: carboxymethyl cellulose; prevents ingredients from separating out, considered safe.

**colours**
orange-yellow beta-carotene and beta-apo-carotene; natural plant derivatives, safe

**artificial sweetener**
saccharin, or ortho-sulpho benzimide; 300 times as sweet as sugar; potentially carcinogenic

---

obesity. In the UK, sucrose may not be used in baby foods.

The main sources of sucrose are tropical sugar cane *Saccharum officinarum*, which accounts for about two-thirds of production, and temperate sugar beet *Beta vulgaris*. Minor quantities are produced from the sap of maple trees, and from sorghum and date palms. Raw sugar crystals obtained by heating the juice of sugar canes are processed to form brown sugars, such as Muscovado and Demerara, or refined and sifted to produce white sugars, such as granulated, caster, and icing. The syrup that is drained away from the raw sugar is *molasses*; it may be processed to form golden syrup or treacle, or fermented to produce rum. Molasses obtained from sugar beet juice is too bitter for human consumption.

**sweetener, artificial** or *noncaloric sweetener* a chemical that adds sweetness to food without providing energy; for example, saccharin and aspartame (Nutrasweet). Artificial sweeteners are used in the food industry and by dieters and diabetics. Thaumatin, aspartame, and acesulfame-K are banned in foods intended for babies and young children. Cyclamate is banned completely in the UK and USA; acesulfame-K is banned in the USA.

**sweets** confectionery made mainly from sucrose sugar. Other ingredients include glucose, milk, nuts, fat (animal and vegetable), and fruit. Boiled-sugar sweets contain sugar, glucose, colour, and flavouring, and are boiled, cooled, and shaped. *Chewing gum* consists of synthetic or vegetable gum with colour, flavouring, and sometimes sweetener added. *Toffee* and *caramel* are made from sugar, glucose, animal fat, milk, and cream or vegetable fat, heated and shaped. The USA is the biggest producer of sweets, though the UK has the highest consumption, with millions of pounds spent each year on advertising.

**tea** beverage made by infusing the dried leaves of the evergreen shrub *Camellia sinensis*. Known in China as early as 2737 BC, tea was first brought to Europe AD 1610 and rapidly became a fashionable drink. In 1823 it was found growing wild in N India, and plantations were later established in Assam and Sri Lanka; producers today include Africa, South America, the USSR, Indonesia, and Iran.

The young leaves and shoots of the tea plant are picked every five years. After 24 hours spread on shelves in withering lofts, they are broken up by rolling machines to release the essential oils, and then left to ferment. This process is halted by passing the leaves through ovens where moisture is removed and the blackish-brown **black tea** emerges ready for sifting into various grades. *Green tea* is steamed and quickly dried before fermentation, remaining partly green in colour.

**vegetable** any food plant, especially leafy plants (cabbage and lettuce), roots and tubers (carrots, parsnips, and potatoes), pulses (peas, lentils, and beans), and even flowers (cauliflower, broccoli, and artichoke). Tomatoes, peppers, aubergines, and cucumbers are generally regarded as vegetables but are technically fruits. Green leafy vegetables and potatoes are good sources of vitamin C, though much is lost in cooking, and pulses are a main source of protein. Cooking softens vegetables by dissolving pectins and hemicellulose and gelatinizing starch.

**vinegar** acidic liquid produced by the souring of alcoholic liquids, such as wine, beer, or cider, and used to flavour food and as a preservative in pickling. The souring yeasts and bacteria oxidize the alcohol to ethanoic (acetic) acid. *Malt vinegar* is brown and made from malted cereals; *white vinegar* is distilled from it. *Balsamic vinegar* is wine vinegar aged in wooden barrels. Other sources of vinegar include sherry and fermented fruits and honey.

**wine** alcoholic beverage, usually made from fermented grape pulp, although wines have also traditionally been made from many other fruits such as damsons and elderberries. *Red wine* is the product of the grape with the skin; *white wine* of the inner pulp of the grape. The sugar content is converted to alcohol (ethanol) by the yeast *Saccharomyces ellipsoideus*, which lives on the skin of the grape. Most wines have an alcohol content of 10–12%. For *dry wine* the fermentation is allowed to go on longer than for *sweet* or *medium* wine. Champagne (sparkling wine from the Champagne region of France) and other, similar, *méthode champenoise* wines are bottled while still fermenting, but other sparkling wines are artificially carbonated. The largest wine-producing countries are Italy, France, the USSR, and Spain; others include almost all European countries, Australia, South Africa, the USA, and Chile.

A *vintage wine* is produced during a good year (as regards quality of wine, produced by favourable weather conditions) in recognized vineyards of a particular area; France has a guarantee of origin (*appellation controlée*), as do Italy (*Denominazione di Origine Controllata*), Spain (*Denominación Controllata*), and Germany (a series of graded qualities running from *Qualitätswein* to *Beerenauslese*).

**wine, fortified** wine that has extra alcohol added to raise its alcohol content to about 20%. Fortified wines keep well because the alcohol kills the microorganisms that spoil natural wines. Port, which originates from Oporto in Portugal, is made by adding brandy to wine before fermentation is complete; sherry, originally made in Jerez in Spain, is a dry wine fortified after fermentation and later blended with sugar for sweet sherry; vermouth is flavoured with bitter herbs. Marsala, from Sicily, is fortified after fermentation and then heated gradually.

**yoghurt** or *yogurt* or *yoghourt* semi-solid, curdlike dairy product made from milk fermented with bacteria. It is drunk plain throughout the Asian and Mediterranean regions, but honey, sugar, and fruit are usually added in Europe and the USA, and the product made solid and creamy, to be eaten by spoon.

Heat-treated, homogenized milk is inoculated with a culture of *Streptococcus lactis* and *Lactobacillus bulgaricus* in equal amounts, which change the lactose in the milk to lactic acid. Acetaldehyde gives yoghurt its characteristic flavour. Commercially, fruit, flavourings, and colouring and thickening agents are added to the fermented yoghurt.

# FOOD TECHNOLOGY

**food technology** the commercial processing of foodstuffs in order to render them more palatable or digestible, or to preserve them from spoilage. Food spoils because of the action of enzymes within the food that change its chemical composition, or because of the growth of bacteria, moulds, yeasts, and other microorganisms. Fatty or oily foods also suffer oxidation of the fats, giving them an unpleasant rancid flavour. Traditional forms of processing include boiling, frying, flour-milling, bread–making, yoghurt- and cheese-making, brewing, and various methods of *food preservation*, such as salting, smoking, pickling, drying, bottling, and preserving in sugar. Modern food technology still employs traditional methods, but also uses many novel processes and additives, which allow a wider range of foodstuffs to be preserved.

**additive** any natural or artificial chemical added to prolong the shelf life of processed foods, alter the colour or flavour of food, or improve its nutritional value. Many additives are used and they are subject to regulation, since individuals may be affected by constant exposure even to traces of certain chemicals, and may suffer side effects ranging from headaches and hyperactivity to cancer. Additives approved for use throughout the European Community are given an official E number.

*flavours* are used to alter or intensify a food's taste. They may be natural or artificial, and include artificial sweeteners.

*enhancers* heighten the flavour or smell of foods without imparting their own taste—for example, monosodium glutamate (MSG).

*colourings* enhance the visual appeal of foods.

*nutrients* enhance food value or replace nutrients lost in processing.

*preservatives* slow down the rate of spoilage by controlling the growth of bacteria and fungi.

*antioxidants* prevent fatty foods from going rancid by inhibiting their natural oxidation.

*emulsifiers* and *stabilizers* modify the texture and consistency of food, and prevent the ingredients of a mixture from separating out.

*leavening agents* are substances other than yeast that lighten the texture of baked products—for example, sodium bicarbonate.

# E Numbers: A Selection of Food Additives

| number | name | typical use |
|---|---|---|
| | COLOURS | |
| E102 | tartrazine | soft drinks |
| E104 | quinoline yellow | |
| E110 | sunset yellow | biscuits |
| E120 | cochineal | alcoholic drinks |
| E122 | carmoisine | jams and preserves |
| E123 | amaranth | |
| E124 | ponceau 4R | dessert mixes |
| E127 | erythrosine | glacé cherries |
| E131 | patent blue V | |
| E132 | indigo carmine | |
| E142 | green S | pastilles |
| E150 | caramel | beers, soft drinks, sauces, gravy browning |
| E151 | black PN | |
| E160 (b) | annatto; bixin; norbixin | crisps |
| E180 | pigment rubine (lithol rubine BK) | |

| | ANTIOXIDANTS | |
|---|---|---|
| E310 | propyl gallate | vegetable oils; chewing gum |
| E311 | octyl gallate | |
| E312 | dodecyl gallate | |
| E320 | butylated hydroxynisole (BHA) | beef stock cubes; cheese spread |
| E321 | butylated hydroxytoluene (BHT) | chewing gum |

| | EMULSIFIERS AND STABILIZERS | |
|---|---|---|
| E407 | carageenan | quick-setting jelly mixes; milk shakes |
| E413 | tragacanth | salad dressings; processed cheese |

| | PRESERVATIVES | |
|---|---|---|
| E210 | benzoic acid | |
| E211 | sodium benzoate | beer, jam, salad cream, soft drinks, fruit pulp |

| E212 | potassium benzoate | fruit-based pie fillings, marinated herring and mackerel |
|---|---|---|
| E213 | calcium benzoate | |
| E214 | ethyl para-hydroxy-benzoate | |
| E215 | sodium ethyl para-hydroxy-benzoate | |
| E216 | propyl para-hydroxy-benzoate | |
| E217 | sodium propyl para-hydroxy-benzoate | |
| E218 | methyl para-hydroxy-benzoate | |
| E220 | sulphur dioxide | |
| E221 | sodium sulphate | dried fruit, dehydrated vegetables, fruit juices and syrups, |
| E222 | sodium bisulphite | sausages, fruit-based dairy desserts, cider, beer, |
| E223 | sodium metabisulphite | and wine; also used to prevent browning of peeled |
| E224 | potassium metabisulphite | potatoes and to condition biscuit doughs |
| E226 | calcium sulphite | |
| E227 | calcium bisulphite | |
| E249 | potassium nitrite | |
| E250 | sodium nitrite | bacon, ham, cured meats, corned beef and |
| E251 | sodium nitrate | some cheeses |
| E252 | potassium nitrate | |

| | OTHERS | |
|---|---|---|
| E450 (a) | disodium dihydrogen diphosphate | buffers, sequestrants, emulsifying salts, |
| | trisodium diphosphate | stabilizers, texturizers |
| | tetrasodium diphosphate | raising agents, used in whipping |
| | tetrapotassium diphosphate | cream, fish and meat products, bread, |
| E450 (b) | pentasodium triphosphate | processed cheese, canned vegetables |
| | pentapotassium triphosphate | |

**acidulants** sharpen the taste of foods but may also perform a buffering function in the control of acidity.

**bleaching agents** whiten flours.

**anticaking agents** prevent powdered products from coagulating into solid lumps.

**humectants** control the humidity of foods by absorbing and retaining moisture.

**clarifying agents** are used in fruit juices, vinegars, and other fermented liquids. Gelatin is the most common.

**firming agents** restore the texture of vegetables that may be damaged during processing.

**foam regulators** may be used in beer to provide a controlled 'head' on top of the poured product.

**canning** preservation of food in hermetically sealed steel, aluminium, or plastic containers (cans) by the application of heat. The high temperature destroys microorganisms and enzymes, and the can's seal prevents recontamination. Beverages may also be canned to preserve the carbon dioxide that makes drinks fizzy.

**curing** method of preserving meat by soaking it in salt (sodium chloride) solution, with saltpetre (sodium nitrate) added to give the meat its pink colour and characteristic taste. The nitrates in cured meats are converted to nitrites and nitrosamines by bacteria, and these are potentially carcinogenic to humans.

**deep freezing** method of preserving food by lowering its temperature to −18°C/0°F or below. It stops almost all spoilage processes, although there may be some residual enzyme activity in uncooked vegetables, which is why these are blanched (dipped in hot water to destroy the enzymes) before freezing. Microorganisms cannot grow or divide while frozen, but most remain alive and can resume activity once defrosted. Commercial techniques freeze foods rapidly in order to prevent the growth

## WHAT'S IN YOUR FOOD?

In the past four years the labelling of food additives has proliferated. Should we be alarmed by additives? Do they matter?

Although the main function of food is nutritional, we require more than this. We expect eating to be an enjoyable experience. A heightened expectation, even subconscious, enhances the flow of salivary juices. It is paradoxical that cooks are allowed to enhance foods by all sorts of additions, none of which are disclosed on the menu, whereas food manufacturers are castigated for the number of additives that appear on their goods' labels.

To what extent is the consumer responsible for the use of certain additives in foods? The soft drinks sector of the food industry highlights a number of interesting aspects. There is nothing natural about the concept of soft drinks, as opposed to fruit juices. Some contain some fruit material but the majority are merely flavoured blends of acids and sweeteners, coloured to satisfy consumer expectations, and sometimes made more palatable by fizzing them up with carbon dioxide. Food colours have come under heavy fire over the last couple of decades and manufacturers have tried to replace synthetic colourants with more natural ones. Tartrazine, once the most commonly used synthetic dye, has become less popular because of frequent allergic reaction. Yet the extensive use of food colours, although in minute quantities, has unwittingly been the fault of the consumers, who have previously expected an orange drink to be the colour of orange peel rather than of its juice. The biggest-selling soft drink in the world has nothing natural to commend it, least of all its colour.

Repeated concerns are expressed about the use of the artificial sweetener saccharin. There is clearly a demand for a sweetener that has no calorific value. This is important for the diabetics in the community, for whom sugar presents a particular problem. In the early 1960s saccharin was rivalled by cyclamates, the sodium and calcium salts of cyclamic acid, which don't leave a bitter aftertaste. But the cyclamates were deposed, almost overnight, in 1969 when tests in the USA showed that large dosages produced tumours in rats. Saccharin

was once more supreme until recent developments threw up a handful of alternatives. The best known of these is aspartame, marketed under the tradename Nutrasweet, which comprises mainly two amino acids, aspartic acid and phenylalanine.

Some additives rarely, if ever, come under the spotlight. These are used for technological advantage. They are emulsifiers and stabilizers, which are used for texture modification or thickeners in, for example, salad creams, bakery products, and cheese spreads. They range from natural gums, although not necessarily from traditional food sources, to chemically tailored substances with specific properties.

There is no doubt that many additives have been developed to satisfy changing consumer requirements, especially 'convenience foods' but not necessarily in response to direct consumer demand. The use of additives is just one of the means whereby food materials can be presented in a variety of appetizing ways. More importantly, they help to prolong the safe life of many food substances.

The major complaint against food additives is in the context of the harm they can do to people with metabolic disorders or allergies. Here they are no different from natural constituents such as lactose (milk sugar) and phenylethylamine (a natural constituent of chocolate), which adversely affect people suffering from lactose-intolerance and migraine respectively. It is not the naturalness or artificiality that is the problem but the physiological response to them.

Comprehensive labelling is intended to provide protection for the consumer. Armed with his/her guide to additives, the shopper is expected to scan the ingredients lists and determine whether there is anything there that might offend. There is an implicit assumption that he/she is up to date with the latest additives and can recognize a hazardous substance. Perhaps it would be better to put the onus on the manufacturer, who has ready access to scientific and medical advice. 'Not recommended for sufferers of phenylketonuria' would be more helpful than 'artificial sweetener (aspartame)' in a contents list.

of large ice crystals, which would damage the food tissue on thawing.

**dehydration** preservation of food by reducing its moisture content by 80% or more. It inhibits the activity of moulds and bacteria, and reduces the mass and volume of foods, thereby lowering distribution costs. Products such as dried milk and instant coffee are made by spraying the liquid into a rising column of dry, heated air.

**freeze-drying** method of preserving food by freezing it and then placing it in a vacuum chamber so that the ice is forced out as water vapour. Many of the substances that give products such as coffee their typical flavour are volatile, and would be lost in a normal drying

process because they would evaporate along with the water. In the freeze-drying process these volatile compounds do not pass into the ice that is to be sublimed, and are therefore largely retained.

**hydrogenation** method by which liquid oils are transformed into solid products, such as margarine. Vegetable oils contain double carbon-to-carbon bonds and are therefore examples of unsaturated compounds. When hydrogen is added to these double bonds, the oils become saturated and more solid in consistency.

**irradiation** method of preserving food by subjecting it to low-level gamma radiation in order to kill microorganisms. Although the process is now legal in several countries,

## GENETICALLY ENGINEERED FOOD—IS IT SAFE?

Square tomatoes and headless chickens are not going to be produced as genetically engineered food. However, what will be on offer are crops that will grow faster and bigger and will resist insects, viruses, drought, and frost damage. Vegetables altered to last longer will soon be on the market. Biological pesticides that will replace toxic chemicals are also a reality. Genetically engineered animals have already been developed in the USA, where mice are being used in cancer research and have been patented. The European Community is introducing a directive to allow the patenting of animals and plants.

In the UK, new genetically engineered foods are scrutinized by the Advisory Committee on Novel Foods and Processes (ACNFP), which is part of the Ministry of Agriculture, Fisheries and Food (MAFF). The committee only investigates food safety, not animal welfare, ethics, or the effects on the environment.

Genetic engineering will allow genes (which contain the information for protein manufacture) from almost any form of life to be introduced into almost any other form of life. By this method the basic blueprint of life can be altered. Genetic engineering is part of biotechnology and involves a number of techniques for introducing foreign genes into plants and animals.

The reason biotechnology is used in agriculture is to reduce crop losses and food production costs, and to alter the quality and flavour of the food.

Examples of genetically engineered food are:
— tomatoes that do not soften with age (the softening gene has been deactivated).
— pest-resistant crop plants. In 1990, a crop of potatoes was produced in Norfolk, England, containing a pea gene that produces a protein fatal to insect pests. The company responsible wants to carry out more trials, which will lead to other plants being protected from pests in the same way. The effect that these plants would have if they spread as weeds is being investigated.
— plants that resist herbicides, so that any herbicides applied to crops will kill weeds only. The first such plant, a new sugar beet, was developed in Denmark.
— 'ice-minus' bacteria. When applied to crops, they prevent the plant tissues from being damaged by ice formation by competing with other bacteria that promote its formation. Their success in preventing frost damage to potatoes and strawberries has been tested.
— pigs have been genetically altered to produce growth hormone, in order to make them grow faster.

Many people are worried that genetic engineering is 'playing God', and upsetting the integrity of plants and animals. There are concerns about the welfare of the laboratory animals undergoing experimentation, and also about the stress that future genetically altered farm animals might experience. Environmental risks are concerning some: genetically engineered organisms could become the pollution of the future. Once released they would be impossible to recall.

The biotechnology industry estimates that we can only feed the world population (which might be as high as 8.5 billion in 2025) by widespread use of biotechnology. However, opponents say that it will further depress the ability of Third-World farmers to feed themselves, when they already suffer from non-economic farming practices in order to produce cash crops for the international market.

New labelling proposals are being considered by the government. The proposals are to label only those foods where genetic engineering has materially altered the nature of the food. Therefore, foods that use genetically engineered organisms in their processing will not be labelled. Meat might not be labelled under these proposals.

Genetically engineered foods are scrutinized by ACNFP under the Food Safety Act 1990. The act does not require that all genetically engineered organisms released into the environment be scrutinized, and it does not make the originator of the organism effectively liable for any damage or injury to the environment. Clearly, some parts of the act need to be tightened up to ensure our environmental safety and to relieve consumer concern.

---

uncertainty remains about possible long-term effects on consumers of irradiated food. The process does not make the food radioactive, but some vitamins, such as vitamin C, are destroyed and many molecular changes take place including the initiation of free radicals, which may be further changed into a range of unknown and unstable chemicals. Irradiation also eradicates the smell, taste, and poor appearance of bad or ageing food products.

**pasteurization** treatment of food to reduce the number of microorganisms it contains and so protect consumers from disease. Harmful bacteria are killed and the development of others is delayed. For milk, the method involves heating it to 72°C/161°F for 15 seconds followed by rapid cooling to 10°C/50°F or lower. However, the process also kills beneficial bacteria and reduces the nutritive property of milk.

**pickling** method of preserving food by soaking it in acetic acid (found in vinegar), which stops the growth of moulds. In sauerkraut, lactic acid, produced by bacteria, has the same effect.

**puffing** method of processing cereal grains. The grains are first subjected to high pressures, and then suddenly ejected into a normal atmospheric pressure, causing each grain to expand sharply. This type of process is used to make puffed wheat cereals and puffed rice cakes.

**refrigeration** method of preserving food by lowering its temperature to below 5°C/41°F (or below 3°C/37°F for cooked foods). It slows the processes of spoilage, but is less effective for foods with a high water content. Although a convenient form of preservation, this process cannot kill microorganisms, nor stop their growth completely, and a failure to realize its limitations causes many cases of food poisoning. Refrigerator temperatures should be checked as the efficiency of the machinery can decline with age.

**smoking** method of preserving fresh oily meats (such as pork and goose) or fish (such as herring and salmon). Before being smoked, the food is first salted or soaked in brine, then hung to dry. Meat is hot-smoked over a fast-burning wood fire, which is covered with sawdust, producing thick smoke and partly cooking the meat. Fish may be hot-smoked or cold-smoked over a slow-burning wood fire, which does not cook it. Modern refrigeration techniques mean that food does not need to be smoked to help it keep, so factory-smoked foods tend to be smoked just enough to give them a smoky flavour, with colours added to give them the appearance of traditionally smoked food.

**ultra-heat treatment** (UHT) preservation of milk by raising its temperature to 132°C/269°F or more. It uses higher temperatures than pasteurization, and kills all bacteria present, giving the milk a long shelf life but altering the flavour.

# AGRICULTURE

**agriculture** the cultivation of land and the raising of animals in order to provide food for human nourishment, fodder for animals, or commodities such as wool and cotton. The units for managing agricultural production vary from small holdings and individually owned farms, to corporate-run farms and collective farms run by entire communities.

The first agricultural communities appeared about 9000 BC in southwest Asia, followed by Egypt, India, and China; in Europe farming began around 6500 BC in the Balkans and Aegean, and then spread north and east. Previously, food had been obtained only by hunting and by gathering wild vegetation. The selective breeding of reliable and productive animals and crop plants, and the improvement of soil by ploughing, irrigation, crop rotation, and the use of organic fertilizers such as manure and ashes meant that communities could become more stable, giving rise to fixed villages and towns and to complicated social systems. Reorganization of farming along more scientific and productive lines took place in Europe in the 18th century in response to dramatic population growth. Mechanization made considerable progress in Europe and the USA

during the 19th century. After World War II, there was a dramatic increase in the use of agricultural chemicals: herbicides (weed-killers), insecticides, fungicides, and inorganic fertilizers. In the 1960s high-yielding species were developed for the *green revolution* of the Third World, and the industrialized countries began intensive farming of cattle, poultry, and pigs. In the 1980s, hybridization of species by genetic engineering, and pest control by the use of chemicals such as pheromones (scents emitted by animals) were developed. However, there was also a reaction against some forms of intensive agriculture because of the pollution and habitat destruction caused. One result of this was a growth of alternative methods, including organic farming.

**agricultural revolution** the sweeping changes that took place in British agriculture over the period 1750–1850 in response to the increased demand for food from a rapidly expanding population. Changes during the latter half of the 18th century include the enclosure of open fields, the introduction of four-year crop rotation, together with new fodder crops such as turnip, and the development of improved breeds of livestock.

**agrochemical** artificially produced chemical used in modern, intensive agricultural systems. Agrochemicals include inorganic nitrate and phosphate fertilizers, pesticides, some animal-feed additives, and drugs. Many are responsible for pollution and almost all are avoided by organic farmers.

**agronomy** the study of crops and soils, a branch of agricultural science. Agronomy includes such topics as selective breeding (of plants and animals), irrigation, pest control, and soil analysis and modification.

**artificial insemination** (AI) mating achieved by mechanically injecting previously collected semen into the uterus without genital contact. It is commonly used with cattle because it allows farmers to select the type and quality of bull required for a herd, and to control the timing and organization of a breeding programme. The practice of artificially inseminating pigs has also become widespread in recent years.

**bovine spongiform encephalopathy** (BSE) or *mad-cow disease* disease of cattle, allied to scrapie, that renders the brain spongy and may drive an animal mad. It has been identified only in the UK, where more than 14,000 cases had been confirmed between the first diagnosis Nov 1986 and June 1990. The source of the disease has been traced to manufactured protein feed incorporating the rendered brains of scrapie-infected sheep. BSE is very similar to, and may be related to, Creutzfeld–Jakob disease and kuru, which affect humans.

**cash crop** crop grown solely for sale rather than for the farmer's own use—for example, coffee, cotton, or sugar beet. Many Third World countries grow cash crops to meet their debt repayments rather than grow food for their people. The price for these crops depends on financial interests, such as those of the

## ORGANIC FARMING: IS IT THE ANSWER?

To judge from the amount of attention given to organic farming, you might think that it was already a major sector of agriculture. Over the past five years, repeated surveys have shown that most consumers would welcome access to more organic food. Organic agriculture has some high-profile advocates, including HRH Prince Charles. Yet organic farmers make up at most 1% of agriculture in most industrialized countries, and there is still great ignorance about what organic farming and growing actually entails.

Many people assume that organic agriculture is the same as the traditional agriculture practised in Europe and North America before 1945. This is not the case. Although organic faming uses some traditional techniques that were abandoned during the boom years of chemical agriculture, it builds on contemporary knowledge of crop breeding, ecology, soil science, and selective innovations in farm machinery and pest control.

Organic farming began at about the same time as the development of modern intensive agriculture, in the early 1940s. It was started by a group of scientists and farmers who believed that some of the contemporary farming innovations, such as the use of agrochemicals and heavy machinery, would prove damaging to ecology and health in the long term.

Today, there are thousands of organic farmers throughout the world. Most of these produce food to one or more recognized certification schemes, which lay down the standards for organic production and inspect symbol holders to ensure that they are following the system correctly. There have, until recently, been many standards, all giving slightly different interpretations of what is meant by 'organic', and leading to a great deal of confusion among consumers. Common standards are coming, though, both within individual countries and internationally—for example, by the European Community.

The basic principle of organic agriculture is ⁻are of the soil's fertility and structure. This is achieved through developing high levels of humus and beneficial soil organisms, avoiding artificial fertilizers and pesticides, and maintaining fertility through crop rotation, and the managed use of manure and some naturally occurring fertilizers.

Another principle of organic farming is the reluctance to use pesticides of any sort. Weeds are kept down by mechanical weeders and a variety of cultural controls, and insect pests through biological control, timing of planting to avoid the pest's life cycle, traps, barriers, and emergency use of a limited range of plant-based insecticides. This means that protection of wildlife on a farm or holding is not just a luxury, but is essential to maintain the pool of natural predators needed for pest control.

Organic farming results in a slight drop in production, but this is less than many people assume. Typically, a fully converted organic farm (one that has been running for some time and has built up levels of soil fertility, pest predators, and so on) produces 10–15% less than a conventional farm. Several influential reports, including one from the US National Academy of Sciences, have stated that a large-scale shift to organic and similar systems would not mean a catastrophic reduction in food production, but would result in substantial reductions in environmental pollution and improvements in resource use in agriculture.

However, it is currently very difficult for farmers to convert to an organic system in most industrialized countries, because of the overt and hidden subsidies paid to conventional farmers, ranging from guaranteed prices to direct subsidy for agrochemicals. It is becoming increasingly clear that, for a major shift to the organic option, some conversion grant will have to be introduced and agricultural subsidy policies rethought.

*Inter-row cultivation of an organic patato crop.*

multinational companies and the International Monetary Fund.

**cattle** large, ruminant, even-toed, hoofed mammals of the genus *Bos*, family Bovidae. Fermentation in the four-chambered stomach allows cattle to make good use of the grass that normally forms the greater part of their diet. They are bred to achieve maximum yields of meat (beef cattle) or milk (dairy cattle). The old established beef breeds are mostly British in origin—for example, the Hereford, the Aberdeen Angus, the Devon, and the Beef Shorthorn. In recent years, more interest has been shown in other European breeds, their tendency to have less fat being more suited to modern tastes. Examples include the Charolais and the Limousin from central France, and the Simmental, originally from Switzerland. For dairying purposes, a breed raised in many countries is variously known as the Friesian, Holstein, or Black and White. It can give enormous milk yields, up to 13,000 l/3,450 gal in a single lactation, and will produce calves ideally suited for intensive beef production. Other dairying types include the Jersey and Guernsey, whose milk has a high butterfat content, and the Ayrshire, a smaller breed capable of staying outside all year.

**cereal** grass grown for its edible, nutrient-rich, starchy seeds. The term refers primarily to wheat, oats, rye, barley, and triticale (a cross between wheat and rye), but may also refer to maize (corn), millet, sorghum, and rice. Cereals contain about 75% complex carbohydrates and 10% protein, plus fats and roughage. They store easily. In 1984, world production exceeded 2 billion tonnes. If all the world's cereal crop were consumed as wholegrain products directly by humans, everyone would obtain adequate protein and carbohydrate; however, a large proportion of cereal production in affluent nations is used as animal feed to boost the production of meat, dairy products, and eggs.

**collective farm** (Russian *kolkhoz*) farm in which a group of farmers pool their land, domestic animals, and agricultural implements, retaining as private property enough only for the members' own requirements. The profits of the farm are divided among its members. Collective farming is practised in the USSR, China, and Israel.

**combine harvester** or *combine* machine used for harvesting cereals and other crops, so called because it combines the actions of reaping (cutting the crop) and threshing (beating the ears so that the grain separates).

**Common Agricultural Policy** (CAP) system that allows the member countries of the European Community (EC) jointly to organize and control agricultural production within their boundaries. The objectives of the CAP were outlined in the Treaty of Rome: to increase agricultural productivity, to provide a fair standard of living for farmers and their employees, to stabilize markets, and to assure the availability of supply at a price that was reasonable to the consumer. The CAP is increasingly criticized

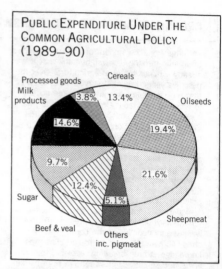

PUBLIC EXPENDITURE UNDER THE COMMON AGRICULTURAL POLICY (1989–90)

Processed goods
Milk products 3.8%
Cereals 13.4%
Oilseeds
19.4%
14.6%
9.7%
21.6%
12.4%
5.1%
Sugar
Sheepmeat
Beef & veal
Others inc. pigmeat

for its role in creating overproduction, and consequent environmental damage, and for the high price of food subsidies.

**crop rotation** the system of regularly changing the crops grown on a piece of land. The crops are grown in a particular order in order to utilize and add to the nutrients in the soil and to prevent the build-up of insect and fungal pests. Including a legume crop (member of the pea family, such as clover or alfalfa) in the rotation helps build up nitrate in the soil because the roots contain bacteria capable of fixing nitrogen from the air. In the 18th century a four-year rotation was widely adopted, in which an autumn-sown cereal such as wheat, was followed by a root crop, a spring cereal such as barley, and a legume crop.

**dairying** the business of producing and handling milk and milk products, such as cream, butter, and cheese. It is now usual for dairy farms to concentrate on the production of milk and for factories to take over the handling, processing, and distribution of milk as well as the manufacture of dairy products. In the UK, the Milk Marketing Board (1933), to which all producers must sell their milk, forms a connecting link between small farms and factories.

**deer farming** method of producing venison through the controlled breeding and rearing of deer on farms rather than hunting them in the wild. British deer-farming enterprises have been growing in number during the 1980s as more farmers seek to diversify into new sources of income. The meat is sold largely to the restaurant trade, and there is a market for the antlers and skin.

**factory farming** the intensive rearing of poultry or other animals for food, usually on high-protein foodstuffs and in confined quarters. Chickens for eggs and meat, and calves for veal are commonly farmed in this way. Some countries restrict the use of antibiotics and growth hormones as aids to factory farming, because they can persist in the flesh of the ani-

## WHY CAN'T WE FEED THE WORLD?

Throughout the 1980s and 1990s, images of famine and starvation have flashed across our television screens in appeal after appeal for relief aid and money. At the same time, we hear of vast surpluses within the European Community, with butter and grain mountains, and wine and milk lakes. Surely something is going very wrong? Why can't we feed the world?

During the 1960s and 1970s, there was a rapid intensification of agriculture in many Third World countries, with the introduction of more productive crop strains, although these needed large inputs of artificial pesticides and fertilizers. This 'green revolution' led to increased productivity, but only for those farmers rich enough to buy the expensive new seeds and agrochemicals. Smaller farmers were doubly disadvantaged: unable to buy into the new agriculture, they also saw the price of their products fall as productivity increased elsewhere. Many were forced off the land, which was then concentrated into the hands of large landowners. The extra food was, in many cases, sold for export rather than circulating within the country.

This illustrates two major reasons for world hunger. In most Third World countries, almost all the productive land is owned by a tiny proportion of the population. And much of this land is used to produce luxury export crops, such as tea, coffee, cocoa, bananas, tobacco, and animal feeds, rather than producing the food needed within the country. In recent years, the drive to produce export crops has been given a new urgency by the enormous foreign debts that most Third World countries have accumulated, largely as a result of changes in international interest rates.

This is by no means the whole story, of course. In many countries there are still enormous problems in transporting food to areas where it is needed. Poor or nonexistent roads meant that the famines in several East African countries continued despite there being a surplus elsewhere. Ethiopia continued to export grain throughout the worst of the famines in the 1980s.

There are wider environmental issues as well. Some agriculture innovations have done more harm than good, such as the poorly designed irrigation schemes that are causing soil to become contaminated with salt water in parts of Africa, and forcing farmers to abandon the land and move on. Deforestation is causing soil erosion, floods, and local changes in weather patterns. Climate change on a larger scale, including global warming caused by air pollution, may be a factor in the rapid increase in desertland in some areas.

This means that simple food aid doesn't help in the long term, if at all. Sending free grain, for example, can simply depress the price of locally produced food, forcing farmers out of business and acting against the interests of permanent agricultural stability. Donated food has often been stolen and sold by corrupt officials. However, the real reasons for Third World hunger are far more difficult to tackle. Land reform movements have, as yet, had little success in many countries. Efforts to write off or defer repayments on huge national debts are blocked by the creditor countries. Building up an adequate infrastructure of roads and other transport systems is difficult, time consuming, and costly. Birth control is a sensitive issue both in many aid-donor countries and in poor countries. The large fluctuations in climate experienced over the last few years add a new uncertainty to the famine problem. But it is certain that something more than aid is going to be required.

*Cuba's tobacco crop is largely destined for export. This factory in Havana exports 20 million cigars a year.*

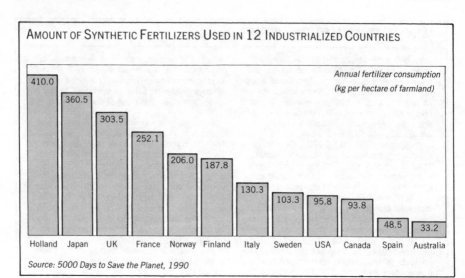

AMOUNT OF SYNTHETIC FERTILIZERS USED IN 12 INDUSTRIALIZED COUNTRIES

Annual fertilizer consumption
(kg per hectare of farmland)

| Holland | Japan | UK | France | Norway | Finland | Italy | Sweden | USA | Canada | Spain | Australia |
|---------|-------|-----|--------|--------|---------|-------|--------|------|--------|-------|-----------|
| 410.0 | 360.5 | 303.5 | 252.1 | 206.0 | 187.8 | 130.3 | 103.3 | 95.8 | 93.8 | 48.5 | 33.2 |

Source: 5000 Days to Save the Planet, 1990

mals after they are slaughtered. The European Commission banned steroid hormones for beef cattle at the end of 1985. Many people object to factory farming for moral as well as health reasons.

**fallow** term describing land that is ploughed and tilled but left unsown for a season to allow it to regain its fertility.

**fertilizer** substance containing some or all of a range of about 20 chemical elements necessary for healthy plant growth, used to compensate the deficiencies of poor or depleted soil. Fertilizers may be *organic*—for example farmyard manure, composts, bonemeal, blood, and fishmeal; or *inorganic*, in the form of compounds, mainly of nitrogen, potassium, and phosphorus, which have been used on a very much increased scale since 1945.

**fibre crop** plant that is grown for the fibres that can be extracted from its tissues. Temperate areas produce flax and hemp; tropical and subtropical areas produce cotton, jute, and sisal. Cotton dominates fibre-crop production.

**field** enclosed area of land used for farming. Twentieth-century developments in agricultural science and technology have encouraged farmers to amalgamate and enlarge their fields, often to as much as 40 hectares/100 acres.

CEREAL PRODUCTION 1989

| Region | Yield (tonnes per hectare harvested) |
|--------|--------|
| World | 2.646 |
| Africa | 1.228 |
| Asia (excl USSR) | 2.686 |
| Europe (excl USSR) | 4.246 |
| North and Central America | 3.627 |
| Oceania | 1.666 |
| South America | 2.073 |
| USSR | 1.905 |

Source: FAO Production, vol 43, 1989

**fish farming** or *aquaculture* raising fish and shellfish (molluscs and crustaceans) under controlled conditions in tanks and ponds, sometimes in offshore pens. It has been practised for centuries in the Far East, where Japan alone produces some 100,000 tonnes of fish a year. In the 1980s one-tenth of the world's consumption of fish was farmed, notably carp, catfish, trout, salmon, turbot, eel, mussels, clams, oysters, and shrimp.

**foot-and-mouth disease** contagious eruptive viral disease of cloven-hoofed mammals (such as cattle and sheep), characterized by blisters in the mouth and around the hooves. In cattle it causes deterioration of milk yield and abortions. In the UK, affected herds are destroyed; inoculation is practised in Europe, and in the USA, a vaccine was developed in the 1980s.

**forage crop** plant that is grown to feed livestock, for example, grass, clover, and kale (a form of cabbage). Forage crops cover a greater area of the world than food crops, and grass, which dominates this group, is the world's most abundant crop, though much of it is still in an unimproved state.

**game farming** protected rearing of gamebirds such as pheasants, partridges, and grouse for subsequent shooting. Game farms provide plenty of woodland and brush, which the birds require for cover, and may also plant special crops for them to feed on.

**green revolution** a popular term for the changes in agricultural methods that have taken place in developing countries since the 1960s and 1970s. The intent is to provide more and better food for their populations, albeit with a heavy reliance on chemicals and machinery. The green revolution was abandoned by some countries in the 1980s. Much of the food produced is exported as cash crops, so that local diet does not always improve.

**harrow** implement used to break up the furrows left by the plough and reduce the soil to a fine

### LIVESTOCK NUMBERS IN THE UK

At June each year - 000s

|  | 1980 | 1986 | 1987 | 1988 | 1989 (provisional) |
|---|---|---|---|---|---|
| Total cattle and calves | 13,426 | 12,533 | 12,158 | 11,872 | 12,016 |
| Total sheep and lambs | 31,446 | 37,016 | 38,701 | 40,942 | 42,885 |
| Total pigs | 7,815 | 7,937 | 7,942 | 7,980 | 7,717 |
| Total fowls | 127,063 | 120,740 | 128,628 | 130,809 | NA |

Source: Ministry of Agriculture, Food and Fisheries

consistency, or tilth, and to cover the seeds after sowing. The traditional harrow consists of spikes set in a frame; modern harrows use sets of discs.

**hay** preserved grass or clover used as a winter feed for livestock. The grass is cut and allowed to dry in the field before being baled and removed for storage in a barn. The optimum period for cutting is when the grass has just come into flower and contains most feed value. One hectare of grass can produce up to 7.5 tonnes/7.3 tons of hay.

**herbicide** or **weedkiller** chemical used to kill plants or check their growth. Herbicides may be nonselective, killing all plants, or selective, killing only broad-leaved weeds and leaving narrow-leaved cereals unharmed. Nonselective herbicides include sodium chlorate and paraquat. The widespread use of weedkillers in agriculture has led to a dramatic increase in crop yield but also to pollution of soil and water supplies.

**horticulture** the growing of flowers, fruit, and vegetables. The growth of industrial towns in the 19th century led to the development of commercial horticulture in the form of nurseries and market gardens, pioneering methods such as glasshouses, artificial heat, herbicides (weedkillers), and pesticides, inorganic fertilizers, and machinery. In the UK, over half a million acres are devoted to commercial horticulture, and vegetables account for almost three-quarters of the produce.

**insecticide** any chemical pesticide used to kill insects. Among the most effective insecticides are synthetic chlorinated organic chemicals such as DDT (dichloro-diphenyl-trichloroethane) and dieldrin. However, these have proved persistent in the environment and are also poisonous to animal life, including humans, and are consequently banned in many countries. Other synthetic insecticides include organic phosphorus compounds such as malathion. Insecticides prepared from plants, such as derris and pyrethrum, are safer to use but need to be applied frequently and carefully.

**irrigation** artificial water supply for dry agricultural areas by means of dams and channels. An example is the channelling of the annual Nile flood in Egypt, which has been done from earliest times to its present control by the Aswan High Dam. Drawbacks to irrigation are that it tends to concentrate salts, ultimately causing infertility, and rich river silt is retained at dams, to the impoverishment of the land and fisheries below them.

**legume** plant of the family Leguminosae, which has a pod containing dry seeds. The family includes peas, beans, lentils, clover, and alfalfa (lucerne). Legumes are widely grown because of their specialized roots, which have nodules containing bacteria capable of fixing nitrogen from the air and increasing the nitrate content of the soil. The edible seeds of legumes are called **pulses**; they provide a concentrated source of vegetable protein, and make a vital contribution to human diets in poor countries where meat is scarce, and among vegetarians. Soya beans are the major temperate pulse crop in the West; most are used for oil production or for animal feed; some are processed into 'meat substitutes'. In Asia, most are processed into soya milk and beancurd. Peanuts dominate pulse production in the tropical world and are generally consumed as human food.

**ley** area of temporary grassland, sown for grazing or to produce hay or silage for a period of one to ten years before being ploughed and cropped. Short-term leys are often incorporated in systems of crop rotation.

**milking machine** machine that uses suction to milk cows. The first milking machine was invented in the USA by L O Colvin in 1860. Later it was improved so that the suction was regularly released by a pulsating device, since it was found that continuous suction is harmful to cows.

**oil crop** plant grown for the oil that can be pressed from its seeds or fruit. Cool temperate areas grow rapeseed and linseed; warm temperate regions produce sunflowers, olives, and soya beans; tropical regions produce groundnuts (peanuts), palm oil, and coconuts. Some of the major vegetable oils, such as soya bean oil, peanut oil, and cottonseed oil, are derived from crops grown primarily for other purposes. Most vegetable oils are used as both edible oils and as ingredients of other products such as soaps, varnishes, printing inks, and paints.

**organic farming** farming without the use of synthetic fertilizers (such as nitrates and phosphates) or pesticides (herbicides, insecticides, and fungicides) or other agrochemicals (such as hormones, growth stimulants, or fruit regulators). In place of synthetic fertilizers, compost, manure, seaweed, or other substances derived from living things are used (hence the name 'organic'). Growing a crop of a nitrogen-fixing legume such as clover, then ploughing it back into the soil, also fertilizes the ground. Organic farming methods produce food without pesticide residues and greatly re-

AGRICULTURAL HOLDINGS BY TYPE OF FARMING IN THE UK (1989)

| | United Kingdom | England | Wales | Scotland | Northern Ireland |
|---|---|---|---|---|---|
| Number of holdings ('000s) by type of farming (a) | | | | | |
| Dairying | 38.5 | 23.9 | 5.4 | 2.7 | 6.6 |
| Hill and upland (LFA) livestock | 47.6 | 8.8 | 9.3 | 14.5 | 15.1 |
| Lowland livestock | 57.0 | 41.0 | 9.6 | 2.6 | 3.9 |
| Cereals | 20.3 | 16.4 | 0.3 | 2.9 | 0.7 |
| Other cropping | 28.9 | 25.2 | 0.5 | 2.5 | 0.8 |
| Pigs and poultry | 11.1 | 9.3 | 0.8 | 0.3 | 0.7 |
| Horticulture | 11.7 | 10.2 | 0.3 | 0.4 | 0.7 |
| Other | 41.4 | 22.8 | 4.5 | 0.6 | 13.5 |
| Total (b) | 256.5 | 157.5 | 30.5 | 26.5 | 42.0 |

(a) The exact definitions of the different types of farming vary slightly between countries.
(b) Figures may not add to totals shown due to roundings.
*Source: Ministry of Agriculture, Fisheries and Food.*

duce pollution of the environment. They are more labour intensive, and therefore more expensive, but use less fossil fuel. Soil structure is greatly improved by organic methods, and recent studies show that a conventional farm can lose four times as much soil through erosion as an organic farm.

**pesticide** any chemical used to combat pests. Pesticides are of three main types: *insecticides* (to kill insects), *fungicides* (to kill fungi), and *herbicides* (to kill plants, mainly those considered weeds). Such chemicals cause a number of pollution problems through spray drift on to surrounding areas, direct contamination of users or the public, and as residues on food. The aid organization Oxfam estimates that the indiscriminate use of pesticides causes about 10,000 deaths worldwide every year.

**pig** even-toed hoofed mammal of the family Suidae. Pigs are omnivorous, and have simple, non-ruminating stomachs and thick hides. Over 400 varieties have been bred over the centuries, many of which have all but disappeared in more recent times with the development of intensive rearing systems. The Berkshire, Chester White, Poland, China, Saddleback, Yorkshire, Duroc, Tamworth, and Razorback are the main surviving breeds. Indoor rearing methods favour the large white breeds, such as the Chester White and the originally Swedish Landrace, over coloured varieties, which tend to be hardier and can survive better outdoors. Since 1960, hybrid pigs, produced by crossing two or more breeds, have become popular for their heavy lean carcasses.

**plough** implement used for tilling the soil. The plough dates from about 3500 BC, when oxen were used to pull a simple wooden blade, or ard. The present tractor-drawn plough consists of many 'bottoms', each comprising a curved ploughshare and angled mouldboard, and designed so that it slices into the ground and turns the soil over.

**poultry** domestic birds such as chickens, turkeys, ducks, and geese. Good egg-laying breeds of chicken are Leghorns, Minorcas, and Anconas; varieties most suitable for eating are Dorkings, Australorps, Brahmas, and Cornish; those useful for both purposes are Orpingtons, Rhode

Island Reds, Wyandottes, Plymouth Rocks, and Jersey White Giants. Most farm poultry are hybrids, selectively crossbred for certain characteristics, including feathers and down. Since World War II, the development of battery-produced eggs and the intensive breeding of broiler fowls and turkeys has doubled egg yields and increased the availability of poultry meat. However, this form of factory farming has also aroused public concern about the conditions in which the birds are kept, and has led to a growing interest in deep-litter and free-range systems. In 1988-89 the UK egg industry suffered a major blow when it was discovered that salmonella was present in large quantities of eggs. Chickens were slaughtered and farmers lost large amounts of money. Eggs were declared safe only if heated to a high enough temperature to kill the bacteria.

**root crop** ambiguous term for several different types of crop, which may or may not be cultivated for their true roots; in agriculture, it usually refers to turnips, swedes, and beets, whereas in trade statistics it refers to the tubers of potatoes, sweet potatoes, cassava, and yams. Roots have a high carbohydrate content, but their protein content rarely exceeds 2%. Consequently, communities relying almost exclusively upon roots may suffer from protein deficiency. Potatoes, cassava, and yams are second in importance only to cereals as human food. Food production for a given area from roots is greater than from cereals.

**scrapie** fatal disease of sheep and goats that attacks the central nervous system, causing deterioration of the brain cells. It is believed to be caused by a submicroscopic organism known as a prion and may be related to bovine spongiform encephalopathy, the disease of cattle known as 'mad-cow disease'.

**scythe** harvesting tool with long wooden handle and sharp, curving blade. It was in common use in the Middle East and Europe from the dawn of agriculture until the early 20th century, by which time it had generally been replaced by machinery.

**seed drill** machine for sowing cereals and other seeds, developed by Jethro Tull in England 1701. The seed is stored in a hopper and delivered by tubes into furrows in the ground. The furrows are made by a set of blades, or coulters, attached to the front of the drill. A harrow drawn behind the drill covers up the seeds.

**sheep** ruminant, even-toed, hoofed mammal of the genus *Ovis*, family Bovidae. Various breeds of sheep are reared worldwide for meat, wool, milk, and cheese, and for rotation on arable land to maintain its fertility. Over 50 breeds were developed in the UK, but only a small proportion are still in full commercial use. They are grouped into three principal categories. The hardy **upland** breeds, such as the Scottish Blackface and Welsh Mountain, are able to survive in a bleak, rugged environment. The **shortwool** varieties, such as the Down breeds of Hampshire and Suffolk, are well adapted to thrive on the lush grassland of lowland areas. **Longwool** breeds, such as the Leicesters and Border Leicesters, were originally bred for their coarse, heavy fleeces, but are now crossed with hill-sheep flocks to produce fat lambs.

**silage** green fodder preserved through controlled fermentation in an airtight tower (silo) or pit. The term also refers to stacked crops that may be preserved indefinitely.

**subsistence farming** farming in which the produce is enough to feed only the farmer and family and there is no surplus to sell.

**tenant farming** system whereby farmers rent their holdings from a landowner in return for the use of agricultural land.

**threshing** process of separating cereal grains from the plant. Traditionally, the work was carried out by hand in winter months using the flail, a jointed beating stick. Today, threshing is done automatically inside the combine harvester at the time of cutting.

**topsoil** the upper, cultivated layer of soil, which may vary in depth from 8–45 cm/3–18 in. It contains organic matter, the decayed remains of vegetation, which plants need for active growth, along with a variety of soil organisms, including earthworms.

**tractor** a powerful motor vehicle, commonly having large rear wheels or caterpillar tracks, used for pulling farm machinery and loads. It is usually powered by a diesel engine and has a power-takeoff mechanism for driving machinery, and a hydraulic lift for raising and lowering implements.

## Eating habits

*How much do you worry about the quality and health aspects of the food you eat?*

| | |
|---|---|
| A great deal | 25 |
| A fair amount | 32 |
| Some | 13 |
| Not too much | 17 |
| Not at all | 13 |

*Overall, how healthy would you say your eating habits are?*

| | |
|---|---|
| Very healthy | 26 |
| Fairly healthy | 59 |
| Not too healthy | 13 |
| Not at all healthy | 2 |
| Don't know | 1 |

*How would you describe your own person weight situation?*

| | |
|---|---|
| Overweight | 41 |
| About right | 52 |
| Underweight | 7 |

## Eating out

*Which, if any, of these is your favourite type of restaurant?*

| | |
|---|---|
| English | 42 |
| Chinese | 18 |
| Italian | 12 |
| Indian | 10 |
| French | 8 |
| Greek | 2 |
| Spanish | 1 |
| Japanese | 1 |
| None of these | 6 |

*And which next? (Excluding English)*

| | |
|---|---|
| Chinese | 35 |
| Italian | 19 |
| French | 16 |
| Indian | 15 |
| Greek | 5 |
| Spanish | 2 |
| Japanese | 1 |
| None of these | 22 |

*Which of these is your favourite take-away meal?*

| | |
|---|---|
| Fish 'n' Chips | 30 |
| Chinese | 28 |
| Curry | 10 |
| Pizza | 8 |
| Hamburger | 4 |
| None of these | 15 |

# EVOLUTIONARY BIOLOGY

**adaptation** any change in the structure or function of an organism that allows it to survive and reproduce more effectively in its environment. In evolution, adaptation is thought to occur as a result of random variation in the genetic make-up of organisms (produced by mutation and recombination) coupled with natural selection.

**artificial selection** selective breeding of individuals that exhibit the particular characteristics that a plant or animal breeder wishes to develop. In plants, desirable features might include resistance to disease, high yield (in crop plants), or attractive appearance. In animal breeding, selection has led to the development of particular breeds of cattle for improved meat or milk production.

**cladistics** a method of biological classification (taxonomy) that uses a formal step-by-step procedure for objectively assessing the extent to which organisms share particular characters, and for assigning them to taxonomic groups. These taxonomic groups (species, genus, family) are termed *clades*.

**competition** the interaction between two or more organisms, or groups of organisms (for example, species), that use a common resource which is in short supply. Competition invariably results in a reduction in the numbers of one or both competitors, and in evolution contributes both to the decline of certain species and to the evolution of adaptations.

**convergent evolution** the independent evolution of similar structures in species (or other taxonomic groups) that are not closely related, as a result of living in a similar way. Thus, birds and bats have wings, not because they are descended from a common winged ancestor, but because their respective ancestors independently evolved flight.

**evolution** slow process of change from one form to another, as in the evolution of the universe from its formation in the Big Bang to its present state, or in the evolution of life on Earth.

**extinction** the complete disappearance of a species. In the past, extinctions are believed to have occurred because species were unable to adapt quickly enough to a naturally changing environment. Today, most extinctions are due to human activity. Some species, such as the dodo of Mauritius, the moas of New Zealand, and the passenger pigeon of North America, were exterminated by hunting. Others become extinct when their habitat is destroyed. (See feature in *Natural History*.)

**human species, origins of** evolution of humans from ancestral primates. The African apes (gorilla and chimpanzee) are shown by anatomical and molecular comparisons to be the closest living relatives of humans. Molecular studies put the date of the split between the human and African ape lines at 5–10 million years ago. There are no ape or *hominid* (of the human group) fossils from this period; the oldest known hominids, found in Ethiopia and Tanzania, date from 3.5 million years ago. These creatures are known as *Australopithecus afarensis*, and they walked upright. They were either direct ancestors or an offshoot of the line that led to modern humans. They might have been the ancestors of *Homo habilis* (considered by some to be a species of *Australopithecus*), who appeared about a million years later, had slightly larger bodies and brains, and were probably the first to use stone tools. *Australopithecus robustus* and *A. gracilis* also lived in Africa at the same time, but these are not generally considered to be our ancestors.

**Lamarckism** theory of evolution advocated during the early 19th century by French naturalist Jean Baptiste de Lamarck (1744–1829). It differed from the Darwinian theory of evolution in that it was based on the idea that acquired characteristics were inherited: he argued that particular use of an organ or limb strengthens it, and that this development may be 'preserved by reproduction'. For example, he suggested that giraffes have long necks because they are continually stretching them to reach high leaves; according to the theory, giraffes that have lengthened their necks by stretching will pass this characteristic on to their offspring.

**mutation** a change in the genes produced by a change in the DNA that makes up the hereditary material of all living organisms. Mutations, the raw material of evolution, result from mistakes during replication (copying) of DNA molecules. Only a few improve the organism's performance and are therefore favoured by natural selection. Mutation rates are increased by certain chemicals and by radiation.

**natural selection** the process whereby gene frequencies in a population change through certain individuals producing more descendants than others because they are better able to survive and reproduce in their environment. The accumulated effect of natural selection is to produce adaptations such as the insulating coat of a polar bear or the spadelike forelimbs of a mole. The process is slow, relying firstly on random variation in the genes of an organism being produced by mutation and the genetic recombination of sexual reproduction. It was recognized by Charles Darwin and Alfred Russel Wallace as the main process driving evolution.

**neo-Darwinism** the modern theory of evolution, built up since the 1930s by integrating Darwin's theory of evolution through natural selection with the theory of genetic inheritance founded on the work of Mendel.

**phylogeny** the historical sequence of changes that occurs in a given species during the course of its evolution. It was once erroneously associated with ontogeny (the process of development of a living organism).

**punctuated equilibrium model** evolutionary theory developed by Niles Eldridge and

## A DINOSAUR ROUND-UP

How did the dinosaurs die out 65 million years ago? Since 1980, when Luis and Walter Alvarez discovered a layer of the chemical iridium marking the division between the Cretaceous period—the end of the dinosaur age—and the Tertiary period—the age of mammals—there has been a dispute between those who see this extinction as a sudden catastrophic event and those who see it as a gradual change. Alvarez postulated that the iridium had come from a giant meteorite that had struck the earth and caused such damage that the dinosaurs could not have survived.

In 1988 late Cretaceous rocks that looked as though they had been formed by a tsunami (what journalists call a 'tidal wave') at the end of the Cretaceous were found in Texas suggesting there was a great explosion in the region of the Caribbean at that time. In 1990 more weight was given to this argument by the discovery, by Alan Hildebrand of the University of Arizona and Glen Penfield of Aero Service in Houston, of a geological structure buried beneath the Yucatan peninsula of Mexico that looks very much like a meteorite impact crater. It is about 60 km/37 mi across but has not yet been dated.

On the other hand the proponents of the gradual change theory were vindicated by the investigations of Art Sweet of the Geological Survey of Canada, Dennis Braman of the Tyrrell Museum in Alberta, and Jack Lerbecko with the University of Alberta. They found evidence for a worldwide change in vegetation between 300,000 and 400,000 years before the end of the Cretaceous, when many of the dinosaurs' food plants had died out. They see this as evidence for a climatic change.

But it seems that there were not as many dinosaurs as was once believed. Peter Dodson of the University of Pennsylvania published some calculations of dinosaur numbers in 1990. He estimated that palaeontologists had discovered about 25% of all dinosaur genera that ever lived. As these discoveries represent 285 genera, then his estimates suggest that there were about a thousand different types of dinosaurs, spread over 160 million years. There were about 100 different genera of dinosaurs existing at any one time, which seems a small number compared with the 175 genera of large mammals existing today. Each dinosaur genus existed for between 5 and 10 million years, compared to a figure of between 7 and 8 million years for a modern large mammal.

North Africa has recently become the site of some spectacular dinosaur discoveries. A series of expeditions into the Sahel mounted by Kingston Polytechnic and the Natural History Museum (London) discovered a veritable dinosaur graveyard in Niger dating from the early Cretaceous. In sandstones that represented flood deposits of a big river they found complete skeletons of animals very similar to the North American long-necked genus *Camarasaurus*. Late Cretaceous rocks from the same area have bones of the meat-eater *Megalosaurus* along with crocodiles and turtles.

In England, where dinosaurs were first discovered 150 years ago, discoveries continue to be made. In 1987 a vertebra found in a quarry in the Cotswolds by amateur geologist Brian Boneham led to the excavation of much of the skeleton of a stegosaur—one of the plated dinosaurs. It has yet to be studied in detail but it seems to be very similar to *Lexovisaurus*, a 5 m/16 ft stegosaur from the middle Jurassic of England and France. A rock-fall in Romania, in 1990, revealed a nest of dinosaur eggs. These were found in rows as if they had been laid while the animal was moving. They were 150 mm/6 in in diameter and probably came from a sauropod—one of the long-necked plant-eaters—called *Magyarsaurus*.

Meanwhile in North America the biggest *Tyrannosaurus* skeleton ever discovered was unearthed by Susan Hendrickson of the Black Hills Institute of Geological Research in South Dakota. It seems to be about 70% complete, making it one of the most complete *Tyrannosaurus* skeletons known. The famous one in the American Museum of Natural History is inaccurately assembled from two different skeletons.

*Excavation of sauropod dinosaur, Niger 1988.*

## BIOLOGY: CHRONOLOGY

| | |
|---|---|
| c 500 BC | First studies of the structure and behaviour of animals, by the Greek Alcmaeon of Creton. |
| c 450 | Hippocrates of Cos undertook the first detailed studies of human anatomy. |
| c 350 | Aristotle laid down the basic philosophy of the biological sciences and outlined a theory of evolution. |
| c 300 | Theophrastus carried out the first detailed studies of plants. |
| c AD 175 | Galen established the basic principles of anatomy and physiology. |
| c 1500 | Leonardo da Vinci studied human anatomy to improve his drawing ability and produced detailed anatomical drawings. |
| 1628 | William Harvey described the circulation of the blood and the function of the heart as a pump. |
| 1665 | Robert Hooke used a microscope to describe the cellular structure of plants. |
| 1672 | Marcelle Malphigi undertook the first studies in embryology by describing the development of a chicken egg. |
| 1677 | Anthony van Leeuwenhoek greatly improved the microscope and used it to describe spermatozoa as well as many microorganisms. |
| 1682 | Nehemiah Grew published the first textbook in botany. |
| 1736 | Carolus (Carl) Linnaeus published his systematic classification of plants, so establishing taxonomy. |
| 1768–79 | James Cook's voyages of discovery in the Pacific revealed an undreamed-of diversity of living species, prompting the development of theories to explain their origin. |
| 1796 | Edward Jenner established the practice of vaccination against smallpox, laying the foundations for theories of antibodies an d immune reactions. |
| 1809 | Jean-Baptiste Lamarck advocated a theory of evolution through inheritance of acquired characters. |
| 1839 | Theodor Schwann proposed that all living matter is made up of cells. |
| 1857 | Louis Pasteur established that microorganisms are responsible for fermentation, creating the discipline of microbiology. |
| 1859 | Charles Darwin published *On the Origin of Species*, expounding his theory of the evolution of species by natural selection. |
| 1866 | Gregor Mendel pioneered the study of inheritance with his experiments on peas, but achieved little recognition. |
| 1883 | August Weismann proposed his theory of the continuity of the germ plasm. |
| 1900 | Mendel's work was rediscovered and the science of genetic s founded. |
| 1935 | Konrad Lorenz published the first of many major studies of animal behaviour, which founded the discipline of ethology. |
| 1953 | James Watson and Francis Crick described the molecular structure of the genetic material, DNA. |
| 1964 | William Hamilton recognized the importance of inclusive fitness, so paving the way for the development of sociobiology. |
| 1975 | Discovery of endogenous opiates (the brain's own painkillers) opened up a new phase in the study of brain chemistry. |
| 1976 | Har Gobind Khorana and his colleagues constructed the first artificial gene to function naturally when inserted into a bacterial cell, a major step in genetic engineering. |
| 1982 | Establishment of gene databases at Heidelberg, Germany for the European Molecular Biology Laboratory, and at Los Alamos, USA for the US National Laboratories. |
| 1985 | Isolation of the first human cancer gene, retinoblastoma, by researchers at the Massachusetts Eye and Ear Infirmary and the Whitehead Institute, Massachusetts. |
| 1988 | Human Genome Organization (HUGO) established in Washington, DC, with the aim of mapping the complete sequence of DNA. |

Stephen Jay Gould in 1972 to explain discontinuities in the fossil record. It claims that periods of rapid change alternate with periods of relative stability (stasis), and that the appearance of new lineages is a separate process from the gradual evolution of adaptive changes within a species.

**saltation** (Latin *saltare* 'to leap') the idea that an abrupt genetic change can occur in an individual, which then gives rise to a new species. The idea has now been largely discredited, although the appearance of polyploid individuals (possessing three or more sets of chromosomes) can be considered an example.

**species** a distinguishable group of organisms that resemble each other or consist of a few distinctive types (as in polymorphism), and that can all interbreed to produce fertile offspring. Species are the lowest level in the system of biological classification.

**variation** difference between individuals of the same species, found in any sexually reproducing population. Variations may be almost unnoticeable in some cases, obvious in others, and can concern many

# MAPPING THE HUMAN RACE—THE GENOME PROJECT

Inside every cell in your body are complex strands of the molecule Deoxyribonucleic Acid. If the strands were untwisted and laid in line, they would measure over a metre in length. Running the length of each strand are chemical building blocks called nucleotides. There are only four different types, but the number of possible combinations is immense. The different combinations of nucleotides produce different proteins in the cell. It is through the arrangements of nucleotides on the molecule that the cells in our bodies are controlled, and it is through the different arrangements of nucleotides that we inherit our differences from other people.

It is this fundamental importance of the sequence of nucleotides that has led to the setting up of the largest research project ever undertaken in the life sciences, the human genome project. The goal of the Human Genome Organization (HUGO), set up in 1988, is the complete mapping of the nucleotide sequence of DNA and the creation of genetic maps for different individuals.

The implications of the project are enormous. Many crippling and lethal diseases, such as cystic fibrosis, muscular dystrophy and haemophilia, result from genetic defects, and the expectation is that these will be more easily treated with the knowledge gained from the project. Perhaps more important is the potential that understanding the control mechanisms of the cell offers for cancer research and treatment. But, alongside the health gains, there are potential ethical problems. Knowledge of a parent's genetic make-up will enable the characteristics of children to be more closely predicted. Knowledge of an individual's genes may make them an unacceptable insurance risk. During 1991 legislation on Human Genome Privacy is to be introduced to the US Congress to ensure that an individual's genome map cannot be disclosed without their permission. In fact, so great are the ethical implications that 3% of HUGOs funds have been set aside for researching and reporting in this area.

You could say 3% does not sound a great deal, but HUGO plans to spend $1 billion dollars over the first five years of its existence. The final estimate for the project is $10 billion dollars, over the next 15 years, but this may be reduced. One of the initial goals of the project was to discover cheaper ways of sequencing DNA, which cost around $4 a nucleotide when HUGO was set up in 1988. However, a team at the University of Wisconsin announced a new technique early in 1991, which is 25 times faster than previous methods and which may eventually halve costs.

The difficulty with sequencing DNA is that the molecule is extremely long. The longest section of DNA that can be dealt with is only about 500 nucleotides. This means that most DNA needs to be broken down into shorter fragments to be sequenced. But even when a fragment has been sequenced, it is difficult to tell what its original position on the DNA strand was. So strands need to be broken into fragments in two or three different ways, so that overlapping sections can be identified and used to place the fragments in the correct order.

The sequencing of so many different fragments is an immense task, and is being carried out by over 20 centres around the world. The initial breaking-up involves the construction of libraries of fragments, which are introduced into rapidly dividing cells of yeast or the bacterium *E. Coli*. These cells then replicate the human DNA fragment along with their own, and cells from these libraries can then be sent to individual centres. Yeast artificial chromosomes containing fragments of the human genome up to 1 million nucleotides long have been created.

At the same time as the human genome is being mapped, other species are being investigated so that comparisons can be made. Yeast and mouse genome are being mapped, and the entire sequence of *Cytomegalivirus* has been determined. This genome is approximately 250,000 nucleotides, whereas the single gene causing muscular dystrophy contains over two million nucleotides.

There are approximately 80,000 different genes in the human genome. Some 2,000 of these had been sequenced by the beginning of 1991.

However, genes only account for a small amount of the DNA sequence. Over 90% of DNA appears not to have a function, although is it perfectly replicated each time the cell divides, and perfectly handed on to the next generation. Many higher organisms have large amounts of redundant DNA and it may be that this is an advantage, in that there is a pool of DNA available to form new genes, rather than an old gene being lost by mutation into something new.

One method of working, increasingly adopted by British workers, is to identify which sections of DNA are genes and which are redundant. The effort then goes into mapping and sequencing the gene sections, rather than the entire genome. Once the section has been identified, the first few hundred nucleotides can be sequenced to see what sort of protein will be produced by the gene. If the protein is deemed important, then further work can be undertaken to sequence the gene. Although this sampling approach will not yield an entire map of the genome, it may produce important medical results more quickly.

aspects of the organism. Typically, variation in size, behaviour, biochemistry, or colouring may be found. The cause of the variation can be genetic (that is, inherited), environmental, or more usually a combination of the two. The origins of variation can be traced to the recombination of the genetic material during the formation of the gametes, and, more rarely, to mutation.

# REPRODUCTION

Reproduction is the process by which a living organism produces other organisms similar to itself. Reproduction may be sexual or asexual. *sexual reproduction* requires the union, or fertilization, of gametes (specialized reproductive cells, such as eggs and sperm). These are usually produced by two different individuals, although self-fertilization occurs in a few hermaphrodites such as tapeworms. Most organisms other than bacteria and cyanobacteria show some sort of sexual process. Except in some lower organisms, the gametes are of two distinct types called eggs and sperm. The organisms producing the eggs are called females, and those producing the sperm, males. The fusion of a male and female gamete produces a *zygote*, from which a new individual develops. *Asexual reproduction* does not involve the manufacture and fusion of sex cells, nor the necessity for two parents. The process carries a clear advantage in that there is no need to search for a mate nor to develop complex pollinating mechanisms; every asexual organism can reproduce on its own. Asexual reproduction can therefore lead to a rapid population build-up.

In evolutionary terms, the disadvantage of asexual reproduction arises from the fact that only identical individuals, or clones, are produced—there is no variation. In the field of horticulture, where standardized production is needed, this is useful, but in the wild, an asexual population that cannot adapt to a changing environment is at risk of extinction.

**binary fission** a type of asexual reproduction, whereby a single-celled organism divides into two smaller 'daughter' cells. It can also occur in a few simple multicellular organisms, such as sea anemones, producing two smaller sea anemones of equal size.

**budding** a type of asexual reproduction in which an outgrowth develops from a cell to form a new individual. Most yeasts reproduce in this way. In a suitable environment, yeasts grow rapidly, forming long chains of cells as the buds themselves produce further buds before being separated from the parent. Simple invertebrates, such as hydra, can also reproduce by budding.

In horticulture, the term is used for a technique of plant propagation whereby a bud (or scion) and a sliver of bark from one plant are transferred to an incision made in the bark of another plant (the stock). This method of grafting is often used for roses.

**parthenogenesis** the development of an ovum (egg) without any genetic contribution from a male. Parthenogenesis is the normal means of reproduction in a few plants (for example,

## MAJOR DATABASES STORING INFORMATION ON THE GENOME

| Location | Sponsor | Work |
|---|---|---|
| Los Alamos National Laboratory New Mexico, USA | Dept of Energy and the National Institutes of Health, Washington DC | Gen Bank (contains the DNA sequences that make up human genes) |
| European Molecular Biology Laboratory, Heidelberg, Germany | 15 European states and the EC | Nucleotide Sequence Data Library (contains the DNA sequences that make up human genes) |
| National Institute of Genetics, Mishima, Japan | Science and Technology Agency, Tokyo | DNA Database of Japan |
| Laboratory of Molecular Biology, Cambridge, UK | Medical Research Council, London | Nematode worm |
| Johns Hopkins University, Baltimore, Maryland, USA | Howard Hughes Medical Institute, Bethesda | Genome Database |
| Johns Hopkins University, Baltimore, Maryland, USA | National Institutes of Health | OMIM, the Online Mendelian Inheritance in Man |
| Brookhaven National Laboratory, Upton, New York, USA | Dept of Energy | Protein DataBank (contains 3-D coordinates associated with each protein) |
| Georgetown University, Washington DC | National Institutes of Health | Protein Identification Resource (contains sequences of the amino acids that make up proteins) |
| Jackson Laboratory, Bar Harbor, Maine, USA | National Institutes of Health | Homology Database and Project (contains genetic data on humans, mice and 23 other species) |

*Source: The New Scientist 1990*

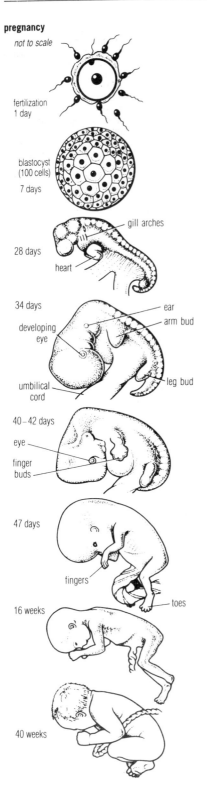

**pregnancy**

*not to scale*

fertilization
1 day

blastocyst
(100 cells)

7 days

gill arches

28 days

heart

34 days — ear

developing — arm bud
eye

umbilical — leg bud
cord

40–42 days

eye

finger
buds

47 days

fingers

toes

16 weeks

40 weeks

dandelions) and animals (for example, certain fish). Some sexually reproducing species, such as aphids, show parthenogenesis at some stage in their life cycle.

In most cases, there is no fertilization at all, but in a few the stimulus of being fertilized by a sperm is needed to initiate development, although the male's chromosomes are not absorbed into the nucleus of the ovum. Parthenogenesis can be artificially induced in many animals (such as rabbits) by cooling, pricking, or applying acid to an egg.

# THE LIFE CYCLE

The life cycle is the sequence of developmental stages through which members of a given species pass. Most vertebrates have a simple life cycle consisting of fertilization of sex cells or gametes, a period of development as an embryo, a period of juvenile growth after hatching or birth, an adulthood including sexual reproduction, and finally death. Invertebrate life cycles are generally more complex and may involve major reconstitution of the individual's appearance (metamorphosis) and completely different styles of life. Thus dragonflies live an aquatic life as larvae and an aerial life during the adult phase. In many invertebrates and protozoa there is a sequence of stages in the life cycle, and in parasites different stages often occur in different host organisms. Plants have a special type of life cycle with two distinct phases, known as alternation of generations.

**birth** is the act of producing live young from within the body of female animals. Both viviparous and ovoviviparous animals give birth to young. In viviparous animals, embryos obtain nourishment from the mother via a placenta or other means. In ovoviviparous animals, fertilized eggs develop and hatch in the oviduct of the mother and gain little or no nourishment from maternal tissues.

**ageing** is the period of deterioration of the physical condition of a living organism that leads to death; in biological terms, the entire life process. Three current theories attempt to account for ageing. The first suggests that the process is genetically determined, to remove individuals that can no longer reproduce. The second suggests that it is due to the accumulation of mistakes during the replication of DNA at cell division. The third suggests that it is actively induced by pieces of DNA that move between cells, or by cancer-causing viruses; these may become abundant in old cells and induce them to produce unwanted proteins or interfere with the control functions of their DNA.

**death** is the cessation of all life functions, so that the molecules and structures associated with living things become disorganized and indistinguishable from similar molecules found in non-living things. Large molecules such as proteins break down into simpler, soluble components. Eventually the organism partly dissolves into the soil or evaporates into the air, leaving behind skeletal material. Living organisms expend large amounts of energy preventing their complex molecules from breaking up; cellular repair and replacement are vital processes in multicellular organisms. At death this energy is no longer available, and the processes of disorganization become inevitable.

Biologists have a problem in explaining the phenomenon of death. If proteins, other complex molecules, and whole cells can be repaired or replaced, why cannot a multicellular organism be immortal? The most favoured explanation is an evolutionary one. Organisms must die in order to make way for new ones, which, by virtue of sexual reproduction, may vary slightly in relation to the previous generation. Most environments change constantly, if slowly; without this variation organisms would be unable to adapt to the changes.

In human beings, death used to be pronounced when a person's breathing and heartbeat stopped. The advent of mechanical aids has made this point sometimes difficult to determine, and in controversial cases a person is now pronounced dead when the brain ceases to control the vital functions.

**alternation of generations** the typical life cycle of terrestrial plants and some seaweeds, in which there are two distinct forms occurring alternately: *diploid* (having two sets of chromosomes) and *haploid* (one set of chromosomes). The diploid generation produces haploid spores by meiosis, and is called the sporophyte, while the haploid generation produces gametes (sex cells), and is called the gametophyte. The gametes fuse to form a diploid zygote which develops into a new sporophyte; thus the sporophyte and gametophyte alternate.

**allele (or *allelomorph*)** one of a pair of genes that occupy the same relative position (locus) on homologous chromosomes, and are responsible for the occurrence of contrasting characteristics—for example, blue and brown eyes in humans are determined by different alleles of the gene for eye colour. Organisms with two sets of chromosomes (diploid) will have two copies of each gene. If the two alleles are identical the individual is said to be homozygous at that locus; if different, heterozygous.

**chromosome** structure in a cell nucleus that carries the genes. Each chromosome consists of one very long strand of DNA, coiled and folded to produce a compact chromosome. The point on a chromosome where a particular gene occurs is known as its locus. Most higher organisms have two copies of each chromosome (they are diploid) but some have only one (they are haploid).

**diploid** having two sets of chromosomes in each cell. In sexually reproducing species, one set is derived from each parent, the gametes, or sex cells, of each parent being haploid (having only one set of chromosomes) due to meiosis (reduction cell division).

**embryo** early development stage of an animal or a plant following fertilization of an ovum (egg cell), or activation of an ovum by parthenogenesis.

In animals the embryo exists either within an egg (where it is nourished by food contained in the yolk), or in mammals, in the uterus of the mother. In mammals (except marsupials) the embryo is fed through the placenta. In humans the term embryo describes the fertilized egg during its first seven weeks of existence; from the eighth week onwards it is referred to as a fetus. The plant embryo is found within the seed in higher plants. It sometimes consists of only a few cells, but usually includes a root; a shoot (or primary bud); and one or two cotyledons, which nourish the growing seedling.

**fertilization** in sexual reproduction, the union of two gametes (sex cells, often called egg and sperm) to produce a zygote, which combines the genetic material contributed by each parent. In self-fertilization the male and female gametes come from the same plant; in cross-fertilization they come from different plants. Self-fertilization rarely occurs in animals; usually even hermaphrodite animals cross-fertilize each other.

**gamete** cell that functions in sexual reproduction by merging with another gamete to form a zygote. Examples of gametes include sperm and egg cells. In most organisms, the gametes are haploid (they contain half the number of chromosomes of the parent), owing to reduction division or meiosis.

**gene** unit of inherited material, encoded by a strand of DNA, and transcribed by RNA. In higher organisms, genes are located on the chromosomes. The term 'gene', coined in 1909 by the Danish geneticist Wilhelm Johannsen (1857–1927), refers to the inherited factor that consistently affects a particular character in an individual—for example the gene for eye colour. Also termed a Mendelian gene, after Gregor Mendel, it occurs at a particular point or locus on a particular chromosome and may have several variants or alleles, each specifying a particular form of that character—for example the alleles for blue or brown eyes. Some alleles show dominance. These mask the effect of other alleles known as recessive.

**genome** the full complement of genes carried by a single (haploid) set of chromosomes in the nucleus of any cell, organism, or species. (See feature on the *Genome Project* in this section.)

**genotype** the particular set of alleles possessed by a given organism. The term is often used in conjunction with the phenotype (physical appearance) of the organism.

**haploid** having a single set of chromosomes in each cell. Most higher organisms are diploid—that is, they have two sets—but some plants, such as mosses, liverworts, and many seaweeds are haploid. Male honey bees are haploid because they develop from eggs that have not been fertilized.

**hermaphrodite** an organism that has both male

and female sex organs. Hermaphroditism is the norm in species such as earthworms and snails, and is common in flowering plants. Cross-fertilization is the rule among hermaphrodites, with the parents functioning as male and female simultaneously, or as one or the other sex at different stages in their development.

**heterozygous** in a living organism, having two different alleles for any one trait. In homozygous organisms, by contrast, both chromosomes carry the same allele. In an outbreeding population (one that produces offspring outside a particular family/tribe/group) an individual organism will generally be heterozygous for some genes but homozygous for others.

**homozygous** in a living organism, having two identical alleles for a given trait. Individuals homozygous for a trait always breed true, that is they produce offspring that resemble them in appearance when bred with a genetically similar individual; inbred varieties or species are homozygous for almost all traits.

**karyotype** the set of chromosomes characteristic of a given species. It is described as the number, shape, and size of the chromosomes in a single cell of an organism. In humans for example, the karyotype consists of 46 chromosomes, in mice 40, crayfish 200, and in fruit flies 8.

The diagrammatic representation of a complete chromosome set is called a *karyogram*.

**larva** the stage between hatching and adulthood in those species in which the young have a different appearance and way of life from the adults. Examples include tadpoles (frogs) and caterpillars (butterflies and moths). Larvae are typical of the invertebrates, and some (for example, shrimps) have two or more distinct larval stages. Among vertebrates, it is only the amphibians and some fishes that have a larval stage. The process whereby the larva changes into another stage, such as a pupa (chrysalis) or adult, is known as metamorphosis.

**meiosis** a process of cell division in which the number of chromosomes in the cell is halved. It only occurs in eukaryotic cells, and is part of a life cycle that involves sexual reproduction because it allows the genes of two parents to be combined without the total number of chromosomes increasing.

**metamorphosis** period during the life cycle of many invertebrates, most amphibians, and some fish, during which the individual's body changes from one form to another through a major reconstitution of its tissues. For example, adult frogs are produced by metamorphosis from tadpoles, and butterflies are produced from caterpillars following metamorphosis within a pupa.

**ovum** (plural *ova*) the female gamete (sex cell) before fertilization. In animals it is called an egg, and is produced in the ovaries. In plants, where it is also known as an egg cell or oosphere, the ovum is produced in an ovule. The ovum is nonmotile. It must be fertilized by a male gamete before it can develop further, except in cases of parthenogenesis.

**phenotype** the physical traits, collectively, displayed by an organism. It is determined both by its genetic constitution (genotype) and the environment.

The phenotype is not a direct reflection of the genotype—for example, two plants may have the same genotype for height, but if one receives less sunlight it will become paler and taller than the other. The phenotype can also differ (in organisms with the same genotype) because some alleles are masked by the presence of other, dominant alleles, in a phenomenon known as penetrance, or the extent to which a gene exhibits its effect. Such variations in the effects of a gene are thought to be influenced by the effect of other genes present and by the environment.

**pollen** the grains of seed plants that contain the male gametes. In angiosperms pollen is produced within anthers; in most gymnosperms it is produced in male cones. A pollen grain is typically yellow and, when mature, has a hard outer wall. Pollen of insect-pollinated plants is often sticky and spiny and larger than the smooth, light grains produced by wind-pollinated species. The study of pollen grains is known as palynology, and the study of fossil grains (well-preserved in many kinds of rock and especially numerous in peat) can reveal the dominant flora—and hence the climate—in past geological eras.

**pregnancy** in humans, the period during which an embryo grows within the womb. It begins at conception and ends at birth, and the normal length is 40 weeks. Menstruation usually stops on conception. About one in five pregnancies fails, but most of these failures occur very early on, so the woman may notice only that her period is late. After the second month, the breasts become tense and tender, and the areas round the nipples become darker. Enlargement of the uterus can be felt at about the end of the third month, and thereafter the abdomen enlarges progressively. Pregnancy in animals is called gestation.

**pupa** the nonfeeding, largely immobile stage of some insect life cycles, in which larval tissues are broken down, and adult tissues and structures are formed. In many insects, it is *exarate*, with the appendages (legs, antennae, wings) visible outside the pupal case; in butterflies and moths, the pupa is called a chrysalis, and is *obtect*, with the appendages developing inside the case.

**replication** production of two identical molecules of DNA from the parent molecule; it occurs during cell division (mitosis and meiosis). The two new single strands that are formed (from the splitting of the double-stranded parent molecule) each control the synthesis of a new strand complementary to itself.

**sperm** or *spermatozoon* the male gamete of animals. Each sperm cell has a head capsule containing a nucleus, a middle portion containing mitochondria (which provide energy), and a long tail (flagellum).

zygote ovum (egg) after fertilization but before it undergoes cleavage to begin embryonic development.

# THE MAINTENANCE OF LIFE

aerobic using molecular oxygen (usually dissolved in water) for the efficient release of energy. Almost all living organisms are aerobic. They use oxygen to convert glucose to carbon dioxide and water, thereby releasing energy. Most aerobic organisms die in the absence of oxygen, but certain organisms and cells, such as muscle cells, can function for short periods anaerobically (without oxygen).

anaerobic not requiring oxygen for the release of energy food. Anaerobic organisms include many bacteria, yeasts, and internal parasites. *Obligate anaerobes* such as archaebacteria cannot function in the presence of oxygen; but *facultative anaerobes*, like the fermenting yeasts and some bacteria, can function with or without oxygen. Anaerobic organisms release 19 times less of the available energy from their food than do aerobic organisms.

autotroph any living organism that synthesizes organic substances from inorganic molecules by using light or chemical energy. Autotrophs are the *primary producers* in all food chains since the materials they synthesize and store are the energy sources of all other organisms. All green plants and many planktonic organisms are autotrophs, using sunlight to convert carbon dioxide and water into sugars by photosynthesis.

basal metabolic rate (BMR) the amount of energy needed by an animal just to stay alive. It is measured when the animal is awake but resting, and includes the energy required to keep the heart beating, sustain breathing, repair tissues, and keep the brain and nerves functioning. Measuring the animal's consumption of oxygen gives an accurate value for BMR, because oxygen is needed to release energy from food.

BMR varies from one species to another, and from males to females. In humans, it is highest in children and declines with age. Disease, including mental illness, can make it rise or fall. Hormones from the thyroid gland control the BMR.

biosynthesis the synthesis of organic chemicals from simple inorganic ones by living cells—for example, the conversion of carbon dioxide and water to glucose by plants during photosynthesis. Other biosynthetic reactions produce cell constituents including proteins and fats.

carnivore animal that eats other animals. Although it is sometimes confined to animals that eat the flesh of vertebrate prey, the term is often used more broadly to include any animal that eats other animals, even microscopic ones. Carrion-eaters may or may not be included.

chemosynthesis method of making protoplasm (contents of a cell) using the energy from chemical reactions, in contrast to the use of light energy employed for the same purpose in photosynthesis. The process is used by certain bacteria, which can synthesize organic compounds from carbon dioxide and water using the energy from special methods of respiration.

decomposer any organism that breaks down dead matter. Decomposers play a vital role in the ecosystem by freeing important chemical substances, such as nitrogen compounds, locked up in dead organisms or excrement. They feed on some of the released organic matter, but leave the rest to filter back into the soil and pass in gas form into the atmosphere. The principal decomposers are bacteria and fungi, but earthworms and many other invertebrates are often included in this group. The nitrogen cycle relies on the actions of decomposers.

food chain or *food web* in ecology, the sequence of organisms through which energy and other nutrients are successively transferred. Since many organisms feed at several different levels (for example, omnivores feed on both fruit and meat), the relationships often form a complex web rather than a simple chain.

The sequence of the food chain comprises the autotrophs, or producers, which are principally plants and photosynthetic microorganisms, and a series of heterotrophs, or consumers, which are the herbivores that feed on the producers; the carnivores that feed on the herbivores; and the decomposers that break down the dead bodies and waste products of all four groups (including their own), ready for recycling.

gas exchange the exchange of gases between living organisms and the atmosphere, principally oxygen and carbon dioxide.

herbivore an animal that feeds on green plants or their products, including seeds, fruit, and nectar. The most numerous type of herbivore is thought to be the zooplankton, tiny invertebrates in the surface waters of the oceans that feed on small photosynthetic algae. Herbivores are more numerous than other animals because their food is the most abundant. They form a link in the food chain between plants and carnivores.

heterotroph any living organism that obtains its energy from organic substances produced by other organisms. All animals and fungi are heterotrophs, and they include herbivores, carnivores, and saprotrophs (those that feed on dead animal and plant material).

nitrogen cycle the process of nitrogen passing through the ecosystem. Nitrogen, in the form of inorganic compounds (such as nitrates) in the soil, is absorbed by plants and turned into organic compounds (such as proteins) in plant tissue. A proportion of this nitrogen is eaten by herbivores, with some of this in turn being passed on to the carnivores, which feed on the herbivores. The nitrogen is ultimately returned to the soil as excrement, and when organisms die and decompose.

**omnivore** animal that feeds on both plant and animal material. Omnivores have digestive adaptations intermediate between those of herbivores and carnivores, with relatively unspecialized digestive systems and gut microorganisms that can digest a variety of foodstuffs.

**photosynthesis** the process by which green plants, photosynthetic bacteria, and cyanobacteria use light energy from the Sun to produce food molecules (carbohydrates) from carbon dioxide and water. There are two stages. During the *light reaction* sunlight is used to split water ($H_2O$) into oxygen ($O_2$), protons (hydrogen ions, $H^+$), and electrons, and oxygen is given off as a by-product. In the second-stage *dark reaction*, where sunlight is not required, the protons and electrons are used to convert carbon dioxide ($CO_2$) into carbohydrates ($CH_2O$). Photosynthesis depends on the ability of chlorophyll to capture the energy of sunlight and to use it to split water molecules.

Photosynthesis by cyanobacteria was responsible for the appearance of oxygen in the Earth's atmosphere 2 billion years ago, and photosynthesis by plants maintains the oxygen level today.

**respiration** biochemical process whereby food molecules are progressively broken down (oxidized) to release energy in the form of ATP. In most organisms this requires oxygen, but in some bacteria the oxidant is the nitrate or sulphate ion instead. In all higher organisms, respiration occurs in the mitochondria. Respiration is also used to mean breathing, although this is more accurately described as a form of gas exchange.

# THE MACROSCOPIC WORLD

## ANIMAL

(or *metazoan*) member of the kingdom Animalia, one of the major categories of living things, the science of which is *zoology*. Animals are all heterotrophs (they obtain their energy from organic substances produced by other organisms); they have eukaryotic cells (the genetic material is contained within a distinct nucleus) bounded by a thin cell membrane rather than the thick cell wall of plants. In the past, it was common to include the single-celled protozoa with the animals, but these are now classified as protists, together with single-celled plants. Thus all animals are multicellular. Most are capable of moving around for at least part of their life cycle.

### Types
*invertebrate*

animal without a backbone. The invertebrates comprise over 95% of the million or so existing animal species and include the sponges, coelenterates, flatworms, nematodes, annelid worms, arthropods, molluscs, echinoderms, and primitive aquatic chordates such as sea squirts and lancelets.

**annelid** any segmented worm of the phylum Annelida. Annelids include earthworms, leeches, and marine worms such as lugworms. They have a distinct head and soft body, which is divided into a number of similar segments shut off from one another internally by mem-

**nitrogen cycle**

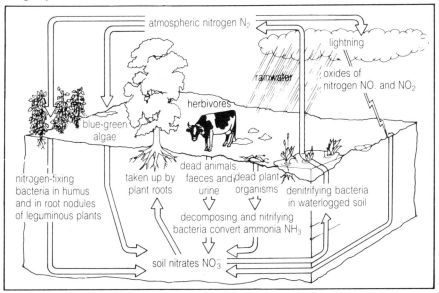

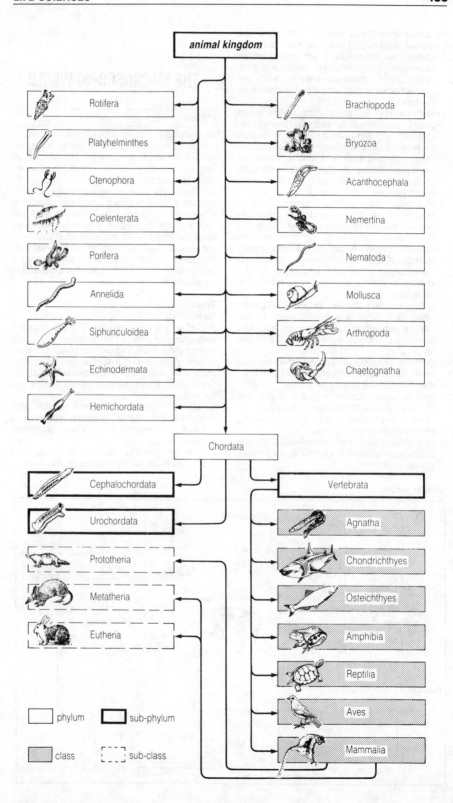

branous partitions, but there are no jointed appendages.

**arachnid** or **arachnoid** type of arthropod, including spiders, scorpions, and mites. They differ from insects in possessing only two main body regions, the cephalophorax and the abdomen.

**arthropod** member of the phylum Arthropoda; an invertebrate animal with jointed legs and a segmented body with a horny or chitinous casing (exoskeleton), which is shed periodically and replaced as the animal grows. Included are arachnids such as spiders and mites, as well as crustaceans, millipedes, centipedes, and insects.

**crustacean** one of the class of arthropods that includes crabs, lobsters, shrimps, woodlice, and barnacles. The external skeleton is made of protein and chitin hardened with lime. Each segment bears a pair of appendages that may be modified as sensory feelers (antennae), as mouthparts, or as swimming, walking, or grasping structures.

**echinoderm** marine invertebrate of the phylum Echinodermata ('spiny-skinned'), with a basic body structure divided into five sectors. Included are starfishes (or sea stars), brittlestars, sea-lilies, sea-urchins, and sea-cucumbers. The skeleton is external, made of a series of limy plates, and echinoderms generally move by using tube-feet, small water-filled sacs that can be protruded or pulled back to the body.

**flatworm** invertebrate of the phylum Platyhelminthes. Some are free-living, but many are parasitic (for example, tapeworms and flukes). The body is simple and bilaterally symmetrical, with one opening to the intestine. Many are hermaphroditic (with both male and female sex organs), and practise self-fertilization.

**insect** any member of the class Insecta among the arthropods or jointed-legged animals. An insect's body is divided into head, thorax, and abdomen. The head bears a pair of feelers or antennae, and attached to the thorax are three pairs of legs and usually two pairs of wings. The scientific study of insects is termed entomology. More than one million species are known, and several thousand new ones are discovered every year. Insects vary in size from 0.02 cm/0.007 in to 35 cm/13.5 in in length.

**jellyfish** marine invertebrate of the phylum Cnidaria (coelenterates) with an umbrella-shaped body composed of a semi-transparent gelatinous substance, with a fringe of stinging tentacles. Most adult jellyfishes move freely, but during parts of their life cycle many are polyp-like and attached. They feed on small animals that are paralyzed by stinging cells in the jellyfishes' tentacles.

**mollusc** any invertebrate of the phylum Mollusca. The majority of molluscs are marine animals, but some inhabit fresh water, and a few are terrestrial. They include bivalves, snails, slugs, and squids. The body is soft, limbless, and cold-blooded. There is no internal skeleton, but most species have a hard shell covering the body. Molluscs vary in diet, the carnivorous species feeding chiefly upon other members of

the phylum. Some are vegetarian. Reproduction is by means of eggs and is sexual; many species are hermaphrodite.

**nematode** unsegmented worm of the phylum Aschelminthes. Nematodes are pointed at both ends, with a tough, smooth outer skin. They include many free-living soil and water forms, but a large number are parasites, such as the roundworms and pinworms that live in humans, or the eelworms that attack plant roots.

*vertebrate*
any animal with a backbone. The 41,000 species of vertebrates include mammals, birds, reptiles, amphibians, and fishes. They include most of the larger animals, but in terms of numbers of species are only a tiny proportion of the world's animals. The zoological taxonomic group Vertebrata is a subgroup of the phylum Chordata.

**amphibian** member of the vertebrate class Amphibia (Greek 'double life'), which generally spend their larval (tadpole) stage in fresh water, transferring to land at maturity and generally returning to water to breed. Like fish and reptiles, they continue to grow throughout life, and cannot maintain a temperature greatly differing from that of their environment. The class includes caecilians, worm-like in appearance; salamanders, frogs, and toads.

**bird** backboned animal of the class Aves, the biggest group of land vertebrates, characterized by warm blood, feathers, wings, breathing through lungs, and egg-laying by the female. Birds are bipedal, with the front limb modified to form a wing and retaining only three digits. The heart has four chambers, and the body is maintained at a high temperature (about 41°C/106°F). Most birds fly, but some groups (such as ostriches) are flightless, and others include flightless members. Many communicate by sounds, or by visual displays, in connection with which many species are brightly coloured, usually the males. Birds have highly developed patterns of instinctive behaviour. Hearing and eyesight are well developed, but the sense of smell is usually poor. Typically the eggs are brooded in a nest and, on hatching, the young receive a period of parental care. There are nearly 8,500 species of birds.

**fish** aquatic vertebrate that uses gills for obtaining oxygen from water. There are three main groups, not closely related: the bony fishes or Osteichthyes (these include goldfish, cod, tuna, and constitute the majority of living fishes, about 20,000 species); the cartilaginous fishes or Chondrichthyes (sharks, rays, of which there are fewer than 600 known species); and the jawless fishes or Agnatha (hagfishes, lampreys).

**mammal** any vertebrate that suckles its young and has hair. Mammals maintain a constant body temperature in varied surroundings. Most mammals give birth to live young, but the platypus and echidna lay eggs. There are over 4,000 species, adapted to almost every way of life. The smallest shrew weighs only 2 g/

# WHEN BIOLOGICAL CONTROL GOES WRONG: THE STORY OF THE CANE TOAD

1990 saw the start of an Australian project to control the cane toad, a poisonous amphibian rapidly spreading through northern and eastern Australia. The irony of the situation is that the A$ 5,000,000 effort is needed to curb an animal that was deliberately introduced into Australia less than 60 years ago.

The cane toad, *Bufo Marinus*, is also known as the giant or marine toad. The threat it poses to Australian wildlife is threefold. It preys voraciously on virtually anything that moves, so threatening species of insects and worms. It reproduces very rapidly, females producing 30,000 eggs in one spawning, and both males and females reaching maturity in one year. This rapid rise in numbers displaces native species. Finally, it is poisonous, so that it is also decimating local populations of predators. Lizards, snakes, koalas and even crocodiles die after eating the toad—small marsupials as rapidly as 20 minutes after their first mouthful.

It is this last threat that has led to its rapid spread. The cane toad has few natural predators, and so is spreading northwards and eastwards from Queensland at a rate of 35 kilometres a year. Only a few species of bird have learned how to cope with the toad—they roll it on its back and peck out its tongue. For the most part, native predators have learned to steer clear of the poisonous toad. So far, the only thing to have checked the toad at all are collectors, who sell the toads to other countries, or to Australian schools and colleges for dissection purposes. Why have the Australians inflicted this pest on themselves? The answer is biological control, an important weapon for the farmer in the attempt to increase crop yields. The cane toad was originally intended to control the numbers of greyback beetles, a beetle that we seriously damaging sugar cane crops in Queensland.

Control of pests by other animals is normally a cheaper and longer-term solution than by using chemicals. It carries less risk to the user and to the environment.

There are many instances of successful biological control. The Vedalia beetle was introduced into Californian orange groves in the 1890s and wiped out the cottony cushion scale which had been threatening the citrus industry with ruin. In the 1920s, nearly 30 million hectares/74 million acres of Australian farmland was cleared of prickly pear cactus by the use of the Argentian moth. Brazilian waterways have been cleared of the weed salvina by the use of a parasitic weevil, discovered by a member of the Australian research team that is now to investigate cane toad control. In Britain plans are under way to use the caterpillars of *conservula cinisigna* to control the growth of bracken on moorland.

The cane toad had been a shining example of such control. Originally from South America, it was imported into Puerto Rico and the West Indies in the 19th century to control sugar cane pests. Such was the success of this venture that plantations in Hawaii and the Philippines followed suit. The Queensland sugar growers followed these later efforts with interest, and when they appeared successful the import of nearly 60,000 toadlets from Hawaii was organized. These were released in the Bundaberg area in 1935. In the short term the operation was a success—the greyback beetle was soon under control. However, the Australian flora and fauna is very different from that of other sugar growing areas. Like other introduced species, such as the dingo and the rabbit, the cane toad revelled in a situation where there were few competitors and even fewer predators. Most of the Australian continent provides ideal habitats for the toad, and if it is not checked it will spread across the entire country. This is why the Australians have initiated the toad control project.

The aim of the project is to study the biology of the toad in greater detail, with the idea of finding a vulnerable point in the life cycle. At present, surprisingly little is known about the toad, despite its wide occurrence. One suggestion is to use another biological control, such as a virus or a bacterium. Not surprisingly the research team are cautious about this approach—there is an obvious danger of the wrong type of microbe spreading rapidly through all types of wildlife. How much money might then be needed to bring the situation under control?

*The Cane Toad (bufo marinus) which has caused destruction in Australia. It can grow as big as a dinner plate.*

**skeleton**

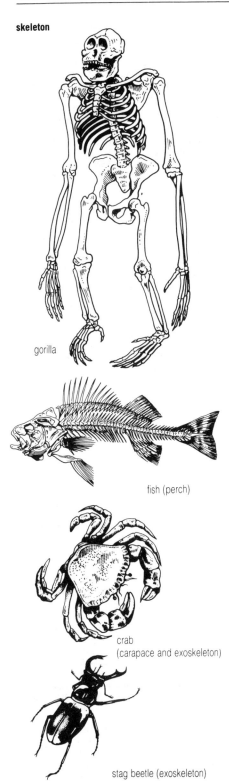

gorilla

fish (perch)

crab
(carapace and exoskeleton)

stag beetle (exoskeleton)

0.07 oz, the largest whale up to 150 tonnes.

**reptile** class (Reptilia) of vertebrates. Unlike amphibians, reptiles have hard-shelled, yolk-filled
eggs that are laid on land and from which fully
formed young are born. Some snakes and lizards retain their eggs and give birth to live
young. Reptiles are cold-blooded, produced
from eggs, and the skin is usually covered
with scales. The metabolism is slow, and in
some cases (some large snakes) intervals between meals may be months. Reptiles date back
over 300 million years. They include snakes,
lizards, crocodiles, turtles, tortoises, and the
tuatara.

**Systems**
**alimentary canal** in animals, the tube through
which food passes; it extends from the mouth
to the anus. It is a complex organ, adapted for
digestion. In human adults, it is about 9 m/
30 ft long, consisting of the mouth cavity,
pharynx, oesophagus, stomach, and the small
and large intestines.

**bone** the hard connective tissue comprising the
skeleton of most vertebrate animals. It consists of a network of collagen fibres impregnated with inorganic salts, especially calcium
phospate. Enclosed within this solid matrix
are bone cells, blood vessels, and nerves. In
strength, the toughest bone is comparable with
reinforced concrete. There are two types of
bone: those that develop by replacing cartilage
and those that form directly from connective
tissue. The latter are usually platelike in shape,
and form in the skin of the developing embryo.
Humans have about 206 distinct bones in the
skeleton. The interior of long bones consists of
a spongy matrix filled with a soft marrow that
produces blood cells.

**brain** in higher animals, a mass of interconnected
nerve cells, forming the anterior part of the
central nervous system, whose activities it
coordinates and controls. In vertebrates, the
brain is contained by the skull. An enlarged
portion of the upper spinal cord, the *medulla
oblongata*, contains centres for the control of
respiration, heartbeat rate and strength, and
blood pressure. Overlying this is the *cerebellum*, which is concerned with coordinating
complex muscular processes such as maintaining posture and moving limbs. The cerebral hemispheres (*cerebrum*) are paired out-
growths of the front end of the forebrain, in
early vertebrates mainly concerned with the
senses, but in higher vertebrates greatly developed and involved in the integration of all sensory input and motor output, and in intelligent
behaviour. In the brain, nerve impulses are
passed across synapses by neurotransmitters,
in the same way as in other parts of the nervous
system.

In mammals the cerebrum is the largest part
of the brain, carrying the *cerebral cortex*. As
cerebral complexity grows, the surface of the
brain becomes convoluted into deep folds. In
higher mammals, there are large unassigned
areas of the brain that seem to be connected

with intelligence, personality, and higher mental faculties. Language is controlled in two special regions usually in the left side of the brain: **Broca's area** governs the ability to talk, and **Wernicke's area** is responsible for the comprehension of spoken and written words.

In 1990, scientists at Johns Hopkins University, Baltimore, succeeded in culturing human brain cells.

**circulatory system** the system of vessels in an animal's body that transports essential substances (blood or other circulatory fluid) to and from the different parts of the body. Except for simple animals such as sponges and coelenterates (jellyfishes, sea anemones, corals), all animals have a circulatory system.

**muscle** contractile animal tissue that produces locomotion and maintains the movement of body substances. Muscle is made of long cells that can contract to between one-half and one-third of their relaxed length. **Striped** muscles are activated by motor nerves under voluntary control; their ends are usually attached via tendons to bones. **Involuntary** or **smooth** muscles are controlled by motor nerves of the autonomic nervous system, and located in the gut, blood vessels, iris, and various ducts. **Cardiac** muscle occurs only in the heart, and is also controlled by the autonomic nervous system.

**nervous system** the system of interconnected nerve cells of most invertebrates and all vertebrates. It is composed of the central and autonomic nervous systems. It may be as simple as the nerve net of coelenterates (for example, jellyfishes) or as complex as the mammalian nervous system, with a central nervous system comprising brain and spinal cord, and a peripheral nervous system connecting up with sensory organs, muscles, and glands.

**skeleton** the rigid or semirigid framework that supports an animal's body, protects its internal organs, and provides anchorage points for its muscles. The skeleton may be composed of bone and cartilage (vertebrates), chitin (arthropods), calcium carbonate (molluscs and other invertebrates, or silica (many protists).

It may be internal, forming an **endoskeleton**, or external, forming an **exoskeleton**. Another type of skeleton, found in invertebrates such as earthworms, is the **hydrostatic skeleton**. This gains partial rigidity from fluid enclosed within a body cavity. Because the fluid cannot be compressed, contraction of one part of the body results in extension of another part, giving peristaltic motion.

## PLANT

an organism that carries out photosynthesis, has cellulose cell walls and complex eukaryotic cells, and is immobile. A few parasitic plants have lost the ability to photosynthesize but are still considered to be plants.

Plants are autotrophs, that is, they make carbohydrates from water and carbon dioxide, and are the primary producers in all food chains, so that all animal life is dependent on them. They play a vital part in the carbon cycle, removing carbon dioxide from the atmosphere and generating oxygen. The study of plants is known as botany.

**algae** (singular **alga**) diverse group of plants (including those commonly called seaweeds) that shows great variety of form, ranging from single-celled forms to multicellular seaweeds of considerable size and complexity.

**angiosperm** flowering plant in which the seeds are enclosed within an ovary, which ripens to a fruit. Angiosperms are divided into monocotyledons (single seed leaf in the embryo) and dicotyledons (two seed leaves in the embryo). They include the majority of flowers, herbs, grasses, and trees except conifers.

**bryophyte** member of the Bryophyta, a division of the plant kingdom containing three classes, the Hepaticae (liverwort), Musci (moss), and Anthocerotae (hornwort). Bryophytes are generally small, low-growing, terrestrial plants with no vascular (water-conducting) system as in higher plants. Their life cycle shows a marked alternation of generations. Bryophytes chiefly occur in damp habitats and require water for the dispersal of the male gametes (antherozoids).

**gymnosperm** in botany, any plant whose seeds are exposed, as opposed to the structurally more advanced angiosperms, where they are inside an ovary. The group includes conifers and related plants such as cycads and ginkgos, whose seeds develop in cones. Fossil gymnosperms have been found in rocks about 350 million years old.

**pteridophyte** simple type of vascular plant. The pteridophytes comprise four classes: the Psilosida, including the most primitive vascular plants, found mainly in the tropics; the Lycopsida, including the club mosses; the Sphenopsida, including the horsetails; and the Pteropsida, including the ferns. They are mainly terrestrial, non-flowering plants characterized by the presence of a vascular system; the possession of true stems, roots, and leaves; and by a marked alternation of generations, with the sporophyte forming the dominant generation in the life cycle. They do not produce seeds.

### Systems

**chlorophyll** green pigment present in most plants; it is responsible for the absorption of light energy during photosynthesis. The pigment absorbs the red and blue-violet parts of sunlight but reflects the green, thus giving plants their characteristic colour.

**chloroplast** structure (organelle) within a plant cell containing the green pigment chlorophyll. Chloroplasts occur in most cells of the green plant that are exposed to light, often in large numbers. Typically, they are flattened and disclike, with a double membrane enclosing the stroma, a gel-like matrix. Within the stroma are stacks of fluid-containing cavities, or vesicles, where photosynthesis occurs.

**flower** the reproductive unit of an angiosperm or flowering plant, typically consisting of four whorls of modified leaves: sepals, petals, stamens, and carpels. These are borne on a central axis or receptacle. The many variations in size, colour, number and arrangement of parts are closely related to the method of pollination. Flowers adapted for wind pollination typically have reduced or absent petals and sepals and long, feathery stigmas that hang outside the flower to trap airborne pollen. In contrast, the petals of insect-pollinated flowers are usually conspicuous and brightly coloured.

In size, flowers range from the tiny blooms of duckweeds scarcely visible with the naked eye to the gigantic flowers of the Malaysian *Rafflesia*, which can reach over 1 m/3 ft across.

**leaf** lateral outgrowth on the stem of a plant, and in most species the primary organ of photosynthesis. The chief leaf types are cotyledons (seed leaves), scale leaves (on underground stems), foliage leaves, and bracts (in the axil of which a flower is produced).

Structurally the leaf is made up of mesophyll cells surrounded by the epidermis and usually, in addition, a waxy layer, termed the cuticle, which prevents excessive evaporation of water from the leaf tissues by transpiration. The epidermis is interrupted by small pores, or stomata through which gas exchange occurs.

**root** the part of a plant that is usually underground, and whose primary functions are anchorage and the absorption of water and dissolved mineral salts. Roots usually grow downwards and towards water (that is, they are positively geotropic and hydrotropic; see tropism). Plants, such as epiphytic orchids that grow above ground, produce aerial roots that absorb moisture from the atmosphere. Others, such as ivy, have climbing roots arising from the stems that serve to attach the plant to trees and walls.

# THE MICROSCOPIC WORLD

**archaebacteria** three groups of bacteria whose DNA differs significantly from that of other bacteria (called the 'eubacteria'). All are strict anaerobes, that is, they are killed by oxygen. This is thought to be a primitive condition and to indicate that the archaebacteria are related to the earliest life forms, which appeared about 4 billion years ago, when there was little oxygen in the Earth's atmosphere.

**bacillus** member of a group of rodlike bacteria that occur everywhere in the soil and air. Some are responsible for diseases such as anthrax or for causing food spoilage.

**bacteria** (singular *bacterium*) microscopic unicellular organisms with prokaryotic cells (lacking true nuclei and other specialized cell structures), divided into groups on the basis of such characteristics as the rigidity and shape of the cell wall, type of colony, and type and products of metabolism. The large majority of bacteria are *eubacteria*, which have a rigid cell wall.

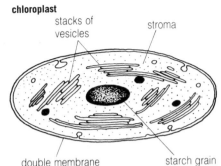

**chloroplast**

stacks of vesicles

stroma

double membrane

starch grain

They usually reproduce by binary fission, and since this may occur approximately every 20 minutes, a single bacterium is potentially capable of producing 16 million copies of itself in a day.

**blue-green algae** single-celled, primitive organisms that resemble bacteria in their internal cell organization, sometimes joined together in colonies or filaments. Blue-green algae are among the oldest known living organisms; remains have been found in rocks up to 3.5 billion years old. They are widely distributed in aquatic habitats, on the damp surfaces of rocks and trees, and in the soil.

Blue-green algae and bacteria are prokaryotic organisms. Some can fix nitrogen and thus are necessary to the nitrogen cycle, while others follow a symbiotic existence—for example, living in association with fungi to form lichens.

**cell** a self-contained portion of living matter bordered by a membrane, the smallest unit capable of an independent existence. All living organisms consist of one or more cells, with the exception of viruses. Bacteria, protozoa and many other microorganisms consist of single cells, whereas a human is made up of billions of cells. Essential features of a cell are the membrane, which encloses it and restricts the flow of substances in and out; the jellylike material within, often known as protoplasm, the ribosomes, which carry out protein synthesis, and the DNA, which forms the hereditary material.

**coccus** (plural *cocci*) member of a group of globular bacteria, some of which are harmful to humans. The cocci contain the subgroups *streptococci*, where the bacteria associate in straight chains, and *staphylococci*, where the bacteria associate in branched chains.

**cytoplasm** the part of the cell outside the nucleus. Strictly speaking, this includes all the organelles (mitochondria, chloroplasts, and so on), but often cytoplasm refers to the jellylike matter in which the organelles are embedded (correctly termed the cytosol). In many cells, the cytoplasm is made up of two parts: the *ectoplasm* (or plasmagel), a dense gelatinous outer layer concerned with cell movement, and the *endoplasm* (or plasmasol), a more fluid inner part where most of the organelles are found.

**eukaryote** an organism whose cells have a distinct nucleus which carries the genetic material on

**Plant kingdom**

taxonomic (classification) levels

1 Kingdom

2 sub-kingdom

3 division

4 class

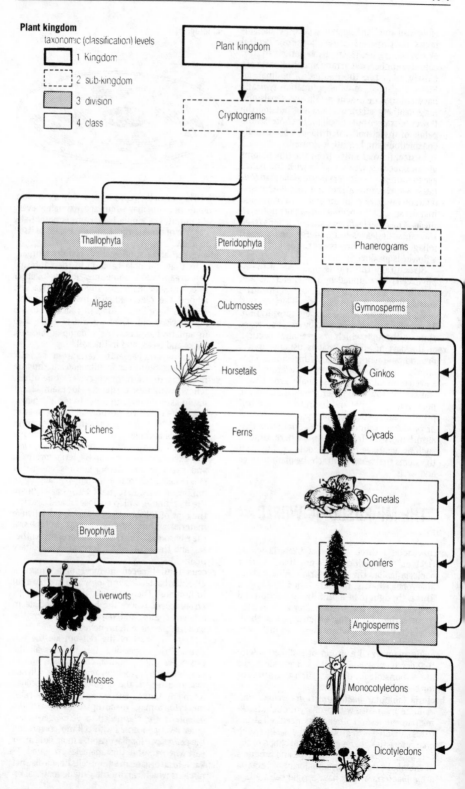

chromosomes. All organisms, except bacteria and blue-green algae, which belong to the prokaryote grouping, are eukaryotes.

**methanogenic bacteria** one of a group of primitive bacteria (archaebacteria). They give off methane gas as a by-product of their metabolism, and are common in sewage treatment plants and hot springs, where the temperature is high and oxygen is absent.

**microorganism** or **microbe** living organism invisible to the naked eye but visible under a microscope. Microorganisms include viruses and single-celled organisms such as bacteria, protozoa, yeasts, and some algae. The term has no taxonomic significance in biology. The study of microorganisms is known as microbiology.

**nucleus** the central, membrane-enclosed part of a eukaryotic cell, containing the genetic material, DNA.

**prokaryote** an organism whose cells lack organelles (specialized segregated structures such as nuclei, mitochondria, and chloroplasts). Prokaryote DNA is not arranged in chromosomes but forms a coiled structure called a *nucleoid*. The prokaryotes comprise only the *bacteria* and *blue-green algae*; all other organisms are eukaryotes.

**protist** a single-celled organism which has a eukaryotic cell, but which is not a member of the plant, fungal, or animal kingdoms. The main protists are protozoa.

**protozoa** group of single-celled organisms without rigid cell walls. Some, such as amoeba, ingest other cells, but most are saprotrophs or parasites. The group is polyphyletic (containing organisms which have different evolutionary origins).

**virus** infectious particle consisting of a core of nucleic acid (DNA or RNA) enclosed in a protein shell. Viruses are acellular and able to function and reproduce only if they can invade a living cell to use the cell's system to replicate themselves. In the process they may disrupt or alter the host cell's own DNA. The healthy human body reacts by producing an antiviral protein, interferon, which prevents the infection spreading to adjacent cells.

Among diseases caused by viruses are canine distemper, chickenpox, common cold, herpes, influenza, rabies, smallpox, yellow fever, AIDS, and many plant diseases.

# THE NEW SYNTHESIS

**amino acid** water-soluble organic molecule, mainly composed of carbon, oxygen, hydrogen, and nitrogen, containing both a basic amine group ($NH_2$) and an acidic carboxyl (COOH) group. When two or more amino acids are joined together, they are known as peptides; proteins are made up of interacting polypeptides (peptide chains consisting of more than three amino acids) and are folded

or twisted in characteristic shapes.

Many different proteins are found in the cells of living organisms, but they are all made up of the same 20 amino acids, joined together in varying combinations, (although other types of amino acid do occur infrequently in nature). Eight of these, the **essential amino acids**, cannot be synthesized by humans and must be obtained from the diet. Children need a further two amino acids that are not essential for adults. Other animals also need some preformed amino acids in their diet, but green plants can manufacture all the amino acids they need from simpler molecules, relying on energy from the sun and minerals (including nitrates) from the soil.

**amylase** one of a group of enzymes that breaks down starches into their component molecules (sugars) for use in their body. It occurs widely in both plants and animals. In humans, it is found in saliva and in pancreatic juices.

**basepair** the linkage of two base (purine or pyrimidine) molecules in DNA. They are found in nucleotides, and form the basis of the genetic code.

One base lies on one strand of the DNA double helix, and one on the other, so that the base pairs link the two strands like the rungs of a ladder. In DNA, there are four bases: adenine and guanine (purines) and cytosine and thymine (pyrimidines). Adenine always pairs with thymine, and cytosine with guanine.

**codon** a triplet of bases in a molecule of DNA or RNA that directs the placement of a particular amino acid during the process of protein synthesis. There are 64 codons in the genetic code.

**cytochrome** protein responsible for part of the process of respiration by which food molecules are broken down in aerobic organisms. Cytochromes are part of the electron transport chain, which uses energized electrons to reduce molecular oxygen ($O_2$) to oxygen ions ($O^{2-}$). These combine with hydrogen ions ($H^+$) to form water ($H_2O$), the end product of aerobic respiration. As electrons are passed from one cytochrome to another energy is released and used to make ATP.

**DNA** *deoxyribonucleic acid* complex two stranded molecule that contains, in chemically coded form, all the information needed to build, control, and maintain a living organism. DNA is a ladderlike double-stranded nucleic acid that forms the basis of genetic inheritance in all organisms, except for a few viruses that have only RNA. In eukaryotic organisms, it is organized into chromosomes and contained in the cell nucleus.

**enzyme** biological catalyst produced in cells, and capable of speeding up the chemical reactions necessary for life. Enzymes are not themselves destroyed by this process. They are large, complex proteins, and are highly specific, each chemical reaction requiring its own particular enzyme. Digestive enzymes include amylases (which digest starch), lipases (which digest fats), and proteases (which digest protein).

## IN SEARCH OF THE MOLECULAR CLOCK

Is there a way of measuring how species have evolved? Of determining how closely related one species is to another? Of telling what were the branching points in the descent of any one particular species?

For the past 30 years, molecular biologists have been looking for such a technique. Ever since the first determination of protein structure, they have been comparing the structure of proteins with the same function from different species of animal. Pork insulin and beef insulin or bacterial cytochrome and human cytochrome—many different molecules have been examined for the light that changes in their biochemical composition can shed upon their evolutionary history.

The method works because proteins consist of long sequences of about 20 different amino acids. This chain of amino acids is known as the primary structure of a protein. Some of the amino acids in the chain react with one another to cause the long straight chain to fold up. The interaction between different amino acids gives the protein its secondary and tertiary structure—its shape. It is because proteins can be formed into so many varied and complex shapes that they are so essential in the maintenance of life.

Not all the amino acids in the primary structure of a protein are involved with shaping it. Many of the amino acids are there simply to pad out the chain, to make the strand between an important interaction long enough to bend in a certain way. It may be of no consequence whether amino acid number 223 in a chain is alanine, glycine, or some other amino acid. And different species of animals do vary as to which amino acids are found in these inconsequential areas, even though the essential ones are identical, to produce the same folded structure.

DNA carries information about protein structure very precisely. All the members of a species will probably have the same primary sequence for a protein, whether the amino acid is of consequence or not. However, mutations occur from time to time, and these lead to changes in the sequence. If this happens to an essential amino acid, the protein cannot function and the organism (and the mutation) will die out. If a mutation occurs to an inconsequential amino acid, the mutation is unimportant and will be passed on. So the number of differences between the amino acid sequence of proteins of different species will be a measure of how much time has elapsed since the two had a common ancestor. The greater the differences between any particular protein from two different animals, the further apart they are in evolutionary terms.

However, this theory is by no means proven.

Can we assume that mutations occur at a steady rate, or are there periods when they occur more rapidly, perhaps at times of increased radiation? Research in 1990 suggested that some organisms may be able to induce mutations in their own DNA in order to increase their chances of survival under conditions of extreme hardship. Mutation of this sort would certainly upset any idea of a steady mutation clock. And it may well be that large, complex organisms have fewer sites that are truly inconsequential. If so, organisms like this would show a slower rate of mutation than less complicated organisms, and, indeed, the mutational rate does seem slower for humans.

To answer these questions, scientists have begun to look one step further back in the biochemical process, to DNA itself. For complete comparison between species we will need the sequence of human DNA and of other organisms. The human genome project is expected to take 15 years, so the prospect of sequencing all but a few other organisms is remote at present.

However, some useful evidence is beginning to emerge from the study of DNA from fossils. Early in 1991 a research team from the University of California managed to recover a fragment of DNA that was at least 17 million years old. The DNA had decomposed into small fragments, but by using a technique known as polymerase chain reaction (PCR), a fragment nearly 800 nucleotides long has been preserved and replicated, so that its sequence can be determined.

The possibility of recovering DNA fragments from long-dead organisms is exciting, but not all fossils will yield such material. Of the four bases that make up DNA, two are easily oxidized, while the other two dissolve readily. If DNA is to be recovered, it needs to be preserved in conditions without oxygen or water.

Some comparison of DNA has already been done. DNA fragments from a museum specimen of the quagga (a horselike animal that became extinct in 1883) have been replicated by cloning—the fragments were introduced into bacteria, which duplicated them along with their own DNA. This technique is less reliable with damaged DNA than PCR, since the bacteria try to repair the DNA and introduce errors. Still, even with the possibility of replication errors, the fragment was found to be only 12 nucleotides different from a similar section of zebra DNA.

The possibility is that, instead of having to make assumptions about the workings of a molecular clock, we shall be able to examine directly the material that has mutated.

Other enzymes play a part in the conversion of food energy into ATP; the manufacture of all the molecular components of the body; the replication of DNA when a cell divides; the production of hormones; and the control of movement of substances into and out of cells.

Enzymes have many medical and industrial uses, from washing powders to drug production, and as research tools in molecular biology. They can be extracted from bacteria and moulds, and genetic engineering now makes it possible to tailor the enzyme for a specific purpose, and greatly increase the rate of production.

**genetic code** the way in which instructions for building proteins, the basic structural molecules of living matter, are 'written' in the genetic material DNA. This relationship between the sequence of bases (the subunits in a DNA molecule) and the sequence of amino acids (the subunits of a protein molecule) is the basis of heredity. The code employs codons of three bases each; it is the same in almost all organisms, except for a few minor differences recently discovered in some protozoa.

**mitochondria** (singular **mitochondrion**) membrane-enclosed organelles within eukaryotic cells, containing enzymes responsible for energy production during aerobic respiration. These rodlike or spherical bodies are thought to be derived from free-living bacteria that, at a very early stage in the history of life, invaded larger cells and took up a symbiotic way of life inside. Each still contains its own small loop of DNA, and new mitochondria arise by division of existing ones.

**molecular biology** the study of the molecular basis of life, including the biochemistry of molecules such as DNA, RNA, and proteins, and the molecular structure and function of the various parts of living cells.

**nucleotide** organic compound consisting of a purine (adenine or guanine) or a pyrimidine (thymine, uracil, or cytosine) base linked to a sugar (deoxyribose or ribose) and a phosphate group. DNA and RNA are made up of long chains of nucleotides.

**operon** group of genes that are found next to each other on a chromosome, and are turned on and off as an integrated unit. They usually produce enzymes that control different steps in the same biochemical pathway. Operons were discovered 1961 (by the French biochemists F Jacob and J Monod) in bacteria; they are less common in higher organisms where the control of metabolism is a more complex process.

**peptide** a molecule comprising two or more amino acid molecules (not necessarily different) joined by **peptide bonds**, whereby the acid group of one acid is linked to the amino group of the other (–CO.NH). The number of amino acid molecules in the peptide is indicated by referring to it as a di-, tri-, or polypeptide (two, three, or many amino acids).

**protein** complex, biologically important substance composed of amino acids joined by peptide bonds. Other types of bond, such as sulphur-sulphur bonds, hydrogen bonds, and cation bridges between acid sites, are responsible for creating the protein's characteristic three-dimensional structure, which may be fibrous, globular, or pleated.

Proteins are essential to all living organisms. As **enzymes** they regulate all aspects of metabolism. Structural proteins such as **keratin** and **collagen** make up the skin, claws, bones, tendons, and ligaments; **muscle** proteins produce movement; **haemoglobin** transports oxygen; and **membrane** proteins regulate the movement of substances into and out of cells.

**ribosome** the protein-making machinery of the cell. Ribosomes are located on the endoplasmic reticulum (ER) of eukaryotic cells, and are made of proteins and a special type of RNA, ribosomal RNA. They receive messenger RNA (copied from the DNA) and amino acids, and 'translate' the messenger RNA by using its chemically coded instructions to link amino acids in a specific order, to make a strand of a particular protein.

**RNA** **ribonucleic acid** nucleic acid involved in the process of translating DNA, the genetic material into proteins. It is usually single-stranded, unlike the double-stranded DNA, and consists of a large number of nucleotides strung together, each of which comprises the sugar ribose, a phosphate group, and one of four bases (uracil, cytosine, adenine, or guanine). RNA is copied from DNA by the formation of base pairs, with uracil taking the place of thymine. Although RNA is normally associated only with the process of protein synthesis, it makes up the hereditary material itself in some viruses, such as retroviruses.

**translation** in living cells, the process by which proteins are synthesized. During translation, the information coded as a sequence of nucelotides in messenger RNA is transformed into a sequence of amino acids in a peptide chain. The process involves the 'translation' of the genetic code. See also transcription.

# NEW TECHNIQUES

**abzyme** an artificially created antibody that can be used like an enzyme to accelerate reactions.

**autoradiography** technique for following the movement of molecules within an organism, especially a plant, by labelling with a radioactive isotope that can be traced on photographs. It is used to study photosynthesis, where the pathway of radioactive carbon dioxide can be traced as it moves through the various chemical stages.

**bacteriophage** virus that attacks bacteria. Such viruses are now of use in genetic engineering.

**biosensor** device based on microelectronic circuits that can directly measure medically significant variables for the purpose of diagnosis or monitoring treatment. One such device measures the blood sugar level of diabetics using a single drop of blood, and shows the result on a liquid crystal display within a few minutes.

**biotechnology** the industrial use of living organisms to manufacture food, drugs, or other products. The brewing and baking industries have long relied on the yeast microorganism for fermentation purposes, while the dairy industry employs a range of bacteria and fungi to convert milk into cheeses and yoghurts. Recent advances include genetic engineering, in which single-celled organisms with modified

**DNA**
*how a cell divides*

1 original double helix

2 forms ladder

3 unzips

4 new bases join onto opened zip teeth

5 two new identical double strands

S P S P S

S P S P S

C G

G C

T A

C G

A T

C

A

C

T A

C G

A T

C G

T A

C G

A T

C G

**Key**

| | |
|---|---|
| S sugars | G guanine |
| P phosphates | A adenine |
| C cytosine | T thymine |

instead of light rays, as in an optical microscope. An *electron lens* is an arrangement of electromagnetic coils that control and focus the beam. Electrons are not visible to the eye, so instead of an eyepiece there is a fluorescent screen or a photographic plate on which the electrons form an image. The wavelength of the electron beam is much shorter than that of light, so much greater magnification and resolution (ability to distinguish detail) can be achieved.

A *high-resolution electron microscope* (HREM) can produce a magnification of 7 million times ($\times$ 7,000,000). The development of the electron microscope has made possible the observation of very minute organisms, viruses, and even large molecules. A *transmission electron microscope* passes the electron beam through a very thin slice of a specimen. A *scanning electron microscope* looks at the exterior of a specimen.

**electroporation** a technique of introducing foreign DNA into pollen with a strong burst of electricity, used in creating genetically-engineered plants.

**fluorescence microscopy** technique for examining samples under a microscope without slicing them into thin sections. Instead, fluorescent dyes are introduced to the tissue and used as a light source for imaging purposes.

**gene bank** collection of seeds or other forms of genetic material, such as tubers, spores, bacterial or yeast cultures, live animals and plants, frozen sperm and eggs, or frozen embryos. These are stored for possible future use in agriculture, plant and animal breeding, or in medicine, genetic engineering, or the restocking of wild habitats where species have become extinct. Gene banks will be increasingly used as the rate of extinction increases, depleting the Earth's genetic variety (biodiversity).

**gene therapy** proposed medical technique for curing or alleviating inherited diseases or defects. Although not yet a practical possibility for most defects, some of the basic techniques are available as a result of intensive research in genetic engineering.

**genetic engineering** the deliberate manipulation of genetic material by biochemical techniques. It is often achieved by the introduction of new DNA, usually by means of a virus or plasmid. This can be for pure research or to breed functionally specific plants, animals or bacteria. These organisms with a foreign gene added are said to be transgenic.

In genetic engineering, the splicing and reconciliation of genes is used to increase knowledge of cell function and reproduction, but it can also achieve practical ends. For example, plants grown for food could be given the ability to fix nitrogen, found in some bacteria, and so reduce the need for expensive fertilizers, or simple bacteria may be modified to produce rare drugs. Developments in genetic engineering have led to the production of human insulin, human growth hormone and a number of other bone-marrow stimulating hormones.

DNA are used to produce insulin and other drugs. Enzymes, whether extracted from cells or produced artificially, are central to most biotechnological applications.

**cosmid** fragment of DNA from the human genome inserted into a bacterial cell. The bacterium replicates the fragment along with its own DNA. In this way the fragments are copied for a gene library. Cosmids are characteristically 40,000 base pairs in length. The most commonly used bacterium is *Escherichia coli*. A yeast artificial chromosome works in the same way.

**electron microscope** instrument that produces a magnified image by using a beam of electrons

## PLAYING GOD OR ADVANCING SCIENCE?

Transgenic organisms are those that have had new genetic material added to them. By genetic engineering, foreign DNA is introduced into the organism, which then replicates and behaves just like the original DNA of the organism. The new DNA will produce proteins and, indeed, complete characteristics that the organism did not have before.

It is this ability to alter the characteristics of organisms in a planned way that is so exciting to genetic engineers. To take just one example, the bacteria *Bacillus thuringiensus* produces a poison that is toxic to insects and is highly specific (so it does not poison other organisms). The gene for this poison has been isolated on bacterial DNA and then introduced into the cells of tobacco plants. The tobacco plants now respond to the new DNA and produce a poison that kills their insect predators. This saves the expense and inefficiency of spraying with synthetic pesticide.

Other recent examples of transgenic organisms include plants that have nitrogen-fixing genes transferred from bacteria and cows with growth-regulators transferred from humans. Mice feature considerably in the catalogue of transgenic organisms, because of their rapid reproductive cycle. Mice that secrete human growth hormone were reported in 1990, as were mice with fragments of human DNA responsible for leukaemia. The latter offer the possibility of being able to study leukaemia without human patients.

Food-storage methods may be more easily studied with the help of genetic engineering. A team at Nottingham University has transferred a gene responsible for the bioluminescence of a marine bacterium into the listeria bacterium. The new organism glows a greeny blue, thus making it much easier to track and monitor.

Genetic engineering involves cutting identified genes from a cell and transplanting them, creating new combinations of DNA. Such DNA is known as recombinant DNA. The cutting is done with enzymes known as restriction endonucleases, which are normally used by bacteria to destroy viruses by chopping up invading DNA. Recombining DNA is done by using the enzyme DNA ligase. A great deal of this work is done with bacteria, because their cells have no nucleus, so the DNA can be easily separated from a broken-up cell. Animal and plant cells, which do have a nucleus, are more difficult to deal with. In these cells, genetic engineers copy genetic information by first isolating messenger RNA, and then producing the DNA it would have come from with an enzyme called reverse transcriptase. Building the new DNA is only one problem. Next, the molecule must be introduced to a cell that will express it—make the proteins for which it codes. With bacteria, this transfer can be achieved with plasmids. These are small loops of DNA that multiply separately from the rest of the cell's DNA. They are readily transferred between bacteria, even of different species. The plasmid can be cut with a restriction enzyme, and new DNA pasted into the loop with DNA ligase. Bacteria are then subjected to high and low temperature treatments so that they take up the new plasmid (even at best, only 4–5% of bacteria take up the plasmid). Colonies of bacteria are then screened to find which are producing the new protein coded for by the plasmid.

Another way of introducing new genetic material is by using bacteriophages. These are viruses that attack bacteria by introducing their own DNA. Using such viruses, DNA of lengths of up to 50,000 nucleotides can be incorporated, whereas the maximum for the plasmid technique is 20,000. Viruses are also used to carry new material into animals.

Some animals have been engineered on a larger scale, with DNA being injected into fertilized eggs through a very fine glass tube. The eggs are then transferred to a suitable foster mother. This technique has been used to rear transgenic farm animals.

New genes can be introduced into plants by using the soil bacterium *Agrobacterium tumefaciens*. This bacterium has a plasmid that induces tumours in plant cells by interfering with the plant's DNA. Genetic engineers use a version of this plasmid to carry new genes from the bacterium to the plant. Unfortunately, many important crops seem to be resistant to the bacteria, so techniques for direct transfer are being developed—perhaps the most remarkable being ballistic impregnation. In this method, DNA is stuck onto minute tungsten particles about 1 micrometre in diameter. These are then fired into the soft plant tissue at a speed that is large enough to let them penetrate the cells without killing them.

New strains of animals have also been produced; a new strain of mouse was patented in the USA 1989 (the application was rejected in the European patent office). A vaccine against a sheep parasite (a larval tapeworm) has been developed by genetic engineering; most existing vaccines protect against bacteria and viruses.

There is a risk that when transplanting genes between different types of bacteria (*Escherichia coli*, which lives in the human intestine, is often used) new and harmful strains might be produced. For this reason strict safety precautions are observed, and the altered bacteria are disabled in some way so they are unable to exist outside the laboratory.

**molecular clock** the use of rates of mutation in genetic material to calculate the length of time elapsed since two related species diverged from each other during evolution. The method can be based on comparisons of the DNA or of widely occurring proteins, such as haemoglobin.

Since mutations are thought to occur at a constant rate, the length of time that must have elapsed in order to produce the difference between two species can be estimated.

**electron microscope**

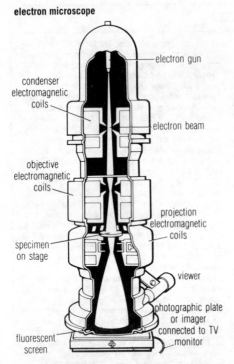

- electron gun
- condenser electromagnetic coils
- electron beam
- objective electromagnetic coils
- projection electromagnetic coils
- specimen on stage
- viewer
- photographic plate or imager connected to TV monitor
- fluorescent screen

This information can be compared with the evidence obtained from palaeontology to reconstruct evolutionary events.(See feature in this section.)

**protein engineering** the creation of synthetic proteins designed to carry out specific tasks. For example, an enzyme may be designed to remove grease from soiled clothes and remain stable at the high temperatures in a washing machine.

**restriction enzyme** enzyme that breaks a chain of DNA into two pieces at a specific point. The point along the DNA chain at which the enzyme can work is restricted to places where a specific sequence of base pairs occurs.

Different restriction enzymes will break a DNA chain at different points. The overlap between the fragments is used in determining the sequence of base pairs in the DNA chain.

**sequencing** determining the sequence of chemical subunits within a large molecule. Techniques for sequencing amino acids in proteins were established in the 1950s, insulin being the first for which the sequence was completed. Major efforts are now being made to determine the sequence of base pairs within DNA.

**transgenic organism** plant, animal, bacterium, or other living organism which has had a foreign gene added to it by means of genetic engineering.(See feature in this section.)

**yeast artificial chromosome** (YAC) fragment of DNA from the human genome inserted into a yeast cell. The yeast replicates the fragment along with its own DNA. In this way the fragments are copied to be preserved in a gene library. YACs are characteristically between 250,000 and 1 million base pairs in length. A cosmid works in the same way.

---

**Animal experiments**

*Do you refuse, on principle, to buy goods which have been tested on animals or that contain animal products?*

| | |
|---|---|
| Yes | 38 |
| No | 62 |

*What comes to mind when you hear the phrase animal experimentation?*

| | |
|---|---|
| A revolting practice that should be banned | 26 |
| An unpleasant practice that should be banned | 30 |
| A necessary evil | 26 |
| Something that is essential for the good of humans | 13 |
| None of these | 2 |
| Don't know | 2 |

# TERMS

**abacus** method of calculating with a handful of stones on 'a flat surface' (Latin *abacus*), familiar to the Greeks and Romans, and used by earlier peoples, possibly even in ancient Babylon; it still survives in the more sophisticated bead-frame form of the Russian *schoty* and the Japanese *soroban*. The abacus has principles in common with the electronic calculator.

**abscissa** in coordinate geometry, the horizontal or $x$ coordinate, that is, the distance of a point from the vertical or $y$-axis. For example, a point with the coordinates (3,4) has an abscissa of 3.

**algebra** system of arithmetic applying to any set of non-numerical symbols, and the axioms and rules by which they are combined or operated upon. It is used in many branches of mathematics, such as matrix algebra and Boolean algebra, the method of algebraic reasoning devised in the 19th century by English mathematician George Boole and used in working out the logic for computers.

**alternate angle** in geometry, one of a pair of angles that lie on opposite sides of a transversal (a line cutting two other lines). If the two other lines are parallel, the alternate angles are equal.

**altitude** in geometry, the perpendicular distance from a vertex (corner) of a triangle to the base (the side opposite the vertex). In ordinary terms, the altitude is the height of the triangle.

**angle** in geometry, an amount of rotation. Angles are measured in degrees or radians. An angle of 90° (90 degrees) is a right angle. Angles of less than 90° are called *acute angles*; angles of more than 90° but less than 180° are *obtuse angles*. A *reflex angle* is an angle of more than 180° but less than 360°. *Complementary angles* are two angles that add up to 90°; *supplementary angles* are two angles that add up to 180°.

**apex** the highest point, or vertex, of a solid or plane (two-dimensional) figure, with respect to a particular base plane or line.

**Arabic numerals** or *Hindu–Arabic numerals* the symbols 0, 1, 2, 3, 4, 5, 6, 7, 8, 9, early forms of which were in use among the Arabs before being adapted by the peoples of Europe during the Middle Ages in place of Roman numerals. They appear to have originated in India, and reached Europe by way of Spain.

**arc** in geometry, a section of a curve. A circle has two types of arc. An arc that is less than a semicircle is called a *minor arc*; an arc that is greater than a semicircle is a *major arc*.

**area** a measure of surface, measured in square units (such as m² or km²).

**arithmetic** branch of mathematics that concerns all questions involving numbers, as in counting, measuring, or weighing. Simple arithmetic already existed in prehistoric times. The fundamental operations are addition and subtraction, and multiplication and division. Fractions, percentages, and ratios are developed from these operations.

**Modular arithmetic** deals with events recurring in regular cycles, and is used in describing the functioning of petrol engines, electrical generators, and so on. For example in the modulo-twelve system, the answer to a question as to what time it will be in five hours if it is now ten o'clock, can be expressed $10 \pm 5 \pm 3$.

**associative operation** an operation that is independent of the grouping of the numbers, terms, or symbols concerned. For example, multiplication is associative, as $4 \times (3 \times 2) = (4 \times 3) \times 2 = 24$; however, division is not, as $12 \div (4 \div 2) = 6$, but $(12 \div 4) \div 2 = 1.5$. Compare commutative operation and distributive operation.

**base** the number of different single-digit symbols used in a particular number system. Thus our usual (decimal) counting system of numbers (with symbols 0, 1, 2, 3, 4, 5, 6, 7, 8, 9) has the base 10. In the binary number system, which has only the symbols 1 and 0, the base is 2.

**bearing** angle that a fixed, distant point makes with true or magnetic north at the point of observation, or the angle of the path of a moving object with respect to the north lines. Bearings are measured in degrees and given as three-digit numbers increasing clockwise. For instance, NW would be denoted as 045M or 045T, depending on whether the reference line were magnetic (M) or true (T) north.

**binomial** in algebra, an expression consisting of two terms, such as $a + b$, $a - b$. The **binomial theorem**, discovered by English mathematician and physicist Isaac Newton (1642–1727) and first published in 1676, is a formula calculating any power of a binomial quantity.

**calculus** branch of mathematics that permits the manipulation of continuously varying quantities, used in practical problems involving such matters as changing speeds, problems

AREAS OF COMMON TWO-DIMENSIONAL SHAPES

| | |
|---|---|
| rectangle | *lb* |
| length *l*, breadth *b*, | |
| square | *l²* |
| side *l* | |
| triangle | 1/2*lh* |
| side *l*, perpendicular height *h* | |
| parallelogram | *lh* |
| side *l*, perpendicular height *h* | |
| circle | $\pi r^2$ |
| radius *r* | |

SURFACE AREAS OF COMMON THREE-DIMENSIONAL SHAPES

| | |
|---|---|
| sphere | $4\pi r^2$ |
| radius *r* | |
| cylinder (closed) | $2\pi r(h + r)$ |
| height *h*, radius of cross section *r* | |
| cube | $6l^2$ |
| side *l* | |

**Circle**

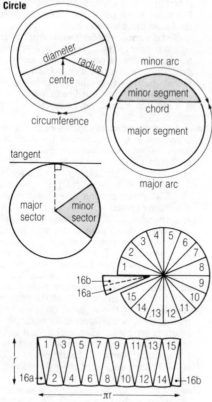

of flight, varying stresses in the framework of a bridge, and alternating current theory. *Integral calculus* deals with the method of summation, or adding together the effects of continuously varying quantities. *Differential calculus* deals in a similar way with rates of change. Many of its applications arose from the study of the gradients of the tangents to curves.

**cardinal number** one of a series of numbers 0, 1, 2, 3, 4 ... Cardinal numbers relate to quantity, whereas ordinal numbers (first, second, third, fourth ...) relate to order.

**chord** a straight line joining any two points on a curve. The chord that passes through the centre of a circle (its longest chord) is the diameter. The longest and shortest chords of an ellipse (a regular oval) are called the major and minor axes.

**circle** a path followed by a point that moves so as to keep a constant distance, the **radius**, from a fixed point, the **centre**. The longest distance in a straight line from one side of a circle to the other is called the **diameter**. It is twice the radius. The ratio of the distance all the way round the circle—the **circumference** —to the diameter is an irrational number called **pi** ($\pi$), roughly equal to 3.14159. A circle of diameter $d$ and radius $r$ has a circumference $C$ equal to $\pi d$, or $2\pi r$, and an area $A$ equal to $\pi r^2$. If a circle is divided up by two radii, then the

resulting divisions of its area are termed major and minor **sectors**. The area of a circle ($\pi r^2$) can be shown by dividing a circle into very thin sectors and reassembling them to make an approximate rectangle.

**circumference** in geometry, the curved line that encloses a plane, or two-dimensional, figure—for example, a circle or an ellipse. Its length varies according to the nature of the curve.

**coefficient** the number part in front of an algebraic term, signifying multiplication. For example, in the expression $4x^2 + 2xy - x$, the coefficient of $x^2$ is 4 (because $4x^2$ means $4 \times x^2$), that of $xy$ is 2 and that of $x$ is $-1$ (because $-1 \times x = -x$). In some algebraic expressions, coefficients are represented by letters called constants, that stand for numbers - for example, in the equation $ax^2 + bx + c = 0$, $a$, $b$ and $c$ are constants.

**commutative operation** an operation that is independent of the order of the numbers or symbols concerned. For example, addition is commutative: the result of adding $4 + 2$ is the same as that of adding $2 + 4$; subtraction is not: $4 - 2 = 2$, but $2 - 4 = -2$. Compare associative operation and distributive operation.

**complement** in set theory, all the members of a universal set that are not members of a particular set. A set and its complement add up to the whole. For example, if the universal set is the set of all positive whole numbers and the set $S$ is the set of all even numbers, then the complement of $S$ (denoted $S\underline{)}$) is the set of all odd numbers.

**concave** (of a surface) curving inwards, or away from the eye. For example, a bowl appears concave when viewed from above. In geometry, a concave polygon is one that has an interior angle greater than 180°. Compare convex.

**concentric** (of two or more circles) having the same centre but different radii.

**cone** in geometry, a solid figure having a plane (two-dimensional) curve as its base and tapering to a point (the vertex). The line joining the vertex to the centre of the base is called the axis of the cone. A circular cone has a circle as its base; a cone that has its axis at right angles to the base is called a right cone. A circular cone of perpendicular height $h$ and base of radius $r$ has a volume $V$ equal to $1/3 \, \pi r^2 h$. The distance from the edge of the base of a cone to the vertex is called the slant height. In a right circular cone of slant height $l$, the curved surface area is $\pi r l$, and the area of the base is $\pi r^2$. Therefore, the total surface area $A = \pi r l + \pi r^2 = \pi r(l + r)$.

**congruent** (of two or more plane or solid figures) having the same shape and size. With plane congruent figures, one figure will fit on top of the other exactly, though this may first require rotation and/or reflection (making a mirror image) of one of the figures.

**conic section** in geometry, curve obtained when a cone is intersected by a plane (two-dimensional surface). If the intersecting plane cuts both extensions of the cone it yields a hyperbola; if it

## THE MATHEMATICS OF CHAOS

Why are tides predictable years ahead, whereas weather forecasts often go wrong within a few days?

Both tides and weather are governed by natural laws. Tides are caused by the gravitational attraction of the Sun and Moon; the weather by the motion of the atmosphere under the influence of heat from the Sun. The law of gravitation is not noticeably simpler than the laws of fluid dynamics; yet for weather the resulting behaviour seems to be far more complicated.

The reason for this is *chaos*, which lies at the heart of one of the most exciting and most rapidly expanding areas of mathematical research, the theory of nonlinear dynamic systems.

It has been known for a long time that dynamic systems—systems that change with time according to fixed laws—can exhibit regular patterns, such as repetitive cycles. Thanks to new mathematical techniques, emphasizing shape rather than number, and to fast and sophisticated computer graphics, we now know that dynamic systems can also behave randomly. The difference lies not in the complexity of the formulae that define their mathematics, but in the geometrical features of the dynamics. This is a remarkable discovery: random behaviour in a system whose mathematical description contains no hint whatsoever of randomness.

Simple geometric structure produces simple dynamics. For example, if the geometry shrinks everything towards a fixed point, then the motion tends towards a steady state. But if the dynamics keep stretching things apart and then folding them together again, the motion tends to be chaotic—like food being mixed in a bowl. The motion of the Sun and Moon, on the kind of timescale that matters when we want to predict the tides, is a series of regular cycles, so prediction is easy. The changing patterns of the weather involve a great deal of stretching and folding, so here chaos reigns.

The geometry of chaos can be explored using theoretical mathematical techniques such as topology—'rubber-sheet geometry'—but the most vivid pictures are obtained using computer graphics. The geometric structures of chaos are *fractals*: they have detailed form on all scales of magnification. Order and chaos, traditionally seen as opposites, are now viewed as two aspects of the same basic process, the evolution of a system in time. Indeed, there are now examples where both order and chaos occur naturally within a single geometrical form.

Does chaos make randomness predictable? Sometimes. If what looks like random behaviour is actually governed by a dynamic system, then short-term prediction becomes possible. Long-term prediction is not as easy, however. In chaotic systems any initial error of measurement, however small, will grow rapidly and eventually ruin the prediction. This is known as the butterfly effect : if a butterfly flaps its wings, a month later the air disturbance created may cause a hurricane.

Chaos can be applied to many areas of science, such as chemistry, engineering, computer sicence, biology, electronics, and astronomy. For example, although the short-term motions of the Sun and Moon are not chaotic, the long-term motion of the Solar System *is* chaotic. It is impossible to predict on which side of the Sun Pluto will lie in 200 million years' time. Saturn's satellite *Hyperion* tumbles chaotically. Chaos caused by Jupiter's gravitational field can fling asteroids out of orbit, towards the Earth. Disease epidemics, locust plagues, and irregular heartbeats are more down-to-earth examples of chaos, on a more human timescale.

Chaos places limits on science: it implies that even when we know the equations that govern a system's behaviour, we may not in practice be able to make effective predictions. On the other hand, it opens up new avenues for discovery, because it implies that apparently random phenomena may have simple, non-random explanations. So chaos is changing the way scientists think about what they do: the relation between determinism and chance, the role of experiment, the computability of the world, the prospects for prediction, and the interaction between mathematics, science, and nature. Chaos cuts right across traditional subject boundaries, and distinctions between pure and applied mathematicians, between mathematicians and physicists, between physicists and biologists, become meaningless when compared to the unity revealed by their joint efforts.

is parallel to the side of the cone it produces a parabola. Other intersecting planes produce a circle or an ellipse. Conic sections were first discovered by the ancient Greeks.

**constant** a fixed quantity or one that does not change its value in relation to variables. For example, in the algebraic expression $y^2 = x$ m2 3, the number 3 is a constant; so too are $a$ and $b$ in the general equation $ax \pm b = 0$.

**converse** the reversed order of a conditional statement; the converse of the statement 'if $a$..., then $b$...' is 'if $b$..., then $a$...'. The converse does not always hold true; for example, the converse of 'if $x = 3$, then $x^2 = 9$' is 'if $x^2 =$ 9, then $x = 3$', which is not true, as $x$ could also be –3.

**convex** curving outwards, or towards the eye. For example, the outer surface of a ball appears convex. In geometry, the term is used to describe any polygon possessing no interior angle greater than 180°. Compare concave.

**coordinate geometry** or *analytical geometry* a system of geometry in which points, lines, shapes, and surfaces are represented by algebraic expressions. In plane (two-dimensional) coordinate geometry, the plane is usually defined by two axes at right angles to each other, the horizontal $x$-axis (abscissa) and the vertical $y$-axis (ordinate), crossing at 0, the origin. A

## MATHEMATICAL SYMBOLS

| | |
|---|---|
| $a \rightarrow b$ | $a$ implies $b$ |
| $x$ | unknown |
| $\infty$ | infinity |
| $a \sim b$ | numerical difference between $a$ and $b$ |
| $a \approx b$ | $a$ approximately equal to $b$ |
| $a = b$ | $a$ equal to $b$ |
| $a \equiv b$ | $a$ identical with $b$ (for formulae only) |
| $a > b$ | $a$ greater than $b$ |
| $a < b$ | $a$ smaller than $b$ |
| $a \neq b$ | $a$ not equal to $b$ |
| $b < a < c$ | $a$ greater than $b$ and smaller than $c$, that is, $a$ lies between the values $b$ and $c$ but cannot equal either |
| $a \geq b$ | $a$ equal to or greater than $b$, that is, $a$ at least as great as $b$ |
| $a \leq b$ | $a$ equal to or less than $b$, that is, $a$ at most as great as $b$ |
| $b \leq a \leq c$ | $a$ lies between the values $b$ and $c$ and could take the values $b$ and $c$ |
| $\lvert a \rvert$ | absolute value of $a$: this is always positive, for example $\lvert -5 \rvert = 5$ |
| $+$ | addition sign, positive |
| $-$ | subtraction sign, negative |
| $\times$ or $.$ | multiplication sign, times |
| $\div$ | division sign, divided by |
| $a + b = c$ | $a + b$, read as '$a$ plus $b$', denotes the addition of $a$ and $b$. The result of the addition, $c$, is also known as the sum. |
| $a - b = c$ | $a - b$, read as '$a$ minus $b$', denotes subtraction of $b$ from $a$<br>$a - b$, or $c$ is the difference. Subtraction is the opposite of addition. |
| $a \times b = c$<br>$ab = c$<br>$a.b = c$ | $a \times b$, read as '$a$ multiplied by $b$', denotes multiplication of $a$ by $b$; $c$ is the product, $a$ and $b$ are factors of $c$ |

| | |
|---|---|
| $a \div b = c$<br>$a/b = c$ | $a \div b$, read as '$a$ divided by $b$', denotes division. $a$ is the dividend, $b$ is the divisor, $c$ is the quotient.<br>In the fraction $a/b$, $a$ is the numerator $b$ the denominator |
| $a : b$ | ratio of $a$ to $b$ |
| $a^b = c$ | $a^b$, read as '$a$ to the power $b$', $a$ is the base, $b$ the exponent, or index |
| $^b\sqrt{a} = c$ | $^b\sqrt{a}$, is the $b$th root of $a$, $b$ being known as the root exponent. In the special case of $^2\sqrt{a} = c$, $c$ is known as the square root of $a$, and the root exponent is usually omitted, that is, $^2\sqrt{a} = \sqrt{a}$ |
| $n!$ | factorial of the positive integer $n$, denotes $n \times (n-1) \times (n-2) \times (n-3) \ldots 3 \times 2 \times 1$ |
| $\int$ | indefinite integral |
| $\int_a^b f(x) dx$ | definite integral, or integral between $x = a$ and $x = b$ |
| $e$ | exponential constant and the base of natural (Napierian) logarithms $= 2.7182818284 \ldots$ |
| $\pi$ | ratio of the circumference of a circle to its diameter $= 3.1415925535 \ldots$ |
| $p \in S$ | $p$ is a member of the set $S$ |
| $p \notin S$ | $p$ is not a member of $S$ |
| $S \subset T$ | $S$ is a subset of $T$, all members of $S$ are also members of the larger set $T$ |
| $T \not\subset S$ | $T$ is not a subset of $S$, not all members of $T$ are members of $S$ |
| $S \cap T$ | intersection of sets $S$ and $T$, denotes all elements that are members of both $S$ and $T$ |
| $S \cup T$ | union of sets $S$ and $T$, denotes all elements that are members of either $S$ or $T$ |
| $S'$ | complement of set $S$, denotes all elements that are not members of $S$ |
| U<br>$\mathscr{E}$ | universal set, the union of any set and its complement |
| $\{ \}$<br>$\varnothing$ | empty set, set that has no members |

point on the plane can be represented by a pair of Cartesian coordinates, which define its position in terms of its distance along the $x$-axis and along the $y$-axis from O. These distances are respectively the $x$ and $y$ coordinates of the point.

Lines are represented as equations; for example, $y = 2x + 1$ gives a straight line, and $y = 3x^2 + 2x$ gives a parabola (a curve). Different lines and curves can be drawn by plotting the coordinates of points that satisfy their equations and joining up the points. One of the advantages of coordinate geometry is that geometrical solutions can be obtained without drawing but by manipulating algebraic expressions. For example, the coordinates of the point of intersection of two straight lines can be determined by finding the unique values of $x$ and $y$ that satisfy both of the equations for the lines, that is, by solving them as a pair of simultaneous equations. The curves studied in simple coordinate geometry are the conic sections (circle, ellipse, parabola, and hyperbola) each of which has its own characteristic equation.

**cosine** in trigonometry, a function of an angle in a right-angled triangle found by dividing the length of the side adjacent to the angle by the length of the hypotenuse (the longest side).

**cube** in geometry, a solid figure whose faces are all squares. It has six equal-area faces and 12 equal-length edges. If the length of one edge is $l$, the volume of the cube $V$ is equal to $l^3$ and its surface area $A$ equals $6l^2$.

**cuboid** in geometry, a solid figure whose faces are all rectangles. A brick is a cuboid.

**curve** in geometry, the locus of a point moving according to specified conditions. The best-known of all curves is the circle, which is the locus of all points equidistant from a given

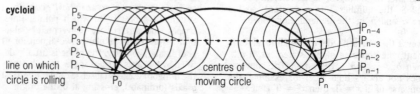

cycloid

line on which circle is rolling

circle is rolling

centres of moving circle

point (the centre). Other common geometrical curves are the ellipse, parabola, and hyperbola, which are also produced when a cone is cut by a plane (two-dimensional surface) at different angles. Many curves have been invented for the solution of special problems in geometry and mechanics—for example, the cissoid and the cycloid.

**cybernetics** (Greek *kubernan*, 'to steer') science concerned with how systems organize, regulate, and reproduce themselves, and also how they evolve and learn. In the laboratory inanimate objects are created that behave like living systems. Uses range from the creation of electronic artificial limbs to the running of the fully automated factory where decision-making machines operate at up to managerial level. Cybernetics was founded and named in 1947 by US mathematician Norbert Wiener.

**cycloid** in geometry, a curve resembling a series of arches traced out by a point on the circumference of a circle that rolls along a straight line. It has such applications as studying the motion of wheeled vehicles along roads and tracks.

**cylinder** in geometry, a tubular solid figure with a circular cross-section, ordinarily understood to be a right cylinder (that is, having its curved surface at right angles to the base). The volume $V$ of a cylinder of radius $r$ and height $h$ is given by $V = \pi r^2 h$. Its total surface area $A$ has the formula $A = 2\pi r \,(h + r)$ where $2\pi r h$ is the curved surface area, and $2\pi r^2$ is the area of both ends.

**decimal fraction** fraction expressed by the use of the decimal point, that is, a fraction in which the denominator is any higher power of 10. Thus 3/10, 51/100, 23/1,000 are decimal fractions and are normally expressed as 0.3, 0.51, 0.023. The use of decimals greatly simplifies addition and multiplication of fractions, though not all fractions can be expressed exactly as decimal fractions. The regular use of the decimal point appears to have been introduced about 1585, but the occasional use of decimal fractions can be traced back as far as the 12th century.

**degree** (symbol °) a unit of measurement of an angle. One complete revolution, or circle, is divided into 360°; a degree is subdivided into 60 minutes (symbol '). A quarter-turn, or right angle is 90°; a half-turn, or the angle on a straight line, is 180°.

**denominator** the number or symbol that appears below the line in a vulgar fraction. For example, the denominator of 3/4 is 4. The denominator represents the fraction's divisor, or the number of equal parts into which the whole may be considered to have been divided. Compare numerator.

**differentiation** a procedure for finding the rate of change of one variable quantity relative to another. Together, differentation and integration of functions make up calculus.

**distributive operation** an operation, such as multiplication, that bears a relationship to another operation, such as addition, such that

**Ellipse**

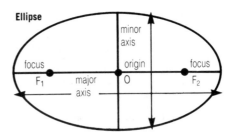

$a \times (b + c) = (a \times b) + (a \times c)$. For example, $3 \times (2 + 4) = (3 \times 2) + (3 \times 4) = 18$. Multiplication may be said to be distributive over addition. Addition is not, however, distributive over multiplication because $3 + (2 \times 4) \neq (3 + 2) \times (3 + 4)$. Compare associative operation and commutative operation.

**ellipse** in geometry, a curve joining all points (loci) around two fixed points (foci) so that the sum of the distances from those points is always constant. The diameter passing through the foci is the major axis, and the diameter bisecting this at right angles is the minor axis. An ellipse is one of a series of curves known as conic sections; a slice across a cone that is not made parallel to, or does not pass through, the base will produce an ellipse.

**epicycloid** in geometry, a curve resembling a series of arches traced out by a point on the circumference of a circle that rolls around another circle of a different diameter. If the two circles have the same diameter, the curve is a **cardioid**. Greek mathematicians thought that planets moved in small circles (epicycles) while completing a large circle (the deferent) round the Earth.

**equation** expression that represents the equality of two expressions involving constants and/or variables, and thus usually includes an equals sign (=). For example, the equation $A = \pi r^2$ equates the area $A$ of a circle of radius $r$ to the product $\pi r^2$. The algebraic equation $y = mx + c$ is the general one in coordinate geometry for a straight line.

If a mathematical equation is true for all variables in a given domain, it is sometimes called an identity and denoted by ≡.

**equilateral** having all sides of equal length. For example, a square and a rhombus are both equilateral four-sided figures. An equilateral triangle, to which the term is most often applied, has all three sides equal and all three angles equal (at 60°).

**exponent** or **power** or **index** a number that indicates the number of times a term is multiplied by itself. It is written a superior small numeral. For example, in $x^2$ the exponent is 2 and signifies $x \times x$; in $4^5$ the exponent is 5 and signifies $4 \times 4 \times 4 \times 4 \times 4$. Exponents obey certain rules. Terms that contain them are multiplied by adding the exponents - for example, $x^2 \times x^5 = x^7$; and divided by subtracting the exponents - for example, $y^5 \div y^3 = y^2$. Any number with an exponent of 0 is equal to 1, for example, $x^0 = 1$ and $99^0 = 1$.

**exponential** a function in which the variable quantity is an exponent (power, or index) to which another number or expression is raised. For example, $f(x) = a^x$ is an exponential function in which $a$ is typically a number, say 5, and $x$ is the exponent (0.1, 0.5, m210, and so on). Such functions are always positive and their values get closer and closer to 0 with increasingly negative values of $x$.

The term **exponential function** usually refers to $f(x) = e^x$, the basis of natural, or Naperian, logarithms and definitive of many natural phenomena of growth and decay (such as the radioactive decay of various isotopes). In this expression $e$ is an irrational number equal to 2.71828... **Exponential growth** is a form of increase in numbers in which the rate of growth is slow at first but then rises sharply. It applies, for example, to uncontrolled population growth.

**factor** a number that divides into another number exactly. For example, the factors of 64 are 1, 2, 4, 8, 16, 32, and 64. In algebra, certain kinds of polynomials (expressions consisting of several or many terms) can be factorized. For example, the factors of $x^2 + 3x + 2$ are $x + 1$ and $x + 2$, since $x^2 + 3x + 2 = (x + 1)(x + 2)$.

**factorial** of a positive number, the product of all the whole numbers (integers) inclusive between 1 and the number itself. A factorial is indicated by the symbol !. For example, 6! $= 1 \times 2 \times 3 \times 4 \times 5 \times 6 = 720$. Zero factorial, 0!, is defined as 1.

**fractal** (Latin *fractus*, 'broken') an irregular shape or surface produced by a procedure of repeated subdivision. Generated on a computer screen, fractals are used in creating models for geographical or biological processes (for example, the creation of a coastline by erosion or accretion, or the growth of plants). They are also used for computer art.

**fraction** a number that indicates one or more equal parts of a whole. The usual way of denoting this is to place below a horizontal line the number of equal parts into which the unit is divided (denominator), and above the line the number of these parts comprising the fraction (numerator); thus 2/3 or 3/4. Such fractions are called **vulgar** or **simple fractions**. The denominator can never be zero.

A **proper fraction** is one in which the numerator is less than the denominator. An **improper fraction** is one in which the numerator is larger than the denominator—for example, 3/2. An improper fraction can therefore be expressed as a mixed number, for example, 11/2. A **decimal fraction** has as its denominator a power of 10 (10, 100, 1,000, and so on), but this is omitted and is expressed instead by the position of the numerator after a dot or point (the decimal point)—for example, 0.4 is 4/10, 0.04 is 4/100, and 0.004 is 4/1,000.

**function** a procedure that defines a relationship between quantities, usually variables. For example, in the algebraic expression $y = 4x^3 \pm 2$, the variable $y$ is a function of the variable $x$, generally written as $f(x)$. Functions are commonly used in applied mathematics, physics, and science generally—for example, the formula $t = 2\pi(l/g)^{1/2}$ shows that, for a simple pendulum, the time of swing $t$ is a function of its length $l$ and of no other variable quantity ($\pi$ and $g$, the acceleration due to gravity, are constants).

**geometry** branch of mathematics concerned with the properties of space, usually in terms of plane (two-dimensional) and solid (three-dimensional) figures. It probably originated in Egypt, in land measurements necessitated by the periodic inundations of the River Nile, and was soon extended into surveying and navigation. Early geometers were Thales, Pythagoras, and Euclid. Analytical methods were introduced and developed by Descartes in the 17th century. The subject is usually divided into **pure geometry**, which embraces roughly the plane and solid geometry dealt with in Euclid's *Elements*, and **analytical** or **coordinate geometry**, in which problems are solved using algebraic methods. A third, quite distinct, type includes the **non-Euclidean geometries**, which proved significant in the development of the theory of relativity and in the formulation of atomic theory.

**group** a finite or infinite set of elements that can be combined by an operation; formally, a group must satisfy certain conditions. For example, the set of all integers (positive or negative whole numbers) forms a group with regard to addition because: (1) addition is associative, that is, the sum of two or more integers is the same regardless of the order in which the integers are added; (2) adding two integers gives another integer; (3) the set includes an identity element 0, which has no effect on any integer to which it is added (for example, $0 + 3 = 3$); and (4) each integer has an inverse (for instance, 7 has the inverse $-7$), such that the sum of an integer and its inverse is 0. **Group theory** is the study of the properties of groups.

**helix** in geometry, a three-dimensional curve resembling a screw thread. It is generated by a line that encircles a cylinder or cone at a constant angle. Formally, a group must satisfy certain conditons $G$ that can be combined by an operation *, provided the following four conditions are satisfied ($a$, $b$, and $c$ are all elements, or members, of $G$): (1) the set is closed under b6, that is, if $a$ b6 $b = p$, then $p$ must be a member of $G$; (2) $G$ contains an identity element $I$ such that $a$ b6 $I = I$ b6 $a = a$; (3) each element $a$ has an inverse $a^{-1}$ such that $a$ b6 $a^{-1} = 1$; (4) the operation is associative, that is, ($a$ b6 $b$) b6 $c = a$ b6 ($b$ b6 $c$). **Group theory** is the study of the properties of groups.

**hyperbola** in geometry, a curve formed by cutting a right circular cone with a plane (two-dimensional surface) so that the angle between the plane and the base is greater than the angle between the base and the side of the cone. It is a member of the family of curves known as conic sections.

**hypotenuse** the longest side of a right-angled triangle, that is, the side opposite the right angle.

**infinity** quantity that is larger than any fixed assignable quantity; symbol $\infty$. By convention, the result of dividing any number by zero is regarded as infinity.

**integer** a positive or negative whole number—for example, 3 and 0. Fractions, such as $\frac{1}{2}$ and 0.35, are known as nonintegral numbers.

**integration** a method in calculus of evaluating definite or indefinite integrals. An example of a definite integral can be thought of as finding the area under a curve (as represented by an algebraic expression or function) between particular values of the function's variable. In practice, integral calculus provides scientists with a powerful tool for doing calculations that involve a continually varying quantity (such as determing the position at any given instant of a space rocket that is accelerating away from Earth). Its basic principles were discovered in the late 1660s independently by the German philosopher Gottfried Leibniz and the British scientist Isaac Newton.

**interest** in finance, a sum of money paid to an investor in return for the loan, usually expressed as percentage per annum. *Simple interest* is interest calculated as a straight percentage of the amount invested. In *compound interest*, the interest earned over a period of time (for example, per annum) is added to the investment, so that at the end of the next period interest is paid on that total.

A sum of £100 invested at 10% per annum simple interest for five years earns £10 a year, giving a total of £50 interest (and at the end of the period the investor receives a total of £150). The same sum of £100 invested for five years at 10% compound interest earns a total of £61.05 interest (with £161.05 returned at the end of the period). Generally, for a sum $S$ invested at $x$% simple interest for $y$ years, the total amount returned is $S + xyS/100$. If it is invested at $x$% compound interest for $y$ years, the total amount returned is $S[(100 + x)/100]^y$.

**linear equation** an equation involving two variables $(x,y)$, of the general form $y = mx + c$, where $m$ and $c$ are constants. In coordinate geometry, such an equation plotted using Cartesian coordinates gives a straight-line graph of slope $m$; $c$ is the value of $y$ where the line crosses the $y$-axis. Linear equations can be used to describe the behaviour of buildings, bridges, and other static structures.

**locus** (Latin 'place') in geometry, the path traced by a moving point. For example, the locus of a point that moves so that it is always at the same distance from another fixed point is a circle; the locus of a point that is always at the same distance from two fixed points is a straight line that perpendicularly bisects the line joining them.

**logarithm** or *log* the exponent of a number to a specified base. If $b^a = x$, then $a$ is the logarithm of $x$ to the base $b$. Before the advent of cheap electronic calculators, the multiplication and division of large numbers could be simplified by substituting respectively the addition and subtraction of those numbers' logarithms. Tables of logarithms and antilogarithms are available (usually to the base 10) that show conversions of numbers to logarithms, and vice versa.

For any two numbers $x$ and $y$ (where $x = b^a$ and $y = b^c$), $x \times y = b^a + b^c = b^{a+c}$. Therefore, the product of $x$ and $y$ can be found by adding their logarithms ($a$ and $b$), and looking up this figure in antilogarithm tables. For example, to multiply $6,560 \times 980$, one would look up the logarithms of these numbers (3.8169 and 2.9912), add them together (6.8081), then look up the antilogarithm of this to get the answer (6,428,000). Natural, or Naperian, logarithms are to the base $e$, an irrational number equal to approximately 2.7183. Log tables (to the base $e$) were first published 1614 by Scottish mathematician John Napier; base-10 logs were introduced from 1624 by Henry Briggs of England and Adriaen Vlacq of the Netherlands.

**magic square** a square array of different numbers in which the rows, columns, and diagonals add up to the same total. A simple example employing the numbers 1 to 9, with a total of 15, is:

$$\begin{array}{ccc} 6 & 7 & 2 \\ 1 & 5 & 9 \\ 8 & 3 & 4 \end{array}$$

**matrix** a square ($n \times n$) or rectangular ($m \times n$) array of elements (numbers or algebraic variables). They are a means of condensing information about mathematical systems and can be used for, among other things, solving simultaneous linear equations and transformations.

**maximum and minimum** points at which the slope of a curve representing a function in coordinate geometry changes from positive to negative (maximum), or from negative to positive (minimum). A tangent to a curve at a maximum or minimum has zero gradient (is horizontal). Maxima and minima can be found by differentiating the function for the curve and setting the differential to zero (the value of the slope at the turning point). For example, differentiating the function for the parabola $y = 2x^2 - 8x$ gives $dy/dx = 4x - 8$. Setting this equal to zero gives $x = 2$, so that $y = -8$ (found by substituting $x = 2$ into the parabola equation). Thus the function has a minimum at the point (2, –8).

**mean** a measure of the average of a number of terms or quantities. The simple *arithmetic mean* is the average value of the quantities, that is, the sum of the quantities divided by their number. The *weighted mean* takes into account the frequency of the terms that are summed; it is calculated by multiplying each term by the number of times it occurs, summing the results and dividing this total by the total number of occurrences. The *geometric mean* is the corresponding root of the product of the quantities.

**modulus** the positive value of a real number, irrespective of its sign, indicated by a pair of vertical lines. Thus $|3|$ is 3; and $|-5|$ is 5.

**number** a symbol used in counting or measuring. In mathematics, there are various kinds of numbers. The everyday number system is the decimal ('proceeding by tens') system, using the base 10. *Real numbers* include all rational numbers (integers, or whole numbers, and fractions) and irrational numbers (those not expressible as fractions). *Complex numbers* are of the form $a + ib$, where $a$ and $b$ are real numbers and $i$ is the square root of $-1$ (an imaginary number). The complex numbers include real numbers (when $b$ is zero).

The numerals, 0, 1, 2, 3, 4, 5, 6, 7, 8, 9, give a counting system which, to the base ten, continues 10, 11, 12, 13, and so on. These are positive whole numbers, with fractions represented as 1/4, 1/2, 3/4 and so on, or as decimal fractions (0.25, 0.5, 0.75 and so on). They are also rational numbers. Irrational numbers cannot be represented as fractions and require symbols, such as $\sqrt{2}$, $\pi$, and $e$: they can be expressed numerically only as the (inexact) approximations 1.414, 3.142 and 2.728 (to three places of decimals) respectively.

**numerator** the number or symbol that appears above the line in a vulgar fraction. For example, the numerator of 5/6 is 5. The numerator represents the fraction's dividend and indicates how many of the equal parts indicated by the denominator (number or symbol below the line) comprise the fraction.

**ordinal number** one of the series first, second, third, fourth,... . Ordinal numbers relate to order, whereas cardinal numbers (1, 2, 3, 4,...) relate to quantity, or count.

**ordinate** in coordinate geometry, the vertical or $y$ coordinate, that is, the distance of a point from the horizontal or $x$-axis. For example, a point with the coordinates (3,4) has an ordinate of 4.

**origin** in coordinate geometry, the point at which the horizontal $x$-axis and vertical $y$-axis cross, and therefore the point at which both $x$ and $y$ equal 0.

**parabola** in geometry, a curve formed by cutting a right circular cone with a plane (two-dimensional figure) parallel to the sloping side of the cone; it is one of the family of curves known as conic sections. A parabola can also be defined as a path traced out by a point that moves in such a way that it is always the same distance from a fixed point (focus) and a fixed straight line (directrix). The corresponding solid figure, the *paraboloid*, is formed by rotating a parabola about its axis. The parabola is a common shape for headlamp reflectors, dish-shaped microwave and radar aerials, and for radiotelescopes. A source of radiation placed at the focus of a paraboloidal reflector is propagated as a parallel beam.

**parallel lines and parallel planes** straight lines or planes (two-dimensional surfaces) that always remain the same perpendicular distance from one another no matter how far they

**Polygon**

| | number of sides | sum of interior angles (degrees) |
|---|---|---|
| triangle | 3 | 180 |
| quadrilateral | 4 | 360 |
| pentagon | 5 | 540 |
| hexagon | 6 | 720 |
| heptagon | 7 | 900 |
| octagon | 8 | 1,080 |
| decagon | 10 | 1,440 |
| duodecagon | 12 | 1,800 |
| icosagon | 20 | 3,240 |

are extended. This is a principle of Euclidean geometry. Some non-Euclidean geometries, such as elliptical and hyperbolic geometry, however, reject Euclid's parallel axiom.

**parallelogram** in geometry, a quadrilateral (four-sided plane figure) with opposite pairs of sides equal in length and parallel, and opposite angles equal. When all four sides are equal in length, the parallelogram is known as a rhombus; when the internal angles are right angles, it is a rectangle or square. The diagonals of a parallelogram bisect each other. Its area is the product of the length of one side and the perpendicular distance between this side and the side parallel to it.

**percentage** a way of representing a number as a fraction of 100. Thus 45 per cent (or 45%) equals 45/100, and 45% of 20 is 45/100 × 20 = 9. In general, if a quantity $x$ changes to $y$, the percentage change is $100(x - y)/x$. Thus, if the number of people in a room changes from 40 to 50, the percentage increase is $(100 \times 10)/40 = 25\%$. To express a fraction as a percentage, its denominator must first be converted to 100, for example, 1/8 = 12.5/100 = 12.5%. The use of percentages often makes it easier to compare fractions that do not have a common denominator.

**perimeter** the line enclosing a plane (two-dimensional) figure, or the distance measured around the figure's boundary. For example, the perimeter of a square is its four sides (or four times the length of one side); the perimeter of a circle is its circumference.

**permutation** a specified arrangement of a group of objects. In general, the number of permutations of $a$ items taken $b$ at a time is given by $a!/(a \text{ m2 } b)!$, where the symbol ! stands for factorial (the product of all the integers (whole numbers) up to and including the number). For example, the number of permutations of four letters taken from any group of six different letters is $6!/2! = (1 \times 2 \times 3 \times 4 \times 5 \times 6)/(1 \times 2) = 360$. The theoretical number of four-letter 'words' that can be made from an alphabet of 26 letters is $26!/22! = 358,800$.

**perpendicular** or *normal* term describing a line that is oriented at right angles (90°) to another line or to a plane (two-dimensional) surface. A vertical line is perpendicular to a horizontal line.

**polygon** in geometry, a plane (two-dimensional) figure with three or more straight-line sides. Common polygons have their own names, which define the number of sides (for example, triangle, quadrilateral, pentagon). These are all convex polygons, having no interior angle greater than 180°. In general, the more sides a polygon has, the larger the sum of its internal angles and, in the case of a convex polygon, the more closely it approximates a circle.

**polyhedron** in geometry, a solid figure with four or more plane, or two-dimensional, faces. Common polyhedra have their own names (for example, pyramid, tetrahedron, cube, cuboid, prism). The more faces there are on a polyhedron, the more closely it approximates a sphere. There are only five types of regular polyhedra (with all faces the same size and shape), as was deduced by early Greek mathematicians; they are the tetrahedron (four equilateral triangular faces), cube (six square faces), octahedron (eight equilateral triangles), dodecahedron (12 regular pentagons) and icosahedron (20 equilateral triangles).

**prime number** a number that can be divided only by 1 or itself, that is, having no other factors. There is an infinite number of primes, the first ten of which are 2, 3, 5, 7, 11, 13, 17, 19, 23, and 29 (by definition, the number 1 is excluded from the set of prime numbers). The number 2 is the only even prime because all other even numbers have 2 as a factor.

In 1989 researchers at Amdahl Corporation, Sunnyvale, California, calculated the largest known prime number. It has 65,087 digits, and is more than a trillion trillion trillion times as large as the previous record holder. It took over a year of computation to locate the number and prove it was a prime.

**prism** in geometry, a solid figure whose cross-section is constant in planes drawn perpendicular to its axis. A cylinder is a prism of circular cross-section.

**probability** the likelihood or chance that something will happen, often expressed as 'odds' or as a fraction. In general, the probability that $n$ particular events will happen out of a total of $m$ possible events is $n/m$. A certainty has a probability of 1; an impossibility has a probability of 0.

In tossing an unbiased coin the chance that it will land heads is the same as the chance that it will land tails, that is, 1 to 1 or 'even'; mathematically this probability is expressed as 1/2 or 0.5. The odds against any chosen number coming up on the roll of an unbiased dice are 5 to 1; the probability is 1/6 or 0.1666... If two dice are rolled there are $6 \times 6 = 36$ different possible combinations. A double (two numbers the same) occurs in six of these combinations; thus the probability is 6/36 or 0.1666...

Probability theory was first developed by French mathematicians Blaise Pascal and Pierre de Fermat, initially in response to a request to calculate the odds of being dealt various hands at cards. Today probability plays a major part in the mathematics of atomic theory and finds application in insurance and statistical studies.

**progression** sequence of numbers each formed by a specific relationship to its predecessor: an **arithmetical progression** has numbers that increase or decrease by a common sum or difference (for example, 2, 4, 6, 8, 10); a **geometric progression** has numbers each bearing a fixed ratio to its predecessor (for example, 3, 6, 12, 24, 48), and a **harmonic progression** is a sequence with numbers whose reciprocals are in arithmetical progression (for example, 1, 1/2, 1/3, 1/4, 1/5).

**proportional** related by a constant ratio. Two variable quantities $x$ and $y$ are proportional if, for all values of $x$, $y = ax$, where $a$ is a constant. This means that if $x$ increases, $y$ increases in a linear fashion. A graph of $x$ against $y$ would be a straight line passing through the origin (the point $x = 0$, $y = 0$). $y$ is **inversely proportional** to $x$ if the graph of $y$ against $1/x$ is a straight line through the origin. The corresponding equation is $y = a/x$. Many laws of science relate quantities that are proportional.

**pyramid** in geometry, a solid figure with triangular side-faces meeting at a common vertex (point) and with a polygon as its base. The volume of a pyramid, no matter how many faces it has, is equal to the area of the base multiplied by one-third of the perpendicular height. A pyramid with a triangular base is called a tetrahedron; the Egyptian pyramids have square bases.

**Pythagoras' theorem** in geometry, theorem stating that in a right-angled triangle, the area of the square on the hypotenuse (the longest side) is equal to the sum of the areas of the squares drawn on the other two sides. If the hypotenuse is $h$ units long and the lengths of the other sides are $a$ and $b$, then $h^2 = a^2 + b^2$. The theorem provides a way of calculating the length of any side of a right-angled triangle if the lengths of the other two sides are known.

**quadratic equation** an equation containing as its highest exponent, or power, the square of a single unknown variable, such as $x$, for example, $3x^2 + 2x + 2 = 0$. The general formula of such equations is $ax^2 + bx + c = 0$, in which $a$, $b$, and $c$ are real numbers, and only the coefficient $a$ cannot equal 0. In coordinate geometry, a quadratic equation represents a parabola.

Depending on the value of $b^2 - 4ac$ (the **discriminant**), the roots, or solutions, of a quadratic equation are either two real roots or two complex roots (when $b^2 - 4ac < 0$, two different real roots; when $b^2 - 4ac = 0$, two equal real roots; and when $b^2 - 4ac > 0$, two different complex roots). Some quadratic equations can be solved by factorization, or the the values of $x$ may be found by using the formula $x = [-b \pm \sqrt{(b^2 - 4ac)}]/2a$.

**radian** in geometry, an alternative unit to the degree for measuring angles. It is the angle at the centre of a circle when the centre is joined to the two ends of an arc (part of the circumference) equal in length to the radius of the circle. There are $2\pi$ (approximately 6.284) radians in a full circle (360°); 1 radian is approximately 57°, and 1° is $\pi/180$ or approximately 0.0175 radians. Radians are commonly used to specify angles in polar coordinates.

**ratio** measure of the relative size of two quantities or of two measurements (in similar units), expressed as a proportion. For example, the ratio of vowels to consonants in the alphabet is 5:21; the ratio of 500 m to 2 km is 500:2,000, or 1:4.

**reciprocal** of a quantity, that quantity divided into 1. Thus the reciprocal of 2 is 1/2 (= 0.5); of 150 is 1/150 (= 0.00666666...); of $x^2$ is $1/x^2$ or $x^{-2}$.

**rectangle** a quadrilateral (four-sided figure) with opposite sides equal and parallel, and with each interior angle a right angle (90°). The diagonals of a rectangle bisect each other. Its area $A$ is the product of its length $l$ and breadth $b$; that is, $A = l \times b$. A rectangle is a special case of a parallelogram. A rectangle with all four sides equal is a square.

**rhombus** a diamond-shaped plane figure, a parallelogram with four equal sides (opposite sides are equal in length and parallel) and no internal angle that is a right angle (otherwise it is a square). Its diagonals bisect each other at right angles. The area of a rhombus is equal to the length of a side multiplied by its height (the perpendicular distance between opposite sides).

**right-angled triangle** a triangle in which one of the angles is a right angle (90°). It is the basic form of triangle for defining trigonometrical ratios (for example, sine, cosine and tangent) and for which Pythagoras' theorem holds true. The longest side of a right-angled triangle is called the **hypotenuse**. Its area is equal to half the product of the other two sides. A triangle constructed on the diameter of a circle with its opposite vertex (corner) on the circumference is a right-angled triangle, a fundamental theorem in geometry first credited to the Greek mathematician Thales about 580 BC.

**Roman numerals** an old number system using different symbols from today's Arabic numerals (the ordinary numbers 1, 2, 3, 4, 5, and so on). The seven key symbols in Roman numerals as represented today (originally they were a little different) are I (= 1), V (= 5), X (= 10), L (= 50), C (= 100), D (= 500), and M (= 1,000). There is no zero. The first fifteen Roman numerals are I, II, III, IV (or IIII), V, VI, VII, VIII, IX, X, XI, XII, XIII, XIV, and XV; the multiples of 10 from 20 to 90 are XX, XXX, XL, L, LX, LXX, LXXX, and XC; and the year 1992 becomes MCMXCII. Although addition and subtraction are fairly straightforward using Roman numerals, the

**topology**

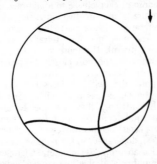

this figure is topologically equivalent to this one

absence of a zero makes other arithmetic operations (such as multiplication) clumsy and difficult.

**scalar quantity** any quantity that has magnitude but no direction, as distinct from a vector quantity, which has direction as well as magnitude. Speed, mass, and volume are scalar quantities.

**set** any collection of defined things (elements), provided the elements are distinct and that there is a rule to decide whether an element is a member of the set. It is usually denoted by a capital letter and indicated by curly brackets { }. For example, $L = \{$letters of the alphabet$\}$ represents the set that consists of all the letters of the alphabet. The symbol $\epsilon$ stands for 'is a member of'; thus $p \epsilon L$ means that p belongs to the set consisting of all letters, and $4 \notin L$ means that 4 does not belong to the set consisting of all letters.

A **finite set** has a limited number of members, such as $\{$letters of the alphabet$\}$; an **infinite set** has an unlimited number of members, such as $\{$all whole numbers$\}$; an **empty** or **null set** has no members, such as the number of people who have swum across the Atlantic Ocean, written as { } or $\varnothing$. Sets with some members in common are **intersecting sets**; for example, if $R = \{$red playing cards$\}$ and $F = \{$face cards$\}$, then $R$ and $F$ share the members that are red face cards. Sets with no members in common are **disjoint sets**, such as $\{$minerals$\}$ and $\{$vegetables$\}$. Sets contained within others are **subsets**; for example, $\{$vowels$\}$ is a subset of $\{$letters of the alphabet$\}$. The set that contains all the elements of all the sets under consideration is known as the **universal set**; the **complement** of a set consists of all elements within the universal set that

**Triangle**

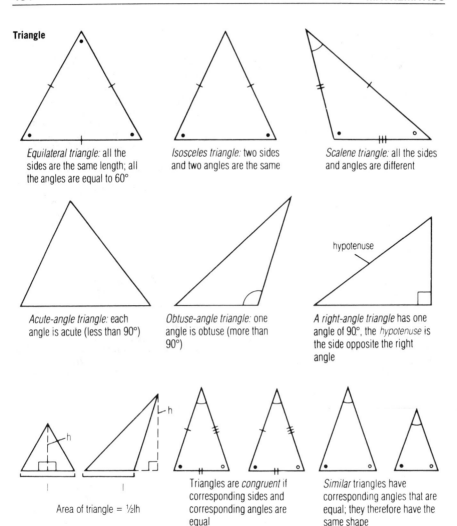

*Equilateral triangle:* all the sides are the same length; all the angles are equal to 60°

*Isosceles triangle:* two sides and two angles are the same

*Scalene triangle:* all the sides and angles are different

*Acute-angle triangle:* each angle is acute (less than 90°)

*Obtuse-angle triangle:* one angle is obtuse (more than 90°)

A *right-angle triangle* has one angle of 90°, the *hypotenuse* is the side opposite the right angle

Area of triangle = ½lh

Triangles are *congruent* if corresponding sides and corresponding angles are equal

*Similar* triangles have corresponding angles that are equal; they therefore have the same shape

are not members of that particular set. For example, if the universal set is the set of all positive whole numbers and the designated set $S$ is the set of all even numbers, then the complement of $S$ (denoted $S'$) is the set of all odd numbers. Sets and their interrelationships are often illustrated by a **Venn diagram.**

**significant figures** the figures in a number that, by virtue of their place value, express the magnitude of that number to a specified degree of accuracy. The final significant figure is rounded up if the following digit is, greater than five. For example, 5,463,254 to three significant figures is 5,460,000; 3.462891 to four significant figures is 3.463.

**simultaneous equations** two or more algebraic equations that contain two or more unknown quantities that may have a unique solution. For example, in the case of two linear equations with two unknown variables, such as (i) $x + 3y = 6$ and (ii) $3y - 2x = 4$, the solution will be those unique values of $x$ and $y$ that are

valid for both equations. Linear simultaneous equations can be solved by using algebraic manipulation to eliminate one of the variables, coordinate geometry, or matrices.

**sine** in trigonometry, a function of an angle in a right-angled triangle found by dividing the length of the side opposite to the angle by the length of the hypotenuse (the longest side). Various properties in physics vary sinsoidally, that is, they can be represented diagramatically by a sine wave (a graph obtained by plotting values of angles against the values of their sines). Examples include simple harmonic motion, such as the way alternating current (AC) electricity varies with time.

**speed** the rate at which an object moves. Speed in kilometres per hour is calculated by dividing the distance travelled in kilometres by the time taken in hours. Speed is a scalar quantity, as the direction of motion is not taken into consideration. This makes it different from velocity, which is a vector quantity.

**Ven diagram**

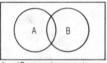

A and B are overlapping sets

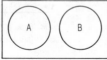

A and B are disjoint sets

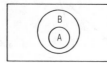

A is the subset of B

**sphere** in geometry, a circular solid figure with all points on its surface the same distance from the centre. For a sphere of radius $r$, the volume $V = 4/3\pi(12)r^3$, and the surface area $A = 4\pi r^2$.

**square root** a number that when squared (multiplied by itself) equals another given number. For example, the square root of 25 (written $\sqrt{25}$) is ±5, because $+5 \times +5 = 25$, and $(-5) \times (-5) = 25$. As an exponent, a square root is represented by 1/2; for example, $16^{1/2} = \pm4$. Negative numbers (less than 0) do not have square roots that are real numbers. Their roots are represented by complex numbers, in which the square root of –1 is given the symbol $i$ (that is, $i^2 = -1$). Thus the square root of –4 is $\pm2i$.

**statistics** the branch of mathematics concerned with the collection and interpretation of data. For meaningful interpretation, there should be a large amount of data to analyse. For example, faced with the task of determining the mean (average) age of the children in a school, an exact mean could be obtained by averaging the ages of every pupil in the school. A statistically acceptable answer might be obtained by calculating the average based on the ages of a representative sample, consisting say of a random tenth of the pupils from each class.

**tangent** in trigonometry, a function of an angle in a right-angled triangle, defined as the ratio of the length of the side opposite the angle (not the right angle) to the length of the side adjacent to it; a way of expressing the gradient of a line. In geometry, a tangent is a straight line that touches a curve and has the same slope as the curve at the point of contact. At a maximum or minimum, the tangent to a curve has zero gradient.

**tetrahedron** in geometry, a solid figure (polyhedron) with four triangular faces; that is, a pyramid on a triangular base. A regular tetrahedron has equilateral triangles as its faces; it can be constructed by joining four points that are equidistant from each other on the surface of a sphere.

**topology** the branch of geometry that deals with those properties of a figure that remain unchanged even when the figure is transformed (bent, stretched)—for example, when a square painted on a rubber sheet is deformed by distorting the sheet. Topology has scientific applications, as in the study of turbulence in flowing fluids. The map of the London Underground system is an example of the topological representation of a network; connectivity (the way the lines join together) is preserved, but shape and size are not. The topological theory, proposed 1880, that only four colours are required in order to produce a map in which no two adjoining countries have the same colour, inspired extensive research, and was proved 1972 by Kenneth Appel and Wolfgang Haken.

**trapezium** (North American **trapezoid**) in geometry, a four-sided plane figure quadrilateral with two of its sides parallel. If the parallel sides have lengths $a$ and $b$ and the perpendicular distance between them is $h$ (the height of the trapezium), its area $A = 1/2h(a + b)$.

**triangle** in geometry, a three-sided plane figure. A *scalene triangle* has no two sides equal; an *isosceles triangle* has two equal sides (and two equal angles); an *equilateral triangle* has three equal sides (and three equal angles of 60°). A right-angled triangle has one angle of 90°. If the length of one side of a triangle is $l$ and the perpendicular distance from that side to the opposite corner is $h$ (the height, or altitude, of the triangle), its area $A = 1/2l \times h$.

**trigonometry** branch of mathematics that solves problems relating to plane and spherical triangles. Its principles are based on the fixed proportions of angles and sides in a right-angled triangle, the simplest of which is the sine, cosine, and tangent (so-called trigonometrical ratios).

It is possible, using trigonometry, to calculate the lengths of the sides and the sizes of the angles of a right-angled triangle as long as one angle (other than the right-angle) and one side are known. Trigonometry is of practical importance in navigation and surveying, and simple harmonic motion in physics.

**variable** a changing quantity (one that can take various values), as opposed to a constant. For example, in the algebraic expression $y = 4x^3 + 2$, the variables are $x$ and $y$, whereas 4 and 2 are constants.

**vector quantity** a physical quantity such as velocity or acceleration that has both magnitude and direction, as distinct from a scalar quantity (such as speed, density, or mass), which has magnitude but no direction. A vector is often represented geometrically by an arrow on a line of length equal to its magnitude and in technical writing it is denoted by **bold type**. Vectors can be added graphically by constructing a parallelogram of vectors.

**velocity** the speed of an object in a given direction. Velocity is a vector quantity, since its direction is as important as its magnitude (or speed).

**Venn diagram** a diagram representing a set or sets and the logical relationships between them. Sets are drawn as circles. An area of overlap between two circles (sets) contains elements that are common to both sets, and thus represents a third set. Circles that do not overlap represent sets with no elements in common (disjoint sets). The method is named after English logician John Venn (1834–1923).

**vertex** a corner of a plane (two-dimensional) or solid shape. In a polygon, it is the point of intersection of two sides; in a polyhedron it is the point where two edges meet. For example, a square has four vertices; a cube has eight.

**volume** the space occupied by a three-dimensional solid object.

VOLUMES OF COMMON THREE-DIMENSIONAL SHAPES

| | |
|---|---|
| cuboid | $lbh$ |
| length $l$, breadth $b$, height $h$ | |
| cube | $l^3$ |
| side $l$ | |
| cylinder | $\pi r^2 h$ |
| height $h$, radius of cross section $r$ | |
| cone | $1/3\pi r^2 h$ |
| height $h$, radius of base $r$ | |
| sphere | $4/3\pi r^3$ |
| radius $r$ | |

# THE GREAT MATHEMATICIANS

**Archimedes** c. 287–212 BC. Greek mathematician who made discoveries in geometry, hydrostatics, and mechanics. He used geometrical techniques to measure the areas and volumes of curved figures, such as the sphere, determined an approximate value for $\pi$, and devised a system of notation for very large numbers. He also formulated a law of fluid displacement (Archimedes' principle), and is credited with the invention of the Archimedes screw, a cylindrical device for raising water.

**Bernoulli** Swiss family that produced many capable mathematicians in the 17th, 18th, and 19th centuries, in particular the brothers **Jakob** (1654–1705) and **Johann** (1667–1748), who were pioneers of Leibniz's calculus. Jakob used calculus to study the forms of many curves arising in practical situations, and studied probability; **Bernoulli numbers**, a complex series of fractions used in higher mathematics, are named after him. Johann discovered exponential calculus and contributed to many areas of applied mathematics, including the problem of a particle moving in a gravitational field. His son **Daniel** (1700–1782) investigated calculus and probability, and made discoveries in hydrodynamics.

**Boole** George 1814–1864. English mathematician whose work *The Mathematical Analysis of Logic* 1847 established the basis of modern mathematical logic, and whose **Boolean algebra** can be used in designing computers.

**Cantor** Georg 1845–1918. German mathematician who followed his work on number theory and trigonometry by considering the foundations of mathematics. He defined real numbers and produced a treatment of irrational numbers using a series of transfinite numbers. Cantor's set theory has been used in the development of topology and real function theory.

**Cauchy** Augustin Louis 1789–1857. French mathematician, celebrated for his rigorous methods of analysis. His prolific output included work on complex functions, determinants, and probability, and on the convergence of infinite series. In calculus, he refined the concepts of the definite integral.

**Descartes** René 1596–1650. French mathematician and philosopher. He believed that commonly accepted knowledge was doubtful because of the subjective nature of the senses, and attempted to rebuild human knowledge using as his foundation *'cogito ergo sum'* ('I think, therefore I am'). He aimed to express the physical sciences in mathematical terms, and founded coordinate geometry as a way of defining and manipulating geometrical shapes by means of algebraic expressions. Cartesian coordinates, the means by which points are represented in this system, were named after him.

**Eratosthenes** c. 276–c. 194 BC. Greek geographer and mathematician whose map of the ancient world was the first to contain lines of latitude and longitude. He calculated the Earth's circumference with an error of about 10%. His mathematical achievements include a method for duplicating the cube, and for finding prime numbers (**Eratosthenes' sieve**).

**Euclid** c. 330–c. 260 BC. Greek mathematician from Alexandria who wrote the *Stoicheia/Elements* in 13 books, of which nine deal with plane and solid geometry, and four with arithmetic. His great achievement lay in the systematic arrangement of previous discoveries, based on axioms, definitions, and theorems.

**Euler** Leonhard 1707–1783. Swiss mathematician. He developed the theory of differential equations and the calculus of variations, and worked in astronomy and optics. He was a pupil of Johann Bernoulli.

**Fermat** Pierre de 1601–1665. French mathematician who with Blaise Pascal founded the theory of probability and the modern theory of numbers, and who made contributions to coordinate geometry. **Fermat's last theorem** states that equations of the form $x^n + y^n = z^n$, where $x$, $y$, $z$, and $n$ are all integers, have no solutions if $n < 2$. There is no general proof of this, so it remains a conjecture rather than a theorem.

**Fibonacci** Leonardo (also known as Leonardo of Pisa) c. 1170–c. 1250. Italian mathematician. In 1202 he published *Liber abaci/Book of the*

## THE ELECTRONIC MATHEMATICIAN

Mathematicians have always dreamed of possessing machines that would remove the drudgery from their work. The inventor of logarithms, John Napier, also invented a system of carved ivory rods for doing multiplication, known as Napier's bones. Blaise Pascal built the first mechanical calculator in 1642. In 1835 Charles Babbage designed a calculating machine that could modify its own instructions, a forerunner of today's computers. Two of the true parents of the computer, John Von Neumann and Alan Turing, were mathematicians.

Until the 1970s, computers were used as glorified calculators, for 'number crunching'—performing what were essentially just long and complicated calculations in arithmetic. Many mathematical problems, however, require understanding, not just a numerical answer. More and more, computers are being used by mathematicians as 'experimental' tools: to investigate aspects of mathematical problems, test predictions, and prove the correctness of theories. Computer scientists have also responded to mathematicians' needs by devising symbolic computation systems. These manipulate algebraic expressions in the same way that a human mathematician would—only faster and more accurately. The result might be called 'computer-assisted mathematics': the computer does not make mathematicians obsolete, but it adds enormously to their power, bringing within their range problems that had hitherto seemed impossible.

A good example is the proof in 1972 of the Four Colour Theorem by Kenneth Appel and Wolfgang Haken. In 1850 Francis Guthrie conjectured that no more than four colours need be used in colouring a map in order to ensure that no two adjacent countries share the same colour. Mathematicians quickly proved that five colours would suffice, but had no success whatsoever in reducing that number to four. A direct attack by computer would not be possible, for how could a computer consider all possible maps? But Appel and Haken came up with a list of 1,936 particular maps, and showed that if each had a rather complicated property, then the conjecture must be true. They then checked this property, case by case, on a computer, taking about 1,200 hours.

There are now many different symbolic computation systems, such as Macsyma, Reduce,

Maple, and Mathematica. Their use is becoming almost routine among reseach mathematicians. Their power is immense. In 1847 the French mathematician Charles Delaunay spent 20 years calculating a formula for the position of the Moon, and the end result occupies an entire book. In 1970 three researchers at the Boeing Laboratories in Seattle checked his calculation by symbolic computation, taking only 20 *hours*. They found that Delaunay had made three errors, none serious.

Symbolic computation has been used to answer long-standing questions about dynamic systems, to help prove new results in number theory, to investigate questions in algebraic geometry, to devise new minimal surfaces, and even in the mathematics of games. In March 1991 Uri Zwick and Mike Patterson of Warwick University, England, used Mathematica to work out a winning strategy for the memory game pelmanism, in which pairs of identical cards are laid face down and players take turns to turn two of them over. If they match, the player removes them and takes an extra turn. The winner is whoever removes the most cards. The strategy is quite simple, but the proof that it works—and the experiments needed to discover it—would not have been possible without the computer.

Computation and mathematics have always been closely related, and as the century draws to a close they are becoming intimately intertwined. This strong interaction between computing and mathematics will let the mathematician of the future spend more time thinking about concepts, and less time performing routine calculations. Computers, moreover, open up a whole new range of problems that mathematicians would not otherwise have thought of, and offer new perspectives from which to find answers.

The technology is not yet perfect. Symbolic computation programs seldom work well without a lot of careful structuring by their human user. Left to their own devices, the programs tend to suffer 'memory explosions', leaving copies of intermediate steps all over the computer's memory, filling it up, and grinding to an ignominious halt. But the technology is improving so fast that by the turn of the century there will be few mathematicians who do not 'collaborate' with a computer on a regular basis.

---

*Abacus* (based in part on his knowledge of the work of the Persian mathematician al-Khwārizmī), which was instrumental in the introduction of Hindu–Arabic numerals into Europe. It also described special sequences of numbers, now called **Fibonacci numbers**, in which each number is the sum of its two predecessors (for example, 1, 1, 2, 3, 5, 8, 13...). From 1960, interest developed in these sequences' unusual characteristics and their possible applications in botany, psychology, and astronomy. For example, the number of petals and sepals on flowers, the spirals in a

spider's web, and the distances between the planets and the Sun, all fit such sequences.

**Galois** Evariste 1811–1832. French mathematician who originated the theory of groups. His attempts to gain recognition for his work were largely thwarted by the French mathematical establishment, critical of his lack of formal qualifications. Galois was killed in a duel before he was 21. The night before, he had hurriedly written out his unpublished discoveries on group theory, the importance of which would come to be appreciated more and more as the 19th century progressed.

**Gauss** Karl Friedrich 1777–1855. German mathematician. He found four different proofs of the fundamental theorem of algebra, which states that every equation has at least one root, and developed a form of non-Euclidean geometry. Gauss also worked on the mathematical development of electric and magnetic theory.

**Gödel** Kurt 1906–1978. Austrian-born US mathematician and philospher who proved that a mathematical system always contains statements that can be neither proved nor disproved within the system; in other words, as a science, mathematics can never be totally consistent and totally complete. He was a friend of Einstein and worked on relativity, constructing a mathematical model of the Universe that made travel back through time theoretically possible.

**Hilbert** David 1862–1943. German mathematician who attempted to put mathematics on a logical foundation through defining it in terms of a number of basic principles, which Kurt Gödel later showed to be impossible; none the less, his attempt greatly influenced 20th-century mathematicians. Hilbert proposed a set of 23 unsolved problems in 1900 for future mathematicians to solve, a programme that has inspired mathematical research ever since.

**Khwārizmī, al-** Muhammad ibn-Mūsāc 780–c.850. Persian mathematician who wrote a book on algebra, from part of whose title (*al-jabr*, 'transposition') comes the word 'algebra'. His work helped to introduce to the West the Hindu–Arabic decimal number system, including the symbol for zero. The word 'algorithm' (the process of steps used to solve mathematical problems) is a corruption of his name.

**Lagrange** Joseph Louis 1736–1813. French mathematician who presided over the commission that introduced the metric system in 1793. His *Mécanique analytique* 1788 applied mathematical analysis, using principles established by Newton to such problems as the movements of planets when affected by each other's gravitational force.

**Leibniz** Gottfried Wilhelm 1646–1716. German mathematician and philosopher. Independently of, but concurrently with, the British scientist Isaac Newton he developed calculus. In his metaphysical works, such as *The Monadology* 1714, he argued that everything consisted of innumerable units, *monads*, whose individual properties determined each thing's past, present, and future.

**Lobachevsky** Nikolai Ivanovich 1792–1856. Russian mathematician who founded non-Euclidean geometry concurrently with, but independently of, Karl Gauss and the Hungarian János Bulyai (1802–1860). Lobachevsky published the first account of the subject in 1829, but his work went unrecognized until Georg Riemann's system was published.

**Lorenz** Ludwig Valentine 1829–1891. Danish mathematician and physicist who developed mathematical formulae to describe various phenomena, such as the relationship between refraction of light and the density of a pure transparent substance, and the relationship between a metal's electrical and thermal conductivity and temperature.

**Mandelbrot** Benoit B 1924– . Polish-born US scientist who coined the term *fractal geometry* to describe 'self-similar' shape, a motif that repeats indefinitely, each time smaller.

**Markov** Andrei 1856–1922. Russian mathematician who formulated the *Markov chain*, a concept that holds that a chain of events is governed only by established probability and is uninfluenced by the past history of earlier links in the chain.

**Möbius** August Ferdinand 1790–1868. German mathematician, considered one of the founders of topology. He discovered the *Möbius strip*, a structure made by giving a half twist to a flat strip of paper and joining the ends together. It has certain remarkable properties, arising from the fact that it has only one edge and one side. If cut down the centre of the strip, instead of two new strips of paper, only one long strip is produced.

**Napier** John 1550–1617. Scottish mathematician who invented logarithms in 1614, and 'Napier's Bones', an early mechanical calculating device for multiplication and division.

**Newton** Isaac 1642–1727. English physicist and mathematician who laid the foundations of physics as a modern discipline. He discovered the law of gravity, showed that white light is composed of many colours, and developed the three standard laws of motion still in use today. In mathematics, Newton discovered differential and integral calculus (although it was Gottfried Leibniz's notation that was finally adopted), and the binomial theorem. Most of the last 30 years of his life were taken up by studies and experiments in alchemy.

**Pascal** Blaise 1623–1662. French mathematician physicist who worked on conic sections and (with Pierre de Fermat) probability theory. *Pascal's triangle* is an array of numbers with 1 at the apex and in which each number is the sum of the pair of numbers above it. Plotted at equal distances along a horizontal axis, the numbers in the rows give the binomial probability distribution with equal probability of success and failure, such as when tossing coins.

**Poincaré** Jules Henri 1854–1912. French mathematician who developed the theory of differential equations and was a pioneer in relativity

**Pascal triangle**

```
                1
              1   1
            1   2   1
          1   3   3   1
        1   4   6   4   1
      1   5  10  10   5   1
    1   6  15  20  15   6   1
  1   7  21  35  35  21   7   1
```

theory. He suggested that Isaac Newton's laws for the behaviour of the universe could be the exception rather than the rule. However, the calculation was so complex and time-consuming that he never managed to realise its full implication. He also published the first paper devoted entirely to topology.

**Pythagoras** c. 580–c. 500 BC. Greek mathematician and philosopher who formulated Pythagoras' theorem. Much of his work concerned numbers, to which he assigned mystical properties. For example, he classified numbers into triangular ones (1, 3, 6, 10,...) which can be represented as a triangular array, and square ones (1, 4, 9, 16,...) which form squares. He also observed that any two adjacent triangular numbers add to a square number (for example, $1 + 3 = 4, 3 = 6 = 9, 6 + 10 = 16$, and so on).

**Riemann** Georg Friedrich Bernhard 1826–1866. German mathematician whose system of non-Euclidean geometry, thought at the time to be a mere mathematical curiosity, was used by Einstein to develop his general theory of relativity.

**Rubik** Erno 1944– . Hungarian architect who invented the **Rubik Cube** 1974, a plastic multi-coloured puzzle that can be manipulated and rearranged in only one correct way and in around 43 trillion wrong ones. Intended to help his students understand three-dimensional design, it became a fad that swept the world.

**Thales** c. 624–c. 547 BC. Greek philosopher and scientist. He advanced geometry as an abstract study, predicted an eclipse of the Sun 585 BC, and as a philosophical materialist, theorized that water was the first principle of all things, that the Earth floated on water, and so proposed an explanation for earthquakes.

**Turing** Alan Mathison 1912–1954. British mathematician and logician. In 1936 he described a 'universal computing machine' that could theoretically be programmed to solve any problem capable of solution by a specially designed machine. This concept, now called the **Turing machine**, foreshadowed the digital computer.

**Von Neumann** John 1903–1957. Hungarian-born US mathematician and scientist. He invented his celebrated 'rings of operators' (called Von Neumann algebras) in the late 1930s, and also contributed to set theory, games theory, cybernetics (with his theory of self-reproducing automata, called **Von Neumann machines**), and the development of the atomic and hydrogen bombs.

**Wiener** Norbert 1894–1964. US mathematician, credited with the establishment of the science of cybernetics in his book *Cybernetics* 1948. He laid the foundation of the study of stochastic processes (those dependent on random events), including Brownian movement (evidence of constant random motion of molecules).

### Can people add up?

*How much would it cost you to buy a cup of coffee at 50p and a sandwich at £1.25p?*

96% got the correct answer

*How much does it cost to buy eight 22p stamps?*

63% got the correct answer

*This is a restaurant bill. If you wanted to leave a 10% tip, how much would the tip be?*

50% got the correct answer when shown a bill for £11.40

*Which is bigger, three hundred thousand or a quarter of a million?*

79% got the correct answer

*Suppose that the rate of inflation had dropped from 20% to 15%. Which one of these results would you have expected?*

32%, given four choices, correctly chose 'prices would still be rising but not as fast as before'

*If you bought a raincoat in the 'summer sales' reduced from £84 to £59.50, how much would you save?*

61% got the correct answer

*This shows you the temperature changes on a day last summer. What was the hottest time of day? And how hot was it then?*

88% got the correct time
72% got the correct temperature

# SOME ENDANGERED SPECIES

## MAMMALS

**African elephant** the world's largest land animal *Loxodonta africana*, ruthlessly hunted by poachers throughout E Africa for the ivory from its tusks. Numbers collapsed during the 1980s owing to overhunting, and elephant populations in several countries are threatened with extinction. A ban on trading ivory introduced 1990 resulted in an apparent drop in poaching but it is too early to be certain what long-term effects this will have.

**American manatee** or *sea cow* ungainly marine mammal *Trichecus manatus*, once widespread in the oceans around the southern USA, the Caribbean, and South America. It has suffered a massive decline through hunting, pollution, drowning in fishing gear, and damage from powerboat propellers. The manatee is said to have been a source of the mermaid legend.

**Arabian oryx** or *white oryx* antelope *Oryx leucoryx* with curved horns up to 70 cm/28 in, formerly found throughout the arid areas of the Middle East. The oryx population was devastated by the advent of motorized hunting in the 1960s; the last wild one is thought to have been killed in 1972. There are breeding colonies in captivity and in fenced reserves, intended for eventual release, in Oman, Israel, and Jordan.

**aye-aye** nocturnal primate *Daubentonia madagascariensis* that lives in trees and feeds on fruit and insect larvae, extracting the latter from rotten wood with an elongated middle finger. One of at least 25 endemic primate species threatened by catastrophic deforestation in Madagascar, it is confined to a few scattered individuals in coastal districts, although a breeding colony has been established on an offshore island from animals raised in zoos.

**Bactrian camel** desert-living, herbivorous mammal *Camelus bactrianus* with two humps, capable of surviving for long periods without water. Domesticated for at least 6,000 years, it remained locally common in desert regions of Eurasia until the 19th century; the camel is now confined to 300–500 animals living on a reserve in the Gobi Desert, on the borders of Mongolia and China.

**blue whale** the world's largest mammal *Balaenoptera musculus*, the largest animal known to have existed at any time. It feeds on plankton, which it filters through its sievelike baleen. Originally found in all seas, with about 200,000 in the rich feeding grounds of the southern oceans, the blue whale suffered badly from commercial whaling, and world populations are thought to be little more than 6,000, although there is a great deal of uncertainty about population levels. Despite full protection, its survival remains in doubt because of the low total numbers.

**bumblebee bat** or *Kitti's hog-nosed bat* the world's smallest mammal, *Craseonycteris thonglongyai* is the size of a bumblebee, discovered in 1973 in a once forested area of N Thailand, now cleared for agriculture. The bat lives deep in limestone caves, which it leaves to hunt at dusk. The known world population is only a few hundred, and is threatened by human disturbance, including the establishment of Buddhist shrines in caves.

**giant panda** bearlike mammal *Ailuropoda melanoleuca* confined to upland forests in central China, where it feeds almost exclusively on bamboo. It has been declining for thousands of years because of hunting and also climatic change. Less than 1000 remained in the wild by the 1980s, and its numbers suffered further through minor poaching for skins. It is now protected by strict laws in China. The panda's success rate for breeding in captivity is extremely low. The panda is the symbol of the World Wide Fund for Nature.

**lemur** prosimian primate of the family *Lemuridae*, inhabiting Madagascar and the Comoro Islands. There are about 16 species, ranging from mouse-sized to dog-sized animals; they are arboreal, and some species are nocturnal. They feed on fruit, insects, and small animals. Many are threatened with extinction owing to loss of their forest habitat and, in some cases, from hunting.

**long-nosed echidna** egg-laying marsupial *Zaglossus bruijni* with spines and a long snout, found in mountain forest in New Guinea. It is threat-

aye-aye

African elephant

# CAN WE LEARN TO LOVE BATS?

Most people think of bats as rather frightening oddities—flying mammals with a sophisticated sonar system that enables them to sense their way in pitch darkness. However, with some 980 species of bats known to science—and bats making up nearly one quarter of the world's mammals—it might be more logical to argue that they represent the norm.

Bats are also unique in the bad press they have received over the years, especially in the West. In the Middle Ages, bats were regarded as the symbol of the Antichrist, and hence the Devil, and paintings often showed Satan and his servants with bat's wings. Even today, there is an unfounded belief that bats can become caught in people's hair. Perhaps for their ability to navigate in the dark, bats were once credited with supernatural powers, and their blood was used in many quack medicines, a practice that is still current in India. In China and Japan, on the other hand, bats have always been a symbol of happiness, and the Chinese word *fu* means both 'bat' and 'good fortune.' In parts of Latin America, such ancient civilizations as the Maya regarded bats as deities.

Bats are the only mammals capable of powered flight, as opposed to the gliding performed by a few other species, such as the flying squirrel. They vary in size from the extremely rare bumblebee bat of Thailand (first discovered in 1973) which, at approximately 3 cm/1.2 in, is the world's smallest mammal, to the flying fox of Malaysia, which has a wingspan of 1.5 m/5 ft. Most bats found in Europe have bodies about the size of mice and voles. Unlike most small mammals, they live a long time, with individuals reaching 30 years or more, and give birth to only one young a year.

Fossils have been found of bats well over 50 million years old. Today, most bats are found in the tropics, with only about 30 species extending into Europe, and 14 in the UK (all of which are protected). Most live in caves, hollow trees, and, increasingly, in the roofs of buildings. In temperate climates bats hibernate during the winter and may congregate in huge numbers; one particularly populated roost is situated in abandoned concrete tunnels in Poland, where 25,000 bats of 12 species spend the winter.

Many species, including all those found in temperate climates, are insectivores, catching flying insects such as moths and mosquitoes on the wing. A bat can eat 3,000 insects in one night. In the tropics many bats visit flowers for nectar and pollen and play an important role in tree pollination; a decline in bat numbers means those plant species which are completely dependent on their bat pollinators for survival will also be faced with extinction. The larger bat species are generally fruit eaters. Bats eat only fruit that is too ripe for commercial use, but owners of orchards often blame bats for damage caused by birds and poison them. Three small Latin American species feed by sucking blood from large sleeping animals, and it is these vampire bats that have been connected with the old European vampire legends; they represent the only real danger to humans from bats, in that they may transmit rabies.

Bats mainly hunt at night, although dusk- or day-flying species are known. They have developed a system of echolocation for hunting and flying in the dark, which involves emitting ultrasonic signals that bounce back off objects and enable the bat to build up a picture of what is ahead. (Whales, dolphins, and some birds also use biosonar.) Different echolocation systems are used by different species of bats. All are extremely sensitive, allowing bats to locate, identify, and capture tiny flying insects while avoiding bumping into any other objects, all undertaken at very high speed.

Today many bat species are threatened with extinction by a range of human activities. Habitat destruction, including deforestation, is putting species at risk throughout the tropics. In the richer countries, the loss of much natural habitat means that bats are increasingly reliant on making use of buildings, tunnels, and other artificial environments. Enduring misconceptions about bats mean that many people try to get rid of them as pests. Chemicals and other pollutants pose an even greater risk—some common pesticides used as wood preservatives can remain toxic to bats for years. One such, lindane or gamma HCH, has been measured as fatally toxic to bats roosting on treated timber more than 20 years after application.

Conservationists are working hard to try to preserve the bats that are left. In Europe, 'bat-friendly' pesticides are becoming more widely available, and volunteers talk to owners of bat-harbouring houses about how to live on friendly terms with their guests or offer them alternative accommodation. International organizations are helping governments set up bat reserves to protect the most endangered species. Welcome though these initiatives are, they may be too late for some of the species now facing imminent risk of extinction.

*Popular misconceptions have contributed to the decline of bat populations. Above, a baby fruit bat.*

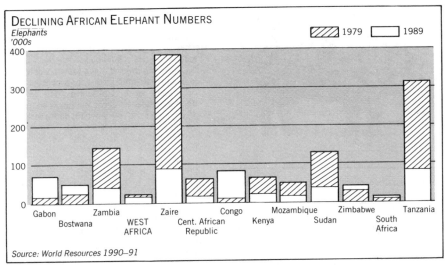

DECLINING AFRICAN ELEPHANT NUMBERS
Elephants '000s

1979  1989

Source: World Resources 1990–91

ened by forest destruction and hunting for food. Listed by CITES (Convention on Trade in Endangered Species) and protected by law in Indonesia and Papua New Guinea, although the latter allows hunting by tribal people. Exact status unknown.

**mandrill** large baboon *Papio sphinx* with spectacular blue and red markings on the male's face. Restricted to forests in W Africa and thought to be one of the continent's most threatened monkeys, it is declining because of forest destruction and international wildlife trade, the latter for both zoos and medical research.

**Mediterranean monk seal** aquatic mammal *Monachus monachus* once widespread in the Mediterranean, the Black Sea, and along part of the W African coast, but now reduced to a total world population of 500–1,000 and facing severe risk of extinction. Hunting is the main cause of its decline, first for skins and later because of alleged damage to fish stocks.

**mountain gorilla** highly endangered ape subspecies *Gorilla gorilla beringei* found in bamboo and rainforest on the Rwanda, Zaire, and Uganda borders in central Africa, with a total population of under 400. It is threatened by deforestation and illegal hunting for skins and the zoo trade.

**pygmy hog** the world's smallest pig *Sus salvanius*, an omnivore living in family groups in swampy grassland. Once found in Nepal, Bhutan, Bangladesh, and NE India, it was believed to have been made extinct in 1960 but about 150 have since been discovered in the Indian state of Assam. The pygmy hog is still threatened by

forest burning and human encroachment.

**snow leopard** or *ounce* large elusive cat *Panthera uncia* that lives in the Himalayas, upland Afghanistan, and Siberia at heights of up to 6,000 m/20,000 ft. Main threats are the displacement of prey species, such as deer, by domestic livestock, and illegal trapping for the fur trade.

**Sumatran rhinoceros** twin-horned, armour-plated rhinoceros *Dicerorhinus sumatrensis* living in forest and hill country. Once found throughout SE Asia, it is now confined to scattered populations numbering a few hundred, as a result of overhunting. The horn and internal organs are used in quack medicines and aphrodisiacs, a use that has created risks for all rhinoceros species.

**Yangtse River dolphin** one of five freshwater dolphin species found worldwide, *Lipotes vexillifer* is confined to the river Chang Jiang, or Yangtse-Kiang, and its tributaries in China. Protected since 1975, the species is still highly at risk through collisions with boats, entanglement in fishing operations, and sedimentation.

lemur

**Mediterranean monk seal**

Sumatran rhinoceros

## BIRDS

**bird of paradise** any of a group of tropical forest-living birds *paradisaeidae* in which the males have spectacular tail feathers used for display and courtship. Found in forests of New Guinea, many species are threatened by overhunting for their feathers, both for export and for use in local ceremonies.

**California condor** a New World vulture *Gymnogyps californianus* is a large bird, with a wingspan up to 3 m/10 ft, weight up to 13 kg/28 lb, and length up to 1.2 m/3.8 ft. It lives in the Andes and along the South American coast, and feeds on carrion. It lays only one egg at a time and may not breed every year. It is on the verge of extinction and the subject of a special conservation effort.

**Hawaiian goose** large goose *Branta sandvicensis* confined to the islands of the Hawaiian group, reduced to a world population of 50 by 1950. Establishment of a captive breeding group at the Wildfowl Trust, Slimbridge, England, allowed numbers to build up, and some have now been returned to the wild.

**houbara bustard** large, desert-living bird *Chalmydotis undulata* of the Middle East, ranging as far as N Africa and Pakistan. Traditionally hunted by Arab peoples with falcons, the bustard is now threatened by a sharp increase in hunting with modern equipment.

**Siberian crane** large white bird *Grus leucogeranus* that breeds on the Siberian tundra and migrates to overwinter sites in India, China, and formerly Iran. Its numbers were thought to have declined to just 33 birds by 1980, when some eggs were taken to the USA to establish a captive-breeding programme. Since then, numbers have built up slightly in the Indian wintering ground of Bharatpur nature reserve, but none have been sighted in Iran. In China, around 800 were spotted, but redevelopment now threatens their habitat there.

## REPTILES

**gharial** or *gavial* long-nosed, fish-eating crocodile *Gavialis gangeticus* once found widely in India and Nepal, living in large, fast-flowing rivers such as the Ganges. It was virtually extinct by the mid-1970s through overhunting for skins and loss of habitat from river damming. Conservation efforts, including collecting wild

eggs for captive rearing, built up a population of some 2,000, with at least 1,200 released back into the wild.

**Hochstetter's frog** one of three species of frog native to New Zealand *Lieopelma hochstetteri* is 4½ cm/1¾ in long, has a brown, warty skin, is nocturnal, and lives near water; it feeds on insects, slugs, and worms. The tadpoles develop inside the eggs, and hatch as froglets 40 days after the eggs are laid. All three species are rare; exact status unknown.

Globally, many frog species are threatened by overcollection for the international trade in frogs' legs, which are eaten as a delicacy. Over 200 million frogs are exported from Asia every year. The decrease in numbers of frogs has resulted in an increase in malaria in humans, as malaria mosquitos are no longer controlled by their natural predators.

**Kemp's Ridley sea turtle** marine turtle *Lepidochelys kempii* one of many species endangered through a combination of habitat destruction and hunting for food. Because turtles haul themselves ashore to lay eggs in sand, they are very vulnerable to egg collectors and to tourist and industrial development of their breeding sites. Adults are also killed to make turtle soup. Kemp's Ridley is among the most threatened turtles: once widely distributed, it now has an estimated population of under 700, down from 5,000 in the 1960s.

## INVERTEBRATES

**coral** any of a range of colonial coelenterates that secrete a skeleton of calcium carbonate, which is made into jewellery and souvenirs and can be burned to produce lime. Coral is also very quickly killed by certain sorts of pollution, including oil and some pesticides. Coral reefs are disappearing fast in areas of Asia, especially in Bali, and are facing threats in virtually all tropical seas.

**irridescent beetle** insect *Carabus olympiae* found in the Italian Alps, much prized by collectors for its attractive appearance. Thought to have become extinct in 1928, it was rediscovered in 1942. Despite a captive breeding programme

California condor

## EXTINCTION OR SURVIVAL: EFFORTS TO SAVE ENDANGERED SPECIES

Once extinct, a species can never be recovered. From the natural disappearance of the dinosaurs to the hunting to destruction of the flightless dodo birds, extinctions have always taken place. However, our generation may well be witness to the largest number of extinctions in the history of the planet. Although no one has any real idea of the numbers involved, scientists believe that we are probably losing several species *every day*, and that rate of extinction could increase rapidly over the next few decades.

Many species, particularly larger animals and birds, become endangered or extinct because of hunting for sport or the wildlife trade. Spotted and striped cats have been killed to make fur coats, and reptiles provide leather for shoes and bags. Until recently, about 2 million snake skins were exported from India every year. Marine turtles are killed for turtle soup. Whales have been hunted to the point of extinction for their blubber, meat, oil, and the baleen used, in the days before plastics, to make women's corsets. Elephants are killed for their ivory and rhinos for their horns. Many birds of prey are captured and 'tamed' for hunting. Coral reefs are destroyed to provide tourist souvenirs. American buffalo were wiped out for food. The list is long.

Serious though these impacts are, they are almost insignificant compared to the effects of habitat destruction. Deforestation, especially in tropical rainforests, loss of wetlands, desertification, and destruction of mangroves and coral reefs threaten to wipe out a far larger number of species of plants and animals. Most of these are small and, especially in the extraordinarily rich rainforest environments, many have not yet been identified by scientists. Contrary to the perspective given in TV films or appeals from wildlife organizations, the greatest threat, numerically, is to plants and invertebrates. Despite their seeming insignificance, they have a part in their ecosystems and with them we lose irreplaceable genetic material.

Belated recognition of the scale of destruction is now slowly developing. An international treaty on biodiversity is planned for introduction at the United Nations Conference on Environment and Development in Rio de Janeiro in 1992. There are also a few hopeful signs that, for some animals at least, protection, active management, and, most important of all, public education

programmes can halt and even reverse the decline. A number of animals that seemed faced with extinction a few years ago are now building up their numbers again. Some of the alligator species of the southern USA, once highly threatened by hunting, have thrived under legal protection. Complicated management systems allow the dangerous polar bears to migrate harmlessly through some townships in Alaska and northern Canada. The highly threatened mountain gorillas of Rwanda have stabilized their population under protection and tourists coming to watch them provide local people with an economic alternative to poaching.

National and international legislation is vital to save species from extinction. Preservation of habitat means, in the short term, establishment of reserves and national parks. Longer-term solutions in fragile areas involve learning land management techniques, directed not only to protecting species but also to preventing soil erosion, flooding, and other forms of environmental degradation.

Just as vital are steps to block the wildlife trade. The most important is an international treaty, the Convention on Trade in Endangered Species (CITES). Once a plant or animal is listed on CITES, signatory countries agree to severe restrictions or a total ban on trade in its products. But it is a slow process; for example, the inclusion of a number of whale species on CITES I, the schedule of most stringent protection, took years of hard debate to achieve.

Some important steps forward have been made in the 1990s. Following the decimation of African elephant populations by ruthless gangs of poachers, who have had a virtually free hand over huge areas of the continent, the elephant was finally listed on CITES. Although it is still too early to say for certain what the effects of this have been, first reports suggest a major falling-off of poaching.

There are no easy answers to extinction, and tragically there seems little chance of averting further massive losses of species over the next couple of decades. However, international efforts are already having limited success in protecting some of the most endangered of the larger plants and animals, and are starting to come to terms with larger problems of maintaining entire threatened habitats.

to build up wild populations, and full legal protection since 1983, the beetle is still endangered by collectors, who will pay several hundred pounds for a specimen.

**medicinal leech** *Hirudo medicinalis* the only European leech able to break through the skin of humans and suck their blood. Leeches were used for hundreds of years for blood-letting in medicine and are still in use today, in part for

their anticoagulant properties. Now seriously threatened in many areas through overhunting and habitat destruction, they are in Britain confined to a few localities in the southern counties.

**South African giant earthworm** the world's biggest earthworm *Microchaetus microchaetus*, reaching a length of 7 m/23 ft with a diameter of 2–3 cm/1 in. Having a rather limited range

## Conventions Concerning the Protection of the Marine Environment and Species

| Convention | State/organization | Date |
|---|---|---|
| Species protection and fishing | | |
| International Convention on the Regulation of Whaling | Washington (USA) | 1946 |
| Establishment of an Inter-American Tropical Tuna Commission | Washington(USA) | 1949 |
| Agreement for the Establishment of a General Fisheries Council for the Mediterranean | Rome (FAO) | 1949 |
| Agreement Concerning Measures for the Protection of the Stocks of Deep-Sea Prawns, etc. | Oslo (Norway) | 1952 |
| International Convention for the High Seas Fisheries of the North Pacific Ocean | Tokyo (INPFC)* | 1952 |
| Interim Convention on the Conservation of North Pacific Fur Seals | Washington (USA) | 1957 |
| Convention on Fishing and the Conservation of the Living Resources of the High Seas | Geneva (UN) | 1958 |
| North-East Atlantic Fisheries Convention | London (UK) | 1959 |
| Convention Concerning Fishing in The Black Sea | Varna (Bulgaria) | 1960 |
| Agreement Concerning Cooperation in Marine Fishing | Warsaw (Poland) | 1962 |
| International Convention for the Conservation of Atlantic | Rio de Janeiro  Tunas(FAO) | 1966 |
| Convention on the Conservation of Living Resources of the South-east Atlantic | Rome (FAO) | 1969 |
| Convention for the Conservation of Antarctic Seals | London (UK) | 1972 |
| Convention on Fishing and Conservation of the Living Resources in the Baltic Sea and Belt | Gdansk (Poland) | 1973 |
| Convention on Future Multilateral Cooperation in the Northwest Atlantic Fisheries | Ottawa (Canada) | 1978 |
| Convention on Future Multilateral Cooperation in the North-East Atlantic Fisheries | London (UK) | 1980 |
| Convention for the Conservation of Salmon in the North Atlantic Ocean | Reykjavik (EEC) | 1982 |

* International North Pacific Fisheries Commission

Source: The Times Guide to the Environment 1990

and unable to stand habitat changes, it is currently threatened by lowering of the water table and desertification caused by overgrazing.

## PLANTS

**mangrove** any tree of the genus *Rhizophora*, *Bruguiera*, or *Avicennia*, found along muddy coastal waters of tropical America and Asia. Worldwide, mangrove trees and the associated habitats support over 2,000 species of invertebrates, fish, and plants. Mangroves are being destroyed everywhere—for example, the mangrove area in the Philippines declined from 5,000 sq km/2,000 sq mi to just 380 sq km/150 sq mi between 1920 and 1980. The trees are felled for timber, woodfuel, wood chips, and urban and agricultural expansion, or accidentally destroyed by pesticides and industrial pollution. Loss of mangroves damages local fisheries and leads to coastal erosion.

**orchid** large, worldwide family *Orchidacea* of monocotyledonous plants, including many exotically shaped and coloured varieties much prized for cultivation. Many species of orchid are thought to have been exterminated by digging up for export and resale, and others are on the brink of extinction. In Britain, there are only about a dozen individuals of the ***monkey orchid*** *Orchis simia* left, and these have to be guarded night and day during their 16-week flowering period.

**teak** tropical hardwood tree *Tectona grandis*, originally found only in Asia but planted elsewhere. The species is by no means in danger of complete extinction, but the unique habitat of the teak forest has already virtually disappeared in many countries through overlogging. The teak forests of Myanmar (formerly Burma) and Laos are currently being felled to meet the timber needs of Thailand, where most of the teak has already disappeared. Although there are efforts to control logging through national laws and the International Tropical Timber Organization, the rate of destruction continues to increase.

**orchid**

## ANIMALS PROTECTED IN UK UNDER THE WILDLIFE AND COUNTRYSIDE ACT 1981

| common name | species | scientific name |
|---|---|---|
| adder [1] | | Vipera berus |
| anemone [4] | Ivell's sea | Edwardsia ivelli |
| | starlet sea | Nematostella vectensis |
| apus [4] | | Triops cancriformis |
| bat | all species | — |
| beetle | rainbow leaf | Chrysolina cerealis |
| | violet click [4] | Limoniscus violaceus |
| burbot | | Lota lota |
| butterfly | heath fritillary | Mellicta athalia or Melitaea athalia |
| | large blue | Maculinea arion |
| | swallowtail | Papilio machaon |
| cat [4] | wild | Felis silvestris |
| cicada [4] | New Forest | Cicadetta montana |
| crayfish [4] [2] | white-clawed | Austropotamobius pallipes |
| cricket | field | Gryllus campestris |
| | mole | Gryllotalpa gryllotalpa |
| dolphin [4] | | Cetacea species |
| dormouse [4] | | Muscardinus avellanarius |
| dragonfly | Norfolk aeshna | Aeshna isosceles |
| frog [1] | common | Rana temporaria |
| grasshopper | wart-biter | Decticus verrucivorus |
| leech [4] | medicinal | Hirudo medicinalis |
| lizard | sand | Lacerta agilis |
| | viviparous [3] | Lacerta vivipara |
| marten [4] | pine | Martes martes |
| moth | barberry carpet | Pareulype berberata |
| | black-veined | Siona lineata or Idaea lineata |
| | Essex emerald | Thetidia smaragdaria |
| | New Forest burnet | Zygaena viciae |
| | reddish buff | Acosmetica caliginosa |
| | viper's bugloss [4] | Hadena irregularis |
| newt | great crested (warty) | Triturus cristatus |
| | palmate [1] | Triturus helveticus |
| | smooth [1] | Triturus vulgaris |
| otter | common | Lutra lutra |
| porpoise [4] | | Cetacea species |
| sandworm [4] | lagoon | Armandia cirrhosa |
| sea mat [4] | trembling | Victorella pavida |
| shrimp [4] | fairy | Chirocephalus diaphanus |
| | lagoon sand | Gammarus insensibilis |
| slowworm [3] | | Anguis fragilis |
| snail | glutinous | Myxas glutinosa |
| | sandbowl | Catinella avenaria |
| snake | grass [3] | Natrix natrix |
| | smooth | Coronella austriaca |
| spider | great raft | Dolomedes plantarius |
| | ladybird | Eresus niger |
| squirrel | red | Sciurus vulgaris |
| toad | common [1] | Bufo bufo |
| | natterjack | Bufo calamita |
| turtle [4] | leatherback | Dermochelyidae |
| | marine (all species) | Chelonidae |
| vendace [4] | | Coregonus albula |
| walrus [4] | | Odobenus rosmarus |
| whale [4] | | Cetacea species |
| whitefish [4] | | Coregonus lavaretus |

It is normally an offence to kill, injure, take, possess, or sell any of the above-mentioned animals (whether live or dead) and to disturb its place of shelter and protection or to destroy that place.
[1] species for which the offence relates to sale only [2] species for/which the offence relates to taking and sale only
[3] species for which the offence relates to killing, injuring, and sale [4] species added to the list in 1986
Sources: *Protecting Britain's Wildlife: A Brief Guide* (DOE), and *IUCN, Red List of Threatened Animals 1988*

## STILL POISONING THE FOOD CHAIN: PESTICIDES AND WILDLIFE

In 1962, US marine biologist Rachel Carson published *Silent Spring*, the book that first drew public attention to the environmental dangers posed by pesticides. In 30 years, have we learned the lesson?

The introduction of various synthetic chemicals to control plant and animal pests came in the 1940s with the intensification of agriculture. Among the earliest pesticides were a group of organochlorine insecticides, including DDT, hailed as a wonder chemical by agricultural scientists. Organochlorines were supremely efficient at killing pests, and remained chemically active for years after just one spraying. This persistence had a destructive effect on wildlife—organochlorines are picked up in sublethal doses and stored in the body fat of animals such as shrews and voles, perhaps through eating poisoned insects. A larger animal, such as a bird of prey, eats the shrews and voles and ends up with a considerable amount of the chemical; in a phenomenon known as 'concentration in the food chain', the top predators accumulate the poison from thousands of invertebrates. The effects of this included failure to reproduce, often because eggs were laid with such thin shells that they broke before the young birds were ready to hatch. Widespread use of pesticides had a catastrophic effect on the populations of many predatory birds. In Norfolk, England, the number of sparrowhawks fell from 400–500 pairs in the late 1940s to a single pair by the 1960s.

*Silent Spring* caused a furore, and Carson was bitterly attacked by the chemical industry. She died soon after she wrote the book, but the modern environmental movement she had helped to launch lived on. Despite protests from the industry, the most persistent chemicals began to be withdrawn—but it is a slow and continuing process: DDT was not finally banned in the UK until 1984, for example, and is still used in many countries. The phasing-out of persistent organochlorine pesticides created the illusion that most of the problems of pesticides and wildlife had now been solved, but recent research has shown this to be untrue.

Throughout the Third World, the use of hazardous pesticides has been increasing. Many of the users are unable to read safety instructions or to afford protective clothing, with a resulting huge toll on human health as well as wildlife. In Ghana, for example, pesticides are still used deliberately to poison fish to eat, rather than catching them alive in nets. Apart from the danger to the consumer of pesticide residues in the fish, this also kills most other aquatic life. In Brazil, chemical defoliants have been used to clear rainforest for development. In the Philippines, misuse of pesticides on crops has led to widespread pollution of fresh water and consequent threats to fisheries. Malaria control in many countries has involved spraying vast areas of fresh water with toxic chemicals to kill the mosquitoes that carry the disease, although the increasing resistance to pesticides among malaria mosquitoes makes this extremely damaging process more and more futile.

Damage is not confined to the South. Widespread pesticide poisoning incidents continue to occur in the rich industrialized world as well. The use of seed treated with pesticides has killed thousands of geese feeding on farmland. Barn owls have declined throughout Europe from accidentally eating rat poison. Illegal use of poisoned bait by gamekeepers takes an annual toll of buzzards, kites, and eagles. In the UK, if current trends continue, the common partridge will be extinct within 20 years. Its decline is due to subtle food-chain effects, which are far harder to identify though of the greatest consequence to wildlife. Research by the Game Conservancy has shown that the survival of young partridge chicks triples if a farmer does not spray herbicide right up to the field margins (this also leads to increases in the numbers of smaller birds, butterflies, and other insects). The herbicide is not directly toxic to the partridge, but spray drift kills wild flowers in hedgerows, thus depleting the food source of many insects that are, in turn, eaten by young partridges. The food-chain effect of the weed killer means the partridges die of starvation: an unseen and hitherto unsuspected side effect.

The hidden losses from pesticides are likely to be far greater than the corpses we see, and account in large part for the continuing depletion of wild species from farmland and forestry areas throughout the world. This increasing toll on wildlife lends even greater urgency to the efforts to find nonchemical alternatives to pesticides (such as biological control and integrated pest management), and to phase out completely the most toxic chemicals on the market.

*The survival of grey partridges in the UK is threatened by herbicides.*

## LEGAL TRADE IN ANIMALS AND ANIMAL PRODUCTS
*World imports (%)*

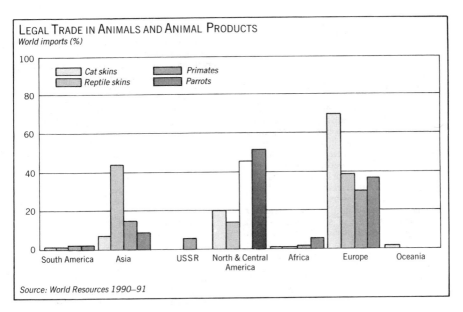

Legend: Cat skins, Reptile skins, Primates, Parrots

*Source: World Resources 1990–91*

### Extinction and greenhouse effect

*Finally, more generally, how concerned or worried are you about the following: a great deal, a fair amount, not very much, or not at all?*

*a) The extinction in the world of some plants and animal species*

|              | Today | Oct 1988 |
|--------------|-------|----------|
| A great deal | 52    | 43       |
| A fair amount| 32    | 36       |
| Not very much| 11    | 14       |
| Not at all   | 4     | 5        |
| Don't know   | 1     | 1        |

*b) The depletion of world forest resources*

|              | Today | Oct 1988 |
|--------------|-------|----------|
| A great deal | 61    | 51       |
| A fair amount| 26    | 31       |
| Not very much| 8     | 11       |
| Not at all   | 4     | 5        |
| Don't know   | 1     | 2        |

*c) The 'greenhouse' effect, that is the possible atmospheric damages affecting the world's weather brought about by the gas (carbon dioxide) emitted from burning coal and oil products, and from ozone depletion*

|              | Today | Oct 1988 |
|--------------|-------|----------|
| A great deal | 59    | 50       |
| A fair amount| 25    | 29       |
| Not very much| 10    | 13       |
| Not at all   | 5     | 5        |
| Don't know   | 2     | 3        |

*Have you heard of the greenhouse effect?*

|            |    |
|------------|----|
| Yes        | 89 |
| No         | 9  |
| Don't know | 2  |

# TERMS

too many neutrons escape from the surface for a chain reaction to carry on; above the critical mass, the reaction may accelerate into a nuclear explosion.

**absolute zero** the lowest temperature theoretically possible, zero kelvin, equivalent to $-273.16°C/-459.67°F$, at which molecules are motionless. Although the third law of thermodynamics indicates the impossibility of reaching absolute zero exactly, a temperature within $3 \times 10^{-8}$ kelvin of it was produced in 1984 by Finnish scientists. Near absolute zero, the physical properties of some materials change substantially; for example, some metals lose their electrical resistance and become superconductive. See cryogenics.

**acoustics** in general, the experimental and theoretical science of sound and its transmission; in particular, that branch of the science that has to do with the phenomena of sound in a particular space such as a room or theatre.

**analogue signal** in electronics, current or voltage that conveys or stores information, and varies continuously in the same way as the information it represents. Analogue signals are prone to interference and distortion.

**centre of mass** or **centre of gravity** the point in or near an object from which its total weight appears to originate and can be assumed to act. A symmetrical homogeneous object such as a sphere or cube has its centre of mass at its physical centre; a hollow shape (such as a cup) may have its centre of mass in space inside the hollow.

**chain reaction** in nuclear physics, a fission reaction that is maintained because neutrons released by the splitting of some atomic nuclei themselves go on to split others, releasing even more neutrons. Such a reaction can be controlled (as in a nuclear reactor) by using moderators to absorb excess neutrons. Uncontrolled, a chain reaction produces a nuclear explosion (as in an atom bomb).

**critical mass** in nuclear physics, the minimum mass of fissile material that can undergo a continuous chain reaction. Below this mass,

**cryogenics** science of very low temperatures (approaching absolute zero), including the production of very low temperatures and the exploitation of special properties associated with them, such as the disappearance of electrical resistance (superconductivity).

**diffraction** the spreading of a wave motion (such as light or sound) as it passes an obstacle and expands into a region not exposed directly to incoming waves behind the obstacle. This accounts for interference phenomena observed at the edges of opaque objects, or discontinuities between different media in the path of a wave train. The phenomena give rise to slight spreading of light into coloured bands at the shadow of a straight edge.

**digital** in electronics and computing, a term meaning 'coded as numbers'. A digital system uses two-state, either on/off or high/low voltage pulses, to encode, receive, and transmit information. A *digital display* shows discrete values as numbers (as opposed to an analogue signal, such as the continuous sweep of a pointer on a dial). *Digital electronics* is the technology that underlies digital techniques. Low-power, miniature, integrated circuits (chips) provide the means for the coding, storage, transmission, processing, and reconstruction of information of all kinds.

**dynamics** in mechanics, the mathematical and physical study of the behaviour of bodies under the action of forces that produce changes of motion in them.

**efficiency** in a machine, the useful work output (work done by the machine) divided by the work input (work put into the machine), usually expressed as a percentage. Because of losses caused by friction, efficiency is always less than 100%, although it can approach this for electrical machines with no moving parts (such as a transformer).

**elasticity** the ability of a solid to recover its shape once deforming forces (stresses modifying its dimensions or shape) are removed. An

## FUNDAMENTAL CONSTANTS

| Constant | Symbol | Value in SI Units |
|---|---|---|
| acceleration of free fall | $g$ | $9.80665$ m s$^{-2}$ |
| Avogadro's constant | $N_A$ | $6.02252 \times 10^{23}$ mol$^{-1}$ |
| Boltzmann's constant | $k = R/N_A$ | $1.380622 \times 10^{-23}$ J K$^{-1}$ |
| electronic charge | $e$ | $1.602192 \times 10^{-19}$ C |
| electronic rest mass | $m_e$ | $9.109558 \times 10^{-31}$ kg |
| Faraday's constant | $F$ | $9.648670 \times 10^4$ C mol$^{-1}$ |
| gas constant | $R$ | $8.31434$ J K$^{-1}$ mol$^{-1}$ |
| gravitational constant | $G$ | $6.664 \times 10^{-11}$ N m$^2$ kg$^{-2}$ |
| Loschmidt's number | $N_L$ | $2.68719 \times 10^{25}$ m$^{-3}$ |
| neutron rest mass | $m_n$ | $1.67492 \times 10^{-27}$ kg |
| Planck's constant | $h$ | $6.626196 \times 10^{-34}$ J s |
| proton rest mass | $m_p$ | $1.672614 \times 10^{-27}$ kg |
| speed of light | $c$ | $2.99792458 \times 10^8$ m s$^{-1}$ |
| standard atmospheric pressure | $P$ | $1.01325 \times 10^5$ Pa |
| Stefan–Boltzmann constant | $\sigma$ | $5.6697 \times 10^{-8}$ W m$^{-2}$ K$^{-4}$ |

# COLD FUSION: THE DISCOVERY THAT NEVER WAS

On 23 March 1989, the scientific world was stunned by an announcement made by two chemists working at the University of Utah, USA. Stanley Pons and Martin Fleischmann, claimed that they could produce nuclear fusion—the process that powers the Sun—in a simple test tube, at room temperature.

In nuclear fusion, atomic nuclei of light elements are joined together, releasing great quantities of energy in the process. Inside the Sun, nuclei of hydrogen atoms are joined together, producing an immense outpouring of heat and light. For decades, scientists have been trying to produce controlled nuclear fusion as a source of cheap, pollution-free power. However, the technical problems to be overcome are immense. This is because all nuclei are electrically charged and repel each other, which makes it difficult to force together and fuse nuclei. Most fusion research involves heating the nuclei to very high temperatures—ten times hotter than those found inside the Sun. At these temperatures, the nuclei are moving very rapidly and occasional collisions between nuclei are so energetic that fusion occurs. Despite the huge amounts of money spent on fusion research, a working fusion reactor is still decades away.

*Stanley Pons and Martin Fleischmann.*

The announcement of Pons and Fleischmann seemed to offer a cheap and quick shortcut to fusion power. Their process involved passing an electric current through heavy water—water containing deuterium or 'heavy hydrogen'—between electrodes made of the metal palladium. After the current had been flowing for some time, large amounts of heat were produced.

The two scientists claimed the heat was produced by fusion of the deuterium nuclei in the water, and they had a theory to explain how the fusion occurred. It was well known that palladium can absorb large amounts of hydrogen. Perhaps the electric current carried the deuterium to the palladium electrodes where it was soaked up like water being absorbed into a sponge. Once the deuterium was crammed inside the palladium, deuterium nuclei would be close enough to fuse.

To prove their case, Pons and Fleischmann firstly claimed that the heat produced could not be explained by any known electrical or chemical effect; there was just too much heat. Secondly, the two chemists claimed to have detected neutrons—subatomic particles produced by fusion—coming from the test tube. Finally, they had found traces of the rare gas helium, the end product of the fusion of helium nuclei.

Excitement spread rapidly through the scientific world as research groups raced to repeat and verify the results. Pons and Fleischmann were treated as stars by the press. Reports appeared in newspapers saying that 'cold fusion' would solve the world's energy crisis, as an endless supply of deuterium can be extracted from sea water.

During the first week of April, there were reports that workers at the Texas A&M University had duplicated Pons and Fleischmann's experiment. One or two other claims were made that small teams of researchers at minor universities had achieved cold fusion. But, at the major research laboratories, with large teams of scientists using the best equipment, nothing was found. Doubts began to creep into many minds.

So began a remarkable process in which the evidence for cold fusion was gradually undermined. Workers at the Texas A&M University discovered that an electrical short circuit in their equipment produced the excess heat that they had seen. Other researchers also found errors in their work and withdrew claims to have seen cold fusion. A group at the California Institute of Technology showed that Pons' claim to have found helium was impossible to support. It was most likely, the team concluded, that any helium detected came from the atmosphere. In the UK, a team at Harwell laboratories announced that after an extensive range of experiments, conducted over a long period and with the best equipment, they had found no evidence for cold fusion. Harwell's reputation for high-quality science meant that the idea of cold fusion was effectively killed off.

The cold fusion story shows that science is a very untidy, very human process. When faced with a glittering prize, such as a source of limitless pollution-free energy, even the most competent scientist is apt to rush ahead too quickly. Wishful thinking takes over. Perhaps greed plays a part. After all, the commercial rewards available if cold fusion had worked would have been immense. And scientists are just as fallible as other people.

elastic material obeys Hooke's law: that is, its deformation is proportional to the applied stress up to a certain point, called the *elastic limit*, beyond which additional stress will deform it permanently. Elastic materials include metals and rubber; however, all materials have some degree of elasticity.

**electric current** the flow of electrically charged particles through a conducting circuit due to the presence of a potential difference. The current at any point in a circuit is the amount of charge flowing per second; it is measured in amperes. Current carries electrical energy from a power supply, such as a battery of electrical cells, to the components of the circuit where it is converted into other forms of energy, such as heat, light, or motion. It may be either direct (DC) or alternating (AC).

**electricity** all phenomena caused by electric charge, whether static or in motion. Electric charge is caused by an excess or deficit of electrons in the charged substance, and an electric current by the movement of electrons around a circuit. Substances may be electrical conductors, such as metals, which allow the passage of electricity through them, or insulators, such as rubber, which are extremely poor conductors. Substances with relatively poor conductivities that can be improved by the addition of heat or light are known as semiconductors.

**electric potential** the relative electrical state of an object. A charged conductor, for example, has a higher potential than the earth, whose potential is taken by convention to be zero. An electric cell (battery) has a potential in relation to emf (electromotive force), which can make current flow in an external circuit. The difference in potential between two points—the *potential difference*—is expressed in volts; that is, a 12V battery has a potential difference of 12 volts between its negative and positive terminals.

**electrodynamics** the branch of physics dealing with electric currents and associated magnetic forces. Quantum electrodynamics (QED) studies the interaction between charged particles and their emission and absorption of electromagnetic radiation. This field combines quantum theory and relativity theory, making accurate predictions about subatomic processes involving charged particles such as electrons and protons.

**electromagnetic waves** oscillating electric and magnetic fields travelling together through space at a speed of nearly 300,000 km/186,000 mi per second. The (limitless) range of possible wavelengths or frequencies of electromagnetic waves, which can be thought of as making up the *electromagnetic spectrum*, includes radio waves, infrared radiation, visible light, ultraviolet radiation, X-rays, and gamma rays.

**energy** the capacity for doing work. Potential energy (PE) is energy deriving from position; thus a stretched spring has elastic PE, and an object raised to a height above the Earth's surface, or the water in an elevated reservoir, has gravitational PE. A lump of coal and a tank of petrol, together with the oxygen needed for their combustion, have chemical energy. Other sorts of energy include electrical and nuclear energy, and light and sound. Moving bodies possess kinetic energy (KE). Energy can be converted from one form to another, but the total quantity stays the same (in accordance with the conservation of energy principle that governs many natural phenomena). For example, as an apple falls, it loses gravitational PE but gains KE.

**engine** a device for converting stored energy into useful work or movement. Most engines use a fuel as their energy store. The fuel is burnt to produce heat energy—hence the name 'heat engine'—which is then converted into movement. Heat engines can be classified according to the fuel they use (petrol engine or diesel engine), or according to whether the fuel is burnt inside (internal combustion engine) or outside (steam engine) the engine, or according to whether they produce a reciprocating or rotary motion (turbine or Wankel engine).

**entropy** in thermodynamics, a parameter representing the state of disorder of a system at the atomic, ionic, or molecular level; the greater the disorder, the higher the entropy. Thus the fast-moving disordered molecules of water vapour have higher entropy than those of more ordered liquid water, which in turn have more entropy than the molecules in solid crystalline ice.

**equilibrium** an unchanging condition in which the forces acting on a particle or system of particles (body) cancel each other, or in which energy is distributed among the particles of a system in the most probable way; or the state in which a body is at rest or moving at constant velocity. A body is in *thermal equilibrium* if no heat enters or leaves it, so that all its parts are at the same temperature as its surroundings.

**field** the region of space by which an object exerts a force on another separate object because of certain properties they both possess. For example, there is a force of attraction between any two objects that have mass, where one is in the gravitational field of the other. Other fields of force include electric fields (caused by electric charges) and magnetic fields (caused by magnetic poles), either of which can involve attractive or repulsive forces.

**force** any influence that tends to change the state of rest or the uniform motion in a straight line of a body. The action of an unbalanced or resultant force results in the acceleration of a body in the direction of action of the force or it may, if the body is unable to move freely, result in its deformation. Force is a vector quantity, possessing both magnitude and direction; its unit is the newton.

**forces, fundamental** the four fundamental interactions believed to be at work in

## SPACEWARPS: THE SEARCH FOR GRAVITATIONAL WAVES

Within the next few years, a new type of 'telescope' will scan the skies, picking up an entirely new kind of signal from space. The new instruments are gravitational wave detectors. They should detect radiation from the most violent events in the universe: supernovae, or colliding neutron stars. These events are so violent that they distort the structure of space itself, and cause 'spacewarps', which ripple outwards like waves on a pond when a stone is dropped in. It is these waves—called gravitational waves—that the new telescopes will detect.

Albert Einstein decided that gravitational waves should exist after developing his theory of gravity—general relativity. One way to visualize Einstein's ideas is to think of space as a thin rubber sheet. If a mass on a rubber sheet is wiggled up and down, ripples will spread across the sheet. This is similar to the way gravitational waves are produced according to Einstein. Space–time is a combination of space and time, and complicated mathematics is needed to describe it properly. Suffice it to say that distortions in space–time are the cause of gravity and gravitational waves.

Any two objects orbiting around each other generate gravitational waves. For instance, the Earth orbiting around the Sun produces gravitational waves, but they are too weak to be detected. The best sources of gravitational waves are likely to be extremely violent events, such as supernovae and the collapse of neutron stars.

When a gravitational wave passes over and through an object, it distorts the shape of that object. The object is squeezed in one direction and stretched in the perpendicular direction. We do not notice these changes because they are too small to detect easily. An object a metre across would change in size less that the diameter of an atomic nucleus.

Despite the formidable difficulties, physicists have been trying to detect gravitational waves. In the 1960s, Joseph Weber of the University of Maryland used a cylindrical bar of aluminium, weighing a tonne, as a detector. Over the years, other researchers have built similar detectors, usually cooled to a few degrees above absolute zero to increase sensitivity. However, these bar detectors have not been successful. Although Weber claims to have found gravitational waves, most astronomers are sceptical of his claims.

However, a new type of detector has recently led to a resurgence of interest in gravitational wave astronomy. The new detectors, developed by Bob Forward of the Hughes Corporation, use laser technology to measure the distance between two widely separated mirrors. This is a refinement of the laser ranging technique routinely used by surveyors. A laser beam is bounced off a distant mirror; the time taken for the beam to return indicates the distance to the mirror. When a gravitational wave passes over the equipment, the distance between the mirrors changes as the wave distorts the space between the mirrors.

In practice, the laser light is beamed at two mirrors in different directions, at right angles. When a gravitational waves passes, one direction is lengthened and the other distance is reduced. This setup means that you do not have to time the light. You let the beams interfere with each other after their trip to the mirrors, producing a pattern of light and dark bands known as an interference pattern. This pattern changes noticeably if even very slight changes in mirror positions occur. A final refinement is to bounce the light beams back and forth between the mirrors many times, up to a hundred times, before forming the interference pattern. This increases the sensitivity of the apparatus as the distance to the mirror is in effect increased.

Prototype detectors of this type have been built at Caltech in California, Munich in Germany, and Glasgow in the UK. Full-scale models are about to be built. It will take about three years to get the full-scale detectors working, and another two years to iron out any problems. When all detectors are working they will act in concert. As a gravitational wave passes through the Earth, at the speed of light, it will pass through different detectors at different times. By noting the time the wave arrives at each detector, astronomers will be able to calculate the direction the wave came from. The more detectors, the more accurately the direction of a source can be established. With a full set of detectors spread across the Earth, the direction of the wave can be established quite accurately, to within about a quarter of the apparent size of the Moon. By the late 1990s, gravitational wave astronomy should be well established, and producing its first results.

the physical universe. There are two long-range forces: **gravity**, which keeps the planets in orbit around the Sun, and acts between all particles that have mass; and the **electromagnetic force**, which stops solids from falling apart, and acts between all particles with electric charge. There are two very short-range forces: the **weak force**, responsible for the reactions that fuel the Sun and for the emission of beta particles from certain nuclei; and the **strong force**, which binds together the protons and neutrons in the nuclei of atoms.

**frequency** the number of periodic oscillations, vibrations, or waves occurring per unit of time. The unit of frequency is the hertz (Hz), one hertz being equivalent to one cycle per second. Human beings can hear sounds from objects vibrating in the range 20—15,000 Hz.

**electromagnetic waves**

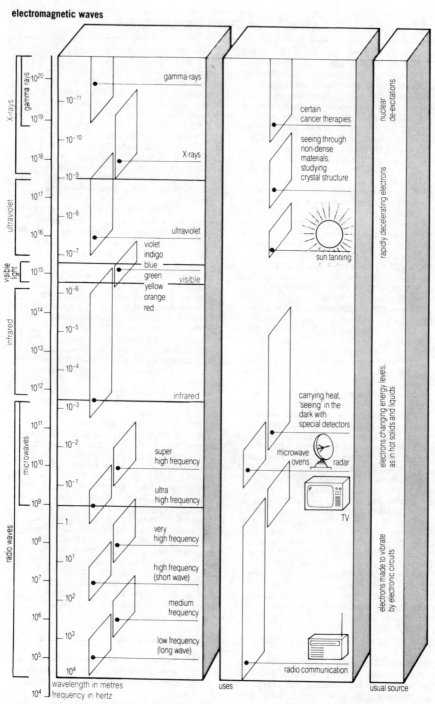

Ultrasonic frequencies well above 15,000 Hz can be detected by mammals such as bats.

**friction** the force that opposes the relative motion of two bodies in contact. The *coefficient of friction* is the ratio of the force required to achieve this relative motion to the force pressing the two bodies together.

**fundamental constant** a physical quantity that is constant in all circumstances throughout the whole universe. Examples are the electric charge of an electron, the speed of light, Planck's constant, and the gravitational constant.

**grand unified theory** (GUT) a sought-for theory that would combine the theory of the strong nuclear force (called quantum chromodynamics) with the theory of the weak and electromagnetic forces. The search for the grand unified theory is part of a larger programme seeking a unified field theory, which would combine all the forces of nature (including gravity) within one framework.

**gravity** the force of attraction that arises between objects by virtue of their masses. On Earth, gravity is the force of attraction between any object in the Earth's gravitational field and the Earth itself.

**half-life** the time taken for the strength of a radioactive source to decay to half its original value. It may vary from millionths of a second to billions of years. Radioactive substances decay exponentially; thus the time taken for the first 50% of the isotope to decay will be the same as the time taken by the next 25%, and by the 12.5% after that, and so on. For example, carbon-14 takes about 5,730 years for half the material to decay; another 5,730 for half of the remaining half to decay; then 5,730 years for half of that remaining half to decay, and so on. Plutonium-239, one of the most toxic of all radioactive substances, has a half-life of about 24,000 years. In theory, the decay process is never complete and there is always some residual radioactivity.

**heat** form of internal energy possessed by a substance by virtue of the kinetic energy in the motion of its molecules or atoms. Heat energy is transferred by conduction, convection, and radiation. It always flows from a region of higher temperature (heat intensity) to one of lower temperature. Its effect on a substance may be simply to raise its temperature, or to cause it to expand, melt (if a solid), vaporize (if a liquid), or increase its pressure (if a confined gas).

**hydrodynamics** the science of nonviscous fluids (such as water, alcohol, and ether) in motion.

**hydrostatics** the branch of statics dealing with the mechanical problems of fluids in equilibrium—that is, in a static condition. Practical applications include shipbuilding and dam design.

**inertia** the tendency of an object to remain in a state of rest or uniform motion until an external force is applied, as stated by Isaac Newton's first law of motion (see Newton's laws of motion).

**interference** the phenomenon of two or more wave motions interacting and combining to produce a resultant wave of larger or smaller amplitude (depending on whether the combining waves are in or out of phase with each other). Interference of white light (multiwavelength) results in spectral coloured fringes, for example, the iridescent colours of oil films seen on water or soap bubbles. Interference of sound waves of similar frequency produces the phenomenon of beats, often used by musicians when tuning an instrument. With monochromatic light (of a single wavelength), interference produces patterns of light and dark bands. This is the basis of holography, for example. Interferometry can also be applied to radio waves, and is a powerful tool in modern astronomy.

**kinetic theory** theory describing the physical properties of matter in terms of the behaviour—principally movement—of its component atoms or molecules. The temperature of a substance is dependent on the velocity of movement of its constituent particles, increased temperature being accompanied by increased movement. A gas consists of rapidly moving atoms or molecules and, according to kinetic theory, it is their continual impact on the walls of the containing vessel that accounts for the pressure of the gas. The slowing of molecular motion as temperature falls, according to kinetic theory, accounts for the physical properties of liquids and solids, culminating in the concept of no molecular motion at absolute zero (0 K/–273°C). By making various assumptions about the nature of gas molecules, it is possible to derive from the kinetic theory the various gas laws (such as Avogadro's law, Boyle's law, and Charles's law).

**laser** (acronym for *light amplification by stimulated emission of radiation*) a device for producing a narrow beam of light, capable of travelling over vast distances without dispersion, and of being focused to give enormous power densities ($10^8$ watts per $cm^2$ for high-energy lasers). It operates on a principle similar to that of the maser (a high-frequency microwave amplifier or oscillator). The uses of lasers include communications (a laser beam can carry much more information than can radio waves), cutting, drilling, welding, satellite tracking, medical and biological research, and surgery.

**lens** in optics, a piece of a transparent material, such as glass, with two polished surfaces—one concave or convex, and the other plane, concave, or convex—that modifies rays of light. A convex lens brings rays of light together; a concave lens makes the rays diverge. Lenses are essential to spectacles, microscopes, telescopes, cameras, and almost all optical instruments.

**lever** a simple machine consisting of a rigid rod pivoted at a fixed point called the fulcrum, used for shifting or raising a heavy load or applying force in a similar way. Levers are classified into orders according to where the effort is applied, and the load-moving force developed, in relation to the position of the fulcrum. A *first-order* lever has the load and the effort on opposite sides of the fulcrum—for example, a see-saw or pair of scissors. A *second-order* lever has the load and the effort on the same side of the fulcrum, with the load nearer the fulcrum—for example, nutcrackers or a

lens

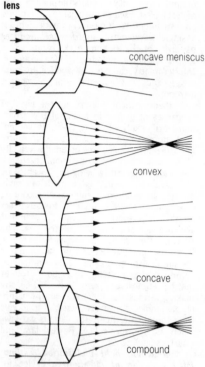

concave meniscus

convex

concave

compound

wheelbarrow. A ***third-order*** lever has the effort nearer the fulcrum than the load with both on the same side of it—for example, a pair of tweezers or tongs.

**light**  electromagnetic waves in the visible range, having a wavelength, from about 400 nanometers in the extreme violet to about 770 nanometers in the extreme red. Light is considered to exhibit particle and wave properties, and the fundamental particle, or quantum, of light is called the photon. The speed of light (and of all electromagnetic radiation) in a vacuum is approximately 300,000 km/186,000 mi per second, and is a universal constant denoted by $c$.

**luminescence**  emission of light from a body when its atoms are excited by means other than raising its temperature. Short-lived luminescence is called fluorescence; longer-lived luminescence is called phosporescence.

**magnetism**  branch of physics dealing with the properties of magnets and magnetic fields. Magnetic fields are produced by moving charged particles: in electromagnets, electrons flow through a coil of wire connected to a battery; in magnets, spinning electrons within the atoms generate the field.

**mass** the quantity of matter in a body as measured by its inertia. Mass determines the acceleration produced in a body by a given force acting on it, the acceleration being inversely proportional to the mass of the body. The mass also determines the force exerted on a body by gravity on Earth, although this attraction

varies slightly from place to place. In the SI system, the base unit of mass is the kilogram.

**mechanics**  branch of physics dealing with the motions of bodies and the forces causing these motions, and also with the forces acting on bodies in equilibrium. It is usually divided into dynamics and statics.

**mirror** any polished surface that reflects light; often made from 'silvered' glass (in practice, a mercury alloy coating of glass). A plane (flat) mirror produces a same-size, erect 'virtual' image located behind the mirror at the same distance from it as the object is in front of it. A spherical concave mirror produces a reduced, inverted real image in front or an enlarged, erect virtual image behind it (as with a shaving mirror), depending on how close the object is to the mirror. A spherical convex mirror produces a reduced, erect virtual image behind it (as with a car's rear-view mirror).

**Newton's laws of motion** three laws that form the basis of Newtonian mechanics. (1) Unless acted upon by an external resultant, or unbalanced, force, an object at rest stays at rest, and a moving object continues moving at the same speed in the same straight line. Put more simply, the law says that, if left alone, stationary objects will not move and moving objects will keep on moving at a constant speed in a straight line. (2) A resultant or unbalanced force applied to an object produces a rate of change of momentum that is directly proportional to the force and is in the direction of the force. (3) When an object A applies a force to an object B, B applies an equal and opposite force to A; that is, to every action there is an equal and opposite reaction.

**nuclear fission**  process whereby an atomic nucleus breaks up into two or more major fragments with the emission of two or three neutrons. It is accompanied by the release of energy in the form of gamma radiation and the kinetic energy of the emitted particles.

**nuclear fusion**  process whereby two atomic nuclei are fused, with the release of a large amount of energy. Very high temperatures and pressures are thought to be required in order for the process to happen. Under these conditions the atoms involved are stripped of all their electrons so that the remaining particles, which together make up plasma, can come close together at very high speeds and overcome the mutual repulsion of the positive charges on the atomic nuclei. At very close range another nuclear force will come into play, fusing the particles together to form a larger nucleus. As fusion is accompanied by the release of large amounts of energy, the process might one day be harnessed to form the basis of commercial energy production. Methods of achieving controlled fusion are therefore the subject of research around the world.

**optics**  the branch of physics that deals with the study of light and vision—for example, shadows and mirror images, lenses, microscopes, telescopes, and cameras. For all

PHYSICS: CHRONOLOGY

| | |
|---|---|
| **c. 400 BC** | The first 'atomic' theory was put forward by Democritus. |
| **c. 250** | Archimedes' principle of buoyancy was established. |
| **45** | The Julian calendar as used in most Western countries was introduced. |
| **AD 1600** | Magnetism was described by English physicist and physician William Gilbert. |
| **c. 1610** | The principle of falling bodies descending to earth at the same speed was established by Italian astronomer Galileo. |
| **1642** | The principles of hydraulics were put forward by French mathematician, physicist, and philosopher Blaise Pascal. |
| **1643** | The mercury barometer was invented by Italian physicist Evangelista Torricelli. |
| **1656** | The pendulum clock was invented by Dutch physicist and astronomer Christiaan Huygens. |
| **1662** | Boyle's law concerning gas was established by Irish physicist and chemist Robert Boyle. |
| **c. 1665** | English physicist Isaac Newton put forward the law of gravity, stating that the Earth exerts a constant force on falling bodies. |
| **1677** | The simple microscope was invented by Dutch microscopist Antoni van Leeuwenhoek. |
| **1690** | The wave theory of light was propounded by Dutch physicist Christiaan Huygens. |
| **1704** | The corpuscular theory of light was put forward by Isaac Newton. |
| **1714** | The mercury thermometer was invented by German physicist Daniel Fahrenheit. |
| **1764** | Specific and latent heats were described by Scottish chemist Joseph Black. |
| **1771** | The link between nerve action and electricity was discovered by Italian anatomist and physiologist Luigi Galvani. |
| **c. 1787** | Charles's law relating the pressure, volume, and temperature of a gas was established by French physicist and physical chemist Jacques Alexandre César Charles. |
| **1795** | The metric system was adopted in France. |
| **1798** | The link between heat and friction was discovered by Anglo-American physicist Benjamin Thomson Rumford. |
| **1800** | Italian physicist Alessandro Volta invented the Voltaic cell. |
| **1801** | Interference of light was discovered by British physicist Thomas Young. |
| **1808** | The 'modern' atomic theory was propounded by British physicist and chemist John Dalton. |
| **1811** | Avogadro's hypothesis relating volumes and numbers of molecules of gases was proposed by Italian physicist and chemist Amedeo Avogadro. |
| **1814** | Fraunhofer lines in the solar spectrum were mapped by German physicist Joseph von Fraunhofer. |
| **1815** | Refraction of light was explained by French physicist Augustin Fresnel. |
| **1819** | The discovery of electromagnetism was made by Danish physicist Hans Oersted. |
| **1821** | The dynamo principle was described by British physicist and chemist Michael Faraday; the thermocouple was discovered by German physicist Thomas Seebeck. |
| **1822** | The laws of electrodynamics were established by French physicist and mathematician André Ampère. |
| **1824** | Thermodynamics as a branch of physics was proposed by French physicist Sadi Carnot. |
| **1827** | Ohm's law of electrical resistance was established by German physicist Georg Ohm; Brownian motion resulting from molecular vibrations was observed by British botanist Robert Brown. |
| **1829** | The law of gaseous diffusion established by Scottish chemist Thomas Graham. |
| **1831** | Electromagnetic induction was discovered by Faraday. |
| **1834** | Faraday discovered self-induction. |
| **1842** | The principle of conservation of energy was observed by German physician and physicist Julius von Mayer. |
| **c. 1847** | The mechanical equivalent of heat was described by English physicist James Joule. |
| **1849** | A measurement of speed of light was put forward by French physicist Armand Fizeau (1819–1896). |
| **1851** | The rotation of the Earth was demonstrated by French physicist Jean Foucault. |
| **1858** | The mirror galvanometer, an instrument for measuring small electric currents, was invented by Scottish mathematician and physicist William Kelvin. |
| **1859** | Spectrographic analysis was made by German chemist Robert Bunsen and German physicist Gustav Kirchhoff. |
| **1861** | Osmosis was discovered. |
| **1873** | Light was conceived as electromagnetic radiation by Scottish physicist James Maxwell. |

## PHYSICS: CHRONOLOGY CONT.

| | |
|---|---|
| 1877 | A theory of sound as vibrations in an elastic medium was propounded by British physicist John Rayleigh. |
| 1880 | Piezoelectricity was discovered by French scientist Pierre Curie. |
| 1887 | The existence of radio waves was predicted by German physicist Heinrich Hertz. |
| 1895 | X-rays were discovered by German physicist Wilhelm Röntgen. |
| 1896 | The discovery of radioactivity was made by French physicist Antoine Becquerel. |
| 1897 | The electron was discovered by Joseph John Thomson. |
| 1899 | New Zealand physicist Ernest Rutherford discovered alpha and beta rays. |
| 1900 | Quantum theory was propounded by German physicist Max Planck; the discovery of gamma rays was made by French physicist Paul-Ulrich Villard (1860–1934). |
| 1902 | British physicist Oliver Heaviside discovered the ionosphere. |
| 1904 | The theory of radioactivity was put forward by Rutherford and British chemist Frederick Soddy. |
| 1905 | German–Swiss physicist Albert Einstein propounded his special theory of relativity. |
| 1911 | The discovery of the atomic nucleus was made by Rutherford. |
| 1913 | The Geiger counter was invented by German physicist Hans Geiger and Walther Müller; the orbiting electron atomic theory was propounded by Danish physicist Niels Bohr. |
| 1915 | X-ray crystallography was discovered by William and Lawrence Bragg. |
| 1916 | Einstein put forward his general theory of relativity; mass spectrography was discovered by British physicist William Aston. |
| 1924 | English physicist Edward Appleton made his study of the Heaviside layer. |
| 1927 | The uncertainty principle of atomic physics was established by German physicist Werner Heisenberg. |
| 1928 | Wave mechanics was introduced by Austrian physicist Erwin Schrödinger. |
| 1931 | The cyclotron was developed by US physicist Ernest Lawrence. |
| 1932 | The discovery of the neutron was made by James Chadwick; the electron microscope was developed by Soviet–American physicist Vladimir Zworykin. |
| 1933 | The positron, the antiparticle of the electron, was discovered by US physicist Carl David Anderson. |
| 1934 | Artificial radioactivity was developed by Frédéric and Irène Joliot-Curie. |
| 1939 | The discovery of nuclear fission was made by German chemists Otto Hahn and Fritz Strassman (1902–   ). |
| 1942 | The first controlled nuclear chain reaction was achieved by US physicist Enrico Fermi. |
| 1956 | The neutrino, an elementary particle, was discovered. |
| 1960 | The Mössbauer effect of atom emissions was discovered by German physicist Rudolf Mössbauer; the first maser was developed by US physicist Theodore Maiman (1927–   ). |
| 1963 | Maiman developed the first laser or light amplification by stimulated emission of radiation. |
| 1964 | US physicist Murray Gell-Mann discovered the quark. |
| 1983 | Evidence of W and Z particles confirmed at CERN, validating the link between the weak and electromagnetic forces. |
| 1986 | First high-temperature superconductor discovered, able to conduct electricity without resistance at a temperature of 35K. |
| 1989 | Stanley Pons of the USA and Martin Fleischmann of the UK claimed to have achieved nuclear fusion at room temperature and pressure (cold fusion). CERN's Large Electron–Positron Collider (LEP), a particle accelerator with a circumference of 27 km/16.8 mi, came into operation. |

practical purposes light rays travel in straight lines, although Einstein demonstrated that they may be 'bent' by a gravitational field. On striking a surface they are reflected or refracted with some absorption of energy, and the study of this is known as geometrical optics.

**power** the rate of doing work or consuming energy. Its SI unit is the watt (joule per second).

**pressure** measure of the force acting normally (at right angles) to a body per unit surface area. Its SI unit is the pascal (newton per square metre). In a fluid (liquid or gas), pressure increases with depth. At the edge of Earth's atmosphere, pressure is zero, whereas at ground level it is about 100 kPa.

**quantum theory** the theory that energy does not have a continuous range of values, but is, instead, absorbed or radiated discontinuously, in multiples of definite, indivisible units called quanta. Just as earlier theory showed how light, generally seen as a wave motion, could also in some ways be seen as composed of discrete particles (photons), quantum mechanics shows how atomic particles such as electrons may also be seen as having wavelike properties. Quantum mechanics is the basis of particle physics, modern theoretical chemistry, and the solid-state physics that describes the behaviour of the silicon chips used in computers.

**radiation** emission of radiant energy as particles or waves—for example, heat, light, alpha particles, and beta particles.

**radioactivity** spontaneous alteration of the nuclei of radioactive atoms, accompanied by the emission of radiation. It is the property exhibited by the radioactive isotopes of stable elements and all isotopes of radioactive elements.

**radioisotope** contraction of *radioactive isotope* a naturally occurring or synthetic radioactive form of an element. Most radioisotopes are made by bombarding a stable element with neutrons in the core of a nuclear reactor. The radiations given off by radioisotopes are easy to detect (hence their use as tracers), can in some instances penetrate substantial thicknesses of materials, and have profound effects on living matter. Although dangerous, radioisotopes are used in the fields of medicine, industry, agriculture, and research.

**reflection** the throwing back or deflection of waves, such as light or sound waves, when they hit a surface. The *law of reflection* states that the angle of incidence (the angle between the ray and a perpendicular line drawn to the surface) is equal to the angle of reflection (the angle between the reflected ray and a perpendicular to the surface).

**refraction** the bending of a wave of light, heat, or sound when it passes from one medium to another. Refraction occurs because waves travel at different velocities in diferent media.

**relativity** the theory of the relative rather than absolute character of motion and mass and the interdependence of matter, time, and space, as developed by Albert Einstein in two phases:

*special theory* (1905) Starting with the premises that (1) the laws of nature are the same for all observers in unaccelerated motion, and (2) the speed of light is independent of the motion of its source, Einstein postulated that the time interval between two events was longer for an observer in whose frame of reference the events occur in different places than for the observer for whom they occur at the same place.

*general theory of relativity* (1915) The geometrical properties of space-time were to be conceived as modified locally by the presence of a body with mass. A planet's orbit around the Sun (as observed in three-dimensional space) arises from its natural trajectory in modified space-time; there is no need to invoke, as Isaac Newton did, a force of gravity coming from the Sun and acting on the planet. Einstein's theory predicted slight differences in the orbits of the planets from Newton's theory, which were observable in the case of Mercury. The new theory also said light rays should bend when they pass by a massive object, owing to the object's effect on local space-time. The predicted bending of starlight was observed during the eclipse of the Sun 1919, when light

from distant stars passing close to the Sun was not masked by sunlight.

**resistance** that property of a substance that restricts the flow of electricity through it, associated with the conversion of electrical energy to heat; also the magnitude of this property. Resistance depends on many factors, such as the nature of the material, its temperature, dimensions, and thermal properties; degree of impurity; the nature and state of illumination of the surface; and the frequency and magnitude of the current. The unit of resistance is the ohm.

**resonance** rapid and uncontrolled increase in the size of a vibration when the vibrating object is subject to a force varying at its natural frequency. In a trombone, for example, the length of the air column in the instrument is adjusted until it resonates with the note being sounded. Resonance effects are also produced by many electrical circuits. Tuning a radio, for example, is done by adjusting the natural frequency of the receiver circuit until it coincides with the frequency of the radio waves falling on the aerial.

**semiconductor** crystalline material with an electrical conductivity between that of metals (good) and insulators (poor).

**SI units** (French *Système International d'Unités*) standard system of scientific units used by scientists worldwide. Originally proposed in 1960, it replaces the m.k.s., c.g.s., and f.p.s. systems. It is based on seven basic units: the metre (m) for length, kilogram (kg) for weight, second (s) for time, ampere (A) for electrical current, kelvin (K) for temperature, mole (mol) for amount of substance, and candela (cd) for luminosity.

**sound** physiological sensation received by the ear, originating in a vibration (pressure variation in the air) that communicates itself to the air, and travels in every direction, spreading out as an expanding sphere. All sound waves in air travel with a speed dependent on the temperature; under ordinary conditions, this is about 330 m/1,070 ft per second. The pitch of the sound depends on the number of vibrations imposed on the air per second, but the speed is unaffected. The loudness of a sound is dependent primarily on the amplitude of the vibration of the air.

**spectroscopy** the study of spectra associated with atoms or molecules in solid, liquid, or gaseous phase. Spectroscopy can be used to identify unknown compounds and is an invaluable tool in science, medicine, and industry (for example, in checking the purity of drugs).

**spectrum** (plural *spectra*) an arrangement of frequencies or wavelengths when electromagnetic radiations are separated into their constituent parts. Visible light is part of the electromagnetic spectrum and most sources emit waves over a range of wavelengths that can be broken up or 'dispersed'; white light can be separated into red, orange, yellow, green, blue, indigo, and violet. The visible spectrum was first studied by Newton, who showed in

## SI Prefixes

| Multiple | Prefix | Symbol | Example | |
|---|---|---|---|---|
| 1,000,000,000,000 ($10^{12}$) | tera | T | TV | (teravolt) |
| 1,000,000,000 ($10^9$) | giga | G | GW | (gigawatt) |
| 1,000,000 ($10^6$) | mega | M | MHz | (megahertz) |
| 1,000 ($10^3$) | kilo | K | Kg | (kilogram) |
| 1/10 ($10^{-1}$) | deci | d | dC | (decicoulomb) |
| 1/100 ($10^{-2}$) | centi | c | cm | (centimetre) |
| 1/1,000 ($10^{-3}$) | milli | m | mA | (milliampere) |
| 1/1,000,000 ($10^{-6}$) | micro | μ | μF | (microfarad) |
| 1/1,000,000,000 ($10^{-9}$) | nano | n | ns | (nanometre) |
| 1/1,000,000,000,000 ($10^{-12}$) | pico | p | ps | (picosecond) |

1672 how white light could be broken up into different colours.

**states of matter** the forms (solid, liquid, or gas) in which material can exist. Whether a material is solid, liquid, or gas depends on its temperature and the pressure on it. The transition between states takes place at definite temperatures, called melting point and boiling point.

**statics** branch of mechanics concerned with the behaviour of bodies at rest and forces in equilibrium, and distinguished from dynamics.

**stress and strain** measures of the deforming force applied to a body (stress) and of the resulting change in its shape (strain). For a perfectly elastic material, stress is proportional to strain (*Hooke's law*).

**surface tension** the property that causes the surface of a liquid to behave as if it were

## SI Units

| Quantity | SI unit | Symbol |
|---|---|---|
| absorbed radiation dose | gray | Gy |
| amount of substance | mole* | mol |
| electric capacitance | farad | F |
| electric charge | coulomb | C |
| electric conductance | siemens | S |
| electric current | ampere* | A |
| energy or work | joule | J |
| force | newton | N |
| frequency | hertz | Hz |
| illuminance | lux | lx |
| inductance | henry | H |
| length | metre* | m |
| luminous flux | lumen | lm |
| luminous intensity | candela* | cd |
| magnetic flux | weber | Wb |
| magnetic flux density | tesla | T |
| mass | kilogram* | kg |
| plane angle | radian | rad |
| potential difference | volt | V |
| power | watt | W |
| pressure | pascal | Pa |
| radiation dose equivalent | sievert | Sv |
| radiation exposure | roentgen | r |
| radioactivity | becquerel | Bq |
| resistance | ohm | Ω |
| solid angle | steradian | sr |
| sound intensity | decibel | dB |
| temperature | °Celsius | °C |
| temperature, thermodynamic | kelvin* | K |
| time | second* | s |

*SI base unit

covered with a weak elastic skin; this is why a needle can float on water. It is caused by the exposed surface's tendency to contract to the smallest possible area because of unequal cohesive forces between molecules at the surface. Allied phenomena include the formation of droplets, the concave profile of a meniscus, and the capillary action by which water soaks into a sponge.

**temperature** the state of hotness or coldness of a body, and the condition that determines whether or not it will transfer heat to, or receive heat from, another body according to the laws of thermodynamics. It is measured in degrees Celsius (before 1948 called centigrade), kelvin, or Fahrenheit.

**tension** reaction force set up in a body that is subjected to stress. In a stretched string or wire it exerts a pull that is equal in magnitude but opposite in direction to the stress being applied at its ends. Tension originates in the net attractive intermolecular force created when a stress causes the mean distance separating a material's molecules to become greater than the equilibrium distance. It is measured in newtons.

**thermodynamics** branch of physics dealing with the transformation of heat into and from other forms of energy. It is the basis of the study of the efficient working of engines, such as the steam and internal combustion engines. The three laws of thermodynamics are (1) energy can be neither created nor destroyed, heat and mechanical work being mutually convertible; (2) it is impossible for an unaided self-acting machine to convey heat from one body to another at a higher temperature; and (3) it is impossible by any procedure, no matter how idealized, to reduce any system to the absolute zero of temperature (0K/–273°C) in a finite number of operations. Put into mathematical form, these laws have widespread applications in physics and chemistry.

**ultrasound** pressure waves similar in nature to sound waves but occurring at frequencies above 20,000 Hz (cycles per second), the approximate upper limit of human hearing (15–16 Hz is the lower limit). Ultrasonics is concerned with the study and practical application of these phenomena.

**viscosity** the resistance of a fluid to flow, caused by its internal friction, which makes it resist flowing past a solid surface or other layers of the fluid. It applies to the motion of an object moving through a fluid as well as the motion of a fluid passing by an object.

**wave** a disturbance travelling through a medium (or space).

There are two types: in a *longitudinal wave* (such as a sound wave) the disturbance is parallel to the wave's direction of travel; in a *transverse wave* (such as an electromagnetic wave) it is perpendicular. The medium (for example the Earth, for seismic waves) is not permanently displaced by the passage of a wave.

**weight** the force exerted on an object by gravity. The weight of an object depends on its mass—the amount of material in it—and the strength of the Earth's gravitational pull, which decreases with height. Consequently, an object weighs less at the top of a mountain than at sea level. On the Moon, an object weighs only one-sixth of its weight on Earth, because the pull of the Moon's gravity is one-sixth that of the Earth.

**work** a measure of the result of transferring energy from one system to another to cause an object to move. Work should not be confused with energy (the capacity to do work, which is also measured in joules) or with power (the rate of doing work, measured in joules per second).

# PARTICLE PHYSICS

The study of the properties of the particles that make up all atoms, and of their interactions. More than 300 subatomic particles have now been identified by physicists, categorized into several classes according to their mass, electric charge, spin, magnetic moment, and interaction. Subatomic particles include the *elementary particles* (quarks, leptons, and gauge bosons), which are indivisible and so can be considered the fundamental units of matter; and the *hadrons* (baryons, such as protons and neutrons, and mesons), which are composite particles made up of two or three quarks. Some subatomic particles have been shown to change from one form to another.

**antimatter** a form of matter in which most of the attributes (such as electrical charge, magnetic moment, and spin) of elementary particles are reversed. Such particles (antiparticles) can be created in particle accelerators, such as those at CERN in Geneva and at Fermilab in the USA.

**baryon** a heavy subatomic particle made up of three indivisible elementary particles called quarks. The baryons form a subclass of the hadrons, and comprise the nucleons (protons and neutrons) and hyperons.

**boson** a subatomic particle whose spin can only take values that are whole numbers or zero. Bosons may be classified as gauge bosons (carriers of the four fundamental forces) or

mesons. All subatomic particles are either bosons or fermions.

**electron** an elementary particle of negative charge, which cannot be subdivided; it is a constituent of all atoms, and a member of the class of particles known as leptons. The electrons in each atom surround the nucleus in shells, the number being equal to the atom's atomic number (the number of protons in the nucleus). This electron structure is responsible for the chemical properties of the atom (see atomic structure).

**fermion** a subatomic particle whose spin can only take values that are half-integers, such as $\frac{1}{2}$ or $1\frac{1}{2}$. Fermions may be classified as leptons, such as the electron, and baryons, such as the proton and neutron. All subatomic particles are either fermions or bosons.

**gauge boson** or *field particle* any of the elementary particles that carry the four fundamental forces. Gauge bosons include the photon, the graviton, the gluons, and the weakons.

**gluon** a gauge boson that carries the strong force responsible for binding quarks together to form the strongly interacting subatomic particles known as hadrons. There are eight kinds of gluon.

**graviton** a gauge boson that is the postulated carrier of the gravitational force.

**hadron** a strongly interacting subatomic particle made up of indivisible elementary particles called quarks. The hadrons are grouped into the baryons (protons, neutrons, and hyperons) and the mesons (particles with masses between those of electrons and protons). Since the 1960s, particle physicists' main interest has been the elucidation of hadron structure.

**lepton** a light elementary particle that does not interact strongly with other particles or nuclei. The leptons include six particles: electron, muon, and tau, and their neutrinos, the electron neutrino, muon neutrino, and tau neutrino, plus their six antiparticles.

**meson** a subatomic particle made up of two indivisible elementary particles called quarks. The mesons have masses intermediate between those of the leptons (such as the electron) and those of the baryons (such as the proton and neutron). They are found in cosmic radiation, and are emitted by nuclei under bombardment by very high-energy particles. The mesons form a subclass of the hadrons and include the kaons, pions, psi, and upsilon.

**neutrino** any of three uncharged elementary particles (and their antiparticles) of the lepton class, having a mass too close to zero to be measured. The most familiar type, the electron neutrino, is emitted in the beta decay of a nucleus. The other two are the muon neutrino and the tau neutrino.

**neutron** one of the three main subatomic particles, the others being the proton and the electron. It belongs to the baryon group of the hadrons. Neutrons have about the same mass as protons but no electric charge, and occur in the nuclei of all atoms except hydrogen. They contribute to the mass of atoms but do not af-

## PROVING EINSTEIN WRONG

Albert Einstein never felt comfortable about quantum theory. He could not accept that, on the subatomic scale, events happen almost by chance. He expressed this by saying, 'God does not play dice'. Many people would agree with him. The concepts of quantum theory seem bizarre; in the subatomic quantum world, a particle does not have an exact position. There is a range of positions where the particle might be found and all we can do is to calculate the probability of it being at a given point. There is a similar uncertainty about other physical quantities, such as energy and momentum.

Common sense says that behind the uncertainties of the quantum world there must be an exact reality. It must be the limitations of our measuring apparatus that obscures the real behaviour of subatomic particles, and forces us to talk in probabilities instead of certainties. Herein lies the nub of the matter; according to quantum theorists, the uncertainties are unavoidable. A subatomic particle really does not have an exact position and momentum.

In 1964 Irish physicist John Bell proposed a test that would show whether there was an exact reality behind the quantum uncertainties. His arguments were based on the behaviour of pairs of particles that were once close together but have since separated. Such pairs are formed when an atom gives out two particles of light, called photons. According to quantum theory, if we observe one photon of such a pair, the other photon instantly 'knows' that we have made an observation and adjusts its behaviour or properties in certain ways. This would happen even if we waited until the photons were millions of kilometres apart before making our observation. Somehow, the photons remain 'in contact' whilst separated by vast distances. In the commonsense world, of course, this could not happen. In fact, Einstein used the impossibility of the particles remaining in contact as one of his arguments against quantum theory; there could be no instantaneous 'action at a

distance', he said. So, according to Bell, if we could check whether pairs of once-close photons behave in a correlated way, we could establish which was correct: Einstein or quantum theory.

It took a long time to convert this idea into a practicable experiment. However, in the early 1980s, a series of tests was carried out by a team of French scientists led by Alain Aspect in Paris. The apparatus used consisted of a source of light—calcium atoms—halfway along a long tube. Pairs of photons emitted by the calcium atoms split so that each photon sped towards opposite ends of the tube. At each end was a detector that could measure a particular property—the polarization—of a photon within 0.00000001 second of the photon reaching it. As the experiment proceeded, the experimenters measured the polarization of the photons arriving at one end of the tube. Then they very quickly checked the polarization of the photon at the other end. This is where the ultra-high speed of the detectors was essential. The measurements had to be done so swiftly that there would be no time for a 'message' to pass from the first observed photon to the other.

The scientists found that, when the polarization of one photon was measured, the polarization of the photon at the other end of the apparatus instantly changed in the manner that quantum theory predicted. So, Einstein was wrong. There is instantaneous 'action at a distance'. Quantum theory is correct, and there is no exact reality behind the uncertainties of the subatomic world.

The implications of the experiment are profound because, according to the Big Bang theory, all particles now in existence originate from a common point at the birth of the universe. Does this mean that there is an hidden connection between all the particles in the universe? How does this web of interconnection manifest itself? Physicists and philosophers are still examining these questions.

*The apparatus used by Alain Aspect and his colleagues to test quantum theory.*

## PRINCIPAL SUBATOMIC PARTICLES

| Group | | Particle | Symbol | Charge | Mass (MeV) | Spin | Lifetime (sec) |
|---|---|---|---|---|---|---|---|
| **elementary particle** | quark | up | u | $2/3$ | 336 | $1/2$ | ? |
| | | down | d | $-1/3$ | 336 | $1/2$ | ? |
| | | (top) | t | $(2/3)$ | (<600,000) | $(1/2)$ | ? |
| | | bottom | b | $-1/3$ | 4,700 | $1/2$ | ? |
| | | strange | s | $-1/3$ | 540 | $1/2$ | ? |
| | | charm | c | $2/3$ | 1,500 | $1/2$ | ? |
| | lepton | electron | $e^-$ | $-1$ | 0·511 | $1/2$ | stable |
| | | electron neutrino | $\nu_e$ | 0 | (0) | $1/2$ | stable |
| | | muon | $\mu^-$ | $-1$ | 105·66 | $1/2$ | $2·2 \times 10^{-6}$ |
| | | muon neutrino | $\nu_\mu$ | 0 | (0) | $1/2$ | stable |
| | | tau | $\tau^-$ | $-1$ | 1,784 | $1/2$ | $3·4 \times 10^{-13}$ |
| | | tau neutrino | $\nu_\tau$ | 0 | (0) | $1/2$ | ? |
| | gauge boson | photon | $\gamma$ | 0 | 0 | 1 | stable |
| | | graviton | g | 0 | (0) | 2 | stable |
| | | gluon | g | 0 | 0 | 1 | ? |
| | | weakon | $W^\pm$ | $\pm 1$ | 81,000 | 1 | ? |
| | | | Z | 0 | 94,000 | 1 | ? |
| **hadron** | meson | pion | $\pi^+$ | 1 | 139·57 | 0 | $2·6 \times 10^{-8}$ |
| | | | $\pi^0$ | 0 | 134·96 | 0 | $8·3 \times 10^{-17}$ |
| | | kaon | $K^+$ | 1 | 493·67 | 0 | $1·2 \times 10^{-8}$ |
| | | | $K_s^0$ | 0 | 497·67 | 0 | $8·9 \times 10^{-11}$ |
| | | | $K_L^0$ | 0 | 497·67 | 0 | $5·18 \times 10^{-8}$ |
| | | psi | $\Psi$ | 0 | 3,100 | 1 | $6·3 \times 10^{-2}$ |
| | | upsilon | Y | 0 | 9,460 | 1 | $\sim 1 \times 10^{-20}$ |
| | baryon | nucleon | | | | | |
| | | proton | p | 1 | 938·28 | $1/2$ | stable |
| | | nucleon | n | 0 | 939·57 | $1/2$ | 920 |
| | | hyperon | | | | | |
| | | lambda | $\Lambda$ | 0 | 1,115·6 | $1/2$ | $2·63 \times 10^{-10}$ |
| | | sigma | $\Sigma^+$ | 1 | 1,189·4 | $1/2$ | $8·0 \times 10^{-11}$ |
| | | | $\Sigma^-$ | $-1$ | 1,197·3 | $1/2$ | $1·5 \times 10^{-10}$ |
| | | | $\Sigma^0$ | 0 | 1,192·5 | $1/2$ | $5·8 \times 10^{-20}$ |
| | | xi | $\Xi^-$ | $-1$ | 1,321·3 | $1/2$ | $1·64 \times 10^{-10}$ |
| | | | $\Xi^0$ | 0 | 1,314·9 | $1/2$ | $2·9 \times 10^{-10}$ |
| | | omega | $\Omega$ | $-1$ | 1,672·4 | $3/2$ | $8·2 \times 10^{-11}$ |

*? indicates that the particle's lifetime has yet to be determined*
*( ) indicates that the property has been deduced but not confirmed*
*MeV = million electron volts*

fect their chemistry. For instance, the isotopes of a single element differ only in the number of neutrons in their nuclei but have identical chemical properties. Outside a nucleus, a free neutron is radioactive, decaying with a half-life of 11.6 minutes into a proton, an electron, and an antineutrino.

**nucleus** the positively charged central part of an atom, which is only one-ten-thousandth the diameter of the atom but constitutes almost all its mass. Except for hydrogen nuclei, which have only protons, nuclei are primarily composed of both protons and neutrons. Surrounding the nuclei are electrons, which contain a negative charge equal to the protons, thus giving the atom a neutral charge.

**photon** the elementary particle or quantum of energy in which light or other forms of electromagnetic radiation is emitted. It has both particle and wave properties; it has no charge, is considered massless, but possesses momentum and energy. It is one of the gauge bosons and is the carrier of the electromagnetic force, one of the fundamental forces of nature.

**proton** (Greek 'first') a positively charged subatomic particle, a constituent of the nucleus of all atoms. It belongs to the baryon subclass of the hadrons. A proton is extremely long-lived, with a lifespan of at least $10^{32}$ years. It carries a unit positive charge equal to the negative charge of an electron. Its mass is almost 1,836 times that of an electron, or $1.67 \times 10^{-24}$ g. The number of protons in the atom of an element is equal to the atomic number of that element.

**quantum chromodynamics** (QCD) a theory describing the interactions of quarks, the elementary particles that make up hadrons (such as protons and neutrons). In quantum chromodynamics, quarks are considered to interact by exchanging gauge bosons called gluons, which carry the strong nuclear force, and whose role is to 'glue' quarks together. The mathematics involved in the theory is complex, and although a number of successful predictions have been made, as yet the theory does not compare in accuracy with quantum

## GETTING TO THE TOP: THE RACE FOR THE TOP QUARK

The race is on to find the top quark! For 20 years, it has been clear that many subatomic particles—the proton and neutron, for example—are made up of even smaller particles called quarks. From the properties of particles like the proton and neutron, physicists have deduced that there are at least five different kinds of quark, called up, down, charm, strange, and bottom. According to the best theory—called the standard model—of the particle world, the quarks occur in pairs—up and down, charm and strange, bottom and ...? Yes, most physicists expect there will be a sixth, as yet undiscovered, quark to pair with the bottom quark. Naturally, the new particle is called the top quark.

Why has the top quark never been seen? There are two possible answers: either it does not exist, or it is difficult to detect. If the top quark does not exist, the standard model is wrong, and theorists will have to rethink much of modern particle physics.

The top quark would be difficult to detect if it were very massive. It would not then show up easily in the experiments that physicists carry out in particle accelerators. In these machines, particles are boosted to speeds approaching the speed of light and directed at a target. In the collision, energy is converted directly into matter and a shower of new particles results. This is in accordance with Einstein's famous equation $E = mc^2$, which shows that energy and matter are interconvertible. It also shows that the more massive a particle is, the more energy is needed to create it. The top quark has not yet been seen in these experiments, so most physicists think, because not enough energy has been available to create its enormous mass.

So, the race to find the top quark has become a race to build bigger and better particle accelerators. At CERN, the European laboratory

for particle physics near Geneva, an accelerator called the Large Electron–Positron collider (LEP) has been used in the search. But the limited energy available on the LEP means that no sign of the top quark has been seen. The Europeans are therefore pressing ahead with plans to build a larger, more powerful accelerator, known as the Large Hadron Collider. The proposed machine would collide protons with their antimatter equivalents, antiprotons, at energies equivalent to 16,000 proton masses. It will cost £600 million to build and should be completed in 1999.

At Fermilab, the US particle physics laboratory near Chicago, a machine called the Tevatron is being used to search for the top quark. The Tevatron collides beams of protons and antiprotons at energies equivalent to 18,000 proton masses. However, because of the particular experimental arrangement used, the full energy of the Tevatron cannot be converted into particles, and no sign of the top quark has yet been found.

If the Tevatron fails to find its quarry then, like their European counterparts, US physicists plan to build an even larger machine, the Superconducting Supercollider (SSC), at Waxahachie in the heart of Texas. The American giant will cost $8 billion and should be completed in the late 1990s. If it performs as its designers expect, the SSC will accelerate protons and antiprotons around an 87 km/54 mi circular tunnel before colliding them with energies equivalent to 40,000 proton masses. At these energies, the SSC seems almost certain to find the top quark. But if the elusive particle is not found, the standard model will be in serious trouble. Physicists will have to look for a new theory of elementary particles.

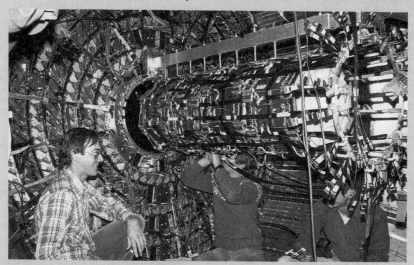

*Fermilab's Tevatron may be the first to find the elusive top quark*

electrodynamics, upon which it is modelled.

**quantum electrodynamics** (QED) a theory describing the interaction of charged subatomic particles within electric and magnetic fields. It combines quantum theory and relativity, and considers charged particles to interact by the exchange of photons. QED is remarkable for the accuracy of its predictions—for example, it has been used to calculate the value of some physical quantities to an accuracy of ten decimal places, a feat equivalent to calculating the distance between New York and Los Angeles to within the thickness of a hair. The theory was developed by US physicists Richard Feynman and Julian Schwinger, and by Japanese physicist Sin-Itiro Tomonaga.

**quark** an elementary particle that is the fundamental constituent of all hadrons (baryons, such as neutrons and protons, and mesons). There are six types, or 'flavours': up, down, top, bottom, strange, and charm, each of which has three varieties, or 'colours': red, yellow, and blue (visual colour is not meant, although the analogy is useful in many ways). To each quark there is an antiparticle, called an antiquark.

**spin** the intrinsic angular momentum of a subatomic particle, nucleus, atom, or molecule, which continues to exist even when the particle comes to rest. A particle in a specific energy state has a particular spin, just as it has a particular electric charge and mass. According to quantum theory, this is restricted to discrete and indivisible values, specified by a spin quantum number. Because of its spin, a charged particle acts as a small magnet and is affected by magnetic fields.

**standard model** the modern theory of elementary particles and their interactions. According to the standard model, subatomic particles are classified as leptons (light particles, such as electrons), hadrons (particles, such as neutrons and protons, that are formed from quarks), and gauge bosons. Leptons and hadrons interact by exchanging gauge bosons, each of which is responsible for a different fundamental force: photons mediate the electromagnetic force, which affects all charged particles; gluons mediate the strong nuclear force, which affects quarks; gravitons mediate the gravitational force; and the weakons mediate the weak nuclear force.

**superstring theory** a mathematical theory developed in the 1980s to explain the properties of elementary particles and the forces between them (in particular, gravity and the nuclear forces) in a way that combines relativity and quantum theory. In string theory, the fundamental objects in the universe are not pointlike particles but extremely small stringlike objects. These objects exist in a universe of ten dimensions, although, for reasons not yet understood, only three space dimensions and one dimension of time are discernable. There are many unresolved difficulties with superstring theory, but some physicists think it may be the ultimate 'theory of everything'

that explains all aspects of the universe within one framework.

**supersymmetry** a theory that relates the two classes of elementary particle, the fermions and the bosons. According to supersymmetry, each fermion particle has a boson partner particle, and vice versa. It has not been possible to marry up all the known fermions with the known bosons, and so the theory postulates the existence of other, as-yet undiscovered fermions, such as the photinos (partners of the photons), gluinos (partners of the gluons), and gravitinos (partners of the gravitons). Using these ideas, it has become possible to develop a theory of gravity—called supergravity—that extends Einstein's work and considers the gravitational, nuclear, and elecromagnetic forces to be manifestations of an underlying superforce. Supersymmetry has been incorporated into the superstring theory, and appears to be a crucial ingredient in the 'theory of everything' sought by scientists.

**uncertainty principle** or **indeterminacy principle** the principle that it is meaningless to speak of a particle's position, momentum, or other parameters, except as results of measurements; measuring, however, involves an interaction (such as a photon of light bouncing off the particle under scrutiny), which must disturb the particle, though the disturbance is noticeable only at an atomic scale. The principle implies that one cannot, even in theory, predict the moment-to-moment behaviour of such a system.

**weakon** a gauge boson that carries the weak force, one of the fundamental forces of nature. There are three types of weakon, the positive and negative W particles and the neutral Z particle.

# THE GREAT PHYSICISTS

**Ampère** André Marie 1775–1836. French physicist and mathematician who made many discoveries in electromagnetism and electrodymanics. He followed up the work of Hans Oersted on the interaction between magnets and electric currents, developing a rule for determining the direction of the magnetic field associated with an electric current. The ammeter and ampere are named after him.

**Bohr** Niels Henrik David 1885–1962. Danish physicist. After work with Ernest Rutherford at Manchester, he became professor at Copenhagen in 1916, and founded there the Institute of Theoretical Physics of which he became director in 1920. He was awarded the Nobel Prize for Physics 1922. Bohr fled from the Nazis in World War II and took part in work on the atomic bomb in the USA. In 1952, he helped to set up CERN, the European nuclear research organization, in Geneva.

**Boyle** Robert 1627–1691. Irish physicist and chemist, who published the seminal *The*

*Skeptical Chymist* 1661. He was the first chemist to collect a sample of gas, formulated **Boyle's law** on the compressibility of a gas in 1662, and was one of the founders of the Royal Society.

**Broglie, de** Louis, 7th Duc de Broglie 1892--1987. French theoretical physicist. He established that all subatomic particles can be described either by particle equations or by wave equations, thus laying the foundations of wave mechanics. He was awarded the 1929 Nobel Prize for Physics.

**Carnot** (Nicolas Leonard) Sadi 1796–1832. French scientist and military engineer who founded the science of thermodynamics; his pioneering work was *Réflexions sur la puissance motrice du feu/On the Motive Power of Fire*, which considered the changes that would take place in an idealized, frictionless steam engine.

**Cavendish** Henry 1731–1810. British physicist. He discovered hydrogen (which he called 'inflammable air') 1766, and determined the compositions of water and of nitric acid.

**Chadwick** James 1891–1974. British physicist. In 1932 he discovered the particle in the nucleus of an atom that became known as the neutron because it has no electric charge. He was awarded a Nobel prize 1935.

**Curie** Marie (born Sklodovska) 1867–1934. Polish scientist who investigated radioactivity with her French husband Pierre (1859–1906). In 1898 she reported the possible existence of a new, powerfully radioactive element in pitchblende ores. Her husband abandoned his own researches to assist her, and in the same year they announced the existence of polonium and radium. They isolated the pure elements in 1902. Both scientists refused to take out a patent on their discoveries and were awarded, with Becquerel, the Nobel Prize for Physics 1903. Marie Curie was awarded the Nobel Prize for Chemistry 1911.

**Dirac** Paul Adrien Maurice 1902–1984. British physicist who worked out a version of quantum mechanics consistent with special relativity. The existence of the positron (positive electron) was one of its predictions. He shared a Nobel Prize for Physics 1933.

**Einstein** Albert 1879–1955. German-born US physicist who formulated the theories of relativity, and worked on radiation physics and thermodynamics. In 1905 he published the special theory of relativity, and in 1915 issued his general theory of relativity. His latest conception of the basic laws governing the universe was outlined in his unified field theory, made public 1953.

**Faraday** Michael 1791–1867. English chemist and physicist. In 1821 he began experimenting with electromagnetism, and ten years later discovered the induction of electric currents and made the first dynamo. He subsequently found that a magnetic field will rotate the plane of polarization of light. Faraday also investigated electrolysis.

**Fermi** Enrico 1901–1954. Italian-born US physicist, who proved the existence of new radioactive elements produced by bombardment with neutrons, and discovered nuclear reactions produced by low-energy neutrons. His theoretical work included study of the weak nuclear force, one of the fundamental forces of nature, and (with Paul Dirac) of the quantum statistics of fermion particles. He was awarded a Nobel prize 1938.

**Feynman** Richard Phillips 1918–1988. US physicist whose work provided the foundations for quantum electrodynamics. For his work on the theory of radiation he was awarded a share of the Nobel Prize for Physics 1965. As a member of the committee investigating the *Challenger* space-shuttle disaster 1986, he demonstrated the lethal faults in the rubber seals on the shuttle's booster rocket. Towards the end of his life he became widely known for his revealing autobiography *Surely you're Joking Mr Feynman!*.

**Foucault** Jean Bernard Léon 1819–1868. French physicist who used a pendulum to demonstrate the rotation of the Earth on its axis, and invented the gyroscope.

**Gabor** Dennis 1900–1979. Hungarian-born British physicist. In 1947 he invented the holographic method of three-dimensional photography and in 1958 invented a type of colour-television tube of greatly reduced depth. He was awarded a Nobel prize 1971.

**Galileo** properly Galileo Galilei 1564–1642. Italian mathematician, astronomer, and physicist. He developed the astronomical telescope and was the first to see sunspots, the four main satellites of Jupiter, mountains and craters on the Moon, and the appearance of Venus going through 'phases', thus proving it was orbiting the Sun. In mechanics, Galileo discovered that freely falling bodies, heavy or light, had the same, constant acceleration (although the story of his dropping cannonballs from the Leaning Tower of Pisa is questionable) and that a body moving on a perfectly smooth horizontal surface would neither speed up nor slow down.

**Gell-Mann** Murray 1929– . US physicist. In 1964 he formulated the theory of the quark as one of the fundamental constituents of matter. He was awarded a Nobel prize 1969.

**Glashow** Sheldon Lee 1932– . US particle physicist. He proposed the existence of a fourth 'charmed' quark 1964, and argued that quarks must have properties analagous with colour. Glashow went on to consider ways in which the weak and the electromagnetic forces (two of the fundamental forces of nature) could be unified as a single force now called the electroweak force. He shared the Nobel Prize for Physics 1979 with Abdus Salam and Steven Weinberg.

**Hawking** Stephen William 1942– . English physicist. He discovered that the strong gravitational field around a black hole can radiate particles of matter. Commenting on Einstein's remark, 'God does not play dice with the universe,' Hawking said: 'God not only plays dice, he throws them where they can't be seen.' Confined to a wheelchair because of a muscular disease, he performs complex mathematical calculations entirely in his head. His books include *A Brief History of Time* 1988.

**Heisenberg** Werner Carl 1901–1976. German physicist who developed quantum theory and formulated the uncertainty principle, which concerns matter, radiation, and their reactions, and places absolute limits on the achievable accuracy of measurement. He was awarded a Nobel prize 1932.

**Hertz** Heinrich 1857–1894. German physicist who studied electromagnetic waves, showing that their behaviour resembles that of light and heat waves.

**Hooke** Robert 1635–1703. English scientist and inventor. *Hooke's law* states that the deformation of a body is proportional to the magnitude of the deforming force, provided that the body's elastic limit is not exceeded. Hooke's inventions included a telegraph system, the spirit-level, marine barometer, and sea gauge. He coined the term 'cell' in biology.

**Josephson** Brian 1940– . British physicist, a leading authority on superconductivity. In 1973 he shared a Nobel prize for his theoretical predictions of the properties of a supercurrent through a tunnel barrier (the Josephson junction).

**Joule** James Prescott 1818–1889. British physicist whose work on the relations between electrical, mechanical, and chemical effects led to the discovery of the first law of thermodynamics.

**Kelvin** William Thomson, 1st Baron Kelvin 1824–1907. Irish physicist who introduced the *kelvin scale*, the absolute scale of temperature. His work on the conservation of energy 1851 led to the second law of thermodynamics.

**Lawrence** Ernest O(rlando) 1901–1958. US physicist. His invention of the cyclotron pioneered the production of artificial radioisotopes. He was awarded a Nobel prize in 1939.

**Maxwell** James Clerk 1831–1879. Scottish physicist. His major achievement was in the understanding of electromagnetic waves: *Maxwell's equations* bring together electricity, magnetism, and light in one set of relations. He contributed to every branch of physical science—gases, optics, and colour sensation. His theoretical work in magnetism prepared the way for wireless telegraphy and telephony.

**Michelson** Albert Abraham 1852–1931. German-born US physicist. In conjunction with Edward Morley, he performed in 1887 the *Michelson–Morley experiment* to detect the motion of the Earth through the postulated ether (a medium believed to be necessary for the propagation of light). The failure of the experiment indicated the nonexistence of the ether, and led Einstein to his theory of relativity. Michelson was the first American to be awarded a Nobel prize 1907.

**Newton** Isaac 1642–1727. English physicist and mathematician who laid the foundations of physics as a modern discipline. He discov-

ered the law of gravity, showed that white light is composed of many colours, and developed the three standard laws of motion still in use today. His *Philosophiae naturalis principia mathematica* (usually referred to as *Principia*) was published in three volumes 1686–87, with the aid of the astronomer and physicist Edmund Halley.

**Ohm** Georg Simon 1787–1854. German physicist who studied electricity and discovered the fundamental law that bears his name. The SI unit of electrical resistance is named after him, and the unit of conductance (the reverse of resistance) was formerly called the mho, which is Ohm spelt backwards.

**Pauli** Wolfgang 1900–1958. Austrian physicist who originated the *exclusion principle*: in a given system no two fermions (electrons, protons, neutrons, or other elementary particles of half-integral spin) can be characterized by the same set of quantum numbers. He also predicted the existence of neutrinos. He won a Nobel prize 1945 for his work on atomic structure.

**Planck** Max 1858–1947. German physicist who framed the quantum theory 1900. His research into the manner in which heated bodies radiate energy led him to report that energy is emitted only in indivisible amounts, called quanta, the magnitudes of which are proportional to the frequency of the radiation. His discovery ran counter to classical physics and is held to have marked the commencement of the modern science. Planck was awarded the Nobel Prize for Physics 1918.

**Powell** Cecil Frank 1903–1969. English physicist, awarded a Nobel prize 1950 for his use of photographic emulsion as a method of tracking charged nuclear particles.

**Rutherford** Ernest 1871–1937. New Zealand physicist, a pioneer of modern atomic science. His main research was in the field of radioactivity, and he discovered alpha, beta, and gamma rays. He named the nucleus, and was the first to recognize the ionizing nature of the atom. Nobel prize 1908.

**Salam** Abdus 1926– . Pakistani physicist. In 1967 he proposed a theory linking the electromagnetic and weak forces, also arrived at independently by Steven Weinberg. In 1979 he was the first person from his country to receive a Nobel prize, which he shared with Weinberg and Sheldon Glashow.

**Schrödinger** Erwin 1887–1961. Austrian physicist who advanced the study of wave mechanics (see quantum theory). Born in Vienna, he became senior professor at the Dublin Institute for Advanced Studies 1940. He shared (with Paul Dirac) a Nobel prize 1933.

**Shockley** William 1910–1989. US physicist and amateur geneticist who worked with John Bardeen and Walter Brattain on the invention of the transistor. They were jointly awarded a Nobel prize 1956. During the 1970s Shockley was criticized for his claim that blacks were genetically inferior to whites in terms of intelligence.

## Nobel Prize For Physics

**Thomson** J(oseph) J(ohn) 1856–1940. English physicist who discovered the electron. He was responsible for organizing the Cavendish atomic research laboratory at Cambridge University. His work inaugurated the electrical theory of the atom, and his elucidation of positive rays and their application to an analysis of neon led to Frederick Aston's discovery of isotopes. He was awarded a Nobel prize 1906.

**Volta** Alessandro 1745–1827. Italian physicist who invented the first electric cell (the voltaic pile), the electrophorus (an early electrostatic generator), and an electroscope.

**Watt** James 1736–1819. Scottish engineer who developed the steam engine. He made Newcomen's steam engine vastly more efficient by cooling the used steam in a condenser separate from the main cylinder.

**Weinberg** Steven 1933– . US physicist, who in 1967 demonstrated, together with Abdus Salam, that the weak force and the electromagnetic force (two of the fundamental forces) are variations of a single underlying force, now called the electroweak force. Weinberg and Salam shared a Nobel prize with Sheldon Glashow in 1979.

### Science history

*Can you tell me who made famous the following laws and theories of physics?*

*a) The laws of gravity*

| | |
|---|---|
| Correct—Newton | 61 |
| Other answers | 7 |
| Don't know | 32 |

*b) The theory of relativity?*

| | |
|---|---|
| 1 Correct—Einstein | 42 |
| 2 Other answers | 6 |
| 3 Don't know | 52 |

# CONSTRUCTION

**bridge** a construction that provides a continuous path or road over water, valleys, ravines, or above other roads. Bridges may be classified into four main groups:

*arch bridges*, for example, Sydney Harbour bridge (steel arch) with a span of 503 m/1,650 ft;

*beam* or *girder bridges*, as at Rio-Niteroi (1974), Guanabara Bay, Brazil, the world's longest continuous box-and-plate girder bridge: centre span 300 m/984 ft; length 13.9 km/8 mi 3,363 ft;

*cantilever bridges*, for example, the Forth rail bridge, which is 1,658 m/5,440 ft long and has two main spans, each consisting of two cantilevers, one from each tower;

*suspension bridges*, such as the Humber bridge, the world's longest-span suspension bridge with a centre span of 1,410 m/4,626 ft.

Steel is pre-eminent in the construction of long-span bridges because of its high strength-to-weight ratio, but in other circumstances reinforced concrete has the advantage of lower maintenance costs.

**canal** a man-made waterway constructed for drainage, irrigation, or navigation.

*irrigation canals* carry water for irrigation from rivers, reservoirs, or wells, and are carefully designed to maintain an even flow of water over the whole length. Irrigation canals fed from the Nile have maintained life in Egypt since the earliest times; the Murray Basin project of Victoria, Australia, and the Imperial and Central Valley project of California, USA, are examples of 19th- and 20th-century irrigation-canal development.

*navigation and ship canals* constructed at one level between locks, canals frequently link with other forms of waterway—natural rivers, modified river channels, and sea links—to

bridge

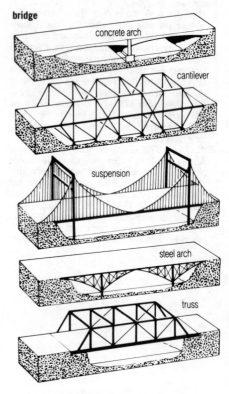

form a waterway system. The world's two major international ship canals are the Suez Canal and the Panama Canal which provide invaluable short cuts for shipping respectively between Europe and the East and between the east and west coasts of the Americas. The first major British canal was the Bridgewater Canal from Worsley to Manchester 1761–76; the engineer was Brindley and the canal was constructed for the 3rd Duke of Bridgewater

## THE WORLD'S MOST REMARKABLE BRIDGES

| | |
|---|---|
| **Angostura** | *Cuidad Bolivar, Venezuela* |
| | Suspension-type bridge; span 712 m/2,336 ft; total length 1,678 m/5,507 ft |
| **Bendorf Bridge** | *Coblenz, Germany* |
| | 3-span cement girder bridge; main span 208 m/682 ft ; total length 1030 m/3,378 ft |
| **Bosphorus Bridge** | *Istanbul, Turkey* (linking Europe to Asia) |
| | Suspension bridge; total length 1,074 m/3,524 ft |
| **Gladesville Bridge** | *Sydney, Australia* |
| | Concrete arch bridge; 305 m/1,000 ft span – world's longest concrete arch |
| **Humber Bridge** | *Kingston upon Hull, England* |
| | Suspension bridge; total span 1410 m/4,626 ft – world's longest suspension span |
| **Lake Pontchartrain Causeway** | *New Orleans, USA* |
| | Multiple span; 38,421 m/126,055 ft – the world's longest multiple span |
| **Oostersceldebrug** | *Flushing/Rotterdam, Netherlands* |
| | Traffic causeway over Zeeland sea arm; total length 19 km 3.125 mi |
| **Rio-Niteroi** | *Guanabara Bay, Brazil* |
| | Continuous box and plate girder bridge; 14 km/8.7 mi length – the world's longest box girder bridge |
| **Tagus River Bridge** | *Lisbon, Portugal* |
| | Main span 1013 m/3,323 ft |
| **Zoo Bridge** | *Cologne, Germany* |
| | Steel box girder bridge; main span 259 m/850 ft |

## ROBOTS OF ALL SHAPES AND SIZES

The 1990 Robot Olympics, held in Glasgow, got off to an umpromising start. Trolleyman, the robot designed to light the Olympic flame, suffered an electrical fault. It was unable to carry the flame from The Parthenon Greek restaurant to the university sports hall where the games were held. Ingloriously, the robot arrived in a Land Rover driven by its creator. Other robots had trouble, too. A six-legged robot from the Massachusetts Institute of Technology refused to start its race. The electronics in one robot failed, and photographer's flashlights blinded the sensors in another.

Nevertheless, the winner of the Olympics, called Yamabico, performed well. Yamabico, from Tsukuba University in Japan, was able to negotiate a path strewn with obstacles without stopping. Most robots need to scan any obstacle and spend time computing the next move each time it encounters anything in its path.

Many of the other robots on display in Glasgow were experimental testbeds, designed to show how the central problems of robotics might be tackled. One of these problems is locomotion; how should a robot get around? A solution on view was the two-legged walking robot from the University of Wales, Cardiff. Each leg of the robot carries pressure and acceleration sensors connected to a computer. After each leg movement, the computer decides what to do next using a mathematical model of walking which is

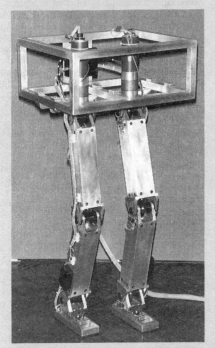

*Walking robot from University College of Wales, Cardiff.*

based on two swinging pendulums. Walking may be simple for us but, for robots, it takes a great deal of thought.

Another problem which is simple for us but difficult for a robot is that of recognizing an object. If robots are to fulfil their promise they must be able to recognize objects such as machine parts to be assembled in a factory. The aim is to produce a robot that will recognize objects without having to refer to a vast bank of rules stored in their electronic memories. Such rule-based recognition is inflexible and inefficient. Instead, 'neural networks' seem to be the key. This approach mimics the way the human brain works. The robot is trained to recognize an object by viewing a variety of objects and, when it identifies them correctly, the computer circuits which led to the correct recognition are reinforced.

The main purpose of the Games was to encourage school children to take an interest in the science of robotics, and to allow the competitors to exchange information. However, the Olympics were also a showcase for a sophisticated technology with increasingly varied applications.

A surgical robot, 'Robodoc', carried out its first operation in the USA in June 1990. It was used to grind a leg bone very precisely to replace the hip of a dog with severe arthritis. 'Robodoc' could be ready to operate on humans within a year. A group of British scientists is planning a robot to perform brain surgery. A surgeon would oversee the robot, but the robot could operate much closer to vital areas of the brain where a human surgeon might not be prepared to work.

An underwater robot was launched into Australian waters in early 1991 to help researchers to find out what goes on in the turbulent waters in lakes, esturies and coastal seas. It resembles a small cactus, weighs roughly 100 kg/220 lb, and is 2 m/6.5 ft from top to toe. Underwater it operates independently, roaming the waters, measuring currents and the movement of sand particles, and analysing sewage effluent.

A Swedish company has developed a robot petrol pump for people too lazy, or unable, to get out of their cars. To fill up, the driver parks next to the machine and inserts a credit card. Guided by sensors, the robot locates the petrol tank, removes the cap, and inserts the petrol nozzle into the tank. The amount of petrol pumped in is displayed on a terminal near the driver. When it is finished the robot withdraws the hose, replaces and locks the cap and the driver can move off.

A wall climbing robot was demonstrated at the South Bank Polytechnic in London in 1990. On its back, the robot carries equipment to clean, paint or inspect buildings. It can move over ceilings as well as walls while gripping the surface with suckers. It is controlled from the ground by an umbilical cord, but also has built-in sensors. The days when a robot looked like a Dalek or a Cyberman are long past.

## THE WORLD'S HIGHEST DAMS

| Rank order | Name | Country | Ht. above lowest formation |
|---|---|---|---|
| 1 | Rogun* | USSR | 335 m/1099 ft |
| 2 | Nurek | USSR | 300 m/984 ft |
| 3 | Grand Dixence | Switzerland | 285 m/935 ft |
| 4 | Inguri | USSR | 272 m/892 ft |
| 5 | Chicoasen | Mexico | 261 m/856 ft |
|   | Tehri* | India | 261 m/856 ft |
| 6 | Kishau* | India | 253 m/830 ft |
| 7 | Ertan | China | 245 m/804 ft |
|   | Sayano-Shushensk* | USSR | 245 m/804 ft |
| 8 | Guavio* | Colombia | 243 m/797 ft |
| 9 | Mica | Canada | 242 m/794 ft |
| 10 | Mauvoisin | Switzerland | 237 m/778 ft |
|   | Chivor | Colombia | 237 m/778 ft |
| 11 | El Cajon | Honduras | 234 m/768 ft |
| 12 | Chirkei | USSR | 233 m/765 ft |
| 13 | Oroville | USA | 230 m/755 ft |
| 14 | Bhakra | India | 226 m/741 ft |
| 15 | Hoover | USA | 221 m/738 ft |
| 16 | Contra | Switzerland | 220 m/772 ft |
|   | Mratinje | Yugoslavia | 220 m/722 ft |

* Under construction.
Source: The World Almanac & Book of Facts 1991

to carry coal from his collieries to Manchester. Brindley overcame great difficulties in the route. Today many of Britain's canals form part of an interconnecting system of waterways some 4,000 km/2,500 mi long. Although most have fallen out of commercial use, many have been restored for recreation and the use of pleasure craft.

Where speed is not a major consideration, the cost-effectiveness of transporting goods by canal has encouraged a revival and Belgium, France, Germany, and the USSR are among countries that have extended and improved their canals.

**dam** a structure built to hold back water in order to prevent flooding, provide water for irrigation and storage, or generate hydroelectric power. The world's largest dam is the Pati dam on the Paraná river, Argentina, which has a volume of 238 million cu m/933 million cu ft. Like all the biggest dams it is an **earth-and-rock-fill dam**, also called an **embankment dam**. Such dams are generally built on broad valley sites. Deep, narrow gorges, however, dictate a concrete dam, the enormous strength of reinforced concrete being able to withstand the enormous water pressures involved. Many concrete dams are triangular in cross-section, with their vertical face pointing upstream. Their sheer weight holds them in position, and they are called **gravity dams**. Some concrete dams, however, are more slight and are built in the shape of an arch, with the curve facing upstream. The **arch dam** derives its strength from its shape, just as an arch bridge does. A valuable development in arid regions, as in parts of Brazil, is the **underground dam**, where water is stored among sand and stones on a solid rock base, with a wall to ground level, so avoiding rapid evaporation.

**tunnel** tunnelling is an increasingly important branch of civil engineering in mining, transport, and other areas. In the 19th century there were two major advances: the use of compressed air within the tunnel to balance the external pressure of water and of the tunnel shield to support the rockface and assist excavation. In recent years there have been notable developments in tunnel linings, such as concrete segments and steel liner plates, and in the use of rotary diggers and cutters, and of explosives. Famous tunnels include the world's longest road tunnel, the St Gotthard (1882), Switzerland, 16.3 km/10.1 mi long; the world's longest rail tunnel, the Seikan (1975), under Tsugaru Strait linking Honshu and Hokkaido, Japan, 53.85 km/33.5 mi long, of which 23.3 km/14.5 mi is under the sea; the Orange-Fish River tunnel (1975), South Africa 82 km/50 mi long, constructed for irrigation; and the Chesapeake Bay Bridge tunnel (1963), USA, 28 km/17.5 mi long.

A tunnel beneath the English Channel was planned as a military measure by Napoleon in 1802. Excavations were made from both shores in the late 1870s and early 1880s, but work was halted by Parliament for security reasons. In 1986 a scheme for a Channel Tunnel (or Chunnel), in the form of twin rail tunnels, was approved by the French and British governments. Excavation began November 1987 and should be completed 1993.

**skyscraper** a building so tall that it appears to 'scrape the sky', developed in New York, USA, where land prices were high and the geology adapted to such methods of construction. Skyscrapers are now found in cities throughout the world. The world's tallest free-standing structure is the CN (Canadian National) Tower, Toronto, 555 m/1,821 ft. The tallest building

## WORLD'S LONGEST RAILWAY TUNNELS

| Tunnel | Date | Km/Mi |
|---|---|---|
| Seikan | 1985 | 54/33.5 |
| Dai-shimizu | 1979 | 23/14 |
| Simplon No. 1 and 2 | 1906, 1922 | 19/12 |
| Kanmon | 1975 | 19/12 |
| Apennine | 1934 | 18/11 |
| Rokko | 1972 | 16/10 |
| Mt MacDonald | 1989 | 15/9.1 |
| Gotthard | 1882 | 14/9 |
| Lotschberg | 1913 | 14/9 |
| Hokuriku | 1962 | 14/9 |
| Mont Canis (Frejus) | 1871 | 13/8 |
| Shin-Shimizu | 1961 | 13/8 |
| Aki | 1975 | 13/8 |
| Cascade | 1929 | 13/8 |
| Flathead | 1970 | 13/8 |
| Keijo | 1970 | 11/7 |
| Lierasen | 1973 | 11/7 |
| Santa Lucia | 1977 | 10/6 |
| Arlberg | 1884 | 10/6 |
| Moffat | 1928 | 10/6 |
| Shimizu | 1931 | 10/6 |

Source: The World Almanac and Book of Facts 1991, 1990 Pharos Books

CHANNEL TUNNEL: CHRONOLOGY

| | |
|---|---|
| 1751 | French farmer Nicolas Desmaret suggested a fixed link across the English Channel. |
| 1802 | French mining engineer Albert Mathieu-Favier proposed to Napoleon I a channel tunnel through which horse-drawn carriages might travel. Discussions with British politicians ceased in 1803 when war broke out between the two countries. |
| 1834 | Aim de Gamond of France suggested the construction of a submerged tube across the channel. |
| 1842 | De la Haye of Liverpool designed an underwater tube, the sections of which would be bolted together underwater by workers without diving apparatus. |
| 1851 | Hector Horeau proposed a tunnel that would slope down towards the middle of the Channel and up thereafter, so that the carriages would be propelled downhill by their own weight and for a short distance uphill, after which compressed air would take over as the motive power. |
| 1857 | A joint committee of British and French scientists approved the aim of constructing a channel tunnel. |
| 1875 | Channel-tunnel bills passed by the British and French parliaments. |
| 1876 | Anglo-French protocol signed laying down the basis of a treaty governing construction of a tunnel. |
| 1878 | Borings began from the French and British sides of the channel. |
| 1882 | British government forced abandonment of the project after public opinion, fearing invasion by the French, turned against the tunnel. |
| 1904 | Signing of the Entente Cordiale between France and the UK enabled plans to be reconsidered. Albert Sartiaux and Francis Fox proposed a twin-tunnel scheme. |
| 1907 | Defeat of a new channel-tunnel bill in British parliament. |
| 1930 | Bill narrowly failed in British parliament. |
| 1930–40 | British prime minister Winston Churchill and the French government supported the digging of a tunnel. |
| 1955 | Defence objections to a tunnel lifted in the UK by Prime Minister Harold Macmillan. |
| 1957 | Channel Tunnel Study Group established. |
| 1961 | Study Group plans for a double-bore tunnel presented to British government. |
| 1964 | Ernest Marples, minister of transport, and his French counterpart gave go-ahead for construction. |
| 1967 | British government invited proposals to build a tunnel from private interests. |
| 1973 | Anglo-French treaty on trial borings signed. |
| 1974 | New tunnel bill introduced in British parliament but was not passed before a general election was called by Harold Wilson. |
| 1975 | British government cancelled project because of escalating costs. |
| 1982 | Intergovernmental study group on tunnel established. |
| 1984 | Construction of a tunnel agreed in principle at an Anglo-French summit. |
| 1986 | Anglo-French treaty signed; design submitted by a consortium called the Channel Tunnel Group accepted. |
| 1987 | Legislation completed; Anglo-French treaty ratified. |
| 1987 (Nov) | Construction began in earnest. |
| 1990 (Dec) | First breakthrough of service tunnel. |
| 1991 (May) | Breakthrough of first rail tunnel. |
| 1991 (June) | Completion of second rail tunnel. |
| 1993 (June) | Tunnel scheduled to be operational. |

in the UK is the office tower of the Canary Wharf development in London Docklands, 259 m/850 ft.

In Manhattan, New York, are the Empire State Building (1931), 102 storeys and 381 m/1,250 ft high, and the twin towers of the World Trade Center, 415 m/1,361 ft, but these were surpassed 1973 by the Sears Tower, 443 m/1,454 ft, in Chicago. Chicago was the home of the first skyscraper, the Home Insurance Building (1885), which was built ten storeys high with an iron and steel frame. Most skyscrapers are constructed around a rigid loadbearing steel frame; the walls simply hang from the frame (curtain walling), and can therefore be made from relatively flimsy materials such as glass and aluminium. Another type of construction, central-core construction, has the lifts and staircases enclosed to form the skyscraper's core. Unit-slab construction involves building each storey on top of the last.

# TELECOMMUNICATIONS AND VIDEO TECHNOLOGY

Telecommunications are communications over a distance. For centuries bonfires have been used as a method of conveying a simple message, such as 'The Armada is coming' (1588). The first mechanical telecommunications systems were the *semaphore* and *heliograph* (which used flashes of sunlight). But the forerunner of the mod-

## CHIPS WITH EVERYTHING

The amazing pace of miniaturization in the electronic industry continues. When the first integrated circuit or chip (a small piece of semiconductor containing a complete electronic circuit)—was made in 1958 by US electrical physicist Jack Kilby, it contained just five components. Kilby's prototype was not elegant. It was a thin wafer of germanium 19 mm long. The five components were linked by tiny wires and the power supply was simply soldered on. The whole thing was held together with wax. Nevertheless, it worked, and from it grew the modern electronics industry. The first microprocessor—or computer on a chip—designed by US electrical physicist Ted Hoff, was produced in 1971. It contained 2,250 components. Three years later, microprocessors contained 4,500 components. In 1979, a typical microprocessor contained 70,000 components. In 1981, the number of components per chip had risen to 450,000. By 1990 memory chips which store information inside computers contained millions of components.

Memory chips, commonly called DRAM chips, are vital for the computer industry. They store and retrieve information almost instantly, as long as the power remains on. This speed of access makes DRAMs vital in computers and many household gadgets. The most widely used DRAMs today hold 1 million bits of information, but 4 million-bit chips are readily available. A 4 million-bit (4 megabit) chip can store the equivalent of 520,000 characters, or 200 typewritten pages. The chip contains 9 million components packed on a piece of silicon less than 15 mm long by 5 mm wide.

Now the race is on to produce the next generations of high capacity DRAMs. A 16 megabit DRAM must contain four times as many circuits as a 4 megabit chip. However manufacturers have found the new chips relatively easy to produce. Only refinement of existing technology is required. The most important technique involves building circuits in three dimensions. Since most manufacturers learnt how to build three-dimensional chips when moving from 1 megabit to 4 megabit chips, no great leap is required to produce 16 megabit chips. Mass production of 16 megabit chips has yet to start, although prototype chips have been produced by several companies, including Texas Instruments in America and Hitachi in Japan.

The next step up to the 64 megabit chip, capable of storing the equivalent of 6,400 typewritten pages, more than the complete works of Shakespeare, is likely to be more difficult. It will be necessary to shrink the size of the components on the chip. However, there seems to be a limit beyond which components will not store electric charge reliably. Engineers hope to get around this problem by designing components with novel shapes. Mitsubishi have developed a cylindrical capacitor, for example. Another problem lies in the thickness of the connecting lines on the chip. These lines must be so fine that there is doubt whether the

*The 1Mbit TSOP and 4Mbit SOJ DRAMs compared to a matchstick.*

methods used on earlier chips can be used. Some experts believe that it will be necessary to use X-rays instead of light for the photographic process which etches the lines onto the chip. Despite these difficulties four Japanese companies, Fujitsu, Matsushita, Mitsubishi, and Toshiba, announced in early 1991 that they had made working prototypes. If all goes well, the 64 megabit chip could be on the market in the mid 1990s.

There has also been progress with chips not based on silicon. In May 1991, the US computer manufacturer Convex unveiled the first supercomputer made without silicon chips. Instead, its processor is built of chips made from gallium arsenide, a semiconductor material which was once tipped to replace silicon in computers. Gallium arsenide uses less power than silicon and is faster because electrons move more freely through it. However, gallium arsenide is expensive to fabricate and applications have been limited to specialized applications, such as weather forecasting and image processing where great speed is needed, and cost is no object. The new computer can do two thousand million mathematical operations per second.

US researchers are also taking tentative steps towards building chips based on the high-temperature superconducting materials discovered in 1986. These materials conduct electricity with almost no resistance at temperatures up to about 120 degrees above absolute zero (−153°C). Unfortunately, the materials are difficult to fabricate. A new approach, however, seems to offer promise. A new type of transistor has been developed at the University of Wisconsin which requires only a single layer of the brittle superconducting material—the transistors normally found in integrated circuits are made up of several layers of semiconducting material. Although these devices are still very crude, it is well to remember Jack Kilby's first simple integrated circuit and its remarkable development, before dismissing them.

**telecommunications**

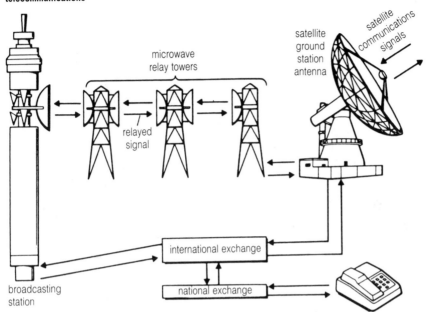

ern telecommunications age was the *electric telegraph*. The earliest practicable instrument was invented by William Cooke and Charles Wheatstone in the UK in 1837, and used by railway companies, the first public line being laid between Paddington and Slough in 1843. In the USA Morse invented a signalling code, Morse code, which is still used, and a recording telegraph, first used commercially between England and France in 1851. As a result of Heinrich Hertz's discoveries using electromagnetic waves, Guglielmo Marconi pioneered a *wireless telegraph*, ancestor of the radio. He established wireless communication between England and France 1899 and across the Atlantic 1901. The modern telegraph uses teleprinters to send coded messages along telecommunications lines. They are keyboard-operated machines that transmit a five-unit baudot code. The receiving teleprinter automatically prints the received message.

Long-distance voice communication was pioneered in 1876 by Alexander Graham Bell, when he invented the *telephone* as a result of Michael Faraday's discovery of electromagnetism. Today it is possible to communicate with most countries by telephone cable, several thousand simultaneous conversations being carried. However, the chief method of relaying long-distance calls on land is *microwave radio transmission*. The drawback to this is that the transmissions follow a straight line from tower to tower, so that over the sea the system becomes impracticable.

A solution was put forward in 1945 by Arthur C Clarke in *Wireless World*, when he proposed a system of *communications satellites* in an orbit 35,900 km/27,300 mi above the equator, where they would circle the Earth in exactly 24 hours, and thus appear fixed in the sky.

Such a system is now in operation internationally, operated by Intelsat. The satellites are called geostationary satellites, or synchronous satellites (syncoms). The first to be successfully launched, by Delta rocket from Cape Canaveral, was *Syncom 2* in July 1963. Numbers of such satellites are now in use, concentrated over heavy traffic areas such as the Atlantic, Indian, and Pacific Oceans. Telegraphy, telephony, and television transmissions are carried simultaneously by high-frequency radio waves. They are beamed to the satellites from large dish antennae or Earth stations, which connect with international networks. The number of stations continues to increase. In the UK Goonhilly and Madley are the main Earth stations.

In 1980 the Post Office opened its first System X (all electronic, digital) telephone exchange in London, a method already adopted in the USA. Other recent advances include the use of fibre-optic cables consisting of fine glass fibres for telephone lines instead of the usual copper cables. The telecommunications signals are transmitted along the fibres on pulses of laser light. Procedures, technical standards, frequencies, and so on, in telecommunications are controlled by the International Telecommunications Union (ITU).

**cellphone** or *cellular radio* mobile radio telephone, one of a network connected to the telephone system by a computer-controlled communication system. Service areas are divided into small 'cells', about 5 km/3 mi across, each with a separate low-power transmitter.

The cellular system allows the use of the same set of frequencies with the minimum risk of interference. Nevertheless, in crowded city areas, cells can become overloaded. This has led to a move away from analogue transmis-

**skyscraper**

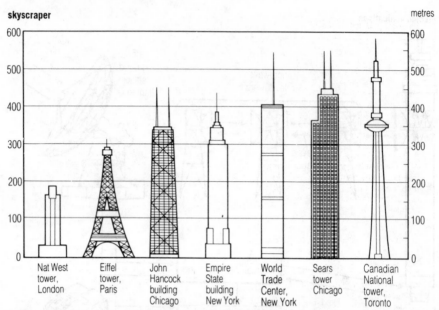

sions to digital methods that allow more calls to be made within a limited frequency range.

**fax** common name for **facsimile transmission** or **telefax**: the transmission of images over a telecommunications link, usually the telephone network. When placed in a fax machine, the original image is scanned by a transmitting device and converted into coded signals, which travel via the telephone lines to the receiving fax machine, where an image is created that is a copy of the original. Photographs as well as printed text and drawings may be sent.

**radio** the transmission and reception of radio waves. The theory of electromagnetic waves was first developed by James Clerk Maxwell 1864, given practical confirmation in the laboratory 1888 by Heinrich Hertz, and put to

practical use by Marconi, who in 1901 achieved reception of a signal in Newfoundland transmitted from Poldhu in Cornwall.

**radio transmission** a microphone converts sound waves (pressure variations in the air) into an audiofrequency electrical signal. An oscillator produces a carrier wave of high frequency; different stations are allocated different transmitting carrier frequencies. A modulator superimposes the audiofrequency signal on the carrier. There are two main ways of doing this: amplitude modulation (AM), used for long- and medium-wave broadcasts, in which the strength of the carrier is made to fluctuate in time with the audio signal; and frequency modulation (FM), as used for VHF broadcasts, in which the frequency of the carrier is made

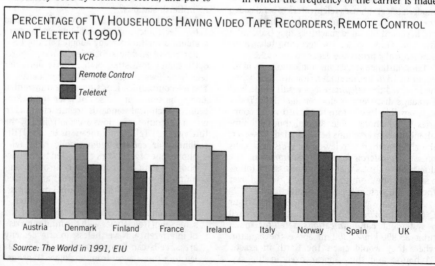

PERCENTAGE OF TV HOUSEHOLDS HAVING VIDEO TAPE RECORDERS, REMOTE CONTROL AND TELETEXT (1990)

*Source: The World in 1991, EIU*

## IMAGE COMPRESSION

To digitize a still picture image, it is first broken down into a large number of individual picture points, or pixels. This is done by overlaying the picture with a stationary mosaic of light sensors, rather like a fine honeycomb, or by moving the picture slowly past a fine strip of sensors. In each case all the picture points are analysed for their light content. The measurements made are then coverted into digital code.

There will always be a large amount of redundant information in any picture. The sea, the sky, or a white shirt will contain less fine detail than a close-up of the human face. 'This makes it possible to compress the image, reducing the number of digital bits needed to represent it. Where there is a lot of fine detail, and adjacent pixels are all different, each is individually coded. Where adjacent points are identical, signifying a wash area of white, black, grey, or single colour, the coding system registers the boundaries of the area. That way, digital bits are not wasted on coding the same information over and over again.

Still-picture compression coding is an established technology with an algorithm, or a set of computer-control instructions, agreed by the Joint Photographic Experts Group (JPEG) of the International Standards Organization and International Electrotechnical Commission and now rapidly becoming standard.

Compressing moving pictures, for recording as digital code on tape or disc or in solid-state memory, is much more challenging. Existing TV and video systems rely on the display of 25 (for Europe) or 30 (for the USA and Japan) individual pictures per second. The cinema gets away with 24 pictures per second, but if there are any fewer, the human eye registers judder.

Without compression, each individual picture (of the 25 or 30 a second) needs at least 64 kilobytes (512,000 bits) when digitally coded, and preferably twice that. A 12 cm/4 in compact disc, originally designed to store an hour or more of digital hi-fi stereo sound, and later adopted to store text, graphic images, still pictures, and many hours of lower-fidelity sound, can only deliver data at a rate of around 150 kilobytes per second. So, to store an hour or more of moving video pictures on a CD requires very heavy compression.

The early, sledgehammer approach was to break each frame of the moving image down into a quarter of a million individual pixel points, compare the pixels in one frame with those in the next, and identify points with no change. In this way, the amount of digital information needed to code each picture image could be reduced to around 5 kilobytes per frame. But picture quality was poor and it took 30 seconds to process each of the 25 or 30 pictures per second. In 1989 the Moving Picture Experts Group (MPEG) began to analyse a score of different proposals for coding moving pictures. This work was made urgent by the explosion of interest in multimedia and interactive compact discs. Agreement was reached in mid-1991 on the basic essentials.

Instead of analysing pixel-by-pixel differences between successive pictures, the encoder now uses a technique called Discrete Cosine Transform encoding to break each picture down into blocks, compare them in successive pictures, and record how these blocks differ. The less change there is, the larger the blocks can be, with less code needed to describe them. The processor also describes and predicts how block patterns move from picture to picture. Imagine a car moving across the screen. Its shape is coded once, but then only the position that it occupies on the screen is coded, along with any change of shape caused by changing perspective.

The system interleaves full or 'key frame' pictures with partially coded pictures that contain only updating information. The ratio of key frames to updating frames can be fixed (say at one key for every four or five updates) or may vary with the programme material. And all the time, the digital code adapts itself to the amount of information to be recorded, with the size of the coding steps changing according to the content of the picture.

Taken together, these techniques reduce the bit rate to well below the CD threshold of 150 kilobytes per second, even with accompanying sound. One penalty is that cuts in the picture content (for example, a change of view from long shot to close up) must be timed to coincide with the transmission of a key frame. Another is that the video sequence cannot easily be run backwards, because update frames then precede key frames.

Similar techniques are used for compressing high-definition TV signals into the frequency bands that have until now been suitable only for conventional TV transmissions. Now that the MPEG-coding algorithms have been agreed, microchip manufacturers around the world can develop integrated circuits that encode and decode moving pictures in real time, so that a one-minute sequence of moving pictures takes one minute to convert into digital code and one minute to display on screen again. Real-time decoding makes it possible for the new generation of interactive multimedia systems to store over an hour of moving pictures (and sound) on a 12 cm/4 in CD for replay on a domestic player and TV set. The moving pictures occupy the full screen area, whereas early multimedia systems displayed motion video only in part of the screen, in a window.

Initially, real-time encoding will be used only by programme makers. But it now looks certain that home computers of the future will incorporate real-time encoding and decoding chips that let the user store moving-picture sequences from a video camera on computer disc, and manipulate the images with graphics software.

### TELECOMMUNICATIONS: CHRONOLOGY

| | |
|---|---|
| 1794 | Claude Chappe in France built a long-distance signalling system using semaphore. |
| 1839 | Charles Wheatstone and William Cooke devised an electric telegraph in England. |
| 1843 | Samuel Morse transmitted the first message along a telegraph line in the USA, using his Morse code of signals—short (dots) and long (dashes). |
| 1858 | The first transatlantic telegraph cable was laid. |
| 1876 | American Alexander Graham Bell invented the telephone. |
| 1877 | Thomas Edison invented the carbon transmitter for the telephone. |
| 1894 | Guglielmo Marconi pioneered wireless telegraphy in Italy, later moving to England. |
| 1900 | Reginald Fessenden in the USA first broadcast voice by radio. |
| 1901 | Marconi transmitted the first radio signals across the Atlantic. |
| 1904 | John Ambrose Fleming invented the thermionic valve. |
| 1907 | American Charles Krumm introduced the forerunner of the teleprinter. |
| 1920 | Stations in Detroit and Pittsburgh began regular radio broadcasts. |
| 1922 | The BBC began its first radio transmissions, for the London station 2LO. |
| 1932 | The Post Office introduced the Telex in the UK. |
| 1956 | The first transatlantic telephone cable was laid. |
| 1962 | Telstar pioneers transatlantic satellite communications, transmitting live TV pictures. |
| 1966 | Charles Kao in England advanced the idea of using optical fibres for telecommunications transmissions. |
| 1969 | Live TV pictures were sent from astronauts on the Moon back to Earth. |
| 1975 | The Post Office announced Prestel, the world's first viewdata system, using the telephone lines to link a computer data bank with the TV screen. |
| 1977 | The first optical fibre cable was installed in California. |
| 1984 | First commercial cellphone service started in Chicago, USA. |
| 1985 | Cellphone services introduced in the UK. |
| 1988 | Videophones introduced in Japan. |
| 1989 | *Voyager 2* transmitted pictures of the planet Neptune over a distance of some 4,400 million km/2,700 million mi, the signals taking 4 hours 6 minutes to reach Earth; the first transoceanic optical-fibre cable, capable of carrying 40,000 simultaneous telephone conversations, was laid between Europe and the USA. |

to fluctuate. The transmitting aerial emits the modulated electromagnetic waves, which travel outwards from it.

**radio reception** a receiving aerial produces minute voltages in response to the waves sent out by a transmitter. A tuned circuit selects a particular voltage frequency, usually by means of a variable capacitor connected across a coil of wire. (The effect is similar to altering the tension in a piano wire, making it capable of vibrating at a different frequency.) A demodulator disentangles the audio signal from the carrier, which is now discarded, having served its purpose. An amplifier boosts the audio signal for feeding to the loudspeaker, which produces sound waves.

**superheterodyne receiver** the most widely used type of radio receiver, in which the incoming signal is mixed with a signal of fixed frequency generated within the receiver circuits. The resulting signal, called the intermediate-frequency (i.f.) signal, has a frequency between that of the incoming signal and the internal signal. The intermediate frequency is near the optimum frequency of the amplifier to which the i.f. signal is passed. This arrangement ensures greater gain and selectivity. The superheterodyne system is also used in basic television receivers.

**telephone** instrument for communicating by voice over long distances, invented by Alexander Graham Bell 1876. The transmitter (mouthpiece) consists of a carbon microphone, with a diaphragm that vibrates when a person speaks into it. The diaphragm vibrations compress grains of carbon to a greater or lesser extent, altering their resistance to an electric current passing through them. This sets up variable electrical signals, which travel along the telephone lines to the receiver of the person being called. There they cause the magnetism of an electromagnet to vary, making a diaphragm above the electromagnet vibrate and give out sound waves, which mirror those that entered the mouthpiece originally.

The standard instrument has a handset, which houses the transmitter (mouthpiece), and receiver (earpiece), resting on a base, which has a dial or push-button mechanism for dialling a telephone number. Some telephones combine a push-button mechanism and mouthpiece and earpiece in one unit. A cordless telephone is of this kind, connected to a base unit not by wires but by radio. It can be used at distances up to about 100 m/330 ft from the base unit. In 1988 Japan and in 1990 Britain introduced an integrated services digital network, providing fast transfer of computerized information.

**television** the reproduction at a distance by radio waves of visual images.

**history** in 1873 it was realized that since the electrical properties of selenium vary according to the amount of light to which it is exposed, light could be converted into electrical impulses, making it possible to transmit such

TELEVISION CHRONOLOGY

| | |
|---|---|
| 1878 | William Crookes in England invented the Crookes tube, which produced cathode rays. |
| 1884 | Paul Nipkow in Germany built a mechanical scanning device, the Nipkow disc, a rotating disc with a spiral pattern of holes in it. |
| 1897 | Karl Ferdinand Braun, also in Germany, modified the Crookes tube to produce the ancestor of the modern TV receiver picture tube. |
| 1906 | Boris Rosing in Russia began experimenting with the Nipkow disc and cathode-ray tube, eventually succeeding in transmitting some crude TV pictures. |
| 1923 | Vladimir Zworykin in the USA invented the first electronic camera tube, the iconoscope. |
| 1926 | John Logie Baird demonstrated a workable TV system, using mechanical scanning by Nipkow disc. |
| 1928 | Baird demonstrated colour TV. |
| 1929 | The BBC began experimental broadcasting of TV programmes, using Baird's system. |
| 1936 | The BBC began regular broadcasting using Baird's system from Alexandra Palace, London. |
| 1940 | Experimental colour TV transmission began in the USA, using the modern system of colour reproduction. |
| 1953 | Successful colour TV transmissions began in the USA. |
| 1956 | The first videotape recorder was produced in California, USA by the Ampex Corporation. |
| 1962 | TV signals were transmitted across the Atlantic via the *Telstar* satellite. |
| 1970 | The first videodisc system was announced by Decca in the UK and by AEG–Telefunken in Germany, but it was not perfected until the 1980s, when laser scanning was used for playback. |
| 1975 | Sony introduced their videocassette tape-recorder system, Betamax, for domestic viewers, six years after their professional U-Matic system; the British Post Office (now British Telecom) announced their Prestel viewdata system. |
| 1973 | The BBC and Independent Television introduced the world's first teletext systems, Ceefax and Oracle, respectively. |
| 1979 | Matsushita in Japan developed a pocket-sized flat-screen TV set, using a liquid-crystal display (LCD). |
| 1986 | Data broadcasting using digital techniques was developed; an enhancement of teletext was produced. |
| 1989 | The Japanese began broadcasting high-definition television; satellite television was introduced in the UK. |
| 1990 | Independent Television introduced a digital stereo sound system (NICAM); MAC, a European system allowing greater picture definition, more data, and sound tracks, was introduced. |

impulses over a distance and then reconvert them into light. The chief difficulty was seen to be the 'splitting of the picture' so that the infinite variety of light and shade values might be transmitted and reproduced. In 1908 Alan Archibald Campbell Swinton pointed out that cathode-ray tubes would best effect transmission and reception. Mechanical devices were used at the first practical demonstration of actual television, given by John Logie Baird in London on 27 Jan 1926, and cathode-ray tubes were used experimentally by the BBC from 1934. The world's first public television service was started from the BBC station at the Alexandra Palace, in N London, on 2 Nov 1936.

**technology** for transmission, a television camera converts the pattern of light it receives into a pattern of electrical charges. This is scanned line-by-line by a beam of electrons from an electron gun, resulting in variable electrical signals that represent the visual picture. These vision signals are combined with a radio carrier wave and broadcast. The TV aerial picks up the wave and feeds it to the receiver (TV set). This separates out the vision signals, which pass to the picture tube (a cathode-ray tube). The broad end of the tube, upon which the scene is to appear, has its inside surface coated with a fluorescent material. The vision signals control the strength of a beam of electrons from an electron gun, aimed at the screen and making it glow more or less brightly. At the same time the beam is made to scan across the screen line-by-line, mirroring the action of the gun in the TV camera. The result is a re-creation spot-by-spot, line-by-line of the pattern of light that entered the camera. 25 pictures are built up each second with interlaced scanning (30 in USA), with a total of 625 lines (in Europe, but 525 lines in the USA and Japan).

**colour television** Baird gave a demonstration of colour television in London in 1928, but it was not until Dec 1953 that the first successful system was adopted for broadcasting, in the USA. This is called the NTSC system, since it was developed by the National Television System Committee, and variations of it have been developed in Europe—for example, the SECAM (sequential and memory) system in France and the PAL (phase alternation by line) in West Germany. All three differ only in the way colour signals are prepared for transmission. When there was no agreement on a universal European system 1964, in 1967 the UK, West Germany, the Netherlands, and Switzerland adopted PAL while France and the USSR adopted SECAM. In 1989 the European Community agreed to harmonize TV channels from 1991, allowing any station to show programmes anywhere in the EC.

The method of colour reproduction in television is related to that used in colour photography and printing. It uses the principle that any colours can be made by mixing the primary colours red, green, and blue in appropriate proportions. In colour television the receiver reproduces only three basic colours: red, green and blue. The effect of yellow, for example, is reproduced by combining equal amounts of red and green light, while white is formed by a mixture of all three basic colours. Signals indicate the amounts of red, green, and blue light to be generated at the receiver.

To transmit each of these three signals in the same way as the single-brightness signal in monochrome (black-and-white) television would need three times the normal bandwidth, and reduce the number of possible stations and programmes to one-third of that possible with monochrome television. The three signals are therefore coded into one complex signal, which is transmitted as a more-or-less normal black-and-white signal, and produces a satisfactory—or compatible—picture on ordinary black-and-white receivers. A fraction of each primary red, green, and blue signal is added together to produce the normal brightness, or luminance, signal. The minimum of extra colouring information is then sent by a special subcarrier signal, which is superimposed on the brightness signal. This extra colouring information corresponds to the hue and saturation of the transmitted colour, but without any of the fine detail of the picture. The impression of sharpness is conveyed only by the brightness signal, the colouring being added as a broad colour wash. The various colour systems differ only in the way in which the colouring information is sent on the subcarrier signal.

The colour receiver has to amplify the complex signal and decode it back to the basic red, green and blue signals; these primary signals are then applied to a colour cathode-ray tube. The colour display tube is the heart of any colour receiver. Many designs of colour picture tube have been invented; the most successful of these is known as the 'shadow mask tube'. It operates on similar electronic principles to the black-and-white television picture tube, but the screen is composed of a fine mosaic of over one million dots arranged in an orderly fashion. One-third of the dots glow red when bombarded by electrons, one-third glow green, and one-third blue. There are three sources of electrons, respectively modulated by the red, green, and blue signals. The tube is so arranged that the shadow mask allows only the red signals to hit red dots, the green signals to hit green dots, and the blue signals to hit blue dots. The glowing dots are so small that from a normal viewing distance the colours merge into one another and a picture with a full range of colours is seen.

**high-definition television** (HDTV) system offering a significantly greater number of scanning lines, and therefore a clearer picture, than the 525/625 lines of established television systems. In 1989 the Japanese broadcasting station NHK and a consortium of manufacturers launched the Hi-Vision system, with 1125 lines and a wide-screen format. The Eureka research project has gathered together 30 European electronics companies, research laboratories, and broadcasting authorities to provide a common 1250-line system for Europe by 1993.

**TV channels** in addition to transmissions received by all viewers, the 1970s and 1980s saw the growth of pay-television cable networks, which are received only by special subscribers, and of devices, such as those used in the Qube system (USA), which allow the viewers' opinions to be transmitted instantaneously to the studio via a response button, so that, for example, a home viewing audience can vote in a talent competition. The number of programme channels continues to increase, following the introduction of satellite television (in the UK, Sky Television 1989 and British Satellite Broadcasting 1990, which merged to form British Sky Broadcasting 1990).

Further use of the television set has been brought about by videotext and the use of video recorders to tape programmes for playback later or to play prerecorded videocassettes, and by their use as computer screens and for security systems. Extended-definition television gives a clear enlargement from a microscopic camera and was first used in 1989 in neurosurgery to enable medical students to watch brain operations.

**video camera** or **camcorder** portable television camera that takes moving pictures electronically on magnetic tape. It produces an electrical output signal corresponding to rapid line-by-line scanning of the field of view. The output is recorded on videotape and is played back on a television screen via a video tape recorder (VTR).

**video disc** disc with pictures (and sounds) recorded on it, played back by laser. It works in the same way as a compact disc. The video disc (originated by Baird 1928; commercially available from 1978) is chiefly used to provide commercial films for private viewing. Most systems use a 30 cm/12 in rotating vinyl disc coated with a reflective material. Laser scanning recovers picture and sound signals from the surface where they are recorded as a spiral of microscopic pits.

**video tape recorder** (VTR) device for recording visuals and sound on cassettes or spools of magnetic tape. The first commercial VTR was launched 1956 for the television broadcasting industry, but from the late 1970s cheaper models developed for home use—to record broadcast programmes for future viewing and to view rented or purchased video cassettes of commercial films.

Video recording works in the same way as audio tape recording: the picture information is stored as a line of varying magnetism, or track, on a plastic tape covered with magnetic material. The main difficulty—the huge amount of information needed to reproduce a picture—is overcome by arranging the video track diagonally across the tape. During recording, the tape is wrapped around a drum in a spiral fashion. The recording head rotates inside the drum. The combination of the forward motion of the tape and the rotation of the head produces a diagonal track. The audio signal accompanying the video signal is recorded as a separate track along the edge of the tape.

Two VTR systems were introduced by Japanese firms in the 1970s. The Sony Betamax was considered technically superior, but Matsushita's VHS (Video Home Service) had larger marketing resources behind it and after some years became the sole system on the market. Super-VHS is an improved version of the VHS system, launched 1989, with higher picture definition and colour quality.

**videotext** system in which information (text) is displayed on a television (video) screen. There are two basic systems, known as teletext and viewdata. In the teletext system information is broadcast with the ordinary television signals, whereas in viewdata information is relayed to the screen from a central data bank via the telephone network. Both systems require the use of a television receiver with special decoder.

# ELECTRONICS

**electronics** the branch of science that deals with the emission of electrons from conductors and semiconductors, with the subsequent manipulation of these electrons, and with the construction of electronic devices. The first electronic device was the thermionic valve, or vacuum tube, in which electrons moved in a vacuum, and led to such inventions as radio, television, radar, and the digital computer. Replacement of valves with the comparatively tiny and reliable transistor in 1948 revolutionized electronic development. Modern electronic devices are based on minute integrated circuits (silicon chips), wafer-thin crystal slices holding tens of thousands of electronic components.

By using solid-state devices such as integrated circuits, extremely complex electronic circuits can be constructed, leading to the development of digital watches, pocket calculators, powerful microcomputers, and word processors.

**electron** stable, negatively charged elementary particle, a constituent of all atoms and the basic particle of electricity. A beam of electrons will undergo diffraction (scattering), and produce interference patterns, in the same way as electromagnetic waves such as light; hence they may also be regarded as waves.

**integrated circuit** popularly called *silicon chip* complete miniaturized electronic circuit produced on a single crystal, or chip, of a semiconducting material such as silicon. It may contain many thousands of transistors, resistors, and capacitors, and yet measure only 5 mm/0.2 in square and 1 mm/0.04 in thick.

The integrated circuit is encapsulated within a plastic or ceramic case, and linked via gold wires to metal pins with which it is connected to a printed circuit board and the other components that make up electronic devices such as computers and calculators. The discovery in

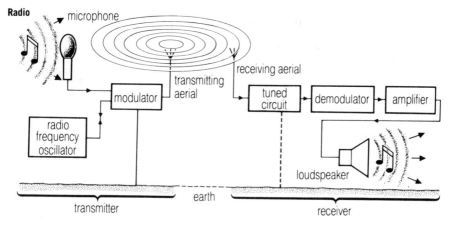

Radio

---

ELECTRONICS: CHRONOLOGY

| | |
|---|---|
| **1897** | Discovery of the electron by English physicist John Joseph Thomson. |
| **1904** | Diode valve, which allows flow of electricity in one direction only, invented by English physicist Ambrose Fleming. |
| **1906** | Triode electron valve, the first device to control an electric current, invented by US physicist Lee De Forest. |
| **1947** | John Bardeen, William Shockley, and Walter Brattain invented the junction germanium transistor at the Bell Laboratories, New Jersey, USA. |
| **1952** | British physicist G W A Dunner proposed the integrated circuit. |
| **1953** | Jay Forrester of the Massachusetts Institute of Technology, USA, built a magnetic memory smaller than existing vacuum-tube memories. |
| **1954** | Silicon transistor perfected by Gordon Teal of Texas Instruments, USA. |
| **1958** | The first integrated circuit, containing five components, built by US electrical physicist Jack Kilby. |
| **1959** | The planar transistor, which is built up in layers, or planes, designed by Robert Noyce of Fairchild Semiconductor Corporation, USA. |
| **1961** | Steven Hofstein designed the field-effect transistor used in modern integrated circuits. |
| **1971** | The first microprocessor, the Intel 4004, designed by Ted Hoff in the USA; it contained 2,250 components and could add two four-bit numbers in 11-millionths of a second. |
| **1974** | The Intel 8080 microprocessor introduced; it contained 4,500 components and could add two eight-bit numbers in 2.5-millionths of a second. |
| **1979** | The Motorola 68000 microprocessor introduced; it contained 70,000 components and could multiply two 16-bit numbers in 3.2-millionths of a second. |
| **1981** | The Hewlett-Packard Superchip introduced; it contained 450,000 components and could multiply two 32-bit numbers in 1.8-millionths of a second. |
| **1985** | The Inmos T414 Transputer introduced, the first microprocessor designed for use in parallel computers. |
| **1988** | The first optical microchip, which uses light instead of electricity, was developed. |
| **1989** | Wafer-scale silicon memory chips introduced: the size of a beer mat, they are able to store 200 million characters. |
| **1990** | Memory chips capable of holding 4 million bits of information began to be mass-produced in Japan. The chips can store the equivalent of 520,000 characters, or the contents of a 16-page newspaper. Each chip contains 9 million components packed on a piece of silicon less than 15 mm long by 5 mm wide. |

---

the early 1970s of the means to produce integrated circuits began the so-called computer revolution.

**microprocessor** a computer's central processing unit, contained on a single integrated circuit. The appearance of the first microprocessors 1971 heralded the introduction of the microcomputer. The microprocessor has led to a dramatic fall in the size and cost of computers and to the introduction of dedicated computers in washing machines, cars, and so on.

**semiconductor** crystalline material with an electrical conductivity between that of metals (good) and insulators (poor). The conductivity of semiconductors can usually be improved by minute additions of different substances or by other factors. Silicon, for example, has poor conductivity at low temperatures, but this is improved by the application of light, heat, or voltage; hence its use in transistors, rectifiers, and integrated circuits (silicon chips).

**transistor** solid-state electronic component, made of semiconducting material and with three or more electrodes, that can regulate a current passing through it. A transistor can act as an amplifier, oscillator, photocell, or switch, and usually operates on a very small amount of power. Transistors commonly consist of a tiny sandwich of germanium or silicon, alternate layers having different electrical properties.

A crystal of pure germanium or silicon would act as an insulator (nonconductor). However, by introducing impurities in the form of atoms of other materials (for example, boron, arsenic, or indium) in minute amounts, the germanium and silicon layers may be made either **n-type**, having an excess of electrons, or **p-type**, having a deficiency of electrons. This enables electrons

**integrated circuit**

*the packaging of a silicon 'chip'*

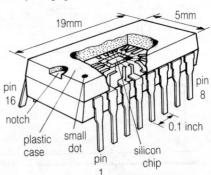

## SEEING THE UNSEEABLE—PROGRESS IN MICROSCOPY

In Jan 1991, the Japanese electronics firm Hitachi produced the smallest writing of all time. The message read 'Peace 91', followed by the initials of the Hitachi Central Research Laboratory where the work was done. The letters were less than 1.5 nanometres (1.5-thousand-millionths of a metre) high. They were written by removing individual sulphur atoms from the surface of a crystal of molybdenum disulphide. This was not the first time that a message had been written with individual atoms. In late 1990, researchers at IBM wrote their company name by placing 35 xenon atoms on the surface of a nickel crystal.

Both teams used scanning tunnelling microscopes (STM) to write their messages. These microscopes belong to a family of remarkable new microscopes developed in the late 1980s. These microscopes, called scanned probe microscopes, run a metal probe, with a tip so fine that it may consist only of a single atom, across the surface of the specimen. In the scanning tunnelling microscope, an electric current that flows through the probe is used to construct an image of the specimen on a computer screen. A related instrument, the atomic force microscope, uses the force felt by the probe to form the image. These microscopes can magnify a million times and can give images of single atoms and molecules.

The STM can also be used to manipulate individual atoms, picking them up and moving them to new positions. The IBM message was written by bringing the tip of the STM probe very close to a xenon atom, and then increasing the current through the probe. This pins the atom down, allowing it to be dragged to a new position. The Japanese technique was to bring the probe tip very close to an atom in the crystal surface and subject the atom to a pulse of electricity. This blasts the atom away, leaving a space in the regular atomic arrangement of the crystal.

The ability to manipulate individual atoms could be used to produce miniature data storage devices. The presence or absence of an atom at a particular site in a regular crystal arrangement could represent the 1s or 0s used in binary computer code. Hitachi claim that one thousand million bits of data could be held on a square 10 millionths of a metre across. Currently a computer disc 10 cm/4 in across would be needed to store this much data.

Probe technology has also produced an optical microscope that is capable of seeing details finer than the wavelength of visible light. Called the photon STM, the new microscope can see details at least ten times smaller than the best conventional optical microscopes. The photon STM has an advantage over the electron STM in that the specimen does not need to be electrically conducting, hence it can be used to examine biological samples. Biological samples examined by electron STMs must be coated with a thin film of conducting material before an image can be obtained. The photon STM, however, can produce images of both conducting and non-conducting materials, as long as they are transparent. Scientists at the Oak Ridge National Laboratory, where the new microscope was developed, have produced images of bacteria and viruses.

In the photon STM, the specimen is placed on the upper surface of a transparent prism. Light is shone upwards so that it reflects from the inside of the prism surface. A fine fibre optic probe is brought close to the specimen, and particles of light—photons—are collected by the probe as it travels across the specimen. The photons are collected by a photomultiplier and converted into an electrical signal. A computer forms an image from these signals.

Researchers expect to be able to increase the power of the photon STM in a number of ways. Firstly, they plan to reduce the wavelength of light used. At present they are using visible light, but plan to change to shorter-wavelength ultraviolet light, and then to X-rays. Another improvement would be to use a probe with a finer tip. This could be achieved by chemically etching the quartz probe until the tip is just 150 nanometres across. Finally, resolution could be increased by improving control of the scanning mechanism. As in all scanned probe microscopes, the distance between the probe and the specimen must be controlled and measured very accurately. These improvements should enable images of individual atoms to be produced, although the resolution of the photon STM will never match that of the electron STM.

to flow from one layer to another in one direction only. Transistors have had a great impact on the electronics industry, and are now made in thousands of millions each year. They perform many of the same functions as the thermionic valve, but have the advantages of greater reliability, long life, compactness, and instantaneous action, no warming-up period being necessary. They are widely used in most electronic equipment, including portable radios and televisions, computers, satellites, and space research, and are the basis of the integrated circuit (silicon chip). They were invented at Bell Telephone Laboratories in the USA in 1948 by John Bardeen and Walter Brittain, developing the work of William Shockley.

**Transputer** electronic device that increases the computing power of a computer, launched 1985 by UK company Inmos. In the circuits of a standard computer the processing of data takes place in sequence. In a Transputer's circuits processing takes place in parallel, greatly reducing computing time for programs written specifically for the Transputer.

**valve** or **electron tube** a glass tube containing gas at low pressure, which is used to control the flow of electricity in a circuit. Three or more metal electrodes are inset into the tube By varying the voltage on one of them, called

**Television**

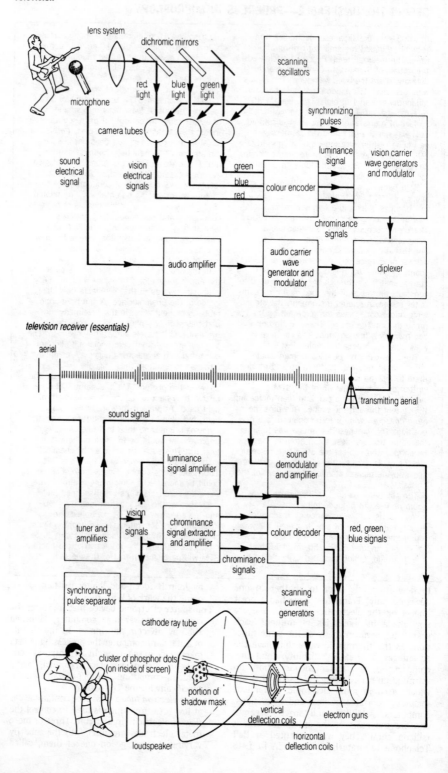

*television receiver (essentials)*

the grid electrode, the current through the valve can be controlled, and the valve can act as an amplifier. They have been replaced for most applications by transistors. However, they are still used in high-power transmitters and amplifiers, and in some hi-fi systems.

## Science and society

*Do you think that Britain is or is not falling behind the rest of the world in scientific innovation and the development and applications of technology?*

| | |
|---|---|
| Is | 61 |
| Is not | 26 |
| Don't know | 13 |

## Science at school

*Which, if any, of these best describes your experience of science lessons in school*

| | |
|---|---|
| Boring | 20 |
| Hard | 9 |
| Badly taught | 17 |
| Irrelevant to everyday life | 14 |
| Interesting | 33 |
| Easy | 5 |
| Well taught | 15 |
| Improved understanding of the outside world | 9 |
| None of these | 3 |
| No experience | 11 |

*Do you think the Government should legislate to ensure that all children are taught some science and technology at school?*

| | |
|---|---|
| Yes | 86 |
| No | 10 |
| Don't know | 4 |

*How strongly do you agree or disagree with the following statements?*

*a) Our national prosperity depends on science and technology?*

| | |
|---|---|
| Agree strongly | 18 |
| Agree | 58 |
| Disagree | 16 |
| Disagree strongly | 1 |
| Don't know | 7 |

*b) Politicians don't know enough about science to*

*judge its importance*

| | |
|---|---|
| Agree strongly | 20 |
| Agree | 57 |
| Disagree | 11 |
| Disagree strongly | 1 |
| Don't know | 11 |

*c) Many of the world's problems can be solved by scientific research*

| | | |
|---|---|---|
| Agree strongly | | 15 |
| Agree | | 59 |
| | Disagree | 15 |
| Disagree strongly | | 1 |
| Don't know | | 10 |

*d) Science and technology play a major role in our daily lives*

| | |
|---|---|
| Agree strongly | 22 |
| Agree | 68 |
| Disagree | 5 |
| Disagree strongly | 1 |
| Don't know | 5 |

*e) It is important for Britain to be a leading nation in science*

| | |
|---|---|
| Agree strongly | 23 |
| Agree | 56 |
| Disagree | 12 |
| Disagree strongly | 1 |
| Don't know | 7 |

*How knowledgeable do you consider yourself to be about science and technology?*

| | |
|---|---|
| Very knowledgeable | 4 |
| Reasonably knowledgeable | 27 |
| Slightly knowledgeable | 43 |
| Baffled | 25 |
| Don't know | 0 |

*Think of the many innovations we take for granted in modern life—television, telephone. aerosols, insecticides, computers, air travel, painkillers etc. How would you summarise the influence that science and technology have had on everyday life during the past 50 years?*

| | |
|---|---|
| Enormously beneficial | 31 |
| Moderately beneficial | 39 |
| No overall benefit or harm | 8 |
| Quite harmful | 14 |
| Disastrous | 6 |
| Don't know | 2 |

# SPORT AND LEISURE

# LEISURE

Leisure can be defined as time spent free from employment, or time that is free to spend as one chooses. It can be spent relaxing in the sun or strenuously repairing a roof. The ways in which people choose to spend their leisure are often related to the type of work in which they are normally engaged. For those who give priority to their work and derive a great deal of satisfaction from it, leisure time is often seen as a means of furthering work-related interests or projects. Whereas those who find their work dull, arduous, or in some way unrewarding, may tend to place more importance on leisure and deliberately seek to make it different from work.

Although attitudes towards leisure vary greatly, it is undoubtedly an important element in the life of any individual, as well as for society as a whole. Leisure, however employed, provides relaxation and diversion from daily routines and from the stress or anxieties that often accompany work. It can create the state of mind that enables individuals to focus on their particular interests, such as education or volunteer work, or to find an escape from drudgery through forms of entertainment, such as film, television, and social activities. The relatively recent phenomenon of tourism stems, to a large extent, from people's need to escape *from* places rather than to travel to places. Surveys show that two-thirds of people feel that work stress has increased. According to anthropologists, tourism has become a form of secular pilgrimage, a therapeutic quest for the freedom that is increasingly denied to people in their daily lives. Employers often provide leisure facilities for their employees because the beneficial effect of leisure is recognized as an essential

## ATTENDANCES AT THE MOST POPULAR UK TOURIST ATTRACTIONS* (1990)

| * Attractions charging admission | Millions |
|---|---|
| Madame Tussaud's, London | 2.5 |
| Tower of London | 2.3 |
| Alton Towers, Staffordshire | 2.1 |
| Natural History Museum, London | 1.5 |
| Chessington World of Adventures, Surrey | 1.5 |
| Blackpool Tower, Lancashire | 1.4 |
| Royal Academy, London | 1.3 |
| Science Museum, London | 1.3 |
| London Zoo | 1.2 |
| Kew Gardens, London | 1.2 |
| Source: British Tourist Authority | |

## SPECTATOR ATTENDANCE AT SELECTED SPORTING EVENTS

| | Thousands 1989/90 |
|---|---|
| Football League (England & Wales) | 19,466 |
| Greyhound racing | 5,400 |
| Horse racing | 4,924 |
| Scottish Football League | 3,575 |
| Rugby Football Union (England) | 2,250 |
| Motor sports | 1,650 |
| Rugby Football League | 1,689 |
| Test and County cricket | 751 |
| English basketball | 203 |
| Motorcycle sports | 25 |
| Scottish basketball | 9 |
| Source: Organisations concerned | |

ingredient in the making of a healthy, productive worker.

Home-based leisure activities include watching television, reading, and listening to radio, records and tapes, as well as more active pastimes, such as gardening and do-it-yourself. Leisure activities away from the home may be devoted to cultural

---

## WEALTH: CAN WE EVER GET ENOUGH OF IT?

The results of a Gallup survey for American Express Gold Card showed that the majority of people earning more than twice the annual national average believe that they would need to earn more than £100,000 a year to be considered wealthy. Seven out of ten of those earning £600,000 or more a year chose a figure between £100,000 and £500,000, while one in five felt they would need an annual income that topped half a million in order to consider themselves rich. Of those earning above £300,000, a quarter are less than happy with their income, claiming to be only 'coping'. Few of the respondents in any of the affluent income groups surveyed describe themselves as rich, and the results indicate that the more people earn the more money they would need to consider themselves rich.

High-income earners live lifestyles that clearly reflect their consumer potential. They own luxury goods—a quarter have a mobile phone and a watch worth more than £500. Travel and

entertainment are two of the most evident rewards of success. On average people in this income bracket take three holidays a year, travel abroad a great deal on business, and entertain in restaurants for pleasure three times a month and twice a month on business.

Most of those surveyed admit to living comfortably and seven out of ten say they have no ambition to become a millionaire. Those who claim such ambitions are mainly the high-earning 18–34 year-olds, of whom half believe they have a realistic chance of achieving this goal. Attitudes towards displaying wealth and success are mixed, with people divided equally between those who feel it is right to show that they have done well and those who believe that success should not be flaunted. There was a similar mixed reaction to possessions and status symbols. Red braces—the essential item for the 80s 'yuppie look'—is now at the top of the list of things that most would be embarrassed to own, followed closely by the filofax.

# TOURISM: CAN THE DAMAGE BE LIMITED?

Tourism will soon be the world's largest industry. During the last four decades the numbers of world tourists have increased relentlessly. In 1950 an estimated 50 million travelled abroad; in 1988 there were more than 400 million travellers; by 2000 it is calculated there could be up to 650 million taking international trips, and four or five times as many travelling in their own countries (3 billion or more in transit). Tourism currently provides 5.7% of the world's payroll, with 6% of all jobs. In the UK, tourism provides more than a million jobs; in southern Europe, 14.4% of jobs are connected with tourism; in the USA, tourism ranks amongst the country's top two or three industries. It is astonishing to learn that these figures are all based on no more than 3% of the world's population having the leisure and the money to become tourists.

As the charter of the International Council on Monuments and Sites declares, 'Tourism is an irreversible social, human, economic and cultural fact.' Yet, one can no longer ignore how the sheer weight of its numbers is taking its toll. The growth of tourism is now accompanied by an ever growing alarm at its destructive potential, a fact that many feel must somehow be reversed. The problem of numbers is one that affects busy urban centres and remote ecosystems alike. The Mediterranean is an area where the overkill of mass tourism is perhaps best known, with the Spanish experience invariably cited as an illustration of its evil effects. The Mediterranean is now not only the dirtiest sea in the world but the most urbanized.

Many of the world's most valued cultural and historical sites and monuments are being eroded or 'polluted' by mass tourism. More stone at the Temple of Zeus in Olympia has been worn away, by millions of pairs of tourists' feet, in the past generation than in the previous 2,000 years. The Lascaux Caves are now closed to the public because the exhaled breath of thousands of visitors was damaging the irreplaceable paintings. Venice has decided to implement a 'visa' system of entry to the city during the high season, whereby people will have to apply to be allowed in. The instances of damage caused by tourism are innumerable and range from the overloading of waste disposal and sewage systems to threatening coral reefs and mangrove forests. Tourism threatens habitats and endangers species as well as human groups. As early as 1976, the Australian Heritage Commission announced that they would no longer publish specific details of Aboriginal sites in danger, because publication would only attract more sightseers and increase that danger.

Many are convinced that tourism's destructive character stems purely from its mismanagement, and that it is potentially the least damaging of the profit-making initiatives, because it is in its interest to preserve the environment.

Tourism can also strengthen conservation and heritage, as in the case of historic houses and gardens. Wildlife in the parks of East Africa, such as Serengeti and Amboseli, owes its survival, however precarious, to the safari market. In Madagascar, although tourism may 'spoil' parts of the island, it could also be a powerful element in saving rainforests. 'Green' tourism aims to minimize the overall impact on the environment, to benefit the host community and the local environment, and to be sustainable. At Cyprus' first National Park, environmentalists are working with the local and national governments to limit nearby tourism development and to offer visitors accommodation in traditional village houses. Although local villagers are angered that they will not see the same profits as others on the island have, the environmental and protection concerns that created the park will not be disrupted.

Increased demand for environmentally positive tourism has given rise to tour operators offering 'green' holidays, and making initiatives to lobby governments, educate consumers, and take part in conservation projects. If managed effectively the tourist industry could provide economic benefits to local people, educate tourists about conservation issues, finance conservation projects, and force tighter environmental legislation. The growth of tourism may be unstoppable, but its negative consequences can certainly be limited.

Venice, July 1989.

## How People Spend Their Time in the UK (1989)

| | Full-time employees | | Part-time employees | | |
| Weekly hours spent on: | Males | Females | Females | Housewives | Retired |
|---|---|---|---|---|---|
| Employment and travel* | 48.9 | 43.6 | 21.0 | 0.4 | 0.7 |
| Essential activities** | 25.9 | 42.2 | 58.6 | 65.3 | 30.8 |
| Sleep*** | 49.0 | 49.0 | 49.0 | 49.0 | 49.0 |
| Free Time | 44.2 | 33.2 | 39.4 | 53.3 | 87.5 |
| Free time per weekday | 4.7 | 3.2 | 4.7 | 7.1 | 12.3 |
| Free time per weekend day | 10.4 | 8.5 | 8.0 | 9.0 | 13.1 |

* Travel to and from place of work **Essential domestic work and personal care, including essential shopping, child care, cooking, washing and getting up and going to bed ***An average of 7 hours sleep per night is assumed

Source: The Henley Centre for Forecasting in Social Trends 21, 1991

interests such as theatre, cinema, libraries, and museums, or to other forms of entertainment, such as eating and drinking out, socializing, and shopping. Sport is another popular way of spending leisure time, whether in the form of participation in indoor or outdoor activities, or of attendance at spectator sports. Increasingly, day trips are made to attractions such as theme parks and shopping malls, which also feature aspects of leisure and entertainment.

At the end of the 1980s the split between in-home and out-of-home leisure was around 35:65, with the in-home sector predicted to grow faster in the 1990s. In-home leisure will be enhanced by the new range of high-quality TV systems, and more sophisticated electronic hardware and software, such as video equipment, home computers, and multi-media compact-disc systems. Some forecasters believe that the increasing pressures of daily work and travel, and growing violence on the streets combined with improvements in information technology, will make it easier for many more people to work at home and spend more of their lives 'cocooned' within their own four walls.

## UK Household Expenditure on Selected Leisure Items (£)

| | 1986 | 1989 |
|---|---|---|
| Average weekly household expenditure | | |
| Alcoholic drink | 5.93 | 6.92 |
| Meals consumed out | 4.38 | 5.51 |
| Books, newspapers, magazines, etc | 2.73 | 3.31 |
| Television, radio and musical instruments | 4.85 | 5.65 |
| Purchase of materials for home repairs, etc | 3.06 | 2.89 |
| Holidays | 5.39 | 7.76 |
| Hobbies | 0.06 | 0.09 |
| Cinema admissions | 0.10 | 0.16 |
| Dance admissions | 0.12 | * |
| Theatre, concert, etc admissions | 0.29 | 0.35 |
| Subscription and admission charges to participant sports | 0.71 | 0.85 |
| Football match admissions | 0.08 | 0.20 |
| Admissions to other spectator sports | 0.04 | ' |
| Sports goods (excluding clothes) | 0.37 | 0.62 |
| Other entertainment | 0.41 | 0.70* |
| Total weekly expenditure on above | 28.52 | 35.01 |
| Expenditure as percentage of total household expenditure | 16.0 | 15.6 |

* For 1989, 'Dance admissions' have been included with 'Other entertainment'.

Source: CSO, Social Trends 21, 1991

Although homes may well become more comfortable places in which to spend time, and the wish to avoid commuting congestion will certainly grow, it is unlikely that 'cocooning' will become a major phenomenon. In any event, out-of-home leisure activities will continue to attract many people, whether they prefer to work at home or not.

Retirement often creates a considerable leisure problem because of the vacuum left by work in terms of time expenditure. The ease with which people adjust to retirement depends, in most instances, on how involved and interested they were in their work. Those involved with creative work tend to be able to occupy themselves with activities similar to those that characterized their professional lives. People who tended to compartmentalize their work and leisure pursuits may concentrate on expanding their established leisure interests and activities, to fill the time once devoted to work. Filling the free time presented by retirement is perhaps most problematical for those who immersed themselves in routine work, because they may have fewer of the interests and inner resources that enable people to lead more active and fulfilling lives after retirement.

The increase in available leisure time over the past few decades has been accompanied by the creation of new and diverse leisure facilities and related products. Leisure has thus become big business, an industry with a strong growth rate. In the UK, leisure accounts for around 30% of all consumer expenditure (around £70 billion in 1989). The growth of interest in and expenditure on in-home leisure activities is strong, and includes not only electronic equipment but also gardening and DIY. In 1989 some £44 billion was spent on out-of-home leisure in the UK, an expenditure fostered to some extent by the development of new retailing and leisure centres, new heritage attractions, and theme parks. These centres, which are often characterized by their controlled, themed, and largely artificial environments, target millions of people from wide catchment areas to spend several hours within their purpose-built structures. The reasons for their success are clear. After all, they offer a variety of leisure activities and, most importantly, they cater to people's needs for fantasy and escapism.

# EVENTS AND RECORDS

**angling** fishing with rod and line. *Freshwater fishing* embraces game fishing, in which members of the salmon family, such as salmon and trout, are taken by spinners (revolving lures) and flies (imitations of adult or larval insects); and coarse fishing, in which members of the carp family, pike, perch, and eels are taken by baits or lures, and (in the UK) are returned to the water virtually unharmed. In *sea fishing* the catch includes flatfish, bass, and mackerel; big-game fishes include shark, tuna or tunny, marlin, and swordfish. World championships take place for most branches of the sport.

WORLD FRESHWATER CHAMPIONSHIP
first held 1957
*individual*
1983 Rudiger Kremkus *(West Germany)*
1984 Bobby Smithers *(England)*
1985 Dave Roper *(England)*
1986 Lud Wever *(Holland)*
1987 Clive Branson *(Wales)*
1988 Jean-Pierre Fouquet *(France)*
1989 Tom Pickering *(England)*
1990 Bob Nudd *(England)*
*team*
1983 Belgium
1984 Luxembourg
1985 England
1986 Italy
1987 England
1988 England
1989 Wales
1990 France

**archery** shooting with a bow and arrow at a circular target made up of ten concentric scoring zones. The highest score (10 points) is obtained by hitting the central, gold-coloured zone. Competitions usually take the form of Double FITA (Fédération Internationale de Tir à l'Arc) rounds—that is, 72 arrows are fired at each of four targets from distances of 90, 70, 50, and 30 m (70, 60, 50, and 30 m for women). The highest possible score is 2,880.

WORLD CHAMPIONSHIP
first held 1931; now contested every two years
*men – individual*
1981 Kyöti Laasonen *(Finland)*
1983 Richard McKinney *(USA)*
1985 Richard McKinney *(USA)*
1987 Vladimir Asheyer *(USSR)*
1989 Stanislav Zabrodsky *(USSR)*
*men – team*
1981 USA
1983 USA
1985 South Korea
1987 South Korea
1989 USSR
*women – individual*
1979 Jin-Ho Kim *(South Korea)*

1981 Natalia Butuzova *(USSR)*
1983 Jin-Ho Kim *(South Korea)*
1985 Irina Soldatova *(USSR)*
1987 Ma Xiagjuan *(China)*
1989 Soo Nyung-Kim *(South Korea)*
*women – team*
1981 USSR
1983 South Korea
1985 USSR
1987 China
1989 South Korea

**athletics** competitive track and field events consisting of running, throwing, and jumping disciplines. *Running events* range from sprint races (100 m/328 ft) and hurdles to the marathon (42.2 km/26.2 mi). *Jumping events* are the high jump and long jump, and, for men only, the triple jump and pole vault. *Throwing events* are javelin, discus, shot put, and hammer throw (men only).

OLYMPIC GAMES
events staged since 1896
*24th Olympics 1988*
*track and field*
*men/women*
100 metres Carl Lewis *(USA)*/Florence Griffith-Joyner *(USA)*
200 metres Joe Deloach *(USA)*/Florence Griffith-Joyner *(USA)*
400 metres Steve Lewis *(USA)*/Olga Bryzgina *(USSR)*
800 metres Paul Ereng *(Kenya)*/Sigrun Wodars *(East Germany)*
1,500 metres Peter Rono *(Kenya)*/Paula Ivan *(Romania)*
3,000 metres – /Tatyana Samolenko *(USSR)*
5,000 metres John Ngugi *(Kenya)*/ –
10,000 metres Brahim Boutaib *(Morocco)*/Olga Bondarenko *(USSR)*
marathon Gelindo Bordin *(Italy)*/Rosa Mota *(Portugal)*
100 metres hurdles – /Jordanka Donkova *(Bulgaria)*
110 metres hurdles Roger Kingdom *(USA)*/ –
400 metres hurdles Andre Phillips *(USA)*/Debbie Flintoff-King *(Australia)*
3,000 metres steeplechase Julius Kariuki *(Kenya)*/–
20,000 metres walk Joseph Pribilinec *(Czechoslovakia)*/–
50,000 metres walk Viacheslav Ivanenko *(USSR)*/–
4 × 100 metres relay USSR/USA
4 × 400 metres relay USA/USSR
high jump Gennadi Avdeyenko *(USSR)*/Louise Ritter *(USA)*
long jump Carl Lewis *(USA)*/Jackie Joyner-Kersee *(USA)*
triple jump Hristo Markov *(Bulgaria)*/ –
pole vault Sergey Bubka *(USSR)*/ –
javelin Tapio Korjus *(Finland)*/Petra Felke *(East Germany)*
hammer Sergey Litvinov *(USSR)*/ –
discus Jurgen Schult *(East Germany)*/Martina Hellmann *(East Germany)*
shot put Ulf Timmermann *(East Germany)*/Natalya Lisovaskaya *(USSR)*
decathlon Christian Schenk *(East Germany)*/ –
heptathlon – /Jackie Joyner-Kersee *(USA)*

WORLD CROSS-COUNTRY CHAMPIONSHIP
*men – individual*
1988 John Ngugi *(Kenya)*
1989 John Ngugi *(Kenya)*
1990 Khaled Skah *(Morocco)*
1991 Khaled Skah *(Morocco)*
*women – individual*
1988 Ingrid Kristiansen *(Norway)*
1989 Annette Sergant *(France)*
1990 Lynn Jennings *(USA)*
1991 Lynn Jennings *(USA)*
*men – team*
1988 Kenya
1989 Kenya
1990 Kenya
1991 Kenya
*women – team*
1988 USSR
1989 USSR
1990 USSR
1991 Kenya/Ethiopia
WORLD RECORDS
at 1 Aug 1990
*men*
100 metres 9.90sec Leroy Burrell *(USA)*
200 metres 19.72 sec Pietro Mennea *(Italy)*
400 metres 43.29 sec Butch Reynolds *(USA)*
800 metres 1 min 41.73 sec Sebastian Coe *(UK)*
1,000 metres 2 min 12.18 sec Sebastian Coe *(UK)*
1,500 metres 3 min 29.46 sec Said Aouita *(Morocco)*
mile 3 min 46.32 sec Steve Cram *(UK)*
2,000 metres 4 min 50.81 sec Said Aouita *(Morocco)*
3,000 metres 7 min 29.45 sec Said Aouita *(Morocco)*
5,000 metres 12 min 58.39 sec Said Aouita *(Morocco)*
10,000 metres 27 min 08.23 sec Arturo Barrios *(Mexico)*
20,000 metres 57 min 18.4 sec Dionisio Castro *(Portugal)*
20,994 metres 1 hr Jos Hermans *(Holland)*
25,000 metres 1hr 13 min 55.8 sec Toshihiko Seko *(Japan)*
30,000 metres 1 hr 29 min 18.8 sec Toshihiko Seko *(Japan)*
110 metres hurdles 12.92 sec Roger Kingdom *(USA)*

400 metres hurdles 47.02 sec Edwin Moses *(USA)*
3,000 metres steeplechase 8 min 5.35 sec Peter Koech *(Kenya)*
4 × 100 metres relay 37.79 sec France
4 × 400 metres relay 2 min 56.16 sec USA
4 × 800 metres relay 7 min 03.89 sec UK
4 × 1,500 metres relay 14 min 38.8 sec West Germany
high jump 2.44 metres Javier Sotomayor *(Cuba)*
pole vault 6.10 metres Sergey Bubka *(USSR)*
long jump 8.90 metres Bob Beamon *(USA)*
triple jump 17.97 metres Willie Banks *(USA)*
shot 23.12 metres Randy Barnes *(USA)*
discus 74.08 metres Jurgen Schult *(East Germany)*
hammer 86.74 metres Yuriy Sedykh *(USSR)*
javelin 96.96 metres Seppo Raty *(Finland)*
decathlon 8,847 points Daley Thompson *(UK)*
marathon 2 hr 6 min 50 sec Belayneh Dinsamo *(Ethiopia)*
*women*
100 metres 10.49 sec Florence Griffith-Joyner *(USA)*
200 metres 21.34 sec Florence Griffith-Joyner *(USA)*
400 metres 47.60 sec Marita Koch *(East Germany)*
800 metres 1 min 53.28 sec Jarmila Kratochvilova *(Czechoslovakia)*
1,500 metres 3 min 52.47 sec Tatyana Kazankina *(USSR)*
mile 4 min 15.61 sec Paula Ivan *(Romania)*
2,000 metres 5 min 28.69 sec Maricica Puica *(Romania)*
3,000 metres 8 min 22.62 sec Tatyana Kazankini *(USSR)*
5,000 metres 14 min 37.33 sec Ingrid Kristiansen *(Norway)*
10,000 metres 30 min 13.74 sec Ingrid Kristiansen *(Norway)*
20,000 metres 1 hr 29 min 29.2 sec Karolina Szabo *(Hungary)*
30,000 metres 1 hr 49 min 5.6 sec Karolina Szabo *(Hungary)*
100 metres hurdles 12.21 sec Yordanka Donkova *(Bulgaria)*
400 metres hurdles 52.94 sec Marina Stepanova *(USSR)*
4 × 100 metres relay 41.37 sec East Germany
4 × 200 metres relay 1 min 28.15 sec East Germany
4 × 400 metres relay 3 min 15.17 sec USSR

## Estimated Numbers Attending Sporting Events

| | 1971/72 | *000s* 1989/90 |
|---|---|---|
| Football League (England and Wales) | 28,700 | 19,466 |
| Greyhound racing | 8,800 | 5,400 |
| Horse racing | 4,200 | 4,924 |
| Scottish Football League | 4,521 | 3,575 |
| Rugby union (England) | 700 | 2,250 |
| Motor sports[1] | | 1,650 |
| Rugby league[2] | 1,170 | 1,689 |
| Test and County cricket | 984 | 751[5] |
| Basketball (England) | 2 | 203 |
| Motorcycle sports[3] | | 25 |
| Basketball (Scotland)[4] | 9 | 9 |

[1] Car and kart racing only. [2] League matches only. [3] Excluding speedway. [4] National league and cup matches only.
[5] 1988 season
*Source: Social Trends, 1991*

**badminton** indoor racket game, similar to lawn tennis, played with a shuttlecock (a half sphere of cork or plastic with a feather or nylon skirt) instead of a ball. It may be played by two or four players. The game takes place on a court 13.4 m/44 ft long and 5.2 m/17 ft wide (6.1 m/20 ft wide for doubles), with a raised net across the middle. The object of the game is to prevent the opponent from being able to return the shuttlecock.

WORLD CHAMPIONSHIP
first held 1977; now contested every two years
*men*
1980 Rudy Hartono *(Indonesia)*
1983 Icuk Sugiarto *(Indonesia)*
1985 Han Jian *(China)*
1987 Yang Yang *(China)*
1989 Yang Yang *(China)*
1991 Zao Zinhua *(China)*
*women*
1980 Wiharjo Verawaty *(Indonesia)*
1983 Li Lingwei *(China)*
1985 Han Aiping *(China)*
1987 Han Aiping *(China)*
1989 Li Lingwei *(China)*
1991 Tang Jiu Hong *(China)*
THOMAS CUP
men's team championship, first held 1949
1970 Indonesia
1973 Indonesia
1976 Indonesia
1979 Indonesia
1982 China
1984 Indonesia
1986 China
1988 China
1990 China
UBER CUP
women's team championship, first held 1957
1972 Japan
1975 Indonesia
1978 Japan
1981 Japan
1984 China
1986 China
1988 China
1990 China

**baseball** bat-and-ball game played between two teams, each of nine players. The field is marked out in the form of a diamond, with a base at each corner. The ball is struck with a cylindrical bat, and the players try to score ('make a run') by circuiting the bases. A 'home run' is a circuit on one hit.

WORLD SERIES
first held 1903 as an end-of-season game between the winners of the two professional leagues, the National League and the American League, and established as a series of seven games 1905
1982 St Louis Cardinals
1983 Baltimore Orioles
1984 Detroit Tigers
1985 Kansas City Royals
1986 New York Mets
1987 Minnesota Twins
1988 Los Angeles Dodgers
1989 Oakland Athletics
1990 Cincinatti Reds

**basketball** ball game between two teams of five players on an indoor enclosed court. The object is, via a series of passing moves, to throw the large inflated ball through a circular hoop and net positioned at each end of the court, 3.05 m/10 ft above the ground.

WORLD CHAMPIONSHIP
first held 1950 for men, 1953 for women; contested every four years
*men*
1954 USA
1959 Brazil
1963 Brazil
1967 USSR
1970 Yugoslavia
1974 USSR
1978 Yugoslavia
1982 USSR
1986 USA
1990 Yugoslavia
*women*
1957 USA
1959 USSR
1964 USSR
1967 USSR
1971 USSR
1975 USSR
1979 USA
1983 USSR
1986 USA
1990 USA

**billiards** indoor game played, normally by two players, with tapered poles (cues) and composition balls (one red, two white) on a rectangular table covered with a green baize cloth. The table has six pockets, one at each corner and in each of the long sides at the middle. Scoring strokes are made by potting the red ball, potting the opponent's ball, or potting another ball off one of these two. The cannon (when the cue ball hits the two other balls on the table) is another scoring stroke.

WORLD PROFESSIONAL CHAMPIONSHIP
instituted 1870, on a challenge basis, and restored as an annual tournament 1980
1982 Rex Williams *(England)*
1983 Rex Williams *(England)*
1984 Mark Wildman *(England)*
1985 Ray Edmonds *(England)*
1986 Robert Foldvari *(Australia)*
1987 Norman Dagley *(England)*
1988 Norman Dagley *(England)*
1989 Mike Russell *(England)*
1990 Mike Russell *(England)*
1991 Mike Russell *(England)*

**bobsleighing** or *bobsledding* racing steel-bodied, steerable toboggans, crewed by two or four people, down mountain ice-chutes at speeds of up to 130 kph/80 mph.

WORLD CHAMPIONSHIP
four-crew championship introduced 1924, two-crew 1931; in Olympic years winners automatically become world champions
*two-person/four-person*
1982 Switzerland/Switzerland
1983 Switzerland/Switzerland
1984 East Germany/East Germany
1985 East Germany/East Germany
1986 East Germany/Switzerland
1987 Switzerland/Switzerland
1988 USSR/Switzerland
1989 East Germany/Switzerland
1990 Switzerland/Switzerland
1991 Germany/Germany

**bowls** outdoor and indoor game popular in Commonwealth countries. The outdoor game is played on a finely cut grassed area called a rink, with biased bowls 13 cm/5 in in diameter. It is played as either singles, pairs, triples, or fours. The object is to position one's bowl (or bowls) as near as possible to the jack (target). **Lawn bowls** is played on a flat surface; **crown green bowls** is played on a rink with undulations and a crown at the centre of the green.

WORLD CHAMPIONSHIP
first held 1966 for men, and 1969 for women
*men: singles/pairs*
1972 Maldwyn Evans *(Wales)*/Hong Kong
1976 Doug Watson *(South Africa)*/South Africa
1980 David Bryant *(England)*/Australia
1984 Peter Bellis *(New Zealand)*/USA
1988 David Bryant *(England)*/New Zealand
*triples/fours*
1972 USA/England
1976 South Africa/South Africa
1980 England/Hong Kong
1984 Ireland/England
1988 New Zealand/Ireland
*women: singles/pairs*
1973 Elsie Wilke *(New Zealand)*/Australia
1977 Elsie Wilke *(New Zealand)*/Hong Kong
1981 Norma Shaw *(England)*/Ireland
1985 Merle Richardson *(Australia)*/Australia
1988 Janet Ackland *(Wales)*/Ireland
*triples/fours*
1973 New Zealand/New Zealand
1977 Wales/Australia
1981 Hong Kong/England
1985 Australia/Scotland
1988 Australia/Australia
CROWN GREEN BOWLS WATERLOO HANDICAP
first held 1907
1981 Roy Nicholson
1982 Dennis Mercer
1983 Stan Frith
1984 Steve Ellis
1985 Tommy Johnstone
1986 Brian Duncan
1987 Brian Duncan
1988 Ingham Gregory

1989 Brian Duncan
1990 John Bancroft

**boxing** fighting with gloved fists, almost entirely a male sport. Contests take place in a square, roped ring 4.3–6.1 m/14–20 ft square. All rounds last three minutes. Amateur bouts last three rounds and professional championship bouts for as many as 12 or 15 rounds. Boxers are classified according to weight and may not fight in a division lighter than their own. The weight divisions in professional boxing range from straw-weight (also known as paperweight and mini-flyweight), under 49 kg/108 lb, to heavyweight, over 88 kg/195 lb.

WORLD CHAMPIONSHIP
(WBC = World Boxing Council; WBA = World Boxing Association; IBF = International Boxing Federation; WBO = World Boxing Organization)
*heavyweight*
1986 Tim Witherspoon *(USA)* (WBA)
1986 Trevor Berbick *Canada* (WBC)
1986 Mike Tyson *(USA)* (WBC)
1986 James Smith *(USA)* (WBA)
1987 Mike Tyson *(USA)* (WBA)
1987 Tony Tucker *(USA)* (IBF)
1987 Mike Tyson *(USA)* (undisputed)
1989 Francesco Damiani *(Italy)* (WBO)
1990 James Douglas *(USA)* (undisputed)
1990 Evander Holyfield *(USA)* (undisputed)
*great heavyweight champions include:*
John L Sullivan (bare-knuckle champion) 1882–92
Jim Corbett (first Marquess of Queensberry champion) 1892–97
Jack Dempsey 1919–26
Joe Louis 1937–49
Rocky Marciano 1952–56
Muhammad Ali 1964–67, 1974–78, 1978–79
Larry Holmes 1978–85
Mike Tyson 1986–1990

**canoeing** propelling a lightweight, shallow boat, pointed at both ends, by paddles or sails. Currently, canoes are made from fibreglass, but original boats were of wooden construction covered in bark or skin. Two types of canoe are used: the *kayak*, and the *Canadian-style* canoe. The kayak, derived from the Eskimo model, has a keel and the canoeist sits. The Canadian style canoe has no keel and the canoeist kneels.

OLYMPIC GAMES
event introduced 1936
*men: kayak singles*
*500 metres*
1980 Vladimir Parfenovich *(USSR)*
1984 Ian Ferguson *(New Zealand)* 1988 Zsolt Gyulay *(Hungary)*
*1,000 metres*
1980 Rudiger Helm *(East Germany)*
1984 Alan Thompson *(New Zealand)*
1988 Greg Barton *(USA)*
*kayak pairs*
*500 metres*
1980 USSR
1984 New Zealand

## UNUSUAL SPORTS

The rise in unusual sports and pastimes has had much to do with the success of such authorities as the *Guinness Book of Records* and the consequent desire of contestants to make a name for themselves. This has got to the point where authorities have been forced to veto some of the more bizarre attempts to gain notoriety. A number of novel, rare, or exotic sports have found appreciative television audiences, as have some well-structured and organized games. Some sports and pastimes in vogue today are:

*arm wrestling* first televised in the UK 1990, the activity had its own TV series 1991;
*chicken flying* the world record in this US-based activity was set in 1989 with a 165 m/542 ft flight, though the winner subsequently had to be encouraged down to earth from its perch on the top of the sponsors' marquee;
*Cluedo* after the success of the 1990 world championships in Torquay, Devon, entries for the 1991 event are oversubscribed;
*ferret racing* world championships are held in Yapton, Sussex, each year, but the 1990 entries numbered just two, both owned by the same trainer;
*frog jumping* official world championships are held every year in Calveras, California. The 1990 event finished in uproar when a contestant brought along several 1 m/3 ft African frogs

from Cameroon. The current world champion, though, is an ordinary frog, which cleared 5.8 m/19 ft 3 in;
*marbles* the UK championship has been run since 1926, when the British Marbles Board of Control was established at the Greyhound Hotel, Tinsley Green, Sussex;
*pigeon racing* the National Homing Union was established in the UK 1898. Edward VII and George V were royal patrons. In 1991 a pigeon beat a fax machine with a message over a one-mile course in W London;
*octopush* or underwater hockey has been flourishing in the UK since the late 1970s;
*robot olympics* were first held in 1990 in Glasgow, Scotland;
*Scrabble* the UK championships were instituted 1971. The highest competitive score is 1,049, set in 1989;
*Subbuteo* the World Cup for this miniature football game was held in 1990 to coincide with association football's World Cup;
*sumo wrestling* this ancient Japanese ritual is now an integral part of the UK Channel 4 sport output. The UK's first champion was Larry Steventon, who won the title in Nov 1990 in a church hall near Stockwell bus garage;
*women's boxing* there are now three divisions in the UK, and six (with world champions) in the USA.

1988 New Zealand
*1,000 metres*
1980 USSR
1984 Canada
1988 USA
*kayak fours*
*1,000 metres*
1980 East Germany
1984 New Zealand
1988 Hungary
*Canadian singles*
*500 metres*
1980 Sergey Postrekhin *(USSR)*
1984 Larry Cain *(Canada)*
1988 Olaf Heukrodt *(East Germany)*
*1,000 metres*
1980 Lubomir Lubenov *(Bulgaria)*
1984 Ulrich Eicke *(West Germany)*
1988 Ivan Klementiev *(USSR)*
*Canadian pairs*
*500 metres*
1980 Hungary
1984 Yugoslavia
1988 USSR
*1,000 metres*
1980 Romania
1984 Romania
1988 USSR
*women: kayak singles*
*500 metres*
1980 Birgit Fischer *(East Germany)*

1984 Agneta Anderson *(Sweden)*
1988 Vania Guecheva *(Bulgaria)*
*kayak pairs*
*500 metres*
1980 East Germany
1984 Sweden
1988 East Germany

**chess** board game originating as early as the 2nd century AD. Two players use 16 pieces each, on a board of 64 squares of alternating colour, to try and force the opponent into a position where the main piece (the king) is threatened, and cannot move to another position without remaining threatened.

WORLD CHAMPIONSHIP
first official world champion recognized 1886
*men*
1957 Vassily Smyslov *(USSR)*
1958 Mikhail Botvinnik *(USSR)*
1960 Mikhail Tal *(USSR)*
1961 Mikhail Botvinnik *(USSR)*
1963 Tigran Petrosian *(USSR)*
1969 Boris Spassky *(USSR)*
1972 Bobby Fischer *(USA)*
1975 Anatoly Karpov *(USSR)*
1985 Gary Kasparov *(USSR)*
*women*
1950 Lyudmila Rudenko *(USSR)*
1953 Elizaveta Bykova *(USSR)*

1955 Olga Runtsova *(USSR)*
1958 Elizaveta Bykova *(USSR)*
1962 Nona Gaprindashvili *(USSR)*
1978 Maya Chiburdanidze *(USSR)*

**cricket** bat-and-ball game between two teams of 11 players each. It is played with a small solid ball and long flat-sided wooden bats, on a round or oval field, at the centre of which is a finely mown pitch, 20 m/22 yd long. At each end of the pitch is a wicket made up of three upright wooden sticks (stumps), surmounted by two smaller sticks (bails). The object of the game is to score more runs than the opposing team. A run is normally scored by the batsman after striking the ball and exchanging ends with his or her partner until the ball is returned by a fielder, or by hitting the ball to the boundary line for an automatic four or six runs.

COUNTY CHAMPIONSHIP
first held officially 1890
1981 Nottinghamshire
1982 Middlesex
1983 Essex
1984 Essex
1985 Middlesex
1986 Essex
1987 Nottinghamshire
1988 Worcestershire
1989 Worcestershire
1990 Middlesex
REFUGE ASSURANCE LEAGUE
(formerly John Player League), first held 1969
1981 Essex
1982 Sussex
1983 Yorkshire
1984 Essex
1985 Essex
1986 Hampshire
1987 Worcestershire
1988 Worcestershire
1989 Lancashire
1990 Derbyshire
NATWEST CUP
(formerly the Gillette Cup), first held 1963
1981 Derbyshire
1982 Surrey
1983 Somerset
1984 Middlesex
1985 Essex
1986 Sussex
1987 Nottinghamshire
1988 Middlesex
1989 Warwickshire
1990 Lancashire
BENSON AND HEDGES CUP
first held 1972
1981 Somerset
1982 Somerset
1983 Middlesex
1984 Lancashire
1985 Leicestershire
1986 Middlesex
1987 Yorkshire
1988 Hampshire

1989 Nottinghamshire
1990 Lancashire
WORLD CUP
first held 1975, contested every four years
1975 West Indies
1979 West Indies
1983 India
1987 Australia

**curling** game resembling bowls that is played on ice, between two teams of four players each. Each player has two disclike stones, of equal size, fitted with a handle. The object of the game is to slide the stones across the ice so that they are positioned as near as possible to a target object (the tee), those nearest scoring. The stone may be curled in one direction or another according to the twist given as it leaves the hand. The match is played for an agreed number of heads or shots, or by time.

WORLD CHAMPIONSHIP
first held 1959 for men, 1979 for women
*men*
1986 Canada
1987 Canada
1988 Norway
1989 Canada
1990 Canada
1991 Scotland
*women*
1986 Canada
1987 Canada
1988 West Germany
1989 Canada
1990 Norway
1991 Norway

**cycling** cycle racing can take place on oval artificial tracks, on the road,or across country (cyclo-cross). *Stage races* are run over gruelling terrain and can last anything from three to five days up to three and a half weeks, as in the Tour de France, Tour of Italy, and Tour of Spain. *Criteriums* are fast, action-packed races around the closed streets of town or city centres. *Road races* are run over a prescribed circuit, which the riders will lap several times. Such a race will normally cover a distance of approximately 100 mi/160 km. *Track racing* takes place on a concrete or wooden banked circuit, either indoors or outdoors. In *time trialling* each rider races against the clock, with all the competitors starting at different intervals.

TOUR DE FRANCE
first held 1903
1982 Bernard Hinault *(France)*
1983 Laurent Fignon *(France)*
1984 Laurent Fignon *(France)*
1985 Bernard Hinault *(France)*
1986 Greg LeMond *(USA)*
1987 Stephen Roche *(Ireland)*
1988 Pedro Delgado *(Spain)*
1989 Greg LeMond *(USA)*
1990 Greg LeMond *(USA)*

1991 Miguel Indurain *(Spain)*
*TOUR OF BRITAIN*
(formerly the Milk Race) first held 1951
1981 Sergey Krivocheyev *(USSR)*
1982 Yuri Kashirin *(USSR)*
1983 Matt Eaton *(USA)*
1984 Oleg Czougeda *(USSR)*
1985 Erik van Lancker *(Belgium)*
1986 Joey McLoughlin *(UK)*
1987 Malcolm Elliott *(UK)*
1988 Vasily Zhdanov *(USSR)*
1989 Brian Walton *(Canada)*
1990 Shane Sutton *(Australia)*
WORLD PROFESSIONAL ROAD RACE CHAMPION-
SHIP
first held 1927
1981 Freddie Maertens *(Belgium)*
1982 Giuseppe Saroni *(Italy)*
1983 Greg LeMond *(USA)*
1984 Claude Criquielon *(Belgium)*
1985 Joop Zoetemelk *(Holland)*
1986 Moreno Argentin *(Italy)*
1987 Stephen Roche *(Ireland)*
1988 Maurizio Fondriest *(Italy)*
1989 Greg LeMond *(USA)*
1990 Rudy Dhaenens *(Belgium)*

**darts**  indoor game played on a circular board. Darts about 13 cm/5 in long are thrown at segmented targets, and score points according to their landing place.

WORLD CHAMPIONSHIP
first held 1978
1982 Jocky Wilson *(Scotland)*
1983 Keith Deller *(England)*
1984 Eric Bristow *(England)*
1985 Eric Bristow *(England)*
1986 Eric Bristow *(England)*
1987 John Lowe *(England)*
1988 Bob Anderson *(England)*
1989 Jocky Wilson *(Scotland)*
1990 Phil Taylor *(England)*
1991 Dennis Priestley *(England)*

**diving**  sport of entering water either from a springboard (3 m/10 ft above the water), or from a platform, or highboard (10 m/33 ft above the water). Various starts are adopted, and twists and somersaults may be performed in midair. Points are awarded and the level of difficulty of each dive is used as a multiplying factor.

OLYMPIC GAMES
*springboard diving*
*men*
1980 Aleksandr Portnov *(USSR)*
1984 Greg Louganis *(USA)*
1988 Greg Louganis *(USA)*
*women*
1980 Irina Kalinina *(USSR)*
1984 Sylvie Bernier *(Canada)*
1988 Gao Min *(China)*
*highboard diving*
*men*
1980 Falk Hoffmann *(East Germany)*

1984 Greg Louganis *(USA)*
1988 Greg Louganis *(USA)*
*women*
1980 Martina Jäschke *(East Germany)*
1984 Zhou Jihong *(China)*
1988 Xu Yanmei *(China)*

**equestrianism**  skill in horse riding, as practised under International Equestrian Federation rules. **Showjumping** is horse-jumping over a course of fences. The winner is usually the competitor with fewest 'faults' (penalty marks given for knocking down or refusing fences), but in timed competitions it is the competitor completing the course most quickly, additional seconds being added for mistakes. **Dressage** tests the horse's obedience skills, and the rider's control. Tests consist of a series of movements at walk, trot, canter, with each movement marked by judges who look for suppleness, balance and the special harmony between rider and horse. **Three-Day Eventing** tests the all-round abilities of a horse and rider in dressage, cross-country, and showjumping.

WORLD CHAMPIONSHIP
show jumping; first held 1953 for men, 1965 for women; since 1978 men and women have competed together
*men*
1953 Francisco Goyoago *(Spain)*
1954 Hans-Günter Winkler *(West Germany)*
1955 Hans-Günter Winkler *(West Germany)*
1956 Raimondo D'Inzeo *(Italy)*
1960 Raimondo D'Inzeo *(Italy)*
1966 Pierre d'Oriola *(France)*
1970 David Broome *(UK)*
1974 Hartwig Steenken *(West Germany)*
*women*
1965 Marion Coakes *(UK)*
1970 Janou Lefebvre *(France)*
1974 Janou Tissot (born Lefebvre) *(France)*
*mixed*
1978 Gerd Wiltfang *(West Germany)*
1982 Norbert Koof *(West Germany)*
1986 Gail Greenough *(Canada)*
1990 Eric Navet *(France)*
EUROPEAN CHAMPIONSHIP
show jumping; first held 1957 with men and women competing separately; since 1975 they have competed together
1977 Johan Heins *(Holland)*
1979 Gerd Wiltfang *(West Germany)*
1981 Paul Schockemöhle *(West Germany)*
1983 Paul Schockemöhle *(West Germany)*
1985 Paul Schockemöhle *(West Germany)*
1987 Pierre Durand *(France)*
1989 John Whitaker *(UK)*
*1991 Eric Navet (France)*
BRITISH SHOWJUMPING DERBY
first held 1961
1981 Harvey Smith *(UK)*
1982 Paul Schockemöhle *(West Germany)*
1983 John Whitaker *(UK)*
1984 John Ledingham *(Ireland)*
1985 Paul Schockemöhle *(West Germany)*
1986 Paul Schockemöhle *(West Germany)*

1987 Nick Skelton *(UK)*
1988 Nick Skelton *(UK)*
1989 Nick Skelton *(UK)*
1990 Joe Turi *(UK)*
THREE–DAY EVENTING WORLD CHAMPIONSHIP
1970 Mary Gordon-Watson *(UK)*
1974 Bruce Davidson *(USA)*
1978 Bruce Davidson *(USA)*
1982 Lucinda Green (born Prior-Palmer) *(UK)*
1986 Virginia Leng (born Holgate) *(UK)*
1990 Blyth Tait *(New Zealand)*
BADMINTON HORSE TRIALS
first held 1949
1982 Richard Meade *(UK)*
1983 Lucinda Green *(UK)*
1984 Lucinda Green *(UK)*
1985 Virginia Holgate *(UK)*
1986 Ian Stark *(UK)*
1987 cancelled
1988 Ian Stark *(UK)*
1989 Virginia Leng *(UK)*
1990 Nicola McIrvine *(UK)*
1991 Rodney Powell *(UK)*

**fencing** sport of fighting with swords including the *foil*, derived from the light weapon used in practice duels; the *épée*, a heavier weapon derived from the duelling sword proper; and the *sabre*, with a curved handle and narrow V-shaped blade. In sabre fighting, cuts count as well as thrusts. Masks and protective jackets are worn, and hits are registered electronically in competitions.

WORLD CHAMPIONSHIP
first held 1921; Olympic winners automatically become world champions
*foil – men*
1981 Vladimir Smirnov *(USSR)*
1982 Aleksandr Romankov *(USSR)*
1983 Aleksandr Romankov *(USSR)*
1984 Mauro Numa *(Italy)*
1985 Mauro Numa *(Italy)*
1986 Andrea Borella *(Italy)*
1987 Mathias Gey *(West Germany)*
1988 Stefano Cerioni *(Italy)*
1989 Alexandr Koch *(West Germany)*
1990 Philippe Onnes *(France)*
*foil – women*
1981 Cornelia Hanisch *(West Germany)*
1982 Naila Giliazova *(USSR)*
1983 Dorina Vaccaroni *(Italy)*
1984 Jujie Luan *(China)*
1985 Cornelia Hanisch *(West Germany)*
1986 Anja Fichtel *(West Germany)*
1987 Elisabeta Tufan *(Romania)*
1988 Anja Fichtel *(West Germany)*
1989 Olga Velichko *(USSR)*
1990 Anja Fichtel *(West Germany)*
*épée–men*
1981 Zoltan Szekely *(Hungary)*
1982 Jenö Pap *(Hungary)*
1983 Ellmar Bormann *(West Germany)*
1984 Philippe Boisse *(France)*
1985 Philippe Boisse *(France)*
1986 Philippe Riboud *(France)*
*1987 Volker Fischer (West Germany)*

1988 Arnd Schmitt *(West Germany)*
1989 Manuel Pereira *(Spain)*
1990 Thomas Gerull *(West Germany)*
*épée–women*
1989 Anja Straub *(Switzerland)*
1990 Taimi Chappe *(Cuba)*
*sabre–men*
1981 Mariusz Wodke *(Poland)*
1982 Viktor Krovopuskov *(USSR)*
1983 Vasiliy Etropolski *(Bulgaria)*
1984 Jean-Francois Lamour *(France)*
1985 György Nebald *(Hungary)*
1986 Sergey Mindirgassov *(USSR)*
1987 Jean-François Lamour *(France)*
1988 Jean-François Lamour *(France)*
1989 Grigoriy Kirienko *(USSR)*
1990 Gyorgy Nebald *(Hungary)*

**football, American** contact sport played between two teams of 11 players, with an inflated oval ball. Players are well padded for protection and wear protective helmets. The game is played on a field 91.4 m/100 yd long and 48.8 m/53.3 yd wide, marked out with a series of parallel lines giving a gridiron effect. There is a goalpost at each end of the field, and beyond this an endzone 9 m/10 yd long. Points are scored by running or passing the ball across the goal line (touchdown, 6 points); by kicking it over the goal's crossbar after a touchdown (conversion, 2 points), or from the field during regular play (field goal, 3 points); or by tackling an offensive player who has the ball in the end zone, or blocking an offensive team's kick so it goes out of bounds from the end zone (safety, 2 points). Games are divided into four quarters of 15 minutes each.

SUPER BOWL
first held 1967
1982 San Francisco 49ers
1983 Washington Redskins
1984 Los Angeles Raiders
1985 San Francisco 49ers
1986 Chicago Bears
1987 New York Giants
1988 Washington Redskins
1989 San Francisco 49ers
1990 San Francisco 49ers
1991 New York Giants

**football, association** or *soccer* form of football originating in the UK, popular in Europe and Latin America. It is played between two teams each of 11 players, on a field 90–120 m/100–130 yd long and 45–90 m/50–100 yd wide, with an inflated spherical ball. The object of the game is to kick or head the ball into the opponents' goal, an area 7.31 m/8 yd wide and 2.44 m/8 ft high. Games are divided into two halves of 45 minutes each, the teams changing ends at half-time.

In the UK the game is played according to the rules laid down by the Football Association, founded 1863. Slight amendments to the rules take effect in certain competitions and overseas matches as laid down by the sport's world governing body, Fédération Internationale de Football Association (FIFA, 1904).

---

WORLD CUP
first held 1930; contested every four years
1954 West Germany
1958 Brazil
1962 Brazil
1966 England
1970 Brazil
1974 West Germany
1978 Argentina
1982 Italy
1986 Argentina
1990 West Germany
EUROPEAN CHAMPIONSHIP
instituted 1958, first final 1960; contested every four years
1960 USSR
1964 Spain
1968 Italy
1972 West Germany
1976 Czechoslovakia
1980 West Germany
1984 France
1988 Holland
EUROPEAN CHAMPIONS CUP
first held 1955
1982 Aston Villa *(England)*
1983 SV Hamburg *(West Germany)*
1984 Liverpool *(England)*
1985 Juventus *(Italy)*
1986 Steaua Bucharest *(Romania)*
1987 FC Porto *(Portugal)*
1988 PSV Eindhoven *(Holland)*
1989 AC Milan *(Italy)*
1990 AC Milan *(Italy)*
1991 Red Star Belgrade *(Yugoslavia)*
EUROPEAN CUP WINNERS' CUP
first held 1960
1982 Barcelona *(Spain)*
1983 Aberdeen *(Scotland)*
1984 Juventus *(Italy)*
1985 Everton *(England)*
1986 Dinamo Kiev *(USSR)*
1987 Ajax *(Holland)*
1988 Mechelen *(Belgium)*
1989 Barcelona *(Spain)*
1990 Sampdoria *(Italy)*
1991 Manchester United *(England)*
UEFA CUP
(formerly Inter Cities Fairs Cup) first held 1955
1982 IFK Gothenburg *(Sweden)*
1983 Anderlecht *(Belgium)*
1984 Tottenham Hotspur *(England)*
1985 Real Madrid *(Spain)*
1986 Real Madrid *(Spain)*
1987 IFK Gothenburg *(Sweden)*
1988 Bayer Leverkusen *(West Germany)*
1989 Napoli *(Italy)*
1990 Juventus *(Italy)*
1991 Internazionale Milan *(Italy)*
UK CHAMPIONSHIPS:
FA CUP
a knockout club competition, first held 1872
1982 Tottenham Hotspur
1983 Manchester United

1984 Everton
1985 Manchester United
1986 Liverpool
1987 Coventry City
1988 Wimbledon
1989 Liverpool
1990 Manchester United
1991 Tottenham Hotspur
FOOTBALL LEAGUE CUP
(currently known as the Rumbelows Cup, formerly the Milk Cup and the Littlewoods Cup) first final 1961 in two stages, now a single game
1982 Liverpool
1983 Liverpool
1984 Liverpool
1985 Norwich City
1986 Oxford United
1987 Arsenal
1988 Luton Town
1989 Nottingham Forest
1990 Nottingham Forest
1991 Sheffield Wednesday
DIVISION ONE CHAMPIONS
Football League founded 1888–89
1981–82 Liverpool
1982–83 Liverpool
1983–84 Liverpool
1984–85 Everton
1985–86 Liverpool
1986–87 Everton
1987–88 Liverpool
1988–89 Arsenal
1989–90 Liverpool
1990–91 Arsenal
SCOTTISH PREMIER DIVISION CHAMPIONSHIP
Scottish League formed 1899–91, reformed into three divisions 1975–76
1981–82 Celtic
1982–83 Dundee United
1983–84 Aberdeen
1984–85 Aberdeen
1985–86 Celtic
1986–87 Rangers
1987–88 Celtic
1988–89 Rangers
1989–90 Rangers
1990–91 Rangers
*SCOTTISH FA CUP*
first final held 1874
1982 Aberdeen
1983 Aberdeen
1984 Aberdeen
1985 Celtic
1986 Aberdeen
1987 St Mirren
1988 Celtic
1989 Celtic
1990 Aberdeen
1991 Motherwell

---

**football, Australian Rules** game that combines aspects of Gaelic football, rugby, and association football; it is played between two teams of 18 players, with an inflated oval ball. It is unique to Australia. The game is played on an oval pitch, 164.4 m/180 yd long and 137 m/150 yd wide, with a pair of goalposts, 6 m/

## BRITAIN'S OLYMPIC BID

For a nation that, in some sports, is still entrenched in the ideal that it is better to take part than succeed, the UK does remarkably well in world sport. When the yearly sporting awards are handed out, a list of British world champions, both individual and team, always feature near the very top. Yet for all the prowess, the major championships to be hosted in the UK are few in number—since World War II, the 1948 Olympics in London and the 1966 World Football Cup are the only events that spring readily to mind.

Many theories have been put forward about the paucity of top-class events (other than the regulars like Wimbledon and the Open golf) in the UK. Certainly hooliganism discouraged football authorities; lack of finance, sponsorship, and interest have also been suggested. Another excuse is antiquated stadiums.

The Hillsborough disaster brought forth the Taylor Report and, with it, many significant changes. The insistence on all-seater stadiums has thrown away the cloth-cap image: clubs have become aware of the need to raise funds in order to improve facilities. The more progressive are now seriously eyeing the hosting of world events. Make no mistake, the English bid for the 1998 World Football Cup is a strong one.

All this makes the British Olympic Association's decision to nominate Manchester for the Olympics in the year 2000 more than just a passing fancy. Birmingham made a serious attempt to host the 1992 Games; Manchester gained 16 votes in its bid to host the 1996 Olympics, and the city's bid for 2000 is firmly based on the experience gained in that attempt.

At the British Olympic Association's nomination meeting in April 1991, the committee decided by a vote of 26 to 7 to endorse the Manchester campaign. London, the other candidate, despite the advantage of being the capital, managed to shoot itself in the foot by failing to curtail a squabble between two rival bids, and then leaving itself no time to attend to the nuts and bolts of its bid.

Although Manchester would be the fulcrum of the proposed Games, the magnitude of the event means that the greater part of Merseyside would be involved. Most of the basic infrastructure is already in place.

Manchester international airport is second only to Heathrow in importance in the UK, and Speake airport is close by. The motorway system in NE England is extensive. Accommodation is plentiful in the university campuses of Salford, Manchester, and Liverpool. Existing sports facilities are sound: the football competition would be at Anfield, Goodison, Maine Road, and Old Trafford; North Wales provides excellent yachting; Chester has an international rowing centre; Haydock Park can cope with equestrian events; and the G-Mex centre has already staged boxing world-title fights. Altogether, the organizing committee say that 90% of the required facilities exist.

Three new construction projects have been given the go-ahead by planners in the event that Manchester should be selected: a stadium, another indoor centre, and an arena for cycling. Barton Cross, on the western outskirts of the city and close to the motorway interchanges, has been approved as the Olympic centre.

Three other cities have formally announced their candidature for the Games of 2000: Berlin, Beijing, and Sydney, with Istanbul, Milan, and Brasília as possible contenders. The reunification of Germany gives Berlin credibility; Beijing's hopes are based on the desire for another Olympics in the Asian or Pacific region after their handling of the recent Asian Games. Australia has been pressing Sydney's claim since 1956.

The International Olympic Committee (IOC) meets in Sept 1993 to select the venue for the 2000 Games. Manchester's representatives are confident that their house is in order to meet the special demands of the Olympic organization. But bear in mind a story from Birmingham's failed 1992 attempt: when asked why Barcelona was selected, the IOC spokesperson pointed to leaden skies. Rain would scupper the Olympics. Will Manchester's bid go up in the clouds? At least test cricket, with its notorious Old Trafford rain, is not an Olympic event.

---

19 ft high, at each end. On either side of each pair of goalposts is a smaller post. Each team is placed in five lines of three persons each, and three players follow the ball all the time. Points are scored by kicking the ball between the goalposts, without its being touched on the way (goal, 6 points), or by passing the ball between a goalpast and one of the smaller posts, or causing it to hit a post (behind, 1 point).

VICTORIA FOOTBALL LEAGUE PREMIERSHIP TROPHY
first contested 1897
1981 Carlton
1982 Carlton

1983 Hawthorn
1984 Essendon
1985 Essendon
1986 Hawthorn
1987 Carlton
1988 Hawthorn
1989 Hawthorn
1990 Collingwood

**football, Gaelic** kicking and catching game played mainly in Ireland, between two teams of 15 players each. It is played with an inflated spherical ball, on a field 76–91 m/84–100 yd long and 128–146 m/140–160 yd wide. At each end is a set of goalposts 4.88 m/16 ft high, with a crossbar 2.44 m/8 ft above the ground, and a net across its lower half. Goals are scored by kicking the ball into the net (3 points) or over the crossbar (1 point).

ALL–IRELAND CHAMPIONSHIP
first played 1887
1983 Dublin
1984 Kerry
1985 Kerry
1986 Kerry
1987 Meath
1988 Meath
1989 Cork
1990 Cork

**golf** outdoor game in which a small rubber-cored ball is hit with a wooden- or iron-faced club. Its objective is to sink the ball in a hole than can be anywhere between 90 m/100 yd and 457 m/500 yd away, using the least number of strokes. The faces of the clubs have varying angles and are styled for different types of shot.

Most golf courses consist of 18 holes and are approximately 5,500 m/6,000 yd in length. Each hole is made up of distinct areas: the **tee**, from where plays start at each hole; the **green**, a finely manicured area where the hole is located; the **fairway**, the grassed area between the tee and the green, not cut as finely as the green; and the **rough**, the perimeter of the fairway, which is left to grow naturally. Natural hazards such as trees, bushes, and streams make play more difficult, and there are additional artificial hazards in the form of sand-filled bunkers.

BRITISH OPEN
first held 1860
1982 Tom Watson (USA)
1983 Tom Watson (USA)
1984 Severiano Ballesteros (Spain)
1985 Sandy Lyle (UK)
1986 Greg Norman (Australia)
1987 Nick Faldo (UK)
1988 Severiano Ballesteros (Spain)
1989 Mark Calcavecchia (USA)
1990 Nick Faldo (UK)
1991 Ian Baker-Finch (Australia)
US OPEN
first held 1895
1982 Tom Watson (USA)
1983 Larry Nelson (USA)
1984 Fuzzy Zoeller (USA)
1985 Andy North (USA)
1986 Ray Floyd USA)
1987 Scott Simpson (USA)
1988 Curtis Strange (USA)
1989 Curtis Strange (USA)
1990 Hale Irwin (USA)

1991 Payne Stewart (USA)
US MASTERS
first held 1934
1981 Tom Watson (USA)
1982 Craig Stadler (USA)
1983 Severiano Ballesteros (Spain)

1984 Ben Crenshaw (USA)
1985 Bernhard Langer (West Germany)
1986 Jack Nicklaus (USA)
1987 Larry Mize (USA)
1988 Sandy Lyle (UK)
1989 Nick Faldo (UK)
1990 Nick Faldo (UK)
1991 Ian Woosnam (UK)
UNITED STATES PGA
first held 1916
1981 Larry Nelson (USA)
1982 Ray Floyd (USA)
1983 Hal Sutton (USA)
1984 Lee Trevino (USA)
1985 Hubert Green (USA)
1986 Bob Tway (USA)
1987 Larry Nelson (USA)
1988 Jeff Sluman (USA)
1989 Payne Stewart (USA)
1990 Wayne Grady (Australia)

**greyhound racing** spectator sport, invented in 1919 in the USA, that has a number of greyhounds pursuing a mechanical hare around a circular or oval track. It is popular in the UK and Australia, attracting much on- and off-course betting.

GREYHOUND DERBY
UK, first held 1927
1982 Laurie's Panther
1983 I'm Slippy
1984 Whisper Wishes
1985 Pagan Swallow
1986 Tico
1987 Signal Park
1988 Hit the Lid
1989 Lartigue Note
1990 Slippy Blue
1991 Ballinderry Ash

**gymnastics** competitive physical exercises. **Men's gymnastics** includes exercises on apparatus such as the horizontal bar, parallel bars, horse vault, pommel horse, and rings, and on an area of floor 12 m/13 yd square. **Women's gymnastics** includes work on the asymmetric bars, side horse vault, and beam, and floor exercises. Each exercise is marked out of ten by a set of judges, who look for suppleness, balance, control, and innovation. **Rhythmic gymnastics**, is choreographed to music and performed by individuals or six-woman teams, with small hand apparatus such as a ribbon, ball, or hoop.

WORLD CHAMPIONSHIP
first held 1903 for men, 1934 for women; contested every two years; Olympic champions automatically become world champions
men: individual/team
1966 Mikhail Voronin (USSR)/Japan
1970 Eizo Kenmotsu (Japan)/Japan
1974 Shigeru Kasamatsu (Japan)/Japan
1978 Nikolai Adrianov (USSR)/Japan
1979 Aleksandr Ditiatin (USSR)/USSR
1981 Yuri Korolev (USSR)/USSR

1983 Dimitri Belozertchev *(USSR)*/China
1985 Yuri Korolev *(USSR)*/USSR
1987 Dimitri Belozertchev *(USSR)*/USSR
1989 Igor Korobichensky *(USSR)*/USSR
*women: individual/team*
1966 Vera Caslavska *(Czechoslovakia)*/Czechoslovakia
1970 Ludmila Tourischeva *(USSR)*/USSR
1974 Ludmila Tourischeva *(USSR)*/USSR
1978 Elena Mukhina *(USSR)*/USSR
1979 Nelli Kim *(USSR)*/Romania
1981 Olga Bitcherova *(USSR)*/USSR
1983 Natalia Yurchenko *(USSR)*/USSR
1985 Elena Shoushounova *(USSR)* and Oksana Omeliantchik *(USSR)*/USSR
1987 Aurelia Dobre *(Romania)*/Romania
1989 Svetlana Boginskaya *(USSR)*/USSR

**handball**  game resembling football, but played with the hands instead of the feet. The indoor game has seven players in a team; the outdoor version (field handball) has 11. The indoor court is 40 m/43.8 yd long and 20 m/21.9 yd wide, with goals 2 m/6.6 ft high and 3 m/9.8 ft wide.

OLYMPIC GAMES
indoor event introduced 1972 for men, 1976 for women
*men*
1972 Yugoslavia
1976 USSR
1980 East Germany
1984 Yugoslavia
1988 USSR
*women* 1976 USSR
1980 USSR
1984 Yugoslavia
1988 South Korea

**hockey** or *field hockey* stick-and-ball game played by two teams of 11 players each. Its object is to strike the solid white ball, by means of a hooked stick, into the opposing team's goal. The game is played on a pitch 91.5 m/100 yd long and 54.9 m/60 yd wide, with a goal, 2.13 m/7 ft high and 3.65 m/4 yd wide, at each end. All shots at goal must be made from within a striking 'circle', a semicircle of 14.64 m/16 yd radius in front of each goal. The game is divided into two 35-minute periods.

OLYMPIC GAMES
event introduced 1908 for men, 1980 for women
*men*
1960 Pakistan
1964 India
1968 Pakistan
1972 West Germany
1976 New Zealand
1980 India
1984 Pakistan
1988 UK
*women*
1980 Zimbabwe
1984 Holland
1988 Australia

**horse racing**  the sport of racing mounted or driven horses. Two popular forms in Britain are *flat racing*, for thoroughbred horses over a flat course, and *National Hunt racing*, in which the horses have to clear obstacles. Forms of National Hunt racing include *steeplechasing*, a development of foxhunting, in which horses jump over fixed fences 0.9–1.2 m/3–4 ft high (the amateur version is point-to-point), and *hurdling*, in which the horses negotiate less taxing, and movable, fences. *Harness racing* is popular in North America. It is for standard-bred horses pulling a two-wheeled 'sulky' on which the driver sits. Leading races include The Hambletonian and Little Brown Jug.

DERBY
first held 1780; 1 mi 4 furlongs long
*horse/jockey*
1982 Golden Fleece/Pat Eddery
1983 Teenoso/Lester Piggott
1984 Secreto/Christy Roche
1985 Slip Anchor/Steve Cauthen
1986 Shahrastani/Walter Swinburn
1987 Reference Point/Steve Cauthen
1988 Kahyasi/Ray Cochrane
1989 Nashwan/Willie Carson
1990 Quest for Fame/Pat Eddery
1991 Generous/Alan Munro
OAKS
first held 1779; 1 mi 4 furlongs long
*horse/jockey*
1982 Time Charter/Billy Newnes
1983 Sun Princess/Willie Carson
1984 Circus Plume/Lester Piggott
1985 Oh So Sharp/Steve Cauthen
1986 Midway Lady/Ray Cochrane
1987 Unite/Walter Swinburn
1988 Diminuendo/Steve Cauthen
1989 Aliysa/Walter Swinburn
1990 Salsabil/Willie Carson
1991 Jet Ski Lady/Christy Roche
1,000 GUINEAS
first held 1814; 1 mi long
*horse/jockey*
1982 On The House/John Reid
1983 Ma Biche/Freddy Head
1984 Pebbles/Philip Robinson
1985 Oh So Sharp/Steve Cauthen
1986 Midway Lady/Ray Cochrane
1987 Miesque/Freddy Head
1988 Ravinella/Gary Moore
1989 Musical Bliss/Walter Swinburn
1990 Salsabil/Willie Carson
1991 Shadayid/Willie Carson
2,000 GUINEAS
first held 1809; 1 mi long
*horse/jockey*
1982 Zino/Freddy Head
1983 Lomond/Pat Eddery
1984 El Gran Senor/Pat Eddery
1985 Shadeed/Lester Piggott
1986 Dancing Brave/Greville Starkey
1987 Don't Forget Me/Willie Carson
1988 Doyoun/Walter Swinburn
1989 Nashwan/Walter Swinburn
1990 Tirol/Michael Kinane

1991 Mystiko/Michael Roberts
ST LEGER
the oldest English classic, first held 1776; 1 mi 6
furlongs 127 yd long
*horse/jockey*
1981 Cut Above/Joe Mercer
1982 Touching Wood/Paul Cook
1983 Sun Princess/Willie Carson
1984 Commanche Run/Lester Piggott
1985 Oh So Sharp/Steve Cauthen
1986 Moon Madness/Pat Eddery
1987 Reference Point/Steve Cauthen
1988 Minster Son/Willie Carson
1989 Michelozza/Steve Cauthen
1990 Snurge/Richard Quinn
GRAND NATIONAL
steeplechase; first held 1847; 4 mi 4 furlongs long
*horse/jockey* (amateurs are shown as Mr)
1982 Grittar/Mr Dick Saunders
1983 Corbiere/Ben De Haan
1984 Hallo Dandy/Neale Doughty
1985 Last Suspect/Hywel Davies
1986 West Tip/Richard Dunwoody
1987 Maori Venture/Steve Knight
1988 Rhyme N'Reason/Brendan Powell
1989 Little Polveir/Jimmy Frost
1990 Mr Frisk/Marcus Armytage
1991 Seagram/Nigel Hawke
PRIX DE L'ARC DE TRIOMPHE
first held 1920; 2,400 m long
*horse/jockey*
1981 Gold River/Gary Moore
1982 Akiyda/Yves Saint-Martin
1983 All Along/Walter Swinburn
1984 Sagace/Yves Saint-Martin
1985 Rainbow Quest/Pat Eddery
1986 Dancing Brave/Pat Eddery
1986 Lieutenant's Lark/Robbie Davis
1987 Trempolino/Pat Eddery
1988 Tony Bin/John Reid
1989 Caroll House/Michael Kinane
1990 Saumarez/Gerald Mosse

**hurling** or ***hurley*** stick-and-ball game played between two teams of 15 players each, popular in
Ireland. Its object is to hit the ball, by means of
a curved stick, into the opposing team's goal.
If the ball passes under the goal's crossbar 3
points are scored; if it passes above the crossbar
1 point is scored.

ALL-IRELAND CHAMPIONSHIP
first held 1887
1986 Cork
1987 Galway
1988 Galway
1989 Tipperary
1990 Cork

**ice hockey** game played on ice between two teams
of six, developed in Canada from hockey. A
rubber disc (puck) is used in place of a ball.
Players wear skates and protective clothing.

OLYMPIC GAMES
event introduced 1920
1960 United States

1964 USSR
1968 USSR
1972 USSR
1976 USSR
1980 United States
1984 USSR
1988 USSR
STANLEY CUP
first held 1916
1982 New York Islanders
1983 New York Islanders
1984 Edmonton Oilers
1985 Edmonton Oilers
1986 Montréal Canadiens
1987 Edmonton Oilers
1988 Edmonton Oilers
1989 Calgary Flames
1990 Edmonton Oilers
1991 Edmonton Oilers

**judo** form of wrestling of Japanese origin. The two
combatants wear loose-fitting, belted jackets
and trousers to facilitate holds, and falls are
broken by a square mat; when one has established a painful hold that the other cannot
break, the latter signifies surrender by slap-
ping the ground with a free hand. Degrees
of proficiency are indicated by the colour of
the belt: for novices, white; after examination,
brown (three degrees); and finally, black (nine
degrees).

WORLD CHAMPIONSHIP
first held 1956 for men, 1980 for women; contested
every two years
*men*
*open class*
1983 Angelo Parisi *(France)*
1985 Yoshimi Masaki *(Japan)*
1987 Noayo Ogawa *(Japan)*
1989 Noayo Ogawa *(Japan)*
1991 Noayo Ogawa *(Japan)*
*over 95 kg*
1983 Yasuhiro Yamashita *(Japan)*
1985 Yong-Chul Cho *(South Korea)*
1987 Grigori Vertichev *(USSR)*
1989 Noayo Ogawa *(Japan)*
1991 S Kosorotov *(USSR)*
*under 95 kg*
1983 Valeriy Divisenko *(USSR)*
1985 Hitoshi Sugai *(Japan)*
1987 Hitoshi Sugai *(Japan)*
1989 Kota Kurtanidze *(USSR)*
1991 S Traineau *(France)*
*under 86 kg*
1983 Detlef Ultsch *(East Germany)*
1985 Peter Seisenbacher *(Austria)*
1987 Fabien Canu *(France)*
1989 Fabien Canu *(France)*
1991 H Okada *(Japan)*
*under 78 kg*
1983 Nobutoshi Hikage *(Japan)*
1985 Nobutoshi Hikage *(Japan)*
1987 Hirotaki Okada *(Japan)*
1989 Kim Byung-ju *(South Korea)*
1991 D Lascau *(Germany)*
*under 71 kg*

1983 Hidetoshi Nakanichi *(Japan)*
1985 Ahn Byeong-keun *(South Korea)*
1987 Mike Swain *(USA)*
1989 Toshihiko Koga *(Japan)*
1991 Toshihiko Koga *(Japan)*
*under 65 kg*
1983 Nikolai Soludkhin *(USSR)*
1985 Yuri Sokolov *(USSR)*
1987 Yosuke Yamamto *(Japan)*
1989 Drago Becanovic *(Yugoslavia)*
1991 G Quellmalz *(Germany)*
*under 60 kg*
1983 Khazret Tletseri *(USSR)*
1985 Shinji Hosokawa *(Japan)*
1987 Jae Yup Kim *(South Korea)*
1989 Amiran Totikashvilli *(USSR)*
1991 T Koshino *(Japan)*
*women*
*open class*
1984 Ingrid Berghmans *(Belgium)*
1986 Ingrid Berghmans *(Belgium)*
1987 Fengliang Gao *(China)*
1989 Estela Rodriguez *(Cuba)*
1991 Y Zhaung *(China)*
*over 72 kg*
1984 Maria-Teresa Motta *(Italy)*
1986 Fengliang Gao *(China)*
1987 Fengliang Gao *(China)*
1989 Fengliang Gao *(China)*
1991 M Ji-yoon *(South Korea)*
*under 72 kg*
1984 Ingrid Berghmans *(Belgium)*
1986 Irene de Kok *(Holland)*
1987 Irene de Kok *(Holland)*
1989 Ingrid Berghmans *(Belgium)*
1991 K Mi-jong *(South Korea)*
*under 66 kg*
1984 Brigitte Deydier *(France)*
1986 Brigitte Deydier *(France)*
1987 Alexandra Schreider *(West Germany)*
1989 Emanuela Pierantozzi *(Italy)*
1991 Emanuela Pierantozzi *(Italy)*
*under 61 kg*
1984 Natasha Hernandez *(Venezuela)*
1986 Diane Bell *(UK)*
1987 Diane Bell *(UK)*
1989 Catherine Fleury *(France)*
1991 S Eickhoff *(Germany)*
*under 56 kg*
1984 Ann-Maria Burns *(USA)*
1986 Ann Hughes *(UK)*
1987 Catherine Arnaud *(France)*
1989 Catherine Arnaud *(France)*
1991 N Blasco *(Spain)*
*under 52 kg*
1984 Kaori Yamaguchi *(Japan)*
1986 Dominique Brun *(France)*
1897 Sharon Rendle *(UK)*
1989 Sharon Rendle *(UK)*
1991 A Grungi *(Italy)*
*under 48 kg*
1984 Karen Briggs *(UK)*
1986 Karen Briggs *(UK)*
1987 Zang Yun Li *(China)*
1989 Karen Briggs *(UK)*
1991 C Nowak *(France)*

**lacrosse** Canadian ball game, adopted from the North American Indians, and named from a fancied resemblance of the lacrosse stick (crosse) to a bishop's crosier. Thongs across the curved end of the crosse form a pocket to carry the small rubber ball. The field is approximately 100 m/110 yd long and a minimum 55 m/60 yd wide in the men's game, which is played with ten players per side; the women's field is larger, and there are 12 players per side. The goals are just under 2 m/6 ft square, with loose nets.

WORLD CHAMPIONSHIP
first held 1967 for men, 1969 for women
*men*
1967 USA
1974 USA
1978 Canada
1982 USA
1986 USA
1990 USA
*women*
1969 UK
1974 USA
1978 Canada
1982 USA
1986 Australia
1989 United States

**motorcycle racing** speed contests on motorcycles. It has many different forms: **road racing** over open roads; **circuit racing** over purpose-built tracks; **speedway** over oval-shaped dirt tracks; **motocross** (or **scrambling**) over natural terrain, incorporating hill climbs; and **trials**, also over natural terrain, but with the addition of artificial hazards. For finely tuned production machines, there exists a season-long world championship Grand Prix series with various categories for machines with engine sizes 125 cc–500 cc.

WORLD CHAMPIONSHIP
Grand Prix racing; first held 1949
*500cc class*
*rider/manufacturer*
1981 Marco Luchinelli/Suzuki *(Italy)*
1982 Franco Uncini/Suzuki *(Italy)*
1983 Freddie Spencer/Honda *(USA)*
1984 Eddie Lawson/Yamaha *(USA)*
1985 Freddie Spencer/Honda *(USA)*
1986 Eddie Lawson/Yamaha *(USA)*
1987 Wayne Gardner/Honda *(Australia)*
1988 Eddie Lawson/Yamaha *(USA)*
1989 Eddie Lawson/Honda *(USA)*
1990 Wayne Rainey/Yamaha *(USA)*
ISLE OF MAN TOURIST TROPHY
road race; first held 1907
*Senior TT*
*rider/manufacturer*
1982 Norman Brown/Suzuki *(UK)*
1983 Rob McElnea/Suzuki *(UK)*
1984 Rob McElnea/Suzuki *(UK)*
1985 Joey Dunlop/Honda *(Ireland)*
1986 Roger Burnett/Honda *(UK)*
1987 Joey Dunlop/Honda *(Ireland)*

1988 Joey Dunlop/Honda *(Ireland)*
1989 Steve Hislop/Honda *(UK)*
1990 Carl Fogarty/Honda *(UK)*
1991 Steve Hislop/Honda *(UK)*
WORLD CHAMPIONSHIP
speedway; first held 1936
*individual*
1981 Bruce Penhall *(USA)*
1982 Bruce Penhall *(USA)*
1983 Egon Müller *(West Germany)*
1984 Erik Gundersen *(Denmark)*
1985 Erik Gundersen *(Denmark)*
1986 Hans Nielsen *(Denmark)*
1987 Hans Nielsen *(Denmark)*
1988 Erik Gundersen *(Denmark)*
1989 Hans Nielsen *(Denmark)*
1990 Per Jonsson *(Sweden)*
*pairs* event introduced 1970
1981 Bruce Penhall and Bobby Schwartz *(USA)*
1982 Dennis Sigalos and Bobby Schwartz *USA)*
1983 Kenny Carter and Peter Collins *(England)*
1984 Peter Collins and Chris Morton *(England)*
1985 Erik Gundersen and Tommy Knudsen *(Denmark)*
1986 Erik Gundersen and Hans Nielsen *(Denmark)*
1987 Erik Gundersen and Hans Nielsen *(Denmark)*
1988 Erik Gundersen and Hans Nielsen *(Denmark)*
1989 Erik Gundersen and Hans Nielsen *(Denmark)*
1990 Hans Nielsen and Jan Pedersen *(Denmark)*
*team* event introduced 1960
1981 Denmark
1982 USA
1983 Denmark
1984 Denmark
1985 Denmark
1986 Denmark
1987 Denmark
1988 Denmark
1989 England
1990 USA
WORLD CHAMPIONSHIP
motocross; first held 1957
*500cc class*
*rider/manufacturer*
1981 André Malherbe/Honda *(Belgium)*
1982 Brad Lackey/Suzuki *(USA)*
1983 Hakan Carlqvist/Yamaha *(Sweden)*
1984 André Malherbe/Honda *(Belgium)*
1985 Dave Thorpe/Honda *(UK)*
1986 Dave Thorpe/Honda *(UK)*
1987 Georges Jobé/Honda *(Belgium)*
1988 Eric Geboers/Honda *(Belgium)*
1989 Dave Thorpe/Honda *(UK)*
1990 Eric Geboers *(Belgium)*

**motor racing** competitive racing of motor vehicles. It has forms as diverse as hill-climbing, stock-car racing, rallying, sports-car racing, and Formula One Grand Prix racing. The first organized race was from Paris to Rouen 1894.

WORLD DRIVER'S CHAMPIONSHIP
Formula One Grand Prix racing; instituted 1950
*driver/manufacturer*
1981 Nelson Piquet/Williams *(Brazil)*
1982 Keke Rosberg/Ferrari *(Finland)*
1983 Nelson Piquet/Ferrari *(Brazil)*
1984 Niki Lauda/McLaren *(Austria)*

1985 Alain Prost/McLaren *(France)*
1986 Alain Prost/Williams *(France)*
1987 Nelson Piquet/Williams *(Brazil)*
1988 Ayrton Senna/McLaren *(Brazil)*
1989 Alain Prost/McLaren *(France)*
1990 Ayrton Senna *(Brazil)*
LE MANS GRAND PRIX D'ENDURANCE
(Le Mans 24-Hour Race) first held 1923
1982 Jacky Ickx *(Belgium)*/Derek Bell *(UK)*
1983 Vern Schuppan *(Austria)*/Al Holbert *(USA)*/Hurley Haywood *(USA)*
1984 Klaus Ludwig *(West Germany)*/Henri Pescarolo *(France)*
1985 Klaus Ludwig *(West Germany)*/'John Winter' *(West Germany)*/Paolo Barilla *(Italy)*
1986 Hans Stuck *(West Germany)*/Derek Bell *(UK)*/Al Holbert *(USA)*
1987 Hans Stuck *(West Germany)*/Derek Bell *(UK)*/Al Holbert *(USA)*
1988 Jan Lammers *(Holland)*/Johnny Dumfries *(UK)*/Andy Wallace *(UK)*
1989 Jochen Mass *(West Germany)*/Manuel Reuter *(West Germany)*/Stanley Dickens *(Sweden)*
1990 John Nielsen *(Denmark)*/Price Cobb *(USA)*/Martin Brundle *(UK)*
1991 Volker Weidler *(Germany)*/John Herbert *(UK)*/Bertrand Gachot *(Belgium)*
INDIANAPOLIS 500
first held 1911
*driver/manufacturer*
1982 Gordon Johncock/Wildcat–Cosworth *(USA)*
1983 Tom Sneva/March–Cosworth *(USA)*
1984 Rick Mears/March–Cosworth *(USA)*
1985 Danny Sullivan/March–Cosworth *(USA)*
1986 Bobby Rahal/March–Cosworth *(USA)*
1987 Al Unser/March–Cosworth *(USA)*
1988 Rick Mears/Penske–Chevrolet *(USA)*
1989 Emerson Fittipaldi/Penske–Chevrolet *(Brazil)*.
1990 Arie Luyendyk/Lola–Chevrolet *(Holland)*
1991 Rick Mears/Penske–Chevrolet *(USA)*
MONTE CARLO RALLY
1982 Walter Röhrl *(West Germany)*
1983 Walter Röhrl *(West Germany)*
1984 Walter Röhrl *(West Germany)*
1985 Ari Vatanen *(Finland)*
1986 Henri Toivonen *(Finland)*
1987 Mikki Biasion *(Italy)*
1988 Bruno Saby *(France)*
1989 Mikki Biasion *(Italy)*
1990 Didier Auriol *(France)*
1991 Carlos Sainz *(Spain)*
LOMBARD–RAC RALLY
(formerly RAC International Rally of Great Britain) first held 1927
1981 Hannu Mikkola *(Finland)*
1982 Hannu Mikkola *(Finland)*
1983 Stig Blomqvist *(Sweden)*
1984 Ari Vatanen *(Finland)*
1985 Henri Toivonen *(Finland)*
1986 Timo Salonen *(Finland)*
1987 Juha Kankkunen *(Finland)*
1988 Markku Alén *(Finland)*
1989 Pentti Arikkala *(Finland)*
1990 Carlos Sainz *(Spain)*

**netball** a women's game, developed from basketball, played by two teams of seven players each.

It is played on a hard court 30.5 m/100 ft long and 15.25 m/50 ft wide. At each end is a goal, consisting of a post 3.05 m/10 ft high, at the top of which is attached a circular hoop and net. The object of the game is to pass an inflated spherical ball through the opposing team's net. The ball is thrown from player to player; no contact is allowed between players, and none may run with the ball.

WORLD CHAMPIONSHIP
first held 1963; contested every four years
1963 Australia
1967 New Zealand
1971 Australia
1975 Australia
1979 Australia, New Zealand, and Trinidad and Tobago
1983 Australia
1987 New Zealand
1991 Australia

**orienteering** sport of cross-country running and route-finding. Competitors set off at one-minute intervals and have to find their way, using map and compass, to various check-points (approximately 0.8 km/0.5 mi apart), where their control cards are marked.

WORLD CHAMPIONSHIP
first held 1966
*individual (men/women)*
1981 Oyvin Thon *(Norway)*/Annichen Kringstad *(Norway)*
1983 Morten Berglia *(Norway)*/Annichen Kringstad *(Norway)*
1985 Kari Sallinen *(Finland)*/Annichen Kringstad *(Norway)*
1987 Kent Olsson *(Sweden)*/Arja Hannus *(Sweden)*
1989 Peter Thoresen *(Norway)*/Marita Skogum *(Sweden)*
*relay (men/women)*
1979 Sweden/Finland
1981 Norway/Sweden
1983 Norway/Sweden
1985 Norway/Sweden
1987 Norway/Norway
1989 Norway/Sweden

**polo** stick-and-ball game played between two teams of four on horseback. It is played on the largest pitch of any game, measuring up to 274m/300yd by 182 m/200yd. A small solid ball is struck with the side of a long-handled mallet through goals at each end of the pitch. A typical match lasts about an hour, and is divided into 'chukkas' of 7 ½ minutes each. No pony is expected to play more than two chukkas in the course of a day.

*COWDRAY PARK GOLD CUP*
British Open Championship; first held 1956
1985 Maple Leafs
1986 Tramontana
1987 Tramontana
1988 Tramontana
1989 Tramontana
1990 Hildon

**rowing** propulsion of a boat by oars, either by one rower with two oars (sculling) or by crews (two, four, or eight persons) with one oar each, often with a coxswain.

WORLD CHAMPIONSHIP
first held 1962 for men, 1974 for women
*men – single sculls*
1981 Peter-Michael Kolbe *(West Germany)*
1982 Rudiger Reiche *(East Germany)*
1983 Peter-Michael Kolbe *(West Germany)*
1985 Pertti Karppinen *(Finland)*
1986 Peter-Michael Kolbe *(West Germany)*
1987 Thomas Lange *(East Germany)*
1989 Thomas Lange *(East Germany)*
1990 Uri Janson *(USSR)*
*women – single sculls*
1981 Sanda Toma *(Romania)*
1982 Irina Fetisova *(USSR)*
1983 Jutta Hampe *(East Germany)*
1985 Cornelia Linse *(East Germany)*
1986 Jutta Hampe *(East Germany)*
1987 Magdalena Georgeyeva *(Bulgaria)*
1989 Elisabeta Lipa *(Romania)*
1990 Birgit Peter *(East Germany)*
THE BOAT RACE
first held 1829; rowed annually by crews from Oxford and Cambridge Universities, between Putney and Mortlake on the river Thames
1986 Cambridge
1987 Oxford
1988 Oxford
1989 Oxford
1990 Oxford
1991 Oxford
*wins*
Cambridge 69
Oxford 67

**rugby league** the professional form of rugby football founded in England 1895 as the Northern Union when a dispute about pay caused northern clubs to break away from the Rugby Football Union. The game is similar to rugby union, but the number of players is reduced from 15 to 13, and other rule changes have made the game more open and fast-moving.

CHALLENGE CUP FINAL
first held 1897
1982 Hull
1983 Featherstone Rovers
1984 Widnes
1985 Wigan
1986 Castleford
1987 Halifax
1988 Wigan
1989 Wigan
1990 Wigan
1991 Wigan
PREMIERSHIP TROPHY
introduced at the end of the 1974–75 season; a knockout competition involving the top eight clubs in the first division

## 1892: SOME SPORTING HIGHLIGHTS

*association football* The league was won by Sunderland, and in 1892 was extended to two divisions for the first time. The 1892 FA Cup was won by West Bromwich Albion, who beat Aston Villa 3–0 in front of a 32,810 crowd at the Kennington Oval in S London (now the home of Surrey County Cricket Club). In Scotland, Dumbarton were league champions. The Scottish FA Cup was won by Celtic, who beat Queens Park 5–1 after the game had to be replayed because of crowd trouble.

*athletics* The first Olympic Games were still four years away, but the Amateur Athletics Association (AAA) Championships had been held since 1880. In 1892, R A Bradley of Huddersfield ran 100 yards in 10.2 seconds (equivalent to 11.3 seconds for 100 metres) and H Wade (London AC) won the mile in 4 minutes 19.2 seconds. By comparison, in 1991 the world records for running 100 metres and one mile were, respectively, 9.9 seconds and 3 minutes 46.32 seconds.

*boxing* On 7 Sept 1892, US boxer James J Corbett became the first world heavyweight champion under Marquess of Queensberry rules, in the first championship bout in which gloves were worn. Robert Fitzsimmons from Helston, Cornwall, won the first of his three world titles.

*cricket* Australia beat England 2–1, and England beat the only other test-playing nation, South Africa, by an innings and 189 runs. Lancashire and Nottinghamshire shared the county championship.

*golf* H H Hilton (of the Royal Liverpool club) won the Open with a four-round total of 305 at Muirfield, Scotland. It was the first time that Muirfield had staged the event, and the first time that golfers had to complete four instead of two rounds. The Amateur Championship was in its eighth season, while the US Open was to begin in 1893.

*horse racing* The 'sport of kings' was more advanced than any rival sport, the Derby having been run since 1780, the Grand National since 1837, and the oldest classic, the St Leger, since 1776. The Jockey Club was founded 1750.

*lawn tennis* Wimbledon started in 1877 and the US Open in 1881. Wimbledon was run on the challenge basis, with the holder meeting the winner of the all-comers competition. The Wimbledon ladies' singles champion was Lottie Dod, her fourth of five titles; she is still the youngest woman champion.

*motor racing* The world was still two years away from the first historic road race, from Paris to Rouen, which would be won by Count de Dion in a De Dion steam car at a speed of 18.7 kph/11.6 mph.

*rowing* Oxford won the Boat Race in a new record 19 minutes 21 seconds. Henley Regatta had started in 1875.

*rugby union* England won the Triple Crown and Grand Slam without conceding a point. Their home grounds were Blackheath, London, and Manchester. The northern teams were gathering momentum for their breakaway to rugby league in 1893.

---

1982 Hull Kingston Rovers
1983 Widnes
1984 Hull Kingston Rovers
1985 St Helens
1986 Warrington
1987 Wigan
1988 Widnes
1989 Widnes
1990 Widnes
1991 Hull

**rugby union** the amateur form of rugby football in which there are 15 players on each side. It is played with an inflated oval ball, on a field 69 m/75 yd long and 100 m/110 yd wide. At each end of the field is an H-shaped set of goalposts 5.6 m/18.5 ft wide, with a crossbar 3 m/10 ft above the ground. Points are scored by 'touching down', or grounding, the ball beyond the goal line (try, 4 points), or by kicking it over the goal's crossbar after a touchdown (conversion, 2 points), from the field during regular play (dropped goal, 3 points), or in response to a penalty against the opposing team (3 points).

WORLD CUP
William Webb Ellis Trophy

1987 New Zealand
INTERNATIONAL CHAMPIONSHIP
instituted 1884, now a tournament between England, France, Ireland, Scotland, and Wales
1982 Ireland
1983 France and Ireland
1984 Scotland
1985 Ireland
1986 France
1987 France
1988 France and Wales
1989 France
1990 Scotland
1991 England
COUNTY CHAMPIONSHIP first held 1889
1982 Lancashire
1983 Gloucestershire
1984 Gloucestershire
1985 Middlesex
1986 Warwickshire
1987 Yorkshire
1988 Lancashire
1989 Durham
1990 Lancashire
1991 Cornwall
PILKINGTON CUP
formerly the *John Player Special Cup* the English club knockout tournament, first held 1971–72

1982 Gloucester and Moseley
1983 Bristol
1984 Bath
1985 Bath
1986 Bath
1987 Bath
1988 Harlequins
1989 Bath
1990 Bath
1991 Harlequins
SCOTTISH CLUB CHAMPIONSHIP
first held 1974
*Division One*
1982 Hawick
1983 Gala
1984 Hawick
1985 Hawick
1986 Hawick
1987 Hawick
1988 Kelso
1989 Kelso
1990 Melrose
1991 Boroughmuir
SCHWEPPES WELSH CUP
the Welsh club knockout tournament, first held
1971–72
1982 Cardiff
1983 Pontypool
1984 Cardiff
1985 Llanelli
1986 Cardiff
1987 Cardiff
1988 Llanelli
1989 Neath
1990 Neath
1991 Llanelli

**shinty** (Gaelic *camanachd*) stick-and-ball game, resembling hurling, popular in the Scottish Highlands. It is played between two teams of 12 players each, on a field 132–183 m/ 144–200 yd long and 64–91 m/70–99 yd wide. A curved stick (caman) is used to propel a leather-covered cork and worsted ball into the opposing team's goal (hail).
CAMANACHD CUP
instituted 1896
1985 Newtonmore
1986 Newtonmore
1987 Kingussie
1988 Kingussie
1989 Kingussie
1990 Skye
1991 Kingussie

**skating** self-propulsion on ice by means of bladed skates, or on other surfaces by skates with small rollers. The chief competitive ice-skating events are figure skating, for singles or pairs, ice-dancing, and simple speed skating.

WORLD CHAMPIONSHIP
ice-skating; first held 1896
*men*
1982 Scott Hamilton *(USA)*
1983 Scott Hamilton *(USA)*
1984 Scott Hamilton *(USA)*

1985 Aleksandr Fadeyev *(USSR)*
1986 Brian Boitano *(USA)*
1987 Brian Orser *(Canada)*
1988 Brian Boitano *(USA)*
1989 Kurt Browning *(Canada)*
1990 Kurt Browning *(Canada)*
1991 Kurt Browning *(Canada)*
*women*
1982 Elaine Zayak *(USA)*
1983 Rosalynn Sumners *(USA)*
1984 Katarina Witt *(East Germany)*
1985 Katarina Witt *(East Germany)*
1986 Debbie Thomas *(USA)*
1987 Katarina Witt *(East Germany)*
1988 Katarina Witt *(East Germany)*
1989 Midoria Ito *(Japan)*
1990 Jill Trenary *(USA)*
1991 Kristi Yamaguchi *(USA)*
*pairs*
1982 Tassilo Thierbach and Sabine Baess *(East Germany)*
1983 Oleg Vasiliev and Yelena Valova *(USSR)*
1984 Paul Martini and Barbara Underhill *(Canada)*
1985 Oleg Vasiliev and Yelena Valova *(USSR)*
1986 Sergey Grinkov and Ekaterina Gordeeva *(USSR)*
1987 Sergey Grinkov and Ekaterina Gordeeva *(USSR)*
1988 Oleg Vasilyev and Yelena Valova *(USSR)*
1989 Sergey Grinkov and Ekaterina Gordeeva *(USSR)*
1990 Sergey Grinkov and Ekaterina Gordeeva *(USSR)*
1991 Artur Dmitriev and Natalya Mishkuteniok*(USSR)*
*ice dance*
1982 Christopher Dean and Jayne Torvill *(UK)*
1983 Christopher Dean and Jayne Torvill *(UK)*
1984 Christopher Dean and Jayne Torvill *(UK)*
1985 Andrei Bukin and Natalia Bestemianova *(USSR)*
1986 Andrei Bukin and Natalia Bestemianova *(USSR*
1987 Andrei Bukin and Natalia Bestemianova *(USSR)*
1988 Andrei Bukin and Natalia Bestemianova *(USSR)*
1989 Sergey Ponomarenko and Marina Klimova *(USSR)*
1990 Sergey Ponomarenko and Marina Klimova *(USSR)*
1991 Paul Duchesnay and Isabelle Duchesnay *(France)*

**skiing** self-propulsion on snow by means of elongated runners (skis) for the feet, slightly bent upward at the tip. Events include downhill; slalom, in which a series of turns between flags have to be negotiated; cross-country racing; and ski jumping, when jumps of over 150 m/ 490 ft are achieved from ramps up to 90 m/ 295 ft high. Speed-skiing uses skis approximately 1/3 longer and wider than normal, with which speeds of up to 200 kmph have been recorded.

ALPINE WORLD CUP
first held 1967
*men – overall*
1982 Phil Mahre *(USA)*
1983 Phil Mahre *(USA)*
1984 Pirmin Zurbriggen *(Switzerland)*
1985 Marc Girardelli *(Luxembourg)*
1986 Marc Girardelli *(Luxembourg)*
1987 Pirmin Zurbriggen *(Switzerland)*
1988 Pirmin Zurbriggen *(Switzerland)*
1989 Marc Girardelli *(Luxembourg)*
1990 Pirmin Zurbriggen *(Switzerland)*
1991 Marc Girardelli *(Luxembourg)*

*women*
1982 Erika Hess *(Switzerland)*
1983 Tamara McKinney *(USA)*
1984 Erika Hess *(Switzerland)*
1985 Michela Figini *(Switzerland)*
1986 Maria Walliser *(Switzerland)*
1987 Maria Walliser *(Switzerland)*
1988 Michela Figini *(Switzerland)*
1989 Vreni Schneider *(Switzerland)*
1990 Petra Krönberger *(Austria)*
1991 Petra Krönberger *(Austria)*

**snooker**  indoor game derived from billiards. It is played with 22 balls: 15 red, one each of yellow, green, brown, blue, pink, and black, and one white cueball. Red balls are worth one point when sunk, while the coloured balls have ascending values from two points for the yellow to seven points for the black.

WORLD PROFESSIONAL CHAMPIONSHIP
first held 1927
1982 Alex Higgins *(Northern Ireland)*
1983 Steve Davis *(England)*
1984 Steve Davis *(England)*
1985 Dennis Taylor *(Northern Ireland)*
1986 Joe Johnson *(England)*
1987 Steve Davis *(England)*
1988 Steve Davis *(England)*
1989 Steve Davis *(England)*
1990 Stephen Hendry *(Scotland)*
1991 John Parrott *(England)*
WORLD AMATEUR CHAMPIONSHIP
first held 1963
1980 Jimmy White *(England)*
1982 Terry Parsons *(Wales)*
1984 O B Agrawal *(India)*
1985 Paul Mifsud *(Malta)*
1986 Paul Mifsud *(Malta)*
1987 Darren Morgan *(Wales)*
1988 James Wattana *(Thailand)*
1989 Ken Doherty *(Republic of Ireland)*
1990 Stephen O'Connell *(Republic of Ireland)*

**softball**  a form of baseball played with similar equipment. The two main differences are the distances between the bases (18.29 m/60 ft) and that the ball is pitched underhand in softball. There are two forms of the game, *fast pitch* and *slow pitch*; in the latter the ball must be delivered to home plate in an arc that must not be less than 2.4 m/8 ft at its height.
WORLD CHAMPIONSHIP
fast pitch; introduced 1965 for women, 1966 for men; now contested every four years
*men*
1966 USA
1968 USA
1972 Canada
1976 Canada, New Zealand, and USA
1980 USA
1984 New Zealand
1988 USA
*women*
1965 Australia
1970 Japan
1974 USA

1978 USA
1982 New Zealand
1986 USA

**squash**  or **squash rackets**  racket-and-ball game usually played by two people on an enclosed court. Each player hits the small rubber ball against the front wall of the court alternately. The object is to win points by playing shots the opponent cannot return to the wall. There are two forms of the game: the American form, which is played in North and some South American countries and the English, which is played mainly in Europe, Pakistan, and Commonwealth countries such as Australia and New Zealand. In English singles, the court is 6.4 m/21 ft wide and 10 m/32 ft long. Doubles squash is played on a larger court.

WORLD OPEN CHAMPIONSHIP
*first held 1975*
*men*
1982 Jahangir Khan *(Pakistan)*
1983 Jahangir Khan *(Pakistan)*
1984 Jahangir Khan *(Pakistan)*
1985 Jahangir Khan *(Pakistan*
1986 Ross Norman *(New Zealand)*
1987 Jansher Khan *(Pakistan)*
1988 Jahangir Khan *(Pakistan)*
1989 Jansher Khan *(Pakistan)*
1990 Jansher Khan *(Pakistan)*
1991 Rodney Martin *(Australia)*
*women*
1981 Rhonda Thorne *(Australia)*
1983 Vicky Cardwell *(Australia)*
1985 Sue Devoy *(New Zealand)*
1987 Sue Devoy *(New Zealand)*
1989 Martine Le Moignan *(UK)*
1990 Sue Devoy *(New Zealand)*

**surfing**  riding on the crest of large waves while standing on a narrow, keeled surfboard, usually of a light synthetic material such as fibreglass, about 1.8 m/6 ft long (or 2.4–7 m/8–9 ft known as the Malibu), as first developed in Hawaii and Australia.

WORLD PROFESSIONAL CHAMPIONSHIP
first held 1970
*men*
1985 Tommy Curren *(USA)*
1986 Tommy Curren *(USA)*
1987 Damien Hardman *(Australia)*
1988 Barton Lynch *(Australia)*
1989 Martin Potter *(UK)*
*women*
1985 Frieda Zamba *(USA)*
1986 Frieda Zamba *(USA)*
1987 Wendy Botha *(South Africa)*
1988 Frieda Zamba *(USA)*
1989 Wendy Botha *(South Africa)*
WORLD AMATEUR CHAMPIONSHIP
first held 1964
*men*
1980 Mark Scott *(Australia)*
1982 Tommy Curren *(USA)*
1984 Scott Farnsworth *(USA)*

1986 Mark Sainsbury *(Australia)*
1988 Fabio Gouveia *(Brazil)*
1990 Heifara Tahutini *(Tahiti)*
*women*
1980 Alisa Schwarzstein *(USA)*
1982 Jenny Gill *(Australia)*
1984 Janice Aragon *(USA)*
1986 Connie Nixon *(Australia)*
1988 Pauline Menczer *(Australia)*
1990 Kathy Newman *(Australia)*

**swimming** self-propulsion of the body through water. There are four strokes in competitive swimming: **freestyle** (or **front crawl**), the fastest stroke; **breaststroke**, the slowest stroke; **backstroke**; and **butterfly**, the newest stroke, developed in the USA from breaststroke. Swimmers enter the water with a 'racing plunge' (a form of dive) with the exception of the backstroke, when competitors start in the water. Distances of races vary between 50 m/54.7 yd and 1,500 m/1,641 yd. Olympic-size pools are 50 m/55 yd long and have eight lanes. **Synchronized swimming** is a form of 'ballet' performed in and under water.

OLYMPIC GAMES
*event introduced 1896 for men, 1912 for women*
*most gold medals*
9 Mark Spitz *(USA)* 1968, 1972
6 Kirstin Otto *(East Germany)* 1988
5 Charles Daniels *(USA)* 1904, 1908
5 Johnny Weissmuller *(USA)* 1924, 1928
5 Don Schollander *(USA)* 1964, 1968
5 Matt Bondi *(USA)* 1984, 1988
4 Henry Taylor *(UK)* 1906, 1908
4 Murray Rose *(Australia)* 1956, 1960
4 Dawn Fraser *(Australia)* 1956, 1960, 1964
4 Roland Matthes *(East Germany)* 1968, 1972
4 John Naber *(USA)* 1976
4 Kornelia Ender *(East Germany)* 1976
4 Vladimir Salnikov *(USSR)* 1980, 1988
*most medals*
11 Mark Spitz *(USA)* 1968, 1972
8 Charles Daniels *(USA)* 1904, 1908
8 Roland Matthes *(East Germany)* 1968, 1972
8 Henry Taylor *(UK)* 1906, 1908, 1912, 1920
8 Dawn Fraser *(Australia)* 1956, 1960, 1964
8 Kornelia Ender *(East Germany)* 1972, 1976
8 Shirley Babashoff *(USA)* 1972, 1976
WORLD CHAMPIONSHIP
introduced 1973, next held 1975, 1978, and every four years since
*most gold medals*
8 Kornelia Ender *(East Germany)* 1973, 1975
7 Kristin Otto *(East Germany)* 1982, 1986
6 Jim Montgomery *(USA)* 1973, 1975
5 Rowdy Gaines *(USA)* 1978, 1982
*most medals*
10 Kornelia Ender *(East Germany)* 1973, 1975
9 Kristin Otto *(East Germany)* 1982, 1986
9 Mary Meagher *(USA)* 1978, 1982
8 Rowdy Gaines *(USA)* 1978, 1982

**table tennis** or **ping pong** indoor game played on a rectangular table by two or four players. Play takes place on a table measuring 2.74 m/9 ft long by 1.52 m/5 ft wide. Across the middle is a 15.25 cm/6 in high net over which the ball must be hit. The players use small, wooden paddles covered in sponge or rubber. Points are scored by forcing the opponent(s) into an error. The first to score 21 wins the game. A match may consist of three or five games. Volleying is not allowed. In doubles play, the players must hit the ball in strict rotation.

WORLD CHAMPIONSHIP
*first held 1926, now contested every two years*
*men's team*
1973 Sweden
1975 China
1977 China
1979 Hungary
1981 China
1983 China
1985 China
1987 China
1989 Sweden
1991 Sweden
*women's team*
1973 South Korea
1975 China
1977 China
1979 China
1981 China
1983 China
1985 China
1987 China
1989 China
1991 Korea
*men's singles*
1973 Hsi En-Ting *(China)*
1975 Istvan Jonyer *(Hungary)*
1977 Mitsuru Kohno *(Japan)*
1979 Seiji Ono *(Japan)*
1981 Guo Yue-Hua *(China)*
1983 Guo Yue-Hua *(China)*
1985 Jiang Jialiang *(China)*
1987 Jiang Jialiang *(China)*
1989 Jan-Ove Waldner *(Sweden)*
1991 Jorgen Persson *(Sweden)*
*women's singles*
1973 Hu Yu-Lan *(China)*
1975 Pak Yung-Sun *(North Korea)*
1977 Pak Yung-Sun *(North Korea)*
1979 Ke Hsin-Ai *(China)*
1981 Ting Ling *(China)*
1983 Cao Yan-Hua *(China)*
1985 Cao Yan-Hua *(China)*
1987 He Zhili *(China)*
1989 Qiuo Hong *(China)*
1991 Deng Yaping *(China)*

**tennis, lawn** racket-and-ball game for two or four players, invented towards the end of the 19th century. It may be played on a grass, wood, shale, clay, or concrete surface. The object of the game is to strike the ball into the prescribed area of the court, with oval-headed rackets (strung with gut or nylon), in such a way that it cannot be returned. The game is won by those first winning four points (called 15, 30, 40, game), unless both sides reach

40 (deuce), when two consecutive points are needed to win. A set is won by winning six games with a margin of two over opponents, though a tie-break system operates, that is at six games to each side (or in some cases eight) except in the final set.

The Grand Slam events are the Wimbledon Championship, the United States Open, French Open, and Australian Open.

---

WIMBLEDON CHAMPIONSHIPS
All England Lawn Tennis Club championships; first held 1877; grass surface
*men's singles*
1982 Jimmy Connors *(USA)*
1983 John McEnroe *(USA)*
1984 John McEnroe *(USA)*
1985 Boris Becker *(West Germany)*
1986 Boris Becker *(West Germany)*
1987 Pat Cash *(Australia)*
1988 Stefan Edberg *(Sweden)*
1989 Boris Becker *(West Germany)*
1990 Stefan Edberg *(Sweden)*
1991 Michael Stich *(Germany)*
*women's singles*
1982 Martina Navratilova *(USA)*
1983 Martina Navratilova *(USA)*
1984 Martina Navratilova *(USA)*
1985 Martina Navratilova *(USA)*
1986 Martina Navratilova *(USA)*
1987 Martina Navratilova *(USA)*
1988 Steffi Graf *(West Germany)*
1989 Steffi Graf *(West Germany)*
1990 Martina Navratilova *(USA)*
1991 Steffi Graf *(Germany)*
UNITED STATES OPEN
first held 1881 as the United States Championship; became the United States Open 1968; concrete surface
*men's singles*
1981 John McEnroe *(USA)*
1982 Jimmy Connors *(USA)*
1983 Jimmy Connors *(USA)*
1984 John McEnroe *(USA)*
1985 Ivan Lendl *(Czechoslovakia)*
1986 Ivan Lendl *(Czechoslovakia)*
1987 Ivan Lendl *(Czechoslovakia)*
1988 Mats Wilander *(Sweden)*
1989 Boris Becker *(West Germany)*
1990 Pete Sampras *(USA)*
*women's singles*
1981 Tracy Austin *(USA)*
1982 Chris Evert *(USA)*
1983 Martina Navratilova *(USA)*
1984 Martina Navratilova *(USA)*
1985 Hana Mandlikova *(Czechoslovakia)*
1986 Martina Navratilova *(USA)*
1987 Martina Navritilova *(USA)*
1988 Steffi Graf *(West Germany)*
1989 Steffi Graf *(West Germany)*
1990 Gabriela Sabatini *(Argentina)*
FRENCH OPEN
first held 1891 (a national championship until 1924); clay surface
*men's singles*
1982 Mats Wilander *(Sweden)*
1983 Yannick Noah *(France)*

1984 Ivan Lendl *(Czechoslovakia)*
1985 Mats Wilander *(Sweden)*
1986 Ivan Lendl *(Czechoslovakia)*
1987 Ivan Lendl *(Czechoslovakia)*
1988 Mats Wilander *(Sweden)*
1989 Michael Chang *(USA)*
1990 Andres Gomez *(Ecuador)*
1991 Jim Courier *(USA)*
*women's singles*
1982 Martina Navratilova *(USA)*
1983 Chris Evert *(USA)*
1984 Martina Navratilova *(USA)*
1985 Chris Evert *(USA)*
1986 Chris Evert *(USA)*
1987 Steffi Graf *(West Germany)*
1988 Steffi Graf *(West Germany)*
1989 Arantxa Sanchez *(Spain)*
1990 Monica Seles *(Yugoslavia)*
1991 Monica Seles *(Yugoslavia)*
AUSTRALIAN OPEN
first held 1905 (a national championship until 1925); clay surface
*men's singles*
1982 Johan Kriek *(South Africa)*
1983 Mats Wilander *(Sweden)*
1984 Mats Wilander *(Sweden)*
1985 Stefan Edberg *(Sweden)*
1986/7 Stefan Edberg *(Sweden)*
1988 Mats Wilander *(Sweden)*
1989 Ivan Lendl *(Czechoslovakia)*
1990 Ivan Lendl *(Czechoslovakia)*
1991 Boris Becker *(Germany)*
*women's singles*
1981 Martina Navratilova *(USA)*
1982 Chris Evert *(USA)*
1983 Martina Navratilova *(USA)*
1984 Chris Evert *(USA)*
1985 Martina Navratilova *(USA)*
1986/7 Hana Mandlikova *(Czechoslovakia)*
1988 Steffi Graf *(West Germany)*
1989 Steffi Graf *(West Germany)*
1990 Steffi Graf *(West Germany)*
1991 Monica Seles *(Yugoslavia)*
DAVIS CUP
first contested 1900
1981 USA
1982 USA
1983 Australia
1984 Sweden
1985 Sweden
1986 Australia
1987 Sweden
1988 West Germany
1989 West Germany
1990 USA

---

**trampolining** gymnastics performed on a sprung canvas sheet that allows the performer to reach great heights before landing again. Marks are gained for carrying out difficult manoeuvres. Synchronized trampolining and tumbling are also popular forms of the sport.

---

WORLD CHAMPIONSHIP
first held 1964
*men*
1972 Paul Luxon *(UK)*

1974 Richard Tisson *(France)*
1976 Richard Tisson *(France)*/Evgeni Janes *(USSR)*
1978 Evgeni Janes *(USSR)*
1980 Stewart Matthews *(UK)*
1982 Carl Furrer *(UK)*
1984 Lionel Pioline *(France)*
1986 Lionel Pioline *(France)*
1988 Vadim Krasonchapka *(USSR)*
1990 Alexandr Moskalenko *(USSR)*
*women*
1972 Alexandra Nicholson *(USA)*
1974 Alexandra Nicholson *(USA)*
1976 Svetlana Levina *(USSR)*
1978 Tatyana Anisimova *(USSR)*
1980 Ruth Keller *(Switzerland)*
1982 Ruth Keller *(Switzerland)*
1984 Sue Shotton *(Great Britian)*
1986 Tatyana Lushina *(USSR)*
1988 Khoperla Rusudum *(USSR)*
1990 Elena Merkulova *(USSR)*

**volleyball** an indoor and outdoor game played between two teams of six players each. The court measures 18 m/59 ft by 9 m/29 ft 6 in, and has a raised net drawn across its centre. Players hit an inflated spherical ball over the net with their hands or arms, the aim being to ground the ball in the opponents' court. The ball may not be hit more than three times on one team's side of the net.

WORLD CHAMPIONSHIP
first held 1949 for men, 1952 for women
*men*
1972 Japan
1974 Poland
1976 Poland
1978 USSR
1980 USSR
1982 USSR
1984 USA
1986 USA
1988 USA
1990 Italy
*women*
1972 USSR
1974 Japan
1976 Japan
1978 Cuba
1980 USSR
1982 China
1984 China
1986 USA
1988 USSR
1990 USSR

**water polo** (formerly ***football-in-water***) sport played in a swimming pool, between two teams of seven players each. An inflated ball is passed among the players, who must swim around the pool without touching the bottom. Goals are scored when the ball is thrown past the opposing team's goalkeeper and into a net.

WORLD CHAMPIONSHIP
first held 1973; contested every four years since 1978
1973 Hungary

1975 USSR
1978 Italy
1982 USSR
1986 Yugoslavia
1990/91 Yugoslavia

**water skiing** sport in which a person is towed across water on a ski or skis, by means of a rope (23 m/75 ft long) attached to a speedboat. Competitions are held for overall performances, slalom, tricks, and jumping.

WORLD CHAMPIONSHIP
first held 1949; contested every two years
*men – overall*
1971 George Athans *(Canada)*
1973 George Athans *(Canada)*
1975 Carlos Suarez *(Venezuela)*
1977 Mike Hazelwood *(UK)*
1979 Joel McClintock *(Canada)*
1981 Sammy Duvall *(USA)*
1983 Sammy Duvall *(USA)*
1985 Sammy Duvall *(USA)*
1987 Sammy Duvall *(USA)*
1989 Patrice Martin *(France)*
*women – overall*
1971 Christy Weir *(USA)*
1973 Lisa St John *(USA)*
1975 Liz Allan-Shetter *(USA)*
1977 Cindy Todd *(USA)*
1979 Cindy Todd *(USA)*
1981 Karin Roberge *(USA)*
1983 Ana-Maria Carrasco *(Venezuela)*
1985 Karen Neville *(Australia)*
1987 Deena Brush *(USA)*
1989 Deena Mapple (née Brush) *(USA)*

**weightlifting** the sport of lifting the heaviest possible weight above one's head to the satisfaction of judges. In international competitions there are two standard lifts: snatch and jerk. In the ***snatch***, the bar and weights are lifted from the floor to a position with the arms outstretched and above the head in one continuous movement. The arms must be locked for two seconds for the lift to be good. The ***jerk*** is a two-movement lift: from the floor to the chest, and from the chest to the outstretched position. The aggregate weight of the two lifts counts.

OLYMPIC GAMES
*24th Olympics 1988*
52 kg Sevdalin Marinov *(Bulgaria)*
56 kg Oxen Mirzoian *(USSR)*
60 kg Naim Suleymanoglu *(Turkey)*
67.5 kg Joachim Kunz *(East Germany)*
75 kg Borislav Guidikov *(Bulgaria)*
82.5 kg Israil Arsanmakov *(USSR)*
90 kg Anatoliy Khrapati *(USSR)*
100 kg Pavel Kouznetsov *(USSR)*
110 kg Yuriy Zacharovich *(USSR)*
110+ kg Aleksandr Kurlovich *(USSR)*

**wrestling** fighting without the use of fists. The two main modern international styles are ***Greco-Roman***, concentrating on above-waist holds, and **freestyle**, which allows the legs to be used to hold or trip; in both the aim is to throw the opponent to the ground. Competitors are categorized according to weight: there are ten weight divisions in each style of wrestling, ranging from light-flyweight (under 48 kg) to super-heavyweight (over 100 kg). The professional form of the sport has become popular, partly due to television coverage, but is regarded by purists as an extension of show-business. Many countries have their own forms of wrestling. **Glima** is unique to Iceland; **Kushti** is the national style practised in Iran; **Schwingen** has been practised in Switzerland for hundreds of years; and **sumo** is the national sport of Japan.

WORLD CHAMPIONSHIP
Olympic champions automatically become world champions
*Greco-Roman* first held 1921
*super-heavyweight*
1980 Aleksandr Kolchinsky *(USSR)*
1981 Refik Memisevic *(Yugoslavia)*
1982 Nikolai Dinev *(Bulgaria)*
1983 Yevgeniy Artioshin *(USSR)*
1984 Jeffrey Blatnick *(USA)*
1985 Igor Rostozotskiy *(USSR)*
1986 Tomas Johansson *(Sweden)*
1987 Igor Rostozotskiy *(USSR)*
1988 Aleksandr Karelin *(USSR)*
1989 Aleksandr Karelin *(USSR)*
1990 Aleksandr Karelin *(USSR)*
*freestyle* first held 1951
*super-heavyweight*
1981 Salman Khasimikov *(USSR)*
1982 Salman Khasimikov *(USSR)*
1983 Salman Khasimikov *(USSR)*
1984 Bruce Baumgartner *(USA)*
1985 David Gobedzhishvilli *(USSR)*
1986 Bruce Baumgartner *(USA)*
1987 Aslan Khadartzev *(USSR)*
1988 David Gobedzhishvilli *(USSR)*
1989 Ali Reza Soleimani *(Iran)*
1990 David Gobedzhishvilli *(USSR)*
*champions with the most world and Olympic titles*
10 Aleksandr Medved *(USSR)* freestyle 1962-72
8 Sergey Beloglazov *(USSR)* freestyle 1980-89
7 Nikolai Balboshin *(USSR)* Greco-Roman 1971–79
7 Valeriy Rezantsev *(USSR)* Greco-Roman 1970–76
6 Ali Aliev *(USSR)* freestyle 1959-68
6 Abdollah Movahed *(Iran)* freestyle 1965-70
6 Levan Tediashvili *(USSR)* freestyle 1971-76
6 Soslan Andiev *(USSR)* freestyle 1973-80

**yachting** racing a small, light sailing vessel. At the Olympic Games, seven categories exist: Soling, Flying Dutchman, Star, Finn, Tornado, 470, and Windglider (or windsurfing/boardsailing), which was introduced at the 1984 Los Angeles games. The Finn and Windglider are solo events; the Soling class is for three-person crews; all other classes are for crews of two.

AMERICA'S CUP
first held 1870; now contested approximately every four years; all winners have been US boats, except for

Australia II
1962 *Weatherly*
1964 *Constellation*
1967 *Intrepid*
1970 *Intrepid*
1974 *Courageous*
1977 *Courageous*
1980 *Freedom*
1983 *Australia II*
1987 *Stars and Stripes*
1988 *Stars and Stripes*
ADMIRAL'S CUP
first held 1957; national teams consisting of three boats compete over three inshore courses and two offshore courses; contested every two years
1971 UK
1973 West Germany
1975 UK
1977 UK
1979 Australia
1981 UK
1983 West Germany
1985 West Germany
1987 New Zealand
1989 UK

# BIOGRAPHIES

**Agostini** Giacomo 1943– . Italian motorcyclist who won a record 122 grand prix and 15 world titles. His world titles were at 350cc and 500cc and he was five times a dual champion. In addition he was ten times winner of the Isle of Man Tourist Trophy (TT) races; a figure only bettered by Mike Hailwood and Joey Dunlop.
CAREER HIGHLIGHTS

*World titles*
350cc: 1968–73 (MV Agusta), 1974 (Yamaha)
500cc: 1966–72 (MV Agusta), 1975 (Yamaha) Isle of Man
*TT wins*
Junior TT: 1966, 1968–70, 1972 (all MV Agusta)
Senior TT: 1968–72 (all MV Agusta)

**Alexeev** Vasiliy 1942– . Soviet weightlifter who broke 80 world records 1970–77, a record for any sport. He was Olympic super-heavyweight champion twice, world champion seven times, and European champion on eight occasions. At one time the most decorated man in the USSR, he was regarded as the strongest man in the world. He carried the Soviet flag at the 1980 Moscow Olympics opening ceremony, but retired shortly afterwards.
CAREER HIGHLIGHTS

Olympic champion: 1972, 1976
world champion: 1970–71, 1973–75, 1977
European champion: 1970–78.

**Ali** Muhammad. Born Cassius Marcellus Clay, Jr. 1942– . US boxer. Olympic light-heavyweight champion 1960, he went on to become world professional heavyweight champion 1964, and was the only man to regain the title twice. Ali had his title stripped from him 1967 for refusing to be drafted into the US Army. He was known for his fast footwork and extrovert nature.

CAREER HIGHLIGHTS

fights: 61
wins: 56 (37 knockouts)
draws: 0
defeats: 5
first professional fight: 29 Oct 1960 v. Tunny Hunsaker (USA)
last professional fight: 11 Dec 1981 v. Trevor Berbick (Canada)

**Aouita** Said 1960– . Moroccan runner. Outstanding at middle and long distances, he won the 1984 Olympic and 1987 World Championship 5,000-metres title. In 1985 he held world records at both 1,500 and 5,000 metres, the first person for 30 years to hold both. He has since broken the 2 miles, 3,000 metres, and 2,000 metres world records.

CAREER HIGHLIGHTS

*Olympic Games*
gold: 5,000 metres (1984)
*world records*
1,500 metres: 1985
2,000 metres: 1987
3,000 metres: 1987; 1989
5,000 metres: 1985; 1987
*world championships*
gold: 5,000 metres 1987
*world best*
2 miles: 1987

**Archer** Frederick 1857–1886. English jockey who rode 2,748 winners in 8,084 races 1870–86, including 21 classic winners. He rode 246 winners in the 1885 season, a record that stood until 1933 (when it was broken by Gordon Richards). Archer shot himself in a fit of depression.

CAREER HIGHLIGHTS

Derby: 1877, 1880, 1881, 1885, 1886
Oaks: 1875, 1878, 1879, 1885
St.Leger: 1877, 1878, 1881, 1882, 1885, 1886
2,000 Guineas: 1874, 1879, 1883, 1885
1,000 Guineas: 1875, 1879
Champion Jockey: 1874–86 (13 times)

**Ashe** Arthur Robert, Jr 1943– . US tennis player and coach renowned for his exceptionally strong serve. He won the US national men's singles title at Forest Hills and the first US Open 1968. He won the Australian men's title 1970 and Wimbledon 1975. Cardiac problems ended his playing career 1979, but he continued his involvement with the sport, serving as captain of the US Davis Cup team.

**Ballesteros** Seve(riano) 1957– . Spanish golfer who came to prominence 1976 and has won several leading tournaments, including the US Masters Tournament and the British Open. Born in Pedrena, N Spain, he is one of four golf-playing brothers.

CAREER HIGHLIGHTS

British Open: 1979, 1984, 1988
US Masters: 1980, 1983
World Match-play: 1981–82, 1984–85

**Bannister** Roger Gilbert 1929– . English track and field athlete, the first person to run a mile in under four minutes. He achieved this feat at Oxford, England, on 6 May 1954 in a time of 3 min 59.4 sec. Bannister also broke the four-minute barrier at the 1954 Commonwealth Games in Vancouver, Canada.

CAREER HIGHLIGHTS

*Commonwealth Games*
1954: gold 1 mile
*European Championship*
1954: gold 1,500 metres
1950: silver 800 metres
*World records*
1953: 4 x 1 mile relay: (member of Great Britain and Northern Ireland squad)
1954: 1 mile

**Becker** Boris 1967– . German lawn-tennis player. In 1985 he became the youngest winner of a singles title at Wimbledon at the age of 17. He has won the title three times and helped West Germany to win the Davis Cup 1988 and 1989. He also won the US Open 1989.

**Best** George 1946– . Irish footballer. He won two League championship medals and was a member of the Manchester United side that won the European Cup in 1968. Best joined Manchester United as a youth and made his debut at 17; seven months later he made his international debut for Northern Ireland. Trouble with managers, fellow players, and the media led to his early retirement.

CAREER HIGHLIGHTS

*Football League*
appearances: 411
goals: 147
League championship: 1965, 1967
Footballer of the Year: 1968
*internationals*
appearances: 37
goals: 9
European Cup: 1968
European Footballer of the Year: 1968

**Border** Allan 1955– . Australian cricketer, captain of the Australian team from 1985. He has played for New South Wales and Queensland, and in England for Gloucestershire and Essex. He has played for Australia since 1978, and

now holds the world record for appearances in test matches (125) and one-day internationals (223).
CAREER HIGHLIGHTS

*test cricket*
appearances (up to April 1991): 125
runs: 9,257
average: 52.29
best: 205 not out (v. New Zealand 1987–88)
wickets: 37
average: 34.91
best: 7 for 46 (v. West Indies 1988–89)

**Borg** Bjorn 1956– . Swedish lawn-tennis player who won the men's singles title at Wimbledon five times 1976–80, a record since the abolition of the challenge system 1922. He also won six French Open singles titles. In 1991 Borg returned to professional tennis.
CAREER HIGHLIGHTS

*Wimbledon*
singles: 1976–80
*French Open*
singles: 1974–75, 1978–81
*Davis Cup*
1975 (member of winning Sweden team)
*Grand Prix Masters*
1980–81
*WCT Champion*
1976
*ITF World Champion*
1978–80

**Botham** Ian (Terrence) 1955– . English cricketer whose test record places him among the world's greatest all-rounders. He has played county cricket for Somerset and Worcestershire (for which he currently plays) as well as playing in Australia. He played for England 1977-89 and returned to the England side in 1991. Botham has raised money for leukaemia research with much-publicized walks from John o'Groats to Land's End in the UK, and across the Alps in the style of Hannibal.
CAREER HIGHLIGHTS

*all first-class matches (to start of 1991 season)*
runs: 17,436
average: 34.05
best: 228 (Somerset v. Gloucestershire 1980)
wickets: 1,082
average: 26.81
best: 8 for 34 (England v. Pakistan 1978)
*test cricket*
appearances (to April 1991): 97
runs: 5,119
average: 34.35
best: 208 (England v. India 1982)
wickets: 376
average: 28.27
best: 8 for 34 (England v. Pakistan 1978)
catches: 112

**Boycott** Geoffrey 1940– . English cricketer who was England's most prolific run-maker, with

8,114 runs in test cricket. He played in 108 test matches. Twice, in 1971 and 1979, his average was over 100 runs in an English season. Boycott was banned as a test player in 1982 for taking part in matches against South Africa. He was released by his county side Yorkshire after a dispute in 1986, and has not played first-class cricket since.

CAREER HIGHLIGHTS

*all first-class matches*
runs: 48,426
average: 56.83
best: 261 not out (MCC v. WIBC President's XI 1973–74)
*test cricket*
runs: 8,114
average: 47.72
best: 246 not out (England v. India 1967)

**Bradman** Donald George 1908– . Australian test cricketer with the highest average in test history. From 52 test matches he averaged 99.94 runs per innings. He only needed four runs from his final test innings to average 100 but was dismissed at second ball. Bradman played for Australia for 20 years and was captain 1936–48. He twice scored triple centuries against England and in 1930 scored 452 not out for New South Wales against Queensland, the highest first-class innings until 1959.

CAREER HIGHLIGHTS

*all first-class matches*
runs: 28,067
average: 95.14
best: 452 not out (New South Wales v. Queensland 1930)
*test cricket*
runs: 6,996
average: 99.94
best: 334 (Australia v. England, 1930)

**Bristow** Eric 1957– . English darts player nicknamed 'the Crafty Cockney'. He has won all the game's major titles, including the world professional title a record five times between 1980 and 1986.
CAREER HIGHLIGHTS

*World professional champion*
1980–81, 1984–86
*World Masters*
1977, 1979, 1981, 1983–84
*World Cup (Team)*
1979, 1981, 1983, 1985, 1987, 1989
*World Cup (Ind)*
1983, 1985, 1987, 1989
*British Open*
1978, 1981, 1983, 1985–86
*News of the World*
1983–84
*World Pairs*
1987 (with Peter Locke)

## People Playing Sports and Exercising

| Great Britain | | | | | Percentages and numbers | | | | | |
|---|---|---|---|---|---|---|---|---|---|---|
| | Males | | | | | Females | | | | |
| | 16–19 | 20–29 | 30–59 | 60 and over | All aged 16 and over | | 16–19 | 20–29 | 30–59 | 60 and over | All aged 16 and over |
| Percentage in each group participating in each activity in the 4 weeks before interview | | | | | | | | | | | |
| Pedal cyling | 28 | 12 | 10 | 5 | 10 | 14 | 8 | 8 | 2 | 7 |
| Track and field athletics | 4 | 1 | – | 0 | 1 | 2 | – | – | 0 | – |
| Jogging, cross-country/ road running | 18 | 17 | 7 | – | 8 | 10 | 5 | 2 | – | 3 |
| Association Football | 40 | 22 | 5 | – | 10 | 2 | 1 | – | 0 | – |
| Rugby union/league | 4 | 2 | – | 0 | 1 | 0 | 0 | 0 | 0 | 0 |
| Cricket | 7 | 5 | 2 | – | 2 | – | – | – | 0 | – |
| Tennis | 6 | 4 | 2 | – | 2 | 4 | 2 | 2 | – | 1 |
| Netball | – | – | – | 0 | – | 6 | 1 | – | 0 | 1 |
| Basketball | 7 | 1 | – | 0 | 1 | 4 | – | – | 0 | – |
| Golf, pitch and putt, putting | 9 | 9 | 7 | 4 | 7 | 1 | 1 | 1 | 1 | 1 |
| Swimming or diving | 24 | 20 | 14 | 3 | 13 | 24 | 20 | 14 | 3 | 13 |
| Fishing | 7 | 5 | 4 | 1 | 4 | 1 | 1 | – | 0 | – |
| Yachting or dinghy sailing | 1 | 1 | 1 | – | 1 | 1 | 1 | – | – | – |
| Other water sports | 4 | 3 | 2 | – | 2 | 2 | 1 | 1 | 0 | 1 |
| Horse riding, show jumping, pony trekking | 1 | – | 1 | – | – | 6 | 3 | 1 | – | 1 |
| Badminton | 11 | 6 | 4 | – | 4 | 12 | 5 | 3 | – | 3 |
| Squash | 8 | 8 | 4 | – | 4 | 4 | 3 | 1 | 0 | 1 |
| Table tennis | 14 | 5 | 3 | 1 | 4 | 6 | 2 | 1 | – | 1 |
| Snooker, pool, billiards | 62 | 49 | 23 | 6 | 27 | 23 | 11 | 3 | – | 5 |
| Darts | 33 | 25 | 13 | 3 | 14 | 11 | 7 | 4 | 1 | 4 |
| Tenpin bowls or skittles | 4 | 3 | 2 | – | 2 | 4 | 2 | 2 | – | 1 |
| Lawn or carpet bowls | 2 | 1 | 2 | 4 | 2 | 1 | 1 | 1 | 1 | 1 |
| Boxing or wrestling | 2 | 1 | – | 0 | – | – | – | 0 | 0 | – |
| Self defence | 5 | 3 | 1 | – | 1 | 1 | 1 | – | 0 | – |
| Weight training/lifting | 22 | 17 | 5 | – | 7 | 9 | 5 | 2 | – | 2 |
| Gymnastics | 1 | – | – | – | – | 1 | – | – | 0 | – |
| Keep fit, yoga, aerobics, dance exercise | 5 | 6 | 5 | 3 | 5 | 24 | 20 | 12 | 5 | 12 |
| Skiing | 2 | 1 | 1 | – | 1 | 1 | 1 | – | 0 | – |
| Ice skating | 4 | 1 | – | – | 1 | 5 | 1 | – | 0 | – |
| Curling | 0 | – | – | 0 | – | 0 | 0 | 0 | 0 | 0 |
| Motor sports | 3 | 2 | 1 | 0 | 1 | – | – | – | 0 | – |
| Sample size (= 100%) numbers) | 706 | 1,725 | 4,476 | 2,179 | 9,086 | 678 | 1,923 | 4,826 | 3,016 | 10,443 |

*Source: Social Trends 1991*

**Bryant** David 1931– . English flat-green (lawn) bowls player. He has won every honour the game has offered, including four outdoor world titles (three singles and one triples) and three indoor titles.

CAREER HIGHLIGHTS

*World outdoor champion*
singles: 1966, 1980 (singles and triples), 1988
*World indoor champion*
1979–81
*Commonwealth Games*
singles: 1962, 1970, 1974, 1978
fours: 1962
*English Bowling Association titles*
singles: 1960, 1966, 1971–73, 1975

pairs: 1965, 1969, 1974
triples: 1966, 1977
fours: 1957, 1968–69, 1971

**Budge** Donald 1915– . US tennis player who was the first to perform the Grand Slam when he won the Wimbledon, French, US, and Australian championships all in 1938. He won 14 Grand Slam events in all, including Wimbledon singles twice.

CAREER HIGHLIGHTS

*Wimbledon*
singles: 1937–38
doubles: 1937–38
mixed: 1937–38

*US Open*
singles: 1937–38
doubles: 1936, 1938
mixed: 1937–38
*French Open*
singles: 1938
*Australian Open*
singles: 1938

---

**Campese** David 1962– . Australian rugby union player who holds the record for the most tries scored in senior international rugby (34 tries in 48 internationals up to May 1990).

**Caslavska** Vera 1943– . Czechoslovak gymnast, the first of the great present-day stylists. She won a record 21 world, Olympic and European gold medals 1959-68; she also won eight silver and three bronze medals.

CAREER HIGHLIGHTS

*Olympic champion*
overall individual: 1964, 1968
beam: 1964, 1968
vault: 1964, 1968
floor exercise: 1968
*World champion*
overall individual: 1966
vault: 1962, 1966.

---

**Cauthen** Steve 1960– . US jockey. He rode Affirmed to the US Triple Crown in 1978 at the age of 18 and won 487 races in 1977. Since 1979 he has ridden in England, and has twice won the Derby, on Slip Anchor in 1985 and on Reference Point in 1987. He was UK champion jockey in 1984, 1985, and 1987.

**Charlton** Bobby (Robert) 1937– . English footballer, younger brother of Jack Charlton, who scored a record 49 goals in 106 appearances. He was an elegant midfield player renowned for his sportsmanlike attitude and the fierce long-range shots in which he specialized. Moore spent most of his playing career with Manchester United. On retiring he had an unsuccessful spell as manager of Preston North End. He later became a director of Manchester United.

CAREER HIGHLIGHTS

*Football League appearances* 644, goals 206
*International appearances* 106, goals 49
*World Cup* 1966
*Football League championship* 1965, 1967
*FA Cup* 1963
*European Cup* 1968
*Footballer of the Year* 1966
*European Footballer of the Year* 1966

---

**Clark** Jim (James) 1936–1968. Scottish-born motor-racing driver who was twice world champion, in 1963 and 1965. He spent all his Formula One career with Lotus. Clark won 25 Formula One Grand Prix races, a record at the time, before losing his life at Hockenheim, West Germany, in April 1968 during a Formula Two race.

CAREER HIGHLIGHTS

*World Champion* 1963, 1965 (both Lotus)
*Formula One Grand Prix* races 72, wins 25
*1st Grand Prix* Dutch Grand Prix (Lotus) 1960
*Last Grand Prix* South African Grand Prix (Lotus) 1968

**Cobb** Ty(rus Raymond), nicknamed 'the Georgia Peach' 1886–1961. US baseball player, one of the greatest batters and base runners of all time. He played for Detroit and Philadelphia 1905–28, and won the American League batting average championship 12 times. He holds the record for runs scored, 2,254, and batting average, .367. He had 4,191 hits in his career—a record that stood for almost 60 years.

**Coe** Sebastian 1956– . English middle-distance runner, Olympic 1,500-metre champion 1980 and 1984. He became Britain's most prolific world-record breaker with eight outdoor world records and three indoor world records 1979–81. In 1990 he announced his retirement after failing to win a Commonwealth Games title and is now pursuing a political career with the Conservative Party.

CAREER HIGHLIGHTS

*Olympic Games*
1980: 1,500 metres gold, 800 metres silver
1984: 1,500 metres gold, 800 metres silver
*World records*
800 metres: 1979, 1981
1,000 metres: 1980, 1981
one mile: 1979, 1981 (twice)
1,500 metres: 1979
4 x 800 metres relay: 1982

---

**Comaneci** Nadia 1961– . Romanian gymnast. She won three gold medals at the 1976 Olympics at the age of 14, and was the first gymnast to record a perfect score of 10 in international competition. Upon retirement she became a coach of the Romanian team. She defected to Canada 1989.

CAREER HIGHLIGHTS

*Olympic Games*
1976: gold: beam, vault, floor exercise
1980: gold: beam, parallel bars

---

**Connolly** Maureen 1934–1969. US lawn-tennis player, nicknamed 'Little Mo' because she was just 91 cm/5 ft 2 in tall. In 1953 she became the first woman to complete the Grand Slam by winning all four major tournaments. All her singles titles (at nine major championships) and her Grand Slam titles were won between 1951 and 1954. Her career ended 1954 after a riding accident.

CAREER HIGHLIGHTS

*Wimbledon*

singles: 1952–54
*US Open*
singles: 1951–53
*French Open*
singles: 1953–54
doubles: 1954
mixed: 1954
*Australian Open*
singles: 1953
doubles: 1953.

---

**Connors** Jimmy 1952– . US lawn-tennis player. He won the Wimbledon title 1974, and has since won ten Grand Slam events. He was one of the first players to popularize the two-handed backhand. A popular and entertaining player, he became well known for his 'grunting' during play.
CAREER HIGHLIGHTS

---

*Wimbledon*
singles: 1974, 1982
doubles: 1973
*US Open*
singles: 1974, 1976, 1978, 1982–83
doubles: 1975
*Australian Open*
singles: 1974

---

**Court** Margaret (born Smith) 1942– . Australian tennis player. The most prolific winner in the women's game, she won a record 64 Grand Slam titles, including 25 at singles. Court was the first from her country to win the ladies title at Wimbledon (1963) and the second woman after Maureen Connolly to complete the Grand Slam (1970).
CAREER HIGHLIGHTS

---

*Wimbledon*
singles: 1963, 1965, 1970
doubles: 1964, 1969
mixed: 1963, 1965–66, 1968, 1975
*US Open*
singles: 1962, 1965, 1968–70, 1973
doubles: 1963, 1968–70, 1973, 1975
mixed: 1961–65, 1969–70, 1972
*French Open*
singles: 1962, 1964, 1969–70, 1973
doubles: 1964–66, 1973
mixed: 1963–65, 1969
*Australian Open*
singles: 1960–66, 1969–71, 1973
doubles: 1961–63, 1965, 1969–71, 1973
mixed: 1963–64

---

**Davis** Steve 1957– . English snooker player who has won every major honour in the game since turning professional 1978. Davis won his first major title 1980 when he won the Coral UK Championship. He has been world champion six times, and has also won world titles at Pairs and with the England team.
CAREER HIGHLIGHTS

---

*World Professional champion*
1981, 1983–84, 1987–89

*World Pairs Championship* (with Tony Meo)
1982–83, 1985–86
*World Team Championship*
1981, 1983, 1988–89.

---

**Dempsey** Jack 1895–1983. US heavyweight boxing champion, nicknamed 'the Manassa Mauler'. He beat Jess Willard 1919 to win the title and held it until losing to Gene Tunney 1926. He engaged in the 'Battle of the Long Count' with Tunney 1927.

CAREER HIGHLIGHTS

---

fights: 79
wins: 64
draws: 9
defeats: 6

---

**DiMaggio** Joe 1914– . US baseball player with the New York Yankees 1936–51. In 1941 he set a record by getting hits in 56 consecutive games. He was an outstanding fielder, hit 361 home runs, and had a career average of .325. He was once married to the actress Marilyn Monroe.

**Edberg** Stefan 1966– . Swedish lawn-tennis player. He won the junior Grand Slam 1983 and his first senior Grand Slam title, the Australian Open, two years later. He has since won three Grand Slam events. At Wimbledon in 1987, he became the first male player in 40 years to win a match in straight sets (without conceding a game).

CAREER HIGHLIGHTS

---

*Wimbledon*
singles: 1988, 1990
*Australian Open*
singles: 1985, 1987
doubles: 1987
*US Open*
doubles: 1987

---

**Edwards** Gareth 1947– . Welsh rugby union player. He was appointed captain of his country when only 20 years old. Edwards appeared in seven championship-winning teams, five Triple Crown-winning teams, and two Grand-Slam-winning teams. He scored 20 tries in 53 international matches.

CAREER HIGHLIGHTS

---

*International Championship*
1969, 1970*, 1971, 1972*, 1975–76, 1978
*Triple Crown*
1969, 1971, 1976–78
*Grand Slam*
1976, 1978
*British Lions Tours*
1968 to South Africa, 1971 to New Zealand, 1974 to South Africa
( *denotes title shared)

---

# THE RETURN OF SOUTH AFRICA TO WORLD-CLASS SPORT

The return of South Africa to international sport is an exciting development. Many enthusiasts will doubtless wonder how their own particular sport will be affected by the athletes from the tip of Africa.

Because the territory was formerly under British influence, the sporting set-up in South Africa, both from the playing and the social angle, is very colonial. Sport dominates many people's lives, to the point where it was once suggested that the only effective sanction against South Africa would be an embargo on Wimbledon, the Open golf, and the Cup Final. The schools of the privileged lay great importance on outdoor activities and exercise, and the facilities for whites at club houses and stadiums are second to none.

In the major sports, it can be assumed that the South Africans will return to world ratings similar to those they previously enjoyed. When South Africa left the world stage in 1970, their cricketers were the best in the world. Graeme Pollock had scored three test centuries by the age of 21; Barry Richards and Mike Procter were, respectively, the best opening bat and and all-rounder on the test scene; Dennis Lindsay had scored 500 runs in a series against Australia; and Peter Pollock was as fine an opening bowler as any team captain could wish for. Today, these names will be familiar to many via the county cricket circuit. English counties were happy to employ South African players, who were of test standard yet never called away for international duty.

Clive Rice (Nottinghamshire), Jimmy Cook (Somerset), and Allan Donald (Warwickshire) will be strong contenders indeed for a place on a South African cricket team. Of the home-based players, Tim Shaw, the Eastern Province spinner, Mark Rushmere, the Eastern Province opening bat, and the Western Province fast bowler Craig Matthews will be almost certain of places. South Africa's batting line-up would be stronger, had not the Smith brothers, Allan Lamb, and Graeme Hick become part of the English scene.

When South Africa returns to international rugby union, the bookies may well put them straight in as co-favourites with New Zealand for a place in any World Cup final. An Afrikaaner-dominated sport, rugby has survived in style in South Africa with palatial stadiums, fanatical following, and an endless supply of talent from the schools and universities. If the likes of Naas Botha and Danie Gerber are getting a little past their best, there is no shortage of players to take their place.

Football, boxing, and athletics have long been totally integrated. Boxing received a tremendous boost when Gerrie Coetzee became world heavyweight champion in 1983. Recently the splendid junior lightweight Brian Mitchell has defended his world title some 13 times, and the International Boxing Foundation junior featherweight champion Welcome Ncita is fast becoming a hero in the townships.

Football commands crowds of 70,000 to the Kaiser Chiefs, Orlando Pirates, and Cosmos matches. Several former English professionals have graced the scene in their later years and if the standard is still that of the lower half of England's second division, South Africa's readmittance into FIFA will cause an explosion.

In athletics, too, there is untapped international talent. The hurdlers Myrtle Bothma and Dries Vorster have world-ranking times, as does the new middle-distance star Elana Meyer. Zola Budd-Pieterze was portly on her return to the track, but her times are coming down as the weight is being shed. When sanctions were introduced, the athletes took up challenges such as the Iron Man (swimming, cycling, and marathon in succession), the Two Oceans race (56 km/35 mi around Cape Town's hills), and the Comrades' Marathon (90 km/56 mi) from Durban to Pietermaritzburg. What is required now is the integration of these athletes back into Olympic disciplines.

Elsewhere South Africans continue to make the news. Mark McNulty, a top European golfer, is more Durban than the Harare flag under which he flies. Michael 'Mouse' Roberts, 11 times champion jockey, is beginning to impinge on the Carson and Eddery monopoly. Incoming sanctions-busting tourists, on the other hand, have usually been has-beens or never-weres, described as 'world-class' by South African newspapers simply because they come from far away. When South Africa re-enters international sport, it may regain a sense of perspective.

*Athlete Zola Budd.*

**Eusebio** Adopted name of Eusebio Ferreira da Silva 1942– . Portuguese footballer. He made his international debut 1961 and played for his country 77 times. He spent most of his league career with Benfica, but also played in the USA. He was European Footballer of the Year 1965.

**Evert** Chris(tine) 1954– . US tennis player. She won her first Wimbledon title 1974, and has since won 21 Grand Slam titles. From 1974–89 at Wimbledon she has never failed to reach the quarter-finals at least. She is renowned for an outstanding two-handed backhand and is a great exponent of baseline technique. She became the first woman tennis player to win $1 million in prize money.

CAREER HIGHLIGHTS

*Wimbledon*
singles: 1974, 1976, 1981
doubles: 1976
*US Open*
singles: 1975–78, 1980, 1982
*French Open*
singles: 1974–75, 1979–80, 1983, 1985–86
doubles: 1974–75
*Australian Open*
singles: 1982, 1984

**Faldo** Nick 1957– . English golfer who was the first Briton in 40 years to win two British Open titles, and the only person after Jack Nicklaus to win two successive US Masters titles (1989 and 1990). He is one of only six golfers to win the Masters and British Open in the same year.

CAREER HIGHLIGHTS

*British Open:* 1987, 1989
*US Masters:* 1989, 1990
*PGA Championship:* 1978, 1980-81, 1989
*Ryder Cup winning team:* 1985, 1987, tie 1989.

**Ferrari** Enzo 1898–1988. Italian founder of the Ferrari car empire, which specializes in Grand Prix racing cars and high-quality sports cars. He was a racing driver for Alfa Romeo in the 1920s, went on to become one of their designers and in 1929 took over their racing division. In 1947 the first 'true' Ferrari was seen. The Ferrari car has won more world championship Grands Prix than any other car.

**Finney** Tom (Thomas) 1922– . English footballer, known as the 'Preston Plumber'. His only Football League club was his home-town team, Preston North End. He played for England 76 times, and in every forward position. Finney was celebrated for his ball control and goal-scoring skills, and was the first person to win the Footballer of the Year award twice.

CAREER HIGHLIGHTS

*Football League appearances:* 433; goals: 187
*international appearances:* 76; goals: 30
*FA Cup (runners-up medal):* 1954

*Footballer of the Year:* 1954, 1957

**Francome** John 1952– . British jockey who holds the record for the most National Hunt winners (over hurdles or fences). Between 1970 and 1985 he rode 1,138 winners from 5,061 mounts—the second person (after Stan Mellor) to ride 1,000 winners. He took up training after retiring from riding.

CAREER HIGHLIGHTS

Cheltenham Gold Cup: 1978
Champion Hurdle: 1981
Hennessy Cognac Gold Cup: 1983–84
King George VI Chase: 1982
Champion Jockey: 1979, 1981–85 (shared title 1982)

**Gavaskar** Sunil Manohar 1949– . Indian cricketer. Between 1971 and 1987 he scored a record 10,122 test runs in a record 125 matches (including 106 consecutive tests).

CAREER HIGHLIGHTS

*all first-class matches*
runs: 25,834
average: 51.46
best: 340 (Bombay v. Bengal 1981–82)
*test cricket*
runs: 10,122
average: 51.12
best: 236 not out (India v. West Indies 1983–84)

**Gooch** Graham Alan 1953– . English cricketer who plays for Essex county and England. He made his first-class cricket debut in 1973, and was first capped for England two years later. Banned for three years for captaining a team for a tour of South Africa in 1982, he was later reinstated as England captain 1989. He scored a world record 456 runs in a test match against India in 1990.

CAREER HIGHLIGHTS

*all first-class matches*
runs: 31,363
average: 46.46
best: 333 (England v. India 1990)
wickets: 213
average: 34.46
best: 7 for 14 (Essex v. Worcestershire 1982)
*test matches*
runs: 5,910
average: 41.62
best: 333 (England v. India 1990)
wickets: 15
average: 47.80
best: 2 for 12 (England v. India 1981–82)

**Gower** David 1957– . English left-handed cricketer who played for Leicestershire 1975-89 and for Hampshire from 1990. England's most capped cricketer, he began the 1991 season needing 34 runs to beat Geoff Boycott's

English test record aggregate (8,114 runs). He scored over 23,000 runs in first-class cricket to 1991.
CAREER HIGHLIGHTS

*test cricket*
appearances (to April 1991): 114
runs: 8,081
average: 44.15
best: 215 (England v. Australia 1985)

**Grace** W(illiam) G(ilbert) 1848–1915. English cricketer. By profession a doctor, he became the best batsman in England. Grace began playing first-class cricket at the age of 16, scored 152 runs in his first test match, and scored the first triple century 1876.

CAREER HIGHLIGHTS

*all first-class matches*
runs: 54,896
average: 39.55
best: 344 (MCC v. Kent 1876)
wickets: 2,876
average: 17.92
best: 10 for 49 (MCC v. Oxford University 1886)
*test cricket*
runs: 1,098
average: 32.29
best: 170 (v. Australia 1886)
wickets: 9
average: 26.22
best: 2 for 12 (v. Australia 1890)

**Graf** Steffi 1969– . German lawn-tennis player who brought Martina Navratilova's long reign as the world's number-one female player to an end. Graf reached the semifinal of the US Open 1985 at the age of 16, and won five consecutive Grand Slam singles titles 1988–89.

CAREER HIGHLIGHTS

*Wimbledon*
singles: 1988–89
doubles: 1988
*US Open*
singles: 1988–89
*French Open*
singles: 1987–88
*Australian Open*
singles: 1988–90

**Green** Lucinda (born Prior-Palmer) 1953– . British three-day eventer. She won the Badminton Horse Trials a record six times 1973–84 and was world individual champion 1982.

**Gretzky** Wayne 1961– . Canadian ice-hockey player, probably the best in the history of the National Hockey League (NHL). He took 11 years to break the NHL scoring record—1,979 points at the beginning of the 1990–91 season (surpassing Gordie Howe's 1,850 points accumulated over 26 years). He plays with the Edmonton Oilers and the Los Angeles Kings.

CAREER HIGHLIGHTS

Stanley Cup winner 1984, 1985, 1987, 1988
Hart Memorial Trophy (NHL's most valuable player) 1988–89
Ross Trophy (most points in regular season) 1981–90

**Griffith-Joyner** (born Griffith) Delorez Florence 1959– . US track athlete, nicknamed 'Flo-Jo', who won three gold medals at the 1988 Seoul Olympics, the 100 and 200 metres and the sprint relay. Her time in the 200 metres was a world record 21.34 seconds.

**Hadlee** Richard John 1951– . New Zealand cricketer. In 1987 he surpassed Ian Botham's world record of 373 wickets in test cricket and went on to set the record at 431 wickets. He played for Tasmania in Australia, and for Canterbury and Nottinghamshire in England; he retired from international cricket in 1990.
CAREER HIGHLIGHTS

*all first-class matches*
runs: 12,052
average: 31.78
best: 210 not out (Nottinghamshire v. Middlesex 1984)
wickets: 1,490
average: 18.11
best: 9 for 52 (New Zealand v. Australia 1985–86)
*test cricket*
appearances: 86
runs: 3,124
average: 27.16
best: 151 not out (New Zealand v. Sri Lanka 1986–87)
wickets: 431
average: 22.29
best: 9 for 52 (New Zealand v. Australia 1985–86)

**Hendry** Stephen 1970– . Scottish snooker player.He replaced Steve Davis as the top-ranking player during the 1989–90 season, and became the youngest ever world champion.
CAREER HIGHLIGHTS

Embassy World Professional Championship 1990
Rothmans Grand Prix 1987
MIM Britannia British Open 1988
Benson and Hedges Masters 1989–90
Stormseal UK Open 1989
555 Asian Open 1989
Dubai Duty Free Classic 1989

**Hick** Graeme 1966– . Rhodesian-born cricketer who became Zimbabwe's youngest professional cricketer at the age of 17. A prolific batsman, he joined Worcestershire, England, in 1984. He achieved the highest score in England in the 20th century in 1988 against Somerset with 405 not out. He made his test debut for England in 1991 after a seven-year qualification period.

CAREER HIGHLIGHTS

*first class cricket*
runs: 15,080

## WHO'D BE A REFEREE?

In these days of sponsorship, big prize money, corporate entertainment, and trial by television, pressure on referees and umpires has become so acute that many sports are seriously considering changing the role of referees and umpires to professional status. Indeed, many sports have already taken the step.

Most officials will tell you that they become referees or umpires to stay in contact with the game they love, rather than for remuneration or keeping fit. But with the implications of a wrong decision—or, indeed, a correct one—tied up in so much finance, honour, and even greed, several associations are putting the role of the officials right at the top of their agendas.

Take, for example, the 1991 Football Association Cup Final between Tottenham Hotspur and Nottingham Forest. Referee Roger Milford is one of the UK's most experienced officials—he began refereeing in 1972 and reached the League lists in 1981—yet he had the sort of afternoon at Wembley that must have tested his sense of humour. Within the first half he had to make split-second judgements on:

—whether to book Paul Gascoigne, the somewhat tarnished national hero, for putting his boot into the stomach of Forest's Garry Parker in the very first minute;

—whether to book Gascoigne or send him off (or neither) when he fouled Gary Charles with an awful tackle that caused a longterm injury;

—the legitimacy of the goal scored by Forest's Stuart Pearce from the subsequent free kick for the foul on Charles, when Lee Glover had clearly manhandled Gary Mabbutt out of the Tottenham defensive wall;

—whether to disallow an equalizing goal by Gary Lineker for offside, when Milford's linesman may have failed him;

—whether to book or send off Forest keeper Mark Crossley for fouling Lineker for Tottenham's penalty award.

The whys and wherefores of those incidents will be discussed in pubs and clubs far beyond the boundaries of north London and Nottingham, and perhaps the last word ought to be with Milford, who said in a TV interview before the final: 'I may make mistakes, but they will all be honest mistakes, and that is why I won't worry'.

In other sports, there is the same concern. Back in 1977, the best rugby-union referee in the world at the time, Norman Sanson, retired, believed to be deeply upset at the lack of official sanction for his decision to send Willie Duggan and Geoff Wheel from the pitch in the Wales v. Ireland match that season. Rugby has made progress from that day: referees now run the touchline at international matches and are given the brief to enter the field of play if they see misdemeanours. It makes one wonder what Sir Denis Thatcher would have thought of it all—he ran the line for England against France in 1956.

*England cricket captain Mike Gatting and umpire Shakhoor Rana.*

Other sports try to offer different solutions. First-class cricket umpires are invariably former international or county players who have years of experience at the top level. The former Fraud Squad police officer Nigel Plews is just about the only umpire at international level who has not been a first-class cricketer. Yet the predominance of former players fails to halt increasing verbal attacks on umpires. Remember when a day's play was lost during the Pakistan–England test after an argument between England cricket captain Mike Gatting and umpire Shakhoor Rana?

Then again, who would want to umpire John McEnroe with a sore head, or Jimmy Connors? Quiz questions often ask who the unfortunate was who was called 'the pits of the world' by an irate McEnroe. The tennis authorities have now appointed professional umpires, which has eased friction. Boxing referees have always had the problem of deciding when to stop a fight; snooker has to deal with Alex Higgins; and a sin bin in rugby league often looks like a crowded bus shelter.

What is the answer? Professional referees and umpires are certainly a step in the right direction. In American football, television evidence is used to make hairline decisions, but would all sports tolerate the stoppage time necessary to discuss the point? The flow of the game would be seriously impaired. Would sponsorship money to performers be better spent on allowances for training of officials? Fortunately, society still breeds brave souls who will enable the sport to survive. Characters such as Dickie Bird, Clive Norling, and 'Ballcrusher' Ganley survive with skill and humour. Perhaps it is more of that mixture that is required.

average: 64.17
best: 405 (Worcestershire v. Somerset 1988)

**Hobbs** Jack (John Berry) 1882–1963. English cricketer who represented his country 61 times. In first-class cricket he scored a world record 61,237 runs, including a record 197 centuries in a career that lasted nearly 30 years.

CAREER HIGHLIGHTS

*all first class matches*
runs: 61,237
average: 50.65
best: 316 not out (Surrey v. Middlesex 1926)
*test cricket*
runs: 5,410
average: 56.94
best: 211 (v. South Africa 1924)

**Howe** Gordie 1926– . Canadian ice-hockey player who played for the Detroit Red Wings (National Hockey League) 1946–71 and then the New England Whalers (World Hockey Association). In the NHL, he scored more goals (801), assists (1,049), and points (1,850) than any other player in ice-hockey history until beaten by Wayne Gretsky. Howe played professional hockey until he was over 50.

**Hutton** Leonard 1916–1990. English cricketer. He captained England in 23 test matches 1952–56 and was England's first professional captain. In 1938 at the Oval he scored 364 against Australia, a world record test score until beaten by Gary Sobers 1958.

CAREER HIGHLIGHTS

*all first class matches*
runs: 40,140
average: 55.51
best: 364 (England v. Australia 1938)
*test cricket*
runs: 6,971
average: 55.51
best: 364 (England v. Australia 1938)

**Irvine** Andy (Andrew Robertson) 1951– . British rugby union player who held the world record for the most points scored in senior international rugby with 301 (273 for Scotland, 28 for the British Lions) between 1972 and 1982.

CAREER HIGHLIGHTS

international appearances: 60 (Scotland 51, British Lions 9)
international championship wins: 1973 (shared title)
British Lions tours: 1974 to South Africa, 1977 to New Zealand and Fiji, 1980 to South Africa (as a replacement)

**Johnson** Ben 1961– . Canadian sprinter. In 1987, he broke the world record for the 100 metres, running it in 9.83 seconds. At the

Olympic Games 1988, he again broke the record, but was disqualified and suspended for using anabolic steroids to enhance his performance.

**Johnson** Jack 1878–1968. US heavyweight boxer. He overcame severe racial prejudice to become the first black heavyweight champion of the world 1908 when he travelled to Australia to challenge Tommy Burns. The US authorities wanted Johnson 'dethroned' because of his colour but could not find suitable challengers until 1915, when he lost the title in a dubious fight decision to the giant Jess Willard.

CAREER HIGHLIGHTS

fights: 107
wins: 86
draws: 11
defeats: 10

**Jones** Bobby (Robert Tyre) 1902–1971. US golfer who was the game's greatest amateur player. He never turned professional but won 13 major amateur and professional tournaments, including the Grand Slam of the amateur and professional opens of both the USA and the UK 1930. Jones finished playing competitive golf 1930, but maintained his contacts with the sport and was largely responsible for inaugurating the US Masters.

CAREER HIGHLIGHTS

British Open: 1926–27, 1930
US Open: 1923, 1926, 1929–30
British Amateur: 1930
US Amateur: 1924–25, 1927–28, 1930
US Walker Cup team: 1922, 1924, 1926, 1928*, 1930*
* indicates playing captain

**Khan** Imran 1952– . Pakistani cricketer. He played county cricket for Worcestershire and Sussex in England, and made his test debut for Pakistan 1971, subsequently playing for his country 82 times. In first-class cricket he has scored over 16,000 runs and taken over 1,200 wickets.

CAREER HIGHLIGHTS

*test cricket*
appearances: 82
runs: 3,541
average: 36.88
best: 136 (Pakistan v. Australia 1989–90)
wickets: 358
average: 22.87
best: 8-58 (Pakistan v. Sri Lanka 1981–82)

**Khan** Jahangir 1963– . Pakistani squash player who won the world open championship a record six times 1981–85 and 1988. He was nine times British Open champion 1982–90, and World Amateur champion 1979, 1983, and 1985. After losing to Geoff Hunt (Australia) in the final of the 1981 British Open he did not lose again until Nov 1986 when he lost to Ross Norman (New Zealand) in the World Open final.

**King** Billie Jean (born Moffitt) 1943– . US lawn-tennis player. She won the Wimbledon singles title six times, the US Open singles title four times, the French Open once, and the Australian Open once. Her 39 Grand Slam events at singles and doubles are third only to Navratilova and Margaret Court.

CAREER HIGHLIGHTS

*Wimbledon*
singles: 1966–68, 1972–73, 1975
doubles: 1961–62, 1965, 1967–68, 1970–73, 1979
mixed: 1967, 1971, 1973–74
*US Open*
singles: 1967, 1971–72, 1974
doubles: 1964, 1967, 1974, 1978, 1980
mixed: 1967, 1971, 1973, 1976
*French Open*
singles: 1972
doubles: 1972
mixed: 1967, 1970
*Australian Open*
singles: 1968
mixed: 1968

**Klammer** Franz 1953– . Austrian skier who won a record 35 World Cup downhill races between 1974 and 1985. He was the combined world champion 1974, Olympic gold medallist 1976, and the World Cup downhill champion 1975–78 and 1983.

**Korbut** Olga 1955– . Soviet gymnast who attracted world attention at the 1972 Munich Olympics with her lively floor routine. She won gold medals for the beam and floor exercises, a silver for the parallel bars, and another gold as member of the winning Soviet team.

**Kristiansen** Ingrid 1956– . Norwegian athlete, an outstanding long-distance runner at 5,000 metres, 10,000 metres, marathon, and cross-country running. She has won all the world's leading marathons. In 1986 she knocked 45.68 seconds off the world 10,000 metres record. She was the world cross-country champion in 1988 and won the London marathon in 1984–1985, 1987–1988.

**Latynina** Larissa Semyonovna 1935– . Soviet gymnast, winner of more Olympic medals than any person in any sport. She won 18 medals between 1956 and 1964, including nine gold medals. During her careeer she won a total of 12 individual Olympic and world championship gold medals.

CAREER HIGHLIGHTS

*Olympic champion*
team: 1956, 1960, 1964
overall individual: 1956, 1960
floor exercise: 1956*, 1960, 1964
vault: 1956
*World champion*

team: 1958, 1962
overall individual: 1958, 1962
vault: 1958
beam: 1958
floor exercise: 1962
asymmetric bars: 1958
* denotes shared title

**Lauda** Niki 1949– . Austrian motor racing driver who won the world championship in 1975, 1977 and 1984. He was also runner-up in 1976 just six weeks after an accident at Nurburgring, West Germany that had left him badly burned. Lauda was Formula Two champion in 1972, and drove for March, BRM, Ferrari, and Brabham before his retirement in 1978. He returned to the sport in 1984 and won his third world title in a McLaren before eventually quitting in 1985 to concentrate on his airline business, Lauda-Air.

CAREER HIGHLIGHTS

*world champion*
1975 Ferrari
1977 Ferrari
1984 McLaren
*Formula One Grand Prix*
races: 171
wins: 25
first: 1974 (Spanish Grand Prix; Ferrari)
last: 1985 (Dutch Grand Prix; McLaren)

**Laver** Rod(ney George) 1938– . Australian lawn tennis player. He was one of the greatest left-handed players, and the only player to perform the Grand Slam twice (1962 and 1969). He won four Wimbledon singles titles, the Australian title three times, the US Open twice, and the French Open twice. He turned professional after winning Wimbledon 1962 but returned when the championships were opened to professionals in 1968.

CAREER HIGHLIGHTS

*Wimbledon*
singles: 1961–62, 1968–69
doubles: 1971
mixed: 1959–60
*US Open*
singles: 1962, 1969
*French Open*
singles: 1962, 1969
doubles: 1961
mixed: 1961
*Australian Open*
singles: 1960, 1962, 1969
doubles: 1959–61, 1969

**LeMond** Greg 1961– . US racing cyclist, the first American to win the Tour de France 1986. Although his career received a setback in 1987 through injury, he recovered sufficiently to regain his Tour de France title in 1989 by seven seconds, the smallest margin ever. He won it again in 1990. He also won the World Professional Road Race in 1983 and 1989.

**Leonard** Sugar Ray 1956– . US boxer. In 1988 he became the first man to have won world titles at five officially recognized weights. He was Olympic light-welterweight champion 1976, and won his first professional title 1979 when he beat Wilfred Benitez for the WBC welterweight title. He later won titles at junior-middleweight (WBA version) 1981, middle-weight (WBC) 1987, light-heavyweight (WBC) 1988, and super-middleweight (WBC) 1988. In 1989 he drew with Thomas Hearns.

**Lewis** Carl (Frederick Carleton) 1961– . US track and field athlete. At the 1984 Olympic Games he equalled the performance of Jesse Owens, winning gold medals in the 100 and 200 metres, sprint relay, and long jump. In the 1988 Olympics, he repeated his golds in the 100 metres and long jump, and won a silver in the 200 metres.

CAREER HIGHLIGHTS

*Olympic Games*
gold: 100 metres 1984, 1988
200 metres 1984
4 x 100 metres relay 1984
long jump 1984, 1988
silver: 200 metres 1988
*World Championships*
gold: 100 metres 1983
4 x 100 metres relay 1983, 1987
long jump 1983, 1987
silver: 100 metres 1987.

**Lopez** Nancy 1957– . US golfer who turned professional 1977 and in 1979 became the first woman to win $200,000 in a season. She has won the US LPGA title three times and has won over 35 tour events, and $3 million in prize money.

**Louis** Joe. Assumed name of Joseph Louis Barrow 1914–1981. US boxer, nicknamed 'the Brown Bomber'. He was world heavyweight champion between 1937 and 1949 and made a record 25 successful defences (a record for any weight). Louis was the longest-reigning world heavyweight champion at 11 years and 252 days before announcing his retirement 1949. He subsequently made a comeback and lost to Ezzard Charles in a world title fight 1950.

CAREER HIGHLIGHTS

Professional fights: 66
wins: 63
knockouts: 49
defeats: 3
1st professional fight: 4 July 1934 v. Jack Kracken *(USA)*
last professional fight: 26 Oct 1951 v. Rocky Marciano *(USA)*

**McBride** Willie John 1940– . Irish Rugby Union player. He was capped 63 times by Ireland, and

won a record 17 British Lions caps. He played on five Lions tours, 1962, 1966, 1968, 1971, and in 1974 as captain when they returned from South Africa undefeated.

**Mantle** Mickey Charles 1931– . US baseball player. Signed by the New York Yankees, he broke into the major leagues 1951. A powerful switchhitter (able to bat with either the left or the right hand), Mantle also excelled as a centre-fielder. In 1956 he won baseball's Triple Crown, leading the American League in batting average, home runs, and runs batted in. He retired 1969 after 18 years with the Yankees and seven World Series championships.

**Maradona** Diego 1960– . Argentine footballer who was voted the best player of the 1980s by the world's press. He helped his country to two successive World Cup finals. Maradona played for Argentinos Juniors and Boca Juniors before leaving South America for Barcelona, Spain, 1982 for a transfer fee of approximately £5 million. He moved to Napoli, Italy, for £9 million 1984, and contributed to their first Italian League title.

CAREER HIGHLIGHTS

World Cup: 1986
UEFA Cup: 1989
Italian League: 1987, 1990
Italian Cup: 1987
Spanish Cup: 1983
South American footballer of the year: 1979, 1980

**Marciano** Rocky (Rocco Francis Marchegiano) 1923–1969. US boxer, world heavyweight champion 1952–56. He retired after 49 professional fights, the only heavyweight champion to retire undefeated. He was killed in a plane crash.

CAREER HIGHLIGHTS

Professional fights: 49
wins: 49
knockouts: 43
defeats: 0
1st professional fight: 17 Mar 1947 v. Lee Epperson *(USA)*
last professional fight: 21 Sept 1955 v. Archie Moore *(USA)*

**Matthews** Stanley 1915– . English footballer who played for Stoke City, Blackpool, and England. An outstanding right-winger, he won the nickname 'the Wizard of the Dribble' because of his ball control. Matthews played nearly 700 Football League games, and won 54 international caps. He continued to play first-division football after the age of 50. He was the first European Footballer of the Year 1956.

CAREER HIGHLIGHTS

Football League appearances: 698, goals: 71
International appearances: 54, goals: 11
FA Cup: 1953
Footballer of the Year: 1948, 1963

European Footballer of the Year: 1956.

**Merckx** Eddie 1945– . Belgian cyclist, known as 'the Cannibal', who won the Tour de France a joint record five times 1969–74. Merckx turned professional 1966 and won his first classic race, the Milan–San Remo, the same year. He went on to win 24 classics as well as the three major tours (of Italy, Spain, and France) a total of 11 times. He was world professional road-race champion three times and in 1971 won a record 54 races in the season. He retired in 1977.

CAREER HIGHLIGHTS

Tour de France: 1969–72, 1974
Tour of Italy: 1968, 1970, 1972–74
Tour of Spain: 1973
world professional champion: 1967, 1971, 1974
world amateur champion: 1964.

**Montana** Joe 1956– . US football player who has appeared in four winning Super Bowls with the San Francisco 49ers 1982, 1985, 1989, and 1990, winning the Most Valuable Player award in 1982, 1985, and 1990. He had five touchdown passes in the 1990 Super Bowl.

**Namath** Joe (Joseph William) 1943– . US football player. An outstanding quarterback, he made his professional debut with the New York Jets 1965, and in the same season passed for a record 4,007 yards. In 1969 he led the team to a momentous upset victory over the Baltimore Colts in the Super Bowl. After leaving the Jets 1977, Namath joined the Los Angeles Rams; however, knee injuries forced his retirement as a player the following year. He later became a sports broadcaster and actor.

**Navratilova** Martina 1956– . Czech tennis player who became a naturalized US citizen 1981. The most outstanding woman player of the 1980s, she had by 1991 won 55 Grand Slam titles, including 18 singles titles. She has won the Wimbledon singles title a record nine times, including six in succession 1982–87.

CAREER HIGHLIGHTS

*Wimbledon*
singles: 1978–79, 1982–87, 1990
doubles: 1976, 1979, 1981–84, 1986
mixed: 1985
*US Open*
singles: 1983–84, 1986–87
doubles: 1977–78, 1980, 1983–84, 1986–90
mixed: 1985, 1987
*French Open*
singles: 1982, 1984
doubles: 1975, 1982, 1984–88
mixed: 1974, 1985
*Australian Open*
singles: 1981, 1983, 1985
doubles: 1980, 1982–85, 1987–89

**Nicklaus** Jack (William) 1940– . US golfer, nicknamed 'the Golden Bear'. He won a record 20 major titles, including 18 professional majors

between 1962 and 1986. When he won the US Masters for a record sixth time 1986 he was the oldest winner at the age of 48 years and 82 days. Nicklaus played for the US Ryder Cup team six times 1969–81 and was nonplaying captain 1983 and 1987 when the event was played over the course he designed at Muirfield Village, Ohio. He was voted the 'Golfer of the Century' 1988.

CAREER HIGHLIGHTS

US Amateur: 1959, 1961
US Open: 1962, 1967, 1972, 1980
British Open: 1966, 1970, 1978
US Masters: 1963, 1965–66, 1972, 1975, 1986
US PGA: 1963, 1971, 1973, 1975, 1980
US Ryder Cup team: 1969, 1971, 1973, 1975, 1977.

**Owens** Jesse (James Cleveland) 1913–1980. US track and field athlete, who excelled in the sprints, hurdles, and the long jump. At the 1936 Berlin Olympics he won four gold medals, and the Nazi leader Hitler is said to have stormed out of the stadium in disgust at the black man's triumph. Owens held the world long jump record for 25 years 1935–60. At Ann Arbor, Michigan, on 25 May 1935, he broke six world records in less than an hour.

CAREER HIGHLIGHTS

*Olympic champion*
100 metres, 200 metres, 4 x 100 metres relay, long jump 1936
*World Records:*
100 metres: 1936
100 yards: 1935, 1936
200 metres: 1935
220 yards: 1935
200 metres hurdles: 1935
220 yards hurdles: 1935
4 x 100 metres relay: 1936 (US National team)
long jump: 1935

**Palmer** Arnold (Daniel) 1929– . US golfer who helped to popularize the professional sport in the USA in the 1950s and 1960s. He won the US amateur title 1954, and went on to win all the world major professional trophies except the US PGA championship. In the 1980s he enjoyed a successful career on the US Seniors Tour.

CAREER HIGHLIGHTS

US Open: 1960
British Open: 1961–62
US Masters: 1958, 1960, 1962, 1964
World Match-Play: 1964, 1967
US Ryder Cup team: 1961, 1963*, 1965, 1967, 1971, 1973, 1975**
* playing captain; ** nonplaying captain

**Pelé** Adopted name of Edson Arantes do Nascimento 1940– . Brazilian soccer player who was celebrated as one of the finest inside-forwards in the history of the game. A prolific goal scorer, he appeared in four World Cup competitions 1958–70 and led Brazil to three championships. He spent most of his playing career with the Brazilian team, Santos, before ending it with the New York Cosmos in the USA.

CAREER HIGHLIGHTS

first-class appearances: 1,363
total first-class goals: 1,281
world cup winner: 1958, 1962, 1970
Brazilian Cup: 1962-64, 1968
World Club Championship: 1962-63

**Piggott** Lester 1935– . English jockey. He is regarded as a brilliant tactician and has adopted a unique high riding style. A champion jockey 11 times between 1960 and 1982, he has ridden a record nine Derby winners. He retired from riding 1985 and took up training, but returned to racing 1990. In 1987 he was imprisoned for tax evasion.

CAREER HIGHLIGHTS

Champion Jockey: 1960, 1964–71, 1981–82
Derby: 1954, 1957, 1960, 1968, 1970, 1972, 1976–77, 1983
Oaks: 1957, 1959, 1966, 1975, 1981, 1984
St Leger: 1960–61, 1967–68, 1970–72, 1984
1,000 Guineas: 1970, 1981
2,000 Guineas: 1957, 1968, 1970, 1985

**Prost** Alain 1955– . French motor-racing driver who was world champion 1985, 1986, and 1989, the first French world drivers' champion. He raced in Formula One events from 1980 and he had his first Grand Prix win 1981 (French Grand Prix) driving a Renault. In 1984 he began driving for the McLaren team. By the beginning of 1991 he had won a record 44 Grands Prix from 169 starts.

He is known as 'the Professor'.

CAREER HIGHLIGHTS

*World champion:*
1985 (Marlboro–McLaren)
1986 (Marlboro–McLaren)
1989 (Marlboro–Honda)
*Formula One Grand Prix*
races: 168
wins: 44 (record)
1st Grand Prix: 1980 Argentine GP (McLaren)

**Rhodes** Wilfred 1877–1973. English cricketer who took more wickets than anyone else in the game—4,187 wickets 1898–1930—and also scored 39,802 first-class runs. Playing for Yorkshire, Rhodes made a record 763 appearances in the county championship. He took 100 wickets in a season 23 times and completed the 'double' of 1,000 runs and 100 wickets in a season 16 times (both records). He played his

58th and final game for England, against the West Indies 1930, when he was 52 years old, the oldest ever test cricketer.

CAREER HIGHLIGHTS

*all first class matches*
runs: 39,802
average: 30.83
best: 267 not out (Yorkshire v. Leicestershire 1921)
wickets: 4,187
average: 16.71
best: 9 for 24 (C I Thornton's XI v. Australia 1899)
*test cricket*
runs: 2,325
average: 30.19
best: 179 (v. Australia 1911–12)
wickets: 127
average: 26.96
best: 8 for 68 (v. Australia 1903–04)

**Richards** Gordon 1905–1986. English jockey and trainer who was champion on the flat a record 26 times between 1925 and 1953. He started riding 1920 and rode 4,870 winners from 21,834 mounts before retiring 1954 and taking up training. He rode the winners of all the classic races but only once won the Derby (on Pinza 1953). In 1947 he rode a record 269 winners in a season.

CAREER HIGHLIGHTS

Derby: 1953
Oaks: 1930, 1942
St Leger: 1930, 1937, 1940, 1942, 1944
1,000 Guineas: 1942, 1948, 1951
2,000 Guineas: 1938, 1942, 1947
Champion Jockey: 1925, 1927-29, 1931-40, 1942-53

**Richards** Viv (Isaac Vivian Alexander) 1952– . West Indian cricketer, captain of the West Indies team from 1986. He has played for the Leeward Islands and, in the UK, for Somerset and Glamorgan. A prolific run-scorer, he holds the record for the greatest number of runs made in test cricket in one calendar year (1,710 runs in 1976). Richards announced that he would retire from the West Indies team at the end of the World Cup in 1992.

CAREER HIGHLIGHTS

*all first-class cricket*
runs: 33,033
average: 54.2
best: 322 (Somerset v. Warwickshire 1985)
wickets: 210
average: 44.52
best: 5 for 88 (West Indies v. Queensland 1981–82)
*test cricket*
runs: 7,990
average: 51.21
best: 291 (v. England 1976)
wickets: 32

average: 58.03
best: 2 for 17 (v. Pakistan 1988)

**Roche** Stephen 1959– . Irish cyclist. One of the outstanding riders in Europe in the 1980s, he was the first British winner of the Tour de France 1987 and the first English-speaking winner of the Tour of Italy the same year, as well as the 1987 world professional road-race champion.

**Rodnina** Irina 1949– . Soviet ice skater. Between 1969 and 1980 she won 23 world, Olympic, and European gold medals in pairs competitions. Her partners were Alexei Ulanov and then Alexsandr Zaitsev.

CAREER HIGHLIGHTS

Olympic champion: 1972, 1976, 1980
World champion: 1969-78
European champion: 1969-78

**Ruth** Babe (George Herman) 1895–1948. US baseball player, regarded by many as the greatest of all time. He played in ten World Series and hit 714 home runs, a record that stood from 1935 to 1974 and led to a nickname as the 'Sultan of Swat'. He is still the holder of the record for most bases in a season: 457 in 1921. The New York Yankee stadium is known as 'the house that Ruth built' because of the money he brought into the club.

CAREER HIGHLIGHTS

games: 2,503
runs: 2,174
home runs: 714
average: 0.342
world series wins: 1915–16, 1918, 1923, 1927–28, 1932

**Sawchuk** Terry (Terrance Gordon) 1929–1970. Canadian ice-hockey player, often regarded as the greatest goaltender of all time. He played for Detroit, Boston, Toronto, Los Angeles, and New York Rangers 1950–67, and holds the National Hockey League (NHL) record of 103 shut-outs (games in which he did not concede a goal).

**Scudamore** Peter 1958– . British National Hunt jockey who was champion jockey 1982 (shared with John Francome) and from 1986–1991. In 1988–89 he rode a record 221 winners, and after the 1990–91 season his total of winners stood at a world record 1,374.

**Senna** Ayrton 1960– . Brazilian motor-racing driver. He had his first Grand Prix win in the 1985 Portuguese Grand Prix, and won world driver's title 1988 and 1990. He started his Formula One career with Toleman 1984, went to Lotus 1985–87, and joined McLaren 1988. By the beginning of the 1991 season he had 26 wins in 100 starts, which he improved early on in the season with a record four consecutive victories.

**Shilton** Peter 1949– . English international footballer, an outstanding goalkeeper. He has set records for the highest number of Football league appearances (over 900) and England caps (125). First capped by England 1970, he announced his retirement from international football in 1990, after the England–West Germany World Cup semifinal.

**Shoemaker** Willie (William Lee) 1931– . US jockey, whose career 1949–90 was outstandingly successful. He rode 8,833 winners from 40,351 mounts and his earnings exceeded $123 million. He retired 3 Feb 1990 after finishing 4th on Patchy Groundfog at Santa Anita, California.

CAREER HIGHLIGHTS

US Triple Crown wins:
Kentucky Derby: 1955, 1959, 1965, 1986
Preakness Stakes: 1963, 1967
Belmont Stakes: 1957, 1959, 1962, 1967, 1975
Leading US money winner: 1951, 1953–54, 1958–64

**Sobers** Gary (Garfield St Aubrun) 1936– . West Indian cricketer. One of the game's great all-rounders, he holds the record for the highest test innings, 365 not out. He played English county cricket with Nottinghamshire and while playing for them against Glamorgan at Swansea 1968, he established a world record by scoring six 6s in one over. He played for the West Indies 93 times.

CAREER HIGHLIGHTS

*all first-class cricket*
runs: 28,315
average: 54.87
best: 365 not out (West Indies v. Pakistan 1957–58)
wickets: 1,043
average: 27.74
best: 9 for 49 (West Indies v. Kent 1966)
*test cricket*
runs: 8,032
average: 57.78
best: 365 not out (v. Pakistan 1957–58)
wickets: 235
average: 34.03
best: 6 for 73 (v. Australia 1968–69)

**Spitz** Mark Andrew 1950– . US swimmer who won a record seven gold medals at the 1972 Olympic Games, all in world record times. He won 11 Olympic medals in total (four in 1968) and set 26 world records between 1967 and 1972. After retiring in 1972 he became a film actor, two of his films being elected candidates for 'The Worst of Hollywood'.

CAREER HIGHLIGHTS

*Olympic medals*
*gold*
4 x 100 metres freestyle relay 1968, 1972
4 x 200 metres freestyle relay 1968, 1972
4 x 100 metres medley relay 1972

100 metres freestyle 1972
200 metres freestyle 1972
100 metres butterfly 1972
200 metres butterfly 1972
*silver*
100 metres butterfly 1968
*bronze*
100 metres freestyle 1968

**Stewart** Jackie (John Young) 1939– . Scottish motor-racing driver. Until surpassed by Alain Prost 1987, Stewart held the record for the most Formula One Grand Prix wins (27). With manufacturer Ken Tyrrell, Stewart built up one of the sport's great partnerships. His last race was the 1973 Canadian Grand Prix. He pulled out of the next race (which would have been his 100th) because of the death of his team-mate Francois Cevert. He is now a motor-racing commentator.

CAREER HIGHLIGHTS

*world champion*
1969: Matra
1971: Tyrrell
1973: Tyrrell
*Formula One Grand Prix*
races: 99
wins: 27
first: 1965 (South African Grand Prix; BRM)
last: 1973 (Canadian Grand Prix; Tyrrell)

**Thompson** Daley (Francis Morgan) 1958– . English decathlete who broke the world record four times after winning the Commonwealth Games decathlon title 1978. He won two more Commonwealth titles (1982, 1986), two Olympic gold medals (1980, 1984), three European medals (silver 1978; gold 1982, 1986), and a world title (1983).

**Torvill and Dean** British ice-dance champions Jayne Torvill (1957–  ) and Christopher Dean (1959–  ), both from Nottingham. They won the world title four times 1981–84 and were the 1984 Olympic champions. They turned professional upon ending their competitive careers.

**Tyson** Mike 1966– . US heavyweight boxer, undisputed world champion from Aug 1987 to Feb 1990. He won the WBC heavyweight title 1986 when he beat Trevor Berbick to become the youngest world heavyweight champion. He beat James 'Bonecrusher' Smith for the WBA title 1987 and later that year became the first undisputed champion since 1978 when he beat Tony Tucker for the IBF title. He was undefeated until 1990 when he lost the championship to an outsider, James 'Buster' Douglas. Of Tyson's first 25 opponents, 15 were knocked out in the first round.

**Witt** Katarina 1965– . East German ice-skater. She was 1984 Olympic champion and by 1990 had won four world titles (1984–85, 1987–88) and six consecutive European titles (1983–88).

**Woosnam** Ian 1958– . Welsh golfer who came to prominence 1987 when he became the first UK player to win the Suntory World Match-play

Championship. He has since won many leading tournaments, including the World Cup 1987, World Match-play 1990, and US Masters 1991. Woosnam was Europe's leading money-winner in 1987 (as a result of winning the one-million-dollar Sun City Open in South Africa) and again in 1990.

## SPORTS

*In what sports or exercise do you take part? (All saying 'very/quite' = 100%)*

| | |
|---|---|
| Brisk walking | 48 |
| Dance/fitness classes | 16 |
| Tennis/squash | 12 |
| Running/jogging | 10 |
| Golf | 9 |
| Sailing watersports | 8 |
| Rugby/football | 6 |
| Cricket | 3 |
| Skiing | 3 |
| Hockey/netball | 1 |
| Other | 44 |
| None of these | 6 |

*How important is active sport or exercise in your life?*

| | |
|---|---|
| Very | 18 |
| Quite | 35 |
| Not at all | 46 |
| Don't know | 1 |

### Governing bodies of Olympic sports affiliated to the British Olympic Association

*Amateur Fencing Association* Gillian Kenneally, The de Beaumount Centre, 83 Perham Road, West Kensington, London W14 9SP Tel: 071-385 7442
*Amateur Rowing Association* The Priory, 6 Lower Mall, London W6 9JD Tel: 081-748 3632
*Amateur Swimming Federation of Great Britain* David Reeves, Harold Fern House, Derby Square, Loughborough, Leicestershire LE11 0AL Tel: (0509) 230431
*British Amateur Athletic Board* Edgbaston House, 3 Duchess Place, Hagley Road, Edgbaston, Birmingham B16 8NM Tel: 021-456 4050
*British Amateur Boxing Association* Clive Howe, Francis House, Francis Street, London SW1P 1DE Tel: 071-828 8571
*British Amateur Gymnastics Association* The Secretary, Ford Hall, Lilleshall NSC, Nr Newport, Shropshire TF10 9NB Tel: (0952) 677137
*British Amateur Weightlifters' Association* Walter Holland, 3 Iffley Turn, Oxford OX4 4DU Tel: (0865) 778319
*British Amateur Wrestling Association* Bert Jacob, 2 Huxley Drive, Bramhall, Stockport, Cheshire Tel: 061-832 9209

*British Badminton Olympic Committee* Arthur Jones, 2 Broadstrood, Loughton, Essex IG10 2SE Tel: 081-508 7218

*British Baseball Federation* East Park Lido, Hull HU8 9AW Tel: (0482) 76169

*British Bobsleigh Association* Paul Pruszynski, 111a Cheyne Walk, London SW10 Tel: 071-351 5120

*British and Irish Basketball Federation* Mel Welch, Calomax House, Lupton Avenue, Leeds LS9 7EE Tel: (0532) 496044

*British Canoe Union* Trevor Bailey, Matterley Hall, Lucknow Avenue, Nottingham NG3 5FA Tel: (0602) 691944

*British Cycling Federation* Jim Hendry, 36 Rockingham Road, Kettering, Northamptonshire NN16 8HG Tel: (0536) 412211

*British Equestrian Federation* Malcolm Wallace, British Equestrian Centre, Stoneleigh, Kenilworth, Warwickshire CV8 2LR Tel: (0203) 696697

*British Handball Association* Bridgefield Forum Leisure Centre, Cartbridge Lane, Halewood, Liverpool L26 6LH Tel: 051-443 2124

*British Ice Hockey Association* David Pickles, 48 Hambleton Road, Bournemouth, Hampshire BH7 6PQ Tel: (0202) 432583

*British Judo Association* The Secretary, 9 Islington High Street, London N1 9LQ Tel: 071-833 4424

*British Ski Federation* The Secretary, Brocades House, Pyrford Road, West Byfleet, Surrey KT14 6RA Tel: (0932) 336488

*British Volleyball Association* George Bulman, 13 Rectory Road, West Bridgeford, Nottingham NG2 6BE Tel: (0602) 816324

*Football Association* Graham Kelly, 16 Lancaster Gate, London W2 3LW Tel: 071-262 4542

*Grand National Archery Society* John Middleton, 7th Street, National Agricultural Centre, Stoneleigh, Kenilworth, Warwickshire CV8 2LG Tel: (0203) 696631

*Great Britain Hockey Board* Freddie Scott, Coventry Farmhouse, Hankins Lane, London NW7 3AJ Tel: 081-959 2339

*Great Britain Luge Association* Chris Dyason, 89 Tenison Road, Cambridge CB1 2DG Tel: (0223) 350800

*Great Britain Target Shooting Federation* Lord Roberts House, Bisley Camp, Brookwood, Woking, Surrey GU24 0NP Tel: (04867) 6969

*Joint United Kingdom Table Tennis Committee* Albert Shipley, Third Floor, Queensbury House, Havelock Road, Hastings, East Sussex TN34 1HF Tel: (0424) 722525

*Lawn Tennis Association* Queens Club, West Kensington, London W14 9EG Tel: 071-385 2366

*Modern Pentathlon Association of Great Britain* Pat Chaffey, Q8 Baughurst Road, Baughurst, Basingstoke, Hampshire Tel: 0734-813 735

*National Skating Association* Eric Waughray, 15-23 Geo Street, London EC1V 3RE Tel: 071-253 3824

*Royal Yachting Association* Robin Duchesne, RYA House, Romsey Road, Eastleigh, Hampshire SO5 4YA Tel: (0703) 629962

## Other governing bodies of sports affiliated to the British Olympic Association

*All England Netball Association* L Nicholl, Francis House, Francis Street, London SW1P 1DE Tel: 071-828 2176

*Amateur Athletic Association* M A Farrell, Edgbaston House, 3 Duchess Place, Hagley Road, Edgbaston, Birmingham B16 8NM Tel: 021-456 4050

*Army Sport Control Board* Clayton Barracks, Thornhill Road, Aldershot, Hampshire GU11 2BG Tel: (0252) 24431 x 2569

*British Association of Sport and Medicine* P Thomson, 10 Eldon Road, Reading RG1 4DH Tel: 0734-502 002

*British Clay Pigeon Shooting Association* K Murray, 107 Epping New Road, Buckhurst Hill, Essex IG9 5TQ Tel: 081-505 6221

*British Colleges Sports Association* The Secretary, 28 Woburn Square, London WC1H 0AA Tel: 071-580 3618

*British Karate Federation* B Whelan, 1 Berwick Place, Coatbridge, Nr Glasgow, Scotland

*British Orienteering Federation* R Mason, 1 Dale Road, Matlock, Derbyshire DE4 3LT Tel: (0629) 3991

*British Taekwondo Control Board (WTF)* J Ingram, 53 Geary Road, London NW10 1HJ Tel: 081-450 3818

*British Tenpin Bowling Association* M Glazer, 19 Canterbury Avenue, Ilford, Essex IG1 3NA Tel: 081-478 1745

*British University Athletic Club* The Secretary, 28 Woburn Square, London WC1H 0AA Tel: 071-580 3618

*British Water Ski Federation* G Hill, 90 City Road, London EC1 Tel: 071-833 2855

*Cambridge University Athletic Club* C Thorne, St Catherine's College, Cambridge

*Central Council of Physical Recreation* P Lawson, Francis House, Francis Street, London SW1P 1DE Tel: 071-828 3163

*Civil Service Sports Council* F P Krinks, Minster House, 272/274 Vauxhall Bridge Road, London SW1V 1BW Tel: 071-630 8100

*English Basketball Association* M D Welch, Calomax House, Lupton Avenue, Leeds LS9 7EE Tel: (0532) 496044

*English Lacrosse Union* R Balls, 70 High Road, Rayleigh, Essex SS6 7AD

*Oxford University Athletic Club* F F Brown, c/o Department of Biochemistry, University of Oxford, South Parks Road, Oxford OX1 3QU Tel: (0865) 511281

*Race Walking Association* R Marlow, 11 Parkland, 234 Peckham Rye, London SE22 0LS

*Royal Air Force Sports Board* E I G Geddes, Room 334, Ministry of Defence, Adastral House, Theobalds Road, London WC1X 8RU Tel: 071-430 7295

*R N & R M Sports Control Board* M F O'Reilly, Orion Block, HMS Nelson, Portsmouth, Hampshire PO1 3HH

*Scottish Amateur Athletic Association* R W Greenoak, 18 Ainslie Place, Edinburgh EH3

6AU Tel: 031-229 4401
*Scottish Amateur Boxing Association* W Cowan, 60 St Andrew's Gardens, Dalry, Ayrshire KA24 4JZ
*Scottish Amateur Swimming Association* W Black, Room E1, Pathfoot Building, University of Stirling, Stirling Tel: (0786) 70544
*Universities Athletic Union* I Grant, 28 Woburn Square, London WC1H 0AA Tel: 071-637 4828

*Welsh Amateur Boxing Association* J K Watkins, 8 Erw Wen, Rhiwbina, Cardiff
*Welsh Cross Country Association* J H Collins, Harries Haunt, 40 Twyni-Teg, Killay, Swansea SA2 7NS
*Women's Amateur Athletic Association* M Hartman, Francis House, Francis Street, London SW1P 1DE Tel: 071-828 4731

# THE WORLD

# CONTINENTS

**Africa** second largest of the continents, three times the area of Europe

**area** 30,097,000 sq km/11,620,451 sq mi

**largest cities** (population over 1 million) Cairo, Algiers, Lagos, Kinshasa, Abidjan, Cape Town, Nairobi, Casablanca, El Gîza, Addis Ababa, Luanda, Dar-es Salaam, Ibadan, Douala, Mogadishu

**physical** dominated by a uniform central plateau comprising a southern tableland with a mean altitude of 1,070 m/3,000 ft that falls northwards to a lower elevated plain with a mean altitude of 400 m/1,300 ft. Although there are no great alpine regions or extensive coastal plains, Africa has a mean altitude of 610 m/2,000 ft, two times greater than Europe. The highest points are Mount Kilimanjaro 5,900 m/19,364 ft, and Mount Kenya 5,200 m/17,058 ft; the lowest point is Lac Assal in Djibouti 144 m/471 ft below sea level. Compared with other continents, Africa has few broad estuaries or inlets and therefore has proportionately the shortest coastline (24,000 km/15,000 mi). The geographical extremities of the continental mainland are Cape Hafun in the E, Cape Almadies in the W, Ras Ben Sekka in the N, and Cape Agulhas in the S. The Sahel is a narrow belt of savanna and scrub forest which covers 700 million hectares of west and central Africa; 75% of the continent lies within the tropics

**features** Great Rift Valley, containing most of the great lakes of E Africa (except Lake Victoria); Atlas Mountains in NW; Drakensberg mountain range in SE; Sahara Desert (world's largest desert) in N; Namib, Kalahari, and Great Karoo deserts in S; Nile, Zaïre, Niger, Zambezi, Limpopo, Volta, and Orange rivers

**products** has 30% of the world's minerals including diamonds (51%) and gold (47%); produces 11% of the world's crude petroleum, 58% of the world's cocoa (Ivory Coast, Ghana, Cameroon, Nigeria), 23% of the world's coffee (Uganda, Ivory Coast, Zaïre, Ethiopia, Cameroon, Kenya), 20% of the world's groundnuts (Senegal, Nigeria, Sudan, Zaïre), and 21% of the world's hardwood timber (Nigeria, Zaïre, Tanzania, Kenya)

**population** (1988) 610 million; more than double the 1960 population of 278 million, and rising to an estimated 900 million by 2000; annual growth rate 3% (10 times greater than Europe); 27% of the world's undernourished people live in sub-Saharan Africa where an estimated 25 million are facing famine

**language** over 1,000 languages spoken in Africa; Niger-Kordofanian languages including Mandinke, Kwa, Lingala, Bemba, and Bantu (Zulu, Swahili, Kikuyu), spoken over half of Africa from Mauritania in the W to South Africa; Nilo-Saharan languages, including Dinka, Shilluk, Nuer, and Masai, spoken in Central Africa from the bend of the Niger river to the foothills of Ethiopia; Afro-Asiatic (Hamito-Semitic) languages, including Arabic, Berber, Ethiopian, and Amharic, N of Equator; Khoisan languages with 'click' consonants spoken in SW by Bushmen, Hottentots, and Nama people of Namibia

**religion** Islam in the N and on the E coast as far S as N Mozambique; animism below the Sahara, which survives alongside Christianity (both Catholic and Protestant) in many central and S areas.

**Antarctica** an ice-covered continent surrounding the South Pole

**area** 13,900,000 sq km/5,400,000 sq mi (the size of Europe and the USA combined)

**physical** formed of two blocks of rock with an area of about 8 million sq km/3 million sq mi, Antarctica is covered by a cap of ice that flows slowly towards its 22,400 km/14,000 mi coastline, reaching the sea in high ice cliffs. The most southerly shores are near the 78th parallel in the Ross and Weddell Seas. E Antarctica is a massive block of ancient rocks that surface in the Transantarctic Mountains of Victoria Land. Separated by a deep channel, W Antarctica is characterized by the mountainous regions of Graham Land, the Antarctic Peninsula, Palmer Land and Ellsworth Land; the highest peak is Vinson Massif (5,139 m/16,866 ft). Little more than 1% of the land is ice-free. With an estimated volume of 24 million cu m/283 million cu ft, the ice-cap has a mean thickness of 1,880 m/6,170 ft and in places reaches depths of 5,000 m/16,000 ft or more. Each annual layer of snow preserves a record of global conditions, and where no melting at the surface of the bedrock has occurred the ice can be a million years old. Occupying 10% of the world's surface, the continent contains 90% of the world's ice and 70% of its fresh water. Winds are strong and temperatures are cold, particularly in the interior where temperatures can drop to –70°C/–100°F and below. Precipitation is largely in the form of snow or hoar-frost rather than rain which rarely exceeds 50 mm/2 in in a year (less than the Sahara Desert). The Antarctic ecosystem is characterized by large numbers of relatively few species of higher plants and animals, and a short food chain from tiny marine plants to whales, seals, penguins, and other sea birds. Only two species of vascular plant are known, but there are about 60 species of moss, 100 species of lichen, and 400 species of algae. The crabeater seal is the most numerous wild large mammal in the world

**features** Mount Erebus on Ross Island is the world's southernmost active volcano; the Ross Ice Shelf is formed by several glaciers coalescing in the Ross Sea

**products** cod, Antarctic icefish, and krill are fished in Antarctic waters. Whaling, which began in the early 20th century ceased during the 1960s as a result of over-whaling. Petroleum, coal, and minerals such as palladium and platinum exist, but their exploitation is prevented

---

### ANTARCTIC EXPLORATION

| | |
|---|---|
| 1773–77 | English explorer James Cook first sailed in Antarctic seas, but exploration was difficult before the development of iron ships able to withstand ice pressure. |
| 1819–21 | Antarctica circumnavigated by Russian explorer Fabian Bellingshausen. |
| 1823 | British navigator James Weddell sailed into the sea named after him. |
| 1841–42 | Scottish explorer James Ross sighted the Great Ice Barrier named after him. |
| 1895 | Norwegian explorer Carsten Borchgrevink was one of the first landing party on the continent. |
| 1898 | Borchgrevink's British expedition first wintered in Antarctica. |
| 1901–04 | English explorer Robert Scott first penetrated the interior of the continent. |
| 1907–08 | English explorer Ernest Shackleton came within 182 km/113 mi of the Pole. |
| 1911 | Norwegian explorer Roald Amundsen reached the Pole, 14 Dec, overland with dogs. |
| 1912 | Scott reached the Pole, 18 Jan, initially aided by ponies. |
| 1928–29 | US naval officer Richard Byrd made the first flight to the Pole. |
| 1935 | US explorer Lincoln Ellsworth first flew across Antarctica. |
| 1946–48 | US explorer Finn Ronne's expedition proved the Antarctic to be one continent. |
| 1957–58 | English explorer Vivian Fuchs made the first overland crossing. |
| 1959 | Soviet expedition from the West Ice Shelf to the Pole. |
| 1959 | International Antarctic Treaty suspended all territorial claims, reserving an area south of 60° S latitude for peaceful purposes. |
| 1961–62 | Bentley Trench discovered, which suggested that there may be an Atlantic-Pacific link beneath the Continent. |
| 1966–67 | Specially protected areas established internationally for animals and plants. |
| 1979 | Fossils of ape-like humanoids resembling E Africa's Proconsul found 500 km/300 mi from the Pole. |
| 1980 | International Convention on the exploitation of resources—oil, gas, fish, and krill. |
| 1982 | First circumnavigation of Earth (2 Sept 1979–29 Aug 1982) via the Poles by English explorers Ranulph Fiennes and Charles Burton. |
| 1990 | Longest unmechanized crossing (6,100 km/3,182 mi) completed by a 6-person international team, using only skis and dogs. |
| 1991 | Antarctic Treaty imposing a 50-year ban on mining activity secured. |

---

by a 50-year ban on commercial mining agreed by 39 nations in 1991

**population** no permanent residents; settlement limited to scientific research stations with maximum population of 2,000 to 3,000 during the summer months. Sectors of Antarctica are claimed by Argentina, Australia, Chile, France, the UK, Norway, and New Zealand

**history** following multi-national scientific co-operation in Antarctica during the International Geophysical Year of 1957–58, 12 countries signed an Antarctic Treaty with a view to promoting scientific research and keeping Antarctica free from conflict. After it came into effect 1961, a further 27 countries acceded to the treaty. In response to overfishing in Antarctic waters, the Conservation of Antarctic Marine Living Resources was agreed 1980. In 1988 the Convention on the Regulation of Antarctic Mineral Resource Activities gave any signatory the right to veto mining activity on environmental grounds. While this provided a means of regulation, environmental pressure groups felt it would not prevent commercial exploitation. In 1991 an agreement was signed extending the Antarctic Treaty and imposing a 50-year ban on mining activity.

**Arctic, the** that part of the northern hemisphere surrounding the North Pole; arbitrarily defined as the region lying N of the Arctic Circle (66° 32'N) or N of the tree line. There is

no Arctic continent—the greater part of the region comprises the Arctic Ocean which is the world's smallest ocean. Arctic climate, fauna, and flora extend over the islands and northern edges of continental land masses that surround the Arctic Ocean (Svalbard, Iceland, Greenland, Siberia, Scandinavia, Alaska, and Canada)

**area** 36,000,000 sq km/14,000,000 sq mi

**physical** pack-ice floating on the Arctic Ocean occupies almost the entire region between the North Pole and the coasts of North America and Eurasia, covering an area that ranges in diameter from 3,000 km/1,900 mi to 4,000 km/2,500 mi. The pack-ice reaches a maximum extent in Feb when its outer limit (influenced by the cold Labrador Current and the warm Gulf Stream) varies from 50°N along the coast of Labrador to 75°N in the Barents Sea N of Scandinavia. In spring the pack-ice begins to break up into ice floes which are carried by the S-flowing Greenland Current to the Atlantic Ocean. Arctic ice is at its minimum area in August. The greatest concentration of icebergs in Arctic regions is found in Baffin Bay. They are derived from the glaciers of W Greenland, then carried along Baffin Bay and down into the N Atlantic where they melt off Labrador and Newfoundland. The Bering Straits are icebound for more than six months each year, but the Barents Sea between Scandinavia and Svalbard is free of ice and is

## ARCTIC EXPLORATION

| | |
|---|---|
| 60,000–35,000 BC | Ancestors of the Inuit and American Indians began migration from Siberia to North America by the 'lost' landbridge of Beringia. |
| 320 BC | Pytheas, Greek sailor contemporary with Alexander the Great, possibly reached Iceland. |
| 9th–10th centuries AD | Vikings colonized Iceland and Greenland, which then had a much warmer climate. |
| c. 1000 | Norwegian sailor Leif Ericsson reached Baffin Island (NE of Canada) and Labrador. |
| 1497 | Genoese pilot Giovanni Caboto first sought the Northwest Passage as a trade route around North America for Henry VII of England. |
| 1553 | English navigator Richard Chancellor tried to find the Northeast Passage around Siberia and first established direct English trade with Russia. |
| 1576 | English sailor Martin Frobisher reached Frobisher Bay, but found only 'fools' gold' (iron pyrites) for Elizabeth I of England. |
| 1594–97 | Dutch navigator Willem Barents made three expeditions in search of the Northeast Passage. |
| 1607 | English navigator Henry Hudson failed to cross the Arctic Ocean, but his reports of whales started the northern whaling industry. |
| 1670 | Hudson's Bay Company started the fur trade in Canada. |
| 1728 | Danish navigator Vitus Bering passed Bering Strait. |
| 1829–33 | Scottish explorer John Ross discovered the North Magnetic Pole. |
| 1845 | Mysterious disappearance of English explorer John Franklin's expedition to the Northwest Passage stimulated further exploration. |
| 1878–79 | Swedish navigator Nils Nordensköld was the first European to discover the Northeast Passage. |
| 1893–96 | Norwegian explorer Fridtjof Nansen's ship *Fram* drifted across the Arctic, locked in the ice, proving that no Arctic continent existed. |
| 1903–06 | Norwegian explorer Roald Amundsen sailed through the Northwest Passage. |
| 1909 | US explorer Robert Peary, Matt Henson, and four Inuit reached the North Pole on 2 April. |
| 1926 | US explorer Richard Byrd and Floyd Bennett flew to the Pole on 9 May. |
| 1926 | Italian aviator Umberto Nobile and Amundsen crossed the Pole (Spitzbergen–Alaska) in the airship *Norge* on 12 May. |
| 1954 | First regular commercial flights over the short-cut polar route by Scandinavian Airlines. |
| 1958 | The US submarine *Nautilus* crossed the Pole beneath the ice. |
| 1960 | From this date a Soviet nuclear-powered icebreaker has kept open a 4,000 km/2,500 mi Asia-Europe passage along the north coast of Siberia 150 days a year. |
| 1969 | First surface crossing, by dog sled, of the Arctic Ocean (Alaska–Spitzbergen) by Wally Herbert, British Transarctic Expedition, Feb–May. |
| 1977 | The Soviet icebreaker *Arktika* made the first surface voyage to the Pole. |
| 1982 | First circumnavigation of the Earth (2 Sept 1979–29 Aug 1982) via the Poles by Ranulph Fiennes and Charles Burton. |
| 1988 | Canadian and Soviet skiers attempted the first overland crossing from the USSR to Canada via the Pole. |

navigable throughout the year. Arctic coastlines, which have emerged from the sea since the last Ice Age, are characterized by deposits of gravel and disintegrated rock

**climate** permanent ice sheets and year-round snow cover are found in regions where average monthly temperatures remain below 0°C/32°F, but on land areas where one or more summer months have average temperatures between freezing point and 10°C/50°F, a stunted, treeless tundra vegetation is found. Mean annual temperatures range from –23°C at the North Pole to –12°C on the coast of Alaska. In winter the sun disappears below the horizon for a time, but the cold is less severe than in parts of inland Siberia or Antarctica. During the short summer season there is a maximum of 24 hours of daylight at the summer solstice on the Arctic Circle and six months constant light at the North Pole. Countries with Arctic coastlines established the International Arctic Sciences Committee in 1987 to study ozone depletion and climatic change

**flora and fauna** the plants of the relatively infertile Arctic tundra (lichens, mosses, grasses, cushion plants, and low shrubs) spring to life during the short summer season and remain dormant for the remaining ten months of the year. There are no annual plants, only perennials. Animal species include reindeer, caribou, musk ox, fox, hare, lemming, wolf, polar bear, seal, and walrus. There are few birds except in summer when insects, especially mosquitoes, are plentiful

**natural resources** the Arctic is rich in coal (Svalbard, USSR), oil and natural gas (Alaska, Canadian Arctic, USSR), and mineral resources including gold, silver, copper, uranium, lead, zinc, nickel, and bauxite. Because of climatic conditions, the Arctic is not well-suited to navigation and the exploitation of these resources. Murmansk naval base on the Kola Peninsula is the largest in the world

*population* there are about one million aboriginal people including the Aleuts of Alaska, North American Indians, the Lapps of Scandinavia and the USSR, the Yakuts, Samoyeds, Komi, Chukchi, Tungus, and Dolgany of the USSR, and the Inuit of Siberia, the Canadian Arctic, and Greenland.

**Asia** largest of the continents, occupying one third of the total land surface of the world

*area* 44,000,000 sq km/17,000,000 sq mi

*largest cities* (population over 5 million) Tokyo, Shanghai, Osaka, Beijing, Seoul, Calcutta, Bombay, Jakarta, Bangkok, Tehran, Hong Kong, Delhi, Tianjin, Karachi

*physical* lying in the eastern hemisphere, Asia extends from the Arctic Circle to just over 10° S of the Equator. The Asia mainland, which forms the greater part of the Eurasian continent, lies entirely in the northern hemisphere and stretches from Cape Chelyubinsk at its N extremity to Cape Piai at the S tip of the Malay Peninsula. From Dezhneva Cape in the E, the mainland extends W over more than 165° longitude to Cape Baba in Turkey. Containing the world's highest mountains and largest inland seas, Asia can be divided into five physical units:

1) at the heart of the continent, a central triangle of plateaux at varying altitudes (Tibetan Plateau, Tarim Basin, Gobi Desert), surrounded by huge mountain chains which spread in all directions (Himalayas, Karakoram, Hindu Kush, Pamirs, Kunlun, Tien Shan, Altai);

2) the W plateaux and ranges (Elburz, Zagros, Taurus Great Caucasus mountains) of Afghanistan, Iran, N Iraq, Soviet Armenia, and Turkey;

3) the lowlands of Turkestan and Siberia which stretch N of the central mountains to the Arctic Ocean and include large areas in which the subsoil is permanently frozen;

4) the fertile and densely populated E lowlands and river plains of Korea, China, and Indochina, and the islands of the East Indies and Japan;

5) the southern plateaux of Arabia, and the Deccan, with the fertile alluvial plains of the Euphrates, Tigris, Indus, Ganges, Brahmaputra, and Irrawaddy rivers.

In Asiatic Russia are the largest areas of coniferous forest (taiga) in the world. The climate shows great extremes and contrasts, the heart of the continent becoming bitterly cold in winter and extremely hot in summer. When the heated air over land rises, moisture-laden air from the surrounding seas flows in, bringing heavy monsoon rain to all SE Asia, China, and Japan between May and Oct

*features* Mount Everest at 8,872 m/29,118 ft, is the world's highest mountain; Dead Sea −394 m/−1,293 ft is the world's lowest point

below sea level; rivers (over 3,200 km/ 2,000 mi) include Chiang Jiang (Yangtze), Huang He (Yellow River), Ob-Irtysh, Amur, Lena, Mekong, Yeni sei; lakes (over 18,000 sq km/7,000 sq mi) include Caspian Sea (the largest inland sea in the world), Aral Sea, Baikal (largest freshwater lake in Eurasia), Balkhash; deserts include the Gobi, Takla Makan, Syrian Desert, Arabian Desert, Negev

*products* 62% of the population are employed in agriculture; Asia produces 46% of the world's cereal crops (91% of the world's rice); other crops include mangoes (India), groundnuts (India, China), 84% of the world's copra (Philippines, Indonesia), 93% of the world's rubber (Indonesia, Malaysia, Thailand), tobacco (China), flax (China, USSR), 95% of the world's jute (India, Bangladesh, China), cotton (China, India, Pakistan), silk (China, India), fish (Japan, China, Korea, Thailand); China produces 55% of the world's tungsten; 45% of the world's tin is produced by Malaysia, China, and Indonesia; Saudi Arabia is the world's largest producer of coal

*population* (1988) 3 billion; the world's largest, though not the fastest growing population, amounting to more than half the total number of people in the world; between 1950 and 1990 the death rate and infant mortality rate were reduced by more than 60%; annual growth rate 1.7%; projected to increase to 3.55 billion by 2000

*language* predominantly tonal languages (Chinese, Japanese) in the E, Indo-Iranian languages (Hindi, Urdu, Persian) in S Asia, Altaic languages (Mongolian, Turkish) in W and Central Asia, Semitic languages (Arabic, Hebrew) in the SW

*religion* the major religions of the world had their origins in Asia—Judaism and Christianity in the Middle East, Islam in Arabia, Buddhism, Hinduism, and Sikhism in India, Confucianism in China, and Shinto in Japan.

**Europe** second smallest continent, occupying 8% of the Earth's surface

*area* 10,400,000 sq km/4,000,000 sq mi

*largest cities* (population over 1.5 million) Athens, Barcelona, Berlin, Birmingham, Budapest, Hamburg, Istanbul, Kiev, Leningrad, London, Madrid, Manchester, Milan, Moscow, Paris, Rome, Vienna, Warsaw, Lisbon, Bucharest, Kharkov

*physical* conventionally occupying that part of Eurasia W of the Ural mountains, N of the Caucasus mountains and N of the Sea of Marmara; Europe lies entirely in the northern hemisphere between 36° N and the Arctic Ocean. About two-thirds of the continent is a great plain which covers the whole of European Russia and spreads westwards through Poland to the Low Countries and the Bay of Biscay. To the north lie the Scandinavian highlands rising to 2,470 m/8,110 ft at Glittertind in the Jotenheim Range of Norway. To the south, a series of mountain ranges stretch from E to W (Caucasus, Balkans, Carpathians, Apennines, Alps, Pyrenees, and Sierra Nevada). The most westerly point of the mainland is Cape Roca in Portugal; the most southerly location is Tarifa Point in Spain; the most northerly point on the mainland is Nordkynn in Norway. A line from the Baltic to the Black Sea divides Europe between an E continental region and a W region characterized by a series of peninsulas that include Scandinavia (Norway, Sweden, and Finland), Jutland (Denmark and Germany), Iberia (Spain and Portugal), Italy and the Balkans (Greece, Albania, Yugoslavia, Bulgaria, and European Turkey). Because of the large number of bays, inlets and peninsulas, the coastline is longer in proportion to its size than that of any other continent. The largest islands adjacent to continental Europe are the British Isles, Novaya Zemla, Sicily, Sardinia, Crete, Corsica, Gotland (in the Baltic Sea), and the Balearic Islands; other more distant islands associated with Europe include Iceland, Svalbard, Franz Josef Land, Madeira, the Azores, and the Canary Islands. The greater part of Europe falls within the northern temperate zone which is modified by the Gulf Stream in the NW; Central Europe has warm summers and cold winters; the Mediterranean coast has comparatively mild winters and hot summers.

**features** Mount Elbruz 5,642 m/18,517 ft in the Caucasus mountains is the highest peak in Europe; Mont Blanc 4,807 m/ 15,772 ft is the highest peak in the Alps; lakes (over 5,100 sq km/2,000 sq mi) include Ladoga, Onega, Vänern; rivers (over 800 km/ 500 mi) include the Volga, Danube, Dnieper, Ural, Don, Pechora, Dneister, Rhine, Loire, Tagus, Ebro, Oder, Prut, Rhône

**products** nearly 50% of the world's cars are produced in Europe (Germany, France, Italy, Spain, USSR, UK); the rate of fertilizer consumption on agricultural land is four times greater than that in any other continent; Europe produces 43% of the world's barley (Germany, Spain, France, UK), 41% of its rye (Poland, Germany), 31% of its oats (Poland, Germany, Sweden, France), and 24% of its wheat (France, Germany, UK, Romania); Italy, Spain, and Greece produce more than 70% of the world's olive oil

**population** (1985) 496 million (excluding Turkey and USSR); annual growth rate 0.3%, projected population of 512 million by 2000

**language** mostly Indo-European, with a few exceptions, including Finno-Ugrian (Finnish and Hungarian) and Basque and Altaic (Turkish); apart from a fringe of Celtic, the NW is Germanic; Letto-Lithuanian languages separate the Germanic from the Slavonic tongues of E Europe; Romance languages spread E-W from Romania through Italy and France to Spain and Portugal

**religion** Christianity (Protestantism, Roman Catholicism, Eastern Orthodox), Islam, (Turkey, Albania, Yugoslavia, Bulgaria), Judaism.

**North America** third largest of the continents (including Greenland and Central America), and more than twice the size of Europe

**area** 24,000,000 sq km/9,400,000 sq mi

**largest cities** (population over 1 million) Mexico City, New York, Chicago, Toronto, Los Angeles, Montreal, Guadalajara, Monterrey, Philadelphia, Houston, Guatemala City, Vancouver, Detroit, San Diego, Dallas

**physical** occupying the N part of the landmass of the western hemisphere between the Arctic Ocean and the tropical SE tip of the isthmus that joins Central America to South America; the northernmost point on the mainland is the tip of Boothia Peninsula in the Canadian Arctic; the northernmost point on adjacent islands is Cape Morris Jesup on Greenland; the most westerly point on the mainland is Cape Prince of Wales, Alaska; the most westerly point on adjacent islands is Attu Island in the Aleutians; the most easterly point on the mainland lies on the SE coast of Labrador; the highest point is Mount McKinley, Alaska 6,194 m/20,320 ft; the lowest point is Badwater in Death Valley –86 m/–282 ft. In Canada and the USA, the Great Plains of the interior separate mountain belts to the E (Appalachians, Laurentian Highlands) and W (Rocky Mountains, Coast Mountains, Cascade Range, Sierra Nevada). The W range extends S into Mexico as the Sierra Madre. The Mississippi river system drains from the central Great Plains into the Gulf of Mexico; low coastal plains on the Atlantic coast are indented by the Gulf of St Lawrence, Bay of Fundy, Delaware Bay, Chesapeake Bay; the St Lawrence and Great Lakes form a rough crescent (with Lake Winnipeg, Lake Athabasca, the Great Bear, and the Great Slave lakes) around the exposed rock of the great Canadian/Laurentian shield, into which Hudson Bay breaks from the north; Greenland (the largest island in the world next to Australia) is a high, ice-covered plateau with a deeply indented coastline of fjords

**features** Lake Superior (the largest body of freshwater in the world); Grand Canyon on the Colorado river; Redwood National Park, California has some of the world's tallest trees; San Andreas Fault, California; deserts: Death Valley, Mojave, Sonoran; rivers (over 1,600 km/1,000 mi) include Mississippi, Missouri, Mackenzie, Rio Grande, Yukon, Arkansas, Colorado, Saskatchewan-Bow, Columbia, Red, Peace, Snake

**products** with abundant resources and an ever-expanding home market, the USA's fast-growing industrial and technological strength has made it less dependent on exports and a dominant economic power throughout the continent. Canada is the world's leading producer of nickel, zinc, uranium, potash, and linseed, and the world's second largest producer of asbestos, silver, titanium, gypsum, sulphur, and molybdenum; Mexico is the world's leading producer of silver and the fourth largest oil producer; the USA is the world's leading producer of salt and the second largest producer of oil and cotton; nearly 30% of the world's beef and veal is produced in North America *population* (1988) 417 million, rising to an estimated 450 million by 2000; annual growth rate from 1980 to 1985: Canada 1.08%, USA 0.88%, Mexico 2.59%, Honduras 3.39%; the native American Indian, Inuit, and Aleut peoples are now a minority within a population predominantly of European immigrant origin. Many Africans were brought in as part of the slave trade

*language* English predominates in Canada, USA, and Belize; Spanish is the chief language of the countries of Latin America and a sizeable minority in the USA; French is spoken by about 25% of the population of Canada, and by people of the French *département* of St Pierre and Miquelon; indigenous non-European minorities, including the Inuit of Arctic Canada, the Aleuts of Alaska, North American Indians, and the Maya of Central America, have their own languages and dialects

*religion* Christian and Jewish religions predominate; 97% of Latin Americans, 47% of Canadians, and 21% of those living in the USA are Roman Catholic

**Oceania** a general term for the islands of the central and S Pacific, including Australia, New Zealand, and the E half of New Guinea; although situated in the world's largest ocean, Oceania is the smallest continent in the world in terms of land surface

*area* 8,500,000 sq km/3,300,000 sq mi (land area)

*largest cities* (population over 500,000) Sydney, Melbourne, Brisbane, Perth, Adelaide, Auckland

*physical* stretching from the Tropic of Cancer in the N to the S tip of New Zealand, Oceania can be broadly divided into groups of volcanic and coral islands on the basis of the ethnic origins of their inhabitants: Micronesia (Guam, Kiribati, Mariana, Marshall, Caroline Islands), Melanesia (Papua New Guinea, Vanuatu, New Caledonia, Fiji, Solomon Islands), and Polynesia (Tonga, Samoa, Line Islands, Tuvalu, French Polynesia, Pitcairn); Australia (the largest island in the world) occupies more than 90% of the land surface; the highest point is Mount Wilhelm, Papua New Guinea 4,509 m/14,793 ft; the lowest point is Lake Eyre, South Australia –16 m/–52 ft; the longest river is the Murray in SE Australia 2,590 km/1,609 mi

*features* the Challenger Deep in the Mariana Trench –11,034 m/–36,201 ft is the greatest known depth of sea in the world; Ayers Rock in Northern Territory, Australia is the world's largest monolith; the Great Barrier Reef is the longest coral reef in the world; Mount Kosciusko 2,229 m/7,316 ft in New South Wales, is the highest peak in Australia; Mount Cook 3,764 m/21,353 ft is the highest peak in New Zealand

*products* with a small home market, Oceania has a manufacturing sector dedicated to servicing domestic requirements and a large export-oriented sector, 70% of which is based on exports of primary agricultural or mineral products. Australia is a major producer of bauxite, nickel, silver, cobalt, gold, iron ore, diamonds, lead, and uranium; New Caledonia is a source of cobalt, chromite, and nickel; Papua and New Guinea produce gold and copper.

Agricultural products include coconuts, copra, palm oil, coffee, cocoa, phosphates (Nauru), rubber (Papua New Guinea), 40% of the world's wool (Australia, New Zealand); New Zealand and Australia are, respectively, the world's second and third largest producers of mutton and lamb; fishing and tourism are also major industries

*population* 26 million, rising to 30 million by 2000; annual growth rate from 1980 to 1985 1.5%; Australia accounts for 65% of the population; 1% of Australia's population is Aboriginal and 9% of the people of New Zealand are Maori

*language* English, French (French Polynesia, New Caledonia, Wallis and Fatuna, Vanuatu); a wide range of indigenous Aboriginal, Maori, Melanesian, Micronesian, and Polynesian languages and dialects (over 700 in Papua New Guinea) are spoken

*religion* predominantly Christian; 30% of the people of Tonga adhere to the Free Wesleyan Church; 70% of the people of Tokelau adhere to the Congregational Church; French overseas territories are largely Roman Catholic.

**South America** fourth largest of the continents, nearly twice as large as Europe, occupying 13% of the world's land surface

*area* 17,864,000 sq km/6,900,000 sq mi

*largest cities* (population over 2 million) Buenos Aires, São Paulo, Rio de Janeiro, Bogotá, Santiago, Lima, Caracas, Janeiro, Belo Horizonte

*physical* occupying the S part of the landmass of the western hemisphere, the South American continent stretches from Point Gallinas on the Caribbean coast of Colombia to Cape Horn at the southern tip of Horn Island which lies adjacent to Tierra del Fuego; the most southerly point on the mainland is Cape Froward on the Brunswick peninsula, S Chile; at its maximum width (5,120 km/3,200 mi) the continent stretches from Point Pariñas, Peru in the extreme W to Point Coqueiros, just N of Recife, Brazil, in the E; five-sixths of the continent lies in the southern hemisphere and two-thirds within the tropics. South America can be divided into the following physical regions: 1) the Andes mountain system which begins as three separate ranges in the N and stretches the whole length of the W coast approximately 7,200 km/4,500 mi; the highest peak is Aconcagua 6,960 m/22,834 ft; the width of the Andes ranges from 40 km/25 mi in Chile to 640 km/400 mi in Bolivia; a narrow coastal belt lies between the Andes and the Pacific Ocean;
2) the uplifted remains of the old continental mass, with interior plains at an elevation of 610–1,520 m/2,000–5,000 ft, are found in the E and NE, in the Brazilian Highlands (half the area of Brazil) and Guiana Highlands;

3) the plain of the Orinoco river is an alluvial tropical lowland lying between the Venezuelan Andes and the Guiana Highlands;

4) the tropical Amazon Plain stretches over 3,200 km/2,000 mi from the E foothills of the Andes to the Atlantic ocean, separating the Brazilian and Guiana highlands; once an inland sea, the Amazon basin was filled with sediment and then uplifted;

5) the Pampa-Chaco plain of Argentina, Paraguay, and Bolivia occupies a former bay of the Atlantic that has been filled with sediment brought down from the surrounding highlands;

6) the Patagonian Plateau in the S consists of a series of terraces that rise from the Atlantic Ocean to the foothills of the Andes; glaciation, wind, and rain have dissected these terraces and created rugged land forms

*features* Lake Titicaca (world's highest navigable lake); La Paz (highest capital city in the world); Atacama Desert; Inca ruins at Machu Picchu; rivers include the Amazon (world's largest and second longest), Parana, Madeira, São Francisco, Purus, Paraguay, Orinoco, Araguaia, Negro, Uruguay

*products* produces 44% of the world's coffee (Brazil, Colombia), 22% of its cocoa (Brazil), 35% of its citrus fruit, meat (Argentina, Brazil), soybeans (Argentina, Brazil), cotton (Brazil), linseed (Argentina); Argentina is the world's second largest producer of sunflower seed; Brazil is the world's largest producer of bananas, its second largest producer of tin, and its third largest producer of manganese, tobacco, and mangoes; Peru is the world's second largest producer of silver; Chile is the world's largest producer of copper

*population* (1988) 285 million, rising to 550 million by 2000; annual growth rate from 1980 to 1985 2.3%

*language* Spanish, Portuguese (chief language in Brazil), Dutch (Surinam), French (French Guiana), Amerindian languages; Hindi, Javanese, and Chinese spoken by descendants of Asian immigrants to Surinam and Guyana; a variety of Creole dialects spoken by those of African descent

*religion* 90–95% Roman Catholic; local animist beliefs among Amerindians; Hindu and Muslim religions predominate among the descendants of Asian immigrants in Surinam and Guyana.

---

### Emigration

*If you were free to do so, would you like to go and settle in another country? If Yes; which country would you settle in if you were to emigrate from Britain?*

| | |
|---|---|
| Australia | 15 |
| Canada | 7 |
| New Zealand | 5 |
| USA | 5 |
| Europe | 4 |
| Other | 7 |
| Don't know | 3 |
| No, would not | 54 |
| 'Speaking a foreign language' | |
| In | 76 |
| Out | 17 |
| Don't know | 7 |

# COUNTRIES

## Afghanistan (Republic of)
(*Jamhuria Afghanistan*)

**area** 652,090 sq km/251,707 sq mi
**capital** Kābul
**towns** Kandahār, Herāt

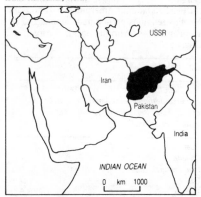

**physical** mountainous in centre and NE, desert in SW
**features** Hindu Kush mountain range (Khyber and Salang passes, Wakhan salient and Panjshir Valley), Helmond River, Lake Saberi
**head of state** Najibullah Ahmadzai (president) from 1986
**head of government** Fazl Haq Khaleqiar (prime minister) from 1990
**political system** military emergency republic
**political parties** Homeland Party (formerly People's Democratic Party of Afghanistan (PDPA) Marxist-Leninist; Hesb-i-Islami and Jamiat-i-Islami, Islamic fundamentalist mujahaddin; National Liberation Front, moderate mujahaddin
**exports** dried fruit, rare minerals, natural gas (piped to USSR), karakul lamb skins, Afghan coats
**currency** afgháni (99.25 = £1 July 1991)
**population** (1989) 15,590,000 (more than 5 million have become refugees since 1979); growth rate 0.6% p.a.
**life expectancy** men 37, women 37
**language** Pushtu
**religion** Muslim: 80% Sunni, 20% Shi'ite
**literacy** men 39%/women 8% (1985 est)
**GNP** $3.3 bn (1985); $275 per head

**chronology**
**1747** Afghanistan became an independent emirate.
**1838–1919** Afghan Wars waged between Afghanistan and Britain to counter the threat to British India from expanding Russian influence in Afghanistan.
**1919** Afghanistan recovered full independence following Third Afghan War.
**1953** Lt-Gen Daud Khan became prime minister and introduced reform programme.
**1963** Daud Khan forced to resign and constitutional monarchy established.
**1973** Monarchy overthrown in coup by Daud Khan.
**1978** Daud Khan ousted by Taraki and the PDPA.
**1979** Taraki replaced by Hafizullah Amin; USSR entered country to prop up government and installed Babrak Karmal in power. Amin executed.
**1986** Replacement of Karmal as leader by Dr Najibullah Ahmadzai. Partial Soviet troop withdrawal.

**1988** New non-Marxist constitution adopted.
**1989** Withdrawal of Soviet troops; state of emergency imposed in response to intensification of civil war.
**1990** PDPA renamed the Homeland Party; President Najibullah elected its president.
**1991** Peace plan accepted by President Najibullah and Mujaheddin.

## Albania (Republic of)

**area** 28,748 sq km/11,097 sq mi
**capital** Tiranë
**towns** Shkodër, Vlorë, chief port Durrës

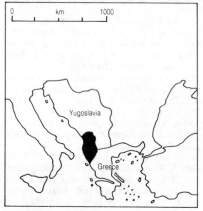

**physical** mainly mountainous, with rivers flowing E to W, and a small coastal plain
**features** Dinaric Alps, with wild boar and wolves
**head of state** Ramiz Alia from 1982
**head of government** Fatos Nano from 1991
**political system** socialist pluralist republic
**political parties** Party of Labour of Albania (PLA), Marxist-Leninist; Democratic Party
**exports** crude oil, bitumen, chrome, iron ore, nickel, coal, copper wire, tobacco, fruit
**currency** lek (10.10 = £1 July 1991)
**population** (1990 est) 3,270,000; growth rate 1.9% p.a.
**life expectancy** men 69, women 73
**language** Albanian, Greek
**religion** Muslim 70%, although all religion banned 1967–90
**literacy** 75% (1986)
**GNP** $2.8 bn (1986 est); $900 per head

**chronology**
**1468** Albania made part of the Ottoman Empire.
**1912** Independence achieved from Turkey.
**1925** Republic proclaimed.
**1928–39** Monarchy of King Zog.
**1939–44** Under Italian and then German rule.
**1946** Communist republic proclaimed under the leadership of Enver Hoxha.
**1949** Admitted into Comecon.
**1961** Break with Khrushchev's USSR.
**1967** Albania declared itself the 'first atheist state in the world'.
**1978** Break with 'revisionist' China.
**1985** Death of Hoxha.
**1987** Normal diplomatic relations restored with Canada, Greece, and West Germany.
**1988** Attendance at conference of Balkan states for the first time since the 1930s.
**1990** One-party system abandoned; first opposition party formed.
**1991** Civil unrest; thousands fled to neighbouring coun-

tries. Albanian Party of Labour (PLA) won a working majority in first free, multi-party assembly elections and PLA leader, Ramiz Alia, re-elected president. Country renamed the Republic of Albania in the new draft constitution. PLA government collapsed after widespread strikes and a coalition 'national salvation' government was formed.

## Algeria (Democratic and Popular Republic of)
(*al-Jumhuriya al-Jazairiya ad-Dimuqratiya ash-Shabiya*)

**area** 2,381,741 sq km/919,352 sq mi
**capital** al-Jazair (Algiers)
**towns** Qacentina/Constantine; ports are Ouahran/Oran, Annaba

**physical** coastal plains backed by mountains in N; Sahara desert in S
**features** Atlas mountains, Barbary Coast, Chott Melrhir depression, Hoggar mountains
**head of state** Benjedid Chadli from 1979
**political system** one-party socialist republic
**political parties** National Liberation Front (FLN), nationalist socialist
**exports** oil, natural gas, iron, wine, olive oil
**currency** dinar (29.26 = £1 July 1991)
**population** (1990 est) 25,715,000 (83% Arab, 17% Berber); growth rate 3.0% p.a.
**life expectancy** men 59, women 62
**language** Arabic (official); Berber, French
**religion** Sunni Muslim
**literacy** men 63%/women 37% (1985 est)
**GDP** $58.0 bn (1986); $2,645 per head

**chronology**
**1954** War for independence from France led by the FLN
**1962** Independence achieved from France, Republic declared. Ben Bella elected president.
**1965** Ben Bella deposed by military, led by Colonel Houari Boumédienne.
**1976** New constitution approved.
**1978** Death of Boumédienne.
**1979** Bendjedid Chadli elected president. Ben Bella released from house arrest. FLN adopted new party structure.
**1981** Algeria helped secure release of US prisoners in Iran.
**1983** Chadli re-elected.
**1988** Riots in protest at government policies; 170 killed. Reform programme introduced. Diplomatic relations with Egypt restored.
**1989** Constitutional changes proposed, leading to limited political pluralism.
**1990** Fundamentalist Islamic Salvation Front win Algerian elections. Ben Bella returned.

**1991** President Chadli promised multi-party elections. Government clamp-down on religious extremists.

## Andorra (Principality of)
(*Principat d'Andorra*)

**area** 468 sq km/181 sq mi
**capital** Andorra-la-Vella
**towns** Les Escaldes

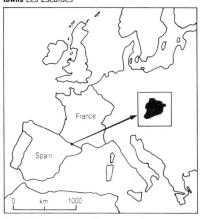

**physical** mountainous, with narrow valleys
**features** the E Pyrenees, Valira River
**heads of state** Joan Marti y Alanis (bishop of Seo de Urgel, Spain) and François Mitterrand (president of France)
**head of government** Josep Pintat Solens from 1986
**political system** feudal co-principality
**political parties** Andorran Democratic Party
**exports** main industries tourism and smuggling; tobacco
**currency** French franc (9.96 = £1 July 1991) and Spanish peseta (184.10 = £1 July 1991)
**population** (1990) 51,000 (30% Andorrans, 61% immigrant Spanish workers, 6% French)
**language** Catalan (official) 30%; Spanish 59%, French 6%
**religion** Roman Catholic
**literacy** 100% (1987)
**GDP** $300 million (1985)

**chronology**
**1278** Treaty signed making Spanish bishop and French count joint rulers of Andorra (through marriage the king of France later inherited the count's right).
**1970** Extension of franchise to third-generation women and second-generation men.
**1976** First political organization (Democratic Party of Andorra) formed
**1977** Franchise extended to first-generation Andorrans.
**1981** First prime minister appointed by General Council.

## Angola (People's Republic of)
(*República Popular de Angola*)

**area** 1,246,700 sq km/481,226 sq mi
**capital** and chief port Luanda
**towns** Lobito and Benguela, also ports; Huambo, under UNITA control
**physical** narrow coastal plain rises to vast interior plateau with rainforest in N; desert in S
**features** Cuanza, Cuito, Cubango, and Cunene rivers; Cabinda exclave
**head of state and government** José Eduardo dos Santos from 1979
**political system** socialist republic

**political parties** People's Movement for the Liberation of Angola-Workers' Party (MPLA-PT), Marxist-Leninist; National Union for the total independence of Angola (UNITA)

**exports** oil, coffee, diamonds, palm oil, sisal, iron ore, fish

**currency** kwanza (104.33 = £1 July 1991)

**population** (1989 est) 9,733,000 (largest ethnic group Ovimbundu); growth rate 2.5% p.a.

**life expectancy** men 40, women 44

**language** Portuguese (official); Bantu dialects

**religion** Roman Catholic 68%, Protestant 20%, animist 12%

**literacy** 20% (1985)

**GDP** $2.7 bn; $478 per head

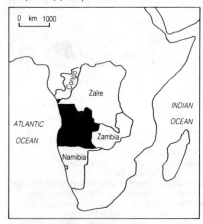

**chronology**
**1951** Angola became an overseas territory of Portugal.
**1956** First independence movement formed, the People's Movement for the Liberation of Angola (MPLA).
**1961** Unsuccessful independence rebellion.
**1962** Second nationalist movement formed, the National Front for the Liberation of Angola (FNLA).
**1966** Third nationalist movement formed, the National Union for the Total Independence of Angola (UNITA).
**1975** Independence achieved from Portugal. Transitional government of independence formed from representatives of MPLA, FNLA, UNITA, and Portuguese government. MPLA supported by USSR and Cuba, FNLA by 'non-left' power groups of southern Africa, and UNITA by Western powers. MPLA proclaimed People's Republic under the presidency of Dr Agostinho Neto. FNLA and UNITA proclaimed People's Democratic Republic of Angola.
**1976** MPLA gained control of most of the country. South African troops withdrawn, but Cuban units remained.
**1977** MPLA restructured to become the People's Movement for the Liberation of Angola-Workers' Party (MPLA-PT).
**1979** Death of Neto, succeeded by José Eduardo dos Santos.
**1980** Constitution amended to provide for an elected people's assembly. UNITA guerrillas, aided by South Africa, continued raids against the Luanda government and bases of the South West Africa People's Organization (SWAPO) bases in Angola.
**1984** The Lusaka Agreement.
**1985** South African forces officially withdrawn.
**1986** Further South African raids into Angola. UNITA continued to receive South African support.
**1988** Peace treaty, providing for the withdrawal of all foreign troops, signed with South Africa and Cuba.

**1989** Ceasefire agreed with UNITA broke down and guerrilla activity restarted.
**1990** Peace offer by rebels. Return to multiparty politics promised.
**1991** Peace agreement signed, civil war between MPLA-PT and UNITA officially ended. Amnesty for all political prisoners.

## Antigua and Barbuda (State of)

**area** Antigua 280 sq km/108 sq mi, Barbuda 161 sq km/62 sq mi, plus Redonda 1 sq km/0.4 sq mi

**capital** and chief port St John's

**towns** Codrington (on Barbuda)

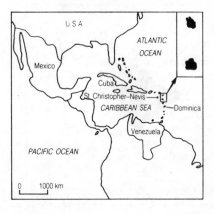

**physical** low-lying tropical islands with volcanic outcrop on W Antigua

**features** Antigua is the largest of the Leeward Islands; Redonda is uninhabited

**head of state** Elizabeth II from 1981 represented by governor general

**head of government** Vere C Bird from 1981

**political system** liberal democracy

**political parties** Antigua Labour Party (ALP), moderate, left-of-centre; Progressive Labour Movement (PLM), left-of-centre

**exports** sea-island cotton, rum, lobsters

**currency** Eastern Caribbean dollar (4.39 = £1 July 1991)

**population** (1989) 83,500; growth rate 1.3% p.a.

**language** English

**religion** Christian (mostly Anglican)

**literacy** 90% (1985)

**GDP** $130 million (1983); $1,850 per head

**chronology**
**1632** Antigua colonized by English settlers.
**1667** Treaty of Breda formally cedes Antigua to Britain.
**1871–1956** Antigua and Barbuda administered as part of the Leeward Islands Federation.
**1967** Antigua and Barbuda became an associated state within the Commonwealth, with full internal independence.
**1971** PLM won general election by defeating the ALP.
**1976** PLM called for early independence, but ALP urged caution. ALP won the general election.
**1981** Independence from Britain achieved.
**1983** Assisted US invasion of Grenada.
**1984** ALP won decisive victory in general election.
**1985** ALP re-elected.
**1989** Another sweeping general election victory for the ALP.

## Argentina (Republic of)
(*República Argentina*)

**area** 2,780,092 sq km/1,073,116 sq mi
**capital** Buenos Aires (to move to Viedma)
**towns** Rosario, Córdoba, Tucumán, Mendoza, Santa Fé; ports are La Plata and Bahía Blanca

**physical** mountains in W, forest in N, pampas (treeless plains) in central area, Patagonian plateau in S; rivers Colorado, Paraná, Uruguay, Rio de la Plata estuary
**territories** Tierra del Fuego; disputed claims to S Atlantic islands; part of Antarctica
**features** Andes mountains, with Aconcagua the highest peak in the W hemisphere
**head of state and government** Carlos Menem from 1989
**political system** emergent democratic federal republic
**political parties** Radical Union Party (UCR), moderate centrist; Justice Party, right-wing Peronist
**exports** beef, livestock, cereals, wool, tannin, peanuts, linseed oil, minerals (coal, copper, molybdenum, gold, silver, lead, zinc, barium, uranium); huge resources of oil, natural gas, hydroelectric power
**currency** austral (16,306.00 = £1 July 1991)
**population** (1989 est) 32,425,000 (mainly of Spanish or Italian origin, only about 30,000 American Indians surviving); growth rate 1.6% p.a.
**life expectancy** men 66, women 73
**language** Spanish (official), English, Italian, German, French
**religion** Roman Catholic (state-supported)
**literacy** men 96%/women 95% (1985 est)
**GDP** $58 bn (1983); $2,350 per head

**chronology**
**1816** Independence achieved from Spain, followed by civil wars.
**1946** Juan Perón elected president, supported by his wife 'Evita'.
**1952** 'Evita' Perón died.
**1955** Perón overthrown and civilian administration restored.
**1966** Coup brought back military rule.
**1973** The Peronist party won the presidential and congressional elections. Perón returned from exile in Spain as president, with his third wife, 'Isabelita', as vice-president.
**1974** Perón died, succeeded by 'Isabelita'.
**1976** Coup resulted in rule by a military junta led by Lt-Gen Jorge Videla. Congress dissolved, and hundreds of people, including 'Isabelita' Perón, detained.

**1976–78** Ferocious campaign against left-wing elements. The start of the 'dirty war'.
**1978** Videla retired. Succeeded by General Roberto Viola, who promised a return to democracy.
**1981** Viola died suddenly. Replaced by General Leopoldo Galtieri.
**1982** With a deteriorating economy, Galtieri sought popular support by ordering an invasion of the British-held Falkland Islands. After losing the short war, Galtieri was removed and replaced by General Reynaldo Bignone.
**1983** Amnesty law passed and 1853 democratic constitution revived. General elections won by Dr Raúl Alfonsín and his party. Armed forces under scrutiny.
**1984** Commission on the Disappearance of Persons (CONADEP) reported on over 8,000 people who had disappeared during the 'dirty war' of 1976–83.
**1985** A deteriorating economy forced Alfonsín to seek help from the IMF and introduce a harsh austerity programme.
**1986** Unsuccessful attempt on Alfonsín's life.
**1988** Unsuccessful army coup attempt.
**1989** Carlos Menem, of the Justice Party, elected president. Alfonsín handed over power before required date of Dec 1989. Thirty-day state of emergency declared, after rioting following price measures and dramatic inflation (120% in June, with an annual rate of approximately 12,000%).
**1990** Full diplomatic relations with the UK restored. Menem elected Justice Party leader. Revolt by army officers thwarted.

## Australia (Commonwealth of)

**area** 7,682,300 sq km/2,966,136 sq mi
**capital** Canberra
**towns** Adelaide, Alice Springs, Brisbane, Darwin, Melbourne, Perth, Sydney, Hobart, Geelong, Newcastle, Townsville, Wollongong
**physical** the world's smallest, flattest, and driest continent (40% lies in the Tropics, one third is desert, and one third is marginal grazing); Great Sandy Desert; Great Victoria Desert; Simpson Desert; Great Dividing Range and Australian Alps in the E; rivers N–S, but Darling River and Murray system E–S; Lake Eyre basin and Nullarbor Plain in S

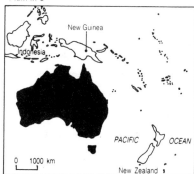

**territories** Norfolk Island, Christmas Island, Cocos (Keeling) Islands, Ashmore and Cartier Islands, Coral Sea Islands, Heard Island and McDonald Islands, Australian Antarctic Territory
**features** Ayers Rock; Arnhem Land; Gulf of Carpentaria; Great Australian Bight; the Great Barrier Reef (largest coral reef in the world, stretching 2000 km/1,250 mi off E coast of Queensland); unique animal species include the kangaroo, koala, platypus, wombat, Tasmanian devil, and spiny anteater; of 800 species of bird, the budgerigar, cassowary, emu, kookaburra, lyre bird, and

black swan are also unique as a result of Australia's long isolation from other continents.

**head of state** Elizabeth II from 1952 represented by governor general

**head of government** Bob Hawke from 1983

**political system** federal constitutional monarchy

**political parties** Australian Labor Party (ALP), moderate left-of-centre; Liberal Party of Australia, moderate, liberal, free-enterprise; National Party of Australia, centrist non-metropolitan

**exports** world's largest exporter of sheep, wool, alumina, coal, refined lead and zinc ores, and mineral sands; other exports include cereals, beef, veal, mutton, lamb, sugar, nickel, bauxite, iron ore; principal trade partners are Japan, the USA, and EC member states

**currency** Australian dollar (2.11 = £1 July 1991)

**population** (1990 est) 16,650,000; growth rate 1.5% p.a.

**life expectancy** men 72, women 79

**language** English, Aboriginal

**religion** Anglican 26%, other Protestant 17%, Roman Catholic 26%

**literacy** 100% (1984)

**GDP** $220.96 bn (1988); $14,458 per head

**chronology**
**1901** Creation of Commonwealth of Australia.
**1911** Site acquired for capital at Canberra.
**1927** Seat of government moved to Canberra.
**1942** Statute of Westminster Adoption Act gave Australia autonomy from UK in internal and external affairs.
**1944** Liberal Party founded by Robert Menzies.
**1951** Australia joined New Zealand and the USA as a signatory to the ANZUS Pacific security treaty.
**1966** Menzies resigned after being Liberal prime minister for 17 years, and was succeeded by Harold Holt.
**1968** John Gorton became prime minister after Holt's death.
**1971** Gorton succeeded by William McMahon, heading a Liberal–National Party coalition.
**1972** Gough Whitlam became prime minister, leading a Labor government.
**1975** Senate blocked the government's financial legislation; Whitlam declined to resign but was dismissed by the governor general, who invited Malcolm Fraser to form a Liberal–National Party caretaker government. The action of the governor general, John Kerr, was widely criticized.
**1977** Kerr resigned.
**1978** Northern Territory attained self-government.
**1983** Australian Labor Party, returned to power under Bob Hawke, convened meeting of employers and unions to seek concensus on economic policy to deal with growing unemployment.
**1986** Australia Act passed by UK government, eliminating last vestiges of British legal authority in Australia.
**1988** Labor foreign minister Bill Hayden appointed governor general designate. Free trade agreement with New Zealand signed.
**1989** Andrew Peacock returned as Liberal Party leader. National Party leader, Ian Sinclair, replaced by Charles Blunt.
**1990** Hawke wins record fourth election victory, defeating Liberal Party by small majority. John Henson elected leader or Liberal Party.
**1991** Hawke defeated challenge for Labor Party leadership from Paul Keating.

---

## Austria (Republic of)
(*Republik Österreich*)

**area** 83,920 sq km/32,393 sq mi

**capital** Vienna

**towns** Graz, Linz, Salzburg, Innsbruck

**physical** mountainous, with the Alps in W and S and the Danube River basin in E

**features** Austrian Alps (including Zugspitze and Brenner and Semmering passes); river Danube; Hainburg, the largest primeval rainforest left in Europe, now under threat from a dam project (suspended in 1990)

**head of state** Kurt Waldheim from 1986

**head of government** Franz Vranitzky from 1986

**political system** democratic federal republic

**political parties** Socialist Party of Austria (SPÖ), democratic socialist; Austrian People's Party (ÖVP), progressive centrist; Freedom Party of Austria (FPÖ), moderate left-of-centre; United Green Party of Austria (VGÖ), conservative ecological; Green Alternative Party (ALV), radical ecological

**exports** manufactured goods, lumber, textiles, chemicals

**currency** schilling (20.64 = £1 July 1991)

**population** (1990 est) 7,595,000; growth rate 0% p.a.

**life expectancy** men 70, women 77

**language** German

**religion** Roman Catholic 85%, Protestant 6%

**literacy** 98% (1983)

**GNP** $94.7 bn (1986); $12,521 per head

**chronology**
**1867** Emperor Franz Josef established dual monarchy of Austria and Hungary.
**1914** Archduke Franz Ferdinand assassinated by Serbian nationalists; Austria-Hungary invaded Serbia, precipitating start of World War I.
**1918** Habsburg empire ended, republic proclaimed.
**1938** Austria incorporated into German Third Reich by Hitler.
**1945** Under Allied occupation, 1920 constitution reinstated and coalition government formed by the SPÖ and the ÖVP.
**1955** Allied occupation ended, and the independence of Austria formally recognized.
**1966** ÖVP in power with Josef Klaus as chancellor.
**1970** SPÖ formed a minority government, with Dr Bruno Kreisky as chancellor.
**1983** Kreisky resigned, was replaced by Dr Fred Sinowatz, leading a coalition.
**1986** Dr Kurt Waldheim elected president. Sinowatz resigned, succeeded by Franz Vranitzky. No party won an overall majority; Vranitzky formed a coalition of the SPÖ and the ÖVP, with ÖVP leader, Dr Alois Mock, as vice-chancellor. Sinowatz denounced the coalition as a betrayal of socialist principles and resigned his SPÖ chair.
**1989** Austria sought European Community membership.
**1990** Vranitzky re-elected.

---

## Bahamas (Commonwealth of the)

**area** 13,864 sq km/5,352 sq mi

**capital** Nassau on New Providence
**physical** comprises 700 tropical coral islands and about
 1,000 cays

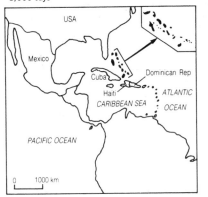

**features** desert islands: only 30 are inhabited; Blue Holes
 of Andros, the world's longest and deepest submarine
 caves
**head of state** Elizabeth II from 1973 represented by governor general
**head of government** Lynden Oscar Pindling from 1967
**political system** constitutional monarchy
**political parties** Progressive Liberal Party (PLP), centrist;
 Free National Movement (FNM), centre-left
**exports** cement, pharmaceuticals, petroleum products,
 crawfish, rum, pulpwood; over half the islands' employment comes from tourism
**currency** Bahamian dollar (1.61 = £1 July 1991)
**population** (1990 est) 251,000; growth rate 1.8% p.a.
**language** English
**religion** 29% Baptist, 23% Anglican, 22% Roman Catholic
**literacy** 95% (1986)
**GDP** $2.7 bn (1987); $11,260 per head

**chronology**
**1964** Independence achieved from Britain.
**1967** First national assembly elections.
**1972** Constitutional conference to discuss full independence.
**1973** Full independence achieved.
**1983** Allegations of drug trafficking by government ministers.
**1984** Deputy prime minister and two cabinet ministers
 resigned. Pindling denied any personal involvement and
 was endorsed as party leader.
**1987** Pindling re-elected despite claims of frauds. penny

---

**Bahrain (State of)**
(*Dawlat al Bahrayn*)

**area** 688 sq km/266 sq mi
**capital** Manama on the largest island (also called Bahrain)
**towns** oil port Mina Sulman
**physical** 35 islands, composed largely of sand-covered
 limestone; generally poor and infertile soil; flat and hot
**features** causeway linking Bahrain to mainland Saudi Arabia; Sitra island is a communications centre for the lower
 Persian Gulf and has a satellite-tracking station; a wildlife park featuring the oryx on Bahrain; most of the south
 of the island is preserved for the ruling family's falconry
**head of state and government** Sheikh Isa bin Sulman al-
 Khalifa (1933– ) from 1961
**political system** absolute emirate
**political parties** none
**exports** oil, natural gas, aluminium, fish

**currency** Bahrain dinar (0.61 = £1 July 1991)
**population** (1990 est) 512,000 (two thirds are nationals);
 growth rate 4.4% p.a.

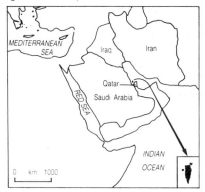

**life expectancy** men 67, women 71
**language** Arabic (official), Farsi, English, Urdu
**religion** Muslim (Shi'ite 60%, Sunni 40%)
**literacy** men 79%/women 64% (1985 est)
**GDP** $4.1 bn (1984); $6,315 per head

**chronology**
**1861** Became British protectorate.
**1968** Britain announced its intention to withdraw its
 forces. Bahrain formed, with Qatar and the Trucial States,
 the Federation of Arab Emirates.
**1971** Qatar and the Trucial States withdrew from the federation and Bahrain became an independent state.
**1973** New constitution adopted, with an elected national
 assembly.
**1975** Prime minister resigned and national assembly dissolved. Emir and his family assumed virtually absolute
 power.
**1986** Gulf University established in Bahrain. A causeway
 (25 km/15 mi long) linking the island with Saudi Arabia
 was opened.
**1988** Bahrain recognizes Afghan rebel government.

---

**Bangladesh (People's Republic of)**
(*Gana Prajatantri Bangladesh* formerly *East Pakistan*)

**area** 144,000 sq km/55,585 sq mi
**capital** Dhaka (formerly Dacca)
**towns** ports Chittagong, Khulna
**physical** flat delta of rivers Ganges and Brahmaputra; an-

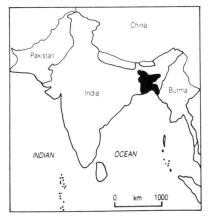

nual rainfall of 2,540 mm/100 in; some 75% of the land
is less than 3 m/10 ft above sea level and vulnerable to
flooding and cyclones; hilly in extreme SE and NE
**head of state** Shahabuddin Ahmad (interim president)
from Dec 1990
**head of government** Khaleda Zia from 1991
**political system** restricted democratic republic
**political parties** Jatiya Dal (National Party), Islamic nationalist; Awami League, secular, moderate socialist; Bangladesh National Party (BNP), Islamic right-of-centre
**exports** jute (50% of world production), tea, garments
**currency** taka (56.00 = £1 July 1991)
**population** (1990 est) 117,980,000; growth rate 2.7%
p.a.
**life expectancy** men 50, women 52
**language** Bangla (Bengali)
**religion** Sunni Muslim 85%, Hindu 14%
**literacy** men 43%/women 22% (1985 est)
**GDP** $11.2 bn (1983); $119 per head

chronology
**1947** Formed into eastern province of Pakistan on partition of British India.
**1970** Half a million killed in flood.
**1971** Bangladesh emerged as independent nation, under
leadership of Sheik Mujibur Rahman, after civil war.
**1975** Mujibur Rahman assassinated. Martial law imposed.
**1976–77** Maj-Gen Zia ur-Rahman assumed power.
**1978–79** Elections held and civilian rule restored.
**1981** Assassination of Maj-Gen Zia.
**1982** Lt-Gen Ershad assumed power in army coup. Martial
law imposed.
**1986** Elections held but disputed. Martial law ended.
**1987** State of emergency declared in response to opposition demonstrations.
**1988** Assembly elections boycotted by main opposition
parties. State of emergency lifted. Islam made state
religion. Monsoon floods and cyclone left 35 million
homeless and thousands dead.
**1989** Power devolved to Chittagong Hill Tracts to end 14-
year conflict between local people and army-protected
settlers.
**1990** Following mass antigovernment protests, Pres
Hussain Mohammad Ershad resigned; replaced by
Shahabuddin Ahmad pending elections.
**1991** Parliamentary elections held; coalition government
formed with BNP dominant. Worst cyclone in country's history left 10 million homeless. Former president
Ershad jailed for 10 years.

## Barbados

**area** 430 sq km/166 sq mi
**capital** Bridgetown
**towns** Speightstown, Holetown, Oistins
**physical** most easterly island of the West Indies; surrounded by coral reefs; subject to hurricanes June–Nov
**features** highest point Mount Hillaby 340 m/1,115 ft
**head of state** Elizabeth II from 1966 represented by governor general Hugh Springer from 1984
**head of government** prime minister Erskine Lloyd
Sandiford from 1987
**political system** constitutional monarchy
**political parties** Barbados Labour Party (BLP), moderate
left-of-centre; Democratic Labour Party (DLP), moderate
left-of-centre; National Democratic Party (NDP), centre
**exports** sugar, rum, electronic parts, clothing
**currency** Barbados dollar (3.27 = £1 July 1991)
**population** (1990 est) 260,000; growth rate 0.5% p.a.
**life expectancy** men 70, women 75
**language** English
**religion** 70% Anglican, 9% Methodist, 4% Roman Catholic

**literacy** 99% (1984)
**GDP** $1 bn (1984); $3,040 per head

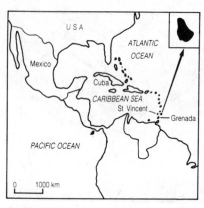

chronology
**1951** Universal adult suffrage introduced. BLP won general election.
**1954** Ministerial government established.
**1961** Independence achieved from Britain. DLP, led by
Errol Barrow, in power.
**1966** Barbados achieved full independence within
Commonwealth. Barrow became the new nation's first
prime minister.
**1972** Diplomatic relations with Cuba established.
**1976** BLP, led by Tom Adams, returned to power.
**1983** Barbados supported US invasion of Grenada.
**1985** Adams died suddenly; Bernard St John became
prime minister.
**1986** DLP, led by Barrow, returned to power.
**1987** Barrow died, succeeded by Erskine Lloyd Sandiford.
**1989** New NDP opposition formed.
**1991** DLP under Erskine Sandifield, won general election.

## Belgium (Kingdom of)
(French *Royaume de Belgique*, Flemish *Koninkrijk België*)

**area** 30,510 sq km/11,784 sq mi
**capital** Brussels
**towns** Ghent, Liège, Charleroi, Bruges, Mons, Namur,
Leuven; ports are Antwerp, Ostend, Zeebrugge

**physical** flat coastal plain in NW, central rolling hills, hills
and forest in SE
**features** Ardennes; rivers Scheldt and Meuse
**head of state** King Baudouin from 1951

**head of government** Wilfried Martens from 1981
**political system** liberal democracy
**political parties** Flemish Social Christian Party (CVP),
centre-left; French Social Christian Party (PSC), centre-
left; Flemish Socialist Party (SP), left-of-centre; French
Socialist Party (PS), left-of-centre; Flemish Liberal Party
(PVV), moderate centrist; French Liberal Reform Party
(PRL), moderate centrist; Flemish People's Party (VU),
federalist; Flemish Green Party (Agalev); French Green
Party (Ecolo)
**exports** iron, steel, textiles, manufactured goods, petrochemicals
**currency** Belgian franc (60.30 = £1 July 1991)
**population** (1990 est) 9,895,000 (comprising Flemings
and Walloons); growth rate 0.1% p.a.
**life expectancy** men 72, women 78
**language** in the N (Flanders) Flemish (a Dutch dialect,
known as *Vlaams*) 55%; in the S (Wallonia) Walloon (a
French dialect 32%; bilingual 11%; German (E border)
0.6%; all are official
**religion** Roman Catholic 75%
**literacy** 98% (1984)
**GDP** $111 bn (1986); $9,230 per head

**chronology**
**1830** Belgium became an independent kingdom.
**1914** Invaded by Germany.
**1940** Again invaded by Germany.
**1948** Belgium became founding member of Benelux Customs Union.
**1949** Belgium became founding member of Council of
Europe and NATO.
**1951** Leopold III abdicated in favour of his son Baudouin.
**1952** Belgium became founding member of European
Coal and Steel Community (ECSC).
**1957** Belgium became founding member of the European
Community (EC).
**1971** Steps towards regional autonomy taken.
**1972** German-speaking members of the cabinet included
for the first time.
**1973** Linguistic parity achieved in government appointments.
**1974** Separate regional councils and ministerial committees established.
**1978** Wilfried Martens succeeded Leo Tindemans as
prime minister.
**1980** Open violence over language divisions. Regional assemblies for Flanders and Wallonia and a three-member
executive for Brussels created.
**1981** Short-lived coalition led by Mark Eyskens was followed by the return of Martens.
**1987** Martens head of caretaker government after breakup
of coalition.
**1988** Following a general election, Martens formed a new
CVP–PS–SP–PSC–VU coalition.

**Belize**
(formerly *British Honduras*)

**area** 22,963 sq km/8,864 sq mi
**capital** Belmopan
**towns** port Belize City
**physical** tropical swampy coastal plain, Maya Mountains
in S, over 90% under forest
**features** world's second longest barrier reef; Cockscomb
jaguar reserve; Maya ruins
**head of state** Elizabeth II from 1981 represented by governor general
**head of government** George Price from 1989
**political system** constitutional monarchy
**political parties** People's United Party (PUP), left-of-
centre; United Democratic Party (UDP), moderate conservative
**exports** sugar, citrus, rice, lobster

**currency** Belize dollar (3.25 = £1 July 1991)
**population** (1990 est) 180,400 (including Mayan minority in the interior); growth rate 2.5% p.a.
**life expectancy** 60 (1988)
**language** English (official), Spanish (widely spoken), native Creole dialects
**religion** Roman Catholic 60%, Protestant 35%
**literacy** 93% (1988)
**GDP** $176 million (1983); $1,000 per head

**chronology**
**1862** Belize became a British colony.
**1954** Constitution adopted, providing for limited internal
self-government. General election won by George Price.
**1964** Self-government achieved from Britain (universal
adult suffrage introduced).
**1965** Two-chamber national assembly introduced, with
Price as prime minister.
**1970** Capital moved from Belize City to Belmopan.
**1974** British Honduras became Belize.
**1975** British troops sent to defend the disputed frontier
with Guatemala.
**1977** Negotiations undertaken with Guatemala but no
agreement reached.
**1980** United Nations called for full independence.
**1981** Full independence achieved. Price became prime
minister.
**1984** Price defeated in general election. Manuel Esquivel
formed the government. Britain reaffirmed its undertaking to defend the frontier.
**1989** Price and the PUP won the general election.

**Benin (People's Republic of)**
(*République Populaire du Bénin*)

**area** 112,622 sq km/43,472 sq mi

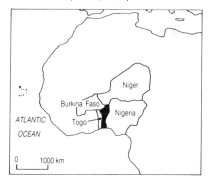

**capital** Porto Novo (official), Cotonou (de facto)
**towns** Abomey, Natitingou; chief port Cotonou
**physical** flat, humid, with dense vegetation
**features** fishing villages on stilts
**head of state and government** Nicephore Soglo from 1991
**political system** socialist pluralist republic
**political parties** Party of the People's Revolution of Benin (PRPB), Marxist-Leninist; other parties from 1990
**exports** cocoa, peanuts, cotton, palm oil, petroleum
**currency** CFA franc (498.25 = £1 July 1991)
**population** (1990 est) 4,840,000; growth rate 3% p.a.
**life expectancy** men 42, women 46
**language** French (official); Fan 47%
**religion** animist 65%, Christian 17%, Muslim 13%
**literacy** men 37%/women 16% (1985 est)
**GDP** $1.1 bn (1983); $290 per head

**chronology**
**1851** Under French control.
**1958** Became self-governing dominion within the French Community.
**1960** Independence achieved from France.
**1960–72** Acute political instability, with switches from civilian to military rule.
**1972** Military regime established by General Mathieu Kerekou.
**1974** Kerekou announced that the country would follow a path of 'scientific socialism'.
**1975** Name of country changed from Dahomey to Benin.
**1977** Return to civilian rule under a new constitution.
**1980** Kerekou formally elected president by the national revolutionary assembly.
**1989** Marxist-Leninism dropped as official ideology. Strikes and protests against his rule mounted; Kerekou banned demonstrations and deployed the army against protesters.
**1990** Referendum support for multiparty politics.
**1991** Multiparty elections held. Kerekou defeated in presidential elections by Nicephore Soglo.

## Bhutan (Kingdom of)
(*Druk-yul*)

**area** 46,500 sq km/17,954 sq mi
**capital** Thimbu (Thimphu)
**towns** Paro, Punakha, Mongar
**physical** occupies S slopes of the Himalayas; cut by valleys formed by tributaries of the Brahmaputra; thick forests in S

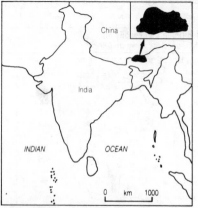

**head of state and government** Jigme Singye Wangchuk from 1972
**political system** absolute monarchy

**political parties** none officially; illegal Bhutan People's Party (BPP)
**exports** timber, talc, fruit, cement
**currency** ngultrum (34.09 = £1 July 1991); also Indian currency
**population** (1990 est) 1,566,000; growth rate 2% p.a.
**life expectancy** men 44, women 43
**language** offical Dzongkha (a Tibetan dialect), Nepali, and English
**religion** 75% Lamaistic Buddhist, 25% Hindu
**literacy** 5%
**GDP** $300 million (1986); $210 per head

**chronology**
**1865** Trade treaty with Britain signed.
**1907** First hereditary monarch installed.
**1910** Anglo-Bhutanese Treaty signed.
**1945** Indo-Bhutan Treaty of Friendship signed.
**1952** King Jigme Dorji Wangchuk installed.
**1953** National assembly established.
**1959** 4,000 Tibetan refugees given asylum.
**1968** King established first cabinet.
**1972** King died and was succeeded by his son Jigme Singye Wangchuk.
**1979** Tibetan refugees told to take Bhutanese citizenship or leave; most stayed.
**1983** Bhutan became a founding member of the South Asian Regional Cooperation organization (SARC).
**1988** King imposed 'code of conduct' suppressing Nepalese customs.
**1989** People's Forum of Human Rights founded.
**1990** Pro-democracy demonstrations took place.

## Bolivia (Republic of)
(*República de Bolivia*)

**area** 1,098,581 sq km/424,052 sq mi
**capital** La Paz (seat of government), Sucre (legal capital and seat of judiciary)
**towns** Santa Cruz, Cochabamba
**physical** high plateau between mountain ridges; forest and lowlands in the E
**features** Andes, lakes Titicaca and Poopó
**head of state and government** Jaime Paz Zamora from 1989

**political system** emergent democratic republic
**political parties** National Revolutionary Movement (MNR), centre-right; Nationalist Democratic Action Party (ADN), extreme right-wing; Movement of the Revolutionary Left (MIR), left-of-centre

**exports** tin (second largest world producer), other non-ferrous metals, oil, gas (piped to Argentina), agricultural products, coffee, sugar, cotton
**currency** boliviano (5.80 = £1 July 1991)
**population** (1990 est) 6,730,000; (Quechua 25%, Aymara 17%, Mestizo 30%, European 14%); growth rate 2.7% p.a.
**life expectancy** men 51, women 54
**language** Spanish, Aymara, Quechua (all official)
**religion** Roman Catholic 95% (state-recognized)
**literacy** men 84%/women 65% (1985 est)
**GDP** $3 bn (1983); $570 per head

**chronology**
**1825** Liberated from Spanish rule by Simón Bolívar; independence achieved (formerly known as Upper Peru).
**1952** Dr Víctor Paz Estenssoro elected president.
**1956** Dr Hernan Siles Zuazo became president.
**1960** Estenssoro returned to power.
**1964** Army coup led by vice president.
**1966** Gen René Barrientos became president.
**1967** Uprising, led by 'Che' Guevara, put down with US help.
**1969** Barrientos killed in plane crash, replaced by vice-president Siles Salinas. Army coup deposed him.
**1970** Army coup put Gen Juan Torres Gonzalez in power.
**1971** Torres replaced by Col Hugo Banzer Suarez.
**1973** Banzer promised a return to democratic government.
**1974** Attempted coup prompted Banzer to postpone elections and ban political and trade union activity.
**1978** Elections declared invalid after allegations of fraud.
**1980** More inconclusive elections followed by another coup, led by Gen Garcia. Allegations of corruption and drug trafficking led to cancellation of US and EC aid.
**1981** Garcia forced to resign. Replaced by Gen Celso Torrelio Villa.
**1982** Torrelio resigned. Replaced by military junta led by Gen Vildoso. Because of worsening economy, Vildoso asked congress to install a civilian administration. Dr Siles Zuazo chosen as president.
**1983** Economic aid from USA and Europe resumed.
**1984** New coalition government formed by Siles. Abduction of president by right-wing officers. The president undertook a five-day hunger strike as an example to the nation.
**1985** Pres Siles resigned. Election result inconclusive. Dr Paz Estenssoro, at the age of 77, chosen by congress.
**1989** Jaime Paz Zamora (MIR) elected president in power-sharing arrangement with Hugo Banzer Suarez; pledged to maintain fiscal and monetary discipline and preserve free-market policies.

## Botswana (Republic of)

**area** 582,000 sq km/225,000 sq mi
**capital** Gaborone
**towns** Mahalpye, Serowe, Tutume, Francistown
**physical** desert in SW, plains in E, fertile lands and swamp in N
**features** the Kalahari Desert; Okavango Swamp in N, remarkable for its wildlife; Makgadikgadi salt pans in E; diamonds mined at Orapa and Jwaneng in partnership with De Beers of South Africa
**head of state and government** Quett Ketamile Joni Masire from 1980
**political system** democratic republic
**political parties** Botswana Democratic Party (BDP), moderate centrist; Botswana National Front (BNF), moderate left-of-centre
**exports** diamonds, copper, nickel, meat
**currency** pula (3.37 = £1 July 1991)
**population** (1990 est) 1,218,000 (80% Bamangwato, 20% Bangwaketse); growth rate 3.5% p.a.

**life expectancy** men 53, women 56
**language** English (official); Setswana (national)
**religion** Christian 50%, animist 50%
**literacy** men 73%/women 69% (1985 est)
**GDP** $905 million (1985); $880 per head

**chronology**
**1885** Became a British protectorate.
**1960** New constitution created a legislative council.
**1963** End of rule by high commission.
**1965** Capital transferred from Mafeking to Gaborone. Internal self-government granted. Seretse Khama elected head of government.
**1966** Independence achieved from Britain. New constitution came into effect; name changed from Bechuanaland to Botswana; Seretse Khama elected president.

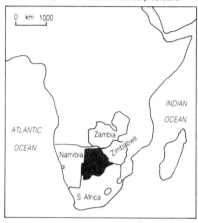

**1980** Seretse Khama died; succeeded by vice president Quett Masire.
**1984** Masire re-elected.
**1985** South African raid on Gaborone.
**1987** Joint permanent commission with Mozambique established, to improve relations.
**1989** The BDP and Masire re-elected.

## Brazil (Federative Republic of)
(*República Federativa do Brasil*)

**area** 8,511,965 sq km/3,285,618 sq mi

**capital** Brasília
**towns** São Paulo, Belo Horizonte, Curitiba, Manaus
Fortaleza; ports are Rio de Janeiro, Belém, Recife, Pôrto
Alegre, Salvador
**physical** the densely forested Amazon basin covers the
northern half of the country with a network of rivers;
the south is fertile; enormous energy resources, both
hydroelectric (Itaipú dam on the Paraná, and Tucurui
on the Tocantins) and nuclear (uranium ores)
**features** Mt Roraima, Xingu National Park; Amazon delta;
Rio harbour; one-third of the world's tropical rainforest is
in Brazil, which has a greater variety of flowering plants
than any other country in the world
**head of state and government** Fernando Affonso Collor de
Mello from 1989
**political system** emergent democratic federal republic
**political parties** Social Democratic Party (PDS), moderate left-of-centre; Brazilian Democratic Movement Party
(PMDB), centre-left; Liberal Front Party (PFL), moderate
left-of-centre; Workers' Party, left-of-centre; National
Reconstruction Party (PRN), centre-right
**exports** coffee, sugar, soybeans, cotton, textiles, timber, motor vehicles, iron, chrome, manganese, tungsten
and other ores, as well as quartz crystals, industrial
diamonds, gemstones; the world's sixth largest arms
exporter.
**currency** cruzado (introduced 1986; value = 100 cruzei-
ros, the former unit) (44.13 = £1 Feb 1990)
**population** (1990 est) 153,770,000 (including 200,000
Indians, survivors of 5 million, especially in Rondonia
and Mato Grosso, mostly living on reservations); growth
rate 2.2% p.a.
**life expectancy** men 61, women 66
**language** Portuguese (official); 120 Indian languages
**religion** Roman Catholic 89%; Indian faiths
**literacy** men 79%/women 76% (1985 est)
**GDP** $352 bn (1988); $2,434 per head

**chronology**
**1822** Independence achieved from Portugal; ruled by
Dom Pedro, son of the refugee King John VI of Portugal.
**1889** Monarchy abolished and republic established.
**1891** Constitution for a federal state adopted.
**1930** Dr Getulio Vargas became president.
**1945** Vargas deposed by the military.
**1946** New constitution adopted.
**1951** Vargas returned to office.
**1954** Vargas committed suicide.
**1956** Juscelino Kubitschek became president.
**1960** Capital moved to Brasília.
**1961** João Goulart became president.
**1964** Bloodless coup made Gen Castelo Branco president;
he assumed dictatorial powers, abolishing free political
parties.
**1967** New constitution adopted. Branco succeeded by
Marshal da Costa e Silva.
**1969** Da Costa e Silva resigned and a military junta
took over.
**1974** Gen Ernesto Geisel became president.
**1978** Gen Baptista de Figueiredo became president.
**1979** Political parties legalized again.
**1984** Mass calls for a return to fully democratic government.
**1985** Tancredo Neves became first civilian president in
21 years. Neves died and was succeeded by the vice
president, José Sarney.
**1988** New constitution approved, transferring power from
the president to the congress. Measures announced to
halt large-scale burning of Amazonian rainforest for cattle grazing.
**1989** Forest Protection Service and Ministry for Land Reform abolished. International concern over how much of
the Amazon has been burned. Fernando Collor (PRN)
elected president Dec, pledging free-market economic
policies.

**1990** Government won the general election offset by mass
abstentions.

---

### Brunei (The Islamic Sultanate of)
(*Negara Brunei Darussalam*)

**area** 5,765 sq km/2,225 sq mi
**capital** and chief port Bandar Seri Begawan
**towns** Tutong, Seria, Kuala Belait
**physical** flat coastal plain with hilly lowland in W and
mountains in E; 75% of the area is forested; the Limbang
valley splits Brunei in two, and its cession to Sarawak
1890 is disputed by Brunei

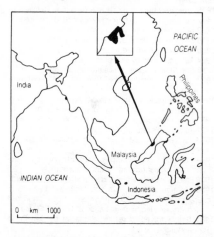

**head of state and of government** HM Muda Hassanal
Bolkiah Mu'izzaddin Waddaulah, Sultan of Brunei, from
1968
**political system** absolute monarchy
**political parties** Brunei National United Party (BNUP),
Brunei National Democratic Party (banned 1988)
**exports** liquefied natural gas (world's largest producer)
and oil, both expected to be exhausted by the year 2000
**currency** Brunei dollar (2.86 = £1 July 1991)
**population** (1990 est) 372,000 (65% Malay, 25% Chinese—few Chinese granted citizenship); growth rate
12% p.a.
**life expectancy** 74
**language** Malay (official), Chinese (Hokkien), English
**religion** 60% Muslim (official)
**literacy** men 75%/women 50% (1971)
**GDP** $3.8 bn (1983); $20,000 per head

**chronology**
**1888** Brunei became a British protectorate.
**1941–45** Occupied by Japan.
**1959** Written constitution made Britain responsible for
defence and external affairs.
**1962** Sultan began rule by decree.
**1963** Proposal to join Malaysia abandoned.
**1967** Sultan abdicated in favour of his son, Hassanal
Bolkiah.
**1971** Brunei given internal self-government.
**1975** UN resolution called for independence for Brunei.
**1984** Independence achieved from Britain, with Britain
maintaining a small force to protect the oil and gas
fields.
**1985** A 'loyal and reliable' political party, the Brunei National Democratic Party (BNDP), legalized.
**1986** Death of former sultan, Sir Omar. Formation of
multi-ethnic Brunei National United Party (BNUP).
**1988** BNDP banned.

## Bulgaria (People's Republic of)
(*Narodna Republika Bulgaria*)

**area** 110,912 sq km/42,812 sq mi
**capital** Sofia
**towns** Plovdiv, Ruse; Black Sea ports Burgas and Varna
**physical** Balkan and Rhodope mountains; Danube River in N

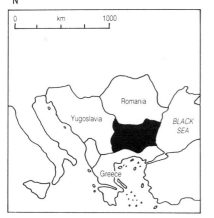

**features** key position on land route from Europe to Asia; Black Sea coast
**head of state** Zhelyo Zhelev from 1990
**head of government** Dimitur Popov from 1990
**political system** socialist pluralist republic
**political parties** Bulgarian Socialist Party (BSP), the former communist party; Bulgarian Agrarian People's Union (BZNS); Union of Democratic Forces (UDF)
**exports** textiles, chemicals, nonferrous metals, timber, minerals, machinery
**currency** lev (31.01 = £1 July 1991)
**population** (1990 est) 8,978,000 including 900,000–1,500,000 ethnic Turks, concentrated in S and NE); growth rate 0.1% p.a.
**life expectancy** men 69, women 74
**language** Bulgarian, Turkish
**religion** Eastern Orthodox Christian 90%, Sunni Muslim 10%
**literacy** men 96%/women 93% (1980 est)
**GNP** $61.2 bn (1986); $6,800 per head

**chronology**
**1908** Bulgaria became a kingdom independent of Turkish rule.
**1944** Soviet invasion of German-occupied Bulgaria.
**1946** Monarchy abolished and communist-dominated people's republic proclaimed.
**1947** Soviet-style constitution adopted.
**1949** Death of Georgi Dimitrov, the communist government leader.
**1954** Election of Todor Zhivkov as Communist Party general secretary; made nation a loyal satellite of USSR.
**1971** Constitution modified; Zhivkov elected president.
**1985–88** Large administrative and personnel changes made haphazardly under Soviet stimulus.
**1987** New electoral law introduced multi-candidate elections.
**1989** 310,000 ethnic Turks fled in opposition to the 'Bulgarianization' campaign of forced assimilation. Zhivkov ousted by Petar Mladenov in Nov and expelled from BCP. Sweeping pluralist reforms instituted, and opposition parties allowed to form; Bulgarianization abandoned.
**1990** Alexander Lilov elected new BCP leader and Andrey Loukanov prime minister in Feb, the latter replaced in

Dec by Popov heading a coalition government.
**1991** Food shortages and price rises accompanied the move to a market economy.

## Burkina Faso (The People's Democratic Republic of)
(formerly *Upper Volta*)

**area** 274,122 sq km/105,811 sq mi
**capital** Ouagadougou
**towns** Bobo-Dioulasso

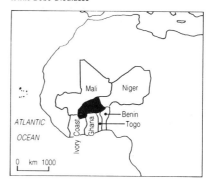

**physical** landlocked plateau with hills in W and SW; headwaters of the river Volta
**features** tropical savanna exposed to overgrazing and deforestation
**head of state and government** Blaise Compaore from 1987
**political system** one-party military republic
**political parties** Organization for Popular Democracy-Workers' Movement (ODP-MT), nationalist left-wing
**exports** cotton, groundnuts, livestock, hides, skins, sesame
**currency** CFA franc (498.25 = £1 July 1991)
**population** (1990 est) 8,941,000; growth rate 2.4% p.a.
**life expectancy** men 44, women 47
**language** French (official); about 50 native Sudanie languages spoken by 90% of population
**religion** animist 53%, Sunni Muslim 36%, Roman Catholic 11%
**literacy** men 21%/women 6% (1985 est)
**GDP** $1.2 bn (1983); $180 per head

**chronology**
**1958** Became a self-governing republic within the French Community.
**1960** Independence achieved from France, with Maurice Yameogo as the first president.
**1966** Military coup led by Col Lamizana. Constitution suspended, political activities banned, and a supreme council of the armed forces established.
**1969** Ban on political activities lifted.
**1970** Referendum approved a new constitution leading to a return to civilian rule.
**1974** After experimenting with a mixture of military and civilian rule, Lamizana reassumed full power.
**1977** Ban on political activities removed. Referendum approved a new constitution based on civilian rule.
**1978** Lamizana elected president.
**1980** Lamizana overthrown in bloodless coup led by Col Zerbo.
**1982** Zerbo ousted in a coup by junior officers. Maj Ouédraogo became president and Thomas Sankara prime minister.
**1983** Sankara seized complete power.
**1984** Upper Volta renamed Burkina Faso, 'land of upright men'.
**1987** Sankara killed in coup led by Blaise Compaore.

**1989** New government party ODP-MT formed by merger of other pro-government parties. Coup against Compoare foiled.

## Burundi (Republic of)
(*Republika y'Uburundi*)

**area** 27,834 sq km/10,744 sq mi
**capital** Bujumbura
**towns** Gitega

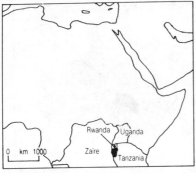

**physical** landlocked grassy highland straddling watershed of Nile and Congo
**features** Lake Tanganyika, Great Rift Valley
**head of state and government** Pierre Buyoya from 1987
**political system** one-party military republic
**political parties** Union for National Progress (UPRONA), nationalist socialist
**exports** coffee, cotton, tea, nickel, hides, livestock; there are 500 million tonnes of peat reserves in the basin of the Akanyaru river
**currency** Burundi franc (287.50 = £1 July 1991)
**population** (1990 est) 5,647,000 (of whom 15% are the Nilotic Tutsi, still holding most of the land and political power, 1% are Pymy Twa, and the remainder Bantu Hutu); growth rate 2.8% p.a.
**life expectancy** men 45, women 48
**language** Kirundi (a Bantu language) and French (official); Kiswahili
**religion** Roman Catholic 62%, Protestant 5%, Muslim 1%, animist 32%
**literacy** men 43%/women 26% (1985)
**GDP** $1 bn (1983); $273 per head

chronology
**1962** Separated from Ruanda-Urundi, as Burundi, and given independence as a monarchy under King Mwambutsa IV.
**1966** King deposed by his son Charles, who became Ntare V; he was in turn deposed by his prime minister, Capt Michel Micombero, who declared Burundi a republic.
**1972** Ntare V killed, allegedly by the Hutu ethnic group. Massacres of 150,000 Hutus by the rival Tutsi ethnic group, of which Micombero was a member.
**1973** Micombero made president and prime minister.
**1974** UPRONA declared the only legal political party, with the president as its secretary general.
**1976** Army coup deposed Micombero. Col Jean-Baptiste Bagaza appointed president by Supreme Revolutionary Council.
**1981** New constitution adopted, providing for a national assembly.
**1984** Bagaza elected president as sole candidate.
**1987** Bagaza deposed in coup in Sept. Maj Pierre Buyoya headed new Military Council for National Redemption.
**1988** Some 24,000 majority Hutus killed by Tutsis. First Hutu prime minister appointed.

## Cambodia (State of)
(formerly *Khmer Republic* 1970–1976 *Democratic Kampuchea* 1976–1979 *People's Republic of Kampuchea* 1979–1989)

**area** 181,035 sq km/69,880 sq mi
**capital** Phnom Penh
**towns** Battambang, the seaport Kompong Som

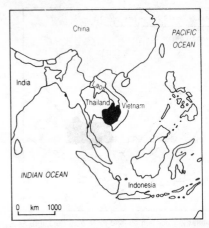

**physical** mostly flat forested plains with mountains in SW and N; Mekong River runs N to S
**features** ruins of ancient capital Angkor
**head of state** Heng Samrin from 1979*
**head of government** Hun Sen from 1985*
* Not internationally recognized. UN seat is held by government-in-exile formed 1982: Son Sann, premier; Norodom Sihanouk, coalition leader.
**political system** communism
**political parties** Kampuchean People's Revolutionary Party (KPRP), Marxist-Leninist; Party of Democratic Kampuchea (Khmer Rouge), exiled ultra-nationalist communist; Khmer People's National Liberation Front (KPNLF), exiled anti-communist; Sihanoukists, exiled prodemocracy forces allied to Prince Sihanouk
**exports** rubber, rice, pepper, wood
**currency** Cambodian riel (975.00 = £1 July 1991)
**population** (1990 est) 6,993,000; growth rate 2.2% p.a.
**life expectancy** men 42, women 45
**language** Khmer (official), French
**religion** Theravada Buddhist 95%
**literacy** men 78%/women 39% (1980 est)
**GDP** $100 per head (1984)

chronology
**1863–1941** French protectorate.
**1941–45** Occupied by Japan.
**1946** Recaptured by France.
**1953** Independence achieved from France.
**1970** Prince Sihanouk overthrown by US-backed Lon Nol.
**1975** Lon Nol overthrown by Khmer Rouge.
**1978–79** Vietnamese invasion and installation of Heng Samrin government.
**1982** The three main anti-Vietnamese resistance groups formed an alliance under Prince Sihanouk.
**1987** Partial withdrawal of Vietnamese troops.
**1988** Vietnamese troop withdrawal continued.
**1989** Name of State of Cambodia readopted and Buddhism declared state religion. Vietnamese forces fully withdrawn in Sept. Civil war intensified; Khmer Rouge captured a provincial capital; Sihanouk declared willingness to consider UN trusteeship pending

elections.
**1991** Some Vietnamese troops believed to have been redeployed to check fresh Khmer advances. Ceasefire agreed and peace talks started but subsequently collapsed.

## Cameroon (Republic of)
(*République du Cameroun*)

**area** 475,440 sq km/183,638 sq mi
**capital** Yaoundé
**towns** chief port Douala

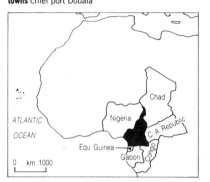

**physical** desert in far N in the Lake Chad basin, mountains in W, dry savanna plateau in the intermediate area, and dense tropical rainforest in S
**features** Mount Cameroon 4,070 m/13,358 ft, an active volcano on the coast, W of the Adamawa Mountains
**head of state and of government** Paul Biya from 1982
**political system** one-party authoritarian nationalism
**political parties** Democratic Assembly of the Cameroon People (RDPC), nationalist left-of-centre
**exports** cocoa, coffee, bananas, cotton, timber, rubber, groundnuts, gold, aluminium
**currency** CFA franc (498.25 = £1 July 1991)
**population** (1990 est) 11,109,000; growth rate 2.7% p.a.
**life expectancy** men 49, women 53
**language** French and English in pidgin variations (official); there has been some discontent with the emphasis on French—there are 163 indigenous peoples with their own African languages
**religion** Roman Catholic 35%, animist 25%, Muslim 22%, Protestant 18%
**literacy** men 68%/women 45% (1985 est)
**GDP** $12.6 bn (1984); $1,230 per head

**chronology**
**1884** Treaty signed establishing German rule.
**1916** Captured by Allied forces in World War I.
**1922** Divided between Britain and France.
**1946** French and British Cameroons made UN trust territories.
**1960** French Cameroon became the independent Republic of Cameroon. Ahmadou Ahidjo elected president.
**1961** N part of British Cameroon merged with Nigeria and S part joined the Republic of Cameroon to become the Federal Republic of Cameroon.
**1966** One-party regime introduced.
**1972** New constitution made Cameroon a unitary state, the United Republic of Cameroon.
**1973** New national assembly elected.
**1982** Ahidjo resigned and was succeeded by Paul Biya.
**1983** Biya began to remove his predecessor's supporters; accused by Ahidjo of trying to create a police state. Ahidjo went into exile in France.
**1984** Biya re-elected; defeated a plot to overthrow him.

Country's name changed to Republic of Cameroon.
**1988** Biya re-elected.
**1991** Widespread public disorder. Biya granted amnesty to political prisoners and promised multi-party elections.

## Canada (Dominion of)

**area** 9,970,600 sq km/3,849,803 sq mi
**capital** Ottawa
**towns** Toronto, Montréal, Vancouver, Edmonton, Calgary, Winnipeg, Québec, Hamilton, Saskatoon, Halifax

**physical** mountains in W, with low-lying plains in interior and rolling hills in E. Climate varies from temperate in S to arctic in N
**features** St Lawrence Seaway, Mackenzie River; Great Lakes; Arctic Archipelago; Rocky Mountains; Great Plains or Prairies; Canadian Shield
**head of state** Elizabeth II from 1952 represented by governor general
**head of government** Brian Mulroney from 1984
**political system** federal constitutional monarchy
**political parties** Progressive Conservative Party, free-enterprise centrist; Liberal Party, nationalist left-of-centre; New Democratic Party, moderate left-of-centre
**exports** wheat, timber, pulp, newsprint, fish (salmon), furs (ranched fox and mink exceed the value of wild furs), oil, natural gas, aluminium, asbestos, coal, copper, iron, nickel, motor vehicles and parts, industrial and agricultural machinery, fertilizers
**currency** Canadian dollar (1.85 = £1 July 1991)
**population** (1990 est) 26,527,000 including 300,000 North American Indians, of whom 75% live on over 2,000 reservations in Ontario and the four western provinces; some 300,000 Métis (people of mixed race) and 19,000 Inuit (or Eskimo, of whom 75% live in the Northwest Territories). Over half Canada's population lives in Ontario and Québec. Growth rate 1.1% p.a.
**life expectancy** men 72, women 79
**language** English, French (both official) (about 70% speak English, 20% French, and the rest are bilingual); there are also North American Indian languages and the Inuit Inuktitut
**religion** Roman Catholic 40%, Protestant 35%
**literacy** 99%
**GDP** $412 bn (1987); $15,910 per head

**chronology**
**1867** Dominion of Canada founded.
**1949** Newfoundland joined Canada.
**1957** Progressive Conservatives returned to power after 22 years in opposition.

**1961** New Democratic Party (NDP) formed.
**1963** Liberals elected under Lester Pearson.
**1968** Pearson succeeded by Pierre Trudeau.
**1979** Joe Clark, leader of the Progressive Conservatives, formed a minority government; defeated on budget proposals.
**1980** Liberals under Trudeau returned with a large majority.
**1982** Canada Act removed Britain's last legal control over Canadian affairs; 'patriation' of Canada's constitution.
**1983** Clark replaced as leader of the Progressive Conservatives by Brian Mulroney.
**1984** Trudeau retired and was succeeded as Liberal leader and prime minister by John Turner. Progressive Conservatives won the federal election with a large majority, and Mulroney became prime minister.
**1988** Conservatives re-elected with reduced majority on platform of free trade with the USA.
**1989** Free trade agreement signed. Turner resigned as Liberal Party leader, and Ed Broadbent as New Democratic Party leader.

## Cape Verde (Republic of)
(*República de Cabo Verde*)

**area** 4,033 sq km/1,557 sq mi
**capital** Praia

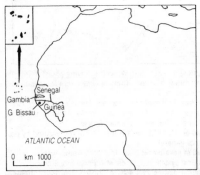

**physical** archipelago of ten volcanic islands 565 km/350 mi W of Senegal
**features** strategic importance guaranteed by its domination of western shipping lanes
**head of state** Mascarenhas Monteiro from 1991
**head of government** Carlos Viega from 1991
**political system** socialist pluralist state
**political parties** African Party for the Independence of Cape Verde (PAICV), African nationalist; Movement for Democracy (MPD)
**exports** bananas, coffee, salt, fish
**currency** Cape Verde escudo (126.94 = £1 July 1991)
**population** (1990 est) 375,000 (including 100,000 Angolan refugees); growth rate 1.9% p.a.
**life expectancy** men 57, women 61
**language** Creole dialect of Portuguese
**religion** Roman Catholic 80%
**literacy** men 61%/women 39% (1985)
**GDP** $135.1 million (1983); $390 per head

### chronology
**1951–74** Ruled as an overseas territory by Portugal.
**1974** Moved towards independence through a transitional Portuguese-Cape Verde government.
**1975** Independence achieved from Portugal. National people's assembly elected. Aristides Pereira became the first president.
**1980** Constitution adopted providing for eventual union with Guinea-Bissau.

**1981** Union with Guinea-Bissau abandoned and the constitution amended; became one-party state.
**1991** First multiparty elections held. New party, Movement for Democracy (MPD) won majority in assembly. Pereira replaced by Mascarenhas Monteiro.

## Central African Republic
(*République Centrafricaine*)

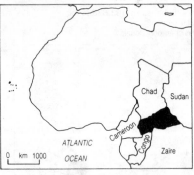

**area** 622,436 sq km/240,260 sq mi
**capital** Bangui
**physical** most of the country is on a plateau, with rivers flowing N and S. Dry in N, rainforest in SW
**head of state and government** André Kolingba from 1981
**political system** one-party military republic
**political parties** Central African Democratic Assembly (RDC), nationalist
**exports** diamonds, uranium, coffee, cotton, timber, tobacco
**currency** CFA franc (498.25 = £1 July 1991)
**population** (1990 est) 2,879,000; growth rate 2.3% p.a.
**life expectancy** men 41, women 45
**language** Sangho (national), French (official)
**religion** animist 35%; Roman Catholic 25%; Protestant 25%; Muslim 15%
**literacy** men 53%/women 29% (1985 est)
**GNP** $690 million (1983); $310 per head

### chronology
**1960** Central African Republic achieved independence from France; David Dacko elected president.
**1962** The republic made a one-party state.
**1965** Dacko ousted in military coup led by Col Bokassa.
**1966** Constitution rescinded and national assembly dissolved.
**1972** Bokassa declared himself president for life.
**1976** Bokassa made himself emperor of the Central African Empire.
**1979** Bokassa deposed by Dacko following violent repressive measures by the self-styled emperor, who went into exile.
**1981** Dacko deposed in a bloodless coup, led by Gen André Kolingba, and an all-military government established.
**1983** Clandestine opposition movement formed.
**1984** Amnesty for all political party leaders announced. Pres Mitterrand of France paid a state visit.
**1985** New constitution promised, with some civilians in the government.
**1986** Bokassa returned from France, expecting to return to power; he was imprisoned and his trial started. Gen Kolingba re-elected.
**1988** Bokassa found guilty and received death sentence, later commuted to life imprisonment.
**1990** Public calls for a return to multi-party politics.
**1991** Further calls for political reform.

## Chad (Republic of)
(République du Tchad)

**area** 1,284,000 sq km/495,624 sq mi
**capital** N'djamena
**towns** Sarh, Moundou, Abéché
**physical** mountains in NW, savanna and part of Sahara Desert in N; rivers in S flow N to Lake Chad in marshy E

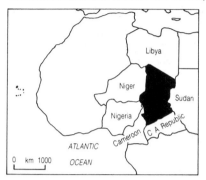

**head of state and government** Idriss Deby from 1990
**political system** emergent democracy
**political parties** National Union for Independence (UNIR), nationalist
**exports** cotton, meat, livestock, hides, skins, bauxite, uranium, gold, oil
**currency** CFA franc (498.25 = £1 July 1991)
**population** (1990 est) 5,064,000; growth rate 2.3% p.a.
**life expectancy** men 42, women 45
**language** French, Arabic (both official), over 100 African dialects spoken
**religion** Muslim 44% (N); Christian 33%; animist 23% (S)
**literacy** men 40%/women 11% (1985 est)
**GDP** $817 million (1986); $160 per head

**chronology**
**1960** Independence achieved from France, with François Tombalbaye as president.
**1963** Violent opposition in the Muslim north, led by the Chadian National Liberation Front (Frolinat), backed by Libya.
**1968** Revolt quelled with France's help.
**1975** Tombalbaye killed in military coup led by Felix Malloum. Frolinat continued its resistance.
**1978** Malloum tried to find a political solution by bringing the former Frolinat leader Hissène Habré into his government but they were unable to work together.
**1979** Malloum forced to leave the country; an interim government was set up under Gen Goukouni. Habré continued his opposition with his Army of the North (FAN).
**1981** Habré now in control of half the country, forcing Goukouni to flee to Cameroon and then Algeria, where, with Libya's support, he set up a 'government in exile'.
**1983** Habré's regime recognized by the Organization for African Unity (OAU), but in north Goukouni's supporters, with Libya's help, fought on. Eventually a ceasefire was agreed, dividing the country into two halves on either side of latitude 16° N.
**1984** Libya and France agreed to a withdrawal of forces.
**1985** Fighting between Libyan-backed and French-backed forces intensified.
**1987** Chad, France, and Libya agreed on ceasefire proposed by OAU.
**1988** Full diplomatic relations with Libya restored.
**1989** Libyan troop movements reported on border. Habré met Col Khaddaffi. In Dec Habré re-elected and new constitution announced.
**1990** Pres Habré ousted in coup led by Idriss Deby. New constitution adopted.

## Chile (Republic of)
(República de Chile)

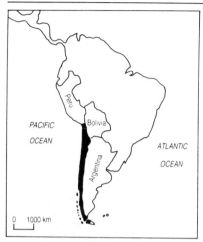

**area** 756,950 sq km/292,257 sq mi
**capital** Santiago
**towns** Concepción, Viña del Mar, Temuco; ports Valparaiso, Antofagasta, Arica, Iquique and Punta Arenas
**physical** Andes mountains along E border, Atacama Desert in N, arable land and forest in S
**territories** Easter Island, Juan Fernandez Islands, half of Tierra del Fuego, part of Antarctica
**head of state and government** Patricio Aylwin Azodar from 1990
**political system** emergent democratic republic
**political parties** Christian Democratic Party (PDC), moderate centrist; National Renewal Party (RN), right-wing
**exports** copper, iron, nitrate (Chile is the chief mining country of South America), pulp and paper
**currency** peso (583.65 = £1 July 1991)
**population** (1990 est) 13,000,000 (the majority mestizo, of mixed American Indian and Spanish descent); growth rate 1.6% p.a.
**life expectancy** men 67, women 73
**language** Spanish
**religion** Roman Catholic 89%
**literacy** 94% (1988)
**GNP** $21.8 bn (1983); $1,950 per head

**chronology**
**1818** Independence achieved from Spain.
**1964** PDC formed government under Eduardo Frei.
**1970** Dr Salvador Allende became the first democratically elected Marxist president; he embarked on an extensive programme of nationalization and social reform.
**1973** Government overthrown by the CIA-backed military, led by Gen Augusto Pinochet. Allende killed. Policy of repression began during which all opposition was put down and political activity banned.
**1983** Growing opposition to the regime from all sides, with outbreaks of violence.
**1988** Referendum on whether Pinochet should serve a further term resulted in a clear 'No' vote.
**1989** Pres Pinochet agreed to constitutional changes to allow pluralist politics. Patricio Aylwin (PDC) elected president. Pinochet remained as army commander.

**1990** Salvador Allende officially restored to favour. Aylwin reaches accord on end to military junta government. Pinochet censured by president.

---

*PEOPLE OF THE YEAR*

In July 1990 Alberto Fujimoro, a comparatively inexperienced politician, who had campaigned on a reformist ticket (Cambio 90/Change 90), took office as president. Fujimoro, of Japanese parentage, had defeated his more experienced Democratic Front opponent in the elections and inherited from Alan Garcia, the retiring president, a nation still struggling to maintain its democracy in the face of widespread violence by extremist groups such as the Maoist Shining Path (Sendero Luminoso) and right wing activists. With no assembly majority, but support from the underprivileged who respected his immigrant origins, the new president immediately called for a government of national unity.

### China (People's Republic of)
(*Zhonghua Renmin Gonghe Guo*)

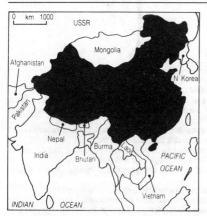

**area** 9,596,960 sq km/3,599,975 sq mi
**capital** Beijing (Peking)
**towns** Chongqing (Chungking), Shenyang (Mukden), Wuhan, Nanjing (Nanking), Harbin; ports Tianjin (Tientsin), Shanghai, Qingdao (Tsingtao), Lüda (Lü-ta), Guangzhou (Canton)
**physical** two-thirds of China is mountains or desert (N and W); the low-lying E is irrigated by rivers Huang He (Yellow River), Chang Jiang (Yangtze-Kiang), Xi Jiang (Si Kiang)
**features** Great Wall of China; Gezhouba Dam; Ming Tombs; Terra-Cotta Warriers (Xi'ein); Gobi Desert
**head of state** Yang Shangkun from 1988
**head of government** Li Peng from 1987
**political system** communist republic
**political parties** Chinese Communist Party (CCP), Marxist-Leninist-Maoist
**exports** tea, livestock and animal products, silk, cotton, oil, minerals (China is the world's largest producer of tungsten), chemicals, light industrial goods
**currency** yuan (8.76 = £1 July 1991)
**population** (1990 est) 1,130,065,000 (the majority are Han or ethnic Chinese; the 67 million of other ethnic groups, including Tibetan, Uigur, and Zhuang, live in border areas). The number of people of Chinese origin outside China, Taiwan, and Hong Kong is estimated at 15–24 million. Growth rate 1.2% p.a.
**life expectancy** men 67, women 69
**language** Chinese, including Mandarin (official), Cantonese and other dialects

**religion** officially atheist, but traditionally Taoist, Confucianist, and Buddhist; Muslim 13 million; Catholic 3–6 million (divided between the 'patriotic' church established 1958 and the 'loyal' church subject to Rome); Protestant 3 million
**literacy** men 82%/women 66% (1985 est)
**GDP** $313 bn (1983); $566 per head

**chronology**
**1949** People's Republic of China proclaimed by Mao Zedong.
**1954** Soviet-style constitution adopted.
**1956–57** Hundred Flowers Movement encouraged criticism of the government.
**1958–60** Great Leap Forward commune experiment to achieve 'true communism'.
**1960** Withdrawal of Soviet technical advisers.
**1962** Sino-Indian border war.
**1962–65** Economic recovery programme under Liu Shaoqi; Maoist 'socialist education movement' rectification campaign.
**1966–68** Great Proletarian Cultural Revolution and overthrow of Liu Shaoqi.
**1969** Ussuri river border clashes with USSR.
**1970–76** Reconstruction under Mao and Zhou Enlai; purge of extreme left.
**1971** Entry into United Nations.
**1972** US president Nixon visited Beijing.
**1975** New state constitution. Unveiling of Zhou's Four Modernizations programme.
**1976** Deaths of Zhou Enlai and Mao Zedong; appointment of Hua Guofeng as prime minister and Communist Party chair. Deng in hiding. Gang of Four arrested.
**1977** Rehabilitation of Deng Xiaoping.
**1979** Economic reforms introduced. Diplomatic relations opened with USA. Punitive invasion of Vietnam.
**1980** Zhao Ziyang appointed prime minister.
**1981** Hu Yaobang succeeded Hua as party chair. Imprisonment of Gang of Four.
**1982** New state constitution adopted.
**1984** 'Enterprise management' reforms for industrial sector.
**1986** Student prodemocracy demonstrations.
**1987** Hu was replaced as party leader by Zhao, with Li Peng as prime minister. Deng left Politburo but remained influential.
**1988** Yang Shangkun became state president. Economic reforms encountered increasing problems; inflation rocketed.
**1989** Following the death of Hu Yaobang, prodemocracy student demonstrations in Tiananmen Square, Beijing, were crushed by army, who killed over 2,000 demonstrators. Some international sanctions imposed in protest. Zhao Ziyang replaced as party leader by Jiang Zemin in swing towards conservatism. Deng retired from remaining army and party posts but received high-level US delegation in Dec.
**1991** Having given considerable support to the US line on the Gulf crisis, China was no longer subject to sanctions from the European Community or Japan. Normal relations with USSR resumed. Jiang Qing died, allegedly committing suicide.

---

*PEOPLE OF THE YEAR*

After spending 386 days in refuge, Professor Fang Lizhi, China's most renowned political dissident, was allowed to leave the US Embassy in Beijing for political exile in June 1990. Fang, a Canton-born astrophysicist, with a long-standing concern for human rights and an advocate of Western-style political pluralism, has been regarded as the conscience of the nation. As vice president of the Hefei Institute of Science and Technology, he encouraged his students to campaign for democracy, sparking off a movement that spread cross-campus and resulted in the resignation of the communist party's liberal-minded leader Hu Yaobang. Victimized in the conservative backlash of 1987–88, he was demoted to a research position at the Beijing Astronomical Observatory. Again, however, in the spring of 1989, Fang and his wife Li Shuxian, an associate-professor of physics at Beijing University, were the catalysts behind a broader pro-democracy spearheaded by students, which was eventually crushed in Tiananmen Square on 3–4 June 1989. In its aftermath, he was branded a 'counter-revolutionary propagandist' and was stripped of his membership of the Chinese Academy of Sciences.

### Colombia (Republic of)
(*República de Colombia*)

**area** 1,141,748 sq km/440,715 sq mi
**capital** Bogotá
**towns** Medellín, Cali, Bucaramanga; ports Barranquilla, Cartagena, Buenaventura

**physical** the Andes mountains run N–S; flat coastland in W and plains in E; Magdalena River runs N to Caribbean Sea
**head of state and government** Virgilio Barco Vargas from 1986
**political system** emergent democratic republic
**political parties** Liberal Party, centrist; April 19 Movement; National Salvation Movement; Conservative Party, right-of-centre
**exports** emeralds (world's largest producer), coffee (second largest world producer), cocaine (country's largest export), bananas, cotton, meat, sugar, oil, skins, hides
**currency** peso (1011.97 = £1 July 1991)
**population** (1990 est) 32,598,800 (mestizo 68%, white 20%, Amerindian 1%); growth rate 2.2% p.a.
**life expectancy** men 61, women 66; Indians 34
**language** Spanish
**religion** Roman Catholic 95%
**literacy** men 89%/women 87% (1985 est); Indians 40%
**GNP** $42.5 bn (1983); $1,112 per head

**chronology**
**1886** Full independence achieved from Spain. Conservatives in power.
**1930** Liberals in power.
**1946** Conservatives in power.
**1948** Left-wing mayor of Bogotá assassinated; widespread outcry.
**1949** Start of civil war, 'La Violencia', during which 280,000 people died.
**1957** Hoping to halt the violence, Conservatives and Liberals agreed to form a National Front, sharing the presidency.
**1970** National Popular Alliance (ANAPO) formed as a

left-wing opposition to the National Front.
**1974** National Front accord temporarily ended.
**1975** Civil unrest because of disillusionment with the government.
**1978** Liberals, under Julio Turbay, revived the accord and began an intensive fight against drug dealers.
**1982** Liberals maintained their control of congress but lost the presidency. The Conservative president, Belisario Betancur, attempted to end the violence by granting left-wing guerrillas an amnesty, freeing political prisoners, and embarking on a large public-works programme.
**1984** Minister of justice assassinated by drug dealers; campaign against them stepped up.
**1986** Virgilio Barco Vargas, Liberal, elected president by record margin.
**1989** Campaign against drug traffickers intensified.
**1990** Liberals maintained control of congress.
**1991** Peace talks with rebel leaders.

### Comoros (Federal Islamic Republic of)
(*Jumhurīyat al-Qumur al-Itthādīyah al-Islāmīyah*)

**area** 1,862 sq km/719 sq mi
**capital** Moroni
**physical** comprises the volcanic islands of Njazídja, Nzwani, and Mwali (formerly Grande Comore, Anjouan, Moheli); at N end of Mozambique Channel
**features** active volcano on Njazídja; poor tropical soil
**head of state and government** Said Mohammad Djohar (interim administration)

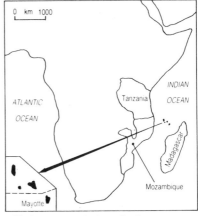

**political system** authoritarian nationalism
**political parties** Comoran Union for Progress (Udzima), nationalist Islamic
**exports** copra, vanilla, cocoa, sisal, coffee, cloves, essential oils
**currency** CFA franc (498.25 = £1 July 1991)
**population** (1990 est) 459,000; growth rate 3.1% p.a.
**life expectancy** men 48, women 52
**language** Comorian (Swahili and Arabic dialect), Makua, French, Arabic (official)
**religion** Muslim (official) 86%, Roman Catholic 14%
**literacy** 15%
**GNP** $163 million (1986); $390 per head

**chronology**
**1975** Independence achieved from France, but Mayotte remained part of France. Ahmed Abdallah elected president. The Comoros joined United Nations.
**1976** Abdallah overthrown by Ali Soilih.
**1978** Soilih killed by mercenaries working for Abdallah. Islamic republic proclaimed and Abdallah elected president.
**1979** The Comoros became a one-party state; powers of

the federal government increased.
**1985** Constitution amended to make Abdallah head of government as well as head of state.
**1989** Abdallah killed by French mercenaries who took control of government; under French and South African pressure mercenaries left Comoros, turning authority over to French administration and interim president Said Mohammad Djohar.
**1990** Anti-government coup foiled.

## Congo (People's Republic of)
(*République Populaire du Congo*)

**area** 342,000 sq km/132,012 sq mi
**capital** Brazzaville
**towns** chief port Pointe-Noire
**physical** narrow coastal plain rises to central plateau then falls into northern basin. Zaïre (Congo) River on the border with Zaïre; half the country is rainforest
**features** 70% of the population lives in Brazzaville, Pointe-Noire or in towns along the railway linking these two places.
**head of state and government** Denis Sassau-Nguesso from 1979
**political system** one-party socialist republic
**political parties** Congolese Labour Party (PCT), Marxist-Leninist
**exports** timber, potash, petroleum, coffee, tobacco
**currency** CFA franc (498.25 = £1 July 1991)
**population** (1990 est) 2,305,000 (chiefly Bantu); growth rate 2.6% p.a.
**life expectancy** men 45, women 48

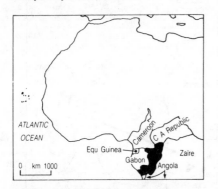

**language** French (official), many African dialects spoken
**religion** animist 50%, Christian 48%, Muslim 2%
**literacy** men 79%/women 55% (1985 est)
**GDP** $2.1 bn (1983); $500 per head

### chronology
**1910** Became part of French Equatorial Africa.
**1960** Achieved independence from France, with Abbe Youlou as the first president.
**1963** Youlou forced to resign. New constitution approved, with Alphonse Massamba-Débat as president.
**1964** The Congo became a one-party state.
**1968** Military coup, led by Capt Marien Ngouabi, ousted Massamba-Débat.
**1970** A Marxist state, the People's Republic of the Congo, was announced, with the PCT as the only legal party.
**1977** Ngouabi assassinated. Col Yhombi-Opango became president.
**1979** Yhombi-Opango handed over the presidency to PCT, who chose Col Denis Sassou-Ngessou as his successor.
**1984** Sassou-Ngessou elected for another five-year term.
**1990** PCT abandoned Marxist-Leninism and promised

multi-party politics.
**1991** 1979 constitution suspended pending the introduction of multi-party democracy. Multi-party elections promised.

## Costa Rica (Republic of)
(*República de Costa Rica*)

**area** 51,100 sq km/19,735 sq mi
**capital** San José
**towns** ports Limón, Puntarenas
**physical** high central plateau and tropical coasts; Costa Rica was once entirely forested, containing an estimated 5% of the Earth's flora and fauna. By 1983 only 17% of the forest remained; half of the arable land had been cleared for cattle ranching, accelerating soil erosion; the massive environmental destruction also caused incalculable loss to the gene pool.

**head of state and government** Rafael Calderón from 1990
**political system** liberal democracy
**political parties** National Liberation Party (PLN), left-of-centre; Christian Socialist Unity Party (PUSC), centrist coalition; 10 minor parties
**exports** coffee, bananas, cocoa, sugar, beef
**currency** colón (200.69 = £1 July 1991)
**population** (1990 est) 3,032,000 (including 1,200 Guaymi Indians); growth rate 2.6% p.a.
**life expectancy** men 71, women 76
**language** Spanish (official)
**religion** Roman Catholic 95%
**literacy** men 94%/women 93% (1985 est)
**GDP** $4.2 bn (1986); $1,530 per head

### chronology
**1821** Independence achieved from Spain.
**1949** New constitution adopted. National army abolished. José Figueres, co-founder of the PLN, elected president; he embarked on ambitious socialist programme.
**1958–73** Mainly conservative administrations.
**1974** PLN regained the presidency and returned to socialist policies.
**1978** Rodrigo Carazo, conservative, elected president. Sharp deterioration in the state of the economy.
**1982** Luis Alberto Monge of the PLN elected president. Harsh austerity programme introduced to rebuild the economy. Pressure from the USA to abandon neutral stance and condemn Sandinista regime in Nicaragua.
**1983** Policy of neutrality reaffirmed.
**1985** Following border clashes with Sandinista forces, a US-trained antiguerrilla guard formed.
**1986** Oscar Arias Sanchez won the presidency on a neutralist platform.
**1987** Oscar Arias Sanchez won Nobel Peace Prize for devising a Central American peace plan.

**1990** Rafael Calderón (PUSC) elected president.

## Cuba (Republic of)
(*República de Cuba*)

**area** 110,860 sq km/42,820 sq mi
**capital** Havana
**towns** Santiago de Cuba, Camaguey
**physical** comprises Cuba, the largest and westernmost of the West Indies, and smaller islands including Isle of Youth; low hills; Sierra Maestra mountains in SE;
**features** 3,380 km/2,100 mi of coastline, with deep bays, sandy beaches, coral islands and reefs; more than 1,600 islands surround the Cuban mainland
**head of state and government** Fidel Castro Ruz from 1959
**political system** communist republic
**political parties** Communist Party of Cuba (PCC), Marxist-Leninist
**exports** sugar (largest producer after USSR), tobacco, coffee, iron, copper, nickel
**currency** Cuban peso (1.29 = £1 July 1991, official rate)

**population** (1990 est) 10,582,000 (plus 125,000 refugees—*marielitos*—from the Cuban port of Mariel in USA); 37% are white of Spanish descent, 51% mulatto, and 11% are of African origin; growth rate 0.6% p.a.
**life expectancy** men 72, women 75
**language** Spanish
**religion** Roman Catholic 45%; also Episcopalians and Methodists
**literacy** men 96%/women 95% (1988)
**disposable national income** $15.8 bn (1983); $1,590 per head

**chronology**
**1898** US defeated Spain in Spanish-American War; Spain gave up all claims to Cuba.
**1901** Cuba achieved independence; Tomás Estrada Palma became first president of the Republic of Cuba.
**1933** Fulgencia Batista seized power.
**1944** Batista retired.
**1952** Batista seized power again to begin an oppressive regime.
**1953** Fidel Castro led an unsuccessful coup against Batista, and again in 1956.
**1959** Batista overthrown by Castro. Constitution of 1940 replaced by a 'Fundamental Law', making Castro prime minister, his brother Raul Castro his deputy, and Ché Guevara his number three.
**1960** All US businesses in Cuba appropriated without compensation; USA broke off diplomatic relations.
**1961** USA sponsored an unsuccessful invasion at the Bay of Pigs. Castro announced that Cuba had become a communist state, with a Marxist-Leninist programme of economic development.

**1962** Cuba expelled from the Organization of American States (OAS). Soviet nuclear missiles removed from Cuba at US insistence.
**1965** Cuba's sole political party renamed Cuban Communist Party (PCC). With Soviet help, Cuba began to make considerable economic and social progress.
**1972** Cuba became a full member of the Moscow-based Council for Mutual Economic Assistance (CMEA).
**1976** New socialist constitution approved; Castro elected president.
**1976–81** Castro became involved in extensive international commitments, assisting Third World countries, particularly in Africa.
**1982** Cuba joined other Latin American countries in giving moral support to Argentina in its dispute with Britain over the Falklands.
**1984** Castro tried to improve US–Cuban relations by discussing the exchange of US prisoners in Cuba with Cuban 'undesirables' in the USA.
**1988** Peace accord with South Africa signed, agreeing to withdrawal of Cuban troops from Angola.
**1989** Reduction in Cuba's overseas military activities. Castro reaffirmed communist orthodoxy.

## Cyprus (Greek Republic of Cyprus)
(*Kypriaki Dimokratia*) in the south, and **Turkish Republic of Northern Cyprus** (*Kibris Cumhuriyeti*) in the north

**area** 9,251 sq km/3,571 sq mi, 37% in Turkish hands
**capital** Nicosia (divided between Greeks and Turks)
**towns** ports Paphos, Limassol, and Larnaca (Greek); Morphou, and ports Kyrenia and Famagusta (Turkish)
**physical** central plain between two E–W mountain ranges
**features** archaeological and historic sites; Mt Olympus 1,953 m/6,406 ft (highest peak); beaches
**heads of state and government** Georgios Vassilou (Greek) from 1988, Rauf Denktaş (Turkish) from 1976
**political system** democratic divided republic
**political parties** Democratic Front (DIKO). centre-left; Progressive Party of the Working People (AKEL), socialist; Democratic Rally (DISY), centrist; Socialist Party (EDEK), socialist; *Turkish zone*: National Unity Party (NUP), Communal Liberation Party (CLP), Republican Turkish Party (RTP), New British Party (NBP)
**exports** citrus, grapes, Cyprus sherry, potatoes, copper, pyrites
**currency** Cyprus pound (0.79 = £1 July 1991) and Turkish lira
**population** (1990 est) 708,000 (Greek Cypriot 78%, Turkish Cypriot 18%); growth rate 1.2% p.a.
**life expectancy** men 72, women 76
**language** Greek and Turkish (official); English
**religion** Greek Orthodox 78%, Sunni Muslim 18%
**literacy** 99% (1984)

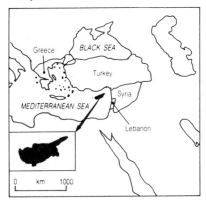

**GNP** $2.11 bn (1983); $3,986 per head

**chronology**
**1878** Came under British administration.
**1955** Guerrilla campaign began against the British for *enosis* (union with Greece), led by Archbishop Makarios and Gen Grivas.
**1956** Makarios and *enosis* leaders deported.
**1959** Compromise agreed and Makarios returned to be elected president of an independent Greek-Turkish Cyprus.
**1960** Independence achieved from Britain, with Britain retaining its military bases.
**1963** Turks set up their own government in northern Cyprus fighting broke out between the two communities.
**1964** UN peacekeeping force installed.
**1971** Grivas returned to start a guerrilla war against the Makarios government.
**1974** Grivas died. Military coup deposed Makarios, who fled to Britain. Nicos Sampson appointed president. Turkish army sent to northern Cyprus to confirm Turkish Cypriots' control; Military regime in southern Cyprus collapsed; Makarios returned. Northern Cyprus declared itself the Turkish Federated State of Cyprus (TFSC), with Rauf Denktaş as president.
**1977** Makarios died; succeeded by Spyros Kyprianou.
**1983** An independent Turkish Republic of Northern Cyprus (TRNC) proclaimed but recognized only by Turkey.
**1984** UN peace proposals rejected.
**1985** Summit meeting between Kyprianou and Denktaş failed to reach agreement.
**1988** Georgios Vassilou elected president. Talks with Denktaş began, under UN auspices.
**1989** Vassilou and Denktaş agreed to draft an agreement for the future reunification of the island, but peace talks were abandoned in Sept.
**1991** Turkish offer of peace talks rejected by Cyprus and Greece.

---

### Czechoslovakia (Czech and Slovak Federative Republic)
(*Česká a Slovenská federativní*)

---

**area** 127,903 sq km/49,371 sq mi
**capital** Prague
**towns** Brno, Bratislava, Ostrava

**physical** Carpathian Mountains, rivers Morava, Labe (Elbe), Vltava (Moldau); hills and plateau; Danube plain in S
**features** divided by valley of the Morava into the densely populated Czech area with good communications in W, and the sparsely populated, mainly agricultural Slovak area in E; summer and winter resort areas in Western

Carpathian, Bohemian, and Sudetes mountain ranges
**head of state** Václav Havel from 1989
**head of government** Marián Čalfa from 1989
**political system** liberal democracy
**political parties** Communist Party of Czechoslovakia (CCP), Marxist-Leninist; Civic Forum, Czech pluralist reform coalition; Public Against Violence, Slovak pluralist reform coalition; Agrarian Party, farmers' party supporting collectivization; Czechoslovak Socialist Party and Czechoslovak Freedom Party (pre-1989 allies of CCP); Green Party
**exports** machinery, timber, ceramics, glass, textiles
**currency** koruna (50.73 commercial rate, 48.90 tourist rate = £1 Feb 1990)
**population** (1990 est) 15,695,000 (63% Czech, 31% Slovak, with Hungarian, Polish, German, Russian, and other minorities); growth rate 0.4% p.a.
**life expectancy** men 68, women 75
**language** Czech and Slovak (official)
**religion** Roman Catholic 75%, Protestant 15%
**literacy** 99% (1981)
**GNP** $143.9 bn (1986); $9,280 per head

**chronology**
**1918** Independence achieved from Austro-Hungarian Empire; Czechs and Slovaks formed Czechoslovakia as independent nation.
**1938** Infamous Munich Agreement gave Sudetenland to Nazi Germany, as 'appeasement', but six months later Hitler occupied entire nation. Benes headed government in exile until 1945.
**1945** Liberation of Czechoslovakia from Nazis by USSR and USA.
**1948** Communists assumed power in coup and new constitution framed.
**1968** 'Prague Spring' experiment with liberalization ended by Soviet invasion and occupation.
**1969** Czechoslovakia became a federal state; Husák elected Communist Party leader.
**1977** Emergence and suppression of Charter 77 human-rights movement.
**1985–86** Criticism of Husák rule by new Soviet leadership.
**1987** Husák resigned as communist leader, remaining president; replaced by Miloš Jakeš.
**1988** Personnel overhaul of party and state bodies, including replacement of Prime Minister Štrougal by the technocrat Adamec.
**1989** Communist regime of Jakeš, Husák, and Adamec overthrown in Nov-Dec bloodless 'gentle revolution', following mass prodemocracy protests in Prague and throughout country, directed by newly formed Civic Forum. Communist monopoly of power ended, with new 'Grand Coalition' government formed; Václav Havel appointed state president and Alexander Dubček chair of national parliament.
**1990** Jan: 22,000 prisoners released. Feb: Havel announced agreement with USSR for complete withdrawal of Soviet troops by May 1991. Dec: devolution of more powers to federal republics.
**1991** Bill of rights passed. Steps taken towards privatization of small businesses and the return of nationalized property to its pre-1948 owners. Splits appeared in reform coalitions.

---

### Denmark (Kingdom of)
(*Kongeriget Danmark*)

---

**area** 43,075 sq km/16,627 sq mi
**capital** Copenhagen
**towns** Aarhus, Odense, Aalborg, Esbjerg, all ports
**physical** comprises the Jutland peninsula and about 500 islands (100 inhabited); the land is flat and cultivated; sand dunes and lagoons on the W coast and long inlets

on the E
**territories** Faeroe Islands and Greenland
**features** fjords along W and E coasts; lakes and rivers;
Kronburg Castle; Tivoli Gardens (Copenhagen); the main
island is Sjælland, where most of Copenhagen is located
(the rest of it is on island of Amager).
**head of state** Queen Margrethe II from 1972
**head of government** Poul Schlüter from 1982
**political system** liberal democracy
**political parties** Social Democrats (SD), left-of-centre;
Conservative People's Party (KF), moderate centre-
right; Liberal Party (V), centre-left; Socialist People's
Party (SF), moderate left-wing; Radical Liberals (RV),
radical internationalist left-of-centre; Centre Democrats
(CD), moderate centrist; Progress Party (FP), radical anti-bureaucratic; Christian People's Party (KrF),
interdenominational, family values
**exports** bacon, dairy produce, eggs, fish, mink pelts,
car and aircraft parts, electrical equipment, textiles,
chemicals
**currency** kroner (11.34 = £1 July 1991)
**population** (1990 est) 5,134,000; growth rate 0% p.a.
**life expectancy** men 72, women 78
**language** Danish (official)
**religion** Lutheran 97%
**literacy** 99% (1983)
**GNP** $78.7 bn (1986); $15,370 per head

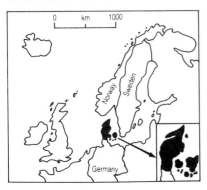

**chronology**
**1940–45** Occupied by Germany.
**1945** Iceland's independence recognized.
**1947** Frederik IX succeeded Christian X.
**1948** Home rule granted for Faeroe Islands.
**1949** Became a founding member of NATO.
**1960** Joined European Free Trade Association (EFTA).
**1972** Margrethe II became Denmark's first queen in
nearly 600 years.
**1973** Left EFTA and joined European Community.
**1979** Home rule granted for Greenland.
**1985** Strong non-nuclear movement in evidence.
**1990** General election; another coalition government
formed.

## Djibouti (Republic of)
(*Jumhouriyya Djibouti*)

**area** 23,200 sq km/8,955 sq mi
**capital** (and chief port) Djibouti
**physical** mountains divide an inland plateau from a coastal
plain; hot and arid
**head of state and government** Hassan Gouled Aptidon
from 1977
**political system** authoritarian nationalism
**political parties** People's Progress Assembly (RPP), nationalist
**exports** acts mainly as a transit port for Ethiopia

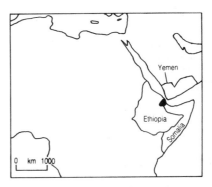

**currency** Djibouti franc (285.00 = £1 July 1991)
**population** (1990 est) 337,000 (Issa 47%, Afar 37%,
European 8%, Arab 6%); growth rate 3.4% p.a.
**life expectancy** 50
**language** Somali, Afar, French (official), Arabic
**religion** Sunni Muslim
**literacy** 17% (1985)
**GNP** $307 (1984); $400 per head

**chronology**
**1977** Independence achieved from France; Hassan
Gouled elected president.
**1979** All political parties combined to form the People's
Progress Assembly (RPP).
**1981** New constitution made RPP the only legal party.
Gouled re-elected. Treaties of friendship signed with
Ethiopia, Somalia, Kenya, and Sudan.
**1984** Policy of neutrality reaffirmed.
**1987** Gouled re-elected for a final term.

## Dominica (Commonwealth of)

**area** 751 sq km/290 sq mi
**capital** Roseau, with a deepwater port
**physical** second largest of the Windward Islands, mountainous central ridge with tropical rainforest

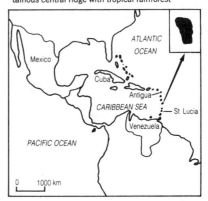

**features** of great beauty, it has mountains of volcanic origin rising to 1,620 m/5,317 ft; Boiling Lake (an effect
produced by escaping subterranean gas)
**head of state** Clarence Seignoret from 1983
**head of government** Mary Eugenia Charles from 1980
**political system** liberal democracy
**political parties** Dominica Freedom Party (DFP), centrist;
Labour Party of Dominica (LPD), left-of-centre coalition
**exports** bananas, coconuts, citrus, lime, bay oil
**currency** E Caribbean dollar (4.38 = £1 July 1991),

pound sterling, French franc
**population** (1990 est) 94,200 (mainly black African in
origin, but with a small Carib reserve of some 500);
growth rate 1.3% p.a.
**language** English (official), but the Dominican *patois* still
reflects earlier periods of French rule
**religion** Roman Catholic 80%
**literacy** 80%
**GNP** $79 million (1983); $460 per head

**chronology**
**1978** Independence achieved from Britain. Patrick John,
leader of DLP, elected prime minister.
**1980** DFP, led by Eugenia Charles, won convincing victory
in general election.
**1981** Patrick John implicated in plot to overthrow government.
**1982** John tried and acquitted.
**1985** John retried and found guilty. Regrouping of left-of-
centre parties resulted in new Labour Party of Dominica
(LPD). DFP, led by Eugenia Charles, re-elected.

## Dominican Republic
(*República Dominicana*)

**area** 48,442 sq km/18,700 sq mi
**capital** Santo Domingo
**physical** comprises eastern two-thirds of island of
Hispaniola; central mountain range; fertile valley in N
**features** Pico Duarte 3,174 m/10,417 ft, highest point
in Caribbean islands
**head of state and government** Joaquín Ricardo Balaguer
from 1986
**political system** democratic republic
**political parties** Dominican Revolutionary Party (PRD),
moderate left-of-centre; Christian Social Reform Party
(PRSC), independent socialist; Dominican Liberation
Party (PLD), nationalist
**exports** sugar, gold, silver, bauxite, tobacco, coffee, ferro-
nickel
**currency** peso (20.75 = £1 July 1991)
**population** (1989 est) 7,307,000; growth rate 2.3% p.a.
**life expectancy** men 61, women 65
**language** Spanish (official)
**religion** Roman Catholic 95%

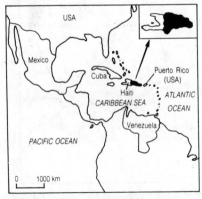

**literacy** men 78%/women 77% (1985 est)
**GNP** $8.7 bn (1983); $1,221 per head

**chronology**
**1844** Dominican Republic established.
**1930** Military coup established dictatorship of Rafael
Trujillo.
**1961** Trujillo assassinated.
**1962** First democratic elections resulted in Juan Bosch,

founder of PRD, becoming president.
**1963** Bosch overthrown in military coup.
**1965** US Marines intervened to restore order and protect
foreign nationals.
**1966** New constitution adopted. Joaquín Balaguer, leader
of the PRSC, became president.
**1978** PRD returned to power, with Silvestre Antonio
Guzmán as president.
**1982** PRD re-elected, with Jorge Blanco as president.
**1985** Blanco forced by International Monetary Fund to
adopt austerity measures to save the economy.
**1986** PRSC returned to power, with Balaguer re-elected
president.

## Ecuador (Republic of)
(*República del Ecuador*)

**area** 270,670 sq km/104,479 sq mi
**capital** Quito
**towns** Cuenca; chief port Guayaquil

**physical** coastal plain rises sharply to Andes Mountains
which are divided into a series of cultivated valleys;
flat, low-lying rainforest in the E; about 25,000 species
became extinct 1965–90 as a result of environmental
destruction
**features** Ecuador is crossed by the equator, from which it
derives its name; Galapagos Islands; Cotopaxi is world's
highest active volcano; rich wildlife in rainforest of Amazon basin
**head of state and government** Rodrigo Borja Cevallos
from 1988
**political system** emergent democracy
**political parties** Progressive Democratic Front coalition,
left-of-centre (composed of six individual parties); Concentration of Popular Forces (CFP), right-of-centre; Social Christian Party (PSC), right-wing; Conservative Party
(PC), right-wing; others
**exports** bananas, cocoa, coffee, sugar, rice, balsa wood,
fish, petroleum
**currency** sucre (1,657.66 = £1 July 1991, official rate)
**population** (1989 est) 10,490,000; (25% Indian, 55%
Mestizo, 10% European, 10% black African); growth
rate 2.9% p.a.
**life expectancy** men 62, women 66
**language** Spanish (official); Quechuan, Jivaroan
**religion** Roman Catholic 95%
**literacy** men 85%/women 80% (1985 est)
**GNP** $13.1 bn (1986); $1,310 per head

**chronology**

**1830** Independence achieved from Spain.
**1925–48** Great political instability; no president completed his term of office.
**1948–55** Liberals in power.
**1956** First conservative president in 60 years.
**1960** Liberals returned, with José Velasco as president.
**1961** Velasco deposed and replaced by the vice president.
**1963** Military junta installed.
**1968** Velasco returned as president.
**1972** A coup put the military back in power.
**1978** New democratic constitution adopted.
**1979** Liberals in power but opposed by right-and left-wing parties.
**1982** Deteriorating economy provoked strikes, demonstrations, and a state of emergency.
**1983** Austerity measures introduced.
**1985** No party with a clear majority in the national congress; Febres Cordero narrowly won the presidency for the conservatives.
**1988** Roderigo Borja elected president for moderate left-wing coalition.
**1989** Guerrilla left-wing group, *Alfaro Vive, Carajo* ('Alfaro lives, Dammit'), numbering about 1,000, lays down arms after 9 years.

### Egypt (Arab Republic of)
(*Jumhuriyat Misr al-Arabiya*)

**area** 1,001,450 sq km/386,990 sq mi
**capital** Cairo
**towns** Giza; ports Alexandria, Port Said, Suez, Damietta
**physical** mostly desert; hills in E; fertile land along river Nile; cultivated and settled area is about 35,500 sq km/13,700 sq mi
**features** Aswan High Dam and Lake Nasser; Sinai; remains of ancient Egypt (Pyramids, Sphinx, Luxor, Karnak, Abu Simbel, El Faiyum)
**head of state and government** Hosni Mubarak from 1981
**political system** democratic republic
**political parties** National Democratic Party (NDP), moderate left-of-centre; Socialist Labour Party, right-of-centre; Socialist Liberal Party, free-enterprise; New Wafd Party, nationalist
**exports** cotton and textiles, petroleum
**currency** Egyptian pound (5.40 = £1 July 1991)
**population** (1989 est) 54,779,000; growth rate 2.4% p.a.
**life expectancy** men 57, women 60
**language** Arabic (official) (ancient Egyptian survives to some extent in Coptic)
**religion** Sunni Muslim 95%, Coptic Christian 5%
**literacy** men 59%/women 30% (1985 est)
**GDP** $32 bn (1983); $686 per head

**chronology**
**1936** Independence achieved from Britain. King Fuad succeeded by his son Farouk.
**1946** Withdrawal of British troops except from Suez Canal Zone.
**1952** Farouk overthrown by army in bloodless coup.
**1953** Egypt declared a republic, with General Neguib as president.
**1956** Neguib replaced by Col Gamal Nasser. Nasser announced nationalization of Suez Canal; Egypt attacked by UK, France, and Israel. Cease-fire agreed because of US intervention.
**1958** Short-lived merger of Egypt and Syria as United Arab Republic (UAR). Subsequent attempts to federate Egypt, Syria, and Iraq failed.
**1967** Six-Day War with Israel ended in Egypt's defeat and Israeli occupation of Sinai and Gaza strip.
**1970** Nasser died suddenly, succeeded by Anwar Sadat.

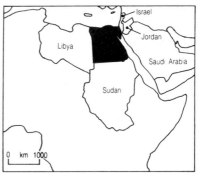

**1973** Attempt to regain territory lost to Israel led to fighting; cease-fire arranged by US secretary of state Henry Kissinger.
**1977** Sadat's visit to Israel to address the Israeli parliament was criticized by Egypt's Arab neighbours.
**1978–79** Camp David talks in the USA resulted in a treaty between Egypt and Israel. Egypt expelled from the Arab League.
**1981** Sadat assassinated, succeeded by Hosni Mubarak.
**1983** Improved relations between Egypt and the Arab world; only Libya and Syria maintained a trade boycott.
**1984** Mubarak's party victorious in the people's assembly elections.
**1987** Mubarak re-elected. Egypt readmitted to Arab League.
**1988** Full diplomatic relations with Algeria restored.
**1989** Improved relations with Libya; diplomatic relations with Syria restored. Mubarak proposed a peace plan.
**1990** Gains for independents in general election.
**1991** Participation in Gulf War on US-led side.

### El Salvador (Republic of)
(*República de El Salvador*)

**area** 21,393 sq km/8,258 sq mi
**capital** San Salvador
**physical** narrow coastal plain, rising to mountains in N with central plateau

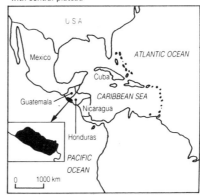

**features** smallest and most densely populated Central American country; Mayan archaeological remains
**head of state and government** Alfredo Cristiani from 1989
**political system** emergent democracy
**political parties** Christian Democrats (PDC), anti-imperialist; National Republican Alliance (ARENA), right-wing; National Conciliation Party (PCN), right-wing
**exports** coffee, cotton, sugar
**currency** colón (13.02 = £1 July 1991)

**population** (1989 est) 5,900,000 (mainly of mixed Spanish and Indian ancestry; 10% Indian); growth rate 2.9% p.a.
**life expectancy** men 63, women 67
**language** Spanish and Nahua
**religion** Roman Catholic 97%
**literacy** men 75%/women 69% (1985 est)
**GDP** $4.3 bn (1984); $854 per head

### chronology
**1821** Independence achieved from Spain.
**1961** Right-wing coup.
**1972** Allegations of human-rights violations and growth of left-wing guerrilla activities. General Carlos Romero elected president.
**1979** A coup replaced Romero with a military-civilian junta.
**1980** Archbishop Oscar Romero assassinated; country on verge of civil war. José Duarte became president.
**1981** Mexico and France recognized the guerrillas as a legitimate political force but the USA actively assisted the government in its battle against them.
**1982** Assembly elections boycotted by left-wing parties and held amid considerable violence.
**1986** Duarte sought a negotiated settlement with the guerrillas.
**1988** Duarte resigned following diagnosis of terminal cancer.
**1989** Alfredo Cristiani (ARENA) elected president, amid allegations of ballot-rigging; rebel attacks intensified; right-wing death-squad activity resurgent.
**1991** UN-sponsored peace talks with the Farabundo Martí Liberation Front (FMLN) began.

### Equatorial Guinea (Republic of)
(*República de Guinea Ecuatorial*)

**area** 28,051 sq km/10,828 sq mi
**capital** Malabo (Bioko)
**towns** Bata and Mbini (Río Muni)
**physical** comprises mainland Rio Muni, plus the small islands of Corisco, Elobey Grande and Elobey Chico, and Bioko (formerly Fernando Po) together with Annobón (formerly Pagalu)
**features** volcanic mountains on Bioko
**head of state and government** Teodoro Obiang Nguema Mbasogo from 1979
**political system** one-party military republic
**political parties** Democratic Party of Equatorial Guinea (PDGE), militarily controlled

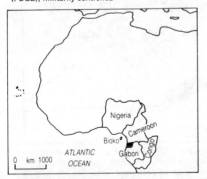

**exports** cocoa, coffee, bananas, timber
**currency** ekuele; CFA franc (498.25 = £1 July 1991)
**population** (1988 est) 336,000 (plus 110,000 estimated to live in exile abroad); growth rate 2.2% p.a.
**life expectancy** men 42, women 48
**language** Spanish (official); pidgin English is widely spoken, and on Annobón (whose people were formerly slaves of the Portuguese) a Portuguese dialect
**religion** nominally Christian, mainly Catholic, but in 1978 Roman Catholicism was banned
**literacy** 55% (1984)
**GDP** $60 million (1983); $250 per head

### chronology
**1778** Bioko Island ceded to Spain.
**1885** Mainland territory came under Spanish rule; colony known as Spanish Guinea.
**1968** Independence achieved from Spain. Francisco Macias Nguema became first president, soon assuming dictatorial powers.
**1979** Macias overthrown and replaced by his nephew, Teodoro Obiang Nguema Mbasogo, who established a military regime. Macias tried and executed.
**1982** Obiang elected president for another seven years. New constitution adopted, promising a return to civilian government.
**1989** Obiang re-elected president.

### Ethiopia (People's Democratic Republic of)
(*Hebretesebawit Ityopia*, formerly also known as *Abyssinia*)

**area** 1,221,900 sq km/471,653 sq mi
**capital** Addis Ababa
**towns** Asmara (capital of Eritrea), Dire Dawa; ports Massawa, Assab
**physical** a high plateau with central mountain range divided by Rift Valley; plains in E; Blue Nile River
**features** Danakil and Ogaden deserts; ancient remains (at Aksum, Gondar, Lalibela, amongst others); only African country to retain its independence during the colonial period
**head of state and government** Tesfaye Gebre Kidan from 1991
**political system** one-party socialist republic
**political parties** Workers' Party of Ethiopia (WPE), Marxist-Leninist; Eritrean People's Liberation Front (EPLE), a guerrilla army fighting for an independent Eritrea; Tigré People's Liberation Front (TPLF), fighting for regional autonomy in Tigré

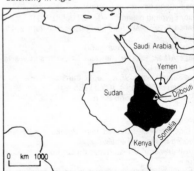

**exports** coffee, pulses, oilseeds, hides, skins
**currency** birr (3.34 = £1 July 1991)
**population** (1989 est) 47,709,000 (Oromo 40%, Amhara 25%, Tigré 12%, Sidama 9%); growth rate 2.5% p.a.
**language** Amharic (official); Tigrinya, Orominga, Arabic
**religion** Christian (Ethiopian Orthodox church, which has had its own patriarch since 1976) 50%, Sunni Muslim 50%
**literacy** 35% (1988)
**GNP** $4.7 bn (1984); $141 per head

### chronology

**1930** Haile Selassie became emperor.
**1962** Eritrea annexed by Haile Selassie; resistance movement began.
**1974** Haile Selassie deposed and replaced by a military government led by Gen Teferi Benti. Ethiopia declared a socialist state.
**1977** Teferi Benti killed and replaced by Col Mengistu Haile Mariam.
**1977–79** 'Red Terror' period in which Mengistu's regime killed thousands of innocent people.
**1984** WPE declared the only legal political party.
**1985** Worst famine in more than a decade; Western aid sent and forcible internal resettlement programmes undertaken.
**1987** New constitution adopted, Mengistu Mariam elected president; provisional Military Administrative Council dissolved, and elected National Assembly introduced. New famine; food aid hindered by guerrillas.
**1988** Mengistu agreed to adjust his economic policies in order to secure IMF assistance. Influx of refugees from Sudan.
**1989** Government forces routed from Eritrea and Tigré, rebels claimed; army accused of bombing civilian targets. Coup attempt against Mengistu foiled; another famine in N feared; peace talks mediated by former US president Carter reported some progress.
**1990** Rebels captured port of Massawa. Mengistu announced new reforms.
**1991** Mengistu overthrown and temporary administration set up by the Ethiopian People's Revolutionary Democratic Front (EPRDF). Independence of Eritrea agreed and access to the Red Sea guaranteed by making Assab a free port.

---

## Fiji (Republic of)

**area** 18,333 sq km/7,078 sq mi
**capital** Suva
**towns** ports of Lavtoka and Levuka
**physical** comprises 844 Melanesian and Polynesian islands and islets (about 110 inhabited), the largest being Viti Levu (10,429 sq km/4,028 sq mi) and Vanua Levu (5,550 sq km/2,146 sq mi); mountainous, volcanic, with tropical rainforest and grasslands
**features** almost all islands surrounded by coral reefs; high volcanic peaks
**head of state** Ratu Sir Penaia Ganilau from 1987
**head of government** Ratu Sir Kamisese Mara from 1987
**political system** democratic republic
**political parties** Alliance Party (AP), moderate centrist Fijian; National Federation Party (NFP), moderate left-of-centre Indian; Fijian Labour Party (FLP), left-of-centre Indian; United Front, Fijian

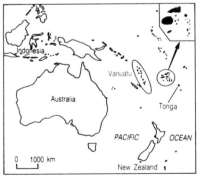

**exports** sugar, coconut oil, ginger, timber, canned fish; tourism is important
**currency** Fiji dollar (2.45 = £1 July 1991)

**population** (1989 est) 758,000 (46% Fijian, holding 80% of the land communally, and 49% Indian, introduced in the 19th century to work the sugar crop); growth rate 2.1% p.a.
**life expectancy** men 67, women 71
**language** English (official); Fijian, Hindi
**religion** Hindu 50%, Methodist 44%
**literacy** men 88%/women 77% (1980 est)
**GDP** $1.2 bn (1984); $1,086 per head

**chronology**
**1970** Independence achieved from Britain; Ratu Sir Kamisese Mara elected as first prime minister.
**1987** April: general election brought to power an Indian-dominated coalition led by Dr Timoci Bavadra. May: military coup by Col Sitiveni Rabuka removed new government at gunpoint; Governor General Ratu Sir Penaia Ganilau regained control within weeks. Sept: second military coup by Rabuka proclaimed Fiji a republic and suspended the constitution. Oct: Fiji ceased to be a member of the Commonwealth. Dec: civilian government restored with Rambuka retaining control of security as minister for home affairs.
**1989** New constitution proposed.

---

## Finland (Republic of)
(*Suomen Tasavalta*)

**area** 338,145 sq km/130,608 sq mi
**capital** Helsinki
**towns** Tampere, port Turku, Oulu, Rovaniemi, Lahti
**physical** most of the country is forest, with low hills and about 60,000 lakes; one-third is within the Arctic Circle; archipelago in S
**head of state** Mauno Koivisto from 1982
**head of government** Esko Ahoi from 1991
**political system** democratic republic
**political parties** Social Democratic Party (SDP), moderate left-of-centre; National Coalition Party (KOK), moderate right-of-centre; Centre Party (KP), centrist, rural-orientated; Finnish People's Democratic League (SKDL), left-wing; Swedish People's Party, independent Swedish-orientated; Finnish Rural Party (SMP), farmers and small businesses; Democratic Alternative, left-wing; Green Party

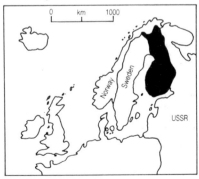

**exports** metal, chemical, and engineering products (icebreakers and oil rigs), paper, timber, textiles, fine ceramics, glass, furniture
**currency** markka (6.96 = £1 July 1991)
**population** (1989 est) 4,990,00; growth rate 0.5% p.a.
**life expectancy** men 70, women 78
**language** Finnish 93%, Swedish 6% (both official), small Lapp- and Russian-speaking minorities
**religion** Lutheran 97%, Eastern Orthodox 1.2%
**literacy** 99%
**GNP** $50.6 bn (1984); $10,477 per head

**chronology**
**1917** Independence achieved from Russia.
**1939** Defeated by USSR in Winter War.
**1941** Allowed Germany to station troops in Finland to attack USSR; USSR bombed Finland.
**1944** Concluded separate armistice with USSR.
**1948** Finno-Soviet Pact of Friendship, Co-operation, and Mutual Assistance signed.
**1955** Finland joined the UN and the Nordic Council.
**1956** Urho Kekkonen elected president; re-elected 1962, 1968, 1978.
**1973** Trade treaty with EEC signed.
**1977** Trade agreement with USSR signed.
**1982** Koivisto elected president; re-elected 1988.
**1989** Finland joined Council of Europe.
**1991** Big swing to the centre in general election. New coalition government formed.

Pompidou became president.
**1974** Giscard d'Estaing elected president.
**1981** François Mitterrand elected Fifth Republic's first socialist president.
**1986** 'Cohabitation' experiment, with the conservative Jacques Chirac as prime minister.
**1988** Mitterrand re-elected. Moderate socialist Michel Rocard became prime minister and continued in this post despite the Socialist Party failing to obtain a secure majority in the National Assembly elections. Matignon Accord on future of New Caledonia approved by referendum.
**1989** Greens gained 11% of vote in elections to European Parliament.
**1991** French forces were part of the US-led coalition in the Gulf War. Edith Cresson became France's first woman prime minister.

---

**France (French Republic)**
(*République Française*)

**area** (including Corsica) 543,965 sq km/209,970 sq mi
**capital** Paris
**towns** Lyons, Lille, Bordeaux, Toulouse, Nantes, Strasbourg; ports Marseilles, Nice, Le Havre
**territories** Guadeloupe, French Guiana, Martinique, Réunion, St Pierre and Miquelon, Southern and Antarctic Territories, New Caledonia, French Polynesia, Wallis and Futuna
**physical** rivers Seine, Loire, Garonne, Rhône, Rhine; mountain ranges Alps, Massif Central, Pyrenees, Jura, Vosges, Cévennes
**features** Ardennes forest, Auvergne mountain region, Riviera, Mount Blanc 4,810 m/15,781 ft, caves of Dordogne with relics of early humans; largest W European nation
**head of state** François Mitterrand from 1981
**head of government** Edith Cresson from 1991
**political system** liberal democracy
**political parties** Socialist Party (PS), left-of-centre; Rally for the Republic (RPR), neo-Gaullist conservative; Union for French Democracy (UDF), centre-right; Republican Party (RP), centre-right; French Communist Party (PCF), Marxist-Leninist; National Front, far-right; Greens, environmentalist
**exports** fruit (especially apples), wine, cheese, automobiles, aircraft, chemicals, jewellery, silk, lace; tourism is very important
**currency** franc (9.96 = £1 July 1991)
**population** (1990 est) 56,184,000 (including 4,500,000 immigrants, chiefly from Portugal, Algeria, Morocco, and Tunisia); growth rate 0.3% p.a.
**life expectancy** men 71, women 79
**language** French (regional dialects include Breton, Catalan, Provençal)
**religion** Roman Catholic 90%, Muslim 1%, Protestant 2%
**literacy** 99% (1984)
**GNP** $568 bn (1983); $7,179 per head

**chronology**
**1944–46** Charles de Gaulle provisional government; start of Fourth Republic.
**1954** Indochina achieved independence.
**1956** Morocco and Tunisia achieved independence.
**1957** Entry into EEC.
**1958** Recall of de Gaulle following Algerian crisis.
**1959** De Gaulle became president; start of Fifth Republic.
**1962** Algeria achieved independence.
**1966** France withdrew from military wing of NATO.
**1968** 'May events' crisis.
**1969** De Gaulle resigned following referendum defeat;

---

**Gabon (Gabonese Republic)**
(*République Gabonaise*)

**area** 267,667 sq km/103,319 sq mi
**capital** Libreville
**towns** Ports Port-Gentil and Owendo; Masuku (Franceville)

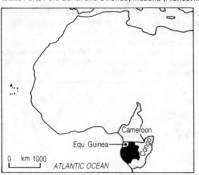

**physical** virtually the whole country is tropical rainforest; narrow coastal plain rising to hilly interior with savanna in E and S; Ogooué River flows S–W
**features** Schweitzer hospital at Lambaréné; Trans-Gabonais railway
**head of state and government** Omar Bongo from 1967
**political system** authoritarian nationalism
**political parties** Gabonese Democratic Party (PDG), nationalist
**exports** petroleum, manganese, iron, uranium, timber
**currency** CFA franc (498.25 = £1 July 1991)

**population** (1988) 1,226,000 including 40 Bantu tribes; growth rate 1.6% p.a.
**life expectancy** men 47, women 51
**language** French (official), Bantu
**religion** animist 60%, Roman Catholic 35%, small Muslim minority
**literacy** men 70%/women 53% (1985 est)
**GNP** $3 bn (1983); $2,613 per head

**chronology**
**1960** Independence from France achieved; Léon M'ba became the first president.
**1967** Attempted coup by rival party foiled with French help. M'ba died; he was succeeded by his protégé, Albert-Bernard Bongo.
**1968** One-party state established.
**1973** Bongo re-elected; converted to Islam, he changed his first name to Omar.
**1986** Bongo re-elected.
**1989** Coup attempt against Bongo defeated.
**1990** Widespread fraud alleged in first multi-party elections since 1964.

## Gambia (Republic of The)

**area** 10,402 sq km/4,018 sq mi
**capital** Banjul
**physical** banks of the river Gambia flanked by low hills

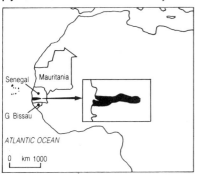

**features** the smallest state in black Africa
**head of state and government** Dawda Kairaba Jawara from 1970
**political system** liberal democracy
**political parties** Progressive People's Party (PPP), moderate centrist; National Convention Party (NCP), left-of-centre
**exports** groundnuts, palm oil, fish
**currency** dalasi (14.26 = £1 July 1991)
**population** (1990 est) 820,000; growth rate 1.9% p.a.
**life expectancy** men 34, women 37
**language** English (official); Mandinka, Fula and other native tongues
**religion** Muslim 90%, with animist and Christian minorities
**literacy** men 36%/women 15% (1985 est)
**GNP** $200 million (1983); $330 per head

**chronology**
**1965** Independence achieved from Britain as a constitutional monarchy within the Commonwealth, with Dawda K Jawara as prime minister.
**1970** Declared itself a republic, with Jawara as president.
**1972** Jawara re-elected.
**1981** Attempted coup foiled with the help of Senegal.
**1982** Formed with Senegal the Confederation of Senegambia; Jawara re-elected.

**1987** Jawara re-elected.
**1989** Confederation of Senegambia dissolved.

## Germany (Federal Republic of)
*(Bundesrepublik Deutschland)*

**area** 357,041 sq km/137,853 sq mi
**capital** Berlin
**towns** Cologne, Munich, Essen, Frankfurt-am-Main, Dortmund, Stuttgart, Düsseldorf, Leipzig, Dresden, Chemnitz, Magdeburg; ports Hamburg, Kiel, Cuxhaven, Bremerhaven, Rostock.
**physical** flat in N, mountainous in S with Alps; rivers Rhine, Weser, Elbe flow N, Danube flows SE, Oder, Neisse flow N along Polish frontier; many lakes, including Müritz
**features** Black Forest, Harz Mountains, Erzgebirge, Bavarian Alps, Fichtelgebirge, Thüringer Forest
**head of state** Richard von Weizsäcker from 1984
**head of government** Helmut Kohl from 1982
**political system** democratic federal republic
**political parties** *formerly West German*: Christian Democratic Union (CDU), right-of-centre; Social Democratic Party (SPD), left-of-centre; Free Democratic Party (FDP), liberal; Christian Social Union (CSU), Bavarian-based conservative; Greens, environmentalist; Republicans, far right; *formerly East German*: Socialist Union Party (SED), Marxist-Leninist; New Forum, opposition umbrella pressure group; Social Democratic Party (SPD), left-of-centre; Liberal Democratic Party, Christian Democratic Union (CDU), National Democratic Party and Democratic Farmers Party, until 1989 allies of the SED; Free Democratic Party (FDP), liberal; Green Party, environmentalist
**exports** machine tools (world's leading exporter), cars, commercial vehicles, electronics, industrial goods, textiles, chemicals, iron, steel, wine, lignite, uranium, cobalt, coal, iron, steel, fertilizers, plastics

**currency** Deutschmark (2.94 = £1 July 1991)
**population** (1990 est) 77,600,000 (including nearly 5,000,000 guest workers, *Gastarbeiter*, of whom 1,600,000 are Turks; the rest are Yugoslavs, Italians, Greeks, Spanish, and Portuguese); growth rate −0.7% p.a.
**life expectancy** men 68, women 74
**languages** German, Serbian
**religion** Protestant 45%, Roman Catholic 37%
**literacy** 99% (1985)
**GNP** $1,016 bn (1988); $13,000 per head

**chronology**
**1945** Germany surrendered; country divided into four occupation zones (US, French, British, Soviet).

**1948** Blockade of West Berlin.
**1949** Establishment of Federal Republic under the 'Basic Law' Constitution with Adenauer as chancellor; establishment of the German Democratic Republic as an independent state.
**1953** Riots in East Berlin suppressed by Soviet troops.
**1954** Grant of full sovereignty to West Germany.
**1957** West Germany entered EC; recovery of Saarland.
**1961** Construction of Berlin Wall.
**1963** Retirement of Chancellor Adenauer.
**1964** Treaty of Friendship and Mutual Assistance signed between East Germany and USSR.
**1969** Willy Brandt became chancellor of West Germany.
**1971** Erich Honecker elected Socialist Unity Party (SED) leader in East Germany.
**1972** Basic Treaty between West Germany and East Germany; treaty ratified 1973, normalizing relations between the two.
**1974** Resignation of Brandt; Helmut Schmidt became chancellor.
**1975** East German friendship treaty with USSR renewed for 25 years.
**1982** Helmut Kohl became West German chancellor.
**1987** Official visit of Honecker to the Federal Republic.
**1988** Death of West German Bavarian CSU leader Franz-Josef Strauss.
**1989** West Germany: rising support for far right in local and European elections, and declining support for Kohl. East Germany: East German visitors to Hungary permitted to enter Austria and the West; mass exodus to West Germany began (344,000 left during 1989). Honecker replaced by Egon Krenz after mass demonstrations. New Forum opposition movement legalized; national borders opened in Nov, including Berlin Wall. Reformist Hans Modrow appointed prime minister. Krenz replaced.
**1990** Jan: Secret-police (*Stasi*) headquarters in East Berlin stormed by demonstrators. Feb: Modrow called for a neutral united Germany. March: multiparty elections won by the right-wing CDU. 3 Oct: official reunification of East and West Germany. 2 Dec: first all-German elections since 1932, resulting in coalition government and the re-election of Chancellor Kohl.
**1991** Taxes increased to finance economic development in the east, while unemployment was rising, as well as a share of the cost of the US-led Gulf War against Iraq. New Deutsche Bundesbank president: Helmut Schlesinger. Berlin voted in as the new capital.

---

### PEOPLE OF THE YEAR

For Hans Dietrich Genscher, the Federal Republic's long-serving foreign minister, 1990–91 was a year of solidly earned success in securing Germany's unification. Born and raised in Halle, East Germany until 1952, Genscher held the reunion of the two Germanies as a lifelong goal. First appointed the Federal Republic's foreign minister in 1974, Genscher was a consistent exponent of Ostpolitik détente. During the 'new Cold War' years of the early 1980s he tirelessly maintained the fracturing lines of East-West communication. As the USSR's attitude began to thaw in the mid-1980s, he soon developed a close relationship with Mikhail Gorbachev, becoming, in 1987, the first major Western diplomat to urge that Gorbachev be taken 'at his word'. Finally, in 1990, despite a deteriorating heart condition, Genscher successfully overcame the USSR's anxieties over German unification. In the Dec 1990 inaugural all-German election, Genscher's Free Democrats recorded their most impressive results for three decades.

---

### Ghana (Republic of)

**area** 238,305 sq km/91,986 sq mi

**capital** Accra
**towns** Kumasi, and ports Sekondi-Takoradi, Tema

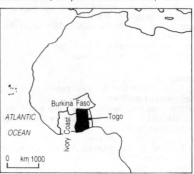

**physical** mostly plains; bisected by river Volta
**features** world's largest artificial lake Lake Volta; relics of traditional kingdom of Ashanti; 32,000 chiefs and kings
**head of state and government** Jerry Rawlings from 1981
**political system** military republic
**political parties** all political parties banned 1981
**exports** cocoa, coffee, timber, gold, diamonds, manganese, bauxite
**currency** cedi (593.10 = £1 July 1991)
**population** (1990 est) 15,310,000; growth rate 3.2% p.a.
**life expectancy** men 50, women 54
**language** English (official) and African languages
**religion** Christian 24%, animist 38%, Muslim 30%
**literacy** men 64%/women 43% (1985 est)
**GNP** $3.9 bn (1983); $420 per head

**chronology**
**1957** Independence achieved from Britain, within the Commonwealth, with Kwame Nkrumah as president.
**1960** Ghana became a republic and a one-party state.
**1966** Nkrumah deposed and replaced by Gen Joseph Ankrah.
**1969** Ankrah replaced by Gen Akwasi Afrifa, who initiated a return to civilian government.
**1970** Edward Akufo-Addo elected president.
**1972** Another coup placed Col Acheampong at the head of a military government.
**1978** Acheampong deposed in a bloodless coup led by Frederick Akuffo; another coup put Flight-Lt Jerry Rawlings in power.
**1979** Return to civilian rule under Hilla Limann.
**1981** Rawlings seized power again, citing the incompetence of previous governments.
**1989** Coup attempt against Rawlings foiled.

---

### Greece (Hellenic Republic)
(*Elliniki Dimokratia*)

**area** 131,957 sq km/50,935 sq mi
**capital** Athens ~
**towns** ports Thessaloniki, Patras, Larisa, Iráklion
**physical** mountainous; a large number of islands, notably Crete, Corfu, and Rhodes
**features** Corinth canal; Mount Olympus; the Acropolis; many archaeological sites; the Aegean and Ionian Islands
**head of state** Christos Sartzetakis from 1985
**head of government** Xenophon Zolotas from 1989
**political system** democratic republic
**political parties** Panhellenic Socialist Movement (PASOK), democratic socialist; New Democracy Party (ND), centre-right; Democratic Renewal (DR); Communist Party;

Greek Left Party
**exports** tobacco, fruit, vegetables, olives, olive oil, textiles
**currency** drachma (321.37 = £1 July 1991)
**population** (1990 est) 10,066,000; growth rate 0.3% p.a.

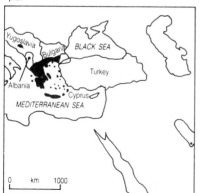

**life expectancy** men 72, women 76
**language** Greek
**religion** Greek Orthodox 97%
**literacy** men 96%/women 89% (1985)
**GNP** $32.4 bn (1984); $3,260 per head

**chronology**
**1829** Independence achieved from Turkish rule.
**1912–13** Balkan Wars; Greece gained much land.
**1941–44** German occupation of Greece.
**1946** Civil war between royalists and communists; communists defeated.
**1949** Monarchy re-established with Paul as king.
**1964** King Paul succeeded by his son Constantine.
**1967** Army coup removed the king; Col George Papadopoulos became prime minister. Martial law imposed, all political activity banned.
**1973** Republic proclaimed, with Papadopoulos as president.
**1974** Former premier Constantine Karamanlis recalled from exile to lead government. Martial law and ban on political parties lifted; restoration of the monarchy rejected by a referendum.
**1975** New constitution adopted, making Greece a republic.
**1980** Karamanlis resigned as prime minister and was elected president.
**1981** Greece became full member of EEC. Andreas Papandreou elected as Greece's first socialist prime minister.
**1983** Five-year defence and economic cooperation agreement signed with USA; ten-year economic cooperation agreement signed with USSR.
**1985** Papandreou re-elected.
**1988** Relations with Turkey improved. Major cabinet reshuffle after mounting criticism of Papandreou.
**1989** Papandreou defeated in elections. Tzannis Tzannetakis, conservative backbencher, became prime minister, heading first all-party government (including communists) for 15 years. This broke up and Xenophon Zolotas formed new unity government. Papandreou charged with illegal wiretapping and bribery.
**1990** Siting of US bases agreed.

---

**Grenada**
---
**area** (including the Grenadines, notably Carriacou) 340 sq km/131 sq mi
**capital** St George's
**physical** southernmost of the Windward Islands; mountainous
**features** Grand-Anse beach; Annandale Falls; the Great Pool volcanic crater

**head of state** Elizabeth II from 1974 represented by governor general
**head of government** Ben Jones from 1989
**political system** emergent democracy
**political parties** New National Party (NNP), centrist; Grenada United Labour Party (GULP), nationalist left-of-centre
**exports** cocoa, nutmeg, bananas, mace
**currency** Eastern Caribbean dollar (4.39 = £1 July 1991)
**population** (1990 est) 84,000, 84% of black African descent; growth rate 1.2% p.a.
**life expectancy** 69
**language** English (official); some French patois spoken
**religion** Roman Catholic
**literacy** 85% (1985)
**GDP** $116 million (1983); $500 per head

**chronology**
**1974** Independence achieved from Britain; Eric Gairy elected prime minister.
**1979** Gairy removed in bloodless coup led by Maurice Bishop; constitution suspended and a people's revolutionary government established.
**1982** Relations with the USA and Britain deteriorated as ties with Cuba and the USSR strengthened. Bishop feared impending US invasion.
**1983** After Bishop's attempt to improve relations with the USA, he was overthrown by left-wing opponents. A coup established the Revolutionary Military Council (RMC), and Bishop and some of his colleagues were executed. The USA invaded Grenada, accompanied by troops from other E Caribbean countries; RMC overthrown, 1974 constitution reinstated.
**1984** The newly formed NNP won 14 of the 15 seats in the house of representatives and its leader, Herbert Blaize, became prime minister.
**1989** Herbert Blaize lost leadership of NNP, remaining as head of government; he died and was succeeded by Ben Jones.

---

**Guatemala (Republic of)**
(*República de Guatemala*)

**area** 108,889 sq km/42,031 sq mi
**capital** Guatemala City
**towns** Quezaltenango, Puerto Barrios (naval base)
**physical** mountainous; narrow coastal plains; limestone plateau in N; frequent earthquakes

**features** Mayan archaeological remains, including site at Tikal
**head of state and government** Jorge Serrano Elias from 1991
**political system** democratic republic
**political parties** Guatemalan Christian Democratic Party (PDCG), Christian centre-left; Centre Party (UCN), centrist; National Democratic Co-operation Party (PDNC), centre-right; Revolutionary Party (PR), radical; Movement of National Liberation (MLN), extreme right-wing; Democratic Institutional Party (PID), moderate conservative

**exports** coffee, bananas, cotton
**currency** quetzal (7.93 = £1 July 1991)
**population** (1990 est) 9,340,000 (Mayaquiche Indians 54%, mestizos 42%); growth rate 2.8% p.a. (87% of under-fives suffer from malnutrition).
**life expectancy** men 57, women 61
**language** Spanish (official); 40% speak 18 Indian dialects
**religion** Roman Catholic
**literacy** men 63%/women 47% (1985 est)
**GDP** $9.9 bn (1984); $1,085 per head

**chronology**
**1839** Independence achieved from Spain.
**1954** Col Carlos Castillo became president in US-backed coup, halting land reform.
**1963** Military coup made Col Enrique Peralta president.
**1966** Cesar Méndez elected president.
**1970** Carlos Araña elected president.
**1974** Gen Kjell Laugerud became president. Widespread political violence.
**1978** Gen Fernando Romeo became president.
**1981** Growth of anti-government guerrilla movement.
**1982** Gen Angel Anibal became president. Army coup installed Gen Ríos Montt as head of junta and then as president; political violence continued.
**1983** Montt removed in coup led by Gen Mejía Victores, who declared amnesty for the guerrillas.
**1985** New constitution adopted; PDCG won congressional elections; Vinicio Cerezo elected president.
**1989** Coup attempt against Cerezo foiled. Over 100,000 people killed, and 40,000 reported missing since 1979.
**1991** Jorge Serrano Elias of the Solidarity Action Movement (MAS) elected president.

### Guinea (Republic of)
(*République de Guinée*)

**area** 245,857 sq km/94,901 sq mi
**capital** Conakry
**towns** Labe, N'Zérékoré, Kankan

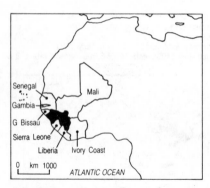

**physical** flat coastal plain with mountainous interior; sources of rivers Niger, Gambia, and Senegal; forest in SE
**features** Fouta Djallon, area of sandstone plateaus, cut by deep valleys
**head of state and government** Lansana Conté from 1984
**political system** military republic
**politisal parties** none since 1984
**exports** coffee, rice, palm kernels, alumina, bauxite, diamonds
**currency** syli or franc (1,007.50 free rate, 487.50 public transaction rate = £1 July 1991)
**population** (1990 est) 7,269,000 (chief peoples are Fulani, Malinke, Susu); growth rate 2.3% p.a.
**life expectancy** men 39, women 42
**language** French (official); African languages spoken
**religion** Muslim 85%, Christian 10%, local 5%
**literacy** men 40%/women 17% (1985 est)
**GNP** $1.6 bn (1983); $305 per head

**chronology**
**1958** Full independence achieved from France; Sékou Touré elected president.
**1977** Strong opposition to Touré's rigid Marxist policies forced him to accept return to mixed economy.
**1980** Touré returned unopposed for fourth seven-year term.
**1984** Touré died. Bloodless coup established a military committee for national recovery, led by Col Lansana Conté.
**1985** Attempted coup against Conté while he was out of the country was foiled by loyal troops.
**1991** Anti-government general strike.

### Guinea-Bissau (Republic of)
(*Republica da Guiné-Bissau*)

**area** 36,125 sq km/13,944 sq mi
**capital** and chief port Bissau
**physical** flat coastal plain rising to savanna in E
**features** the archipelago of Bijagos
**head of state and government** João Bernardo Vieira from 1980
**political system** socialist pluralist republic
**political parties** African Party for the Independence of Portuguese Guinea and Cape Verde (PAIGC), nationalist socialist
**exports** rice, coconuts, peanuts, fish, salt, timber
**currency** peso (1,056.25 = £1 July 1991)
**population** (1989 est) 929,000; growth rate 2.4% p.a.
**life expectancy** 39; 1990 infant mortality rate was 14.8%.
**language** Portuguese (official), Crioulo (Cape Verdean dialect of Portuguese), African languages
**religion** Muslim 40%, Christian 4%
**literacy** men 46%/women 17% (1985 est)
**GDP** $177 million (1982); $165 per head

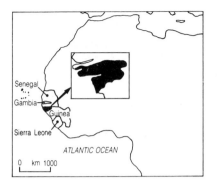

**chronology**
**1956** PAIGC formed to secure independence from Portugal.
**1973** Two-thirds of the country declared independent, with Luiz Cabral as president of a state council.
**1974** Independence achieved from Portugal.
**1980** Cape Verde decided not to join a unified state. Cabral deposed, and João Vieira became chair of a council of revolution.
**1981** PAIGC confirmed as the only legal party, with Vieira as its secretary-general.
**1982** Normal relations with Cape Verde restored.
**1984** New constitution adopted, making Vieira head of government as well as head of state.
**1989** Vieira re-elected.
**1991** Other parties legalized. Multi-party elections promised.

## Guyana (Cooperative Republic of)

**area** 214,969 sq km/82,978 sq mi
**capital** and port Georgetown

**physical** coastal plain rises into rolling highlands with savanna in S; mostly tropical rainforest
**features** Mount Roraima; Kaietur National Park, including Kaietur Fall on the Potaro (tributary of Essequibo) 250 m/821 ft
**head of state and government** Desmond Hoyte from 1985
**political system** democratic republic
**political parties** People's National Congress (PNC), Indian nationalist socialist; People's Progressive Party (PPP), Afro-Indian Marxist-Leninist
**exports** sugar, rice, rum, timber, diamonds, bauxite
**currency** Guyanese dollar (206.37 = £1 July 1991)
**population** (1989 est) 846,000 (51% E Indians, intro-

duced to work the sugar plantations after the abolition of slavery, 30% black, 5% Amerindian); growth rate 2% p.a.
**life expectancy** men 66, women 71
**language** English (official), Hindi, Amerindian
**religion** Christian 57%, Hindu 33%, Sunni Muslim 9%
**literacy** men 97%/women 95% (1985 est)
**GNP** $419 million (1983); $457 per head

**chronology**
**1961** Internal self-government granted.
**1966** Independence achieved from Britain.
**1970** Guyana became a republic within the Commonwealth.
**1980** Forbes Burnham became first executive president under new constitution.
**1985** Burnham died; succeeded by Desmond Hoyte.

## Haiti (Republic of)
(*République d'Haïti*)

**area** 27,750 sq km/10,712 sq mi
**capital** Port-au-Prince
**physical** mainly mountainous and tropical; occupies W third of Hispaniola Island in Caribbean Sea; seriously deforested
**features** oldest black republic in the world; only French-speaking republic in the Americas; island of La Tortuga off N coast was formerly a pirate lair
**head of state and government** Jean-Bertrand Aristide from 1991
**political system** transitional
**political parties** National Progressive Party (PNP), right-wing military
**exports** coffee, sugar, sisal, cotton, cocoa, rice
**currency** gourde (8.12 = £1 July 1991)
**population** (1990 est) 6,409,000; growth rate 1.7% p.a.; one of highest population densities in the world; about 1.5 million Haitians live outside Haiti (in USA and Canada); about 400,000 live in virtual slavery in the Dominican Republic, where they went or were sent to cut sugar cane

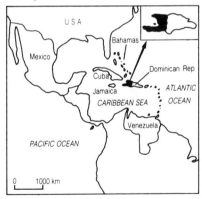

**life expectancy** men 51, women 54
**language** French (official, spoken by literate 10% minority), Creole (spoken by 90% black majority)
**religion** voodoo; also Christianity
**literacy** men 40%/women 35% (1985 est)
**GNP** $1.6 bn (1983); $300 per head

**chronology**
**1804** Independence achieved from France.
**1915** Haiti invaded by USA; remained under US control until 1934.
**1957** Dr François Duvalier (Papa Doc) elected president.

**1964** Duvalier pronounced himself president for life.
**1971** Constitution amended to allow president to nominate his successor. Duvalier died, succeeded by his son, Jean-Claude (Baby Doc); thousands murdered during Duvalier era.
**1986** Duvalier deposed; replaced by Lt-Gen Henri Namphy as head of a governing council.
**1988** Leslie Manigat became president in Feb despite allegations of fraudulent elections. Namphy staged a military coup in June, but another coup in Sept led by Prosper Avril replaced him with a civilian government under military control.
**1989** Coup attempt against Avril foiled; US aid resumed.
**1990** Opposition elements expelled; Pascal-Trouillot acting president.
**1991** Newly elected president Aristide dismissed the army high command. President Aristide tightened grip on army by sacking all high command officers other than Gen Herard Abraham.

---

### PEOPLE OF THE YEAR

A charismatic left-wing priest, Jean-Bertrand Aristide made the cause of the poor and the oppressed the basis for his successful campaign for the presidency. He campaigned for the National Front for Change and Democracy, representing a loose coalition of peasants, trade unionists, and clerics, and won 70% of the vote in the Dec 1990 elections. After thirty years of corrupt Duvalier rule, 'Papa Doc' being succeeded by his son 'Baby Doc' until his overthrow in 1986, Aristide faced the difficult task of returning the country to democracy and social equality.

---

### Honduras (Republic of)
(*República de Honduras*)

**area** 112,100 sq km/43,282 sq mi
**capital** Tegucigalpa
**towns** San Pedro Sula; ports Henecan (on Pacific), La Ceiba Puerto Cortés

**physical** narrow tropical coastal plain with mountainous interior, Bay Islands
**features** archaeological sites; Mayan ruins at Copán
**head of state and government** Rafael Leonardo Callejas from 1990
**political system** democratic republic
**political parties** Liberal Party of Honduras (PLH), centre-left; National Party (PN), right-wing
**exports** coffee, bananas, sugar, timber (including mahogany, rosewood)
**currency** lempira (9.16 = £1 July 1991)
**population** (1989 est) 5,106,000 (90% mestizo, 10% Indians and Europeans); growth rate 3.1% p.a.

**life expectancy** men 58, women 62
**language** Spanish, Indian dialects
**religion** Roman Catholic 97%
**literacy** men 61%/women 58% (1985 est)
**GNP** $2.8 bn (1983); $590 per head

**chronology**
**1838** Independence achieved from Spain.
**1980** After more than a century of mostly military rule, a civilian government was elected, with Dr Roberto Suazo as president; the commander in chief of the army, Gen Gustavo Alvarez, retained considerable power.
**1983** Close involvement with the USA in providing naval and air bases and allowing Nicaraguan counter-revolutionaries ('contras') to operate from Honduras.
**1984** Alvares ousted in coup led by junior officers, resulting in policy review towards USA and Nicaragua.
**1985** José Azcona elected president after electoral law changed, making Suazo ineligible for presidency.
**1989** Government and opposition declared support for Central American peace plan to demobilize Nicaraguan Contras based in Honduras; Contras and their dependents in Honduras in 1989 thought to number about 55,000.
**1990** Rafael Callejas (PN) elected president.

---

### Hungary (Republic of)
(*Magyar Köztársaság*)

**area** 93,032 sq km/35,910 sq mi
**capital** Budapest
**towns** Miskolc, Debrecen, Szeged, Pécs
**physical** Great Hungarian Plain covers E half of country; Bakony Forest; Transdanubian Highlands in the W; rivers Danube, Tisza; Lake Balaton
**head of state** Matyas Szuros (acting) from 1989
**head of government** Károly Grosz from 1988
**political system** socialist pluralist republic
**political parties** over 50, including Hungarian Socialist Party (HSP), left-of-centre; Hungarian Democratic Forum (MDF), umbrella prodemocracy grouping; Alliance of Free Democrats (SzDSz), radical free-market opposition group heading coalition with Alliance of Young Democrats, Social Democrats, and Smallholders Party, right-wing
**exports** machinery, vehicles, chemicals, textiles
**currency** forint (126.15 = £1 July 1991)
**population** (1990 est) 10,546,000 (Magyar 92%, Romany 3%, German 2.5%; Hungarian minority in Romania has caused some friction between the two countries); growth rate 0.2% p.a.
**life expectancy** men 67, women 74
**language** Hungarian (or Magyar), one of the few lan-

guages of Europe with non-Indo-European origins; it is grouped with Finnish and Estonian in the Finno-Ugric family
**religion** Roman Catholic 67%, other Christian denominations 25%
**literacy** men 99.3%/women 98.5% (1980)
**GNP** $18.6 bn (1983); $4,180 per head

**chronology**
**1918** Independence achieved from Austro-Hungarian Empire.
**1919** A communist state formed for 133 days.
**1920–44** Regency formed under Admiral Hartley, who joined Hitler's attack on the USSR.
**1945** Liberated by USSR.
**1946** Republic proclaimed; Stalinist regime imposed.
**1949** Soviet-style constitution adopted.
**1956** Hungarian national uprising; workers' demonstrations in Budapest; democratization reforms by Imre Nagy overturned by Soviet tanks, Kádár installed as party leader.
**1968** Economic decentralization reforms.
**1983** Competition introduced into elections.
**1987** VAT and income tax introduced.
**1988** Kádár replaced by Károly Grosz. First free trade union recognized; rival political parties legalized.
**1989** May: border with Austria opened. July: new four-man collective leadership of HSWP. Oct: new 'transitional constitution' adopted, founded on multiparty democracy and new presidentialist executive. HSWP changed name to Hungarian Socialist Party, with Nyers as new leader. Kádán 'retired', later died; Nagy rehabilitated.
**1990** HSP reputation damaged by 'Danubegate' bugging scandal.
**1991** Devaluation of currency.

## Iceland (Republic of)
(*Lýdveldid Ísland*)

**area** 103,000 sq km/39,758 sq mi
**capital** Reykjavik
**physical** warmed by the Gulf Stream; glaciers and lava fields cover 75% of the country; active volcanoes (Hekla was once thought the gateway to Hell), geysers, hot springs, and new islands created offshore (Surtsey in 1963); subterranean hot water heats Iceland's homes

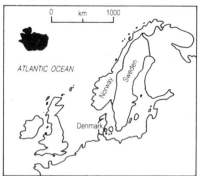

**features** the most westerly European country; Thingvellir, where the oldest parliament in the world first met AD 930
**head of state** Vigdís Finnbogadóttir from 1980
**head of government** David Oddsson from 1991
**political system** democratic republic
**political parties** Independence Party (IP), right-of-centre; Progressive Party (PP), radical socialist; People's Alliance (PA), socialist; Social Democratic Party (SDP), moderate, left-of-centre; Citizen's Party, centrist; Wom-

en's Alliance, women and family orientated
**exports** cod and other fish products, aluminium, diatomite
**currency** krona (102.25 = £1 July 1991)
**population** (1990 est) 251,000; growth rate 0.8% p.a.
**life expectancy** men 74, women 80
**language** Icelandic, the most archaic Scandinavian language, in which some of the finest sagas were written
**religion** Evangelical Lutheran 95%
**literacy** 99.9% (1984)
**GDP** $3.9 bn (1986); $16,200 per head

**chronology**
**1944** Independence achieved from Denmark.
**1949** Joined NATO and Council of Europe.
**1953** Joined Nordic Council.
**1976** 'Cod War' with UK.
**1979** Iceland announced 200-mile exclusive fishing zone.
**1983** Steingrímur Hermannsson appointed to lead a coalition government.
**1985** Iceland declared itself nuclear-free zone.
**1987** New coalition government formed by Thorsteinn Palsson after general election.
**1988** Vigdís Finnbogadóttir re-elected president for a third term; Hermannsson led new coalition.
**1991** David Oddsson led new IP-SDP (Independence Party and Social Democratic Party) centre-right coalition, becoming prime minister in the general election.

## India (Republic of)
(Hindi *Bharat*)

**area** 3,166,829 sq km/1,222,396 sq mi
**capital** New Delhi
**towns** Bangalore, Hyderabad, Ahmedabad; ports Calcutta, Bombay, Madras, Kanpur, Pune, Nagpur
**physical** Himalaya mountains on N border; plains around rivers Ganges, Indus, Brahmaputra; Deccan peninsula S of the Narmada River forms plateau between W and E Ghats mountain ranges; desert in W; Andaman and Nicobar Islands, Lakshadweep (Laccadive Islands)
**features** Taj Mahal monument; Golden Temple, Amritsar; archaeological sites and cave paintings (Ajanta); world's second most populous country
**head of government** P V Narasimha Rao from 1991
**political system** federal democratic republic
**political parties** Janata Dal, left-of-centre; Congress Party–Indira (Congress (I)), cross-caste and religion left-of-centre; Bharatiya Janata Party (BJP), conservative Hindu-chauvinist; Communist Party of India

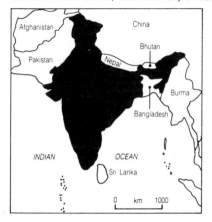

## INDIA—CAN PARLIAMENTARY DEMOCRACY SURVIVE?

For four decades India has been a conspicuous oasis of liberal democracy and political stability within South Asia. In favourable contrast to neighbouring Pakistan and Bangladesh, a clear division has been upheld between the political and military spheres, and a secular state structure preserved. The Congress Party, a 'catch-all', cross-caste, and cross-community coalition dating back to the nationalist struggle, provided crucial continuity and cohesion, monopolizing national power for all but two years between 1947–89. So did the Nehru-Gandhi family dynasty, which, during this period, provided all but one of the Congress's leaders.

In recent years, however, the fabric of India's democratic stability has begun to progressively unravel. This has been brought about through direct pressure exerted by the peoples of its periphery, by the increasing challenges to the secularist compact of 1947, by the Congress Party's step-by-step fracturing, and, with the assassination of Rajiv Gandhi in 1991, by the apparent ending of the Nehru-Gandhi political dynasty.

The pressure exerted from the periphery has, since the early 1980s, taken the form of an escalating scourge of inter-ethnic strife and secessionist insurgencies in the northern fringe states of Kashmir, Punjab, Assam, and the northeastern hills. The bloody Tamil-Sinhala struggle in Sri Lanka has also proved destabilizing for the south. More generally, there has been growing religious intolerance as well as a desecularization of politics, brought about by the emergence of Sikh fundamentalism and the revival of an increasingly militant militant Hinduism. The battle for jobs, as the country's population increased by a staggering 160 million during the 1980s, and control of scarce water resources added a material edge to these religious and caste rivalries.

The Congress Party's decline as an all-embracing, popular national force has been gradual and somewhat masked by the peculiarities of the first-past-the-post electoral system. The party's splintering commenced during the leadership of Indira Gandhi, but continued under her son Rajiv, with the defection of the former finance and defence minister, V P Singh, who maintained that the prime minister was implicated in the Bofors corruption scandal. Presenting himself as the new 'Mr Clean' of Indian politics, Singh (a respected raja's son) assembled the broad-church National Front which, with the support of allies from the left and right, successfully unseated Congress, for only the second time since 1947, in the general election of November 1989.

Like the Janata government of 1977–79, which came to power after Indira Gandhi's anti-constitutional 1975–77 Emergency, this coalition administration was, however, to prove short-lived. It was beset, from the outset, by intense personal rivalry among its ruling troika—V P Singh, Devi Lal, the middle peasant leader from Haryana, and Chandra Shekhar, an incessantly scheming socialist. It faced worsening ethnic unrest in Kashmir, Punjab, and Assam. It encountered, from September 1990, the most serious Hindu–Muslim communal conflict witnessed in the nation since partition, as the Hindu militants of the Vishwa Hindu Parishad pressed for the construction of a temple to the warrior-god Rama on the site of a 16th century Muslim mosque, in the holy city of Ajodhya. In addition, through controversially deciding to implement the eight-year-old recommendations of the Mandal Commission on job reservations for disadvantaged castes, the government itself helped to provoke an unprecedented and bloody caste war in north India's cities.

On 7 November 1990, shortly after troops fired on Hindu fanatics in Ajodhya, the Singh government was voted from office and Chandra Shekhar, supported by Devi Lal, took over as premier. His minority administration, kept in power by the puppet-master support of Rajiv Gandhi's Congress (I), was to last just 115 days. Through shelving the proposals of the Mandal Commission, the new government did quell inter-caste conflict. However, regional and communal strife continued, claiming at least 5,000 lives during 1990. Indeed, the campaign for the general election of May–June 1991 was the most violent in the Republic's history, culminating in the murder of Rajiv Gandhi at a rally in south India. This assassination, and the refusal of Rajiv's Italian-born wife Sonia to take Congress (I)'s helm, effectively closed the forty-year reign of the Nehru–Gandhi dynasty. However, the subsequent upswell of popular sympathy was sufficient for Congress (I) to return to power—despite the strong challenge of the Hindu chauvinist Bharatiya Janata Party (BJP)—albeit as a minority administration.

Despite the pressures of the last decade, India's democracy has successfully endured and, outside such regional blackspots as Assam, Kashmir, and Punjab, seems likely to continue to do so during the 1990s. The country possesses a well-entrenched free press, a popular respect for legal norms, and a non-politicized, professional army corps. But whether the British-imposed parliamentary system, based on a strong centre and assembly-selected executive, will (or indeed should) survive is less certain. A more full-blooded federal system, founded upon a greater devolution of authority to the state governments but concurrently united by a directly-elected charismatic president, might be a preferable institutional structure for the pluralistic subcontinent.

(CPI), pro-Moscow Marxist-Leninist; Communist Party of India—Marxist (CPI-M), West Bengal-based moderate socialist
**exports** tea, coffee, fish, iron ore, leather, textiles, polished diamonds

**currency** rupee (34.09 = £1 July 1991)
**population** (1989 est) 833,422,000; growth rate 2.0% p.a.
**life expectancy** men 56, women 55
**language** Hindi, English, and 14 other official languages:

Assamese, Bengali, Gujarati, Kannada, Kashmiri, Malayalam, Marathi, Oriya, Punjabi, Sanskrit, Sindhi, Tamil, Telugu, Urdu; Hindustani widely spoken in N India
**religion** Hindu 80%, Sunni Muslim 10%, Christian 2.5%, Sikh 2%
**literacy** men 57%/women 29% (1985 est)
**GNP** $200 bn (1983); $250 per head

**chronology**
**1947** Independence achieved from Britain.
**1950** Federal republic proclaimed.
**1962** Border skirmishes with China.
**1964** Death of Prime Minister Nehru. Border war with Pakistan over Kashmir.
**1966** Indira Gandhi became prime minister.
**1971** War with Pakistan leading to creation of Bangladesh.
**1975–77** State of emergency proclaimed.
**1977–79** Janata party government in power.
**1980** Indira Gandhi returned in landslide victory.
**1984** Indira Gandhi assassinated; Rajiv Gandhi elected with record majority.
**1987** Signing of 'Tamil' Colombo peace accord with Sri Lanka; Indian Peacekeeping Force (IPKF) sent there. Public revelation of Bofors scandal.
**1988** New opposition party, Janata Dal, established by former finance minister V P Singh. Indian paratroopers foiled attempted coup in Maldives. Voting age lowered from 21 to 18.
**1989** Congress (I) lost majority in general election, after Gandhi associates implicated in financial misconduct, and Janata Dal minority government formed, with V P Singh prime minister.
**1990** Central rule imposed in Jammu and Kashmir following Muslim separatist violence. V P Singh resigned; new minority Janata Dal government formed by Chandra Shekhar.
**1991** Central rule imposed in Tamil Nadu. Interethnic and religious violence in Punjab, Andhra Pradesh, and elsewhere. Shekhar resigned; elections called for May. Rajiv Gandhi assassinated in May. Elections resumed in June, resulting in a Congress (I) minority government led by P V Narasimha Rao.

## Indonesia (Republic of)
(*Republik Indonesia*)

**area** 1,919,443 sq km/740,905 sq mi
**capital** Jakarta
**towns** Bandung, ports Surabaya, Semarang

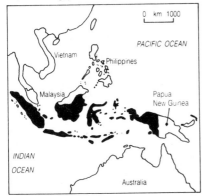

**physical** comprises 13,677 tropical islands, of the Greater Sunda group (including Java and Madura, part of Kalimantan/Borneo, Sumatra, Sulawesi and Belitung), and the Lesser Sundas/Nusa Tenggara

(including Bali, Lombok, Sumba, Timor), as well as Malaku/Moluccas and part of New Guinea (Irian Jaya)
**features** world's largest Islamic population; Java is one of the world's most densely populated areas
**head of state and government** T N J Suharto from 1967
**political system** authoritarian nationalist republic
**political parties** Golkar, military-bureaucrat-farmers ruling party; United Development Party (PPP), moderate Islamic; Indonesian Democratic Party (PDI), nationalist Christian
**exports** coffee, rubber, palm oil, coconuts, tin, tea, tobacco, oil, liquid natural gas
**currency** rupiah (3,175.66 = £1 July 1991)
**population** (1989 est) 187,726,000 (including 300 ethnic groups); growth rate 2% p.a.
**life expectancy** men 52, women 55
**language** Indonesian (official), closely allied to Malay; Javanese is the most widely spoken local dialect
**religion** Muslim 90%; Buddhist, Hindu, and Pancasila (a secular official ideology)
**literacy** men 83%/women 65% (1985 est)
**GNP** $87 bn (1983); $560 per head

**chronology**
**1942** Occupied by Japan; nationalist government established.
**1945** Japanese surrender; nationalists declared independence under Sukarno.
**1949** Formal transfer of Dutch sovereignty.
**1950** Unitary constitution established.
**1963** Western New Guinea (Irian Jaya) ceded by the Netherlands.
**1965–66** Attempted communist coup; Gen Suharto imposed emergency administration, carried out massacre of hundreds of thousands.
**1967** Sukarno replaced as president by Suharto.
**1975** Terrorists seeking independence for S Moluccas seized train and Dutch Embassy, held Western hostages.
**1976** Forced annexation of former Portuguese colony of East Timor.
**1986** Institution of 'transmigration programme' to settle large numbers of Javanese on sparsely populated outer islands, particularly Irian Jaya.
**1988** Partial easing of travel restrictions to East Timor. Suharto re-elected for fifth term.
**1989** Foreign debt reached $50 billion; Western creditors offer aid on condition that concessions are made to foreign companies and that austerity measures are introduced.
**1991** Democracy Forum launched to promote political dialogue.

## Iran (Islamic Republic of)
(*Jomhori-e-Islami-e-Irân*; until 1935 **Persia**)

**area** 1,648,000 sq km/636,128 sq mi
**capital** Tehran
**towns** Isfahan, Mashhad, Tabriz, Shiraz, Ahvaz; chief port Abadan
**physical** plateau surrounded by mountains, including Elburz and Zagros; Lake Rezayeh; Dasht-Ekavir Desert; occupies islands of Abu Musa, Greater Tunb and Lesser Tunb in the Gulf
**features** ruins of Persepolis; Mt Demavend 5,670 m/18,603 ft
**Leader of the Revolution** Ali Khamenei from 1989
**head of government** Ali Akbar Rafsanjani from 1989
**political system** authoritarian Islamic republic
**political parties** Islamic Republican Party (IRP), fundamentalist Islamic
**exports** carpets, cotton textiles, metalwork, leather goods, oil, petrochemicals, fruit

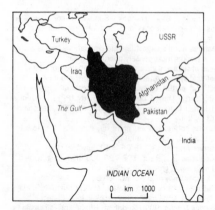

**currency** rial (112.50 = £1 July 1991)
**population** (1989 est) 51,005,000 (including minorities in Azerbaijan, Baluchistan, Khuzestan/Arabistan, and Kurdistan); growth rate 3.2% p.a.
**life expectancy** men 57, women 57
**language** Farsi, Kurdish, Turkish, Arabic, English, French
**religion** Shi'ite Muslim 93% (official), Sunni Muslim 5%, Zoroastrian 2%, Jewish, Baha'i and Christian
**literacy** men 62%/women 39% (1985 est)
**GDP** $86.4 bn (1987); $1,756 per head

**chronology**
**1946** British, US, and Soviet forces left Iran.
**1951** Oilfields nationalized by Prime Minister Mohammad Mossadeq.
**1953** Mossadeq deposed and the US-backed shah took full control of the government.
**1975** The shah introduced single-party system.
**1978** Opposition to the shah organized from France by Ayatollah Khomeini.
**1979** Shah left the country, Khomeini returned to create Islamic state. Revolutionaries seized US hostages at embassy in Tehran; US economic boycott.
**1980** Start of Gulf War against Iraq.
**1981** US hostages released.
**1984** Egyptian peace proposals rejected.
**1985** Gulf War fighting intensified; UN secretary-general's peace moves unsuccessful.
**1988** Ceasefire in Gulf War, talks with Iraq began.
**1989** Khomeini called for the death of British writer Salman Rushdie. June: Khomeini died; Ali Khamenei elected interim Leader of the Revolution; speaker of Iranian parliament Ali Akbar Rafsanjani elected president. Secret oil deal with Israel revealed.
**1990** Generous peace terms with Iraq accepted.
**1991** Normal relations with UK restored. Imprisoned British businessman, Roger Cooper, released.

## Iraq (Republic of)
*(al Jumhouriya al 'Iraqia)*

**area** 434,924 sq km/167,881 sq mi
**capital** Baghdad
**towns** Mosul and port of Basra
**physical** mountains in N, desert in W; wide valley of rivers Tigris and Euphrates NW–SE
**features** reed architecture of the marsh Arabs; ancient sites of Eridu, Babylon, Nineveh, Ur, Ctesiphon
**head of state and government** Saddam Hussein al-Takriti from 1979
**political system** one-party socialist republic
**political parties** Arab Ba'ath Socialist Party, nationalist socialist
**exports** dates (80% of world supply), wool, oil

**currency** Iraqi dinar (0.59 = £1 July 1991)
**population** (1989 est) 17,610,000; growth rate 3.6% p.a.
**life expectancy** men 62, women 63
**language** Arabic (official), Kurdish, Assyrian, Armenian
**religion** Shi'ite Muslim 60%, Sunni Muslim 37%, Christian 3%
**literacy** men 68%/women 32% (1980 est)
**GNP** $40 bn (1987); $2,400 per head

**chronology**
**1920** Iraq became a British League of Nations protectorate.
**1921** Hashemite dynasty established, with Faisal I as king.
**1932** Independence achieved from British protectorate status.
**1958** Monarchy overthrown; Iraq became a republic.
**1968** Military coup put Gen al-Bakr in power.
**1979** Al-Bakr replaced by Saddam Hussein.
**1980** War between Iraq and Iran broke out.
**1985** Fighting intensified.
**1988** Cease-fire; talks began with Iran. Iraq used chemical weapons against Kurdish rebels seeking greater autonomy.
**1989** Unsuccessful coup against President Hussein.
**1990** Generous peace treaty with Iran agreed. Aug: Iraq invaded and annexed Kuwait, precipitating another Gulf crisis. US forces massed in Saudi Arabia at request of King Fahd. UN resolutions ordered Iraqi withdrawal from Kuwait and imposed total trade ban on Iraq; UN resolution sanctioning force approved. All foreign hostages released.
**1991** 16 Jan: US-led forces began aerial assault on Iraq; Iraq's infrastructure destroyed by bombing. 23–28 Feb: land-sea-air offensive to free Kuwait successful. Uprisings of Kurds and Shias brutally suppressed by surviving Iraqi troops. Talks between Kurdish leaders and Saddam Hussein about Turkish autonomy. Allied troops withdrew after establishing 'safe havens' for Kurds in the North. A rapid reaction force left near the Turkish border. Allied troops threatened to bomb strategic targets in Iraq if full information about nuclear facilities denied to United Nations.

## Ireland (Republic of)
*(Irish Éire)*

**area** 70,282 sq km/27,146 sq mi
**capital** Dublin
**towns** ports Cork, Dún Laoghaire, Limerick, Waterford
**physical** central plateau surrounded by hills; rivers Shannon, Liffey, Boyne
**features** Bog of Allen, source of domestic and national

power; Magillicuddy's Reeks, Wicklow Mountains; Lough Corrib, lakes of Killarney; Galway Bay and Aran Islands
**head of state** Mary Robinson from 1990
**head of government** Charles Haughey from 1987
**political system** democratic republic
**political parties** Fianna Fail (Soldiers of Destiny), moderate centre-right; Fine Gael (Irish Tribe), moderate centre-left; Labour Party, moderate left-of-centre; Progressive Democrats, radical free-enterprise

**exports** livestock, dairy products, Irish whiskey, microelectronic components and assemblies, mining and engineering products, chemicals, tobacco, clothing; tourism is important
**currency** punt (1.10 = £1 July 1991)
**population** (1989 est) 3,734,000; growth rate 0.1% p.a.
**life expectancy** men 70, women 76
**language** Irish and English (both official)
**religion** Roman Catholic 94%
**literacy** 99% (1984)
**GNP** $21.7 (1986); $6,130 per head

**chronology**
**1916** Easter Rising: nationalists against British rule seized the Dublin general post office and proclaimed a republic; the revolt was suppressed by the British army and most of the leaders executed.
**1918–21** Guerrilla warfare against British army led to split in rebel forces.
**1921** Anglo-Irish Treaty resulted in creation of the Irish Free State (Southern Ireland).
**1937** Independence achieved from Britain.
**1949** Eire left the Commonwealth and became the Republic of Ireland.
**1973** Fianna Fáil defeated after 40 years in office; Liam Cosgrave formed a coalition government.
**1977** Fianna Fáil returned to power, with Jack Lynch as prime minister.
**1979** Lynch resigned, succeeded by Charles Haughey.
**1981** Garret FitzGerald formed a coalition.
**1983** New Ireland Forum formed, but rejected by the British government.
**1985** Anglo-Irish Agreement signed.
**1986** Protests by Ulster Unionists against the agreement.
**1987** General election won by Charles Haughey.
**1988** Relations with UK at low ebb because of disagreement over extradition decisions.
**1989** Haughey failed to win majority in general election. Progressive Democrats (a breakaway party of Fianna Fáil) given cabinet positions in coalition government.
**1990** Mary Robinson elected president; John Bruton became Fine Gael leader.

### PEOPLE OF THE YEAR

Mary Robinson successfully defeated Fianna Fàil frontrunner, Brian Lenihan, Nov 1990 to become president. As Trinity College, Dublin's youngest professor of law, at 25, an academic career seemed promising, but a strong social conscience made her campaign for women's rights in Ireland. As a Labour candidate, she tried unsuccessfully to enter the Dail (parliament) 1990, and then, unexpectedly, won the presidency. She offered herself as a modern president, independent of the government of the day.

### Israel (State of)
*(Medinat Israel)*

**area** 20,800 sq km/8,029 sq mi (as at 1949 armistice)
**capital** Jerusalem (not recognized by the United Nations)
**towns** ports Tel Aviv, Jaffa, Haifa, Acre, Eilat, Bat-Yam, Holon, Ramat Gan, Petach Tikva, Beersheba
**physical** coastal plain of Sharon between Haifa and Tel Aviv noted since ancient times for fertility; central mountains of Galilee, Samariq and Judea; river Jordan Rift Valley along the E is below sea level; Negev desert in the S occupies Golan Heights, West Bank and Gaza
**features** Dead Sea, Lake Tiberias, Negev Desert, Golan Heights; historic sites: Jerusalem, Bethlehem, Nazareth, Masada, Megiddo, Jericho; caves of the Dead Sea scrolls
**head of state** Chaim Herzog from 1983
**head of government** Itzhak Shamir from 1986
**political system** democratic republic
**political parties** Israel Labour Party, moderate left-of-centre; Consolidation Party (Likud), right-of-centre
**exports** citrus and other fruit, avocados, chinese leaves, fertilizers, plastics, petrochemicals, textiles, electronics (military, medical, scientific, industrial), electro-optics, precision instruments, aircraft and missiles
**currency** shekel (4.01 = £1 July 1991)
**population** (1989 est) 4,477,000 (including 750,000 Arab Israeli citizens and over 1 million Arabs in the occupied territories); under the Law of Return 1950, 'every Jew shall be entitled to come to Israel as an immigrant'; those from the East and E Europe are *Ashkenazim*, and from Mediterranean Europe (Spain, Portugal, Italy, France, Greece) and Arab N Africa are *Sephardim* (over 50% of the population is now of Sephardic descent). An Israeli-born Jew is a *Sabra*; about 500,000 Israeli Jews are resident in the USA. Growth rate 1.8% p.a.

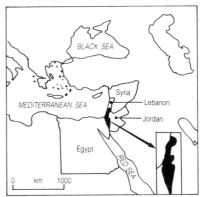

**life expectancy** men 73, women 76
**language** Hebrew and Arabic (official); Yiddish, European and W Asian languages
**religion** Israel is a secular state, but the predominant faith is Judaism 83%; also Sunni Muslim, Christian,

and Druse
**literacy** men 97%/women 93% (1985 est)
**GNP** $23 bn (1983); $5,609 per head

**chronology**
**1948** Independent State of Israel proclaimed with Ben-Gurion as prime minister; attacked by Arab nations, Israel won the War of Independence.
**1963** Ben-Gurion resigned, succeeded by Levi Eshkol.
**1964** Palestine Liberation Organization (PLO) founded with the aim of overthrowing the state of Israel.
**1967** Israel victorious in the Six-Day War.
**1968** Israel Labour Party formed, led by Golda Meir.
**1969** Golda Meir became prime minister.
**1974** Yom Kippur War: Israel attacked by Egypt and Syria. Golda Meir succeeded by Itzhak Rabin.
**1977** Menachem Begin elected prime minister. Egyptian president addressed the Knesset.
**1978** Camp David talks.
**1979** Egyptian-Israeli agreement signed.
**1982** Israel pursued PLO fighters into Lebanon.
**1983** Agreement reached for withdrawal from Lebanon.
**1985** Israeli prime minister Shimon Peres had secret talks with King Hussein of Jordan.
**1986** Itzhak Shamir took over from Peres under power-sharing agreement.
**1988** Criticism of Israel's handling of Palestinian uprising in occupied territories; PLO acknowledged Israel's right to exist.
**1989** New Likud–Labour coalition government formed under Shamir. Limited progress achieved on proposals for negotiations leading to elections in occupied territories.
**1990** Coalition threatened by differences over peace process; international condemnation of Temple Mount killings.
**1991** Shamir gave cautious response to US Middle East peace proposals.

---

## Italy (Republic of)
(*Repubblica Italiana*)

---

**area** 301,300 sq km/116,332 sq mi
**capital** Rome
**towns** Milan, Turin; ports Naples, Genoa, Palermo, Bari, Catania, Trieste

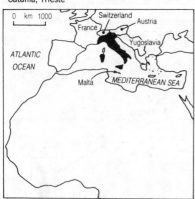

**physical** mountainous (Maritime Alps, Dolomites, Apennines); rivers Po, Adige, Arno, Tiber, Rubicon; islands of Sicily, Sardinia, Elba, Capri, Ischia, Lipari, Pantelleria; lakes Como, Maggiore, Garda
**features** continental Europe's only active volcanoes: Vesuvius, Etna, Stromboli; historic towns include Venice, Florence, Siena, Rome; Greek, Roman, Etruscan

archeological sites
**political parties** Christian Democratic Party (DC), Christian, centrist; Democratic Party of the Left (PDS), pro-European socialist; Italian Socialist Party (PSI), moderate socialist; Italian Social Movement–National Right (MSI-DN), neo-fascist; Italian Republican Party (PRI), social democratic, left-of-centre; Italian Social Democratic Party (PSDI), moderate left-of-centre; Liberals (PLI), right-of-centre
**exports** wine (world's largest producer), fruit, vegetables, textiles (Europe's largest silk producer), leather goods, motor vehicles, electrical goods, chemicals, marble (Carrara), sulphur, mercury, iron, steel
**head of state** Francesco Cossiga from 1985
**head of government** Giulio Andreotti from 1989
**political system** democratic republic
**currency** lira (2,187.00 = £1 July 1991)
**population** (1990 est) 57,657,000; growth rate 0.1% p.a.
**life expectancy** men 73, women 80 (1989)
**language** Italian; German, French, Slovene minorities
**religion** Roman Catholic 90%
**literacy** 97% (1989)
**GNP** $825 bn; $14,383 per head (1988)

**chronology**
**1946** Monarchy replaced by a republic.
**1948** New constitution adopted.
**1954** Trieste returned to Italy.
**1976** Communists proposed establishment of broad-based, left–right government, the 'historic compromise'; rejected by Christian Democrats.
**1978** Christian Democrat Aldo Moro, architect of the historic compromise, kidnapped and murdered by Red Brigade guerrillas.
**1983** Bettino Craxi, a Socialist, became leader of broad coalition government.
**1987** Craxi resigned; succeeding coalition fell within months.
**1988** Christian Democrats leader Ciriaco de Mita, established a five-party coalition including the Socialists.
**1989** De Mita resigned after disagreements within his coalition government; succeeded by Giulio Andreotti. De Mita lost leadership of Christian Democrats; Communists formed 'shadow government'.
**1991** Referendum approved electoral reform.

---

### PEOPLE OF THE YEAR

In 1989, at the age of 70, Giulio Andreotti formed his sixth government. Andreotti has served in more governments over a longer period of time than any other Italian politician: in addition to being prime minister, he has been defence minister eight times and foreign minister five. He owes much to his friendship with Alcide de Gasperi, who led eight of Italy's postwar governments—Andreotti served as prime minister in two of them. In 1990 it was Italy's turn to take the European Community's presidency, and Andreotti, a fervent European, made full use of it. It was the summit meeting in Rome, October 1990, that proved to be a turning point for Margaret Thatcher's political career, for in the following month her strong anti-European stance eventually forced her out of office.

---

## Ivory Coast (Republic of)
(*République de la Côte d'Ivoire*)

---

**area** 322,463 sq km/124,471 sq mi
**capital** Abidjan; capital designate Yamoussoukro
**towns** Bouaké, Daloa, Man; port San Pedro
**physical** tropical rainforest (diminishing as exploited) in

S; savanna and low mountains in N
**head of state and government** Félix Houphouët-Boigny
from 1960
**political system** one-party presidential republic (since
1960)
**political parties** Democratic Party of the Ivory Coast
(PDCI), nationalist, free-enterprise
**exports** coffee, cocoa, timber, petroleum products
**currency** franc CFA (498.25 = £1 July 1991)
**population** (1990 est) 12,070,000; growth rate 3.3%
p.a.
**life expectancy** men 52, women 55 (1989)

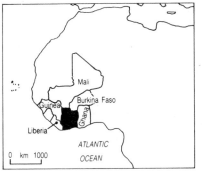

**language** French (official), over 60 native dialects
**religion** animist 65%, Muslim 24%, Christian 11%
**literacy** 35% (1988)
**GNP** $10.3 bn (1987); $921 per head

**chronology**
**1958** Achieved internal self-government.
**1960** Independence achieved from France, with Félix
Houphouët-Boigny as president of a one-party state.
**1985** Houphouët-Boigny re-elected, unopposed.
**1986** Name changed officially to Côte d'Ivoire.
**1990** Houphouët-Boigny and PDCI re-elected.

---

**Jamaica**

**area** 10,957 sq km/4,230 sq mi
**capital** Kingston
**towns** Montego Bay, Spanish Town, St Andrew
**physical** mountainous tropical island

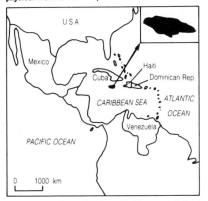

**features** Blue Mountains (so called because of the haze
over them; renowned for their coffee); partly undersea
ruins of pirate city of Port Royal, destroyed by an earthquake in 1692

**head of state** Elizabeth II from 1962 represented by
governor-general
**head of government** Michael Manley from 1989
**political system** constitutional monarchy
**political parties** Jamaica Labour Party (JLP), moderate,
centrist; People's National Party (PNP), left-of-centre
**exports** sugar, bananas, bauxite, rum, coffee, coconuts,
liqueurs, cigars, citrus
**currency** Jamaican dollar (J$16.16 = £1 July 1991)
**population** (1990 est) 2,513,000 (African 76%, mixed
15%, Chinese, Caucasian, East Indian); growth rate
2.2% p.a.
**life expectancy** men 75, women 78 (1989)
**language** English, Jamaican creole
**religion** Protestant 70%, Rastafarian
**literacy** 82% (1988)
**GNP** $2.9 bn (1987); $1,160 per head

**chronology**
**1944** Internal self-government introduced.
**1962** Independence achieved from Britain, with Alexander Bustamante of the JLP as prime minister.
**1967** JLP re-elected under Hugh Shearer.
**1972** Michael Manley of the PNP became prime minister.
**1980** JLP elected, with Edward Seaga as prime minister.
**1983** JLP re-elected, winning all 60 seats.
**1988** Island badly damaged by Hurricane Gilbert.
**1989** PNP won a decisive victory with Michael Manley
returning as prime minister.

---

**Japan**
(*Nippon*)

**area** 377,535 sq km/145,822 sq mi
**capital** Tokyo
**towns** Fukuoka, Kitakyushu, Kyoto, Sapporo; ports Osaka,
Nagoya, Yokohama, Kobe, Kawasaki

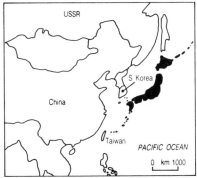

**physical** mountainous, volcanic; comprises over 1,000
islands, including Hokkaido, Honshu, Shikoku, Kyushu,
Ryukyu
**features** Mount Fuji, Mount Aso (volcanic)
**head of state** (figurehead) Emperor Akihito from 1989
**head of government** Toshiki Kaifu from 1989
**political system** constitutional monarchy
**political parties** Liberal Democratic Party (LDP), right-
of-centre; Japan Socialist Party (JSP), left-of-centre;
Komeito (Clean Government Party), Buddhist-centrist;
Democratic Socialist Party, centrist; Japanese Communist Party (JCP), socialist
**exports** televisions, cassette and video recorders, radios,
cameras, computers, robots, other electronic and electrical equipment, motor vehicles, ships, iron, steel, chemicals, textiles
**currency** yen (223.50 = £1 July 1991)

**population** (1990 est) 123,778,000; growth rate 0.5% p.a.
**life expectancy** men 76, women 82 (1989)
**language** Japanese
**religion** Shinto, Buddhist (often combined), Christian; 30% claim a personal religious faith
**literacy** 99% (1989)
**GNP** $1.8 tri (1989); $15,030 per head

**chronology**
**1871** Feudal system abolished.
**1894–95** War with China; Taiwan gained.
**1902** Formed alliance with Britain.
**1904–05** War with Russia; Russia ceded southern half of Sakhalin.
**1910** Japan annexed Korea.
**1914** Joined Allies in World War I.
**1918** Received German Pacific islands as mandates.
**1931–32** War with China; renewed 1937.
**1941** Japan attacked US fleet at Pearl Harbor Dec 7.
**1945** World War II ended with Japanese surrender. Allied control commission took power.
**1946** Framing of 'peace constitution'.
**1952** Full sovereignty regained.
**1958** Joined United Nations.
**1972** Ryukyu Islands regained.
**1974** Prime Minister Tanaka resigned over Lockheed bribes scandal.
**1982** Yasuhiro Nakasone elected prime minister.
**1987** Noboru Takeshita chosen to succeed Nakasone.
**1988** Recruit corporation insider-trading scandal cast shadow over government and opposition parties.
**1989** Emperor Hirohito died; succeeded by his son Akihito. Two cabinet ministers resigned over Recruit, many more implicated. Takeshita resigned because of Recruit scandal; succeeded by Sosuke Uno in June. Uno resigned Aug after sex scandal; succeeded by Toshiki Kaifu.
**1990** New house of councillors' elections (Feb) won by LDP. Public-works budget increased by 50% to encourage imports.
**1991** Japan contributed billions of dollars to the Gulf war and its aftermath.

**Jordan (Hashemite Kingdom of)**
(*Al Mamlaka al Urduniya al Hashemiyah*)

**area** 89,206 sq km/34,434 sq mi (West Bank, incorporated into Jordan 1950 but occupied by Israel since 1967, area 5,879 sq km/2,269 sq mi)

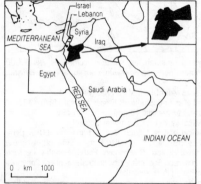

**capital** Amman
**towns** Zarqa, Irbid, Aqaba (the only port)
**physical** desert plateau in E; Rift valley separate E and W banks of the Jordan

**features** Dead Sea, river Jordan, archaeological sites at Jerash and Petra
**head of state and government** King Hussein ibn Talai from 1952
**political system** absolute monarchy
**political parties** none (banned 1976)
**exports** potash, phosphates, citrus
**currency** Jordanian dinar (JD1.09 = £1 July 1991)
**population** (1990 est) 3,065,000 (including Palestinian refugees); West Bank (1988) 866,000; growth rate 3.6% p.a.
**life expectancy** men 67, women 71
**language** Arabic (official); English
**religion** Sunni Muslim 92%, Christian 8%
**literacy** 71% (1988)
**GNP** $4.3 bn (1987); $1,500 per head (1988)

**chronology**
**1946** Independence achieved from Britain as Transjordan.
**1949** New state of Jordan declared.
**1953** Hussein ibn Talai became king of Jordan.
**1958** Jordan and Iraq formed Arab Federation that ended when the Iraqi monarchy was deposed.
**1976** Lower house dissolved, elections postponed until further notice.
**1982** Hussein tried to mediate in Arab-Israeli conflict.
**1984** Women voted for the first time.
**1985** Hussein put forward framework for Middle East peace settlement. Secret meeting between Hussein and Israeli prime minister.
**1988** Hussein announced a decision to cease administering the West Bank as part of Jordan, passing responsibility to Palestine Liberation Organization, and the suspension of parliament.
**1989** Prime minister Zaid al-Rifai resigned; Hussein promised new parliamentary elections following criticism of economic policies. Riots over price increases up to 50% following fall in oil revenues. 80-member parliament elected and Mudar Badran appointed prime minister. First parliamentary elections for 22 years; Muslim Brotherhood won 25 of 80 seats but exiled from government; martial law provisions lifted.
**1990** Hussein unsuccessfully tried to mediate after Iraq's invasion of Kuwait. Massive refugee problems as thousands fled to Jordan from Kuwait and Iraq.
**1991** Ban on political parties removed. 24 years of martial law lifted.

**Kenya (Republic of)**
(*Jamhuri ya Kenya*)

**area** 582,600 sq km/224,884 sq mi
**capital** Nairobi
**towns** Kisumu, port Mombasa

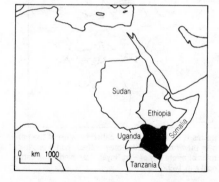

**physical** mountains and highlands in W and centre; coastal plain in S; N arid

**features** Great Rift Valley, Mount Kenya, Lake Nakuru (flamingos), Lake Turkana (Rudolf), national parks with wildlife, Malindini Marine Reserve, Olduvai Gorge

**head of state and government** Daniel arap Moi from 1978

**political system** authoritarian nationalism

**political parties** Kenya African National Union (KANU), nationalist, centrist; National Democratic Party (NDP), centrist

**exports** coffee, tea, pineapples, petroleum products

**currency** Kenya shilling (46.57 = £1 July 1991)

**population** (1990 est) 25,393,000 (Kikuyu 21%, Luo 13%, Luhya 14%, Kelenjin 11%; Asian, Arab, European); growth rate 4.2% p.a.

**life expectancy** men 59, women 63 (1989)

**language** Kiswahili (official); English

**religion** Protestant 38%, Roman Catholic 26%, Muslim 6%; indigenous

**literacy** 50% (1988)

**GNP** $8.1 bn (1987); $360 per head (1988)

**chronology**

**1895** British East African protectorate established.

**1920** Kenya became a British colony.

**1944** African participation in politics began.

**1950** Mau Mau campaign began.

**1953** Nationalist leader Jomo Kenyatta imprisoned.

**1956** Mau Mau campaign defeated, Kenyatta released.

**1963** Achieved internal self-government, with Kenyatta as prime minister.

**1964** Independence achieved from Britain as a republic, within the Commonwealth, with Kenyatta as president.

**1978** Death of Kenyatta. Succeeded by Daniel arap Moi.

**1982** Attempted coup against Moi foiled.

**1983** Moi re-elected.

**1984** Over 2,000 people massacred by government forces at Wajir.

**1985–86** Thousands of forest villagers evicted by army and police and their homes destroyed to make way for cash crops.

**1988** Moi re-elected. 150,000 evicted from state-owned forests.

**1989** Moi announced the release of all known political prisoners. Confiscated ivory burned in attempt to stop elephant poaching.

**1990** Despite anti-government riots, Moi refused multi-party politics.

**1991** Opposition National Democratic Party launched by Oginga Odinga in the face of Moi's refusal to accept it.

### Kiribati (Republic of

**area** 717 sq km/277 sq mi

**capital** and port Bairiki (on Tarawa Atoll)

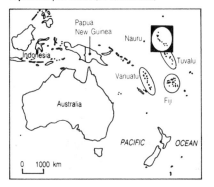

**physical** comprises 33 Pacific coral islands: the Gilbert, Phoenix, and Line Islands, and Banaba (Ocean Island)

**head of state and government** Ieremia Tabai from 1979

**political system** liberal democracy

**political parties** Christian Democratic Party, opposition faction within assembly; National Party, governing faction

**exports** copra, fish

**currency** Australian dollar (A$2.11 = £1 July 1991)

**population** (1990 est) 65,600 (Micronesian); growth rate 1.7% p.a.

**language** English, Gilbertese (official)

**religion** Roman Catholic 48%, Protestant 45%

**literacy** 90% (1985)

**GNP** $24 million (1987); $650 per head (1988)

**chronology**

**1892** Gilbert and Ellice Islands proclaimed a British protectorate.

**1937** Phoenix Islands added to colony.

**1975** Ellice Islands separated to become Tuvalu.

**1977** Gilbert Islands granted internal self-government.

**1979** Independence achieved from Britain, within the Commonwealth, as the Republic of Kiribati, with Ieremia Tabai as president.

**1983** Tabai re-elected.

**1985** Fishing agreement with Soviet state-owned company negotiated, prompted formation of Kiribati's first political party, the opposition Christian Democrats.

**1987** Tabai re-elected.

### Korea, North (Democratic People's Republic of)
(*Chosun Minchu-chui Inmin Konghwa-guk*)

**area** 120,538 sq km/46,528 sq mi

**capital** Pyongyang

**towns** Chorgjin, Nampo, Wonsan

**physical** wide coastal plain in west rising to mountains cut by deep valleys in the interior

**features** the richer of the two Koreas in mineral resources

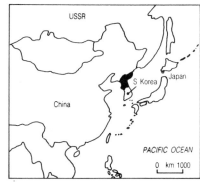

**head of state** Kim Il Sung from 1972 (also head of Communist Party)

**head of government** Yon Hyong Muk from 1988

**political system** communism

**political parties** Korean Workers' Party (KWP), Marxist-Leninist-Kim Il Sungist

**exports** coal, iron, copper, textiles, chemicals

**currency** won (1.58 = £1 July 1991)

**population** (1990 est) 23,059,000; growth rate 2.5% p.a.

**life expectancy** men 67, women 73 (1989)

**language** Korean

**religion** traditionally Buddhist, Confucian

**literacy** 99% (1989)

**GNP** $20 bn (1988); $3,450 per head

**chronology**
**1910** Korea formally annexed by Japan.
**1945** Russian and US troops entered Korea, forced surrender of Japanese, and divided the country in two.
**1948** Democratic People's Republic of Korea declared.
**1950** North Korea invaded South Korea to unite the nation, beginning the Korean War.
**1953** Armistice agreed to end Korean War.
**1961** Friendship and mutual assistance treaty signed with China.
**1972** New constitution, with executive president, adopted. Talks took place with South Korea about possible reunification.
**1980** Reunification talks broke down.
**1983** Four South Korean cabinet ministers assassinated in Rangoon, Burma (Myanmar), by North Korean army officers.
**1985** Increased relations with the USSR.
**1989** Increasing evidence shown of nuclear-weapons development.
**1990** Diplomatic contacts with South Korea and Japan suggested the beginning of a thaw in North Korea's relations with the rest of the world.

**Korea, South (Republic of Korea)**
(*Daehan Minguk*)

**area** 98,799 sq km/38,161 sq mi
**capital** Seoul
**towns** Taegu, ports Pusan, Inchon
**physical** southern end of a mountainous peninsula separating the Sea of Japan from the Yellow Sea
**head of state** Roh Tae-Woo from 1988
**head of government** Ro Jai Bong from 1990
**political system** emergent democracy
**political parties** Democratic Liberal Party (DLP), right-of-centre; New Democratic Union (NDU), left-of-centre

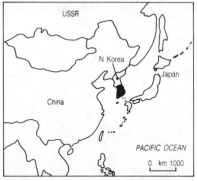

**exports** steel, ships, chemicals, electronics, textiles, plastics
**currency** won (1,172.52 = £1 July 1991)
**population** (1990 est) 43,919,000; growth rate 1.4% p.a.
**life expectancy** men 66, women 73 (1989)
**language** Korean
**religion** traditionally Buddhist and Confucian
**literacy** 92% (1989)
**GNP** $171bn (1988); $2,180 per head (1986)

**chronology**
**1910** Korea formally annexed by Japan.
**1945** Russian and US troops entered Korea, forced surrender of Japanese, and divided the country in two.
**1948** Republic proclaimed.
**1950–53** War with North Korea.
**1960** President Syngman Rhee resigned amid unrest.

**1961** Military coup by General Park Chung-Hee. Industrial growth programme.
**1979** Assassination of President Park.
**1980** Military coup by General Chun Doo-Hwan.
**1987** Adoption of more democratic constitution following student unrest. Roh Tae Woo elected president.
**1988** Former president Chun, accused of corruption, publicly apologized and agreed to hand over his financial assets to the state. Seoul hosted Summer Olympic Games.
**1989** Roh reshuffled cabinet, threatened crackdown on protesters.
**1990** Two minor opposition parties united with Democratic Justice Party to form ruling Democratic Liberal Party. Diplomatic relations established with the USSR.
**1991** Violent mass demonstrations against the government. New opposition grouping, New Democratic Union (NDU) formed.

**Kuwait (State of)**
(*Dowlat al Kuwait*)

**area** 17,819 sq km/6,878 sq mi
**capital** Kuwait (also chief port)
**physical** hot desert and islands of Bubiyan and Warba at NE corner of Arabian Peninsula
**features** oil revenues make it one of the world's best-equipped states in public works and medical and educational services

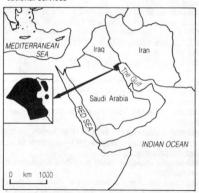

**head of state and government** Jabir al-Ahmad al-Jabir al-Sabah from 1977
**political system** absolute monarchy
**political parties** none
**exports** oil
**currency** Kuwaiti dinar (KD0.48 = £1 July 1991)
**population** (1990 est) 2,080,000 (Kuwaitis 40%, Palestinians 30%); growth rate 5.5% p.a.
**life expectancy** men 72, women 76 (1989)
**language** Arabic 78%, Kurdish 10%, Farsi 4%
**religion** Sunni Muslim 45%, Shi'ite minority 30%
**literacy** 71% (1988)
**GNP** $19.1 bn (1988); $10,410 per head

**chronology**
**1914** Britain recognized Kuwait as an independent sovereign state.
**1961** Full independence achieved from Britain, with Sheik Abdullah al-Salem al-Sabah as emir.
**1965** Sheik Abdullah died; succeeded by his brother, Sheik Sabah.
**1977** Sheik Sabah died; succeeded by Crown Prince Jabir.
**1983** Shi'ite guerrillas bombed targets in Kuwait; 17 arrested.

# THE GULF CONFLICT—A NECESSARY WAR?

As a matter of principle, and sometimes expediency, wars are to be avoided wherever possible and historians have identified some as clearly unnecessary. Was the Gulf Conflict avoidable or inevitable? Was it a necessary war?

In the months following the invasion of Kuwait, on 2 August 1990, there were widespread calls for economic sanctions to force Saddam Hussein to withdraw his forces. The UN accepted this argument and within four days the Security Council had, in Resolution 661, authorized the imposition of sanctions and set up a committee to monitor their implementation. On 25 August, in Resolution 665, the Council called on member states to take active measures to intercept ships in the Gulf area to ensure enforcement. A month later Resolution 670 extended the blockade to aircraft.

During this period of 'economic warfare' the UN secretary-general, Perez de Cuellar, embarked on diplomacy, which he described as a 'long haul for peace', and King Hussein of Jordan attempted to act as an 'honest broker' in search of a peaceful solution. At the same time, Saddam Hussein was consolidating his position in Kuwait, claiming it as Iraq's nineteenth province, installing his own officials and strengthening his defences against possible military action by the growing coalition, led by the United States. This coalition was building up a massive presence to match the might of the 'fourth biggest army in the world.'

On 29 November 1990, following intensive diplomatic activity by US secretary of state James Baker, the UN Security Council approved, in Resolution 678, a deadline of 15 January 1991 for Iraq's withdrawal from Kuwait, after which all 'necessary means' could be used by the coalition to enforce a withdrawal, in compliance with Resolution 660, passed on the date of the initial invasion.

The UN secretary-general's peace initiative had met with little success but the Soviet president, Mikhail Gorbachev, was still urging US president, George Bush, to continue to give peace a chance and on 3 January 1991 Bush proposed talks between his officials and their Iraqi conterparts in Switzerland for 'one last attempt' at peace. Talks between Iraq's foreign minister, Tariq Aziz, and James Baker proved fruitless and were broken off after six hours and within six days of the Resolution 678 deadline, Perez de Cuellar embarked on a last-ditch peace mission to Baghdad but returned disconsolate, saying 'Only God Knows' if there will be war. A final peace initiative by the Soviet Union seemed doomed to failure from the start.

Given the entrenched positions on both sides, it seemed that by January 1991, and possibly before, war had become inevitable. But inevitability does not always equate with necessity and we return to the question, was the conflict a necessary war? There are three possible approaches towards an answer : first, from the standpoint of the instigator of the conflict, Saddam Hussein; second from the viewpoint of the coalition assembled against him, and particularly the United States; third, using the benefits of hindsight, and evaluating, on a 'profit and loss' basis, whether the end justified the means.

Saddam Hussein's record as Iraq's leader since 1979 suggests that he saw the invasion of Kuwait just as necessary as the war with Iran in 1980. He viewed the takeover of Iran by religious fundamentalists as a threat, fearing that Islamic fervour might spread, like an infection, to Iraq. For a long time he had felt it essential to gain better access to the Gulf, and occupation of the the Kuwaiti islands of Bubiyan and Warba was a logical first step. If this meant war with Kuwait, then a war was necessary. However, the necessity of war with the large multi-national coalition which was eventually assembled against him was probably not anticipated. He seriously miscalculated their will, and particularly that of the United States, to fight.

From George Bush's viewpoint, once, with Margaret Thatcher's encouragement, he had decided to stand firm, war with Iraq was probably necessary. International economic sanctions had not, historically, a great track record and would be likely to take years, rather than months, to bite. He saw Saddam Hussein's vast war machine as a threat to long-term stability in the region and he was mindful of the strong pro-Israeli lobby in his own country. There was also intelligence of Iraq's potential nuclear capability, arguing that a war now was preferable to one a year or two later.

With the advantage of hindsight, and because coalition casualties were so light, a convincing case can be made out for the necessity of the Gulf War, but only if the chance of securing greater peace and stability in the Middle East, described so graphically by James Baker as a 'window of opportunity', is seized and acted upon.

Was it, then, a necessary war? The case for either side of the argument has yet to be proven and the final answer may well have to wait until the enormous environmental damage to the region, and possibly the whole world, can be fully assessed.

---

**1984** Shi'ite bombers convicted.
**1987** Kuwaiti oil tankers reflagged, received US Navy protection; missile attacks by Iran.
**1988** Aircraft hijacked by pro-Iranian Shi'ites demanding release of convicted bombers; Kuwait refused.
**1990** Pro-democracy demonstrations suppressed. Kuwait annexed by Iraq. Emir set up government in exile in Saudi Arabia.
**1991** (Feb) Kuwait liberated by US-led coalition forces; extensive damage to property and environment. New government omits any opposition representatives. Trials of alleged Iraqi collaborators criticized. Promised elections

postponed.

## PEOPLE OF THE YEAR

Until its invasion by Iraq in Aug 1990, the Emir of Kuwait was little known outside his own country. Even now he is recognized by his title rather than as an individual. Sheik Jabir al Ahmadal Jabir al Sabah succeeded his uncle Sheikh Sabah as emir Dec 1977. He suspended Kuwait's National Assembly 1986, after mounting parliamentary criticism, but was generally considered to be receptive to Kuwait's progressive thinkers. The Iraqi invasion of Kuwait Aug 1990 forced him to flee into exile in Saudi Arabia; he was reluctant to return to his country until some semblance of the comfort he had previously enjoyed reappeared. Despite his attempts to retain his feudal, if paternalistic rule, it seems certain that the principle of popular participation in public life will be reestablished.

### Laos (Lao People's Democratic Republic)
(*Saathiaranagroat Prachhathippatay Prachhachhon Lao*)

**area** 236,790 sq km/91,400 sq mi
**capital** Vientiane
**towns** Luang Prabang, the former royal capital, Pakse, Savannakhet
**physical** high mountains in E; Mekong River in W; jungle

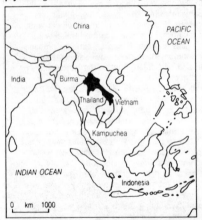

**features** hydroelectric power from the Mekong is exported to Thailand; Plain of Jars, where prehistoric people carved stone jars large enough to hold a person; formerly known as the Land of a Million Elephants
**head of state** Prince Souphanouvong from 1975; Phoumi Vongvichit acting president from 1986
**head of government** Kaysone Phomvihane from 1975
**political system** communism, one-party state
**political parties** Lao People's Revolutionary Party (only legal party)
**exports** tin, teak, coffee, electricity
**currency** new kip (K.1,137.50 = £1 July 1991)
**population** (1990 est) 4,024,000 (Lao 48%, Thai 14%, Khmer 25%, Chinese 13%); growth rate 2.2% p.a.
**life expectancy** men 48, women 51 (1989)
**language** Lao (official), French
**religion** Theravada Buddhist 85%
**literacy** 41% (1986)
**GNP** $500 million (1987); $180 per head (1988)

#### chronology
**1893–1945** Laos a French protectorate.
**1945** Temporarily occupied by Japan.
**1946** Retaken by France.

**1950** Granted semi-autonomy in French Union.
**1954** Independence achieved from France.
**1960** Right-wing government seized power.
**1962** Coalition government established; civil war continued.
**1973** Vientiane ceasefire agreement.
**1975** Communist-dominated republic proclaimed with Prince Souphanouvong as head of state.
**1987** Phoumi Vongvichit became acting president.
**1988** Plans announced to withdraw 40% of Vietnamese forces stationed in the country.
**1989** First assembly elections since communist takeover.
**1990** Draft constitution published.

### Lebanon (Republic of)
(*al-Jumhouria al-Lubnaniya*)

**area** 10,452 sq km/4,034 sq mi
**capital** and port Beirut
**towns** ports Tripoli, Tyre, Sidon
**physical** narrow coastal plain; Bekka valley N–S between Lebanon and Antilebanon mountain ranges
**features** few of the cedars of Lebanon remain; Mount Hermon; Chouf Mountains; archaeological sites at Baalbeck, Byblos, Tyre; until the civil war, the financial centre of the Middle East

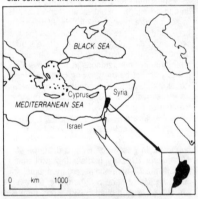

**head of state** Elias Hrawi from 1989
**head of government** Umar Karami from 1990
**political system** emergent democratic republic
**political parties** Phalangist Party, Christian, radical, right-wing; Progressive Socialist Party (PSP), Druze, moderate, socialist; National Liberal Party (NLP), Maronite, centre-left; Parliamentary Democratic Front, Sunni Muslim, centrist; Lebanese Communist Party (PCL), nationalist, communist
**exports** citrus and other fruit; industrial products to Arab neighbours
**currency** Lebanese pound (Leb.1469.00 = £1 July 1991)
**population** (1990 est) 3,340,000 (Lebanese 82%, Palestinian 9%, Armenian 5%); growth rate -0.1% p.a.
**life expectancy** men 65, women 70 (1989)
**language** Arabic, French (both official); Armenian, English
**religion** Muslim 57% (Shi'ite 33%, Sunni 24%), Christian (Maronite and Orthodox) 40%, Druse 3%
**literacy** 75% (1989)
**GNP** $1.8 bn (1986); $690 per head

#### chronology
**1920–41** Administered under French mandate.
**1944** Independence achieved.
**1964** Palestine Liberation Organization (PLO) founded in Beirut.
**1975** Outbreak of civil war between Christians and Mus-

lims.
**1976** Cease-fire agreed.
**1978** Israel invaded S Lebanon in search of PLO fighters. International peacekeeping force established. Fighting broke out again.
**1979** Part of S Lebanon declared an 'independent free Lebanon'.
**1982** Bachir Gemayel became president but was assassinated before he could assume office; succeeded by his brother Amin Gemayel.
**1983** Agreement reached for the withdrawal of Syrian and Israeli troops but abrogated under Syrian pressure.
**1984** Most of international peacekeeping force withdrawn.
**1985** Lebanon nearing chaos; many foreigners taken hostage.
**1987** Syrian troops sent into Beirut.
**1988** Agreement on a Christian successor to Gemayel failed; he established a military government; Selim al-Hoss set up rival government; threat of partition hung over the country.
**1989** Arab Peace Plan accepted by Muslims but rejected by Maronite Christians led by General Michel Aoun; National Assembly appointed René Muawad as president, in place of Aoun; Muawad killed by car bomb, succeeded by Elias Hrawi; Hrawi formally made Selim al-Hoss prime minister; Aoun continued his defiance.
**1990** Irish hostage Brian Keenan released. General Aoun surrendered and legitimate government restored, with Umar Karami as prime minister.
**1991** Government extended control to the whole country. Treaty of cooperation with Syria signed.

---

## Lesotho (Kingdom of)

**area** 30,355 sq km/11,717 sq mi
**capital** Maseru

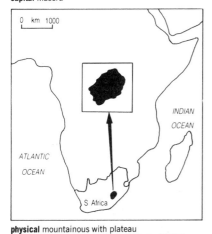

**physical** mountainous with plateau
**features** Lesotho is an enclave within South Africa
**head of state** King Letsie I from 1990
**head of government** Elias Tutsoane Ramaema from 1991
**political system** military-controlled monarchy
**political parties** Basotho National Party (BNP), traditionalist, nationalist, Basutoland Congress Party (BCP)
**exports** wool, mohair, diamonds
**currency** maluti (4.68 = £1 July 1991)
**population** (1990 est) 1,757,000; growth rate 2.7% p.a.
**life expectancy** men 59, women 62 (1989)
**language** Sesotho, English (official); Zulu, Xhosa
**religion** Protestant 42%, Roman Catholic 38%
**literacy** 59% (1988)
**GNP** $408 million (1988); $410 per head

**chronology**
**1966** Independence achieved from Britain, within the Commonwealth, as the Kingdom of Lesotho, with Chief Leabua Jonathan as prime minister.
**1970** State of emergency declared and constitution suspended.
**1973** Pro-government interim assembly established.
**1975** Members of the ruling party attacked by guerrillas backed by South Africa.
**1986** South Africa imposed border blockade, forcing deportation of 60 African National Congress members. Gen Lekhanya ousted Chief Jonathan in coup. National Assembly abolished.
**1990** Moshoeshoe II dethroned by ruling military council; replaced by his son Mohato.
**1991** Lekhanya ousted in military coup led by Col Elias Tutsoane Ramaema. Political parties permitted to operate.

---

## Liberia (Republic of)

**area** 111,370 sq km/42,989 sq mi
**capital** and port, Monrovia
**towns** ports Buchanan, Greenville

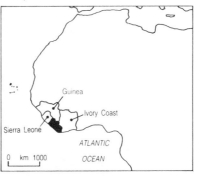

**physical** forested highlands; swampy coast where six rivers enter the sea
**features** nominally the world's largest merchant navy as minimal registration controls make Liberia's a flag of convenience; the world's largest rubber plantations
**head of state and government** Amos Sawyer from 1990
**political system** emergent democratic republic
**political parties** National Democratic party of Liberia (NDLP), nationalist; Liberian Action Party; Liberian Unity Party; United People's Party; Unity Party
**exports** iron ore, rubber, diamonds, coffee, cocoa, palm oil
**currency** Liberian dollar (1.61 = £1 July 1991)
**population** (1990 est) 2,644,000 (95% indigenous); growth rate 3% p.a.
**life expectancy** men 53, women 56 (1989)
**language** English (official); over 20 Niger-Congo languages
**religion** Muslim 20%, Christian 15%, traditional 65%
**literacy** 47% male/23% female (1985 est)
**GNP** $973 million (1987); $410 per head

**chronology**
**1847** Founded as an independent republic.
**1944** William Tubman elected president.
**1971** Tubman died and was succeeded by William Tolbert.
**1980** Tolbert assassinated in coup led by Samuel Doe, who suspended the constitution and ruled through a People's Redemption Council.
**1984** New constitution approved. National Democratic

Party of Liberia (NDPL) founded by Doe.
**1985** NDPL won decisive victory in general election. Unsuccessful coup against Doe.
**1990** Doe killed during a bloody civil war between rival rebel factions. Amos Sawyer became interim head of government.
**1991** Amos Sawyer re-elected president. Rebel leader, Charles Taylor agreed to work together.

### PEOPLE OF THE YEAR

On the tenth anniversary of the coup he had led against President William Tolbert, making him head of state of Liberia, Samuel Doe was himself killed in a rebel uprising. In 1981 he raised himself from the rank of master sergeant to general and commander-in-chief of the army. Having, as he thought, made himself secure as leader of the National Democratic Party, ethnic unrest and economic problems threatened his position. After surviving a number of attempted coups, Doe found himself surrounded by rebel forces in the presidential palace of the capital, Monrovia. In September 1990 he was captured, tortured, and killed.

### Libya (Great Socialist People's Libyan Arab Jamahiriya)
(*al-Jamahiriya al-Arabiya al-Libya al-Shabiya al-Ishtirakiya al-Uzma*)

**area** 1,759,540 sq km/679,182 sq mi
**capital** Tripoli
**towns** ports Benghazi, Misurata, Tobruk

**physical** desert with plateaux and depressions; mountains in N and S
**features** Gulf of Sirte; rock paintings of *c.* 3000 BC in the Fezzan; Roman city sites include Leptis Magna, Sabratha; plan to pump water from below the Sahara to the coast risks rapid exhaustion of non-renewable supply
**head of state and government** Moamer Khaddafi from 1969
**political system** one-party, socialist state
**political parties** Arab Socialist Union (ASU), radical, left-wing
**exports** oil, natural gas
**currency** Libyan dinar (LD0.48 = £1 July 1991)
**population** (1990 est) 4,280,000 (including 500,000 foreign workers); growth rate 3.1% p.a.
**life expectancy** men 64, women 69 (1989)
**language** Arabic
**religion** Sunni Muslim 97%
**literacy** 60% (1989)
**GNP** $20 bn; $5,410 per head (1988)

**chronology**

**1911** Conquered by Italy.
**1934** Colony named Libya.
**1942** Divided into 3 provinces: Fezzan (under French control); Cyrenaica, Tripolitana (under British control).
**1951** Achieved independence as the United Kingdom of Libya, under King Idris.
**1969** King deposed in a coup led by Col Moamer Khaddhafi. Revolution Command Council set up and the Arab Socialist Union (ASU) proclaimed the only legal party.
**1972** Proposed federation of Libya, Syria, and Egypt abandoned.
**1980** Proposed merger with Syria abandoned. Libyan troops began fighting in Chad.
**1981** Proposed merger with Chad abandoned.
**1986** US bombing of Khaddhafi's headquarters, following allegations of his complicity in terrorist activities.
**1988** Diplomatic relations with Chad restored.
**1989** USA accused Libya of building a chemical-weapons factory and shot down two Libyan planes; reconciliation with Egypt.

### Liechtenstein (Principality of)
(*Fürstenum Liechtenstein*)

**area** 160 sq km/62 sq mi
**capital** Vaduz
**physical** Alpine; includes part of Rhine Valley in W

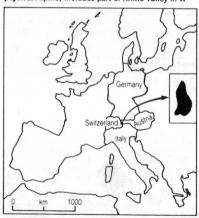

**features** only country in the world to take its name from its reigning family; easy tax laws make it an international haven for foreign companies and banks
**head of state** Prince Hans Adam 11 from 1989
**head of government** Hans Brunhart from 1978
**political system** constitutional monarchy
**political parties** Fatherland Union (VU); Progressive Citizens' Party (FBP)
**exports** microchips, dental products, processed foods, postage stamps
**currency** Swiss franc (2.52 = £1 July 1991)
**population** (1990 est) 30,000 (33% foreign); growth rate 1.4% p.a.
**life expectancy** men 78, women 83 (1989)
**language** German (official), Alemannic dialect
**religion** Roman Catholic 87%, Protestant 8%
**literacy** 100% (1989)
**GNP** $450 million (1986)

**chronology**
**1342** Became a sovereign state.
**1434** Present boundaries established.
**1719** Former counties of Schellenberg and Vaduz constituted as the Principality of Liechtenstein.
**1921** Adopted Swiss currency.

**1923** United with Switzerland in a customs union.
**1938** Prince Franz Josef II came to power.
**1984** Vote extended to women in national elections.
**1989** Prince Franz Joseph II died; Hans Adam II succeeded him as prince. Liechtenstein sought admission to UN.

## Luxembourg (Grand Duchy of)
(*Grand-Duché de Luxembourg*)

**area** 2,586 sq km/998 sq mi
**capital** Luxembourg
**physical** on the river Moselle; part of the Ardennes (Oesling) forest in N
**features** seat of the European Court of Justice, Secretariat of the European Parliament, international banking centre; economically linked with Belgium
**head of state** Grand Duke Jean from 1964
**head of government** Jacques Santer from 1984
**political system** liberal democracy
**political parties** Christian Social Party (PCS), moderate, left-of-centre; Luxembourg Socialist Workers' Party (POSL), moderate, socialist; Democratic Party (PD), centre-left; Communist Party of Luxembourg, pro-European left-wing

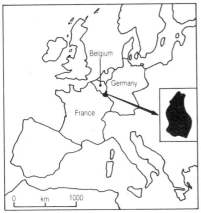

**exports** pharmaceuticals, synthetic textiles
**currency** Luxembourg franc (60.30 = £1 July 1991)
**population** (1990 est) 369,000; growth rate 0% p.a.
**life expectancy** men 71, women 78 (1989)
**language** French (official); local Letzeburgesch; German
**religion** Roman Catholic 97%
**literacy** 100% (1989)
**GNP** $4.9 bn (1988); $13,380 per head

**chronology**
**1815** Treaty of Vienna created Luxembourg a grand duchy, ruled by the king of the Netherlands.
**1830** With Belgium, revolted against Dutch rule.
**1890** Link with Netherlands ended with accession of Grand Duke Adolphe of Nassau-Weilburg.
**1948** With Belgium and the Netherlands, formed the Benelux customs union.
**1958** Benelux became economic union.
**1961** Prince Jean became acting head of state on behalf of his mother, Grand Duchess Charlotte.
**1964** Grand Duchess Charlotte abdicated, and Prince Jean became grand duke.

## Madagascar (Democratic Republic of)
(*Repoblika Demokratika n'i Madagascar*)

**area** 587,041 sq km/226,598 sq mi

**capital** Antananarivo
**towns** chief port Toamasina
**physical** central highlands; humid valleys and coastal plains; arid in S
**features** one of the last places to be inhabited, it evolved in isolation with unique animals (e.g. the lemur, now under threat from deforestation)
**head of state and government** Didier Ratsiraka from 1975

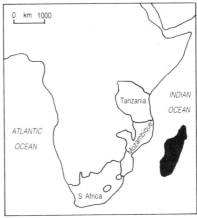

**political system** one-party socialist republic
**political parties** National Front for the Defence of the Malagasy Socialist Revolution (FNDR)
**exports** coffee, cloves, vanilla
**currency** Malagasy franc (2,968.50 = £1 July 1991)
**population** (1990 est) 11,802,000; growth rate 3.2% p.a.
**life expectancy** men 50, women 53 (1989)
**language** Malagasy (official); French, English
**religion** animist 50%, Christian 40%, Muslim 10%
**literacy** 53% (1988)
**GNP** $2.1 bn (1987); $280 per head (1988)

**chronology**
**1960** Independence achieved from France, with Philibert Tsiranana as president.
**1972** Army took control of the government.
**1975** Martial law imposed under a national military directorate. New constitution proclaimed the Democratic Republic of Madagascar, with Didier Ratsiraka as president.
**1976** Front-Line Revolutionary Organisation (AREMA) formed.
**1977** National Front for the Defence of the Malagasy Socialist Revolution (FNDR) became the sole legal political organization.
**1983** Ratsiraka re-elected, despite strong opposition from radical socialist National Movement for the Independence of Madagascar (MONIMA) under Monja Jaona.
**1989** Ratsiraka re-elected for third term.
**1991** Anti-government demonstrations.

## Malawi (Republic of)
(*Malaŵi*)

**area** 118,000 sq km/45,560 sq mi
**capital** Lilongwe
**towns** Blantyre-Limbe
**physical** rolling plains; mountainous W of Lake Malawi
**features** Livingstonia National Park on the Nyika Plateau in N; orchids, arthropods, elephants; Shiré Highlands grows tea and tobacco, rising to 1,750 m/5,750 ft
**head of state and government** Hastings Kamusu Banda from 1966 for life

**political system** one-party republic
**political parties** Malawi Congress Party (MCP), multi-racial, right-wing
**exports** tea, tobacco, cotton, peanuts, sugar
**currency** kwacha (K.4.75 = £1 July 1991)
**population** (1990 est) 9,080,000 (nearly 1 million refugees from Mozambique); growth rate 3.3% p.a.
**life expectancy** men 46, women 50 (1989)
**language** English, Chichewa (both official)
**religion** Christian 75%; Muslim 20%
**literacy** 25% (1989)
**GNP** $1.2 bn (1987); $160 per head (1988)

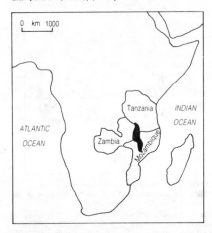

**chronology**
**1964** Independence achieved from Britain, within the Commonwealth, as Malawi.
**1966** Became a one-party republic, with Hastings Banda as president.
**1971** Banda was made president for life.
**1977** Banda started a programme of moderate liberalization, releasing some political detainees and allowing greater freedom of the press.
**1986–89** Influx of nearly 1 million refugees from Mozambique.

## Malaysia

**area** 329,759 sq km/127,287 sq mi
**capital** Kuala Lumpur
**towns** Johor Baharu, Ipoh, Geogetown (Penang), Kuching in Sarawak, Kota Kinabalu in Sabah
**physical** comprises Peninsular Malaysia (the nine Malay states—Perlis, Kedah, Johore, Selangor, Perak, Negri Sembilan, Kelantan, Trengganu, Pahang—plus Penang and Malacca); and E Malaysia (Sarawak and Sabah); 75% tropical jungle; central mountain range; swamps in E
**head of state** Rajah Azlan Muhibuddin Shah (sultan of Perak) from 1989
**head of government** Mahathir bin Mohamad from 1981
**political system** liberal democracy
**political parties** New United Malay's National Organization (UMNO Baru) Malay-orientated nationalist; Malaysian Chinese Association (MCA), Chinese-orientated conservative; Gerakan, Chinese-orientated left-of-centre; Malaysian Indian Congress (MIC), Indian-orientated; Democratic Action Party (DAP), left-of-centre multi-racial, but Chinese dominated; Pan-Malayan Islamic Party (PAS), Islamic; Semangat '46, moderate, multi-racial
**exports** pineapples, palm oil, rubber, timber, petroleum (Sarawak), bauxite

**currency** ringgit (4.52 = £1 July 1991)
**population** (1990 est) 17,053,000 (Malaysian 47%, Chinese 32%, Indian 8%, others 13%); growth rate 2% p.a.
**life expectancy** men 65, women 70 (1989)
**language** Bahasa Malaysia (official); English, Chinese, Indian languages
**religion** Muslim (official)
**literacy** 80% (1989)
**GNP** $34.3 bn; $1,870 per head (1988)

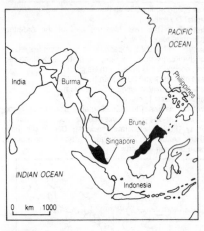

**chronology**
**1963** Federation of Malaysia formed, including Malaya, Singapore, Sabah (N Borneo), and Sarawak (NW Borneo).
**1965** Secession of Singapore from federation.
**1969** Anti-Chinese riots in Kuala Lumpur.
**1971** Launch of Bumiputra 'new economic policy'.
**1981** Election of Dr Mahathir bin Mohamad as prime minister.
**1982** Mahathir bin Mohamad re-elected.
**1986** Mahathir bin Mohamad re-elected.
**1987** Arrest of opposition leader DAP leader as Malay-Chinese relations deteriorate.
**1988** Split in ruling UMNO party over Mahathir's leadership style; new UMNO formed.
**1989** Semangat '46 set up by former members of UMNO inluding ex-premier Tunku Abdul Rahman.
**1990** Mahathir bin Mohamad re-elected.

## Maldives (Republic of)
(*Divehi Jumhuriya*)

**area** 298 sq km/115 sq mi
**capital** Malé
**towns** Seenu
**physical** comprises 1,200 coral islands, grouped into 12 clusters of atolls, largely flat, none bigger than 13 sq km/5 sq mi
**features** only about 200 of the islands are inhabited
**head of state and government** Maumoon Abdul Gayoom from 1978
**political system** authoritarian nationalism
**political parties** none; candidates elected on the basis of personal influence and clan loyalties
**exports** coconuts, copra, bonito (fish related to tuna)
**currency** Rufiya (16.20 = £1 July 1991)
**population** (1990 est) 219,000; growth rate 3.7% p.a.
**life expectancy** men 60, women 63 (1989)
**language** Divehi (Sinhalese dialect), English
**religion** Sunni Muslim
**literacy** 36% (1989)

**GNP** $69 million (1987); $410 per head (1988)

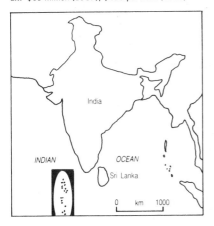

**chronology**
**1953** Long a sultanate, the Maldive Islands became a republic within the Commonwealth.
**1954** Sultanate restored.
**1965** Achieved full independence outside the Commonwealth.
**1968** Sultan deposed; republic reinstated with Ibrahim Nasir as president.
**1978** Nasir retired; replaced by Maumoon Abdul Gayoom.
**1983** Gayoom re-elected.
**1985** Rejoined the Commonwealth.
**1988** Gayoom re-elected. Coup attempt by mercenaries thought to have the backing of former president Nasir was foiled by Indian paratroops.

## Mali (Republic of)
(*République du Mali*)

**area** 1,240,142 sq km/478,695 sq mi
**capital** Bamako
**towns** Mopti, Kayes, Ségou, Timbuktu

**physical** river Niger and savanna in S; part of the Sahara in N; hills in NE
**features** ancient town of Timbuktu; railway to Dakar is the only outlet to the sea
**head of state and government** Amadou Toumani Toure from 1991
**political system** one-party republic
**political parties** Malian People's Democratic Union (UDPM)), nationalist
**exports** cotton, peanuts, livestock
**currency** franc CFA (498.25 = £1 July 1991)
**population** (1990 est) 9,182,000; growth rate 2.9% p.a.

**life expectancy** men 44, women 47 (1989)
**language** French (official), Bambara
**religion** Sunni Muslim 90%, animist
**literacy** 10% (1989)
**GNP** $1.6 bn (1987); $230 per head (1988)

**chronology**
**1898** Came under French rule.
**1959** With Senegal, formed the Federation of Mali.
**1960** Became the independent Republic of Mali, with Mobido Keita as president.
**1968** Keita replaced in an army coup by Moussa Traoré.
**1974** New constitution made Mali a one-party state.
**1976** New national party, the Malian People's Democratic Union, announced.
**1983** Agreement between Mali and Guinea for eventual political and economic integration signed.
**1985** War with Burkina Faso lasted 5 days, mediated by International Court of Justice.
**1991** Demonstrations against one-party rule. Moussa Traore ousted in a coup led by Lt Col Amadou Toumani Toure.

## Malta (Republic of)
(*Repubblika Ta'Malta*)

**area** 320 sq km/124 sq mi
**capital** and port Valletta
**towns** Rabat; port of Marsaxlokk
**physical** includes islands of Gozo 67 sq km/26 sq mi and Comino 2.5 sq km/1 sq mi
**features** occupies strategic location in central Mediterranean; large commercial dock facilities

**head of state** Vincent Tabone from 1989
**head of government** Edward Fenech Adami from 1987
**political system** liberal democracy
**political parties** Malta Labour Party (MLP), moderate, left-of-centre; Nationalist Party, Christian, centrist, pro-European
**exports** vegetables, knitwear, handmade lace, plastics, electronic equipment
**currency** Maltese lira (Lm 0.55 = £1 July 1991)
**population** (1990 est) 373,000; growth rate 0.7% p.a.
**life expectancy** men 72, women 77 (1987)
**language** Maltese, English
**religion** Roman Catholic 98%
**literacy** 90% (1988)
**GNP** $1.6 bn (1988); $4,750 per head

**chronology**
**1947** Achieved self-government from UK.
**1955** Dom Mintoff of the Malta Labour Party (MLP) became prime minister.
**1956** Referendum approved proposal for integration with

the UK. Proposal opposed by the Nationalist Party.
**1958** MLP rejected the integration proposal.
**1962** Nationalists elected, with Borg Olivier as prime minister.
**1964** Independence achieved from Britain, within the Commonwealth. Ten-year defence and economic-aid treaty with UK signed.
**1971** Mintoff re-elected. 1964 treaty declared invalid and negotiations began for leasing the NATO base in Malta.
**1972** Seven-year NATO agreement signed.
**1974** Became a republic.
**1979** British military base closed.
**1984** Mintoff retired and was replaced by Mifsud Bonnici as prime minister and MLP leader.
**1987** Edward Fenech Adami (Nationalist) elected prime minister.
**1989** Vincent Tabone elected president. US–USSR summit held offshore.
**1990** Formal application made for EC membership.

## Mauritania (Islamic Republic of)
(*République Islamique de Mauritanie*)

**area** 1,030,700 sq km/397,850 sq mi
**capital** Nouakchott
**towns** port of Nouadhibou
**physical** valley of river Senegal in S; remainder arid and flat

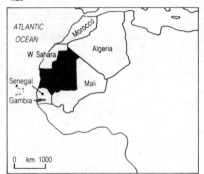

**features** part of the Sahara Desert
**head of state and government** Moaouia Ould Sidi Mohamed Taya from 1984
**political system** military republic
**political parties** none
**exports** iron ore, fish, gypsum
**currency** ouguiya (134.97 = £1 Mar 1990)
**population** (1990 est) 2,038,000 (30% Arab-Berber, 30% black Africans, 30% Haratine—descendants of black slaves, who remained slaves until 1980); growth rate 3% p.a.
**life expectancy** men 43, women 48 (1989)
**language** French (official), Hasaniya Arabic
**religion** Sunni Muslim 99%
**literacy** 17% (1987)
**GNP** $843 million (1988); $480 per head

**chronology**
**1960** Independence achieved from France, with Moktar Ould Daddah as president.
**1975** Western Sahara ceded by Spain. Mauritania occupied the southern part and Morocco the rest. Polisario Front formed in Sahara to resist the occupation by Mauritania and Morocco.
**1978** Daddah deposed in bloodless coup; replaced by Mohamed Khouni Ould Haidalla. Peace agreed with Polisario Front.
**1981** Diplomatic relations with Morocco broken.

**1984** Haidalla overthrown by Moaouia Ould Sidi Mohamed Taya. Polisario regime formally recognized.
**1985** Relations with Morocco restored.
**1989** Violent clashes between Mauritanians and Senegalese in Nouakchott and Dakar over disputed border grazing rights. Arab-dominated government expelled thousands of Africans into N Senegal; governments had earlier agreed to repatriate each other's citizens (about 250,000).
**1991** Amnesty for political prisoners. Multi-party elections promised. Calls for resignation of President Taya.

## Mauritius (State of)

**area** 1,865 sq km/720 sq mi; the island of Rodrigues is part of Mauritius; there are several small island dependencies
**capital** Port Louis
**towns** Beau Bassin-Rose Hill, Curepipe, Quatre Bornes
**physical** mountainous, volcanic island surrounded by coral reefs
**features** geologically part of Gondwanaland; unusual wildlife includes flying fox and ostrich; it was home of the dodo (extinct from *c.* 1680)
**head of state** Elizabeth II represented by governor-general
**head of government** Aneerood Jugnauth from 1982
**political system** constitutional monarchy
**political parties** Mauritius Socialist Movement (MSM), moderate socialist-republican; Mauritius labour Party (MLP), centrist Hindu-orientated; Mauritius Social Democratic Party (PMSD), conservative, Francophile; Mauritius Militant Movement (MMM), Marxist-republican
**exports** sugar, knitted goods, tea

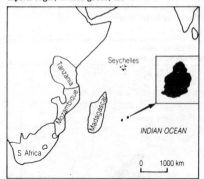

**currency** Mauritius rupee (27.05 = £1 July 1991)
**population** (1990 est) 1,141,900; growth rate 1.5% p.a.
**life expectancy** men 64, women 71 (1989)
**language** English (official); French, Creole
**religion** Hindu 51%, Christian 30%, Muslim 17%
**literacy** 94% (1989)
**GNP** $1.4 bn (1987); $1,810 per head (1988)

**chronology**
**1968** Independence achieved from Britain within the Commonwealth, with Seewoosagur Ramgoolam as prime minister.
**1982** Aneerood Jugnauth prime minister.
**1983** Jugnauth formed a new party, the Mauritius Socialist Movement, pledged to make Mauritius a republic within the Commonwealth, but Assembly refused. Ramgoolam appointed governor general. Jugnauth formed a new coalition government.
**1985** Ramgoolam died, succeeded by Ringadoo.
**1987** Jugnauth's coalition re-elected.

**1990** Attempt to create a republic failed.

## Mexico (United States of)
(*Estados Unidos Mexicanos*)

**area** 1,958,201 sq km/756,198 sq mi
**capital** Mexico City
**towns** Guadalajara, Monterrey; port Veracruz

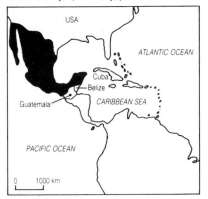

**physical** partly arid central highlands; Sierra Madre mountain ranges E and W; tropical coastal plains
**features** Rio Grande; 2,000 mi frontier with USA; resorts Acapulco, Mexicali, Tijuana; Baja California, Yucatan peninsulas; volcanoes, including Popocatepetl; pre-Columbian archaeological sites
**head of state and government** Carlos Salinas de Gortari from 1988
**political system** federal democratic republic
**political parties** Institutional Revolutionary Party (PRI), moderate, left-wing; National Action Party (PAN), moderate Christian socialist
**exports** silver, gold, lead, uranium, oil, natural gas, handicrafts, fish, shellfish, fruits and vegetables
**currency** peso (free rate 4,900.00 = £1 July 1991)
**population** (1990 est) 88,335,000 (10% Spanish descent, 30% Indian, 60% mixed descent; 50% under 20 years of age); growth rate 2.6% p.a.
**life expectancy** men 67, women 73
**language** Spanish (official) 92%; Náhuatl, Maya, Mixtec
**religion** Roman Catholic 97%
**literacy** men 92%/women 88% (1989)
**GNP** $126 bn (1987); $2,082 per head

**chronology**
**1821** Independence achieved from Spain.
**1846–48** Mexico at war with USA; loses territory.
**1848** Maya Indian revolt suppressed.
**1917** New constitution introduced, designed to establish permanent democracy.
**1983–84** Financial crisis.
**1985** Institutional Revolutionary Party (PRI) returned to power. Earthquake in Mexico City.
**1986** IMF loan agreement signed to keep the country solvent until at least 1988.
**1988** PRI candidate Carlos Salinas Gotari elected president. Debt reduction accords negotiated with USA.

## Monaco (Principality of)

**area** 1.95 sq km/0.75 sq mi
**capital** Monaco-Ville
**towns** Monte Carlo; heliport Fontvieille
**physical** steep and rugged; surrounded landward by French territory, being expanded by filling in the sea;

**features** aquarium and oceanographic centre; Monte Carlo film festival, motor races, and casinos
**head of state** Rainier III from 1949
**head of government** Jean Ausseil from 1986
**political system** constitutional monarchy under French protectorate
**political parties** National and Democratic Union; Democratic Union Movement; Monaco Action; Monagasque Socialist Party
**exports** some light industry; economy dependent on tourism and gambling
**currency** French franc (9.96 = £1 July 1991)
**population** (1989) 29,000; growth rate -0.5% p.a.
**language** French
**religion** Roman Catholic 95%
**literacy** 99% (1985)
**GNP**

**chronology**
**1861** Became an independent state under French protection.
**1918** France given a veto over succession to the throne.
**1949** Prince Rainier III ascended the throne.
**1956** Prince Rainier married US actress Grace Kelly; male heir born 1958.
**1959** Constitution of 1911 suspended.
**1962** New constitution adopted.

## Mongolia (Mongolian People's Republic)
(*Bügd Nayramdakh Momgol Ard Uls*)

**area** 1,565,000 sq km/604,480 sq mi
**capital** Ulaanbaatar

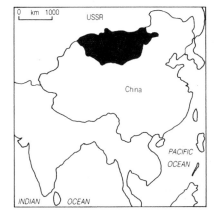

**towns** Darkhan, Choybalsan
**physical** high plateau with steppe (grasslands)
**features** Altai Mountains in southwest; salt lakes; part of Gobi Desert in southeast
**head of state** Punsalmaagiyn Ochirbat from 1990
**head of government** Dashiyn Byambasuren from 1990
**political system** communism
**political parties** Mongolian People's Revolutionary Party; Mongolian Democratic Union
**exports** meat and butter; minerals; furs
**currency** tugrik (5.45 = £1 July 1991)
**population** (1990 est) 2,185,000; growth rate 2.8% p.a.
**life expectancy** men 63, women 67 (1989)
**language** Khalkha Mongolian (official), Chinese, Russian
**religion** officially none (Tibetan Buddhist Lamaism suppressed 1930s)
**literacy** 89% (1985)
**GNP** $3.6 bn (1986); $1,820 per head

### chronology
**1911** Outer Mongolia gained autonomy from China.
**1915** Chinese sovereignty reasserted.
**1921** Chinese rule overthrown with Soviet help.
**1924** People's Republic proclaimed.
**1946** China recognized Mongolia's independence.
**1966** 20-year friendship, cooperation, and mutual-assistance pact signed with USSR. Relations deteriorated with China.
**1984** Yumjaagiyn Tsedenbal, effective leader, deposed and replaced by Jambyn Batmonh.
**1987** Soviet troops reduced; Mongolia's external contacts broadened.
**1989** Further Soviet troop reductions.
**1990** Democratization campaign launched by Mongolian Democratic Union. Ochirbat's Mongolian People's Revolutionary Party elected in free multiparty elections.
**1991** Country's name changed to Mongolia. Massive privatization programme launched.

### Morocco (The Kingdom of)
(*al-Mamlaka al-Maghrebia*)

**area** 458,730 sq km/177,070 sq mi

**capital** Rabat
**towns** Marrakesh, Fez, Mekinès; ports Casablanca, Tangier, Agadir
**physical** mountain ranges NE–SW; fertile coastal plains in W
**features** Atlas Mountains; the towns Ceuta (from 1580), Melilla (from 1492) are held by Spain; tunnel crossing the Strait of Gibraltar to Spain proposed 1985
**head of state** Hassan II from 1961
**head of government** Mohamed Karim Lamrani from 1984
**political system** constitutional monarchy

**political parties** Constitutional Union (UC), right-wing; National Rally of Independents (RNI), royalist; Popular Movement (MP), moderate socialist; Istiqual, nationalist, right-of-centre; Socialist Union of Popular Forces (USFP), progressive socialist; National Democratic Party (PND), moderate, nationalist
**exports** dates, figs, cork, wood pulp, canned fish, phosphates
**currency** dirham (DH) (14.76 = £1 July 1991)
**population** (1990 est) 26,249,000; growth rate 2.5% p.a.
**life expectancy** men 62, women 65 (1989)
**language** Arabic (official) 75%, Berber 25%, French, Spanish
**religion** Sunni Muslim 99%
**literacy** men 45%/women 22% (1985 est)
**GNP** $18.7 bn (1988); $750 per head

### chronology
**1912** Morocco established as a French and Spanish protectorate.
**1956** Independence achieved from France as the Sultanate of Morocco.
**1957** Sultan restyled king of Morocco.
**1961** Hassan II came to the throne.
**1969** Former Spanish province of Ifni returned to Morocco.
**1972** Major revision of the constitution.
**1975** Western Sahara ceded by Spain to Morocco and Mauritania.
**1976** Guerrilla war in the Sahara by the Polisario Front. Sahrawi Arab Democratic Republic (SADR) established in Algiers. Diplomatic relations between Morocco and Algeria broken.
**1979** Mauritania signed a peace treaty with Polisario.
**1983** Peace formula for the Sahara proposed by the Organization of African Unity (OAU) but not accepted by Morocco.
**1984** Hassan signed an agreement for cooperation and mutual defence with Libya.
**1987** Ceasefire agreed with Polisario, but fighting continued.
**1988** Diplomatic relations with Algeria restored.
**1989** Diplomatic relations with Syria restored.

### Mozambique (People's Republic of)
(*República Popular de Moçambique*)

**area** 799,380 sq km/308,561 sq mi
**capital** and chief port Maputo
**towns** Beira, Nampula
**physical** mostly flat tropical lowland; mountains in W

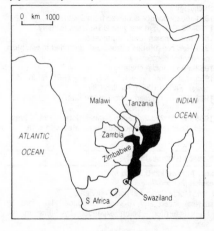

**features** rivers Zambezi, Limpopo
**head of state and government** Joaquim Alberto Chissano from 1986
**political system** one-party socialist republic
**political parties** National Front for the Liberation of Mozambique (Frelimo), Marxist-Leninist
**exports** prawns, cashews, sugar, cotton, petroleum products, copra
**currency** metical (replaced escudo 1980) (2,462.87 = £1 July 1991
**population** (1990 est) 14,718,000 (mainly indigenous Bantu peoples; Portuguese 50,000); growth rate 2.8% p.a.
**life expectancy** men 45, women 48 (1989)
**language** Portuguese (official), 16 African languages
**religion** animist 60%, Roman Catholic 18%, Muslim 16%
**literacy** men 55%/women 22% (1985 est)
**GDP** $4.7 bn (1987); $319 per head

**chronology**
**1951** Mozambique became an overseas province of Portugal (Portuguese East Africa).
**1962** Frelimo (liberation front) established.
**1975** Independence achieved from Portugal as a Socialist republic, with Samora Machel as president and Frelimo as the sole legal party.
**1983** Re-establishment of good relations with Western powers.
**1984** Nkomati Accord of nonagression signed with South Africa.
**1986** Machel killed in air crash; succeeded by Joaquim Chissano.
**1988** Tanzania announced withdrawal of its troops. South Africa provided training to Mozambiquan forces.
**1989** Frelimo offered to abandon Marxist-Leninism; Chissano re-elected. Renamo continued attacks on government facilities and civilians.
**1990** One-party rule ended. Partial ceasefire agreed.
**1991** Peace talks resumed in Rome. Attempted antigovernment coup thwarted.

## Myanmar (Union of)

(Union of *Thammada Myanmar Naingngandaw*, formerly *Burma*)

**area** 676,577 sq km/261,228 sq mi
**capital** and chief port Yangon (formerly Rangoon)
**towns** Mandalay, Karbe

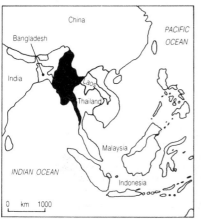

**physical** over half is rainforest; rivers Irrawaddy and Chindwin; mountains in N, W, and E
**features** ruined cities of Pagan and Mingun

**head of state and government** General Saw Maung from 1988
**political system** military republic
**political parties** National Unity Party, military-socialist ruling party; National League for Democracy (NLD), pluralist opposition grouping
**exports** rice, rubber, jute, teak, jade, rubies, sapphires
**currency** kyat (K 10.79 = £1 July 1991)
**population** (1990 est) 41,279,000; growth rate 1.9% p.a.
**life expectancy** men 53, women 56 (1989)
**language** Burmese
**religion** Hinayana Buddhist 85%; animist, Christian
**literacy** 66% (1989)
**GNP** $9.3 bn (1988); $210 per head (1989)

**chronology**
**1886** United as province of British India.
**1937** Became crown colony in the British Commonwealth.
**1942–45** Occupied by Japan.
**1948** Independence achieved from Britain. Left the Commonwealth.
**1962** General Ne Win assumed power in army coup.
**1973–74** Adopted presidential-style 'civilian' constitution.
**1975** Opposition National Democratic Front formed.
**1986** Several thousand supporters of opposition leader Suu Kyi arrested.
**1988** Government resigned after violent demonstrations. General Saw Maung seized power in military coup Sept; over 1,000 killed.
**1989** Martial law declared; thousands arrested including advocates of democracy and human rights.
**1990** Breakaway opposition group formed 'parallel government' on rebel-held territory.
**1991** Martial law and human-rights abuses continued.

## Namibia

**area** 824,300 sq km/318,262 sq mi
**capital** Windhoek
**towns** Swakopmund, Rehoboth, Rundu
**physical** mainly desert; includes the enclave of Walvis Bay (area 1,120 sq km/432 sq mi)

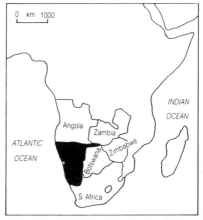

**features** Namib and Kalahari deserts; Orange River
**head of state and government** Sam Nujoma from 1990
**political system** democratic republic
**political parties** South West African People's Organization of Namibia (SWAPO), socialist Ovambo-orientated; Democratic Turnhalle Alliance (DTA), moderate, multiracial coalition; United Democratic Front (UDF), disaf-

fected ex-SWAPO members; National Christian Action (ACN), white conservative
**exports** diamonds, uranium
**currency** South African rand (R 4.68 = July 1991)
**population** (1990 est) 1,372,000 (85% black African, 6% European)
**life expectancy** black 40, whites 69
**language** Afrikaans, German, English (all official)
**religion** Lutheran 51%, Roman Catholic 19%, Dutch Reformed Church 6%, Anglican 6%
**literacy** whites 100%, non-whites 16%
**GNP** $1.6 bn (1988); $1,300 per head

**chronology**
**1920** Administered by South Africa, under League of Nations mandate, as British South Africa.
**1946** Full incorporation in South Africa refused by United Nations (UN).
**1958** South West African People's Organization (SWAPO) set up to seek racial equality and full independence.
**1966** South Africa's apartheid laws extended to the country.
**1968** Redesignated Namibia by UN.
**1978** UN Security Council Resolution 435 for the granting of full sovereignty accepted by South Africa and then rescinded.
**1988** Peace talks between South Africa, Angola, and Cuba led to agreement on full independence for Namibia.
**1989** Unexpected incursion by SWAPO guerrillas from Angola into Namibia threatened agreed timetable for independence from South Africa; transitional constitution created by elected representatives; SWAPO dominated party
**1990** Liberal multi-party 'independence' constitution adopted; Independence achieved from South Africa. Sam Nujoma elected president.

## Nauru (Republic of)
(*Naoero*)

**area** 21 sq km/8 sq mi
**capital** seat of government Yaren District
**physical** tropical island country in W Pacific

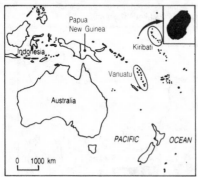

**features** plateau circled by coral cliffs and sandy beaches
**head of state and government** Hammer DeRoburt from 1987
**political system** liberal democracy
**political parties** Democratic Party of Nauru (DPN)
**exports** phosphates
**currency** Australian dollar ($A2.11 = £1 July 1991)
**population** (1990 est) 8,100 (mainly Polynesian; Chinese 8%, European 8%); growth rate 1.7% p.a.
**language** Nauruan (official), English
**religion** Protestant 45%
**literacy** 99% (1988)
**GNP** $160 million (1986); $9,091 per head (1985)

**chronology**
**1920** Administered by Australia, New Zealand, and UK until independence, except 1942–45, when it was occupied by Japan.
**1968** Independence achieved from Australia, New Zealand, and Britain with 'special member' Commonwealth status. Hammer DeRoburt elected president.
**1976** Bernard Dowiyogo elected president.
**1978** DeRoburt elected.
**1986** DeRoburt briefly replaced as president by Kenneth Adeang.
**1987** DeRoburt elected; Adeang established the Democratic Party of Nauru.
**1989** DeRoburt replaced by Kensas Aroi, who was later succeeded by Bernard Dowiyogo.

## Nepal

**area** 147,181 sq km/56,850 sq mi
**capital** Kátmándu
**towns** Pátan, Moráng, Bhádgáon
**physical** descends from the Himalayan mountain range in N through foothills to the river Ganges plain in S
**features** Mount Everest, Mount Kangchenjunga, the only Hindu kingdom in the world; Lumbini, birthplace of Buddha
**head of state** King Birendra Bir Bikram Sháh Dev from 1972
**head of government** Girija Prasad Koirala from 1991
**political system** constitutional monarchy
**political parties** banned from 1961; four opposition parties function unofficially: the United Nepal Communist Party (UNCP), Marxist-Leninist-Maoist; the Nepali Congress Party (NCP), left-of-centre; the United Liberation Torchbearers; the Democratic Front, radical republican
**exports** jute, rice, timber
**currency** Nepalese rupee (54.29 = £1 July 1991)
**population** (1990 est) 19,158,000 (mainly known by name of predominant clan, the Gurkhas; the Sherpas are a Buddhist minority of NE Nepal); growth rate 2.3% p.a.
**life expectancy** men 50, women 49 (1989)
**language** Nepali (official); 20 dialects spoken

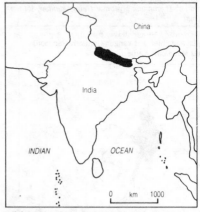

**religion** Hindu 90%; Buddhist, Muslim, Christian
**literacy** men 39%/women 12% (1985 est)
**GNP** $3.1 bn (1988); $160 per head (1986)

**chronology**
**1923** Independence achieved from Britain.
**1951** Monarchy restored.
**1959** Constitution created elected legislature.
**1960–61** Parliament dissolved by king; political parties

banned.
**1980** Constitutional referendum held following popular agitation.
**1981** Direct elections held to national assembly.
**1983** Overthrow of monarch-supported prime minister.
**1986** New assembly elections returned a majority opposed to *panchayat* system of partyless government.
**1988** Strict curbs placed on opposition activity; over 100 supporters of banned opposition party arrested; censorship imposed.
**1989** Border blockade imposed by India in treaty dispute.
**1990** *Panchayat* system collapsed; new constitution introduced; elections set for May 1991.
**1991** Nepali Congress Party, led by Girija Prasad Koirala, won the general election.

---

## Netherlands (Kingdom of the)
(*Koninkrijk der Nederlanden*),
popularly referred to as **Holland**

---

**area** 41,863 sq km/16,169 sq mi
**capital** Amsterdam
**towns** The Hague (seat of government), Utrecht; chief port Rotterdam
**physical** flat; rivers Rhine, Schelde (*Scheldt*), Maas; Frisian Islands
**territories** Aruba, Netherlands Antilles (Caribbean)
**features** land reclamation has turned former Zuider Zee inlet into the freshwater IJsselmeer
**head of state** Queen Beatrix Wilhelmina Armgard from 1980
**head of government** Ruud Lubbers
**political system** constitutional monarchy
**political parties** Christian Democratic Appeal (CDA), Christian, right-of-centre; Labour party (PvdA), moderate, left-of-centre; People's Party for Freedom and Democracy (VVD), free enterprise, centrist
**exports** dairy products, flower bulbs, vegetables, petrochemicals, electronics
**currency** guilder (3.31 = £1 July 1991)
**population** (1990 est) 14,864,000 (including 300,000 of Dutch-Indonesian origin absorbed 1949–64 from former colonial possessions); growth rate 0.4% p.a.
**life expectancy** men 74, women 81 (1989)
**language** Dutch

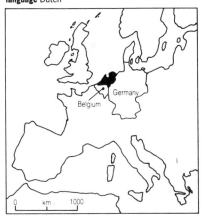

**religion** Roman Catholic 35%, Protestant 28%
**literacy** 99% (1989)
**GNP** $223 bn (1988); $13,065 per head (1987)

**chronology**
**1940–45** Occupied by Germany during World War II.
**1947** Joined Benelux Union.

**1948** Queen Juliana succeeded Queen Wilhelmina to the throne.
**1949** Founding member of NATO.
**1953** Dykes breached by storm; nearly 2,000 people and tens of thousands of cattle died in flood.
**1958** Joined European Community.
**1980** Queen Juliana abdicated in favour of her daughter Beatrix.
**1981** Opposition to cruise missiles averted their being sited on Dutch soil.
**1989** Prime minister Lubbers resigned; new Lubbers-led coalition elected.
**1991** Netherlands Communist Party wound up.

---

## New Zealand

---

**area** 268,680 sq km/103,777 sq mi
**capital** Wellington
**towns** Hamilton, Palmerston North, Christchurch, Dunedin; ports Wellington, Auckland
**physical** comprises North Island, South Island, Stewart Island, Chatham Islands, and minor islands; mainly mountainous
**overseas territories** Tokelau (three atolls transferred 1926 from former Gilbert and Ellice Islands colony); Niue Island (one of the Cook Islands, separately administered from 1903: chief town Alafi); Cook Islands are internally self-governing but share common citizenship with New Zealand; Ross Dependency in Antarctica
**features** Ruapehu on North Island, 2,797 m/9,180 ft, highest of three active volcanoes; geysers and hot springs of the Rotorua district; Lake Taupo (616 sq km/238 sq mi), source of Waikato River; Kaingaroa state forest. On South Island are the Southern Alps and Canterbury Plains.

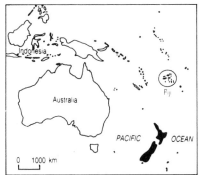

**head of state** Elizabeth II from 1952 represented by Governor General Catherine lizard from 1990
**head of government** Prime Minister Jim Bolger from 1990
**political system** constitutional monarchy
**political parties** Labour Party, moderate, left-of-centre; New Zealand National Party, free enterprise, centre-right
**exports** lamb, beef, wool, leather, dairy products, processed foods, kiwi fruit; seeds and breeding stock; timber, paper, pulp, light aircraft
**currency** New Zealand dollar ($NZ2.90 = £1 July 1991)
**population** (1990 est) 3,397,000 (European (mostly British) 87%; Polynesian (mostly Maori) 9%) ; growth rate 0.9% p.a.
**life expectancy** men 72, women 78 (1989)
**language** English (official); Maori
**religion** Protestant 50%, Roman Catholic 15%
**literacy** 99% (1989)
**GNP** $37 bn; $11,040 per head (1988)

**chronology**

**1931** Granted independence from Britain.
**1947** Independence within the Commonwealth confirmed by the New Zealand parliament.
**1972** National Party government replaced Labour Party, with Norman Kirk as prime minister.
**1974** Kirk died; replaced by Wallace Rowling.
**1975** National Party returned, with Robert Muldoon as prime minister.
**1984** Labour Party returned under David Lange.
**1985** Non-nuclear military policy created disagreements with France and the USA.
**1987** National Party declared support for the Labour government's non-nuclear policy. Lange re-elected. New Zealand officially became a 'friendly' rather than 'allied' country to the USA because of its non-nuclear military policy.
**1988** Free-trade agreement with Australia signed.
**1989** Lange resigned over economic differences with finance minister; replaced by Geoffrey Palmer.
**1990** Palmer replaced by Mike Moore. Labour Party defeated by National Party in general election.

## Nicaragua (Republic of)
(*República de Nicaragua*)

**area** 127,849 sq km/49,363 sq mi
**capital** Managua
**towns** León, Granada; chief port Corinto
**physical** narrow Pacific coastal plain separated from broad Atlantic coastal plain by volcanic mountains and lakes Managua and Nicaragua
**features** largest state of Central America and most thinly populated

**head of state and government** Violeta Barrios de Chamorro from April 1990
**political system** emergent democracy
**political parties** Sandinista National Liberation Front (FSLN), Marxist-Leninist; Democratic Conservative Party (PCD), centrist; National Opposition Union (UNO), loose, US-backed coalition;
**exports** coffee, cotton, sugar, bananas
**currency** cordoba (C$8.12 = £1 July 1991)
**population** (1990) 3,606,000 (70% mestizo, 15% Spanish descent, 10% Indian or black); growth rate 3.3% p.a.
**life expectancy** men 61, women 63 (1989)
**language** Spanish (official), Indian, English
**religion** Roman Catholic 88%
**literacy** 66% (1986)
**GNP** $2.1 bn; $610 per head (1988)

**chronology**
**1838** Independence achieved from Spain.
**1926–1933** Occupied by US marines.
**1962** Sandinista National Liberation Front (FSLN) formed to fight Somoza regime.
**1979** Somoza government ousted by FSLN.
**1982** Subversive activity against the government promoted by the USA. State of emergency declared.
**1984** The USA mined Nicaraguan harbours.
**1985** Denunciation of Sandinista government by US president Reagan. FSLN won assembly elections.
**1987** Central American peace agreement co-signed by Nicaraguan leaders.
**1988** Peace agreement failed. Nicaragua held talks with Contra rebel leaders. Hurricane left 180,000 people homeless.
**1989** Demobilization of rebels and release of former Somozan supporters; cease-fire ended.
**1990** FSLN defeated by UNO, a US-backed coalition; Violeta Chamorro elected president. Anti-government riots.

### PEOPLE OF THE YEAR

In February 1990 Violeta de Chammoro, the candidate for the National Opposition Union (UNO), emerged from relative obscurity to defeat the Sandinista National Liberation Front's Daniel Ortega, and wrest the presidency from him. Her political life did not begin until after the assassination of her husband Pedro Joaquín Chamorro in 1978. His murder sparked off the Sandinista revolution, and saw the end of the infamous regime of Gen Anastasio Somoza. The smooth transfer of power from Ortega to Chammoro was an indication of the maturity of Nicaraguan politics. Chamorro's strong US backing will help her bid for US aid in strengthening Nicaragua's weakened economy.

## Niger (Republic of)
(*République du Niger*)

**area** 1,186,408 sq km/457,953 sq mi
**capital** Niamey
**towns** Zinder, Maradi
**physical** desert plains between hills in N and savanna in S; River Niger in SW, Lake Chad in SE

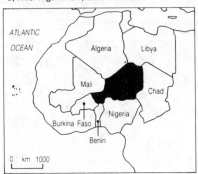

**features** part of the Sahara Desert and subject to Sahel droughts
**head of state and government** Ali Seybou from 1987
**political system** military republic
**political parties** banned from 1974
**exports** peanuts, livestock, gum arabic, tin, uranium
**currency** franc CFA (498.25 = £1 July 1991)
**population** (1990 est) 7,691,000; growth rate 2.8% p.a.
**life expectancy** men 48, women 50 (1989)
**language** French (official), Hausa, Djerma
**religion** Sunni Muslim 85%, animist 15%
**literacy** men 19%/women 9% (1985 est)
**GNP** $2.2 bn; $310 per head (1987)

**chronology**
**1960** Achieved full independence from France; Hamani Diori elected president.
**1974** Diori ousted in army coup led by Seyni Kountché.
**1977** Cooperation agreement signed with France.
**1987** Kountché died and was replaced by Col Ali Seybou.
**1990** Multi-party politics promised.

## Nigeria (Federal Republic of)

**area** 923,773 sq km/356,576 sq mi
**capital** and chief port Lagos; Abuja (capital-designate)
**towns** administrative headquarters Abuja; Ibadan, Ogbomosho, Kano; ports Port Harcourt, Warri, Calabar
**physical** arid in N; savanna; tropical rainforest in S, with mangrove swamps along the coast; river Niger forms wide delta
**features** harmattan (dry wind from the Sahara); rich artistic heritage; for example, Benin bronzes
**head of state and government** Ibrahim Babangida from 1985
**political system** military republic pending promised elections
**political parties** Social Democratic Party (SDP), left-of-centre; National Republican Convention (NRC), right-of-centre

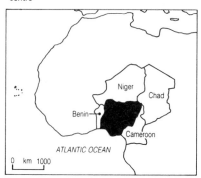

**exports** petroleum (largest oil resources in Africa), cocoa, peanuts, palm oil, cotton, rubber, tin
**currency** naira (16.98 = £1 July 1991)
**population** (1990 est) 118,865,000 (Yoruba in W, Ibo in E, and Hausa-Fulani in N); growth rate 3.3% p.a.
**life expectancy** men 47, women 49 (1989)
**language** English (official), Hausa, Ibo, Yoruba
**religion** Sunni Muslim (50%) in N, Christian (40%) in S
**literacy** men 54%/women 31% (1985 est)
**GNP** $78 bn (1987); $790 per head (1984)

**chronology**
**1914** N Nigeria and S Nigeria united to become Britain's largest African colony.
**1954** Nigeria became a federation.
**1960** Independence achieved from Britain within the Commonwealth.
**1963** Became a republic, with Nnamdi Azikiwe as president.
**1966** Military coup, followed by a counter-coup led by Gen Yakubu Gowon. Slaughter of many members of the Ibo tribe in N.
**1967** Conflict over oil revenues led to declaration of an independent state of Biafra and outbreak of civil war.
**1970** Surrender of Biafra and end of civil war.
**1975** Gowon ousted in military coup; second coup puts Gen Obasanjo in power.
**1979** Shehu Shagari became civilian president.
**1983** Shagari's government overthrown in coup by Maj-

Gen Buhari.
**1985** Buhari replaced in a bloodless coup led by Maj-Gen Ibrahim Babangida.
**1989** Two new parties approved. Babangida promised a return to pluralist politics; date set for 1992.

## Norway (Kingdom of)
(*Kongeriket Norge*)

**area** 387,000 sq km/149,421 sq mi (includes Svalbard and Jan Mayen)
**capital** Oslo
**towns** Bergen, Trondheim
**physical** mountainous; forests cover 25%; extends N of Arctic Circle
**territories** dependencies in the Arctic (Svalbard and Jan Mayen) and in Antarctica (Bouvet and Peter I Island, and Queen Maud Land)
**features** fjords, including Hardanger and Sogne, longest 185 km/115 mi, deepest 1,245 m/4,086 ft; glaciers in north; midnight sun and northern lights
**head of state** Harald V from 1991
**head of government** Prime Minister Gro Harlem Brundtland from 1990
**political system** constitutional monarchy
**political parties** Norwegian Labour Party (DNA), moderate, left-of-centre; Conservative Party, progressive, right-of-centre; Christian People's Party (KrF), Christian, centre-left; Centre Party (SP), left-of-centre, rural-oriented

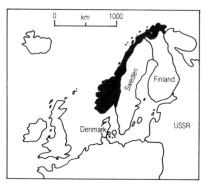

**exports** petrochemicals from North Sea oil and gas, paper, wood pulp, furniture, iron ore and other minerals, high-tech goods, sports goods, fish
**currency** krone (11.43 = £1 July 1991)
**population** (1990 est) 4,214,000; growth rate 0.3% p.a.
**life expectancy** men 73, women 80 (1989)
**language** Norwegian (official); Lapp
**religion** Evangelical Lutheran (endowed by state) 94%
**literacy** 100% (1989)
**GNP** $89 bn (1988); $13,790 per head (1984)

**chronology**
**1814** Became independent from Denmark.
**1905** Links with Sweden ended.
**1940–45** Occupied by Germany.
**1949** Joined NATO.
**1952** Joined Nordic Council.
**1957** King Haakon VII succeeded by his son Olaf V.
**1960** Joined EFTA.
**1972** Accepted into membership of European Community; application withdrawn after a referendum.
**1988** Gro Harlem Brundtland awarded Third World Prize.
**1989** Jan P Syse became prime minister.
**1990** Brundtland returned to power.
**1991** King Olaf V succeeded by his son Harald V.

## Oman (Sultanate of)
(*Saltanat 'Uman*)

**area** 272,000 sq km/105,000 sq mi
**capital** Muscat
**towns** Salalah
**physical** mountains and a high arid plateau; fertile coastal strip
**features** Jebel Akhdar highlands; Kuria Muria islands; Masirah Island is used in aerial reconnaissance of the Arabian Sea and Indian Ocean
**head of state and government** Qaboos bin Said from 1970
**political system** absolute monarchy
**exports** oil, dates, silverware
**currency** rial Omani (0.62 = £1 July 1991)
**population** (1990 est) 1,305,000; growth rate 3.0% p.a.
**life expectancy** men 55, women 58 (1989)
**language** Arabic (official); English, Urdu
**religion** Ibadhi Muslim 75%; Sunni Muslim
**literacy** 20% (1989)
**GNP** $7.5 bn (1987); $5,070 per head (1988)

**chronology**
**1951** The Sultanate of Muscat and Oman achieved full independence from Britain. Treaty of Friendship with Britain signed.
**1970** After 38 years' rule, Sultan Said bin Taimur replaced in coup by his son Qaboos bin Said. Name changed to Sultanate of Oman.
**1975** Left-wing rebels in S defeated.
**1982** Memorandum of Understanding with UK signed, providing for regular consultation on international issues.
**1985** Diplomatic ties established with USSR.

## Pakistan (Islamic Republic of)

**area** 796,100 sq km/307,295 sq mi; ⅓ of Kashmir under Pakistani control
**capital** Islamabad
**towns** Karachi, Lahore
**physical** fertile Indus plain in E; Baluchistan plateau in W, mountains in N and NW
**features** the 'five rivers' (Indus, Jhelum, Chenab, Ravi, and Sutlej) feed a large irrigation system; K2 mountain; Khyber Pass; sites of the Indus Valley civilization
**head of state** Ghulam Ishaq Khan from 1988
**head of government** Nawaz Sharif from 1990
**political system** emergent democracy
**political parties** Pakistan People's Party (PPP), moderate, Islamic, socialist; Islamic Democratic Alliance (IJI), including the Pakistan Muslim League (PML), Islamic conservative; Mohajir National Movement (MQM), Sind-based *mohajir* settlers

**exports** cotton textiles, rice, leather, carpets

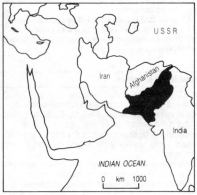

**currency** Pakistan rupee (39.00 = £1 July 1991)
**population** (1990 est) 113,163,000 (66% Punjabi, 13% Sindhi); growth rate 3.1% p.a.
**life expectancy** men 54, women 55 (1989)
**language** Urdu and English (official); Punjabi, Sindhi, Pashto, Baluchi
**religion** Sunni Muslim 75%, Shi'ite Muslim 20%, Hindu 4%
**literacy** men 40%/women 19% (1985 est)
**GDP** $39 bn (1988); $360 per head (1984)

**chronology**
**1947** Independence achieved from Britain, Pakistan formed following partition of India.
**1956** Proclaimed a republic.
**1958** Military rule imposed by General Ayub Khan.
**1969** Power transferred to General Yahya Khan.
**1971** Secession of East Pakistan (Bangladesh). After civil war, power transferred to Zulfiqar Ali Bhutto.
**1977** Bhutto overthrown in military coup by General Zia ul-haq; martial law imposed.
**1979** Bhutto executed.
**1981** Opposition Movement for Restoration of Democracy formed. Islamization process pushed forward.
**1985** Non-party elections held, amended constitution adopted, martial law and ban on political parties lifted.
**1986** Agitation for free elections launched by Benazir Bhutto.
**1988** Zia introduced Islamic legal code, the *Shariah*. He was killed in a military plane crash in Aug; Benazir Bhutto elected prime minister in Nov.
**1989** Pakistan rejoined the Commonwealth.
**1990** Army mobilized in support of Muslim separatists in Indian Kashmir. Bhutto dismissed.

## Panama (Republic of)
(*República de Panamá*)

**area** 77,100 sq km/29,768 sq mi
**capital** Panama City
**towns** Cristóbal, Balboa, Colón
**physical** mountain ranges; tropical rainforest; Pearl Islands in Gulf of Panama
**features** Panama Canal; Barro Colorado Island in Gatun Lake (reservoir suppling the canal), a tropical forest reserve since 1923; Smithsonian Tropical Research Institute
**head of state and government** Guillermo Endara from 1989
**political system** emergent democratic republic
**political parties** Democratic Revolutionary Party (PRD), right-wing; Labour Party (PALA), right-of-centre; Republican Party (PR), right-wing; National Liberal Repub-

lican Movement (MOLIRENA), left-of-centre; Authentic Panama Party (PPA), centrist; Christian Democratic Party (PDC), centre-left

**exports** bananas, petroleum products, copper, shrimps, sugar
**currency** balboa (1.61 = £1 July 1991)
**population** (1990 est) 2,423,000; growth rate 2.2% p.a.
**life expectancy** men 71, women 75 (1989)
**language** Spanish (official), English
**religion** Roman Catholic 93%, Protestant 6%
**literacy** 87% (1989)
**GNP** $4.2 bn (1988); $1,970 per head (1984)

**chronology**
**1821** Achieved independence from Spain; joined Columbia
**1903** Full independence achieved on separation from Colombia.
**1974** Agreement to negotiate full transfer of the Panama Canal from the USA to Panama.
**1977** USA-Panama treaties transferred the canal to Panama, effective 1999, with the USA guaranteeing its protection and an annual payment.
**1984** Nicolas Ardito Barletta elected president.
**1985** Barletta resigned; replaced by Eric Arturo del Valle.
**1987** Gen Noriega resisted calls for his removal, despite suspension of US military and economic aid.
**1988** Del Valle replaced by Manuel Solis Palma. Noriega, charged with drug smuggling by the US, declared a state of emergency.
**1989** Opposition won election; Noriega declared results invalid; coup attempt failed; Noriega declared 'maximum leader' by assembly; 'state of war' with the USA announced; US invasion deposed Noriega; installed Guillermo Endara; Noriega surrendered to US forces. Several hundred people were killed during the invasion.

## Papua New Guinea

**area** 462,840 sq km/178,656 sq mi
**capital** Port Moresby (on E New Guinea)
**towns** Lae, Rabaul, Madang
**physical** mountainous; includes islands of New Ireland, New Britain, and Bougainville; Admiralty Islands, D'Entrecasteaux Islands, and Louisiade Archipelago
**features** tropical; annual rainfall 100 cm/39 in; rare birds of paradise, the world's largest butterfly, orchids
**head of state** Elizabeth II, represented by governor general
**head of government** Rabbie Namaliu from 1988
**political system** constitutional monarchy
**political parties** Papua New Guinea Party (Pangu Pati: PP), urban-and-coastal-oriented nationalist; People's Democratic Movement (PDM), 1985 breakaway from the

PP; National Party (NP), highlands-based; Melanesian Alliance (MA), Bougainville-based autonomy; People's Progress Party (PPP), conservative

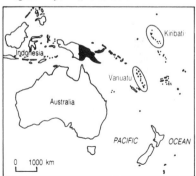

**exports** copra, coconut oil, palm oil, tea, copper
**currency** kina (K1.56 = £1 July 1991)
**population** (1989 est) 3,613,000 (Papuans, Melanesians, Pygmies, various minorities); growth rate 2.6% p.a.
**life expectancy** men 53, women 54 (1987)
**language** English (official); pidgin English, 715 local languages
**religion** Protestant 63%, Roman Catholic 31%, local faiths
**literacy** men 55%/women 36% (1985 est)
**GNP** $2.5 bn; $730 per head (1987)

**chronology**
**1883** Annexed by Queensland; became the Australian Territory of Papua.
**1884** NE New Guinea annexed by Germany; southeast claimed by Britain.
**1914** NE New Guinea occupied by Australia.
**1921–42** Held as a League of Nations mandate.
**1942–45** Occupied by Japan.
**1975** Independence achieved from Australia, within the Commonwealth, with Michael Somare as prime minister.
**1980** Julius Chan became prime minister.
**1982** Somare returned to power.
**1985** Somare challenged by deputy prime minister, Paias Wingti, who later formed a five-party coalition government.
**1988** Wingti defeated on no-confidence vote and replaced by Rabbie Namaliu, who established a six-party coalition government.
**1989** State of emergency imposed in Bougainville in response to separatist violence.
**1991** Peace accord signed with Bougainville secessionists.

## Paraguay (Republic of)
(*República del Paraguay*)

**area** 406,752 sq km/157,006 sq mi
**capital** Asunción
**towns** Presidente Stroessner, Pedro Juan Caballero; port Concepción
**physical** flat; divided by Paraguay River; Paraná River in S
**features** Itaipú dam on border with Brazil; Gran Chaco plain with huge swamps
**head of state and government** Andrés Rodriguez from 1989
**political system** military republic
**political parties** National Republican Association (Colorado Party), right-of-centre; Liberal Party (PL), right-of-centre; Radical Liberal Party (PLR), centrist
**exports** cotton, soya beans, timber, vegetable oil, maté

**currency** guaraní (2,145.28 = £1 July 1991)
**population** (1990 est) 4,660,000 (95% mixed Guaraní Indian–Spanish descent); growth rate 3.0% p.a.
**life expectancy** men 67, women 72 (1989)
**language** Spanish 6% (official); Guaraní 90%
**religion** Roman Catholic 97%
**literacy** men 91%/women 85% (1985 est)
**GNP** $7.4 bn; $1,000 per head (1987)

**chronology**
**1811** Independence achieved from Spain.
**1865–70** War with Argentina, Brazil, and Uruguay; much territory lost.
**1932–35** Territory won from Bolivia during the Chaco War.
**1940–48** Gen Higino Morinigo elected president.
**1948–54** Political instability; six different presidents.
**1954** Gen Alfredo Stroessner seized power.
**1989** Stroessner ousted in coup led by Gen Andrés Rodriguez. Rodriguez elected president; Colorado Party won the congressional elections.

---

**Peru (Republic of)**
(*República del Perú*)

**area** 1,285,200 sq km/496,216 sq mi

**capital** Lima, including port of Callao
**towns** Arequipa, Iquitos, Chiclayo
**physical** Andes mountains N–S cover 27%; Amazon river-basin jungle in NE; coastal plain in W; desert along coast N–S
**features** Lake Titicaca; Atacama Desert; Nazca lines; monuments of Machu Picchu, Chanchan, Charín de Huantar
**head of state and government** Alberto Fujimoro from 1990
**political system** democratic republic
**political parties** American Popular Revolutionary Alliance (APRA), moderate, left-wing; United Left (IU), left-wing
**exports** coca, coffee, alpaca, llama and vicuna wool, fish meal, lead, copper, iron, oil
**currency** new sol (1.38 = £1 July 1991)
**population** (1990 est) 21,904,000 (46% Indian, mainly Quechua and Aymara; 43% mixed Spanish–Indian descent); growth rate 2.6% p.a.
**life expectancy** men 61, women 66
**language** Spanish 68%, Quechua 27% (both official), Aymará 3%
**religion** Roman Catholic 90%
**literacy** men 91%/women 78% (1985 est)
**GNP** $19.6 bn (1988); $940 per head (1984)

**chronology**
**1824** Independence achieved from Spain.
**1902** Boundary dispute with Bolivia settled.
**1927** Boundary dispute with Colombia settled.
**1942** Boundary dispute with Ecuador settled.
**1948** Army coup, led by Gen Manuel Odria, installed a military government.
**1963** Return to civilian rule, with Fernando Belaúnde Terry as president.
**1968** Return of military government in a bloodless coup by Gen Juan Velasco Alvarado.
**1975** Velasco replaced, in a bloodless coup, by Gen Morales Bermudez.
**1980** Return to civilian rule, with Fernando Belaúnde as president.
**1981** Boundary dispute with Ecuador renewed.
**1985** Belaúnde succeeded by Social Democrat Alan García Perez.
**1987** President García delayed the nationalization of Peru's banks after a vigorous campaign against the proposal.
**1988** García pressured to seek help from the International Monetary Fund.
**1989** Mario Vargas Llosa entered presidential race; his Democratic Front won municipal elections Nov.
**1990** Alberto Fujimoro defeated Vargas Llosa in presidential elections. Assassination attempt on president failed.

---

### PEOPLE OF THE YEAR

In his nine years as secretary-general of the United Nations, Javier Pérez de Cuéllar has significantly raised the reputation of the organization. His one weakness perhaps, has been in his reluctance to appoint a deputy. Nevertheless, his successes, particularly in his second term, were important: ending the Iran-Iraq war; negotiating a ceasefire in Angola; and overseeing the independence of Namibia. However his efforts to find a peaceful solution to the Gulf Crisis failed and, although the authority of the United Nations was enhanced, Pérez de Cuéllar found himself, eventually, a spectator, rather than a leader of events in the Gulf War that followed.

---

**Philippines (Republic of the)**
(*Republica de Filipinas*)

**area** 300,000 sq km/115,800 sq mi

**capital** Manila (on Luzon)
**towns** Quezon City
**ports** Cebu, Davao (on Mindanao) and Iloilu
**physical** comprises over 7,000 islands; volcanic mountain ranges traverse main chain N–S; 50% still forested. The largest islands are Luzon 108,172 sq km/41,754 sq mi and Mindanao 94,227 sq km/36,372 sq mi; others include Samar, Negros, Palawan, Panay, Mindoro, Leyte, Cebu, and the Sulu group

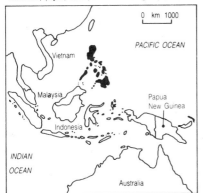

**features** Luzon, site of Clark Field, US air base used as a logistical base in Vietnam War; Subic Bay, US naval base; Mindanao has active volcano Apo (2,855 m/9,370 ft) and mountainous rainforest
**head of state and government** Corazón Aquino from 1986
**political system** emergent democracy
**political parties** People's Power, includings the PDP-Laban Party and the Liberal Party, centrist pro-Aquino; Nationalist Party, Union for National Action (UNA), and Grand Alliance for Democracy (GAD), conservative opposition groupings; Mindanao Alliance, Island-based decentralist body
**exports** sugar, copra and coconut oil, timber, iron ore, copper concentrates
**currency** peso (43.00 = £1 July 1991)
**population** (1990 est) 66,647,000 (93% Malaysian); growth rate 2.4% p.a.
**life expectancy** men 63, women 69 (1989)
**language** Filipino; English and Spanish
**religion** Roman Catholic 84%, Protestant 9%, Muslim 5%
**literacy** 88% (1989)
**GNP** $38.2 bn; $667 per head (1988)

**chronology**
**1898** Ceded to the USA by Spain after Spanish-American War.
**1935** Granted internal self-government.
**1942–45** Occupied by Japan.
**1946** Independence achieved from USA.
**1965** Ferdinand Marcos elected president.
**1983** Opposition leader Benigno Aquino murdered by military guard.
**1986** Marcos overthrown by Corazón Aquino's People's Power movement.
**1987** 'Freedom constitution' adopted; People's Power won majority in congressional elections. Attempted right-wing coup suppressed. Communist guerrillas active. Government in rightward swing.
**1988** Land Reform Act gave favourable compensation to large estateholders.
**1989** Referendum on southern autonomy failed; Marcos died in exile; Aquino refused compensation in Philippines. Sixth coup attempt suppressed with US aid; Aquino declared state of emergency.
**1990** Seventh coup attempt survived by President

Aquino.

---

**Poland (Republic of Poland)**
(*Polska Rzeczpospolita*)

**area** 312,700 sq km/120,733 sq mi

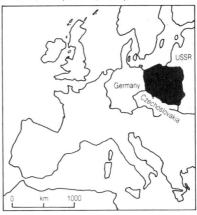

**capital** Warsaw
**towns** Lódź, Kraków, Wroclaw, Poznań, Katowice, Bydgoszcz, Lublin; ports Gdánsk, Szczecin, Gdynia
**physical** part of the great plain of Europe; Vistula, Oder, and Neisse rivers; Sudeten, Tatra, and Carpathian mountains
**head of state** Lech Walesa from 1990
**head of government** Jan Krzysztof Bielecki from 1991
**political system** socialist pluralist republic
**political parties** Social Democratic Party of the Polish Republic, 1990 successor to Polish United Worker's Party (PUWP), social democratic; Union of Social Democrats, radical breakaway from PUWP formed 1990; Solidarność (Solidarity) Parliamentary Club (OKP), anti-communist coalition
**exports** coal, softwood timber, chemicals, machinery, ships
**currency** zloty (18,684.00 = £1 July 1991)
**population** (1990 est) 38,363,000; growth rate 0.6% p.a.
**life expectancy** men 66, women 74 (1989)
**language** Polish
**religion** Roman Catholic 95%
**literacy** 98% (1989)
**GNP** $276 bn (1988); $2,000 per head (1986)

**chronology**
**1918** Poland revived as independent republic.
**1939** German invasion and occupation.
**1944** Germans driven out by Soviet forces.
**1945** Polish boundaries redrawn at Potsdam Conference.
**1947** Communist people's republic proclaimed.
**1956** Poznań riots. Gomulka installed as Polish United Workers' Party (PUWP) leader.
**1970** Gomulka replaced by Gierek after Gdańsk riots.
**1980** Solidarity emerged as a free trade union following Gdańsk disturbances.
**1981** Martial law imposed by Gen Jaruzelski.
**1983** Martial law ended.
**1984** Amnesty for political prisoners.
**1985** Zbigniew Messner became prime minister.
**1987** Referendum on economic reform rejected.
**1988** Solidarity strikes and demonstrations called off after pay increases. Messner resigned; replaced by the reformist Mieczyslaw Rakowski.
**1989** Solidarity relegalized; new 'socialist pluralist' constitution reached in church-state-union negotiations

(April). Solidarity swept board in national assembly elections (June). Jaruzelski elected president (July). 'Grand coalition' formed headed by Solidarity's Mazowiecki (Sept).
**1990** PUWP dissolved; replaced by Social Democratic Party and breakaway Union of Social Democrats (Jan). Lech Walesa elected head of state; Prime Minister Mazowiecki resigned (Dec).
**1991** Multiparty general election scheduled for Oct.

## Portugal (Republic of)
(*República Portuguesa*)

**area** 92,000 sq km/35,521 sq mi (including Azores and Madeira)
**capital** Lisbon
**towns** Coimbra, ports Porto, Setúbal
**physical** mountainous in the north, plains in south
**features** rivers Minho, Douro, Tagus, Guadiana; Serra da Estrélla mountains
**head of state** Mario Alberto Nobre Lopes Soares from 1986
**head of government** Cavaco Silva from 1985
**political system** democratic republic
**political parties** Social Democratic Party (PSD), moderate, left-of-centre; Socialist Party (PS), progressive socialist; Democratic Renewal Party (PRD), centre-left; Democratic Social centre Party (CDS), moderate, left-of-centre

**exports** port wine, sherry, olive oil, resin, cork, sardines, textiles, pottery, pulpwood
**currency** escudo (254.10 = £1 July 1991)
**population** (1990 est) 10,528,000; growth rate 0.5% p.a.
**life expectancy** men 71, women 78 (1989)
**language** Portuguese
**religion** Roman Catholic 97%
**literacy** men 89%/women 80% (1985)
**GNP** $33.5 bn (1987); $2,970 per head (1986)

**chronology**
**1928–68** Military dictatorship under Antonio de Oliveira Salazar.
**1968** Salazar succeeded by Marcello Caetano.
**1974** Caetano removed in military coup led by General Antonio Ribeiro de Spinola. Spinola replaced by General Francisco da Costa Gomes.
**1975** African colonies became independent.
**1976** New constitution, providing for return to civilian rule, adopted. Minority government appointed, led by Socialist Party leader Mario Soares.
**1978** Soares resigned.
**1980** Francisco Balsemão formed centre-party coalition after two years of political instability.

**1982** Draft of new constitution approved, reducing powers of presidency.
**1983** Centre-left coalition government formed.
**1985** Cavaco Silva became prime minister.
**1986** Mario Soares elected first civilian president in 60 years. Portugal joined European Community.
**1988** Portugal joined Western European Union.
**1989** Constitution amended to allow state enterprises to be denationalized.
**1991** Mario Soares re-elected president.

## Qatar (State of)
(*Dawlat Qatar*)

**area** 11,400 sq km/4,402 sq mi
**capital** and chief port Doha
**towns** Dukhan, centre of oil production
**physical** mostly flat desert with salt flats in S
**features** negligible rain and surface water, only 3% is fertile, but irrigation allows self-sufficiency in fruit and vegetables; extensive oil discoveries since World War II
**head of state and government** Sheik Khalifa bin Hamad al-Thani from 1972
**political system** absolute monarchy
**political parties** none
**exports** oil, natural gas, petrochemicals, fertilizers, iron, steel
**currency** riyal (5.89 = £1 July 1991)
**population** (1990 est) 498,000 (half in Doha); growth rate 3.7% p.a.
**life expectancy** men 68, women 72 (1989)
**language** Arabic (official), English
**religion** Sunni Muslim 95%
**literacy** 60% (1987)
**GNP** $5.9 bn (1983); $35,000 per head

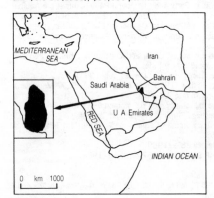

**chronology**
**1970** Constitution adopted, confirming the emirate as an absolute monarchy.
**1971** Independence achieved from Britain. New Treaty of friendship with UK signed.
**1972** Emir Sheik Ahmad replaced in bloodless coup by his cousin, Crown Prince Sheik Khalifa.

## Romania

**area** 237,500 sq km/91,699 sq mi
**capital** Bucharest
**towns** Brasov, Timişoara, Cluj, Iasi; ports Galati, Constanta, Brăila
**physical** mountains surrounding a plateau, with river plains S and E
**features** Carpathian Mountains, Transylvanian Alps; river Danube; Black Sea coast; mineral springs

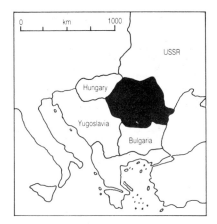

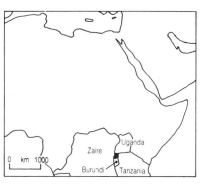

**head of state** Ion Iliescu from 1989
**head of government** Petre Roman from 1989
**political system** emergency provisional government from Dec 1989
**exports** petroleum products and oilfield equipment, electrical goods, cars
**currency** leu (101.48 = £1 July 1991)
**population** (1990 est) 23,269,000 (Romanians 89% Hungarians 7.9%, Germans 1.6%); growth rate 0.5% p.a.
**life expectancy** men 67, women 73 (1989)
**language** Romanian (official); Hungarian, German
**religion** Romanian Orthodox 80%, Roman Catholic 6%
**literacy** 98% (1988)
**GNP** $151 bn (1988); $6,400 per head

**chronology**
**1944** Pro-Nazi Antonescu government overthrown.
**1945** Communist-dominated government appointed.
**1947** Boundaries redrawn. King Michael abdicated and People's Republic proclaimed.
**1949** New constitution adopted. Joined Comecon.
**1952** New Soviet-style constitution.
**1955** Romania joined Warsaw Pact.
**1958** Soviet occupation forces removed.
**1965** New constitution adopted.
**1974** Ceauşescu created president.
**1985–86** Winters of austerity and power cuts.
**1987** Workers demonstrated against austerity programme.
**1988–89** Relations with Hungary deteriorated over 'systematization programme'.
**1989** Bloody overthrow of Ceauşescu regime in 'Christmas Revolution'; power assumed by new military-dissident-reform communist National Salvation Front, headed by Ion Iliescu. Ceauşescu tried and executed.
**1990** Securitate replaced by new Romanian Intelligence Service (RIS); religious practices resumed; mounting strikes and protests against effects of market economy.

## Rwanda (Republic of)
*(Republika y'u Rwanda)*

**area** 26,338 sq km/10,173 sq mi
**capital** Kigali
**towns** Butare, Ruhengeri
**physical** high savanna and hills, with volcanic mountains in NW
**features** part of lake Kivu; highest peak Mount Karisimbi 4,507 m/14,792 ft; Kagera River (whose headwaters are the source of the Nile) and National Park
**head of state and government** Juvenal Habyarimana from 1973

**political system** one-party military republic
**political parties** National Revolutionary Movement for Development (MRND), nationalistic, socialist
**exports** coffee, tea, pyrethrum, tin, tungsten
**currency** franc (213.03 = £1 July 1991)
**population** (1990 est) 7,603,000 (Hutu 90%, Tutsi 9%); growth rate 3.3% p.a.
**life expectancy** men 49, women 53 (1989)
**language** Kinyarwanda, French (official); Kiswahili
**religion** Roman Catholic 54%, animist 23%, Protestant 12%; Muslim 9%
**literacy** men 50% (1989)
**GNP** $2.3 bn (1987); $323 per head (1986)

**chronology**
**1916** Belgian troops occupied Rwanda; League of Nations mandated Rwanda and Burundi to Belgium as Territory of Ruanda-Urundi.
**1959** Tribal warfare between Hutu and Tutsi.
**1962** Independence from Belgium achieved, with Gregoire Kayibanda as president.
**1972** Renewal of tribal fighting.
**1973** Kayibanda ousted in a military coup led by Maj-Gen Juvenal Habyarimana.
**1978** New constitution approved; Rwanda remained a military-controlled state.
**1980** Civilian rule adopted.
**1988** Refugees from Burundi massacres streamed into Rwanda.
**1990** Rwandan Patriotic Army attacked government. Constitutional reforms promised.

## St Christopher (St Kitts)-Nevis (Federation of)

**area** 269 sq km/104 sq mi
**capital** Basseterre (on St Kitts)

**towns** Charlestown (largest on Nevis)
**physical** two volcanic islands in the Lesser Antilles
**features** first British West Indian island to be colonized
**head of state** Elizabeth II from 1983; represented by governor-general
**head of government** Kennedy Alphonse Simmonds from 1980
**political system** federal constitutional monarchy
**political parties** People's Action Movement (PAM), centre-right; Nevis Reformation Party (NRP), Nevis-separatist; Labour Party, moderate, left-of-centre
**exports** sugar, molasses, cotton
**currency** E Caribbean dollar (EC$4.39 = £1 July 1991)
**population** (1990 est) 40,000; growth rate 0.2% p.a.
**life expectancy** men 69/women 72
**language** English
**religion** Anglican 36%, Methodist 32%, other protestant 8%, Roman Catholic 10% (1985 est)
**literacy** 90% (1987)
**GNP** $40 million (1983); $870 per head

**chronology**
**1871–56** Part of the Leeward Islands Federation.
**1958–62** Part of the Federation of the West Indies.
**1967** St Christopher, Nevis, and Anguilla granted internal self-government, within the British Commonwealth, with Robert Bradshaw, Labour Party leader, as prime minister.
**1971** Anguilla left the federation.
**1978** Bradshaw died; succeeded by Paul Southwell.
**1979** Southwell died; succeeded by Lee L Moore.
**1980** Coalition government led by Kennedy Simmonds.
**1983** Full independence achieved within the Commonwealth.
**1984** Coalition government re-elected.
**1989** Prime minister Simmonds won a third successive term.

## St Lucia

**area** 617 sq km/238 sq mi
**capital** Castries
**towns** Vieux-Fort, Soufrière
**physical** mountainous; mainly tropical forest
**features** volcanic peaks; Gros and Petit Pitons
**head of state** Elizabeth II from 1979 represented by governor-general
**head of government** John G M Compton from 1982
**political system** constitutional monarchy
**political parties** United Worker's Party (UWP), moderate, left-of-centre; St Lucia Labour Party (SLP), moderate, left-of-centre; Progressive Labour Party (PLP), moderate, left-of-centre
**exports** coconut oil, bananas, cocoa, copra

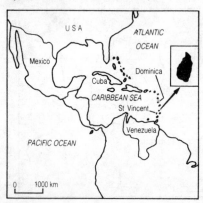

**currency** E Caribbean dollar (EC$4.39 = £1 July 1991)
**population** (1990 est) 153,000; growth rate 2.8% p.a.
**life expectancy** 68 men, 73 women (1989)
**language** English; French patois
**religion** Roman Catholic 90%
**literacy** 78% (1989)
**GNP** $166 min; $1,370 per head (1987)

**chronology**
**1967** Granted internal self-government as a West Indies associated state.
**1979** Independence achieved from Britain within the Commonwealth, with John Compton, leader of the United Workers' Party (UWP), as prime minister. Allan Louisy, leader of the Saint Lucia Labour Party (SLP), replaced Compton as prime minister.
**1981** Louisy resigned; replaced by Winston Cenac.
**1982** Compton returned to power at the head of a UWP government.
**1987** Compton re-elected with reduced majority.

## St Vincent and the Grenadines

**area** 388 sq km/150 sq mi, including Northern Grenadines 43 sq km/17 sq mi
**capital** Kingstown
**physical** volcanic mountains, thickly forested
**features** Mustique, one of the Grenadines, a holiday resort

**head of state** Elizabeth II from 1979 represented by governor-general
**head of government** James Mitchell from 1984
**political system** constitutional monarchy
**political parties** New Democratic Party (NDP), moderate, left-of-centre; St Vincent Labour Party (SVLP), moderate; left-of-centre
**exports** bananas, tarros, sweet potatoes, arrowroot, copra
**currency** E Caribbean dollar (EC$4.39 = £1 July 1991)
**population** (1990 est) 106,000; growth rate -4% p.a.
**life expectancy** men 69, women 74 (1989)
**language** English; French patois
**religion** Anglican 47%, Methodist 28%, Roman Catholic 13%
**literacy** 85% (1989)
**GNP** $188 min; $1,070 per head (1987)

**chronology**
**1783** Became a British Crown Colony.
**1958–62** Part of the West Indies Federation.
**1969** Granted internal self-government.
**1979** Achieved full independence from Britain within the Commonwealth, with Milton Cato as prime minister.
**1984** James Mitchell replaced Cato as prime minister.
**1989** Mitchell decisively re-elected.

## Samoa, Western (Independent State of)
(*Samoa i Sisifo*)

**area** 2,830 sq km/1,093 sq mi
**capital** Apia (on Upolu island)
**physical** comprises South Pacific islands of Savai'i and Upolu, with two smaller tropical islands and islets; mountain ranges on main islands
**features** lava flows on Savai'i

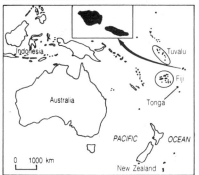

**head of state** King Malietoa Tanumafili II from 1962
**head of government** Tofilau Eti Alesana from 1988
**political system** constitutional monarchy
**political parties** Human Rights Protection Party (HRPP), led by Tofilau Eti Alesana; the Va'ai Kolone Group (VKG); Christian Democratic Party (CDP), led by Tupuola Taisi Efi. All 'parties' are personality-based groupings.
**exports** coconut oil, copra, cocoa, fruit juice, cigarettes
**currency** talā (3.84 = £1 July 1991)
**population** (1989) 169,000; growth rate 1.1% p.a.
**life expectancy** men 64, women 69 (1989)
**language** English, Samoan (official)
**religion** Protestant 70%, Roman Catholic 20%
**literacy** 90% (1989)
**GNP** $110 min (1987); $520 per head

**chronology**
**1899–1914** German protectorate.
**1920–61** Administered by New Zealand.
**1959** Local government elected.
**1961** Referendum favoured independence.
**1962** Independence achieved within the Commonwealth, with Fiame Mata'afa Mulinu'u as prime minister.
**1975** Mata'afa died; succeeded by Tupuola Taisi Efi, first non-royal prime minister.
**1982** Va'ai Kolone became prime minister; replaced by Tupuola Efi. Assembly failed to approve budget; Tupuola Efi resigned; replaced by Tofilau Eti Alesana.
**1985** Tofilau Eti resigned; head of state invited Va'ai Kolombe to lead the government.
**1988** Elections produced a hung parliament, with first Tupuola Efi as prime minister and then Tofilau Eti Alesana.

## San Marino (Republic of)
(*Republica di San Marino*)

**area** 61 sq km/24 sq mi
**capital** San Marino
**towns** Serravalle
**physical** on the slope of Mount Titano
**features** surrounded by Italian territory; one of the world's smallest states
**head of state and government** two captains-regent, elected for a six-month period

**political system** direct democracy
**political parties** San Marino Christian Democrat Party (PDCS), right-of-centre; San Marino Communist Party (PCS), moderate Euro-communist; Socialist Unity Party (PSU) and Socialist Party (PSS), both left-of-centre
**exports** wine, ceramics, paint, chemicals
**currency** Italian lira (2,187.00 = £1 July 1991)
**population** (1990 est) 23,000; growth rate 0.1% p.a.
**life expectancy** men 70, women 77
**language** Italian
**religion** Roman Catholic 95%
**literacy** 97% (1987)

**chronology**
**1862** Treaty with Italy signed; independence recognized under Italy's protection.
**1947–86** Governed by a series of left-wing and centre-left coalitions.
**1986** Formation of Communist and Christian Democrat 'grand coalition'.

## São Tomé e Príncipe (Democratic Republic of)

**area** 1,000 sq km/386 sq mi
**capital** São Tomé
**towns** Trinidad, Santana
**physical** comprises two main islands and several smaller ones, all volcanic; thickly forested and fertile
**head of state and government** Manuel Pinto da Costa from 1975
**political system** one-party socialist republic
**political parties** Movement for the Liberation of São Tomé and Príncipe (MLSTP ), nationalist socialist
**exports** cocoa, copra, coffee, palm oil and kernels
**currency** dobra (303.87 = £1 July 1991)
**population** (1990 est) 125,000; growth rate 2.5% p.a.

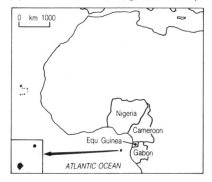

**life expectancy** men 62, women 62
**language** Portuguese (official)
**religion** Roman Catholic 80%, animist
**literacy** men 73%/women 42% (1981)
**GNP** $32 min (1987); $384 per head (1986)

chronology
**1973** Granted internal self-government from Portugal.
**1975** Independence achieved from Portugal, with Manuel Pinto da Costa as president.
**1984** Formally declared itself a nonaligned state.
**1987** President now popularly elected.
**1988** Unsuccessful coup attempt against Pinto da Costa.
**1990** New constitution approved.
**1991** First multi-party elections held.

### Saudi Arabia (Kingdom of)
(*al-Mamlaka al-'Arabiya as-Sa'udiya*)

**area** 2,200,518 sq km/849,400 sq mi
**capital** Riyadh
**towns** Mecca, Medina, Taif; ports Jidda, Dammam
**physical** desert, sloping to the Persian Gulf from a height of 2,750 m/9,000 ft in the W
**features** Nafud desert in N and the Rub'al Khali (Empty Quarter) in S, area 650,000 sq km/250,000 sq mi

**head of state and government** King Fahd Ibn Abdul Aziz from 1982
**political system** absolute monarchy
**political parties** none
**exports** oil, petroleum products
**currency** rial (6.07 = £1 July 1991)
**population** (1990 est) 16,758,000 (16% nomadic); growth rate 3.1% p.a.
**life expectancy** men 64, women 67 (1989)
**language** Arabic
**religion** Sunni Muslim; Shi'ite minority
**literacy** men 34%/women 12% (1980 est)
**GNP** $70 bn (1988); $6,170 per head (1988)

chronology
**1926–32** Territories united and kingdom established.
**1953** King ibn-Saud died and was succeeded by his eldest son, Saud.
**1964** King Saud forced to abdicate; succeeded by his brother, Faisal.
**1975** King Faisal assassinated; succeeded by his half-brother, Khalid.
**1982** King Khalid died of a heart attack; succeeded by his brother, Crown Prince Fahd.
**1987** Rioting by Iranian pilgrims caused 400 deaths in Mecca; diplomatic relations with Iran severed.
**1990** Iraqi troops invaded and annexed Kuwait and massed on Saudi Arabian border. King Fahd called for help from US and UK forces.

**1991** Calls from religious leaders for consultative assembly.

### Senegal (Republic of)
(*République du Sénégal*)

**area** 196,200 sq km/75,753 sq mi
**capital** and chief port Dakar
**towns** Thiès, Kaolack

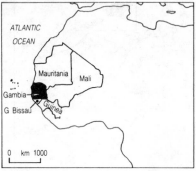

**physical** plains rising to hills in SE; swamp and tropical forest in SW
**features** river Senegal; Gambia forms an enclave within Senegal
**head of state and government** Abdou Diouf from 1981
**political system** emergent socialist democratic republic
**political parties** Senegalese Socialist Party (PS), democratic socialist; Senegalese Democratic Party (PDS), left-of-centre
**exports** peanuts, cotton, fish, phosphates
**currency** franc CFA (498.25 = £1 July 1991)
**population** (1990 est) 7,740,000; growth rate 3.1% p.a.
**life expectancy** men 51, women 54 (1989)
**language** French (official); African dialects
**religion** Muslim 80%, Roman Catholic 10%, animist
**literacy** men 37%/women 19% (1985 est)
**GNP** $2 bn (1987); $380 per head (1984)

chronology
**1659** Became a French colony.
**1854–65** Interior occupied.
**1902** Became a territory of French West Africa.
**1959** Formed the Federation of Mali with French Sudan.
**1960** Independence achieved from France, but withdrew from the federation. Léopold Sedar Senghor, leader of the Senegalese Progressive Union (UPS), became president.
**1966** UPS declared the only legal party.
**1974** Pluralist system re-established.
**1976** UPS reconstituted as Senegalese Socialist Party (PS). Prime Minister Abdou Diouf nominated as Senghor's successor.
**1980** Senghor resigned; succeeded by Diouf. Troops sent to defend Gambia.
**1981** Military help again sent to Gambia.
**1982** Confederation of Senegambia came into effect.
**1983** Diouf re-elected. Post of prime minister abolished.
**1988** Diouf decisively re-elected.
**1989** Violent clashes between Senegalese and Mauritanians in Dakar and Nouakchott, killed more than 450 people; over 50,000 people repatriated from both countries. Senegambia federation abandoned.

### Seychelles (Republic of)

**area** 453 sq km/175 sq mi
**capital** Victoria (on Mahé island)
**physical** comprises two distinct island groups, one concentrated, the other widely scattered, totalling over 100 islands and islets

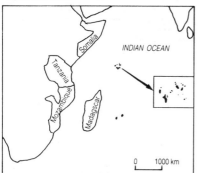

**features** Aldabra atoll, containing world's largest tropical lagoon; the unique 'double coconut' (coco-de-mer)
**head of state and government** France-Albert René from 1977
**political system** one-party socialist republic
**political parties** Seychelles People's Progressive Front (SPPF), nationalistic socialist
**exports** copra, cinnamon
**currency** Seychelles rupee (8.80 = £1 July 1991)
**population** (1990) 71,000; growth rate 2.2% p.a.
**language** Creole 95%, English, French (all official)
**religion** Roman Catholic 90%
**literacy** 80% (1989)
**GNP** $175 min; $2,600 per head (1987)

**chronology**
**1768** Colonized by French settlers.
**1794** Captured by British.
**1814** Incorporated as dependency of Mauritius.
**1903** Became a separate colony.
**1975** Internal self-government granted.
**1976** Independence achieved from Britain as a republic within the Commonwealth, with Mancham as president.
**1977** René ousted Mancham in an armed coup and took over presidency.
**1979** New constitution adopted; Seychelles People's Progressive Front (SPPF) sole legal party.
**1981** Attempted coup by South African mercenaries thwarted.
**1984** René re-elected.
**1987** Coup attempt foiled.
**1989** René re-elected.

### Sierra Leone (Republic of)

**area** 71,740 sq km/27,710 sq mi
**capital** Freetown
**towns** Bo, Kenema, Makeni
**physical** mountains in E; hills and forest; coastal mangrove swamps
**features** hot and humid climate (3,500 mm/138 in rainfall p.a.)
**head of state and government** Joseph Saidu Momoh from 1985
**political system** one-party republic
**political parties** All People's Congress (APC), moderate socialist
**exports** palm kernels, cocoa, coffee, ginger, diamonds, bauxite, rutile

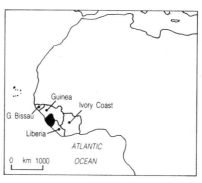

**currency** leone (371.45 = £1 July 1991)
**population** (1990 est) 4,168,000; growth rate 2.5% p.a.
**life expectancy** men 41, women 47 (1989)
**language** English (official); local languages
**religion** Muslim 39%, animist 52%, Protestant 6%, Roman Catholic 2% (1980 est)
**literacy** men 38%/women 21% (1985 est)
**GNP** $965 min (1987); $320 per head (1984)

**chronology**
**1896** Hinterland declared a British protectorate.
**1961** Independence achieved from Britain within the Commonwealth, with Milton Margai, leader of Sierra Leone People's Party (SLPP), as prime minister.
**1964** Milton succeeded by his half-brother, Albert Margai.
**1967** Election results disputed by army, who set up a National Reformation Council and forced the governor general to leave.
**1968** Army revolt made Siaka Stevens, leader of the All-People's Congress (APC), prime minister.
**1971** New constitution adopted, making Sierra Leone a republic, with Stevens as president.
**1978** APC declared only legal party. Stevens sworn in for another seven-year term.
**1985** Stevens retired; succeeded by Maj-Gen Joseph Momoh.
**1989** Attempted coup against president Momoh foiled.
**1991** Momoh 'welcomes' multi-party democracy.

### Singapore (Republic of)

**area** 620 sq km/239 sq mi
**capital** Singapore City

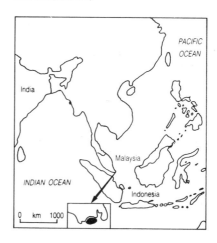

**towns** Jurong, Changi

**physical** comprises Singapore Island, low and flat, and 57 small islands

**features** Singapore Island is joined to mainland by causeway across Strait of Johore; temperature range 21°–34°C/69°–93°F

**head of state** Wee Kim Wee from 1985

**head of government** Goh Chok Tong from 1990

**political system** liberal democratic republic

**political parties** People's Action Party (PAP) conservative; Worker's Party (WP), socialist; Singapore Democratic Party (SDP), liberal pluralist

**exports** electronics, petroleum products, rubber, machinery, vehicles

**currency** Singapore dollar (S$2.86 = £1 July 1991)

**population** (1990 est) 2,703,000 (Chinese 75%, Malay 14%, Tamil 7%); growth rate 1.2% p.a.

**life expectancy** men 71, women 77 (1989)

**language** Malay, Chinese, Tamil, English (all official)

**religion** Buddhist, Taoist, Muslim, Hindu, Christian

**literacy** men 93%/women 79% (1985 est)

**GNP** $23.7 bn (1984); $6,200 per head (1985)

**chronology**

**1858** Singapore placed under crown rule.

**1942** Invaded and occupied by Japan.

**1945** Japanese removed by British forces.

**1959** Independence achieved from Britain; Lee Kuan Yew became prime minister.

**1963** Joined new Federation of Malaysia.

**1965** Left federation to become independent republic.

**1984** Opposition made advances in parliamentary elections.

**1986** Opposition leader convicted of perjury, prohibited from standing for election.

**1988** Ruling conservative party elected to all but one of available assembly seats; increasingly authoritarian rule.

**1990** Lee Kuan Yew resigned as prime minister; replaced by Goh Chok Tong.

---

### Solomon Islands

**area** 27,600 sq km/10,656 sq mi

**capital** Honiara (on Guadalcanal)

**physical** comprises all but the northernmost islands (which belong to Papua New Guinea) of a Melanesian archipelago stretching nearly 1,500 km/900 mi. The largest is Guadalcanal (area 6,500 sq km/2,510 sq mi); others are Malaita, San Cristobal, New Georgia, Santa Isabel, Choiseul; mainly mountainous and forested

**features** rivers ideal for hydroelectric power

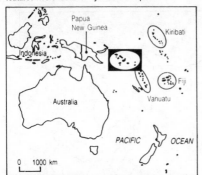

**head of state** Elizabeth II, represented by governor-general

**head of government** Solomon Mamaloni from 1989

**political system** constitutional monarchy

**political parties** People's Alliance Party (PAP), centre-left; Solomon Islands United Party (SIUPA), right-of-centre

**exports** fish products, palm oil, copra, cocoa, timber

**currency** Solomon Island dollar (SI$4.44 = £1 July 1991)

**population** (1990 est) 314,000 (Melanesian 95%, Polynesian 4%); growth rate 3.9% p.a.

**life expectancy** men 66, women 71

**language** English (official); 120 Melanesian dialects

**religion** Anglican 34%, South Sea Evangelical 17%, Roman Catholic 19%

**literacy** 60% (1989)

**GNP** $141 min; $420 per head (1987)

**chronology**

**1893–99** Soloman Islands placed under British protection.

**1978** Independence achieved from Britain within the Commonwealth, with Peter Kenilorea as prime minister.

**1981** Solomon Mamaloni replaced Kenilorea as prime minister.

**1984** Kenilorea returned to power, heading a coalition government.

**1986** Kenilorea resigned after allegations of corruption; replaced by his deputy, Ezekiel Alebua.

**1988** Kenilorea elected deputy prime minister. Joined Vanuatu and Papua New Guinea to form the Spearhead Group, aiming to preserve Melanesian cultural traditions and secure independence for the French territory of New Caledonia.

**1989** Solomon Mamaloni (People's Action Party) elected prime minister; formed PAP-dominated coalition.

---

### Somalia (Somali Democratic Republic)

(*Jamhuriyadda Dimugradiga Somaliya*)

**area** 637,700 sq km/246,220 sq mi

**capital** Mogadishu

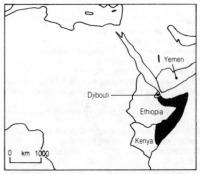

**towns** Hargeisa, Kismayu, port Berbera

**physical** mainly flat, with hills in the N

**features** occupies a strategic location on the Horn of Africa

**head of state** Ali Mahdi Mohammed from 1991

**head of government** Mohammed Ali Samantar from 1987

**political system** one-party socialist republic

**political parties** Somali Revolutionary Socialist Party (SRSP), nationalist, socialist

**exports** livestock, skins, hides, bananas

**currency** Somali shilling (4,257.50 = £1 July 1991)

**population** (1990 est) 8,415,000 (including 350,000 refugees from Ethopia and 50,000 in Djibouti); growth rate 3.1% p.a.

**life expectancy** men 53, women 53 (1989)

**language** Somali, Arabic (both official), Italian, English

**religion** Sunni Muslim 99%

**literacy** 40% (1986)

**GNP** $1.5 bn; $290 per head (1987)

## SOUTH AFRICA: ON THE ROAD TO DEMOCRACY

The ascendancy of F W de Klerk to the presidency of South Africa in 1989 may, in retrospect, prove as momentous as the arrival on to the world stage of Mikhail Gorbachev four years before. Gorbachev's two-pronged attack of *perestroika* and *glasnost* on the Soviet Union's ossified political and economic system has had far-reaching effects, eventually changing the political map of Eastern Europe, replacing one-party rule with pluralism, and breaking up the empire of Soviet satellite states.

De Klerk's arrival has not had the same dramatic effect, even within South Africa, but he has opened the door to change and the wind now rushing through is unlikely to be subdued. His problem now is to allow this wind to blow in a controlled fashion by nullifying extreme elements and supporting moderates in both the white and the black communities. If he can do this successfully then his contribution to racial harmony and democratic government in Africa will be considerable.

Some recent events give encouragement to the hope that de Klerk will succeed. The release of Nelson Mandela from prison, of course; the reinstatement of the ANC in Johannesburg; the growth of moderate white political parties; the smooth transition to independence in Namibia; the moves towards multi-party politics in neighbouring Zambia, Angola and Mozambique; the rapprochement between Mandela and the Zulu Chief Buthelezi; and, most importantly, the ending of apartheid legislation. The latter move, while ending all racial discrimination laws relating to property, registration of birth, and communal intermixing, did not however give blacks the franchise.

On the debit side is the threat of a backlash against the moderation of de Klerk by the white extremists, such as Andries Treurnicht, and a similar reaction gainst the ANC leaders by extreme blacks, impatient for faster progress in dismantling the apparatus of apartheid.

The question posed is whether real democracy can be achieved in South Africa. It is a question which should be widened to the whole of the continent. Democracy, on the Western liberal model, is not traditional to Africa. Tribal patterns and methods of decision making do not easily accommodate the compromise and give-and-take which typify pluralistic politics in the West. Real democracy, in the sense of free and active participation in the political process and the acceptance of an opposition party as well as the government in power, demands an informed and politically sophisticated electorate, if it is not to be exploited by an unscrupulous minority. The black population in South Africa has been deliberately denied the opportunity of exercising those political rights which are taken for granted in most Western countries. The whites, too, have lived in an unreal world, where the dominance won by their ancestors was bequeathed to them, without their having to justify or defend it.

The future of democracy in South Africa, as in the rest of Africa, depends on the wisdom and courage of a minority, white and black. It is fortunate that de Klerk and Mandela have emerged at this particular time, despite all the pressures that might have prevented this happening. The progress towards majority rule must be steady, and not a headlong rush. It must be accompanied, or preceded by economic and social reforms, which, to the ordinary citizen are more important in the short term than political freedoms. Lessons can be learned from recent events in the Soviet Union, where political progress is threatened by economic mismanagement.

Real democracy can, and will, come to South Africa, but whether it comes during the remaining years of this century without bloodshed depends on the good sense and farsightedness of its present leaders, black and white.

**chronology**
**1884–87** British protectorate of Somaliland established.
**1889** Italian protectorate of Somalia established.
**1960** Independence achieved from Italy and Britain.
**1963** Border dispute with Kenya, diplomatic relations with the UK broken.
**1968** Diplomatic relations with the UK restored.
**1969** Army coup led by Maj-Gen Mohammad Siyad Barre; constitution suspended, Supreme Revolutionary Council set up; name changed to Somali Democratic Republic.
**1978** Defeated in eight-month war with Ethiopia. Armed insurrection began in north.
**1979** New constitution for socialist one-party state adopted.
**1982** Somali National Movement, anti-government formed. Oppressive countermeasures by government.
**1987** Barre re-elected president.
**1989** Dissatisfaction with government and increased guerrilla activity in north.
**1990** Civil war intensified. Constitutional reforms promised.
**1991** Mogadishu captured by rebels. Ali Mahdi Mohammed named president; free elections promised. Secession of north-east Somalia, as the Somaliland Republic,

announced. Peace talks commenced. Ceasefire agreed.

### South Africa (Republic of)
(*Republiek van Suid-Afrika*)

**area** 1,223,181 sq km/472,148 sq mi
**capital** Cape Town (legislative), Pretoria (administrative), Bloemfontein (judicial)
**towns** Johannesburg; ports Cape Town, Durban, Port Elizabeth, East London
**physical** southern end of large plateau, fringed by mountains and lowland coastal margin
**territories** Prince Edward Island in the Antarctic
**features** Drakensberg Mountains; Table Mountain; Limpopo and Orange rivers; the Veld and the Karroo; part of Kalahari Desert; Kruger National Park
**head of state and government** F W de Klerk from 1989
**political system** racist, nationalist republic, restricted democracy; state of emergency
**political parties** White: National Party (NP), right-of-centre, racist; Conservative Party of South Africa (CPSA), extreme right, racist; Democratic Party (DP), left-of-centre, multiracial. Coloureds: Labour Party of South Africa, left-of-centre; People's Congress Party, right-of-centre.

Indian: National People's Party, right-of-centre; Solidarity Party, left-of-centre
**exports** maize, sugar, fruit; wool; gold, platinum, diamonds
**currency** rand (R4.68, commercial rate = £1 July 1991)
**population** (1990 est) 39,550,000 (73% Black: Zulu, Xhosa, Sotho, Tswana; 18% White: 3% mixed, 3% Asiatic); growth rate 2.5% p.a.
**life expectancy** Whites 71, Asians 67, Blacks 58
**language** Afrikaans and English (both official); Bantu
**religion** Dutch Reformed Church 40%, Anglican 11%, Roman Catholic 8%, other Christian 25%; Hindu, Muslim
**literacy** Whites 99%, Asians 69%, Blacks 50% (1989)
**GNP** $81 bn; $1,890 per head (1987)

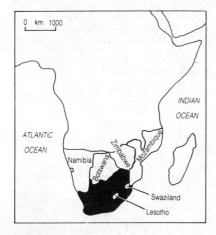

**chronology**
**1910** Union of South Africa formed from two British colonies and two Boer republics.
**1912** African National Congress (ANC) formed.
**1948** Apartheid system of racial discrimination initiated by Daniel Malan, leader of National Party (NP).
**1955** Freedom Charter adopted by African National Congress (ANC).
**1958** Malan succeeded as prime minister by Hendrik Verwoerd.
**1960** ANC banned.
**1961** South Africa withdrew from Commonwealth and became a republic.
**1962** ANC leader Nelson Mandela jailed.
**1964** Mandela, Walter Sisulu, Govan Mbeki, and five other ANC leaders sentenced to life imprisonment.
**1966** Verwoerd assassinated and succeeded by B J Vorster.
**1976** Soweto uprising.
**1977** Death in custody of Pan African Congress activist Steve Biko.
**1978** Vorster resigned and was replaced by Pieter W Botha.
**1984** New constitution adopted, giving segregated representation to coloureds and Asians and making Botha president. Nonaggression pact with Mozambique signed but not observed.
**1985** Growth of violence in black townships.
**1986** Commonwealth agreed on limited sanctions. US Congress voted to impose sanctions. Some major multinational companies closed down their South African operations.
**1987** Government formally acknowledged the presence of its military forces in Angola.
**1988** Peace agreement with Angola and Cuba, recognizing independence for Namibia.
**1989** Botha gave up NP leadership and state presidency.

Democratic Party (DP) launched. F W de Klerk became president. Walter Sisulu and other ANC activists released.
**1990** ANC ban lifted; Nelson Mandela released from prison. National Party membership opened to all races. Oliver Tambo returned. Daily average of 35 murders and homicides recorded.
**1991** Meeting between Mandela and Zulu leader Buthelezi resulted in agreement to end fighting between ANC and Inkatha. Mandela elected ANC president. Revelations of government financial support for Inkatha threatened ANC cooperation. De Klerk announced repeal of remaining apartheid laws and introduced legislation to abolish racial controls on land ownership. South Africa readmitted to international sport.

## Spain
(*España*)

**area** 504,750 sq km/194,960 sq mi
**capital** Madrid
**towns** Zaragoza, Seville, Murcia, Córdoba; ports Barcelona, Valencia, Cartagena, Málaga, Cádiz, Vigo, Santander, Bilbao
**physical** central plateau with mountain ranges; lowlands in S
**features** includes Balearic and Canary Islands, and Ceuta and Melilla; rivers Ebro, Douro, Tagus, Guadiana, Guadalquivir; Iberian Plateau (Meseta); Pyrenees, Cantabrian Mountains, Andalusian Mountains, Sierra Nevada
**head of state** Juan Carlos I from 1975
**head of government** Felipe González Marquez from 1982
**political system** constitutional monarchy
**political parties** Socialist Worker's Party (PSOE), democratic socialist; Popular Alliance (AP), centre-right; Christian Democrats (DC), centrist; Liberal Party (PL), left-of-centre
**exports** citrus fruits, grapes, pomegranates, vegetables, wine, sherry, olive oil, canned fruit and fish, iron ore, cork, vehicles, leather goods, ceramics
**currency** peseta (184.10 = £1 July 1991)
**population** (1990 est) 39,623,000; growth rate 0.2% p.a.
**life expectancy** men 74, women 80 (1989)
**language** Spanish (Castilian, official), Basque, Catalan, Galician, Valencian, and Majorcan
**religion** Roman Catholic 90%
**literacy** 97% (1989)
**GNP** $288 bn (1987); $4,490 per head (1984)

**chronology**
**1936–39** Civil war; Gen Francisco Franco became head of state and government; facist party Falange declared only legal political organization.
**1947** Gen Franco announced return to the monarchy after his death, with Prince Juan Carlos as his successor.
**1975** Franco died; succeeded as head of state by King Juan Carlos I.
**1978** New constitution adopted with Adolfo Suárez, leader of the Democratic Centre Party, prime minister.
**1981** Suárez resigned; succeeded by his deputy, Calvo-Sotelo. Attempted military coup thwarted.
**1982** Socialist Workers' Party (PSOE), led by Felipe González, won a sweeping electoral victory. Basque separatist organization (ETA) stepped up its guerrilla campaign.
**1985** ETA's campaign spread to holiday resorts.
**1986** Referendum confirmed NATO membership. Spain joined the European Community.
**1988** Spain joined the Western European Union. PSOE lost seats to hold only parity after general election.
**1989** Talks between government and ETA collapsed and truce ended.

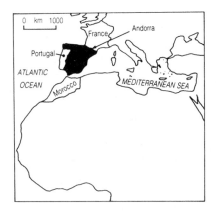

**1948** Ceylon achieved independence from Britain within the Commonwealth.
**1956** Sinhalese established as official language.
**1959** Prime Minister Solomon Bandaranaike assassinated.
**1972** Socialist Republic of Sri Lanka proclaimed.
**1978** Presidential constitution adopted by new Jayawardene government.
**1983** Tamil guerrilla violence escalated; state of emergency imposed.
**1987** Violence continued despite cease-fire policed by Indian troops.
**1988** Left-wing guerrillas campaigned against Indo-Sri Lankan peace pact. Prime Minister Premadasa elected president.
**1989** Premadasa became president; Wijetunge, prime minister. Leaders of the TULF and JVP assassinated.
**1990** IPKF withdrawn by March. Violence continued. People's Libration Front (JVP), Sinhala-extremist organization, banned from 1983

## Sri Lanka (Democratic Socialist Republic of)
(*Prajathanrika Samajawadi Janarajaya Sri Lanka*)
(until 1972 **Ceylon**)

**area** 65,600 sq km/25,328 sq mi
**capital** and chief port Colombo

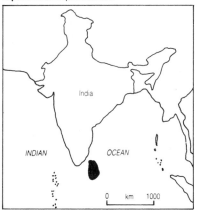

**towns** Kandy; ports Jaffna, Galle, Negombo, Trincomalee
**physical** flat in N and around the coast; hills and mountains in S and central interior
**features** Adam's Peak (2,243 m/7,538 ft); ruined cities of Anuradhapura, Polonnaruwa
**head of state** Ranasinghe Premadsa from 1989
**head of government** Dingiri Banda Wijetunge from 1989
**political system** liberal democratic republic
**political parties** United National Party (UNP), right-of-centre; Sri Lanka Freedom Party (SLFP), left-of-centre; Tamil United Liberation Front (TULF), Tamil autonomy; Eelam People's Revolutionary Liberation Front (EPLRF), Indian-backed Tamil-secessionist *Tamil Tigers*
**exports** tea, rubber, coconut products, graphite, sapphires, rubies, other gemstones
**currency** Sri Lanka rupee (Rs 66.00 = £1 July 1991)
**population** (1990 est) 17,135,000 (Sinhalese 74%, Tamils 17%, Moors 7%); growth rate 1.8% p.a.
**life expectancy** men 67, women 72 (1989)
**language** Sinhala, Tamil (both official); English
**religion** Buddhist 69%, Hindu 15%, Muslim 8%, Christian 7%
**literacy** men 87% (1988)
**GNP** $7.2 bn; $400 per head (1988)

**chronology**

## Sudan (Democratic Republic of)
(*Jamhuryat es-Sudan*)

**area** 2,505,800 sq km/967,489 sq mi
**capital** Khartoum
**towns** Omdurman, Juba, Wadi Medani, al-Obeid, Kassala, Atbara, al-Qadarif, Kosti; chief port Port Sudan
**physical** fertile valley of river Nile separates Libyan Desert in W from high rocky Nubian Desert in E
**features** Sudd swamp; largest country in Africa

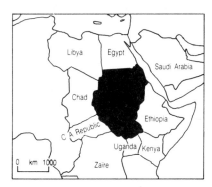

**head of state and government** Gen Omar Hasan Ahmed el-Bashir from 1989
**political system** military republic
**political parties** New National Umma Party (NNUP), Islamic, nationalist; Democratic Unionist Party (DUP), moderate, nationalist; National Islamic Front, Islamic nationalist
**exports** cotton, gum arabic, sesame seed, peanuts, sorghum
**currency** Sudanese pound (S7.31 official rate, 18.60 financial rate = £1 July 1991)
**population** (1990 est) 25,164,000; growth rate 2.9% p.a.
**life expectancy** men 51, women 55 (1989)
**language** Arabic 51% (official); tribal languages
**religion** Sunni Muslim 73%, animist 18%, Christian 9%
**literacy** 30% (1986)
**GNP** $8.5 bn (1988); $330 per head (1988)

**chronology**
**1820** Sudan ruled by Egypt.
**1885** Revolt led to capture of Khartoum.

**1896–98** Anglo-Egyptian offensive led by Lord Kitchener subdued revolt.
**1899** Sudan administered as an Anglo-Egyptian condominium.
**1955** Civil war between Muslim N and non-Muslim S broke out.
**1956** Sudan achieved independence from Britain and Egypt as a republic.
**1958** Military coup replaced civilian government with Supreme Council of the Armed Forces.
**1964** Civilian rule reinstated.
**1969** Coup led by Col Gaafar Mohammed Nimeri established Revolutionary Command Council (RCC); name changed to Democratic Republic of Sudan.
**1970** Union with Egypt agreed in principle.
**1971** New constitution adopted; Nimeri confirmed as president; Sudanese Socialist Union (SSU) declared only legal party.
**1972** Proposed Federation of Arab Republics, comprising Sudan, Egypt, and Syria, abandoned. Addis Ababa conference proposed autonomy for southern provinces.
**1974** National assembly established.
**1983** Nimeri re-elected. *Sharia* (Islamic law) introduced.
**1985** Nimeri deposed in a bloodless coup led by Gen Swar al-Dahab; transitional military council set up. State of emergency declared.
**1986** More than 40 political parties fought general election; coalition government formed.
**1987** Virtual civil war with Sudan People's Liberation Movement (SPLM).
**1988** Al-Mahdi formed a new coalition. Another flare-up of civil war between N and S created tens of thousands of refugees. Floods made 1.5 million people homeless. Peace pact signed with Sudan People's Liberation Movement.
**1989** Sadiq Al-Mahdi overthrown in coup led by Gen Omar Hasan Ahmed el-Bashir.
**1990** Civil war continued with new SPLM offensive.

## Suriname (Republic of)

**area** 163,820 sq km/63,243 sq mi
**capital** Paramaribo
**towns** Nieuw Nickerie, Brokopondo, Nieuw Amsterdam
**physical** hilly and forested, with flat coast

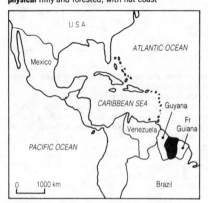

**features** Surinam River
**head of state and government** (interim) Johan Kraag from 1991
**political system** emergent democratic republic
**political parties** Party for National Unity and Solidarity (KTPI)*, Indonesian, left-of-centre; Suriname National Party (NPS)*, Creole, left-of-centre; Progressive Reform Party (VHP)*, Indian, left-of-centre; *members of Front for Democracy and Development (FDD); National Demo-

cratic Party (NDP)
**exports** allumina, alluminium, bauxite, rice, timber
**currency** Suriname guilder (2.90 = £1 July 1991)
**population** (1990 est) 408,000 (Hindustani 37%, Creole 31%, Javanese 15%) growth rate 1.1% p.a.
**life expectancy** men 66, women 71 (1989)
**language** Dutch (official); Sranan (Creole), English, others
**religion** Christian 25%, Hindu 27%, Muslim 23%
**literacy** 65% (1989)
**GNP** $1.1 bn (1987); $2,920 per head (1985)

**chronology**
**1814** Became a Dutch colony.
**1954** Achieved internal self-government as Dutch Guiana.
**1975** Independence achieved from the Netherlands, with Dr Johan Ferrier as president and Henck Arron as prime minister; 40% of the population emigrated to the Netherlands.
**1980** Arron's government overthrown in army coup; Ferrier refused to recognize military regime; appointed Dr Henk Chin A Sen to lead civilian administration. Army replaced Ferrier with Dr Chin A Sen.
**1982** Army, led by Lt-Col Desi Bouterse, seized power, setting up a Revolutionary People's Front.
**1985** Ban on political activities lifted.
**1986** Anti-government rebels brought economic chaos to Suriname.
**1987** New constitution approved.
**1988** Ramsewak Shankar elected president.
**1989** Bouterse rejects peace accord reached by President Shankar with guerrilla insurgents, vows to continue fighting.
**1990** Shankar deposed in army coup.
**1991** Johan Kraag became interim president. New Front for Democracy and Development (FDD) won assembly majority.

## Swaziland (Kingdom of)

**area** 17,400 sq km/6,716 sq mi
**capital** Mbabane
**towns** Manzini, Big Bend
**physical** central valley; mountains in W

**features** landlocked enclave between South Africa and Mozambique
**head of state and government** King Mswati III from 1986
**political system** near-absolute monarchy
**political parties** Imbokodvo National Movement (INM), nationalistic monarchist
**exports** sugar, canned fruit, woodpulp, asbestos
**currency** lilangeni (4.68 = £1 July 1991)

**population** (1990 est) 779,000; growth rate 3% p.a.
**life expectancy** men 47, women 54 (1989)
**language** Swazi 90%, English (both official)
**religion** Christian 57%; animist
**literacy** men 70%/women 66% (1985 est)
**GNP** $539 min; $750 per head (1987)

**chronology**
**1903** Swaziland became a special High Commission territory.
**1967** Achieved internal self-government.
**1968** Independence achieved from Britain, within the Commonwealth, as the Kingdom of Swaziland, with King Sobhuza II as head of state.
**1973** The king suspended constitution and assumed absolute powers.
**1978** New constitution adopted.
**1982** King Sobhuza died, and his place was taken by one of his wives, Dzeliewe, until his son, Prince Makhosetive, reached the age of 21.
**1983** Queen Dzeliewe ousted by another wife, Ntombi.
**1984** After royal power struggle, it was announced that the crown prince would become king at 18.
**1986** Crown prince formally invested as King Mswati III.
**1987** Power struggle developed between advisory council Liqoqo and Queen Ntombi over accession of king. Mswati dissolved parliament; new government elected with Sotsha Dlamini as prime minister.

---

**Sweden (Kingdom of)**
(*Konungariket Sverige*)

**area** 450,000 sq km/173,745 sq mi
**capital** Stockholm
**towns** Göteborg, Malmö, Uppsala, Norrköping, Västerås
**physical** mountains in NW; plains in S; thickly forested; more than 20,000 islands off the Stockholm coast
**features** lakes, including Vänern, Vättern, Mälaren, Hjälmaren; islands of Öland and Gotland; wild elk
**head of state** Carl XVI Gustaf from 1973
**head of government** Ingvar Carlsson from 1986
**political system** constitutional monarchy
**political parties** Social Democratic Labour party (SAP), moderate, left-of-centre; Moderate Party, right-of-centre; Liberal Party, centre-left; Centre Party, centrist; Christian Democratic Party, Christian, centrist; Left (Communist) Party, European, Marxist; Green, ecological
**exports** aircraft, vehicles, ballbearings, drills, missiles, electronics, petrochemicals, textiles, furnishings, ornamental glass
**currency** krona (10.58 £1 July 1991)
**population** (1990 est) 8,407,000 (including 17,000 Lapps and 1.2 million postwar immigrants from Finland, Turkey, Yugoslavia, Greece, Iran, other Nordic countries); growth rate 0.1% p.a.
**life expectancy** men 74, women 81 (1989)

**language** Swedish; Finnish
**religion** Lutheran (official) 95%
**literacy** 99% (1989)
**GNP** $179 bn; $11,783 per head (1989)

**chronology**
**12th century** United as an independent nation.
**1397–1520** Under Danish rule.
**1914–45** Neutral in both world wars.
**1951–76** Social Democratic Labour Party (SAP) in power.
**1969** Olof Palme became SAP leader and prime minister.
**1971** Constitution amended, creating a single-chamber *Riksdag*, the governing body.
**1975** Monarch's constitutional powers reduced.
**1976** Thorbjörn Fälldin, leader of the Centre Party, became prime minister, heading centre-right coalition.
**1982** SAP, led by Palme, returned to power.
**1985** SAP formed minority government, with Communist support.
**1986** Olof Palme murdered. Ingvar Carlsson became prime minister and SAP party leader.
**1988** SAP re-elected with reduced majority; Green Party increased its vote dramatically.
**1990** SAP government resigned. Sweden to apply for European Community membership.
**1991** Formal application for EC membership submitted.

---

**Switzerland (Swiss Confederation)**
(German **Schweiz**, French **Suisse**, Italian **Svizzera**)

**area** 41,300 sq km/15,946 sq mi
**capital** Bern
**towns** Zürich, Geneva, Lausanne; river port Basel (on the Rhine)
**physical** most mountainous country in Europe (Alps and Jura Mountains); highest peak Dufourspitze 4,634 m/15,203 ft in Appenines
**features** winter sports area of the upper valley of the river Inn (Engadine); lakes Maggiore, Lucerne, Geneva, Constance
**head of state and government** Flavio Cotti from 1991
**government** federal democratic republic
**political parties** Radical Democratic Party (FDP), radical, centre-left; Social Democratic party (SPS), moderate, left-of-centre; Christian Democratic Party (PDC), Christian, moderate, centrist; People's Party (SVP), centre-left; Liberal Party (PLS), federalist, centre-left; Green Party, ecological
**exports** electrical goods, chemicals, pharmaceuticals, watches, precision instruments, confectionery
**currency** Swiss franc (2.53 = £1 July 1991)
**population** (1990 est) 6,628,000; growth rate 0.2% p.a.
**life expectancy** men 74, women 82 (1989)

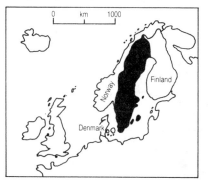

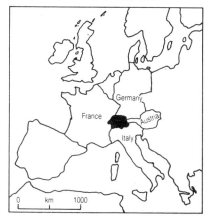

**language** German 65%, French 18%, Italian 12%, Romansch 1% (all official)
**religion** Roman Catholic 50%, Protestant 48%
**literacy** 99% (1989)
**GNP** $111 bn (1988); $26,309 per head (1987)

chronology
**1648** Became independent of the Holy Roman Empire.
**1798–1815** Helvetic Republic established by French Revolutionary armies.
**1847** Civil war resulted in greater centralization.
**1971** Women given the vote in federal elections.
**1984** First female cabinet minister appointed.
**1986** Referendum rejected proposal for membership of United Nations.
**1989** Referendum supported abolition of citizen army and military service requirements.

---

**Syria (Syrian Arab Republic)**
(al-Jamhuriya al-Arabya as-Suriya)

---

**area** 185,200 sq km/71,506 sq mi
**capital** Damascus
**towns** Aleppo, Homs, Hama; chief port Latakia
**physical** mountains alternate with fertile plains and desert areas; Euphrates River
**features** Mount Hermon, Golan Heights; crusader castles (Krak des Chevaliers); Phoenician city sites (Ugarit), ruins of ancient Palmyra
**head of state and government** Hafez al-Assad from 1971
**political system** socialist republic
**political parties** National Progressive Front (NPF), pro-Arab, socialist; Communist Action Party, socialist
**exports** cotton, cereals, oil, phosphates, tobacco
**currency** Syrian pound (Syr 34.12 = £1 July 1991)
**population** (1990 est) 12,471,000; growth rate 3.5% p.a.

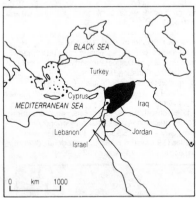

**life expectancy** men 67, women 69 (1989)
**language** Arabic 89% (official), Kurdish 6%, Armenian 3%
**religion** Sunni Muslim 74%; ruling minority Alawite, an Islamic sect; Druse; Christian 10%
**literacy** men 76%/women 43% (1985 est)
**GNP** $17 bn (1986); $702 per head

chronology
**1946** Achieved full independence from France.
**1958** Merged with Egypt to form the United Arab Republic (UAR).
**1961** UAR disintegrated.
**1967** Six-Day War resulted in the loss of territory to Israel.
**1970–71** Syria supported Palestinian guerrillas against Jordanian troops.

**1971** Following a bloodless coup, Hafez al-Assad became president.
**1973** Israel consolidated its control of the Golan Heights after the Yom Kippur War.
**1976** Substantial numbers of troops committed to the civil war in Lebanon.
**1978** Assad re-elected.
**1981–82** Further military engagements in Lebanon.
**1982** Islamic militant uprising suppressed; 5,000 dead.
**1984** Presidents Assad and Gemayel approved a plan for government of national unity in Lebanon.
**1985** Assad secured the release of US hostages held in an aircraft hijacked by extremist Shi'ite group. Assad re-elected.
**1987** Improved relations with USA and attempts to secure the release of western hostages in Lebanon.
**1989** Diplomatic relations with Morocco restored. Continued fighting in Lebanon.
**1990** Diplomatic relations with Britain restored.
**1991** President Assad agreed to US Middle East peace plan.

---

**Taiwan (Republic of China)**
(Chung Hua Min Kuo)

---

**area** 36,179 sq km/13,965 sq mi
**capital** Taipei
**towns** ports Keelung, Kaohsiung

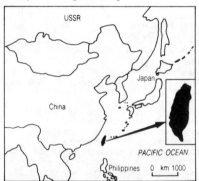

**physical** island (formerly Formosa) off People's Republic of China; mountainous, with lowlands in west
**features** Penghu (Pescadores), Jinmen (Quemoy), Mazu (Matsu) islands
**head of state** Lee Teng-hui from 1988
**head of government** Lee Huan from 1989
**political system** emergent democracy
**political parties** Nationalist Party of China (Kuomintang: KMT), anticommunist, Chinese nationalist; Democratic Progressive Party (DPP), centrist-pluralist, pro-self-determination grouping; Workers' Party (Kungtang), left-of-centre
**exports** textiles, steel, plastics, electronics
**currency** New Taiwan dollar (NT$44.12 = £1 July 1991)
**population** (1990) 20,454,000 (84% Taiwanese, 14% mainlanders); growth rate 1.4% p.a.
**life expectancy** 70 men, 75 women (1986)
**language** Mandarin Chinese (official); Taiwan, Hakka dialects
**religion** officially atheist; Taoist, Confucian, Buddhist, Christian
**literacy** 90% (1988)
**GNP** $119.1 bn; $6,200 per head (1988)

chronology
**1683** Taiwan (Formosa) annexed by China.
**1895** Ceded to Japan.
**1945** Recovered by China.

**1949** Flight of Nationalist government to Taiwan after Chinese communist revolution.
**1954** US-Taiwanese mutual defence treaty.
**1971** Expulsion from United Nations.
**1972** Commencement of legislature elections.
**1975** President Chiang Kai-shek died; replaced as Kuomintang leader by his son, Chiang Ching-kuo.
**1979** USA severed diplomatic relations and annulled security pact.
**1986** Opposition party to the nationalist Kuomintang formed.
**1987** Martial law lifted.
**1988** President Chiang Ching-kuo died; replaced by Taiwanese-born Lee Teng-hui.
**1989** Kuomintang won first free assembly elections.
**1990** Formal move towards normalization of relations with China.

## Tanzania (United Republic of)
(*Jamhuri ya Muungano wa Tanzania*)

**area** 945,000 sq km/364,865 sq mi
**capital** Dodoma
**towns** Zanzibar Town, Mwanza; chief port Dar es Salaam
**physical** central plateau; lakes in N and W; coastal plains; lakes Victoria, Tanganyika, and Niasa

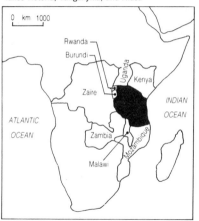

**features** comprises islands of Zanzibar and Pemba; Mount Kilimanjaro, 5,895 m/19,340 ft, the highest peak in Africa; Serengeti National Park, Olduvai Gorge; Ngorongoro Crater 14.5 km/9 mi across, 762 m/2,500 ft deep
**head of state and government** Ndugu Ali Hassan Mwinyi from 1985
**political system** one-party socialist republic
**political parties** Revolutionary Party of Tanzania (CCM), African, socialist
**exports** coffee, cotton, sisal, cloves, tea, tobacco
**currency** Tanzanian shilling (371.64 = £1 July 1991)
**population** (1990 est) 26,070,000; growth rate 3.5% p.a.
**life expectancy** men 49, women 54 (1989)
**language** Kiswahili, English (both official)
**religion** Muslim 35%, Christian 35%, traditional 30%
**literacy** 85% (1987)
**GNP** $4.9 bn; $258 per head (1987)

### chronology
**1920–46** Administered as a British League of Nations mandate.
**1946–62** Came under United Nations (UN) trusteeship.
**1961** Independence achieved from Britain, within the Commonwealth, with Julius Nyerere as prime minister.

**1962** Tanganyika became a republic with Nyerere as president.
**1964** Tanganyika and Zanzibar became the United Republic of Tanzania with Nyerere as president.
**1967** East African Community (EAC) formed. Arusha Declaration.
**1977** Revolutionary Party of Tanzania (CCM) proclaimed the only legal party. EAC dissolved.
**1979** Tanzanian troops sent to Uganda to help overthrow the president, Idi Amin.
**1984** Nyerere announced his retirement but stayed on as CCM leader. Prime Minister Edward Sokoine killed in a road accident.
**1985** Ali Hassan Mwinyi elected president.
**1990** Nyerere surrendered party leadership.

## Thailand (Kingdom of)
(*Prathet Thai* or *Muang-Thai*)

**area** 513,100 sq km/198,108 sq mi
**capital** and chief port Bangkok
**towns** Chiangmai, Nakhon Sawan river port
**physical** mountainous, semi-arid plateau in NE, fertile central region, tropical isthmus in S
**features** rivers Chao Phraya, Mekong, Salween; ancient ruins of Sukhothai and Ayurrhaya
**head of state** King Bhumibol Adulyadej from 1946

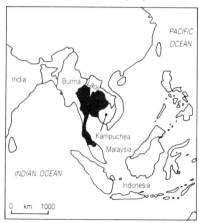

**head of government** Anand Panyarachun from 1991
**political system** emergent democracy
**political parties** Thai Nation (Chart Thai), conservative, pro-business; Democratic Party (Prachipat), right-of-centre, pro-monarchist; Social Action Party (Kij Sangkhom), right-of-centre; Citizen's Party (Rassadorn), conservative
**exports** rice, textiles, rubber, tin, rubies, sapphires
**currency** baht (41.00 = £1 July 1991)
**population** (1990 est) 54,890,000 (Thai 75%, Chinese 14%); growth rate 2% p.a.
**life expectancy** men 62, women 68 (1989)
**language** Thai and Chinese (both official); region dialects
**religion** Buddhist 95%, Muslim 4%
**literacy** 89% (1988)
**GNP** $52 bn (1988); $771 per head (1988)

### chronology
**1782** Siam absolutist dynasty commenced.
**1896** Anglo-French agreement recognized Siam as independent buffer state.
**1932** Constitutional monarchy established.
**1939** Name of Thailand adopted.
**1941–44** Japanese occupation.
**1947** Military seized power in coup.
**1972** Withdrawal of Thai troops from South Vietnam.

**1973** Military government overthrown.
**1976** Military reassumed control.
**1980** General Prem Tinsulanonda assumed power.
**1983** Civilian government formed; martial law maintained.
**1988** Prime Minister Prem resigned; replaced by Chatichai Choonhavan.
**1989** Thai pirates continued to murder, pillage, and kidnap Vietnamese 'boat people' at sea.
**1991** Military seized power in coup. Martial law ended.

## Togo (Republic of)
(*République Togolaise*)

**area** 56,800 sq km/21,930 sq mi
**capital** Lomé
**towns** Sokodé, Kpalimé
**physical** two savanna plains, divided by range of hills NE–SW; coastal lagoons and marsh

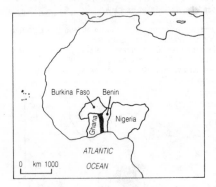

**features** mineral deposits (phosphates, bauxite, marble, iron ore, limestone); dry plains, forest, and arable land
**head of state and government** Etienne Gnassingbé Eyadéma from 1967
**political system** one-party socialist republic
**political parties** Assembly of the Tongolese People (RPT), nationalist, socialist
**exports** phosphates, cotton, cocoa, coffee,
**currency** franc CFA (498.25 = £1 July 1991)
**population** (1990 est) 3,566,000; growth rate 3% p.a.
**life expectancy** men 53, women 57 (1989)
**language** French (official), local languages
**religion** animist 46%, Catholic 28%, Muslim 17%, Protestant 9%
**literacy** men 53%/women 28% (1985 est)
**GNP** $1.3 bn (1987);     per head (1985)

**chronology**
**1885–1914** Togoland was a German protectorate until captured by Anglo-French forces.
**1922** Divided between Britain and France under League of Nations mandate.
**1946** Continued under United Nations trusteeship.
**1960** Independence achieved from France as the Republic of Togo with Sylvanus Olympio as head of state.
**1963** Olympio killed in a military coup. Nicolas Grunitzky became president.
**1967** Grunitzky replaced by Lt-Gen Etienne Gnassingbé Eyadéma in bloodless coup.
**1973** Assembly of Togolese People (RPT) formed as sole legal political party.
**1979** Eyadéma returned in election.
**1986** Attempted coup failed.
**1991** Constitutional talks promised, but progress restricted.

## Tonga (Kingdom of)
(*Pule'anga Fakatu'i 'o Tonga*)
or **Friendly Islands**

**area** 750 sq km/290 sq mi
**capital** Nuku'alofa (on Tongatapu island)
**physical** three groups of islands in SW Pacific, mostly coral formations, but actively volcanic in W
**features** of 170 islands in Tonga group, 36 are inhabited
**head of state and government** King Taufa'ahau Tupou IV from 1965
**political system** absolute monarchy
**political parties** none
**currency** Tongan dollar or pa'anga (T$2.11 = £1 July 1991)
**population** (1988) 95,000; growth rate 2.4% p.a.
**life expectancy** men 69, women 74 (1989)
**language** Tongan (official), English
**religion** Wesleyan 47%, Roman Catholic 14%, Free Church of Tonga 14%, Mormon 9%, Church of Tonga 9%
**literacy** 93% (1988)
**GNP** $65 million (1987); $430 per head

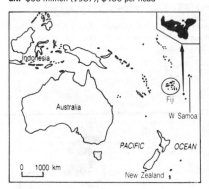

**chronology**
**1831** Tongan dynasty founded by Prince Taufa'ahau Tupou
**1900** Became a British protectorate.
**1965** Queen Salote died; succeeded by her son, King Taufa'ahau Tupou IV.
**1970** Independence achieved from Britain within the Commonwealth.

## Trinidad and Tobago (Republic of)

**area** Trinidad 4,828 sq km/1,864 sq mi and Tobago 300 sq km/116 sq mi
**capital** Port-of-Spain
**towns** San Fernando, Arima
**physical** comprises two main islands and some smaller ones; coastal swamps and hills E–W
**features** Pitch Lake, a self-renewing source of asphalt used by 16th-century explorer Walter Raleigh to repair his ships
**head of state** Noor Hassanali from 1987
**head of government** Arthur Robinson from 1986
**political system** democratic republic
**political parties** National Alliance for Reconstruction (NAR), nationalistic, left-of-centre; People's National Movement (PNM), nationalistic, moderate, centrist
**exports** oil, petroleum products, chemicals, sugar, cocoa
**currency** Trinidad and Tobago dollar (TT$6.90 = £1 July 1991)
**population** (1990 est) 1,270,000 (40% African descent, 40% Indian, 16% European, Chinese and others 2%), 1.2 million on Trinidad; growth rate 1.6% p.a.
**life expectancy** men 68, women 72 (1989)
**language** English (official), Hindi, French, Spanish

**religion** Roman Catholic 32%, Protestant 29%, Hindu 25%, Muslim 6%
**literacy** 97% (1988)
**GNP** $4.5 bn; $3,731 per head (1987)

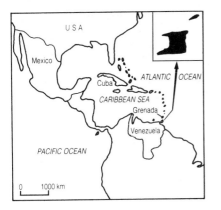

## chronology
**1888** Trinidad and Tobago united as a British colony.
**1956** People's National Movement (PNM) founded.
**1959** Granted internal self-government, with PNM leader Eric Williams as chief minister.
**1962** Independence achieved from Britain, within the Commonwealth, with Williams as prime minister.
**1976** Became a republic, with Ellis Clarke as president and Williams as prime minister.
**1981** Williams died and was succeeded by George Chambers, with Arthur Robinson as opposition leader.
**1986** Arthur Robinson became prime minister.
**1987** Noor Hassanali became president.
**1990** Attempted anti-government coup defeated.

## Tunisia (Tunisian Republic)
(al-Jumhuriya at-Tunisiya)

**area** 164,150 sq km/63,378 sq mi
**capital** and chief port Tunis
**towns** ports Sfax, Sousse, Bizerta
**physical** arable and forested land in N graduates towards desert in S

**features** fertile island of Jerba, linked to mainland by causeway (identified with island of lotus-eaters); Shott el Jerid salt lakes; holy city of Kairouan, ruins of Carthage
**head of state and government** Zine el Abdin Ben Ali from 1987
**political system** emergent democratic republic

**political parties** Constitutional Democratic Rally (RDC), nationalist, moderate, socialist
**exports** oil, phosphates, chemicals, textiles, food
**currency** dinar (1.61 = £1 July 1991)
**population** (1990 est) 8,094,000; growth rate 2% p.a.
**life expectancy** men 68, women 71 (1989)
**language** Arabic (official), French
**religion** Sunni Muslim 95%, Jewish, Christian
**literacy** men 68%/women 41% (1985 est)
**GNP** $9.6 bn (1987); $1,163 per head (1986)

## chronology
**1956** Independence achieved from France as a monarchy, with Habib Bourguiba as prime minister.
**1957** Became a republic with Bourguiba as president.
**1975** Bourguiba made president for life.
**1985** Diplomatic relations with Libya severed.
**1987** Bourguiba removed Prime Minister Rashed Sfar and appointed Zine el Abdin Ben Ali. Ben Ali declared Bourguiba incompetent and seized power.
**1988** Constitutional changes towards democracy announced. Diplomatic relations with Libya restored.
**1989** Government party, RCD, won all assembly seats in general election.
**1991** Crackdown on religious fundamentalists.

## Turkey (Republic of)
(Türkiye Cumhuriyeti)

**area** 779,500 sq km/300,965 sq mi
**capital** Ankara
**towns** ports Istanbul and Izmir
**physical** central plateau surrounded by mountains

**features** Bosporus and Dardanelles; Mount Ararat; Taurus Mountains in SW (highest peak Kaldi Dağ, 3,734 m/ 12,255 ft); sources of rivers Euphrates and Tigris in E; archaeological sites include Catal Hüyük, Ephesus, and Troy; rock villages of Cappadocia; historic towns (Antioch, Iskenderun, Tarsus)
**head of state** Turgot Ozal from 1989
**head of government** Vildirim Akbulut from 1989
**political system** democratic republic
**political parties** Motherland Party (ANAP), Islamic, nationalist, right-of-centre; Social Democratic Populist Party (SDPP), moderate, left-of-centre; True Path Party (TPP), centre-right
**exports** cotton, hazelnuts, citrus, tobacco, dried fruit, chromium ores
**currency** Turkish lira (7,027.94 = £1 July 1991)
**population** (1990 est) 56,549,000 (85% Turkish, 12% Kurdish); growth rate 2.1% p.a.
**life expectancy** men 63, women 66 (1989)
**language** Turkish (official); Kurdish, Arabic
**religion** Sunni Muslim 98%

**literacy** men 86%/women 62% (1985)
**GNP** $62 bn (1987); $1,160 per head (1986)

**chronology**
**1919–22** Turkish War of Independence provoked by Greek occupation of Izmir. Mustafa Kemal (Atatürk), leader of nationalist congress, defeated Italian, French, and Greek forces.
**1923** Treaty of Lausanne established Turkey as independent republic under Kemal. Westernization began.
**1950** First free elections; Adnan Menderes became prime minister.
**1960** Menderes executed after military coup by Gen Cemal Gürsel.
**1965** Suleyman Demirel became prime minister.
**1971** Army forced Demirel to resign.
**1973** Civilian rule returned under Bulent Ecevit.
**1974** Turkish troops sent to protect Turkish community in Cyprus.
**1975** Demirel returned to head a right-wing coalition.
**1978** Ecevit returned, in the face of economic difficulties and factional violence.
**1979** Demeril returned. Violence grew.
**1980** Army took over, and Bulent Ulusu became prime minister. Harsh repression of political activists attracted international criticism.
**1982** New constitution adopted.
**1983** Ban on political activity lifted. Turgut Ozal became prime minister.
**1987** Ozal maintained majority in general election.
**1988** improved relations and talks with Greece.
**1989** Turgot Ozal elected president. Application for EC membership refused.

## Tuvalu (South West Pacific State of)

**area** 25 sq km/9.5 sq mi
**capital** Funafuti
**physical** low coral atolls forming a chain of 579 km/650 mi in the SW Pacific
**features** the name means 'cluster of eight' islands (there are actually nine, but one is very small)
**head of state** Elizabeth II from 1978 represented by governor-general
**head of government** Bikenibeu Paeniu from 1989
**political system** liberal democracy
**political parties** none, members are elected to parliament as independents
**exports** phosphates, copra, handicrafts, stamps
**currency** Australian dollar (2.11 = £1 July 1991)
**population** (1990 est) 9,000 (Polynesian); growth rate 3.4% p.a.
**life expectancy** 60 men, 63 women (1989)
**language** Tuvaluan, English
**religion** Christian, (Protestant)
**literacy** 96% (1985)

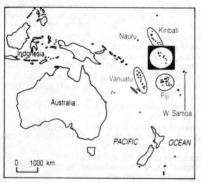

**GNP** $3.2 m (1985); $372 per head

**chronology**
**1892** Became a British protectorate called the Ellice Islands.
**1978** Independence achieved from Britain within the Commonwealth with Toaripi Lauti as prime minister.
**1981** Dr Tomasi Puapua replaced Lauti as premier.
**1986** Islanders rejected proposal for republican status.
**1989** Bikenibeu Paeniu elected new prime minister.

## Uganda (Republic of)

**area** 236,600 sq km/91,351 sq mi
**capital** Kampala
**towns** Jinja, M'Bale, Entebbe, Masaka

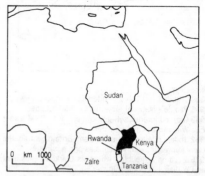

**physical** plateau with mountains in W; forest and grassland; arid in NE
**features** Ruwenzori Range (Mt Margherita 5,110 m/16,765 ft); national parks with wildlife (chimpanzees, crocodiles, Nile perch to 70 kg/160 lb); Owen Falls on White Nile where it leaves Lake Victoria; Lake Albert in W
**head of state and government** Yoweri Museveni from 1986
**political system** emergent democratic republic
**political parties** National Resistance Movement (NRM), left-of-centre; Democratic Party (DP), centre-left; Conservative Party (CP), centre-right; Uganda People's Congress (UPC), left-of-centre; Uganda Freedom Movement (UFM), left-of-centre
**exports** coffee, cotton, tea, copper
**currency** Uganda new shilling (1,136.59 = £1 July 1991)
**population** (1990 est) 17,593,000 (largely the Baganda, from whom the country is named; also Langi and Acholi, some surviving Pygmies); growth rate 3.3% p.a.
**life expectancy** men 49, women 51 (1989)
**language** English (official); Kiswahili, Luganda
**religion** Roman Catholic 33%, Protestant 33%, Muslim 6%, animist
**literacy** men 70%/women 45% (1985 est)
**GNP** $3.6 bn (1987); $220 per head

**chronology**
**1962** Independence achieved from Britain within the Commonwealth with Milton Obote as prime minister.
**1963** Proclaimed a federal republic with King Mutesa II as president.
**1966** King Mutesa ousted in coup led by Obote, who ended the federal status and became executive president.
**1969** All opposition parties banned after assassination attempt on Obote.
**1971** Obote overthrown in army coup led by Maj-Gen Idi Amin; ruthlessly dictatorial regime established; nearly 49,000 Ugandan Asians expelled; over 300,000 oppo-

nents of regime killed.
**1978** Amin forced to leave country by opponents backed by Tanzanian troops. Provisional government set up with Yusuf Lule as president. Lule replaced by Godfrey Binaisa.
**1978–79** Fighting broke out against Tanzanian troops.
**1980** Binaisa overthrown by army. Elections held and Milton Obote returned to power.
**1985** After opposition by National Resistance Army (NRA), and indiscipline in army, Obote ousted by Brig Basilio Okello; power-sharing agreement entered into with NRA leader Yoweri Museveni.
**1986** Agreement ended; Museveni became president, heading broad-based coalition government.

---

## Union of Soviet Socialist Republics (USSR)
(*Soyuz Sovyetskikh Sotsialisticheskikh Respublik*)

---

**area** 22,402,200 sq km/8,590,274 sq mi
**capital** Moscow
**towns** Kiev, Tashkent, Kharkov, Gorky, Novosibirsk, Minsk, Sverdlovsk, Kuibyshev, Chelyabinsk, Dnepropetrovsk, Tbilisi; ports Leningrad, Odessa, Baku, Archangel, Murmansk, Vladivostok, Vostochny, Rostov, Riga
**physical** Ural Mountains separate European and Asian plain; Caucasus Mountains in S between Black Sea and Caspian Sea, mountain ranges in SE; coniferous forests and tundra in Siberia; desert in Central Asia
**features** Pamirs and Altai mountains; Kara Kum Desert; Aral Sea; rivers (in Europe) Don, Dnieper, Volga, Dvina, Pechora, Dneister, Neva, Kuban, and (in Asia) Ob, Yenisei, Lena, Amur, Amu Darya and Syr Darya; lakes Ladoga, Onega, Baikal, and Balkhash; largest country in the world
**head of state and government** Mikhail Gorbachev from 1988
**political system** communism
**political parties** Communist Party of the Soviet Union (CPSU); Russian United Workers' Front, conservative; Democratic Union in Moscow, pluralist, intelligentsialed

**exports** cotton, timber, iron and steel, non-ferrous metals electrical equipment, machinery, oil and natural gas
**currency** rouble (0.99 official rate, 2.97 commercial rate = £1 July 1991)
**population** (1990 est) 290,939,000 (125 nationalities; 52% Russian, 17% Ukrainian); growth rate 1% p.a.
**life expectancy** men 64, women 74 (1989)
**language** Slavic 75% (Russian, Ukrainian, Byelorussian), Altaic 12% (Turkish, Mongolian, others), Uralian 3%, Caucasian 2%
**religion** atheist 60%; Russian Orthodox 22%, Sunni Muslim 11% Protestant 2%, Roman Catholic 1%, Jewish 1%
**literacy** 99% (1989)
**GNP** $734 bn (1984); $3,000 per head (1987)

### chronology
**1917** Revolution: provisional democratic government established by Mensheviks. Communist takeover by Bolsheviks under Lenin.

**1922** Soviet Union established.
**1924** Death of Lenin.
**1928** Stalin emerged as absolute ruler after ousting Trotsky.
**1930s** Purges of Stalin's opponents took place.
**1939** Nonaggression pact signed with Germany.
**1941–45** Great Patriotic War against Germany.
**1949** Comecon created.
**1953** Stalin died. Beria removed. 'Collective leadership' in power.
**1955** Warsaw Pact created.
**1956** Khrushchev made February 'secret speech'. Hungarian uprising.
**1957–58** Ousting of 'anti-party' group and Bulganin.
**1960** Sino-Soviet rift.
**1962** Cuban missile crisis.
**1964** Khrushchev ousted by new 'collective leadership'.
**1968** Czechoslovakia invaded.
**1969** Sino-Soviet border war.
**1972** Salt I arms-limitation agreed with USA.
**1977** Brezhnev elected president.
**1979** Salt II. Soviet invasion of Afghanistan.
**1980** Kosygin replaced as prime minister by Tikhonov.
**1980–81** Polish crisis.
**1982** Deaths of Suslov and Brezhnev. Andropov became Communist Party leader.
**1984** Chernenko succeeded Andropov.
**1985** Gorbachev succeeded Chernenko and introduced wide-ranging reforms. Gromyko appointed president.
**1986** Gorbachev's power consolidated at 27th Party Congress. Chernobyl nuclear disaster.
**1987** USSR and USA agreed to scrap intermediate-range nuclear missiles. Boris Yeltsin, Moscow party chief, dismissed for criticizing the slow pace of reform.
**1988** Nationalists challenged in Kazakhstan, Baltic republics, Armenia, and Azerbaijan. Earthquake killed 100,000 in Armenia. Constitution radically overhauled; private sector encouraged at Special All-Union Party Conference. Gorbachev replaced Gromyko as head of state.
**1989** Troops withdrew from Afghanistan. General election held, with candidate choice for new congress of People's Deputies. 20 killed in nationalist riots in Georgia. 74 members of CPSU Central Committee removed, 1/4 of the total. Gorbachev elected state president; conservative communist regimes in Eastern Europe overthrown. Relations with Chinese normalized. Lithuania allowed multiparty elections. Gorbachev and US president Bush declared end of Cold War; Gorbachev renounced 'Brezhnev doctrine'; Soviet Union admitted invasion of Afghanistan and intervention in Czechoslovakia to have been mistakes; Gorbachev opposed calls to modify Soviet constitution; economic problems mounted; Lithuanian Communist Party declared independence from Moscow.
**1990** Troops sent to Azerbaijan during civil war with Armenia. CPSU Central Committee agreed to end one-party rule. Gorbachev opposed independence of Baltic republics; sanctions imposed on Lithuania; elections showed strength of liberal Communists. Summit meeting with President Bush.
**1991** Pact between Moscow and 9 of the 15 republics, aimed at achieving stable relations. Boris Yeltsin elected president of the Russian Federation. Gorbachev and Yeltsin agreed to cooperate. Eduard Shevardnadze left the government and the Communist Party. Leningrad changed its name back to St Petersburg. Gorbachev addressed the G7 leaders and obtained promise of technical help from the West. **19 Aug:** right-wing coup staged by eight senior government officials (including vice president Gennady Yanayev and prime minister Valentine Pavlov); Gorbachev placed under house arrest in the Crimea; Boris Yeltsin led the resistance in Moscow. **21 Aug:** the coup collapsed in the face of public defiance; Gorbachev returned to Moscow; coup leaders arrested. **23 Aug:** Gorbachev resigned as head of the CPSU. CPSU dissolved itself. Estonia, Lithuania

## NATIONALISM IN THE USSR—THE UNION FRACTURES

Incorporating one-sixth of the world's land surface and embracing more than 100 language groups, the Soviet Union has existed as a vast multi-ethnic federation which, according to its 1977 constitution, was formed through the 'free self-determination ... and ... voluntary union of equal Soviet Socialist Republics'. In truth, however, it represents the last of the great European continental empires. The southernmost territories of Central Asia and Transcaucasia were secured through Tsarist military conquest during the 18th and 19th centuries, while the Baltic states, Moldova (formerly Moldavia), and the western Ukraine were acquired in 1939–40, through a combination of cynical diplomacy and power politics. The tight rein imposed upon nationalist dissent meant that the USSR escaped the wave of decolonization that engulfed the British, French, Dutch, Belgian, and Portuguese empires. But with the accession to power of the reformist Mikhail Gorbachev in 1985, the 'nationality question' came increasingly to dominate the Soviet political scene.

Two factors accounted for this development. First, with the new *glasnost* (openness) initiative, hitherto suppressed ethnic grievances and feelings of national identity came to be publicly voiced. Second, Gorbachev's promotion of gradual democratization enabled nationalist organizations to be formed openly and to secure a measure of local authority.

Gorbachev, while willing to sanction increased decentralization of political and economic power, was resolutely opposed to any rupturing of the inherited union. As a 'reform communist', he looked down on nationalism as an archaic 'bourgeois reactionary' philosophy. He believed that his reforms would win sufficient support to outflank the nationalist challenge. Events proved his optimism misplaced.

Mounting inter-ethnic tension first flared up early in 1988, with the outbreak of violence between Christian Armenians and Muslim Azerbaijanis in the enclave of Nagorno-Karabakh. So serious was this conflict that for much of 1989 the autonomous region had to be placed under Moscow rule and subsequently, in Jan 1990, Red Army forces were sent to reimpose order in the Azerbaijani capital of Baku, at the cost of more than 70 civilian lives. Inter-ethnic conflicts also arose in South Ossetia and Abkhazia in Transcaucasia, in the Gagauz and Dnetsr valley areas of Moldova, in Crimea, and across Turkestan.

Even more serious was the growing strength, from 1988, of independence-minded 'popular front' groupings at the republic level, particularly in the three Baltic states of Lithuania, Latvia, and Estonia, whose citizens had long contested their forced annexation by Stalin in 1940. The Baltics' parliaments, led by Lithuania in March 1990, issued independence declarations, adopted new national flags, renamed streets and cities, and built up autonomous paramilitary forces, discouraging conscription into the Red Army.

Moscow responded by formally annulling these independence declarations, imposing an economic blockade on Lithuania from April 1990, and then, in Jan 1991, unleashing military force in the Lithuanian capital, Vilnius. Despite these actions, other republics, including Armenia, Georgia, and Moldova, made it clear that they were determined to follow the Baltics' lead and make a bid for separate statehood. By the close of 1990 all fifteen Soviet republics, as well as the autonomous republics, had formally placed their laws above those of the federation.

From 1989 a second problem emerged, the increasing divergence of economic and social policies. In the Baltics, legislation was adopted to reinstall private ownership of land and property, and in the giant Russian Federation (RSFSR), led by the lapsed communist Boris Yeltsin, an ambitious programme, entailing a 500-day transition to a market economy, was approved. More generally, there were moves towards economic isolation, with restrictions placed upon the movement of goods between republics, financial contributions to the centre reduced, and plans framed for separate currencies. All this exacerbated the mounting economic crisis in what had previously been a tightly integrated federation.

As 1991 progressed, the nationalities dispute and 'war of laws' between Moscow and the republics moved to crisis point. In the spring, after briefly siding with conservative forces, Gorbachev framed a new Union Treaty and federalized government structure, based upon a much fuller devolution of economic and political policy-making to the republics. Though rejected by the Baltics, Armenia, Georgia, and Moldova, it was approved by the people of the Slavic and Central Asian core of the USSR in a March referendum. So concerned were 'old guard' elements within the Communist Party (CPSU), military, and KGB that on 19 Aug 1991, a day before the new Union Treaty was to be signed, a centralizing *coup d'état* was desperately launched. It was, however, abortive.

In large measure the coup was thwarted because the USSR's federal structure (by now partially democratized) provided rival centres of power (most notably the RSFSR) around which popular resistance could coalesce. Its failure dramatically accelerated the union's fracturing. The CPSU, the Soviet empire's essential glue, was ignominiously disbanded; Byelorussia and the Ukraine joined the list of states declaring their independence; and the Baltics began to be accorded international recognition. What remained uncertain was the form that any successor federation of the remaining republics of the USSR would take, and whether those republics that had chosen independence would seek to uphold residual economic and security ties with their former federal partners. But of greatest concern was the fate of ethnic minorities, particularly Russian, within the republics, since it was feared that their mistreatment might provide the pretext for forced 'boundary redrawing'.

and Latvia declared themselves independent and were recognized by the EC countries. Declarations of independence by other republics signalled the dissolution of the USSR, a process formally recognized by the Congress of People's Deputies voting itself out of existence 5 Sept.

## PEOPLE OF THE YEAR

Eduard Shevardnadze's dramatic departure from the Soviet government, Dec 1990, signalled the seriousness of the power struggle that was taking place between reform-democrats, nationalists, and old-guard conservatives within the USSR. From the summer of 1990, as inter-ethnic conflict and economic crisis worsened, the conservatives and the KGB launched a concerted counterthrust. It was so successful that as the winter of 1990–91 approached, glasnost, perestroika, and the more relaxed approach to foreign affairs were beginning to slide. In its place a new authoritarianism was emerging, with President Gorbachev becoming a prisoner of the right. Increasingly blamed by resurgent conservatives for 'losing' Eastern Europe and for allowing, as witnessed during the Gulf Conflict, the re-establishment of a new US global hegemony, and opposed to the anti-nationalist military crackdown in the Baltic States, Shevardnadze decided to resign. The legacy he left behind was, however, outstanding: that of a far less politically and militarily divided world, as a cooperative new world order replaced the dangerous bipolarity of the Cold War era.

## United Arab Emirates (UAE)

(*Ittihad al-Imarat al-Arabiyah* federation of the emirates of Abu Dhabi, Ajman, Dubai, Fujairah, Sharjah, Umm al Qaiwain, Ras al Khaimah)

**total area** 83,657 sq km/32,292 sq mi
**capital** Abu Dhabi
**towns** chief port Dubai

**physical** desert and flat coastal plain; mountains in E
**features** linked by their dependence on oil revenues
**head of state and of government** Zayed Bin Sultan al-Nahayan of Abu Dhabi from 1971
**political system** absolutism
**political parties** none
**exports** oil, natural gas, fish, dates
**currency** UAE dirham (5.95 = £1 July 1991)
**population** (1990 est) 2,250,000 (10% nomadic); growth rate 6.1% p.a.
**life expectancy** men 68, women 72 (1989)
**language** Arabic (official); Farsi, Hindi, Urdu
**religion** Muslim 96%, Christian, Hindu
**literacy** 68% (1989)
**GNP** $22 bn (1987); $11,900 per head

## chronology
**1952** Trucial Council established.
**1971** Federation of Arab Emirates formed; later dissolved. Six Trucial States formed United Arab Emirates, with ruler of Abu Dhabi, Sheik Zayed, as president.
**1972** The seventh state joined.
**1976** Sheik Zayed threatened to relinquish presidency unless progress towards centralization became more rapid.
**1985** Diplomatic and economic links with USSR and China established.
**1987** Diplomatic relations with Egypt restored.

## United Kingdom of Great Britain and Northern Ireland (UK)

**area** 244,100 sq km/94,247 sq mi
**capital** London
**towns** Birmingham, Glasgow, Leeds, Sheffield, Liverpool, Manchester, Edinburgh, Bradford, Bristol, Belfast, Newcastle-upon-Tyne, Cardiff

**physical** became separated from European continent c. 6000 BC; rolling landscape, increasingly mountainous towards the N, with Grampian Mountains in Scotland, Pennines in N England, Cambrian Mountains in Wales; rivers include Thames, Severn, and Spey
**territories** Anguilla, Bermuda, British Antarctic Territory, British Indian Ocean Territory, British Virgin Islands, Cayman Islands, Falkland Islands, Gibraltar, Hong Kong (until 1997), Montserrat, Pitcairn Islands, St Helena and Dependencies (Ascension, Tristan da Cunha), Turks and Caicos Islands
**features** milder climate than N Europe because of Gulf Stream; considerable rainfall. Nowhere further than 120 km/74.5 mi from sea; indented coastline, various small islands
**head of state** Elizabeth II from 1952
**head of government** John Major from 1990
**political system** liberal democracy
**political parties** Conservative and Unionist Party, right-of-centre; Labour Party, moderate, left-of-centre; Social and Liberal Democrats, centre-left; Scottish National Party (SNP), Scottish nationalist; Plaid Cymru (Welsh Nationalist Party), Welsh nationalist; Official Ulster Unionist Party (OUP), Northern Ireland moderate right-of-centre; Democratic Unionist Party (DUP), Northern Ireland, right-of-centre; Social Democratic Labour Party (SDLP), Northern Ireland, moderate, left-of-centre; Ulster People's Unionist Party (UPUP), Northern Ireland, militant right-of-centre; Sinn Féin, Northern Ireland, pro-united Ireland; Green Party, ecological
**exports** cereals, rape, sugar beet, potatoes, meat and meat products, poultry, dairy products, electronic and

telecommunications equipment, engineering equipment and scientific instruments, oil and gas, petrochemicals, pharmaceuticals, fertilizers, film and television programmes
**currency** pound sterling (£)
**population** (1990 est) 57,121,000 (81.5% English, 9.6% Scottish, 1.9% Welsh, 2.4% Irish, 1.8% Ulster); growth rate 0.1% p.a.
**religion** Christian (55% Protestant, 10% Roman Catholic); Muslim, Jewish, Hindu, Sikh
**life expectancy** men 72, women 78 (1989)
**language** English, Welsh, Gaelic
**literacy** 99% (1989)
**GNP** $758 bn; $13,329 per head (1988)

**chronology**
**1707** Act of Union between England and Scotland under Queen Anne.
**1721** Robert Walpole unofficially first prime minister, under George I.
**1783** Loss of North American colonies that form USA; Canada retained.
**1801** Act of Ireland united Britain and Ireland.
**1819** Peterloo massacre: cavalry charged a meeting of supporters of parliamentary reform.
**1832** Great Reform Bill became law, shifting political power from upper to middle class.
**1846** Corn Laws repealed by Robert Peel.
**1848** Chartist working-class movement formed.
**1851** Great Exhibition in London.
**1867** Second Reform Bill, extending the franchise, introduced by Disraeli and passed.
**1906** Liberal victory; programme of social reform.
**1911** Powers of House of Lords curbed.
**1914** Irish Home Rule Bill introduced.
**1914–18** World War I.
**1916** Lloyd George became prime minister.
**1920** Home Rule Act incorporated NE of Ireland (Ulster) into the United Kingdom of Great Britain and Northern Ireland.
**1921** Ireland, except for Ulster, became a dominion (Irish Free State, later Eire, 1937).
**1924** First Labour government led by Ramsay MacDonald.
**1926** General Strike.
**1931** National government; unemployment reached 3 million.
**1939** World War II began.
**1940** Winston Churchill became head of coalition government.
**1945** Labour government under Clement Attlee; welfare state established.
**1951** Conservatives defeated Labour.
**1956** Suez crisis.
**1964** Labour victory under Harold Wilson.
**1970** Conservatives under Edward Heath defeated Labour.
**1972** Parliament prorogued in Northern Ireland; direct rule from Westminster began.
**1973** UK joined European Community.
**1974** Three-day week, coal strike; Wilson replaced Heath.
**1976** James Callaghan replaced Wilson as prime minister.
**1977** Liberal-Labour pact.
**1979** Victory for Conservatives under Margaret Thatcher.
**1981** Formation of Social Democratic Party (SDP). Riots occurred in inner cities.
**1982** Unemployment over 3 million. Falklands War.
**1983** Thatcher re-elected.
**1984–85** Coal strike, the longest in British history.
**1986** Abolition of metropolitan counties.
**1987** Thatcher re-elected for third term.
**1988** Liberals and most of SDP merged into the Social and Liberal Democrats, leaving a splinter SDP. Inflation and interest rates rose.
**1989** The Green Party polled 2 million votes in the European elections.
**1990** Riots as poll tax introduced in England. Troops sent to the Persian Gulf following Iraq's invasion of Kuwait. British hostages held in Iraq, later released. Britain joined European exchange-rate mechanism. Thatcher replaced by John Major as Conservative leader and prime minister.
**1991** British troops took part in US-led war against Iraq under United Nations umbrella.

## United States of America (USA)

**area** 9,368,900 sq km/3,618,770 sq mi
**capital** Washington DC
**towns** New York, Los Angeles, Chicago, Philadelphia, Detroit, San Francisco, Washington, Dallas, San Diego, San Antonio, Houston, Boston, Baltimore, Phoenix, Indianapolis, Memphis, Honolulu, San José

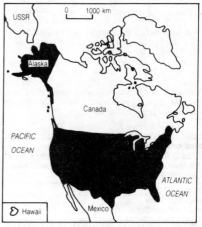

**physical** topography and vegetation from tropical (Hawaii) to arctic (Alaska); mountain ranges parallel with E and W coasts, and the Rocky Mountains separate rivers emptying into the Pacific from those flowing into the Gulf of Mexico; Great Lakes in N; rivers include Hudson, Mississippi, Missouri, Colorado, Columbia, Snake, Rio Grande, Ohio; Death Valley (282 ft/86 m below sea level, the lowest point in the W hemisphere)
**features** Grand Canyon National Park (AZ); Yosemite and Sequoia national parks, Hollywood (CA); Everglades National Park, John F Kennedy Space Center at Cape Canaveral, Disney World theme park (FL); Niagara Falls, Adirondacks (NY); the White House, Lincoln Memorial, Smithsonian Institute, Library of Congress (Washington DC)
**territories** the commonwealths of Puerto Rico and Northern Marianas; the federated states of Micronesia; Guam, the US Virgin Islands, American Samoa, Wake Island, Midway Islands, Marshall Islands, Belau, and Johnston and Sand Islands
**head of state and of government** George Bush from 1989
**political system** liberal democracy
**political parties** Democratic Party liberal, centre; Republican Party, centre-right
**currency** US dollar (US$1.61 = £1 July 1991)
**population** (1990 est) 250,372,000 (ethnic minorities include 26,500,000 black, c. 20,000,000 Hispanic, and 1,000,000 American Indians, of whom 50% concentrated in Arizona, California, New Mexico, North Carolina, Oklahoma); growth rate 0.9% p.a.
**life expectancy** men 72, women 79 (1989)
**language** English; Spanish
**religion** Protestant 52%; Roman Catholic 37%; Jewish

4%; Mormons 3%; Eastern Orthodox churches 3%
**literacy** 99% (1989)
**GNP** $3,855 bn (1983); $13,451 per head

**chronology**
**1776** Declaration of Independence.
**1787** US constitution drawn up.
**1789** Washington elected as first president.
**1803** Louisiana Purchase.
**1812–14** War of 1812 with England, arising from commercial disputes caused by Britain's struggle with Napoleon.
**1819** Florida purchased from Spain.
**1836** The battle of the Alamo, Texas, won by Mexico.
**1841** First wagon train left Missouri for California.
**1846–48** Mexican War resulted in cession to USA of Arizona, California, Colorado (part), Nevada, New Mexico, Texas, and Utah.
**1846** Mormons, under Brigham Young, founded Salt Lake City, Utah.
**1848** California gold rush.
**1860** Lincoln elected president.
**1861–65** Civil War between North and South.
**1865** Slavery abolished. Lincoln assassinated.
**1867** Alaska bought from Russia.
**1890** Battle of Wounded Knee, the last major battle between American Indians and US troops.
**1898** War with Spain ended with the Spanish cession of Philippines, Puerto Rico, and Guam; it was agreed that Cuba be independent.
**1898** Hawaii annexed.
**1917–18** USA entered World War I.
**1919–1921** Wilson's 14 Points become base for League of Nations.
**1920** Women achieved the vote.
**1924** American Indians made citizens by Congress.
**1929** Wall Street stock-market crash.
**1933** F D Roosevelt's New Deal to alleviate the Depression put into force.
**1941–45** The Japanese attack on Pearl Harbor Dec 1941 precipitated US entry into World War II.
**1945** The USA ends war in the Pacific by dropping A-bombs on Hiroshima and Nagasaki, Japan.
**1950–53** US involvement in Korean war. McCarthy anti-Communist investigations (HUAC) became a 'witch hunt'.
**1954** Civil Rights legislation began with segregation ended in public schools.
**1957** Civil Rights bill on voting.
**1958** First US satellite in orbit.
**1961** Bay of Pigs abortive CIA-backed invasion of Cuba.
**1963** Kennedy assassinated; L B Johnson assumed the presidency.
**1964–68** 'Great Society' civil-rights and welfare measures in the Omnibus Civil Rights bill.
**1964–75** US involvement in Vietnam War.
**1965** US intervention in Dominican Republic.
**1969** First human on the Moon.
**1973** OPEC oil embargo almost crippled US industry and consumers. Inflation began.
**1973–74** Watergate scandal began in effort to re-elect Nixon and ended just before impeachment; Nixon resigned as president; replaced by Gerald Ford, who 'pardoned' Nixon.
**1975** Final US withdrawal from Vietnam.
**1979** US-Chinese diplomatic relations normalized.
**1979–80** Iranian hostage crisis; relieved by Reagan concessions and released on his inauguration day Jan 1981.
**1981** Space shuttle mission was successful.
**1983** US invasion of Grenada.
**1986** 'Irangate' scandal over secret US government arms sales to Iran, with proceeds to anti-government Contra guerrillas in Nicaragua.
**1987** Reagan and Gorbachev signed INF treaty. Wall Street stock-market crash caused by programme trad-

ing.
**1988** USA became world's largest debtor nation, owing $532 billion, in Republican bid to control Congress under Reagan and Bush.
**1989** Bush met Gorbachev at Malta, declared end to Cold War; high-level delegation sent to China amid severe criticism; large troop reductions and budget cuts announced for US military; US invaded Panama, Noriega taken into custody.
**1990** Bush and Gorbachev met. South Africa's Nelson Mandela freed in South Africa and toured USA. Troops sent to Middle East following Iraq's invasion of Kuwait.
**1991 Jan:** USA led UN-backed coalition forces against Iraq; liberation of Kuwait achieved in Feb. **July:** Presidents Bush and Gorbachev signed START treaty; **Aug:** President Bush recognized independence of Baltic nations.

---

### PEOPLE OF THE YEAR

The US has a special regard for success in battle. In 1991 a new American military hero was acclaimed: General H Norman Schwarzkopf. Set for retirement in the summer of 1991 after 35 distinguished years, which earned him two Purple Hearts and Three Silver Stars during two tours of Vietnam, 'Stormin' Norman' became a household name during the Gulf War. As Supreme Commander of the Allied forces (a disparate 28-member military coalition), he planned and executed a blitzkrieg campaign: 'Desert Storm', which sustained remarkably few allied casualties. With victory secured, he emerged in March 1991 with a national approval rating in excess of 90%, higher than that of President Bush. Above all, Schwarzkopf was popular with his troops and belying his 'Stormin'' image, was a cautious, calculating commander determined to avoid a 'second Vietnam'.

---

**Uruguay (Oriental Republic of)**
(*República Oriental del Uruguay*)

**area** 176,200 sq km/68,031 sq mi
**capital** Montevideo
**physical** grassy plains (pampas) and low hills

**features** rivers Negro, Uruguay, Rio de la Planta
**head of state and of government** Luis Lacalle Herrera from 1989
**political system** democratic republic
**political parties** Colorado Party (PC), progressive, centre-left; National (Blanco) Party (PN), traditionalist, right-of-

centre; Amplio Front (FA), moderate, left-wing
**exports** meat and meat products, leather, wool, textiles
**currency** nuevo peso (3,198.30 = £1 July 1991)
**population** (1990 est) 3,002,000 (Spanish, Italian; mestizo, mulatto, black); growth rate 0.7% p.a.
**life expectancy** men 68, women 75 (1989)
**language** Spanish
**religion** Roman Catholic 66%
**literacy** 96% (1984)
**GNP** $7.5 bn; $2,470 per head (1988)

**chronology**
**1825** Independence declared from Brazil.
**1930** First constitution adopted.
**1956** Blanco party in power, with Jorge Pacheco Areco as president.
**1972** Colorado Party returned, with Juan Maria Bordaberry Arocena as president.
**1976** Bordaberry deposed by army; Dr Méndez Manfredini became president.
**1984** Violent anti-government protests after ten years of repressive rule.
**1985** Agreement reached between the army and political leaders for return to constitutional government. Colorado Party won general election; Dr Julio Maria Sanguinetti became president.
**1986** Government of national accord established under President Sanguinetti's leadership.
**1989** Luis Lacalle elected president.

## Vatican City State
(*Stato della Città del Vaticano*)

**area** 0.4 sq km/109 acres
**physical** forms an enclave in the heart of Rome, Italy
**features** Vatican Palace, official residence of the pope; basilica and square of St Peter's; churches in and near Rome; the pope's summer villa at Castel Gandolfo; the world's smallest state

**head of state and government** John Paul II from 1978
**political system** absolute Catholic
**currency** Vatican City lira; Italian lira (2,187.00 = £1 July 1991)
**population** (1985) 1,000
**language** Latin (official), Italian
**religion** Roman Catholic

**chronology**
**1929** Three treaties recognized sovereignty of the pope.
**1947** New Italian constitution confirmed the sovereignty of the Vatican City State.
**1978** John Paul II became the first non-Italian pope for more than 400 years.
**1985** New concordat signed under which Roman

Catholicism ceased to be the state religion.

## Venezuela (Republic of)
(*República de Venezuela*)

**area** 912,100 sq km/352,162 sq mi
**capital** Caracas
**towns** Barquisimeto, Valencia; port Maracaibo
**physical** Andes Mountains and Lake Maracaibo in NW; central plains (llanos); delta of river Orinoco in E; Guiana Highlands in SE
**features** Angel Falls, world's highest waterfall
**head of state and of government** Carlos Andrés Pérez from 1988
**government** federal democratic republic
**political parties** Democratic Action Party (AD), moderate, left-of-centre; Christian Social Party (COPEI), Christian centre-right; Movement towards Socialism (MAS), left-of-centre
**exports** coffee, timber, oil, aluminium, iron ore, petrochemicals

**currency** bolívar (Bs.88.90 = £1 July 1991)
**population** (1990 est) 19,753,000 (mestizos 70%, white (Spanish, Portuguese, Italian) 20%, black 9%, amerindian 2%); growth rate 2.8% p.a.
**life expectancy** men 67, women 73 (1989)
**religion** Roman Catholic 96%, Protestant 2%
**language** Spanish (official), Indian languages 2%
**literacy** 88% (1989)
**GNP** $47.3 bn (1988); $2,629 per head (1985)

**chronology**
**1961** New constitution adopted, with Rómulo Betancourt as president.
**1964** Dr Raúl Leoni became president.
**1969** Dr Rafael Caldera became president.
**1974** Carlos Andrés Pérez Rodríguez became president.
**1979** Dr Luis Herrera became president.
**1984** Dr Jaime Lusinchi became president; social pact established between government, trade unions, and business; national debt rescheduled.
**1987** Widespread social unrest triggered by inflation; student demonstrators shot by police.
**1988** Andrés Pérez elected president. Payments suspended on foreign debts (increase due to drop in oil prices).
**1989** Economic austerity programme enforced by $4.3 billion loan from International Monetary Fund. Price increases triggered riots in which 300 people were killed; martial law declared Feb. General strike May; elections boycotted by opposition groups.

## Vietnam (Socialist Republic of)

*(Công Hòa Xã Hôi Chu Nghĩa Viêt Nam)*

**area** 329,600 sq km/127,259 sq mi
**capital** Hanoi
**towns** ports Ho Chi Minh City (formerly Saigon), Da Nang,
and Haiphong
**physical** Red River and Mekong deltas, centre of cultivation and population; tropical rainforest; mountainous in
N and NW
**head of state** Vo Chi Cong from 1987
**head of government** Do Muoi from 1988
**political system** communism
**political parties** Communist Party of Vietnam (CPV)
**exports** rice, rubber, coal, iron, apatite
**currency** dong (13,406.25 = £1 July 1991)
**population** (1990 est) 68,488,000 (750,000 refugees,
majority ethnic Chinese left 1975–79, some settled in
SW China, others fled by sea (the 'boat people') to Hong
Kong and elsewhere); growth rate 2.4% p.a.
**life expectancy** men 62, women 66 (1989)
**language** Vietnamese (official), French, English, Khmer,
Chinese, tribal
**religion** Buddhist, Taoist, Confucian, Christian

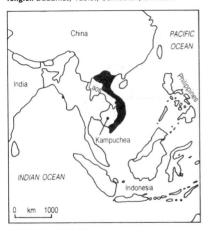

**literacy** 78% (1989)
**GNP** $12.6 bn; $180 per head (1987)

**chronology**
**1945** Japanese removed from Vietnam.
**1946** Commencement of Vietminh war against French.
**1954** France defeated at Dien Bien Phu. Vietnam divided
along 17th parallel.
**1964** US troops entered Vietnam War.
**1973** Paris ceasefire agreement.
**1975** Saigon captured by North Vietnam.
**1976** Socialist Republic of Vietnam proclaimed.
**1978** Admission into Comecon. Invasion of Cambodia.
**1979** Sino-Vietnamese border war.
**1986** Retirement of old-guard leaders.
**1987–88** Over 10,000 political prisoners released.
**1988–89** Troop withdrawals from Cambodia continued.
**1989** 'Boat people' leaving Vietnam murdered and robbed
at sea by Thai pirates. Troop withdrawal from Cambodia
completed. Hong Kong forcibly repatriated some Vietnamese refugees.

**Yemen (Republic of Yemen)**
*(al Jamhuriya al Yamaniya)*

**area** 531,900 sq km/205,367 sq mi
**capital** San'a
**towns** Ta'iz; and chief port Aden
**physical** hot moist coastal plain, rising to plateau and

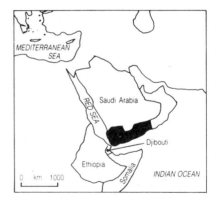

desert
**features** once known as *Arabia felix* because of its fertility,
includes islands of Perim (in strait of Bab-el-Mandeb, at
S entrance to Red Sea), Socotra, and Kamaran
**head of state and of government** Ali Abdullah Saleh from
1978
**political system** authoritarian republic
**political parties** none
**exports** cotton, coffee, grapes
**currency** rial (19.58 = £1 July 1991)
**population** (1990 est) 11,000,000; growth rate 2.7%
p.a.
**life expectancy** men 47, women 50
**language** Arabic
**religion** Sunni Muslim 63%, Shi'ite Muslim 37%
**literacy** men 20%/women 3% (1985 est)
**GNP** $4.9 bn (1983); $520 per head

**chronology**
**1918** Yemen became independent
**1962** North Yemen declared the Arab Republic of Yemen
(YAR), with Abdullah al-Sallal as president. Civil war
broke out between royalists and republicans.
**1967** Civil war ended with the republicans victorious.
Sallal deposed and replaced by a Republican Council.
The People's Republic of South Yemen was formed.
**1971–72** War between South Yemen and YAR; union
agreement not kept.
**1974** Ibrahim al-Hamadi seized power in North Yemen
and a Military Command Council was set up.
**1977** Hamadi assassinated and replaced by Ahmed ibn
Hussein al-Ghashmi.
**1978** Constituent People's Assembly appointed and Military Command Council dissolved. Ghashmi killed by
envoy from South Yemen; succeeded by Ali Abdullah
Saleh. War broke out again between the two Yemens.
**1979** Ceasefire agreed with commitment to future union.
**1983** Saleh elected president of North Yemen for a further
five-year term.
**1984** Joint committee on foreign policy for the two Yemens met in Aden.
**1988** President Saleh re-elected.
**1989** Draft constitution for single Yemen state published.
**1990** Border with South Yemen opened; formally united
May 22.
**1991** New constitution approved.

**Yugoslavia (Socialist Federal Republic of)**
*(Socijalistička Federativna Republika Jugoslavija)*

**area** 255,800 sq km/98,739 sq mi
**capital** Belgrade
**towns** Zagreb, Skopje, Ljubljana; ports Split, Rijeka
**physical** mountainous, with river Danube plains in N and

E; limestone (Karst) features in NW
**features** constituent republics of Bosnia and Herzegovina, Croatia, Macedonia, Montenegro, Serbia (including the autonomous provinces of Kosovo and Vojvodina), and Slovenia; scenic Dalmatian coast and Dinaric Alps; Lake Shkodër

**head of state** vacant from 15 March 1991
**head of government** Ante Marković from 1989
**political system** socialist pluralist republic
**political parties** League of Communists of Yugoslavia (SKJ), Marxist-Leninist-Titoist; nationalist parties in the republics
**exports** machinery, electrical goods, chemicals
**currency** dinar (38.11 = £1 July 1991)
**population** (1990 est) 24,107,000 (Serbs 36%, Croats 20%, Muslims 9%, Slovenes 8%, Albanians 8%, Macedonians 6%, Montenegrins 3%, Hungarians 2%, 5.5% declared 'Yugoslavs'); growth rate 0.6% p.a.
**life expectancy** men 69, women 75 (1989)
**language** Serbo-Croat, Macedonian, Slovenian
**religion** Eastern Orthodox 41% (Serbs), Roman Catholic 12% (Croats), Muslim 3%
**literacy** 90% (1989)
**GNP** $154.1 bn; $6,540 per head (1988)

**chronology**
**1917–18** Creation of Kingdom of the Serbs, Croats, and Slovenes.
**1929** Name of Yugoslavia adopted.
**1941** Invaded by Germany.
**1945** Communist federal republic formed under leadership of Tito.
**1948** Split with USSR.
**1953** Self-management principle enshrined in constitution.
**1961** Nonaligned movement formed under Yugoslavia's leadership.
**1974** New constitution adopted.
**1980** Tito died; collective leadership assumed power.
**1987** Threatened use of army to curb unrest.
**1988** Economic difficulties: 1,800 strikes, inflation 250%, 20% unemployment. Ethnic unrest in Montenegro and Vojvodina; party reshuffles and resignation of government.
**1989** Reformist Croatian Ante Markovic became prime minister. 29 died in ethnic riots in Kosovo province; state of emergency imposed. Inflation to May 490%; tensions with ethnic Albanians rose.
**1990** Multiparty systems established in Slovenia and Croatia.
**1991** Several republics called for secession. President resigned. Clashes between Serbs and Croats in Croatia. Slovenia declared itself independent, and the federal army intervened. Slovenia accepted EC-sponsored peace pact. Fighting continued in Croatia.

---

**Zaïre (Republic of)**
(*République du Zaïre*) (formerly Congo)

**area** 2,344,900 sq km/905,366 sq mi
**capital** Kinshasa
**towns** Lubumbashi, Kananga, Kisangani; ports Matadi, Boma
**physical** Zaïre river basin has tropical rainforest and savanna; mountains in E and W
**features** lakes Tanganyika, Mobutu Sésé Séko, Edward; Ruwenzori mountains
**head of state and of government** Mobuto Sésé Séko Kuku Ngbendu wa Zabanga from 1965
**political system** socialist pluralist republic
**political parties** Popular Movement of the Revolution (MPR), African socialist
**exports** coffee, copper, cobalt (80% of world output), industrial diamonds
**currency** zaïre (7,564.00 = £1 July 1991)

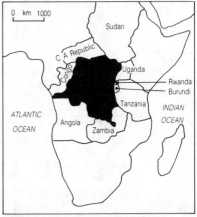

**population** (1990 est) 35,330,000; growth rate 2.9% p.a.
**life expectancy** men 51, women 54 (1989)
**language** French (official), Swahili, Lingala
**religion** Christian 70%, Muslim 10%
**literacy** men 79%/women 45% (1985 est)
**GNP** $5 bn (1987); $127 per head

**chronology**
**1907** Congo Free State annexed to Belgium.
**1960** Independence achieved from Belgium as Republic of the Congo. Civil war broke out between central government and Katanga province.
**1963** Katanga war ended.
**1967** New constitution adopted.
**1970** Col Mobutu elected president.
**1971** Country became the Republic of Zaïre, with the Popular Movement of the Revolution (MPR) the only legal political party.
**1974** Foreign-owned businesses and plantations seized by Mobutu and given in political patronage.
**1977** Original owners of confiscated properties invited back. Mobutu re-elected; Zaïrians invaded Katanga province from Angola, repulsed by Belgian paratroops.
**1978** Second unsuccessful invasion from Angola.
**1988** Potential rift with Belgium avoided.
**1991** Multiparty elections planned for 1992.

---

**Zambia (Republic of)**

**area** 752,600 sq km/290,579 sq mi
**capital** Lusaka
**towns** Kitwe, Ndola, Kabwe, Chipata, Livingstone
**physical** forested plateau cut through by rivers
**features** Zambezi River, Victoria Falls, Kariba Dam
**head of state and government** Kenneth Kaunda from 1964
**political system** socialist pluralist republic
**political parties** United National Independence Party (UNIP), African socialist; Movement for Multiparty Democracy (MMD); National Democratic Alliance (Nada)
**exports** copper, cobalt, zinc, emeralds, tobacco
**currency** kwacha (103.76 = £1 July 1991)
**population** (1990 est) 8,119,000; growth rate 3.3% p.a.
**life expectancy** men 54, women 57 (1989)
**language** English (official); Bantu dialects
**religion** Christian 66%, animist, Hindu, Muslim
**literacy** 54% (1988)
**GNP** $2.1 bn (1987); $304 per head (1986)

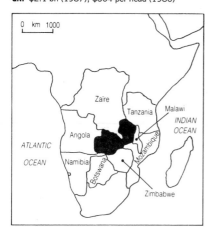

**chronology**
**1899–1924** As Northern Rhodesia, under administration of the British South Africa Company.
**1924** Became a British protectorate.
**1964** Independence achieved from Britain, within the Commonwealth, as the Republic of Zambia with Kenneth Kaunda as president.
**1972** United Independence Party (UNIP) declared the only legal party.
**1976** Support for the Patriotic Front in Rhodesia declared.
**1980** Unsuccessful coup against President Kaunda.
**1985** Kaunda elected chair of the Front Line States.
**1987** Kaunda elected chair of the Organization of African Unity (OAU).
**1988** Kaunda re-elected unopposed for sixth term.
**1990** Multiparty system announced for 1991.

---

## Zimbabwe (Republic of)

**area** 390,300 sq km/150,695 sq mi
**capital** Harare
**towns** Bulawayo, Gweru, Kwekwe, Mutare, Hwange
**physical** high plateau with central high veld and mountains in E; rivers Zambezi, Limpopo
**features** Hwange National Park, part of Kalahari Desert; ruins of Great Aimbabwe
**head of state and government** Robert Mugabe from 1987
**political system** effectively one party socialist republic
**political parties** Zimbabwe African National Union-Patriotic Front (ZANU-PF), African socialist.

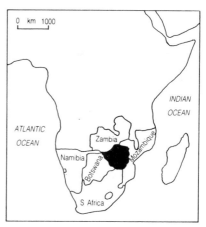

**exports** tobacco, asbestos, cotton, coffee, gold, silver
**currency** Zimbabwe dollar (Z$5.22 = £1 July 1991)
**population** (1990 est) 10,205,000 (Shona 80%, Ndbele 19%; c. 100,000 whites); growth rate 3.5% p.a.
**life expectancy** men 59, women 63 (1989)
**language** English (official); Shona, Sindebele
**religion** Christian, Muslim, Hindu, animist
**literacy** men 81%/women 67% (1985 est)
**GNP** $5.5 bn (1988); $275 per head (1986)

**chronology**
**1880s–1923** As Southern Rhodesia, under administration of British South Africa Company.
**1923** Became a self-governing British colony.
**1961** Zimbabwe African People's Union (ZAPU) formed, with Joshua Nkomo as leader.
**1962** ZAPU declared illegal.
**1963** Zimbabawe African National Union (ZANU) formed, with Robert Mugabe as secretary general.
**1964** Ian Smith became prime minister. Nkomo and Mugabe imprisoned.
**1965** ZANU banned. Smith declared unilateral independence.
**1966–68** Abortive talks between Smith and UK prime minister Harold Wilson.
**1974** Nkomo and Mugabe released.
**1975** Geneva conference set date for constitutional independence.
**1979** Smith produced new constitution and established a government with Bishop Abel Muzorewa as prime minister. New government denounced by Nkomo and Mugabe. Conference in London agreed independence arrangements (Lancaster House Agreement).
**1980** Independence achieved from Britain, with Robert Mugabe as prime minister.
**1981** Rift between Mugabe and Nkomo.
**1982** Nkomo dismissed from the cabinet, leaving the country temporarily.
**1984** ZANU-People's Front (PF) Party Congress agreed to create a one-party state in future.
**1985** Relations between Mugabe and Nkomo improved. Troops sent to Matabeleland to suppress rumoured insurrection; 5,000 civilians killed.
**1986** Joint ZANU-PF rally held amid plans for merger.
**1987** White-roll seats in the assembly were abolished. President Banana retired; Mugabe combined posts of head of state and prime minister with the title executive president.
**1988** Nkomo returned to the cabinet and appointed vice president.
**1989** Opposition party, the Zimbabwe Unity Movement, formed by Edgar Tekere; draft constitution renouncing

Marxism-Leninism as an ideology; ZANU and ZAPU formally merged;
**1990** Opposition to creation of one-party state.

## Attitudes towards Europe

*When you hear people use the word 'Europe', do you think they are thinking of Britain as being part of Europe or as being separate from Europe?*

| | |
|---|---|
| Part of . | 45 |
| Separate | 50 |
| Don't know | 6 |

*What about yourself? Do you think of yourself as being European as well as British, or not?*

| | |
|---|---|
| European and British | 43 |
| Not | 56 |
| Don't know | 2 |

*If, for any reason, you could not live in Britain and had to go and live on the Continent, which country would you choose to live in?*

| | |
|---|---|
| France . | 16 |
| Germany | 13 |
| Spain | 11 |
| Holland | 11 |
| Switzerland | 9 |
| Italy | 6 |
| Austria | 4 |
| Greece | 4 |
| Belgium | 3 |
| Ireland | 3 |
| Portugal | 1 |
| Other | 8 |
| Don't know | 12 |

*Do you have friends, acquaintances or business contacts on the Continent? If yes; In which countries?*

| | |
|---|---|
| France | 16 |
| Germany | 16 |
| Spain | 9 |
| Holland | 8 |
| Italy | 6 |
| Belgium | 5 |
| Ireland | 5 |
| Switzerland | 3 |
| Greece | 3 |
| Austria | 2 |
| Portugal | 1 |
| Other | 4 |
| No, none | 59 |

# THE ANCIENT WORLD

## Africa

**14 million** BC Africa, which is considered the 'cradle-continent', probably produced the first human-like creatures

**3–5 million** direct line of descent of modern humans established from E Africa

**c. 60000** American Indians entered N America from Asia

**15000** agriculture first practised in Egypt

**10000–2000** the originally fertile Sahara became a barrier desert between northern and southern Africa

**9000** Marmes man, earliest human remains found in N America

**5450–2500** era of Saharan rock and cave paintings, as in the Tassili

**c. 3000** first dynasties of Mesopotamia: King Gilgamesh; Bronze Age civilizations: Minoan, Mycenaean

**2800–2205** Sage kings in China, earliest Chinese dynasty; civilization spread to all of China

**2500–1500** Indus valley civilization

**1950** first Babylonian Empire established

**625** birth of Buddha

**550** birth of Confucius

**246** Shi Huangdi, Emperor of China, succeeded to the throne of Qin. He had reunited the country as an empire by 221, and built the Great Wall of China

## Egypt

**5000** BC Egyptian culture already well established in the Nile Valley

**3200** Menes united Lower Egypt (the Delta) with his own kingdom of Upper Egypt to form the Egyptian state

**2800** Imhotep built step pyramid at Sakkara

**c. 2600** Old Kingdom reached the height of its power and the kings of the 4th Dynasty built the pyramids at Gîza

**c. 2200–1800** Middle Kingdom, under which the unity lost towards the end of the Old Kingdom was restored

**1730** invading Asiatic Hyksos established their kingdom in the Delta

**c. 1580** New Kingdom established by the 18th Dynasty, following the eviction of the Hyksos, with its capital at Thebes; high point of Egyptian civilization

**c. 1321** 19th Dynasty

**1191** Ramses III defeated the Indo-European 'Sea Peoples', but after him there was decline and eventual anarchy

**8th–7th centuries** brief interlude of rule by kings from Nubia

**666** the Assyrians under Ashurbanipal occupied Thebes

**525** after a brief resurgence of independence, Egypt became a Persian province following conquest by Cambyses

**332** conquest by Alexander; on the division of his empire, Egypt went to Ptolemy, whose descendants ruled until Cleopatra's death in 30 BC

**30** conquest by the Roman Emperor Augustus: Egypt a province of the Roman and Byzantine empires

**641** AD conquest by the Arabs, so that the Christianity of later Roman rule was replaced by Islam

## Greece

**c. 1600–1200** BC Mycenean civilization

**c. 1180** Siege of Troy

**c. 1100** Dorian invasion, and the rise of the Greek city states, of which the greatest were Athens and Sparta

**750–550** trading colonies founded round the Mediterranean, Black Sea, and elsewhere

**5th century** Persian Empire sought to establish its rule over the Greeks

**490** Persians defeated at Marathon

**480** The Spartans defended Thermopylae to the death against a fresh invasion by Xerxes, but the Persians were defeated at sea (Salamis 480) and on land (Plataea 479)

**461–429** Pericles attempted to convert the alliance against the Persians into the basis of a Greek empire

**431–404** Peloponnesian War prompted by Sparta's suspicion of Pericles's ambitions, with the resultant destruction of the political power of Athens

**378–371** Sparta, successor to Athens in the leadership, overthrown by Thebes

**358–336** Philip II of Macedon seized his opportunity to establish supremacy over Greece

**334–331** Philip's son Alexander the Great defeated the decadent Persian Empire, and went on to found his own

**3rd century** BC Greek cities formed the Achaean and Aetolian Leagues to try and maintain their independence against Macedon, Egypt, and Rome

**146** BC Greece annexed by Rome

**330** AD capital of Roman Empire transferred to Constantinople

**529** closure of the University of Athens by Justinian ended Greek cultural dominance

## Persia

**550** BC Cyrus II became king of the Medes and Persians, founding the Persian Empire, which at its height was to include Babylonia, Assyria, Asia Minor, Egypt, Thrace, and Macedonia

**521** Darius I became king of Persia

**499** revolt of the Ionian Greeks against Persian rule

**490** Darius I defeated by the Greeks at Marathon

**480** Xerxes I victorious at Thermopylae, which Leonidas, king of Sparta, and 1,000 men defended to the death against the Persians; Athens captured but Greek navy victorious at Salamis

**479** Greeks under Spartan general Pausanias victorious at Plataea, driving the Persians from the country

**334–326** conquest by Alexander the Great

## Rome

**753** BC traditional date for the foundation of Rome

*510* the Etruscan dynasty of the Tarquins was expelled, and a republic was established, governed by two consuls, elected annually by the popular assembly, and a council of elders or senate. The concentration of power in the hands of the aristocracy aroused the opposition of the plebeian masses

*390* Rome sacked by Gauls

*367* the plebeians secured the right to elect tribunes, the codification of the laws, and the right to marry patricians; it was enacted that one consul must be a plebeian

*338* the cities of Latium formed into a league under Roman control

*343–290* the Etruscans to the north were subdued during the 5th and 4th centuries, and the Samnites to the southeast

*280–272* the Greek cities of the south were conquered

*264–241* first Punic War, ending in a Roman victory and the annexation of Sicily

*238* Sardinia seized from Carthage and became a Roman province

*226–222* Roman conquest of Cisalpine Gaul (Lombardy); conflict with Carthage, which was attempting to conquer Sicily

*218* Hannibal invaded Italy and won a brilliant series of victories

*202* victory over Hannibal at Zama, followed by surrender of Carthage and relinquishing of its Spanish colonies

*148* three wars with Macedon were followed by its conversion into a province

*146* after a revolt Greece became in effect a Roman province. In the same year Carthage was annexed. On the death of the king of Pergamum, Rome succeeded to his kingdom in Asia Minor

*133* Tiberius Gracchus put forward proposals for agrarian reforms and was murdered by the senatorial party

*123* Tiberius's policy was taken up by his brother Gaius Gracchus, who was likewise murdered

*109–106* the leadership of the democrats passed to Marius

*91–88* Social War: a revolt of the Italian cities compelled Rome to grant citizenship to all Italians

*87–84* while Sulla was repelling an invasion of Greece by Mithridates, Marius seized power

*82* on his return Sulla established a dictatorship and ruled by terror

*70* Sulla's changes were reversed by Pompey and Crassus

*66–62* defeat of Mithridates and annexation of Syria and the rest of Asia Minor

*60* Pompey formed an alliance with the democratic leaders Crassus and Julius Caesar

*51* Gaul conquered by Caesar as far as the Rhine

*49* Caesar's return to Italy (crossing the Rubicon) led to civil war between Caesar and Pompey

*48* defeat of Pompey at Pharsalus

*44* Caesar's dictatorship ended by his assassination

*32* the Empire divided between Caesar's nephew Octavian in the west, and Antony in the east; war between them

*31* defeat of Antony at Actium

*30* with the deaths of Antony and Cleopatra Egypt was annexed

*27* Octavian took the name Augustus; he was by now absolute ruler, although in title only *Princeps* (first citizen)

*43* AD Augustus made the Rhine and the Danube the frontiers of the Empire; Claudius added Britain

*96–180* under the Flavian emperors Nerva, Trajan, Hadrian, Antoninus Pius, and Marcus Aurelius the Empire enjoyed a golden age

*115* Trajan conquered Macedonia; peak of Roman territorial expansion

*180* death of Marcus Aurelius. A century of war and disorder followed, during which a succession of generals were placed on the throne by their armies

*284–305* Diocletian reorganized the Empire as a centralized autocracy

*324–37* Constantine I realized the political value of Christianity and became a convert

*330* Constantine removed the capital to Constantinople, and the Empire was divided

*410* the Goths overran Greece and Italy, sacked Rome, and finally settled in Spain. The Vandals conquered Italy

*451–2* the Huns raided Gaul and Italy

*476* the last Western emperor was deposed

# MEDIEVAL AND EARLY MODERN

*300–1500* AD period of the great medieval states in Africa: Ghana, Mali, Songhai, Benin, Ife

*320–550* Gupta dynasty in India

*4th century* Christianity became the established religion of the Roman Empire

*4th–6th centuries* Western Europe overrun by Anglo-Saxons, Franks, Goths, and Lombards

*570* birth of Muhammad

*7th–8th centuries* Islamic expansion began in N, E, and Central Africa. Christendom threatened by Moorish invasions

*800* Charlemagne given title of Emperor by the Pope

*c. 1000* Leif Ericsson traditionally reached N America

*1073* Gregory VII began 200 years of conflict between the Empire and the Papacy

*1096–1291* the Crusades were undertaken to recover the Holy Land from the Muslims

*1192* first Muslim kingdom of India established

*12th century* setting up of German, Flemish, and Italian city states in Europe, which in the 14th and 15th centuries fostered the Renaissance

*12th–14th centuries* height of Moundbuilder and Pueblo cultures in N America

*12th–15th centuries* era of Arab travellers in Africa, such as Ibn Batuta, and of trade (for example Kilwa)

*1280* Kublai Khan became emperor of China

*1395* Tamerlane defeated the Golden Horde, the invading Mongol-Tartar army which had terror-

ized Europe from 1237
*1398* Tamerlane captured Delhi
*1453* Constantinople captured by the Turks
*1488* Diaz rounded the Cape of Good Hope
*1492, 12 Oct* Columbus first sighted land in the Caribbean
*16th century* arrival of Europeans in S America, with the Spanish (Pizarro) and Portuguese conquest. American Indians were either killed, assimilated, or, where unsuitable as slave labour, replaced by imported slaves from Africa
*1526* Babur established the Mogul Empire in India
*1565* first Spanish settlements in N America
*16th–17th centuries* Europe dominated by rivalry of France and the Hapsburgs, the Protestant Reformation, and the Catholic Counter-Reformation
*1607* first permanent English settlement in N America at Jamestown, Virginia
*17th century* beginnings of the British East India Company in India. Era of absolute monarchies in Europe (notably Louis XIV)
*18th century* War of Austrian Succession and Seven Years' War ended in loss of French colonial empire to Britain and the emergence of Prussia as a leading European power. Height of the Atlantic and Indian Ocean slave trade
*1789–95* French Revolution and the overthrow of Louis XVI

# REVOLUTIONS

**REVOLUTION**
The word can be used to describe any rapid, far-reaching or violent change in the political, social or economic structure of society. It has usually been applied to different forms of political change; the American Revolution (War of Independence) where colonists broke free from their colonial ties and established a sovereign, independent state; the French Revolution where an absolute monarchy was overthrown by opposition from inside the country and a popular rising; and the Russian Revolution where a repressive monarchy was overthrown by those seeking to institute widespread social and economic changes in line with a socialist model. While political revolutions are often associated with violence, there are other types of change which often have just as much impact on society. Most notable is the Industrial Revolution, a process which has imposed massive changes on economies and societies since the mid-18th century. In the 1980s, a 'silicon' revolution was underway, involving the increasing use of computers to undertake tasks formerly done 'by hand'.
**American Revolution** the revolt 1775–83 of the British North American colonies that resulted in the establishment of the United States of America. It was caused by colonial resentment at the contemporary attitude that commercial or industrial interests of any colony should be subordinate to those of the mother country;

and by the unwillingness of the colonists to pay for a standing army. It was also fuelled by the colonists anti-monarchist sentiment and a desire to participate in the policies affecting them.
*1773* a government tax on tea which led citizens disguised as N American Indians to board the ships carrying the tea and throw it into the harbour (the **Boston Tea Party**)
*1774–75* the **First Continental Congress** held in Philadelphia to call for civil disobedience in reply to British measures
*1775* 19 April hostilities began at Lexington and Concord, Massachusetts, the first shots being fired when British troops, sent to seize illegal military stores, were attacked by the local militia. The first battles was **Bunker Hill** Massachusetts, 17 June 1775, in which the colonists were defeated; George Washington was appointed colonial commander soon afterwards
*1776* the **Second Continental Congress** on 4 July issued the **Declaration of Independence**. 27 Aug at **Long Island** Washington was defeated, forced to evacuate New York and retire to Pennsylvania, but re-crossed the Delaware to win successes at **Trenton** (26 Dec) and **Princeton** (3 Jan 1777)
*1777* a British plan, for Sir William Howe (advancing from New York) and General Burgoyne (from Canada) to link up, miscarried. Burgoyne surrendered at **Saratoga** (17 Oct) but Howe invaded Pennsylvania, defeating Washington at **Brandywine** (11 Sept) and **Germantown** (4 Oct), and occupying Philadelphia; Washington wintered at Valley Forge 1777–78
*1778* France and Spain entered the war on the American side
*1780* 12 May capture of **Charleston**, the most notable of a series of British victories in American south, but they alienated support by attempting to enforce conscription
*1781* 19 Oct Cornwallis, besieged in **Yorktown** by Washington and the French fleet, surrendered
*1782* peace negotiations opened
*1783* 3 Sept **Treaty of Paris** American independence recognized.
**Industrial Revolution** the sudden acceleration of technical development which occurred in Europe from the late 18th century, and which transferred the balance of political power from the landowner to the industrial capitalist, and created an organized industrial working class. The great achievement of the first phase (to 1830) was the invention of the steam engine in Britain, originally developed for draining mines, but rapidly put to use in factories and in the railways. In the second phase, from 1830 to the early 20th century, the Industrial Revolution enlarged its scope from Europe to the world, with some initial exploitation of 'colonial' possessions by European powers as a preliminary to their independent development, and the internal combustion engine and electricity were developed. Then in 1911

Rutherford split the atom at Manchester and the prospect of nuclear power opened, and electronic devices were developed which made possible automation, with the eventual prospect of even managerial decision-making being in the hands of 'machines'.

**French Revolution** the forcible abolition of the *Ancien Régime* 'old order of things' (feudalism and absolute monarchy) 1789–99.

*1789* 5 May the States General (an assembly of the three 'estates', nobles, clergy, and commons) met at Versailles, bent on establishing a new constitution; 17 June National Assembly formed by the Third Estate (commons); 14 Jul Bastille was taken by the mob when Louis XVI attempted repressive moves

*1791* 20 June flight of the royal family to Varennes; 14 Sept Louis, brought back as a prisoner, accepted the new constitution

*1792* 20 April war declared on Austria, which threatened to suppress the revolution; 10 Aug royal palace stormed by the French mob; 21 Sept First Republic proclaimed

*1793* 21 Jan Louis XVI executed; 2 June overthrow of the moderate Girondins by the Jacobins; rule of the dictatorial Committee of Public Safety; 5 Sept the mass executions of the Terror began

*1794* 27 July (9 Thermidor under the Revolutionary calendar) fall of Robespierre and end of the Terror; the Directory (a body of five directors) established to hold a middle course between Royalism and Jacobinism. It ruled until Napoleon seized power in 1799.

**Bastille** a fortress prison in Paris, stormed by the mob at the beginning of the revolution on 14 July 1789, when it was found to contain only seven prisoners. The governor and most of the garrison were killed and the building razed.

**Commune of Paris** first body which took this name between 1789–1794 and acted as the municipal government of Paris from the storming of the Bastille to the fall of Robespierre.

**Jacobins** extremist republican club founded at Versailles in 1789, which later used a former Jacobin (Dominican) friary as its headquarters in Paris. It was led by Robespierre and closed after his execution in 1794.

**Girondins** right wing republicans of the French Revolution whose leaders came from the Gironde departement of France.

**Robespierre** Maximilien. French politician, 'the Sea Green Incorruptible'. As Jacobin leader in the National Convention, he supported the execution of Louis XVI and the overthrow of the Girondins, and as dominant member of the Committee of Public Safety instituted the Reign of Terror in 1793. His extremist zeal made him enemies on both left and right, resulting in his overthrow and death by guillotining in July 1794.

**Danton** Georges Jacques. French lawyer and leading revolutionary. Influential in the early years of the revolution in Paris, he was instrumental in organizing the rising of 10 Aug 1792 which overthrew the monarchy. He also helped to instigate the revolutionary tribunal

and the Committee of Public Safety in 1793. He led the Committee until July 1793 but was then superseded by Robespierre. An attempt to reassert his power failed and he was guillotined in 1794.

**Marat** Jean Paul 1743–93. French revolutionary leader and journalist. He was the idol of the Paris revolutionary crowds, and was elected in 1792 to the National Convention, where he carried on a long struggle with the Girondins, ending in their overthrow in May 1793. In Jul he was murdered by Charlotte Corday.

**Revolutions of 1848** a series of revolts in various parts of Europe against monarchial rule. While some of the revolutionaries had republican ideas, many more were motivated by economic grievances. The revolution began in France and then spread to Italy, the Austrian Empire, and to Germany where the short-lived Frankfurt Parliament put forward ideas about German political unity. None of the revolutions enjoyed any lasting success, and most were violently suppressed within a few months.

**Indian Mutiny (1857–58)** the revolt of the Bengal Army against the British in India. The movement was confined to the North, from Bengal to the Punjab, and Central India. Most support came from the army and recently dethroned princes, but in some areas it developed into a peasant rising or general revolt. Outstanding episodes were the seizure of Delhi by the rebels, and its seige and recapture by the British, and the defence of Lucknow by a British garrison. The mutiny led to the end of rule by the East Indian Co. and its replacement by direct Crown administration.

**Paris Commune** the second body to bear this name. A provisional government of Socialist and left-wing Republicans, elected in March 1871 after an attempt by the right-wing National Assembly at Versailles to disarm the Paris National Guard, it held power until May, when the Versailles troops captured Paris and massacred at least 20,000 people. It is famous as the first socialist government in history.

**Chinese Revolution** a series of major political upheavals which began in 1911 with a nationalist revolt which overthrew the Chiing imperial dynasty in 1912. Led by Sun Yat-Sen (1923–5) and then by Chiang Kai-Shek (1925–49), the nationalists came under increasing pressure from the growing communist movement. The 6,000 mile 'Long March' of the Chinese communists (1934–5) to escape from the nationalist forces saw Mao Tse-Tung emerge as leader. After World War II, the conflict expanded into open civil war (1946–9) with the nationalists finally being defeated at Nanking. This effectively established communist rule in China under the leadership of Mao.

**Sun Yat-Sen** or **Sun Zhong Shan** 1867–1925. Chinese revolutionary, founder of the Guomindang, and moving spirit behind the revolution of 1911 which overthrew the Manchu dynasty. He was briefly president 1912, but the reactionaries gained the ascendant, and he broke away to try to establish an independent republic in S China based on Canton. He lacked organizational ability, but his three 'people's principles' of nationalism, democracy, and social reform were influential.

**Chiang Kai-Shek** Chinese statesman (Pinyin: *Jiang Jie Shi*). He took part in the Revolution of 1911, and after the death of Sun Yat-sen was made Commander-in-Chief of the Guomindang armies in S China in 1925. The initial collaboration with the communists, broken in 1927, was resumed following the Xi An incident, and he nominally headed the struggle against the Japanese invaders, receiving the Japanese surrender in 1945. Civil War then resumed between communists and nationalists, and ended in the defeat of Chiang in 1949, and the limitation of his rule to Taiwan.

**Mao Zedong** or **Mao Tse-Tung** 1893–1976. Chinese statesman, the 'Great Helmsman'. Born in Hunan, he became the leader of the communists in 1927. After the rupture with the nationalists, led by Chiang Kai-shek, Mao Zedong and his troops undertook the 'Long March' of 10,000 km/6000 mi 1934–5 from SE to NW China, the prelude to his ascent to power. Again in nominal alliance with Chiang against the Japanese 1937–45, he subsequently defeated him, and proclaimed the People's Republic of China in 1949. As Chairman of the Communist Party, he provided the pattern for the development of the country through the Great Leap Forward of 1959, and the Cultural Revolution of 1966 based on his thoughts contained in the *Little Red Book*. His reputation plunged after his death, but was later somewhat restored.

**Russian Revolution** the name given to the two revolutions of March and Nov 1917 which began with the overthrow of the Romanov Imperial dynasty and ended with the the establishment of a state run by Lenin and the Bolsheviks. The revolution of March 1917 arose in part from the repressive nature of Tsarist government but primarily as a result of the mismanagement of the war after 1914. Riots in St Petersburg led to the abdication of Tsar Nicholas II and the formation of a provisional government under Kerensky. The Provisional government ruled until Oct 1917 but found its power increasingly undermined by the soldiers' and workers' soviets in Petrograd (St Petersburg) and Moscow. During this period, the Bolsheviks under Lenin's guidance, had concentrated on gaining control of the soviets and advocating an end to the war and land reform. Under the slogan 'All power to the Soviets', they staged a coup on the night of 6–7 Nov which overthrew the government. The second All-Russian Congress of Soviets, which met the following day, proclaimed itself the new government of Russia. The Bolshevik seizure of power led to peace with Germany through the Treaty of Brest-Litovsk, but also to civil war as anti-Bolshevik elements within the army attempted to seize power. The war lasted until 1920, when the Red Army, organized by

Trotsky, finally overcame 'white' opposition.

**Lenin** Vladimir Ilich Ulyanov 1870–1924. Born 22 April 1870 at Simbinsk (Ulyanovsk), Vladimir Ilich Ulyanov was converted to Marxism in 1889 and exiled to Siberia in 1895 as a result of subversive activity. After 1900, he spent most of his time in Western Europe, emerging as the leader of the more radical Bolshevik section of Russian Social Democracy. Returning to Russia in April 1917 with German help, Lenin assumed control of the Bolshevik movement and was instrumental in organizing the coup of 6–7 Nov. From then until his death in 1924, he effectively controlled Russia, establishing Bolshevik rule and the beginnings of communism. In addition he consolidated his position as a great Marxist theoretician, modifying traditional Marxist doctrine to fit the objective conditions prevailing in Russia, a doctrine known as Marxism-Leninism which became the basis of communist ideology.

**Trotsky** Leon 1879–1940. Born 7 Nov 1879 at Yanovka. Communist theorist, agitator, and collaborator with Lenin after the two met in exile in London in 1902. Trotsky was a leading member of the Bolshevik movement in 1917 and helped organize the overthrow of the Provisional Government. He was instrumental in building up the Red Army to the point where it could win the Civil War and acted as Commissioner for Foreign Affairs until 1924. He was ousted during the power struggle which followed Lenin's death, but he remained active in opposing Stalin's rule until he was assassinated in Aug 1940.

**Cuban Revolution** 1959 name given to the overthrow of the Batista regime in Jan 1959 by Fidel Castro and the 26 July Movement. Having led abortive coups in 1953 and 1956, Castro succeeded in overthrowing Batista with a force of only 5,000 men. Politically non-aligned, Castro was increasingly forced to seek Eastern Bloc help for government as a result of US opposition—which culminated in the abortive 'Bay of Pigs' invasion of 1961 sponsored by the CIA. The missile crisis of 1962 highlighted Russian involvement in Cuba. Between 1959 and 1974, Cuba, led by Castro, his brother Raúl, and initially Che Guevara, adopted economic and social policies based on the principles of Marxism-Leninism and relied almost exclusively on communist help. After 1974, in an attempt to stabilize the economy, Castro reintroduced incentives into society with the maxim that each 'should receive according to his work' rather than according to his need.

**Castro Ruz** Fidel 1927– . Cuban Prime Minister. Of wealthy parentage Castro was educated at Jesuit schools and, after studying law at the University of Havana, he gained a reputation through his work for poor clients. He strongly opposed the Batista dictatorship, and with his brother Raúl took part in an unsuccessful attack on the Army barracks at Santiago de Cuba in 1953. After spending some time in exile in the USA and Mexico, Castro attempted a secret landing in Cuba in 1956

## CHINESE DYNASTIES

| | |
|---|---|
| *c.* 2200–*c.* 1500 BC | The *Xia dynasty*, a bronze age early civilization, with further agricultural developments, including irrigation, and the first known use of writing in this area. |
| *c.* 1500–*c.* 1066 BC | The *Shang dynasty* is the first of which we have documentary evidence. Writing became well-developed; bronze vases survive in ceremonial burials. The first Chinese calendar was made. |
| *c.* 1066–221 BC | During the *Zhou dynasty*, the feudal structure of society broke down in a period of political upheaval, though iron, money, and written laws were all in use, and philosophy flourished. The dynasty ended in the 'Warring States' period (403–221 BC), with the country divided into small kingdoms. |
| 221–206 BC | The *Qin* dynasty corresponds to the reign of Shih Huang Ti, who curbed the feudal nobility and introduced orderly bureaucratic government; he had roads and canals built and began the Great Wall of China to keep out invaders from the north. |
| 206 BC–AD 220 | The *Han dynasty* was a long period of peace, during which territory was incorporated, the keeping of historical records was systematized, and an extensive civil service set up. Art and literature flourished, and Buddhism was introduced. The first census was taken in AD 2, registering a population of 57 million. Chinese caravans traded with the Parthians. |
| 220–581 | The area was divided under *Three Kingdoms*: the Wei, Shu, and Wu. Confucianism was superseded by Buddhism and Taoism; glass was introduced from the West. Following prolonged fighting, the Wei became the most powerful kingdom, eventually founding the *Jin dynasty* (265–304), which expanded to take over from the barbarian invaders who ruled much of China at that time, but from 305 to 580 lost the territory they had gained to the Tatar invaders from the north. |
| 581–618 | Reunification came with the *Sui dynasty* when the government was reinstated, the barbarian invasions stopped, and the Great Wall refortified. |
| 618–907 | During the *Tang dynasty* the system of government became more highly developed and centralized, and the empire covered most of SE and much of central Asia. Sculpture, painting, and poetry flourished again, and trade relations were established with the Islamic world and the Byzantine Empire. |
| 907–960 | The period known as the *Five Dynasties and Ten Kingdoms* held war, economic depression, and loss of territory in N China, central Asia, and Korea, but printing was developed, including the first use of paper money, and porcelain traded to Islamic lands. |
| 960–1279 | The *Sung dynasty* was a period of calm and creativity. Central government was restored, and movable type was invented. At the end of the dynasty, the northern and western frontiers were neglected, and Mongol invasions took place. Marco Polo visited the court of the Great Khan in 1275. |
| 1279–1368 | The *Yuan dynasty* saw the beginning of Mongol rule in China, with Kublai Khan on the throne in Beijing 1293; there were widespread revolts. Marco Polo served the Kublai Khan. |
| 1368–1644 | The Mongols were expelled by the first of the native Chinese *Ming dynasty*, who expanded the empire. Chinese ships sailed to the Sunda Islands 1403, Ceylon 1408, and the Red Sea 1430. Mongolia was captured by the second Ming emperor. Architecture developed and Beijing flourished as the new capital. Portuguese explorers reached Macao 1516 and Canton 1517; other Europeans followed. Chinese porcelain arrived in Europe 1580. The Jesuits reached Beijing 1600. |
| 1644–1912 | The last of the dynasties was the *Manchu* or *Ching*, who were non-Chinese nomads from Manchuria. Initially trade and culture flourished, but during the 19th century it seemed that China would be partitioned among the US and European imperialist nations, since all trade was conducted through treaty ports in their control. The *Boxer Rebellion* 1900 against Western influence was suppressed by European troops. |
| 1911–12 | Revolution broke out, and the infant emperor Henry P'u-i was deposed. |

in which all but 11 of his supporters were killed. He eventually gathered an army of over 5,000 which overthrew Batista in 1959 and he became Prime Minister a few months later. He became president in 1976, and in 1979 also president of the Non-Aligned Movement. His brother Raúl was appointed Minister of Armed Forces in 1959.

**Guevara** Ernesto 'Che' 1928–67. Revolutionary. Born in Argentina, he was trained as a doctor, but in 1953 left the country because of his opposition to Peron. In effecting the Cuban revolution of 1959, he was second only to Castro and his brother, but in 1965 moved on to fight against white mercenaries in the Congo, and then to Bolivia, where he was killed in an unsuccessful attempt to lead a peasant rising. His revolutionary technique using minimum resources has been influential, but his orthodox Marxism has been obscured by romanticizing disciples.

**Chilean Revolution** 1970–73. Name given to the period between 1970 and 1973 and the Presidency of Salvador Allende, the world's first democratically elected Marxist head of state. Allende was brought to power in 1970 as the head of the Popular Unity alliance of socialists, communists, and radicals, a victory which owed more to the disunity of the Christian Democrat opposition than a major shift in voter preferences. Allende was committed to extensive social and economic reforms to be carried out within the existing political structure—the so-called 'peaceful road to socialism'. Nationalization of key industries and increased contacts with Eastern Bloc countries strained Chile's traditional economic relations with the USA and the West. His failure to stabilize the economy created widespread opposition; Allende was unable to fulfil the expectations of his supporters or quell the fears of his opponents about the pace of change. This led to increasing political polarization which culminated in a military coup in Sept 1973. The Allende regime was overthrown and replaced by a four-man junta led by General Pinochet.

***Allende Gossens*** Salvador 1908– . Born in Valparaiso, Chile, Allende became a Marxist activist in the 1930s and rose to prominence as a left-wing presidential candidate in 1952, 1958, and 1964. In each election he had the support of the socialist and communist movements but was defeated by the Christian Democrats and Nationalists. Elected in 1970 as the candidate of the Popular Front alliance, Allende never succeeded in keeping the electoral alliance together in government. His failure to solve the country's economic problems or to deal with political subversion allowed the army to stage the 1973 coup which brought about Allende's death, and those of many of his supporters.

**Nicaraguan Revolution** the revolt led by the FSLN (Sandinist National Liberation Front, named after Augusto Cesar Sandino, killed by the National Guard in 1934) against the dictatorship established by the father of the president Anastasio 'Tacho' Somoza. The dictatorship of the Somoza family had been underwritten by US support but this was of little help in 1978–9 when the Sandinistas mounted a full scale challenge to the regime and the hated National Guard. Somoza was forced into exile and assassinated in Paraguay in 1980. Since the revolution, the Sandinistas have taken political control of the country, introducing socialist policies and receiving help from Eastern Bloc countries and US aid dried up. The Sandinista government has had to contend with severe economic problems and also the activities of a counter-revolutionary movement, the Contras, operating in the north of the country with US monetary and technical support.

**Iranian Revolution** the revolution in Iran 1979 which deposed the shah 15 Jan and led to the popular return of Ayatollah Khomeini 1 Feb. Opposition to the shah's one-party regime (introduced 1975) became so great that he was forced to quit the country, leaving the way open for Khomeini's return. Khomeini, exiled for 25 years, had led an effective campaign from France. He appointed Mehdi Bazargan as prime minister 1979–80; real power however, remained with Khomeini's Islamic Revolutionary Council. Revolutionary forces took control of the country, and Khomeini announced the establishment of the Islamic Republic, in which a return was made to the strict observance of Muslim principles and tradition. The harshness of the Islamic codes caused increasing opposition to Khomeini's regime, which led to a power struggle after his death 1989. The more moderate Hoshemi Rafsanjani became president.

**Revolutions of 1989** a series of revolutions in various countries of Eastern Europe against communist rule. By 1990 most had moved from monist to pluralist political systems.

Mikhail Gorbachev's official encouragement of *perestroika* (radical restructuring), and *glasnost* (greater political openness), largely for economic reasons, unleashed a wave of simmering discontent: both within the USSR (notably in the Baltic states of Estonia, Latvia, and Lithuania, and in Byelorussia, the Ukraine, and Moldova) and in several East European countries. Until the late 1980s, any potentially damaging discontent, however widespread, had been kept in check by the use of, or threat of military force controlled from Moscow—as in the termination of the Prague Spring experiment 1968 in Czechoslovakia.

Bulgaria, Czechoslovakia, East Germany, Hungary, Poland, Romania, Albania, and Yugoslavia were not as 'reluctantly content' with their lot as had been supposed, though they still subscribed to a form of one-party communism. Though many of the countries achieved bloodless coups (Bulgaria, Czechoslovakia, and Hungary), some were more dramatic: Romania's 'Christmas Revolution' 1989, in which Nicolae Ceauşescu was shot, was short and bloody. East Germany's revolution witnessed the symbolic dismantling of the Berlin Wall Nov 1989, with formal unification of East and West Germany Oct 1990. In Yugoslavia, the multi-party systems established in Slovenia and Croatia led to several republics calling for secession, and fighting between Serbs and Croats in Croatia 1991.

# HOLY ROMAN EMPERORS

*Carolingian Kings and Emperors*

Charlemagne, Charles the Great          800–14

| | |
|---|---|
| Louis I, the Pious | 814–40 |
| Lothair I | 840–55 |
| Louis II | 855–75 |
| Charles II, the Bald | 875–77 |
| Charles III, the Fat | 881–87 |
| Guido of Spoleto | 891–94 |
| Lambert of Spoleto (co-emperor) | 892–98 |
| Arnulf (rival) | 896–901 |
| Louis III of Provence | 901–05 |
| Berengar | 905–24 |
| Conrad I of Franconia (rival) | 911–18 |

*Saxon Kings and Emperors*

| | |
|---|---|
| Henry I, the Fowler | 918–36 |
| Otto I, the Great | 936–73 |
| Otto II | 973–83 |
| Otto III | 938–1002 |
| Henry II, the Saint | 1002–24 |

*Franconian (Salian) Emperors*

| | |
|---|---|
| Conrad II | 1024–39 |
| Henry III, the Black | 1039–56 |
| Henry IV | 1056–1106 |
| Rudolf of Swabia (rival) | 1077–80 |
| Hermann of Luxembourg (rival) | 1081–93 |
| Conrad of Franconia (rival) | 1093–1101 |
| Henry V | 1106–25 |
| Lothair II | 1126–37 |

*Hohenstaufen Kings and Emperors*

| | |
|---|---|
| Conrad III | 1138–52 |
| Frederick Barbarossa | 1152–90 |
| Henry VI | 1190–97 |
| Otto IV | 1198–1215 |
| Philip of Swabia (rival) | 1198–1208 |
| Frederick II | 1215–50 |
| Henry Raspe of Thuringia (rival) | 1246–67 |
| William of Holland (rival) | 1247–56 |
| Conrad IV | 1250–54 |
| *The Great Interregnum* | 1254–73 |

*Rulers from Various Noble Families*

| | |
|---|---|
| Richard of Cornwall (rival) | 1257–72 |
| Alfonso X of Castile (rival) | 1257–73 |
| Rudolf I, Habsburg | 1273–91 |
| Adolf I of Nassau | 1292–98 |
| Albert I, Habsburg | 1298–1303 |
| Henry VII, Luxembourg | 1308–13 |
| Louis IV of Bavaria | 1314–47 |
| Frederick of Habsburg (co-regent) | 1314–25 |
| Charles IV, Luxembourg | 1347–78 |
| Wenceslas of Bohemia | 1378–1400 |
| Frederick III of Brunswick | 1400 |
| Rupert of the Palatinate | 1400–10 |
| Sigismund, Luxembourg | 1411–37 |

*Habsburg Emperors*

| | |
|---|---|
| Albert II | 1438–39 |
| Frederick III | 1440–93 |
| Maximilian I | 1493–1519 |
| Charles V | 1519–56 |
| Ferdinand I | 1556–64 |

| | |
|---|---|
| Maximilian II | 1564–76 |
| Rudolf II | 1576–1612 |
| Matthais | 1612–19 |
| Ferdinand II | 1619–37 |
| Ferdinand III | 1637–57 |
| Leopold I | 1658–1705 |
| Joseph I | 1705–11 |
| Charles VI | 1711–40 |
| Charles VII of Bavaria | 1742–45 |

*Habsburg-Lorraine Emperors*

| | |
|---|---|
| Francis I of Lorraine | 1745–65 |
| Joseph II | 1765–90 |
| Leopold II | 1790–92 |
| Francis II | 1792–1806 |

# ENGLISH SOVEREIGNS
# FROM 900

| Name | Date of accession | Relationship |
|---|---|---|
| *West Saxon Kings* | | |
| Edward the Elder | 901 | son of Alfred the Great |
| Athelstan | 925 | son of Edward I |
| Edmund | 940 | half-brother of Athelstan |
| Edred | 946 | brother of Edmund |
| Edwy | 955 | son of Edmund |
| Edgar | 959 | brother of Edwy |
| Edward the Martyr | 975 | son of Edgar |
| Ethelred II | 978 | son of Edgar |
| Edmund Ironside | 1016 | son of Ethelred |
| *Danish Kings* | | |
| Canute | 1016 | son of Sweyn |
| Hardicanute | 1040 | son of Canute |
| Harold I | 1035 | son of Canute |
| *West Saxon Kings (restored)* | | |
| Edward the Confessor | 1042 | son of Ethelred II |
| Harold II | 1066 | son of Godwin |
| *Norman Kings* | | |
| William I | 1066 | |
| William II | 1087 | son of William I |
| Henry I | 1100 | son of William I |
| Stephen | 1135 | grandson of William II |
| *House of Plantagenet* | | |
| Henry II | 1154 | son of Matilda (daughter of Henry I) |
| Richard I | 1189 | son of Henry II |
| John | 1199 | son of Henry II |
| Henry III | 1216 | son of John |
| Edward I | 1272 | son of Henry III |
| Edward II | 1307 | son of Edward I |
| Edward III | 1327 | son of Edward II |
| Richard II | 1377 | son of the Black Prince |

(son of Edward III)

*House of Lancaster*

| | | |
|---|---|---|
| Henry IV | 1399 | son of John of Gaunt |
| Henry V | 1413 | son of Henry IV |
| Henry VI | 1422 | son of Henry V |

*House of York*

| | | |
|---|---|---|
| Edward IV | 1461 | son of Richard, Duke of York |
| Edward V | 1483 | son of Edward IV |
| Richard III | 1483 | brother of Edward IV |

*House of Tudor*

| | | |
|---|---|---|
| Henry VII | 1485 | son of Edmund Tudor, Earl of Richmond |
| Henry VIII | 1509 | son of Henry VII |
| Edward VI | 1547 | son of Henry VIII |
| Mary I | 1553 | daughter of Henry VIII |

*House of Stuart*

| | | |
|---|---|---|
| Elizabeth I | 1558 | daughter of Henry VIII |
| James I | 1603 | great-grandson of Margaret (daughter of Henry VII) |

*The Commonwealth*

| | | |
|---|---|---|
| Charles I | 1625 | son of James I |

*House of Stuart (restored)*

| | | |
|---|---|---|
| Charles II | 1660 | son of Charles I |
| James II | 1685 | son of Charles I |
| William III and Mary | 1689 | son of Mary (daughter of Charles I)/ daughter of James II |
| Anne | 1702 | daughter of James II |

*House of Hanover*

| | | |
|---|---|---|
| George I | 1714 | son of Sophia (granddaughter of James I) |
| George II | 1727 | son of George I |
| George III | 1760 | son of Frederick (son of George II) |
| George IV | 1820 | son of George III |
| William IV | 1830 | son of George III |
| Victoria | 1837 | daughter of Edward (son of George III) |

*House of Saxe-Coburg*

| | | |
|---|---|---|
| Edward VII | 1901 | son of Victoria |

*House of Windsor*

| | | |
|---|---|---|
| George V | 1910 | son of Edward VII |
| Edward VIII | 1936 | son of George V |
| George VI | 1936 | son of George V |
| Elizabeth II | 1952 | daughter of George VI |

# KINGS OF FRANCE

*Valois Kings of France*

| | |
|---|---|
| Philip VI | 1328–50 |
| John | 1350–64 |
| Charles V | 1364–80 |
| Charles VI | 1380–1422 |
| Charles VII | 1422–61 |
| Louis XI | 1461–83 |
| Charles VIII | 1483–98 |
| Louis XII | 1498–1515 |
| Francis I | 1515–47 |
| Henry II | 1547–59 |
| Francis II | 1559–60 |
| Charles IX | 1560–74 |
| Henry III | 1574–89 |

*Bourbon Kings of France*

| | |
|---|---|
| Henry IV | 1589–1610 |
| Louis XIII | 1610–43 |
| Louis XIV | 1643–1715 |
| Louis XV | 1715–74 |
| Louis XVI | 1774–93 |

# KINGS OF ITALY

| | |
|---|---|
| Vittorio Emanuele II | 1861–78 |
| Umberto I | 1878–1900 |
| Vittorio Emanuele III | 1900–46 |
| Umberto II | 1946 (abdicated) |

# HABSBURGS

*Emperors of Austria*

| | |
|---|---|
| Franz I and II | 1804–35 |
| Ferdinand I | 1835–48 |

*Emperors of Austria-Hungary*

| | |
|---|---|
| Franz Josef | 1848–1916 |
| Karl | 1916–18 (abdicated) |

# RUSSIAN RULERS
# 1547–1917

*House of Rurik*

| | |
|---|---|
| Ivan 'the Terrible' | 1547–84 |
| Theodore I | 1548–98 |
| Irina | 1598 |

| House of Gudonov | |
|---|---|
| Boris Gudonov | 1598–1605 |
| Theodore II | 1605 |

| Usurpers | |
|---|---|
| Dimitri III | 1605–06 |
| Basil IV | 1606–10 |
| Interregnum | 1610–13 |

| House of Romanov | |
|---|---|
| Michael Romanov | 1613–45 |
| Alexis | 1645–76 |
| Theodore III | 1676–82 |
| Peter I and Ivan V (brothers) | 1682–96 |
| Peter I 'Peter the Great' (Tsar) | 1689–1721 |
| Peter I (Emperor) | 1721–25 |
| Catherine I | 1725–27 |
| Peter II | 1727–30 |
| Anna Ivanovna | 1730–40 |
| Ivan VI | 1740–41 |
| Elizabeth | 1741–62 |
| Peter III | 1762 |
| Catherine II 'Catherine the Great' | 1762–96 |
| Paul I | 1796–1801 |
| Alexander I | 1801–25 |
| Nicholas I | 1825–55 |
| Alexander II | 1855–81 |
| Alexander III | 1881–94 |
| Nicholas II | 1894–1917 |

# LEADERS OF THE MODERN WORLD

**Adenauer** Konrad 1876–1967. German Christian Democrat politician, chancellor of West Germany 1949–63. With the French president de Gaulle he achieved the postwar reconciliation of France and Germany and strongly supported all measures designed to strengthen the Western bloc in Europe.

**Allende Gossens** Salvador 1908–1973. Chilean Marxist politician, president from 1970 until his death during a military coup in 1973.

**Amin Dada** Idi 1926– . Ugandan politician, president 1971–79. He led the coup that deposed Milton Obote 1971, expelled the Asian community 1972, and exercised a reign of terror over his people. He fled to Libya when insurgent Ugandan and Tanzanian troops invaded the country 1979.

**Aquino** (Maria) Corazón (born Cojuangco) 1933– . President of the Philippines from 1986, when she was instrumental in the nonviolent overthrow of President Ferdinand Marcos. She has sought to rule in a conciliatory manner, but has encountered opposition from left (communist guerrillas) and right (army coup attempts), and her land reforms have been seen as inadequate.

**Arafat** Yassir 1929– . Palestinian nationalist politician, cofounder of al-Fatah 1956 and president of the Palestine Liberation Organization (PLO) from 1969. In the 1970s his activities in pursuit of an independent homeland for Palestinians made him a prominent figure in world politics, but in the 1980s the growth of factions within the PLO effectively reduced his power. He was forced to evacuate Lebanon 1983, but remained leader of most of the PLO and in 1990 persuaded it to recognize formally the state of Israel. His support for Saddam Hussein after Iraq's invasion of Kuwait 1990 weakened his international standing.

**Attlee** Clement (Richard), 1st Earl 1883–1967. British Labour politician. In the coalition government during World War II he was Lord Privy Seal 1940–42, dominions secretary 1942–43, and Lord President of the Council 1943–45, as well as deputy prime minister from 1942. As prime minister 1945–51 he introduced a sweeping programme of nationalization and a whole new system of social services.

**Babangida** Ibrahim 1941– . Nigerian politician and soldier, president from 1985. He became head of the Nigerian army in 1983 and in 1985 led a coup against President Buhari, assuming the presidency himself.

**Balfour** Arthur James, 1st Earl of Balfour 1848–1930. British Conservative politician, prime minister 1902–05 and foreign secretary 1916–19, when he issued the Balfour Declaration 1917 and was involved in peace negotiations after World War I, signing the Treaty of Versailles.

**Banda** Hastings Kamuzu 1902– . Malawi politican, president from 1966. He led his country's independence movement and was prime minister of Nyasaland (the former name of Malawi) from 1963. He became Malawi's first president in 1966 and in 1971 was named president for life; his rule has been authoritarian.

**Bandaranaike** Sirimavo (born Ratwatte) 1916– . Sri Lankan politician, who succeeded her husband Solomon Bandaranaike to become the world's first female prime minister 1960–65 and 1970–77, but was expelled from parliament 1980 for abuse of her powers while in office. She was largely responsible for the new constitution 1972.

**Bandaranaike** Solomon West Ridgeway Dias 1899–1959. Sri Lankan nationalist politician. In 1951 he founded the Sri Lanka Freedom party and in 1956 became prime minister, pledged to a socialist programme and a neutral foreign policy. He failed to satisfy extremists and was assassinated by a Buddhist monk.

**Begin** Menachem 1913– . Israeli politician, born in Poland. He was a leader of the extremist Irgun Zvai Leumi organization in Palestine from 1942; was prime minister of Israel 1977–83, as head of the right-wing Likud party; and in 1978 shared a Nobel Peace Prize with President Sadat of Egypt for work on the Camp David Agreements for a Middle East peace settlement.

**Ben Bella** Ahmed 1916– . Algerian leader of

the National Liberation Front (FLN) from 1952; prime minister of independent Algeria 1962–65, when he was overthrown by Boumédienne and detained until 1980. He founded a new party, Mouvement pour la Démocratie en Algérie, in 1985. In 1990 he returned to Algeria.

**Beneš** Eduard 1884–1948. Czechoslovak politician. He worked with Thomas Masaryk towards Czechoslovak nationalism from 1918 and was foreign minister and representative at the League of Nations. He was president of the republic from 1935 until forced to resign by the Germans; he headed a government in exile in London during World War II. He returned home as president 1945 but resigned again after the Communist coup 1948.

**Ben-Gurion** David. Adopted name of David Gruen 1886–1973. Israeli statesman and socialist politician, one of the founders of the state of Israel, the country's first prime minister 1948–53, and again 1955–63.

**Bevan** Aneurin 1897–1960. British Labour politician. Son of a Welsh miner, and himself a miner at 13, he became member of Parliament for Ebbw Vale 1929–60. As minister of health 1945–51, he inaugurated the National Health Service (NHS); he was minister of labour Jan–Apr 1951, when he resigned (with Harold Wilson) on the introduction of NHS charges and led a Bevanite faction against the government. In 1956 he became chief labour spokesman on foreign affairs, and deputy leader of the Labour party 1959. He was a good speaker.

**Bevin** Ernest 1881–1951. British Labour politician. Chief creator of the Transport and General Workers' Union, he was its general secretary from 1921 to 1940, when he entered the war cabinet as minister of labour and National Service. He organized the 'Bevin boys', chosen by ballot to work in the coal mines as war service, and was foreign secretary in the Labour government 1945–51.

**Bhutto** Benazir 1953– . Pakistani politician, leader of the Pakistan People's Party (PPP) from 1984 (in exile until 1986), and prime minister of Pakistan 1988–90, when the opposition manoeuvred her from office and charged her with corruption. She was the first female leader of a Muslim state.

**Bhutto** Zulfikar Ali 1928–1979. Pakistani politician, president 1971–73; prime minister from 1973 until the 1977 military coup led by Gen Zia ul Haq. In 1978 he was sentenced to death for conspiring to murder a political opponent and was hanged the following year.

**Bismarck** Otto Eduard Leopold, Prince von 1815–1898. German politician, prime minister of Prussia 1862–90 and chancellor of the German Empire 1871–90. He pursued an aggressively expansionist policy, waging wars against Denmark 1863–64, Austria 1866, and France 1870–71, which brought about the unification of Germany.

**Bokassa** Jean-Bédel 1921– . President and later self-proclaimed emperor of the Central African

Republic 1966–79. Commander in chief from 1963, in Dec 1965 he led the military coup that gave him the presidency. On 4 Dec 1976 he proclaimed the Central African Empire and one year later crowned himself as emperor for life. His regime was characterized by arbitrary state violence and cruelty. Overthrown in 1979, Bokassa was in exile until 1986. Upon his return he was sentenced to death, but this was commuted to life imprisonment 1988.

**Bolger** Jim (James) Brendan 1935– . New Zealand politician and prime minister. A successful sheep and cattle farmer, Bolger was elected as a member of Parliament 1972. He held a variety of cabinet posts under Robert Muldoon's leadership 1977–84, and was an effective, if uncharismatic leader of the opposition from March 1986, leading the National Party to electoral victory Oct 1990.

**Botha** P(ieter) W(illem) 1916– . South African politician. Prime minister from 1978, he initiated a modification of apartheid, which later slowed in the face of Afrikaner (Boer) opposition. In 1984 he became the first executive state president. In 1989 he unwillingly resigned both party leadership and presidency after suffering a stroke, and was succeeded by F W de Klerk.

**Boumédienne** Houari. Adopted name of Mohammed Boukharouba 1925–1978. Algerian politician who brought the nationalist leader Ben Bella to power by a revolt 1962, and superseded him as president in 1965 by a further coup.

**Brandt** Willy. Adopted name of Karl Herbert Frahm 1913– . West German socialist politician, federal chancellor (premier) 1969–74. He played a key role in the remoulding of the Social Democratic Party (SPD) as a moderate socialist force (leader 1964–87). As mayor of West Berlin 1957–66, Brandt became internationally known during the Berlin Wall crisis 1961. He received the Nobel Peace Prize 1971.

**Brezhnev** Leonid Ilyich 1906–1982. Soviet leader. A protégé of Stalin and Khrushchev, he came to power (after he and Kosygin forced Khrushchev to resign) as general secretary of the Soviet Communist Party (CPSU) 1964–82 and was president 1977–82. Domestically he was conservative; abroad the USSR was established as a military and political superpower during the Brezhnev era, extending its influence in Africa and Asia.

**Brundtland** Gro Harlem 1939– . Norwegian Labour politician. Environment minister 1974–76, she briefly took over as prime minister 1981, and was elected prime minister in 1986 and again in 1990. She chaired the World Commission on Environment and Development which produced the *Brundtland Report* 1987.

**Bush** George 1924– . 41st president of the USA from 1989, a Republican. He was director of the Central Intelligence Agency (CIA) 1976–81 and US vice president 1981–89. He faced economic recession in the USA and was the driving force behind international opposition to Iraq's invasion of Kuwait 1990. Evidence came to light

## PRESIDENTS OF THE UNITED STATES OF AMERICA

| name | party | took office |
|------|-------|-------------|
| 1. George Washington | (Federalist) | 1789 |
| 2. John Adams | (Federalist) | 1797 |
| 3. Thomas Jefferson | (Democratic Republican) | 1801 |
| 4. James Madison | (Democratic Republican) | 1809 |
| 5. James Monroe | (Democratic Republican) | 1817 |
| 6. John Quincy Adams | (Democratic Republican) | 1825 |
| 7. Andrew Jackson | (Democrat) | 1829 |
| 8. Martin Van Buren | (Democrat) | 1837 |
| 9. William Henry Harrison | (Whig) | 1841 |
| 10. John Tyler | (Whig) | 1841 |
| 11. James Knox Polk | (Democrat) | 1845 |
| 12. Zachary Taylor | (Whig) | 1849 |
| 13. Millard Fillmore | (Whig) | 1850 |
| 14. Franklin Pierce | (Democrat) | 1853 |
| 15. James Buchanan | (Democrat) | 1857 |
| 16. Abraham Lincoln | (Republican) | 1861 |
| 17. Andrew Johnson | (Democrat) | 1865 |
| 18. Ulysses Simpson Grant | (Republican) | 1869 |
| 19. Rutherford Birchard Hayes | (Republican) | 1877 |
| 20. James Abram Garfield | (Republican) | 1881 |
| 21. Chester Alan Arthur | (Republican) | 1881 |
| 22. Grover Cleveland | (Democrat) | 1885 |
| 23. Benjamin Harrison | (Republican) | 1889 |
| 24. Grover Cleveland | (Republican) | 1893 |
| 25. William McKinley | (Republican) | 1897 |
| 26. Theodore Roosevelt | (Republican) | 1901 |
| 27. William Howard Taft | (Republican) | 1909 |
| 28. Woodrow Wilson | (Democrat) | 1913 |
| 29. Warren Gamaliel Harding | (Republican) | 1921 |
| 30. Calvin Coolidge | (Republican) | 1923 |
| 31. Herbert C Hoover | (Republican) | 1929 |
| 32. Franklin Delano Roosevelt | (Democrat) | 1933 |
| 33. Harry S Truman | (Democrat) | 1945 |
| 34. Dwight D Eisenhower | (Republican) | 1953 |
| 35. John F Kennedy | (Democrat) | 1961 |
| 36. Lyndon B Johnson | (Democrat) | 1963 |
| 37. Richard M Nixon | (Republican) | 1969 |
| 38. Gerald R Ford | (Republican) | 1974 |
| 39. James Earl Carter | (Democrat) | 1977 |
| 40. Ronald Reagan | (Republican) | 1981 |
| 41. George Bush | (Republican) | 1989 |

in 1987 linking him with the Irangate scandal. His responses as president to the Soviet leader Gorbachev's diplomatic initiatives were initially criticized as inadequate, but sending US troops to depose his former ally, General Noriega of Panama, proved a popular move at home. Success in the 1991 Gulf War against Iraq further raised his standing.

**Buthelezi** Chief Gatsha 1928– . Zulu leader and politician, chief minister of KwaZulu, a black 'homeland' in the Republic of South Africa from 1970. He is founder and president of Inkatha 1975, a paramilitary organization for attaining a nonracial democratic political system.

**Callaghan** (Leonard) James, Baron Callaghan

1912– . British Labour politician. As chancellor of the Exchequer 1964–67, he introduced corporation and capital-gains taxes, and resigned following devaluation. He was home secretary 1967–70 and prime minister 1976–79 in a period of increasing economic stress.

**Carlsson** Ingvar (Gösta) 1934– . Swedish socialist politician, leader of the Social Democratic Party, deputy prime minister 1982–86 and prime minister from 1986.

**Carter** Jimmy (James Earl) 1924– . 39th president of the USA 1977–81, a Democrat. In 1976 he narrowly wrested the presidency from Gerald Ford. Features of his presidency were the return of the Panama Canal Zone to Panama, the Camp David Agreements for peace in the Middle East, and the Iranian seizure of US embassy hostages. He was defeated by Ronald Reagan 1980.

**Castro (Ruz)** Fidel 1927– . Cuban Communist politician, prime minister 1959–76 and president from 1976. He led two unsuccessful coups against the right-wing Batista regime and led the revolution that overthrew the dictator 1959. From 1979 he was also president of the nonaligned movement, although promoting the line of the USSR, which subsidized his regime.

**Cavaco Silva** Anibal 1939– . Portuguese politician, finance minister 1980–81, and prime minister and Social Democratic Party (PSD) leader from 1985. Under his leadership Portugal joined the European Community 1985 and the Western European Union 1988.

**Cavour** Camillo Benso di, Count 1810–1861. Italian nationalist politician. Editor of *Il Risorgimento* from 1847. As prime minister of Piedmont 1852–59 and 1860–61, he enlisted the support of Britain and France for the concept of a united Italy achieved in 1861; after expelling the Austrians 1859, he assisted Garibaldi in liberating Southern Italy 1860.

**Ceauşescu** Nicolae 1918–1989. Romanian politician, leader of the Romanian Communist Party (RCP), in power 1965–89. He pursued a policy line independent of and critical of the USSR. He appointed family members, including his wife *Elena Ceauşescu*, to senior state and party posts, and governed in an increasingly repressive manner, zealously implementing schemes that impoverished the nation. The Ceauşescus were overthrown in a bloody revolutionary coup Dec 1989 and executed.

**Chamberlain** (Arthur) Neville 1869–1940. British Conservative politician, son of Joseph Chamberlain. He was prime minister 1937–40; his policy of appeasement towards the fascist dictators Mussolini and Hitler (with whom he concluded the Munich Agreement 1938) failed to prevent the outbreak of World War II. He resigned 1940 following the defeat of the British forces in Norway.

**Chiang Kai-shek** Pinyin *Jiang Jie Shi* 1887–1975. Chinese Nationalist Guomindang (Kuomintang) general and politician, president of China 1928–31 and 1943–49, and of Taiwan from 1949, where he set up a US-supported right-wing government on his expulsion from the mainland by the Communist forces. He was a commander in the civil war that lasted from the end of imperial rule 1911 to the Second Sino-Japanese War and beyond, having split with the Communist leader Mao Zedong 1927.

**Chirac** Jacques 1932– . French conservative politician, prime minister 1974–76 and 1986–88. He established the neo-Gaullist Rassemblement pour la République (RPR) 1976, and became mayor of Paris 1977.

**Chissano** Joaquim 1939– . Mozambique nationalist politician, president from 1986; foreign minister 1975–86.

**Churchill** Winston (Leonard Spencer) 1874–1965. British Conservative politician. In Parliament from 1900, as a Liberal until 1923, he held a number of ministerial offices, including First Lord of the Admiralty 1911–15 and chancellor of the Exchequer 1924–29. Absent from the cabinet in the 1930s, he returned Sept 1939 to lead a coalition government 1940–45, negotiating with Allied leaders in World War II; he was again prime minister 1951–55. Nobel Prize for Literature 1953.

**Craxi** Bettino 1934– . Italian socialist politician, leader of the Italian Socialist Party (PSI) from 1976, prime minister 1983–87.

**Dalai Lama** 14th incarnation 1935– . Spiritual and temporal head of the Tibetan state until 1959, when he went into exile in protest against Chinese annexation and oppression. Tibetan Buddhists believe that each Dalai Lama is a reincarnation of his predecessor and also of Avalokiteśvara.

**de Gaulle** Charles André Joseph Marie 1890–1970. French general and first president of the Fifth Republic 1959–69. He organized the Free French troops fighting the Nazis 1940–44, was head of the provisional French government 1944–46, and leader of his own Gaullist party. In 1958 the national assembly asked him to form a government during France's economic recovery and to solve the crisis in Algeria. He became president at the end of 1958, having changed the constitution to provide for a presidential system, and served until 1969.

**de Klerk** F(rederik) W(illem) 1936– . South African National Party politician, president from 1989. Trained as a lawyer, he entered the South African parliament in 1972. He served in the cabinets of B J Vorster and P W Botha 1978–89, and in Feb and Aug 1989 successively replaced Botha as National Party leader and state president. Projecting himself as a pragmatic conservative who sought gradual reform of the apartheid system, he won the Sept 1989 elections for his party, but with a reduced majority. In Feb 1990 he ended the ban on the African National Congress opposition movement and released its effective leader, Nelson Mandela. All racial descrimination laws relating to property, registration of birth, and communal intermixing were removed 1991. However, black people are still denied the franchise.

**Delors** Jacques 1925– . French socialist politi-cian, finance minister 1981–84. As president of the European Commission from 1984 he has overseen significant budgetary reform and the move towards a free European Community market in 1992, with increased powers residing in Brussels.

**Deng Xiaoping** or **Teng Hsiao-ping** 1904– . Chinese political leader. A member of the Chinese Communist Party (CCP) from the 1920s, he took part in the Long March 1934–36. He was in the Politburo from 1955 until ousted in the Cultural Revolution 1966–69. Reinstated in the 1970s, he gradually took power and introduced a radical economic modernization programme. He retired from the Politburo in 1987 and from his last official position (as chair of State Military Commission) March 1990, but remained influential behind the scenes.

**Diouf** Abdou 1935– . Senegalese politician, president from 1980. He became prime minister 1970 under President Leopold Senghor and, on his retirement, succeeded him, being re-elected in 1983 and 1988.

**Douglas-Home** Alec, Baron Home of the Hirsel 1903–. British Conservative politician. He was foreign secretary 1960–63, and succeeded MacMillan as prime minster 1963. He renounced his peerage (as 14th Earl of Home) to fight (and lose) the general election 1964, and resigned as party leader 1965. He was again foreign secretary 1970–74, when he received a life peerage. His brother is the playwright William Douglas-Home.

**Dubček** Alexander 1921– . Czechoslovak politician, chair of the federal assembly from 1989. He was a member of the resistance movement during World War II, and became first secretary of the Communist Party 1967–69. He launched a liberalization campaign (called the Prague Spring) that was opposed by the USSR and led to the Soviet invasion of Czechoslovakia in 1968. He was arrested by Soviet troops and expelled from the party 1970.

In 1989 he gave speeches at pro-democracy rallies, and in Dec, after the fall of the hardline regime, he was elected speaker of the National Assembly in Prague.

**Duvalier** François 1907–1971. Right-wing president of Haiti 1957–71. Known as **Papa Doc**, he ruled as a dictator, organizing the Tontons Macoutes ('bogeymen') as a private security force to intimidate and assassinate opponents of his regime. He rigged the 1961 elections in order to have his term of office extended until 1967, and in 1964 declared himself president for life. He was excommunicated by the Vatican for harassing the church, and was succeeded on his death by his son Jean-Claude Duvalier.

**Duvalier** Jean-Claude 1951– . Right-wing president of Haiti 1971–86. Known as **Baby Doc**, he succeeded his father François Duvalier, becoming, at the age of 19, the youngest president in the world. He continued to receive support from the USA but was pressured into moderating some elements of his father's regime, yet still tolerated no opposition. In 1986, with Haiti's economy stagnating and with increasing civil disorder, Duvalier fled to France, taking much of the Haitian treasury with him.

**Eden** Anthony, 1st Earl of Avon 1897–1977. British Conservative politician, foreign secretary 1935–38, 1940–45, and 1951–55; prime minister 1955–57, when he resigned after the failure of the Anglo-French military intervention in the Suez Crisis.

**Eisenhower** Dwight David ('Ike') 1890–1969. the 34th president of the USA 1953–60, a Republican. A general in World War II, he commanded the Allied forces in Italy 1943, then the Allied invasion of Europe, and from Oct 1944 all the Allied armies in the West. As president he promoted business interests at home and conducted the Cold War abroad. His vice president was Richard Nixon.

**Ershad** Hussain Mohammad 1930– . Military ruler of Bangladesh 1982–90. He became chief of staff of the Bangladeshi army 1979 and assumed power in a military coup 1982. As president from 1983, Ershad introduced a successful rural-oriented economic programme. He was re-elected 1986 and lifted martial law, but faced continuing political opposition, which forced him to resign in Dec 1990. In 1991 he was sentenced to ten years in prison for illegal possession of arms.

**Farouk** 1920–1965. King of Egypt 1936–52. He succeeded his father Fuad I. In 1952 a coup headed by General Muhammed Neguib and Colonel Gamal Nasser compelled him to abdicate, and his son Fuad II was temporarily proclaimed king in his place.

**Franco** Francisco (Paulino Hermenegildo Teódulo Bahamonde) 1892–1975. Spanish dictator from 1939. As a general, he led the insurgent Nationalists to victory in the Spanish Civil War 1936–39, supported by Fascist Italy and Nazi Germany, and established a dictatorship. In 1942 Franco reinstated the Cortes (Spanish parliament), which in 1947 passed an act by which he became head of state for life.

**Gandhi** Indira (born Nehru) 1917–1984. Indian politician. Prime minister of India 1966–77 and 1980–84, and leader of the Congress Party 1966–77 and subsequently of the Congress (I) party. She was assassinated 1984 by members of her Sikh bodyguard, resentful of her use of troops to clear malcontents from the Sikh temple at Amritsar.

**Gandhi** Mohandas Karamchand, called **Mahatma** ('Great Soul') 1869–1948. Indian Nationalist leader. A pacifist, he led the struggle for Indian independence from the UK by advocating nonviolent noncooperation (*satyagraha*, defence of and by truth) from 1915. He was imprisoned several times by the British authorities and was influential in the Nationalist Congress Party and in the independence negotiations 1947. He was assassinated by a Hindu nationalist in the violence that followed the partition of British India into India and Pakistan.

**Gandhi** Rajiv 1944–1991. Indian politician, prime minister from 1984, following his mother Indira Gandhi's assassination, to Nov 1989.

As prime minister, he faced growing discontent with his party's elitism and lack of concern for social issues. He was assassinated by a bomb at an election rally, for which the Tamil Tigers are believed to have been responsible.

**García Perez** Alan 1949– . Peruvian politician, leader of the moderate, left-wing APRA party; president 1985–90.

**Garibaldi** Giuseppe 1807–1882. Italian soldier who played a central role in the unification of Italy by conquering Sicily and Naples 1860. From 1834 a member of the nationalist Mazzini's Young Italy society, he was forced into exile until 1848 and again 1849–54. He fought against Austria 1848–49, 1859, and 1866, and led two unsuccessful expeditions to liberate Rome from papal rule in 1862 and 1867.

**Geingob** Hage Gottfried 1941– . Namibian politician and prime minister. He played a major role in the South West Africa's People's Organization (SWAPO), acting as a petitioner to the United Nations 1964–71, to obtain international recognition for SWAPO. He was appointed founding director of the United Nations Institute for Namibia in Lusaka, 1975. Geingob became first prime minister of an independent Namibia March 1990.

**Giscard d'Estaing** Valéry 1926– . French conservative politician, president 1974–81. He was finance minister to de Gaulle 1962–66 and Pompidou 1969–74. As leader of the Union pour la Démocratie Française, which he formed in 1978, Giscard sought to project himself as leader of a 'new centre'.

**Goh Chok Tong** 1941–. Singapore politician, prime minister from 1990. A trained economist, Goh became a member of Parliament for the ruling People's Action Party 1976. Rising steadily through the party ranks, he was appointed deputy prime minister 1985, and subsequently chosen by the cabinet as Lee Kuan Yew's successor.

**González Márquez** Felipe 1942– . Spanish socialist politician, leader of the Socialist Workers' Party (PSOE), prime minister from 1982.

**Gorbachev** Mikhail Sergeyevich 1931– . Soviet president, in power from 1985. He was a member of the Politburo from 1980 and, during the Chernenko administration 1984–85, was chair of the Foreign Affairs Commission. As general secretary of the Communist Party (CPSU) from 1985, and president of the Supreme Soviet from 1988, he introduced liberal reforms at home (*perestroika* and *glasnost*), and attempted to halt the arms race abroad. He became head of state 1989 and in March 1990 he was formally elected to a five-year term as executive president with greater powers. At home, his plans for economic reform failed to avert a food crisis in the winter of 1990–91 and his desire to preserve a single, centrally controlled USSR met with resistance from Soviet republics seeking more independent government systems. He was awarded the Nobel Peace Prize 1990, but his international reputation suffered in the light of the harsh repression of nationalist demonstrations in the Baltic states early in 1991. An attempted coup by communist hardliners 19–21 Aug 1991 threw a question mark over his ability to continue a reform programme;on 23 Aug he resigned as general secretary of the Communist Party.

**Havel** Vaclav 1936– . Czech playwright and a leader of Civic Forum movement. As a playwright in Prague, his works, which criticised the Communist regime, were banned throughout Eastern Europe from 1968 and he was subsequently either imprisoned or placed under house arrest. In 1988 he founded the monthly dissident publication, the 'People's Newspaper'.

In 1989, he became a presidential candidate after the resignation of the Communist Gustav Husak. Following the overthrow of the communist regime, he was elected state president by the federal assembly Dec 1989.

**Hawke** Bob (Robert) 1929– . Australian Labor politician, on the right wing of the party. He was president of the Australian Council of Trade Unions 1970–80 and became prime minister 1983.

**Heath** Edward (Richard George) 1916– . British Conservative politician, party leader 1965–75. As prime minister 1970–74 he took the UK into the European Community but was brought down by economic and industrial relations crises at home. In 1990 he undertook a mission to Iraq in an attempt to secure the release of British hostages.

**Hitler** Adolf 1889–1945. German Nazi dictator, born in Austria. Führer (leader) of the Nazi party from 1921, author of *Mein Kampf/My Struggle* 1925–27. As chancellor of Germany from 1933 and head of state from 1934, he created a dictatorship by playing party and state institutions against each other and continually creating new offices and appointments. His position was not seriously challenged until the 'Bomb Plot' 20 July 1944 (See July plot) to assassinate him. In foreign affairs, he reoccupied the Rhineland and formed an alliance with the Italian Fascist Mussolini 1936, annexed Austria 1938, and occupied the Sudetenland under the Munich Agreement. The rest of Czechoslovakia was annexed March 1939. The Hitler–Stalin pact was followed in Sept by the invasion of Poland and the declaration of war by Britain and France. He committed suicide as Berlin fell.

**Ho Chi Minh** adopted name of Nguyen That Tan 1890–1969. North Vietnamese Communist politician, premier and president 1954–69. Having trained in Moscow shortly after the Russian Revolution, he headed the communist Vietminh from 1941 and fought against the French during the Indochina War 1946–54, becoming president and prime minister of the republic at the armistice. Aided by the Communist bloc, he did much to develop industrial potential. He relinquished the premiership 1955, but continued as president. In the years before his death, Ho successfully led his country's fight against US-aided South Vietnam in the Vietnam War 1954–75.

**Honecker** Erich 1912– . German communist politician, in power 1973–89, elected chair of the council of state (head of state) 1976. He governed in an outwardly austere and efficient manner and, while favouring East–West détente, was a loyal ally of the USSR. In Oct 1989, following a wave of pro-democracy demonstrations, he was replaced as leader of the Socialist Unity Party (SED) and head of state by Egon Krenz, and in Dec expelled from the Communist Party.

**Hoxha** Enver 1908–1985. Albanian Communist politician, the country's leader from 1954. He founded the Albanian Communist Party 1941, and headed the liberation movement 1939–44. He was prime minister 1944–54, combining with foreign affairs 1946–53, and from 1954 was first secretary of the Albanian Party of Labour. In policy he was a Stalinist and independent of both Chinese and Soviet communism.

**Hun Sen** 1950–. Cambodian political leader, prime minister from 1985. Originally a member of the Khmer Rouge army, he defected in 1977 to join Vietnam-based anti-Khmer Cambodian forces.

**Hussein** Saddam 1937– . Iraqi left-wing politician, in power from 1968, president from 1979. Ruthless in the pursuit of his objectives, he fought a bitter war against Iran 1980–88 and dealt harshly with Kurdish rebels seeking a degree of independence, using chemical weapons against civilian populations.

In 1990 he ordered the invasion and annexation of Kuwait, provoking an international crisis and a United Nations embargo, followed by military reprisal. Iraq's defeat in the Gulf War by a UN coalition undermined his position as the country's leader; when the Kurds rebelled again, following the end of the Gulf War, he sent the remainder of his army to crush them, bringing international charges of genocide against him and causing hundreds of thousands of Kurds to flee their homes in northern Iraq.

**Iliescu** Ion 1930– . Romanian president. Iliescu was elected a member of the Romanian Communist Party (PCR) central committee 1968, becoming its propaganda secretary 1971. Conflict over the launching of a 'cultural revolution', and the growth of Nicolae Ceauşescu's personality cult led to Iliescu's removal from national politics: he was sent to Timişoara as chief of party propaganda. At the outbreak of the 'Christmas revolution' 1989, Iliescu was one of the first leaders to emerge, heading the National Salvation Front (NSF), and becoming president of the Provisional Council of National Unity Feb 1990. He won an overwhelming victory in the presidential elections in May, despite earlier controversy over his hard line

**Jaruzelski** Wojciech 1923– . Polish general, communist leader from 1981, president from 1985. He imposed martial law for the first year of his rule, suppressed the opposition, and banned trade-union activity, but later released many political prisoners. In 1989, elections in favour of the free trade union Solidarity forced Jaruzelski to speed up democratic reforms, overseeing a transition to a new form of 'socialist pluralist' democracy, stepping down as president 1990.

**Jayawardene** Junius Richard 1906– . Sri Lankan politician. Leader of the United Nationalist Party from 1973, he became prime minister 1977 and the country's first president 1978–88.

**Jiang** Zemin 1926– . Chinese political leader. The son-in-law of Li Xiannian, he joined the Chinese Communist Party's politburo in 1987 after serving in the Moscow embassy and as mayor of Shanghai. He succeeded Zhao Ziyang as party leader after the Tiananmen Square massacre of 1989. A cautious proponent of economic reform coupled with unswerving adherence to the party's 'political line', he subsequently replaced Deng Xiaoping as head of the influential central military commission.

**Jinnah** Muhammad Ali 1876–1948. Indian politician, Pakistan's first governor general from 1947. He was president of the Muslim League from 1934, and by 1940 was advocating the need for a separate state of Pakistan; at the 1946 conferences in London he insisted on the partition of British India into Hindu and Muslim states.

**Johnson** Lyndon Baines 1908–1973. 36th president of the USA 1963–69, a Democrat. He was born in Stonewall, Texas, elected to Congress 1937–49 and the Senate 1949–60. His persuasive powers and hard work on domestic issues led J F Kennedy to ask him to be his vice presidential running mate 1960. Johnson brought critical Southern support which won a narrow victory.

**Kádár** János 1912–1989. Hungarian Communist leader, in power 1956–88, after suppressing the national uprising. As Hungarian Socialist Workers' Party (HSWP) leader and prime minister 1956–58 and 1961–65, Kádár introduced a series of market-socialist economic reforms, while retaining cordial political relations with the USSR.

**Kaifu** Toshiki 1932– . Japanese conservative politician, prime minister from 1989. A protégé of former premier Takeo Miki, he was selected as a compromise choice as Liberal Democratic Party president and prime minister in Aug 1989, following the resignation of Sosuke Uno.

**Kaunda** Kenneth (David) 1924– . Zambian politician. Imprisoned in 1958–60 as founder of the Zambia African National Congress, he became in 1964 first prime minister of Northern Rhodesia, then first president of Zambia. In 1973 he introduced one-party rule. He supported the nationalist movement in Southern Rhodesia, now Zimbabwe, and survived a coup attempt 1980 thought to have been promoted by South Africa. He was elected chair of the Organization of African Unity 1987. In 1990 his popularity fell and he was faced with wide anti-government demonstrations, leading to the

acceptance of a multiparty political system.

**Kennedy** John F(itzgerald) 1917–1963. 35th president of the USA 1961–63, a Democrat. Kennedy was the first Roman Catholic and the youngest person to be elected president. In foreign policy he carried through the unsuccessful Bay of Pigs invasion of Cuba, and in 1963 secured the withdrawal of Soviet missiles from the island. His programme for reforms at home, called the *New Frontier*, was posthumously executed by Lyndon Johnson. Kennedy was assassinated while on a state visit to Dallas, Texas, on 22 Nov 1963 by Lee Harvey Oswald (1939–1963), who was in turn shot dead by Jack Ruby.

**Kenyatta** Jomo. Assumed name of Kamau Ngengi c. 1894–1978. Kenyan nationalist politician, prime minister from 1963, as well as first president of Kenya from 1964 until his death. He led the Kenya African Union from 1947 (*KANU* from 1963) and was active in liberating Kenya from British rule.

**Khaddhafi** or *Gaddafi* or *Qaddafi*, Moamer al 1942– . Libyan revolutionary leader. Overthrowing King Idris 1969, he became virtual president of a republic, although he nominally gave up all except an ideological role 1974. He favours territorial expansion in N Africa reaching as far as Zaïre, has supported rebels in Chad, and proposed mergers with a number of countries. His theories, based on those of the Chinese communist leader Mao Zedong, are contained in a *Green Book*.

**Khomeini** Ayatollah Ruhollah 1900–1989. Iranian Shi'ite Muslim leader, born in Khomein, central Iran. Exiled for opposition to the Shah from 1964, he returned when the Shah left the country 1979, and established a fundamentalist Islamic republic. His rule was marked by a protracted war with Iraq, and suppression of opposition within Iran, executing thousands of opponents.

**Khrushchev** Nikita Sergeyevich 1894–1971. Soviet politician, secretary general of the Communist Party 1953–64, premier 1958–64. He emerged as leader from the power struggle following Stalin's death and was the first official to denounce Stalin, in 1956. His destalinization programme gave rise to revolts in Poland and Hungary 1956. Because of problems with the economy and foreign affairs (a breach with China 1960; conflict with the USA in the Cuban missile crisis 1962), he was ousted by Leonid Brezhnev and Alexei Kosygin.

**Kim Il Sung** 1912–. North Korean Communist politician and marshal. He became prime minister 1948 and president 1972, retaining the presidency of the Communist Workers' party. He likes to be known as the 'Great Leader' and has campaigned constantly for the reunification of Korea. His son *Kim Jong Il* (1942– ), known as the 'Dear Leader', has been named as his successor.

**King** Martin Luther Jr 1929–1968. US civil-rights campaigner, black leader, and Baptist minister. He first came to national attention as leader of the Montgomery, Alabama, bus boycott 1955, and was one of the organizers of the massive (200,000 people) march on Washington DC 1963 to demand racial equality. An advocate of nonviolence, he was awarded the Nobel Peace Prize 1964. He was assassinated in Memphis, Tennessee by James Earl Ray. King's birthday (15 Jan) is observed on the third Monday in Jan as a public holiday in the USA.

**Kinnock** Neil 1942– . British Labour politician, party leader from 1983. Born and educated in Wales, he was elected to represent a Welsh constituency in Parliament 1970 (Islwyn from 1983). He was further left than prime ministers Wilson and Callaghan, but as party leader (in succession to Michael Foot) adopted a moderate position, initiating a major policy review 1988–89.

**Kissinger** Henry 1923– . German-born US diplomat. Following a brilliant academic career at Harvard University, he was appointed assistant for National Security Affairs in 1969 by President Nixon, and was secretary of state 1973–77. His missions to the USSR and China improved US relations with both countries, and he took part in negotiating US withdrawal from Vietnam 1973 and in Arab-Israeli peace negotiations 1973–75. Nobel Peace Prize 1973.

**Kohl** Helmut 1930– . German conservative politician, leader of the Christian Democratic Union (CDU) from 1976, West German chancellor 1982–90 and chancellor of the newly united Germany from 1990.

**Lange** David (Russell) 1942– . New Zealand Labour Party prime minister 1983–89. Lange, a barrister, was elected to the House of Representatives in 1977. Labour had a decisive win in the 1984 general election on a non-nuclear military policy, which Lange immediately put into effect, despite criticism from the USA. He introduced a free-market economic policy and was re-elected 1987. He resigned Aug 1989 over a disagreement with his finance minister.

**Lee Kuan Yew** 1923–. Singapore politician, prime minister from 1959. Lee founded the anticommunist Socialist People's Action Party 1954 and entered the Singapore legislative assembly 1955. He was elected the country's first prime minister 1959, and took Singapore out of the Malaysian federation 1965. He remained in power until his resignation in 1990. He was succeeded by Goh Chok Tongo.

**Lenin** Vladimir Ilyich. Adopted name of Vladimir Ilyich Ulyanov 1870–1924. Russian revolutionary, first leader of the USSR, and communist theoretician. Active in the 1905 Revolution, Lenin had to leave Russia when it failed, settling in Switzerland 1914. He returned to Russia after the February revolution of 1917. He led the Bolshevik revolution in Nov 1917 and became leader of a Soviet government, concluded peace with Germany, and organized a successful resistance to White Russian (pro-tsarist) uprisings and foreign intervention 1918–20. His modification of traditional Marxist doctrine to fit conditions prevailing in Russia became known as *Marxism-Leninism*,

the basis of communist ideology.

**Lincoln** Abraham 1809–1865. 16th president of the USA 1861–65. In the US Civil War, his chief concern was the preservation of the Union from which the Confederate (Southern) slave states had seceded on his election. In 1863 he announced the freedom of the slaves with the Emancipation Proclamation. He was re-elected 1864 with victory for the North in sight, but assassinated at the end of the war.

**Li Peng** 1928–. Chinese communist politician, a member of the Politburo from 1985, and head of government from 1987. During the pro-democracy demonstrations 1989 he supported the massacre of students by Chinese troops and the subsequent executions of others. He favours maintaining firm central and party control over the economy, and seeks improved relations with the USSR.

**Lloyd George** David 1863–1945. Welsh Liberal politician, prime minister 1916–22. A pioneer of social reform, as chancellor of the Exchequer 1908–15 he introduced old-age pensions 1908 and health and unemployment insurance 1911. High unemployment, intervention in the Russian Civil War, and use of the military police force the Black and Tans in Ireland eroded his support as prime minister, and creation of the Irish Free State 1921 and his pro-Greek policy against the Turks caused the collapse of his coalition government.

**Lumumba** Patrice 1926–1961. Congolese politician, prime minister of Zaïre 1960. Imprisoned by the Belgians, but released in time to attend the conference giving the Congo independence 1960, he led the National Congolese Movement to victory in the subsequent general election. He was deposed in a coup d'état, and murdered some months later.

**MacDonald** (James) Ramsay 1866–1937. British politician, first Labour prime minister Jan–Oct 1924 and 1929–31. He joined the Independent Labour Party 1894, and became first secretary of the new Labour Party 1900. In Parliament he led the party 1906–14 and 1922–31 and was prime minister of the first two Labour governments. Failing to deal with worsening economic conditions, he left the party to form a coalition government 1931, which was increasingly dominated by Conservatives, until he was replaced by Stanley Baldwin 1935.

**Machel** Samora 1933–1986. Mozambique nationalist leader, president 1975–86. Machel was active in the liberation front Frelimo from its conception 1962, fighting for independence from Portugal. He became Frelimo leader 1966, and Mozambique's first president from independence 1975 until his death in a plane crash near the South African border.

**Macmillan** (Maurice) Harold, 1st Earl of Stockton 1894–1986. British prime minister 1957–63. Conservative MP for Stockton 1924–29 and 1931–45; and for Bromley 1945–64. As minister of housing 1951–54 he achieved the construction of 300,000 new houses a year. He became foreign secretary 1955 and was chancellor of the Exchequer from 1955 to 1957. He became prime minister on the resignation of Anthony Eden after the Suez crisis. Macmillan led the Conservative Party to victory in the 1959 elections on the slogan 'You've never had it so good' (the phrase was borrowed from a US election campaign). Internationally, his realization of the 'wind of change' in Africa advanced the independence of former colonies. In 1963 he attempted to negotiate British entry to the European Economic Community, but was blocked by the French president de Gaulle. Much of his career as prime minister was spent trying to maintain a UK nuclear weapon, and he was responsible for the purchase of US Polaris missiles 1962. Macmillan's nickname Supermac was coined by the cartoonist Vicky. Created Ist Earl of Stockton 1984.

**Major** John 1943– . British Conservative politician, foreign secretary 1989, chancellor of the Exchequer 1989–90, and elected prime minister in the Conservative party leadership election in Nov 1990.

**Makarios III** 1913–1977. Cypriot politician, Greek Orthodox archbishop 1950–77. A leader of the Resistance organization EOKA, he was exiled by the British to the Seychelles 1956–57 for supporting armed action to achieve union with Greece (*enosis*). He was president of the republic of Cyprus 1960–77 (briefly deposed by a Greek military coup July– Dec 1974).

**Mandela** Nelson (Rolihlahla) 1918– . South African politician and lawyer. As organizer of the banned African National Congress (ANC), he was acquitted of treason 1961, but was given a life sentence 1964 on charges of sabotage and plotting to overthrow the government. In prison he became a symbol of unity for the worldwide anti-apartheid movement. In Feb 1990 he was released, the ban on the ANC having been lifted.

**Manley** Michael 1924– . Jamaican politician, prime minister 1972–80 and from 1989, adopting more moderate socialist policies. His father, *Norman Manley* (1893–1969), was founder of the People's National Party and prime minister 1959–62.

**Mao Zedong** or *Mao Tse-tung* 1893–1976. Chinese political leader and Marxist theoretician. A founder of the Chinese Communist Party (CCP) 1921, Mao soon emerged as its leader. He organized the Long March 1934–36 and the war of liberation 1937–49, following which he established a People's Republic and Communist rule in China; he headed the CCP and government until his death. His influence diminished with the failure of his 1958–60 Great Leap Forward, but he emerged dominant again during the 1966–69 Cultural Revolution. Mao adapted communism to Chinese conditions, as set out in the *Little Red Book*.

**Marcos** Ferdinand 1917–1989. Filipino right-wing politician, president from 1965 to 1986, when he was forced into exile in Hawaii. He was backed by the USA when in power, but in 1988 US authorities indicted him and his wife *Imelda Marcos* (1931– ) for racketeering, embezzlement,

and defrauding US banks; she was acquitted after his death.

**Masire** Quett Ketumile Joni 1925– . President of Botswana from 1980. In 1962, with Seretse Khama, he founded the Botswana Democratic Party (BDP) and in 1965 was made deputy prime minister. After independence, in 1966, he became vice president and, on Khama's death in 1980, president, continuing a policy of nonalignment.

**Mazowiecki** Tadeusz 1927– . Polish politician, founder member of Solidarity, and Poland's first postwar noncommunist prime minister 1989–1990. Forced to introduce unpopular economic reforms, he was knocked out in the first round of the Nov 1990 presidential elections, resigning in favour of his former colleague, Lech Walesa.

**Mazzini** Giuseppe 1805–1872. Italian nationalist. He was a member of the revolutionary society, the Carbonari, and founded in exile the nationalist movement Giovane Italia (Young Italy) 1832. Returning to Italy on the outbreak of the 1848 revolution, he headed a republican government established in Rome, but was forced into exile again on its overthrow 1849. He acted as a focus for the movement for Italian unity.

**Meir** Golda 1898–1978. Israeli Labour (*Mapai*) politician. Born in Russia, she emigrated to the USA 1906, and in 1921 went to Palestine. She was foreign minister 1956–66 and prime minister 1969–74. Criticism of the Israelis' lack of preparation for the 1973 Arab-Israeli War led to election losses for Labour and, unable to form a government, she resigned.

**Menem** Carlos Saul 1935– . Argentine politician, president from 1989; leader of the Peronist (Justice Party) movement. As president, he improved relations with the UK.

**Milosevic** Slobodan 1941– . Serbian communist politician. A leading figure in the Yugoslavian Communist Party (LCY) in the republic of Serbia, he became Serbian party chief and president in 1986 and campaigned to reintegrate Kosovo and Vojvodina provinces into 'greater Serbia'.

**Mitterrand** François 1916– . French socialist politician, president from 1981. He held ministerial posts in 11 governments 1947–1958. He founded the French Socialist Party (PS) 1971. In 1985 he introduced proportional representation, allegedly to weaken the growing opposition from left and right.

**Mobutu** Sese-Seko-Kuku-Ngbeandu-Wa-Za-Banga 1930– . Zaïrean president from 1965. He assumed the presidency by coup, and created a unitary state under his centralized government. He abolished secret voting in elections 1976 in favour of a system of acclamation at mass rallies. His personal wealth is estimated at $3–4 billion, and more money is spent on the presidency than on the entire social-services budget. The harshness of some of his policies and charges of corruption have attracted widespread international criticism.

**Moi** Daniel arap 1924– . Kenyan politician, president from 1978. Originally a teacher,

## PRIME MINISTERS OF BRITAIN

| | | | | | | |
|---|---|---|---|---|---|---|
| Sir Robert Walpole | (Whig) | 1721 | Lord J Russell | (Liberal) | 1865 |
| Earl of Wilmington | (Whig) | 1742 | Earl of Derby | (Conservative) | 1866 |
| Henry Pelham | (Whig) | 1743 | Benjamin Disraeli | (Conservative) | 1868 |
| Duke of Newcastle | (Whig) | 1754 | W E Gladstone | (Liberal) | 1886 |
| Duke of Devonshire | (Whig) | 1756 | Benjamin Disraeli | (Conservative) | 1874 |
| Duke of Newcastle | (Whig) | 1757 | W E Gladstone | (Liberal) | 1880 |
| Earl of Bute | (Tory) | 1762 | Marquess of Salisbury | (Conservative) | 1885 |
| George Grenville | (Whig) | 1763 | W E Gladstone | (Liberal) | 1886 |
| Marquess of Rockingham | (Whig) | 1765 | Marquess of Salisbury | (Conservative) | 1886 |
| Duke of Grafton | (Whig) | 1766 | W E Gladstone | (Liberal) | 1892 |
| Lord North | (Tory) | 1770 | Earl of Roseberry | (Liberal) | 1894 |
| Marquess of Rockingham | (Whig) | 1782 | Marquess of Salisbury | (Conservative) | 1895 |
| Earl of Shelbourne | (Whig) | 1782 | Sir H Campbell-Bannerman | (Liberal) | 1905 |
| Duke of Portland | (Coalition) | 1783 | H H Asquith | (Liberal) | 1908 |
| William Pitt | (Tory) | 1783 | H H Asquith | (Coalition) | 1915 |
| Henry Addington | (Tory) | 1801 | D Lloyd George | (Coalition) | 1916 |
| William Pitt | (Tory) | 1804 | A Bonar Law | (Conservative) | 1922 |
| Lord Grenville | (Whig) | 1806 | Stanley Baldwin | (Conservative) | 1923 |
| Duke of Portland | (Tory) | 1807 | Ramsay MacDonald | (Labour) | 1924 |
| Spencer Percival | (Tory) | 1809 | Stanley Baldwin | (Conservative) | 1924 |
| Earl of Liverpool | (Tory) | 1812 | Ramsay MacDonald | (Labour) | 1929 |
| George Canning | (Tory) | 1827 | Ramsay MacDonald | (National) | 1931 |
| Viscount Goderich | (Tory) | 1827 | Stanley Baldwin | (National) | 1935 |
| Duke of Wellington | (Tory) | 1828 | N Chamberlain | (National) | 1937 |
| Earl Grey | (Whig) | 1830 | Sir Winston Churchill | (Coalition) | 1940 |
| Viscount Melbourne | (Whig) | 1834 | Clement Attlee | (Labour) | 1945 |
| Sir Robert Peel | (Conservative) | 1834 | Sir Winston Churchill | (Conservative) | 1951 |
| Viscount Melbourne | (Whig) | 1835 | Sir Anthony Eden | (Conservative) | 1955 |
| Sir Robert Peel | (Conservative) | 1841 | Harold Macmillan | (Conservative) | 1957 |
| Lord J Russell | (Liberal) | 1846 | Sir Alec Douglas-Home | (Conservative) | 1963 |
| Earl of Derby | (Conservative) | 1852 | Harold Wilson | (Labour) | 1964 |
| Lord Aberdeen | (Peelite) | 1852 | Edward Heath | (Conservative) | 1970 |
| Viscount Palmerston | (Liberal) | 1855 | Harold Wilson | (Labour) | 1974 |
| Earl of Derby | (Conservative) | 1858 | James Callaghan | (Labour) | 1976 |
| Viscount Palmerston | (Liberal) | 1859 | Margaret Thatcher | (Conservative) | 1979 |
| | | | John Major | (Conservative) | 1990 |

he became minister of home affairs in 1964, vice president in 1967, and succeeded Jomo Kenyatta as president.

**Mubarak** Hosni 1928– . Egyptian politician, president from 1981. He commanded the air force 1972–75 (and was responsible for the initial victories in the Egyptian campaign of 1973 against Israel), when he became an active vice president to Anwar Sadat, and succeeded him on his assassination. He has continued to pursue Sadat's moderate policies, and has significantly increased the freedom of the press and of political association, while trying to repress the growing Islamic fundamentalist movement.

**Mugabe** Robert (Gabriel) 1925– . Zimbabwean politician, prime minister from 1980 and president from 1987. He was in detention in Rhodesia for nationalist activities 1964–74, then carried on guerrilla warfare from Mozambique. As leader of ZANU he was in an uneasy alliance with Joshua Nkomo of ZAPU (Zimbabwe African People's Union) from 1976. The two parties merged 1987.

**Muldoon** Robert David 1921– . New Zealand National Party politician, prime minister 1975–84.

**Mulroney** Brian 1939– . Canadian politician. A former businessman, he replaced Joe Clark

as Progressive Conservative Party leader 1983 and achieved a landslide victory in the 1984 election to become prime minister. He won the 1988 election on a platform of free trade with the US, and by the end of 1988 the Canada–US trade agreement was approved.

**Mussolini** Benito 1883–1945. Italian dictator from 1925 to 1943. As founder of the Fascist Movement 1919 and prime minister from 1922, he became known as *Il Duce* ('the leader'). He invaded Ethiopia 1935–36, intervened in the Spanish Civil War 1936–39 in support of Franco, and conquered Albania 1939. In June 1940 Italy entered World War II supporting Hitler. Forced by military and domestic setbacks to resign 1943, Mussolini established a breakaway government in N Italy 1944–45, but was killed trying to flee the country.

**Najibullah** Ahmadzai 1947– . Afghan communist politician, a member of the Politburo from 1981, and leader of the ruling People's Democratic Party of Afghanistan (PDPA) from 1986, later state president. His attempts to broaden the support of the PDPA regime had little success, but his government survived the withdrawal of Soviet troops Feb 1989.

**Nakasone** Yasuhiro 1917– . Japanese conservative politician, leader of the Liberal Democratic

Party (LDP) and prime minister 1982–87. He stepped up military spending and increased Japanese participation in international affairs, with closer ties to the USA. He was forced to resign his party post May 1989 as a result of having profited from insider trading in the Recruit scandal.

**Napoleon III** 1808–1873. Emperor of the French 1852–70, known as *Louis-Napoleon*. After two attempted coups (1836 and 1840) he was jailed, then went into exile, returning for the revolution of 1848, when he became president of the Second Republic but soon turned authoritarian. In 1870 he was manoeuvred by the German chancellor Bismarck into war with Prussia; he was forced to surrender at Sedan, NE France, and the empire collapsed.

**Nasser** Gamal Abdel 1918–1970. Egyptian politician, prime minister 1954–56 and from 1956 president of Egypt (the United Arab Republic 1958–71). In 1952 he was the driving power behind the Neguib coup, which ended the monarchy. His nationalization of the Suez Canal 1956 led to an Anglo-French invasion and the Suez Crisis), and his ambitions for an Egyptian-led union of Arab states led to disquiet in the Middle East (and in the West). Nasser was also an early and influential leader of the nonaligned movement.

**Nehru** Jawaharlal 1889–1964. Indian nationalist politician, prime minister from 1947. Before the partition (the division of British India into India and Pakistan) he led the socialist wing of the Nationalist Congress Party, and was second in influence only to Mohandas Gandhi. He was imprisoned nine times by the British 1921–45 for political activities. As prime minister from the creation of the dominion (later republic) of India Aug 1947, he originated the idea of nonalignment (neutrality towards major powers). His daughter was Prime Minister Indira Gandhi.

**Ne Win** Adopted name of Maung Shu Maung 1911- - . Myanmar (Burmese) politician, prime minister 1958–60, ruler from 1962 to 1974, president 1974–81.

**Nixon** Richard (Milhous) 1913– . 37th president of the USA 1969–74, a Republican. He attracted attention as a member of the Un-American Activities Committee 1948, and was vice president to Eisenhower 1953–61. As president he was responsible for US withdrawal from Vietnam, and forged new links with China, but at home his culpability in the cover-up of the Watergate scandal and the existence of a 'slush fund' for political machinations during his re-election campaign 1972 led to his resignation 1974 after being threatened with impeachment.

**Nkomo** Joshua 1917– . Zimbabwean politician, president of ZAPU (Zimbabwe African People's Union) from 1961 and a leader of the black nationalist movement against the white Rhodesian regime. He was a member of Robert Mugabe's cabinet in 1980–82 and from 1987.

**Nkrumah** Kwame 1909–1972. Ghanaian nationalist politician, prime minister of the Gold Coast (Ghana's former name) 1952–57 and of newly independent Ghana 1957–60. He became Ghana's first president 1960 but was overthrown in a coup 1966. His policy of 'African socialism' led to links with the Communist bloc.

**Noriega** Manuel Antonio Morena 1940– . Panamanian soldier and politician, effective ruler of Panama from 1982 until arrested by the USA 1989 and detained for trial on drug-trafficking charges.

**Nujoma** Sam 1929– . Namibian left-wing politician, president from 1990, founder and leader of SWAPO (the South-West Africa People's Organization) from 1959. He was exiled in 1960 and controlled guerrillas from Angolan bases until the first free elections were held 1989, taking office early the following year.

**Nyerere** Julius (Kambarage) 1922– . Tanzanian socialist politician, president 1964–85. Originally a teacher, he devoted himself from 1954 to the formation of the Tanganyika African National Union and subsequent campaigning for independence. He became chief minister 1960, was prime minister of Tanganyika 1961–62, president of the newly formed Tanganyika Republic 1962–64, and first president of Tanzania 1964–85.

**Obote** (Apollo) Milton 1924– . Ugandan politician who led the independence movement from 1961. He became prime minister 1962 and was president 1966–71 and 1980–85, being overthrown by first Idi Amin and then Lt-Gen Tito Okello.

**Ortega (Saavedra)** Daniel 1945– . Nicaraguan socialist politician, head of state 1981–90. He was a member of the Sandinista Liberation Front (FSLN), which overthrew the regime of Anastasio Somoza 1979. US-sponsored Contra guerrillas opposed his government from 1982.

**Ozal** Turgut 1927– . Turkish Islamic right-wing politician, prime minister 1983–89, president from 1989.

**Palme** (Sven) Olof 1927–1986. Swedish social-democratic politician, prime minister 1969–76 and 1982–86. He entered government 1963, holding several posts before becoming leader of the Social Democratic Labour Party (SAP) 1969. He was assassinated Feb 1986.

**Papandreou** Andreas 1919– . Greek socialist politician, founder of the Pan-Hellenic Socialist Movement (PASOK), and prime minister 1981–89, when he became implicated in the alleged embezzlement and diversion of funds to the Greek government of $200 million from the Bank of Crete, headed by George Koskotas, and lost the election.

**Pérez de Cuéllar** Javier 1920– . Peruvian diplomat, secretary-general of the United Nations from 1982. A delegate to the first UN General Assembly 1946–47, he subsequently held several ambassadorial posts. He raised the standing of the UN by his successful diplomacy in ending the Iran-Iraq war in 1988 and securing the independence of Namibia 1989. He was, however, unable to resolve the Gulf conflict resulting from Iraq's invasion of Kuwait 1990.

**Perón** Juan (Domingo) 1895–1974. Argentine politician, dictator 1946–55 and from 1973 until his death. He took part in the military coup 1943, and his popularity with the *descamisados* ('shirtless ones') led to his election as president 1946. He instituted social reforms, but encountered economic difficulties. After the death of his second wife Eva Perón he lost popularity, and was deposed in a military coup 1955. He returned from exile to the presidency 1973, but died in office 1974, and was was succeeded by his third wife Isabel Perón.

**Pinochet (Ugarte)** Augusto 1915– . Military ruler of Chile from 1973, when a coup backed by the US Central Intelligence Agency ousted and killed President Salvador Allende. Pinochet took over the presidency and governed ruthlessly, crushing all opposition. He was voted out of power when general elections were held in Dec 1989 but remains head of the armed forces until 1997. In 1990 his attempt to reassert political influence was firmly censured by President Patricio Aylwin.

**Pol Pot** (also known as *Saloth Sar, Tol Saut,* and *Pol Porth*) 1925– . Cambodian politician and Communist party leader; a member of the anti-French resistance under Ho Chi Minh in the 1940s. As leader of the Khmer Rouge, he overthrew the government 1975 and proclaimed Democratic Kampuchea with himself as premier. His policies were to evacuate cities and put people to work in the countryside. The Khmer Rouge also carried out a systematic large-scale extermination of the Western-influenced educated and middle classes (3–4 million) before the regime was overthrown by a Vietnamese invasion 1979. Pol Pot continued to help lead the Khmer Rouge until their withdrawal in 1989; in that year too he resigned from his last position within the Khmer Rouge.

**Primo de Rivera** Miguel 1870–1930. Spanish soldier and politician, dictator from 1923 as well as premier from 1925. He was captain-general of Catalonia when he led a coup against the ineffective monarchy and became virtual dictator of Spain with the support of Alfonso XIII. He resigned 1930.

**Rafsanjani** Hojatoleslam Ali Akbar Hashemi 1934– . Iranian politician and cleric, president from 1989. After training as a mullah (Islamic teacher) under Ayatollah Khomeini in Qom, he acquired considerable wealth through his construction business but kept in touch with his exiled mentor. When the Ayatollah returned after the revolution of 1979–80, Rafsanjani became the speaker of the Iranian parliament and, after Khomeini's death, state president and effective political leader.

**Ramphal** Shridath Surendranath ('Sonny') 1928– . Guyanese politician. He was minister of foreign affairs and justice 1972–75 and secretary-general of the British Commonwealth 1975–90.

**Reagan** Ronald (Wilson) 1911– . 40th president of the USA 1981–89, a Republican. He was governor of California 1966–74, and a former Hollywood actor. Reagan was a hawkish and popular president. He adopted an aggressive policy in Central America, attempting to overthrow the government of Nicaragua, and invading Grenada 1983. In 1987, Irangate was investigated by the Tower Commission; Reagan admitted that USA–Iran negotiations had become an 'arms for hostages deal', but denied knowledge of resultant funds being illegally sent to the Contras in Nicaragua. He increased military spending (sending the national budget deficit to record levels), cut social programmes, introduced deregulation of domestic markets, and cut taxes. His Strategic Defense Initiative, announced 1983, proved controversial owing to the cost and unfeasibility. He was succeeded by George Bush.

**Robinson** Mary 1944– . Irish Labour politician, president from 1990. She became a professor of law at 25 and has campaigned for women's rights in Ireland.

**Rocard** Michel 1930– . French socialist politician, prime minister from 1988. A former radical, he joined the Socialist Party (PS) 1973, emerging as leader of its moderate social-democratic wing. He held ministerial office under Mitterrand 1981–85.

**Roh Tae-woo** 1932–. South Korean right-wing politician and general. He held ministerial office from 1981 under President Chun, and became chair of the ruling Democratic Justice Party 1985. He was elected president 1987, amid allegations of fraud and despite being connected with the massacre of about 2,000 anti-government demonstrators 1980.

**Roosevelt** Franklin Delano 1882–1945. 32nd president of the USA 1933–45, a Democrat. He served as governor of New York 1929–33. Becoming president amid the Depression, he launched the *New Deal* economic and social reform programme, which made him popular with the people. After the outbreak of World War II he introduced Lend-Lease for the supply of war materials and services to the Allies and drew up the Atlantic Charter of solidarity. Once the USA had entered the war 1941 he spent much time in meetings with Allied leaders (including the Québec, Tehran, and Yalta conferences).

**Sadat** Anwar 1918–1981. Egyptian politician. Succeeding Nasser as president 1970, he restored morale by his handling of the Egyptian campaign in the 1973 war against Israel. In 1974 his plan for economic, social, and political reform to transform Egypt was unanimously adopted in a referendum. In 1977 he visited Israel to reconcile the two countries, and shared the Nobel Peace Prize with Israeli prime minister Menachem Begin 1978. He was assassinated by Islamic fundamentalists.

**Salazar** Antonio de Oliveira 1889–1970. Portuguese prime minister 1932–68 who exercised a virtual dictatorship. A corporative constitution on the Italian model was introduced 1933, and until 1945 Salazar's National Union, founded 1930, remained the only legal party. Salazar was also foreign minister 1936–47 and during World War II he maintained Portuguese neutrality. But he fought long colonial wars in Africa (Angola and Mozambique) that impeded his country's economic development.

**Sarney (Costa)** José 1930– . Brazilian politician, member of the Democratic Movement (PMDB), president 1985–90.

**Schmidt** Helmut 1918– . German socialist politician, member of the Social Democratic Party (SPD), chancellor of West Germany 1974–83. As chancellor, Schmidt introduced social reforms and continued Brandt's policy of Ostpolitik. With the French president Giscard d'Estaing, he instigated annual world and European economic summits. He was a firm supporter of NATO and of the deployment of US nuclear missiles in West Germany during the early 1980s.

**Shamir** Yitzhak 1915– . Israeli right-wing politician, born in Poland; prime minister 1983–84 and from 1986; leader of the Likud (Consolidation Party). He was foreign minister under Menachem Begin 1980–83, and again foreign minister in the Peres unity government 1984–86.

**Smith** Ian Douglas 1919– . Rhodesian politician. He was a founder of the Rhodesian Front 1962 and prime minister 1964–79. In 1965 he made a unilateral declaration of Rhodesia's independence and, despite United Nations sanctions, maintained his regime with tenacity. In 1979 he was succeeded as prime minister by Bishop Abel Muzorewa, when the country was renamed Zimbabwe. He was suspended from the Zimbabwe parliament in April 1987 and resigned in May as head of the white opposition party.

**Soares** Mario 1924– . Portuguese socialist politician, president from 1986. Exiled in 1970, he returned to Portugal in 1974, and, as leader of the Portuguese Socialist Party, was prime minister 1976–78. He resigned as party leader in 1980, but in 1986 he was elected Portugal's first socialist president.

**Stalin** Joseph. Adopted name (Russian 'steel') of Joseph Vissarionovich Djugashvili 1879–1953. Soviet politician. A member of the October Revolution Committee 1917, Stalin became general secretary of the Communist Party 1922. After Lenin's death 1924, Stalin sought to create 'socialism in one country' and clashed with Trotsky, who denied the possibility of socialism inside Russia until revolution had occurred in W Europe. Stalin won this ideological struggle by 1927, and a series of five-year plans was launched to collectivize industry and agriculture from 1928. All opposition was eliminated in the Great Purge 1936–38. During World War II, Stalin intervened in the military direction of the campaigns against Nazi Germany. His role was denounced after his death by Khrushchev and other members of the Soviet regime.

**Stroessner** Alfredo 1912– . Military leader and president of Paraguay 1954–89. As head of the armed forces from 1951, he seized power in a coup in 1954 sponsored by the right-wing ruling Colorado Party. Accused by his opponents of harsh repression, his regime spent heavily on the military to preserve his authority. He was overthrown by a military coup and gained asylum in Brazil.

**Suharto** Raden 1921– . Indonesian politician and general. He ousted Sukarno to become president in 1967. He ended confrontation with Malaysia, invaded East Timor in 1975, and reached a cooperation agreement with Papua New Guinea 1979. His authoritarian rule has met domestic opposition from the left. He was re-elected in 1973, 1978, 1983, and 1988.

**Sukarno** Achmed 1901–1970. Indonesian nationalist, president 1945–67. During World War II he cooperated in the local administration set up by the Japanese, replacing Dutch rule. After the war he became the first president of the new Indonesian republic, becoming president-for-life in 1966; he was ousted by Suharto.

**Tambo** Oliver 1917– . South African nationalist politician, in exile 1960–90, president of the African National Congress (ANC) from 1977.

**Thatcher** Margaret Hilda (born Roberts) 1925– . British Conservative politician, prime minister 1979–1990. She was education minister 1970–74 and Conservative party leader from 1975. In 1982 she sent British troops to recapture the Falkland Islands from Argentina. She confronted trade-union power during the miners' strike 1984–85, sold off majority stakes in many public utilities to the private sector, and reduced the influence of local government through such measures as the abolition of metropolitan councils, the control of expenditure through 'rate-capping', and the introduction of the community charge or poll tax from 1989. In 1990 splits in the cabinet over the issues of Europe and consensus government forced her resignation. An astute Parliamentary tactician, she tolerated little disagreement, either from the opposition or from within her own party.

**Tito** adopted name of Josip Broz 1892–1980. Yugoslav soldier and communist politician, in power from 1945. In World War II he organized the National Liberation Army to carry on guerrilla warfare against the German invasion 1941, and was created marshal 1943. As prime minister 1946–53 and president from 1953, he followed a foreign policy of 'positive neutralism'.

**Trotsky** Leon. Adopted name of Lev Davidovitch Bronstein 1879–1940. Russian revolutionary. He joined the Bolshevik party and took a leading part in the seizure of power 1917 and raising the Red Army that fought the Civil War 1918–20. In the struggle for power that followed Lenin's death 1924, Stalin defeated Trotsky, and this and other differences with the Communist Party led to his exile 1929. He settled in Mexico, where he was assassinated with an ice pick at Stalin's instigation. Trotsky believed in world revolution and in permanent revolution, and was an uncompromising, if liberal, idealist.

**Trudeau** Pierre (Elliott) 1919– . Canadian Liberal politician. He was prime minister 1968–79 and won again by a landslide Feb 1980. In 1980 his work helped to defeat the Québec independence movement in a referendum. He repatriated the constitution from Britain 1982, but by 1984 had so lost support that he resigned.

**Truman** Harry S 1884–1972. 33rd president of the USA 1945–53, a Democrat. In Jan 1945 he became vice president to F D Roosevelt, and president when Roosevelt died in Apr that year. He used the atom bomb against Japan, launched the Marshall Plan to restore W Europe's economy, and nurtured the European Community and NATO (including the rearmament of West Germany).

**Tutu** Desmond (Mpilo) 1931– . South African priest, Anglican archbishop of Cape Town and general secretary of the South African Council of Churches 1979–84. One of the leading figures in the struggle against apartheid in the Republic of South Africa, he received the 1984 Nobel Peace Prize.

**Ulbricht** Walter 1893–1973. East German communist politician, in power 1960–71. He lived in exile in the USSR during Hitler's rule 1933–45. A Stalinist, he became first secretary of the Socialist Unity Party in East Germany 1950 and (as chair of the Council of State from 1960) was instrumental in the building of the Berlin Wall 1961. He established East Germany's economy and recognition outside the Eastern European bloc.

**U Thant** 1909–1974. Burmese diplomat, secretary general of the United Nations 1962–71. He helped to resolve the US-Soviet crisis over the Soviet installation of missiles in Cuba, and he made the controversial decision to withdraw the UN peacekeeping force from the Egypt–Israel border 1967 (see Arab-Israeli Wars).

**Waldheim** Kurt 1918– . Austrian politician and diplomat, president from 1986. He was secretary general of the United Nations 1972–81, having been Austria's representative there 1964–68 and 1970–71. He was elected president of Austria despite revelations that during World War II he had been an intelligence officer in an army unit responsible for transporting Jews to death camps.

**Walesa** Lech 1943– . Polish trade-union leader and president of Poland from 1990, founder of Solidarity (Solidarność) in 1980, an organization, independent of the Communist Party, which forced substantial political and economic concessions from the Polish government 1980–81 until being outlawed. Nobel Peace Prize 1983.

**Weizmann** Chaim 1874–1952. Zionist leader, the first president of Israel (1948–52), and chemist. Born in Russia, he became a naturalized British subject, and as director of the Admiralty laboratories 1916–19 discovered a process for manufacturing acetone, a solvent. He conducted the negotiations leading up to the Balfour Declaration, by which Britain declared its support for an independent Jewish state. He became head of the Hebrew University in Jerusalem, then in 1948 became the first president of the new republic of Israel.

**Wilson** (Thomas) Woodrow 1856–1924. 28th president of the US 1913–21, a Democrat. He kept the US out of World War I until 1917 and in Jan 1918 issued his Fourteen Points as a basis for a just peace settlement. At the peace conference in Paris he secured the inclusion of the League of Nations covenant in individual peace treaties, but these were not ratified by Congress, so the US did not join the League. He was awarded the Nobel Peace Prize 1919.

**Wilson** (James) Harold, Baron Wilson of Rievaulx 1916– . British Labour politician, party leader from 1963, prime minister 1964–70 and 1974–76. His premiership was dominated by the issue of UK admission to membership of the European Community, the social contract (unofficial agreement with the trade unions), and economic difficulties.

**Yeltsin** Boris Nikolayevich 1931– . Soviet 're-form' communist politician, president of the Russian Republic from 1990. He was Moscow party chief 1985–87, when he was dismissed after criticizing the slow pace of political and economic reform. He was re-elected in Mar 1989 with a 89% share of the vote, defeating an 'official Communist Party' candidate, and was elected to the Supreme Soviet in May 1989. He supported the Baltic states in their calls for greater independence and has demanded increasingly more radical economic reform. In April 1991 the Russian Republic congress voted him emergency powers. Yeltsin's strong reformist stance was immeasurably strengthened by leading a staunch, successful opposition to the attempted coup 19–21 Aug 1991.

**Zhao Ziyang** 1918–. Chinese politician, prime minister from 1980, and secretary of the Chinese Communist Party (CCP) 1987–89. His reforms included self-management and incentives for workers and factories. He lost his secretaryship and other posts after the Tiananmen Square massacre in Beijing June 1989.

**Zia ul-Haq** Mohammad 1924–1988. Pakistani general, in power from 1977 until his death, probably an assassination, in an aircraft explosion. He became army chief of staff 1976, led the military coup against Zulfiqar Ali Bhutto 1977, and became president 1978. Zia introduced a fundamentalist Islamic regime and restricted political activity.

## THE THIRD WORLD

One of the major political changes to have taken place in recent history has been the break-up of the European overseas empires. Apart from the Spanish colonies in south and central America which achieved their independence in the early 19th century, nearly all of this decolonization has taken place since the end of World War II, either by negotiation or by force. This has created many new, independent, sovereign states in South and Central America, Africa and Asia—all of whom share the experience of having been colonized as part of the Third World (where the USA and USSR form the First World, and the industrialized European states together with Canada and Japan the Second World). While the term Third World may indicate a colonial past, it also indicates the present economic situation of those countries, industrially underdeveloped and dependent on the developed world for many essential products. This relationship between the industrialized nations and the Third World has created a severe debt crisis for many of the underdeveloped nations, which have to raise loans internationally merely in order to pay off existing debts rather than for industrial or agricultural development projects.

The table below outlines the colonial origins of the major Third World states and their current political orientation.

## From Colonialism to Independence: The Break-up of the Empires

### Belgium

| current name | colonial names and history | colonized | independent |
|---|---|---|---|
| Zaïre | Belgian Congo | 1885 | 1960 |

### France

| current name | colonial names and history | colonized | independent |
|---|---|---|---|
| Cambodia | Kampuchea 1970–89 | 1863 | 1953 |
| Laos | French Indochina (protectorate) | 1893 | 1954 |
| Vietnam | Tonkin, Annam, Cochin-China to 1954 | 1858 | 1954 |
| | North and South Vietnam 1954–76 | | |
| Burkina Faso | Upper Volta to 1984 | 1896 | 1960 |
| Central African Republic | Ubangi-Shari | 19th century | 1960 |
| Chad | French Equatorial Africa | 19th century | 1960 |
| Côte d'Ivoire | Ivory Coast to 1986 | 1883 | 1960 |
| Madagascar | | 1896 | 1960 |
| Mali | French Sudan | 19th century | 1960 |
| Niger | | 1912 | 1960 |
| Algeria | colonized in 19th century; incorporated into France 1881 | c. 1840 | 1962 |

### The Netherlands

| current name | colonial names and history | colonized | independent |
|---|---|---|---|
| Indonesia | Netherlands Indies | 17th century | 1949 |
| Suriname | British colony 1650–67 | 1667 | 1975 |

### Portugal

| current name | colonial names and history | colonized | independent |
|---|---|---|---|
| Brazil | | 1532 | 1822 |
| Uruguay | province of Brazil | 1533 | 1828 |
| Mozambique | | 1505 | 1975 |
| Angola | | 1491 | 1975 |

### Spain

| current name | colonial names and history | colonized | independent |
|---|---|---|---|
| Paraguay | viceroyalty of Buenos Aires | 1537 | 1811 |
| Argentina | viceroyalty of Buenos Aires | 16th century | 1816 |
| Chile | | 1541 | 1818 |
| Costa Rica | | 1563 | 1821 |
| Mexico | viceroyalty of New Spain | 16th century | 1821 |
| Peru | | 1541 | 1824 |
| Bolivia | | 16th century | 1825 |
| Ecuador | Greater Colombia 1822–30 | 16th century | 1830 |
| Venezuela | captaincy-general of Caracas to 1822 | 16th century | 1830 |
| | Greater Colombia | 1822–30 | |
| Honduras | federation of Central America 1821–38 | 1523 | 1838 |
| El Salvador | federation of Central America 1821–39 | 16th century | 1839 |
| Guatemala | federation of Central America 1821–39 | 16th century | 1839 |
| Dominican Republic | Hispaniola to 1821 | 16th century | 1844 |
| | ruled by Haiti to 1844 | | |
| Cuba | | 1512 | 1898 |
| Colombia | viceroyalty of New Granada to 1819 | 16th century | 1903 |
| | Greater Colombia to 1830 | | |
| Panama | part of Colombia to 1903 | 16th century | 1903 |
| Philippines | Spain 1565–1898, US 1898–1946 | 1565 | 1946 |

### United Kingdom

| current name | colonial names and history | colonized | independent |
|---|---|---|---|
| India | British E India Co. 18th century–1858 | 18th century | 1947 |
| Pakistan | British E India Co. 18th century–1858 | 18th century | 1947 |
| Sri Lanka | Portuguese, Dutch 1602–1796; Ceylon 1802–1972 | 16th century | 1948 |
| Ghana | Gold Coast | 1618 | 1957 |

## FROM COLONIALISM TO INDEPENDENCE: THE BREAK-UP OF THE EMPIRES (Cont.)

| current name | colonial names and history | colonized | independent |
|---|---|---|---|
| Nigeria | | 1861 | 1960 |
| Cyprus | Turkish to 1878, then British rule | 1878 | 1960 |
| Sierra Leone | British protectorate | 1788 | 1961 |
| Tanzania | German E Africa to 1921; British mandate from League of Nations/UN as Tanganyika | 19th century | 1961 |
| Jamaica | Spanish to 1655 | 17th century | 1962 |
| Trinidad & Tobago | Spanish 1532–1797; British 1797–1962 | 1532 | 1962 |
| Uganda | British protectorate | 1894 | 1962 |
| Kenya | British colony from 1920 | 1895 | 1963 |
| Malaysia | British interests from 1786; Federation of Malaya 1957–63 | 1874 | 1963 |
| Malawi | British protectorate of Nyasaland 1907–53; Federation of Rhodesia & Nyasaland 1953–64 | 1891 | 1964 |
| Malta | French 1798–1814 | 1798 | 1964 |
| Zambia | N Rhodesia – British protectorate; Federation of Rhodesia & Nyasaland 1953–64 | 1924 | 1964 |
| The Gambia | | 1888 | 1965 |
| Singapore | Federation of Malaya 1963–65 | 1858 | 1965 |
| Guyana | Dutch to 1796; British Guiana 1796–1966 | 1620 | 1966 |
| Botswana | Bechuanaland – British protectorate | 1885 | 1966 |
| Lesotho | Basutoland | 1868 | 1966 |
| Bangladesh | British E India Co. 18th cent–1858; British India 1858–1947; E Pakistan 1947–71 | 18th century | 1971 |
| Zimbabwe | S Rhodesia from 1923; UDI under Ian Smith 1965–79 | 1895 | 1980 |

# MISCELLANEOUS

# ABBREVIATIONS, SYMBOLS, AND ACRONYMS

**A** in physics, symbol for *ampere*, a unit of electrical current.

**A1** abbreviation for *first class* (of ships).

**AA** abbreviation for the British *Automobile Association*.

**abb** abbreviation for *abbreviation*.

**ab init** abbreviation for *ab initio* (Latin 'from the beginning').

**ABM** abbreviation for *anti-ballistic missile*.

**a/c** abbreviation for *account*.

**AC** in physics, abbreviation for *alternating current*.

**ACAS** abbreviation for *Advisory, Conciliation and Arbitration Service*.

**ACT** abbreviation for *Australian Capital Territory*.

**AD** in the Christian calender, abbreviation for *Anno Domini* (Latin 'in the year of the Lord'); used with dates.

**ADB** abbreviation for *Asian Development Bank*.

**ADC** in electronics, abbreviation for analogue-to-digital converter.

**ADH** abbreviation for *antidiuretic hormone*, part of the system maintaining a correct salt/water balance in vertebrates.

**adj** in grammar, abbreviation for *adjective*.

**ADP** abbreviation for *adenosine diphosphate*, a raw material in the manufacture of ATP, the molecule used by all cells to drive their chemical reactions.

**adv** abbreviation for *adverb*.

**aet** abbreviation for *aetatis* (Latin 'of the age').

**AEW** abbreviation for *airborne early warning*, a military surveillance system.

**AFD** abbreviation for *accelerated freeze drying*, a common method of food preservation. See food technology.

**AFL-CIO** abbreviation for *American Federation of Labor and Congress of Industrial Organizations*.

**AG** abbreviation for *Aktiengesellschaft* (German 'limited company').

**AH** with reference to the Muslim calendar, abbreviation for *anno hegirae* (Latin 'year of the flight'—of Muhammad, from Mecca to Medina).

**AIDS** abbreviation for *acquired immune deficiency syndrome*, the newest and gravest of sexually transmitted diseases or STDs.

**AK** abbreviation for *Alaska*.

**AL** abbreviation for *Alabama*.

**ALADI** abbreviation for *Asociacion Latino-Americana de Integration* or Latin American Integration Association, organization promoting trade in the region.

**AM** in physics, abbreviation for amplitude modulation, one way in which radio waves are altered for the transmission of broadcasting signals.

**am** or *A.M.* abbreviation for *ante meridiem* (Latin 'before noon').

**AMF** abbreviation of *Arab Monetary Fund*.

**amp** in physics, abbreviation for *ampere*, a unit of electrical current.

**ANC** abbreviation for *African National Congress*; South African nationalist organization.

**ANZUS** acronym for *Australia, New Zealand, and the United States* (Pacific Security Treaty), a military alliance established 1951. It was replaced 1954 by the Southeast Asia Treaty Organization , (SEATO).

**ap** in physics, abbreviation for *atmospheric pressure*.

**APC** abbreviation for *armoured personnel carrier*, a battlefield vehicle.

**approx** abbreviation for *approximately*.

**AR** abbreviation for *Arkansas*.

**ASA** abbreviation for *Association of South East Asia* (1961–67), replaced by ASEAN, *Association of Southeast Asian Nations*.

**a.s.a.p** abbreviation for *as soon as possible*.

**ASAT** acronym for *antisatellite weapon*.

**ASPAC** abbreviation of *Asian and Pacific Council*.

**ASSR** abbreviation for *Autonomous Soviet Socialist Republic*.

**AWACS** acronym for *Airborne Warning and Control System*. The system incorporates a long-range surveillance and detection radar mounted on a Boeing E-3 sentry aircraft. It was used with great success in the 1991 Gulf War.

**AZ** abbreviation for *Arizona*.

**BA** in education, abbreviation for *Bachelor of Arts* degree.

**BAFTA** abbreviation for *British Academy of Film and Television Arts*.

**BBC** abbreviation for *British Broadcasting Corporation*.

**BC** in the Christian calendar, abbreviation for *before Christ*; used with dates.

**BCE** abbreviation for *before the Common Era*; used with dates (instead of BC) particularly by non-Christians, and some theologians in recognition of the multiplicity of belief worldwide.

**BCG** abbreviation for *bacillus of Calmette and Guérin*, used as a vaccine to confer active immunity to tuberculosis (TB).

**Beds** abbreviation for *Bedfordshire*.

**Berks** abbreviation for *Berkshire*.

**BFI** abbreviation for the *British Film Institute*.

**BFPO** abbreviation for *British Forces Post Office*.

**bhp** abbreviation for *brake horsepower*.

**biog** abbreviation for *biography*.

**BIS** abbreviation for *Bank for International Settlements* based in Basel, Switzerland.

**BMA** abbreviation for *British Medical Association*.

**BNF** abbreviation for *British Nuclear Fuels*.

**BOT** abbreviation for *Board of Trade*, former UK government organization, merged in the Department of Trade and Industry from 1970.

**BP** abbreviation for *British Pharmacopoeia*; also *British Petroleum*.

**BR** abbreviation for *British Rail*.

**BSc** abbreviation for *Bachelor of Science* degree. The US abbreviation is *B.S.*.

**BST** abbreviation for *British Summer Time; bovine somatotropin.*

**BT** abbreviation for *British Telecom.*

**Btu** symbol for *British thermal unit.*

**Bucks** abbreviation for *Buckinghamshire.*

**c** abbreviation for *circa* (Latin 'about'); used with dates that are uncertain.

**C** abbreviation for *centum* (Latin 'hundred'); *century; centigrade; Celsius.*

**°C** symbol for degrees Celsius (temperature scale).

**CA** abbreviation for *California* (USA).

**CACM** abbreviation for *Central American Common Market.*

**CAD** abbreviation for *computer-aided design.*

**cal** symbol for *calorie.*

**CAM** abbreviation for *computer-aided manufacture.*

**Cambs** abbreviation for *Cambridgeshire.*

**Cantab** abbreviation for *Cantabrigiensis* (Latin 'of Cambridge').

**cap** abbreviation for *capital.*

**CAP** abbreviation for *Common Agricultural Policy.*

**CARICOM** abbreviation for *Caribbean Community* and Common Market.

**CB** abbreviation for *citizens' band* (radio).

**CBI** abbreviation for *Confederation of British Industry.*

**CC** abbreviation for *county council; cricket club.*

**cc** symbol for *cubic centimetre*; abbreviation for *carbon copy/copies.*

**CCASG** abbreviation of *Cooperative Council for the Arab States of the Gulf.*

**CD** abbreviation for *Corps Diplomatique* (French 'Diplomatic Corps'); *compact disc; certificate of deposit.*

**CDU** abbreviation for the centre-right *Christian Democratic Union* in the Federal Republic of Germany.

**CE** abbreviation for *Common Era; Church of England* (often *C of E*).

**CEGB** abbreviation for the former (until 1990) *Central Electricity Generating Board.*

**CentCom** abbreviation for US *Central Command,* a military strikeforce.

**CENTO** abbreviation for *Central Treaty Organization.*

**CET** abbreviation for *Central European Time.*

**cf** abbreviation for *confer* (Latin 'compare').

**CFC** abbreviation for *chlorofluorocarbon.*

**CFE** abbreviation for *conventional forces in Europe.*

**Ches** abbreviation for Cheshire.

**CIA** abbreviation for the US *Central Intelligence Agency.*

**CID** abbreviation for *Criminal Investigation Department.*

**cif** in economics, abbreviation for *cost, insurance, and freight* or *charged in full.*

**cm** symbol for *centimetre.*

**CND** abbreviation for *Campaign for Nuclear Disarmament.*

**c/o** abbreviation for *care of.*

**co** abbreviation for *company.*

**CO** abbreviation for *Commanding Officer.*

**CO** abbreviation for *Colorado* (USA).

**COD** abbreviation for *cash on delivery.*

**COI** abbreviation for *Central Office of Information.*

**COIN** acronym for *counter insurgency,* the suppression by a state's armed forces of uprisings against the state.

**Comintern** acronym for *Communist International.*

**CPP** abbreviation for *current purchasing power.*

**CPVE** abbreviation for *Certificate of Pre-Vocational Education* in the UK, educational qualification introduced 1986 for students over 16 in schools and colleges who want a one-year course of preparation for work or further vocational study.

**CRT** abbreviation for *cathode-ray tube.*

**CSCE** abbreviation for *Conference on Security and Cooperation in Europe,* popularly known as the Helsinki Conference.

**CSE** abbreviation for *Certificate of Secondary Education* in the UK, the examinations taken by the majority of secondary school pupils who were not regarded as academically capable of GCE O level, until the introduction of the common secondary examination system, GCSE, 1988.

**CT** abbreviation for *Connecticut* (USA).

**cu** abbreviation for *cubic* (measure).

**CV** abbreviation for *curriculum vitae.*

**cwo** abbreviation for *cash with order.*

**cwt** symbol for *hundredweight,* a unit of weight equal to 112 pounds (50.802 kg).

**cwt** symbol for *hundredweight,* a unit of weight equal to 100 lb (45.36 kg) in the US and 112 lb (50.8 kg) in the UK and Canada.

**d** abbreviation for *day; diameter; died;* in the UK, d was the sign for a *penny* (Latin *denarius)* until decimalization of the currency in 1971.

**D** abbreviation for *500* in the Roman numeral system.

**DA** abbreviation for *district attorney.*

**DBE** abbreviation for *Dame (Commander of the Order) of the British Empire.*

**DC** in music, abbreviation for *da capo* (Italian 'from the beginning'); in physics, for *direct current* (electricity); *the District of Columbia.*

**DD** abbreviation for *Doctor of Divinity.*

**DE** abbreviation for *Delaware* (USA).

**DES** abbreviation for *Department of Education and Science.*

**DHSS** abbreviation for *Department of Health and Social Security,* UK government department until divided 1988.

**diag** abbreviation for *diagram.*

**DM** abbreviation for *Deutschmark,* the unit of currency in Germany.

**DMus** abbreviation for *Doctor of Music.*

**DNA** abbreviation for *deoxyribonucleic acid.*

**do** abbreviation for *ditto.*

**DPhil** abbreviation for *Doctor of Philosophy.*

**DPP** abbreviation for *Director of Public Prosecutions.*

**DSO** abbreviation for *Distinguished Service Order,* British military medal.

**DTI** abbreviation for *Department of Trade and Industry,* UK government department.

**E** abbreviation for *east.*

**EC** abbreviation for *European Community.*

**ECM** abbreviation for *electronic countermeasures*, military jargon for disrupting telecom-£munications.

**ECOWAS** acronym for *Economic Community of West African States.*

**ECSC** abbreviation for *European Coal and Steel Community.*

**ECT** abbreviation for *electroconvulsive therapy.*

**ECTU** abbreviation for *European Confederation of Trade Unions.*

**ECU** abbreviation for *European Currency Unit,* official monetary unit of the EC. It is based on the value of the different currencies used in the European Monetary System.

**EEC** abbreviation for *European Economic Community.*

**EFTA** acronym for *European Free Trade Association.*

**EFTPOS** abbreviation of *electronic funds transfer at point of sale* the transfer of funds from one bank account to another by electronic means.

**eg** abbreviation for *exempli gratia* (Latin 'for the sake of example').

**emf** in physics, abbreviation for *electromotive force.*

**EMS** abbreviation for *European Monetary System.*

**ENT** in medicine, abbreviation for *ear, nose, and throat.* It is usually applied to a specialist clinic or hospital department.

**E & O E** abbreviation for *errors and omissions excepted.*

**EOKA** acronym for *Ethnikí Organósis Kipriakóu Agónos* (National Organization of Cypriot Struggle) an underground organization formed by General George Grivas 1955 to fight for the independence of Cyprus from Britain and ultimately its union (*enosis*) with Greece.

**EPLF** abbreviation for *Eritrean People's Liberation Front.*

**EPNS** abbreviation for *electroplated nickel silver.*

**ERM** abbreviation for *Exchange Rate Mechanism.*

**ERNIE** acronym for *electronic random number indicator equipment*, machine designed and produced by the UK Post Office Research Station to select a series of random 9-figure numbers to indicate prizewinners in the government's national lottery.

**ESA** abbreviation for *European Space Agency.*

**est** abbreviation for *estimate(d).*

**et al** abbreviation for *et alii* (Latin 'and others'); used in bibliography.

**etc** abbreviation for *et cetera* (Latin 'and the rest').

**Euratom** acronym for *European Atomic Energy Commission*, forming part of the European Community organization.

**Eutelsat** acronym for *European Telecommunications Satellite Organization.*

**ex lib** abbreviation for *ex libris* (Latin 'from the library of').

**°F** symbol for degrees *Fahrenheit.*

**FA** abbreviation for *Football Association.*

**fao** abbreviation for *for the attention of.*

**FAO** abbreviation for *Food and Agriculture Organization.*

**FBI** abbreviation for *Federal Bureau of Investigation*, agency of the US Department of Justice.

**FDN** abbreviation for *Nicaraguan Democratic Front.*

**fem** in grammar, abbreviation for *feminine.*

**ff** abbreviation for *folios*; and *the following*; used in reference citation and bibliography.

**fig** abbreviation for *figure.*

**fl** abbreviation for *floruit* (Latin 'he/she flourished').

**FL** abbreviation for *Florida* (USA).

**FM** in physics, abbreviation for *frequency modulation.* Used in radio, FM is constant in amplitude and varies the frequency of the carrier wave.

**FNLA** abbreviation for *Front National de Libération de l'Angola* (French 'National Front for the Liberation of Angola').

**FO** abbreviation for *Foreign Office*, British government department.

**FRS** abbreviation for *Fellow of the Royal Society.*

**ft** abbreviation for *foot*, a measure of distance.

**FTC** abbreviation for *Federal Trade Commission*, US anti-monopoly organization.

**g** symbol for *gram.*

**GA** abbreviation for *Georgia* (USA).

**gal** symbol for *gallon.*

**GATT** acronym for *General Agreement on Tariffs and Trade.*

**GCC** abbreviation for *Gulf Cooperation Council.*

**GCE** abbreviation for *General Certificate of Education*, in the UK, the public examination formerly taken at the age of 16 at Ordinary level (O level) and at 18 at Advanced level (A level).

**GCHQ** abbreviation for *Government Communications Headquarters* (UK).

**GCSE** abbreviation for *General Certificate of Secondary Education* in the UK, from 1988, examination for 16-year old pupils, superseding both GCE O level and CSE, and offering qualifications for up to 60% of school leavers in any particular subject.

**GDP** abbreviation for *Gross Domestic Product.*

**GDR** abbreviation for *German Democratic Republic* (former East Germany).

**gen** in grammar, abbreviation for *genitive.*

**ger** in grammar, abbreviation for *gerund.*

**GHQ** abbreviation for *general headquarters.*

**GI** abbreviation for *government issue*; hence (in the USA) a common soldier.

**Glos** abbreviation for *Gloucestershire*, county in SW England.

**GmbH** abbreviation for *Gesellshaft mit beschrankter Haftung* (German 'limited liability company').

**GNP** abbreviation for *Gross National Product.*

**GP** in medicine, abbreviation for *general practitioner.*

**GPU** former name (1922–23) for KGB, the Soviet security service.

**GRP** abbreviation for *glass-reinforced plastic*, a plastic material strengthened by glass fibres, usually erroneously known as fibreglass.

**GU** abbreviation for *Guam*.

**ha** symbol for *hectare*.

**Hants** abbreviation for *Hampshire*.

**Herts** abbreviation for *Hertfordshire*.

**HF** in physics, abbreviation for *high frequency*.

**HGV** abbreviation for *heavy goods vehicle*.

**HI** abbreviation for *Hawaii* (USA).

**HMSO** abbreviation for *His/Her Majesty's Stationery Office*.

**Hon** abbreviation for *Honourable*.

**hp** symbol for *horsepower*.

**HQ** abbreviation for *headquarters*.

**HRH** abbreviation for *His/Her Royal Highness*.

**ht** abbreviation for *height*.

**HWM** abbreviation for *high water mark*.

**Hz** in physics, symbol for *hertz*.

**IA** abbreviation for *Iowa* (USA).

**IADB** abbreviation for *Inter-American Development Bank*.

**IAEA** abbreviation for *International Atomic Energy Agency*.

**IBA** abbreviation for *Independent Broadcasting Authority*, former name of the Independent Television Commission, UK regulatory body for commercial television and radio.

**ibid** abbreviation for *ibidem* (Latin 'in the same place'); used in reference citation.

**ICBM** abbreviation for *intercontinental ballistic missile*.

**id** abbreviation for *idem* (Latin 'the same'); used in reference citation.

**ID** abbreviation for *Idaho* (USA).

**IDA** abbreviation for *International Development Association*.

**ie** abbreviation for *id est* (Latin 'that is').

**IEEE** abbreviation for *Institute of Electrical and Electronic Engineers*, which sets technical standards for electrical equipment and computer data exchange.

**IKBS** abbreviation for *intelligent knowledge-based system*; in computing, an alternative name for the more usual KBS, knowledge-based system.

**ILEA** abbreviation for *Inner London Education Authority*, former UK educational body which administered education in London. It was abolished 1990 and replaced by smaller borough-based education authorities.

**IL** abbreviation for *Illinois* (USA).

**IMF** abbreviation for *International Monetary Fund*.

**in** abbreviation for *inch*, a measure of distance.

**IN** abbreviation for *Indiana* (USA).

**Inc** abbreviation for *Incorporated*.

**INF** abbreviation for *intermediate nuclear forces*, as in the Intermediate Nuclear Forces Treaty.

**IOM** abbreviation for *Isle of Man*.

**IOW** abbreviation for *Isle of Wight*.

**ir** in physics, abbreviation for *infrared*.

**IRCAM** abbreviation for the French *Institut de Recherche et de Coordination Acoustique-Musique*, organization in Paris for research into electronic music and synthesizers, founded 1976.

**ISBN** abbreviation for *International Standard Book Number*, used for ordering or classifying book titles.

**ITU** abbreviation for *intensive therapy unit*, a high-technology facility for treating the critically ill or injured; in the USA *ICU*, for *intensive care unit*.

**IUCN** abbreviation for *International Union for the Conservation of Nature*.

**IUPAC** abbreviation for *International Union of Pure and Applied Chemistry*.

**IWW** abbreviation for *Industrial Workers of the World*.

**J** in physics, symbol for *joule*, SI unit of energy.

**jnr, jr** abbreviation for *junior*.

**JP** abbreviation for *justice of the peace*.

**KBE** abbreviation for *Knight (Commander of the Order) of the British Empire*.

**KC** abbreviation for *King's Counsel*.

**kcal** symbol for *kilocalorie*.

**Kcal** abbreviation for *kilocalorie*.

**kg** abbreviation for *kilogram*.

**KG** abbreviation for *Knight of the Order of the Garter*.

**KGB** abbreviation for *Komitet Gosudarstvennoye Bezhopaznosti* (Russian 'Committee of State Security').

**km** symbol for *kilometre*.

**kph** or *km/h* symbol for *kilometres per hour*.

**KS** abbreviation for *Kansas* (USA).

**kW** abbreviation for *kilowatt*.

**KY** abbreviation for *Kentucky* (USA).

**L** Roman numeral for 50.

**l** symbol for *litre*, a measure of liquid volume.

**LA** abbreviation for *Louisiana* (USA); *Los Angeles*.

**Lab** abbreviation for *Labour* or *Labrador*, Canada.

**Lancs** abbreviation for *Lancashire*.

**lat** abbreviation for *latitude*.

**lb** symbol for *pound* (weight).

**lbw** abbreviation for *leg before wicket* (cricket).

**lc** in typography, abbreviation for *lower case*, or 'small' letters, as opposed to capitals.

**LCD** abbreviation for *liquid crystal display*.

**LDR** abbreviation for *light-dependent resistor*.

**LEA** in the UK, abbreviation for *local education authority*.

**Leics** abbreviation for *Leicestershire*.

**LF** in physics, abbreviation for *low frequency*.

**Lib** abbreviation for *Liberal*.

**LIFFE** acronym for *London International Financial Futures Exchange*, one of the exchanges in London where futures contracts are traded.

**LDR** abbreviation for light-dependent resistor, component of electronic circuits whose resistance varies with the level of illumination on its surface.

**Lincs** abbreviation for *Lincolnshire*.

**loc cit** abbreviation for *loco citato* (Latin 'at the place cited'); used in reference citation.

**log** in mathematics, abbreviation for *logarithm*.

**long** abbreviation for *longitude*.

**Ltd** abbreviation for *Limited*.

**LW** abbreviation for *long wave*, a radio wave with a wavelength of over 1,000 m/3,300 ft; one of the main wavebands into which radio frequency transmissions are divided.

**LWM** abbreviation for *low water mark.*

**m** symbol for *metre.*

**M** Roman numeral for *1,000.*

**MA** abbreviation for *Master of Arts* degree of education; the state of *Massachusetts* (USA).

**MAD** abbreviation for *mutual assured destruction*; the basis of the theory of deterrence by possession of nuclear weapons.

**MAFF** abbreviation for *Ministry of Agriculture, Fisheries and Food.*

**Man** abbreviation for *Manitoba,* Canadian province.

**masc** in grammar, abbreviation for *masculine.*

**max** abbreviation for *maximum.*

**MBE** abbreviation for *Member (of the Order) of the British Empire.*

**MCC** abbreviation for *Marylebone Cricket Club.*

**MD** abbreviation for *Doctor of Medicine*; the state of *Maryland* (USA).

**ME** abbreviation for *Maine* (USA).

**ME** abbreviation for *Middle English,* the period of the English language from 1050 to 1550.

**MEP** abbreviation for *Member of the European Parliament.*

**Messrs** abbreviation for *messieurs* (French 'sirs' or 'gentlemen') used in formal writing to address an organization or group of people.

**MFA** abbreviation for *Multi-Fibre Arrangement.*

**mg** symbol for *milligram.*

**Mgr** abbreviation for *manager*; in the Roman Catholic Church, abbreviation for *Monsignor.*

**MHz** symbol for *megahertz.*

**mi** symbol for *mile.*

**MI** abbreviation for *Michigan* (USA).

**MICV** abbreviation for *mechanized infantry combat vehicle.*

**Middx** abbreviation for *Middlesex,* former county of England.

**MIDI** abbreviation for *Musical Instrument Digital Interface,* a manufacturer's standard allowing different pieces of digital music equipment used in composing and recording to be freely connected.

**min** abbreviation for *minute* (time); *minimum.*

**MIRV** abbreviation for *multiple independently targeted re-entry vehicle,* used in nuclear warfare.

**ml** symbol for *millilitre.*

**MLR** abbreviation for *minimum lending rate.*

**mm** symbol for *millimetre.*

**mmHg** symbol for *millimetre of mercury.*

**MN** abbreviation for *Minnesota* (USA).

**MO** abbreviation for *Missouri* (USA).

**MOD** abbreviation for *Ministry of Defence.*

**MOH** abbreviation for *Medical Officer of Health.*

**mp** in chemistry, abbreviation for *melting point.*

**MP** abbreviation for *member of Parliament.*

**mpg** abbreviation for *miles per gallon.*

**mph** abbreviation for *miles per hour.*

**MPhil** in education, abbreviation for *Master of Philosophy* degree.

**Mr** abbreviation for *mister*; title used before a name to show that the person is male.

**MRBM** abbreviation for *medium-range ballistic missile.*

**Mrs** title used before a name to show that the person is married and female; partly superseded by Ms, which does not indicate marital status. Mrs was originally an abbreviation for *mistress.*

**Ms** title used before a woman's name; pronounced 'miz'. Unlike Miss or Mrs, it can be used by married or unmarried women, and was introduced by the women's movement in the 1970s to parallel Mr, which also does not distinguish marital status.

**MS** abbreviation for *Mississippi* (USA).

**MSc** in education, abbreviation for *Master of Science* degree. The US abbreviation is *MS.*

**MSC** abbreviation for *Manpower Services Commission.*

**MS(S)** abbreviation for *manuscript(s).*

**MT** abbreviation for *Montana* (USA).

**MU** in economics, abbreviation for *monetary unit.*

**n** abbreviation for *noun.*

**N** abbreviation for *north, newton,* and the chemical symbol for *nitrogen.*

**NASA** acronym for *National Aeronautics and Space Administration,* US government agency for spaceflight and aeronautical research.

**NATO** acronym for *N*orth *A*tlantic *T*reaty *Or*ganization.

**NB** abbreviation for *New Brunswick; nota bene* (Latin 'note well'), used in references and citations.

**NBS** abbreviation for *National Bureau of Standards,* the US federal standards organization, on whose technical standards all US weights and measures are based.

**NC** abbreviation for *North Carolina* (USA).

**ND** abbreviation for *North Dakota* (USA).

**NE** abbreviation for *Nebraska* (USA).

**NEDC** abbreviation for *National Economic Development Council.*

**nem con** abbreviation for *nemine contradicente* (Latin 'with no one opposing').

**nem diss** abbreviation for *nemine dissentiente* (Latin 'with no one dissenting').

**NERC** abbreviation for *Natural Environment Research Council.*

**NF** abbreviation for *Newfoundland* (Canada).

**NH** abbreviation for *New Hampshire* (USA).

**NHS** abbreviation for *National Health Service,* the UK state-financed health service.

**NIEO** abbreviation for *New International Economic Order.*

**NJ** abbreviation for *New Jersey* (USA).

**NKVD** the Soviet secret police 1934–38, replaced by the KGB. The NKVD was reponsible for Stalin's infamous purges.

**NM** abbreviation for *New Mexico* (USA).

**n o** abbreviation for *not out* (cricket).

**no** or *No* abbreviation for *number.*

**nom** in grammar, abbreviation for *nominative.*

**Northants** abbreviation for *Northamptonshire.*

**Northd** abbreviation for *Northumberland.*

**Notts** abbreviation for *Nottinghamshire.*

**NPA** abbreviation for *New People's Army* (Philippines).

**NS** abbreviation for *Nova Scotia* (Canada).

**NSW** abbreviation for *New South Wales* (Australia).

**NT** abbreviation for *Northern Territory* (Australia).

**NTP** abbreviation for *normal temperature and pressure*, former name for STP (standard temperature and pressure).

**NV** abbreviation for *Nevada* (USA).

**NY** abbreviation for *New York* (USA).

**NZ** abbreviation for *New Zealand*.

**o/a** abbreviation for *on account*.

**OAPEC** abbreviation for *Organization of Arab Petroleum Exporting Countries*.

**ob** abbreviation for *obiit* (Latin 'he/she died').

**OBE** abbreviation for *Officer (of the Order) of the British Empire*.

**OCAM** acronym for *Organisation Commune Africaine et Mauricienne*, body for economic cooperation in Africa.

**ODA** abbreviation for *Overseas Development Administration*.

**OE** abbreviation for *Old English*, the period of the English language from the 5th century to *c.* AD 1100.

**OGPU** former name 1923–34 of the Soviet secret police, now the KGB.

**OH** abbreviation for *Ohio* (USA).

**OHMS** abbreviation for *On Her (His) Majesty's Service*.

**OIC** abbreviation for *Organization of the Islamic Conference*, international Muslim solidarity association.

**OK** abbreviation for *Oklahoma* (USA).

**o n** abbreviation for *or near(est) offer*.

**Ont** abbreviation for *Ontario* (Canada).

**op cit** abbreviation for *opere citato* (Latin 'in the work cited'), used in reference citation.

**OPEC** abbreviation for *Organization of Petroleum-Exporting Countries*.

**OR** abbreviation for *Oregon* (USA).

**OT** abbreviation for *Old Testament*.

**OU** abbreviation for *Open University*.

**OXFAM** abbreviation for *Oxford Committee for Famine Relief*.

**Oxon** abbreviation for *Oxoniensis* (Latin 'of Oxford').

**oz** symbol for *ounce*.

***p*** in music, abbreviation for *piano* (Italian 'softly').

**p(p)** abbreviation for *page(s)*.

**pa** abbreviation for *per annum* (Latin 'yearly').

**PA** abbreviation for *Pennsylvania* (USA).

**part** in grammar, abbreviation for *participle*.

**PAYE** abbreviation for *pay as you earn*.

**PC** abbreviation for *police constable*; *Privy Councillor, personal computer*.

**PCB** abbreviation for *polychlorinated biphenyl; printed circuit board*.

**PCM** abbreviation for *pulse-code modulation*.

**PEN** abbreviation for *Poets, Playwrights, Editors, Essayists, Novelists*, literary association established 1921 by C A ('Sappho') Dawson Scott, to promote international understanding among writers.

**per pro** abbreviation for *per procurationem* (Latin 'by the agency of').

**PhD** abbreviation for *Doctor of Philosophy* degree.

**plc** abbreviation for *public limited company*.

**PLO** abbreviation for *Palestine Liberation Organization*.

**plur** in grammar, abbreviation for *plural*.

**PM** abbreviation for *prime minister*.

**pm** or *PM* abbreviation for *post meridiem* (Latin 'after noon').

**PO** abbreviation for *Post Office*.

**pp** abbreviation for *per procurationem* (Latin 'by proxy').

**ppm** abbreviation for *parts per million*. An alternative (but numerically equivalent) unit used in chemistry is milligrams perlitre (mg l$^{-1}$).

**PR** abbreviation for *public relations*; *proportional representation*.

**PR** abbreviation for *Puerto Rico*.

**pref** in grammar, abbreviation for *prefix*.

**pro tem** abbreviation for *pro tempore* (Latin 'for the time being').

**PS** abbreviation for *post scriptum* (Latin 'after writing').

**pt** abbreviation for *pint*.

**PTO** abbreviation for *please turn over*.

**PX** abbreviation for *Post Exchange*, a US organization that provides shopping and canteen facilities for armed forces at home and abroad. The British equivalent is the NAAFI.

**QB** abbreviation for *Queen's Bench*.

**QC** abbreviation for *Queen's Counsel*.

**QED** abbreviation for *quod erat demonstrandum* (Latin 'which was to be proved').

**Qld** abbreviation for *Queensland* (Australia).

**quant suff** abbreviation for *quantum sufficit* (Latin 'as much as suffices').

**Que** abbreviation for *Québec* (Canada).

**qv** abbreviation for *quod vide* (Latin 'which see').

**RA** abbreviation for *Royal Academy of Art*, London, founded 1768.

**RAC** abbreviation for the UK *Royal Automobile Club*.

**RAF** abbreviation for *Royal Air Force*.

**RC** abbreviation for *Red Cross; Roman Catholic*.

**re** abbreviation for Latin *'with regard to'*.

**RI** abbreviation for *Rhode Island* (USA).

**RIBA** abbreviation for *Royal Institute of British Architects*.

**RIP** abbreviation for *requiescat in pace* (Latin 'may he/she rest in peace').

**RN** abbreviation for *Royal Navy*.

**RNLI** abbreviation for *Royal National Lifeboat Institution*.

**RPI** abbreviation for *retail price index*.

**rpm** abbreviation for *revolutions per minute*.

**RPV** abbreviation for *remotely piloted vehicle*, a flying TV camera for military use.

**RSFSR** abbreviation for *Russian Soviet Federal Socialist Republic*, popularly known as the Russian Federation, the largest constituent republic of the USSR.

**RSPB** abbreviation for *Royal Society for the Protection of Birds*.

**RSPCA** abbreviation for *Royal Society for the Prevention of Cruelty to Animals*.

**RSV** abbreviation for *Revised Standard Version* of the Bible.

**RSVP** abbreviation for *répondez s'il vous plaît* (French 'please reply').

**Rt Hon** abbreviation for *Right Honourable*, the title of British members of Parliament.

**S** abbreviation for *south*.

**SA** abbreviation for *South Africa*; *South Australia*.

**SAARC** abbreviation for *South Asian Association for Regional Cooperation*.

**SADCC** abbreviation for *Southern African Development Coordination Conference*.

**sae** abbreviation for *stamped addressed envelope*.

**SALT** acronym for *Strategic Arms Limitation Talks*, a series of US-Soviet negotiations 1969–79.

**SAS** abbreviation for *Special Air Service*; also for *Scandinavian Airlines System*.

**Sask** abbreviation for *Saskatchewan* (Canada).

**SBS** abbreviation for *Special Boat Service*, the British Royal Navy's equivalent of the Special Air Service.

**sc** abbreviation for *scilicet* (Latin 'let it be understood').

**SC** abbreviation for *South Carolina* (USA).

**SD** abbreviation for *South Dakota* (USA).

**SDI** abbreviation for *Strategic Defense Initiative*.

**SDLP** abbreviation for *Social Democratic and Labour Party* (Northern Ireland).

**SDP** abbreviation for *Social Democratic Party* (UK).

**SDR** abbreviation for *special drawing right*.

**SEATO** abbreviation for *Southeast Asia Treaty Organization*.

**sec** or *s* abbreviation for *second*, a unit of time.

**SELA** abbreviation for *Sistema Economico Latino-Americana* or Latin American Economic System.

**seq** abbreviation for *sequentes* (Latin 'the following').

**SERC** abbreviation for *Science and Engineering Research Council*.

**SERPS** abbreviation for *State Earnings-Related Pension Schemes*, the UK state pension scheme.

**SFSR** abbreviation for *Soviet Federal Socialist Republic*.

**SHAPE** abbreviation for *Supreme Headquarters Allied Powers Europe*, situated near Mons, Belgium, and the headquarters of NATO's Supreme Allied Commander Europe (SACEUR).

**SHF** in physics, abbreviation for *superhigh frequency*.

**SI** abbreviation for *Système International [d'Unités]* (French 'International System [of Metric Units]').

**SIB** abbreviation for *Securities and Investments Board*, UK regulating body.

**sing** abbreviation for *singular*.

**SIS** abbreviation for *Special Intelligence Service*.

**SJ** abbreviation for *Society of Jesus*.

**SLBM** abbreviation for *submarine-launched ballistic missile*.

**SLD** abbreviation for *Social and Liberal Democrats*.

**SLR** abbreviation for *single-lens reflex*, a type of camera in which the image can be seen through the lens before a picture is taken.

**SOS** internationally recognized distress signal, using letters of the Morse code (... – ...).

**SPF** abbreviation for *South Pacific Forum*, organization of countries in the region.

**SPQR** abbreviation for *Senatus Populusque Romanus*. (Latin 'the Senate and the Roman People').

**sq** abbreviation for *square* (measure).

**Sr** abbreviation for *senior*; also for *señor*.

**SSR** abbreviation for *Soviet Socialist Republic*.

**Staffs** abbreviation for *Staffordshire*.

**START** acronym for *Strategic Arms Reduction Talks*.

**suff** in grammar, abbreviation for *suffix*.

**t** symbol for *ton* or *tonne*.

**tal qual** abbreviation for *talis qualis* (Latin 'just as they come').

**Tas** abbreviation for *Tasmania*.

**TASM** abbreviation for *tactical air-to-surface missile*.

**Tass** acronym for the Soviet news agency *Telegrafnoye Agentstvo Sovyetskovo Soyuza*.

**TB** abbreviation for the infectious disease *tuberculosis*.

**TD** abbreviation for *Teachta Dála* (Irish 'a member of the Irish parliament').

**temp** abbreviation for *temperature*; *temporary*.

**TIR** abbreviation for *Transports Internationaux Routiers* (French 'International Road Transport').

**TM** abbreviation for *transcendental meditation*.

**TN** abbreviation for *Tennessee* (USA).

**TT** abbreviation for *Tourist Trophy*; *teetotal*; *tuberculin tested*.

**TTL** abbreviation for *transistor-transistor logic*, a family of integrated circuits with fast switching speeds commonly used in building electronic devices.

**TUC** abbreviation for *Trades Union Congress*.

**TX** abbreviation for *Texas* (USA).

**UDC** abbreviation for *urban district council*.

**UFO** abbreviation for *unidentified flying object*.

**UHT** abbreviation for *ultra heat treated*.

**UK** abbreviation for the *United Kingdom*.

**UKAEA** abbreviation for *United Kingdom Atomic Energy Authority*.

**UN** abbreviation for the *United Nations*.

**UNCTAD** acronym for *United Nations Commission on Trade and Development*.

**UNEP** acronym for *United Nations Environmental Programme*.

**UNHCR** abbreviation for *United Nations High Commission for Refugees*.

**UNICEF** acronym for *United Nations International Children's Emergency Fund*.

**UNITA** acronym for *National Union for the Total Independence of Angola*.

**US** abbreviation for the *United States of America* (popular and most frequent name used by speakers of American English for the nation).

**USA** abbreviation (official) for the *United States of America*; *US Army*.

**USDA** abbreviation for the *US Department of Agriculture*.

**USGS** abbreviation for the *US Geological Survey*, part of the Department of the Interior.

**USIA** abbreviation for *US Information Agency*.

**USO** abbreviation for *United Service Organizations*.

**USS** abbreviation for *US Ship*.

**USSR** abbreviation for the *Union of Soviet Socialist Republics*.

**UV** in physics, abbreviation for *ultraviolet*.

**V** Roman numeral for *five*; in physics, symbol for *volt*.

**v** in physics, symbol for *velocity*.

**VAT** abbreviation for *value-added tax*.

**vb** in grammar, abbreviation for *verb*.

**VDU** (abbreviation for *visual display terminal*) an electronic output device for displaying the data processed by a computer on a screen.

**vi** in grammar, abbreviation for *verb intransitive*.

**VI** abbreviation for *Virgin Islands*; *Vancouver Island* (Canada).

**VIP** abbreviation for *very important person*.

**viz** abbreviation for *videlicet* (Latin 'that is to say', 'namely').

**VLF** in physics, abbreviation for *very low frequency*.

**voc** in grammar, abbreviation for *vocative*.

**vol** abbreviation for *volume*.

**VR** abbreviation for *velocity ratio*.

**VSTOL** abbreviation for *vertical/short takeoff and landing*.

**vt** in grammar, abbreviation for *verb transitive*.

**VT** abbreviation for *Vermont* (USA).

**W** abbreviation for *west*; in physics, symbol for *watt*.

**WA** abbreviation for *Washington* (state) (USA); *Western Australia*.

**wc** abbreviation for *water closet*, another name for a toilet.

**WCC** abbreviation for *World Council of Churches*.

**WHO** acronym for *World Health Organization*.

**WI** abbreviation for *West Indies*; *Wisconsin* (USA).

**Wilts** abbreviation for *Wiltshire*.

**Worcs** abbreviation for *Worcestershire*.

**wpm** abbreviation for *words per minute*.

**wt** abbreviation for *weight*.

**WV** abbreviation for *West Virginia* (USA).

**WWF** abbreviation for *World Wide Fund for Nature* (formerly World Wildlife Fund).

**WY** abbreviation for *Wyoming* (USA).

**X** Roman numeral *ten*; a person or thing unknown.

**x** in mathematics, an unknown quantity.

**yd** abbreviation for *yard*.

**YHA** abbreviation for *Youth Hostels Association*.

**YMCA** abbreviation for *Young Men's Christian Association*.

**Yorks** abbreviation for *Yorkshire*.

**YWCA** abbreviation for *Young Women's Christian Association*.

**Z** in physics, the symbol for *impedance* (electricity and magnetism).

**zB** abbreviation for *zum Beispiel* (German 'for example').

**ZST** abbreviation for *zone standard time*.

# FOREIGN WORDS AND PHRASES

**Abbé** (French 'abbot') a title of respect used to address any clergyman.

**addendum** (Latin) something to be added, usually in writing, which qualifies a foregoing thesis or statement.

**ad infinitum** (Latin) to infinity, endlessly.

**ad lib(itum)** (Latin) 'freely' interpreted.

**ad nauseam** (Latin) to the point of disgust.

**aide-de-camp** (French) officer who acts as private secretary to a general and would normally accompany the general on any duty.

**al fresco** (Italian 'in the cool') in the open air.

**avant-garde** (from French) in the arts, those artists or works that are in the forefront of new developments in their media.

**ballet blanc** (French 'white ballet') a ballet, such as *Giselle*, in which the female dancers wear calf-length white dresses.

**belles lettres** (French 'fine letters') literature that is appreciated more for its aesthetic qualities than for its content.

**bête noire** (French 'black beast') something particularly disliked.

**Bildungsroman** (German 'education novel') novel that deals with the psychological and emotional development of its protagonist, tracing his or her life from inexperienced youth to maturity. The first example of the type is generally considered to be Wieland's *Agathon* 1765–66.

**billabong** (Australian Aboriginal *billa bung* 'dead river') a stagnant pond.

**billet doux** (French 'sweet note') a letter to or from one's lover.

**Blitzkrieg** (German 'lightning war') swift military campaign, as used by Germany at the beginning of World War II 1939–41. The abbreviated form Blitz was applied to the German air raids on London 1940–41.

**bloc** (French) a group, generally used to describe politically allied countries, as in 'the Soviet bloc'.

**bona vacantia** (Latin 'empty goods') in law, the property of a person who dies without making a will and without relatives or dependants who would be entitled or might reasonably expect to inherit.

**bon marché** (French) cheap.

**bon mot** (French) a witty remark.

**bonsai** (Japanese) the art of producing miniature trees by selective pruning.

**bon ton** (French 'good tone') fashionable manners.

**bon voyage** (French) have a good journey.

**bourgeois** (French) a member of the middle class, implying that a person is unimaginative, conservative, and materialistic.

**bric-à-brac** (French) odds and ends, usually old, ornamental, less valuable than antiques.

**cahier** (French 'notebook') usually the working

notes or drawings of a writer or artist.

**caïque** (French, from Turkish) long, narrow, light rowing boat.

**canaille** (French) the mob, rabble.

**carpe diem** (Latin 'seize the day') live for the present.

**carte blanche** (French 'white paper') no instructions, complete freedom to do as one wishes.

**casus belli** (Latin) a justification for war, grounds for a dispute.

**caveat emptor** (Latin) dictum that professes the buyer is responsible for checking the quality of nonwarrantied goods purchased.

**cave canem** (Latin) beware of the dog.

**céad míle fáilte** (Irish 'a hundred thousand welcomes') a conventional form of greeting.

**c'est la vie** (French) that's life.

**chacun à son goût** (French) each to their own taste.

**chambré** (French) (of wine) at room temperature, as opposed to chilled.

**chef d'oeuvre** (French) a masterpiece.

**cicisbeo** (Italian) 18th-century term for an aristocratic married woman's lover, similar to *cavaliere servente*.

**cogito, ergo sum** (Latin) 'I think, therefore I am'; quotation from French philosopher René Descartes.

**comme il faut** (French 'as it should be') socially correct and acceptable.

**compos mentis** (Latin) of sound mind.

**conquistador** (Spanish for 'conqueror'), applied to such explorers and adventurers in the Americas as Cortés (Mexico) and Pizarro (Peru).

**corrigendum** (Latin) something to be corrected.

**coup d'état** or **coup** (French literally 'stroke of state') forcible takeover of the government of a country by elements from within that country, generally carried out by violent or illegal means.

**coûte que coûte** (French) whatever the cost.

**crème de la crème** (French 'the cream of the cream') the elite, the very best.

**cri de coeur** (French) a cry from the heart.

**cuius regio, eius religio** (Latin) those who live in a country should adopt the religon of its ruler.

**cul-de-sac** (French, literally 'bottom of the bag') a street closed off at one end; an inescapable situation.

**curriculum vitae** or **CV** (Latin, literally 'the course of one's life') an account of a person's education and previous employment, attached to a job application.

**de bene esse** (Latin 'of wellbeing') in law, doing what is the best possible in the circumstances; the term usually relates to evidence.

**decree nisi** (Latin) conditional order of divorce. A *decree absolute* is normally granted six weeks after the decree nisi, and from the date of the decree absolute the parties cease to be husband and wife.

**de die in diem** (Latin) day after day.

**de facto** (Latin) in fact.

**de gustibus non est disputandum** (Latin) there is no accounting for taste.

**Dei gratia** (Latin) by the grace of God.

**déjà vu** (French 'already seen') the feeling that something encountered for the first time has in fact been seen before.

**de jure** (Latin) according to law; legally.

**de novo** (Latin) from the beginning; anew.

**Deo (ad)juvante** (Latin) with God's help.

**Deo gratias** (Latin) thanks to God.

**Deo volente** (Latin) God willing.

**de profundis** (Latin 'from the depths') a cry from the depths of misery. From the Bible, Psalm 130: *De profundis clamavi ad te*; 'Out of the depths have I cried to thee'.

**de rigueur** (French 'of strictness') demanded by the rules of etiquette.

**détente** (French) a reduction of political tension and the easing of strained relations between nations; for example, the ending of the Cold War 1989–90.

**de trop** (French 'of too much') not wanted, in the way.

**deus ex machina** (Latin 'a god from a machine') a far-fetched or unlikely event that resolves an intractable difficulty.

**Dieu et mon droit** (French 'God and my right') motto of the royal arms of UK.

**doppelgänger** (German 'double-goer') a ghostly apparition identical to a living person; a twin soul.

**double entendre** (French 'double meaning') an ambiguous word or phrase, usually one that is coarse or impolite.

**dramatis personae** (Latin) the characters in a play.

**dulce et decorum est pro patria mori** (Latin 'it is sweet and noble to die for one's country') quotation from Horace's *Odes*, also used by English poet Wilfred Owen as the title for his poem denouncing World War I.

**Ecce Homo** (Latin 'behold the man') the words of Pontius Pilate to the accusers of Jesus; the title of paintings showing Jesus crowned with thorns, presented to the people (John 19:5).

**emeritus** (Latin) someone who has retired from an official position but retains their title on an honorary basis, for example a *professor emeritus*.

**éminence grise** (French, literally 'grey eminence') a power behind a throne; that is, a manipulator of power without immediate responsibility. The nickname was originally applied (because of his grey cloak) to the French monk François Leclerc du Tremblay (1577–1638), also known as Père Joseph, who in 1612 became the close friend and behind-the-scenes adviser of Cardinal Richelieu.

**enfant terrible** (French 'terrible child') one whose rash and unconventional behaviour shocks and embarrasses others.

**en masse** (French) as a group, in a body, all together.

**enosis** (Greek) the movement, developed from 1930, for the union of Cyprus with Greece, which took place 1974.

**en plein air** (French) in the open air.

**en route** (French) on the way.

**entente cordiale** (French 'cordial understanding'), specifically, the agreement reached by

Britain and France 1904 recognizing British interests in Egypt and French interests in Morocco. It formed the basis for Anglo-French cooperation before the outbreak of World War I 1914.

**ergo** (Latin) therefore; hence.

**erratum** (Latin) an error.

**ersatz** (German) artificial, substitute, inferior.

**espadrille** (French) a type of shoe made with a canvas upper and a rope sole.

**et in arcadia ego** (Latin 'I also in Arcadia') death exists even in Arcadia (a fabled land).

**ex cathedra** (Latin, literally 'from the chair') term describing a statement by the pope, taken to be indisputably true, and which must be accepted by Catholics.

**exeunt** (Latin 'they go out') a stage direction.

**exit** (Latin 'he/she goes out') a stage direction.

**ex parte** (Latin 'on the part of one side only') in law, term indicating that an order has been made after hearing only the party that made the application; for example, an ex parte injunction.

**factotum** (Latin 'do everything') someone employed to do all types of work.

**fait accompli** (French 'accomplished fact') something that has been done and cannot be undone.

**faute de mieux** (French) for want of better.

**faux pas** (French 'false step') a social blunder.

**fellah** ( Arabic, plural *fellahin*) in Arab countries, a peasant farmer or farm labourer. In Egypt, approximately 60% of the fellah population live in rural areas, often in villages of 1,000–5,000 inhabitants.

**fin de siècle** (French 'end of century') the art and literature of the 1890s; decadent.

**force majeure** (French 'superior force') in politics, the use of force rather than the seeking of a political or diplomatic solution to a problem.

**Gesellschaft** (German 'society') a group whose concerns are of a formal and practical nature.

**glasnost** (Russian 'speaking aloud') Soviet leader Mikhail Gorbachev's policy of liberalizing various aspects of Soviet life, such as introducing greater freedom of expression and information and opening up relations with Western countries.

**Götterdämmerung** (German 'twilight of the gods') in Scandinavian mythology, the end of the world.

**gulag** (Russian) term for the system of prisons and labour camps used to silence dissidents and opponents of the Soviet regime.

**hic jacet** (Latin 'here lies') an epitaph.

**honi soit qui mal y pense** (French 'shamed be he who thinks evil of it') the motto of England's Order of the Garter.

**hors de combat** (French) out of action.

**incunabula** (Latin, originally from swaddling clothes) the birthplace, or early stages of anything; printed books produced before 1500, when printing was in its infancy.

**in loco parentis** (Latin) in a parental capacity.

**in situ** (Latin) in place, on the spot, without moving from position.

**inter alia** (Latin) among other things.

**ipso facto** (Latin) by that very fact.

**j'adoube** (French 'I adjust') used in chess to show that a player is touching a piece in order to correct its position rather than to move it.

**je ne sais quoi** (French 'I don't know what') a certain indescribable quality.

**joie de vivre** (French) finding pleasure in simply being alive.

**kindergarten** (German) another term for nursery school.

**kohl** (Arabic) powdered antimony sulphide, used in Asia and the Middle East to darken the area around the eyes.

**Kyrie eleison** (Greek 'Lord have mercy') the words spoken or sung at the beginning of the mass in the Catholic, Orthodox, and Anglican churches.

**laissez faire** (French) theory that the state should not intervene in economic affairs, except to break up a monopoly. The phrase originated with the Physiocrats, 18th-century French economists whose maxim was *laissez faire et laissez passer*, (leave the individual alone and let commodities circulate freely).

**lakh** or *lac* or *lak* (from Hindi) in India or Pakistan, the sum of 100,000 (rupees).

**Land** (German; plural *Länder*) federal state of Germany or Austria.

**Landtag** (German) legislature of each of the *Länder* (states) that form the federal republics of Germany and Austria.

**Lebensphilosophie** (German) philosophy of life.

**Lebensraum** (German 'living space') theory developed by Hitler for the expansion of Germany into E Europe, and in the 1930s used by the Nazis to justify their annexation of neighbouring states on the grounds that Germany was overpopulated.

**lingua franca** (Italian, literally 'Frankish tongue') any language that is used as a means of communication by groups who do not themselves normally speak that language; for example, English is a lingua franca used by Japanese doing business in Finland, or by Swedes in Saudi Arabia.

**locus standi** (Latin 'a place to stand') in law, the right to bring an action.

**Lumpenproletariat** (German 'ragged proletariat') the poorest of the poor: beggars, tramps, and criminals (according to Karl Marx).

**Machtpolitik** (German) power politics.

**magnum opus** (Latin) a great work of art or literature.

**Mardi Gras** (French 'fat Tuesday' from the custom of using up all the fat in the household before the beginning of Lent) Shrove Tuesday. A festival was traditionally held on this day in Paris, and there are carnivals in many parts of the world, including New Orleans, Louisiana, Italy, and Brazil.

**mare nostrum** (Latin 'our sea') Roman name for the Mediterranean.

**matzo** or *matzoh* (from Hebrew) unleavened bread eaten during the Passover.

**mea culpa** (Latin 'my fault') an admission of guilt.

**memento mori** (Latin) a reminder of death.

**menhir** (Breton 'long stone') a prehistoric standing stone.

**mens sana in corpore sano** (Latin) a healthy mind in a healthy body.

**Messrs** abbreviation for *messieurs* (French 'sirs' or 'gentlemen') used in formal writing to address an organization or group of people.

**mise en scène** (French 'stage setting') in cinema, the composition and content of the frame in terms of background scenery, actors, costumes, props, and lighting.

**modus operandi** (Latin) a method of operating.

**modus vivendi** (Latin 'way of living') a compromise between opposing points of view.

**mores** (Latin) the customs and manners of a society.

**mot juste** (French) the right word, just the word to suit the occasion.

**muezzin** (Arabic) a person whose job is to perform the call to prayer five times a day from the minaret of a Muslim mosque.

**née** (French 'born') followed by a surname, indicates the name of a woman before marriage.

**nemo me impune lacessit** (Latin 'no one injures me with impunity') the motto of Scotland.

**nil desperandum** (Latin) never despair.

**noblesse oblige** (French) the aristocracy ought to behave honourably. The phrase is often used sarcastically to point out how removed this idea is from reality.

**nom de plume** (French 'pen name') a writer's pseudonym.

**non sequitur** (Latin 'it does not follow') a statement that has little or no relevance to the one that preceded it.

**nuit blanche** (French 'white night') a night without sleep.

**nulli secundus** (Latin) second to none.

**obiit** (Latin 'he/she died') found, for example, in inscriptions on tombstones, followed by a date.

**ombudsman** (from Swedish 'commissioner') official who acts on behalf of the private citizen in investigating complaints against the government. The post is of Scandinavian origin; it was introduced in Sweden 1809, Denmark 1954, and Norway 1962, and spread to other countries from the 1960s.

**onus** (Latin) a burden or responsibility.

**outré** (French) extreme, beyond the bounds of acceptability.

**pace** (Latin) with deference to, followed by a name, used to acknowledge contradiction of the person named.

**padre** (Italian 'father') a priest.

**parvenu** (French 'arrived') a social upstart.

**passé** (French) out of date.

**passim** (Latin 'in many places') indicates that a reference occurs repeatedly throughout the cited work.

**perestroika** (Russian 'radical restructuring') in Soviet politics, the wide-ranging economic and political reforms initiated during Mikhail Gorbachev's leadership of the Soviet state.

**per se** (Latin) in itself.

**pièce de résistance** (French) the most outstanding item in a collection; the main dish of a meal.

**pied-à-terre** (French 'foot on the ground') a convenient second home, usually small and in a town or city.

**pique** (French) a feeling of slight irritation or resentment.

**plus ça change, plus c'est la même chose** (French) the more things change, the more they stay the same.

**poste restante** (French) a system whereby mail is sent to a certain post office and kept there until collected by the addressee.

**post hoc, ergo propter hoc** (Latin) after this, therefore on account of this.

**postmortem** (Latin) dissection of a dead body to determine the cause of death. It is also known as an *autopsy*.

**post scriptum** (abbreviation PS; Latin) something written below the signature on a letter.

**prêt-à-porter** (French) ready-to-wear clothes.

**prima facie** (Latin) at first sight.

**pro rata** (Latin) in proportion.

**pro tem(pore)** (Latin) for the time being.

**putsch** (Swiss German) term for a violent seizure of political power, such as the abortive attempt by the Soviet 'Gang of Eight' to wrest power from President Gorbachev Aug 1991.

**quasi** (Latin 'as if') apparently but not actually.

**quid pro quo** (Latin 'something for something') an exchange of one thing in return for another.

**quod erat demonstrandum** (abbreviation QED; Latin 'which was to be proved') added at the end of a geometry proof.

**quod vide** (abbreviation qv; Latin 'which see') indicates a cross-reference.

**quo vadis?** (Latin) where are you going?

**raison d'être** (French) a reason for existence.

**réchauffé** (French 're-heated') warmed up (as of leftover food); old, stale.

**recherché** (French 'sought after') rare.

**revenons à nos moutons** (French 'let us return to our sheep') let us get back to the subject.

**ruat coelum** (Latin 'though the heavens may fall') whatever happens.

**rus in urbe** (Latin) urban retreat where one could imagine oneself in the countryside.

**Sachlichkeit** (German) objectivity, matter-of-factness.

**samovar** (Russian) urn, heated by charcoal, used for making tea.

**sang-froid** (French 'cold blood') coolness, composure.

**sans souci** (French) without cares or worries.

**savoir-faire** (French) knowing what to do, how to behave.

**Schadenfreude** (German) malicious enjoyment at the misfortunes of others.

**scilicet** (Latin) namely, that is.

**secrétaire** (French) a small writing desk.

**sic** (Latin 'thus', 'so') sometimes found in brackets within a printed quotation to show that an apparent error is in the original.

**si monumentum requiris, circumspice** (Latin 'if you seek his monument, look about you') the epitaph of Christopher Wren in St Paul's Cathedral, London.

**sine die** (Latin 'without a day being appointed') indefinitely.

**sine qua non** (Latin 'without which not') absolutely essential.

**soupçon** (French 'suspicion') a very small amount, a dash.

**sovkhoz** (Russian) state-owned farm in the USSR where the workers are state employees. The sovkhoz differs from the *kolkhoz* where the farm is run by a collective.

**status quo** (Latin 'the state in which') the current situation, without change.

**Sturm und Drang** (German, literally 'storm and stress') German early Romantic movement in literature and music, from about 1775, concerned with the depiction of extravagant passions. Writers associated with the movement include Herder, Goethe, and Schiller.

**sub judice** (Latin) not yet decided by a court of law.

**Sûreté** (French) the criminal investigation department of the French police.

**tabula rasa** (Latin 'scraped tablet', from the Romans' use of wax-covered tablets which could be written on with a pointed stick and cleared by smoothing over the surface) a mind without any preconceived ideas.

**tant mieux** (French) so much the better.

**tant pis** (French) so much the worse.

**tempus fugit** (Latin) time flies.

**terra firma** (Latin) dry land; solid earth.

**terra incognita** (Latin) an unknown region.

**terza rima** (Italian 'third line') poetical metre used in Dante's *Divine Comedy*, consisting of three-line stanzas in which the second line rhymes with the first and third of the following stanza.

**tête-à-tête** (French '-to-head') private meeting between two people.

**texte intégral** (French 'the complete text') unabridged.

**tour de force** (French 'feat of strength') a remarkable accomplishment.

**tout de suite** (French) immediately.

**tout ensemble** (French 'all together') the overall effect.

**trahison des clercs** (French 'the treason of the intellectuals') the involvement of intellectuals in active politics.

**tricoteuse** (French 'knitter') in the French Revolution, one of the women who sat knitting in the National Convention and near the guillotine.

**ultra** (Latin) extreme.

**uomo universale** (Italian 'universal man'), someone who is at home in all spheres of knowledge; one of the ideals of the Renaissance.

**urbi et orbi** (Latin 'to the city and to the world') a papal proclamation.

**ut pictura poesis** (Latin) a poem is as a picture.

**vade mecum** (Latin 'go with me') a useful handbook carried about for reference.

**veni, vidi, vici** (Latin 'I came, I saw, I conquered') Julius Caesar's description of his victory over King Pharnaces II (63–47 BC) at Zela in 47 BC.

**vérité** (French 'realism'), as in *cinéma vérité*, used to describe a realistic or documentary style.

**versus** (abbreviation vs; Latin) against.

**vice versa** (Latin) the other way around.

**vis-à-vis** (French 'face-to-face') with regard to.

**viva voce** (Latin 'with living voice') an oral examination.

**Völkerwanderung** (German 'nations wandering') the migration of peoples, usually with reference to the Slavic and Germanic movement in Europe 2nd–11th centuries AD.

**Weltanschauung** (German 'worldview') a philosophy of life.

**yeti** (Tibetan) another term for the abominable snowman.

**Zeitgeist** (German 'time spirit') spirit of the age.

**zenana** (Hindi) the part of a house used by the female members of the household.

**Zugzwang** (German) a position in chess from which it is impossible to move without worsening one's situation.

## Exchange Rates

World Exchange Rates (as of 1 July 1991)

| country | currency | sterling |
|---|---|---|
| Afghanistan | afgháni | 99.25 |
| Albania | lek | 10.10 |
| Algeria | dinar | 29.26 |
| Andorra | French franc | 9.96 |
| | Spanish peseta | 184.10 |
| Angola | kwanza | 104.33 |
| Antigua | East Caribbean dollar | 4.39 |
| Argentina | austral | 16306.00 |
| Aruba | florin | 2.91 |
| Australia | Australian dollar | 2.11 |
| Austria | schilling | 20.64 |
| Azores | port escudo | 254.10 |
| Bahamas | Bahamian dollar | 1.61 |
| Bahrain | dinar | 0.61 |
| Balearic Islands | Spanish peseta | 184.10 |
| Bangladesh | taka | 56.00 |
| Barbados | Barbados dollar | 3.27 |
| Belgium | Belgian franc | 60.30 |
| Belize | Belize dollar | 3.25 |
| Benin | CFA franc | 498.25 |
| Bermuda | Bermudian dollar | 1.61 |
| Bhutan | ngultrum | 34.09 |
| Bolivia | boliviano | 5.80 |
| Botswana | pula | 3.37 |
| Brazil | cruzeiro | 508.20 |
| Brunei | Brunei dollar | 2.86 |
| Bulgaria | lev | 31.01 |
| Burkina Faso | CFA franc | 498.25 |
| Burma | kyat | 10.80 |
| Burundi | Burundi franc | 287.50 |
| Cambodia | riel | 975.00 |
| Cameroon | CFA franc | 498.25 |
| Canada | Canadian dollar | 1.85 |
| Canary Islands | Spanish peseta | 184.10 |
| Cape Verde | Cape Verde escudo | 126.94 |
| Cayman Islands | Cayman Island dollar | 1.35 |
| Central African Rep | CFA franc | 498.25 |
| Chad | CFA franc | 498.25 |
| Chile | Chilean peso | 583.65 |
| China | Renminbi yuan | 8.76 |
| Colombia | Colombian peso | 1011.97 |
| Comoros | CFA franc | 498.25 |
| Congo | CFA franc | 498.25 |
| Costa Rica | colón | 200.69 |
| Côte d'Ivoire | CFA franc | 498.25 |
| Cuba | Cuban peso | 1.29 |
| Cyprus | Cyprus pound | 0.79 |
| Czechoslovakia | koruna | 50.73c |
| | | 48.90t |
| Denmark | Danish kroner | 11.34 |
| Djibouti Republic | Djibouti franc | 285.00 |
| Dominica | East Caribbean dollar | 4.38 |
| Dominican Republic | Dominican peso | 20.75 |
| Ecuador | sucre | 1657.66o |
| | | 1821.36a |
| Egypt | Egyptian pound | 5.40 |
| El Salvador | colón | 13.02 |
| Equatorial Guinea | CFA franc | 498.25 |
| Ethiopia | Ethiopian birr | 3.34 |
| Falkland Islands | Falkland pound | 1.00 |
| Faroe Islands | Danish kroner | 11.34 |
| Fiji Islands | Fiji dollar | 2.45 |
| Finland | markka | 6.96 |
| France | franc | 9.96 |
| French Community/ Africa | CFA franc | 498.25 |
| French Guiana | local franc | 9.96 |
| French Pacific Is | CFP franc | 180.00 |
| Gabon | CFA franc | 498.25 |
| Gambia | dalasi | 14.26 |
| Germany | Deutschmark | 2.94 |
| Ghana | cedi | 593.10 |
| Gibraltar | Gibraltar pound | 1.00 |
| Greece | drachma | 321.37 |
| Greenland | Danish krone | 11.34 |
| Grenada | East Caribbean dollar | 4.39 |
| Guadaloupe | local franc | 9.96 |
| Guam | US dollar | 1.61 |
| Guatemala | quetzal | 7.93 |
| Guinea | franc | 1007.50a |
| | | 487.50n |
| Guinea-Bissau | peso | 1056.25 |
| Guyana | Guyanese dollar | 206.37 |
| Haiti | goude | 8.12 |
| Honduras | lempira | 9.16 |
| Hong Kong | Hong Kong dollar | 12.61 |
| Hungary | forint | 126.15 |
| Iceland | Icelandic krona | 102.25 |
| India | Indian rupee | 34.09 |
| Indonesia | rupiah | 3175.66 |
| Iran | rial | 112.50 |
| Iraq | Iraqi dinar | 0.60 |
| Irish Republic | punt | 1.10 |
| Israel | shekel | 4.01 |
| Italy | lira | 2187.00 |
| Jamaica | Jamaican dollar | 16.16 |
| Japan | yen | 223.50 |
| Jordan | Jordanian dinar | 1.10 |
| Kenya | Kenyan shilling | 46.57 |
| Kiribati | Australian dollar | 2.11 |
| Korea, North | won | 1.58 |
| Korea, South | won | 1172.52 |
| Kuwait | Kuwaiti dinar | 0.48 |
| Laos | new kip | 1137.50 |
| Lebanon | Lebanese pound | 1469.00 |
| Lesotho | maluti | 4.68 |
| Liberia | Liberian dollar | 1.61 |
| Libya | Libyan dinar | 0.48 |
| Liechenstein | Swiss franc | 2.52 |
| Luxembourg | Luxembourg franc | 60.30 |
| Macao | pataca | 13.00 |
| Madagascar | Malagasy franc | 2968.50 |
| Madeira | port escudo | 254.10 |
| Malawi | kwacha | 4.75 |
| Malaysia | ringgit | 4.52 |
| Maldive Islands | rufiya | 16.20 |
| Mali Republic | CFA franc | 498.25 |
| Malta | Maltese pound | 0.56 |
| Martinique | local franc | 9.96 |
| Mauritania | ougiya | 134.97 |
| Mauritius | Mauritian rupee | 27.05 |
| Mexico | Mexican peso | 4900.00a |
| | | 4894.17d |
| Miquelon | local franc | 9.96 |
| Monaco | French franc | 9.96 |
| Mongolia | tugrik | 5.45 |

| | | |
|---|---|---|
| Montserrat | East Caribbean dollar | 4.39 |
| Morocco | dirham | 14.76 |
| Mozambique | metical | 2462.87 |
| Namibia | South African Rand | 4.68 |
| Nauru Island | Australian dollar | 2.11 |
| Nepal | Nepalese rupee | 54.29 |
| Netherlands | guilder | 3.31 |
| Netherland Antilles | Antillian guilder | 2.90 |
| New Zealand | New Zealand dollar | 2.85 |
| Nicaragua | gold cordoba | 8.12 |
| Niger Republic | CFA franc | 498.25 |
| Nigeria | naira | 16.98 |
| Norway | Norwegian krone | 11.43 |
| Oman | Omani rial | 0.62 |
| Pakistan | Pakistani rupee | 39.00 |
| Panama | balboa | 1.61 |
| Papua New Guinea | kina | 1.56 |
| Paraguay | guarani | 2145.28 |
| Peru | new sol | 1.38 |
| Philippines | peso | 43.00 |
| Pitcairn Islands | pound sterling | 1.00 |
| | New Zealand dollar | 2.85 |
| Poland | zloty | 18684.00 |
| Portugal | escudo | 254.10 |
| Puerto Rico | US dollars | 1.61 |
| Qatar | riyal | 5.90 |
| Réunion Islands | French franc | 9.96 |
| Romania | leu | 101.48 |
| Rwanda | franc | 213.03 |
| St Christopher | East Caribbean dollar | 4.39 |
| St Helena | pound sterling | 1.00 |
| St Lucia | East Caribbean dollar | 4.39 |
| St Pierre | French franc | 9.96 |
| St Vincent | East Caribbean dollar | 4.39 |
| San Marino | Italian lira | 2187.00 |
| São Tomé e Principe | dobra | 303.87 |
| Saudi Arabia | riyal | 6.07 |
| Senegal | CFA franc | 498.25 |
| Seychelles | rupee | 8.80 |
| Sierra Leone | leone | 371.45 |
| Singapore | dollar | 2.86 |
| Solomon Islands | dollar | 4.44 |
| Somali Republic | shilling | 4257.50 |
| South Africa | rand | 4.69c |
| | | 5.41g |
| Spain | peseta | 184.10 |
| Sri Lanka | rupee | 66.00 |
| Sudan Republic | Sudanese pound | 7.31o |
| | | 18.61g |
| Suriname | guilder | 2.90 |
| Swaziland | lilangeni | 4.68 |
| Sweden | krona | 10.59 |
| Switzerland | Swiss franc | 2.53 |
| Syria | Syrian pound | 34.12 |
| Taiwan | dollar | 44.12 |
| Tanzania | shilling | 371.63 |
| Thailand | baht | 41.00 |
| Togo Republic | CFA franc | 498.25 |
| Tonga Islands | pa'anga | 2.11 |
| Trinidad and Tobago | dollar | 6.91 |
| Tunisia | dinar | 1.61 |
| Turkey | lira | 7027.94 |

| | | |
|---|---|---|
| Turks and Caicos Islands | US dollar | 1.61 |
| Tuvalu | Australian dollar | 2.11 |
| Uganda | new shilling | 1136.59 |
| United Arab Emirates | dirham | 5.95 |
| United Kingdom | pound sterling | 1.00 |
| United States | US dollar | 1.61 |
| Uruguay | peso | 3198.30 |
| USSR | rouble | 0.99o |
| | | 2.97c |
| Vanuatu | vatu | 179.00 |
| Vatican City State | lira | 2187.00 |
| Venezuela | bolivar | 88.90 |
| Vietnam | dong | 13406.25 |
| Virgin Islands, British | US dollar | 1.61 |
| Virgin Islands, US | US dollar | 1.61 |
| Western Samoa | taia | 3.84 |
| Yemen, North | rial | 19.58 |
| Yemen, South | dinar | 0.74 |
| Yugoslavia | dinar | 38.12 |
| Zaïre Republic | zaïre | 7564.00 |
| Zambia | kwacha | 103.76 |
| Zimbabwe | dollar | 5.22 |

Abbreviations: (a) free rate; (b) banknote rate; (c) commercial rate; (d) controlled rate; (g) financial rate; (h) exports; (i) non commercial rate; (j) business rate; (k) buying rate; (l) luxury goods; (m) market rate; (n) public transaction rate; (o) official rate; (p) preferential rate; (q) convertible rate (s) selling rate; (t) tourist rate; (u) currencies fixed against the US dollar.

Data supplied by Bank of America, Economics Department, London Trading Centre.

# WEIGHTS AND MEASURES

*Imperial, with Metric Equivalents*

*Linear Measure*

| | |
|---|---|
| 1 inch (in) | = 25.4 millimetres |
| 1 foot (ft) = 12 inches | = 0.3048 metre |
| 1 yard (yd) = 3 feet | = 0.9144 metre |
| 1 (statute) mile = 1,760 yards | = 1.609 kilometres |

*Square Measure*

| | |
|---|---|
| 1 square inch (in$^2$ or sq in) | = 6.45 sq centimetres |
| 1 square foot (ft$^2$) = 144 sq in | = 9.29 sq decimetres |
| 1 square yard (yd$^2$ = 9 sq ft | = 0.836 sq metre |
| 1 acre = 4,840 sq yd | = 0.405 hectare |
| 1 square mile (mile$^2$) = 640 acres | =259 hectares |

*Cubic Measure*

| | |
|---|---|
| 1 cubic inch (in$^3$ or cu in) | = 16.4 cu centimetres |
| 1 cubic foot (ft$^3$) = 1,728 cu in | = 0.0283 cu metre |
| 1 cubic yard (yd$^3$) = 27 cu ft | = 0.765 cu metre |

*Capacity Measure British*

| | |
|---|---|
| 1 pint (pt) = 20 fluid oz = 34.68 cu in | = 0.568 litre |
| 1 quart = 2 pints | = 1.136 litres |
| 1 gallon (gal) = 4 quarts | = 4.546 litres |
| 1 peck = 2 gallons | = 9.092 litres |
| 1 bushel = 4 pecks | = 36.4 litres |
| 1 quarter = 8 bushels | = 2.91 hectolitres |

*American dry*

| | |
|---|---|
| 1 pint = 33.60 cu in | = 0.550 litre |
| 1 quart = 2 pints | = 1.101 litres |
| 1 peck = 8 quarts | = 8.81 litres |
| 1 bushel = 4 pecks | = 35.3 litres |

*American liquid*

| | |
|---|---|
| 1 pint = 16 fluid oz = 28.88 cu in | = 0.473 litre |
| 1 quart = 2 pints | = 0.946 litre |
| 1 gallon = 4 quarts | = 3.785 litres |

*Avoirdupois Weight*

| | |
|---|---|
| 1 grain | = 0.065 gram |
| 1 dram | = 1.772 grams |
| 1 ounce (oz) = 16 drams | = 28.35 grams |
| 1 pound (lb) = 16 ounces = 7,000 grains | = 0.4536 kilogram |
| 1 stone (st) = 14 pounds | = 6.35 kilograms |
| 1 quarter = 2 stones | = 12.70 kilograms |
| 1 hundredweight (cwt) 4 quarters | = 50.80 kilograms |
| 1 (long) ton = 20 hundredweight | = 1.016 tonnes |
| 1 short ton = 2,000 pounds | = 0.907 tonne |

*Metric, with Imperial (British) Equivalents*

*Linear Measure*

| | |
|---|---|
| 1 millimetre (mm) = 0.039 inch | |
| 1 centimetre (cm) = 10 mm | = 0.394 inch |
| 1 decimetre (dm) = 10 cm | = 3.94 inches |
| 1 metre (m) = 10 dm | = 1.094 yards |
| 1 decametre (dam) = 10 m | = 10.94 yards |
| 1 hectometre (hm) = 100 m | = 109.4 yards |
| 1 kilometre (km) = 1,000 m | = 0.6214 mile |

*Square Measure*

| | |
|---|---|
| 1 square centimetre (cm$^2$ or sq cm) = 0.155 sq in | |
| 1 square metre (m$^2$) | = 1.196 sq yards |
| 1 are = 100 sq metres | = 119.6 sq yards |
| 1 hectare (ha) = 100 ares | = 2.471 acres |
| 1 square kilometre (km$^2$) | = 0.386 sq mile |

*Cubic Measure*

| | |
|---|---|
| 1 millilitre (ml) | = 0.002 pint (British) |
| 1 centilitre (cl) = 10 ml | = 0.018 pint |
| 1 decilitre (dl) = 10 cl | = 0.176 pint |
| 1 litre (l) = 10 dl | = 1.76 pints |
| 1 decalitre (dal) = 10 l | = 2.20 gallons |
| 1 hectolitre (hl) = 100 l | = 2.75 bushels |
| 1 kilolitre (kl) = 1,000 l | = 3.44 quarters |

*Weight*

| | |
|---|---|
| 1 milligram (mg) = 0.015 grain | |
| 1 centigram (cg) = 10 mg | = 0.154 grain |
| 1 decigram (dg) = 10 cg | = 1.543 grain |
| 1 gram (g) = 10 dg | = 15.43 grain |
| 1 decagram (dag) = 10 g | = 5.64 drams |
| 1 hectogram (hg) = 100 g | = 3.527 ounces |
| 1 kilogram (kg) = 1,000 g | = 2.205 pounds |
| 1 tonne (metric ton) = 1,000 kg | = 0.984 (long) ton |

*Temperature*

Fahrenheit: water boils (under standard conditions) at 212° and freezes at 32°

Celsius or Centigrade: water boils at 100° and freezes at 0°.

Kelvin: water boils at 373.15 and freezes at 273.15.

$°C = 5/9(°F-32)$
$°F = (9/5°C) + 32$
$K = °C = 273.15$

## WEDDING ANNIVERSARIES

*In many Western countries, different wedding anniversaries have become associated with gifts of different materials. There is variation between countries.*

| anniversary | material |
|---|---|
| 1st | cotton |
| 2nd | paper |
| 3rd | leather |
| 4th | fruit, flowers |
| 5th | wood |
| 6th | sugar |
| 7th | copper, wool |
| 8th | bronze, pottery |
| 9th | pottery, willow |
| 10th | tin |
| 11th | steel |
| 12th | silk, linen |
| 13th | lace |
| 14th | ivory |
| 15th | crystal |
| 20th | china |
| 25th | silver |
| 30th | pearl |
| 35th | coral |
| 40th | ruby |
| 45th | sapphire |
| 50th | gold |
| 55th | emerald |
| 60th | diamond |
| 70th | platinum |

## MAJOR HOLIDAYS 1992

| | |
|---|---|
| New Year | 1 Jan |
| Shrove Tuesday | 3 March |
| Ash Wednesday | 4 March |
| Ramadan begins | 5 March |
| 1st Sunday in Lent | 8 March |
| Commonwealth Day | 9 March |
| Mothers Day (UK) | 29 March |
| Palm Sunday | 12 April |
| Maundy Thursday | 16 April |
| Good Friday | 17 April |
| Easter Day | 19 April |
| Bank Holiday (UK) | 4 May |
| Bank Holiday (UK) | 25 May |
| Ascension Day | 28 May |
| Sunday after Ascension | 31 May |
| Pentecost | 7 June |
| Trinity Sunday | 14 June |
| Corpus Christi | 18 June |
| Fathers Day (UK) | 21 June |
| Muslim New Year (1413) | 2 July |
| Bank Holiday (UK) | 31 Aug |
| Jewish New Year (5753) | 28 Sept |
| Day of Atonement | 7 Oct |
| Remembrance Sunday (UK) | 8 Nov |
| 1st Sunday in Advent | 29 Nov |
| Christmas Day | 25 Dec |
| New Year's Eve | 31 Dec |

## BIRTHSTONES

| month | stone | quality |
|---|---|---|
| January | garnet | constancy |
| February | amethyst | sincerity |
| March | bloodstone | courage |
| April | diamond | innocence and lasting love |
| May | emerald | success and hope |
| June | pearl | health and purity |
| July | ruby | love and contentment |
| August | agate | married happiness |
| September | sapphire | wisdom |
| October | opal | hope |
| November | topaz | fidelity |
| December | turquoise | harmony |

# INDEX